MW01698296

Media Studies

Volume 2

Content, Audiences and Production

Media Studies

Volume 2

Content, Audiences and Production

Edited by

Pieter J Fourie

JUTA

First published 2001

ISBN 0 7021 5656 6

P O Box 24309, Lansdowne, 7779
South Africa

Subediting: Pat Hanekom
DTP and design: Charlene Bate
Cover design: Dallas du Toit
Printed and bound by: Creda Communications

This volume is part of a two-volume series:

Volume 1: Media studies: Institutions, Theories and Issues
Edited by Pieter J Fourie

Volume 2: Media studies: Content, Audiences and Production
Edited by Pieter J Fourie

Contents

Part A: Media Content

Unit 1: Text Analysis

Unit 2: Genre Analysis

Unit 3: Media and Language

Unit 4: Narrative Analysis

Part B: Film Theory

Unit 5: Film Theory and Criticism

Part C: Media Audiences

Unit 6: Reception Theory

Unit 7: Ethnography

Unit 8: The Social Psychology of Media Consumption

Unit 9: Audience Research

Unit 10: Media and Psychoanalysis

Part D: Media Production

Unit 11: Newspaper Production

Unit 12: Television Production

Unit 13: Radio Production

Unit 14: Film Production

Unit 15: Educational Media: Television

Unit 16: Educational Media: Radio

List of Figures

UNIT 1

UNIT 13

UNIT 15

UNIT 16

List of Tables

UNIT 15

UNIT 16

Case Studies

Copyright

FOR UNIT 1

Copyright previously granted for photographs and drawings as published in:

Fourie, PJ (ed). 1996. *Introduction to communication – course book 3: communication and the production of meaning.* Kenwyn: Juta.

Fourie, PJ (ed). 1997. *Introduction to communication – course book 6: film and television studies.* Kenwyn: Juta.

Copyright permission granted by Stefan Sonderling for photographs in figures 1.1 to 1.8, 1.14, 1.17 to 1.29 and 1.36 to 1.43.

FOR UNIT 2

Edmunds, M. 1996. The payment that put paid to Abe. *Mail & Guardian* 12(8):1&4, for which copyright was previously granted and published in Oosthuizen, LM (ed). 1996. *Introduction to communication – course book 5: journalism, press and radio studies.* Kenwyn: Juta:184–186.

FOR UNIT 5

Copyright previously granted for photographs as published in:

Fourie, PJ (ed). 1997. *Introduction to communication – course book 6: film and television studies.* Cape Town: Juta:89–147.

- The Russian director and film theorist, Sergei Eisenstein, directs a scene from his film *October*, 1928
- Expressionism: a scene from the *Odessa Steps* sequence in Sergei Eisenstein's film *The Battleship Potemkin*, 1925
- Expressionism: Vera Baranovskaia and Nikolai Batalov in V I Pudovkin's *The Mother*, 1926
- Expressionism: Max Schreck as the vampire Nosferatu in Friedrich Murnau's film *Nosferatu*, 1922
- (Neo)Realism: a scene from Vittorio de Sica's film *Miracle in Milan*, 1951
- Realism: Orson Welles as Kane in his film *Citizen Kane*, 1941
- Realism: a scene from DW Griffith's film *The Birth of a Nation*, 1915

FOR UNIT 15

The Pareto principle represents a number of assumptions and implications that are worth considering when designing training courses (or designing ETV programmes) for specific occupations. Although the discussion in this unit is adapted for the purposes of discussing what should be taught/learned, full credit is given to Jordan (1978), with whose permission this adaptation is published.

Jordan, Y. 1978. *Training officer's operating manual. Industrial Training Unit.* Durban: Technikon Natal.

Authors

GM (Trudie) du Plooy is a professor in communication science in the Department of Communication, University of South Africa.

Pieter J Fourie is a professor in communication science and head of the Department of Communication, University of South Africa.

Dr Corrie Faure is a senior lecturer in communication science in the Department of Communication, University of South Africa.

Beschara Karam is a lecturer in communication science in the Department of Communication, University of South Africa.

Magriet Pitout is an associate professor in communication science in the Department of Communication, University of South Africa.

Stefan Sonderling is a senior lecturer in communication science in the Department of Communication, University of South Africa.

David Wigston is a senior lecturer in communication science in the Department of Communication, University of South Africa.

Introduction

Volume 1

In the introduction to Volume 1 the need for and the growth of media studies as an academic field of inquiry was motivated. It was argued that the remarkable growth of media studies can, amongst other reasons, be attributed to:

- the prominent role of the media in society, culture, economics and politics
- the media's impact on everyday life
- the media as flagship of the late twentieth and early twenty-first centuries' (popular) culture
- the media industry's own acknowledgement of the need for workers to have a sound theoretical and methodological foundation, and all this leading to
- students' and academics' growing interest in the field.

On a macro level it was argued that the growth and importance of media studies could be attributed to:

- the need for institutions of higher learning to be more "relevant" in terms of society and industry's needs
- the role of globalisation, including the central role of the media and information and communication technology in globalisation
- the growth of the media industry itself.

Our answer to the question "Why media studies"? was that the media are integral parts of our lives. This necessitates critical inquiry into the ways in which the media work. In short, the media are omnipresent. As such they impact on our perceptions and experiences of reality, of life, and on our relationships with each other. Secondly, the media have become major economic and political role players. An understanding of their power and responsibilities is essential for all citizens, politicians, the business sector, educators, in short, for all media users. Finally, workers in the media and communications industry should have a sound knowledge of the nature and working of the media. They are, after all, the people producing the popular meanings with which we are confronted on a daily basis. They are the people responsible for framing our ways of thinking about everyday matters, about products and about people. A critical understanding of how the media work can contribute to a more responsible approach to what they are doing, and hopefully to an improvement in the quality of media products.

In Volume 1 we addressed questions related to:

- the nature and practices of the media as power institutions
- the political economy of the media
- the functions, effects and power of the media, and
- the media as producers and disseminators of meaning.

This was done mainly from a social science perspective in the following nineteen units:

Unit 1: A South African media map
Unit 2: Characteristics, trends and the political economy of the media
Unit 3: Media ownership and control
Unit 4: The external media policy framework: from restrictive policy to the democratisation of communication
Unit 5: The internal media policy framework
Unit 6: Mass communication theory
Unit 7: The role and functions of the media: functionalism
Unit 8: The effects and power of mass communication
Unit 9: Media and ideology
Unit 10: Media and the production of meaning: semiotics
Unit 11: Media and culture
Unit 12: Feminist media theory
Unit 13: Media imperialism: the New World Information and Communication Order
Unit 14: A critical assessment of news
Unit 15: Representation: race, gender and sexual orientation
Unit 16: Media and violence
Unit 17: Media and terrorism
Unit 18: Censorship and the media
Unit 19: Globalisation, the information superhighway and development

Volume 2

To a certain extent Volume 2 is a revision of the textbook Fourie, PJ (ed). 1997. *Introduction to communication - course book 6: film and television studies*. Kenwyn: Juta.

In this volume our focus is on media content, media audiences and media production. Although these topics are inseparable from those discussed in Volume 1, we separate them for analytical and academic reasons. We say inseparable, because the learner must keep in mind that the institutions discussed in Volume 1 are responsible for producing the content of the media for audiences who "read" and interpret the content in specific ways. A discussion of institutions, mass communication and media theories and of burning issues related to the media cannot take place without taking cognisance of media content, audiences and production techniques. Similarly, a discussion of content, audiences and production presupposes the existence and functioning of media institutions and is based on the same theories underlying a discussion of media institutions as a mass communication phenomenon.

Whereas our approach in Volume 1 was mainly from a social science perspective, our approach in this volume, in other words in dealing with content, audiences and production, is mainly from a semiotic, structuralist and post-structuralist perspective. In audience analysis we focus mainly on qualitative analysis. The reason for this is that we approach media mainly as producers and disseminators of meaning. How do the media produce meaning in media content/texts? How do audiences (the recipients) attach meaning to media content? As far as production is concerned, our approach is mainly descriptive of certain (key) aspects in media production.

Volume 2 is divided into four parts: media content, film theory, audiences, and production.

Media content

Media content can be described and analysed in many ways. One of the classic and frequently used techniques is quantitative content analysis. This boils down to the counting and measurement of certain aspects of media content, for example the occurrence of specific themes in a newspaper's coverage, for example, of crime, politics, or themes in soap operas and situation comedies. This technique is dealt with in other parts of Unisa's programme in communication science.

Here, following a semiotic approach, we opted in Unit 1 for the visual literacy approach - an approach that contributes to our understanding of visual and audiovisual texts (in general). It is often argued that media culture is mainly a visual culture, especially with television being the dominant mass communication medium of our time.

Thus, in Unit 1 (Text analysis) the emphasis is on visual and audiovisual texts communicated by means of film and television. The unit consists of several sections and subsections, which can conceptually be grouped into two "parts". In part 1 of the unit, Trudie du Plooy deals with the theoretical issues related to the notion of visual (media) literacy, as well as the perceptual approach to visual communication. In the second part of the unit she deals with the

- application and analysis of pictorial codes in a static filmic shot and photograph
- the creation of picturisation through movements, and
- the combination of audiovisual codes.

An underlying point of departure in the unit is that an understanding of the use of audiovisual codes contributes to an increased awareness of their manipulation in the construction of meaning. Such an understanding contributes to an informed aesthetic appreciation of the content and form of photographic, filmic and televisual texts.

In Unit 2 (Genre analysis) Trudie du Plooy argues that all the media communicate with agreed-upon categorisations of their content: news, drama, religion, education, games, sport and so forth, and, within these categories, a number of subcategories. All of them make use of repetitive conventions in order to meet audience expectations. She defines genre, provides the learner with a conceptual framework for the analysis of genre conventions and provides examples of genre analysis of film, television, radio and journalism. The purpose with this unit is to provide the learner with the parameters and theoretical assumptions to do a genre analysis.

Apart from visual codes, the media communicate primarily with and through the means of language (linguistic codes). The aim of Stefan Sonderling in Unit 3 (Media and language) is to provide the learner with a basic understanding of the role of language in mass communication. He discusses

- the relationship between language and society
- two definitions of language
- the formal aspects of language as a text
- language as social interaction, and the
- social context for the use of language.

Media content comprises stories or narratives. It narrates reality and all the different aspects of reality, be it a society's politics, economics, or whatever. Everything is presented to us in the form of a story. How do we analyse media content from the perspective of seeing it as a narrative?

In Unit 4 (Narrative analysis) David Wigston investigates how stories, or more correctly narratives, are constructed and how we interpret them in order to gain meaning from them. The study of narrative is approached in two ways. In the first, the focus is on what happens in the narrative in order to move the story forwards. In the second approach he establishes how meaning is generated by probing the various levels of meaning found within the narrative.

Film theory

Although we offer Unit 5 (Film theory and criticism) as a separate segment, as with the first four units it concerns media content, in this case the content and form of film. The description and evaluation of film content and form, as practised in the field of film theory, is often seen as the foundation of approaches to the analysis of media representations. The key issues are realistic versus expressionistic representations and the production of meaning and ideology in film texts. I begin with the question: What is film theory? Thereafter, the following are discussed:

- different kinds of film theory
- the difference between film history, film criticism and film analysis
- the value of film theory
- the distinction between expressionism and realism in film art and communication
- the *auteur* theory
- film semiotics, including levels of meaning in film and the communicative functions of film
- contemporary film theory in which the emphasis is on ideology and feminist criticism, and on the psychoanalytical approach to the experience of film.

Media audiences

As far as audience research is concerned, reception theory and analysis is one of the most prolific new areas of studying audiences and their interpretation of messages. As a technique, reception theory has its roots in German reception aesthetics and the encoding/decoding model of reception developed by the Centre for Contemporary Cultural Studies. In this unit (Unit 6) Magriet Pitout explains how the German version of reception theory has been adjusted to study mass media texts with the purpose of illustrating the dialectical relationship between readers and texts. This is followed by a discussion of the polysemic nature of television texts, Stewart Hall's model of preferred reading, Burke's narrative model for the analysis of the mythical functions of a narrative, and the social character of media use.

A popular qualitative form of observation in audience research is ethnography (Unit 7), with its roots in anthropology and urban sociology. Magriet Pitout discusses:

- the assumptions shared by audience ethnography and classic ethnography
- a critical view of the first audience ethnographic studies
- how to plan and conduct ethnographic research
- a critical appraisal of ethnography as a form of observation in media studies.

Unit 8 (The social psychology of media consumption) addresses the psychological and social aspects of media consumption. Magriet Pitout discusses Grossberg, Wartella and Whitney's (1998) view that because researchers have failed to adequately describe the psychological relationship between media products and audience members, we should have a closer look at the psychological state of audiences. These "mind" states include the affective state dimensions such as emotions, moods and pleasures. Furthermore Höijer's (1992; 1998) cognitive dimension, and his emphasis on mental experiences, is considered. This is followed by a discussion of the sociology of media consumption, which includes the physical contexts where we consume messages, and the influence thereof on our interaction with and interpretation of media messages.

In Unit 9 (Audience research) Pitout argues that the previous three units dealt mainly with audience research conducted at universities and colleges and are thus theory-driven. In this unit the emphasis is on pragmatic (practical) attempts to solve specific problems rather than to construct theory. She deals with the focus-group interview and survey research as the most popular standard research methods used to investigate mass media audiences, media workers (e.g. journalists, scriptwriters), employers and employees in organisations, and the users and buyers (audiences) of specific media products.

In the last unit of this section (Media and psychoanalysis) Stefan Sonderling explains the rather esoteric psychoanalytical approach to our understanding of how audiences (or the individual recipient) gain meaning from media texts.

Media production

We conclude the volume with introductions to aspects of media production. As referred to earlier, the aim of this book (both volumes) is not to provide learners with a practical guide but to introduce them to critical theories and analytical approaches in media studies. Thus, the four units on production do not pretend to teach learners practical skills. The purpose is to provide them with a basic knowledge about selected aspects of media production and key concepts in media production.

Corrie Faure divides her introduction to newspaper production (Unit 11) into four sections: a classification and definition of the newspaper; newspaper design; the newspaper organisation; and modern newspaper production. She discusses, amongst others, the following topics:

- the classification of newspapers
- the development of the newspaper industry
- newspaper design and layout
- newspaper organisation
- key personnel in the newsroom
- the functions of newspaper journalists
- the news-gathering process
- the interviewing process, and
- the writing of newspaper reports.

Under newspaper production she also discusses new technological developments and the electronic newspaper. To end the unit, and given South Africa's community media needs, she addresses the importance of community journalism.

For Stefan Sonderling the purpose of Unit 12 (Television production) is to provide the learner with an understanding of the:

- stages of television production
- planning activities undertaken during preproduction
- roles of the people involved in television production
- functions of the television studio
- basics of the television camera
- basics of editing, and
- the basics of video and television programme distribution.

In Unit 13 (Radio production) David Wigston takes a closer look at how radio programmes are put together. His case study is music programmes featured on commercial radio stations, which, according to him, provides the learner with the basic principles of radio programming. He discusses the:

- various sound elements that make up the programmes we hear
- factors that determine programme content
- criteria for the analysis of the structure of a radio programme
- how radio stations create a unique image
- thirteen factors that can be used to improve the success rate of any radio programme
- the unique nature of community radio including the programming requirements of a community station
- the economic viability of the radio station and in this regard the importance and value of programme format.

In Unit 14 (Film production) Beschara Karam introduces the learner to the six fundamentals of film production: production, form, style, cinematographic properties, editing and sound. At the most, the purpose of this unit is to make learners aware of some of the basic concepts in film production. It is important to note that this unit is based predominantly on the following works: David Bordwell and Kristin Thompson's *Film art: an introduction* (1993) and Louis Giannetti's *Understanding movies* (1996).

The volume concludes with two units on how to use television and radio for educational purposes. We decided to include these two units against the background of South Africa's yearning educational needs.

In Unit 15 (Educational media: television), based predominantly on the work of Du Plooy (1997), Beschara Karam investigates different learning theories and approaches applicable to mediated teaching and learning. From a development perspective, she deals with suggested goals or aims; learners; different types of interactions; criteria that ought to be considered when determining the scope and sequence of what is taught/learned; the importance of formulating aims and objectives; and an application of the Pareto principle. Thereafter the adaptability of television as a communication medium is investigated with the focus on four issues, namely the means of distributing educational television (ETV); the educational implications of the means of distribution; the encoding (medium) characteristics; and the importance of television-mediated experiences. A distinction is drawn between the formative and summative evaluation of educational television, with the emphasis on the purpose and value of especially formative evaluation. The unit ends with a discussion of the planning, implementing and evaluating of educational television as a continuous cycle.

Finally, David Wigston explores seven factors that influence education by radio in Unit 16 (Educational media: radio). He defines educational broadcasting by distinguishing between the concepts "educational" and "educative". These concepts are then applied to radio programming. In addition, he distinguishes between formal, informal and nonformal education, with each type making use of a particular strategy. Within informal education by radio he considers using two broad strategies to present programmes - that of open broadcasting versus the use of radio listening groups. The latter is of special importance in a developing context, such as in South Africa. To end the unit, he discusses the procedures to be followed in organising an educational campaign that makes use of radio listening groups as a strategy.

Contextualisation

Although this volume can stand on its own, its full value as a prescribed text in media studies can only be judged in coherence with the preceding volume on institutions, theories and issues. As argued previously, media content, audiences and production can not be isolated from the institutions responsible for the production of media content, and vice versa.

Furthermore, the authors are fully aware of some repetition that may occur. This is mainly due to the same underlying point of departure or perspective on media studies followed by the different authors. The most obvious point of departure throughout this volume is structuralism and semiotics with their emphasis on the production of meaning. This becomes evident in the units on text analysis, genre analysis, language, narrative analyses and film theory, in which, although from different perspectives, the topic of signs, codes, levels of meaning, different kinds of meaning and especially the question of ideology features time and again. Even in the part on audiences, meaning and especially ideological meaning are central topics.

Finally, we are aware of some omissions. In this regard we need to emphasise that this volume together with Volume 1 constitute the learning material of only two of the Department of Communication of the University of South Africa's modules in media studies. Other related modules, within the context of Unisa's broader syllabus in communications science, are media ethics, new media technology, international communication, end-user computing and writing skills for the communication industry.

It further needs to be said that more illustrative material, case studies and detailed research activities could have been included. All this would have influenced the production cost of the book and eventually the price to be paid by learners. For these limitations we try to make good in the two Unisa study guides based on the two volumes of this book. For non-Unisa lecturers and learners, the challenge is to bridge the limitations of this and the preceding volume with their own interpretations, knowledge, illustrations, case studies and research activities and exercises.

In the final analysis, the book is only a beginning; a stepping-stone towards more knowledge and a better understanding of the fascinating world of the media.

In conclusion, the authors are much indebted to the authors of other works on media studies, especially to the seminal works of prominent scholars in the field such as Denis McQuail, Lawrence Grossberg, W James Potter, Herbert Zettl, John-Marie Peters, Stuart Hall, Tim O'Sullivan, Melvin DeFleur, Everette Dennis, John Fiske, Julia T Wood, David Bordwell, Kristin Thomspon, Louis D Giannetti, Arnold de Beer, Keyan Tomaselli, and many others as acknowledged in our lists of sources.

Pieter J Fourie
November 2001

Part A
Media Content

Unit 1
Text Analysis

Unit 2
Genre Analysis

Unit 3
Media and Language

Unit 4
Narrative Analysis

Text Analysis

1

GM (Trudie) du Plooy

Overview

This first unit of Part A focuses on text analysis of mass-media content, with specific emphasis on visual and audiovisual texts communicated by means of films and television. The unit consists of several sections and subsections, which can conceptually be grouped into two "parts". The first part deals with the theoretical issues related to the notion of visual (media) literacy, as well as the perceptual approach to visual communication. The second part deals with the application and analysis of pictorial codes in a static filmic shot and photograph, the creation of picturisation through movements, as well as the combination of audiovisual codes. This second part therefore also includes signs and codes as they are used in films and television.

A point of departure that is centrally argued throughout this unit is that an understanding of the use of audiovisual codes contributes to an increased awareness of their manipulation in the construction of meaning, and that such an understanding contributes to an informed aesthetic appreciation of the content and form of photographic, filmic and televisual texts.

Learning outcomes

At the end of this unit you should be able to conduct research by doing a textual analysis of the signs and codes that are used to create meaning in a

- static filmic shot and photograph, and
- filmic or televisual extract.

1.1 INTRODUCTION

The word text can take on different meanings. On the one hand it refers to the mass-media messages as experienced by a reader. For example, a television soap opera becomes a text when it is watched and enjoyed by the viewers. However, for the purpose of this unit, the word text refers to the form and content of the message itself, which could be in oral, written or graphic languages, using still and moving images, or using multimedia, including computers. Although the terms "text" and "message" are often used interchangeably, O'Sullivan, Hartley, Saunders, Montgomery and Fiske (1996:317) emphasise that "*text* usually refers to a message that has a physical existence of its own". In other words, a text stands detached or separate from the communicator and from the mass-media audiences. Therefore, by having referred to oral languages above as an example of a text, such oral language has to be recorded on an audiotape or transcribed in a written form in order to be treated as a "text".

Having qualified the meaning of text in terms of a message with a physical existence, raises the question: What do we need to know or experience in order to become textually literate?

We present our answers to this question by dividing this unit into two "parts", as stated. First, we deal with the *conceptual* issues and theoretical debates about the notion of literacy as it applies to visual and media literacy. These issues and debates are covered in sections 1.2 and 1.3 below. The second "part" deals with the *application* of the basic codes of contextual media aesthetics, namely lighting, colour, two- and three-dimensional space, time and movement, and sound. Although these codes influence the encoding (or production) of the content of messages, the focus in this unit is on the *analysis* of these codes. This second "part" is dealt with in sections 1.4–1.6.

Based on theoretical models developed by British, Canadian and Australian scholars, the Media Literacy National Leadership Conference, in the United States of America identified the following concepts that ought to be included and considered in the textual analysis of media messages:

1 media messages are constructed;
2 media messages are produced within economic, social, political, historical and aesthetic contexts;
3 the interpretative meaning-making process involved in message reception consists of an interaction between the reader, the text and the culture;
4 media have unique "languages", characteristics which typify various forms, genres and symbol systems of communication;
5 media representations play a role in people's understanding of social reality.

(Aufderheide 1993:2)

The above-listed concepts to a certain extent summarise the units that are found in Part A of this publication. This unit therefore essentially serves as an introduction to the majority of the concepts listed, and deals especially with how media messages are constructed by means of auditory, and especially visual codes.

1.2 MEDIA LITERACY

The diversity of arguments about the meaning of the term literacy, especially as it applies to the mass media, have since the 1980s given rise to the following kinds of questions: Is it a skill? Is it an accumulation of knowledge? Is it a particular cultural perspective of the world? Is it the ability to critically analyse media texts as creators of our view of the world? Or is it an understanding of how media texts reduce readers to becoming consumers of social and other values?

Any attempt to debate and answer the above diverse questions and issues within the confines of a few pages would be superficial. Instead, and with reference to works published by the following scholars: Masterman (1997); Messaris (1994; 1998); Zettl (1990; 1998); Meyrowitz (1998); as well as Evans and Hall (1999), we first deal with different types of media literacy and end this section with the most important assumptions on which media literacy are based.

According to Meyrowitz (1998:96–108), three types of media literacy can be distinguished on the basis of how researchers and analysts view the mass media. Each of these three views will lead to different research questions being asked about the media; will lead to different methods used when doing media research; and consequently will lead to different ways of defining media literacy. These three views of the mass media focus on the content, the form (or grammar), and the medium on a micro-level, as well as in a macro- or *societal* context.

1.2.1 Media content literacy

Content literacy is not necessarily limited to specific communication media, because it focuses on those message elements that can be found in settings that involve interpersonal communication, small-group communication, as well as mass communication and the Internet. These content elements refer to topics, themes, values, ideologies, settings, objects, characters, narratives and genres found in different texts. Accordingly, basic media content literacy requires of a scholar and critic to be able to access and analyse the content of messages in a variety of media.

The kind of research questions that can be asked when undertaking a text analysis, based on this view of media literacy, include the following:

- What is the manifest (or overt) message and what is the latent (or covert) message being communicated?
- How do different content genres influence the construction of content in certain ways? (This research question is addressed in Unit 2.)
- How can the same content (text) be read differently by different individuals? (This research question is addressed from different perspectives, in Part C of this publication.)

Religious leaders, politicians and media critics who address issues such as violence, stereotyping, bias, as well as the manifest and latent content of news, are essentially viewing media texts in terms of their content. This is understandably a popular approach to text analysis, for the following reasons:

1 The content is manifestly accessible and can be broken down into smaller manageable units or codes, which – for the purpose of both quantitative and qualitative text analyses – can be coded, in some instances counted, as well as analysed, using categories such as paragraphs, sentences and verbal phrases or categories such as televisual sequences, scenes and individual camera shots.

2 Content that deals with themes and behaviours (e.g. related to sexism, racism and ideological bias) is not limited to a particular communication medium. For example, evidence of stereotyping may be found to occur in a verbal text recorded during an interpersonal interview or recorded during a public speech, as well as in the way in which a character is portrayed and treated in a television drama.
3 A text analysis that focuses on media literacy in terms of the content of messages therefore enables us to formulate research questions and hypotheses, and investigate any aspect of social life. (In Unit 2, for example, we investigate how genre conventions influence the content of texts and how they also serve as overt and covert forms of persuasion.)

By concentrating only on the content of messages, we deny the relevance of the encoding characteristics of different media. Therefore the second type of media literacy is concerned with how these characteristics contribute to the construction of texts, as well as the construction of meaning.

1.2.2 Media grammar literacy

The use of the term "grammar" in the above subheading suggests that this type of media literacy regards communication media as each having its own so-called "language" – or what Zettl (1998:84) prefers to refer to as "the basic elements of contextual media aesthetics".

Table 1.1 below contains examples of these encoding variables as they apply to the *visual* "languages" that are used in print media and film/television.

Table 1.1 Examples of visual "language" variables: print media versus film/television

Print media	Film/Television
page size and shape	sequence, scene, shot
paper: colour, thickness, texture	still versus moving camera
typeface: designs, size(s), colours	focus versus defocus
column widths	objective versus subjective shots
spacing	zoom versus dolly
paragraph breaks	pan versus track
blank spaces	tilt up versus tilt down
page layout	fade in versus fade out
graphics	cuts versus dissolves
cropping of photographs	single screen versus split-screens
size and shape of images	single image versus multiple-images

Table 1.1 illustrates how each medium has a unique combination of encoding and production variables. Yet some variables can operate in more than one medium. For example, when designing the opening titles for a film or television programme, the attributes of the typeface would have to be considered; when selecting a photograph for the front page of a newspaper, variables such as whether it should be a close-up shot versus long shot or objective versus subjective shot, as well as camera angles have to be considered.

Readers and critics are media grammar literate if they are able to analyse how the encoding characteristics of a particular medium are manipulated to convey a particular perception of the message content. For example, even if a message's content is kept constant (*bomb blast in city centre*), readers' perception of the event, as well as the causes and consequences of the event would differ, depending on whether it is shown from the perspective of the victims, of the perpetrator, of the eye-witnesses, of the rescue team or even from the perspective of a local politician.

Therefore, in order to answer the "how" question (posed above) requires a knowledge and awareness of these production variables, with which we deal in greater detail in sections 1.4–1.6 in this unit.

According to Meyrowitz (1998:102), media grammar has in the past not received as much attention as has media content. One of the main reasons being that in order to analyse the grammar of media texts, an understanding of the workings of the medium as well as a vocabulary which is unique to that medium, is required. For example, in the absence of being educated to recognise and name the different camera shots, a television viewer is not only unaware of their uses, but can also not be expected describe or analyse how these shots influence their perceptions of particular content.

This is an ironic situation, because if the encoding characteristics of a particular text have been used effectively, they will be less noticeable to us as readers or researchers and will inadvertently shift our attention and analyses to the content. The learning outcomes set for this unit are specifically aimed at counteracting the latter tendency.

1.2.3 Medium literacy

Medium literacy – "medium" being used in the singular form – deals with how the nature of a medium influences communication on a micro- and macro-level. Although an in-depth discussion of this approach to media literacy is beyond the scope of this unit, some of its concerns and questions are addressed throughout this module.

On a micro-level, questions are prompted as to why certain interactions (e.g. selling a house) work differently depending on the medium of communication used (e.g. an advertisement that is printed, versus one disseminated via electronic mail)? Or, in an attempt to resolve international conflict, why are face-to-face, round-table discussions preferred as a medium of communication, rather then audio- or video conferencing? What are the differences?

On a macro- or societal level, medium analysis has to consider how social forces, including political and economic forces, contribute to the development of certain media, as well as their effects. For example: How does the increasing use of the Internet influence the organisational structures of corporations and other institutions? How is the promotion of globalisation through the use of the World Wide Web changing the function and role of national governments? What effect is the Internet having on individual users' language and social skills?

These questions address broad social changes and are clearly more abstract than the "content" and "grammar" of texts. However, as Zettl (1998:81–95) argues, we can obtain access to these intellectual and cultural frameworks of media criticism by starting with analyses of the encoding characteristics in relation to the content (and therefore context) of message texts.

1.2.4 Assumptions

Against the background of the above brief overview of three types of media literacy, we conclude this subsection by summarising the assumptions on which media literacy, and especially visual media literacy are based.

- A familiarity with the conventions of a particular medium – so-called media literacy – is a prerequisite for analysing media texts.

  When considering visual communication (e.g. photographs and films) we can argue that making sense of visual images comes naturally – unlike having to be taught how to read and write verbal texts. In other words, the average television viewer ascribes meanings to visual images broadcast during the news, without having learned to differentiate between different camera shots or editing techniques.

  In contrast to the above view, the argument that visual images have an arbitrary relationship with appearances in reality, implies, as Gombrich (1982) does, that if someone has not previously been exposed to a visual image, such as a photograph, he or she may not necessarily make sense of it.
- Media literacy may have general (or wider) cognitive consequences for the reader as scholar and researcher.

  According to this assumption, and in terms of development that occurs as a form of life-long learning, the cognitive knowledge acquired from analysing one type of media text (e.g. television) can contribute to a reader's sensitivity and awareness of how meaning is produced in other texts and settings. These wider cognitive consequences may in addition contribute to the ability to make informed decisions when applying audiovisual codes in formative research of media texts and production situations.
- Media literacy contributes to readers' awareness of how meaning is produced by the media, and consequently minimises the manipulative effects of these media.

  In other words, by acquiring an increased awareness of the manipulation of codes in the construction (production and interpretation) of meaning, this assumption is based on the argument that readers will be less vulnerable when receiving messages with a persuasive or propagandistic intent.

- The above three assumptions (knowledge of conventions, cognitive development and an increased awareness) are prerequisites for an aesthetic evaluation of the content and form of texts, as well as an analysis of mass media on a macro- or societal level.

The conceptual issues about the notion of literacy, especially media literacy, can also be debated from different theoretical perspectives or approaches. In the next section we deal with one such approach, which we apply specifically to visual communication.

1.3 PERCEPTUAL APPROACH TO VISUAL COMMUNICATION

Sensation is something we experience when stimuli from the outside world activate the nerve cells in our sense organs, such as hearing a dog bark or smelling food cooking on the stove in the kitchen. Perception refers to the meanings we almost instantaneously ascribe to the noises, smells, temperatures or sights – as raw stimuli. For example, the barking dog can be perceived as a threat to our safety or the smells from the kitchen may automatically make us realise that the food is in fact burning.

When considering a perceptual approach to visual communication, a distinction can be made between the semiotic approach and the cognitive approach. Both these approaches, according to Lester (1995:61), share two assumptions, namely that

- meaning is influenced by the nature of sensual stimuli (such as the content of a visual image); and
- readers have the ability to assign complex meanings to such images.

We first consider the semiotic approach to visual communication.

1.3.1 The semiotic approach

During the Sydney Olympics in 2000, television viewers throughout the world were greeted by images of the Olympic flame; different uniforms, flags and anthems representing different countries; roaring crowds next to the athletics track; referees' gestures during soccer and hockey matches; and even performers wearing traditional Aboriginal dress – to mention just a few. Each of these sounds, objects, actions or images is a sign if it has meaning beyond the sound, object, action or image. For example, one gesture by a referee is a sign that a goal has been awarded, whereas another gesture signifies that a penalty has been awarded.

Semiotics (called *semiology* in Europe) is derived from the Greek word for a sign (*Semeion*). Contemporary semiotics emerged from the work of two linguists, Ferdinand De Saussure (1959) – a Swiss, and Charles Sanders Peirce (1931–58) – an American, who concentrated on studying how words, through narrative structures, communicate meanings. Further studies of semiotics have since then also been undertaken by the Americans Charles Morris and Thomas Sebeok (1991), the Italian, Umberto Eco (1982) and the French, Roland Barthes (1972; 1977; 1999). The application of semiotics over the years has been diverse and varied, from an analysis of signs and symbols in theatrical performances and in television advertisements, to an analysis of cities as examples of social symbols.

As the meaning of media semiotics is dealt with in greater detail in Fourie (2001: Volume 1, Part B, Unit 10), we briefly mention the main points and assumptions on which this approach to visual communication is based.

Three types of visual signs used to communicate

The meaning of all signs must be learned, of which an iconic sign (or icon) is probably the easiest, because it most closely resembles the "thing" that it represents. An identity photograph is an example of an iconic sign because it contains a direct resemblance to the person's face and therefore forms a representational connection with that person.

Indexical signs, however, do not have a direct resemblance to the object or idea being represented and therefore have to be learned through everyday experiences. The connection between an indexical sign and that which it represents, is often based on logic or common sense. For example, a high temperature registered on a thermometer is an indexical sign that the patient has a fever and is ill. Footprints of a wild animal in the sand are indexical signs that the animal has recently walked through that area. However, in order to assign these meanings to a thermometer or to footprints, we would have had to have previously experienced these signs and their meanings.

The meanings conveyed by symbolic signs, because they are more abstract and rooted in our social and cultural past, have to be taught and usually represent stronger emotional meanings than in the case of iconic or indexical signs. The colours and symbols that appear on the national flags of different countries are examples of symbolic signs that represent the heritages of those nations. In view of the powerful effect created by the symbolism of flags and the loyalties they stimulate, an almost spiritual quality is attributed to them – a national flag becomes the people.

Relationships between a sign and meaning communicated

Different relationships exist between a sign and the meaning that it communicates. An understanding of these relationships is essential, if we are to critically analyse media texts, especially visual texts.

The denotative meaning conveyed by a sign refers to its common-sense meaning. For example, a picture of books on a table as iconic signs, denote the meanings "books" and "table". In contrast, connotative meaning is deduced by the individual reader, which – due to factors such as age, past experience, gender and cultural background – may result in many different meanings. For example, the picture of books on a table can have connotations, such as *learning, authority* and *high culture*. A table is usually found in the centre of many television dramas, such as the gaming table in a *Western*, or the operating table in a hospital series. However, when having books on it, the table can on a connotative level (for some readers) represent a symbol of *intellectual life*.

Connotative meanings are very often described as mythical meanings because they are meanings constructed by society, in support of a particular viewpoint, approach, culture or ideology. The portrayal of women in advertisements as (brainless) sex objects, is an example of a stereotypical myth. Because photographs, films and television are visual media, they tell their mythic stories of good versus evil, or social order versus lawlessness, or group dependence versus individual freedom, by means of visual symbolism. Examples of the ideological values and beliefs of a particular culture can very often be found in comic books and cartoons, such as *Madam & Eve* (Francis, Dugmore & Schacherl 2000), which, by means of both visual and verbal symbols comment on pre- and post-apartheid myths in South Africa.

Based on the above distinction between denotation and connotation, it becomes clear that if a reader interprets a sign differently from the meaning as intended by the communicator, the message will be misunderstood. When such poor or ineffective communication takes place, a relationship of aberrant decoding has taken place.

Signs used as codes

In verbal (spoken or written) texts, one word follows the previous words in a particular order, which means that the narrative is linear. In visual texts, however, a picture's narrative is created by combining and presenting signs in different ways – usually called codes. Visual communication therefore enables communicators to combine signs (as codes) in different ways, to communicate complicated and often abstract ideas. Berger (1991:20–27) suggests that two types of codes can be distinguished, namely metonymic and analogic codes.

- A metonymic code consists of a collection of signs that prompts the reader to interpret meanings on the basis of their associations or assumptions. For example, a character in a local soapie that is portrayed in a living-room with expensive paintings and furniture, would communicate that she is an upper-class citizen. If the same character were situated in a dirty back-street setting, a different image would be communicated – based on readers' assumptions and associations. In other words, a metonymic code implies that the code (e.g. expensive furniture equals upper-class citizenship) already exists in readers' minds, which enables them to make the intended connection.

  A common form of metonymy – called synecdoche – which is often used in visual communication, is created when a part (or partial image) represents a whole. For example, a close-up shot of a hand holding a gun represents the person as a whole, as well as the action which is about to take place. To take two further examples: news items that show the maltreatment of farm workers, or the destruction caused by a street bomb in Cape Town, function as metonyms for crime in our society. A documentary television programme that deals with the problems experienced by two black children during their integration in a previously whites-only school in a particular town, serves as a metonymic code – the two children stand for the whole local black community.

- An analogic code consists of a collection of signs that prompts the reader to make mental comparisons. These codes are usually applied, either as *metaphors* or *similes*.

  A metaphor is based on a relationship between two things, which is suggested through the use of analogy. A metaphor transposes characteristics of one thing onto another, and by suggesting equivalence it *symbolically stands for something else*. For example, a cowboy hat has become a metaphor for the Wild West; the soft drink Coca-Cola has become a metaphor for enjoyment; and an umbrella used as a logo by a South African insurance firm has become a metaphor for protection.

  A simile creates meaning by suggesting that a sign is "as" or "like" something else. *Granny is like an angel* is a verbal example, whereas a picture of pencils bundled together can serve as a simile for a crowd of people. Through personification, human qualities are attributed in this example to the inanimate objects (the pencils). In other words, a simile suggests that the two signs have similar characteristics, namely the *togetherness* of the pencils visually representing and suggesting the *cohesion* of a group of people.

The above two types of codes can further be used and analysed, depending on whether or not they are displaced codes and condensed codes. Displaced codes include those codes that are used to transfer meaning from one sign, or collection of signs, to another (of which above pencils is an example). Advertisements of cigarettes, bottles of liquor and lipsticks, as well as certain cover designs of sex magazine, often displace images of penises with other phallic symbols, based on the assumption that readers will make the link between the product and sexual regeneration.

Condensed codes are produced by combining several signs and in so doing creating a new collective sign. Television advertisements and music videos, in which multiple images are portrayed, often combined with fast cuts, graphics and colours, are examples of condensed codes being used to produce often complex messages.

In the above subsection we have given a brief overview of the semiotic approach, as part of a perceptual approach to visual communication. In the next section we consider the cognitive approach, which is also closely related to the perceptual approach.

1.3.2 The cognitive approach

The cognitive approach to visual perception treats perception as a process involving mental events or actions. According to this approach, we perceive and ascribe meanings to that which we perceive (e.g. see or hear) on the basis of association. Such associations can be based on past experiences (learned behaviour) or assumptions. For example, some of us may interpret the meaning of an image of a pipe with security and authority, based on our association with father figures in our past. Whereas, others may interpret the same image to mean complacency and peace, based on an association with traditions of smoking a peace pipe.

As no two people have experienced exactly the same lives, it stands to reason that visual perception is personalised and subjective. However, we argue that such differences are being minimised as we grow older, because we are exposed to the same mass-media texts. In other words, those memories and associations that are based on our experiences via mass-media texts may be different, but will not necessarily be highly personalised or uniquely subjective.

The relevance of mental activities to textual analysis has to be emphasised. These activities show that meaning is not only situated in the manipulation of visual and other codes, but that meaning is also situated in what (e.g. selective perception) readers bring to the mediated experience.

In addition to memory, projection, expectations, selectivity, habituation, salience, dissonance, cultural influences and words are other mental activities, which – according to the cognitive approach – can influence our visual perception. These mental activities are briefly dealt with below.

- Psychologists use (Rorschach) ink blot tests to uncover an individual's personality traits, based on the assumption that we project something of ourselves (e.g. state of mind, characteristic ways of perceiving the world or behaving in it) on to these oddly shaped ink blots. This mental activity – called *projection* – means that some readers make sense and ascribe meanings to vague, ambiguous, and unstructured objects or images, whereas others find the same objects or images meaningless. (This explains why some people can read a person's *fortune* on the basis of tealeaves in a cup, whereas others perceive nothing more than just tealeaves.) Whilst watching a card game being played in a television programme, one viewer may read the cards as being a King, Queen or Knave, whilst another viewer may read them as representing the Father, Mother and the Ego. Projective techniques, involving a series of pictures about which a subject must tell a story, or various forms of play, involving objects such as a doll's house, are often used in formative mass-media research. Such techniques are also sometimes used during the concept testing for advertisements or educational programmes.
- Readers' visual perception can also be impaired if their preconceived *expectations* and/or *selectivity* in perceiving, result in focusing on certain aspects of a visual message and ignoring others. For example, television viewers have a preconceived expectation of how a news presenter should conventionally be dressed. Therefore, unless that expectation is contradicted, viewers do not really notice the dress worn each evening. Most of our visual perception is an unconscious act that takes place automatically. It is therefore not an uncommon experience to travel to work and to selectively concentrate on the traffic and road signs, without processing other visual images. This selectivity of focusing only on important details is also reinforced by a mental activity called *habituation*. We develop habits, which through prolonged practice become activities that become relatively automatic. For example, when shopping for groceries we expect to find a particular brand of beans in its usual place. We selectively ignore the competing brands on either side of the shelves and habitually add the tin of beans to our shopping basket. In so doing, we have selectively ignored many other visual stimuli.

- People who are trained as graphic artists or engineers may read more meanings into graphic drawings and other visual designs than the average person may. For example, only someone with training in architecture will be able to differentiate between the various structural parts of a drawing or picture of a church, such as the flying buttress, clerestory, triforium, spandrel and nave. This example illustrates how *salience* can affect our perception, because a stimulus that has meaning for a person will be noticed more by that person.
- *Dissonance* is a term that originated in music, which refers to an unpleasant noise that is created when two notes are sounded together and do not form a harmonious sound. When applied to perception, dissonance is created when two or more stimuli compete for our attention, such as following a television programme and reading the evening newspaper at the same time. Visual messages in which condensed codes are used, are apt to minimise our perceptual abilities because they have the potential of causing dissonance.
- *Cultural influences*, as manifested in the way we talk, eat, dress, behave socially and practise different religious beliefs, also influence our visual perception. Random, idiosyncratic and shared meanings are three possible ways in which we can ascribe different meanings to visual codes. *Random* communication means that it does not necessarily convey any specific meaning, such as the physical contact being shown between a dentist and a patient in a television drama. Idiosyncratic communication is normally unique to an individual, such as stroking something to relieve tension. Despite the fact that actions, such as rubbing one's nose or scratching one's head, are performed unintentionally, when observed they can be incorrectly interpreted as signs of stress, discomfort or irritation. *Shared* meanings are often culture-specific. Examples are found in proxemics (especially the distance between two people while they are conversing) and haptics (e.g. physical contact as part of greeting rituals). If unaware of these shared meanings in another culture, we could easily misinterpret such behaviour in filmic texts as *distant and aloof*, or *too close for comfort*.
- Although visual perception concentrates on ascribing meaning to visual images, most of our thoughts are formulated in verbal language. Therefore, when *words* are combined with visual images, they may directly influence the meaning ascribed to and remembered of mediated images.

Based on the above overview, we need to remind ourselves that the following are questions that we may not ignore whilst analysing details found in the content and especially in the encoding characteristics of a text:

- Does the text (overtly or covertly) make provision for or even manipulate the influence which culture and previously learned behaviour may have on a reader's perception? For example, is the association between certain objects (e.g. expensive jewellery) and certain meanings (e.g. an élite social status) perpetuated?
- To what extent do words support, accentuate and therefore complement and elaborate on the visual communication; or to what extent do words regulate or even contradict the visual communication?

We are continuously surrounded by a visual environment that could vary from clothes, furniture, buildings, people and moving vehicles, to the plants, birds and other animals found in nature. Being surrounded by such visually perceivable artefacts in almost every aspect of our lives, implies that they can reflect and affect our attitudes towards happiness, politics, health, success, culture, business and whatever else may be significant in our lives. The meanings that we ascribe to perceptions of our visual environment may range from a condition or state, an action or an event, to a quality. However, to ensure that effective communication takes place requires us (as readers and analysts) to make the same transfer, from the visual image to the intended meaning, as premeditated by the communicator. The nature of this transfer process is dependent on many variables, such as our perceptual abilities, cognitive thought, memory, emotions, expectations, attitudes, involvement, the context in which communication occurs, and our past experiences.

A premise of this unit is that perception, or the reception of visual sensory data, is an active process that involves the processes of searching, selecting and comparing. It is therefore acknowledged that the transference of meaning by means of visual codes can be influenced by the reader's attitude and expectations; how selectively s/he perceives, which may be linked to defence mechanisms; and his/her projections, which can be linked to fantasy and gratifications sought. It is against this background that the relevance of aspects such as figure-ground perception and psychological closure are dealt with in the sections that follow. Nevertheless, the one variable which can also influence the communication process, and which is the main focus in the next sections, is the properties (or characteristics) of the mediated codes by means of which film and television as mass media communicate.

1.4 PICTORIAL CODES IN A STATIC FILMIC SHOT AND PHOTOGRAPH

In this section the following codes are dealt with in terms of the conceptual (not technical) aspects of production, with the primary focus on their meaning construction when conducting a text analysis: lighting, colour, field forces within the shot or frame (main directions, magnetism of the frame and attraction of mass, asymmetry of the shot or frame, figure-ground perception, psychological closure, vectors), balance, depth and volume; area orientation (aspect ratio, size of the object), lenses and focus, basic camera shots and camera viewpoint.

A single shot or photograph of a person is an icon that represents the person according to the principle of *similitude*. In other words, a *similarity* exists between the sign and the person. However, from a semiotic perspective, the meaning created, even by a single, static shot, is governed by a complex set of rules and codes.

Codes organise our perceptions and create structures of meaning, which sometimes means that film and television producers draw on meaning systems that already exist among their mass audiences. Because of the existence of shared-meaning systems, and because mediated messages draw on codes found in other similar messages, certain rules that guide interpretation have been established over the years. Communicators who use a camera as medium can and do convert existing meaning systems into modified meanings to suit their particular intentions. The production of meanings (sign values) is best illustrated in advertising, where it is the communicator's intention to create or reinforce an association between a product or service and abstract meanings (e.g. between a particular beer and friendship). In other words, mediated visual codes sell moods, feelings, lifestyles and shape readers' self-concepts. (This so-called selling of values is further discussed in Unit 2.)

In this discussion, and with reference to Fourie (1988:32–34), we make an artificial distinction between codes of represented form; and codes of visual representation, or codes of content. The most important visual code of form – in the case of a static shot or photograph – is that of the camera point of view. Content codes include thematic, *mise-en-scène*, colour and lighting codes; in addition to nonverbal behavioural codes such as kinesics and proxemics.

1.4.1 Lighting as a code of content

When thinking about light and darkness, we often associate light with clarity, warmth and/or security, whereas darkness can be associated with resting, coldness, unpredictability and/or tension. When considering lighting as a visual code of content, we exclude internal light sources, such as the electronic television beam, which makes the perception of projected impulses possible, and we deal specifically with the light captured by the lens.

When key, back or fill lights are used to create artificial lighting effects, this may be done for various reasons, for example to distinguish the actual shape of an object, contours and/or texture. The tonality of a film is also determined by the proportions of *light and dark* in a scene. The latter is an important code in creating emotional connotations, atmosphere and suspense. For example, a simplistic distinction may be made between low-key lighting (e.g. drama) versus high-key lighting (e.g. comedy, a musical or news broadcasts).

Notan and chiaroscuro are traditionally distinguished (Zettl 1990: 39) as two types of external lighting. Notan lighting is characteristically low in contrast, with all the areas captured by the shot being equally bright, including the background (see Figure 1.1 for an illustration). Due to the nonselectiveness of notan lighting, visual images and settings portrayed in this manner are usually associated with neutrality and objectivity, such as a television news studio.

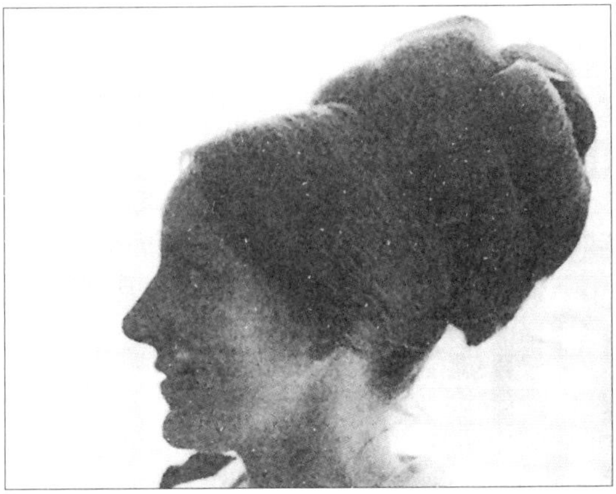

Figure 1.1 Notan lighting

Figure 1.2 Rembrandt lighting

Figure 1.3 Cameo lighting

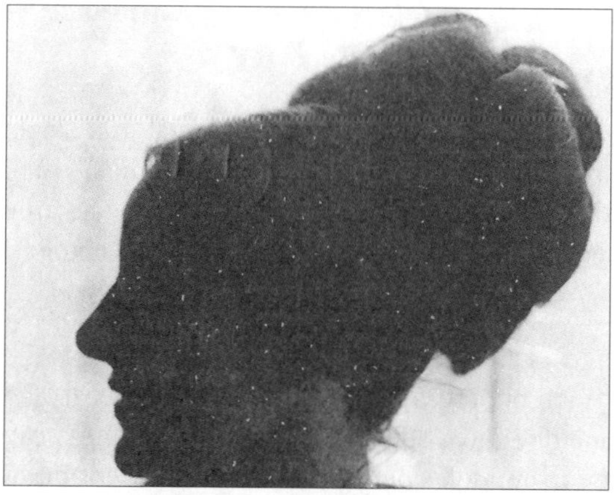

Figure 1.4 Silhouette lighting

Chiaroscuro lighting, on the other hand, refers to *selectively* lighting certain areas of the content. Three types can be distinguished. The first is Rembrandt lighting, named after the Dutch painter Harmens Rembrandt's (1606–1669) dramatic and compositional use of contrasts of light, shadows and half tones. When Rembrandt lighting is used, it means that certain areas are illuminated, whereas others are left either in semi- or complete darkness (see Figure 1.2 for an illustration).

The second type of chiaroscuro lighting is called cameo lighting, which means that a figure or object in the foreground is well lit – like a cameo – against a dark background (see Figure 1.3 for an illustration). Just as gestures are frequently used as indexical signs, so too Rembrandt and cameo lighting often function as indexical signs – pointing to and focusing attention on selective elements of the content within the frame.

The third type is called silhouette lighting, whereby the frame or contours of a figure or shape is made visible against a brighter background (see Figure 1.4 for an illustration).

Unlike the objectivity and neutrality associated with content depicted by means of notan lighting, chiaroscuro lighting tends to draw the audience's attention to the thematic or emotive meaning of the content. Compare for example Figure 1.1 (notan lighting) with Figure 1.4 (silhouette lighting). Because the content is *not* evenly lit, chiaroscuro lighting can be used to make a scene appear more realistic and/or it can be used to add to a compositional orientation by balancing the different visual elements in relation to one another.

1.4.2 Colour as a code of content

Colour is part of our daily life-world. For example, according to international road traffic sign systems, *yellow* signifies temporary signs such as those used at roadworks and to indicate changes in the roadways; while *brown* signifies tourism signs that deal with facilities, services and tourist attractions. These examples clearly show that colours can be used to convey and clarify *information*.

However, colours work on our subconscious and each colour can produce an emotional reaction of its own. For example, in Western cultures *red* usually attracts attention and indicates strength and warmth. This also shows that colours are associated with temperatures (such as warmth and coldness). Our perception of colours and their meanings (moods, energies or dramatic qualities) are influenced by attributes such as hue, saturation and brightness, as well as factors such as surface reflection, surrounding colours and lighting techniques (Zettl 1990:55–68).

Preferences for certain colours are also influenced by demographics, such as gender, age, social group and past experiences. It has been said that lower social classes prefer stronger or brighter colours, whereas upper classes prefer lighter colours. Particularly in advertising (in Western cultures) it is assumed that the use of certain colours can influence consumers' reactions to the product being advertised, as well as their perceptions of symbolic meanings (abstract concepts) such as quality, value and purity. Studies have shown (Russell & Verrill 1986:516) that coffee would be perceived to be *mild*; a *weaker blend; too strong;* and *rich and full-bodied*, depending on whether the coffee is brewed and poured from a blue, a yellow, a brown or a red pot respectively. These examples, however, refer to the symbolic meanings that we learn to associate with certain colours; and because the meanings have to be *learned*, they are subject to traditions – traditions which may vary from one context, period or culture to another.

1.4.3 Field forces within the shot, or frame

Whether the purpose is to clarify and/or to intensify the meaning visualised in a single shot, according to Zettl (1990:101–127), six field forces influence the way in which visual codes are used: main directions; magnetism of the frame and attraction of mass; the asymmetry of the frame; figure-ground perception; psychological closure; and vectors.

Main directions

The main directions within a single shot or photograph are horizontal (X-axis) and vertical (Y-axis). If the content stresses one direction, such as horizontal, calmness can be conveyed (see Figure 1.5), in contrast to the high energy, dynamism, power and/or excitement suggested by the vertical directions as illustrated in Figure 1.6.

Figure 1.5 Horizontal balance, conveying calmness

If we were to tilt the horizontal plane, this could convey meanings such as energy, progress, failure or even a feeling of discomfort. (Compare Figure 1.7, which, due to the tilted *horizon*, conveys a feeling of greater instability than Figure 1.6.)

Figure 1.6 Vertical balance, conveying high energy

Figure 1.7 A tilted horizon

Magnetism of the frame and attraction of mass

The top and side edges, as well as corners of a frame, tend to exert a *magnetic pull* on elements positioned closest. For example, in Figure 1.8 the wedding couple are standing at a comfortable distance (proxemics) from one another, *because* space has been left on the sides, and especially because *looking room* (or nose room) has been included on the left-hand side (that is, the direction in which they are looking).

Figure 1.8 A comfortable space between the people and the frame

However, by moving to a closer shot (and in so doing *removing* the spaces on the sides), the magnetism of the side edges is increased, as shown in Figure 1.9, almost pulling the couple apart. The magnetism of the left-hand side is particularly prominent, because of the limited looking room (or space) in front of the bridegroom. The magnetism of the frame is a significant force when doing a text analysis of camera shots and is further discussed below.

Figure 1.9 Magnetism of the sides of the frame

Asymmetry of the shot or screen

In cultures where pictures are read from left to right, then, according to Zettl (1990:110–111), Figure 1.10 represents a graphic up-diagonal; and Figure 1.11 a graphic down-diagonal.

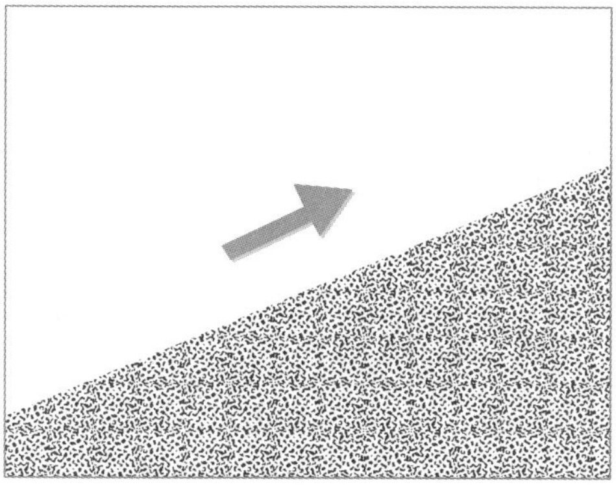

Figure 1.10 Up-diagonal

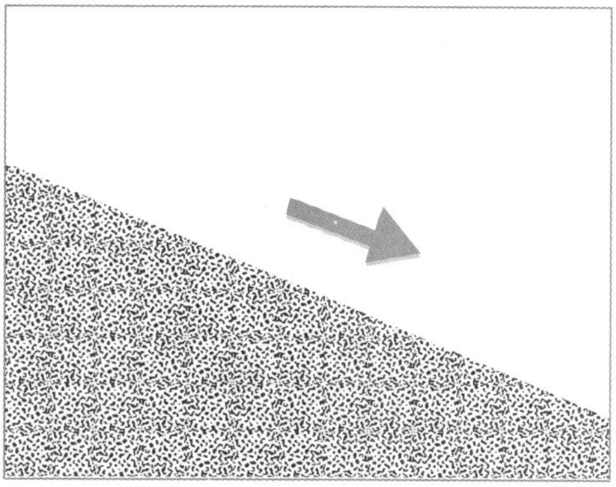

Figure 1.11 Down-diagonal

In other words, if communicators want to reflect the power and stamina which a mountaineer requires, or the effort and struggle which a refugee is experiencing while pushing all his belongings on a home-made wagon, they would reflect the climber or refugee moving and facing *against* the down-diagonal (see Figure 1.12). By having to work against or having to overcome the down-diagonal, the meaning conveyed is that the person depicted as moving from right-to-left *uphill*, requires strength, effort or courage.

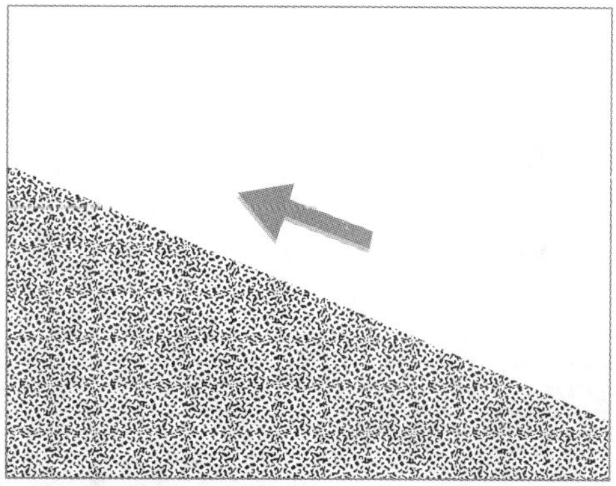

Figure 1.12 Challenging the down-diagonal

Figure-ground perception

Look at Figure 1.13: are these stone pillars or are they the outlines of nude figures? This is an illustration of the figure-ground phenomenon of perception and interpretation, which means that we tend to see (perceive) a figure as if it appears in front of a background. Therefore, in the example in Figure 1.13, what we regard to be the *figure* and what we regard to be the *ground* (or background) will determine whether we see stone pillars (as the figures) or whether we see nude figures (as the figures).

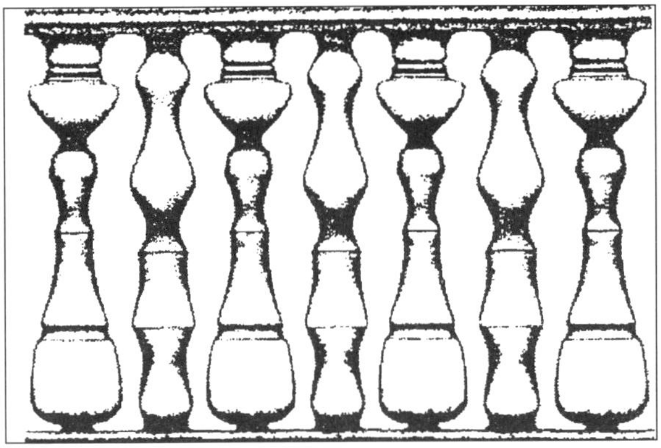

Figure 1.13 Figure and ground (Adapted from McDermott [sa])

When interpreting Figure 1.14 the woman is perceived as the figure and the building as the background. However, a closer shot changes the figure and background relationship. Figure 1.15, for example, shows that the woman (who was previously the figure) now becomes the background, with the mug as the figure. The change in figure-ground relations created by Figure 1.15 alters the meaning presented because the focus shifts to a new figure.

Figure 1.14 Woman-and-building as figure-ground

Figure 1.15 Mug-and-woman as figure-ground

Psychological closure

When presented with visual information that contains gaps or missing details, we tend to fill in the missing parts to obtain a complete image. This perceptual activity is called psychological closure, which is based on the Gestalt principle, in terms of which our eyes naturally tend to organise, for example a series of dots into a coherent pattern.

According to Lester (1995:53–57), psychological closure is based on the principles of proximity, similarity and continuity. According to these principles we will combine those elements which appear closer to one another (*proximity*); we will group similarly shaped elements together (*similarity*); and we will try to make connections between letters or symbols to create a dominant line, shape or pattern (a *continuity*), rather than detached sections. In Figure 1.16, for example, we see four narrow columns, rather than three fat columns, due to the proximity of the lines (and attraction of mass).

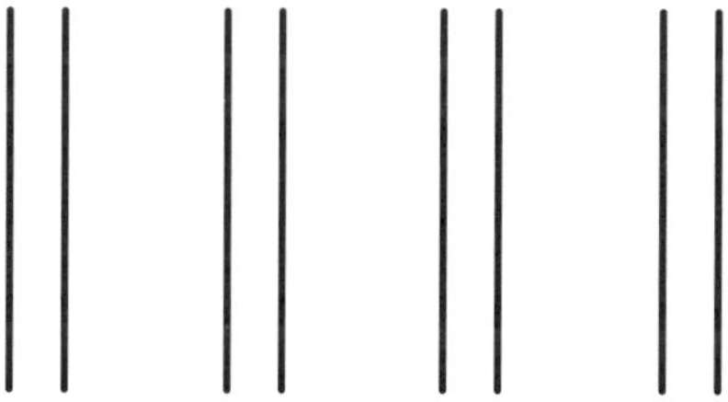

Figure 1.16 Proximity as a principle of psychological closure

Vectors

Vectors are directional forces which are placed within the frame in such a way that readers' eyes are led from one point to another; or to some directional orientation, inside or outside the frame. Zettl (1990:119–125) distinguishes between graphic, index and motion vectors, as three main types of vectors.

Graphic vectors are created by lines or objects. For example, the pole in Figure 1.7 represents a graphic vector, which guides readers' eyes upwards to the sky or downwards to the person in the foreground. Index vectors are created by something (e.g. an arrow) or someone pointing (or looking) in a specific direction. In Figure 1.17 the direction in which the man is looking and pointing leads readers' eyes beyond the frame to the left. According to the Peircean typology of signs (icon, index and symbol), such index vectors are indexical signs, because through contiguity the thing or person pointing relates to the person or object that is being pointed at.

Figure 1.17 Pointing and looking as index vectors

Figure 1.18 Graphic and index vectors combined

In Figure 1.18 the rifle (graphic vector) leads readers' eyes to the space above. The lines of the wall tiles, paper towel, curtains and open oven door (more graphic vectors) lead our eyes horizontally to the woman, and the direction in which she is looking (index vector) returns our attention to the rifle.

A motion vector cannot be illustrated by means of a still picture, and is created by something or someone actually moving in front of a camera and/or by the camera's movement (discussed in section 1.5 below).

The meanings which readers ascribe to vectors can differ, depending on what types of vectors are used (graphic, index or motion) and in the case of index and motion vectors, whether their *directions* continue, converge or diverge.

Figure 1.19 illustrates *continuing* index vectors, as both people are *looking* (index vector) in the *same* direction. Continuous index vectors are also displayed in Figure 1.17 because the directions in which the man points and looks are the same. Continuing vectors, as are found in these two examples, emphasise the importance of what is being looked at, even if the object or person is outside the frame. In the case of film/television, that object or person would in all likelihood be shown in the subsequent shot.

Converging vectors are best illustrated by a shot of two people facing one another whilst conversing, because the fact that they are looking *towards* one another means that the index vectors point at each other. The use of converging vectors can contribute to creating closure, or conveying a feeling of togetherness. However, if the context is confrontational then converging vectors can contribute to the fact that conflict between the elements or people is heightened.

Figure 1.19 Continuing (index) vectors

In contrast to converging vectors, diverging vectors are illustrated in Figure 1.20. The woman sitting on the ground is looking in the *opposite* direction from the women who appear behind her. Depending on the context in which such diverging vectors are used, they could emphasise separation, opposition or disagreement between the elements or parties depicted.

Two or more index vectors can be structured or positioned in such a way so as to create vector structures, which are referred to as *direct focus* or *indirect focus*. A shot of two people (who appear in the same shot) looking at the same object, is an example of direct focus. In the case of indirect focus, one or more index vectors are *redirected* by an intermediary before reaching the target object. For example, in Figure 1.21 the two women on the left are looking at the woman on the right (intermediary) who is looking at the ballot paper (target object).

Figure 1.20 Diverging vectors

Figure 1.21 Index vectors structured as indirect focus

Direct focus is used to guide a reader's eyes to the target object, such as a product being advertised. Whereas indirect focus, although it could be used for the same purpose (to focus attention on the target object), can also contribute to prolonging conflict or to increasing tension between the individuals depicted.

1.4.4 Balance as a code of content

The changes in lighting, colour and the shape and location of the content of a shot in relation to factors such as main directions, magnetism of the frame and attraction of mass, the asymmetry of the frame, figure-ground perception, psychological closure, and vectors, all contribute to structuring the balance. For example, Figure 1.5 illustrates what Zettl (1990:155) calls "stabile balance", because the graphic elements are structured symmetrically. On the other hand, Figure 1.6 illustrates a neutral balance, because the elements are arranged asymmetrically, yet quite ordinarily, in the frame. However, in the third type of balance (labile balance) the elements of the content are extremely tilted and unbalanced, such as illustrated in Figure 1.22.

The balance created by the framing of a shot must correspond with the particular visual moment in a particular context. The choice of one of these three types of balance would therefore be motivated by whether the communicator wants to convey stability, neutrality or instability.

1.4.5 Depth and volume as content codes

In contrast with television and film, a photograph represents a *static* event (people and artefacts). When considering the codes of content, a number of codes can be manipulated to artificially create a feeling of depth (Z-axis) and volume on a surface that is two-dimensional (without any depth), namely volume duality and graphic depth factors.

Figure 1.22 Labile balance

Volume duality

When reconsidering Figure 1.14 the woman and building represent *positive* volume in that their appearance has substance – it can be touched, whereas the cloudless sky in the background represents *negative* space. Volume duality, therefore refers to the way in which positive and negative volumes are combined, with the intention of creating the illusion of depth.

Graphic depth factors

Factors that create the illusion of depth (without movement) on a two-dimensional surface, for example a photograph, are referred to as graphic depth factors.

The most obvious graphic factor contributing to the creation of depth is the positioning of elements so that they *overlap* one another: the element that is partially covered is interpreted as being behind the one in front. A second factor, closely related to the latter overlapping of planes, is the *relative size* of the elements or images. If the normal size of an element is known (such as that of the human body), those images which appear smaller will be perceived to be further away; while those which are larger will seem to be closer. Figure 1.23 illustrates how both these graphic factors contribute to our perception of depth. Notice how the drum majorettes' bodies overlap and how their relative sizes differ.

Height in plane is the third graphic factor that contributes to readers' depth perception and refers to an interpretation of an object or element as being further away, or more distant, the higher it is positioned in the picture in relation to the horizon. Figure 1.24 illustrates this graphic factor: the positioning of the mounds of earth high in the picture field makes them appear to be distant and also helps to emphasise the difference in size compared with the railway trucks. The fourth factor, linear perspective, is shown by the way in which the vertical and horizontal lines converge and seem to move closer to one another in the distance (as in Figure 1.24). The point where these

Figure 1.23 Overlapping planes and relative sizes

lines converge is called the *vanishing point*, which will be either below the horizon (bird's-eye view), or above the horizon, if the camera's position and angle is changed to a worm's-eye view.

Look at Figure 1.24 again, and observe how much more detail we can see in the foreground (e.g. the patterns on the dunes and the texture of the trucks); this clarity diminishes and becomes greyer as we look into the distance. These differences in the clarity of detail and in brightness (called aerial perspective) can also enhance the illusion of depth when skilfully manipulated.

In addition to the manipulation of colours, such as using less saturated colours to signify distance, light and *shadows* are very often used to create the illusion of depth. In Figure 1.1, for example, the *absence* of any shadows minimises the volume or depth. It makes the picture look "flat" (which is another way to describe notan lighting). In Figure 1.23, the shadows are *attached* to the people depicted, which adds to readers' perception of depth. (Notice how the shadows are attached to their feet.) The *cast* shadows in Figure 1.14, on the other hand, give greater prominence to volume and depth. (Notice, in Figure 1.14, how far removed the figure's cast shadow is from her body, when compared with the attached shadows in Figure 1.23.)

Lastly, one other graphic code needs to be considered, namely adding lines and lettering to a photograph. In news reportage and advertising, for example, it is particularly important to realise that the headline, slogan or caption which is added to a static shot, can signify and define different relationships between the *images* of the event depicted or product being advertised, and the *meanings* conveyed. (These relationships are further discussed in section 1.6.2, in this unit, as well as in Unit 2.)

Figure 1.24 Height in plane, relative sizes and linear perspective

1.4.6 Area orientation as a code of form

A still photographer can exercise a number of choices in the orientation of a single shot or image, including two structural codes, namely *aspect ratio* and *size of the object.*

Aspect ratio

The form or shape of a photograph, in addition to its aspect ratio (the height and width), could be square, vertical, horizontal, round or even irregular. The shape or frame in Figure 1.5, for example, is horizontal in order to accommodate the horizontal orientation of the building, in contrast to the vertical shape or frame used in Figure 1.6 to accommodate the vertical nature of the content.

Size of the object

When interpreting the size of visualised objects, readers use previous knowledge of the object (e.g. the size of a normal chair); the clues reflected by the environment that surrounds the object and, more particularly, the human body.

For example, we know the normal size of a petrol pump. It is only when a human hand clasps the pump and a child is shown looking down at the pump, that we are able to interpret the real size of the object. The size of a person or object is also directly influenced by the use of different lenses, and by changing the focus and the framing of the actual shot.

1.4.7 Lenses and focus as codes of form

In addition to the graphic depth factors discussed above, the use of a camera lens in a normal, narrow-angle or wide-angle position also influences our perception of positive and negative volumes and, more particularly, our perception of depth. The narrow-angled lens position (long focal length lens) reflected in Figure 1.25, tends to intensify the close proximity of the stables, thereby suggesting cramped conditions.

The normal lens position used in Figure 1.26, on the other hand, reflects the perspective and relative sizes of the stables and horses as we would normally see them.

In contrast, a wide-angle (short focal length) lens distorts readers' normal depth perception by placing more emphasis on elements or people in the foreground (as shown in Figure 1.27).

Figure 1.25 Narrow-angle shot

Figure 1.26 Normal lens position

Figure 1.27 Wide-angle shot

As discussed above, when analysing a photograph according to the principles of aerial perspective (whereby the brightness and clarity of detail diminishes in the background), we may find that selective focus has been used to counteract the natural aerial perspective. In other words, the communicator can use the camera's focus to place emphasis on or isolate the foreground (as in Figure 1.28), or the middle ground, or the background (as in Figure 1.29).

Figure 1.28 Focus on the foreground

In Figure 1.28 the camera focus differentiates the person and rifles in the foreground from the persons behind. Despite the fact that they all share the same proximity, this camera technique differentiates between the person in the foreground and the others and, depending on the context in which this shot is used, could (in addition) signify that the person in focus in the most important. However Figure 1.28 also contains an interesting combination of codes of content. The focus on the person in the foreground is not obvious at first glance, because it is counteracted by the selective *lighting* of one of the people in the background, and because of the vertical graphic vectors created by the rifles – pointing at the person in the background. Consequently, *despite* the camera's focus on the person in the foreground, readers' attention is initially drawn to the person (out of focus) in the background.

Selective focus is also used in Figure 1.29, but to create a different effect. The focus is on the person in the *background*, which – depending on the context – could be to

- differentiate between the person focused on in the background and the two people who appear in the foreground, or
- signify importance, conflict or superiority of the person in the background.

Figure 1.29 Focus on the background

From a semiotic perspective, we could say that focus (in contrast to out-of-focus) is a spatial (symbolic) metaphor for *significance*. Nevertheless, our interpretations cannot solely be determined by camera focus, because – as illustrated in Figure 1.29 – the denotative, connotative and symbolic meanings conveyed would depend on the indexical and symbolic meanings that readers assign to these signs. In both the pre- and post-apartheid eras in South Africa, the icons of a white uniformed man and a black man (with a clenched fist) still convey symbolic meanings, such as oppression and liberation.

From the above discussion and illustrations it becomes clear that lighting, colour, field forces within the frame, balance, depth and volume, area orientation, as well as camera lenses and focus, are codes of content and form, which can be used to *differentiate* between elements or sections of a shot or to *connect* the content and form into a whole.

1.4.8 Basic camera shots as visual codes of form

Figures 1.30–1.35 illustrate the names and characteristics of basic camera shots used when framing shots (and which are conventionally also used in film and television productions). The *closer* shots (see Figures 1.30, 1.31 and 1.32) convey meaning according to the principle of synecdoche, in terms of which the whole, whether it be a person, an object or scene, is represented by a part. (See section 1.3.1, in this unit, for a further discussion of the latter principle.)

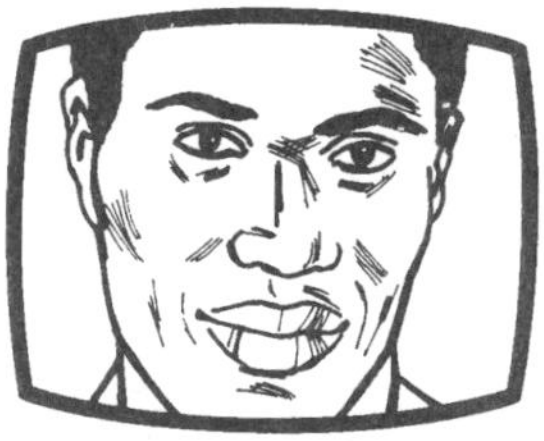

Figure 1.30 Extreme close-up (or big close-up) shot

ECU – an extreme close-up shot (also called *BCU* – big close-up shot) shows a person's lips, nose, eyes; or a logo in an advertisement; or a small section of an artefact, such as a door handle. This shot is used mainly for impact and/or to show detail.

Figure 1.31 Close-up shot

CU – A close-up shot is a tight shot which shows a person's face, including the shoulder line and the top of the head; or the whole product in an advertisement; or a larger section of an artefact, such as a door. Based on the assumption that the eyes reflect the emotions of the soul, this shot is often used to convey emotion. As every blemish on the skin is clearly perceptible, it can also be a cruel shot.

Figure 1.32 Medium close-up shot

MCU – A medium close-up shot frames a person from about the chest level with room above the head; or shows the whole product with some background in an advertisement; or shows a still larger section of an artefact, such as the door and adjacent window of a building. When used to frame a person on television, it is frequently referred to as a *talking-head shot*.

Figure 1.33 Medium shot

MS – A medium shot usually shows a person from the waist upwards and shows more details of the setting or background than in the case of an MCU. Since this shot combines someone's facial expression with the background, it should allow for *looking room* (also called *nose room*).

Figure 1.34 Medium-long shot

MLS – In this shot, a person's head is placed in the hypothetical upper third, without touching the upper edge of the frame, with the lowest point of the frame being above or below the knees. This shot includes more visual information of the setting and allows room or space in which a person can move.

Figure 1.35 Long shot

LS – A long shot (also known as the *far shot*) shows the full length of a person; or shows a product in an advertisement from a distance; or an artefact such as a house as a whole. This shot (or *XLS – extra-long shot*) is normally used to establish the location, hence the label, an *establishing shot*.

1.4.9 Building screen space – camera viewpoint

When building screen space, we are dealing with a particular *viewpoint*, which can be influenced by the actual shot or frame (e.g. a close-up shot versus a long shot) and by the event or context of the particular shot. In other words, the camera viewpoint can vary according to the field view and the amount of visual information that is in/excluded in the shot and the *positioning* of the camera in relation to object/person/scene which is filmed.

By adjusting the camera's viewpoint, a variety of angles can be created, which not only provides a particular point of view but which also intensifies the emotive qualities of the visual event. For example, Figure 1.36 reflects a viewpoint which enables readers to "look at" people (called objective camera).

In comparison, in Figure 1.37 (subjective camera) readers no longer look at the people, but, due to the camera's position, readers feel as if they actively participate in what the people in the shot are doing. A subjective camera view means that the content (that which appears in front of the camera) is shown from one or more of the character's point of view. This camera position is frequently used for instructional and marketing purposes (e.g. in demonstrations of how a machine works), or to increase the tension in a dramatic scene, because it increases the readers' involvement.

Qualities such as superiority and inferiority can also be suggested by placing the camera *below* or *above* the eye-level position in relation to the subject that is being filmed. For example, Figure 1.38 shows a shot of two people at eye-level, while in Figure 1.39 the same people are depicted far above eye-level, literally looking down on them. The importance, power or authority of objects, persons or events can be diminished by positioning the camera *above* eye-level (bird's-eye view) and by looking down with the camera. On the other hand, the reverse impression or emotive qualities can be created when positioning the camera *below* the eye-level position (worm's-eye view).

Figure 1.36 Objective camera

Figure 1.37 Subjective camera

When comparing Figure 1.38 with Figure 1.39, it is clear how a change in camera angle and position – as codes of form – enables the communicator to manipulate the meanings conveyed by the represented content.

Figure 1.38 Positioning a camera on eye-level

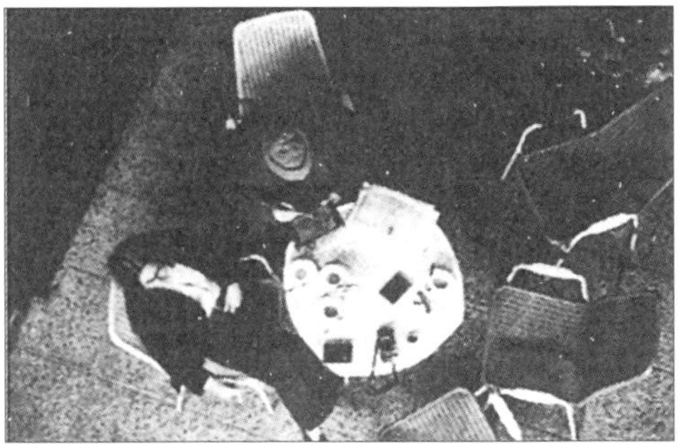

Figure 1.39 Positioning a camera above eye-level

The codes and conventions that are particularly important in television news, are the selection of particular camera shots, and the syntagmatic combination of shots and sequences. By, for example, selecting an eye-level camera position when recording an interview with a national leader, the camera conveys the impression of being a passive onlooker, which in turn implies "objectivity". Nevertheless, the mere selection of a particular shot, means that an element of subjectivity enters the news report, because other visual information that is excluded from the framed shot (and which is not seen or known by the viewer) could have been more relevant.

Both codes of content and of form contribute to the composition of a single shot and, unless its purpose is to convey disequilibrium or incoherence, *unity* and *balance* are two of the most important compositional codes. A bisymmetric *formal* (but static) *balance* is usually created by framing the shot in such a way that elements on the right-hand side are matched in size, shape, intensity of colour and/or dark-light contrasts with those on the left-hand side. *Informal balance*, which is more imaginative and distinctive, is created by arranging elements according to the *golden ratio*. The optical centre of the shot differs from the mathematical centre and is based on the *see-saw principle*, in terms of which a lighter weight on a see-saw can easily balance a heavier weight if the lighter weight is further away from the fulcrum. (Weight, in this compositional sense, refers to any of the codes of content and of form discussed above.)

1.5 PICTURISATION THROUGH MOVEMENT IN FILM AND TELEVISION

In addition to the codes of content and form dealt with in section 1.4, visual codes in film and television not only deal with the visual image as a spatial field, but also more specifically with a *space-time (moving) image*.

1.5.1 Objective versus subjective time

The relevance of time in film and television becomes obvious when we consider the distinction between objective and subjective time. Objective time refers to time as measured by a clock. Zettl (1990:278–295) distinguishes between the following types of objective time:

- *spot* time – the actual time when a television programme is broadcast;
- *running* time – the duration of a film or television programme;
- *story* time – the time span of an event, such as 75 years, if the story deals with the life of an important figure.

Suspense in detective and police genres, for example, relies characteristically on a double temporal tension; that is the time/story of the crime; the time/story of the investigation together with the temporal process of the programme itself. However, running time (e.g. 28 minutes) and story time (e.g. 75 years) are seldom identical. Running time can also be divided into *sequence* time, *scene* time and smaller units, namely *shot time*. In a film, a single frame is often regarded as the smallest unit, whereas in television it is represented by the interval between two distinct visual transitions, that is between one cut and another cut/wipe/dissolve. (These editing techniques are discussed below in section 1.5.4.)

Subjective time, however, cannot be measured or subdivided into different types because it is dependent on a number of contextual variables, such as whether or not the message is interesting, funny or dull. For example, the central themes in soap operas, such as births, marriages, divorces and deaths, are usually treated in multiple plot-structures and the narrative structures are characteristically open-ended (that is, open to different interpretations, including that of subjective time, by mass audiences). On the other hand, despite cliffhanger endings in continuous soap operas, the passage of time generally seems to keep pace with the passage of "real" time.

1.5.2 Picturisation through primary movement

If the film or television camera remains stationary and merely records what happens in front of it (that is, the camera is objective and passive), readers are observing primary movement, which occurs along any one or more of the X-(horizontal), Y-(vertical), or Z-(depth) axes. Movement, or the creation of a motion vector, along the Z-axis, by a person or object moving towards or away from a passive camera, is one of the strongest indexical signs of depth. (See also the discussion of indexical signs above, in section 1.3.1.)

The meanings that can be conveyed by a person who challenges the down-diagonal are discussed above with reference to Figure 1.12. It would make for an interesting textual analysis if we were to research how often the meanings of binary opposition, such as the fight for integrity (versus corruption), humanity (versus savagery), freedom (versus restriction) and equal rights (versus domination) are depicted in film/television by shots of people whose primary movements are shown to challenge such a down-diagonal. The significance of primary movements as motion vectors has been revealed in a study (Sammur 1990:81–92) investigating preschoolers' viewing patterns of nineteen *Sesame Street* pre-reading and pre-science segments. (The South African adaptation of American *Sesame Street*, ETV programmes broadcast on SABC since 2000, is entitled *Takalani Sesame*.) The study revealed that the use of kinesics by the Muppets behind or below printed letters on the television screen is one of the most effective visual codes to encourage left-to-right reading.

1.5.3 Picturisation through secondary movement

Secondary movement refers to the movements made by the camera lens (zoom in or out), or made by the *camera head*, usually whilst its tripod or base remains stationary (pan left/right; tilt or crane up/down); or made by the *camera together with its base* (dolly and track in/out/left/right/around).

The zoom – a lens movement – is normally used as a transition from a long shot to a close-up shot (zoom in), or from a close-up shot to a long shot (zoom out). A series of studies (Salomon 1974:499–511; Comstock 1978:22) that investigated how the relationship between television viewing and the stimulation and development of children's skills in doing cognitive tasks, showed, for example, that the zoom-in lens movements (to isolate sections of art works) increase children's abilities to undertake such tasks on their own. Zooming in/out creates a motion vector along the Z-axis, which, in addition, reinforces the illusion of depth on a two-dimensional screen.

To *pan left* or *right* means that the camera head moves along the X-axis on a horizontal plane. This secondary movement is often used to follow the primary movement of an object or person. However, if no primary movement occurs, a horizontal pan can also be used to reveal a contrast, similarity or relation between two objects, persons or actions.

The camera head can *tilt upwards* or *downwards* (e.g. the downward tilt can be used to frame something at a level lower than the horizon). On the other hand, when using a *crane* movement, the framed shot remains at the same horizontal level of the person or object being framed. For example, while an actor proceeds to climb down a flight of stairs, a crane down means that the framed shots remains at the same horizontal level as the actor's face or body. If a tilt down is used, the camera will also follow the actor's primary movements, but will ultimately be positioned above eye-level in relation to the actor.

The dolly or *track* means that the camera in its entirety (on a tripod, track or some form of mounting) changes position completely. To *dolly in* means moving the camera towards the person or event and to *dolly out* means to move away in the opposite direction. When moving the camera as a whole to the left or right is also sometimes called to *crab*, whereas a *dolly track* usually signifies that the camera moves parallel to the primary movement of the actor or object. As in the case of a lens movement (zooming in/out), the dolly in/out along the Z-axis is frequently used to create or to reinforce the illusion of depth by means of a motion vector.

1.5.4 Picturisation through tertiary movement

Tertiary movement is produced by means of editing techniques that are used to combine individual shots into scenes, and scenes into sequences. *Instantaneous editing* occurs while an event occurs, such as during a direct television broadcast of a soccer game.

In contrast, postproduction editing means that the paradigmatic selection and syntagmatic sequencing of prerecorded filmed or videotaped material occurs after the event has occurred.

The most common editing techniques used are cut, dissolve and fade (in or out). The cut is an instantaneous transition which, to a certain extent, corresponds with the way in which we look at something. Our eyes blink (or cut) rather than pan when we change field or focus. The fade is generally used either at the beginning (fade in) or at the end (fade out) of a film or television programme. When used between sequences, this could signify a long transition of time or place; or could be a marker for a commercial break. Emotionally, a fade out/fade in provides a moment of relief after a climax in a preceding scene or sequence. The dissolve is a transition in which elements or parts of two different shots are seen simultaneously on the screen. In other words, while one image is being faded out, another is gradually faded in *before* the first one disappears from the screen. The dissolve signifies a shorter lapse of time (than a fade out/fade in) and – depending on the context – can signify the introduction of the actor's thoughts or dreams. According to Zettl (1990:296) a dissolve can "provide continuity, follow or establish a smooth event rhythm, bridge large space and time intervals, and show structural or thematic relationships".

In addition to the cut, fade and dissolve, the following are techniques not only used for editing purposes, but also to create special effects. The *wipe*, where one image is pushed off the screen, while another moves in, is a technique that can hardly occur unnoticed. It disrupts the reader's illusion of reality because it is so obvious. The *focus/defocus*, where one shots ends out of focus and the next comes into focus; the *wash*, where the screen seems to ripple as if water were washing over it; and *photographic effects*, where, for example, one shot ends in smoke and the subsequent one starts in smoke or steam, are all editing techniques which focus the reader's attention directly on the technique itself. Special effects, such as slow-motion visuals can, for example, convey meanings of softness, tenderness and freedom, because just like extended dissolves, a slow-motion visual involves the reader's kinaesthetic sense. For example, South African audiences frequently see this technique used in advertisements for fabric softeners and in the sensory appeal being made when margarine melts into the porridge or slowly runs down a mealie.

The narrative of both fictional and factional films and television programmes is largely determined by building an iconographic (visual) event by means of different combinations of individual camera shots. Zettl (1990:299–330) distinguishes between two categories of editing (in which above editing techniques are used), namely continuity and complexity editing.

Continuity editing

The structuring of the vector field, in the case of film and television, is usually bigger than the screen area. If a target object is not visible in one shot, but followed up in the next shot, the vector field has been expanded into a syntagmatic combination of shots. For example, two people look screen-right in one shot (as in Figure 1.19), which is followed by a shot of the target object at which they are looking.

Simultaneity, as a type of montage, developed from the Hollywood film tradition where two actions are developed simultaneously and the outcome of one depends on the outcome of the other. Simultaneity is a temporal relation, which is sometimes also called parallel action, and which is frequently applied in chase scenes in police and detective television programmes. When used for purposes of *elaboration*, the syntagmatic combination of shots can either enlarge the event (e.g. a close-up shot is followed by a long shot of the same action or event), or introduce concentration on detail (e.g. a long shot is followed by a close-up shot of something that appeared in the long shot). For example, if the shot depicted in Figure 1.14 is followed by the shot depicted in Figure 1.15, this combination illustrates this latter form of concentrated elaboration. (This combination also illustrates a metonymic – part-whole – relation, which is further discussed above in section 1.3.1).

As vectors can be extended over several shots, to form a total image, the use of tertiary movement lends itself to creating meanings such as continuity, convergence and divergence. Tertiary movement (or editing) is used to clarify and intensify the screen event, with the main purpose being to establish *continuity* (e.g. between vector fields, positions of objects or persons within and off screen, and between actions). In other words, when shots are combined to *clarify* an event, the *continuity* among the selected shots is an important filmic and television convention. Such continuity can be established by manipulating a number of iconographic (visual) codes, of which the following are three examples:

- the graphic, index and motions vectors continue from one to the next shot (e.g. a long shot of a character running screen right should be shown to continue running screen right in the following medium shot);
- a cut from one shot to the next occurs during the action (not before or thereafter) to ensure visual action continuity (e.g. a subjective shot showing a person opening a door is cut – whilst the door is being opened – to an objective shot of the person who knocked on the door);
- a character's appearance, lighting, colour, and other codes of content are preserved from shot to shot (e.g. when the production of a film occurs over a period of time, the scenery such as furniture and curtains in a room must remain the same).

Complexity editing

Complexity editing is primarily but not exclusively concerned with *intensifying* an event, the purpose being to convey inner emotions, conflicts and/or confusions. Montage is the main convention that is manipulated in this type of editing.

In the early days of silent films, *visual conjunction* was conveyed explicitly (by means of verbal titles, such as "*meanwhile*" ... or "*later*"...), whereas today visual conjunction is realised more implicitly by means of dissolves and cuts. In film theory and film aesthetics considerable attention has been devoted to the concept of editing (or montage), notably by the theories of Eisenstein, Pudovkin, Timoshenko, Bazin and Metz (Van Leeuwen 1991:76–113). Complexity editing is based on the artistic principle of montage, by means of which two or more separate images – when juxtaposed – create a more intense whole or Gestalt.

Three types of montage can be distinguished (Zettl 1990:318–329), depending on *how* these separate images or shots are combined. *Metric montage* is created when a series of images is combined in approximately equally spaced intervals. In so doing, a tertiary motion rhythm is created, irrespective of whether the actual shots are related to the same event, or whether they are unrelated.

Analytical montage is created when important (structural or thematic) elements of an event are selected and combined in order to intensify the screen event.

For example:

Shot 1	A boy runs across a road (cut)	A motion vector – from screen left to screen right
Shot 2	A car approaches (cut)	A motion vector – from screen right to screen left, which is a converging vector in relation to above left-to-right motion vector
Shot 3	The same boy lies motionless in front of the same car	The implied result of the two converging vectors having collided

The above example illustrates *sequential analytical montage*, because the essential elements of the theme (an accident) are combined in their original cause-and-effect sequence. One of the conventions that characterises sequential analytical montage is that the main event is *implied* and not explicitly shown. (In the example above, viewers do not actually see the boy being hit by the car and therefore have to apply psychological closure to fill in the missing visual information.)

Suspense does not depend only on the story line as the manipulation of any *encoding techniques* must also be in keeping with the *content* (unless the purpose is to create comedy or satire). For example: suspense can be created or heightened through the manipulation and combination of different *camera shots*, as illustrated on the next page.

A textual analysis of a fictional television programme often reveals patterns of *action* → *reaction* → *action* being depicted. However, the gradual and progressive increase in conflict or suspense, and development of a story line, which is characteristic of many films, has been altered by television. Mainly due to a time limit and competition from other stations, television must capture the interest and involve the emotions of the

Syntagmatic combination of shots	Creating/heightening suspense through a combination of camera shots
Shot 1	medium-long shot of a blind girl running (cut)
Shot 2	medium-long shot of her killer searching (cut)
Shot 3	medium shot of girl hiding zoom in to a close-up shot of her face (SFX [sound effects] of killer approaching) (cut)
Shot 4	close-up shot of killer's face

viewers at the beginning of the programme and maintain their interest throughout. Therefore, a textual analysis of fictional programmes will often reveal instances where *only reaction* is portrayed, in the *absence* of *action*, such as discovering a corpse without having witnessed the crime. In so doing, communicators rely on the principle of psychological closure (discussed above in section 1.4.2) and assume that readers will "fill in" the criminal action.

In contrast to condensing the progression of an event, sectional analytical montage is created when isolated moments or viewpoints from one event are selected for the purpose of focusing on the quality, detail and/or complexity of the moment.

Figure 1.40 A political rally as event

For example, the political rally as an event, which is reflected in Figure 1.40, can be reconstructed into a special event by isolating and focusing on different viewpoints. The montage of three shots in Figure 1.41 illustrates how the filmic version of an event can contribute to the complexity of an event, depending on the viewpoints selected and combined. Note how the kinesics (gestures and facial expressions) in the first two shots convey jubilation, in contrast to the facial expression in the third shot. More importantly, notice how the way in which these three shots have been combined creates conflict or disagreement that is not reflected in the original event, in Figure 1.40.

Syntagmatic combination of shots	Examples of field forces within the shot	Meanings created
Shot 1	Continuing index vectors (screen right to left)	Challenging the down-diagonal and conveying jubilation
Shot 2	Continuing index vectors (screen right to left)	Supporting and reinforcing the jubilation in shot 1
Shot 3	Diverging index vector (screen left to right)	Opposing or disagreeing with shot 1 and shot 2
	Magnetism of the frame, attracting the mass to the right	Supporting the opposition created by the diverging index vector

In addition to field forces, other visual codes also reinforce the conflict or opposition created between the first two shots and the third shot. Let us analyse two of these visual codes:

- *Volume* – The positive volume in shot 3 is more prominent (than in the other two shots) and therefore emphasises the importance of the person.
- *Camera shots* – Shot 3 is framed in a medium close-up shot, which brings the person and his facial expression closer to the viewer than the medium shots in shot 1 and 2 – which assign importance to both the people as well as the setting or background.

Figure 1.41 Sectional analytical montage

The third type of montage which is conventionally used in complexity editing is called "idea-associative montage" (Zettl 1990:324). In an idea-associative montage, two images that are seemingly unrelated are combined and, by means of this combination, a third idea or meaning is created. However, the combination of unrelated visuals does not occur at random. The combination is conventionally guided by two criteria, namely *comparison* and *collision*.

The juxtaposition (combination) of two visual events which are unrelated, but which do relate to the same theme can, by means of comparison, reinforce that theme or idea. Figure 1.42, for example, illustrates idea-associative montage that is based on comparison, in that the combination of a deserted building and a derelict farm reinforces the idea or theme of decay.

Figure 1.42 Idea-associative montage based on comparison

The (third) idea of decay is further supported by the *absence* of people in both shots; an absence of normality and calmness is suggested by the vertical aspect ratio and vertical graphic vectors in both shots. The dominance of positive volume in the shot of the building suggests a confinement of movement and makes the reader experience a restricted feeling – perhaps a restriction on life. In contrast, the shot of the farm and windmill reflects spaciousness and a cloudless sky and, although it differs from the overwhelming positive volume in the other shot, the spaciousness can also promote feelings of emptiness, of being isolated and lost – perhaps of lifelessness.

A second criterion that is conventionally applied in idea-associative montage, is based on *collision*. The dialectic principle on which this montage is based (Flew 1984:94–95; Peters 1977:14) argues that by juxtaposing a thesis (e.g. a poor condition) with an antithesis (e.g. an opposite condition), a synthesis (e.g. a new idea) can be created.

When editing is based on the selection of actions and reactions to construct a story, it also fulfils a structural function. However, as indicated above, editing can also be used to establish or to convey relational meanings: montage can contrast, convey simultaneity; and construct symbolic meanings. For example, when a shot shows a starving child, followed by an image of a well-to-do man wasting food, a collision is created through negative comparison, which can create a new Gestalt symbolising social injustice.

Figure 1.43 Idea-associative montage based on collision

When considering the two shots that are collided in Figure 1.43, the dialectic principle mentioned above can be analysed and explained as follows:

Thesis	Shot 1 – women and children	⟶	Synthesis	New idea (depending on the context, e.g. conflict)
Antithesis	Shot 2 – deserted burial site			

The collision between these two shots becomes more meaningful if we do a text analysis with reference to the codes of content (that are dealt with above in section 1.4).

In shot 1, the following are examples of codes of content that convey *life*:

- *Magnetism of the frame* – The frame attracts the people, especially on the left and right, thereby suggesting a wider setting in which other people (not seen) are present.
- *Figure-ground perception* – As the figures (positive volume) fill most of the frame, their presence dominates the shot.
- *Psychological closure* – The cast shadows that are projected onto the women and children, signify that other people are watching the procession and although they are not shown, readers can fill in such missing information.
- *Index vectors* – The continuity created by everyone looking and pointing from screen left to right, suggests progress and implies movement from on-screen space to off-screen space on the right-hand side.
- *Graphic depth factors* – The overlapping of planes signifies a three-dimensional depth and therefore a living reality.

All these codes reinforce the idea of "life" and convey a message that these people are moving towards a particular destination with a specific purpose in mind.

In shot 2, on the other hand, the above codes have also been used, but resulting in meanings that contradict "life". Apart from the crosses in the foreground which in Western cultures symbolise death or a burial site, the following are examples of the codes of content that are presented:

- *Magnetism of the frame* – The frame does not exert any meaningful pull on the mass (crosses), thereby emphasising the isolation of the crosses from a world beyond the frame.
- *Figure-ground perception* – The background and sky (negative volume) fill most of the frame and, through this domination, contribute to an idea of emptiness.
- *Vectors* – Graphic vectors that emphasise a vertical direction, lead the readers' focus upward towards the emptiness of the sky.
- *Graphic depth factors* – Aerial perspective is the most important graphic depth factor, which diminishes clarity as readers look into the distance.

The above codes therefore signify an absence of a future, of purpose – of life.

Having dealt with picturisation through primary, secondary and tertiary movement, in the next section we consider how auditory and audiovisual codes contribute to the construction of meaning via film and television.

1.6 AUDITORY CODES AND THE COMBINATION OF AUDIOVISUAL CODES

One of the easiest ways to experience the meanings conveyed by auditory codes is to view a television programme or a film without any sound. Whether it is a drama, the news, a documentary, sport or a children's programme, with the sound turned off, the film or television programme will lack information and its essential dramatic quality will be greatly diminished.

1.6.1 Auditory codes

There are three auditory codes: human voice, music and sound effects (SFX). Each of these codes consists of four basic elements that are manipulated to convey or elicit certain emotions or descriptive associations. The variations of these elements and their typical associations are given in Table 1.2 in tabulated form.

Table 1.2 Examples of auditory variations and typical associations

Elements	Examples of variations	Typical associated meanings
Pitch	high	lightness, excitement, tension, anger
	low	solemnity, depression, affection
Timbre	thin (e.g. flute)	purity
	percussion (e.g. drums)	drama, power
Volume	loud	definiteness, importance, energy, anger
	soft	weakness, subdual, tranquility, affection
	sudden increase (fade up)	climax, impatience, suspense, aggressiveness, conflict
	sudden decrease (fade down)	defeat, lack of purpose, fear
	gradual increase (fade up)	pursuit, increased intensity, gathering strength
	gradual decrease (fade down)	reorientation, temporary defeat, casualness
Tempo	fast	excitement, instability, tension
	slow	peacefulness, stability, melancholy

From Table 1.2 it is clear that a particular variation of an element (e.g. loud volume) may express different descriptive associations – depending on the context and type of audiovisual text in which it is used. When doing a text analysis, a direct relation may, therefore, be sought between the *nature* of the elements (irrespective of whether the codes used are voice, music or sound effects) and the *context* of the specific scene being analysed. For example: during a chase scene in a detective television drama, the voice, music and sound effects used will very likely have a fast tempo and a loud volume.

Human voice

Much of the research into the functions of vocal (paralanguage) variations of the human voice has been concerned with their expressive or emotive capacities. Tests regarding the emotional connotations attached to vocal features have, for example, found (Elam 1980:80) that high pitch, moderately blaring timbre, loudness, a fast tempo and regular rhythm combine to connote "joy". Such research suggests that expressive or emotional connotative meanings conveyed, are not arbitrary, and when mediated, the expression of attitudes and emotions by means of paralanguage features appears to be rule-bound.

Apart from manipulating the paralanguage elements of the human voice, this code is also used according to different *types of address*, namely direct address and indirect address.

- *Direct address* – The communicator, via the text, addresses the readers directly by means of words such as "you" and "your". Direct address is conventionally used in advertisements, political speeches, game shows and educational texts, with the purpose of involving the viewing audience by speaking to them directly.
- *Indirect address* is divided into three types of address. Dialogue takes place when two people address each other in the text. Mediated dialogue, in order to be natural, must be written to be heard (not to be read) and must characteristically consist of interruptions, and incomplete phrases and sentences. Soliloquy takes place when a person or character muses to him- or herself – as if thinking out loud. Narration occurs when a person describes a certain topic, such as during a television broadcast of a soccer game. Verbal narration is the conventional type of address used in documentary genres, and as a convention is written for the ear (to be heard); is in the active (rather than the passive) voice; consists of short simple sentences; and does not repeat what is visually obvious to the viewer. The dialogue during a soapie, the soliloquy during a fictional film and/or the narration during a documentary programme, therefore, addresses the readers indirectly.

The use of specific types of address is largely dictated by the communicator's objective and the genre. For example, in an advertisement broadcast by means of television, the primacy will alternate between the words and the visual images; hence the verbal speech and the visual action jointly assist the communicator's intention to persuade. (The combination of auditory and visual codes is further discussed below in section 1.6.2.)

Clarity of speech sounds and *economy of words* are two of the most important criteria when using the human voice – irrespective of the type of address used. In the case of dialogue, words must sound natural and spontaneous; whereas in soliloquy and narration, the address is structured as a carefully planned, condensed form of the dialogue in real life.

Sound effects

Sound effects (SFX) differ from noise in that they are intentional and are used with a communicative purpose in mind. Sound effects can be produced by electronic or mechanical means and can consist of *literal* sounds that convey denotative meanings. Examples of sources of sound effects include animals (e.g. dogs barking), nature (e.g. the wind, thunder, crashing waves), artefacts created by humans (e.g. a clock ticking, the siren of an ambulance, a car crashing), a person (e.g. coughing), or a group of persons (e.g. an audience applauding).

Descriptive sound effects, on the other hand, do not have a literal meaning and include those sound effects that can not be linked to the sound emitting source, such as the "boings", "hisses" and "bangs" that accompany cartoon characters' actions. Sound effects, as signs, are often used in a process that Elam (1980:15) calls "transcodification". In other words, instead of verbalising "*I'm afraid*" in a dramatised children's programme, the message is signified by the sounds of a howling wind, which in narrative terms means that sound effects can be manipulated to represent and symbolise an antagonist.

Music

Music as a communication code is often a recourse in periods of emotional stress, probably because it is simultaneously "more nurturing of reverie and introspection, and also more emotionally stimulating" (Comstock 1978:31). From a semiotic perspective, the meaning of music is not sought on the first order of signification, or level of meaning, as a self-contained sign conveying representational meaning. When music is regarded as an iconic sign, it should exhibit the properties of the thing being represented, such as birdcalls.

However, Merriam (1964:235) points out that the relation between the musical sound and that which it represents "can only be made through ascription of meaning which is culturally defined". As a connotative agent for the expression of moods, and other affective states, music is expressive of "subjective rather than objective experience" (Fiske & Hartley 1978:44), within the framework of specific cultures. However, music is not only indicative of behaviour and myths in a particular culture. Through repetition via the mass-communication media, some of the symbolic meanings have become universally applicable. For example, a visual country scene recorded in England is accompanied by the sounds of African tribal drums; hence the viewers accept that the scene depicted, is in fact in Africa. Other examples of such musical clichés that function as a short-cut to express certain denotative information and simultaneously connote affective associations are also found in the traditional *Western* film, where the sound of a tom-tom drum signifies native American Indians.

Music can be divided into several structural elements, of which the following two – in *addition* to the elements identified in Table 1.2 above – are worthy of consideration, namely *mode* and *distinct melody*.

- *Mode* – In music a melody can be composed in several modes, of which the major and minor modes are the best known. Modality can be described as the arrangements of eight diatonic tones (of an octave) according to certain intervals. In addition to tempo and volume, the major mode is usually equated with "happiness", whereas the minor mode is usually associated with "sadness".
- *Melody* – A melody is composed of a succession of notes, for example by ascending (increasing in pitch) or by decreasing (going down in pitch). Any suggestion that music is the mere sum of structural elements such as timbre, pitch, volume, tempo, mode and melody, would be erroneous. The functions which music fulfils as a communication code also depend on the objective of the message, for example the use of music in a historical documentary programme versus its use to stress the climax in a television drama. In a text analysis of advertisements, for example, the meanings conveyed could also vary, depending on whether a jingle is used, whether the music is readily identified with a particular brand, and whether lyrics are used to convey the message of the relevant product or service.

1.6.2 The combination of auditory and visual codes

All auditory and visual codes used to construct a screen event can be classified as "operationalizing either *screen event density* or *viewer involvement density*" (Barbatsis & Guy 1991:73 – own emphasis). The interrelatedness among various audiovisual codes (e.g. human voice, kinesics and aspect ratio) is well illustrated by the fact that the small screen space of television requires that action be expressed through kinesics (gestures and especially facial expressions). This is particularly relevant in television soapies, where action is constructed by means of dialogue, rather than through extensive physical movement.

Due to the 3:4 aspect ratio of a regular television screen, it is basically a medium in which close-up shots are used, as the screen is too small to convey extraneous details which are more easily accommodated by motion picture screens (with aspect ratios that vary between 3:6 and 3:8). As a result, television advertisements frequently consist of a syntagmatic combination of close-up shots using a *predicament + solution = happiness* formula, with off-screen narration. A text analysis (Du Plooy 1981) of the use of music in South African television programmes showed that the use of music as a semiotic and structural code in documentaries differs significantly from the use of music in other programmes, particularly dramas, children's programmes, and situation comedies.

Furthermore, Grimes (1990:762) found that a translation process apparently occurs when television viewers confuse what they see on a television screen with what they actually hear. The two examples cited below, illustrate how the *images* described in the *middle* column influenced the translated interpretation in the right-hand columns.

Auditory channel		Visual channel		Translated interpretation
Recent studies show that many people are susceptible to stress during dating.	+	SHOT OF UNDERGRA-DUATE MEN SITTING ON A BENCH	=	Recent studies show that many men are susceptible to stress during dating.
There are some groups that seem to be more successful with first dates.	+	SHOT OF BLACK COUPLE WALKING HAND-IN-HAND DOWN A HALLWAY	=	Blacks seem to be more successful with first dates.

Findings such as these, as well as arguments that recipients visualise the semantic content of sentences (Slack 1983:631–640), or that the imaging of words may be automatic and involuntary (Bagnara, Simion, Tagliabue & Ultima 1988:138–146), means that when undertaking a text analysis, we should *not* treat the auditory and visual codes of film and television as two distinctive codes, but as *integrated* components of one information medium.

By way of illustrating how the auditory codes form an integral part of the visual content and form of film and television, we briefly deal with four communicative *functions* which the different auditory codes fulfil: to inform, to pace, to bridge and to create a mood.

To inform

- *Human voice* – Any of the types of address is a more effective auditory code for transmitting information (than sound effects or music) – be it about a locality, a place, a period, a time of day, a quality, a condition, an event or an action. The off-screen narration in a documentary, for example, gives information about the topic being presented visually, but, in addition, projects information beyond the confines of the visual images.
- *Sound effects* – Sounds of heavy traffic in the city, or the cock's crow announcing a new dawn, are unseen sound effects that serve to inform readers of the locality or time of day.
- *Music* – The music that accompanies the opening and closing titles of regular television programmes, informs viewers both of the commencement of their favourite programme and in fact also its nature. Compare, for example, the type of music used at the commencement of a news programme, versus a children's programme. Music is also used to fulfil a *Leitmotiv* function, whereby the recurrence of a musical phrase, when linked with a character, event or action, informs viewers (through a process of association) of what they may expect.

To pace

Tempo, as an element of sound, forms an integral part in the pacing function. However, when used, together with visual codes of content and form, the pacing function goes beyond the manipulation of tempo.

- *Human voice* – Certain topics can be described more economically in words than visually, thus saving time. In fictional dramas, dialogue or soliloquy is often used to uncover or advance the plot, just as narration can accelerate the pace of certain sections or the whole of a documentary, games or educational programme.
- *Sound effects* – Sound effects are used more often to support than to create the pace or movement that already exists visually, such as the sounds of sirens and screeching tyres that accompany a car chase scene.
- *Music* – Although every musical phrase has a certain pace (tempo) built into it, its most effective use as a pacer is when the text contains emotional movement. In other words, music can superimpose an emotional consistency or counterpoint, either in relation to the visual codes, or to the other auditory codes used, or to a combination of both.

To bridge

Any of the three auditory codes can be effectively used to link or bridge two or more visual shots or scenes, or to link other sounds into a cohesive whole. For example, music can bridge two scenes of a narrative structure, which visually represent a change of time (e.g. from morning to evening) or place (e.g. from workplace to home), so that they form a whole.

To create a mood

A mood has definite emotional connotations, such as happiness, fear, sadness, tension or shock.

- *Human voice* – Dialogue can reveal the emotions that two persons feel towards each other; and this type of address, just like soliloquy, can also be very expressive of emotions and internal conflicts, which cannot readily be expressed visually.
- *Sound effects* – The ominous sounds of a howling wind or of dangerous animals, together with a dark scene in the woods, are examples of how sound effects can contribute to expressing the fear experienced by a young actor in a children's programme.
- *Music* – As the meanings conveyed by music are not limited to the denotative meanings of words, it is used more effectively to establish, heighten, maintain or even change a mood. In the words of Stout, Leckenby and Hecker (1990:898): "music augments pictures and colors words and can be a form of energy available through no other source".

Although the above four functions are dealt with separately, it is important to realise that all four functions are frequently fulfilled simultaneously. Let us take the music in a filmic advertisement for Coca-Cola as an example. The theme of the music and the song may be aimed primarily at identifying the product (information), but, simultaneously, the relative fast tempo lends an energetic pace to the scenes portrayed, the visual shots are linked to form a whole and the mood created by the music intensifies the advertising slogan: *enjoy – the real thing.*

Ways in which to create an audiovisual Gestalt

From the above discussion it becomes clear that the combination of visual images and sound in film or television programmes does not imply the mere combination of separate parts. As the visual images and sounds are structured to form an audiovisual Gestalt, a text analysis will reveal that such a Gestalt – depending on the objective of the message and intended aesthetic impact – has been created in one of the following ways:

- *(V/a)* – The visuals dominate and the audio fulfils a supporting function (e.g. in a chase scene, a man runs along a deserted road and is chased by a speeding car, and fast music supports the action).
- *(A/v)* – The audio dominates and the visuals fulfil a supporting function (e.g. a Government spokesperson makes an important announcement during a news broadcast, and he is visualised by means of an MCU shot).
- *(Va/Av)* – The visuals and audio alternately dominate and support (e.g. visual images set the scene of a story by showing a couple walking in a park, together with music – *Va*; followed by a dialogue between the couple who introduce the initial conflict in the story – *Av*).
- *(V/A)* – The visuals and audio are independent of one another and yet, when combined, equally contribute to forming an audiovisual Gestalt (e.g. a slow-motion replay of a controversial moment in a cricket game, together with voice-over commentary interpreting the visual action).

Contextual variables

From the discussion and examples described above, it becomes clear that *context* plays a significant role when we ascribe meaning during a text analysis of films and television programmes. Context must be understood in two senses; firstly in terms or our different cultural roots, and secondly in terms of the immediate actualities as contained in observable content and mediated codes. In an investigation of the role of culture in the work of foreign correspondents, Starck and Villanueva (1993:27), for example, emphasise the importance of the cultural context, by concluding as follows:

> Without a sensitive eye searching for cultural context, stories can result that convey invalid information or misguided meanings ... interpretations can be erroneous, possibly enforcing stereotypes and ethnocentrism.

Therefore, when conducting a text analysis, meaning must be sought in terms of auditory and visual *codes in context*, or audiovisual *communication-in-use* relationships. In both film and television, the visualised setting and social space are two of the most important contextual variables. In soapies, living-rooms and bedrooms are the main environments in which action takes place – as "real" settings in which "real-life" issues occur. The "room", situated within the family's "home" has become an index for everyday life. These settings, including *mise-en-scène*, reflect on the characters' social positions, almost as extensions of their lives, and function as metaphors for their personalities. The purposeful use of these settings and visual artefacts therefore contributes to conveying what Williams (1965:141) calls "a whole way of life".

Summary

This unit commenced by considering the conceptual issues related to the notion of media literacy, and differentiated between media content literacy, media grammar literacy, and medium literacy on a micro-level, as well as on a macro- societal level. This was followed by dealing with the perceptual approach to visual communication, by concentrating on the assumptions of the semiotic approach and the cognitive approach to visual perception and interpretation.

The sections that followed, dealt with audiovisual codes (of content and form) in terms of the conceptual aspects of production, with the primary focus on their meaning construction, when conducting a text analysis. Pictorial codes in a static film shot and photograph were analysed, including lighting, colour, field forces, balance, depth and volume, area orientation, lenses and focus, basic camera shots and camera viewpoint. This discussion was extended to the visual codes that apply to television and filmic messages, with the emphasis placed on movement (primary, secondary and tertiary), as well as the human voice, types of address, sound effects and music as auditory codes. In addition to picturisation through movement in film and television, this unit ended with a discussion of how auditory codes and the combination of audiovisual codes can be manipulated to create particular meanings.

An argument that was threaded throughout this unit is that the meanings which readers ascribe to audiovisual signs and symbols can change, depending on the context and culture in which communication takes place.

Research activities

If studying in a group, involve a fellow-scholar as co-analyst and report on the extent and why your text analyses corresponded and/or differed.

1 Select a photograph (e.g. used in a press report or in an advertisement) and do a text analysis by explaining how the codes of content and of form were manipulated to clarify the visual information and/or intensify the thematic or emotional meanings that are represented.

2 Access a recording of a film or television programme and conduct a text analysis of an extract of at least one sequence, by following this procedure:
- refer to and use the headings and subheadings in sections 1.4–1.6 as an analytical scheme;
- identify the use of these codes in your analytical scheme in the sampled extract;
- describe in approximately eight pages how these codes were used to produce and influence the meaning(s) presented.

Further reading

Evans, J & Hall, S (eds). 1999. *Visual culture: the reader.* London: Sage in association with the Open University.

Lester, PM. 1995. *Visual communication: images with messages.* Belmont, CA: Wadsworth.

Masterman, L. 1997. A rationale for media education, in *Media literacy in the information age: current perspectives*, edited by R Kubey. New Brunswick, NJ: Transaction.

Messaris, P. 1994. *Visual "literacy". Image, mind, & reality.* Boulder: Westview.

Metallinos, N. 1996. *Television aesthetics.* Mahwah, NJ: Erlbaum.

Meyrowitz, J. 1998. Multiple media literacies. *Journal of Communication* 48(1):96–108.

O'Sullivan, T, Hartley, J, Saunders, D, Montgomery, M & Fiske, J. 1996. *Key concepts in communication and cultural studies.* 2nd, reprinted edition. London: Routledge.

Zettl, H. 1990. *Sight, sound, motion: applied media aesthetics.* 2nd edition. Belmont, CA: Wadsworth.

Zettl, H. 1998. Contextual media aesthetics as the basis for media literacy. *Journal of Communication* 48(1):81–95.

Bibliography

Althusser, L. 1999. Ideology and ideological state apparatuses, in *Visual culture: the reader*, edited by J Evans & S Hall. London: Sage in association with the Open University.

Alvarado, M, Gutch, R & Wollen, T. 1987. *Learning the media.* London: Macmillan.

Andrews, I. 1995. Sandwiched between cultures: the translation of advertisements. *Language Matter. Studies in the Language of Southern Africa* 26:22–39.

Ang, I. 1985. *Watching Dallas: soap opera and the melodramatic imagination.* London: Methuen.

Aufderheide, P (ed). 1993. *Media literacy: a report of the national leadership conference on media literacy.* Aspen, CO: Aspen Institute.

Bagnara, S, Simion, F, Tagliabue, ME & Ultima, C. 1988. Comparison processes on visual mental images. *Memory & Cognition* 16(2):138–146.

Barbatsis, G & Guy, Y. 1991. Analyzing meaning in form: soap opera's compositional construction of "realness". *Journal of Broadcasting & Electronic Media* 35(1):59–74.

Barnouw, E, Gerbner, G, Schramm, W, Worth, TL & Gross, L (eds). 1989. *International encyclopaedia of communications.* Volumes 1–4. New York: Oxford University Press.

Barthes, R. 1972. *Mythologies.* London: Paladin.

Barthes, R. 1977. *Image, music, text.* Glasgow: Fontana.

Barthes, R. 1999. Rhetoric of the image, in *Visual culture: the reader*, edited by J Evans & S Hall. London: Sage in association with the Open University.

Bennett, T, Boyd-Bowman, S, Mercer, C & Woollacott, J (eds). 1981. *Popular television and film.* London: British Film Institute.

Berger, AA. 1991. *Media analysis techniques*. Revised edition. Newbury Park, CA: Sage.
Berger, AA. 1992. *Popular culture genres*. London: Sage.
Biocca, F. 1993. Communication research in the design of communication interfaces and systems. *Journal of Communication* 43(4):59–68.
Burrows, TD, Wood, DN & Gross, LS. 1989. *Television production; disciplines and techniques*. 4th edition. Dubuque, IA: Wm C Brown.
Bywater, T & Sobchack, T. 1989. *Introduction to film criticism: major critical approaches to narrative film*. New York: Longman.
Christ, WG & Potter, WJ. 1998. Media literacy, media education, and the academy. *Journal of Communication* 48(1):5–15.
Cole, B. 1981. *Readings from TV guide*. New York: Oxford University Press.
Comstock, G. 1978. *Trends in the study of incidental learning from television viewing*. Syracuse, NY: Syracuse University Press.
Corner, J. 1991. Meaning, genre and context: the problematics of "public knowledge" in the new audience studies, in *Mass media and society*, edited by J Curran & M Gurevitch. London: Edward Arnold.
Davies, MM. 1997. *Fake, fact, and fantasy: children's interpretations of television reality*. Mahwah, NJ: Erlbaum.
De Saussure, F. 1959. *A course in general linguistics*. New York: Philosophical Library.
Deacon, D, Pickering, M, Gelding, P & Murdoch, G. 1999. *Research communication: a practical guide to methods in media and cultural analysis*. London: Arnold.
DeVito, JA. 1992. *The interpersonal communication book*. 6th edition. New York: HarperCollins.
Dondis, DA. 1973. *A primer of visual literacy*. Cambridge, MA: Massachusetts Institute of Technology.
Du Plooy, GM. 1981. The use of music as communication code in television. MA dissertation, University of South Africa, Pretoria.
Du Plooy, GM. 1989. *Understanding television: guidelines for visual literacy*. Kenwyn: Juta.
Dyer, G. 1982. *Advertising as communication*. London: Methuen.
Eco, U. 1982. Critique of the image, in *Thinking photography*, edited by V Burgin. London: Macmillan.
Eidsvik, C. 1978. *Cineliteracy: film among the arts*. New York: Random House.
Ekman, P & Friesen, WV. 1969. The repertoire of nonverbal behavior: categories, origins, usage, and coding. *Semiotica* 1:49–98.
Elam, K. 1980. *The semiotics of theatre and drama*. New York: Methuen.
Evans, J & Hall, S (eds). 1999. *Visual culture: the reader*. London: Sage in association with the Open University.
Feyen, S & Wigal, D (eds). 1969. *Screen experience: an approach to film*. Dayton, OH: Pflaum.
Fiske, J. 1979. Semiotics: its contribution to the study of intercultural communication. *Educational Broadcasting International* 12:51–57.
Fiske, J. 1987. *Television culture*. London: Methuen.
Fiske, J & Hartley, J. 1978. *Reading television*. London: Methuen.
Flew, A (ed). 1984. *A dictionary of philosophy*. 2nd, revised edition. London: Pan & Macmillan.
Fourie, PJ. 1983. *Beeldkommunikasie. Kultuurkritiek, ideologiese kritiek en 'n inleiding tot die beeldsemiologie*. Johannesburg: McGraw-Hill.
Fourie, PJ. 1985. Betekenis en betekeniskonstruksie in beeldkommunikasie. *Communicare* 4(1):33–40.
Fourie, PJ. 1988. *Aspects of film and television communication*. Kenwyn: Juta.
Fourie, PJ (ed). 1991. *Critical television analyses: an introduction*. Kenwyn: Juta.
Fourie, PJ (ed). 1997. *Introduction to communication – course book 6: film and television studies*. Kenwyn: Juta.

Fourie, PJ (ed). 2001. *Media studies. Volume 1: Institutions, theories and issues.* Kenwyn: Juta.
Francis, S, Dugmore, H & Schacherl, R. 2000. *The madams are restless. A new Madam & Eve collection.* Johannesburg: Rapid Phase.
Fullerton, JA & Kendrick, A. 2000. Portrayal of men and women in U.S. Spanish-language television commercials. *Journalism & Mass Communication Quarterly* 77(1):128–142.
Gettas, GJ. 1990. The globalization of *Sesame Street*: a producer's perspective. *Educational Technology Research and Design* 38(4):55–63.
Giannetti, LD. 1976. *Understanding movies.* 2nd edition. Englewood Cliffs, NJ: Prentice-Hall.
Gombrich, EH. 1982. *The image and eye.* Ithaca, NY: Cornell University Press.
Grimes, T. 1990. Encoding TV news messages into memory. *Journalism Quarterly* 67(4):757–766.
Grossberg, L, Wartella, E & Whitney, DC. 1998. *Media making. Mass media in a popular culture.* Thousand Oaks: Sage.
Hall, ET. 1966. *The hidden dimension.* Garden City, NY: Doubleday.
Hall, ET. 1988. The hidden dimensions of time and space in today's world, in *Cross-cultural perspectives in nonverbal communication*, edited by F. Poyatos. Toronto: Hogrefe.
Hall, S. 1970. A world at one with itself. *New Society* 18 June:1056–1058.
Hawkins, RP, Yong-Ho, K & Pingree, S. 1991. The ups and downs of attention to television. *Communication Research* 18(1):53–76.
Hudson, W. 1962. Cultural problems in pictorial perception. *South African Journal of Science/Suid-Afrikaanse Joernaal vir Wetenskap* 58(7):189–196.
Janeke, C. 1995. Language, cognition, and metaphor. *Language matters. Studies in the languages of Southern Africa* 26:129–146.
Johnston, TF. 1973. The social determinants of Tsonga musical behavior. *International Review of the Aesthetics and Sociology of Music* 4:108–130.
Kantor, L & Bird, E. 1995. Innocent or guilty? Media coverage of the OJ Simpson trial. *Media Mask* 1(4):20–24.
Katz, E & Liebes, T. 1990. Interacting with "Dallas": cross-cultural readings of American TV. *Canadian Journal of Communication* 15(1):45–66.
Kinghorn, E. 1996. The independent imagineer returns from the future with clear directions. *The Sunday Independent* 14 January:18.
Lester, PM. 1995. *Visual communication: images with messages.* Belmont, CA: Wadsworth.
Lovelace, V. 1990. "Sesame Street" as a continuing experiment. *Educational Technology Research and Development* 38(4):17–24.
Lustig, MW & Koester, J. 1993. *Intercultural competence: interpersonal communication across cultures.* New York: HarperCollins.
Masterman, L. 1997. A rationale for media education, in *Media literacy in the information age: current perspectives*, edited by R Kubey. New Brunswick, NJ: Transaction.
McDermott, J. [Sa]. The magic of vision. *Topic* 166:32–39.
McMillan, SJ. 2000. The microscope and the moving target: the challenge of applying content analysis to the World Wide Web. *Journalism & Mass Communication Quarterly* 77(1):80–98.
McQuail, D. 2000. *McQuail's mass communication theory.* 4th edition. London: Sage.
Merriam, AP. 1964. *The anthropology of music.* New York: North-western University Press.
Messaris, P. 1994. *Visual "literacy". Image, mind, & reality.* Boulder: Westview.
Messaris, P. 1998. Visual aspects of media literacy. *Journal of Communication* 48(1):96–108.
Metallinos, N. 1996. *Television aesthetics.* Mahwah, NJ: Erlbaum.
Meyrowitz, J. 1998. Multiple media literacies. *Journal of Communication* 48(1):96–108.
Mohale, B. 2000. Africa: a brand to reckon with. *City Press Supplement,* December 3:7.

Okigbo, C. 1995. National images in the age of the information superhighway: African perspectives. *Africa Media Review* 9(2):105–121.

O'Sullivan, T, Hartley, J, Saunders, D, Montgomery, M & Fiske, J. 1996. *Key concepts in communication and cultural studies.* 2nd, reprinted edition. London: Routledge.

Parrott, AC. 1982. Effects of paintings and music, both alone and in combination, on emotional judgments. *Perceptual and Motor Skills* 54:634–641.

Peirce, CS. 1931–58. The icon, index and symbol, in *Collected works, 8 volumes*, edited by C Hartshorne & P Weiss. Cambridge, MA: Harvard University Press.

Peters, JM. 1977. *Pictorial communication*, revised and translated by M Coombes. Cape Town: David Philip.

Roth, L. 1993. Humanity, technology, and comedy in *Microbi*, a Hungarian animate science fiction television series. *World Communication* 22(2):74–79.

Russell, T & Verrill, G. 1986. *Otto Kleppner's advertising procedure.* 9th edition. Englewood Cliffs, NJ: Prentice-Hall.

Salomon, G. 1974. Internalization of filmic schematic operations in interaction with learners' aptitudes. *Journal of Educational Psychology* 66:499–511.

Sammur, GB. 1990. Selected bibliography of research on programming at the Children's Television Workshop. *Educational Technology Research and Design* 38(4):81–92.

Schramm, W & Porter, WE. 1982. *Men, women, messages and media: understanding human communication.* 2nd edition. New York: Harper & Row.

Sebeok, TA. 1991. *Semiotics in the United States.* Bloomington: Indiana University Press.

Seeco, LI. 2000. Local is lekker, but tread warily if you want to tackle world markets. *City Press Supplement*, 3 December:7.

Slack, JM. 1983. Imagery effects and semantic similarity in sentence recognition memory. *Memory & Cognition* 11(6):631–640.

Starck, K & Villanueva, E. 1993. Foreign correspondents and cultural framing. *Ecquid Novi* 14(1):3–35.

Stout, PA, Leckenby, JD & Hecker, S. 1990. Viewer reactions to music in television commercials. *Journalism Quarterly* 67(4):887–898.

Van Nierop, L. 1998. *Seeing sense: on film analysis.* Pretoria: Van Schaik.

Van Dijk, TA (ed). 1985. *Handbook of discourse analysis: discourse analysis in society.* Volume 4. London: Academic.

Van Leeuwen, T. 1991. Conjunctive structure in documentary film and television. *Continuum* 5(1):76–113.

Walker, AK, Kruger, A & Andrew, IC. 1995. Translation as transformation: a process of linguistic and cultural adaptation. *South African Journal of Linguistics Supplement* 26:99–115.

Walker, JA & Chaplin, S. 1997. *Visual culture: an introduction.* New York: Manchester University Press.

Whillock, RK. 1993. Winning their hearts and minds: strategies for victory in American political campaigns. *World Communication* 22(2):62–67.

Williams, R. 1965. *The long revolution.* Harmondsworth: Penguin.

Wilson, T. 1996. Television's everyday life: towards a phenomenology of the "Televisual Subject". *Journal of Communication Inquiry* 20(1):49–66.

Zettl, H. 1984. *Television production handbook.* 4th edition. Belmont, CA: Wadsworth.

Zettl, H. 1990. *Sight, sound, motion: applied media aesthetics.* 2nd edition. Belmont, CA: Wadsworth.

Zettl, H. 1995. *Video basics.* Belmont, CA: Wadsworth.

Zettl, H. 1998. Contextual media aesthetics as the basis for media literacy. *Journal of Communication* 48(1):81–95.

2 Genre Analysis

GM (Trudie) du Plooy

Overview

The term *genre*, as it applies in media studies, can be defined as an agreed code between the communicator and the audience, which represents systems of orientations. These systems of orientations develop and preserve textual forms through repetitive conventions, in order to meet a double-layered set of expectations.

This unit starts by unravelling the above comprehensive definition by explaining the meanings of assumptions, such as "agreed code", "systems of orientations", the "development and preservation of textual forms" and "double-layered set of expectations". These explanations are followed by a conceptual framework of genre conventions, in which the purposes of genres, as well as the construction of meaning through content and/or form are investigated. Thereafter, the assumptions and conceptual framework are applied to selective genres as they occur in films, television, radio and print media.

Learning outcomes

At the end of this unit you should be able to

- apply the parameters and theoretical assumptions of genre analysis, as a research method by conducting a qualitative content analysis of mass-media texts;
- evaluate how meanings may be constructed through the repetition of conventions found in the content and form of media texts that represent different genres.

2.1 INTRODUCTION

When we page through a newspaper to decide which film to watch or to determine which television programmes are broadcast on a particular day, we as viewers are inadvertently acting as genre critics. The same occurs when we tune to a particular radio station or if we habitually buy certain newspapers and magazines. The reasons for these preferences are linked to the differences between and similarities among mass-media texts – which is the focus of this unit.

The relevance of this unit, in terms of media studies, is summarised in the two learning outcomes set above. The achievement of the first outcome enables us to ask research questions and formulate hypotheses that are relevant to mass communication, and enables us to analyse and evaluate texts that are disseminated by means of films, television, radio and/or the print media.

By developing an awareness and understanding of how *genre* analysis can be used to research and evaluate mass-media content and forms, we also develop a sensitivity towards issues such as the relation between the so-called trueness to reality versus implicit *bias* in mass-media content. Genre analysis, in other words enables us to research how the mass media deal with issues such as maintaining the *status quo*, disseminating cultural values, marginalisation of minorities, representation of violence, globalisation, stereotyping and freedom of expression. These and other related issues are dealt with throughout this module.

By using genre analysis, as a qualitative content analysis, we inevitably become more critical consumers of mass communication and can in the process also develop an appreciation of the importance of lifelong learning.

In the next section, we first consider what is meant by the concept "genre", after which we consider a conceptual (theoretical) framework of characteristics and *conventions* that a genre shares, and which can be applied in practical research activities.

2.2 DEFINING "GENRE"

The meaning of "genre", when applied in researching the mass media is not usually controversial, if both the communicator (media producers) and the audience (readers, listeners, viewers and/or consumers) recognise its identity and its correspondence with other similar content and forms. For example, all television soaps focus mainly on adults (as characters), and personal conflict and sexual identification (as thematic content). According to the above characteristic, as an agreed code, "genre" can be defined as patterns, forms, styles, structures, *narratives* and content that supervise both the encoding/expression of communication by means of the mass media, as well as its decoding/interpretation by the audience.

In order to understand the above relationship between the producers of meaning and the consumers of meaning, we have to consider at least the following additional assumptions that contribute to the definition of a genre.

- *Genres represent systems of orientations* – This assumption refers to orientations that circulate between a particular media industry (e.g. radio broadcasting), the text (e.g. radio news) and the audience (e.g. listeners). In other words, both the communicator and the audience are aware of similarities between a specific text (e.g. a phone-in programme) and other similar texts (other phone-in programmes). The above orientations can therefore not be separated from the fact that genres are determined by the economic factors involved in the production, distribution and reception of mass-media messages. A genre is therefore an integral part of a media industry that cannot be separated from a historical reality – including its economic, sociocultural, ideological, political, language, religious and/or technological milieu.

- *Genres contribute to the development and preservation of textual forms* – This assumption is based on the argument that the communicator consciously works within certain established genre parameters (or conventions) by repeating the formulas that have marked previous financial successes. For example, television game shows share the following conventions: the structure of the programme, the uncertainty of the outcome, and the spontaneity of the participants. In addition, the audience's orientation (e.g. film viewers) is that of approaching the interpreting (e.g. viewing) experience of a particular text (e.g. film) with certain expectations.
- *Genres represent expectations* – This assumption is based on the argument that a double layer of expectations exists when we analyse media texts from a genre perspective. On the one hand, the text has to meet a set of basic conventional requirements to which an audience has become accustomed. Simultaneously, however, the text has to contain novelty and difference in order to lure the audience to return to the same mass medium and particular genre in future. Such conventional patterns, as well as novelties, are usually found in the narrative structures, subject matter and thematic content, and in the case of the visual media, in its *iconography*.

  As expectations are personal variables, their influence on the interpretation and evaluation of a particular genre may be further influenced by an audience member's past experience, attitude, mood, affective state and cognitive abilities.

Against the background of defining a genre as (1) an agreed code between the communicator and audience; as (2) systems of orientations; as (3) a development and preservation of textual forms; and (4) as a double-layered set of expectations, one thread runs though all these assumptions, and can, for purposes of discussion be treated as a fifth assumption, namely: a text can be demarcated as a genre when it *adheres to specific conventions*.

This last assumption brings us to a conceptual (theoretical) framework of characteristics and conventions that a genre shares.

2.3 A CONCEPTUAL FRAMEWORK OF GENRE CONVENTIONS

In this section we concentrate on two "groups" of variables that contribute to the identification or demarcation of a genre, with the aim that they be used as a conceptual framework when researching mass-media texts. The variables are grouped according to (1) the purposes or functions of a text as a genre; and (2) the construction of meaning by the form and/or content of a text. The distinction between two main "groups" is made for purpose of discussion only, because in most instances a variable (e.g. the narrative sequence of a news broadcast) is not limited only to the construction of meaning by means of a narrative form. This narrative sequence is simultaneously determined by the main purpose of a news broadcast, namely to report or comment on current events.

2.3.1 The purposes of a genre

When considering the purpose(s) of mass-media texts, we are inevitably reminded of the functions that the mass media fulfil. These functions are also discussed in Unit 7 (The role and functions of the media: functionalism) in Fourie (2001: Media Studies Volume 1). Nevertheless, we briefly consider them by concentrating on purposes, as intentions from the communicators' point of view and as they are contained in the form and content of the text.

A genre critic's focus is not so much on the active involvement or interpretation processes of the audience. However, although the latter audience's needs, expectations and involvement cannot be totally ignored, a genre critic's focus is on the media texts (e.g. newspapers). We therefore briefly consider the purposes from the media industry and societal points of view, keeping in mind that from a genre approach, the main purposes of all genres is first to *minimise economic risk* on the part of media owners, producers, authors, advertisers and other stakeholders. Simultaneously, genres fulfil the purpose of meeting the *double layer of expectations*, held by audiences. Therefore, although our focus is on the media texts, as genre critics, we are also moving back and forth between the media as integral parts of society and the individual audience member.

When considering society from a political point of view, we are reminded of the views held by a pioneer in communication science, Harold Lasswell (1948). If combined with the views of a sociologist, such as Charles Wright (1960), we can differentiate four classes of purposes which mass-communication texts fulfil.

- *Surveillance* of the environment – From an economic point of view, surveillance includes information on services and goods, plus buying-selling opportunities. From a sociopolitical point of view, surveillance includes information conveyed by politicians, diplomats and foreign correspondents, as well as information related to the acceptance or rejection of certain social roles and norms.
- Correlation or *coordination* of different subgroups in society – Coordination involves the interpretation, dissemination, enforcement and/or operation of economic and political policies to promote public understanding and socio-economic control (e.g. by editors, producers, filmmakers, politicians, journalists and public speakers).
- The *transmission* of a social-economic heritage – Transmission concentrates on initiating and transferring economic behaviour and a social heritage of laws and customs from one generation to the next (e.g. nonformal and informal education by means of the mass media); which in sociological terms could be called socialisation.
- *Entertainment* – Media texts that fulfil the main purpose of play or pleasure, rather than to inform or enlighten, offer audiences relief from problems and represent leisure activities.

Whilst keeping in mind that human communication involves both individual behaviour as well as social relationships, we must also be aware that the above four classes of purposes are *not* mutually exclusive and they tend to blur. For example, a particular genre (e.g. television interviews) can fulfil different purposes, depending on whether we analyse them from the perspective of the individual audience member, or from the view of a particular subgroup (e.g. political, economic or gender) and/or from the viewpoint of a wider sociocultural system. The main purpose of an interview can also depend on whether it is an opinion interview, an information interview or a personality interview. From the industry's point of view, the purpose of television interviews is either to convey expert opinions and information and/or they are "wrapped" around an important personality or celebrity. From the individual viewer's point of view, however, such broadcasts could simply become part of the so-called *wallpaper*. The latter means that the audience member does not actively listen to the interview, which also means that the intended purposes are not necessarily realised.

To take another example: although we accept that television soap operas are intended to entertain, many audience members use them for guidance, insight and reassurance in their personal lives, in addition to enjoying them as leisure activities and for purposes of escapism.

In view of the social transformations and technological changes and developments that have taken place in South Africa since the 1990s, the above four classes of purposes can be elaborated and refined to include many others, of which the following are examples. Namely to provide:

- information, education, comment, service, development;
- entertainment, infotainment, edutainment,
- advertising, propaganda, influence, persuasion, manipulation;
- social upliftment, democratisation;
- a gatekeeper, a watchdog;
- routinisation, wallpaper, white noise, companionship.

If we were to humanise the above purposes and label them as mass-media texts that function as watchdogs, leaders in cooperation and policymaking, teachers and entertainers, then the following two questions arise:

1 Is there a difference in how well films, television, radio and the different print media fulfil these roles?
2 Is there a difference in the way in which different genres contained in one of these mass media (e.g. different radio programmes) fulfil one or more of these principal roles?

The answers to both questions are "yes" and "no", on which we elaborate in the remainder of this unit.

A differentiation between intended purpose (from the communicator's point of view) and realised purpose (from the audience's point of view) has an important implication when doing a genre analysis of media texts. As we are unable to observe the behaviour of mass-media audiences – usually by means of audience ethnography – our focus has to be on the media texts. In other words, when analysing a particular genre, we have to derive the purposes on the basis of conventions contained in the form, content and meaning of those texts. Before we consider these conventions in greater detail, we focus on entertainment as one of the main purposes of mass communication.

Entertainment – a purpose of all genres?

The term entertainment is usually associated with relaxation, amusement and enjoyment. Since the development of the mass-communication media, and especially since the increase in globalisation by means of television, larger and more diverse audiences are able to share the same entertainment on an international level. Under these circumstances certain television genres, such as sport and popular music videos, have acquired commercial significance, in addition to being entertaining.

Entertainment has, in other words, become a marketable commodity. Labelling a particular television soap opera, such as *Egoli*, as entertainment, implies that its primary purpose or intention is not to educate, inform or persuade. Yet, from our perspective as genre critics, we argue that repeated exposure to the same and similar genre formula cumulatively influences the way in which the audience forms expectations about and interpretations of the social world. In addition to providing viewers with the means to escape from reality (escapism), the ideological field of play as reflected or created by such television genres, amounts to a reproduction of society's dominant values.

2.3.2 The construction of meaning through content and/or form

A distinction between content ("what messages are conveyed"?) and form ("how are these messages conveyed"?) is somewhat artificial, because very often the "what" is directly influenced by the "how". For example, a half-page photograph of a victim of crime on a newspaper's front page will convey a different message from a small photograph on the bottom left-hand corner of the second page. In other words, the form (in this example the size of the photograph and selected page) determines the meaning of the content (i.e. relevance, intensity, human interest, "publicness" and news-worthiness) found in the story. However, despite the artificiality of the distinction between form and content, it serves as a useful analytical tool when doing a genre analysis.

The *form* of messages is directly linked to the type of mass medium being researched. For example, in the case of films and television the visual form is determined by the following aesthetic and production codes: lighting, colour, area, vectors, depth, volume, different lenses, camera shots, camera angles, camera positions, camera movements and editing. These two mass media, as well as radio, also use auditory codes, such as language used in different types of verbal address, sound effects, music and silences. Whereas in the case of the printed media (e.g. magazines and newspapers) other visual codes determine the form, such as the size of the pages, layout, photographs, line spacing, margins, columns and different letter fonts.

The relevance of these visual and auditory codes lies therein that when repeatedly used, they become conventions – which in turn enable us to use them to *demarcate* and analyse a particular text as a genre.

When analysing the *content* of a media text, a distinction may be made between content that is more fictional versus content that is more real (factional).

Fictional content deals with a (re-)presentation of a reality that does not exist in real life. Examples of genres that are generally considered to be more fictional than others, are printed cartoons, television sitcoms, musical films and radio soap operas. The main purpose of these genres is to entertain. However, as pointed out in section 2.3.1, these genres could simultaneously fulfil other purposes, such as to convey acceptance or rejection of certain social behaviour.

Factional content deals with the presentation of reality, as it exists in real life. Examples of genres that are generally considered to be more factual than others, are printed news, television sport, documentary films and educational radio programmes. The main purposes of these genres can be traced back to the surveillance, coordination and transmission purposes that are discussed in section 2.3.1. In addition to conveying factual information (e.g. daily news), these genres are usually also aimed at:

- creating understanding (e.g. by means of comparisons); and
- clarifying issues (e.g. by showing cause-and-effect relationships).

The above distinction between fictional and factual content is based on the argument that factional content offers a so-called window on the world – that is, it reflects reality by presenting the audience a view of the outside (real) world, whereas fictional texts deal with imaginary content. This argument is, however, debatable and disputed by the counter-argument that a mass-medium text (e.g. a film) does not simply reflect reality as is. Instead, certain aspects of the recording, editing and production processes influence and mediate the (re-)construction of reality as it is conveyed to the audience.

When considering the blurring between fact and fiction, certain genres, such as radio docudramas and advertisements, cannot be clearly categorised as either factional or fictional. For example, in a docudrama, factual data are conveyed as a dramatisation, often using actors and re-enactments, whereas advertisements may be based on factual data, but they are portrayed by means of persuasive appeal techniques found in fictional genres. In other words, advertisements are factual in the sense that the content (e.g. name and attributes of the product or service being advertised) must be provable, and fictional in the sense that factual information is presented, for example, in a dramatised form.

Irrespective of whether advertisements are shown in a cinema, broadcast via television and radio, or printed in a magazine or newspaper, they share certain conventions; and for this reason we take a closer look at examples of such conventions.

Conventions found in advertisements as genre

One message that (on an overt or covert level) is central to all advertisements, is: *Here is a perfect world and you should be part of it.* The focus is on some aspect of human aspiration, related to health, wealth and popularity. Glamour is manufactured and, by means of appeal techniques, the audience is persuaded to believe the promise: *You are what you have!*

When the overt content of an advertisement consists only or mainly of facts and provable information, this means that the advertiser is addressing the audience's cognitive abilities, as well as rational thoughts and behaviours. Whereas, when use is made of persuasive appeal techniques, the audience's emotions and affective needs are addressed. The following are examples of persuasive techniques conventionally found in advertisements:

- The *slice-of-life* technique becomes a convention when it is repeatedly used to depict everyday situations. For example, the setting can be that of a family environment where members of the family are shown enjoying the product. The product therefore becomes an integral part of that togetherness and thereby addresses the audience's need to belong.
- *Promising rewards* are conventionally found in all advertisements. A promise is made that the product or service will give the audience a feeling of wellbeing, goodness or greater satisfaction. The rewards promised include, for example, greater comfort, safety, removal of danger, companionship, health, a longer life, social acceptance and/or greater self-esteem. The promised reward of a special feeling is also conventionally linked to an elevated status, social class and intelligence; and the before-and-after usage is often linked to a problem-solving narrative (e.g. *After using this cough mixture, your child will ...*). When promises are linked to status appeals, these advertisement as usually aimed at the élite market (e.g. the rewards enjoyed when owning and driving an expensive car).
- *Lifestyle techniques* – usually aimed at the mass market – are used when an advertisement reflects contemporary society or a contemporary lifestyle, by means of the type of language used, choice of dress, hairstyle, music and choice of characters (actors or well-known personalities). The use of this technique addresses the audience's need to identify with the product or service and especially the user of the product or service. Towards this end, advertisers conventionally use testimonials as a persuasive technique. A testimonial (e.g. *It works for me ...*) adds prestige, authority and credibility to the product, especially when endorsed by a well-known personality. Advertisements that focus on motherhood also address this need, because a mother is a family's guardian and therefore knows best what advice to give (e.g. what food to prepare for a balanced diet).
- The *verbal types of address* and verbal *statements* used in advertisements are unique because advertisers, in the case of film, television and radio advertisements, are limited by the cost of time; and in the case of printed advertisements, they are limited by the cost of space in which to arouse audiences' interest and persuade them to buy or use a product or service. A distinction is conventionally made between *direct address* and *indirect address*. The following are examples of statements that illustrate *direct address*:
  - *If the breadwinner of your family were to pass away suddenly ...* (also illustrates a scare statement);
  - *If you cannot trust us, who can you trust?* (also illustrates a question);
  - *A medical aid scheme you'll feel part of* (also illustrates a noninformative statement);

- *Think how it'll work for you* (also illustrates a self-evident statement);
- *Everything you need to know* (also illustrates an exclusive statement);
- *Helps you to the top* (also illustrates the use of weasel words – in this case *helps* – that diminishes the forcefulness or meaningfulness of the statement).

The use of *indirect address* differs, depending on which mass medium is being researched. Interpersonal dialogue is conventionally found in film, television and radio advertisements. Dialogue, on a confidential level, enables the audience to identify with the problem (e.g. dandruff, skin problems, tooth decay or bad breath) and addresses the audience's need for empathy. In addition to dialogue, the above three mass media also make use of monologue (in which the speaker thinks aloud) and narration (in which the speaker may or may not appear on the film or television screen). The following are examples of indirect types of address, used in all the mass media:

- *Nine out of every ten doctors prescribe ...* (also illustrates a universal declaration);
- *Enjoy now ... pay later* (also illustrates an incomplete comparison of product gratification, or an incomplete promise);
- *Always Coca-Cola* (also illustrates a conclusive statement);
- *Anglo-Alpha, The human touch in concrete solutions* (also illustrates an inventive statement);
- *With Iscor, the game is on* (also illustrates a non-comparable comparative statement);
- *Finger lickin' good* (also illustrates a catch phrase);
- *Esso with HTA* (also illustrates a secretive type of statement, because the average audience member does not know the meaning of *HTA*).

• When a *similarity-diversity* dichotomy is repeatedly used in advertisements, the convention involves the following. On the one hand *reinforcement* has to take place, which means that the name of the product/service is repeated by means of visual, verbal and/or auditory (e.g. a musical jingle) codes, with brand-name identification as objective. In so doing, a similar message is also repeatedly conveyed to an audience. However, at the same time advertisers have to cater for diversity, variety and flexibility in order to balance that to which audiences have become accustomed, with *novelty*. South African examples of advertisements that are future directed and fluid in realigning their brands with customers' needs, are the fashion retailer, Edgars, Nando's chicken chain, talk radio station 702 and BMW.

Genres as paradigms

Based on the points raised in the sections above, it becomes clear that it is virtually impossible to isolate exact characteristics of a particular genre, whether for one medium, or across all the mass media. It is not only a matter of the purpose, or form or content, or even the repetition of conventions – a genre is all of these. Therefore, when considering the *meaning potential* of a given text, it makes more sense to consider genres as *paradigms*, and as properties of *signification*.

A paradigm is defined by O'Sullivan, Hartley, Saunders, Montgomery & Fiske (1996:216) as "a set of units which have an overall generic similarity". Let us illustrate this definition with reference to four similar properties (conventions) found in the *traditional Western* (cowboy) film, namely the setting, tension, conflict and characterisation.

- The *setting* is traditionally the unknown, Wild West, where conditions are primitive and lawlessness is rife.
- In contrast to other fictional genres, *tension* is expressed by maximising movement and physical action, and by limiting dialogue. It is not unusual to see an entire cast on the move, using horses and wagons.
- *Conflict* usually arises between *binary opposition* of a sheriff versus a gun fighter; a group of people versus the uncivilised wilderness; the cavalry versus the Indians; the cowboys versus the farmers, and/or the railway developers and workers versus the cowboys. Conflict is resolved by means of explicit (physical) actions (violence), rather than through inner reflection.
- The binary opposition of good versus bad, or guilt versus innocence also finds expression in the *characterisation*, which conventionally includes the following. Innocence is represented by a child or an elderly person who admires the *protagonist's* bravery and combat skills, without necessarily understanding the hero's moral conflicts or motives. The *good woman* usually symbolises civil values, whilst the *bad woman* does not uphold respectable values and is often used to increase the tension and conflict. The villain symbolises miserliness and cruelty and is conventionally surrounded by supporters who share similar barbarous and brutal characteristics. In contrast, the hero is conventionally a competent, white male and a lonely outsider who stops over on his way somewhere. The typical hero is a wanderer.

The above four properties are put forward as illustrations of conventions by means of which we can identify a typical *Western*. However, having said that, we have to remain sensitive to the fact that nowadays "typical" *Westerns* are no longer produced. Although we may recognise a fictional film or television programme as a *Western*, they are constantly transformed. For example, the hero may now be an American Indian man or a woman as a medical practitioner; and the stereotypical *bad woman* may turn out to uphold moral values which the audience respects.

This brings us to the central issue when undertaking a genre analysis, namely that a mass-media text can only be identified and defined as a genre in relation to how it:

- differs from other texts that belong to different genre paradigms; and
- corresponds with other texts that belong to the same genre paradigm.

Signification conveyed as public versus private realities

When considering the construction of meaning from a genre perspective, we focus on a relationship between the properties of a genre (e.g. conventions) to their referential reality. The blurred borderline between fact and fiction, as well as the mixture of genre forms, make it necessary to investigate *signification* by looking at the interaction between private and public discourses, which are disseminated via the mass media.

The growing tendency of audiences being linked "live" to the world stage by the intermediacy of the Internet and broadcast media, means that the very concepts "public" and "private" are changing. As common knowledge and everyday experiences are increasingly playing a larger role in mass communication, a new mixed public sphere is being created. For example, radio and television talk shows and audience participation programmes (e.g. *Oprah Winfrey, Felicia Mabuza-Suttle* and the *Two way – talk show* by Caesar Molebatsi) serve to illustrate how personal and private stories are brought to the public forum.

Similarly, whereas *soft news* and human-interest stories were usually last on the list of *newsworthy* information in the 1980s and 1990s, this is changing. Items that deal with lifestyles, alcoholism, divorce, homosexuality, culture, family problems, private life, AIDS and issues that affects the so-called "losers" in society, are increasingly involved in talk shows and talk-format magazine programmes as adaptations of the traditional filmic documentary genre. Even in well-known (factual) programmes, such as *Rescue 911*, which reconstruct and dramatise real accidents, the (public) professional rescuers are treated as ordinary (private) people.

As a further illustration of the interaction between private and public discourses that are disseminated via the mass media, we briefly consider Dr Taylor Hayes, who plays in *The Bold and the Beautiful* (watched by an estimated 350 million viewers daily). Press reviews describe her as "the most captivating actress on day-time television"; and at the same time credit her as Hunter Tylo "a mother of four and champion of family values", as well as "a frequent guest to the Hollywood Bible Study" because "it has helped her to discover who she is in God" (Bold and Beautiful's Tylo ... 2000:9).

Genres as consumer vehicles

Lifestyle techniques were discussed in the above section, as an example of a persuasive technique that has become a convention in many advertisements. The meaning conveyed by using this technique probably best sums up *consumerism* as a form of pleasure, because what we use and consume (clothing, cars, food, leisure-time activities, etc.) is equated with how we live, or our way of life. Advertisements emphasise the pleasure of consumerism through their structure (form) and appeals. In other words, advertisements sell relief (not cough mixture); sex appeal (not soap); vitality (not breakfast food); comfort (not alkaliser); prestige (not cricket bats) and comradeship (not beer).

By linking a commercial product, a persuasive political campaign or even a news event to individuals whom the audiences admire or who possess qualities which audiences value, uses a genre convention which is based on a need of *identity*, together with the need "*to win*". The source of motivation is not factual, but the emotional appeal of becoming like such-and-such a person. This convention is based on applying motivators which in Maslow's (1962) terms can be described as a high evaluation of the self and the esteem held for others. In other words, audiences will not become healthier by eating a specific breakfast cereal, or richer by voting for a specific political party; nor more knowledgeable by reading a specific magazine. Instead, through experiencing a sense of identity with the prestigious individual who does eat this breakfast cereal, or who does support a certain political party, or who writes a personal account of his or her life, audiences acquire a feeling of satisfaction.

The above combined need to identify and to win explains the reaction of shock and disbelief which cricket fans of Hansie Cronje experienced during 2000 when court hearings about his involvement in receiving bribe money was publicised in the mass media. Not only was Hansie Cronje put on trial. So too were audiences' identification with his public image, as a winning South African cricket captain and a public figure, being questioned. This example also illustrates the difficulty of distinguishing between public (front stage) and private (back stage) behaviour. By making the private side of a well-known public figure, such as Hansie Cronje, accessible by means of television broadcasts, forced audiences to view him in another way than before, when his public and private lives were separated. Such televised broadcasts in other words made his human (private) qualities (bad or good) visible and open to (public) inspection.

When considering genres as consumer vehicles, a direct relation exists between how the form and content of texts create and reflect meaning, and sensitivity towards lifestyles, appeals and cultural values. For example, in a television soap advertisement – aimed at an Afrikaans and English-speaking target in South Africa, a young woman is shown taking a bath, with a man (presumably her husband) entering the bathroom towards the end of the advertisement. In a translated version – aimed at a Zulu-speaking target – the man is substituted by a young girl. In other words, in order to sell, South African advertisements are sensitive to different lifestyles and respect cultural *ethos* and traditions as genre conventions. Sensitivity towards language and translations is equally important. For example, according to Seeco (2000:7), Pepsi's campaign "*Come alive with Pepsi*", translates into German and Chinese to mean "*Come alive out of the grave*", and the name "*Schweppes Tonic Water*" was translated in Italy to "*Schweppes Toilet Water*".

Approaches from the researcher's point of view

When drawing a sample and analysing particular mass-media texts, we have to spell out the research goal or purpose of the analysis (as we would do in any other research study). Such research goals will in turn point to the use of one or more of the following perspectives or approaches:

- When undertaking a genre analysis from a literary approach, our research goal would be to sample and classify the texts in terms of certain principles of *coherence*, such as the use of stereotypes. For example, the rich protagonist in a film must be seen to be rich with reference to appearance, motor car, house, jewellery, and the like. The time dimensions according to which such texts are sampled, could therefore be either *cross-sectional* or *longitudinal.* This approach is limited in its capacity to allow for ambiguity (or differences of opinion) and is mainly concerned with whether genres reassert the *status quo.*

- If the goal of our analysis is aimed at determining how genres contributed to the development of textual forms, such as adaptations to the basic *Western* film recipe, our approach would be from a historical perspective. The *historical approach* therefore enables us to give an overview of the longitudinal development of a genre.
- A semiological perspective of genre deals with texts as a sign system, and our research goal would be to analyse how signs (e.g. close-up shots in a television documentary) are used.
- An ideological perspective is concerned with genre in terms of the analysis of the dissemination of attitudes and values via the mass media in a particular society. When following this approach, our research goal would be to establish how genres are used as instruments of control. Whilst regarding genre as part of a *dominant ideology,* this approach requires audiences (and researchers) to distinguish between the constant conflict and contradictions found in the production and re-presentation of ruling ideas.
- Whereas, if our goal is to determine how genres are used to maintain social order or to assist society in adapting to change, a ritual perspective is more applicable. The *ritual approach* sees genre as an exchange between mass-media industries and audiences. This exchange is essentially a cultural exchange, which facilitates society's ability to accommodate order or change.

From the above brief overview, it becomes clear that our research goal will direct the one or more approaches that we would follow. For example, we could start an analysis using a semiological analysis of sign systems and progress to incorporate an *ideological approach* by analysing the different levels of meaning conveyed by these signs. Any genre analysis would therefore be directed by how we provide operational definitions for conceptual categories. For example, when considering the last approach above, the definitions of the concept "cultural" need not be limited to the creative or artistic products of a society or the traditions learned and passed on to new generations. On a connotative level it could be exemplified by a variety of definitions, such as: *individualism* promoted by sport genres, or *conformity* endorsed by persuasive genres, such as advertisements.

In concluding this section, we are reminded that although a genre analysis of a mass-media text may involve evaluating certain properties of a text, such as the values certain characters convey in a fictional text, the overall meaning is contained in the *Gestalt* of the text. In other words, the meaning of each code, convention or property is dependent on the interrelationship with other codes, conventions and properties found in the text. It is therefore important to keep in mind that the concept *text* (in mass communication) is, according to Fiske (1987:14), used in two ways (see overleaf).

- A text consists of visual and auditory signs and codes disseminated via a physical medium, such as television or the printed page; and
- a text is the meaningful result of an encounter between the content and form of the message, and the decoding/interpretation by the audience.

In the remainder of this unit, we reconsider the above conceptual framework of genre conventions, as well as the two uses of the concept text, by selectively dealing with some of the genres found in the different mass media.

2.4 GENRE ANALYSIS OF FILMS AND TELEVISION

2.4.1 The purposes

We go to a cinema to be entertained, because every aspect of the experience (high-definition, large and coloured visual images, quality sound, comfortable chairs, absence of interruptions) contributes to our involvement and heightens the effect of the experience. However, when tracing the history of films, we find that three purposes can be distinguished which motivated filmmakers, namely to exploit the *aesthetics*, the political and the economic advantages. Traditionally films were identified or linked to eras or styles, such as *Westerns*, musicals or science fiction. With its roots in theatre, David Griffith is given the credit for being the first to take raw film material in the early 1900s and to create a unique visual medium, through the manipulation of editing, camera movements and camera angles (Hiebert, Ungurait & Bohn 1985:358).

Based on the assumptions of different film theories, historically the purpose of films of the 1920s can also be differentiated, depending on where the emphasis was placed. For example:

- *Expressionistic* film theorists regarded films as unique ways which can and should be used to give expression to and an interpretation of the so-called reality. For example, an expressionist documentary film would characteristically experiment with the form of the film, would re-enact and restage historical situations and would *syntagmatically* combine different camera angles.
- Closely related to expressionists, *formalist* film theorists were more exact in how filmic codes, such as the composition of the individual filmic shot, as well as *montage* can be used to restructure our view of reality in a predetermined way.
- In contrast, *realist* film theorists regarded film as a way in which reality, as it presents itself, should be conveyed as objectively as possible. Thereby implying that any form of manipulation, such as lighting techniques, studio sets, changing camera angles or editing, were avoided. Accordingly a realist documentary film would try to imitate reality as closely as possible and avoid the manipulation of iconographic codes.

The above theoretical approaches are further discussed in Unit 5. Nevertheless, the purposes in the first two cases are mainly to interpret and comment on the content, through the manipulation of filmic form. Whereas, realists' purpose was to convey content objectively.

In the tradition of Hollywood of the 1930s and 1940s, so-called *genre* films included the *Western*, musicals, comedies, gangster films, horror films romantic films and thrillers. They were often contrasted by what was called *auteur* films, which did not follow the predictable styles of the above films, but instead represented personal style of individualists, such as Alfred Hitchcock and Orson Welles.

Although contemporary films are difficult to typecast as unique and specific genres, Lester (1995:314–316) argues that the following filmic genres can be distinguished if we analyse films as a reflection of *archetypes* and *myths* that are popular at a particular time and in a particular culture:

- Comedy (e.g. *Dennis the Menace* – 1993; *Bosse Nova* – 2000);
- Crime (e.g. *Basic Instinct* – 1992; *Legions of the Night* –1995);
- Epic (e.g. *Malcolm X* – 1992);
- Horror (e.g. *The Final Nightmare: Freddy's Dead* – 1991);
- Musical (e.g. *What's Love Got to Do with It* – 1993; *Love's Labour's Lost* – 2000);
- Romance (e.g. *Sleepless in Seattle* – 1993; *The Road Home* – 2000);
- Science fiction (e.g. *Terminator 2: Judgment Day* – 1991; *My Favorite Martian* – 1999);
- Social impact (e.g. *Boyz N the Hood* – 1991; *Bringing out the Dead* – 2000);
- Thriller (e.g. *Jurassic Park* – 1993; *In Dreams* – 1999);
- War (e.g. *Glory* – 1989; *Three Kings* –1999);
- *Western* (e.g. *Unforgiven* – 1992).

When considering television programmes, the focus has historically been more on technological advancements, economic viability and control measures, rather than genre as such. Any attempt to categorise television programmes according to established film genres, or according to specific purposes, is a frustrating exercise. The reason for the latter is because television programming consists of a multiplicity of types and forms, such as advertisements, announcements, news, editorials and commentaries, talk/interview programmes, music and variety programmes, magazine programmes, special events, special audience-focused programmes, game shows, documentaries, dramas, situation comedies and soap operas. In fact the list can be extended to include religious programmes, children's programmes, investigative reporting, instructional, educational, industrial and corporate presentations. However, it is not our aim to enumerate an exhaustive list of programme categories or types of films. Instead, we are interested in conventions that unify certain groups or classes and at the same time differentiate amongst certain films and television programmes.

Although films were in the past a major source of entertainment, today they serve as a primary source of recreational content for television. For example, at the time of writing, these films were being broadcast on South African television channels: *Dead Men Don't Wear Plaid* (a private-eye thriller, mixed with comedy); *Good News* (a musical); *Six Days, Seven Nights* (a romantic adventure); *Bruce Lee: The Master* (a documentary); *The Spanish Prisoner* (a thriller); and *The Arrival* (science fiction).

Just as Hollywood's genres borrowed from one another, so television categories borrow from film and other television programmes. For example, *Annie get your gun* is traditionally regarded as a musical, but as it contains certain conventions found in *Westerns*, it can also be analysed as a *Western*. Therefore, although pure examples of filmic and television genres are the exception rather than the rule, it is a worthwhile exercise to consider examples of conventions that relate to the form and/or content of filmic and televised narratives.

2.4.2 The construction of meaning through content and/or form

When regarding films and television programmes as industrial products that are based on a capitalist mode of production, the necessity for *standardisation* becomes understandable. We may accordingly be justified in arguing that such films do not have merit in an artistic sense in terms of originality. However, we also argue (from a *mimetic* point of view) that, instead of constricting or limiting a director's or producer's creativity, genre can contribute to and make provision for original expression.

Various factors influence the genre conventions of a particular type of film or television programme. For the purposes of discussion, we make an artificial distinction between external factors and internal factors.

External factors relate to film (or the cinema) and television as media institutions and include the following:

- economic factors related to the production and distribution of films or the broadcasting of television programmes;
- the relation between films (and television programmes) and the socio-ideological, political and economic reality in which they function; and
- in a historical sense, the influence of previous directors' and/or producers' (*auteurs*) and the relevance of presenters or actors as celebrities.

As indicated above in section 2.2, genre represents systems of orientations. Therefore, in addition to the content of a film, its success is codetermined by a number of factors, including word of mouth, critical reviews and ratings in newspapers, trade advertising, box-office results in other countries, the weather, the season of the year, as well as the quality and number of films competing in the area.

Although films and television are audiovisual mass media, the essence of their fictional stories is told through visual symbolism that is structured in a narrative form. Therefore, when analysing the form and/or content as *internal factors*, we have chosen to concentrate on these visual and structural conventions: the theme of the story; the differences between a series and a serial; characters; and visually perceptible objects and actions. (Although we concentrate on films and television, these internal factors can also be applied in analyses of other mass media, such as fictional radio programmes, or in the analyses of factual genres, such as television news.)

The theme of the story

A useful starting point is to identify the *theme* of any story. Love, hate, excitement, desperation, heroism or cowardice, unrealistic fantasies, violence are examples of emotional elements which form the basis of the themes and appeals conventionally found in fictional films and television programmes. The universal themes or motifs of human existence – birth, death, hope, fear, failure – usually underlie the symbols that are used in myths.

When considering the themes found in television dramas, they conventionally centre on violence, tragedy, conflict, danger or kidnapping. Whereas the television soap opera's themes centre on adults, personal conflicts and sex identification.

How is the theme structured? A distinction needs to be made between a *story structure* and *narrative structure*. A *story* refers to a chronological order of events that take place. Whereas a *narrative* can make use of the following encoding conventions in order to select and shape elements of the story:

- The use of parallel editing (which enables viewers to experience two events that occur simultaneously in so-called "real" time).
- The use of flashbacks and flashforwards.
- The construction of shots, sequences and scenes in such a way as to reduce "real" time (even many years) to 28 minutes broadcast time. Real time is therefore condensed, for example, by only selecting and including the action, events and dialogue which are essential to the story structure.

The following basic narrative structure is found in filmic and television (and in fact also in radio genres) which are based on fiction: exposition, development and resolution.

Exposition: The situation and/or theme is given in the exposition, where the following elements are made known to the audience:

- the locality (e.g. the country and place);
- the era and time (i.e. the time period, such as the 1990s; the seasonal time, such as winter; the occasion, such as Christmas; as well as the time of day);
- the main characters (e.g. the hero, heroine or villain);
- the cause and/or nature of underlying conflict.

In other words, by analysing the exposition, or in the case of television, the introductory title sequence, we are able to obtain some idea of the type of genre that is to follow. For example, the exposition of daily television soap operas is usually given by means of dialogue between two characters and/or flashbacks to the previous episode, to

- highlight events that occurred prior to that particular episode;
- remind the audience of one or more subplots;
- summarise the essence of unresolved conflicts in a previous part of the story;
- give a historical reminder of who the protagonist and the villain are; and
- reintroduce one of the themes in the story.

Development: The following variables influence the development of the *plot*: the *duration* (e.g. length of the film); the degree of *character development* required; and the *complexity* of the story. The plot is the framework of incidents on which the narrative is constructed. The dynamic nature of plot structures in narrative genres facilitates the identification and intensification of themes, values and attitudes towards abstract issues in a particular society. Simultaneously, denotative, connotative and symbolic meanings (also discussed in Unit 1 and in Unit 10 "Media and the production of meaning: semiotics" in Volume 1) are conveyed by raising social, political, intellectual or moral issues.

Having introduced the main characters, conflict and themes during the exposition, a plot develops through the development of themes and characterisation in a particular setting or circumstances, with elements of friction, mystery, tension and/or contradiction.

Resolution: The resolution contains the final *climax*, which is the action that determines the decisive moment in the dramatic conflict. In some texts, the *denouement* and *catharsis* follow immediately after the climax and entails the unravelling of the complications of the plot. The narrative structure of a plot usually allows subplots to reach their final climaxes either before or after the climax of the main plot.

Due to the fact that audiences have become accustomed to the above conventions, *narrative prediction* can occur. For example, the last few minutes of a programme in a police series are not broadcast and viewers who are familiar with the narrative structure of the series would be able to predict that the criminals who were shown to have been caught, would be found guilty and punished.

Differences between a series and a serial

Two narrative differences exist when analysing and comparing a television series versus serials. A *series* consists of different stories that end at the end of each episode. The continuity in both series and serials is obtained by the reappearance of the main characters in each episode. In a series, however, the same characters find themselves in different stories. For example, in the fantasy television series *Touched by an Angle*, Tess and Monica appear as two of the angelic characters in each episode – with each episode containing a different story.

In contrast, in a *serial*, several stories continue from one episode to the next, without an ending. A serial therefore consists of a continuation of the same (main) characters in a continuing story, with more than one subplot. In this way an illusion is created that these characters continue with their lives between each episode.

A second difference between a series and a serial is found in the narrative structure of the stories. In a series, the structure of the stories is based on the principle of *linear processing*. In other words there is a change of story line, actions, events and characters (apart from the main characters) which change with each episode. In contrast, in a serial, the structure of the stories is based on the principle of *parallel processing*. This means that transitions from one story line to another take place within one episode, which involve the different subgroups among the main characters. The continuing serial is often regarded as television's *paradigmatic genre*, of which other programmes are argued to be definable departures. For example, the narrative consisting of open-endings found in a serial, is also a convention of news, breakfast, current affairs and discussion programmes.

Characters

The *personality* (e.g. an extrovert) and traits (e.g. altruistic) of a character are presented or revealed through the manipulation of various codes and conventions, of which the following five are briefly dealt with:

- *action*, including visually perceptible behaviour and verbal dialogue (especially when the character is challenged by adversity or temptation);
- *consistency*, such as always reacting or behaving in a predictable manner;
- *other characters' visualised reactions* towards this particular character, which include kinesics, proxemics, haptics and paralanguage;
- *what other characters say* to and about this particular character (especially in his or her absence);
- *camera techniques*, where weakness (versus strength) can, for example, be implied through a high (versus low) camera angle.

The development of a credible character occurs in three dimensions simultaneously, namely with regard to the character's psychological, physical and environmental traits. A character's *psychological* traits can be analysed by asking whether and to what extent the character's behaviour pattern in a wide range of circumstances is consistent. *Physical* traits include characteristics, such as appearance, height, weight, racial group, posture, kinesic mannerisms, such as gesturing, make-up, hairstyle and the gender of the character. *Environmental* traits include numerous characteristics, such as leisure time activities, manner of speech, and likes and dislikes in terms of food, music, modes of transport, type of work and accommodation.

Because audiences see characters in terms of interpersonal and interspatial relations, a useful method of analysing these relationships is to undertake a structural analysis of their visualisation in films and television. An analysis of visual information, such as appearance, overt behaviour, as well as motivation for actions and reactions, gives us access to the emotional nature of relationships and attitudes between characters. In other words, such analyses will answer questions such as whether the attitudes and emotions shared by two characters are positive, ambivalent or negative towards one another.

The stereotypical portrayal of characters relies on the viewers' needs to be told how to behave so that they too may be socially accepted. For example, not too far removed from the hero in a classic *Western*, the main characters in police, detective and adventure series portray images of men and women who are free, independent and daring. In other words, actors and celebrities become a source of pleasure, because they represent a fictional reality which the average viewer would want to share. It has also become a convention during the past few years to include women in the above types of programmes who are not motherly or sexually erotic. A series, such as *La Femme Nikita*, the aggressive and independent portrayal of women, illustrates how television can simultaneously *unify* and *contradict* dominant values.

The creation of a "star" involves two levels of characterisation, namely the construction of a character and the notion of a character (Bennett, Boyd-Bowman, Mercer & Woollacott 1981:241–267). The *construction* of a character is codetermined by the audience's foreknowledge of the character, such as his/her name, appearance, speech characterics and behaviour patterns. The myths surrounding the nature and qualities of an actor as a "star", and consequently his/her entertainment value, are frequently challenged by their appearances in different roles, in different programmes – which frequently occurs in locally produced programmes in South Africa. The myth surrounding these actors is also usually hampered or even destroyed by press reports or articles about them as private individuals. The restraint which reality places on the believability of the mythical illusion represented by the character, also illustrates the overlapping of private and public realities discussed above in section 2.3.2.

The *notion* of a character, on the other hand, relates to the believable qualities by means of which a character may be identified. A character needs to be *unique* in that he/she is given a "real" name and lives in particular circumstances in a specified geographic area and time (period). Autonomy is also a quality that may be linked with the above uniqueness. This concerns the ability which actors have to create an illusion of life. The characters which historically well-known actors such as John Wayne and Fred Astaire portrayed, were real, and not consciously experienced by viewers as being part of a carefully constructed narrative structure.

One of the main reasons why the general viewing public enjoys fictional films and television programmes is because of the way in which the fictional character's behaviour and relationships legitimise the aspirations or emotions experienced by the average viewer. The character – as a *normative figure* – acts as a model for acceptable and unacceptable behaviour and provides patterns of behaviour with apparent consistency. Identification with the celebrity's way of dress, achievements, interests and especially eventful lives enables viewers to escape – if only temporarily – from their personal hardships and problems.

The pleasure derived from watching soap operas, such as *Egoli – Place of Gold, Isidingo – The Need, Generations, Sunset Beach*, or *The Bold and the Beautiful*, can therefore be found in the conventional fantasy created by lifestyles that are different from those experienced by the average viewer. Nevertheless, identifying "being like" the celebrity is facilitated by the celebrity being shown behaving normally, such as getting married, expecting a child, having to deal with a divorce, feeling depressed or going to bed with a headache.

Visually perceptible objects and actions

Visually perceptible objects and actions can be observed and analysed on an overt and a covert level. On an *overt* level, the iconography of what appears or occurs in front of a film or television camera, include décor, style of clothes, buildings, locations or settings – also called codes of content.

The iconography can also be created by camera shots, camera angles and different types of editing techniques, that are also repeated as conventions – also called codes of form. As an example, let us consider the kind of iconography found in television *sitcoms* and the meanings it conveys.

The codes of content consist of using the same set in each episode. This convention does not differ irrespective of whether the sitcom was produced in South Africa (e.g. *Suburban Bliss*) or in the Unites Sates of America (e.g. *The Bill Cosby Show*). The meanings that these codes signify are that the time setting of the themes is the present (a convention) and that the contemporaneous setting is supported by modern-day furniture, characters' clothing and hairstyles (another convention). In fact, the symbols of a wealthy lifestyle, such as a two-storey house, original artwork against the walls, magazines on a coffee table and well-made furniture, in the case of *The Bill Cosby Show*, have (according to Lester 1995:111) prompted some critics to complain that the sitcom was mainly intended for an Anglo-audience. These complaints illustrate that even the *realness* of sitcoms is based on myths, because in this specific example, the critics argued that these visual symbols of wealth were not characteristic of a typical African-American family home.

The fact that the visual setting focuses on home or work, signifies also that we need not go beyond our home or workplace to find examples of causes of disruption. Examples of such causes are conflict due to age differences, or due to different value systems and other related themes, which have to be resolved to reach equilibrium at the end of each episode.

The codes of form that are conventionally *not* found in sitcoms are the use of outside-filmed footage. Instead, scenes are predictably visualised using indoor shots. In fact, an analysis of these shots often reveals a pattern of starting each new scene with a long (establishing) shot, to notify viewers of a change of scene, followed by a series of medium and medium close-up shots to visualise the dialogue (speaking and listening reactions) of two or more characters.

Visually perceptible objects and actions can also be analysed on a *covert* level. This means that as genre critics we can, in addition to an analysis of the overt level, analyse how sociocultural meanings are expressed, reflected, unified, contradicted or created by these visualisations. An analysis on a covert level can also be treated as a second-order level of meaning, or ideological meaning. For example, if a love affair or a marriage takes place between a man and a woman from different racial or ethnic backgrounds, this could on a latent level not only signify racial harmony, but also democratisation. Let us consider two further examples: A single church in a small town could signify religious unity. If the church building is also used as a meeting place for town councillors, this could signify a close cooperation between religion and local government. This is also why the saloon is the most important building in a *Western*. In addition to showing drinking and gambling activities, the saloon functions on a latent level as the social centre of the town and as centre for the climax of the story – the final gunfight. (We return to this second-order or ideological level of meaning in section 2.6.2 when we discuss news as genre.)

Having dealt with the purposes as well as the construction of meaning in different film and television genres, in the next section we concentrate on radio as a mass medium.

2.5 A GENRE ANALYSIS OF RADIO AND ITS PROGRAMMING

Radio has survived the competition it globally faced from television in the 1950s and which it faced in South Africa between the 1970s and 1990s. As a mass medium radio has developed into a highly fragmented audience and revenue base. In many instances the audiences, programming and sources of income have become local, rather than national. These changes have affected the purposes and functions fulfilled by radio.

2.5.1 The purposes

Radio, as in the case of television, essentially serves a socialisation purpose, of mediating the world around us. In addition to inculcating shared values and defining culture, television and especially radio are particularly effective – due to the *omnipresence* of a human voice – in creating new needs and fulfilling individual needs.

The following six purposes can be distinguished and are in fact unique to the encoding characteristics of the texts broadcast by means of radio as a mass medium:

- *Radio serves local and community needs* – Although we acknowledge that international and national radio broadcasts contribute to crossing geographic boundaries, the past decade has seen a shift to serving *local needs*, rather than national needs. This has led to the emergence of local disc jockeys and other radio personalities operating within a community frame of reference.
- *Radio has become personalised* – Gone are the days when a family would gather around a radio to enjoy a radio programme as a group activity. Listening to a radio has become a *personalised* and individualised activity, which means that an important purpose of radio is to satisfy the personal entertainment and information gratifications sought by individuals.
- *Radio forms an integral part of the daily routine* – The mobility of radio enables listeners to listen whilst undertaking other daily activities, such as when driving to work, washing dishes, enjoying a day at the beach or even whilst studying.
- *Radio stations provide diversity* – By aiming the programming (such as news, current affairs, religion, music, sport, drama, education and magazines) at a particular segment of the listener-consumer market, radio stations programme selectively to serve a certain portion of the population. South African examples of stations which also serve a particular language group, include *RSG* (Afrikaans), *LESEDI FM*, (Sesotho), *UNKHOZI FM* (iziZulu) and *UMHLOBO WENENE FM* (isiXhosa).

- *Radio provides white noise* – A radio is often left switched on, not to be used by a listener to obtain information nor to be entertained, but as a companion. In other words, radio creates a *pervasive* auditory environment and although artificial, it serves a *caressing* function by providing never-ending company.
- *Radio is real* – Unlike the other mass media, radio does not in all genres require expensive production equipment or lengthy production procedures. For example, a newsreader or announcer can be given a note to warn listeners about a disaster almost as it occurs. Due to the characteristics of *immediacy* and *actuality*, radio is experienced as being true and authentic – as being real. Another reason why listeners treat radio content as "real" can be found in the absence of visual images, which results in listeners (consciously or unconsciously) filling-in or adding to the content, based on different variables. These variables could be past experience, loneliness, background knowledge, or numerous other needs that underlie the gratifications that are realised because of the "filling-in" process. The latter is one of the reasons why radio is generally referred to as the *theatre of the mind*.

2.5.2 The construction of meaning through content and/or form

Contemporary radio programming is based on format broadcasting, in which a station identifies a segment of the listening audience and structures its mixture of programmes to reach that segment throughout an entire day's schedule. The identification of the profiles of these segments is usually based on research into factors such as the audience's age, income, geographical location, as well as lifestyles – opinions, attitudes, habits, values and tastes.

As a result of format broadcasting, different radio formats have evolved, which directly influence both the content and form of a radio station's programmes. The following are examples of such formats:

- A station based on an *adult contemporary format* targets its programmes at adults in the 25–49 age group, and includes a mixture of programmes that can vary from experts giving financial advice, to long musical *sweeps* (musical inserts broadcast without interruption).
- Stations that follow the *top-40 contemporary format* target their programmes at listeners in the 12–24 age group, and concentrate of broadcasting popular music, which is repeated during a daily schedule. Promotions by the music industry, together with research into the ranking of music preferences by listeners, therefore directly influence the content of programmes.
- *All-talk formats* are targeted at the 25–55 age group and their programme content includes frequent time checks, weather forecasts, market prices, short features, interviews, news, news commentary and phone-in programmes.
- Radio stations that feature up-tempo jazz, folk, blues and rock music (but excluding rap dance music) follow an *urban contemporary format*, aimed at the 12–34 age group in highly ethnic communities.

- *A full-spectrum format* is usually associated with public radio, in which programmes are diverse and the targeted age groups could vary, depending on the type of programme and the time of the day.

Most radio programming consists mainly of the following genres, namely: recorded music; news and weather; sport; educational programmes; advertising and phone-in programmes.

Continuity announcers or disc jockeys link these genres into a cohesive unit. Due to the absence of visual imagery, the story line in fictional programmes, and the content and structure of factual programmes (such as news), can more easily be compressed in terms of narrative time and space. Instead of using the filmic term *montage*, the musical term *segue* is more applicable in radio. This means that an uninterrupted transition from one auditory segment to the next, without a break, is maintained. *Dead space*, except when purposefully used for effect, is disliked and therefore avoided.

Although each of the genres listed above can be analysed separately, we have decided to concentrate on phone-in programmes to investigate how meaning is constructed by both the content and form of the programmes. Our decision was prompted by the increased use that radio stations make of this genre to fill airtime, as well as realising the socialisation and others functions that this genre fulfils.

Phone-in programmes

As indicated above, in section 2.5.1, radio has become a personalised medium. This directly affects programming formats that have become popular conventions in recent years. These formats include the development of listening relationships between disc jockeys and/or presenters and audiences, in the form of musical request shows, and especially the talk-show concept.

The form of all phone-in programmes share two conventions, namely a host (who answers telephone calls whilst sitting in a radio studio) and the callers (listeners who telephone the host on one or more telephone numbers). Whenever these two conventions are present, both the radio broadcasters and we as listeners have no difficulty in identifying a phone-in programme as a separate genre – which again illustrates the first assumption made in section 2.2, that of an "agreed code".

When evaluating these programmes as being representative of systems of orientations – the second assumption discussed in section 2.2 – a number of important aspects are found to be applicable. In terms of economic factors this is an inexpensive programme – in fact the cost of the call is borne by the listeners as callers. When considering the other variables (listed in section 2.2) the following are not only worth noting, but are also unique to phone-in programmes as a genre:

- As a medium for interpersonal communication, this genre has contributed to radio's ethos becoming more equal, open and accessible, thus enhancing relationships between the mass medium and its audience.
- Phone-in programmes function as a forum for the expression of different subject positions and of multiple voices, which are both private and public.

- This genre is intrinsically reflective on personal experience. In other words, the programmes offer callers opportunities for reflective criticism, as well as for sincere responses to a host or guest – responses which are validated because they are the experiences of ordinary (real) people.

When considering the fourth assumption (i.e. genres represent a double layer of expectations), research studies during the past 30 years have revealed that callers develop an alliance with their favourite hosts and expect to be treated as a good friend. In addition to sharing common interests, experiences and concerns on a regular basis, and fulfilling the need to have their views and values reinforced, listeners, according to Zerbinos (1995:17), expect a phone-in programme to provide information, entertainment, therapy and to function as an ombudsman.

As the social and political impact of phone-in programmes is often based on inconclusive evidence, more research is required to determine whether and how they influence public debate. Such research involves audience research (not a genre analysis) and would have to take into account whether the listeners are simply curious about the programme, whether they are regular listeners who are mostly passively involved, and whether listeners actively participate as callers. According to Dauncey and Hare (1999:103), if editorial control ensures quality information as content and simultaneously allows callers to experience the psychological benefit of participating, it is possible that both empowerment and education can merge in radio phone-in programmes.

Various *formats* have been created around the talk-show concepts, especially involving the radio phone-in programme. However, three formatic characteristics that are shared by all radio phone-in programmes are their predetermined duration (e.g. 30 minutes), a fixed time-slot (e.g. 14:00–14:30) and a predetermined regularity of being broadcast in a daily or weekly schedule. For example, radio *RSG* (Afrikaans) – at the time of writing – has three phone-in programmes on a weekly basis between 00:00 and 05:00. The first consists of a *help-line*; followed by a *market place* phone-in programme; thereafter a phone-in programme that caters specifically for the so-called *association of early risers* (these three titles are freely translated from Afrikaans).

In addition to the above three variables (duration, time-slot and regularity), the following are examples of other variables that also influence the format and content of radio phone-in programmes:

- *Geographic area and radio station* – Phone-in programmes are broadcast on a national level, or in a regional (breakaway) slot.
- *Purpose* – Listeners phone with the purpose of sending messages to family or friends, to sell or exchange goods, to raise questions, to contribute to the topic being discussed, and/or to respond to the host or a previous caller. The option of remaining anonymous, offers troubled callers the opportunity to deal with personal or sensitive issues, which they would be reluctant to share if their identities were known.
- *Topic* – Either a different topic is introduced in each new programme, to which listeners are invited to question/comment; or a similar topic (e.g. medical care) is

repeated on a daily or weekly basis; and/or listeners are free to introduce and comment on topics of their individual choice.

- *Segue* – The broadcast of phone-in calls consists of a dialogue between the host and the caller; or a dialogue combined with musical inserts; and/or it involves a three-way discussion between the caller, the host and a guest (e.g. a medical practitioner) who is present in the studio or linked telephonically to another venue.
- *Pivotal role of the host* – A host's speech acts conventionally consist of opening and terminating the dialogue. In between, the host regulates the dialogue as text, by replying; acknowledging; adding information; evaluating through approval/disapproval; and/or directing, by continuing or changing the subject. A seven-second audio delay also permits the host, or a sound engineer, to screen incoming calls. Similar to hosts in radio and television genres, such as variety programmes or game shows, the hosts of phone-in programmes may be regarded as celebrities, but they are allowed to be freed from artificial, fictional or mythical roles and can "play" and be themselves.

In addition to using the duration, fixed time-slot, regularity of broadcasts, area, purpose, topic, segue, the pivotal role of the host and/or presence of a guest, as an analytical scheme, three components can be added. These three components, which were identified by Halliday (1978) and subsequently applied by Moss and Higgins (1981), are as follows:

- the nature of the social action involved in the conversation (which is referred to as the *field*);
- the role structure identifiable in the interaction, including demographics, such as age and gender (also called the *tenor*); and
- the way in which the discourse text is organised (or *mode*).

The mode could include verbal reactions in the form of explicit statements of anger, denial, rejection, affection, fear, surprise, embarrassment, shame, hurt or apology, either from the caller and/or from the host or guest.

For the purpose of compiling an analytical scheme, based on the distinction made in section 2.4.2 between external factors and internal factors (codes of content and codes of form), the above factors can be applied in such an analysis by first considering research questions that relate to *external factors*, namely:

- Is the phone-in programme broadcast in a national or regional area?
- Do any of the following factors influence the form or the content of the programme: socio-ideological, political, economic, historical and/or the influence of previous phone-in programme formats or hosts?
- Which radio station broadcasts the programme?
- Who is the target audience of the radio station?
- In what type of social situation (or field) does dialogue take place?

In addition, the following research questions can be asked as part of the analytical scheme, based on *internal factors*.

Codes of form

- What is the duration of the programme?
- Does the programme have a fixed time-slot?
- Is the programme broadcast on a daily or a weekly schedule?
- Which kind of segue applies in the programme?
- How does the format of the programme influence the topic?
- How does the pivotal role of the host influence the purpose and topic of the programme?
- If a guest is involved, how is interaction with and/or feedback from the guest integrated in the programme format?
- What are the roles adopted during the interaction (or tenor)?
- What are the demographics of the host, callers generally and (if applicable) the guest?
- How is the mode or format of the text structured?

Codes of content

- What are the main purposes of messages exchanged during a programme?
- Are different topics introduced in each new programme?
- Is a similar topic addressed on a daily or weekly basis?
- Who determines and introduces the topic (the host or the callers)?
- How does the host use any of the following speech acts to regulate dialogue: replying, acknowledging, adding information, evaluating through approval/ disapproval; or directing by continuing or changing the subject?

Phone-in programmes offer a special kind of interpersonal interaction, because the normal cues, such as kinesics, found in face-to-face conversations, are absent. Therefore meaning resides in the verbal text itself.

By answering the above questions, a genre critic determines how meanings are expressed, constructed, confirmed or contradicted by this genre. We usually distinguish between at least two levels of meaning, namely on an overt (or denotative) level and on a latent (or connotative and/or ideological) level. (These different levels of meaning are discussed in Unit 10, Media and the production of meaning: semiotics, in Volume 1.)

In concluding this section on radio, it is important to note that although we focused mainly on phone in programmes, the latter illustrates that when undertaking a genre analysis of a radio programme, the conceptual scheme to be used in such research will depend on four factors (that have repeatedly been dealt with above and are again summarised below):

1 the external environment (e.g. economic conditions) in which the radio station functions;
2 the purpose of the genre;
3 the encoding conventions (form) of radio as a mass medium (language, music, sound effects and silences); and

4 the conventions that are typical of the content of the particular programme being analysed.

Having dealt with genre analyses of film, television and radio in the above sections, we now turn our attention to journalism, with specific attention to an analysis of news as a genre.

2.6 A GENRE ANALYSIS OF JOURNALISM

"Journalism", in its broadest sense, includes newspapers, news magazines, trade magazines, radio and television newscasts, press services and corporate in-house publications – in short, the variety of mass media that describe or comment on current events. When dealing with "journalism" in this section we are doing so by focusing on *news* as one form of journalism, after which we consider more specifically the conventions found in news in general and as disseminated by means of newspapers.

2.6.1 The purposes

News is treated differently by the different mass media, mainly due to the differences between listening (to news broadcast by means of television and radio) and reading (the printed words). That is why broadcast news usually contains the main points or headlines of news events, using fewer words and broadcasting fewer stories, than newspapers. In contrast, one newspaper can cover many different news events, and has the space to interpret, explain and analyse events in greater depth.

Traditionally, the purposes of news genres can be described as being *informative*, *interpretative* and *entertaining*. However, other related purposes or functions can also be fulfilled, namely creating awareness of events that occur in the audience's environment; background information can provide a measure of education; guidance and even persuasion can take place if audiences are guided and persuaded to adopt a particular attitude; and human interest items can function as an inspiration to become involved in community affairs.

The purpose of disseminating information via the *print media*, can also differ depending on one or more of the following variables:

- whether they are once-only publications, such as books, posters, brochures, pamphlets and handbills;
- whether they are regular publications, such as newspapers and magazines;
- the rate of publication, such as daily newspapers versus weekly newspapers;
- the geographic distribution of publications, such as community newspapers versus newspapers distributed nationally;
- whether or not they deal with a specific type of content, such as comic books; and
- whether, by addressing a particular audience, they fulfil different functions, such as consumer magazines that deal with topics of general interest versus specialised magazines, such as children's, professional and trade publications.

Some of the above variables are discussed in Unit 11 (Newspaper production) and in Unit 14 (A critical assessment of news) in Media Studies Volume 1, and are therefore not further elaborated here. From a genre perspective it is important to note that any *one* of the above variables would determine the purpose of the particular print medium, as well as the conventions followed with reference to its content and form.

2.6.2 The construction of meaning through content and/or form

As indicated above, in section 2.4.2, the narratives in news are open-ended, similar to the never-ending convention found in soap operas as serials. However, contrary to the narrative form of exposition, development and resolution found in fictional stories (discussed in section 2.4.2), the narratives of news stories are usually based on the following conventions:

1 The narrative links events in a cause-and-effect sequence, or in a logical beginning-and-end sequence.
2 The narrative consists of events that do not follow a chronological order, but which are structured according to their *news values* and therefore the relevance is determined by the journalist or editor.
3 In the case of a still pictorial image (e.g. a press photograph) the narrative is implicit, because it is taken before, during or after a newsworthy event occurred.

In addition to the order in which news items are arranged to form a narrative, in the case of television, the presentation of news also depends on how the camera is used to visualise (or dramatise) the information, and how the content of the narration or voice-over commentary compares with the content of what is portrayed visually. Television news broadcasts, however, very often do not have live videotaped or filmed inserts, in which case use is made of drawings (e.g. of an accused in a criminal trial), mug shots (e.g. from police records) or other still photographic images. As indicated above, it is paradoxical that a narrative can be implicit in such still images, as it becomes newsworthy because of what is about to occur, or what has occurred before, is implied in the codes of content and form. However, the use of still visual images (in television and newspapers) is based on the assumption that the audience recognises the implied passage of time (before and after) to make sense of the image.

Television also tends to exert an indirect bias on news, because as a mass medium it is mainly devoted to dramatised entertainment. For example, a debate between two politicians, becomes a lawsuit; or a demonstration becomes a dominant form of a social action, instead of a petition.

Conventions that apply to verbal language

In the case of printed news, the readers' eyes are attracted to the main heading, or first paragraph of the printed news story, which summarises the essence of an event. Whereas radio news has to be written for the ear, and in addition to the actual words used, aspects such as the tone of the news presenter, pauses and emphasis of certain words can influence the meanings and sense of urgency of individual items. A news item written for the ear also has to lead into the essence of an item.

For example, a heading in a newspaper report may read:

Microloan move hurts, says bank;

whereas when written for the ear, it could read (sound) as follows:

African Bank Investments – which is known as a J-S-E listed micro-lender – has warned of the adverse consequences for credit providers ...

The meaning of words is socially evolved, because the relation between a word (e.g. clock) and the instrument that denotes time, is *arbitrary*. The distinctions between denotative, connotative and mythical meanings of verbal language are discussed in Unit 3. Nevertheless, although we could argue that the so-called "facts" of an event should determine the reporting thereof, journalists can and do slant, restrict or introduce a *preferred reading* of the meaning of the event by:

- the paradigmatic choice of words (e.g. different meanings are conveyed if a *criminal* is labelled in a news story as *swindler, thief, convict, outlaw, prisoner, gangster, hoodlum* or *mobster*);
- the syntagmatic combination of words into sentences (e.g active voice: *Angolan civil war spreads AIDS*, tends to involve the reader more directly than passive voice: *AIDS is being spread by Angolan civil war*).

When reporting sporting successes (e.g. during the Olympic games) or achievements in international relations (e.g. the release of the Strydom couple in 2000) we could expect that words which connote positive preferred readings would be used as adverbs, adjective or nouns. Whereas we could expect words with negative connotations to be used in reporting on deviant behaviour, misconduct, crime and violence. However, in order to establish what qualities are conventionally ascribed to topics that deal with religion, politics, education, health, freedom of speech or human rights, would require a genre analysis of news disseminated by different media, over a longitudinal time-dimension.

News involves copywriters, announcers, editors and in the case of television, directors. Therefore news has to be written and structured in such a way that others can easily edit, change or abbreviate the copy.

A convention usually followed in news stories printed in newspapers, is the *inverted pyramid* structure. This means that the most important part of the story is placed at the beginning, less important details in the middle, and the least important details at the end. The lead, or opening paragraph, contains a summary of the most important elements of the news story, which is often guided by answering: *who?, what?, when?, where?, why?* and *how?*

The inverted pyramid structure serves two purposes. First, if space is limited, it enables the editor to cut the end of a story, knowing that essential information would not be lost. In contrast to television and radio, the print media do not have a human presence of their own. The messages conveyed by means of print media are decoded and read by readers, which means that these readers are in control of when and how communication is experienced. Therefore, secondly the inverted pyramid structure enables readers to scan the newspaper's headlines and leads to determine the most important events, without having to read each report in its entirety.

Conventions that apply to visual (printed) images

The average reader is seldom aware that codes, such as *typography* and *layout*, are a vital link between how words are seen and what they mean. When looking at this publication, the typographic designer had to make decisions about the following conventions:

- The style of the *typeface* that reflects the content.
- The sizes of heading and subheadings in the body of the text, as well as *captions* for photographs, tables or graphic figures.
- The colour of the words (black) and attributes, such as *italics* and **bold**.
- The length and width of text blocks (paragraphs).
- The style of margin *justification* (left, right, centred or fully justified).
- The white space between individual letters (kerning); between lines of type (leading) and between columns of type (alleys).

When considering the layout of a printed page, the following variables conventionally guide the graphic design:

- *Contrast* – Differences in the colour, size and symbolic images on printed pages determine the extent to which contrast is used. Generally, print media that are aimed at a younger audience tend to make use of much contrast to create a busy design. Whereas a more conservative design would contain little contrast among these elements. Size is relative to the use of typographic white space (kerning and leading). In addition, white space is conventionally used around the edges of a page and not placed in the centre. A layout that consists of a lot of white space is generally interpreted as being modern, whereas a crowded design tends to convey the message that the content is historically dated, traditional and/or serious. The actual content can also be used to create contrast and in so doing to create emphasis. For example, an image or familiar face, which is symbolically significant, will attract more attention, than an image that the reader does not know.
- *Balance* – In film, television and print media, a design is balanced if all the elements in the frame (or on a page) are arranged so that the X (horizontal) weight or axis is equal to the Y (vertical) weight or axis. If elements (paragraphs, photographs, graphics) are arranged in a square, rectangle or circle in the middle between the X- and Y-axis, this results in perfect symmetry. The latter type of design is conventionally used when the content is serious or conservative. (Balance – as a code of content – is also further discussed in Unit 1.)

- *Rhythm* – Rhythm is usually associated with the combination of filmic frames or television shots in sequences (discussed in Unit 1). When applied to print media, sequences are created by placing messages on different pages. However, rhythm also refers to the way in which visual elements are arranged to lead the readers' eyes in a particular direction. The front pages of newspapers are often arranged to accommodate the inverted-6 reading pattern (in societies where it is customary to read from left to right). For example, a large banner headline leads the readers' eyes from left to right, and down the right-hand side to an advertisement place at the bottom-right. Or a large banner heading leads the readers' eyes to an adjacent photograph and accompanying story, both placed close to the headline.
- *Unity* – Unity is acquired when the appearance of a newspaper or magazine is stylistically consistent. In other words, the typographical and pictorial elements have been arranged throughout a publication, in a similar way. The latter can best be illustrated by comparing two publications (e.g. *Reader's Digest* and *Time International*) which use different size paper and express different visual styles. A journalistic convention which is often followed by newspapers, is to use one dominant image (e.g. a photograph which is larger than any of the other visual elements) per page

Conventions that apply to both verbal language and visual images

Visual and verbal codes (in news genres) do not necessarily convey the same message. So, for example, the verbal message may contain negative adverbs, adjectives or nouns (e.g. *severe clashes took place between unruly dissidents at the mine and the police*), whereas the visual shots may consist of neutral shots of miners leaving a mine.

The following are five principles that guide the selection and combination of visual inserts, together with verbal texts: striving to be objective, fair, accurate, clear and complete. However, despite these guiding principles, this does not mean that news is always or only factual. For example, an eyewitness account of an accident is included because of the human-interest value. Such an account is clearly based on the views held by the individual and are not necessarily factual.

Visual images used in news are often extended by verbal language, either in the form of captions, or headlines in accompanying printed texts, or superimposed in the form of voice-over commentary.

Barthes (1999:33–40) distinguishes two functions which the verbal text fulfils in relation to the visual image. If the visual image conveys numerous connotative meanings, the verbal text fulfils an *anchorage function* by selecting some meanings and rejecting others. Whereas, the verbal text fulfils a *relay function* if it is complementary to the visual image. In this case the verbal text would explain, develop or expand on the meaning of the visual image.

According to social psychologists (e.g. Marcuse 1964) we, as mass audiences, tend to protect ourselves from pain and tragedy by dulling our sensitivity towards adversities.

People want relief from their suffering; they want to hope that their dreams will come true; and their dreams renew their hopes. Therefore, in communities that are saturated by the noise created by many mediated messages, the mass media intrude into our dulled sensitivity and complacency, by appealing to emotions, fantasies and dreams. In addition, the news genres do so by inducing an illusion of proof. Examples of such proof are found in the factors listed as news values, such as reporting an event that involves an élite person.

Although literary figures of metaphor, simile and metonymy are usually found in advertising, these formal conventions are also found in visual images of news. Such literary figures enable (especially) television to deal with complex news events that cannot be conveyed in short time spans. For example, metaphors are effective because they link the known with the unknown, or they link that which is visible and tangible to that which is intangible. In addition, they need not be limited to verbal language but can be encoded in visual signs and symbols.

Despite the above differences among print, radio and television, according to McQuail (2000:344–346), the elements of form which are shared by these mass media are found in the recurrence, neutrality and facticity of the news genre' content.

- *Recurrence* refers to the constancy in which the same type of content (e.g. foreign, national, political, economic, disasters, weather, sport, local and human-interest news) is repeated. The latter also highlights *redundancy* as a genre characteristic of news because the news media focus on the same events. Despite superficial differences, the news media – especially television – do not deal with in-depth analyses of conflicting issues.
- *Neutrality* and *facticity* imply that news represents an unbiased truth. The extent to which neutrality and facticity can be verified, depends on variables such as the following: Whether both sides of a controversial issue are given equal representation (e.g. in print); how the camera is used to visualise, or even dramatise, the information (e.g. in television and press photography); and how the use of adjectives and adverbs *colour* the verbal language used (in any of the news media).

The construction of meaning through news values

Two basic conventions, which relate to the content of news, influence whether or not an issue or event is selected and included in a news genre. First, the event or occurrence must be *known*. For example, corruption in a government department is not news until it has been made public (or known). Secondly, the event must be newsworthy. The *news values* of events according to Cohen and Young (1974:68–70) will depend on the extent to which they satisfy the conditions summarised by the following factors (F).

F1 The condition of *frequency*. Negative events tend to occur at greater frequency and over a shorter period of time (e.g. killing a child), than positive events (e.g. the growth and development of a child).

F2 If the size or volume of an event exceeds the *threshold* of newsworthiness. Such intensity is determined by the number of people affected or the extent of the implications of the event.

F3 The *unambiguity* of the event. In other words the meaning conveyed by the nature of the event, people involved and consequences are *not* open to different interpretations.

F4 The *meaningfulness* of the event in terms of the cultural *proximity* or cultural relevance. Proximity refers to the nearness of the actual geographic setting of an event to the audience, and by implication the potential identification and involvement and concern which the audience will have with the event.

F5 The condition of *consonance* between the event and a predictable demand or need. In other words, this factor is based on the assumption that negative news will fulfil latent or manifest needs, and that audiences in fact have such needs.

F6 The *unexpectedness* of the event, either because it was unpredictable and/or because of its scarcity. An unexpected event therefore contains an element of surprise.

F7 The *continuity* of the event. For example, a criminal offence committed by a celebrity is reported and will be reported on again while the legal processes of proving guilt/innocence continue.

F8 A condition which is necessary for *composition*. For example, one occurrence of nepotism is reported in combination with other previous incidents of nepotism.

F9 A reference to *élite nations*. What happens in a country such as the USA, such as the election of a new President, could have important repercussions in other parts of the world.

F10 A reference to *élite people*. Audiences identify with and are interested to read about important people, such as sport heroes, politicians, as well as entertainment celebrities.

Élitism (factors 9 and 10) is usually represented by national leaders, nobility and other important people who are successful in fields that vary from sport to economy. Therefore an event (statements, decisions or actions) that involves such an élite person (or nation) will direct its selection and inclusion in the news.

F11 A reference to *individual persons* (e.g. Hansie Cronje) rather than institutions (e.g. South African United Cricket Board).

F12 A reference to something which is *negative* (bad news).

In addition to these 12 factors listed above, three additional factors (or news values) can be added that may direct the selection of an event:

F13 The condition of *actuality* and whether the event is of current interest. Time is therefore of the essence, because an event that occurred a few hours ago, days, or even weeks prior to the dissemination as news, becomes stale and diminishes in actuality. In television news, actuality can be implied by showing filmed or videotaped shots of actual events taking place, thereby verifying that the event is real.

F14 A condition of *threat*. An event that contains any form of conflict, such as abducting tourists and making certain demands for a religious cause, can be newsworthy. This implies that the event (conflict) can have a negative or a positive side.

F15 A condition of *human interest*. Emotive qualities such as love, hate, grief, empathy or joy can either be an integral part of the event and/or an event is selected as news due to the anticipated emotive response by the audience.

The more of the above conditions or factors an event contains, the greater its likelihood of being selected as news, by journalists and editors.

The construction of meaning through ideological news values

In addition to the above news values, the meaning in news is also constructed according to *ideological news values*. These values refer to ideological themes such as moral and political issues found in the society in which the mass medium operates. For example, the death of Princess Diana was newsworthy, not only because she was an élite in society, but also because it occurred unexpectedly and in tragic (dramatic) circumstances. In fact, when thinking about her death, the event met factors 2, 3, 4, 6, 10, 11, 12 and 15 of the news values. On an ideological level, however, the connotative and mythical meanings were attached by the different new media. These messages included: *The people's princess; The princess who cared for the underprivileged; The Princess who helped to fight the spreading of AIDS; she fought against landmines; she was beautiful; she was innocent; she was a caring mother who was protective of her sons; she was one of us.*

Her death, the funeral ceremony (which became a global news event) and speculations regarding events that led up to that fatal crash, were presented from different angles – all of which bridged the ideological theme: *contrary to the British monarchy, Princess Di cared for ordinary people (and she showed she cared).*

News reports on famine, war, unrest or suppression in a particular region or country, often include visual shots (in television and newspapers) of babies or very young children. The inclusion of pictures of these children may be prompted by the news values contained in the last four factors described above. However, on an ideological (second-order) level, children are mythically equated with innocence (and as a universal symbol), which does not distinguish between gender, racial or class distinctions. Their inclusion ideologically conveys a *we care* message, as part of the interpretation of an inhumane reality. The innocence and symbolic universalism of children, also explains why celebrities, royal families and politicians are often photographed with young children when, or example, visiting foreign countries.

When doing a genre analysis of both denotative and ideological meanings conveyed by news, despite the fact that it represents a so-called factional genre, we can follow the similar steps as when we analyse a *Western* film, a television soap opera, or even a radio phone-in programme (see overleaf).

1 The genre (news) is a narrative in which the characters (people), the story (news event) and detail are repeated again and again.
2 The story comprises, sets forth and/or comments on meanings about what is right and wrong, what is good and bad – meanings that are regarded to be important to those who produce the film or programme (select the news), as well as the audiences who receive the story (news).
3 Some of the meanings are ambiguous because they are hidden by the story (news event) and especially by the way in which the story (news) is told.

The deciphering of these so-called hidden meanings is precisely the genre critic's most challenging task. To this end it is worthwhile to briefly consider the difference between what is "good" and what is "bad". An action or event is treated as bad, if the characters (people) fail to resist temptation. In contrast, an action or event is good, if the characters (people) – in the presence of temptation – maintain control of their desires and behaviour. If we accept these distinctions, then our analysis of a news (or any other genre) should question whether any one or more of the following activities which construct temptation, are present (in the story or news event): drinking, gambling, money, sex or violence. If present, the question arises: how do characters (or real people) deal with these temptations?

Against the background of *external factors* that apply to news genres (such as: competition from other news providers; news and information agencies; advertisers; legal and political control, including censorship) the following research questions can be used as an *analytical scheme* based on *internal factors*.

Codes of form

- Based on the inverted pyramid, what part of the story appears in headline and first paragraph; what appears in the middle and what appears at the end? Based on the answer, which part of the story is given the greatest significance?
- Where in the report (beginning, middle or end) are the following questions answered: *who?, what?, when?, where?, why?, how?* and *with what effects?* Based on the answer, which of the following are given the greatest significance: the person or institution involved; the topic; when the event took place; where it took place, the cause of the event or action; the circumstances surrounding the event or action; or the outcomes or effects of the event or action?
- In printed news: How does the typographical style differentiate between important and less important content? Does the typographical style ascribe a formal or informal quality to the content? Do conventions, such as contrast, balance, rhythm or unity ascribe a modern and youthful quality to the report, or a serious and formal quality? Based on the page number (e.g. front page) and position on the page (e.g. top right) – how important/unimportant is the news report, compared with other reports? In broadcast news, other questions can be posed, such as: how important/unimportant is a news item, based on the chronological order of the narrative structure (e.g. first item versus fourth item)?

Codes of content

- What paradigmatic choice of words is used to label the person or institution in the story? (What denotative and connotative meanings are conveyed by these labels? Is the quality of labels used positive, neutral or negative?)
- Is the syntagmatic combination of words based on active or passive voice? On the basis of the verb used, what is the action or the implied action that the person or institution performs (or what action is connected or associated with the person or institution)?
- What quality (positive, neutral or negative) is associated with the adverbs or adjectives used to describe the actions or which are associated with the event?
- In instances where photographs, video and filmed inserts or graphic drawings are used, do the verbal captions and/or verbal text serve to fulfil an anchorage or a relay function?

On the basis of answers to the above research questions related to form and content, which of the 15 conditions or factors that underlie news values would have prompted the journalist or editor to select and treat the event as being newsworthy?

The ultimate challenge of the genre critic is to be able to reach a motivated conclusion as to what ideological messages are conveyed on a connotative level by means of news genres, by carefully analysing each of the conventions found in the variables that are contained in the above questions.

Summary

In this module we introduced genre analysis as a qualitative content analysis of mass-media texts by identifying the following five assumptions:

- genre is identified (by the producers and consumers of mass communication) on the basis of its correspondence with other similar texts;
- genre represents systems of orientations;
- genre represents the development and preservation of textual forms;
- genre represents a double layer of expectations; and
- genre adheres to specific conventions found in the content and/or form of texts.

These assumptions were followed by an overview of a conceptual framework of conventions which are repeated in texts as genres, with reference to the purposes, as well as the construction of meaning by the form and/or content of texts. This conceptual framework illustrates that genres are characterised by their own narrative structures, themes, formats and iconography. Thereafter we applied the conceptual framework by considering specific genres in more detail, namely:

- advertisements;
- the *Western* film;
- fictional films/television programmes;

- radio programmes, with the emphasis on phone-in programmes; and
- journalism, with the emphasis on news as a genre.

The four classes of purposes differentiated above in section 2.3.1 highlight the fact that genres are created and maintained to support the exchanges of influence in human society. By situating research of mass-media texts (by means of a genre analysis) in the wider context of these exchanges of influence, should bring us closer to finding answers to the following questions:

- How are the norms of a particular subgroup in society expressed, supported or criticised?
- How is social control (e.g. over minorities) shown to be exerted?
- How are social roles defined, allocated or rejected (e.g. through characterisation)?
- Who are the élites of today?
- How are sociopolitical coordination and cooperation obtained and secured, as reflected in specific mass-media genres (e.g. news)?
- Which of the audiences' expectations are addressed overtly and which are addressed covertly?
- Which current topics and events define the human interests of a twenty-first century society?
- What social, moral or ideological values are being "sold" in specified mass-media genres?

A content analysis, in this case by means of a genre analysis, not only enables us to research the characteristics and conventions of communication, it also enables us "to make inferences as to the antecedents of communication, and to make inferences as to the effects of communication" (McMillan 2000:81). This approach to the analysis of mass-media content poses many challenges for current and future scholars who apply it to media, such as the World Wide Web. The challenge lies therein that the assumptions discussed in this unit have yet to be tested with reference to conventions, such as organisational tools (e.g. search engine; site map) or interactive feature (e.g. bulletin boards or chat rooms).

Research activities

1 Select and record the following:
   - a fictional film, or a television advertisement, or soap opera or sitcom;
   - a radio phone-in programme;
   - a print medium that reports news (or refer to the news report reproduced below).

2 Do a genre analysis of these texts by answering the following research questions:
   - Based on an agreed code between the communicator and the audience, which genre is represented by the selected text?
   - Which systems of orientations are represented by the text?
   - Which double-layered set of expectations can be read into the text?

- What purpose(s) does (do) this genre meet?
- Which fictional versus factual content does the text contain?
- Which conventions are used to construct meaning through content and/or form? As additional guidance, use the questions posed as analytical schemes in the subsections above that deal with specific mass media, and specific genres.
- Which conventions are repeated as a preservation of other similar textual forms, and which conventions represent a development or change from other similar genres?
- Which denotative and latent (ideological) meanings are conveyed in the text?

Case study 2.1: The payment that put paid to Abe

Abe Williams' departure from the Cabinet was brought about by a provincial MEC, whose year-long investigation unveiled extraordinary facts, writes Rehana Roussouw

ABE WILLIAMS is being investigated in connection with allegations that he had accepted a large bribe from a company tendering to disburse pension funds.

The Office for Serious Economic Offences (OSEO) raided his house on Wednesday to establish whether claims that he has banked these funds in a front company were true.

The raid on his home and office was a result of a year-long investigation by the Western Cape MEC for Health and Social Services, Ebrahim Rasool, who in 1994 inherited a five-year contract between his administration and a private company Nisec, to pay R1,7-billion a year to Cape pensioners. Nisec is owned by Denel, a former Armscor subsidiary.

And Nisec had access to interest on R100-million for 17 days before pensions and disability grants were paid out.

Following the disclosure last year by national government that the Western Cape was losing R240-million a year in welfare fraud, Rasool launched an investigation, which he said this week unveiled facts "beyond my expectation".

Information he received from informants allegedly fingered Williams, former welfare minister in the House of Representatives.

Rasool said he had believed from the start that the levels of fraud inherited could not simply be the work of officials. "I believed then that political sanction must have been available through commission or omission."

Rasool's breakthrough came when he appealed to the public for further information. He received telephone calls and personal visits from Williams' former staffers and bank officials, who provided information that Williams had allegedly received large sums of money to promote particular companies tendering to pay out pensions. He passed all the information he received to the OSEO investigators.

"My alarm grew when, at a Minmec meeting

The show's over
The
fat man
sang
PAGE 4

in December last year between the national minister (Williams), the deputy minister, the provincial MECs and officials of welfare from across the country, Minister Williams proposed that we all listen to a presentation by Nisec on pension payouts," Rasool said.

"I was the one to raise objections to this proposal by Minister Williams on the basis that Nisec is being investigated in the Western Cape and was a competitor for the tenders of some other provinces, and that the minister's proposal was highly irregular.

"Minister Williams acceded but again tried to have the MECs have lunch with him in his office where Nisec could speak to us.

"This confirmed the stories related to me by informants and I am confident that (the) raid may have the effect of putting at the disposal of OSEO the necessary evidence which may prove, or is likely to prove, corruption, fraud or bribery."

Rasool's forensic investigation into the social security unit of his department has already yielded serious allegations of fraud and corruption, as well as weaknesses in the contract with Nisec.

Investigators found that Nisec enjoyed a monthly "windfall" where it was allowed to hold R100-million a month for 17 days before making pension and disability grant payments. This has since been corrected, and the company receives the money two days before the payments are due.

The investigation also uncovered a variety of fraudulent and corrupt practices among junior clerks and senior management in the Department of Social Services. For instance, transport was procured from a company which did not own a single vehicle, but was paid R80 000 to transport files for the department.

This is not the first time Williams has been in the thick of political controversy.

His appointment to Cabinet was met with howls of protest from ANC members in Cape Town who had felt the bite of Williams' staunch support of attempts to quell anti-apartheid activity.

He first reached Parliament as a Labour Party representative for the House of Representatives in 1984. Five years later, he was appointed HoR deputy minister of education and culture and in 1991 the additional portfolio of welfare minister was added.

Williams did not endear himself to educators and parents in the Western Cape during his tenure, as he was the first Western Cape politician to propose large-scale retrenchments of teachers.

His appointment by De Klerk as minister of welfare and population development in 1994 was seen by many in the ANC as a token of appreciation to Western Cape coloured voters for their support in the elections.

Williams scandal blurs the Nats' new vision

Marion Edmunds

The National Party had hoped to spend this coming weekend romancing the media at the Marine Hotel in the picturesque Cape village of Hermanus. The resignation of Welfare Minister Abe Williams, following the investigation by the Office for Serious Economic Offences, has put an end to that prospect.

The National Party will have to spend its first-ever media *bosberaad* on the defensive, doing damage control to convince a highly sceptical press corps that yes, the Nats are a good, clean and well-intentioned lot, with a future in a democratic society.

The Williams "*skandaal*" could not have hit the Nats at a worse time. It has spoiled the afterglow of the Nats February 2 announcement of a new vision, it has damaged the NP's prospects in the local government elections in Cape Town, to be held at the end of May.

Political scientist Professor Robert Schrire of the University of Cape Town believes that the sought-after coloured vote will be affected by the allegations made against Williams: "The moderate, conservative middle-class coloured voters will hesitate before voting NP now. Not that they will vote for the ANC, they will rather sit on their hands," he said.

This is disputed by another National Party coloured leader, the Western Cape's Local Government MEC Peter Marais, who said after hearing the news: "After Boesak was investigated, the ANC actually improved its position in the Cape; why should the National Party coloured vote be damaged by Williams's resignation?"

The comparison between Boesak and Williams is damning and raises questions about Marais's ambitions. After all, a national Cabinet seat has been freed up by William's resignation and there are eager new Nationalists waiting in the wings.

As Schrire puts it: "A politician is motivated by a mixture of idealism and self-interest. In the case of the black NP members, the motivation is mostly self-interest because they were prepared to be part of a party that once discriminated against them. The NP attracts shady characters because black members in particular see it as an easy way to power and privilege."

Certainly, Williams, through his long association with the National Party and the tricameral parliamentary system, has known both power and privilege. And as political scientist Jannie Gagiano from the University of Stellenbosch points out, there were and still are a lot more like him who played a part in black local government and in the homeland governments in the old days. Many of these co-optees have found a political home in the new NP and these new recruits could ironically do the party more damage than good, if more of their skeletons come tumbling out of the warehouse of the past.

Williams's resignation has placed the spotlight firmly on the black Nationalists and it has raised the stark question: how straight are they? While nobody is giving an answer, the only NP member who has been prepared to comment honestly and authoritatively on the impact of this question is Senator David Malatsi, a politician who has over last few weeks gained some credibility as the new NP's black voice.

"I am terribly disappointed," he said in reaction to the news. "And this hampers our new vision. It undermines all our efforts to try and bring credible people of colour into the NP."

Malatsi said what the secretary general designate of the party, Roelf Meyer, could not allow himself to say for fear of damaging his image before taking on the mantle of his new job.

A NP source said Meyer wanted the old guard "to mop up the mess" so that it did not taint him before he starts as secretary general on March 1. By midnight Wednesday, they were doing their best.

The Nats communication director, Marthinus van Schalkwyk, had swung into damage control mode: "Remember it is not the NP we are dealing with here, it is an individual ... if Mr de Klerk had not acted decisively then there might have been more damage done ... of course the ANC through Ebrahim Rasool staged the whole thing as part of the election campaign in the Western Cape," he said.

To De Klerk's credit, he has acted quickly, and he settled the Williams resignation the day the news hit the street. It will be in his interest to keep up the momentum and raise the media's interest in who will replace Williams, rather than what he did wrong.

The jury is out on the former. Pundits say that Williams' replacement, if from the National Party, ought to be a woman. There are three contenders: MP Sheila Camerer whose big plusses are her experience, and her sophistication. The Northern Cape's MEC for Public Works, Peggy Hollander – who is on the point of coming to national government to swop positions with NP MP PW Saaiman – is another option. She lacks Camerer's skill and political acumen, but she is what the National Party so desperately want and what they lost when Williams went down, a Nationalist leader of colour. And to date, she has no black marks next to her name.

Western Cape Housing MEC Gerald Morkel, as a foremost coloured Nat, must also stand a chance.

Further reading

Evans, J & Hall, S (eds). 1999. *Visual culture: the reader.* London: Sage in association with the Open University.

Feuer, J. 1987. Genre study and television, in *Channels of discourse: television and contemporary criticism*, edited by RC Allen. London: Methuen.

Fourie, PJ (ed). 1997. *Introduction to communication – course book 6: film and television studies.* Kenwyn: Juta.

Grant, BK (ed). 1977. *Film genre: theory and criticism.* London: Scarecrow.

Grossberg, L, Wartella, E & Whitney, DC. 1998. *Media making. Mass media in a popular culture.* Thousand Oaks: Sage.

Lester, PM. 1995. *Visual communication. Images with messages.* Belmont, CA: Wadsworth.

McQuail, D. 2000. *McQuail's mass communication theory.* 4th edition. London: Sage.

O'Sullivan, T, Hartley, J, Saunders, D, Montgomery, M & Fiske, J. 1996. *Key concepts in communication and cultural studies.* 2nd, reprinted edition. London: Routledge.

Van Nierop, L. 1998. *Seeing sense: on film analysis.* Pretoria: Van Schaik.

Bibliography

Alvarado, M, Gutch, R & Wollen, T. 1987. *Learning the media.* London: Macmillan.

Andrews, I. 1995. Sandwiched between cultures: the translation of advertisements. *Language Matter. Studies in the Language of Southern Africa* 26:22–39.

Asam, RH. 1986. A genre analysis of television docudrama. Doctorate of Philosophy. University of Georgia. Ann Arbor, MI: University Information Service.

Barnouw, E, Gerbner, G, Schramm, W, Worth, TL & Gross, L (eds). 1989. *International encyclopaedia of communications.* Volumes 1–4. New York: Oxford University Press.

Barthes, R. 1999. Rhetoric of the image, in *Visual culture: the reader*, edited by J Evans & S Hall. London: Sage in association with the Open University.

Bennett, T, Boyd-Bowman, S, Mercer, C & Woollacott, J (eds). 1981. *Popular television and film.* London: British Film Institute.

Berger, AA. 1991. *Media analysis techniques.* Revised edition. Newbury Park, CA: Sage.

Berger, AA. 1992. *Popular culture genres.* London: Sage.

Bold and Beautiful's Tylo lives for God. 2000. *City Press*, 25 June:9

Bywater, T & Sobchack, T. 1989. *Introduction to film criticism: major critical approaches to narrative film*. New York: Longman.

Chalmers, R. 1990. Black & White television ... . *TV World* 13(2):44–48.

Chanan, M. 2000. The documentary chronotope. *Jump Cut* 43:56–61.

Cohen, S & Young, J (eds). 1974. *The manufacture of news. Social problems, deviance and the mass media*. Reprinted edition. London: Constable.

Cole, B. 1981. *Readings from TV guide*. New York: Oxford University Press.

Corner, J. 1991. Meaning, genre and context: the problematics of "public knowledge" in the new audience studies, in *Mass media and society*, edited by J Curran & M Gurevitch. London: Edward Arnold.

Dauncey, H & Hare, G. 1999. French youth talk radio: the free market and free speech. *Media, Culture & Society* 21(1):93–108.

Du Plooy, GM. 1989. *Understanding television: guidelines for visual literacy*. Kenwyn: Juta.

Du Plooy, GM. 1991. Genre criticism, in *Critical television analyses: an introduction*, edited by PJ Fourie. Kenwyn: Juta.

Dyer, G. 1982. *Advertising as communication*. London: Methuen.

Edmunds, M. 1996. The payment that put paid to Abe. *Mail & Guardian*, 12(8):1&4.

Eidsvik, C. 1978. *Cineliteracy: film among the arts*. New York: Random House.

Evans, J & Hall, S (eds). 1999. *Visual culture: the reader*. London: Sage in association with the Open University.

Feuer, J. 1987. Genre study and television, in *Channels of discourse: television and contemporary criticism*, edited by RC Allen. London: Methuen.

Feyen, S & Wigal, D (eds). 1969. *Screen experience: an approach to film*. Dayton, OH: Pflaum.

Fiske, J. 1987. *Television culture*. London: Methuen.

Flew, A (ed). 1984. *A dictionary of philosophy*. 2nd revised edition. London: Pan & Macmillan.

Fourie, PJ. 1983. *Beeldkommunikasie. Kultuurkritiek, ideologiese kritiek en 'n inleiding tot die beeldsemiologie*. Johannesburg: McGraw-Hill.

Fourie, PJ. 1985. Betekenis en betekeniskonstruksie in beeldkommunikasie. *Communicare* 4(1):33–40.

Fourie, PJ (ed). 1997. *Introduction to communication – course book 6: film and television studies*. Kenwyn: Juta.

Fourie, PJ (ed). 2001. *Media Studies, Volume 1: Institutions, theories and issues*. Kenwyn: Juta.

Frye, N. 1966. *Anatomy of criticism*. New York: Atheneum.

Galtung, J & Ruge, M. 1974. Structuring and selecting news, in *The manufacture of news. Social problems, deviance and the mass media*, edited by S Cohen & J Young. Reprinted edition. London: Constable.

Giannetti, LD. 1976. *Understanding movies*. 2nd edition. Englewood Cliffs, NJ: Prentice-Hall.

Grant, BK (ed). 1977. *Film genre: theory and criticism*. London: Scarecrow.

Grossberg, L, Wartella, E & Whitney, DC. 1998. *Media making. Mass media in a popular culture*. Thousand Oaks: Sage.

Hall, S. 1970. A world at one with itself. *New Society* 18:1056–1058.

Halliday, MAK. 1978. *Language as social semiotic*. London: Edward Arnold.

Hickey, N. 1981. What do you mean it's only a game? in *Readings from TV guide*, edited by B Cole. New York: Oxford University Press.

Hiebert, RE, Ungurait, DF & Bohn, T. 1985. *Mass media IV. An introduction to modern communication*. 4th edition. New York: Longman.

Janeke, C. 1995. Language, cognition, and metaphor. *Language matters. Studies in the languages of Southern Africa* 26:129–146.

Jenkins, H. 1988. "Star Trek" rerun, reread, rewritten: fan writing as textual poaching. *Critical Studies in Mass Communication* 5(2):85–107.

Kantor, L & Bird, E. 1995. Innocent or guilty? Media coverage of the O J Simpson trial. *Media Mask* 1(4):20–24.

Katz, E & Liebes, T. 1990. Interacting with "Dallas": cross-cultural readings of American TV. *Canadian Journal of Communication* 15(1):45–66.

Kinder, M & Houston B. 1972. *Close-up: a critical perspective on film.* New York: Harcourt Brace Jovanovich.

Kinghorn, E. 1996. The independent imagineer returns from the future with clear directions. *The Sunday Independent*, 14 January:18.

Lasswell, H. 1948. The structure and function of communication in society, in *The communication of ideas*, edited by L Bryson. New York: Harper & Row.

Leiss, W, Kline, S & Jhally, S. 1988. *Social communication in advertising.* 2nd edition. London: Methuen.

Lester, PM. 1995. *Visual communication. Images with messages.* Belmont, CA: Wadsworth.

Madsen, RP. 1973. *The impact of film: how ideas are communicated through cinema and television.* New York: MacMillan.

Marcuse, H. 1964. *One dimensional man.* Boston, MA: Beacon.

Maslow, AH. 1962. *Toward a psychology of being.* New York: Litton Educational Publishing.

Mayeux, PE. 1985. *Writing for the broadcast media.* London: Allyn & Bacon.

McMillan, SJ. 2000. The microscope and the moving target: the challenge of applying content analysis to the World Wide Web. *Journalism & Mass Communication Quarterly* 77(1):80–98.

McQuail, D. 2000. *McQuail's mass communication theory.* 4th edition. London: Sage.

Mead, GH. 1934. *Mind, self, and society from the standpoint of a social behaviourist.* Chicago: University of Chicago Press.

Messaris, P. 1994. *Visual "literacy". Image, mind, & reality.* Boulder: Westview.

Moss, P & Higgins, C. 1981. A discourse analysis of talk-back radio: some cultural implications. *Australian Review of Applied Linguistics* 4:32–48.

Neale, S. 1980. Genre. London: British Film Institute.

Nelson, RP. 1989. *The design of advertising.* 6th edition. Dubuque, IA: Wm C Brown.

Noelle-Neumann, E. 1980. Mass media and social change in developed societies, in *Mass communication review yearbook*, volume 1, edited by GC Wilhoit & H de Bock. Beverly Hills, CA: Sage.

Okigbo, C. 1995. National images in the age of the information superhighway: African perspectives. *Africa Media Review* 9(2):105–121.

Oosthuizen, LM (ed). 1996. *Introduction to communication – course book 5: journalism, press and radio studies.* Kenwyn: Juta.

O'Sullivan, T, Hartley, J, Saunders, D, Montgomery, M & Fiske, J. 1996. *Key concepts in communication and cultural studies.* 2nd, reprinted edition. London: Routledge.

Parks, R. 1982. *The western hero in film and television: mass media mythology.* Michigan: UMI Research.

Peters, JM. 1977. *Pictorial communication*, revised and translated by M Coombes. Cape Town: David Philip.

Ross, A. 1987. "Miami Vice": selling in. *Communication* 9:305–334.

Roth, L. 1980. Bergsonian comedy and the human machines in "Star Wars". *Film Criticism* 4(2):1–8.

Roth, L. 1993. Humanity, technology, and comedy in *Microbi*, a Hungarian animate science fiction television series. *World Communication* 22(2):74–79.

Rulashe, L. 1996. Plan to stub out smoking 'pimps'. *Sunday Times*, 13 January:7.

Seeco, Ll. 2000. Local is lekker, but tread warily if you want to tackle world markets. *City Press Supplement*, 3 December:7.

Shaw, L. 1990. Addicted to "Loving". *Sunday Times Magazine*, 30 September:26 & 28.

Stephenson, W. 1967. *The play theory of mass communication*. Chicago: University of Chicago Press.

Van Nierop, L. 1998. *Seeing sense: on film analysis*. Pretoria: Van Schaik.

Vivian, J. 1991. *The media of mass communication*. Boston: Allyn & Bacon.

Walker, AK, Kruger, A & Andrew, IC. 1995. Translation as transformation: a process of linguistic and cultural adaptation. *South African Journal of Linguistics Supplement* 26:99–115.

Whillock, RK. 1993. Winning their hearts and minds: strategies for victory in American political campaigns. *World Communication* 22(2):62–67.

Wilson, T. 1996. Television's everyday life: towards a phenomenology of the "Televisual Subject". *Journal of Communication Inquiry* 20(1):49–66.

Wright, CR. 1960. Functional analysis and mass communication. *Public Opinion Quarterly* 24:606–620.

Zerbinos, E. 1995. The talk radio phenomenon: an update. *Journal of Radio Studies* 3:10–22.

Zettl, H. 1990. *Sight sound motion. Applied media aesthetics*. 2nd edition. Belmont, CA: Wadsworth.

Zettl, H. 1998. Contextual media aesthetics as the basis for media literacy. *Journal of Communication* 48(1):81–95.

Media and Language

3

Stefan Sonderling

Overview

The aim of this unit is to provide you with a critical understanding of the role of language, mass media and society. You will gain knowledge about the role of language in society and in your own life, explain two definitions and describe the formal aspects of language as text, language as social interaction and the social context for the use of language. You will be able to apply your understanding of language to a critical evaluation of the use of language by the mass media.

Learning outcomes

At the end of this unit you should be able to

- provide two definitions of language;
- explain the role of language in society;
- describe the relationship between language and thought;
- recognise three levels of language analysis;
- identify the main elements of a text, the rules of discursive practice and the social context of language;
- describe the relationship between language and social power; and
- write your own case study on the language used by mass media.

3.1 INTRODUCTION

In this unit you are introduced to the study of communication through natural language. Language has two main forms: *speech* and *writing* which are our most common and important means for *oral* and *literary* communication. You will be introduced to the role of language in society and in all our personal and social activities and how language determines the way we think and experience the world. You are then introduced to the different approaches to the study and analysis of language.

3.2 LANGUAGE AND SOCIETY

Language is the most highly developed and most frequently used medium of communication that we possess. We encounter language as spoken (oral) and as written (literary) forms of communication. Language is important and central in all aspects of our lives, from face-to-face situations to communication through the mass media. Our lives depend on language: understanding the language spoken in our society makes us acceptable to our friend; our ability to speak persuasively gets us things done and the respect of our peers; and speaking the right way at a job interview gets us the job we desire.

In our society the mass media have become important industries producing linguistic goods such as texts, books, newspapers, television programmes; and employing a large number of people, such as journalists, editors, and advertising copywriters who almost exclusively earn their living by working with language. The introduction of new information and communication technologies, such as the computer into all aspects of our society results in language gaining importance, for example we communicate with more people and work situations demand efficient communication and linguistic skills. In politics, language has also become a target for planning and change, such as enforcing *political correctness*, the use of non-sexist language, and eradication of hate speech and verbal aggression.

In a fundamental way language makes it possible for us to understand and make sense of the world by providing us with *words* and *meanings* to name things and interpret the world, to represent it to our mind, talk about it and exchange information with other people. Our knowledge and experience of the world are *mediated* by language. The way we organise and articulate our experiences is an interpretative process that takes place mainly in, and through language. Stated differently, language stands between our world and us. By using words to describe objects in our world we *re-present* the world to our mind and such re-presentation influences, shapes and also distorts our view of the world. Thoughts do not exist independently of language; on the contrary, language makes our thoughts possible. For example, we know what things in the world are because they have *names* and are *meaningful*. Indeed, philosophers have always suggested that language is our environment – a symbolic universe – in which human beings live. The American linguist, Edward Sapir (1957:69) said that we cannot grasp our world directly but are dependent on a *symbolic universe* of meanings provided by language. It is also only through *language* that all other forms of nonverbal communication can be understood, interpreted and made meaningful. For example, the French literary scholar, Roland Barthes (1982:28) explains that our ability to understand visual images, such as drawings, photographs and the cinema is dependent on our ability to *verbalise* them. What he means is that we only notice or see the things for which we have words to name and describe them.

Learning how to use language is part of a socialisation process through which we become members of society. It is through such a process that we acquire words and their meanings, and obtain the values, attitudes and *ideology* of our culture. (Ideology and its relations to language is discussed in Unit 9, Volume 1.) As Edward Sapir (1957:69) put it: we are at the mercy of the particular language that has become the medium of expression for our society and we see, hear and experience the world as we do because the language habits of our community provide us with certain choices of interpretation and meanings. Canadian communications scholar Marshall McLuhan (1969), even goes so far as to suggest that the dominant form of linguistic communication such as speech, the written and printed word, and the electronic media, each in turn have created distinct cultures. For example, our dependence on writing and print gave us a literate mentality or *logic* that is different from the logic of past oral societies that only used speech. Research done in the United States of America by Kochman (1974:92), seems to confirm the view that there is a distinct difference between the behaviour of people whose communication is predominately through spoken language (*oral*) as against those who have been socialised through prolonged education and are accustomed to written communication (*literary*), and that such differences are the main causes of many intercultural misunderstandings and conflicts.

Yet for most of us, language is like water for the fish or like the air we breathe: we are surrounded by language but do not pay much attention and think that it is a transparent and natural means for communication. We only take notice of language when we have problems communicating, expressing ourselves; when we misunderstand what someone says, or struggle to write letters and reports. From such experiences it becomes clear that language is not a simple medium for communication but is a powerful and complex social communication system that requires better understanding.

3.3 APPROACHES TO THE STUDY AND ANALYSIS OF LANGUAGE

Approaches to the study and analysis of language have changed over the centuries. In ancient times it was believed that language was given to people by the gods and had magical powers. For example, it was believed that if we use a correct word to name an object we would have power to control it, or if we could guess a person's true name, it would put that person under our control. Even today there are people who believe in the magical power of words: for example, they avoid talking about certain illnesses or misfortunes lest such talk cause an illness or bad luck.

There are a number of competing ways to define, study and analyse language. Philosophers, psychologists, linguists, sociolinguists and communication scholars study language from different perspectives and focus on different aspects that they consider important. Lewis and Slade (1994:26–27) classify the different definitions and approaches to language into two main categories:

- Language is defined as a system of signs for the communication of meaning. From this perspective language is described as a code or a rule-governed system of signs.
- Language is defined as a social phenomenon.

These definitions are reflected in the traditional division in linguistics where the study of language proceeds from the smallest units of sounds and words and grammar, the meaning of words, and the use of language in the wider context of society. These aspects are studied respectively by semiotics, semantics and pragmatics.

Semiotics considers language as a system of signs, rules and conventions and explains how such signs can communicate meaning.

Semantics is concerned with the study of meaning of words and sentences.

Pragmatics is concerned with the study of the functions of language and how it is used to do things in social context.

While such division is useful for linguists, for the study of language as a communication system we need a wider and more comprehensive communication framework. For the purpose of our study we need to consider language as a system of signs, such as sounds, words, sentences and texts that are used according to specific rules of grammar, that provide resources to give meanings to words, sentences and texts and are used in social interaction.

In our verbal communication, the language we encounter is not simply the *raw* material such as sounds or single words; communication takes place through articulated language, that is, language organised into the form of verbal messages. Therefore, we can consider *verbal messages* as our basic units that are created, exchanged and interpreted during any communication encounter (Kress 1983:3; 1988:86). Messages are made up of linguistic *signs* – such as spoken or written words – that have already been selected and organised into meaningful sentences and paragraphs. In verbal communication, people usually do not interpret the meaning of single words or even individual sentences but look at the *message* that is communicated in sentences, paragraphs or in the overall story in a newspaper article. Similarly, when we speak or write we always have a message in mind. Verbal messages can be analysed on three dimensions or levels (Kress 1983:3; Hodge & Kress 1988:5–6; Fairclough 1990:20–25; 1992a:3; 1992b:10; 1997; Van Dijk 1997):

- *Text* – the linguistic and formal aspects of the verbal message; the text of a message is constructed from *written* or *spoken* language signs, such as sounds, spoken or written words, sentences, paragraphs and whole segments of texts (also know as extended discourse). At this level the study focuses on these significant sounds, letters, words and sentences. Methods from both *semiotics* and *semantics* are used for such analysis.
- *Discursive practice* – the rules and conventions that are used to produce the text of verbal messages and determine the linguistic interaction between people. Discursive practice refers to the fact that the use of language is a practical and social phenomenon; it is a particular type of social action or practice, for example conversation or dialogue. Discursive practice also refers to specialised and formal styles of speaking and writing used by the discursive practice of poetry, religion, academic disciplines, and so forth. The study of discursive practice draws on the insights of *pragmatics*, sociolinguistics and social sciences studies.
- *Social context of the use of language* – both text and discursive practice are socially situated; they are communicative acts taking place in different social settings. The social contexts of text and discursive practice are the social conditions such as class and power relations within a society that influence and organise the production, circulation and interpretation of texts; determine who may speak and who must remain silent and listen; where and when one may speak; and determine the values to be placed on a person's speech. Here both pragmatics and a variety of social analyses inform the study of language in social context.

3.4 LANGUAGE IN THE TEXT

The text of verbal messages is composed of many signs and has a formal structure, coherence and organisation. The word *text* comes from the Latin *textus*, meaning something woven together (cf. Hodge & Kress 1988:6). For example, a look at any printed page such as a newspaper or a book creates the impression of a tapestry made from words. Texts can be *spoken* or *written* segments of language (such extended segments of text are also known as *discourse*). We consider texts as the *material product* of a particular *discursive practice*. Different discursive practices produce different and distinct types (or *genre*) of text (cf. Fairclough 1990:20). For example, the discourse of literature produces novels and poetry while the discourse of journalism produces news reports. One type of text may be used for different purposes, for example, the text of the Bible can be used as a document of divine revelation within religious discursive practice, while for literary criticism it is an exemplar of poetic style.

The formal structure of a text reflects the process of its production. For example, the text of a newspaper is characterised by a particular *style* of presenting the information. The text of the news story printed in a newspaper has a particular form, traditionally known as the inverted pyramid. Text written according to the inverted pyramid format begins with the climax of the story and presents all the important facts in the first paragraph. The following is an example of a first paragraph of a news report:

> City runner Simon Mamabolo, who was shot twice by a policeman before the Two Oceans Marathon in Cape Town on Saturday, is back in Pretoria with his friends – but unable to run and in great pain.
>
> (Shot runner back ... 1995:1)

In such a paragraph the facts are arranged to satisfy the readers' curiosity regarding *whom, what, when, where, why,* and *how* of a newsworthy occurrence. While such a formal presentation is considered self-evident today, it originated in the American Civil War period when journalists used the telegraph for the first time. Fearing that their stories would not be transmitted all at once, the journalists crowded as much information as possible into the first paragraph. Subsequently, such a practice has become institutionalised and accepted as a formal requirement for journalistic writing (cf. MacDougall 1969:50). Indeed, the form of presentation or style is an important aspect of media news reporting. Media news reporting is considered as an objective re-presentation of facts, as if the reporter allows the facts to *speak for themselves*. Such a mode of writing is thought to have a zero-degree signification by itself, as if language was a transparent form that did not influence the content it communicated (Barthes 1984:5–6). The belief in objectivity of language is still common among journalists and television reporters and their viewing publics who believe that the medium can re-present reality without *mediation*. However, *content* and *form* or the techniques of presentation are interrelated and do not exist independently. There is no escape from the distortions imposed by language, and *realistic* writing is still a form of mediation or re-presentation, or staging of reality through language.

Some of the important elements of language in texts that we need to know, and understand how they communicate, are *sounds, words and vocabulary, sentences, rules and grammar, cohesion* and *text structure* (Fairclough 1992a:75; Van Dijk 1988:170).

Sounds, words, sentences and text structure

The basic elements of spoken language consist of sounds while written language consists of graphic *signs* such as the *letters* of the alphabet. The basic element of spoken language that makes a significant difference is a phoneme (as a unit of sound that distinguishes it from another), for example we notice that the sound 'p' is different from the sound 'b'. Morphemes are sounds or a combination of sounds that are meaningful, such as words or parts of words. The Swiss linguist Ferdinand De Saussure (1981), who introduced the science of *semiotics*, considered language as a system of *signs* such as words and the *rules* or *conventions* for using them (*langue*, as distinct from actual speech, *parole*). The material aspect of the word as a sign, such as the *sound* of a spoken word or the *graphic* marks on a piece of paper of a written word – is termed the signifier and the corresponding mental image or concept is called the signified. Thus, for me to communicate an idea that I have in my mind, I need to express it in a linguistic sound or written mark (such as a word) with which it is associated. When I address my message to you, the sound of the word will evoke a concept in your mind that corresponds to my idea. In this way, signs do not refer to things in reality but rather to ideas or concepts of such a reality in our mind.

In order to communicate, the writer or speaker of language needs words and a vocabulary before he or she can represent reality. A vocabulary consists of words for *naming* things. There are also specific vocabularies such as *technical terminology*, the *key concepts*, or jargon that have specific meaning and value within a certain type of formal and specialised discursive practice. The meaning of a concept is related to, and is dependent on other concepts and their use, thus forming a network of related concepts. For example, in the discourse of geography we cannot use the word *north* without reference to the corresponding words *south, east* and *west* (Williams 1993:345).

Words or concepts represent categorisation of the world from a particular point of view as they exist within a system organised by ideological assumptions (Kress 1984:124–125). Put differently, the vocabulary of a language or a particular discursive practice is a *map* of objects, concepts, processes and relationships about which the members of the culture or discursive community need to communicate (Fowler 1991:80). All writing, from personal letters to news reporting in the mass media are acts of *mediation*. That is, an event is mediated through language from perceiver to someone who did not witness the event. However, perception is selective and directed by a framework of ideas or schemata about what is important (Kress 1984:120). The writer or speaker, who reports, looks at the world and notices only those things that correspond with the schemata. A writer would only write what he or she already knows and interprets everything according to such knowledge (Gombrich 1986:73). Words or concepts can be considered as labels that structure perception by classifying objects, people and situations and such a classification depends upon the ideological assumptions of the writer and not on any quality of the object, situation or behaviour being classified. For example, imagine that you are a psychologist and you are having a conversation with a person when suddenly you notice that he or she is getting agitated. You could interpret and describe the agitation as an indication that the person gets *angry* or gets *aggressive*. Each description refers to the same event but implies a different evaluation and classification that carry different meanings and justification for subsequent responses. For example, if the person you are talking to is a friend you would probably say that he *gets angry*, but if the person is a mental patient you would say that he *gets aggressive* (Edelman 1974:300). Indeed, such classification of activities and categorisation of people are performed by the practice, talk and writing of psychiatrists and other members of the *helping professions* who have constructed a vocabulary of concepts such as *mental illness, deviance, help* and *therapy* to label certain common activities as demanding professional intervention. Edelman (1974:297) shows the logic behind the use of the concept *therapy* by psychiatrists. In psychiatrists' discourse ordinary people may hold dances, but mental patients have *dance therapy*; engaging in sport is *recreation therapy*; group discussion is *group therapy*, and reading activity is *bibliotherapy*. The use of such a vocabulary has political implications, as Edelman (1974:297) puts it: "To label a common activity as though it were a medical one is to establish superior and subordinate roles, to make it clear who gives orders and who takes them, and to justify in advance the inhibitions placed upon the subordinate classes".

Case study 3.1: The political use of professional vocabulary

According to Edelman (1974:295), psychiatrists often ignore the demands and requests made by mental patients because to grant them would not be in line with *helping* but rather *reinforce deviant behaviour*, and in line with the helping ideology, demanding mental patients are sometimes *punished*. Is the psychiatrist's action punishment or help? Or, for example, how should one interpret the following description for treatment of mental patients, recommended by psychiatric textbooks?

> Deprivation of food, bed, walks in open air, visitors, mail, or telephone calls; solitary confinement; deprivation of reading or entertainment material; immobilizing people by tying them into wet sheets and then exhibiting them to staff and other patients; other physical restraints on body movement; drugging the mind against the client's will; incarceration in locked wards; a range of public humiliations such as the prominent posting of alleged intentions to escape or commit suicide, the requirement of public confessions of misconduct or guilt, and public announcement of individual misdeeds and abnormalities.
>
> (Edelman 1974:300)

Depending on the specific professional ideological perspective, psychiatric treatment could be described as either *help* and *therapy* or *punishment* and *sadism*. For persons not trained in the perspective of the discourse of psychiatry, such language would evoke the horror of torture and repression while for the trained professionals subscribing to the accepted ideology these are necessary means to achieve rehabilitation.

The professional and nonpolitical classification and language of the *helping professions* fulfils a political function. As society becomes more complex and more people become discontented, more types of behaviour become labelled as *deviant* by psychiatrists, medical doctors and social workers, who gain authority and the power to apply such labels. These "professionals create and reinforce popular beliefs about which kinds of people are worthy and which are unworthy: about who should be rewarded through government action and who controlled or repressed" (Edelman 1974:297). The mass media are important in promoting labels that become the "official vocabulary" by being constantly repeated in general usage. The use of such *technical labels* prevents discussion and critical thought as it authoritatively defines *good and evil* and communicates decisions, dictums and commands that must be unquestionably accepted (Marcuse 1970:89). Increasingly, the uses of technical vocabularies of *experts* in the service of government agencies comes to dominate the political decision-making process. Such a *scientisation of politics* (Habermas 1972:62), or the *rationalisation* and *programming* of society through the *medical, psychiatric, "correctional services" techniques* of intervention (Foucault 1980; 1988), eliminates open public debate on social policy characteristic of democratic politics, replacing it with bureaucratic domination (cf. Habermas 1972:62–80).

The use of such vocabulary makes it easy to accept without questioning the fact that an increasing number of legitimate political activities are criminalised. For example, consider the concept *unemployment*. If, in a large city, one man or woman were unemployed, we would consider this to be the individual's *personal trouble* resulting from some personal failing. But if in a nation of 50 million people, 15 million are unemployed and living in poverty then this is no longer individual trouble but a *public issue* requiring economic and political solution (Mills 1978:15). Indeed, attempts by individuals to make political statements can be easily subverted by the use of professional vocabulary. For example, a woman whose poverty makes her angry or despondent becomes a symbol of individual sickness, rather than a victim of a malfunctioning economy, after a psychiatrist defines her as *hysteric* (Edelman in Fourie 1991:4). This way, *public issues of social structure* over which the individual has no control are transformed by definition into *personal troubles* attributed to the private faults of the individual (Mills 1978:14). A case in point would be that political opposition from the powerless classes in South Africa during the era of apartheid was often classified as *deviance* justifying violent reaction from the state. The *helping professions* have become part of the new *social science police* –

effective agents of social control and through their professional language they help "manipulate the discontented into conformity and docility and to isolate or incarcerate those who refuse to be 'rehabilitated'" (Edelman 1974:310).

Words and concepts are essentially metaphors that translate sense experience into vocal and visual symbols (McLuhan 1969:67). Metaphors are concepts that allow us to understand and experience one kind of thing in terms of another and are useful means for understanding a new or problematic situation in terms of situations that are already familiar. As ideas and concepts become more abstract, metaphors are used to translate them into more concrete basic domains that are already understood. Metaphors influence and structure the way we think and behave. Lakoff and Johnson (1980:4) show how the metaphor "argument is war" influences our understanding and conduct of everyday arguments. In our everyday language the use of this metaphor is common, for example:

Your claims are *indefensible*.
He *attacked* my arguments.
Her criticism was right *on target*.
I *demolished* her argument.
He *shot down* my arguments.
I have never *won* an argument with him.

Of course, arguments and war are different kinds of actions, but because of the prevalence of the metaphor in our everyday language we tend to think of, and argue as if, we were conducting war. The metaphor provides a limited perspective through a related framework of concepts on the activity and has the ability to highlight one aspect while concealing other ways of thinking about it. As a result, we do not only use the war metaphor to talk about arguments in terms of war but we actually conduct our arguments as if we were engaged in real combat. The war metaphor is a favourite in mass media discourse to describe politics (So 1987:624; Chilton & Ilyin 1993:10). Identifying the various metaphors should make us aware of their influence on our thinking and acting.

Sentences and grammar

Traditionally, grammar is considered as "the art of speaking and writing correctly", and the grammarian's task is to identify "good usage". Grammar does much more than dictate good usage of language; it provides a theory of reality for a culture as it provides categories for distinction between *subject* and *object* for constructing a sentence and also provides explanations for an event by linking a *deed* to a doer. In the production of text, the writer or speaker makes choices and selects words and grammatical constructions and each choice affects the meaning communicated by presenting a different perspective of the world. For example, reporting on an action, a writer can present it from various perspectives: by using *transitive* or *intransitive* verbs or using the active voice or passive voice and each choice *transforms* the meanings and presents a different perspective that usually reflects an ideological commitment (Fowler 1991:70–78). For example, consider the following sentences:

1 Police kill prisoner in a cell.
2 Prisoner found dead in a police cell.

While the two sentences have similar meanings, they imply different perspectives on the situation on which they report. In the first sentence the focus is on an *actor/agent* ("police") who performs a transitive action affecting someone or something, here, the action ("kill") is performed on someone – the *affected participant/object* of the sentence ("prisoner"). The sentence focuses attention on the actor/agent, providing an explanation and placing the responsibility for the action on the actor. In the second sentence the point of view is that of the affected participant/object and the emphasis is no longer on the action or actor but on a *state of affairs* – "prisoner found dead". Such a transformation displaces the responsibility from the actor to the object. A similar transformation is done by a change from *active* to *passive* voice. Compare the following two newspaper headlines:

1 Police shoot 11 dead in Salisbury riot.
2 Rioting blacks shot dead by police as ANC leaders meet.

In the first headline, the emphasis is squarely on the agent performing the action, identifying the police as responsible for the deaths. The use of the passive in the second headline places the emphasis not on those who did the act of shooting but on those on the receiving end. The change of emphasis displaces the responsibility for the action from the police to their victims (Montgomery 1986:186–187; Kress 1984:127; Fowler 1991:78). The grammatical choices made by the mass media could be explained if linked to the discursive practice of the particular newspapers, their assumptions about society, and their professional or institutional ideology (McQuail 1980:174–182). We may discover, for example, that headline (2) above is derived from a conservative and pro-government publication while headline (1) is from an opposition newspaper. Such examples of grammatical manipulation motivated by ideological assumptions could be found in the use of language by the South African Broadcasting Corporation (SABC) television news broadcasts during the 1980s. Because South African television was controlled by the regime, all news reports on police activity were actively manipulated, and reporting on police shooting of protesters was almost exclusively in the passive voice. For example: "Nine people died and almost 200 injured" or "Country-wide unrest cost the lives of two rioters last night" (Posel 1989:264). By removing the grammatical acting agents of the sentence, the television viewer was prevented from considering the police as the agents who were responsible for the death of protesters. Instead, attention was directed to the abstract concept *unrest* as being responsible for death, and the protesters (presented as *rioters*) who *paid* with their lives.

Texts produced by scientists are also characterised by the passive voice and the absence of the reporting subject. For example, scientists report that "it was decided to use this method" rather than "we decided to use this method", or "the test indicates there is a significant difference" rather than "based on the test, we concluded" (Gusfield 1976:20). The choice of the passive voice is a convention of the discourse of science and "implies that to be scientific is to exercise a definite form over language in use and to write in a particular way which shows the audience that the writer is *doing science*" (Gusfield 1976:17). The impersonal style of scientific discourse combined with a technical vocabulary serves to establish a position of superiority and power for the scientist.

Structures of text segment

Text structure refers to larger segments of the text such as the *topics, themes, perspectives* and overall *meaning* of the text (Fairclough 1992a:75; Van Dijk 1988:170). Words, individual sentences or sequences of sentences are organised into a coherent unity, and form the particular text. Such a framework or *text structure* gives us the overall *topic* or theme represented in the text. Selection of particular topics and the avoidance of others give an insight into assumptions, beliefs and systems of knowledge and ideologies of the discursive practice. For example, South African English language newspapers during the 1980s reported on an increase in the number of black children imprisoned by the authorities. However, almost none of the government-aligned Afrikaans media reported on such matters, but instead deflected attention by constructing a new *social problem* by discovering a new concept of sexual abuse of children.

Rhetorical devices such as argumentative structure are another means to provide cohesion and provide an insight into the assumptions and ideologies of the communicator. Simple cohesive devices such as the conjunctions *since, if, and,* can be used to create coherence and explain connections between different and unrelated things or situations that we would not usually perceive as being related. Such a method is commonly found in advertising text (Fairclough 1992a:77, 176), as in the following example from the *Sunday Times*: "The road through life is full of bumps and unexpected twists and turns. Toyota has always been committed to making the journey as smooth as possible" (Everything keeps going ... 1995:17). The advertisement makes a connection between life and a motorcar journey by using a metaphor to describe life as a bumpy road, followed by a statement that the car manufacturer is committed to making the journey through life as smooth as possible.

Having discussed the main elements of the text we can turn to the rules and convention for producing texts.

3.5 DISCURSIVE PRACTICE: RULES AND CONVENTIONS FOR THE USE OF LANGUAGE AND PRODUCTION OF TEXTS

The use of language is a practical activity or a social performance called a *speech act*. For example, in the first place, when we speak or write we are doing something, and by speaking we also attempt to do something. As the English philosopher John Austin (1984) suggests, we use language for a variety of purposes, such as to make statements, to ask questions, or to give orders. The linguist Roman Jakobson (1964) explains that language can function for a variety of purposes and lists these as the following:

Referential function refers to our ability to use language to provide information to people about things of which they did not know, and to talk about things in our world. For example, to inform and describe are referential uses of language.

Expressive function refers to our ability to express our emotions, beliefs and opinions, for example, to apologise for a mistake or to praise someone.

Conative function refers to our ability to use language to influence people, to direct them to follow our wishes or orders.

Phatic function refers to our use of language to make and maintain contact with other people. For example, small talk, idle chatter and greetings such as "How are you?" "Hello" and "It's a nice day" show other people that we take notice of them and welcome their communication.

Poetic function refers to our ability to use language for the pleasure of such use. For example, we enjoy the sound of words rhyming in a poem, or find delight in the sound of a particular word.

Metalinguistic function refers to our ability to use language in order to talk about language, or other aspects of our verbal communication. For example, when we say, "I don't follow what you are saying" or "What do you mean?" we are talking about the use of language and communication.

It is clear that the use of language, which we call *discursive practice*, is a distinct form of social activity that involves social interaction in the production of texts. As such, we can consider the use of language a distinct social activity and it can be distinguished from nonlinguistic activities such as production of goods and action. The act of speaking, rather than what is said, has important social significance, as is illustrated by the following newspaper report:

> History was made in Parliament yesterday when a deaf MP addressed the National Assembly in sign language. ANC MP Wilma Newhoudt-Druchen drew a respectful silence from members in the House as they listened attentively to her maiden speech, delivered through an interpreter. The whole Assembly and the public gallery broke into applause once she had completed her address, made during debate on the communication budget vote.
>
> (*The Pretoria News*, 10 May 2000:3)

The most significant aspect that is made in the report above is the fact that the person made a speech, and not what was said by the person; as you may note there is not a single word that tells us what the MP said in her speech.

Because acts of speech are social performances they are not simply subjective and individual expressions but are socially shaped. In other words, the type of language we speak and how we speak is largely determined by our social context, social role, identity, and membership of a social group (Fairclough 1990:21).

Language is not homogeneous and uniformly used by the entire linguistic community, rather, language is used in various ways. For example, the language spoken by South Africans is a particular national variety of the English language. Within any large linguistic community there are different regional dialects, slang and formal discourses of social groups. Culture also provides specific rules to a discursive practice. For example there are distinctive communicative behaviours between social class or sub-cultures that are less educated and predominantly use oral communication as against the more educated and literate for whom writing and printed texts have more importance. Such differences are acquired by different socialisation and education (Botha 1991; Kochman 1974; McLuhan 1969; Ong 1982).

Besides national and regional varieties in language use, there are also specialised discursive practices such as science, law, religion, journalism, art, and so on, regulated by formal rules, conventions, and institutional constraints that determine what qualifications a person should have before he or she may speak, who may speak with authority, and who is excluded, how a person may or may not speak, and what should or should not be said.

Scientific writing is an example of a discursive practice that has many formal rules and convention for producing text. Whenever a scientist has something to say about his subject of study, his or her way of saying it is determined by conventions laid down in style manuals and such conventions are learned during the process of entering the scientific community. The specific rules and convention determine the grammatical constructions, vocabulary and the general layout of the text. Thus, a scientist wanting to publish an article in an academic journal needs to conform to the conventions and style that the editorial board believes is appropriate (Crystal 1974:29). Orwell (1975:149) provides an example of how to transform everyday language into scientific text. Orwell takes the following Biblical text:

> I returned and saw under the sun, that the race is not to the swift, nor the battle to the strong, neither yet the bread to the wise, nor yet riches to men of understanding, nor yet favour to men of skill; but time and chance happeneth to all.
> (Orwell 1975:149)

The Biblical writer provides important observations on social phenomena but the personal style and details do not conform to the requirements of scientific writing. For such an observation to be accepted as a scientific report it needs to be transformed and given a particular style, as Orwell shows by rewriting the sentence thus:

> Objective considerations of contemporary phenomena compel the conclusion that success or failure in competitive activities exhibits no tendency to be commensurate with innate capacity, but that a considerable element of the unpredictable must invariably be taken into account.
> (Orwell 1975:149)

By changing the personal style into an impersonal style and transforming concrete examples into generalisations, the Biblical text is easily translated into the language of scientific discourse. Similar translations and rhetorical re-codification of popular superstitions into scientific vocabulary are conducted today by the mass media, social psychology and other helping professions (Harré 1985:141).

The discursive practice of journalism in particular, with its formal and informal rules has become important for constructing and communicating ideology in contemporary society. To understand how such ideological work is performed we can examine how journalists construct texts.

A news article that appears in the newspaper confirms the institutional assumptions and professional ideologies of the journalists (McQuail 1980:174–182). The selection of the topic is the result of assumptions regarding what is considered newsworthy. Events do not make their way into the news simply because they happen but because they are recognised as fitting-in with a category predefined by the media as *news*. To be accepted within such a category the event must fulfil certain criteria of *news values* before it is selected by the media. For example, for an event to be considered newsworthy it needs occur frequently, take short time to unfold and its meaning should be quickly discerned. In addition, the newsworthy event also needs to be dramatic and involve many people; for example a neighbour's argument is less newsworthy than a war (Hartley 1982:76).

Once the topic of the news article has been acknowledged as newsworthy there is a further complex process of reporting, writing and rewriting. For example, a press statement from a government department is delivered to the news editor. The news editor assigns a journalist to the story. After reading the press release the journalist may consult other related reports on the issue to familiarise himself or herself with the background. The journalist then sets up interviews with people involved, to gain more information and will then write the report. The journalist's report is in turn handed to the news editor who may make some corrections or changes. The text is then delivered to a sub-editor for "cutting", tightening, clarifying, and making the text conform to the official style and policy of the newspaper. The edited version of the original story may again be read by the newspaper editor who may suggest additional changes. Should there be some legal issues involved, the editor may obtain legal advice and make the appropriate changes to the story. The final version is sent to the printers and once printed the newspaper is delivered to the public. Thus a newspaper article is the result of a collective effort by journalist, editors, managers, technical personnel, and others, working within a complex institution.

3.6 THE SOCIAL CONTEXT OF LANGUAGE

As we saw above, language and discourse have their own rules and convention. However, the use of language is also influenced by the social situations or context within which it is used. Texts and discursive practices are socially determined, through the various formal conventions that influence the way we communicate. For example, the manner in which we conduct interpersonal conversations with close friends or family members differs greatly from the manner in which we communicate in formal contexts such as delivering a speech in public. Within a particular society, the different and distinct *types of discursive practices* and the texts produced by them are given different values, prestige and authority. Such differences in values of discourses are termed orders of discourse (Fairclough 1992a:69). For example, *slang* is considered inferior to the *official* and *correct* language; the discursive practice of the law courts and judges is given greater prestige, value and power than the discursive practices of poetry.

The authority of an individual to speak socially and to be taken seriously is institutionalised throughout society according to membership in different discursive practices. For example, in our society particular professional discursive practices have acquired a privileged position and people such as doctors and psychologists are authorised to define health and illness, as Foucault (1986:51) puts it: "Medical statements cannot come from anybody; their value, efficacy, even their therapeutic powers, and, generally speaking, their existence as medical statements cannot be dissociated from the statutorily defined person who has the right to make them, and to claim for them the power to overcome suffering and death". It is evident that to speak meaningfully and to be taken seriously in any society is limited and not everyone has the right to speak everywhere or on any topic; some people in society speak with authority while some are silent and only listen. Such a hierarchy of roles is determined by the culture of a society. For example, gender in many societies determines that the words of men are taken more seriously than are those of women, because women are considered inferior to men. Consider the meaning of the word *professional* in the following two sentences:

1 He is a professional.
2 She is a professional.

The word *professional* should have the same meaning in both sentences. However, it is not so. Most speakers of English would conclude that in sentence (1) *he* refers to someone who is a doctor or lawyer while in sentence (2) it would be assume that *she* is a prostitute (Spender 1980:19).

In addition to ascribing value to people according to their sex or gender, membership of social class, ethnic group and race are also important valuation criteria. For example, in South Africa the mass media labelled black minibus-taxi drivers as *Third World drivers* and such label implied that they were *bad, reckless, murderous* drivers responsible for most road-death because as inferior drivers they were unable to master *First World* driving conditions (Sonderling 1992). The use of such First World/Third World dichotomy conceals an underlying racist evaluation and devaluation (Janks & Ivanic 1992:326–329).

The social hierarchy of discursive practices – or *orders of discourse* – is the result of a long history of social and political struggles. From such struggles, particular types of discourses and the people authorised to use them are given privilege and authority to define social reality. The following case study is an example of a historical power struggle to establish the value and power of different discursive practices in South Africa.

Case study 3.2: The power to speak in society

During the apartheid era, the South African government enforced repressive censorship legislation. A government censorship body had almost a free hand to ban publications deemed undesirable by the government. However, many attempts by the government to censor and ban publications were frustrated because people could appeal to the Supreme Court that often overruled the decisions of the censorship board. Government ministers and ministers of the Afrikaner churches claimed that the discourse of the government-appointed censorship body should not be challenged by the courts because *there is no one in South Africa, from the Chief Justice down ... who is better able to decide on these matters than the Publications Control Board itself.* Subsequently, the government appointed a commission of inquiry whose main task was to remove the Supreme Court from the censorship process. The Commission stated that the Supreme Court's decisions were of no greater value than those of other *authorities* sanctioned by the government. According to the Commission, the court *substitutes its opinion for that of the Publications Control Board.* If *the Court was just as competent as a board of experts to give an opinion on ethical norms*, then it was also true *that the board of experts is just as competent as the Court to give an opinion on ethical norms.* In making the case against the courts, the Commission also objected that the Supreme Court rejected the opinion of authoritative religious persons closely linked to the ruling party:

> To quote an example ... an attempt was made to lodge with the Court affidavits made by ... a minister of the Stellenbosch Nederduitse Gereformeerde Kerk, (who was also) Vice-Chancellor of the University of Stellenbosch, has been the moderator of the Cape Synod of that Church since 1965 and was Moderator of the General Synod of the Nederduitse Gereformeerde Kerk in Suid-Afrika from 1966 to 1970 ... Legally speaking, the Court was quite right in refusing to admit these affidavits and it proceeded to give an opinion finding which was opposite to that of the clergyman. In the Commission's opinion this kind of thing tends to involve our courts in controversy, since in cases such as this the public would attach great value to the opinions of clergymen and would not be able to understand why their opinions should be rejected.
>
> (Kruger Commission in Sonderling 1996a:40)

Because the government had the ultimate power to substitute one discursive practice for another, the right of appeal to the Supreme Court against the decision of the Publications Control Board was replaced with appeal to *a prestige body* of government-appointed experts. These experts then legitimise their specialised discursive practice by making a distinction between their superior opinion and knowledge and that of the lesser members of society. As the chairman of the Publications Appeal Board puts it:

> It appears unlikely that much value could be attached to ... the opinions of laymen regarding the question of obscenity, since the latter is an intricate legal concept. To ask a man to state his opinion on a specific blend of coffee is one thing, to ask him for his opinion on whether something is 'obscene' is a far more complex question, one which requires some understanding of the legal issues involved.
>
> (Van Rooyen 1987:47 in Sonderling 1996a:42)

Having legitimated its power, the censorship board went on to define its discursive practice, make policy and provide guidelines regarding the use of some trivial words considered potentially offensive, as the following example indicates:

> After the few cases in 1980 in which the word 'fuck' was allowed in films with military theme it was also allowed in films whose settings warrant its use ... The main consideration in deciding whether or not to cut these words are their frequency, audibility, the identity of the person uttering them, the identity of the person to whom they are spoken, and the age restriction imposed ... Some expletives, such as 'cunt', 'motherfucker', and 'cocksucker' are decidedly risqué and must in most cases be functional if they are not to be cut. If terms such as 'fuck', 'cunt', 'shit' and 'pussy' are used in their primary sense stricter rules are applied ... In general the word 'fuck' is not allowed in films with an age restriction lower than 2–14 ... Occasionally, though never as a matter of policy, the expletive 'fuck' has been left in films with age restrictions lower than 2–14 ... Such instances were usually, however, barely audible ... Words less vulgar than 'fuck' are, however, usually left in films.
>
> (Van Rooyen 1987:78–79 in Sonderling 1996a:42)

3.7 LANGUAGE, POWER AND IDEOLOGY

The ability of certain discursive practices to define our reality should make us aware of the close relationship between language, social relations of power and *ideology*. Ideology can be considered as *meaning in the service of power* (Thompson 1992:7), and refers to the ways in which particular meanings or significations serve to establish and maintain relations of social domination. Such meanings are constructed and communicated through the social use of language – from our everyday conversations to the complex texts of the various discursive practices (Thompson 1990:5; 1992:7). Ideology operates most effectively when it becomes naturalised and achieves the status of a common-sense explanation for the ways the world and society operate. The use of language by the powerful social groups is a strategy for *symbolic violence* – the exercise of power and social control through the manipulation of language (Bourdieu 1992:51). (See Unit 9, Volume 1 for a discussion on ideology and the media.)

Many examples of ideological assumptions are found in discursive practice of the mass media. For example, from a journalist's point of view, a good interview is one that contains interesting opinion. To make the interview more interesting for the readers of a newspaper or viewer of a television show, a good journalist will attempt to introduce personal aspects or a *human factor* of the people being interviewed by asking for the interviewees' first names, having them say something about themselves and asking for their opinion on the current topic of the interview (Mey 1985:68–69). This is evident in particular when journalists interview striking workers or their families, and questions such as the following are considered *interesting*:

> Tell me what you feel about this situation, how does it affect you and your family, is there anything in it for you, why are you doing this, how come you and your children put up with all these hardships, what does your wife/husband say about it, how do you relate to the other people here, how about this particular strike and the union, do they help you at all, what do the bosses say, do you think the strike is going to be a success, et cetera.
>
> (Mey 1985:69)

However, while such questions are taken for granted by the discursive practice of journalism, they, nevertheless, reflect the ideology of individualism of our Western society. By adding such a *personal touch* the journalist manipulates and distorts the situation because the workers' decision to go on strike and their motives are not the individual worker's alone, but express the motives of the labour community as a whole and are based on collective consciousness of the labour situation (Mey 1985:69–70). Asking striking workers for their personal opinion is inappropriate, but such an individualist perspective is enforced by the mass media and propagated as the only legitimate position regarding labour disputes. This is further motivated by the rules of journalistic discursive practices that perpetuate such a perspective for news reporting on labour relations. In many instances reporters' ignorance about labour issues are common (Burton 1987:192). Further, most reporting on labour disputes is biased in favour of big business, as the media usually strive not to offend this economic sector that pays good advertising money. The media's insistence on quoting *authoritative sources* who are easy to reach for comment, results in representatives of big business, employers, and management being first to be contacted by the media. By the time the media interview the workers, the story angle has already been fixed (Burton 1987:193; Tomaselli & Tomaselli 1987:68). Story angles favoured by the media to represent labour disputes present them as *unnatural* activities that are not in the *national interest* (Burton 1987:191). With such underlying bias it is not unusual to find traces of managerial persuasive communication reproduced by the media. For example, statements by management that combine two or more imperatives connecting and purposefully conflating unrelated issues such as: "The employment, housing, health and feeding schemes are specifically for you", so why strike? or the use of unanswerable negative questions such as: "Isn't the security of employment and a pension fund more important than questioning new appointments?" (Du Plooy 1995:25).

Having discussed the nature of language, the important elements of texts, the rules of discursive practice for producing texts and the social context of language, in the next section we will apply these concepts and insight in a case study.

3.8 LANGUAGE AND THE SOUTH AFRICAN MASS MEDIA

In this critical analysis, a text of an editorial commentary from the *Sunday Times*, 18 December 1994 (We can all reap ... 1994:24) (Sonderling 1996b:107–110), is read within the larger context of other media texts, discursive practices and sociopolitical context of South African journalism after the transition to democracy under the newly elected ANC government (cf. Sonderling 1998).

We can all reap fruits of democracy

President Nelson Mandela's call yesterday for the country to put itself on a moral footing strikes a deeply resonant note for many South Africans now caught in the half-light of doubt after the euphoria created by the miracle of political rebirth earlier this year. ... But the task of dragging the country from that morass lies firmly with the ANC, the majority party in the government of national unity ...

The key to defending this very fragile democracy lies in good governance. That can only be achieved by, first, making all South African believe they are beneficiaries of that democracy and, second, forging a patriotism that goes well beyond flags and simple rhetoric.

There can be no half measures and Mr Mandela is right to warn his more clamorous supporters and allies that concepts like fiscal discipline, economic growth and stability are not luxuries – they are critical to the success of the democracy.

If morality and good governance is to flourish it is crucial that South Africans drop the pernicious zero-sum view that blacks can only be advantaged by taking away from whites or, put the other way, whites must suffer to subsidise blacks.

A growing economy driven by good government would make the argument irrelevant: all will benefit. The current debate about whether the ANC is inclining towards "white" interests at the expense of "black" interests would then be exposed for what it is – spurious ...

The central challenge confronting the ANC, said Mr Mandela, is the deracialising of South African society.

It is necessary to keep this in mind because as the new government goes through successive crises of authority and delivery in the future, there will be an undoubted tendency by recidivists in the organisation to fall back on racial scapegoating to hide failure. This continued racialising of the country, similar to what is happening now in Zimbabwe, would be fatal to all hopes of reconciliation.

> This raises the second essential element for good and moral governance: the need for a broader national patriotism.
>
> There is, sadly, little evidence of it at present. Too many private agendas, too many lobbies, too much special pleading whether by truck drivers, wildcat strikers, public servants, rebellious soldiers and policemen, magnates (black or white), teachers or spokesmen for single-issue interest groups.
>
> It is the successful accommodation of these narrow, sometimes excessive, sectarian interests within the new democracy without damaging the society as a whole that will require a toughness of mind, a steel in the belly, that has not been abundantly in evidence in the ANC's stewardship of the country in the last seven months.
>
> The generous view is that it is still a period of settling in and that as government confidence grows, so will authority. The less generous view is that the ANC is attempting to govern the country as it does its own vast and diverse organisation – by trade-offs and deals, compromises and diversions, all aimed at ducking rather than solving problems.
>
> The ANC needs to take heart at its 49th conference. It has a leader who enjoys unchallengeable moral authority here and abroad and, if recent opinion polls are anything to go by, presides over a deeply supportive electorate which genuinely believes that a better life is within grasp.
>
> The ANC can afford to be decisive, even tough.

The *Sunday Times* (We can all reap ... 1994:24) editorial is an example of a particular type of text or genre, known as an editorial opinion that can be contrasted with a news report considered factual and objective and has its own particular formal structures. An editorial opinion clearly presents the newspaper's own view of reality and the newspaper's ideology. That is, mostly editorial opinion takes the form of moralising as it puts forward what the newspaper thinks reality *ought to be* rather than *what it is* (Braham 1982:269–270). Characteristically, such opinion is presented in an authoritative style of a lecture, claiming to represent social consensus, exhibiting definitive knowledge regarding what is good or right, common-sense wisdom, and offering rebuttal of other peoples ideas (Fowler 1991:211, 221). The editorial commentary reproduced above is an example of the discursive practice of most white, English-speaking South African journalists and their mainly white English reading public. Economically, the newspaper depends on advertising money derived mainly from white enterprise that traditionally enjoyed a position of privilege in South Africa.

The headline of the *Sunday Times* (1994) editorial directs the reader's attention to the topic of the article: democracy. Democracy is presented in terms of an organic or natural metaphor – as if it were a tree or plant that needs nourishment and it bears fruits that everyone can reap.

The first two paragraphs present politics as a morality play by defining *good and evil, darkness and light/half-light, mess and order*. The article's moralising is clear by the repeated use of the word *morality*: a call "for the country to put itself on a moral footing" ... "if morality and good governance are to flourish" ... "good and moral governance" ... and "a leader who enjoys unchallengeable moral support". According to the editorial writer, the newly gained democracy needs to be defended, and the *key* to defending this very fragile democracy lies in *morality* and *good governance*. But behind such frequent use of moral vocabulary by the editorial writer there is a basic misunderstanding and misrepresentation of the applicability of morality to an evaluation of politics (Niebuhr 1960:xx–xxiv). There is also an expression of self-serving interest: by claiming the moral high ground, the media substitute themselves for the democratically elected politicians who are the true representatives of the public (Braham 1982:269–271). Indeed, the exercise of political power is mostly expressed in statements about *values* and talk about morality (Bell 1975:83). By moralising public life there is a desire to place politics under a common moral rule – under the control of a consensus – resulting in all conflicts, contests and differences being eliminated, thus making politics unimportant and marginal. Such an outdated idea is essentially based on a desire to escape politics (Connolly 1983:213). Indeed, the attempts to escape politics – to remove politics from the political sphere – was familiar to the old apartheid regime: escaping politics by enforced consensus, installing a powerful bureaucracy and keeping black South Africans disenfranchised. Such enforced consensus was also supported by press censorship and the use of moral and religious vocabularies in politics. The legacy of the apartheid discursive framework is used today by the South African media to report on the new democracy and leads to curiously distorted texts. For example, a headline in *The Pretoria News* (Politics sneaks ... 1994:3) proclaims that "*Politics sneaks into council meeting*", and goes on to report that:

> It was good while it lasted, but Pretoria City Councillors could not keep politics out of their monthly council meeting. Councillors managed to keep politics out of main agenda debates, but when it came to the discussion of a management committee decision on holding a civic banquet to honour visiting heads of state attending the inauguration of the new State President on May 10, things changed.

What is curious in this report is the misrecognition that city councils are primarily political forums and councillors are representatives of political parties. Indeed, there is such a tacit acknowledgement of the council's political nature when the newspaper identifies the councillors firstly by their political party affiliations and then by their names.

Not only do the media show a misunderstanding of politics but they also misrecognise democracy. With the elections in 1994 South Africa entered a process of democratisation. It is a process through which the exercise of political power by a regime or a state becomes less arbitrary, exclusive and authoritarian. Bargaining, as opposed to command, takes on increasing importance in public life and alternative power centres begin to emerge in society. There is an increase in the expression of opposing views and criticism. The people who hold political power begin to recognise that government must proceed through persuasion and reward rather than through coercion and threat. The political leaders also recognise that political, economic and social goals can be achieved by allowing different social groups greater autonomy and participation in decision making. Wider participation in political life by various groups enhances the legitimacy of the government and the state. A culture of democracy demands tolerance of opposition and willingness to compromise with political opponents. Thus, democracy does not demand a powerful government and an autonomous apparatus of the state but a government that can accommodate the demands of various sections of the population. Democracy means that groups of people organise themselves and demand their individual and group interests. At the centre of democratic politics we always find conflict between numerous groups with different views. Democracy is thus seen as "government by discussion" involving public conversations, disputations and persuasions (Schudson 1997:297). In today's democratic society, *politics is talk* as most political deeds are built of and around words; politics more appropriately can be defined as *who talks to whom, when and how* (Bell 1975:10–12).

However, the South African media see democracy differently. According to the *Sunday Times* editorial writer, democracy can be achieved by "first, making all South African believe they are beneficiaries of that democracy and, second, forging a patriotism that goes well beyond flags and simple rhetoric". Democracy is a matter of creating an illusion – *making all South Africans believe* – rather than creating a reality.

The economy is also considered important for democracy. The *economy* is presented in terms of an organic metaphor in a similar manner to the way *democracy* was presented in the headline. The choice of metaphor is not coincidental but reflects an ideological position: the capitalist economy is the *natural* order of things. There are of course other metaphors for presenting the economy, such as a *building structure*, or a *performance* (Nelson 1990:18–20). Indeed, in the financial and business sections of South African media, the economy is presented in terms of the *war* or *boxing match* metaphors, for example (*The Pretoria News, Business Report* 2 and 3 July 1998):

Fight for full payout on your endowment policy
Big guns help rand claw back
Double blow puts rand on the canvas

However, by presenting the economy in organic terms, the *Sunday Times* (1994) readers' attention is distracted from the fact that an economy is a social institution dominated by the powerful interests of dominant social and racial classes. The South African economy based on a racial imbalance has not advanced the disadvantaged classes in the past.

Seen against this background it may seem that *democracy* means something different to the South African media for whom free expression of plurality of opinions, free contestations, and conflictual verbal politics are unfamiliar features of the new society. Such unfamiliarity gives rise to paradoxical pronouncements such as the following headline in *The Star* (Brand 1996:3): "*Verdict on constitution could usher in new era of democracy – or more political wrangling*".

It is as if the concepts *democracy* and *political wrangling* did not belong to the same discourse. And indeed, for the writer of *The Star* article, democracy seems to exclude political wrangling and *negotiations* when he states that "political observers [i.e. journalists] have expressed fears that some parties may be tempted to reopen negotiations on clauses relating to the death penalty ... ". Such a conceptual framework directs the media to reject the free and open exchange of challenges between opposing parties by defining them disapprovingly as *verbal brawls* (Battle marked by ... 1996:23), or war of words (End the circus ... 1996a:11). In a headline for another editorial opinion, a newspaper orders politicians to *Stop the war of words and talk* (Stop the war of ... 1996b:11). Another headline for an editorial opinion in *The Pretoria News* condemns political contestations and demands that politicians *End the circus*; it goes on to suggest that the

> deputy minister of environment affairs ... now fully appreciates how his very public spat with the ANC during the past few weeks had degenerated into theatre ... Nevertheless, the war of words between himself and the ANC, ... had dissolved into an ugly scene which was doing neither side credit.
>
> (End the circus ... 1996a:11)

The newspaper's ideology and assumptions become evident when the editorial writer reports that the former deputy minister "wanted to see an end to the public confrontation and has now instructed his attorneys to act on his behalf in any further dealings with the ANC". Such an escape from public debate is applauded by the editorial writer who proclaims that:

> This is the correct avenue to follow. Airing of dirty linen in public only serves to get backs up and cloud real issues ... lawyers will know what to do. Meanwhile, it's time for the circus to end.
>
> (End the circus ... 1996a:11)

In similar manner the *Sunday Times* editorial (1994) misrecognises democracy but unwittingly presents the ANC as a democratic party when it reports that "the ANC is attempting to govern the country as it does its own vast and diverse organisation – by trade-off and deals, [and] compromises". But such a democratic government is then rejected by the editorial writer and readers of the newspaper as being a "less generous view" of the ANC government. According to the editorial writer, the ANC is simply "ducking rather than solving problems". Democratic politics are further rejected by the editorial as having "too many private agendas, too many lobbies, too much special pleading whether by truck drivers, wildcat strikers, public servants, rebellious soldiers and policemen, magnates (black or white), teachers or spokesmen for single-issue interest groups". The underlying assumption of the editorial writer seems as if implying that democracy should be avoided because "successful accommodation" of these interests cannot be accomplished "without damaging the society as a whole".

The vocabulary of the *Sunday Times* (1994) editorial demonstrates the use of words of power usually associated with the old dictatorial apartheid regime. Thus, while the editorial begins by promoting democracy, it ends up promoting the old paternalistic dictatorships: it sees democracy in "good governance"; in the "forging" of unquestioning "patriotism"; "a deeply supportive electorate"; "a leader" who has "unchallengeable moral authority"; a government that knows "no half-measures", is "decisive" and "even tough", and capable of "dragging the country" to its destination, and in place of negotiation and accommodation it proposes "toughness of mind" and "steel in the belly" when "solving problems".

It is as if South African journalists having lived for so long in a society that was neatly (literally) divided into black and white, now seem confused when confronted with the complexity of democratic political talk. For the South African media the new democratic complexity and social and cultural plurality are difficult to accommodate within the reductionist media discourse. The multiplicity of publicly expressed and contested political perspectives does not fit neatly into the schemata and conventions of media discursive practice that reduces complex issues to the two-dimensional, *two sides of a story*. This *two-valued orientation* ideology animates much of the media's views on political life: the world is divided into two camps: *good* versus *evil*, *right* versus *wrong*, you are *for* or *against* the ruling political party, and the fact that there may possibly be a third neutral position is entirely ignored (Hayakawa 1973:230). Of course, such *binary opposition* is at the heart of language and originates in the primitive mind where quick classification of situations as *fight or flight* was imperative for survival, but in the complex modern society such dichotomous thinking is stifling (Hayakawa 1973:230–231, 253).

South African journalists, having lived for a long time under white dictatorship, have unconsciously absorbed an ideological position of the apartheid era and such position prevents them from seeing the new and changing reality. According to Janks (1997:340), while journalists and other producers of text by their conscious linguistic selection attempt to represent the post-transformation discourse of democracy, unconsciously the racial and paternalistic discourse of pre-transformation era speaks through the text and the writer. As Janks suggests (1997:338), while writers may consciously elect to avoid *apartheid-speak*, nevertheless language and discourse speak through them, or speak them more than they speak language. Such a frame of reference was also evident in the way media reported on a clash of opinion between the South African Communist Party (SACP) and the African National Congress (ANC) government. This debate demonstrated the democratic character of South African politics and of the ANC government, but for most South African newspapers the debate was an attack on democracy and freedom of the press.

The SACP during its 1998 national congress voiced criticism of the ANC government's economic policy. According to the SACP such an economic policy demonstrated that the

ANC abandoned the mass of the population. In itself the criticism was an attempt by the SACP to position itself as the champion of the workers and the underprivileged masses in order to gain votes in the forthcoming elections. President Nelson Mandela, delivering a speech to congress delegates rejected much of the SACP criticism and challenged the party to choose its position: either to remain a partner in the government or exit. Thabo Mbeki, also speaking at the congress, took issue with the SACP critique and reportedly refuted each point of criticism. Following these exchanges the SACP softened its critique of the government in order to preserve its position within the ANC ruling alliance, but nevertheless, the party reasserted its right to criticise the government's economic policy. As Ronnie Kasrils, Deputy Minster of Defence in the ANC governing alliance and also a member of the SACP put it: "I feel a great deal of tact is required, but this doesn't mean changing the party's right to speak or form independent position" (Paton 1998:1).

The South African media's editorial opinion was different and the image represented on the editorial pages seemed as if the media were talking about a different reality. A headline for an editorial opinion in the *Sunday Times* (Watershed speech ...1998:18) proclaimed: "Watershed speech has changed our politics". Commenting on Mbeki's speech at the SACP congress, the editorial writer claimed that "after years of suffering in silence" insults from the SACP and Cosatu, "Mbeki finally responded in kind". Then the editorial cautions that "the speech also showed that Mbeki still clings to the unfortunate notion that all criticism, wittingly or unwittingly, plays into the hands of those who want to topple democracy". According to the newspaper's binary logic:

> Mbeki's frank address was a blast of fresh air that promised to push into the public arena the economic policy debate that has simmered behind the closed doors of the alliance for the past decade. But this promise of open debate was undermined in the very same speech when Mbeki reverted once more to tarring the government's critics with the brush of disloyalty.
> (Watershed speech ... 1998:18)

According the editorial writer, Mbeki's attack on the critics was inspired by his assertion that "many of the forces we use to wage war against one another, including some members of the media, co-operate with us only because they want us to tear each other apart". Mbeki's statements were taken by the *Sunday Times* (1998:18) as a declaration of war against the press:

> In these statements, Mbeki reveals a dangerous paranoia about the crucial role that civil society and the media must play to keep government from abusing its power. He wrongly contends that all criticism is driven by the desire to bring democracy to its knees.

According to the *Sunday Times* (1998:18), Mbeki's failure "to appreciate the role of criticism in democratic debate" is a disservice to all because the "legitimacy and credibility of the government can only improve if its errors and weaknesses are publicly exposed". A similar interpretation of the debate was evident in the text of a more radical newspaper, the *Mail & Guardian*. In an editorial article under the heading *Cracking down on critical allies*, the newspaper argued:

> President Nelson Mandela's comments at the opening of the South African Communist Party conference that the growth, economic and redistribution (Gear) strategy is the fundamental policy of the African National Congress and that he will brook no opposition to it is just the last sign of the ANC's irritation at public criticism from its own allies. This concerns us not because we see conflict within the alliance as a bloodsport, but because there are serious and valid reasons for questioning some of what the government is doing. If the SACP can't debate the government's macro-economic policy, what is there to talk about?
>
> (Cracking down ... 1998:24)

According to the *Mail & Guardian* editorial (1998:24), the government's policy is questionable but "Mandela insists that his critics should remain silent about it". Turning to Mbeki's rebuke of some ANC activists' protest about the government inaction at the arrest of South African government official, Robert McBride by Mozambican authorities, the *Mail & Guardian* editorial writer contends that the "McBride saga is just a further sign of a leadership that appears determined to crack down on democracy within the movement".

Meanwhile within the ANC and the SACP the conflict of opinion was considered as a legitimate political strategy in an effort to gain positions of power and an indication of the lively contest characteristic of democratic politics, whereby parties battle against each other, win, lose or compromise. According to the Secretary General of the SACP the "ANC is a contested terrain, with different strands fighting for supremacy" (Gumede 1998:5). Peter Mokaba of the ANC sees the debate and differences of opinion as an indication of a thriving democracy. As he puts it: "At least now the differences are out there in the open and not under covers – the whole world knows this can only strengthen the alliance partners" (Gumede 1998:5). Even President Mandela in his critical speech at the SACP congress acknowledged that "each member of the alliance has the right to state his or her views", because "we have won the right to state our views freely without fear" after the demise of apartheid. But President Mandela cautions that an attack on, and ridicule of a fundamental government policy by members of the same government are politically unbecoming (Madiba gets tough ... 2 July 1998:1). President Mandela reiterated his commitment to democracy during a reportedly "tough" meeting with editors of the South African National Editors' Forum in 1997. President Mandela voiced his criticism of the white-owned media's inability to reflect the aspirations of the black majority of people, and gave the media a "tongue lashing" for their selective reporting and censorship when publishing the views of the ANC (Tough talk ... 1997:34). While the President in his "gloves-off diplomacy" criticised the media, he also accepted their criticism, as he put it: "I respect you. If you feel that I am wrong, you will say so, as you do in the press. But give us the latitude to say what we think too" (ibid).

Considered against this background, why do the *Sunday Times* (1998:18) and the *Mail & Guardian* (1998:24) editorials express fear and paranoia, as if the political battle between the SACP and the ANC was a war against the press? Why such an obvious *misrecognition* of democratic politics by the mainly white South African media? Professor Kader Asmal, Minister of Water Affairs and Forestry, who argues that South African Liberals, the self-appointed moralist and formally self-appointed champions of free speech have become "increasingly soft with self-pity" because the new democracy brought forth uninhibited and open debate that is now the prerogative of all, and not the exclusive preserve of the media. According to Asmal (1998:28) "integral to free speech is the right to criticise the critic", but Liberal politicians and the media would deny such a right to others. When the media come under criticism they cry foul and claim that such criticism is aimed at curtailing democracy. Thus, Liberal politicians and the media pose as defenders of free speech in order, ironically, to curtail debate (Asmal 1998:28).

The misrecognition of democracy, the desire to escape politics and the distaste for confrontational political discourse could be explained by reference to the rules and conventions of the discursive practice of South African journalists. Thus, the media's fears and paranoia reflect their past experience of the apartheid regime's reign of terror and suppression of opposition media. The media interpret the ANC government statements as attempts to restrict criticism and a possible move towards a one-party dictatorship. Such view is shared by many white South Africans who consider all African governments as heading towards dictatorship.

The discursive practice of Western journalism is also responsible for the South African media's distaste and rejection of legitimate and open expression of conflicting political opinion. Thus, while *news* (as a textual genre) is traditionally considered dramatic and interesting when involving conflict and fitting within the media's binary mode of the *two-sides to a story*; the texts of the editorial opinion columns present a different image. If news reports claim to present *news as it is* – based on conflict and drama – the editorial opinion texts present *news as they would like it to be* – an image of a calm consensus devoid of conflict (Braham 1982:270). Thus, the media claim to represent the wisdom of the *common-sense* view in society; they claim to represent *consensus* that is supposedly beyond and above politics; they represent a supposedly *rational discourse* of the *cool-headed*, practical men and women pronouncing the *truth* to politicians and other lesser mortals (Fowler 1991:49, 212).

The desire to escape politics and eschew the conflicts and the hustle-and-bustle of the new South African reality is, however, also motivated by another more covert influence deeply embodied in the rules of journalistic discourse. This unarticulated discursive convention operating behind the South African media's backs is the socialised attitude and disposition of members of a *literate culture* (or discourse) confronting members of a predominately *oral culture*. The clue to this *literate/oral* dichotomy is found in vocabularies, *logics*, and styles of media texts and discourses, made visible by the critical discourse analysis above. The cultural logic of the literate South African journalists biases their perception of oral culture. "Many, if not all, oral or residually oral cultures strike literates as extraordinarily agonistic in their verbal performance and indeed in their lifestyle" (Ong 1982:43). Communicative interactions in oral culture are *agonistic*, seemingly violent and antagonistic in nature (1982:45). Characteristic of politics in oral culture are the verbal combats, "reciprocal name-calling" and stylised "verbal tongue lashings"; these are not real fights but stylised arts forms. However, these are misinterpreted by the members of the literate culture as if they were violent fights or at best preludes to real combat (1982:44). Journalists, like other members of literate culture are conditioned by education and through the use of writing and printing technologies have fostered abstractions and distance from the arena where human beings struggle with one another. Their culturally ethnocentric bias and professional ideologies are propagated by them as *the universal norm*. Such bias determines their modes of thought and interaction and they insist on calmness, unemotional climate, cooperation and avoidance of dynamic opposition. However, within oral culture "confrontation, or dynamic opposition, is regarded as the appropriate means by which disagreements are expressed, issues developed and debated, and resolutions proposed". In turn, such *hot* discursive interaction is rejected by the scribal logic of members of the literate culture who insist on calm, and unemotional climate for debate (Kohman 1974:101). In the loud, heated, and emotionally expressive confrontational modes of communication characteristic of oral cultures, words are alternative to actual fighting and enmity is dissipated through verbal battles and real bloodshed is avoided (Farb 1977:107; Ong 1982:44; Kochman 1974:98). But such a mode of communication is misunderstood by the literate as if it were real violence or as logically leading to real violence.

For members of the literate culture, *democracy* is "government by discussion" or "government by rational and free public discussion among legally equal citizens" (Schudson 1997:297). Accordingly, at the heart of democracy is the concept of *conversation*, based on the ideal model of the Platonic dialogic discussion, or *rational discourse* (Roelofse 1983:18). This ideal conversation, a "free and open discussion by reasonable people" is thought to be a precondition for democracy, and needs to be safeguarded against the intrusion of other forms of *discussion* of the seemingly *unreasonable* people. Such *rationality* was taken in the past as the justification for the discourse of apartheid and motivated the *permanent removal from society* (i.e. murder in apartheid-speak) of opponents of the regime who threatened to disrupt the *rational* discussion of the white minority. However, the insistence by members of the literate culture that democracy is dependent on the ideal of rational discourse, conceived by them as a *sociable* Platonic dialogue is a distortion as it emphasises consensus, cooperation, and egalitarian inclusion in conversation. However in practice, democracy is characterised by public discussions between people of *different* backgrounds, who hold *different* values, *do not share* the same views and speak from unequal positions of power. This more appropriate model of democracy is full of risk, competitive, conflictual and profoundly *uncomfortable* because it is public (Schudson 1997:299). Schudson

(1997:298–300) suggests that the *conversation* model of rational discourse is "not the soul of democracy", as it only presents one aspect of conversation. A more coherent and realistic view of conversation would be to conceive of two aspects that are intertwined and in tension: the sociable, intimate and pleasurable egalitarian conversation of a *rational discourse* and the more utilitarian public and political conversation aimed at problem-solving and motivated by dissensus. Thus, in a democracy, public discourse is both a discussion *and* a disputation; it is a tension between competition *and* cooperation, equality *and* hierarchy, inclusion *and* exclusion, spontaneity *and* formality (Schudson 1997:299).

> Democracy may sometimes require that your interlocutor does not wait politely for you to finish but shakes you by the collar and cries "Listen! ..." We call these situations social movements, strikes, demonstrations. We call the people who initiate such departures from civility driven, ambitious, unreasonable, self-serving, rude, hot-headed, self-absorbed ... All of these are people willing to engage in democratic conversation but also pugnacious beyond the point of civility, even willing to make their case to opt out of conversation altogether, at least temporarily and strategically.
>
> (Schudson 1997:308)

Political dialogue and public conversation are aimed at *consensus* and *dissensus* (Lyotard 1984:60–61; 65–66). Such an idea of conversation would consider politics more realistically as *war conducted by other means* (Foucault 1980:90), and the model of political conversation and dialogue as being based on the agonistic model of war and battle (1980:114). Thus, if *politics is talk* and *word politics dominates world politics* (Bell 1975:10, 98), political battles are battles fought in and through language and discourse.

Summary

In this unit we examined the importance of language in society and ways we can analyse the language used by the mass media. We suggested that verbal messages were the basic units of linguistic communication and analysed messages on three levels: the formal structure of the text and the elements that make such text; the discursive practice that determines the rules and conventions for the use of language; and the social context of language in society. We concluded with a case study of mass media use of language.

Research activities

1 Do you think that it is possible to think without the help of language? Can you think about any situation in your life were you do not use language?

2 Read the first paragraph of a number of newspaper articles. Is every article structured according to the inverted pyramid?

3 Select a number of newspaper articles on topic such as political protest or labour disputes and identify the words that are used to describe these activities. Can you find instances where political protest and labour dispute are described as criminal activities? Is such a description justified?

4 Describe an argument using the "argument is a dance" metaphor. Does this metaphor provide a different perspective than "the argument is war" metaphor?

5 Read a number of newspaper articles and identify instances of the use of passive and active voice. Rewrite the passive voice sentence into active voice and the active voice into passive voce. Can you notice the change of meaning?

6 Observe the organisation where you work or study or any other organisation where you are a member and identify the rules that determine where and how people may talk to each other.

7 In your workplace or in your family, can everyone express his or her opinion on any issue? In the above situation identify the people who have authority to speak and express their views and those that remain silent, and explain the reason for this situation.

8 Select a number of newspaper articles on labour disputes. Identify how the workers are represented in the articles; what words are used to describe the dispute? What ideology is represented in the article?

9 Select a newspaper article and conduct your own case study of the use of language by the media. Your study should be guided by the following questions:
   - What type or genre does the text represent?
   - What are the main concept, words or jargon that you can identify in the text?
   - What metaphors are used and to what effect?
   - What grammatical structures are used?
   - What type of discursive practice produced the text?
   - Who is the audience for the text?
   - What ideology is evident in the text?
   - How does the text relate to other media text on the particular topic?

Further reading

Fairclough, N. 1990. *Language and power*. London: Longman.

Fairclough, N. 1992a. *Discourse and social change*. Cambridge: Polity.

Fairclough, N (ed). 1992b. *Critical language awareness*. London: Longman.

Fairclough, N & Wodak, R. 1997. Critical discourse analysis, in *Discourse as social interaction, discourse studies: a multidisciplinary introduction, Volume 2*, edited by T van Dijk. London: Sage.

Fowler, R. 1991. *Language in the news: Discourse and ideology in the press*. London: Routledge.

Van Dijk, T (ed). 1997. *Discourse as social interaction, discourse studies: a multidisciplinary introduction, Volume 2*. London: Sage.

Bibliography

Altheide, DL. 1991. The impact of television news formats on social policy. *Journal of Broadcasting and Electronic Media* 35(1):3–21.

Asmal, K. 1998. A second look: Squeals from the free speech symphony. *Mail & Guardian* 14(31)7–13 August: 28.

Austin, JL. 1984. *How to do things with words.* 2nd edition. New York: Oxford University Press.

Barthes, R. 1982. *Image, music, text.* London: Fontana.

Barthes, R. 1984. *Writing degree zero & Elements of semiology.* London: Jonathan Cape.

Bell, A. 1991. *The language of news media.* Oxford: Blackwell.

Bell, DVJ. 1975. *Power, influence, and authority: An essay in political linguistics.* New York: Oxford University Press.

Belsey, C. 1986. *Critical practice.* London: Methuen.

Bennett, WL. 1990. Toward a theory of press-state relations in the United States. *Journal of Communication* 40(2):103–125.

Berger, PL. 1980. *Invitation to sociology: a humanistic perspective.* Harmondsworth: Penguin.

Best, S & Kellner, D. 1991. *Postmodern theory: Critical interrogation.* New York: Guilford.

Botha, PJJ. 1991. Orality, literacy and worldview: exploring the interaction. *Communicatio,* 17(2):2–15.

Bourdieu, P. 1992. *Language and symbolic power.* Cambridge: Polity Press.

Braham, P. 1982. How the media report race, in *Culture, society and the media,* edited by M Gurevitch, T Bennett, J Curran & J Woollacott. London: Methuen.

Brand, R. 1996. Verdict on constitution could usher in new era of democracy – or more political wrangling. *The Star,* 5 September:3.

Burton, S. 1987. Ideology on the beat: labour and the English-language press, in *Narrating the crisis: hegemony and the South African press,* edited by K Tomaselli, R Tomaselli & J Muller. Johannesburg: Richard Lyon.

Chilton, P (ed). 1985. *Language and the nuclear arms debate: Nukespeak today.* London: Pinter.

Chilton, P & Ilyin, M. 1993. Metaphor in political discourse: the case of the 'common European house'. *Discourse and Society* 4(1):7–31.

Connolly, WE. 1983. *The terms of political discourse.* 2nd edition. Oxford: Robertson.

Corcoran, PE. 1979. *Political language and rhetoric.* Austin: University of Texas Press.

Coward, R & Ellis, J. 1986. *Language and materialism: developments in semiology and the theory of the subject.* London: Routledge & Kegan Paul.

Crystal, D. 1974. *Linguistics.* Harmondsworth: Penguin.

Davis, D. 1974. *The grammar of television production.* 3rd edition. London: Barrie and Jenkins.

Davis, H & Walton, P (eds). 1984. *Language, image, media.* Oxford: Blackwell.

De Saussure, F. 1981. *Course in general linguistics.* London: Fontana/Collins.

Du Plooy, GM. 1995. The role of formative research and supportive communication in affirmative action. *Communitas* 2:21–33.

Edelman, M. 1974. The political language of the helping professions. *Politics and Society* 4(3):295–310.

Ellis, DG. 1992. *From language to communication.* Hillsdale: Erlbaum.

Fairclough, N. 1990. *Language and power.* London: Longman.

Fairclough, N. 1992a. *Discourse and social change.* Cambridge: Polity.

Fairclough, N (ed). 1992b. *Critical language awareness.* London: Longman.

Farb, P. 1977. *Word play: What happens when people talk.* London: Coronet Books.

Finegan, E. 1994. *Language: its structure and use.* 2nd edition. Orlando: Harcourt Brace.

Fiske, J. 1982. *Introduction to communication studies.* London: Methuen.

Foucault, M. 1980. *Power/knowledge: selected interviews & other writings 1972–1977.* New York: Pantheon.

Foucault, M. 1986. *The archaeology of knowledge.* London: Tavistock.

Foucault, M. 1988. *Politics, philosophy, culture: interviews and other writings 1977–1984.* New York: Routledge.

Fourie, PJ. 1991. Media, mites, metafore en die kommunikasie van apartheid. *Communicatio* 17(1): 2–6.

Fowler, R. 1991. *Language in the news: Discourse and ideology in the press.* London: Routledge.

Gombrich, EH. 1986. *Art and illusion: A study in the psychology of pictorial representation.* Oxford: Phaidon Press.

Gumede, WM. 1998. Alliance fallout puts spotlight on ANC's tug-o'-war. *The Sunday Independent,* 5 July:5.

Gusfield, J. 1976. The literary rhetoric of science: comedy and pathos in drinking driver research. *American Sociological Review* 41(1):16–34.

Habermas, J. 1972. *Toward a rational society: student protest, science and politics.* London: Heineman.

Hardy, WG. 1978. *Language, thought, and experience: a tapestry of the dimensions of meaning.* Baltimore: University Park Press.

Harré, R. 1985. Persuasion and manipulation, in *Discourse and communication*, edited by TA Van Dijk. New York: De Gruyter.

Hartley, J. 1982. *Understanding news.* London: Methuen.

Hawkes, T. 1985. *Structuralism and semiotics.* London: Methuen.

Hayakawa, SI. 1973. *Language in thought and action.* 2nd edition. London: Allen & Unwin.

Hodge, R & Kress, G. 1988. *Social semiotics.* Cambridge: Polity.

Hollingdale, RJ. 1978. Appendices, in F. Nietzsche, *Twilight of the idols and the Anti-Christ.* Translated by RJ Hollingdale. Harmondsworth: Penguin.

Janks, H. 1997. Critical discourse analysis as a research tool. *Discourse: studies in the cultural politics of education,* 18(3):329–342.

Janks, H & Ivanic, R. 1992. CLA and emancipatory discourse, in *Critical language awareness,* edited by N Fairclough. London: Longman.

Jakobson, R. 1964. Concluding statement: Linguistics and poetics, in *Style in language*, edited by TA Sebeok. Cambridge, MA: Massachusetts Institute of Technology.

Kassin, SM & McNall, K. 1991. Police interrogation and confessions: Communicating promises and threats by pragmatic implication. *Law and Human Behavior* 15(3):233–251.

Kepplinger, HM & Köcher, R. 1990. Professionalism in the media world? *European Journal of Communication* 5(2/3):285–311.

Kochman, T. 1974. Orality and literacy as factors of 'black' and 'white' communicative behavior. *International Journal of the Sociology of Language* 3:91–115.

Kress, G. 1983. Media analysis and the study of discourse. *Media Information Australia* 28:3–17.

Kress, G. 1984. Linguistic and ideological transformation in news reporting, in *Language, image, media,* edited by H Davis & P Walton. Oxford: Blackwell.

Kress, G (ed). 1988. *Communication and culture: an introduction.* Kensington: New South Wales University Press.

Kress, G & Hodge, R. 1979. *Language as ideology.* London: Routledge & Kegan Paul.

Lakoff, G & Johnson, M. 1980. *Metaphors we live by.* Chicago: University of Chicago Press.

Lyons, J. 1977. *Introduction to theoretical linguistics.* Cambridge: Cambridge University Press.

Lyotard, J-F. 1984. *The postmodern condition: a report on knowledge.* Manchester: Manchester University Press.

MacDougall, CD. 1969. *Interpretative reporting*. 5th edition. New York: Macmillan.
Marcuse, H. 1970. *One dimensional man*. London: Sphere Books.
McLuhan, M. 1969. *Understanding media*. London: Sphere Books.
McQuail, D. 1980. *Communication*. London: Longman.
McQuail, D. 1987. *Mass communication: an introduction*. London: Sage.
Mey, J. 1985. *Whose language? A study in linguistic pragmatics*. Amsterdam: John Benjamins.
Mills, CW. 1978. *The sociological imagination*. Harmondsworth: Penguin.
Montgomery, M. 1986. *An introduction to language and society*. London: Methuen.
Nelson, NL. 1990. Metaphor and the media, in *Studies in communication, Volume 4*, edited by S Thomas. Norwood, NJ: Ablex.
Niebuhr, R. 1960. *Moral man and immoral society. A study in ethics and politics*. New York: Scribner.
Nietzsche, F. 1978. *Twilight of the idols and the Anti-Christ*. Translated by RJ Hollingdale. Harmondsworth: Penguin.
Ong, WJ. 1982. *Orality and literacy: the technologizing of the word*. London: Methuen.
O'Sullivan, T, Hartley, J, Saunders, D, Montgomery, M & Fiske, J. 1994. *Key concepts in communication and culture studies*. 2nd edition. London: Routledge.
Orwell, G. 1975. *Inside the whale and other stories*. Harmondsworth: Penguin.
Paton, C. 1998a. Battered SACP retreats after Mbeki onslaught. *Sunday Times*, 5 July:1.
Paton, C. 1998b. Waving a red rag to the ANC. *Sunday Times*, 5 July:4.
Posel, D. 1989. A 'battlefield of perceptions': state discourse on political violence, 1985–1988, in *War and society: the militarisation of South Africa*, edited by J Cock & L Nathan. Cape Town: David Philip.
Poster, M. 1990. *The mode of information: poststructuralism and social context*. Cambridge: Polity.
Poster, M. 1994. The mode of information and postmodernity in *Communication theory today*, edited by D Crowley & D Mitchell. Cambridge: Polity.
Ricoeur, P. 1979. *The conflict of interpretations*. Evanston: Northwestern University Press.
Roelofse, JJ. 1983. *Towards rational discourse: an analysis of the report of the Steyn Commission of Inquiry into the Media*. Pretoria: Van Schaik.
Rossi-Landi, F. 1990. *Marxism and ideology*. Oxford: Oxford University Press.
Sapir, E. 1957. *Culture, language and personality: selected essays*. Berkeley: University of California Press.
Schudson, M. 1997. Why conversation is not the soul of democracy. *Critical Studies in Mass Communication* 14(4):297–309.
So, CYK. 1987. The summit as war: how journalists use metaphors. *Journalism Quarterly* 64(2/3):623–626.
Sonderling, S. 1991. Psychoanalysis and television, in *Critical television analyses: an introduction*, edited by PJ Fourie. Cape Town: Juta:141–162.
Sonderling, S. 1992. Murder of the combi-taxi industry by the mass media: perceptions and realities of road safety. *Communicatio* 18(2):57–63.
Sonderling, S. 1993. Power of discourse and the discourse of power in making an issue of sexual abuse in South Africa: The rise and fall of social problems. *Critical Arts* 6(2):1–26.
Sonderling, S. 1994. An exploration of poststructuralist discursive critique and its implication for the study of communication. *Communicatio* 20(2):9–24.
Sonderling, S. 1996a. Knowledge and power in the South African debate on pornography 1900s–1990s: a discursive critique. *Communicatio* 22(2):33–50.
Sonderling, S. 1996b. Language, in *Introduction to communication – course book 3: communication and the production of meaning*, edited by PJ Fourie. Juta: Cape Town:88–111.

Sonderling, S. 1997a. Psychoanalysis and television, in *Introduction to communication – course book 6: film and television studies*, edited by PJ Fourie. Cape Town: Juta:237–250.

Sonderling, S. 1997b. Development Support Communication (DSC): A change-agent in support of popular participation or a double-agent of deception? *Communicatio* 23(2):34–42.

Spender, D. 1980. *Man made language*. London: Routledge.

Thompson, JB. 1990. *Studies in the theory of ideology*. Cambridge: Polity.

Thompson, JB. 1992. *Ideology and modern culture*. Cambridge: Polity.

Tomaselli, R & Tomaselli, K. 1987. The political economy of the South African press, in *Narrating the crisis: hegemony and the South African press*, edited by K Tomaselli, R Tomaselli & J Muller. Johannesburg: Richard Lyon.

Tough talk from the president. Extract from a meeting of Sanef editors and Nelson Mandela. 1997. *Rhodes Journalism Review* November 15:34.

Van Dijk, T. 1988. *News analysis: case studies of international and national news in the press*. Hillsdale, NJ: Lawrence Erlbaum.

Weedon, C. 1987. *Feminist practice and poststructuralist theory*. Oxford: Blackwell.

Whatmough, J. 1957. *Language: a modern* synthesis. New York: Mentor.

Williams, R. 1993. Texts and discourses, in *Mass media for the nineties: The South African handbook of mass communication*, edited by AS de Beer. Pretoria: Van Schaik.

Williams, R. 1985. *Marxism and literature*. Oxford: Oxford University Press.

Newspaper articles

Battle marked by accusations, verbal brawls. 1996. *The Star*, 7 November:23.

Cracking down on critical allies. 1998. *Mail & Guardian*, 14(26) 3–9 July: 24.

End the circus. 1996a. *The Pretoria News*, 18 September:11.

Everything keeps going right. 1995. *Sunday Times*, 30 April:17.

History was made in Parliament. 2000. *The Pretoria News*, 10 May:3.

Madiba gets tough with SACP. 1998. *The Pretoria News*, 2 July:1.

Politics sneaks into council meeting. 1994. *Pretoria News*, 31 March:3.

Shot runner back in city. 1995. *The Pretoria News*, 19 April:1.

Stop the war of words and talk. 1996b. *The Pretoria News*, 9 October:11.

Watershed speech has changed our politics. 1998. *Sunday Times*, 5 July:18.

We can all reap fruits of democracy. 1994. *Sunday Times*, 18 December:24.

4

Narrative Analysis

David Wigston

Overview

This unit is about telling stories, particularly those we find in the media. We investigate how stories, or more correctly narratives, are constructed and how we interpret them in order to gain meaning from the text. We approach our study of narrative in two ways. In the first, we look at the syntagmatic arrangement of the narrative, where the focus is on what happens in the narrative in order to move the story forwards. This concerns the linear arrangement of the narrative where the temporal chain-effect relationship between events in the narrative is important. This syntagmatic approach is represented by the models of Tzvetan Todorov and Vladimir Propp. Our second approach considers the narrative paradigmatically, where we establish how meaning is generated by probing the various levels found within the narrative. This paradigmatic approach is represented by Umberto Eco's more complex model. These three models of narrative are supported and explained by the theoretical views of Seymour Chatman, Roland Barthes and Claude Lévi-Strauss. But, to start, we look at the four distinct phases that can be identified in the linear progress of a narrative. Two case studies are presented using the models of Propp and Eco to illustrate the applicability of their respective models to our understanding of how television narratives are constructed. Although the contents of this unit are inclusive of all media messages, for the sake of convenience an emphasis has been placed on television narratives. However, this does not imply that all mediated narratives are synonymous in their construction as the nature of the medium can influence the structure of the discourse.

Learning outcomes

By the end of this unit you should be able to

- identify the basic components and elements that make up a narrative;
- describe Roland Barthes' narrative theory;
- summarise Claude Lévi-Strauss' concept of binary opposition;
- explain Tzvetan Todorov's elementary narrative model;
- explain Vladimir Propp's and Umberto Eco's narrative model; and
- analyse the narrative of a media text.

4.1 INTRODUCTION

Why study narrative? Hobbs (1989:264) comments that, as individuals, we need no instruction in to how to watch a film or television. We simply either like or dislike what we see. Chances are that we arrange our daily schedule around those television programmes we enjoy watching. It is also likely that we discuss some of those programmes with our friends, family or colleagues the next day. This points to the pervasive nature of the media and its unique powers which go unnoticed since the media are such a part of our daily lives. But as students of communication, we need to think critically about what we read and see. A critical analysis of media content is not particularly easy owing to the sheer omnipotence of the media. Because of its visual basis, we particularly tend to treat film and television as we do the rest of the world. Film and television have acquired so much power simply because they appear to be genuine, authentic and real. This has led to an "As-Seen-on-TV" syndrome, where, because it was seen on television, it must be so. Unlike our direct experiences, we have to remind ourselves that film and television are merely representations "carefully and expensively designed for our consumption" (Hobbs 1998:264).

In this unit we are not going to enter the debate on whether film and television represent a window on the world or if they are a mirror of society. Instead we opt for the position where film and television are seen as skilfully manufactured products. Within the context of this discussion, the broad purpose of this unit is then to develop our critical skills about the media so that we can function effectively and efficiently in the current information age. We consider ways in which we can analyse and deconstruct some of the messages put out by film and television, in particular the narrative contained in those messages.

Narrative is not limited to film and television as it can be found in any text that contains language, images, gestures or aspects of these. The French literary philosopher, Roland Barthes (1977:79), who provides us with the dominant thinking on narrative (which we discuss in more detail in a later section), indicates that narratives are not limited to the media, but exist in a variety of genres, such as myths, legends, fables, tales, novellas, epics, history, tragedy, comedy, mime, film, the news, and even in paintings and stained-glass windows. Basically this comes down to the fact that as humans, we all have narratives and we like sharing these with other people. Initially stories were passed down through the ages by word-of-mouth as folk tales. Inventions such as the printing press and film have helped to preserve and record these tales for us. But with the development of the media there has been an increase in the number of stories at our disposal. This commonplace nature of storytelling often means that we are unaware of the fact that we are constantly surrounded by a variety of stories throughout the day. Amongst many others, stories form part of the advertisements we see on breakfast-time television. We refer to items in news bulletins as stories. The cartoon strip we so avidly turn to in the newspaper tells a story. Of all the media, one of the most prodigious in the production of stories today must surely be that of television. It is for this reason that we emphasise televison narratives in this unit.

But how do stories work? Is there any similarity in the way that television tells a story to that of a paperback novel? Although we know how an action drama series shown on television will end – the hero always wins so that he/she can return in next week's episode – yet we still sit glued to the edge of our seats. Why? In order to answer these questions about how television (as being representative of all mediated narratives) works, it becomes necessary for us "to step out of its magnetic pull and take it apart piece by piece" (Kozloff 1987:45). This then is the gist of narrative analysis.

The development of the Critical School during the twentieth century provided us, over time, with some of the tools necessary to broaden our understanding of storytelling. Slowly a new field, known collectively as narrative theory, took shape, drawing on the work of many diverse scholars, beginning with the work of Vladimir Propp in the late 1920s. The vast field of narrative theory has received input from different subjects such as linguistics, anthropology, film theory and semiology, where the common binding agent is structuralism. We attempt to bring all these theoretical strands together so that we can study the nature of narratives in mediated texts and explain how these narratives function. We introduce you to the work of some well-known scholars in this field, particularly the theoretical explanations of Seymour Chatman, Roland Barthes and Claude Lévi-Strauss, followed by the narrative models of Tzvetan Todorov, Vladimir Propp and Umberto Eco.

Our study of narrative is based on three important assumptions regarding messages in the media. These are (Hobbs 1998:266–269):

- *Media messages are constructions.* All media messages are created by a variety of people with distinct and varied purposes, which complicate the construction from other media sources. Internal forces include company policies, budgets and process. The visual nature of film and television means that we, as the audience, find the content easy to interpret with little awareness of its constructed nature. We take the conventions used in that construction to be natural and normal.
- *Media messages have economic and political contexts.* The organisation of television as an institution has a large influence on the way in which the programme content is constructed. External forces at work include aspects such as regulation of the broadcasting environment, legislation and competition bureaucracy. We also have to take into account market forces, such as the role played by advertising, which are central to the operation of any broadcaster today. These forces are invariably covert and long term in nature.
- *Individuals negotiate meaning in media texts.* We now recognise that meaning is a result of the interaction between the individual and the content of media messages. The process governing this interaction is a complex one involving a number of variables unique to each individual. We bring to the text our own unique circumstances and knowledge when interpreting those messages. These circumstances and knowledge can either complement or contradict the information in the message so aiding in the construction of the final meaning. The implication of this point of view is that we can no longer assume a universal interpretation of any message.

Much of what we learn in this unit is derived from linguistics, where some of the theories and models of narrative were initially developed. A peculiar convention that has carried over to media studies from the study of literature, is our use of the term "read" when we view, and subsequently interpret, a film or television programme; and the use of the term "text" when we refer to the content of that film or programme. As Hobbs (1998:260) elaborates, "'reading' a film or television program [sic] is not substantially different from reading a newspaper or a novel." She substantiates her argument by saying that the visual images in film and television are symbolic like those we use for representing the printed word. We, as the readers, have to learn those symbols in order to interpret the meaning of any particular image.

To conclude this introduction we need to return to the question we posed at the beginning: why study narrative? A succinct answer to this would be so that we can appreciate how it was put together in the first place. Such an understanding would provide us with a competency in evaluating the relevance of mediated messages, and with such insight we can then start creating our own meaningful messages.

4.2 THE BASIC NARRATIVE PARADIGM

The basic progress of a narrative is a linear one, "A" is the cause of "B", which in turn is the cause of "C" and so on (Butler 1994:20). This is known as the cause-effect chain, where one event causes the next, which in turn cause the next. There are exceptions to this rule, but we do not concern ourselves with these here.

The narrative undergoes a certain development as part of its linear progress, in which we can identify distinct phases. The generalised location of these within the duration of a narrative is illustrated in Figure 4.1 and is outlined briefly below.

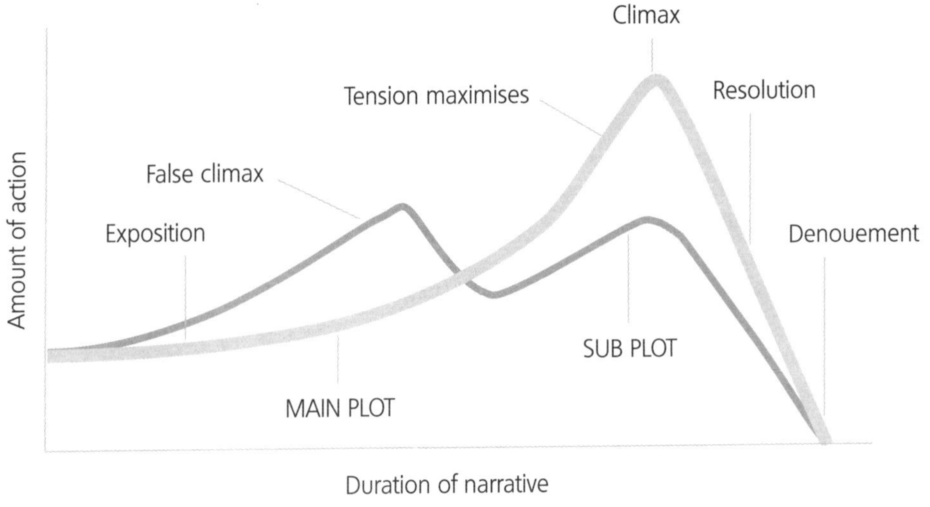

Figure 4.1 The linear progress of a narrative in a generalised text

- *Exposition:* The exposition introduces the reader to the two basic components that make up the story, that is the principal characters and the space or environment that they occupy (see also Figure 4.2). Every narrative must have an exposition, but it is not necessarily always located at the beginning of the narrative as suggested in Figure 4.1 (Butler 1994:19). In television series, the constant recurring nature of certain characters means that the exposition phase of the narrative is usually very brief, because it is assumed that we, as regular viewers, are already familiar with those characters. The usual technique is to reintroduce the characters as part of the title sequence. If the narrative opens with the action already in progress then we say the narrative is *in media res* (Butler 1994:19). The enigma or problems to be resolved in the narrative are usually stated in the exposition.
- *Climax:* The climax occurs when conflict in the story reaches its peak. While the climax is considered to be the most concentrated moment of the entire narrative, its does not signal the end of that narrative (Butler 1994:21). In television programmes we usually find a number of smaller climaxes, where the plot peaks prior to cutting away for an advertising break. The purpose of these mini-climaxes is not to resolve tension, but rather the opposite: to heighten interest in the narrative so as to ensure that the audience returns to the programme following the break.
- *Resolution:* Following the climax comes the resolution, where the enigmas posed at the beginning of the narrative are resolved.
- *Denouement:* The denouement brings about closure to the narrative by rounding out the story. If a narrative ends without a resolution and denouement then we have an open narrative. Open narratives abound in certain film and television genres, such as the soap opera and the sitcom, since this technique facilitates a continuance of the narrative at a later time, either as a sequel or as a continuing episode.

When studying the narratives of mediated messages, we have to remember that, while the principles governing those messages remain the same, no two narratives are alike. We also need to keep in mind that narrative is closely allied with genre, and that television genres are constantly evolving. One of the relatively more recent developments in television genres is the introduction of multiple plots within the narrative. A groundbreaking programme in this field is considered to be *Hill Street Blues*, which aired for the first time in the United States on 15 January 1981 (Deming 1985:1). Up to five distinct plots can be identified in any episode of *Hill Street Blues*, where each plot has its own exposition, climax, resolution and denouement. However, only one of these can be singled out as the main plot, the rest being subplots, which are indicated by the thinner, darker line in Figure 4.1.

In narrative analysis the literary work of a text is not the object of the exercise. Barthes (1977:79) succinctly phrases it as "Caring nothing for the division between good and bad literature, narrative is international, transhistorical, transcultural: it is simply there like life itself." To quote Chatman (1987:17), in narrative analysis, the question we need to ask is not "What makes Macbeth great?" but rather "What makes Macbeth a tragedy?" Narrative analysis does not concern itself with the empirical content, literary merits or quality of production and performances in a text. It does concern itself with the structure and functioning of a discourse in order to establish a grid of possibilities by identifying constant features. A grid is established and each text is plotted on the grid; not to adjust the text, but to adjust the grid (Chatman 1978:18–19). Structuralist theories of narrative thus seek to explain the laws that govern narrative structure, not the accuracy of its representation of reality (Fiske 1987:131).

4.3 ROLAND BARTHES' THEORY OF NARRATIVE

Where, then, does one start looking for the structure of a narrative? Obviously in the narrative itself. But the tools needed to analyse this structure are provided by a model; the findings are explained by a theory. In order to construct a suitable model and accompanying theory, the French structuralist Roland Barthes (1915–1980) (1977:82) suggests we look at linguistics, from which structuralism originally evolved. Barthes' assumption was that language is made up of a system of signs that reflect the beliefs of a particular society at a particular time. Narratives found in media texts differ little, if at all, from those found in literature. Thus, we can begin our study of media narratives by looking at how narratives function in literary texts. Then we can make the necessary analogies regarding the way narratives function in a media text.

Before we continue further with Barthes' theory of narrative, we need to first identify the elements that make up a narrative. These various elements are summarised in Figure 4.2. From a structuralist point of view, all narratives consist of two layers. The first layer

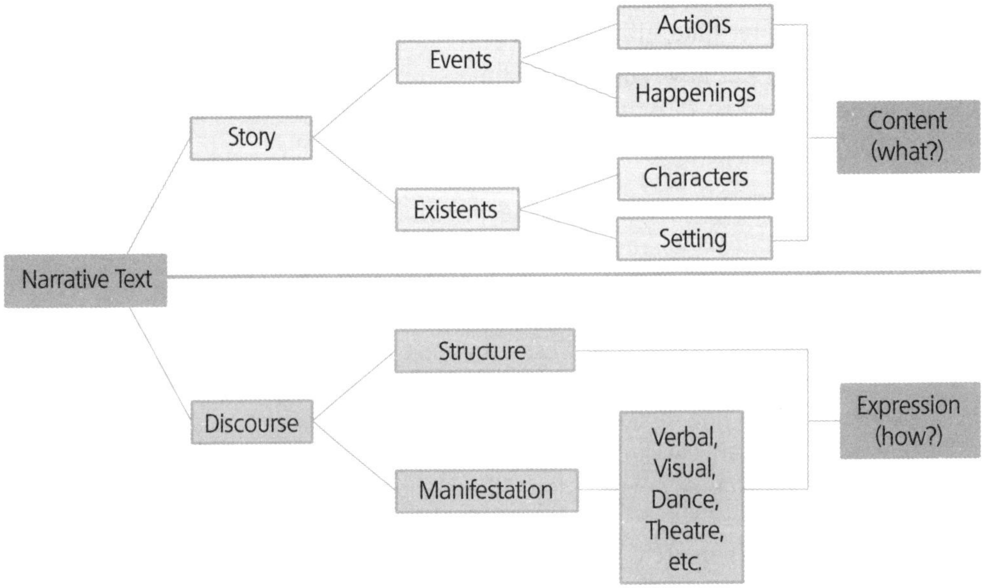

Figure 4.2 A structuralist model of a narrative (adapted from Chatman 1978:26)

is the story, which sets out the content or the chain of events (i.e. the action and happenings) together with the existents (i.e. the characters and setting). The second layer is the discourse, which is the expression, or form, of the story. Chatman (1978:19) explains these components in simple terms when he says "the story is the *what* in a narrative ... , discourse is the *how*." This distinction between the two layers of a narrative is a synthetic one, as in reality a story cannot exist without a discourse and vice versa.

Because there is such a clear distinction between story and discourse, we can take the story element of a narrative and easily transpose it on to different media. Thus, as an example, the same Agatha Christie who-done-it narrative can be presented to us as a novel, a film, serialised on radio or presented on the stage as a play. Instead of following the story through words printed in a book, we can alternatively follow that same story through other codes. We can say this because the story element of a narrative is not made up exclusively of words or images, but events and existents that are manifest and signified by words and images. Thus we can say that stories can exist independently of any particular medium (Chatman 1978:20).

On the second level we also need to distinguish clearly between the structure of the discourse and the manner in which it is manifest, or presented to us. Why do we say that narratives are structured? To qualify as a structure, a narrative requires three attributes (Chatman 1978:21). These are as follows:

- *Wholeness:* a narrative is whole because it is made up of distinct elements that differ from what those elements constitute. This attribute is clearly illustrated in Figure 4.2. These elements are not randomly selected, but as we discuss later in this section, tend to be related in an organised manner and in so doing produce a unique chain of events.
- *Self-regulation:* a narrative maintains and closes itself. This basically means that events or existents that do not belong to the story do not enter the narrative. While the appearance of certain events or existents may not be immediately obvious to us, as recipients of the narrative, their relevance must be revealed at some point in the discourse.
- *Transformation:* to manifest events in a particular medium, the event needs to be physically represented by signs specific to that medium, such as the words in a book. This process is known as transformation.

Having established the elements that make up a narrative, we can return to our explanation of how narrative functions. We have established that a narrative is made up of a number of elements that are all interrelated and hierarchical in nature. In linguistics the sentence is the smallest unit that is wholly representative of the discourse. Beyond the sentence are more sentences. The discourse is organised by all the sentences that make up a particular text. Through this discourse, or organisation of sentences, can be seen a message which operates at a higher level than the language in which it was written. The discourse is then made up of a number of units that are fitted together according to specific codes, which in the case of linguistics are the rules of grammar.

This means that if we want to undertake a narrative analysis of a text, it is necessary that we first establish the relationships between the sentences and the discourse, since a formal organisation orders all semiotic systems, whatever their substance and dimension. Structurally, television narratives share the same characteristics as the sentence, except that television narratives make use of different and far more complex signs and signifiers.

It is from linguistics that we have learned that in order to analysis the narrative of a media text we need to make explicit every system of meaning through its organisation. The narrative is not a simple sum of the propositions that constitute the dialogue. In other words, merely retelling the story that makes up the narrative, is not a narrative analysis. In order to analyse the narrative we need to begin by classifying the enormous number of elements that make up that narrative. This embodies the concept of a level of description. A sentence can be described hierarchically on several levels, for example, it can be described phonetically, grammatically or contextually. Each of these levels has its own unit and correlation, which require a second description. What Barthes is saying here, is that on its own a unit has no meaning. A unit only takes on meaning if we integrate that unit into a higher level. For instance, in language, syllables give meaning only when we consider them on the higher level of words, and words only give meaning when integrated into a sentence, and so on. In this integrational system of creating meaning we find two types of relationship between the signs we use – distribution, which occurs on the same level and integration, which occurs on the next higher level.

To follow the unfolding of a story, it is not enough to understand the narrative. We need to project the horizontal links of the narrative onto a vertical axis. To read a narrative means not only moving horizontally from one unit to the next, but also moving vertically from one descriptive level to the next. Barthes (1977:87) distinguishes three levels of description in a narrative:

- the level of function
- the level of action of characters
- the level of narration in the discourse.

These three levels are fully integrated. A function only has meaning in so far as it has a place in the action of a character, and this action in turn receives meaning when it is narrated.

Therefore, to begin a narrative analysis, we need to define the smallest unit that we can find in the narrative. Meaning must be the creation of such a unit. Its contribution to the story makes it a unit and these first-level units are called functions. As Barthes (1977:89) says, "the essence of a function is, so to speak, the seed that it sows in the narrative, planting an element that will come to fruition later – on the same level or elsewhere, on another level". In narrative, everything has a meaning. Every action must contribute to the narrative and this, rather than the manner in which it is said or done, makes it a functional unit. Some functions can be represented by small units. For example, in a James Bond film, the telephone rings during the night shift at Secret

Service headquarters. James Bond picks up one of the four receivers. The *four* constitutes a functional unit, referring connotatively to a concept necessary to the story – that of a highly developed bureaucratic technology. This narrative unit is not the linguistic unit, which is one word, *four*, but rather the connoted value. This explains how short functional units can be, yet still be an integral part of the discourse. Such units, although incredibly short, extend beyond the level of denotation, and become indexical to a higher order meaning (Barthes 1977:91).

At this point it is necessary that we return to Barthes' concepts of distribution and integration in order to consider the different levels of meaning. Some units correlate to other units on the same level, which is distribution, while others relate to a higher level, which is integration. On the first level, an example of a distributional function in a film or television narrative would be the picking up of a telephone receiver, as this corresponds to the moment of putting it down. On the second level, an example of an integrational function would be the purchase of a revolver, which correlates later in the narrative with the moment it is used. Integrational units also function as indices, since the unit refers not to a complementary and consequential act, but to a more diffuse concept that is necessary to the understanding of the story. The relationship between the unit and its correlate is now no longer distributional. To illustrate this aspect we take as our example, an episode of *MacGyver* titled *The Lost Amadeus*. The casual integration of an invitation to a "Roaring 20's Bash" (a theme party) at the beginning of the episode, leads to a major setting at the resolution of the narrative in a nightclub known as "The Speakeasy" (see also Table 4.1 for more detail).

Several indices can refer to the same signified, but the order of their occurrence is not pertinent. For example, from later on in the same episode of *MacGyver*, Lulu agrees to hand over the violin to the villains, Tubbs and Ginko, in a place with a lot of people to ensure her own safety. This function also points towards the "Roaring 20's Bash" at "The Speakeasy", but in a different way. In order to understand these indexical units, we have to move to a higher level, that of the characters' actions and narration, for only on this higher level is the index clarified by being given meaning. Unlike functions which refer to a signified, indices become semantic units because of the vertical nature of their relationships. Indexical meanings are paradigmatically confirmed higher up the narrative through integration, while that of their function is confirmed syntagmatically by distribution. Some narratives, like folk tales, tend to be heavily functional, while others, such as psychological thrillers, are mainly indexical.

This simple classification can then be further subdivided. Not all units are of the same importance. Some form hinge points in the narrative. To return to our episode of *MacGyver* for an example, if MacGyver had not dropped his newspaper at the front gate to Izzy's home, Lulu's musician boss (having got out of the Lulu's car because of her erratic driving), and found Lulu's invitation to the "Roaring 20's Bash" lodged inside his newspaper, he would not have gone back into the house in order to return the invitation. In this manner MacGyver becomes embroiled in the villains' attempt to extort the Amadeus violin out of Izzy and Lulu who are inside the house at that moment. Other functions act as fillers to merely occupy narrative space between hinge points. Fillers play an important role, particularly in television narratives, where exact timing is essential. A programme has to run for a set time, and fillers provide a convenient way in which the narrative can be expanded, or collapsed, to fit an allotted space of time.

Barthes (1977:93) refers to hinge points as cardinal functions, while fillers are referred to as catalysers because of their complementary nature. To qualify as a cardinal function, the action must have a direct consequence on the development of the story. Between two cardinal functions we can find any number of catalyser functions, which then do not modify the story. This is illustrated graphically in Figure 4.3.

Catalyser functions are consecutive units only, while cardinal functions are both consecutive and consequential; what comes after the unit is caused by that unit.

Table 4.1 illustrates the position of the first few cardinal and catalyser functions in *The Lost Amadeus* episode of *MacGyver*. The fact that Lulu insists on taking MacGyver home, leads directly to MacGyver's becoming involved with the villains. Barthes (1977:94) described catalysers as being parasitic. Their function is merely chronological and they only serve to separate two moments in the story. Cardinal functions have a dual, yet simultaneous, function. They are both chronological and logical. If we were to isolate the cardinal functions in a narrative, as in Table 4.1, we would be left with the structural framework of that narrative. This is what Eco did in his model of narrative analysis, which we discuss in detail later in this unit. On catalyser and cardinal functions, Barthes (1977:95) says, "Cardinal functions are the risky moments of a narrative. Between these points of alternative, these 'dispatchers', the catalysers lay out the areas of safety, rests, luxuries." There are distinct rules that we need to follow when stringing together the different paradigmatic functional units into the narrative syntagm.

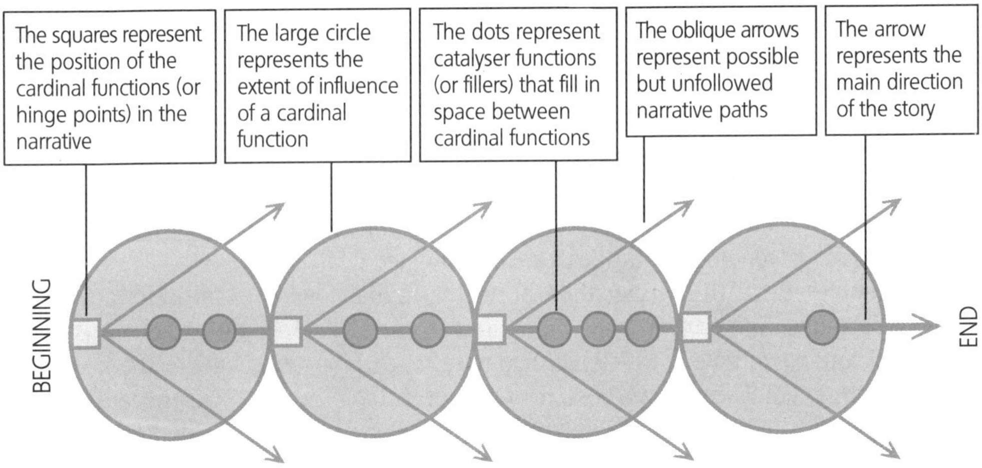

Figure 4.3 Graphic illustration of the position of cardinal and catalyser functions in a narrative (adapted from Chatman 1978: 54)

They are as follows.

- Indices always point to a higher level in the narrative.
- Cardinal and catalyser functions link by implication.
- A catalyser function implies the existence of a cardinal function, but not vice versa.
- Catalyser functions (or fillers) can be removed from the narrative, cardinal functions (or hinge points) cannot.
- Cardinal functions are bound together by reciprocity and this defines the framework of the narrative.

Table 4.1 Cardinal functions and catalysers in *The Lost Amadeus* episode of *MacGyver*

Cardinal functions	Catalysers
	• MacGyver and his friend, Wilt, are out for a Sunday morning bicycle ride. • MacGyver stops to buy a newspaper.
• MacGyver meets Lulu when she knocks him over and crushes his bicycle as a result of her erratic driving.	
• Lulu insists on taking MacGyver home ...	
	• ... but has to fulfil an errand en route for Izzy, her boss.
• A pothole in the road, and Lulu's erratic driving, cause the glove compartment in the car to spill its contents on to the floor of the car, which includes an invitation to a "Roaring 20's Bash"	
	• Lulu stops at a pawnbroker to redeem an item for Izzy. The pawnbroker's shop is closed because it is Sunday.
	• MacGyver argues with Lulu about her erratic driving style and refuses to travel any further with her. • Lulu enters the house
• MacGyver turns to leave, but drops his newspaper at the front gate, where the invitation to the "Roaring 20's Bash" spills out. He returns into the house to give Lulu her invitation back.	

In any narrative there can be a large number of cardinal functions, but it would prove too cumbersome to measure all of these using the techniques discussed here. Each and every shot in a television programme or film would have to be accounted for as either a cardinal or catalyser function. We need to make provision for a description that we can use to collectively describe a number of narrative units simultaneously. For example, cardinal functions are determined not by their importance, but by their inter-relationship. Thus a telephone call is made up of several functional events: the telephone rings; the receiver is picked up; a conversation takes place; the receiver is put down. These actions can be grouped together and collectively referred to as sequence, which is a logical succession of units bound together by a relationship. The sequence opens when one of its units has no antecedent and continues until it reaches a unit with no consequence. The sequence can then be labelled, as in the case of our elementary example, a telephone call. If we group the cardinal functions from *The Lost Amadeus* in terms of Eco's narrative model (which we discuss in section 4.7), we find the following sequences:

- hero meets girl
- girl attempts to seduce hero
- hero meets villain.

Barthes later work focuses more on a macro level, where he considers the structure of the narrative above that of the sentence. Here Barthes examines the macro processes by which meaning is structured into the narrative; where the reader's interpretation becomes an important part of the process (Fiske 1987:142). It is here where the cultural context in which a narrative is created, and ultimately read, strongly influences the interpretive process. For us to make sense of a narrative, certain conventions are used which we interpret from our accumulated cultural knowledge (Whitehead 1992:47; Watson 1998:137). In this way we, as the readers of a particular text, not only make sense of the narrative, but simultaneously anticipate its development. To Barthes, behind the apparently fixed and stable structure of beginning, middle and end in a story, lies a process which produces meaning that is extremely unstable. This process is unstable because it is made up of a set of elements with a very loose relationship between them. Within this relationship Barthes identifies a set of five codes that work towards producing meaning. By identifying these codes within a text, and the many links between them, we can determine how a narrative achieves meaning (Palmer 1991:57). Unlike the codes we discussed earlier, these codes are not derived from linguistics. Barthes considers these codes rather as "the place where there is some form of transfer of meaning, of interaction between signs ..." (Palmer 1991:58). This is in addition to the meaning derived from the linguistic codes that we discussed earlier in this section. The five codes identified by Barthes are:

- *Hermeneutic* or *enigma code:* this code sets and resolves the enigmas (a riddle or mystery) of a narrative. The hermeneutic code controls the pace and style of the discourse by controlling the flow of information we receive from the narrative in order to resolve the enigma. An enigma is created at the beginning of the narrative, which is then held is suspense awaiting final resolution. Various techniques are used to delay resolution of the narrative in order to heighten tension on our part, as readers. Often a number of false clues to the resolution of the mystery are provided. The purpose of this code is to create a tension in the narrative that in turn holds our attention. Resolution is rather important in a narrative as it brings about closure. Barthes suggests that the hermeneutic code is the motor that drives the narrative and works through ten stages, in any combination or order. These stages are (Fiske 1987:143):

- thematisation
- proposal of the enigma
- formulation of the enigma
- request for an answer
- snare
- equivocation
- jamming
- suspended answer
- partial answer
- disclosure.

- *Semic code:* this is the way the iconography of existents and events take on a collective symbolic meaning that points to the general theme of the narrative. For example, the way characters are dressed points to a particular lifestyle that forms the theme of the narrative. Other attributes that contribute to the generation of meaning include speech, gestures and actions (Fiske 1987:142). Semic codes then work connotatively within the context of the narrative in order to generate images of characters, objects or places (Whitehead 1992:47–48). To generalise, we can say these are the cultural stereotypes that are created in the narrative, such as the Western cultural expectation for the hero to be physically perfect while the villain is portrayed as degenerate (Lacey 2000:73). These images are not determined by any needs of the narrative, but rather by the needs of the culture in which the narrative has been created (Fiske 1987:142).
- *Symbolic code*: these are the fundamental oppositions on which the narrative is based (Fiske 1987:142). It is through these oppositions that the identity of an individual character is created within the narrative, where existents and events are interpreted symbolically at a connotative level. Lacey (2000:73) suggests a good method of interpreting the symbolic codes in a narrative is to establish the binary oppositions at work in the narrative. We discuss this aspect in more detail in the next section.
- *Proairetic* or *action code:* this is the portrayal and sequence of events in the narrative, and is closely related to the cardinal functions we discussed earlier. Propp and Eco's models, which we discuss later, provide us with a method of illustrating the sequence found in a narrative. Proairetic codes can also be a form of shorthand to represent

what is not shown. For example, a shot of characters boarding a bus would signify a journey without actually showing that journey.

- *Referential code*: rather than making reference to meanings within the text, referential codes extend meaning beyond the text. In other words, in order for us to understand the text we need to bring a certain body of generalised knowledge to that text. Often this knowledge comprises predetermined stereotypes that we bring to the text. For example, in order to fully contextualise *Doctor Quinn, Medicine Woman*, we need to have some prior understanding of life in Frontier America, such as the relationship between the pioneers and native Americans Indians.

Trying to identify these five codes within a text is not a particularly easy task, on one hand because of the closeness between each of the codes, and on the other hand the interdependence in the functioning of these codes.

4.4 THE ROLE OF BINARY OPPOSITION IN A NARRATIVE

Claude Lévi-Strauss, considered the father of structuralism, investigated tribal culture by analysing 800 American Indian myths. Lévi-Strauss concluded that a single logic underlies all these myths. The myth is a mechanism that deals with unresolvable contradictions by depending on simple and recognisable meanings within a culture that reinforces and challenges social understanding. These contradictions are expressed in terms of oppositional pairs (Fiske 1987:132). Seemingly different aspects of society, such as art, religion and customs, can all be reduced to oppositional pairs which produce meaning. These codes operate in all cultures, from the primitive to the most sophisticated.

Lévi-Strauss theorised that "when two characters are opposed in a binary structure, their symbolic meaning is virtually forced to be both general and easily accessible because of the simplicity of the difference between them" (Bywater & Sobchack 1989:95). Structuralism relies on binary opposition in order to transfer meanings in the easiest way. We make sense of concepts and ideas by contrasting them with their opposites. Thus in a narrative we would, as an example, automatically contrast *rich* against *poor*. Berger (1997:29–30) explains "If everyone has a great deal of money, *rich* loses its meaning; *rich* means something only in contrast to *poor*." Other examples of binary oppositions are light : dark, virtuous : evil, individual : community. In the *Western*, as an example of a particular film genre, the contradictions between culture and nature are manifested in an indoors : outdoors opposition and can be associated with other oppositions such as law and order : lawlessness; white : Indian; humane : inhumane; cowboy : homesteader, and so on.

> So a scene of Indians attacking a white homestead is a concrete metaphorical transformation of the opposition between nature and culture, and the narrative is an argument ... about the characteristics and consequences of this opposition.
> (Fiske 1987:132)

In television programmes, we find a deep common structure in each episode that can be shared with similar programmes in the same genre. For example, *Hart to Hart* shares the same deep structure as *Remington Steele* and *The Scarecrow and Mrs King* which all have male : female hero pairs. Fiske (1987:132) provides a model of the deep structures manifest in *Hart to Hart*, which is illustrated in Figure 4.4.

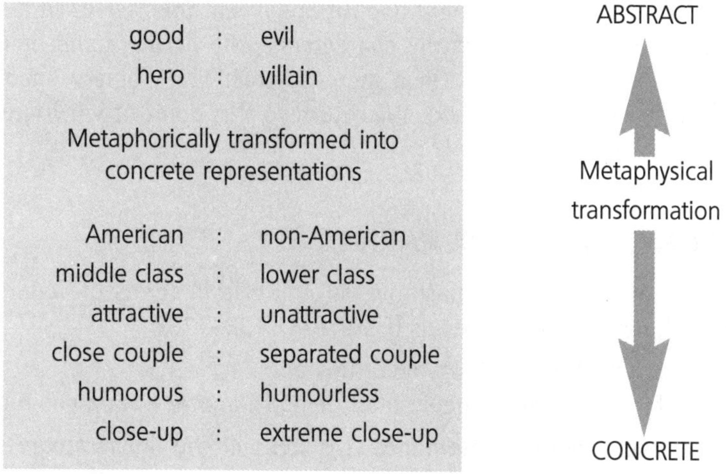

Figure 4.4 Binary oppositions found in *Hart to Hart* (adapted from Fiske 1987:132)

The opposed values are then given the narrative consequences of successful : unsuccessful. Parallelling this set of oppositions is a deeper second structure of oppositions between the hero pair, which is illustrated in Figure 4.5.

masculine	:	feminine
active	:	passive
thinking	:	object of look
controller	:	controlled

Figure 4.5 Deep second binary opposition found in *Hart to Hart* (adapted from Fiske 1987:132)

Characters are therefore also presented as pairs of opposites, with each pair having a different meaning. For example, in the *Western* genre, Wright (1975) has identified oppositions like the gunfighter : homesteader which represents a contrast between individual independence and social domesticity. We can also have the homesteader in opposition to the rancher, which forms a binary opposition on a different level. Binary oppositions are kept fairly general since this allows for complex action to take place in the narrative.

From this description we can see that Lévi-Strauss is not interested in the sequential development of the narrative, but rather in the relationships between the various characters and their settings. Binary opposition then provides us with a means of undertaking a paradigmatic analysis of a text where we can determine these relationships. One way in which binary oppositions reveal themselves in a narrative is through the physical appearance of the characters – the hero is handsome while the villain is ugly (Lacey 2000:66–67). On a more abstract level, binary oppositions can reveal ideological positions in the text. We return to this point of view later when we discuss Eco's model of narrative.

4.5 TODOROV'S MODEL OF NARRATIVE

The simplest way of explaining a narrative structure is in terms of Todorov's model. Todorov's model functions on two levels (Fiske 1987:138–139):

- A state of being which is either stable or unstable
- A causal transformation from one state of being to another, via a chain of events.

From these two levels Todorov determines five steps in the linear progression of the narrative (Lacey 2000:29). These steps are:

- a state of equilibrium
- a disruption of that equilibrium by some action
- recognition there has been a disruption
- attempts to restore the equilibrium
- a reinstatement of equilibrium.

The narrative begins with a state of equilibrium or social harmony. This harmony is disrupted by the villain early on in the narrative, which then charts the course of the disequilibrium. Matters are finally resolved when the disequilibrium is returned to equilibrium and the narrative draws to a close. However, the second equilibrium differs from the initial equilibrium, in that the action is usually divergent where the characters begin moving off in differing directions and go their separate ways. This is opposed to the convergent nature of the initial equilibrium where the action brings characters together. This interconnectivity of events at the beginning with those at the end and those in between, provides the narrative with a temporal axis and causal logic (Young 1990:198). This basic elementary framework supports most narratives.

When analysing a narrative using Todorov's model we need to define the initial equilibrium, or beginning, in terms of its relationship to the disequilibrium, or middle, and the new equilibrium, or end. This requires us to identify the significant chain of events that brought about the disequilibrium and the restoration of the equilibrium. However, at the beginning of a narrative we cannot be sure of the significance of events, nor of the direction they will take the narrative. To establish the sequence of events in a narrative it is best to work backwards, retracing the sequence that lead up to the end in order to arrive at the beginning. A simplified version of Todorov's model is illustrated in Figure 4.6.

To illustrate Todorov's model, we analyse an episode from the television series *MacGyver.* MacGyver is a superhero specialising in the use of clever, self-made, innovative technology and mechanical means to save himself and various victims from a whole range of criminals and their activities. For our analysis we have selected an episode titled *The Lost Amadeus.* In terms of Todorov's model, the narrative structure is as follows:

- Step 1 – *State of equilibrium* at the outset: the initial equilibrium is established in the opening shots where MacGyver is cycling with a friend, Wilt, on a Sunday morning.
- Step 2 – A *disruption* of the initial equilibrium: when MacGyver stops to buy a newspaper, his bicycle is crushed by a car driven by a girl, Lulu. Lulu insists on taking MacGyver home, but stops en route at her employer, Izzy, a concert violinist, after unsuccessful trying to fulfil an errand for him. It is at this point that we get a second disruption entering the narrative, which changes the direction of the story. Izzy is at that moment being molested by two thugs who are after a special violin, once owned by Mozart. The two thugs then beat-up MacGyver before rushing out of the house. This incident marks the beginning of the disequilibrium in this narrative.
- Step 3 – *Recognition of the disruption*: MacGyver decides to help Lulu and Izzy to retrieve the violin.
- Step 4 – *Attempts to restore the equilibrium*: Izzy is kidnapped by the thugs and his safe return is only guaranteed by payment in the form of the Amadeus violin. The exchange is set to take place at a theme party, where the thugs are double-crossed by Lulu and MacGyver. So the disequilibrium continues until the villains are apprehended.
- Step 5 – *Reinstatement of the equilibrium*: a new equilibrium is created when the violin is returned to its rightful owner, and MacGyver and Lulu go their separate ways so that MacGyver can be ready for his next adventure in the following episode.

In television narratives, step 1, establishing the initial equilibrium, is usually very short, or omitted altogether, since it is assumed by the producers that we are already familiar with the characters and their setting. Steps 2 and 3 can be presented in combination, with a limited duration of several minutes, so that the rest of the programme can be devoted to step 4. Step 5 is also given only a few minutes at the conclusion of the programme. This is a good example of how the organisational requirements of television can influence the development of a narrative (Lacey 2000:33).

4.6 VLADIMIR PROPP'S NARRATIVE MODEL

The structural approach to narrative analysis was initially used by Vladimir Propp when he analysed hundreds of Russian folk tales in order to find their underlying structure. Attempts before 1928 to classify Russian folk tales were along the lines of fairy tales, animal tales, tales of daily life, and so on. These attempts at classification did not have much success as these categories overlap too much. For instance, an animal tale often makes much the same point as a tale from any other category. Propp searched for some basic content structure underlying the wide variety of themes, actors and settings, which we early referred to as existents.

Table 4.2 Folk tale scenarios according to Vladimir Propp

- A tsar gives an eagle to a hero. The eagle carries the hero away to another kingdom.
- An old man gives Súčenko a horse. The horse carries Súčenko away to another kingdom.
- A sorcerer gives Iván a little boat. The boat takes Iván to another kingdom.
- A princess gives Iván a ring. Young men appear out of the ring and carry Iván away into another kingdom.

Propp (1968:19–20) presents several folk tales scenarios, illustrated in Table 4.2. From reading these scenarios, it is quite clear that, in spite of the fact that the characters change, all the sequences have something in common. Each scenario has the same action and function: a gift is given to someone, who is then transported to some other place. Because the action is similar in each scenario, Propp termed this constants. Different actions may produce identical constants, not on the basis of surface familiarities, but in so far as they fulfil the same function in a sequence of events. On the other hand, the existents, that is the gift and the transported person, the motives behind the gift and so on, more often than not differ from scenario to scenario. These differences Propp termed as variables.

Propp was able to compile a sequence of thirty-two constant functions in the folk tales he analysed. Propp termed these constants functions because he wanted to emphasise that what characters do to advance the narrative is more important that who they are (Fiske 1987:136). These functions are sequential and common to all folk tales. Although every function identified by Propp need not be part of the narrative, each function that is present must contribute to the general development of the plot. From his analyses, Propp (1968:21–24) was able to formulate four laws that govern functions in folk tales. These laws are as follows (Kozloff 1992:71):

- The functions of characters serve as stable, constant elements in a tale, independent of how and by whom they are fulfilled. They constitute the fundamental component of a tale.
- The number of functions known to the folk tale is limited.
- The sequence of functions is always identical – in other words, Propp's scheme is chronological and the sequence cannot be varied.
- All folk tales are of one type in regard to their structure.

The functions Propp identified are indicated in Table 4.3. Although the number of functions totals 32, for some unknown reason Propp decided to introduce an extra function following function 8, without adjusting the numbering sequence. The initial sequence α is not allocated a number.

Table 4.3 Functions of characters in Russian folk tales according to Vladimir Propp (adapted from Lacey 2000:47; Berger 1997:26)

Preparation		
α	initial situation	Members of the family and hero are introduced.
1	absentation	One of the members of a family absents himself and leaves home.
2	interdiction	An interdiction is addressed to the hero.
3	violation	The interdiction is violated (the villain enters the tale).
4	reconnaissance	The villain makes an attempt at reconnaissance.
5	delivery	The villain received information about his victim.
6	trickery	The villain attempts to deceive his victim in order to take possession of him or his belongings.
7	complicity	The victim submits to deception thus unwittingly helping his enemy.
Complication		
8	villainy	The villain causes harm or injury to a member of the family.
8a	lack	One member of the family either lacks or desires to have something.
9	mediation	Misfortune or a lack is made known; the hero is approached with a request or command; he is allowed to go or he is dispatched.
10	counteraction	The seeker agrees to or decides upon counteraction.
Transference		
11	departure	The hero leaves home.
12	1st donor function	The hero is tested, interrogated, attacked, et cetera, which prepares the way for his receiving either a magical agent or helper.
13	hero's reaction	The hero reacts to the actions of the future donor.
14	receipt of agent	The hero acquires the use of a magical agent.
15	spatial change	The hero is transferred, delivered, or led to the whereabouts of the object of the search.
Struggle		
16	struggle	The hero and the villain join in direct combat.
17	branding	The hero is branded.
18	victory	The villain is defeated.
19	liquidation	The initial misfortune or lack is liquidated.

☞

Return		
20	return	The hero returns.
21	pursuit, chase	The hero is pursued.
22	rescue	The hero is rescued from pursuit.
23	unrecognised arrival	The hero, unrecognised, arrives home or in another country.
24	unfounded claims	A false hero presents unfounded claims.
25	difficult task	A difficult task is proposed to the hero.
26	solution	The task is resolved.
Recognition		
27	recognition	The hero is recognised.
28	exposure	The false hero or villain is exposed.
29	transfiguration	The hero is given a new appearance.
30	punishment	The villain is punished.
31	achievement	The hero is married and ascends the throne.

Figure 4.6 shows there is a striking similarity between Propp's model and that of Todorov. We need to read Figure 4.6 in conjunction with Table 4.3 which explains the action in each of the numbered functions. Both models are chronological in their structure, using the action of characters to take the narrative forward, unlike Eco's model, which is based on the encounters of characters in opposition to one another to advance the narrative.

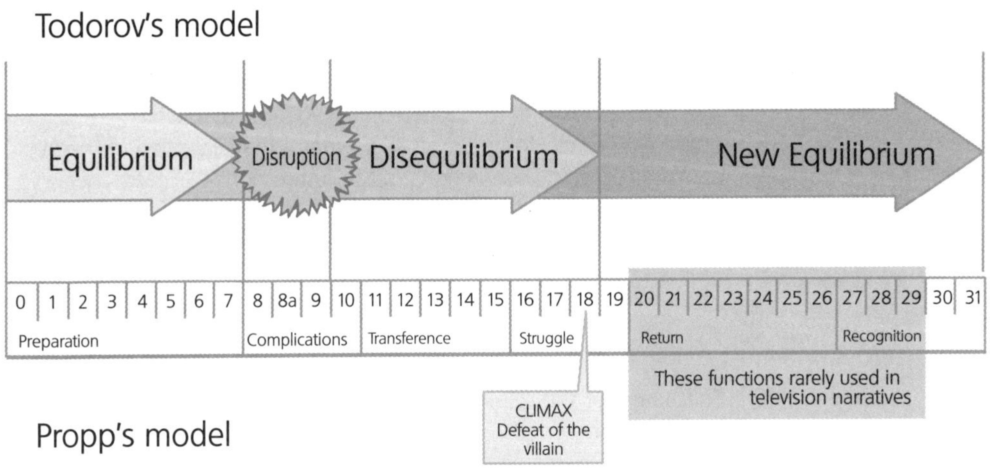

Figure 4.6 Similarities between the narrative models of Todorov and Propp (based on a discussion by Lacey 2000:48)

While Propp admittedly limits his analyses to Russian folk tales, the significance of his work extends far beyond the folk tale as such. Any folk tale, whether Russian or any other language is more than a folk tale – it is a narrative. According to Chatman's (1978:26) breakdown of the narrative which we illustrated in Figure 4.2, the manifestation of a story is not limited to folk tales, but can include any mediated form, such as television programmes, novels, mime, cartoon strips, advertising, films, sports commentaries and news reports. They all contain narrative messages. What Propp did was to identify the narrative character of a particular kind of message and to devise a method of analysis that is applicable not just to the folk tale but to many types of narrative messages, and therefore by implication to most messages found in the media, however they are expressed.

Although function forms an important part of the narrative structure, it is also necessary to look at the characters or as Propp terms them, the *dramatis personae.* Characters set a particular problem for narrative analysis. Without the characters the action simply could not happen, and there is no narrative without any characters. Yet narrative analysis is not concerned with the definition of characters in the psychological terms of "beings", but rather as participants in the discourse (Barthes 1977:105–106). Every character can be the agent of a sequence of actions which then belong to that character. Thus Propp's classification of characters, illustrated in Table 4.4, is concerned more with what the character does to advance the narrative than with whom he or she is as an individual. The characters are defined in terms of the spheres of action assigned that character by the narrative (extent and nature of action evidenced by a character in the narrative). It is possible that one character can be placed in several categories simultaneously. Propp (1968:78–80) identified seven constantly recurring *dramatis personae.*

Television characters can easily be classified using Propp's *dramatis personae.* Some examples are illustrated in Table 4.5. In television narratives new villains and princesses appear regularly in each episode in order to provide the hero with fresh challenges. The donor and false hero have been omitted as it is rare to find them, especially in American television narratives. Exceptions to the rule can always be noted. In *JAG* the hero has two helpers supported by a legal team, while in *18 Wheels of Justice* we find a recurring character (character that appears regularly in a narrative) in the part of the arch-villain Jacob Calder, who has a henchman, played by the guest star, to do his dirty work in each episode. In *Relic Hunter*, the position of the dispatcher is filled by a bit-player (a minor actor in a film or television programme). The interchangeability of the *dramatis personae* is well illustrated by the characters found in *JAG*, where in certain episodes, instead of acting as helpers, Colonel MacKenzie and Lieutenant Roberts are pitted against the hero, Commander Rabb, in this popular naval court-room drama series.

Table 4.4 Propp's *dramatis personae* categories (adapted from Tilley 1991:58; Watson 1998:141; and Lacey 2000:51)

Character role	Sphere of Action	Purpose	Function
Hero	Departs on search, reacts to demands of donor	Seeks to restore the equilibrium	10, 13, 31
Donor	Gives or provides the hero with the magic agent	Sends the object, which helps to restore the equilibrium	12, 14
Helper	Moves the hero, makes good a lack, rescues from pursuit, solves difficult tasks, transforms the hero	Aids and moves the action towards resolution	15, 19, 22, 26, 29
Princess	A sought-after person who assigns difficult tasks, brands, exposes, and recognises, with her father, who punishes the false hero	Leads to the climax of the narrative by being threatened by the villain	17, 25, 28, 30, 31
Dispatcher	Sends hero on journey/ mission/quest	Sends the subject (hero)	9
Villain	Fights or struggles with the hero	Blocks the action, so complicating the narrative	8, 16, 21
False hero	Unfounded claims to hero's sphere of action	Appears as good, but eventually revealed as bad	10, 13, 24

Propp's model, with some adaptation, has a universality about it that can be used to analyse the structure of the narrative in media messages. Look at the elementary examples below by Kozloff (1992:71–72) who made use of Propp's model to analyse the narratives found in television advertisements.

Consider the following:

1 Housewife X's sink is clogged. Josephine the plumber suggests Liquid Plumr The drain cleaner cuts through the clog and the housewife's problem is solved.

2 Customer Y has dry, chapped hands from washing dishes. Madge the manicurist suggests Palmolive dishwashing detergent. Customer Y returns to the beauty parlour with restored hands.

3 Housewife Z makes bad coffee and husband complains. Mrs Olson recommends Folger's coffee. Housewife Z tried Folger's and wins husband's praise and approval.

In each of the above scenarios, the heroine has a lack or misfortune (Propp's function no. 8a), that is noticed (no. 9). She comes into contact with a donor (no. 13), who suggests the use of a magical agent (no. 14). The initial misfortune or lack is liquidated (no. 19). Often the heroine is then praised and thanked by family members (figuratively no. 31).

Some adaptations have been made here to Propp's model so that we can use it in analysing television narratives. In these examples it is science and technology, in the guise of the product being advertised, that assumes the qualities of the "magical agent". We need to keep in mind that the purpose of the "magical agent" is to effect a transition on the part of the hero and in so doing achieve some or other goal. In example one, the blocked drain is cleared, in example two Customer Y gains beautiful hands, while in example three Housewife Z gains praise and approval, all brought about by using a particular product, or "magical agent". Similarly, it is also rare for contemporary narratives to end with a wedding and ascension to the throne. So this function needs to be seen in allegorical terms of achieving some or other particular goal. Other examples that use Propp's model to analyse narratives include the following:

- Peter Wollen's (1976) analysis of Alfred Hitchcock's film *North by Northwest*
- Roger Silverstone's analysis of an episode of the British soap opera *Intimate Strangers* (1976) and his analysis of the scientific documentary *Death of the Dinosaurs* (1987) from the *Horizon* series
- Arthur Berger's (1989) analysis of the pilot episode of the sitcom *Cheers* which is described in more detail as Case study 4.1
- Will Wright's (1975) analysis of the structure of the *Western* as a film genre.

Table 4.5 ***Dramatis personae*** **found in television narratives** (adapted from Kozloff 1987:50)

Programme	Hero	Helper	Dispatcher	Villain	Princess
JAG	Commander Harmon "Harm" Rabb, Jr	Colonel Sarah "Mac" MacKenzie, Lieutenant Bud Roberts	Admiral AJ Chegwidden	Guest star	Guest star
Relic Hunter	Sydney Fox	Nigel Bailey	Implied	Guest star	Guest star
MacGyver	MacGyver	Jack Dalton	Pete Thornton	Guest star	Guest star
18 Wheels of Justice	Chance Bowman	Cie Baxter	Burton Hardesty	Jacob Calder, Guest star	Guest star

Case study 4.1: A syntagmatic analysis of the sitcom *Cheers*

This syntagmatic analysis of *Cheers* by Berger (1989) provides us with some indication of how meaning has been generated and conveyed in the popular sitcom television programme. This is achieved by placing the focus on such aspects as signs and codes, binary oppositions from Lévi-Strauss and the chronological structure determined by using Propp's narrative model. This is but a simplified study – the text of *Cheers* is an extremely complex one requiring deep semiological analysis – the purpose of which is to show how we can analyse a narrative text.

The episode selected by Berger (1989:89–101) for his analysis was the pilot programme, first screened by NBC on 30 September 1982. The series was screened in South Africa by the SABC over many years and still enjoys a number of equally successful re-runs some twenty years after the show's initial debut. The cast for the episode analysed here was Shelly Long as Diane Chambers, Ted Danson as Sam Malone, Rhea Perlman as Carla Tortelli, John Retzenberg as Cliff, George Wendt as Norm, and Nicholas Colosante as Coach. Shelly Long left the cast after the 1987 season to be replaced by Kirstie Alley as Rebecca Howe.

Binary oppositions are a tool by which we can find meaning in a text, based on the simple premise that nothing has meaning in itself. It is through binary oppositions that we come to understand the various characters in the text. As an example, Table 4.6 illustrates the oppositions between Diane and Carla.

Table 4.6 Binary opposition of Diane and Carla in the pilot episode of *Cheers* (adapted from Berger 1989:95)

DIANE CHAMBERS	CARLA TORTELLI
tall	short
blond	dark hair
single (to be married)	was married (now single)
cool and reserved	hot and bitchy
middle class	working class
WASP	ethnic
innocent	experienced
SCHOOLMARM	BAR GIRL

It is apparent that these two characters are opposites in many important ways. While there are many other oppositions between characters found in *Cheers*, let us focus on the oppositions that are crucial to the series; that between the two central characters of Sam Malone and Diane Chambers.

Table 4.7 Binary opposition of main characters from the pilot episode of *Cheers* (adapted from Berger 1989:96)

DIANE CHAMBERS	SAM MALONE
female	male
blond	dark hair
middle class	working class
education	common sense
vulnerable	worldly
beauty	beast
useless	handy

These oppositions are of central importance in moving the narrative along, not only in this particular episode, but in the whole series. The binary oppositions between the two main characters denote the theme of the programme as, not only a battle of the sexes, but also a battle between the classes. We have to be careful when analysing main characters based on a single episode. Characters tend to be discussed in more stereotypical terms, whereas after viewing a number of episodes, we establish a history for each character and can therefore interpret nonfilmic codes with a greater depth of understanding. Thus, says Berger (1989:98), a regular viewer of a series like *Cheers* sees more in a given episode than a casual viewer does.

Berger (1989:89) considers *Cheers* as a modernised fairy tale, based on the fact that the narrative can be analysed in terms of a number of specific functions. Table 4.8 provides a breakdown of the pilot episode of *Cheers* in terms of Propp's narrative functions.

Table 4.8 Proppian functions in the pilot episode of *Cheers* (adapted from Berger 1989:99)

Proppian function		Events in *Cheers*
α	Initial situation	Sam, Diane and Sumner are introduced
1	Absentation	Sumner leaves the bar to get the ring
2	Interdiction	Sumner tells Diane to stay in the bar
7	The victim submits to deception	Sumner goes to his ex-wife, Barbara's home; Diane lets him go
8	The villain causes harm	Barbara "casts a spell" on Sumner ☞

	Proppian function	Events in *Cheers*
8a	Lack or desire to have something	Diane "lacks" Sumner, and waits for his return
9	Misfortune is made known	Diane discovers Sumner has gone to the Bahamas with Barbara
11	The hero(ine) leaves home	Diane cannot return to Boston University
13	The hero(ine) reacts to the action of a future donor	Diane tells Sam she doesn't talk with bartenders
14	The hero(ine) acquires the use of a magical agent	Various characters sympathise with Diane
19	The initial misfortune of lack is liquidated	Sam offers Diane a job at his bar
29	The hero(ine) is given a new appearance	Diane becomes a waitress and dons a uniform
31	The hero(ine) is married and ascends the throne	Diane starts a relationship with Sam

The algorithm for this particular episode of *Cheers* is

1 + 2 + 7 + 8 + 8a + 9 + 11 + 13 + 14 + 19 + 29 + 31

This algorithm represents a highly simplified form of the narrative, which can then be used to compare this episode with other episodes in the same series or with other similar sitcoms. Berger (1989:100) concludes that, although highly camouflaged and modernised, there are elements of the folk tale in our contemporary story forms which then help to carry important social messages. In this brief synopsis, we illustrate how meaning can be created through the use of symbols, binary oppositions and chronological structures.

Kozloff (1987:49) draws two conclusions from the application of Propp's model to television narrative.

- American television evidences a structure not unlike the Russian folk tale. Certain motifs, situations and characters feature again and again in popular television programmes.

- Television stories are governed by a set of unwritten rules acquired by storytellers and received in much the same way that they acquired the basic rules of grammar, that is they are culturally determined. This explains the variability, yet consistency, present in television narrative.

Propp's model, as with that of Todorov, provides us with a means of identifying the conventional narrative structure in a text. From this perspective, the model is useful if we want to compare texts (Lacey 2000:53). But to gain deeper insight into the structure of a text, we need to add other analytical devices, such as Lévi-Strauss' binary opposition, as seen in Case study 4.1.

4.7 UMBERTO ECO'S NARRATIVE MODEL

In 1953, Ian Fleming (1908–1964), a British author, published his first James Bond novel, *Casino Royale*, largely influenced by the work of Mickey Spillane, author of the successful Mike Hammer novels. A total of thirteen novels were written over a twelve-year period from 1953 to 1965. It did not take long for Fleming to gain celebrity status as a best-selling author. This was the problem that Eco set out to investigate. What were the reasons for the success of the James Bond novels? To resolve this problem Eco started by looking at the narrative structure used by the author. Eco considered Fleming's writing style to be that of a machine that functioned along very simple and straight lines, conforming to strict rules of combination. It is this "writing machine" that became the basis for the success of the James Bond novels (Eco 1966:244).

As part of his research on the Bond novels, Eco developed a narrative model. In this model of the typical James Bond novel, Eco makes the assumption that the narrative of a text, which in the context of this unit includes that of television programmes with a closed narrative (a narrative that contains a resolution and denouement), can also function as a model of the world, setting out the wider social and cultural forms of organisation and behaviour. Narrative is then a basic way in which we can make sense of our experience of the real world. A narrative is built up from various paradigmatic (a set from which a choice is made) and syntagmatic (combination of selections from varous paradigms into a meaningful sequence) structures that function to link events together in a relationship so as to render those events meaningful at an ideological level. The Bond novels became popular in the Anglo-Saxon world simply because of the positive and superior way in which Fleming portrayed the British and negatively stereotyped the popular "enemies" of the time. Identification with this view of the world on the part of the reader can then partly explain the phenomenal success Ian Fleming had with his novels.

We now need to look a little closer at Eco's narrative model, which uses three interrelated levels to reveal the narrative structure.

- The binary oppositions of characters and values found in the narrative.
- Play situations and the plot as a game, based on the functions.
- A Manichean ideology based on the stereotypes evident in the text.

We discuss each level in turn. Eco used twelve of Fleming's novels for his investigation, stretching from *Casino Royale* (1953) up to and including *The Man with the Golden Gun* (1965), but excluded *The Spy Who Loved Me* (1962) as being the exception to the rule.

4.7.1 Binary oppositions

Eco (1982:245) identified 14 oppositional sets in the Bond novels, the first four of which relate to characters, while the remaining ten relate to values. These oppositions are given in Table 4.9.

Table 4.9 The binary oppositions of characters and values found in the James Bond novels (Eco 1982:245)

Characters	(a)	Bond : M
	(b)	Bond : Villain
	(c)	Villain : Woman
	(d)	Woman : Bond
Values	(e)	Free World : Soviet Union
	(f)	Great Britain : Countries not Anglo Saxon
	(g)	Duty : Sacrifice
	(h)	Cupidity : Ideals
	(i)	Love : Death
	(j)	Chance : Planning
	(k)	Luxury : Discomfort
	(l)	Excess : Moderation
	(m)	Perversion : Innocence
	(n)	Loyalty : Disloyalty

For Eco, binary oppositions are indicative of a specific relationship between two characters. In the case of the Bond : M opposition we find a dominated : dominant relationship. M is superior to Bond in all respects and sets the limits and possibilities of Bond (Eco 1982:245). M is the equivalent of the dispatcher in Propp's narrative structure. As a result of this dominated : dominant relationship between Bond and M we can identify a number of subsidiary oppositions, as indicated in Table 4.10

Table 4.10 Subsidiary oppositions found in the primary Bond : M opposition

Bond	M
dispatched	dispatcher
obedient	authority
improvisation	religion of duty, country and order
possessed of exceptional qualities	moderation
DOMINATED	DOMINANT

Fleming saw "Bond as an absolutely ordinary person" (Eco 1982:246) despite what we may interpret from the books or subsequent film versions thereof. Eco (ibid) explains that it is only "in contrast with M that the real stature of 007 emerges, endowed with physical attributes, with courage and fast reflexes, without possessing any other quality in excess". The narrative machine needs M to start Bond on the road to duty, which then leads into the next opposition, Bond : Villain.

On the Bond : Villain opposition, Eco (1982:246–252) has much to say. In simple terms, Bond is seen to represent beauty and virility, while the villain is often represented as monstrous and sexually impotent. For example, Eco (1982:247) explains:

> In *Moonraker*, Hugo Drax is six feet tall, with 'exceptionally broad' shoulders, has a large and square head, red hair. The right half of his face is shiny and wrinkled from unsuccessful plastic surgery, the right eye different from the left and larger because of a contraction of the skin and eyelashes ... , has heavy moustaches, whiskers to the lobes of his ears, and patches of hair on his cheekbones: the moustaches concealed with scant success a prognathous upper jaw with a marked protrusion of his upper teeth.

The qualities, or values, of the villain are also opposed to Bond. For example, Eco writes (1982:251):

> ... Bond characterises, in particular Loyalty to the Service, Anglo-Saxon Moderation opposed to the excess of the halfbreeds, the selection of Discomfort and the acceptance of Sacrifice as against the ostentatious luxury of the enemy, the stroke of opportunistic genius (Chance) opposed to the cold Planning which it defeats, the sense of an Ideal opposed to Cupidity (Bond in various cases wins from the Villain in gambling, but as a rule returns the enormous sums won to the Service ...).

As the Bond : M opposition leads to the Bond : Villain combination, so this opposition in turn leads to the Villain : Woman and Woman : Bond oppositions. We can consider these latter two oppositional pairs together since the Woman is dominated first by the Villain, and then by Bond. Eco (1982:252) explains the role of the Woman in the narrative:

> The general scheme is (1) the girl is beautiful and good; (2) has been made frigid and unhappy by severe trials suffered in adolescence; (3) this has conditioned her to the service of the Villain; (4) through meeting Bond she appreciates human nature in all its richness; (5) Bond possesses her but in the end loses her.

4.7.2 Play situations

The various oppositional pairs then combine regularly throughout the narrative. But, we as the reader do not know at what point(s) in the narrative these oppositional pairs will meet and react with each other. These interactions go to make up a prearranged pattern that Eco (1982:253) calls the "algebra" of the narrative structure: M beats Bond, Bond beats the Villain, the Villain beats the Woman, the Free World beats the Soviet Union, moderation beats excess, and so on. In this manner, the Bond narratives are dominated by a variety of play situations. These game situations take the form of a challenge of some or other sort. Eco (1982:254–255) identified nine generalised game situations that kept recurring in all the Bond novels he analysed. These nine generalised game situations provide us with the basic narrative scheme for the Bond novels and are listed in Table 4.11. Each play situation is allocated a letter so that we can easily identify that specific play situation. To summarise, where the Bond : M oppositional pair interact with each other in the narrative, the result of that interaction produces play situation "A", and so on for all nine play situations.

Table 4.11 The basic narrative scheme for the James Bond novels (Eco 1982:254–255)

A	M sends Bond on a mission
B	The Villain (or someone representing the Villain) acts, and is introduced to Bond
C	Bond beats the Villain, or the Villain beats Bond
D	Bond meets the Woman
E	Bond attempts to seduce the Woman and either succeeds or is well on the way to doing so
F	The Villain captures Bond (with or without the Woman)
G	The Villain tortures Bond (with or without the Woman)
H	Bond finally defeats the Villain (or those representing him) completely
I	Bond convalesces with the Woman, who he will eventually lose

This basic narrative scheme represents all the elements that could possibly be present in the Bond novels. However, these nine generalised game situations need not occur in the sequence indicated in Table 4.11. In addition, any one of these game situations can be repeated several times in each novel, giving us inversions and variations. For example, it is possible that Bond meets with the Villain before he receives instructions from M, as is the case in *Goldfinger*. Thus, by merely writing down the letters representing the various play situations we have identified, we can come up with a pattern that represents the narrative of any one of the Bond novels. For *Goldfinger* we have the following pattern

B – C – D – E – A – C – D – F – G – H – E – H – I

Here play situations "C", "D", "E" and "H" are repeated twice. We have two encounters with the Villain ("C"), two meetings with the Woman ("D"), two attempts at seducing her ("E") and an initial defeat of the Villain where he flees and then a second where he is killed ("H"). In *From Russia with Love* the combination becomes more complicated

B – B – B – B – D – A – B – B – C – E – F – G – H – G – H – I

Eco (1982:255) terms the pattern made up from the individual play situations in the narrative as the fundamental scheme. In addition to this fundamental scheme, Eco also distinguishes a number of side issues which "enrich the narrative by unforeseen events, without, however, altering the basic scheme" (ibid), which he calls incidental moves. The functions within the fundamental scheme are akin to the cardinal functions of Roland Barthes that we discussed in section 4.3, while incidental moves are similar in nature to catalysers – refer back to Figure 4.3 for a graphic illustration of the relationship between these two types of function.

4.7.3 A Manichean ideology

The narrative structure invariably indicates an ideological (the social production of meaning according to the beliefs of a particular group) position. However, these ideological positions are not derived from the contents, but from the method of constructing the contents into a discourse (refer back to Figure 4.2 for an illustration of the various elements that make up a narrative). In order to write an effective narrative Fleming made use of the basic principles found in traditional tales. M is the king, Bond the cavalier with a mission to rescue the beautiful princess and the Villain is the dragon that needs to be slain. Fleming is Manichean (a theory of dualism where the forces of good and evil are in opposition) for operational reasons. In his writing Fleming sees the world in the binary terms of black and white, where good and evil forces are in conflict. The Soviet Union and non-Anglo-Saxon countries represent the Lower Race while the Free World is representative of the Chosen Race. From this point of view Fleming is dogmatic and intolerant.

> Fleming is a racialist in the sense that any artist is one if, to represent the devil, he depicts him with oblique eyes; in the sense that a nurse is one who, wishing to frighten children with the bogey-man, suggests that he is black.
> (Eco 1982:260)

When studying the Bond novels, it does not take long to realise that Fleming considers the British as superior to oriental or Mediterranean races, while being rather anti-Communist. Yet, before we accuse Fleming of being a racist, Eco (1982:260) reminds us that he wrote from a popularist perspective, making use of popular opinion in establishing his oppositions. In times of international tension, popular notions such as that of a "wicked Communist" and the "Nazi criminal" develop and Fleming draws on these notions in an uncritical manner (Eco 1982:260).

Even the very names of the protagonists suggest a stereotyped image of the character of the person, so building up elementary associations. For example:

> He is working for the Reds? He will be called *Red* and *Grant* if he works for money, duly granted. A Korean professional killer by unusual means will be *Oddjob*, one obsessed with gold *Auric Goldfinger* ...
> (Eco 1982:261)

Based on the findings provided by his narrative model, Eco (1982) came to the conclusion that Fleming purposely portrayed the British and the British Empire in a superior manner to that of other races and cultures. Identification with this superior image by the British public ensured the popularity of the books. Eco also noted that the way in which Bond's enemies were portrayed in the series of novels changed. For example as general public opinion changed regarding that of Communism, so Fleming ceased to identify Russians with doing fiendish deeds, thus making Russia appears less menacing as a nation. Eco maintains that the ideology of a text is derived not so much from the contents but rather from the way those contents are structured. In this way the use of binary oppositions in a narrative can reveal political or racist stereotypes which carry ideological implications – in the case of the Bond novels this is the ideology of the Cold War. While the deep structure of opposing values remains permanently embedded in the text, the specific ideological messages vary in meaning according to historical contexts. For example, if we were to read a Bond novel today, long after the Cold War has ended, our interpretation of that novel would be from a historical perspective rather than from when the events were contemporary at the time of publication some forty or more years ago. In other words, how do we identify, if at all, with the worldview as presented by that text?

4.7.4 Eco's narrative model and television

The complexity of a narrative can be compared to that of an organisation chart, capable of integrating backwards or forwards, up or down. Narrative appears as a succession of highly interlocking elements requiring a horizontal reading superimposed on a vertical reading. Each unit that makes up the narrative needs to be interpreted horizontally as well as vertically. This, simply, is how a narrative works. A narrative can be identified in terms of its fundamental scheme in terms of Eco's model, or cardinal functions in terms of Barthes' theoretical explanation. This process leads to a summary of the narrative without altering the meaning of the story.

Eco's narrative model, derived from his investigation into the Bond novels, is flexible and therefore useful in isolating the narrative structure of television programmes, particularly those programmes that we can refer to, in Eco's (1982:256) terms, as an "escape machine geared for the entertainment of the masses". However, Eco's narrative model does not work well for media content considered as high art (work considered to have intellectual qualities) forms. Nor can it be applied to programmes with an open narrative such as in soap operas and sitcoms. But it is most effective when applied, in a modified form to the closed narrative found in action-drama genres. The effectiveness of the model is based on the presence of binary oppositions in the text. Eco's model rests on the basic oppositions present in the programme, which then generates the fundamental scheme, incidental moves and stereotypes.

In analysing the narrative of an action-drama series on television, we need to make some adaptations to Eco's model. As the model stands, it has been specifically developed to analyse the structure of James Bond narratives. Since the binary oppositions refer specifically to Bond by name, we need to make some substitutions to Eco's original binary oppositions of characters in order to make the model applicable to television and film narratives. In so doing, we need to establish a set of binary oppositions that are generic in nature. Thus, we can swap the term Hero for Bond in the binary opposition. Since it is what a character does that is important, rather than who that character is, the gender of the character is unimportant. Therefore, by using the term Hero, it does not imply that the Hero has to be a male and an individual. As the character descriptors become generic concepts, the term Hero could describe an individual person, or a team, which in turn will produce its own subsidiary binary oppositions within the team as we discussed in section 4.4, or an object or even an organisation. As an example, in *18 Wheels of Justice*, the concept of the Hero is a team comprising Chance Bowman (male), Cie Baxter (female) and a truck (object).

In Eco's model, M is the character that sends Bond on his various missions. As M is then the dispatcher that Propp refers to in his model, we can substitute Dispatcher for M. Following the same line of argument, we can substitute Woman with Victim. In television and film narratives the concept Victim could comprise a range of people either as individuals or as a group, such as families, children or the elderly. In the context of television and film narratives we can define the Victim as being someone or some group subjected to unfair treatment. The binary oppositions of characters in a generic version of Eco's model would read as given in Table 4.12

Table 4.12 The binary oppositions of characters in a generic version of Eco's narrative model

	Bond version	Generic version
(a)	Bond : M	Hero : Dispatcher
(b)	Villain : Bond	Hero : Villain
(c)	Woman : Villain	Villain : Victim
(d)	Bond : Woman	Victim : Hero

We now need to turn our attention to the remaining ten binary oppositions that relate to values. The values expressed in Eco's model are unique to the ideology present at the time and place when Fleming wrote the novels. If we try and analyse the values in a contemporary action-drama series, the Free World : Soviet Union dichotomy would not be applicable as the Soviet Union ceased to exist in the early 1990s. Similarly, if the programme is made in the United States, then the Great Britain : Countries not Anglo-Saxon dichotomy is also not appropriate. Thus, when we use Eco's model to analyse a contemporary television or film narrative, we need to modify the opposing values accordingly, based on those values evident in the text. This means we need to know when and where the narrative was originally constructed in order to determine the relevant values. When discussing how these values are expressed in order to determine the Manichean ideology, we have to keep the manifestation of the narrative in mind. Fleming's original Bond narratives were limited to words, but in film and television we have considerably many more codes in addition to words. We then need to distinguish between the verbal and visual codes used in the narrative. Visual codes are, in turn, made up of filmic (codes of form which occur behind the camera lens) and nonfilmic codes (codes of content which occur in front of the camera lens). We need to give our attention to how each of these codes is used to generate meaning in the text.

What then, is the value of Eco's model to us today, as researchers of contemporary media texts? The model serves as a point of departure for the interpretation of the relationships between that text and the social context in which that text was produced on one hand, and read on the other. This is achieved by allowing us to reveal the deeper underlying ideology of a text as in Case study 4.2 where an episode of the *MacGyver* series has been analysed. And the popularity of a text can then be influenced by positive public identification with that ideology, since it forms part of the viewer's greater worldview.

Case study 4.2: A narrative analysis of *MacGyver* (Wigston 1997:215–219)

By establishing binary oppositions in a text we can uncover the ideological and manipulative structure of the values embodied in that message. We can also use binary oppositions to reveal deep structures below the surface message that are not immediately clear but are implied in every opposition. These hidden structures together with the visual text then reflect and appeal to the basic values of the audience, without them being aware of such structuring. This textual structuring may account for the tremendous popularity of certain television programmes. In television action-drama series we have to keep in mind that one member of a binary pair may be suppressed and not be overtly present, but merely implied. This is the case in *Runners* where the dispatcher only features briefly at the very beginning of the programme. Although Pete Thornton does not allocate this particular assignment to MacGyver, MacGyver's extraordinary abilities are covertly emphasised through his historical opposition to Pete Thornton in the Hero : Dispatcher opposition.

Table 4.13 Binary opposition of characters in the *Runners* episode from the *MacGyver* series (adapted from Wigston 1997:217)

MacGyver (Hero)	:	Pete Thornton (Dispatcher)
MacGyver (Hero)	:	Snakeskin (Villain)
Snakeskin (Villain)	:	Jennifer (Victim)
Jennifer (Victim)	:	MacGyver (Hero)

In Table 4.14 we have the expanded narrative scheme giving both the fundamental scheme and incidental moves.

Table 4.14 Expanded narrative scheme for the *Runners* episode from the *MacGyver* series (adapted from Wigston 1997:216)

Fundamental scheme	Incidental moves
	• Pete Thornton, head of the Phoenix Foundation and MacGyver install a Phoenix Foundation exhibition at a hotel convention
D MacGyver meets the girl, Jennifer, a prostitute who works for the Villain	
E Jennifer attempts, unsuccessfully to seduce MacGyver	• MacGyver protects Jennifer from being arrested by the hotel authorities
A MacGyver embarks on a self-appointed mission to rescue the girl from the Villain, a pimp and drug dealer	• MacGyver suggests taking Jennifer to a place of safety
B MacGyver is introduced to the Villain, Snakeskin	
C MacGyver beats the Villain for the first time in a knife attack	• MacGyver takes Jennifer to the Challenger's Club, a place of refuge, where she steals MacGyver's money and returns to the Villain
B MacGyver is reintroduced to the Villain	
C MacGyver beats the Villain by setting of the alarm on Snakeskin's car	☞

Fundamental scheme	Incidental moves
D MacGyver meets the girl	• MacGyver rescues Jennifer from the Villain and takes her to his home • Jennifer's father inquires about her at the Challenger's Club • MacGyver returns Jennifer to her father • Jennifer and her father argue • Jennifer returns to the Villain
F The Villain holds Jennifer captive	• MacGyver devises a plan to rescue the girl • Jennifer"s father arrives with the intention to kill the Villain
G The Villain tortures Jennifer	
H MacGyver finally beats the Villain	• Jennifer's father arrives but does not kill the Villain
I MacGyver wins Jennifer's trust and gratitude and they eventually go their own ways	

The narrative pattern for this particular episode is

D – E – A – B – C – B – C – D – F – G – H – I

In this episode of MacGyver there is no opposition between two political value systems. The episode takes place entirely within a Western democratic framework. MacGyver works for the Phoenix Foundation which represents the Free World. Although there is no evil organisation which opposes him in this episode, there is an evil villain, aptly named Snakeskin. MacGyver is driven by his sense of duty and endeavours to help mankind. In this episode, MacGyver exhibits a sense of duty in his determination to save Jennifer from the clutches of Snakeskin. Snakeskin, as the Villain, has no sense of duty to society. His only duty is to himself and his personal enrichment as a pimp and drug dealer. MacGyver and the Phoenix Foundation represent certain puritan values. For example, MacGyver does not smoke nor drink, nor attempt to seduce women, although towards the end of the series it was revealed that he had an illegitimate son. His aim is to bring murderers, drug dealers and pimps to justice. By contrast, the Villain, Snakeskin, has no moral values as he lives off the immoral earning of women. In his attempts to resolve problems, MacGyver avoids the use of violence. To this end, he refuses to carry a gun or resort to using weapons of any sort. On the other hand, Snakeskin carries a gun and threatens to shoot the girl.

MacGyver is portrayed as macho, strong, independent, intelligent and fairly young. He possesses the physical appearance of the all-American football player whom women supposedly find irresistibly attractive. MacGyver exhibits the archetypal characteristics of the handsome prince found in traditional fairy tales. He is also the knight sent on a mission where the Villain is the dragon. It is MacGyver's duty to rescue the damsel in distress and restore her to her senses as well as to her real self. At the same time, MacGyver represents the arch-stereotype of American success, he is white, young and male. The *MacGyver* series thus endorses and perpetuates these ideological values. Unless you possess these three attributes, your chance of success along the American-way is limited.

4.8 AN EVALUATION OF NARRATIVE ANALYSIS

Like all research methods, narrative analysis has its limitations. Kozloff (1987:42–43) sums up these limitations when she says "Because this field is concerned with general mappings of narrative structure, it is inescapably 'formalist' and largely unconcerned with questions about 'content' ...". Since narrative analysis focuses directly on the text itself, other aspects regarding that text, such as effects on the audience, regulation and organisation of the production industry are left to other critical methods. Nor is narrative analysis concerned about the audience and any possible effects the message may have. On the limitations of narrative Barthes (1977:115–116) says "Just as linguistics stops at the sentence, so narrative analysis stops at discourse – from there it is necessary to shift to another semiotics". Beyond that of narrative, fields such as sociology, economy and ideology take over.

What values does narrative theory then have for us, as scholars of mass communication? Narrative analysis presents us with a critical research tool, which should not be underestimated. Media messages, particularly those found in film and television, are steeped in the culture which created them. The various genres that emerge are obviously narrative in nature as they all basically tell a story, from the news bulletin to the accompanying advertisements. Narration can only receive meaning from the world which creates and makes use of it.

It would seem that popular culture, such as television, is more rigidly patterned and formulaic than high art forms. Even television programmes that do not outwardly display any element of either Propp or Eco's models still display a recognisable framework. For example, if we take each episode of the *Star Trek* series, the USS Enterprise will encounter some form of alien life, members of the crew will become separated from the ship, a crew member will become romantically involved, with either the ship or the crew placed in jeopardy. Kozloff (1987:49) argues that such predictability in television has lead to a deficiency in one of the major forces driving narrative, that of suspense. Each event in the narrative should open up a number of possibilities, with the viewer anticipating what should happen next.

Barthes (1977:119) considers suspense as a privileged form of distortion, created by keeping a sequence open by making use of techniques like delay and renewal, which we now find in the serialised format of many television programmes. However, genuine suspense cannot really occur in television narratives, perhaps with the exception factual genres such as news and documentaries. In such genres, the narrative is complicated because of the high number of unpredictable turns in the plot with no guarantee that the good guys will win in the end. For fictional genres, the hero will always be back, if not next week then in the next season. So the narrative is not a question of whether the hero will survive the episode, but rather a question of how he survives.

To compensate for this lack of suspense, certain television genres develop a proliferation of story lines. Two or more story lines can run simultaneously extended over several episodes. Soap operas can have up to six different story lines with different characters at any one time. Each story line carries its own narrative, but they combine, parallel and complement each other in a unique way. Thus we can come to the conclusion that while "television stories may be formulaic, ... the ways in which they are told can vary considerably" (Kozloff 1987:54).

Summary

In narrative analysis we are not concerned with the quality of a text, but rather with how it generates meanings. To discover how meaning is created, we need to look at the structure of the narrative. From Seymour Chatman we learned about the layered structure of a narrative, which we can divide into the story and the discourse. Roland Barthes then provided us with the necessary theoretical understanding of the relationships that exist between the elements that make up a narrative. Every single item present in the narrative has to contribute in some way to the meaning of that narrative. This generation of meaning is achieved either by distribution or integration. Barthes also distinguishes two types of functions: cardinal functions, which are responsible for moving the narrative along, and catalyser functions that simply fill in the gaps. On a macro level, Barthes identified five codes that we use to generate a culturally determined meaning in the narrative.

A key element to our understanding of the deeper meanings in a narrative is that of Claude Lévi-Strauss' binary opposition. Meaning is created through the simply expedient of creating a contrast between two elements in the narrative. This is based on the premise that values, attitudes and characteristics only emerge when contrasted against an equal opposite. Binary oppositions work on abstract as well as concrete levels.

We concluded this unit by looking at three models of narrative. We began with Tzvetan Todorov's elementary model, which explained the construction of a narrative in the simplistic terms of equilibrium – disruption – disequilibrium – new equilibrium. Vladimir Propp derived his model from an analysis of Russian folk tales, where he identified thirty-two sequential functions. These functions are determined by what the characters do to advance the narrative. Umberto Eco devised a narrative model to explain the popularity of the James Bond novels. Eco's model consists of three interrelated levels, beginning with the binary oppositions of characters and values found in the narrative. The interaction between opposing characters gives rise to nine recurring functions, which Eco terms play situations. When contextualised, the binary oppositions present in the text produce a Manichian ideology from which stereotypes emerge. By analysing these three levels, a deep understanding of the narrative within the text emerges. With some adaptation, the models of Propp and Eco can be used to analyse the narratives found in media texts, particularly that of television. This was demonstrated in the two case studies where Propp's model was used to analyse the sitcom *Cheers*, and Eco's model was used to analyse the action-drama series *MacGyver*.

Research activities

1 You are training a group of broadcasters for a local community radio station. The students are required, as an assignment, to write and present a short radio talk of two minutes about a meaningful event in their lives. The students' efforts turn out to be exceeding poor and bland. You then realise that they have no understanding of the importance of narrative to a story. What practical advice concerning narrative would you give these students so that they can improve on their stories?

2 Describe Roland Barthes' contribution to narrative theory and the analysis of television texts with reference to the following concepts:
- function
- catalyser
- integration
- cardinal function
- distribution
- indices

3 Select a single episode of a television soap opera, sitcom and action-drama series. Deconstruct that episode according to Barthes' five codes of narrative, that is:
- hermeneutic or enigma code
- semic code
- symbolic code
- proairetic or action code
- cultural or referential code

Compare your findings for each programme genre. How are they similar and how do they differ?

4 Explain the value of Lévi-Strauss' concept of binary opposition to our understanding of the narrative to a text. Demonstrate how we can use binary opposition as an analytical tool by analysing several news items in a televised news bulletin.

5 Select several advertisements flighted during prime time on television and analyse these advertisements by identifying the following aspects, based on Propp's narrative model:
- the *hero/subject* whose function is to seek
- the *object* that is sought
- the *donor* of the object
- the *receiver*, where it is sent
- the *helper* who aids the action
- the *villain* who blocks the action

6 Write a modern short story based on Propp's functions of narrative. Remember to use past tense when writing your story, and to include descriptions and dialogue and make sure there is action and conflict. Structure your story according to the following functions:
- *Initial situation:* members of the family, hero introduced
- *Absentation:* one family member absents him- or herself
- *Interdiction:* interdiction addressed to the hero, or the other way around
- *Violation:* the interdiction is violated
- *Villainy:* the villain causes harm to members of the family
- *Mediation:* a misfortune is made known and the hero is dispatched
- *Receipt of magical agent:* the hero acquires use of a magical agent
- *Spatial change:* the hero is led to the object of his search
- *Struggle:* the hero and villain join in combat
- *Branding:* the hero is branded
- *Victory:* the villain is defeated
- *Unfounded claims:* the false hero is exposed
- *Wedding:* the hero is 'married' and 'ascends the throne'

As this is a modern story, you need to adapt some of the functions accordingly. For example, at the end of your story, the hero need not literally marry a princess and ascend the throne. This is the reason why the word 'married' and the phrase 'ascends the throne' are placed inside inverted commas. When writing your story, you can also use the fuller descriptions of each function given in Table 4.3.

7 Select the first three items that feature in a news bulletin, either on radio or television. List the oppositions that feature in these particular stories. From your list of oppositions, what conclusions can you come to regarding the bias of the news reports you used for this activity?

8 Select an action-drama series that is currently being screened on television. Using a suitably modified form of Umberto Eco's model, analyse your selected programme(s) in order to establish the underlying ideology that supports that particular programme series. How suitable do you consider that ideology to the community? Can you explain what hidden values within that ideology make the programme appealing to television viewers despite possible cultural differences?

Further reading

Barthes, R. 1964. *Elements of semiology.* London: Jonathan Cape.

Berger, AA. 1997. *Narratives in popular culture, media and everyday life.* Thousand Oaks, CA: Sage.

Chatman, S. 1978. *Story and discourse: narrative structure in fiction and film.* Ithaca, NY: Cornell University Press.

Hawkes, T. 1997. *Structuralism and semiotics.* Revised edition. London: Routledge.

Lacey, N. 2000. *Narrative and genre: key concepts in media studies.* London: Macmillan.

Martin, W. 1986. *Recent theories of narrative.* Ithaca, NY: Cornell University Press.

Nash, C. 1990. *Narrative in culture: the use of storytelling in the sciences, philosophy, and literature.* London: Routledge.

Onega, S & Landa, JAG (eds). 1996. *Narratology: an introduction.* London: Longman.

Phelan, J. 1989. *Reading narrative: form, ethics, ideology.* Columbus, OH: Ohio State University Press.

Propp, V. 1968. *Morphology of the folktale.* Austin, TX: University of Texas Press.

Scholes, R. 1974. *Structuralism in literature: an introduction.* New Haven, CT: Yale University Press.

Wright, W. 1975. *Six guns and society: a structural study of the Western.* Berkeley, CA: University of California Press.

Bibliography

Agard, R. 1999. Existing in other worlds: how to locate indigenous narratives. *Media Development* 46(1):47–51.

Alvardo, M, Gutch, R & Wollen, T. 1987. *Learning the media: an introduction to media teaching.* Houndsmill, Basingstoke: Macmillan.

Barthes, R. 1964. *Elements of semiology.* London: Jonathan Cape.

Bennett, WL & Edelman, M. 1985. Toward a new political narrative. *Journal of Communication* 35(3):156–171.

Berger, AA. 1989. "He's everything you're not ...": a semiological analysis of "Cheers", in *Television studies, textual analysis,* edited by G Burns & J Thompson. New York: Praeger:89–101.

Berger, AA. 1991. *Media analysis techniques.* Newbury Park, CA: Sage.

Berger, AA. 1997. *Narratives in popular culture, media and everyday life.* Thousand Oaks, CA: Sage.

Bird, SE & Dardenne, RW. 1988. Myth, chronicle, and story: exploring the narrative qualities of news, in *media, myths and narratives: television and the press,* edited by JW Carey. Newbury Park, CA: Sage:67–86.

Brown, MH & McMillan, JJ. 1991. Culture as text: the development of an organisational narrative. *Southern Communication Journal* 57:49–60.

Bruner, J. 1991. The narrative construction of reality. *Critical Inquiry* 18(1):1–21.

Butler, JG. 1994. *Television: critical methods and applications.* Belmont, CA: Wadsworth.

Buxton, D. 1990. *From* The Avengers *to* Miami Vice: *form and ideology in television series.* Manchester: Manchester University Press.

Bywater, T & Sobchack, T. 1989. *Introduction to film criticism: major critical approaches to narrative film.* New York: Longman.

Calisi, R. 1966. Myths and history in the Epic of James Bond, in *The Bond affair,* edited by OD Buono & U Eco. London: Macdonald:76–85.

Chanan, M. 2000. The documentary chronotope. *Jump Cut* 43:56–61.

Chatman, S. 1978. *Story and discourse: narrative structure in fiction and film.* Ithaca, NY: Cornell University Press.

Danow, DK. 1997. *Models of narrative: theory and practice.* New York: St Martin's.

Dayan, D & Katz, E. 1992. *Media events: the live broadcasting of history.* Cambridge, MA: Harvard University Press.

Deming, CJ. 1985. *Hill Street Blues* as narrative. *Critical Studies in Mass Communication* 2(1):1–22.

Eco, U. 1982. The narrative structure in Fleming, in *Popular culture: past and present,* edited by B Waites, T Bennett & G Martin. London: Croom Helm:242–262.

Feuer, J. 1986. Narrative form in American network television, in *High theory/low culture: analysing popular television and film,* edited by C MacCabe. Manchester: Manchester University Press:101–114.

Fisher, WR. 1985. The narrative paradigm: an elaboration. *Communication Monographs* 52(4):347–367.

Fisher, WR. 1987. *Human communication as narration: toward a philosophy of reason, value, and action.* Columbia, SC: University of South Carolina Press.

Fisher, WR. 1989. Clarifying the narrative paradigm. *Communication Monographs* 56:55–58.

Fiske, J. 1987. *Television culture.* London: Routledge.

Fleckenstein, KS. 1996. Images, words, and narrative epistemology. *College English* 58(8)914–933.

Garrand, T. 1997. Scripting narrative for interactive multimedia. *Journal of Film and Video* 49(1–2):66–79.

Gjedde, L. 2000. Narrative, genre and context in popular science. *Nordicom Review* 21(1):51–57.

Grossberg, L, Wartella, E & Whitney, DC. 1998. *MediaMaking: mass media in a popular culture.* Thousand Oaks, CA: Sage.

Hansen, A, Cottle, S, Negrine, R & Newbold. 1998. *Mass communication research methods.* Washington Square, NY: New York University Press.

Hartley, J. 1982. *Understanding news.* London: Methuen.

Hawkes, T. 1997. *Structuralism and semiotics.* Revised edition. London: Routledge.

Hellmann, J. 1981. *Fables of fact: the new journalism as new fiction.* Urbana, Ill: University of Illinois Press.

Hobbs, R. 1998. Teaching with and about film and television. Integrating media literacy concepts into management education. *Journal of Management Development* 17(4):259–272.

Jules-Rosette, B. 1990. Semiotics and cultural diversity: entering the 1990s. *The American Journal of Semiotics* 7(12):5–26.

Kaplan, TJ. 1993. Reading policy narratives: beginnings, middles, and ends, in *The argumentative turn in policy analysis and planning,* edited by F Fischer & J Forester. Durham, NC: Duke University Press.

Kelly, C & Zak, M. 1999. Narrativity and professional communication: folktales and community meaning. *Journal of Business and Technical Communication* 13(3):297–317.

Koch, T. 1990. *The news as myth: fact and context in journalism.* New York: Greenwood.

Kozloff, S. 1978. Narrative theory and television, in *Channels of discourse: television and contemporary criticism,* edited by RC Allen. London: Methuen.

Kozloff, S. 1992. Narrative theory and television, in *Channels of discourse, reassembled: television and contemporary criticism.* 2nd edition, edited by RC Allen. London: Routledge:67–100.

Lacey, N. 2000. *Narrative and genre: key concepts in media studies.* London: Macmillan.

Larsen, P. 1991. Textual analysis of fictional media content, in *A handbook of qualitative methodologies for mass communication research,* edited by KB Jensen & NW Jankowski. London: Routledge:121–134.

Lucaites, JL & Condit, CM. 1985. Re-constructing narrative theory: a functional perspective. *Journal of Communication* 35(4):90–108.

Luthar, B. 1997. Exploring moral fundamentalism in tabloid journalism. *Javnost – the Public Journal of the European Institute for Communication and Culture* 4(1):49–64.

Margolin, U. 2000. Models for, of, and in literary narrative, literary narrative(e)ity as a model: disentangling the web. *Semiotica* 128(1/2):167–185.
Martin, W. 1986. *Recent theories of narrative.* Ithaca, NY: Cornell University Press.
McComas, K & Shanahan, J. 1999. Telling stories about global climate change: measuring the impact of narratives on issue cycles. *Communication Research* 26(1):30–57.
McMahon, B & Quin, R. 1987. Stories and stereotypes. *Metro* (72):40–45.
Nash, C. 1990. *Narrative in culture: the use of storytelling in the sciences, philosophy, and literature.* London: Routledge.
Oltean, T. 1993. Series and seriality in media culture. *European Journal of Communication* 8(1):5–31.
Onega, S & Landa, JAG (eds). 1996. *Narratology: an introduction.* London: Longman.
Palmer, J. 1991. *Potboilers: methods, concepts and case studies in popular fiction.* London: Routledge.
Phelan, J. 1989. *Reading narrative: form, ethics, ideology.* Columbus, OH: Ohio State University Press.
Pietilä, V. 1992. Beyond the news story: news as discursive composition. *European Journal of Communication* 7(1):37–67.
Prince, G. 1992. Remodeling narratology. *Semiotica* 90(3/4):259–266.
Prinsloo, J. 1991. Telling tales – considerations of narrative, in *Media matters in South Africa*, edited by J Prinsloo & C Criticos. Durban: Media Resources Centre:130–141.
Propp, V. 1968. *Morphology of the folktale.* Austin, TX: University of Texas Press.
Raunsbjerg P & Sand, H. 1998. TV sport and rhetoric: the mediated event. *Nordicom Review* 19(1):159–173.
Reid, I. 1992. *Narrative exchanges.* London: Routledge.
Ricoeur, P. 1981. Narrative time, in *On narrative*, edited by WJT Mitchell. Chicago: University of Chicago Press:165–186.
Rivera-Perez, L. 1996. Rethinking ideology: polysemy, pleasure and hegemony in television culture. *Journal of Communication* 20(2):37–56.
Scholes, R. 1974. *Structuralism in literature: an introduction.* New Haven, CT: Yale University Press.
Selby, K & Cowdery, R. 1995. *How to study television.* London: Macmillan.
Sheenan, RJ & Rode, S. 1999. On scientific narrative: stories of light by Newton and Einstein. *Journal of Business and Technical Communication* 13(3):336–358.
Silverstone, R. 1976. An approach to the structural analysis of the television message. *Screen* 17(2):9–40.
Silverstone, R. 1987. Narrative strategies in television science, in *Impacts and influences: essays on media power in the twentieth century*, edited by J Curran, A Smith & P Wingate. London: Methuen:291–330.
Silverstone, R. 1988. Television myth and culture, in *Media, myths and narratives: television and the press*, edited by JW Carey. Newbury Park, CA: Sage:20–47.
Silverstone, R. 1989. Let us then return to the murmuring of everyday practices: a note on Michel de Certeau, television and everyday life. *Theory, Culture & Society* 6(1):77–94.
Tait, DH. 1997. *Meaning and the listener's mind: an application of linguistic and cognitive concepts to radio news storytelling.* Ann Arbor, MI: UMI Dissertation Services. (Master of Journalism thesis, Carlton University, Ottawa, 1995.)
Tambling, J. 1991. *Narrative and ideology.* Milton Keynes: Open University Press.
Tilley, A. 1991. Narrative, in *The media studies book*, edited by D Lusted. London: Routledge:53–79.
Tornabuoni, T. 1966. A popular phenomenon, in *The Bond affair*, edited by OD Buono & U Eco. London: Macdonald:13–34.
Vincent, RC, Crow, BK & Davis DK. 1989. *When technology fails: the drama of airline crashes in network television news.* Columbia, SC: Association for Education in Journalism and Mass Communication.

Watson, J. 1998. *Media communication: an introduction to theory and process.* Houndsmill: Macmillan.

Whitehead, F. 1992. Roland Barthes's narratology. *Cambridge Quarterly* 21(1):41–64.

Wigston, DJ. 1997. Narrative theory and analysis, in *Introduction to communication – course book 6: film and television studies*, edited by PJ Fourie. Kenwyn: Juta:197–219.

Wollen, R. 1976. North by north-west: a morphological analysis. *Film Forum* 1(1):19–34.

Woollacott, J. 1982. Messages and meanings, in *Culture, society and the media*, edited by M Gurevitch, T Bennett, J Curran & J Woollacott. London: Routledge:91–111.

Wright, W. 1975. *Six guns and society: a structural study of the Western.* Berkeley, CA: University of California Press.

Young , K. 1999. Narratives of indeterminacy: breaking the medical body into its discourses; breaking the discursive body out of postmodernism, in *Narratologies: new perspectives on narrative analysis*, edited by D Herman. Columbus, OH:Ohio State University:197–217.

Part B
Film Theory

Unit 5
Film Theory and Criticism

Film Theory and Criticism

5

Pieter J Fourie

Overview

In this unit you are introduced to the broad and complex field of film theory. We begin with the question: what is film theory? We look at different kinds of film theory, the questions asked in film theory and the difference between film history, film criticism, film analysis and film theory. We conclude this part of the unit with questions about the value of film theory.

In the second part we discuss classic film theory. The emphasis is on the distinction between expressionism and realism in film art and communication. With reference to the work of a few key theorists we distinguish between expressionist, formalist and realist film theory and theorists. We conclude this part with a discussion of *auteur* theory.

This is followed with an introduction to film semiotics. Because you have already studied the basics of semiotics in the first volume of this book (Unit 10), we briefly concentrate on a few key aspects in film semiotics, such as film as a sign, denotation and connotation in film, film codes, the paradigmatic and syntagmatic nature of film, levels of meaning in film and the communicative functions of film.

The last part of the unit deals with contemporary film theory and thus with ideological criticism, feminist criticism and the psychoanalytical approach.

Learning outcomes

At the end of this unit you should be able to

- explain what film theory and its value and importance are;
- give an overview of the key assumptions in classic film theory with reference to the distinction between expressionism and realism and to the work of key theorists in this period;
- describe the shift in emphasis between classic film theory and the semiotic approach;
- give an overview of the contribution of film semiotics to our understanding of film;
- apply some of the aspects of film semiotics in an analysis of a film;
- describe the shift in emphasis between film semiotics and contemporary film theory;
- describe and explain the assumptions in ideological film criticism;
- apply Lacan's psychoanalytical theory to the viewer's (subject's) experience of film;

- give an overview of the origin and development of feminist film criticism and its basic assumptions; and
- view a film critically from
  - an ideological perspective,
  - a psychoanalytical perspective,
  - a feminist perspective.

5.1 INTRODUCTION

A director requires no knowledge of film theory to produce a film. Indeed, until recently people working in the field showed no interest in film theory. The argument was that film directors instinctively knew (or did not know) what to do. The gradual growth and rise of film as an art form has, however, brought theory and practice closer together. Nowadays the leading directors are thoroughly conversant with film theory. In other words, the work of the most prominent modern directors has a specific theoretical basis.

Consider the work of well-known directors such as Woody Allen (e.g. *Annie Hall* 1977), Steven Spielberg (e.g. *Jaws* 1975), David Lynch (e.g. *Blue Velvet* 1986), Wim Wenders (e.g. *Paris, Texas* 1984), Ingmar Bergman (e.g. *Fanny and Alexander* 1982), Martin Scorsese (e.g. *Taxi Driver* 1976), Francis Ford Coppola (e.g. *Apocalypse Now* 1979), Robert Altman (e.g. *Short Cuts* 1993), Quentin Tarantino (e.g. *Pulp Fiction* 1994), Almodovar (*All About my Mother* 1998) and the Iranian director Majid Majidi (*Children of Heaven* 1997), to mention a few.

The above does not include the classic work, now forming the canon of filmmaking, of directors such as Eisenstein, Pudovkin, Griffith, Murnau, Hitchcock, Wiene, Hawkes, Welles, Kazan, Ford, Fellini, Buñuel, and others.

Initially the argument was that the "Hollywood style", which today still largely governs cinematic style, was not underpinned by any theory of what a film is or can be. Nevertheless, ever since films began to be produced, certain theoretical ideas have been current. Think, for example, of the view of one of the first American directors, DW Griffith (whose films stimulated a considerable number of theoretical views) that for film to succeed, the tempo of a film should essentially be in tune with the average human heartbeat, which, of course, increases in rapidity under influences of excitement, and almost stops in moments of pregnant suspense (cf. Monaco 1984:323).

Many of the first casual theoretical comments, such as the one above, show an underlying need to elevate the film medium, which was originally viewed as popular entertainment for the masses, to the level of art, to place it on the same level as the other art forms and to develop a sound understanding of film as an aesthetic and communication phenomenon. The need to command respect for an art form as well as an academic understanding of a phenomenon may therefore be seen as the chief reasons for the development of theories about film. But what is film theory?

5.2 WHAT IS FILM THEORY?

Film theory is an intellectual and critical activity dealing with divergent questions about the nature of the film as a phenomenon. Answering these questions leads to insight and a better understanding of the phenomenon. The questions and answers are probably not essential to the viewer's pleasurable experience of the film, or the producer's potential financial gain. Yet the insight gained from the questions asked and the answers sought, is vitally important to critics, film actors, film directors and viewers because it contributes to their understanding of, approach to and experience of the film medium.

Just as theories, philosophies and history of art enrich our experience and practice of art, so film theory enriches our experience and practice of film(s) as a form of art and communication.

5.2.1 Establishment, medium and close-up theories

Based on the questions which are and may be asked in film theory, Sergei Eisenstein (1898–1948), the Russian director and one of the first and most eminent of the film theorists, distinguished (in film terminology) between three types of film theories:

- Establishing-shot theories
- Medium-shot theories
- Close-up theories

In establishing-shot theories (an establishing-shot provides us with an overall picture of a scene) the emphasis is on the social context of a film and/or the social context in which films are made. In medium-shot theories (the demarcation of a specific aspect of a scene, but still not detail) the emphasis is on the relationship between a film and its public (or films and their publics) and human relationships in the film as such. In the close-up theories (focus on detail) the emphasis is on the different components of a film and the ways in which the film conveys meaning, as in the semiotics of the film. Typical contemporary questions that might be asked in each of these approaches are the following:

Establishing-shot theories

- What effect did apartheid have on the content and form of South African films?
- What effect did apartheid have on the South African film industry as a whole?
- How are films affected by a social institution such as censorship?
- How does the public's literacy level influence films?
- How are films influenced by religion?
- How is religion influenced by films?
- How are the contents of films influenced by the American culture and way of life?
- What effect does the economy have on films?
- How does politics affect films?
- How are films affected by technology?

Medium-shot theories

- How are people depicted in films?
- What kind of human relationships are depicted in films?
- How are groups or a group such as the Jews, women, gays, blacks, Afrikaners and so on depicted in films?
- How does the viewer experience a film?

Close-up theories

- What is a film?
- What does a film consist of?
- What are the hidden components of a film?
- How do films create and convey meaning?

The questions above are a few examples of the type of questions asked in film theory. In short, they amount to a consideration of the classical distinction between **form, content** and **function**. Questions about what a film is and how it comes into being are related to its form. Questions concerning what the film depicts are related to content. Questions regarding the effect of films on viewers and society and how social factors influence films and the producers/directors of films are related to the functions of films.

Figure 5.1 The Russian director and film theorist, Sergei Eisenstein, directs a scene from his film *October*, 1928

Form is the way in which a film depicts something – it consists in the codes and techniques and the way the film gives shape to the content. Content is the actual content of the film – what the viewer sees. It comprises the theme and narrative and the way the actors portray the theme and narrative. Function is the value of the film for the producer and director, other film artists – in short, the film communicator – and for the viewer or recipients.

5.2.2 Normative and descriptive film theory

A further distinction between different kinds of film theory is made between *normative* and *descriptive* film theory (cf. Monaco 1984:322–323).

The approach to the questions above is mainly normative and/or descriptive. Normative theories are concerned with idealistic views on what films as a phenomenon can and ought to be. Normative theory operates inductively, that is, it starts by creating a set of values or rules with which, ideally, films should comply and then proceeds to apply these rules to a film in order to determine its value. If a film does not comply with these rules (norms), it is a failure. Normative theory is essentially a qualitative judgement.

Descriptive theory adopts the deductive method: the theorist first collects data on the entire field of film activity and only then arrives at preliminary findings on the nature of a film.

The following is a practical example: if normative theory were used to assess a South African film, that is, if it were evaluated inductively, then the theorist/critic would apply generally valid rules/norms and assess the film accordingly. If operating descriptively, the critic would take into account the circumstances, including the economic, political, production and social circumstances surrounding the production of the South African film (the field of film activity) and probably arrive at the conclusion that for economic reasons it is impossible to judge the South African film by the standards which apply to large internationally produced films.

5.2.3 Film history, film theory, film criticism and film analysis

To delineate the broad field of film theory, we furthermore distinguish between film history and film theory (as such). Under film theory we also include film criticism and film analysis. In the next few paragraphs we explain the distinctions in more detail.

Film historians organise the questions concerning film history along a diachronic axis. Hommel (1991:45) explains that film historians attempt to explain a film phenomenon (e.g. a certain film in a certain time period) in a chronological order. They do not only ask why something happens in film history and try to describe this, but also attempt to fathom why something occurs in a certain way and not in any other; why certain changes in film history occur and how these changes affect the nature of film in a certain time period.

In this way, film historians reconstruct, for example, the complicated production history (e.g. developments in technology and the development of the Hollywood industry) underlying a film such as *Gone with the Wind* (Fleming 1939). Or they try to understand the origin and meaning of a certain movement, such as the Italian neo-realism of the Forties, or the French new wave of the Fifties, against the background of developments in social, political, economic, art, media and existential spheres.

Film history is thus concerned with the context in which the film phenomenon (e.g a specific film or movement) originates and develops. The investigation can focus on the production or the reception of the film (or group of films). The most important is that the investigator looks at the film from an historical perspective. What does a film such as *Pulp Fiction* (1994) and its maker (Tarantino) say about late twentieth century society, for example, or about violence, humankind, production techniques and the influence of something such as postmodernism on techinique and narrative structure? What do Tarantino and his films say about the film industry as such, about viewers and what they like or don't like and why? How do all these things influence the eventual form and content of a film such as *Pulp Fiction*?

Based on the work of Allen and Gomery (1985), four forms of film historiography (or film history writing) are generally distinguished today:

- Aesthetic film historiography
- Technological film historiography
- Economic film historiography
- Social film historiography

Aesthetic film historiography (or history writing) deals with the historian's definition and description of how certain codes are aesthetically employed at a certain point in the history of film, for example, in a certain time period, or in the work of a certain director, to convey a specific effect. For example, how is direction, composition, lighting, and so on, handled in order to create a certain impression in the French new wave, Italian realism or in *film noir*. What were the reasons for using these and related codes in that specific manner, and how did this usage relate to similar applications in other art forms, social trends at that stage, the economy of the entertainment industry, political trends in society, and so on? In short, the emphasis falls on aesthetic style.

A good example is *film noir*. The concept *film noir* was used by French critics to describe a characteristic dark ("noir" = night/black) dramatic thriller that was fashionable especially during the period of the Second World War, and which is today still a stylistic characteristic of certain films. Historians on *film noir* attempt to discover why the films made at this time and in this style were "dark", and what techniques were used to visualise this "darkness". Can this darkness be traced back to German expressionism in painting, and how does it relate to the artist's need to visualise people's psychic anguish during the Second World War? How does this compare with the nineteenth century British tradition in thriller fiction? Today, we recognise stylistic elements of *film noir* (dark lighting, dark streets, misty and smoky scenes, rain, shots filmed from behind barred windows, and so on) in films such as *Pulp Fiction* (1994), *Basic Instinct* (1992), and *Natural Born Killers* (1994). The historian would try to learn why there is a tendency for contemporary directors to return to this style. Does this say something about the era in which we live?

Technological film historiography deals with the history of film technology. The origin and development of various sorts of film material (8mm, 16mm, cinerama, synchronised sound and image), cameras, projectors, production studios, animation, special effects, the influence of television and video on film and vice versa, sound equipment, and so forth, are described and investigated historically. This kind of historiography reveals a close relationship between the history of film and related technological developments at a given stage in history. Also examined is how this technology dictated and still dictates the form and content of film. Would Spielberg have made ET (1982), for example, if he had not had the technology to do so?

Economic film historiography is concerned with the questions of who provides the money for the production of films, and why and how they do so. In short, it is the history of production companies and the motion picture business or separate film businesses in various countries. How did Hollywood, as the leading manufacturer of films, originate, and what is the influence of Hollywood right around the world? How is it run economically, and why is it successful as a business? In South Africa, the focus would be on the history of the South African film industry. How did it begin, why has the film industry produced only flashes-in-the-pan, and why has it been unsuccessful up until now? A good example of economic historiography in the South African economy (although it may also be categorised as social film historiography) is Thelma Gutsche's (1972) classic work *The history and social significance of motion pictures in South Africa: 1895–1940* and Keyan Tomaselli's *The South African film industry* (1979). How are film industries in various countries financed and how does film regulation (including censorship) and film policy influence this?

Allen and Gomery (1985) (see also Hommel 1991:129) describe social film historiography in terms of:

- Who makes film and why?
- Who watches films, how and why? and
- What was showing at given stages in the history of film, how and why?

Social film historiography investigates film in a historical-social context, as a social phenomenon among other social phenomena in a specific time period and environment.

For example, who began making films in South Africa, when and why? How do some of the first South African films such as *Sarie Marais* (1931) and *Moedertjie* (1931) relate to the Afrikaner as poor white and with the urbanisation of the Afrikaner in the Thirties? How does *Hans en die Rooinek* (1961) by Jamie Uys, doyen of the South African film industry, relate to the Boer/Brit relationship in South Africa and how do films such as *Die Bou van 'n Nasie* (1939) relate to the rise of Afrikaner nationalism? Who went to see films in those days and in that time period, how were the bioscope theatres influenced by this, who built them, who was responsible for the distribution of films then? Why did South African films show such promise in the Sixties and why did critical questions on apartheid begin to crop up in films such as Jans Rautenbach's *Katrina* (1969)? Why did this movement fade? Was it as a result of apartheid censorship? Why did black South Africans still not truly join the production of South African films, and why can we still not talk of a unique South African film style? Is it a result of apartheid? These are the questions that are addressed in social film historiography. A good example of South African film historiography is Keyan Tomaselli's (1989) *The cinema of apartheid: race and class in South African cinema*; the work, already mentioned, of Gutsche and Botha and Van Aswegen's (1992) *Beelde van Suid Afrika: 'n alternatiewe rolprentoplewing.*

Along with the above mentioned forms and/or methods of film historiography, we differentiate between *classical* and *revisionistic film historiography.* The former is a chronological documentation of films and the work of directors and artists (e.g. actors) since the beginning of film up until today, or of a specific period, or of the work of a specific director or film artist. This often appears as a list of films, directors, actors, scriptwriters and other film artists, margin notes on the production as such, the date of production and usually a short summary of the plot of the film. It may be generally typified as an overview.

Hommel (1991:149) believes that classical film historiography, which was the dominant form of film historiography up until the Seventies especially, is a macrohistory. It attempts to present a chronologically holistic picture of the development of film in general, of a period, a genre, or of the work of a specific artist. In contrast to this, revisionistic film historiography is a microhistory. It looks in greater detail at a certain aspect of a film, or at a director or other film artist's work, and places it in historical perspective, for example, the relationship between the music of a specific pop group and its use in films of a certain historical period; the relationship between the themes of a film and the particular spirit of the era, and so on. Revisionistic historiography *revises* classical (macro-) historiography, and focuses in on more detail. It thus usually considers a work from an aesthetic, social, technological or economic viewpoint.

Unlike film history, film theory investigates the film phenomenon along a synchronic axis. Film theorists view a film apart from its historical links and purely as a manifestation of film art and as the exploitation of film as a communication medium. The angle is not the historical perspective, but the nature and function of film art or aspects of this. *Gone with the Wind* is thus not important because it reflects something of Hollywood or even American history, but because it says something of the nature and possibility of film as art and communication. The result is, according to Hommel (1991:45), a view in which abstract characteristics and functions of film are explained according to examples.

As mentioned above, we further divide the subdiscipline film theory into film criticism and film analysis.

The most important function of *film criticism* is to educate viewers in terms of a specific film. De Putter (1991:166) distinguishes between two kinds of criticism: film criticism that focuses on the story of a film and film criticism that looks at technical aspects (production aspects such as camera use, lighting, sound, and so on). The former is what we usually find in newspaper reviews, while the latter is a more advanced form of criticism, and is usually found in film and academic journals.

Another distinction is made by Bordwell (1989), who distinguishes between film criticism that is directed towards the interpretation of a film, and film criticism that focuses on the discovery of hidden meanings of a film. In both cases, it is the critic's aim to explain the film to readers, and to establish links with other films and literary works, to expose the relationship of the film to reality and to describe the deeper, underlying meanings of a film in terms of this.

In summary, film criticism aims to describe a specific film against the background of knowledge of the medium of film, and on the basis of this to develop a set of criteria and to deliver a value-judgement. Usually, the success of a film for the majority of (newspaper) reviews depends on whether or not the story is told in a logical, consistent manner. Newspaper reviews seldom contain the ideal form of criticism, namely, a combination of

- information on a film (the story, actors, director),
- opinions on the technical and artistic construction of a film (the success of the film as art and communication that is dependent on the use of the camera, direction and lighting), and
- interpretation and establishment of relationships.

Where a report merely provides information and discusses the plot, we talk of a "review". Where this is coupled with an evaluation of the artistic quality of a film and an explanation and interpretation of a film, we refer to film criticism.

In contrast to film criticism, which is chiefly a personal description and value-judgement, film analysis is an exact and rational description of the role of the filmic medium in bringing about meaning in a film. In other words, a careful inventory is made of how the depiction of a story derives meaning through the actors, décor, lighting, sound, camera shots and direction (this is the filmic medium); what this meaning is; what the plot construction is and how it plays on the (un)consciousness of the viewer (cf. De Putter 1991:167).

The analysis may be undertaken from a single or many viewpoints, for example, a feminist, ideological, psychoanalytical perspective, and so on. In film analysis, several analytical methods exist that may be employed, such as narratology (to systematically describe and analyse the plot), ideology criticism (to describe and analyse the ideological meaning of a film), semiotics (to describe and analyse the meaning construction of a film, and film as a unique grammar), rhetorical analysis (to analyse the rhetorical workings of a film), content analysis (making a quantitative analysis of the incidence of certain aspects, e.g. violence), psychoanalysis (to analyse how film plays on the (un)conscious of the viewer), and so on.

As already stated, film theory includes both film criticism and film analysis and places the opinions expressed in film criticism and the findings of film analysis in a broader context. It especially examines the social, political and philosophical implications of criticism and analysis, and how film differs from other arts and communication forms, on the basis of what is unique to the medium. Whereas film criticism is practical, film analysis operates on a more abstract level.

In film theory's often abstract association with the meaning, value and function of the phenomenon of film, several different perspectives may be currently distinguished. Originally, film theory dealt with the difference between realism and expressionism (expressionism is often also referred to as formalism in film theory). Since then, the emphasis has shifted to film as a unique "language" – *film semiotics*. After this, the ideological workings of film were emphasised. At present, the viewer's experience of film is the focal point of film theory. In 5.3, 5.4 and 5.5 an overview of these film theories is presented.

To conclude: we differentiate between film history and film theory for academic purposes, and distinguish film criticism and film analysis within the field of film theory. However, keep in mind that, in practice, these fields converge, they overlap and link up with each other; indeed, not one of these fields may exist without the others.

5.2.4 Why film theory?

Against the background of the above, it may appear as if film theory occupies itself on an abstract level with things that most people experience as commonplace; that it abstracts, rather than explains, the phenomenon of film. This is in fact not the case. What film theory tries to convey is that

- film is a unique and complex form of art and communication;
- various factors play a role in the production and experience of a film;
- a film is always created from a certain perspective;
- we always look at a film from a certain perspective, or experience it from within a certain context.

Film theory concentrates on four subjects in different ways and from different perspectives:

- the fundamental nature and properties of film as an art and communication medium;
- the film artist and communicator;
- the film viewer/audience; and
- the wider context of the medium – the social, political, economic and ideological implications of film.

Film theory organises all the views and opinions on the above and at the same time develops new ideas on film by always posing new questions on these issues.

Film theory is thus a scientific process of organising, through which we learn to be disciplined and as objective as possible in our judgements about films. As such, it is a complete academic discipline that delineates its field of investigation in much the same way as other disciplines, and which poses questions based on the uniqueness of this field of investigation (film, film artists and communicators, film viewers and film in general). These questions then open up new perspectives. Film theory further develops analytical instruments for the investigation of these questions. Although many of these instruments (such as semiotics, psychoanalysis, ideology criticism, feminist criticism and analysis, plot analysis, reception theory, and so on) link up with and originate from disciplines such as linguistics and literary theory, they are revised and adapted for this unique field of study (film) for application to the subject of investigation. In this way, film theory also contributes to the development of the methodology and paradigmatic trends that relate to studies in the human sciences on symbolic forms and humankind's understanding of these.

Summary

To summarise this part of the unit, the following: In the preceding pages, we looked at some of the questions asked in film theory. We distinguished between film history, together with the different kinds of film historiography, and film theory, which includes film criticism and film analysis. We concluded by defining film theory, its value and our reasons for studying it, and discovered that it provides us with perspectives which allow us to order our observations and experiences concerning the properties of film, its producers, its audiences and its wider contexts. In the process of answering the questions posed in and by film theory, film theory develops and tests different methodologies. As such, it not only improves our knowledge of film as an object of study, but also contributes to the epistemology of the human sciences in our endeavour to understand the human mind and its symbolic forms of expression.

5.3 CLASSIC FILM THEORY

5.3.1 Introduction

Classic film theory was mainly concerned with film's representation of reality and whether this should be realistic or expressionistic/formalistic. The dichotomy between *expressionism/formalism* and *realism* in classic film theory (from about 1915) can be traced back to the classic Greek philosophers Plato's (427–347 BC) and Aristotle's (384–322 BC) ideas on the nature and purpose of art, and their respective interpretations of *mimesis* (imitation or *representation*).

Plato saw art largely as an inferior copy or replica of reality. In his view of art, the *copyist* (artist, communicator) contributed no individual creative vision and, since a copy can never possess all the attributes of the original, the product was merely a feeble imitation (mimesis) of the real thing or nature.

Compared to Plato, Aristotle regarded mimesis as a unique process, entailing more than just a copy or replica of nature. Art, although an imitation of reality, is not inferior but requires the craftsmanship of an artist.

The history of painting – from the early Renaissance works of the Italian painter Giotto (1266–1267) to the French impressionist painter Claude Monet (1840–1926) –

supports the Aristotelian conception of art. The nineteenth-century French and Russian novelists Honoré Balzac (1799–1850) and Leo Tolstoi (1883–1945) achieved a more accurate, realistic reproduction of reality than anything produced previously in the history of literature. The Norwegian and Russian dramatists Henrik Ibsen (1828–1906) and Anton Chekhov (1860–1904) perfected realism in the theatre, which portrayed life and reality in a naturalistic, realistic manner.

The period from the late Middle Ages to the end of the nineteenth century could be described as the *age of naturalism*. During this period Western art strove to depict reality as faithfully as possible. True, the romantics of the late eighteenth century, and in due course the *impressionists* as well, departed somewhat from the naturalist view of art. Thus the impressionists set greater store by beauty than by realism and introduced unconventional uses of line and colour. Nevertheless the overriding view was naturalistic: art was seen as a life-like rendering of reality, a mimesis.

After World War I these realistic approaches underwent a radical change. One factor that put paid to this tradition was the emergence of photography, which helped to trigger a revolution in the arts. After all, if photography reproduced reality mimetically (imitatively), what remained for the other art forms?

The quest for solutions to this problem gave rise to expressionism, cubism, abstraction, conceptionalism, surrealism and other trends in the fine arts. In theatre there were forms such as happenings, street theatre and theatre of the absurd. These new forms all suggested that artists should not merely imitate reality but should express their own feelings about the world, interpreting, idealising and/or distorting it. The accent was on emotion and the capacity of the creative person to give unique form and stature to reality, thus investing it with new meaning.

The expressionists rejected illusions about reality. They consciously distorted natural objects and did not attempt to reproduce reality. The movement from realism to expressionism (leaving photography, film and later television to imitate reality mimetically) meant that photographic media were not and could not be viewed as art forms. This led to reflection on whether film (and television) as a technical medium could and should be confined to realistic imitation, or whether – as in the arts – the director could use photographic media to interpret reality expressionistically.

This debate crystallised in the film theories of Sergei Eisenstein (1898–1948), André Bazin (1919–1958), Rudolf Arnheim, V I Pudovkin (1893–1953), Siegfried Kracauer (1989–1966) and others – the so-called classic film theorists and theories. Before long a clear distinction was made between realism and expressionism in filmic art. The controversy was conducted between adherents of Russian formalism and supporters of the French cinema journal *Cahiers du cinéma*. It profoundly influenced filmmakers and was reflected in such movements as Russian social realism, German expressionism, the French "new wave" and Italian neo-realism. Particularly in our time the productions of what are known as *auteur* directors show clear evidence of these theoretical considerations.

Some definitions

Expressionism and **formalism:** In film theory the concepts expressionism and formalism are often used interchangeably to refer to views distinct from realism. Expressionism also refers to a specific period during the 1920s in theatre, art and film, especially in Germany. An outstanding characteristic of expressionism is its emotionalism and the desire of the artist (whether writers, painters or filmmakers) to experiment with the form (techniques) of his/her medium in order to give a new meaning to the content of the work and thus to the topic of the expression. In painting, the work of the painter Van Gogh is a good example of expressionism, and in film the work of the Russian directors Sergei Eisenstein and V I Pudovkin. Expressionism presents physical reality on the screen as a projection, or expression, of the subjective world, generally of a character in the film (cf. Konigsberg 1987:108).

Formalism: Formalism refers to a cultural revival, especially in literature and film, in Russia of the 1920s. There is a small but nevertheless important difference between formalism and expressionism. Expressionism represents the global and theoretical idea of film as a unique form of artistic expression and communication – unique in the sense that film is capable of interpreting reality or an aspect thereof in specific ways. Formalism is more exact and pronounced in its description(s) of how film is capable of doing this. It gives a more concrete and "scientific" description of film's codes (techniques) enabling film to be a unique form of expression. A good example of formalism is early narrative analysis (see Unit 4) and formalist semiotics (see the later discussion in this unit).

Realism: Realism refers to art (symbolic forms in general) which tries to imitate reality as closely as possible. The artist's techniques and methods disappear in the background and the reader/viewer (subject) becomes so involved with the content of the work that he/she is hardly aware of the artist's own interpretation and techniques. Apart from this form of realism, which is known as psychological realism, we also distinguish aesthetic realism. Aesthetic realism has as its goal the true expression of emotion or an emotional quality. Realism in film refers to a direct and truthful view of the real world through the presentation of characters and their physical surroundings with minimal distortion from either the filmmaker's point of view or from filmic techniques. In this respect film realism is related to the traditional mimetic school of criticism in literature and painting, which argues that art should be a representation of reality, heightening our consciousness about the world that surrounds us (cf. Konigsberg 1987:285).

Reality: When we use the concept *reality* in this unit, we do not refer to reality in the sense of what is real or in terms of the visual documentation of something that is real, such as that of documentary films or in the news, but we refer to the *representation* of something. This representation creates the impression of reality and/or imitates reality or an aspect thereof, for instance in feature films. In feature films (dramatic films) the film artist(s) creates something that imitates reality, for example a love affair or a crime. The artist gives form to this by using actors, sets and the numerous techniques of the film medium. What we as viewers eventually see on the screen is not reality, but an imitation thereof. This imitation can be of a realistic or expressionistic nature.

Raw material: Depending on the context in which it is used, *raw material* can either refer to the subject matter of a film, that is the topic, or to the film stock. The latter is the kind of film used, e.g. 16 mm or 35 mm, colour or black and white.

The following overview of classic film theory is based on discussions in seminal works by authors such as Giannetti (1972; 1990); Monaco (1977); Eidsvik (1978); Andrew (1976; 1984); Eberwein (1978); Stromgren and Norden (1984); Peters (1974); Bordwell and Thompson (1980); and Mast and Cohen (1985).

5.3.2 Expressionist film theory

Introduction

The cardinal argument of expressionist film theory is that film, like all art, should introduce structure and order into the chaos and meaninglessness of the world around us. It holds that the camera and editing techniques should be used to add something to reality. A feature film should not simply imitate real life or some scene from it; through imitation of the real-life scenes the director should say something about the world and human existence. Hence the film should present a fresh angle on reality.

Expressionistic film theorists are primarily interested in film methods and techniques. They expound the view that the film should not merely imitate events as they occur in real life, but should use film techniques or technology (filmic codes: camera point of view and editing) to produce an expressionistically edited version of reality.

Expressionist directors prefer to use the camera subjectively and concentrate on individual interpretation and self-expression as opposed to literal renditions of reality. The camera is consciously and deliberately used to interpret reality rather than merely to record and reproduce it.

On expressionism Giannetti (1972:186) says the following:

> Expressionists show a marked preference for form over content, for subjectivity and self-expression over factuality and literalness. The camera is used in a self-conscious manner to interpret reality, not only to record it. Expressionists are concerned with inner and psychological truths, which they feel can be captured by distorting the outer surfaces on the natural world.
>
> ... Technically this emphasis is achieved through the number of stylized techniques: symbolic and artificial lighting, fragmentary editing techniques, nonsynchronous sound, extreme angles, and special-effects cinematography.

In the following parts we focus on the theories of some of the classical theorists labelled as expressionists/formalists.

Vachel Lindsay

The expressionist tradition in film theory dates roughly to the period 1915–1935. In his book, *The art of the moving picture* (1932), Vachel Lindsay advocates the acceptance of the film as a synthesis of the arts. Soon after the publication of this book a movement arose in France which concentrated exclusively on the parallels between film and music and film and poetry. The surrealist and experimental films of such French directors as Germain Dulac (*La souriant Madame Beudet*, 1923), Jean Epstein (*Coeur fidè le*, 1923) and Abel Gance (*Napoleon vu par Abel Gance*, 1927) demonstrated that film, like music, could *cast reality into a particular form*. Like poetry, it offered human beings a dream experience.

At about the same time the expressionist movement arose in Germany. In this movement the emphasis was placed on the portrayal of people's *inner experience*, that is, of the invisible and the abstract.

Hugo Münsterberg

Hugo Münsterberg, one of the first expressionist film theorists, believed that the art of filmmaking lay not in its technology but in people's aesthetic experience of the medium. A Kantian disciple and a thorough-going aesthete, he maintained that the art object (including the film) has a purpose but no function. It (film) is *distinct* and *separate* from reality and all other human experience. In experiencing a film, human beings are cut off from all other events. In the process both the human mind and the art object are liberated to a new experience, in which the viewer is not interested in relating the art object and the experience of it to anything else, or even in evaluating it. The art object and the experience of it become ends in themselves.

Rudolf Arnheim

In line with this view Rudolf Arnheim formulated his film theory in his book, *Film as art* (1933). Like Münsterberg, he was a Gestalt psychologist who maintained that the purpose of the film (as of all art) is to express human existence. In normal perception, human beings are chiefly observing the material world. The aim of a film is not to present a mirror image of material reality, but to alienate reality to the extent that its *metaphysical meaning* will address the viewer. Arnheim claimed that photography and the film cannot imitate or reflect reality as it is, but can only reproduce a part of it. In this sense they are essentially abstractions of reality. Because of their very limitations the electronic and mechanical visual media are art forms.

Arnheim's theory can be summarised as follows:

- A work of art (and film as art) has value to the extent that the artist *manipulates* his material (both content and form).
- The artistic potential of a medium is enriched by its very *limitations*.

In Arnheim's view, the main limitations of film (and hence its artistic potential) reside in the *difference* between *normal human perception* of reality and *human perception of images*, or of reality through the lens of a camera.

These differences include the fact that human perception of reality is not demarcated by and confined to the boundaries of frames. By contrast, the vista of reality afforded by images is a limited perception from a given perspective (angle), confined to the image frame. The film viewer can do nothing about this perspective on reality. The spatiotemporal continuum of ordinary perception is delimited, in contrast to film images that have no boundaries of time and space. This difference between normal perception and perception of images formed the basis of the expressionist principle of *viewer manipulation.*

At the same time, visual communication is the crux of the problem in reception aesthetics. The images perceived by film viewers are not their own experience but a *representation* of reality as experienced and interpreted by the director. The director's choices and presentations in fact assign meanings to reality on behalf of the viewer, leaving the latter defenceless against the director's unlimited power. The director has full command of all the techniques of the visual medium in order to impose a given image of reality on the viewer.

5.3.3 Formalist film theory

Although related to expressionism in the sense that they emphasise that film should not merely imitate events as they occur in real life, but should produce an expressionistically edited version of nature and reality, the Russian theorist and director Sergei M Eisenstein together with Pudovkin are seen to be the most prominent formalist film theorists.

Sergei Eisenstein

Eisenstein regarded the *single camera shot* as the primary semantic unit of the film. In addition he emphasised the meanings which originate from the combination and *juxtapositioning* of single shots by means of editing or *montage.*

Eisenstein's ideas on film were influenced and shaped by the following art forms, movements and theories:

- Japanese Kabuki theatre, characterised by stylised acting and a succession of emotions.
- Italian futurism, launched by Martinelli round 1907. This movement was a revolt against convention and traditionalism in the arts.
- Russian formalism which developed mainly among literary critics in the 1920s and spread to the other arts. The formalists held that a work of art is characterised by certain universal formal properties. These, rather than its other qualities, determine its artistic merit.

- The American director David Wark Griffith, still regarded as one of the outstanding figures in film history. He was the first Western director to experiment with such techniques as cross-fading (or mixing), changing camera perspective within single shots and close-ups. As a result the film medium began to move away from the static, theatrical style that had characterised the early films. He also helped to shape the style of narrative films (i.e. the way in which stories are narrated in films). His best-known films were *The birth of a nation* (1915) and *Intolerance* (1916).
- Intellectually, Eisenstein was influenced mainly by Hegelian dialectical philosophy, which formed the basis of his montage technique. Hegel's theory boiled down to the unity of all intellectual, spiritual, historical and political experiences and activities. The various spheres of human life contained divergent and contrasting elements which, on closer analysis, are linked in polarised relations. These are seen as *thesis* and *antithesis*, with the whole of reality as a *synthesis* between the various polarities. In other words, unity is seen as the product or aggregate of divergent elements and relations within a given subject. Conflict develops when these disparate elements cannot be synthesised.

Figure 5.2 Expressionism: a scene from the *Odessa Steps* sequence in Sergei Eisenstein's film *The Battleship Potemkin*, 1925

As pointed out, this last principle underlies Eisenstein's approach to both his theory about *conflict* in the single shot and montage. Montage consists in organic relations between the different elements both within single shots and between separate shots that are combined. Eisenstein's montage theory which influences filmmaking till today, briefly comes to the following:

The single shot (shot A) is comparable to a cell in which various forms of conflict are operative. This conflict forms the basis of the conjunction of shot A with a subsequent shot (shot B), which is likewise torn by inner conflict. The combination of shot A with shot B is not simply an arbitrary concatenation (linking) of shots. The two are antithetical. This is the crux of film communication – the idea and meaning created by the combination of shot A with shot B.

Eisenstein distinguishes between the following real and potential conflicts both within single shots and between different shots that are combined.

Conflict montage within a *single shot*

- Graphic conflict: The eye is confronted with contrasting lines, and therefore with opposing trends within the same shot. (See Figure 5.2.)
- Conflict of planes: By way of example he cites his production of *Battleship Potemkin* (1925). In one single shot the foreground is filled with a large group of active soldiers shooting at the solitary figure of a mother to the right, beyond the centre plane of the shot. (See Figure 5.2.)
- Conflict of volume: A single shot containing objects of varying volume and magnitude. (See Figure 5.2.)
- Spatial conflict: The screen space is filled by several shapes which together form a composition guiding the eye to a focal point towards the back of the shot. (See Figure 5.2.)
- Conflict of lighting: Some objects in the shot are brightly illuminated – even overlighted – whereas others are underlighted.
- Conlict in tempo: The movement of objects within the single shot conflict with the tempo of the camera movement and/or musical accompaniment.
- Camera-created conflict: This refers to spatial distortion created by camera point of view, as well as optical distortion by the camera lens. The conflict is caused because these effects are not in keeping with normal human perception.
- Conflict created by the frame: Conflict is created by activities within the frame of a single shot which is too confined to accommodate all the activities. In other words, the viewer senses that the activities are too much (or too great) for the parameters of the frame of the single shot, and that they may well continue beyond the shot.

Conflict montage between *different shots*

- Attraction montage: In its simplest form this type of montage (or combination of single shots/editing) amounts to a shock effect on the viewer created by the succession of images and the idea or meaning this may generate. A well-known example from his film *Strike* is the images of strikers who are pursued and shot down by soldiers. These images alternate with images of oxen being slaughtered at an abattoir. Eisenstein feels that this kind of montage is made meaningful by the *idea* that it conveys – in this case that the workers are being slaughtered like animals. He uses images which, in respect of content, have nothing to do with the events being portrayed. The conflict between two images which form an emotional rather than an intellectual association gives rise to new *meaning*.

- Metric montage: Here the criterion is the duration of single shots, which are combined on this basis according to a scheme that matches the beat of the musical accompaniment. Metric montage has a physiological effect in that it constitutes the pulse/*beat* of a film.
- Rhythmic montage: The content of the shot determines its duration and its combination with other shots.
- Tonal montage: The lighting contrasts and colour in one shot form the basis for its combination with the next shot.
- High-tone montage: This refers to the aggregate of the conflicts discussed under conflict montage in a single shot. The composition, lines, colours, lighting and the like provide a basis for the combination with other shots.

Eisenstein therefore used montage techniques to "edit" reality in a premeditated way. Apart from dialectical philosophy, the basis of his montage theory may be traced to the view that realism effects an artistic experience which lulls the recipients: they can feel like heroes or martyrs without actually doing anything about it. Who will bother to perform heroic acts if one can share in and experience the glorification of one's ideals in the cinema? Eisenstein sought to analyse and fully control the power that art exercises over the beholder, so as to harness art (images) in the advancement of a cause.

V I Pudovkin

The theories of Eisenstein's fellow Russian, V I Pudovkin, were not fundamentally different. Pudovkin formulated a carefully considered theory of montage which greatly influenced film directors in the twenties and thirties. He propagated a theory of *construction montage*: the viewer should be shown only what is essential and constructive. Details are components constituting the whole. By concentrating on detail an idea and meaning are shaped and communicated.

Whereas Eisenstein's attraction montage used shots which, content-wise, had nothing to do with the events he was portraying, Pudovkin's construction montage concentrated exclusively on the content of the events portrayed. His premise was that *the camera lens replaces the eye of the viewer and therefore has to imitate the latter's "normal perception"*.

He gave the following example: A horse-drawn carriage is trundling along a muddy road. The driver is impatient. Inside the carriage is a passenger donning a military coat to protect himself against a cold wind. They pass a pedestrian. The driver asks him the distance to the next town (written subtitle). The pedestrian points with his hand. The carriage proceeds jerkily. The pedestrian follows its progress with his eyes.

Pudovkin maintains that these events should not be shown in a single shot, but should emerge step by step in several detailed shots: (1) the wheels of the carriage; (2) the mud; (3) the wheels in the mud; (4) the driver's face; (5) the passenger; (6) the coat; (7) the passenger putting on the coat; (8) the dismal winter landscape; (9) the pedestrian; and so on. *From the characteristic detail the whole can be construed.*

DW Griffith likewise believed that details were the constituents of a whole, but he used them to build suspense or to present the viewer with a consistently "ideal" image. To Pudovkin, construction montage was a means of constructing a sphere, an overall impression, and to portray the cognitive content of a scene.

His assumption of what constitutes or ought to constitute the viewer's normal perception is, in terms of expressionist tradition, a denial of the individuality and freedom of the viewer. Like Eisenstein, he *guides the viewer* to perceive what he (the communicator) wishes or expects his viewers to see. As will be seen in due course, this is in direct contrast to André Bazin's view concerning sequence shots and depth focus.

Figure 5.3 Expressionism: Vera Baranovskaia and Nikolai Batalov in V I Pudovkin's *The Mother*, 1926

Béla Balázs

In his *Theory of film: character and growth of a new art* (1970), Béla Balázs considers how the techniques of visual media may be harnessed to guide the viewer to *identify* with the content.

He maintains that the viewer sees the world through the eyes of the communicator and has no personal viewpoint or perspective. The viewer can and must be guided to identify with the content of the image. This is done by deploying the *formal elements* of the image to this end. Accordingly he is one of the few theorists who discusses the formal elements in detail. He elaborates on close-ups, variations of camera point of view and montage and identification techniques. In his view, the expressive value of the various camera movements and punctuation techniques such as fading and cross-fading is to guide the viewer towards identification.

FILMS TO VIEW

The viewing of the following films should help the learner towards a better understanding of the above discusssed assumptions in expressionist and formalist film theory:

Expressionism/formalism

V I Pudovkin: *The Mother* (1926); *The End of St Petersburg* (1927); *Storm over Asia* (1928); *Deserter* (1933)

Sergei Eisenstein: *The Battleship Potemkin* (1925); *October* (1927/28); *Old and New* (1929); *Alexander Nevsky* (1938); *Ivan the Terrible* (1944)

German expressionism

Paul Wegener: *Der Golem* (1914)
Robert Wiene: *Das Kabinet des Dr Caligari* (1919)
Fritz Lang: *Der müde Tod* (1921)
Friedrich Murnau: *Nosferatu* (1922)

The purpose of the above discussion is to illustrate how expressionist and formalist theorists were all concerned with "the belief that the art of cinema is possible precisely because a movie is unlike everyday reality" (Giannetti 1990:374) and "... how they were all concerned with patterns and methods of restructuring reality into aesthetically appealing designs" (Giannetti 1990:377). Underlying their work was the need to show that film does not only imitate reality or provide us with iconic representations of reality or an aspect thereof, but that it inherently provides us with an expressionistic interpretation and evaluation of reality. As such it is an art similar to all other recognised forms of art.

Figure 5.4 Expressionism: Max Schreck as the vampire Nosferatu in Friedrich Murnau's film *Nosferatu*, 1922

5.3.4 Realist film theory

Realist film theorists are primarily concerned with the raw material – that is, reality itself. They argue in favour of film that reproduces reality undiluted, *imitating* it as closely as possible. The director (communicator) and film techniques should not interfere with the viewer's own interpretation of the events.

Realist theorists advocate a relatively conservative use of the camera, which is seen as an instrument that should objectively record the events enacted. Film should reproduce life very much as it physically is rather than create a world of its own. Technically this is achieved by using natural environments rather than décor and sets. *Natural lighting* is preferred, as well as *long shots, sequence shots* and *depth focus*. On the whole realist film stays clear of special effects.

Realist theorists are concerned with the capacity of film to convey reality intact to the recipients, thus giving them a new awareness of life (reality or a piece of reality as re[presented] by film). Film should not impose an interpretation of something on the viewer, but should lead the viewer to interpret reality or an aspect thereof him/herself and thus bring the viewer in closer contact with reality.

Realist theory is best illustrated by the work of Italian neo-realist directors such as Visconti, Rossellini, De Sica and Fellini. Italian neo-realism, and thus the techniques thereof favoured by realist theorists, is characterised by

- a predilection for neutral, objective renditions of the ordinary life of ordinary people;
- a democratic spirit with emphasis on the values of ordinary people like labourers, peasants and factory workers;
- a refusal to make moral judgements;
- an emphasis on emotion rather than abstract ideas;
- an avoidance of neatly plotted stories in favour of loose, episodic structures that evolve from the situations of the characters;
- a documentary visual style;
- the use of actual locations, usually exteriors, rather than studio sets;
- the use of nonprofessional actors (or unknown actors);
- an avoidance of literary dialogue in favour of conversational speech, including dialects;
- an avoidance of artifice in the editing, camerawork and lighting in favour of a simple style.

Figure 5.5 (Neo)Realism: a scene from Vittorio de Sica's film *Miracle in Milan*, 1951

The camerawork and editing are not poetic or abstract, and the viewer is seldom aware of aesthetic image compositions. The camera is objective and the viewer rarely perceives the action subjectively "through the eyes of the character" (cf. Giannetti 1990:369).

The aim of the neo-realists was to expose anew the details that always form part of real life, and to make the viewer aware of them.

The above are also the characteristics of most of contemporary European (especially French and Italian) films, compared to most of American films which tend to be more expressionist.

If manipulation of viewer perception is the key to expressionist film theory, then neutrality and objectivity are the keys to realist theories. The art of the film consists in its ability to present an imitation of reality. The camera should record the existing reality.

Siegfried Kracauer and André Bazin distinguish between two types of film communicators: those who use the medium to *amplify the meaning* of reality, and those who render reality *purely for its own sake*. The second type does not impose a particular, interpreted version of the world on the viewer but merely sensitises the latter to reality. A film should put viewers in touch with reality and make them perceive aspects of it that they might otherwise have overlooked.

Siegfried Kracauer

The German theorist Siegfried Kracauer was less concerned with producing a realistic portrayal and recording of reality than with using film to convey the meaning of reality, or an aspect of it, realistically. Thus a director may use an unrealistic film portrayal or recording of a scene or an action to convey the untrammelled meaning of that reality to the recipient.

The sole purpose of the film is to put the recipient in touch with reality and with real human beings. Kracauer maintained that twentieth-century technology and science have alienated people from real life, and that the film can serve to make them aware of its true meaning once more. The camera should therefore be an instrument to record *unstaged reality – nature caught in the act.*

Giannetti (1990:371–372) lists the following as key aspects illustrating Kracauer's argument for realism in film:

- The subject matter must give the illusion that it has been found rather than arranged – in other words the narrative structure and the fact that the film is telling a story, must be hidden. The viewer should not constantly be aware of that he/she is looking at a story.
- With the expression "nature caught in the act" Kracauer means that film is best suited to recording events and objects that might be overlooked in life. The realistic cinema is a cinema of "found moments" and poignant revelations of humanity (cf. Giannetti 1990:371).
- To be realistic a film should suggest endlessness. It must imply a slice-of-life, a fragment of a larger reality rather than a self-contained whole. By refusing to tie up

all the loose ends at the conclusion of the movie, the filmmaker can suggest the limitlessness of reality (Giannetti 1990:371).

- Stylistic self-consciousness best illustrated in film adaptations of literary and dramatic works, historical films and fantasies, stands in the way of film realism and is, according to Kracauer, uncinematic.

André Bazin

In his discussion of the ontology of film, André Bazin makes a clear distinction between film and reality, subordinating the former to the latter. Nevertheless the film is a unique phenomenon in that it is freed from spatiotemporal constraints.

To Bazin the outstanding quality of reality is its ambiguity or the multiple meanings of everything. In his opinion the expressionist approach, particularly its use of montage, eclipses this ambiguity. Montage does not permit the viewer to observe the multiple meanings of reality, offering instead a synthetic reality in and through which truth is corrupted: it only generates images, unconnected in the real world, with the result that we as viewers are denied the active intellectual potential of choice to make the connections within the image which we view (Bazin 1967:15).

Instead of montage, he advocates *sequence shots* and *depth perspective*, arguing that by these means one can emphasise the union of humanity and reality, their interdependence and the *multiple meanings* of things. Awareness of the multiple meanings of reality is the essence of people's aesthetic experience of films.

In support of his arguments concerning sequence shots and depth perspective he refers specifically to the films of Orson Welles, Robert Flaherty, Jean Renoir, William Wyler, the Italian neo-realists and directors of the French New Wave.

On the Canadian director Flaherty's classic film *Nanook of the North* (1922), Bazin, for instance, says:

> The camera cannot see everything at once but at least it tries not to miss anything of what it has chosen to see. For Flaherty, the important thing to show when Nanook hunts the seal is the relationship between the man and the animal and the true proportions of Nanook's lying in wait. Editing could have suggested the passage of time; Flaherty is content to show the waiting, and the duration of the hunt becomes the very substance and object of the image. In the film this episode consists of a single shot. Can anyone deny that it is in this way much more moving than "editing by attraction" would have been?
> (Bazin 1967:29)

To illustrate his argument concerning sequence shots, Bazin (1967:39) says the following of Orson Welles' *The Magnificent Ambersons* (1942):

> Anyone who can use his eyes must realize that Welles' sequence shots in The magnificent Ambersons are by no means the passive "recording" of an action photographed within a single frame, but that on the contrary this reluctance to

> break up an event or analyse its dramatic reverberations within time is a positive technique which produces better results than a classical breakdown [like in construction of conflict montage – PJF] of shots could ever have done.

He concedes that because of the emphasis on sequence shots and depth perspective as opposed to montage, the communicator has to omit certain things that could have helped viewers to understand the message – that is, understand it in the way the communicator wants them to understand it. He calls these omissions the ellipses in film communication, the things that are not shown. These ellipses are not defects but in fact an acknowledgement of the potential multiple meanings of reality and the intelligence and experience of the viewer:

> ... the empty gaps, the white spaces, parts of the event that we are not given, are themselves of a concrete nature. It is the same in life: we do not know everything that happens to others.
>
> (Bazin 1967:66)

The viewers themselves have to supply the omissions on the basis of their knowledge and experience of reality.

To Eisenstein, the essence of film communication is the combination of shot A with shot B to constitute shot C. To Bazin, on the other hand, the single shot has its own phenomenological integrity.

Bazin believes that the communicator should not interfere with reality, but should render or recreate it intact on film. The sole aim of the film is to bring the recipients *closer to reality*, to make them *aware* of it *anew*. Film should not recreate reality analytically and in the process interpret it to the viewers: they should be left to do their own interpretation.

Giannetti (1990:144–153) notes the following as some of the key issues in Bazin's theory:

- Influenced by the philosophical movement called Personalism, Bazin emphasised the individualistic and pluralistic nature of truth. Therefore film should not try to impose a reality, interpretation of reality or a truth on the viewer. The viewer will decide for him/herself what the truth is. In film there are many ways of portraying the real. The essence of reality lies in its ambiguity. To capture this ambiguity, the filmmaker must be modest and self-effacing, a patient observer willing to follow where reality leads (cf. Giannetti 1990:144).
- Thematic editing violates the complexities of reality. Montage superimposes a simplistic ideology over infinite variability of actual life.
- Being aware that cinema, like all art, involves a certain amount of selectivity, organisation and interpretation, and thus distortion, Bazin did not advocate a simple-minded theory of realism (cf. Giannetti 1990:147). The values of the filmmaker will always influence the manner in which reality is perceived. However, the filmmaker must try to keep in balance his personal vision with the objective nature of the medium. Certain aspects of reality must be sacrificed for the sake of

artistic coherence, but Bazin felt that abstraction and artifice ought to be kept to a minimum. The materials should be allowed to speak for themselves (cf. Giannetti 1990:147). This the filmmaker can do by including all the dramatic variables within the same frame – that is, by exploiting the resources of the long shot, the lengthy take, deep focus, and wide screen. He/she can preserve actual time and space by panning, craning, tilting or tracking rather than cutting (montage) to individual shots (cf. Giannetti 1990:148).

To summarise Bazin's theory, Giannetti (1990:144) writes:

> Bazin's realist aesthetic is based on his belief that photography, TV, and cinema, unlike the traditional arts, produce images of reality automatically, with a minimum of human interference. This technological objectivity connects the moving image with the observable physical world. A novelist or a painter must represent reality by re-presenting it in another medium – through language [prose and poetry – PJF] and color pigments [painting – PJF]. The filmmaker's image, on the other hand, is essentially an objective recording of what actually exists. No other art, Bazin felt, can be as comprehensive in the presentation of the physical world. No other art can be as realistic, in the most elementary sense of the word.

Figure 5.6 Realism: Orson Welles as Kane in his film *Citizen Kane*, 1941

Jean-Luc Godard

Although the names of Jean-Luc Godard and Bazin are usually linked as representative of the realistic and neo-realistic approach to films, they differ in their evaluations of montage – Godard's being positive (cf. Monaco 1984:343–352).

Godard developed a synthesis of montage and *mise-en-scène*. In the first place he maintains that if a director is dishonest in his choice of images recorded in sequence shots and depth focus (*mise-en-scène*), it could distort reality in the same way that montage does. The very choice of certain images (and image content) is an act of abstraction.

Secondly, he argues that montage does not have to entail a distortion of reality, nor does it necessarily imply dishonesty on the part of the communicator. Although he agrees with Bazin that reality is better rendered by *mise-en-scène* than by montage, he gives a broader definition of realism. Unlike Bazin, Godard does not see it purely as the communicator's untrammelled rendering of reality. Neither does he, like Kracauer, concern himself with the psychological realism which the director creates for the viewer with the aid of montage. To Godard, realism resides not in the content and form of the images, but in the *intellectual reality* that the director creates with his message – the *dialogue* that he conducts with the viewer. Is this dialogue conducted in good faith? If so, the film is realistic. Is the director *sincere*, does he address the recipient directly – or does he try to manipulate the viewer?

Eisenstein sees montage preeminently as the means used by the director to alienate reality for the sake of reconceptualising it. Bazin sees *mise-en-scéne* (including sequence shots and depth perspective) as the communicator's cardinal technique for showing the recipient an unstaged reproduction of reality. Godard, by contrast, does not favour either of these techniques: he takes both for granted as basic filmic codes. To his mind, film communication should aim at a *particular effect*, at creating a *lasting impression* on the viewer (*effect* and *impression* here refer to the meaning a film has for the viewer, rather than its emotional impact).

The effect of a film resides in what it reveals about people's *inner experience* and their *relation* with and to reality. For this reason Godard's theory and films are described as *human-centred cinema*.

Film techniques are employed for the sake of *emotion*. The creative and expressive plane is that of emotional truth. The aim is not simply to present a plausible rendering of reality or some situation, but to render the complete emotional experience of human beings, the emotional quality of events. This should be done in such a way that the images radiate this truth. They should portray the *spirit* of a nation, of human beings, of an individual. Art is not a replica of what we see and hear around us. It should strive to visualise that which is not perceptible to the human senses.

To the director, says Godard, the film is a means of self-expression. In and through this medium the viewer discovers the world, *humanity*, him/herself. It makes the viewer aware of *beauty*, but also of the evil that threatens beauty. In and through the film the viewer elevates the essence of his/her conviction to a symbol, thus giving reality new meaning and form.

To the viewers the film offers a *new perspective* on reality. It is for them to accept or reject it. Either way, the very awareness of a different perspective on life and the world helps to shape their minds and enrich their knowledge, understanding and experience of life.

To Godard, then, film, like theatre, is essentially emotional. The effectiveness of film depends on rhythm, phrasing and intensity. At every level the communicator constructs the film *theatrically* by means of dialogue, *mise-en-scène*, camera point of view and the like, in order to achieve the desired emotional impact.

Figure 5.7 Realism: a scene from DW Griffith's film *The Birth of a Nation*, 1915

FILMS TO VIEW

The viewing of the following films should help the learner towards a better understanding of the above discussed assumptions of realist film theory:

Luchino Visconti: *Obsessions* (1942); *La Terra Trema* (1948); *Senso* (1954)

Roberto Rossellini: *Rome Open City* (1945); *Paisà* (1947); *Germania, Anno Zero* (1947)

Jean Renoir: *La Grande Illusion* (1937)

Jean-Luc Godard: *Une Femme est une Femme* (1961); *Le Gai Savoir* (1968)

DW Griffith: *The Birth of a Nation* (1915); *Intolerance* (1916)

Orson Welles: *Citizen Kane* (1941)

Robert Flaherty: *Nanook of the North* (1922)

The purpose of the above discussion was to introduce you to some of the ideas of some of the realist theorists and their emphasis on film's ability to record and reflect reality; that

> ... cinema is essentialy an extension of photography and shares with it a pronounced affinity for recording the visible world around us ... [that] unlike other art forms, photography and cinema tend to leave the raw material of reality more or less intact.
>
> (Giannetti 1990:368)

5.3.5 *Auteur* theory

The early realist film theories of Bazin and Godard were the direct precursors of and impetus for the development of the *auteur* theory. In this theory it is postulated that the relation between the image and reality can only be described in terms of a specific director's individual interpretation of reality: how this individual discloses, describes, experiences and ultimately visualises reality in the image. In this sense *auteur* theory is related to existentialist philosophy and should be studied against that background.

The film theorist Alexander Astruc initially used the term *caméra-style* (camera pen) to refer to a director whose work is thematically and stylistically recognisable. Although this term never caught on, the term *auteur* from the influential French cinema journal *Cahiers du cinéma* is its equivalent. *Auteur theory* places the emphasis on the director (the communicator), who is equated with the serious writer, the artist whose personality is *inscribed* in the work of art. The most eminent exponents of *auteur* criticism were the cinema journals *Cahiers du cinéma* in France, *Movie* in Britain and the critic Andrew Sarris in the USA.

One of the factors that contributed to the origin and development of this theory was, like in the debate between expressionists and realists, the controversy about the film as an art form. By placing directors on a par with great writers, and by applying to their productions the same analytical methods used for literature, *auteur* theory indicated that the director can be an artist. The emphasis on the director as an *auteur* relates to the romantic view that art cannot be the result of a collective production process. Despite the collective character of film production, *auteur* criticism shows that it is possible to isolate an individual artist in the electronic pictorial media.

Although film production is a collective activity, a film only has value if it is essentially a communication by a director. The presence of a director (who is actually an artist, an *auteur*) will permeate the film with that individual personality. This personality can be traced, both *thematically* and *stylistically*, in virtually all the work of a specific director. On this basis it is possible to distinguish between an *auteur* and a *metteur en scène*. The *auteur* is "consistently expressing his own unique obsessions, the other [is] a competent, even highly competent, filmmaker, but lacking the consistency which betrays the profound involvement of a personality" (Caughie 1981:9).

Originally the emphasis in *auteur theory* was on those Hollywood directors working in a *studio system* but still being able to leave their distinguishable trademarks on the films they directed, for instance directors such as Alfred Hitchcock, Charles Chaplin, John Ford, Howard Hawkes and Orson Welles.

A good example of *auteur* criticism is the work of the American critic Andrew Sarris. He used the *auteur* philosophy to rank American directors according to their *technical competence* (a basic requirement) and on two other levels: their identity as stylists, and their ability to convey their *own interpretation* of the material, reflecting some personal vision or outlook on the world. These criteria were also followed in Europe where the work of directors such as Ingmar Bergman, Frederico Fellini and Luis Buñuel has been elevated to the rank of *auteur*.

At its most basic level, *auteur* criticism provides a means of classification and analysis according to the characteristics common to many films directed by the same filmmaker. It is based on the assumption that any one film can be better understood and appreciated by considering it in relation to the qualities and concerns evident in the other films made by the same director.

The *value* of the theory is that it is a means for identifying and understanding the basic components of style and structure in a director's work. It functions as a systematic but flexible means of placing a film within a class and some historical context.

Auteur theory should not be seen as an aggrandisement of the director and the latter's power over the recipient – rather as if the director is the sublime creator using various techniques to "play" with reality. The emphasis is wholly on the director's mental world and the way this is communicated. When analysing a director's work one should not concentrate on the techniques used, but on his/her description of his/her chosen theme and the images he/she chooses to present to his/her viewers. This is where one can discern a director's attitude to reality. By determining what images a director has chosen "we can talk about reality as it is filtered through the consciousness of the authors" (Caughie 1981:84).

The main criticism from prominent film critics such as Pauline Kael and Dwight Macdonald is that *auteur* theory tends to grade art and the work of an individual artist. This kind of grading is impossible in art. Art is an individual and subjective expression of the artist. This makes the grading of art or a work of art impossible. Structuralists have condemned *auteur* theory as conservative and neo-Romantic. They question the notion that an individual director can somehow avoid or transcend the deep structures of society by virtue of his or her intense creative inner visions. The director always remains part of society. Furthermore, *auteur* theory and criticism can become a cult of personalities in which poor films made by recognised *auteurs* are preferred to better films made by directors not afforded *auteur* status (cf. Stromgren & Norden 1984:260–262).

In our brief discussion of the *auteur* theory we referred to the relation between the theory and realist film theory, the origin of the theory, concern about the collective nature of film production and how this was an impetus for the *auteur* theory, the theory's emphasis on the theme and style in a director's work, Sarris' ranking of directors, the value of the theory and criticism against the theory.

Summary

This part of the unit dealt with premises of the expressionist and realistic film theory. The main emphasis was on the nature, value, method and technique of the film as communication media. It was pointed out that film can, by virtue of its iconic and technological character, offer a mimetic reflection of reality. The question facing film theorists is whether the director should use the film simply to imitate reality, or whether he/she should interpret and evaluate it as well. If he/she imitates reality, the object of the film is to put the viewer in touch with reality or some aspect of it (including the nature and existence of human beings) in a unique and startling way. In this regard we can identify two techniques: sequence shots and depth focus.

If, on the other hand, the aim is to present an interpretation of reality or some aspect of it, the director has to use techniques like montage and close-ups to accentuate certain features for the viewer.

5.4 FILM SEMIOTICS

After the debate on expressionism/realism settled down, the next major movement in film theory was semiotics. (For an overview, a definition and discussion of semiotics see Unit 10, Volume 1 of this book).

The main figure in *film semiotics* was the French theorist Christian Metz. In his book *Film Language: a semiotics of the cinema* (1974) he used semiotics as a systematic and scientific method to analyse the ways in which film produces meaning. This development in film theory is in line with the so-called structuralist movement in linguistics and literature studies during the sixties and seventies (Fourie 1996).

Originally Christian Metz (1974), Peter Wollen (1972), Roland Barthes (1977) and Umberto Eco (1979) argued that film communicates according to a specific set of *grammatical* rules. The accent was on the nature of the image as an iconic sign, the way in which camera and editing codes produce meaning, paradigmatic and syntagmatic structures in visual communication, and the way in which film creates different kinds of meaning.

Apart from the theory underlying film semiotics and which also concerns the relationship between film and reality, or the relation between film as signifier, reality and signified, semiotic theory and analysis also provided us with the analytical tools to analyse the working of film (moving images) as a *signifying practice*. Some of the key insights gained through semiotics in the nature of film as a signifying practice are summarised here in a more general way.

5.4.1 Film as a sign

A *sign* is never the real object. It is not reality, but represents and serves as a means of referring to reality. In their daily communication people use linguistic signs in order to refer to things, to express their feelings, their desires, their thoughts and attitudes. How could one refer to something like a dog, for example, unless one knew the linguistic sign D-O-G? One could draw a dog, but that would simply be to use a pictorial or iconic sign as opposed to a linguistic one. In the same way, film uses images (pictorial signs) to refer to reality. Film is never reality but a semiotic representation of reality. Nevertheless, people readily experience film as real – hence the *credibility* of film.

Film is both iconic and indexical. Here the signifier (the image) resembles the referent. An image (the signifier) of a dog looks like a dog. It is immediately recognisable and the recipient does not need any special knowledge to interpret the sign. Because of the directly identifiable resemblance between an iconic sign and reality, it is possible that the recipient will treat the iconic sign as the real thing. This can explain the persuasive power of film.

Film is indexical in the sense that the image as an effect of a photochemical process (the celluloid strip projected on a screen) is caused by what it represents (the prefilmic referent in reality) (cf. Easthope 1993:7).

5.4.2 Film, denotation and connotation

Film (all photographic and moving images) does not only denote a literal meaning. The image is iconic, indexical and symbolic in the sense that the interpretation and meaning of an image is not untouched by cultural and social codes. In order to understand a film or an image, viewers fill it with their own knowledge, which cannot be separate from their own cultural and ideological background. Thus, apart from the image being or containing iconic, indexical and symbolic features, the viewer and what the viewer does with the image must be kept in mind. An image of a cow (although iconic and indexical) will/can portray different meanings in, for instance, Western and Eastern cultures. The image is both denotative and connotative.

In addition, there is in film a distinction between *paradigmatic connotation* and *syntagmatic connotation*. Paradigmatic connotation refers to the connotative meanings which viewers attach to an image on the basis of their own experience of various objects in the image and the resultant associations. A dog shown with a boy may remind a viewer of his/her childhood, and he/she might associate it connotatively with carefreeness. Advertisements afford good examples of paradigmatic connotation. Advertising agencies usually trade on the possibility that viewers will form pleasant associations with the objects shown in advertisements. The combination of a bottle of suntan lotion next to a bathing beauty lying on an idyllic beach is used to prompt an association with health, pleasure, gratification, carefreeness and sexuality.

Syntagmatic connotation refers to the semantic associations formed by the *interrelationship* of various shots. For example:

Shot 1: Soldiers being shot in battle
Shot 2: Cattle being shot at an abattoir

This combination of shots may give rise to a syntagmatic connotation that people are shot like animals.

5.4.3 Codes in film

Semiotics, and this is especially valuable for the purpose of film analysis, emphasises the difference between *codes of content* and *codes of form*. Codes of content refers to what the viewer perceives (sees and hears) in an image: the theme, the story, the *mise-en-scène* (décor, costumes, props), lighting, music, sound effects, acting and the like.

Consequently, we can distinguish between narrative codes, thematic codes, codes of the *mise-en-scène*, acting codes, production codes, lighting codes and so forth. Consider, for example, the various lighting codes used in a film in order to create a certain atmosphere and convey a particular meaning. What role does colour (e.g. in the costumes and décor) play in the communication of meaning? What is the contribution of the actor's performance, the style of production, the presentation style of the newsreader, composition and so forth.

These codes are not peculiar to film (and television). Film in a sense inherited them from literature (narrative codes), the theatre (lighting codes, costume codes, décor codes), painting, architecture and the other arts. Consequently these codes are also referred to as nonfilmic codes. These techniques, although "borrowed" from other media, are nonetheless vital for the transmission of meaning in film.

Codes of form are the actual *filmic* or *visiolinguistic* codes – specifically those of the *camera point of view and editing*. These are the distinctive codes of film (and television), in the sense that they impart meaning to images in a unique manner.

In the case of camera point of view (cf. Peters 1974:16–19), the following *theoretical* possibilities can be distinguished:

- active and passive camera point of view;
- the camera as a point of view and as a mere reflection of reality; and
- objective and subjective camera point of view.

In the case of active and subjective camera points of view, as well as that of the camera as a point of view, the scene enacted before the camera is seen from a specific perspective (chosen by the director). In the case of the passive, objective use of the camera, as well as that of the camera as the reflector of reality, a purely mimetic version of the scene is produced – it merely records.

In the first case the use of the camera expresses how the communicator (director) perceives and interprets the events enacted. In the second case the camera serves to reproduce a realistic version of those events.

In the case of the camera as point of view and subjective and active camera points of view, the codes used include varying camera distances (close-ups, long shots, zoom shots) and camera movements (panning, dolly, crane, lens changes, filters, camera heights). In the case of camera point of view as mere reproduction, the camera remains predominantly static. In the first case the camera is used to impart *form* to the events enacted; in the second the main concern is with the *content* of those events.

When describing, interpreting and evaluating film from a semiotic perspective, one has to ask how these codes contribute to the meaning of the message conveyed. Does the difference between a long shot and a close-up signify something in terms of the meaning conveyed? If the camera-person takes a shot from below, thus producing an unflattering image of, say, a politician, does it affect the meaning (interpretation) that recipients attach to that image and, ultimately, their image of the politician?

Among codes of form one could also list *optic-acoustic effects*. These make up the *substance* of the image. Does the choice of film or video type, the choice between black-and-white or colour film, synchronised or nonsynchronised sound influence the meaning that the communicator conveys? Could the substance influence the meaning that viewers will attach to an image and the nature of their aesthetic experience?

5.4.4 The paradigmatic-syntagmatic nature of film

A *paradigm* represents the choices at the communicator's disposal when formulating a message. The *syntagm* is the formulated message/statement/film shot. In language, the smallest semantic unit is the word. To be able to conduct a conversation, words have to be combined into sentences according to certain grammatical rules. Sentences are in turn combined into larger units to form paragraphs, and so on.

In film, the smallest unit of meaning is the (single) shot. In order to tell a story, single shots are combined into scenes and scenes into sequences by means of editing techniques to tell the eventual story. The single shot, as the smallest semantic unit, is only one component of a series of semantic units that convey the eventual meaning of the film. In "formulating" a shot, the director has a choice of paradigms offering different options. The director who wants to take a shot of a man walking down a street has such options as the following: camera distance (e.g. a close-up, a medium shot, a long shot); camera movement (e.g. panning, crane, dolly); filter; and speed.

Choice is therefore a key factor, without which communication would not be possible. In people's daily spoken and written communication they are constantly choosing, albeit often unwittingly. Depending on their communication need(s) (to inform, tell a story, persuade, express emotions, and so on), they choose among a range of words and syntactic constructions. The same thing happens in film, where the communicator's means of expression include not only words but also images.

In film we can furthermore distinguish between three paradigmatic *articulations of meaning*:

- First articulation of meaning: the director's choice of what to represent (the eventual *content* of the image)
- Second articulation of meaning: the way the director presents or portrays the chosen content (camera point of view as a means of creating *form*)
- Third articulation of meaning: the way in which the director combines single shots into sequences and scenes (editing as a means of creating *form*).

The decisions at each of these levels of articulation influence and determine the eventual meaning conveyed in and by an image.

Levels of meaning

For purposes of analysis, film semiotics distinguish between five *levels of meaning* in film:

- Topic, theme and story
- Presentation of topic, theme and story
- Filming and editing of topic, theme, story
- Sound
- Optic-acoustic level.

Together, these five levels constitute the meaning that is conveyed. The level of the *topic/theme/story* is concerned exclusively with the narrative and/or topic and the narrative structures it contains. Here one would look at literary factors such as exposition, crisis, climax, denouement, characterisation and the like. *Presentation* relates to the previously mentioned nonfilmic codes such as director's style, acting, costuming, lighting and composition. *Filming and editing* concerns filmic codes – camera point of view and editing. At the level of *sound* there are, for instance, music and sound effects to reinforce a particular meaning. The *optic-acoustic* level has to do with the substance of the image (the material of which it is composed, e.g. type of film stock, colour, synchronised sound, and so on), and the way this contributes to the overall meaning conveyed.

5.4.5 Communicative possibilities of film

On the strength of the qualities outlined above, film has the following *communicative possibilities*:

- it portrays and represents;
- it acts for both the communicator and the recipient (viewer) as a means of observation and experience;
- it acts for both the communicator and the recipient as a means of expression and visualisation (cf. Peters 1974).

Film can portray and represent reality both factually (documentary) and fictionally (feature films). In the second case a reality first has to be created before it can be presented, filmed and structured with the aid of the camera and editing techniques. Because directors have certain techniques at their disposal (such as close-ups and microscopic techniques), they can show things which people cannot observe with the naked eye, such as the germination of a seed. In this sense the electronic image is a means of observation.

At the same time it enables people to observe events that they could not have witnessed personally – a bomb explosion in London, a demonstration in Soweto, a sporting event in Cape Town. Feature films, again, offer people experiences that they could never have in their own lives. In this sense film and television are a means of experience.

As a means of expression and visualisation, images in the first place permit communicators to express themselves through images rather than through verbal (linguistic) signs. Consequently, film – like the plastic arts, music, literature and the theatre – are art forms that require the communicator to have some expertise in handling the medium. As a means of visualisation, images can, through editing techniques, express abstractions.

5.4.6 Communication functions in an image

Another aspect emphasised in film semiotics is the linguist Roman Jakobson's (1960) six communication functions. They were first applied to film by the Dutch linguist JM Peters (1974). The functions are as follows:

- a *referential function*
- a *phatic function*
- an *expressive function*
- a *conative function*
- a *poetic function*
- a *metalinguistic function.*

Referential functions of the messsage are those that refer to the theme or topic of the communication. They concern the content or topic matter of the image – people, fauna, flora, objects and the like.

The phatic functions are those that seek to establish contact by capturing the attention and fascinating the recipient. It could include the size of the object portrayed, colour, composition or dramatic camera point of view.

The communicator expresses each message in a distinctive way. That is, the topic matter or content of the message is formulated in a particular way. The expressive functions refer to this formulation which, in the case of film, entails camera work and editing.

Conative functions of an image are those which are designed to persuade the recipient to accept and share the communicator's point of view – in effect, those things which make an impression on the viewer. These could include anything from the subject and the story to the acting, camera work and *mise-en-scène.*

If the aesthetic qualities of an image emerge clearly, the poetic functions will address the recipient. The viewer is explicitly conscious of the formulation (the way the communicator uses the camera and editing techniques).

A message is always formulated and conveyed by means of various sign systems. A newspaper predominantly uses written language, although it also contains photographs. Film does not rely exclusively on images to convey messages but also makes use of spoken and even written language (consider the use of subtitles). Dialogue comprises not only spoken language, but also gestures, facial expressions, eye contact and the like. In the case of newspapers, the photographs represent the metalinguistic functions of the message; in film communication these are the language and in dialogue the nonverbal behaviour. We could describe metalinguistic functions as those *things* used by the communicator to communicate more intelligibly.

None of these functions occur in isolation. They overlap and can only be separated for analytical purposes.

Summary

To summarise this part of the unit, the following: The above aspects of film semiotics have been dealt with by different authors in different ways, ranging from practical applications and intricate analyses, to abstract treatments on theoretical and philosophical levels. What they all have in common is a concern about the formal qualities of film – what constitutes a film and how this enables a film to produce and convey meaning.

The main value of the semiotic activity in film theory is that it succeeded in "... pushing film theory beyond the naturalist [realist – PJF] fallacy" (Easthope 1993:7). The one thing film semiotics made clear is that film, although it might be a mechanical and electronic reproduction of reality and although it is in its very nature iconic, is also symbolic and thus arbitrary. Although its raw material (reality and the selection of images from reality) is iconic, film as a sign, is constructed by its communicators. Such constructions always imply interpretation against the background of the communicator's culture, experience and knowledge. In the same way, the viewer interprets and understands film against the background of his/her culture, knowledge and experience. The signifier is never closed in the sense of having a fixed meaning. The signifier (image) is open to many interpretations and possibilities. This makes the notion of film being a realistic portrayal of either physical or mental reality, a fallacy.

5.5 CONTEMPORARY FILM THEORY

5.5.1 Introduction

Whereas in classic film theory the emphasis was on the relationship between film and reality, and in the first phase of film semiotics on the formal qualities of film, the emphasis in contemporary theory is on the role of the *subject* (viewer) and on film as an *ideological practice*.

According to Lapsley and Westlake (1988:32–66), film semiotics is no longer concerned with the formal qualities of an image or even with the nature of film as an iconic sign, but with Lacan's conception of meaning as produced in the exchange between subject and a set of signifiers. In the tradition of poststructuralism, film semiotics has also accepted that meaning is not at all the stable relationship between signifier and referent presumed by De Saussure (1959). What fixes meaning is the punctuation of the signifying chain by the action of the subject.

This "new" insight based on the linguist Emile Benveniste's contention that the analysis of discourse can no longer afford to ignore the role of the subject within signification (because language is deeply marked by subjectivity), has, according to Lapsley and Westlake (1988), forced film semioticians like Christian Metz (1974), Umberto Eco (1979) and Stephen Heath (1981) to re-evaluate their former writings on the nature of film as a language, and to follow Julia Kristeva (1974) in her call for a theory of the speaking subject constituted within language. The emphasis is thus on the *relation* between the viewer and film, between text and subject and the text's power to determine the subject's response.

Watching a film necessarily entails adopting the viewer position that is inscribed in the text, in other words the position the communicator (producer/director) wants the subject to take on a specific topic. In accordance with this dictum the second (present) phase of the "new" film semiotics is, according to Lapsley and Westlake (1988), concerned with the following question:

How do the codes in a film (especially the use of the camera and montage) position the subject to take a specific view on a topic, for instance on romance, corruption, crime, sex and such like? To answer this question, semiotic analysis has shifted away from the text as a system (the analysis of specific aspects in a text, such as signs) towards the text as a process; away from the "*object cinema*" towards the "*operation cinema*" and into a theoretical discussion and analysis of the ideological nature and role of film.

According to Lapsley and Westlake (1988), semiotics has, in its fixation on the formal attributes of texts, risked blocking an understanding of how cinema is related to other practices as well as the more general relations between signification, ideology and history. Semiotics itself ran the risk of becoming an obstacle rather than the road to the analysis of the text's political functioning. To circumvent this danger, a conception of film as a specific *signifying practice* was proposed.

Signifying indicates the recognition of film as a system or series of systems of meaning, of film as an articulation of a specific meaning. The term practice entails that film is not some neutral medium transmitting a pre-given ideology, but is the active production of meaning. The term also carries the further implication that, since film produces meanings, the question of the positioning of the viewer enters into the analysis of film.

As a specific signifying practice, film is now not studied in terms of *langue* and *parole* but of *discourse*, thereby implying a subject. Under such a conception, cinema is furthermore viewed as one of a number of "machines" generating ideology: through its mechanism "... the viewer is moved, and related as subject in the process and images of that movement" (Lapsley & Westlake 1988:33). Film is seen as a work of *semiosis*; a work that produces effects of meaning and perception, self-images and subject positions for all those involved, makers and viewers (1988:33–66).

It is against this background that the work of more contemporary theorists such as Stephen Heath (1981), Paul Willemen (1978) and Colin MacCabe (1978/1979) and theories concerning film as ideology as well as the later discussed feminist criticism and psychoanalytical theories must be seen.

For the purpose of this discussion we only summarise some of the assumptions of these approaches in contemporary film theory. We mainly rely on the works of Lapsley and Westlake (1988) and Easthope (1993).

5.5.2 Ideological criticism

The fact that film is a construction against the background of the culture, experience and knowledge of both the communicator (producer/director/artists) and the subject (viewer), places it within the realm of ideology and *ideological criticism*. Our culture, experience and knowledge underlie our view of life, of reality and of humanity and cannot be separated from existential and political beliefs and orientations. In this sense each and every film can be viewed as an ideological construct.

Although this may be a deterministic argument, every film, whether it is a drama, a thriller, a war movie, a comedy or even a musical, embodies the communicator's interpretation of the theme, topic and content against the background of his/her culture, knowledge and experience, and thus ideology (the way in which we see and understand something).

In the same way, the meaning(s) subscribed to a film by a viewer is ideological in the sense that the viewer brings to the movie an understanding based on his/her culture, knowledge and experience.

With this as point of departure, central questions in contemporary film theory and analysis emphasising ideology are as follows:

- How does *mainstream cinema* contribute to maintaining the existing social structure?
- What is the appropriate form for an *oppositional cinema* that will break the ideological hold of mainstream cinema and transform film from a commodity to an instrument for social change?

Mainstream cinema is usually associated with and seen as the product of a dominant production industry in a society; the productions of Hollywood, for example. Oppositional cinema sets itself the goal of analysing and interpreting dominant ideology.

For instance, in South Africa, film production, for decades, was dominated by the mainstream cinema of a few production companies set in the mode of apartheid ideology. Since the eighties these films were questioned by so-called oppositional cinema or alternative films, such as *Jobman* and *Taxi to Soweto*, which set itself the goal of questioning apartheid ideology.

Some definitions

Ideology: According to its popular definition, ideology refers to ideas, attitudes, values, belief systems, or interpretive and conceptual frameworks held by members of a particular social group or culture (Geuss 1981:5). Significantly, our own ideology is seldom if ever recognised as being ideological. Ideology is thus used to describe a system of beliefs held by others (not by ourselves nor those agreeing with us), which is regarded as fundamentally untrue. Ideology thus refers to the assumptions through which groups or societies conceptualise the values and beliefs that enable them to operate effectively (Dupre 1983:240), and can be broadly defined as the total system of beliefs, which selectively provide limited perceptions of reality. In this sense every human group, society or culture has an ideology (Lemon 1991).

Mainstream cinema: By mainstream cinema we mean (1) films produced by the big studios, (2) the so-called big box-office movies and thus popular films, and (3) films produced against the background of capitalist considerations and thus with the emphasis on commercial success.

Oppositional cinema: This refers to those films that challenge the underlying ideology of mainstream cinema. Ideology here means both production practices as well as the political and existential content of films. Whereas, for instance in South Africa, the majority of films for years were part of the hegemony of apartheid and reflected this ideology in their content and form, and whereas these films were produced by a few so-called big production houses, oppositional South African film (also referred to as alternative film) began to question this ideology.

Subject: The concept subject can have a political meaning, a grammatical meaning or a philosophical meaning, implying the thinking recipient. We use the concept in terms of its last meaning. The political meaning relates to the citizen as a subject of the state. It implies, within the context of Marxist ideology, the subject's lack of freedom of the state. The grammatical meaning refers to the subject of a sentence (as in subject-verb-predicate). The notion of the thinking subject is the site of the consciousness. Against the background of poststructuralism, the recipient (viewer/reader) is no longer seen as passive, but using all his/her senses in the interpretation of a text.

For a further discussion of what ideology is, Althusser's theory, and so forth, you are referred to Unit 9 (Ideology and the media) and Unit 11 (Media and culture) in Volume 1 of this book. Here it suffices to say that ideology theory (as discussed in the above mentioned units) has resulted in numerous theoretical studies of the ideological nature of film. It produced numerous analyses of specific films with the aim of showing how the political-economic structure of a given society at a given point in time, determines to a large extent the form and content of that society's films. Every film may be interpreted as an ideological statement, because it was determined by, and hence reflects, the dominant ideology of the society that produced it.

For instance, in South Africa a number of studies were done to show how apartheid influenced South African film and how apartheid (as an ideology) determined the content and form of films. Even the so-called *alternative films* of the late eighties and early nineties, such as *Taxi to Soweto* (1991), were analysed as ideological constructs of apartheid ideology (cf. Tomaselli 1989; Botha & Van Aswegen 1992).

Against this theoretical background, ideological analysis of film sets itself the goal to analyse the relationship between a given film, its society and the ideology of that society, en route to determining the specific ways that the film either supports or attacks the dominant ideology of the society that produced it. For instance, critics claim that Hollywood presented and still presents an incredibly distorted view of the world, masquerading as truth. Most Hollywood films, they assert, do not prompt the audience to question what it is perceiving, or even to think about it. Instead, the audience is encouraged to react passively and lose itself in the story of the film or television production, while concomitantly accepting the purveyed capitalist and conservative dogma. Hollywood is not about to question the society of which it is a part, because it is an industry that literally profits heavily from that very specific society (cf. Stromgren & Norden 1984:266–267).

The main criticism against ideological film criticism and theory is that it tends to be biased and subjective. The very nature of ideological criticism is to downplay or ignore the artistic and technical aspects of film; to ignore the complexities of film production and of film's audiences, in favour of questioning its ideological stance.

We can conclude by saying that film theorists, critics and analysts who emphasise the ideological nature and content of films, warn the public that film is not an innocent form of entertainment. To the contrary, the fact that it is usually produced by big production studios operating in terms of capitalist criteria, or otherwise produced and/or subsidised by government-controlled agencies with the purpose of propagating certain political ideas and values, makes it a powerful ideological instrument. In terms of Althusser's vocabulary it is a powerful Ideological State Apparatus. The danger with this form of analysis and criticism is its heavy-handedness and polemical simplification, with a simplistic application of the concept class struggle to the work of art (cf. Konigsberg 1987:204).

5.5.3 Psychoanalysis

The *psychoanalytical theories* on the *subject/object* relationship (object = in this case a film) in film communication originate from the French theorist Jacques Lacan's adaptation of Sigmund Freud's theory on the unconscious psychological structures that operate in man. These structures are said to characterise the acquisition of the self-image and motivate behaviour. (For a complete overview of Lacan and Freud's psycho-analytical theories and its application in film theory, see Lapsley & Westlake 1988:67–104. See also the discussion on psychoanalysis in Unit 10 of this volume.)

The Freudian and Lacanian view on the workings of the unconscious, the acquisition of a self-image and the enquiry into the symbolic opened up new perspectives on the subject/object relationship in film communication.

In the first place, this approach makes a meaningful shift from the formalistic study of film as a discrete entity on the screen to a deep contemplation on the relationship between the film (object) and the viewer (subject). In this regard, there is an important emphasis on the concept "*absence*" and the idea that the filmic signifier is an absent signifier, and therefore an *imaginary* signifier.

Imaginary signifier means, among other things, that besides the fact that a motion picture, especially, is a product of the imagination for the imagination, what one sees on the screen is essentially absent (thus, the signifier is absent). In other words, the actors, the events, in short, the depicted content is physically absent and exists merely as light and sound on celluloid; that exists only in and through the camera and projector signals, which are themselves empty forms that have no existence outside of the total *filmic apparatus*.

In the second place, the psychoanalytic perspective initiates inspection, albeit of a speculative nature, into the unconscious processes at play during the perception of a film, and upon which the filmic apparatus focuses. Put differently: the filmic apparatus directs itself towards imitating processes of the human unconscious.

Filmic apparatus refers to a complex interwoven structure of which the viewer forms a central part, and which includes the following:

- the technical nature of film communication, including the effects that may be obtained with the camera, editing, sound, lighting, projection, and so on (the filmic design which is implemented with technical apparatus);
- the conditions for the showing of a film (dark theatre, filmic circumstances of the viewer, size of screen, projector, and so on);

- the image in itself (or the image as text) and its inherent quality, for example, the iconic and mimetic nature of the image that leads to the illusion of reality;
- the mental processes of the viewer.

In the third place, the psychoanalytical approach ascribes the viewer's enjoyment (and therefore the popularity of film as a mass communication medium) to the fact that it succeeds in, and is tuned into, reactivating the deep and universal structural processes of the human psyche in an enjoyable way.

To clarify this assumption, psychoanalytical film theory theorises about, among other things, approximately five explanations for the viewer's enjoyment of film, and how the filmic apparatus is tuned into bringing about this enjoyment through identification. The explanations are that:

- viewers identify with their action of perception;
- viewers identify with imagined emotions;
- there is a correspondence between viewers' experience of a film and a dream experience;
- there is a correspondence between the perception of a film and voyeurism; and that
- the viewing of a film is a form of fetishism.

These five explanations are discussed more fully below.

Some definitions

Fetish: A pathological and sexually determined attachment to objects associated with a sexual object.

Voyeur: A person who obtains sexual gratification from observing others' sexual actions or organs.

Psychoanalysis: A therapeutic method of treating mental disorders by investigating the interaction of conscious and unconscious elements in the mind and bringing repressed fears and conflicts into the conscious mind (cf. Allen 1990).

Oedipus: In the Greek mythology Oedipus was the son of Laïus, king of Thebes, and of Jacosta. Laïus was warned by an oracle that he would perish at the hands of his son. Oedipus was brought up in Corinth. When he had grown up Oedipus was told by the Delphic oracle not to return home, as he must inevitably be the murderer of his father. He consequently fled from Corinth and on his way to Thebes slew Laïus in a quarrel, being ignorant of Laïus's identity. Oedipus then delivered the country from the Sphinx and was rewarded with the hand of Jacosta (his mother), by whom he had four children. As a punishment for this incest, Thebes was devastated by a plague. The oracle declared that the country could only by saved if the murderer of Laius was expelled. Oedipus made inquiries and discovered to his horror that he was the guilty man. His mother/wife Jacosta hanged herself and Oedipus, having put out his eyes, left Thebes. The story of Oedipus is the topic of many dramas and was set forth by the classic Greek dramatists Euripides, Aeschylus and Sophocles.

Oedipus complex: The German psychoanalyst Sigmund Freud believed that the causes of psychoneurotic disorders are generally found to lie in early emotional relationships with the parents. The typical form of this relationship is called the *Oedipus complex* in the case of men and the *Electra complex* in the case of women, and concerns the strong emotional attachment to the parent of the opposite sex and jealousy and hatred of the parent of the same sex. Both the love and the hate are normally unconscious and the conscious attitudes may be very different. The unwillingness of a patient to recognise this source of his/her troubles is attributed by Freud to repression: the active banishment of the underlying cause for psychoneurotic behaviour from the conscious mind into the region of the unconscious. The cure depends on the removal of this repression and the consequent emergence of the repressed into the conscious mind, where it can be dealt with in a rational manner.

Identification with the action of perception

Film presents images of something that is absent. Instead of the presence of actual actors, décor sets, theatrical property, and so forth, such as one would find in a play theatre, the film screen confronts the viewer with a world that is physically absent and exists merely of light and sound impressions (cf. Lapsley & Westlake 1988: 81).

The outstanding quality of film is therefore *absence*. This implies that the filmic signifier (what a person looks at on the screen, e.g. a man or woman performing an action) is not there – only the light and sound impressions, and the things projected by the mechanisms of a projector, are present. Film thus involves the viewer in a play of absence/presence.

The *presence* of a rich visual image on the screen and the *absence* of what the image refers to or conveys, defines the fundamental nature of film communication.

The question is now: as the signifier is merely an imaginary signifier, what does the viewer *identify* with during the showing of a film? The French film semiologist, Christian Metz (1982) argues that although the viewer identifies with the fictional character(s) or star(s), and although such identification is part of the enjoyment of the film, it is a *secondary identification*. Prior to this secondary identification, however, *primary identification* must occur. This enables the viewer to identify with the projected image on the screen.

Metz argues that viewers identify with their action of perception. His explanation (cf. also Lapsley & Westlake 1988:83) is as follows:

- Firstly, viewers are always aware that they are in a theatre and in the presence of something that is imaginary and absent.
- Secondly, viewers are also aware of their own absence on the screen; that they find themselves outside that screen in a position of *all-seeing mastery*.
- Thirdly, viewers are aware of the conditions for the viewing of a film, namely, that the film has no existence outside of the view as a present seeing, hearing subject in the auditorium.

This consciousness of absence, of all-seeing mastery and of the non-existence of the film outside of the viewer constitutes primary identification and enables viewers to identify with their own actions of seeing and hearing as an act of perception – as a kind of *transcendental subject* that precedes all that happens on the screen.

Stephen Heath (1981:120) states it perhaps more simply by saying that:

> ... the apparatus of look and identification institutes the viewer in the totalising *security of looking at looking* (own emphasis)

while John Ellis (1982:44) adds that

> identification with the cinematic apparatus involves the *fantasy of self as a pure perceiving being* (own emphasis).

Primary identification (that is, identification with the action of perception) is powerfully *reinforced* by the viewer's simultaneous identification with the camera, whose monocular perspective approaches the quality of almost godlike omniscience. The *viewer is the camera* who actively directs his or her vision towards certain objects, but who at the same time passively receives the results of this perception.

Identification with imagined emotions

A second reason for viewers' enjoyment, according to the psychoanalytical perspective, is that they do not experience real emotions with which they may identify, but rather experience and identify with *imagined emotions*.

Viewers' experience of film shows clearly that they are or can be moved by it: they can, for example, feel sexually aroused, aggressive, compassionate, experience heartache or joy, and so on. But are these emotions genuine? It is also a fact that viewers can indeed watch films where they are confronted with unpleasant experiences like grief, death, disappointment and failure. The question is: is the viewer's grief, anxiety, hate and anguish real?

The French philosopher Sartre (1969:237), who was also concerned with the relationship between emotions and imagination, reasons that an object that exists only in and for the imagination is incapable of evoking genuine emotion. The imagined object (such as a film) is unreal and can therefore not be the cause of a real effect. If someone presents you with a delicious meal, he argues, and your mouth begins to water, it is not the suggestion of the food that prompts the secretion in the mouth, but the already existing feeling of hunger. If a pin-up picture sexually arouses a viewer, it is not the pin-up that leads to the arousal, but an already existing feeling of sexual desire.

The world of film, too, is an unreal world (imagined signifier) that is given "life" by viewers themselves, with their own feelings. Furthermore, the imagined characters, things and events on the screen resemble so closely real people, things and events – real people did in fact appear in front of the camera – that viewers can easily conceive that these imagined people, things and events touch them emotionally.

In reality then, the process runs in two stages:

- Viewers colour the images with their own subjective feelings, or project themselves into the image; and
- because these images so closely resemble real objects, they impress themselves on viewers who can identify with the feelings that the images portray.

However, this identification is also an identification with imagined emotions. Viewers do not actually experience grief over a dying heroine, for example, but imagine sorrow within themselves. In other words, viewers pretend that they are filled with grief. In short, although viewers make believe that the actions on the screen are real, they know throughout that this is not reality.

Although viewers get emotionally involved, they are aware that theirs is a limited experience and that, should they wish it, they can distance themselves from the events unfolding on the screen. Viewers know that they will not be seriously hurt by the emotions that they feel during this time (e.g. lingering heartache and pain) nor sustain persisting feelings of happiness or enjoyment. The crux of the experience is that viewers, although they may become emotionally involved, nevertheless retain a distance.

This *distance* between the viewer and the events on the screen means that viewers never become completely part of the action – they remain, so to speak, safe. The film provides the chance for viewers to acknowledge the loves and heartbreaks of the characters and the events in which they find themselves, *outside* of themselves and others. This always occurs outside of the self, and the viewer is never a participant, but always an observer – essentially, a spy, a quasi-voyeur. For the voyeur, to spy or peep means enjoyment, satisfaction and the experience of a sublime state.

Dream experience

A third reason for viewers' enjoyment is that the perception of a film corresponds to people's "perception" and experience of their own dreams. In both dream and film, viewers have no hold on the image itself.

As in film, the imaginary world of the dream offers viewers no perceptual freedom. Dreamers, in an imaginary world of danger cannot think "Do I have a gun with me?", for as soon as the thought appears, the gun is immediately there. Sartre (1969) calls this the *fatality* of dream events. In film, events have the same fatality – viewers cannot do anything to change them, and they are not free in terms of what is shown to them. Another similarity between the dream and the film is that viewers can see the imagined events from a different standpoint (albeit the director's chosen standpoint): the all-seeing or all-knowing outsider who perceives events from an external position, and from the perspective of the subject who performs the actions. A typical example is as follows:

In a dream, I arrive just too late at the station to catch the last train. Rather distraught, I ask the stationmaster if there are no more trains that leave that evening – I have to be at my destination the following morning. The stationmaster answers that there are no more trains as it is New Year's Eve, and very few trains are running. "Oh, yes", I answer, "I didn't think of that".

The significance of this is that I, who am myself the maker of the dream, am also the subject in the dream and who is not aware that there are fewer trains running as a result of it being New Year's Eve; however, the stationmaster, who is also the product of *my* dream, is aware of this (cf. Peters 1976:12).

The same occurs in the film experience. For example, viewers see the murderer carefully turn the doorknob; next they see the unsuspecting victim in the bed. Both the murderer and the victim know less than the viewers. But now the man in the bed wakes up; he heard a noise; he grabs his revolver and creeps to the door where he takes up his position. He waits tensely; the viewers wait anxiously with him (and identify with the victim's tension). Consequently, the viewers do not see that in the meantime the murderer has come in through the window. They do not see because they, with the victim, feel for that moment of tension like the victim – and yet, viewers do see it as well because they, as viewers and as outsiders, can adopt an all-seeing viewpoint.

The alternation of neutral and subjective camera positions reinforces the character of a film experience. In our example then, viewers see the victim through the keyhole together with the murderer. However, viewers (as the murderer) do not see that a policeman has appeared behind the murderer, while as neutral spectators they can indeed see this. The continual displacement or interchange of the viewers' perspective, and the fact that they constantly share an emotional life with other characters, accentuates the association between dream and film.

In spite of this illusion of *all-knowingness* and *omniscience*, or rather because of it, viewers are caught up in a process of alienation and distancing: a process that shows correlations with *voyeurism* and *fetishism*, as mentioned below in the last two reasons for viewers' enjoyment.

Voyeurism

From a psychoanalytic perspective, Metz (1982) relates the preceding arguments to *voyeurism* and *fetishism*. He also uses the imagined signifier as a point of departure in this regard. Metz begins with the notion that viewers' experience of film images can be related to two basic needs: *scopophilia* or the need to see, and the need to hear.

These two drives are distinguished from other human drives by their reliance on absence, not only in the sense that these drives give rise to a fruitless desire to see and hear that (the original completed self-image) which can never be regained, but also in the sense that these needs can only be satisfied if there is a distance between the subject and the object.

Although maintaining distance is a diagnostic characteristic of all the arts, film differs from the other arts in that the object from which the distance is maintained is effectively absent. In drama, opera and ballet, the physical-being togetherness ensures a sort of assumed complicity in what is happening on the stage: the viewer's voyeurism is paired with the artist's exhibitionism. Contrary to this, the artist in film communication is present (during the making of a film) while the viewer is absent; and the viewer is present (during the screening) when the artist is absent. The reciprocal recognition of the existence of the other is less clear, even absent: a characteristic of film communication that is further strengthened by the fact that film actors seldom look directly into the camera, an act that would confront viewers with their own voyeurism.

This voyeurism involves looking at something that allows itself to be looked at without presenting itself to be seen. Metz (1982) believes that the enjoyment that viewers obtain from this is related to people's unconscious yet fundamental observation of their parents' copulation, which determines the nature and structure of voyeurism as such, and which shows clear correlation with the viewer's situation and the act of looking. Various characteristics of film communication emphasise this relationship: the viewer sits in the dark in front of a lighted screen – a situation that is nearly like peeping through a keyhole; although viewers are part of an audience, they retain their individuality and separateness; actors are neither aware of nor acknowledge the viewer's existence; and, finally, the events of the film unfold in a place where viewers are both closed in and inaccessible. All these characteristics make the experience of voyeurism in the film theatre one of "trangression".

Fetishism

In the last reason (for the purposes of this discussion) provided by Metz (1982) for the enjoyment experience, fetishism is the topic discussed. Like the filmic signifier itself, this mental process is related to the interaction between absence and presence.

Psychoanalytically, fetishism is defined as follows: anxiety is created due to the child's becoming conscious of sexual differences and the accompanying awareness that the mother does not possess a phallus. To ward off this anxiety and the threat that it presents, the child rejects the existence of sexual differences and so with it the mother's "defect". The result is a contradiction: "I know a lot, but nevertheless ..." The child replaces this "defect" with another object, one that both fills the gap created by that loss and denies that anything is missing – but which, by its very presence, acknowledges this absence. When this happens, rejection takes the form of fetishism.

Metz (1982) argues that something similar occurs in the viewer (subject)/film (object) relationship. Viewers know that what they watch is fiction, but they nevertheless believe that it is real – indeed, their enjoyment depends on this belief. Film communication thus depends on the fact that viewers know one thing and, at the same time, completely believe the opposite. This is the exact structure of rejection and fetishism. Further, as the fetishist rejects an object and yet in so doing acknowledges its existence, so the film apparatus, in this case the camera eye, becomes in itself a kind of substitute for the absence of the filmic signifier. The camera shot confirms the presence of that which is absent and, in so doing, emphasises the fact of its absence. The technical ingenuity of the film lies precisely in the fact that the absent is made convincingly present so that the viewer's absence is almost, but never completely, forgotten.

If an awareness of absence is not maintained, viewers cannot appreciate what is present. Viewers' enjoyment depends, as in classical fetishism, on a simultaneous awareness of what is absent and what is present. The fetishist derives enjoyment from the object that replaces the rejected thing; the viewer finds enjoyment in the awareness of the gap that exists between imagined presence and actual absence.

The question "How does the film produce enjoyment and the desire for more?" is answered according to a psychoanalytical perspective as follows: in film communication, attribution of meaning is based on and is ascribed to a process of absence. The image, which is in itself an imagined signifier (impulses in light and sound), steps forward to fill this absence, but cannot ever completely succeed in doing this. The viewer unconsciously experiences this gap between absence and presence as a constant defect, which evokes a continuous need to see more.

5.5.4 Feminist criticism

Related to ideological film theory and criticism the key assumptions in *feminist criticism* is that film and television are products of a sexist society, and that they frequently present biased and stereotyped depictions of women's roles.

In general (cf. Stromgren & Norden 1984:267–268), feminist critics are concerned with three broad areas:

- the ways women have been depicted and treated in film throughout the years;
- the qualities and concerns of films made by women;
- the ways that women in society have been affected by the sex roles presented in film.

One of the main critiques is that men are often presented in films as the people in and of history, who shape the destinies of both their own lives and the societies they inhabit. Women, on the other hand, are typically in supportive roles, and they are presented as eternal, unchanging and without much historical significance.

Following these fundamental assumptions, feminist critics classify women appearing in for instance American films up till the mid-thirties, in one or more of the following categories:

- the *Mother* (whose nurturing, selfless image offends many feminist critics),
- the *Virginal*, unworldly women,
- the streetwise *Whore* or Vamp, and
- for lack of a better term, *Window Dressing*.

Most women appearing in the immediate postwar period of American cinema could generally be classified as one of two types: the *malehungry* woman who desired nothing more than marriage, children and a clean suburban home; and the *strong-willed*, independent woman who by the end of the film was shown to be neurotic, psychotic, or both (cf. Stromgren & Norden 1984:267–268).

According to feminist critics it is clear that Hollywood, along with many other postwar American institutions, sought to discourage women from acting in an independent fashion. Little had changed until the 1970s since when women are portrayed as more assertive.

In feminist criticism it is argued that films are products of a sexist society, and that they frequently present biased and stereotyped depictions of women's roles.

For a further exposition of feminism and feminist media theory see Unit 12 in Volume 1 of this book.

Summary

We began this unit by asking the question and providing some answers to the question: What is film theory? This was followed by a discussion of classic film theory and the distinction between expressionists and realist film theory. We briefly introduced you to the *auteur* theory whereafter some of the main propositions about film as a language (film semiotics) were discussed. The unit then continued with introductory notes about contemporary film theory in which the emphasis moved from a formalist description of film to the ideological nature, working and content of film, an investigation into the nature of the experience of film from a psychoanalytical perspective and feminist film theory.

Research activities

1 Summarise the following theories and describe the differences between them:
   a) establishing-shot theories
   b) medium-shot theories
   c) close-up theories
   d) normative theory
   e) descriptive theory

2 Formulate on the basis of the difference between the theories and the questions asked in them, five of your own questions about the nature, content and form of film and its relation with reality. Apply the questions you have formulated to a recent film you have seen, either on television or in a film theatre.

3 Explain the difference between each of the following areas of film study:
   a) aesthetic film historiography (history writing)
   b) technological film historiography
   c) economic film historiography
   d) social film historiography
   e) classic film historiography
   f) revisionist film historiography

4 Explain the difference between
   a) film criticism
   b) film analysis

5 Design a critical framework for your future viewing of films. Base your framework on the discussion of what film theory is, the different kind of theories and the distinction between film history and film theory. Your framework should consist of at least five points or parameters. For example, are you, in future, going to concentrate your viewing on one or more of the following:
   - the relation between film and social reality
   - the content of a film
   - the form of a film
   - the portrayal of a specific group
   - the industry responsible for the production of the film and the influence of this industry on the content and form of the film, or
   - any of the other topics and/or parameters discussed in the preceding pages.

6 Write an essay in which you give an overview of the expressionist and formalist film theories. Apply the underlying assumptions to a film you have seen recently and which you would describe as expressionist in terms of the underlying assumptions of expressionist film theory.

7 Explain in detail and with reference to his theory of conflict montage, Eisenstein's formalist film theory.

8 Explain V I Pudovkin's theory of construction montage.

9 Write an essay on realist film theory. Substantiate your discussion with examples from a recent film you have seen and which you would describe as realist in terms of the underlying assumptions of realist film theory.

10 Summarise the *auteur* theory in terms of the following: its relation to realist film theory; the origin of the theory; concerns about the collective nature of film production; its emphasis on the theme and style in a director's work; Sarris' ranking of directors; the value of the theory and criticism against the theory.

11 Design a framework for the analysis of the work of a director of your choice. Base your framework on Sarris' distinction between the technical competence of a director, his/her identity as stylist and the director's ability to convey an own interpretation.

12 Explain with your own examples taken from a film(s), the following semiotic concepts:
   a) film as a sign
   b) denotation and connotation in film
   c) codes in film

d) the levels of meaning in film
e) the communicative functions of film

13 Describe the assumptions of ideological criticism. Apply them to a film of your choice.

14 Summarise the psychoanalytical approach to the questions why and how people experience film as a pleasure. Pay attention to the following:
- identification with the act of perception
- identification with imagined emotions
- film and dream experience
- the comparison of the film experience and voyeurism
- the comparison of the film experience and fetishism

Further reading

Allen, R. & Gomery, D. 1985. *Film history: theory and practice*. New York: Knopf.
Andrew, D. 1984. *Concepts in film theory*. Oxford: Oxford University Press.
Bordwell, D & Thompson, K. 1997. *Film art: an introduction*. 5th edition. New York; McGraw-Hill.
Botha, M & Van Aswegen, A. 1992. *Images of South Africa: the rise of the alternative film*. Pretoria: Human Sciences Research Council.
Easthope, A (ed). 1993. *Contemporary film theory*. London: Longman.
Lapsley, R & Westlake, M. 1988. *Film theory: an introduction*. Manchester: Manchester University Press.
Nelmes, J (ed). 1996. *An introduction to film studies*. London: Routledge.
Tomaselli, K. 1989. *The cinema of apartheid: race and class in South African film*. Sandton: Radix.

Bibliography

Allen, R (ed). 1990. *The concise Oxford dictionary of current English*. 8th edition. Oxford: Clarendon.
Allen, R & Gomery, D. 1985. *Film history: theory and practice*. New York: Knopf.
Althusser, L. 1971. *Lenin and philosophy and other essays*, translated by B Brewster. New York: Monthly Review.
Andrew, D. 1976. *The major film theories: an introduction*. London: Oxford University Press.
Andrew, D. 1984. *Concepts in film theory*. Oxford: Oxford University Press.
Arnheim, R. 1933. *Film as art*. Berkeley, CA: University of California Press.
Balazs, B. 1970. *Theory of film: character and growth of a new art*. New York: Dover.
Barthes, R. 1977. *Image, music, text*. Glasgow: Fontana.
Bazin, A. 1967. *What is cinema?* Volume 1. Berkeley, CA: University of California Press.
Bordwell, D & Thompson, K. 1980. *Film art: an introduction*. Reading, MA: Addison-Wesley.
Bordwell, D. 1989. *Making meaning. Inference and rhetoric in the interpretation of cinema*. Cambridge: Harvard University Press.
Botha, M & Van Aswegen, A. 1992. *Beelde van Suid-Afrika: 'n alternatiewe rolprentoplewing*. Pretoria: Raad vir Geesteswetenskaplike Navorsing.
Caughie, J (ed). 1981. *Theories of authorship: a reader*. London: Routledge & Kegan Paul.

Clarke, S, Seidler, VJ, McDonnel, K, Robins, K & Lovell, T. 1980. *One-dimensional Marxism. Althusser and the politics of culture*. London: Allison & Busby.
Cook, P (ed). 1985. *The cinema book*. London: British Film Institute.
De Putter, J. 1991. Theorievorming rond de filmkritiek, in *Filmkunde: een inleiding*, edited by P Bosma, Heerlen: Open Universiteit.
De Saussure, F. 1959. *A course in general linguistics*. New York: Philosophical Library.
De Saussure, F. 1981. *Course in general linguistics*. London: Fontana/Collins.
Dupre, L. 1983. *Marx's social critique of culture*. New Haven: Yale University Press.
Easthope, A (ed). 1993. *Contemporary film theory*. London: Longman.
Eberwein, R. 1979. *A viewer's guide to film theory and criticism*. Metuchen, NJ: Scarecrow.
Eco, U. 1979. *A theory of semiotics*. Bloomington: Indiana University Press.
Eidsvik, C. 1978. *Cineliteracy. Film among the arts*. New York: Random House.
Ellis, J. 1982. *Visible fictions. Cinema, television, video*. London: Routledge & Kegan Paul.
Fiske, J. 1987. British cultural studies and television, in *Channels of discourse. Television and contemporary criticism*, edited by RC Allen. London: Methuen.
Flitterman-Lewis, S. 1987. Psychoanalysis, film and television, in *Channels of discourse. Television and contemporary criticism*, edited by RC Allen. London: Methuen.
Fourie, PJ. 1983. *Beeldkommunikasie. Kultuurkritiek, ideologiese kritiek en 'n inleiding tot die beeldsemiologie*. Johannesburg: McGraw-Hill.
Fourie, PJ. 1988. *Aspects of film and television communication*. Cape Town: Juta.
Fourie, PJ (ed). 1991. *Critical television analyses: an introduction*. Cape Town: Juta.
Fourie, PJ (ed). 1996. *Introduction to communication – course book 3: communication and the production of meaning*. Cape Town: Juta.
Geuss, R. 1981. *The idea of a critical theory. Habermas and the Frankfurt School*. Cambridge: Cambridge University Press.
Giannetti, L. 1972. *Understanding movies*. Englewood Cliffs, NJ: Prentice Hall.
Giannetti, L. 1990. *Understanding movies*. 5th edition. Englewood Cliffs, NJ: Prentice Hall.
Gurevitch, M, Bennett, T, Curran, J & Woollacott, J (eds). 1982. *Culture, society and the media*. London: Methuen.
Gutsche, T. 1972. *The history and social significance of motion pictures in South Africa: 1895–1940*. Cape Town: Howard Timmins.
Hall, S. 1982. The rediscovery of ideology: the return of the repressed in media studies, in *Culture, society and the media*, edited by M Gurevitch, T Bennett, J Curran & J Woollacott. London: Methuen.
Heath, S. 1981. *Questions of cinema*. London: Macmillan.
Hommel, M. 1991. Hartstocht voor film, in *Filmkunde: een inleiding*, edited by P Bosma. Heerlen: Open Universiteit.
Hunter, JE. 1976. Images of woman. *Journal of Social Issues* 32(3):7–17.
Jakobson, R. 1960. Closing statement: linguistics and poetics, in *Style in language*, edited by TA Sebeok. Cambridge, MA: Massachusetts Institute of Technology.
Kaplan, EA. 1990. *Psychoanalysis and cinema*. London: Routledge.
Koch, G. 1982. Why women go to the movies. *Jump Cut* 27:51–53.
Konigsberg, I. 1987. *The complete film dictionary*. New York: Penguin.
Kristeva, J. 1974. The system and the speaking subject. *Times Literary Supplement*, 12 October:1249. 1974.
Lapsley, R & Westlake, M. 1988. *Film theory: an introduction*. Manchester: Manchester University Press.

Lemon, J. 1991. Ideological criticism and analyses, in *Critical television analyses: an introduction*, edited by PJ Fourie. Cape Town: Juta.
Lindsay, V. 1932. *The art of the moving picture*. New York: Liveright.
MacCabe, C. 1978/79. The discursive and the ideological in film – notes on the conditions of political intervention. *Screen* 19(4):35–48.
Mast, G & Cohen, M. 1985. *Film theory and criticism: introductory readings*. New York: Oxford University Press.
Metz, C. 1974. *Film language: a semiotics of the cinema*. New York: Oxford University Press.
Metz, C. 1982. *The imaginary signifier: psychoanalysis and the cinema*. Bloomington: Indiana University Press.
Monaco, J. 1977. *How to read a film. The art, technology, language, history and theory of film and media*. New York: Oxford University Press.
Monaco, J. 1984. *Film. Taal, techniek, geschiedenis*, translated by M Seton & A Van den Bogaard. Antwerpen: Standaard.
Mulvey, L. 1975. Visual pleasure and narrative cinema. *Screen* 16(3):6–18.
Peters, JM. 1972. *Theorie van de audiovisuele communicatie*. Groningen: HD Tjeenk Willink.
Peters, JM. 1974. *Principes van beeldcommunicatie*. Groningen: HD Tjeenk Willink.
Peters, JM. 1976. *Fictioneel beeldamusement. Het amusementskarakter van de bioscoop en televisiefilm*. Leuven: Centrum voor Communicatiewetenschappen.
Peters, JM. 1978. *Semiotiek van de beeld*. Leuven: Centrum voor Communicatiewetenschappen.
Ricoeur, P. 1986. *Lectures on ideology and utopia*. New York: Columbia University.
Sartre, J-P. 1969. *Het imaginaire: fenomenologische psychologie van de verbeelding*. Amsterdam: Meppel.
Sorlin, P. 1980. *The film history: restaging the past*. Oxford: Blackwell.
Stromgren, R & Norden, M. 1984. *Movies: a language in light*. Englewood Cliffs, NJ: Prentice Hall.
Tomaselli, K. 1979. *The South African film industry*. Johannesburg: University of the Witwatersrand.
Tomaselli, K. 1989. *The cinema of apartheid: race and class in South African film*. Sandton: Radix.
White, M. 1987. Ideological analysis and television, in *Channels of discourse. Television and contemporary criticism*, edited by RC Allen. London: Methuen.
Willemen, P. 1978. Notes on subjectivity – on reading "Subjectivity under siege". *Screen* 19(1):45–69.
Wollen, P. 1972. *Signs and meaning in the cinema*. London: Secker & Warburgh.

Part C
Media Audiences

Reception Theory 6

Magriet Pitout

Overview

In this unit we provide a brief overview of important theories of audiences. We then focus on a discussion of reception theory and analysis because this is one of the most prolific new areas of studying audiences and their interpretation of messages. Reception theory as applied to media studies, has it roots both in German reception aesthetics, also called reception theory, and the encoding/decoding model of reception developed by the Centre for Contemporary Cultural Studies (also known as the cultural studies approach). We first explain how the German version of reception theory has been adjusted to study mass media texts by using the conventions of the soap opera genre to illustrate the dialectical relationship between readers and texts. We then discuss the following important themes/issues on the research agenda of the cultural studies approach: the polysemic nature of television texts; Hall's (1980) model of preferred reading; Burke's (1970) narrative model which consists of four discrete stages that contain the key mythical functions of a narrative; and the social character of media use. We illustrate these issues with examples from everyday communication situations to explain our interaction with and interpretation of media messages.

Learning outcomes

After completing this study unit you should be able to demonstrate your knowledge and understanding of

- adapting reception theory to analyse media audiences;
- how to apply reception theory to practical examples;
- the application of structural models to analyse media texts in reception research; and
- the social character of media use with specific reference to your own experience and use of the media.

6.1 INTRODUCTION

Research into audiences has, until quite recently, been largely confined to determine the effects of exposure to the mass media. In the early days of audience effects research there was the tendency to treat the media as "all-powerful" in determining the way audiences think and act ... like robots responding to electronic impulses from the media. This was the first phase of mainstream audience research in the United States of America (USA).

The second phase of mainstream research was introduced in the 1960s with the birth of the uses and gratifications theory. This theory was a turning point in the history of effect studies because of its basic assumption that audience members are actively involved in selecting messages to gratify individual needs. These needs may include a need to relax, to be entertained, to escape from daily routine or worry, to be informed about the immediate and more distant world and the need for advice about how to deal with personal problems. The active recipient assumption thus nullified the assumptions of the great influence of the media on helpless, mindless audiences.

However, to grant audiences unlimited freedom to choose and without taking into account the context within which media use takes place, is individualism in a pure form, thus a view which completely ignores the notion of contextualisation (Reiner 1998:137). Another point of criticism against uses and gratifications theory is that it offers us no understanding of the connection between our individual psychological needs and the influence of cultural and social contexts on our media use and interpretation of media messages (Grossberg, Wortella & Whitney 1998). Although uses and gratifications research helps us to investigate media functions on a macro level, it is not sensitive enough to explain and investigate micro processes such as interpretation.

For quite a long time, uses and gratifications research has dominated the social sciences, especially in the USA. Quite recently however, this theory has been followed by a range of new theories and traditions to study audiences. As Reimer (1998:134) says, uses and gratifications theory and research has been challenged by more humanistic, critical (qualitative) traditions such as reception analysis and ethnography. Reimer (1998) refers to this challenge as "a qualitative" turn in audience studies.

Above we pointed out that reception theory as applied to mass communication has its roots in two schools of thought: German reception aesthetics (also called reception theory) as well as the encoding/decoding model of reception developed by one of the founding fathers of the Centre for Contemporary Cultural Studies, Stuart Hall.

6.2 RECEPTION THEORY

The concept of reception in media audience studies indicates that we are interested in the way readers interpret media texts. In other words, when we use reception theory to investigate readers, we investigate theoretically and empirically the process of interpretation (sense-making). Against this background, we can define interpretation as the result of the process of negotiation between texts (e.g. television programmes) and readers (e.g. viewers) situated within specific social and cultural contexts. When we apply reception theory to the mass media, we substitute the concept "reader" for "user, audience, viewer" while texts refer to "newspapers, television programmes, radio or any other mass medium".

6.2.1 Assumptions of reception theory

The next concept we need to explain is negotiation. We all understand that we negotiate or bargain with people, but is it possible to negotiate with apparently "lifeless" texts? We can explain the process of negotiation by highlighting some of the basic assumptions of reception theory.

- When readers interpret messages there is interaction between them and the text. Poulet (1969:54), a phenomenologist, gives a very good description of the relationship between readers and a text: "You are inside it (the text); it is inside you; there is no longer either inside or outside" (1969:54). Although this may sound far-fetched and ethereal (airy-fairy), it is not so, because very few messages are self-explanatory and transparent – we must engage with or act upon a text to produce meaning. In other words, we must internalise and appropriate a message in order to make it our own. When watching a film, for example the *Titanic*, we are transferred to the time (1912) the ship was built, the luxurious first class accommodation on the ship, the elegantly dressed people and the two lovers who met by chance. We get a visual presentation of the history of the *Titanic*, the horrific way the ship sank, and the gruesome way many of the passengers died in the icy waters of the North Atlantic Ocean. We get engrossed with the happenings in the film to the extent that we lose track of time (objective time ceases to exist) and we become "one" with the text (perhaps shed a tear) as we experience the plight of the passengers and the two young lovers on the ship.
- A text always contains blanks (gaps) which only readers can fill. The act of interpretation requires that we fill these blanks with our knowledge, our private and public experiences and our frame of reference, which is an inescapable part of our social and cultural life-world. Eagleton (1989:433–434) explains that during the act of reading – that is when we appropriate messages – there is a fusion or encounter between our own "historical horizon" and the alien "horizon" of the text itself. Say, for example, we read a newspaper article dealing with the land claims of the Nama people (descendants of the Khoisan) living in the Richtersveld, South Africa. According to the article the Nama people were the rightful owners of the Richtersveld, but they were dispossessed of their land in the nineteenth century. Many of us may for the first time become aware of the Nama people as a cultural group. Depending on our political orientations, frame of reference and cultural and social circumstances we can fill the gaps in our knowledge about the Nama by asking questions about their historical roots, why they had been dispossessed of their land, which language they speak and their way of life. Our horizons of knowledge expand as we become aware of another cultural group in South Africa, their needs and whether their claims are justified or not.
- When studying readers' involvement with and interpretation of texts, their horizons of expectation should also be considered. As readers we have certain expectations about ways television programmes or newspaper items will develop. We then

interpret the content based on our experience of the same types of programmes in the past. Horizons of knowledge and expectation enable us to recognise things as familiar in this world (Wilson 1993). The interpretation of texts is linked to the concept of horizons of expectations in specific ways because we must know (recognise) the genre characteristics. For example, in a soap opera such as *Isidingo – The Need* (a South African multicultural soap opera), the emphasis is to great extent on the melodramatic – tears, pain and suffering. In *Isidingo*, the melodramatic is especially apparent in the story line dealing with the love relationship (and the implications of this relationship) between a black mine manager and a white, upper middle class white woman. Viewers who watch this soap and who are familiar with the characteristic of the soap opera genre, know that this relationship will cause the couple a lot of heartache. Viewers will therefore not expect to have a good laugh – humour and laughter are associated with comedies. In other words, we have expectations regarding the programme type or genre we are going to watch/read.

Another example is our expectations about documentaries: when we watch a documentary we accept that it is based on the truth. Thus, the horizons of expectation generated by the documentary genre imply that we will accept its claims as an authentic and truthful depiction (Harindranath 1998:285). Say, for instance, we read a newspaper article dealing with the manhandling of the Thuli elephants by their owners, we will accept the plight of the elephant as the truth, especially if the claims about the battered elephants are supported by pictures in newspapers, television footage, and interviews on radio programmes.

- The fusion of horizons (those of the reader and those horizons being presented by a text) makes identification possible. To identify with a character in a text, we must appropriate a character's social role, together with the rules of behaviour that are associated with that role. Jauss (1982:40, 161) says that identification with a character (e.g. the hero) affords the reader the opportunity to take part in the actions and emotional life of that character. For example, one respondent said during a focus-group interview, that she identifies with Nenna, one of the female characters in the South African multicultural soap opera, *Egoli: Place of Gold*.

  "I imitate Nenna to the 'Nth' degree ... and if I want to say something that I mean, I say it just the way Nenna would have said it ..."

  The respondent also indicated that she experiences the same emotions as Nenna does: "When Nenna is sad, I feel like crying ..."

  (Pitout 1996:170)

Identification thus allows us to experience the same events as the characters and to feel the same emotions – feelings such as joy, happiness, sadness and heartache.

From the discussion of these assumptions, we can deduce that reception theory rejects any ideas of passive viewers being dominated by powerful texts, or the opposite – powerful viewers having complete control over obscure texts. Reception theory provides us with a basis to explain that media use is a process of negotiation between readers and texts.

6.2.2 Wolfgang Iser and reception theory

We can further explain the interaction/confrontation between a text and a reader by means of concepts such as wandering viewpoint, protention and retention. Iser (1978), one of the main exponents of reception theory, says it is difficult to experience and understand a text as a whole while reading it, because we wander inside the flow of the text. We can therefore experience and understand a text only *after* reading it. Iser (1978) uses the following metaphor to explain wandering viewpoint: a traveller, while within a moving vehicle, can never experience the journey as a whole. Like the traveller, the reader is always inside the flow of the story and can at no time have a complete or total view of that journey.

Wandering viewpoint has two dimensions, namely protention and retention; whilst "travelling" through a text, we continuously alternate between these two dimensions.

- Protention means that we develop certain expectations based on our memories (retention) of characters and events. Our viewpoints constantly "wander" backwards and forwards between different story lines, sequences and episodes. This dialectical interaction between protention and retention encourages us to form links and to fill the gaps in the text with our own imagination based on our social and cultural background. For example, when we read a "whodunit" thriller (that is, we do not know the identity of the killer until the last chapter) we wander backwards and forwards in the text to find clues of who the real murderer is. After many red herrings (how often do we suspect the wrong person!) the killer is brought to book and receives the punishment he/she deserves. The norms of society are upheld because justice has been done.
- Iser's theory of active reading is also based on a semiotic distinction, a distinction between syntagmatic and paradigmatic levels of a text.
- The syntagmatic level refers to the horizontal arrangements of story elements. For example, the syntagmatic elements of a plot or story line lead us from exposition (the beginning), to the rising action to the climax, then downwards to the resolution when the conflict is resolved (the ending) (Schrag & Rosenfeld 1987:363).
- The way these elements are arranged allows us to make a paradigmatic connection between them. In other words, when we read, we only see the syntagmatic combinations (the different story lines and their relating scenes), therefore we have to fill in the paradigmatic connections ourselves by means of protention and retention. As indicated above, a narrative consists of many paradigmatic teasers or unresolved questions which "force" us to move through the text in order to find answers. By looking/searching for answers and resolutions, we remain involved while reading a text. After many interruptions, apparent confusions and red herrings, the final solution unfolds and all enigmas and problems are resolved. We can now see

that the paradigmatic structure of a text together with protention and retention, invite readers to become actively involved with a text (see more examples in Case study 6.1 below).

6.2.3 Application of reception theory to mass media texts

In our discussion of Iser's (1978) version of reception theory we provided examples of the relationship and interaction between readers and literary texts (books). In the next section we explain how reception theory *can be adjusted and applied to study the relationship and interaction between mass media messages (texts) and audiences (readers, viewers, listeners)*.

We focus on the television soap opera genre as an example to illustrate how elements in a text enhance viewers' involvement and pleasure. As has been said, familiarity with genre conventions helps us to understand and interpret a text, that is, we are able to make connections and associations between story lines and characters. These connections and associations to a great extent determine our involvement with and interpretation of programme types (genres). Allen's (1987) analysis of the television soap opera within the framework of reception analysis, indicates that the conventions of the soap opera as genre provide us with the opportunities and positions from which we can create meanings and get actively involved in the process of reading (interpretation).

Case study 6.1: Reception analysis: the television soap opera

- Abrupt segmentation between different story lines in an episode of a soap opera (we also use soap(s) when referring to soap operas) is the norm which creates gaps in soaps to ensure viewers' involvement. Viewers thus constantly wander between the different story lines – just when the viewer's attention has been captured by the characters and circumstances of a given plot, the text suddenly shifts the attention to another set of characters and plots. Viewers familiar with the structure of the soap opera text know that in any given episode there are usually three to five nonlinear story lines unfolding, and these story lines can stretch over months or even years. Guessing and second-guessing the outcomes of story lines keeps viewers glued to the screen.

  For example, in *Isidingo* there were four major story lines unfolding over the period February 2000 to November 2000. The story lines dealt with the super-bitch Cheryl and her relationship with a young schoolboy; the unfolding of Cheryl's dubious past (her involvement with a murder); the teenage girl Dusty, who could not decide whether she was ready to lose her virginity; and the much-talked about inter-racial love relationship between a black man, Derrick, and a white woman, Philippa. Each of these story lines unfolded at its own pace which caused viewers to constantly wander between the story lines, guessing and predicting for example, when Cheryl will drop her young teenage boyfriend for someone else (she usually does); whether Dusty would go to bed with her boyfriend (who later turned out to be homosexual); and whether the love relationship between Derrick and Philippa would last. When the two lovers broke up, viewers held their breath to find out whether they would make up again. These story lines (and subsidiary ones) kept viewers glued to the screen, "forcing" them to watch each episode in case they might miss out on possible resolutions. And soap fans get involved with the happenings in a soap to the extent that when they miss an episode they ask co-viewers to fill them in and together they speculate about possible outcomes of story lines.

We may now begin to understand why viewers get hooked on a particular soap – they cannot but keep on watching faithfully even if a soap stretches over years. In fact, the longer viewers watch a soap(s), the better it gets!

- Each scene in an episode ends with a close-up or big close-up camera shot which draws viewers nearer and nearer the action and gives them an intimate view of the characters' emotions (fear, sadness, a mean smile) and inner conflicts. For example, when Derrick and Philippa in *Isidingo* broke up, a big close-up shot was taken of her distorted grief-stricken face. Although both were involved with other partners after they had broken off their relationship, their desire and feelings for one another were shown by means of close-up shots, lingering on their unhappy faces. Viewers then watched with heightened attention for clues that might support their expectations of a possible reconciliation between the two lovers and the implications of an interracial marriage.
- Use of flashforwards and flashbacks also ensure viewer involvement. Some soap operas offer flashforwards to whet viewers' appetites for the forthcoming action. For instance, prior to transmission of an episode of the soap *Generations*, snippets of major events in that episode are shown on television during the week. Flashbacks may also be used to orientate viewers and bring them up to date with what has been happening over days, weeks, and even years. In *Isidingo* for example, Cheryl is haunted by memories of the murder in which she was involved. These memories are shown by means of flashbacks to remind viewers what happened in the past, but in such a way that they cannot be certain whether Cheryl killed her ex-lover or hired a hit man to do her dirty work. In this way another opportunity is created for viewers to get involved with the story line and to fill in the gaps with their own imagination (did she or did she not pull the trigger?).
- Gap filling relies on paradigmatic and syntagmatic organisation and this is especially true for the soap opera genre. The paradigmatic and syntagmatic components in the soap opera are reversed forms of the narrative scheme of programmes such as sitcoms, police/detective, and hospital genres. In these genres the syntagmatic elements of a story (that which we see on the screen) lead us from exposition (the beginning of a story), up the rising action to a climax and then down the falling action to resolution (ending) of the story (narrative).

The soap opera, on the other hand, concentrates more on paradigmatic complexity (the range of possible choices available to the viewer expressed through the interrelationship between characters) than on the syntagmatic juxtaposition or narrative sequencing of two or more plot lines in an episode of this genre. The paradigmatic complexity of characters' relationships encourages the viewer to imagine all sorts of possible connections.

For example, in *Egoli: Place of Gold* viewers may speculate about Tim and his mistress, and when is Jane (Tim's wife) going to find out about the affair? When will Tim find out that Monica is his biological mother? Who murdered Walt Vorster? Many questions can thus be asked about the story lines unfolding over months before a solution or answer is found.

- Soaps are open narratives that stretch over years to build up a large loyal audience (we can also talk of the longevity of soaps) because they daily come in to contact with a regular group of archetypical characters that we find in almost all soap operas. The following are examples of archetypical characters around which main story lines unfold:

  The young, vulnerable romantic heroine: This character is very popular with viewers. She is pretty, though naive and trusts men too readily. She is vulnerable, gets hurt quite often and therefore has a history of relationships with men that came to naught. Soars (1979:59) says that viewers see this coming and that is where the hand wringing comes in "and it is not all done on the screen ...". In *Egoli*, Lynette is an example of the romantic heroine: her husband died in a car accident and she has had disastrous relationships with Adriaan and Chris Edwards, a married man.

  The romantic hero (Mr Right): He has all the qualities that make him the ideal husband: he is hardworking, shows upward mobility and has a good job. He is tall, good looking, a romantic at heart and a gentleman. He is the kind of man every mother would like to have as a son-in-law. Derrick in *Isidingo* is a good example of the romantic hero. He is the managing director of the mine, attractive and always smartly and neatly dressed. While he and Philippa lived together, he treated her with respect and affirmed her by taking her on romantic outings.

  The female antagonist (super-bitch): This female character destroys people's lives without thinking twice. She is selfish and loves men, especially older wealthy men. These men are usually married, which makes her a natural opponent for "good" female characters. Cheryl in *Isidingo* is the archetypical lying, conniving antagonist, who toys with men without showing any remorse. Even murder is not beyond her.

  The arch-villains: These are "black characters" who hurt and blackmail people, tell lies and are guilty of the most unforgivable sin in soaps, namely pure and premeditated selfishness (Soares 1978:61). In *Egoli*, Spider (his name indicates his characteristics) was such a black character: he did not hesitate to murder and blackmail people. The same applies to Georgie in *Isidingo*.

The loving, caring mother/grandmother: These women have had their fair share of hardship in life. Therefore, they have great understanding for the problems of others. They believe in marriage as a social institution and the family as a core unit. They are caring, loving mothers/grandmothers. Stephanie in the *Bold and the Beautiful* is an example of the archetypical mother/grandmother who shows great commitment to ensure the wellbeing of her family.

The meddling and sometimes mean mothers: Elsa in *Egoli* is perhaps not mean, but she is the archetype of the meddling mother. She is always interfering with Deon (her son) and her daughter-in-law. Elsa loves to gossip, especially about her own family and people living in the Mansions (an apartment block).

The Cinderella clone: In this category we find the beautiful, talented daughters of low social standing who marry older, super-rich men who live in mansions and maintain a jet-set lifestyle. Brooke in *The Bold and the Beautiful* and Louwna in *Egoli* are examples of Cinderella clones. As children they were poor – determined however, not to remain miserable and poor, both married wealthy and powerful men.

The family man/patriarch: This character is kind but strict. He is a combination of idealism and pragmatism. Although he may have a roving eye, he puts the interests of his family first. Eric Forrester in the *Bold and the Beautiful* can be regarded as a patriarch: although he has been involved with many women (even with his daughter-in-law), he is a caring and loving father. His children and his wife regard him as the head of the family.

- Because of the never-ending story lines, soap opera viewing becomes a ritual: year after year, every weekday, at the same time, fans gather in front of the television set – they disconnect the phone and the doorbell, pour a drink and sit back to escape for half an hour into a fantasy world of the soap community. One woman in the focus-group interviews said that when she watches *Egoli* she disconnects the phone and doesn't answer the doorbell – not even for the deacon of the church. And her children know not to speak with her while she is watching *Egoli* (Pitout 1996).
- Because devoted soap fans see soap characters every weekday, they bond with characters. Soap characters therefore "... become everyday friends ... they are part of our lives ... and we sometimes know them better than our neighbours" said some of the female respondents (Pitout 1998:269–300.) As we shall discuss in section 6.3.3 of this unit, soap viewers derive great pleasure from talking about characters and story lines with other viewers.

To summarise our discussion of the application of reception theory to the soap opera genre: the soap opera provides ample opportunity for viewers to get actively involved with the events on the screen. This active involvement is heightened by textual gaps, strategic interruptions, and the paradigmatic and syntagmatic aspects of the soap opera text. The never-ending story lines keep soap fans glued to the screen and eventually fans become so intimately involved with characters that they "bond" with them to the extent that the characters become like best friends.

6.2.4 Reception theory and non-serialised programmes

With a few adjustments we can also use reception theory to analyse several other types of television genres. The reason is that even non-serialised programmes (genres) tend to lack a final narrative closure or solution. We take the following television genres as examples:

- In a series such as a hospital drama, a seriously wounded patient may be saved by the skills of the hero, the famous surgeon. Yet the central problem – illness, suffering and death in society – will not be resolved. Illness, suffering and death exist and so the enigma, a problem related to health, is carried over from week to week.
- Similarly, in police and detectives series the criminal will be caught and brought to justice, but the central problem underlying the programme – crime and justice in society – is not resolved.
- The lack of a final resolution is even more obvious in situation comedies; for instance what would *The Cosby Show* be if the parents get divorced? The stable family situation, which is the basis for this sitcom, will then be destroyed (Fourie 1997: 230).

In the next section we deal with important key themes/issues in reception as they are addressed by the cultural studies approach.

6.3 CULTURAL STUDIES APPROACH: ISSUES IN RECEPTION RESEARCH

Firstly we pay attention to the implications of the polysemic nature of television texts. Secondly, we discuss Hall's model as an example of studying encoding and decoding, Thirdly, we consider the dramatic process model proposed by Burke (1970) to analyse the structural characteristics and underlying meaning of media messages. Finally we address the social character of television viewing.

6.3.1 Polysemic nature of television text

Fiske (1987) proposed the idea of polysemy, that is, the notion that television texts are relatively open and sometimes even contradictory, which means that we can read (interpret) them in various ways. Indeed, according to Fiske (1987), that is what makes television programmes popular – social groupings (or subcultures to use Fiske's term) can attach different meanings to the same text. For example, when we ask a group of adolescent girls who watch *Friends* (a television situation comedy) who their favourite character in this programme is, they will probably show great differences in their preferences.

Because the majority of television texts (e.g. news) are agents for or carriers of the dominant ideology, texts typically try to limit their meanings to ones that promote the dominant ideology. For example, SABC3 news in South Africa supports the African National Congress (ANC) ideology and will therefore endorse the initiatives of President Mbeki and the ideology of an Africa Renaissance. However, tension may develop between the messages underlying the texts and the social positions of the viewers/readers whose opinions may to a great extent differ from the dominant ideology upheld by the ANC. For example, a radical, rightwing newspaper supporting the AWB (*Afrikaanse Weerstandsbeweging* – Afrikaans Resistant Movement) may interpret the initiatives and ideology of the ANC as pie in the sky, an African nightmare of poverty, lawlessness, and political corruption (Fourie 1997:183).

In tandem with the polysemic nature of texts, Fiske (1987) emphasises active, interpreting audiences who enjoy watching programmes, responding to them and talking with other viewers about what they have seen on television. Put another way, Fiske (1987) points out the importance of *talk* or *oral* gossip in reception research. In this way Fiske underscores the social character of television and the way it circulates in society (see 6.3.3 of this unit for a discussion of the social character of television).

Although Fiske's (1978) views elicited favourable responses, he was also criticised for exaggerating the interpretive freedom of audiences as well as the polysemic nature of media texts: although viewers interpret specific programmes in different ways, they are to an extent limited by their own social positions and also the limitations and closures of the texts itself (Dalgren 1998:300; Gray 1998:28). Put differently, texts do not have fixed and absolute meanings, for what the text means to one person is not necessarily the same as it means for someone from another group – even close friends disagree in their interpretation of the same text.

With the above theory of the polysemy of television texts, we now turn to ideological interpretations. Two ways to analyse ideological interpretations are by means of Hall's theory of preferred reading and Burke's dramatic process model.

6.3.2 Hall's model of preferred reading and Burke's dramatic process model

A founding father of reception studies in media studies, is Stewart Hall (1980) who developed a model for preferred reading (also see Volume 1, Part B: Unit 9 with regard to media and ideology). This model shows how television messages are encoded and decoded according to three possible coding positions (also called reading or interpretation strategies). The first position is

- a dominant reading (interpretation) where viewers accept the dominant ideology produced by the text. Or, as McQueen (1998) puts it, viewers accept the assumptions of the encoder (the person who composes the message).

- Then follows a negotiated reading, which is produced by viewers who agree to an extent with the dominant ideology but reserve the right to modify their views. In other words, they can negotiate a position somewhere between accepting and rejecting the ideological messages of a text.
- The third position is an oppositional reading where viewers "see through" the dominant ideology to allow them to reject the dominant ideology encoded in the text. Oppositional readers thus make decodings (interpretations) that defy or work against the dominant ideology.
- According to Grossberg et al (1998), these categories/positions work well where messages contain explicit political messages. They are, however, more difficult to apply to audiences' decoding of texts which contain fewer explicit political messages. Furthermore, in practice there are few purely dominant or oppositional decodings. As explained, using media is usually a process of negotiation between readers situated within various social positions and texts.
- To illustrate Hall's theory in practice, we use the Hansie Cronje saga, which rocked the cricket world in April 2000. Hansie, the South African cricket captain, was fired from the team because it was implied that he was guilty of match fixing. While South African cricket fans (and the cricket world as a whole) held their breath, the drama of deception unfolded on television, radio, in newspapers and magazines. We first apply Hall's theory of preferred reading to explain viewers' interpretation of the Cronje saga (Case study 6.2) and the way their frames of reference and worldview influence their interpretation.

Case study 6.2: Practical illustration of Hall's model of preferred reading: the Hansie Cronje saga

- The first position is the *dominant reading* and when applied to our example, we can say that those readers who support the dominant ideology agreed that Hansie's acceptance of money and his deception of the South African public was shameful. They condemn any weaknesses and are dead set against dishonesty, greed, and thus any behaviour and values that are opposed to the dominant ideological norms of honesty, patriotism and integrity. They might have argued that "he let us down, he deceived us ... Isn't he paid more than enough? He abused his position and responsibility as a role model ... he took advantage of his position ... he should be banned for life from any involvement with cricket". In a sport-mad South Africa, a sportsman has as much social responsibility towards his supporters as a politician, a church leader and other authority figures.
- *Negotiated readings* are produced by the audience members who are situated neither in positions of total conformity nor in total opposition to the dominant ideology. The negotiated readings they produce modify the meanings preferred by the dominant ideology to take into account the social differences between

people. Although people might have initially been shocked to learn about Hansie's dishonesty, they soon compromised between condemning his actions (behaviour) but at the same time made allowances for human weaknesses. They argued "it is human to err but divine to forgive" or "If God forgives us our sins, who are we to throw stones?" People from this position might have argued that Cronje should be forgiven but on condition that he will not be allowed to play cricket for South Africa again.

- An *oppositional reading* puts readers in a position opposite to the dominant ideology. People who use this position might argue that Hansie's transgression was not so serious – he never "threw" any matches but only accepted money for information about pitch conditions. Furthermore, all blame was laid on the Indians who bribed Hansie – they are the corrupt ones. People in this position might also have argued: "Why kick a man when he is down? We should stand by him. There are rapists in the cricket team but they kicked Hansie out just because he made a mistake ... After all, few people would have been able to resist the temptation to receive bribes. Hansie was too honest, he should never have admitted that he received money from the Indians ... after all there is nothing wrong with match fixing".

Another analytical model for the use of textual analyses in reception research is the dramatic process model proposed by Burke (1970). In the case study below, we discuss Burke's process model and illustrate each stage with examples from the Cronje saga.

Case study 6.3: Textual analysis: the application of Burke's dramatic process model

Burke (1970) maintains that the majority of genres, factual and fiction (thus all human drama), consist of (or follow) four discrete stages which contain the key mythical functions of narrative (story which can be fictional or factional):

- *Pollution/disruption*
  A story (or narrative e.g. a fairy tale, a romantic novel, a television entertainment programme, or even "stories" of our lives) and many news events usually begin with a state of equilibrium or social harmony and provide background information on the composition of the elements of the story (e.g. think how a fairy tale or "stories" of our lives begin). Then something happens to disrupt the social harmony. When applied to the Cronje saga, the social harmony (the "good" reputation of the cricket team in general and Hansie in particular) was disturbed and dramatic tension was created when news became public that South Africa's cricket captain might have been involved in match fixing. We can also say that

the norms of our social order of honesty, loyalty, integrity and responsibility were disrupted and threatened by the news of Cronje's fall from grace.

- *Guilt*
  During this phase we must try and find answers to who or what caused the pollution/disruption or disequilibrium. As the Cronje saga unfolded in the mass media, it became evident that Indian police had bugged the cellphone of Cronje. Initially the impression was created that the Indian police were falsely accusing the golden boy of South African cricket, of match fixing. However, the disequilibrium became worse when Cronje publicly admitted that he was indeed guilty of receiving money for either match predicting or match fixing.

  South Africa's own trusted captain was now the guilty party and responsible for having disrupted the social norms of society. Dr Ali Bacher the president of the National Cricket Board, publicly condemned Hansie's dishonesty, dismissed him as captain and expelled him from playing cricket for the South African national team. The social problems of disloyalty, dishonesty, greed, and the abuse of responsibility were highlighted as the social implications became evident.
- *Purification/restitution*
  This phase deals with actions that are put into operation to eliminate pollution and guilt. Hansie was punished for disrupting the social norms of honesty, integrity and loyalty by being stripped of his captaincy and banished from the cricket team. Hansie publicly – on television and in court – apologised for letting down his family, fans, teammates and the National Cricket Board. He acknowledged that his addiction to money was the actual cause as to why he threw overboard all moral principles and codes of conduct.
- *Redemption*
  The cyclic nature of the narrative as manifested in the media, perpetuates and celebrates the social system above the individual. Having seen the punishment and repentance of the previous stages, audiences are shown that disruption of social ethics does not pay. The social system is reinstated once audiences realise the personal and social implications following the disruption of the system. Having seen that crime does not pay and how moral issues of dishonesty, greed and disloyalty have been overcome, the public is encouraged to develop a greater appreciation for the *status quo*. Cronje was publicly executed by television, where the slow truck-in and truck-out camera movements and the use of close-up and extreme close-up shots brought viewers closer and closer to the emotions Cronje experienced; eventually millions of viewers witnessed his emotional breakdown.

In the next case study we use Allan Boesak's fall from grace to further illustrate the application of Burke's model.

Case study 6.4: Textual analysis: the Allan Boesak saga

- Allan Boesak, former ANC icon, former president of the World Alliance of Reformed Churches, and South Africa's ambassador-designate to the United Nations in Geneva, embezzled funds donated by Scandinavian donors to the Foundation for Peace and Justice (Boesak was the main trustee of this foundation). His dishonest behaviour *disrupted the social harmony* and dramatic tension was created when it became public that Boesak "has enriched himself substantially at the expense of the foundation" (Laurence 1999:1).
- Boesak initially put the blame for the misuse of funds on the secretary of the foundation, Ferdie Steenkamp who was found guilty and sent to jail. However, as the investigation continued, and the media reported in detail how Boesak misused the money entrusted to him, it became clear that he was indeed *guilty* of embezzling the funds of the now defunct Foundation for Peace and Justice.
- Because his guilt was proven in a court of law, Boesak was convicted on three counts of theft, one of fraud and was sentenced to six years imprisonment (the *purification* stage). In spite of the support from ANC propagandists who believed in his innocence and the ANC who preferred to assume that Boesak was innocent until proven guilty (Laurence 1999), the democratic system of justice took its course.
- In the end, the Boesak saga illustrates that crime does not pay and that immoral and dishonest behaviour will not be tolerated – not even if the person is a highly regarded comrade of the ruling party (the *redemption* phase).

In conclusion, the central message of the narrative of the Cronje and Boesak sagas is that immoral behaviour – dishonesty and disloyalty – does not pay. Furthermore, these sagas serve as examples of how news narratives of the media emphasise the ideology of moral codes of conduct in South Africa. The cyclic nature of television (and other media) narratives, perpetuates and celebrates the moral values of the social system above the individual. South African news items not only warn us against immoral behaviour but also emphasise themes against racism, violence and anarchy, expressing ideologies of non-violence and democracy as rule of law. As we have illustrated with the fall from grace of Hansie Cronje and Allan Boesak, we can use Burke's model to analyse the majority of news (and entertainment) stories (narratives).

6.3.3 The social character of television viewing

The aim of our discussion of the social character of television viewing is to familiarise you with the following concepts:

- Interpretive community
- Parasocial and social dimensions of television viewing
- Identification

Interpretive community

Interpretation includes the process of negotiation within specific social and cultural circumstances. We generally accept that television viewing is primarily a family activity, yet the social context in which television viewing takes place is not only limited to the immediate family setting, but also involves our social group membership (or interpretive communities to which we belong), which influences our interpretation of messages.

We can therefore argue that viewers will draw on knowledge as informed by various "social positionings", whether in a family setting or the workplace (Roscoe, Marshall & Gleeson 1995:90). In other words, because interpretation is also a social process, different social contexts may influence the process of interpretation. For example, in one family different "interpretive communities" may exist: the husband may be addicted to sports programmes while the wife detests this genre. He will then have to turn to another interpretive community to share his experience of that programme. The same applies to music: parents and children usually listen to different kinds of music, for instance children listen to hard rock while their parents give preference to golden oldies or classical music.

Parasocial and social dimensions of television viewing

When studying audiences, we should also investigate the parasocial and social dimensions of television viewing, because these two dimensions explain why we get involved with television characters and how we make imaginary friends with them. Pitout (1998) investigated the social and parasocial dimensions of television viewing by means of focus-group interviews. The results of her investigation show that viewers built up a parasocial relationship with soap characters whom they regard as their friends; friends they can talk to and of whose daily joy or hardship they can partake. It is this daily encounter with soap characters that feeds the imaginary relationship between viewers and characters. Parasocial interaction spills over to social interaction, that is, when participants discuss soaps with family members, friends and colleagues.

Because television programmes are popular topics for discussion, they serve as a cultural forum for social discourse about aspects of the represented reality. The following research results illustrate social and parasocial interaction:

- In a research study concerning oral gossip, the results indicate that a group of working women find it rewarding to discuss their favourite soap *Egoli*, with their colleagues. This has led to soap opera culture at the workplace. Furthermore, the participants admit that they discuss *Egoli* during office hours, usually during tea and lunch breaks. And it is often social issues and humour in *Egoli* that stimulate discussions. From the results of this study it is evident that the participants successfully combined the private sphere of their lives with their everyday life at the workplace. Their conversations often take the form of gossip sessions and the participants succeed in convincing uninitiated or non-viewers to start watching *Egoli* (Pitout 1996).

- Furthermore, the research results reveal that the participants also recognise aspects of a character similar to those of an important person – also called the "significant other" – in their own lives and then engage in parasocial interaction which leads to "intimacy at a distance". This means that viewers interact with characters as if they are real-live people. Parasocial interaction is thus based on a process of recognition. That is, there are similarities between the everyday lives of viewers and the reality presented in a soap opera. In this way, viewers enter the fantasy world of the soaps by playing opposite a character that resembles someone they know in real life (Pitout 1998).

Identification

Identification with television characters is especially true for those viewers who watch serials (soaps) and series (sitcoms, detective programmes, and the like) over years. We should therefore pay attention to television characters because they mediate the different effects of television through processes such as identification, imitation, role modelling and parasocial interaction. The nature of the relationship we build up with characters over the years is quite intense – we may identify with a particular character by putting ourselves in that character's shoes or we may regard characters as role models and imitate their behaviour. Role models, however, are not limited to entertainment programmes – television sports programmes are also very popular and by watching tennis, cricket, soccer and rugby, sport stars become role models and often fans imitate their heroes' dress code and mannerisms.

As viewers we can identify with many of the themes in television programmes because in real life we are confronted with the same problems, such as divorce, loss of friendship, and death to name but a few. Identification with television characters and their problems heightens our involvement with them and contributes to the pleasure we derive from watching television. In terms of reception theory, identification with television themes and characters carries us into an imaginary world that is far superior and preferred to dreary everyday existence. On the other hand, television viewing also has a reassuring function in the sense that we realise that we are not the only ones with problems – television characters also have their fair share of pain and disappointments. Television programmes may thus enable us to get a new perspective on life.

Summary

In this unit we have discussed reception theory and how it can be applied to study media audiences. Our emphasis was mainly on television. We began the unit by pointing out that the uses and gratifications theory has been challenged by more humanistic, critical traditions such as reception theory and analysis. When we look at the origin of reception theory in media studies, it is interesting to note that although the term "reception" had not been officially used in audience studies until the early 1980s, reception studies have always been conducted in mass communication research but just under different banners (Hoijer 1998:166–167). For example, effects and audience analyses have been conducted within the mainstream research paradigm since the early 1920s. Furthermore, although we may get the impression that the study of interpretation belongs exclusively to reception theory and analysis, it is not the case. For instance, in his review of thirty years of audience research, Klapper (1960) came to the conclusion that one of the first audience studies conducted by Herzog (1944) did indeed investigate how female radio listeners interpret and recall media messages in ways which correspond with their existing frame of reference, values and beliefs.

Hoijer (1998) further points out that the emphasis on play and pleasure is not a unique invention of reception analysis – in 1964 Stephenson already conducted empirical research to test his play theory of news reading on real audiences. We agree with Hoijer (1998) that researchers on both sides of the research spectrum – qualitative and quantitative – should begin to take note and seriously look at the vast audience research that has been done on both sides of the spectrum.

After our discussion of the history of reception theory, we defined interpretation as the result of the process of negotiation between texts and readers situated within specific social and cultural contexts. We explained the assumptions of reception theory, the theoretical points of departure of Wolfgang Iser and how reception theory has been adapted to study the interaction between mass media messages and audiences. We took the television soap opera as a case study to explain how open texts stimulate viewer involvement.

We then discussed and illustrated by means of examples, important issues being addressed by the cultural studies approach in reception research: the polysemic nature of television texts; Hall's (1980) theory of preferred reading; the dramatic process model of Burke (1970) and the social nature of television viewing. Investigating these issues enables us to explain how viewers can interpret messages from different positions, that narratives (factual and fictional) consist of discrete phases, and the pleasure viewers derive from their interaction with media texts by means of processes such as identification, parasocial and social interaction.

Although reception theory acknowledges the active role assumed by readers, it is criticised in that it does not study actual audiences. In other words, we should also study real audiences in order to determine how they create meaning and pleasure in their daily interaction with television programmes and other mass media. We must remember that the communication process is not complete until audience members interpret messages. The way audiences talk about television programmes indicates that a further stage in communication takes place when they talk about programmes in a context completely removed from the primary site of viewing (Seiter, Borchers, Kreutzner & Warth 1991:167).

A research approach that studies real audiences and their daily encounter with mass media, is ethnography. The basic objective of ethnography is to study the way people "live" their culture, and the mass media as integral part of that culture (Fiske 1987:63). We discuss media ethnography in Unit 7.

Research activities

1 Explain in one paragraph the difference and similarities between the uses and gratification theory and reception theory.

2 What is meant by the term "reception"?

3 Name the basic assumptions of reception theory. Describe each assumption in about three sentences and illustrate each with examples from your interaction with media texts.

4 Explain Wolfgang Iser's contribution to reception theory, by means of examples from your reading of texts.

5 How has reception theory been adjusted to explain the interaction between media texts and audiences? Choose one of your favourite soaps to illustrate your explanation.

6 Explain by means of examples from television programmes, the difference between the organisation of paradigmatic and syntagmatic elements in closed and open texts.

7 Is it possible to apply reception theory to genres other than soaps? Illustrate your answer with examples from a television programme(s).

8 Explain the polysemic nature of television programmes by means of your own experience of a television programme(s).

9 Do you agree with Grossberg et al (1998) that it is difficult to apply Hall's model of preferred reading to texts that do not contain explicit political messages? Answer this question by applying Hall's decoding positions to any **one** of the following television genres: situation comedy; soap opera; nature or wild life programme; documentary programme; police/detective series or any other entertainment genre of your choice.

10 *According to Burke's (1970) dramatic process model the majority of genres – factual and fictional – consists of four stages.* Respond to this statement by applying Burke's model to the analysis of factual events (e.g. television news, radio news, newspapers, and so forth) and fictional genres (e.g. soaps, sitcoms, police/detective, science fiction, thrillers, and the like). Use one news event (it may stretch over months before it reaches the redemption phase) and one fictional narrative (you may select any story being told in a magazine, a television entertainment programme or over the radio).

11 Answer the following questions and illustrate your answers with examples from your own personal viewing experience:

a) Do you belong to an "interpretive" community that differs from the one that your parents/partner/children/family/friends belong to?

b) Do you get involved in parasocial interaction with characters whilst watching a television programme(s)?

c) Do you discuss television programmes with people?
d) Do you have role models based on your experience with media characters?
e) Have you ever imitated behaviour and/or dress codes of people you have seen on television or any other mass media?

Further reading

Alasuutari, P (ed). 1999. *The media audience*. London: Sage.

Dickinson, R, Harindranath, R & Linne, O (eds). 1998. *Approaches to audiences: a reader*. London: Harper.

Fiske, J. 1987. *Television culture*. London: Routledge.

Fourie, PJ (ed). 1996. *Introduction to communication: course book 6 – film and television studies*. Cape Town: Juta.

McQueen, D. 1998. *Television: a media student's guide*. London: Arnold.

McQuail, D. 1997. *Audience analysis*. London: Sage.

Pitout, M. 1998. Reception analysis: a qualitative investigation of the parasocial and social dimensions of soap opera viewing. *Communicatio* 24(2):39–47.

Reimer, B. 1998. Crisis? What crisis? Analysing audience studies. *Nordicom Review* 19(1):135–142.

Bibliography

Allen, RC. 1985. *Speaking of soap operas*. Chapel Hill: University of North Carolina Press.

Allen, RC. 1987. Reader-oriented criticism, in *Channels of Discourse*, edited by RC Allen. London: Methuen.

Burke, K. 1970. *The rhetoric of religion: studies in logology*. Berkley, CA: University of California Press.

Dalgren, P. 1998. Critique: elusive audiences, in *Approaches to audiences: a reader*, edited by R Dickinson, R Harindranath & O Linne. London: Harper.

Eagleton, T. 1989. Reading theory, in *International encyclopaedia of communication*, Volume 4, edited by BE Barnow, G Gerbner, W Schramm, T Worth & L Gross. New York: Oxford.

Fiske, J. 1987. *Television culture*. London: Routledge.

Gadamer, H-G. 1975. *Truth and method*. New York: Seabury.

Gray, A.1999. Audience and reception research in retrospect: the trouble with audiences, in *The media audience*, edited by P Alasuutari. London: Sage

Harindranath, R. 1998. Documentary meanings and interpretive contexts: observations on Indian 'repertoires', in *Approaches to audiences: a reader*, edited by R Dickinson, R Harindranath & O Linne. London: Harper.

Grossberg, L, Wartella, E & Whitney, D. 1998. *Mediamaking: mass media in a popular culture*. California: Sage.

Hall, S. 1980. Encoding/decoding, in *Culture, media, language*, edited by S Hall, D Hobson, A Lowe & P Willis. Birmingham: University of Birmingham.

Herzog, H. 1944. What do we really know about day-time serial listeners? In *Radio research 1942–1943*, edited by P Lazarsfeld & FN Stanton. New York: Duell, Sloan & Pearce.

Hobson, D. 1991. Soap operas at work, in *Remote control: television, audiences, & cultural power*, edited by E Seiter, G Borchers, G Kreutzner & E Warth. London: Routledge.

Hoijer, B. 1998. Social psychological perspectives in reception analysis, in *Approaches to audiences: a reader*, edited by R Dickinson, R Harindranath & O Linne. London: Harper.

Holub, RC. 1984. *Reception theory: a critical introduction.* London: Methuen.
Horton, D & Wohl, RR. 1956. Mass communication and parasocial interaction. *Psychiatry* 19(3):215–229.
Iser, W. 1978. *The act of reading. A theory of aesthetic response.* London: Routledge & Kegan Paul.
Jauss, HR. 1982. *Towards an aesthetic of reception.* Brighton: Harvester.
Klapper, JT. 1960. *The effects of mass communication.* Glencoe, ILL: Free Press.
Livingstone, S. 1998. *Making sense of television: the psychology of audience interpretation.* 2nd edition. London: Routledge.
Laurence, P. 1999. *In defence of Boesak.*
Available: http://www.hst.org.za/focus_14/boesak.html
Accessed on 00/11/24
McQueen, D. 1998. *Television: a media student's guide.* London: Arnold.
Moores, S. 1993. *Interpreting audiences: the ethnography of media consumption.* London: Sage.
Pitout, M. 1996. Televisie en resepsiestudie: 'n analise van kykersinterpretasie van die seep-opera "Egoli: Plek van Goud". Ongepubliseerde doktorale proefskrif. Pretoria: Universiteit van Suid-Afrika.
Pitout, M. 1997. Reception theory and analysis, in *Introduction to communication – course book 6: film and television studies*, edited by PJ Fourie. Cape Town: Juta.
Pitout, M. 1998. Reception analysis: a qualitative investigation of the parasocial and social dimensions of soap opera viewing. *Communicatio* 24(2):39–47.
Poulet, G. 1969. Phenomenology of reading. *New Literary History* 1(1):53–68.
Reimer, B. 1998. Crisis? What crisis? Analysing audience studies. *Nordicom Review* 19(1):35–142.
Roscoe, J, Marshall, H & Gleeson, K. 1995. The television audience: a reconsideration of the taken-for-granted terms 'active', 'social' and 'critical'. *European Journal of Communication* 10(1):87–108.
Schrag, RL & Rosenfeld, LB. 1987. Assessing the soap opera frame: audience perceptions of value structures in soap operas and prime-time serial dramas. *The Southern Speech Communication Journal* 52(4):362–376.
Seiter, E, Borchers, G, Kreutzner & Warth, E (eds). 1991. *Remote control: television, audiences, & cultural power.* Paperback edition. London: Routledge.
Stephenson, W. 1964. The ludenic theory of news reading. *Journalism Quarterly* 41:367–374.
Wilson, T. 1993. *Watching television: hermeneutics, reception and popular culture.* Cambridge: Polity.

Ethnography

7

Magriet Pitout

Overview

We are regularly involved in one or other form of observation. For example, when we sit in our cars during a traffic jam and watch (observe) frustrated motorists' nonverbal behaviour; or observe spectators' involvement in a sports game; or watch children playing; or when we discuss television programmes with other viewers, we are involved in observation. This is of course non-academic observation, but it gives us an idea of what observation entails. A popular qualitative form of observation in communication research is ethnography with its roots in anthropology and urban sociology.

In this unit we discuss ethnography in detail because of its popularity with researchers who conduct qualitative audience research. One of the reasons for the popularity of ethnography is that it permits us to zoom in and study media behaviour in more depth than quantitative research methods, such as surveys, allow. Surveys provide us only with one-dimensional accounts of audience members' relationship with the media, for example, how many television sets are switched on, what viewers' favourite programmes are, the activities they engage in while watching television, the number of hours they watch television, and so on. However, such empirical data does not tell us much about what people think while using the media, their relationship with the media, how they interpret messages and the social context of media use, for example who in a family decides what to watch, when and why. In our discussion of ethnography in this unit, we emphasise *conducting research in natural settings* because it is one of the core assumptions of ethnographic research.

We give a brief overview of the relation between reception research and ethnography in audience studies. Because audience ethnography has its roots in classic ethnography, we discuss the assumptions shared by audience ethnography and classic ethnography.

We then provide you with a critical view of the way the first audience ethnographic studies were conducted and illustrate our discussion with research examples. In addition, we explain by means of examples, how to plan and conduct ethnographic research. As a case study, we also include an example of an actual ethnographic study conducted by Daphna Lemish (1985). We conclude this unit by presenting a critical appraisal of ethnography as a form of observation in media studies.

Learning outcomes

At the end of this unit you should be able to demonstrate your knowledge and understanding of

- the historical roots of ethnography;
- the assumptions of ethnography;
- the steps to be followed when planning ethnographic research;
- analysis and evaluation of an actual example of ethnographic research; and
- the advantages and disadvantages of the use of ethnography in audience research.

7.1 INTRODUCTION

In Unit 6 (Reception theory), we worked through approaches in reception research and pointed out that one of the shortcomings of reception theory is that researchers using this theoretical framework concentrate to a large extent on the analysis of the structural characteristics of texts (media messages). These results are used to make deductions about how audiences are influenced by and interpret media messages. Put another way, the text is regarded as the only source of meaning, thereby ignoring how real people interact with and interpret media messages.

This form of textual determinism was unacceptable to audience researchers such as Morley (1980) and Fejes (1984) who set the ball rolling for the empirical investigation of how actual audiences receive and interpret messages. These two authors firmly believe that audiences have the ability to act upon a text, thus to interact with a text to produce their own meanings.

The first researcher to test Hall's (1980) encoding/decoding model using real audiences, was Morley (1980), a proponent of the cultural studies approach (see Unit 6: Reception theory). He used this model to investigate how groups of viewers from different educational and social backgrounds (which Morley calls "interpretive communities") interpreted the British *Nationwide* public affairs television programme. As Livingstone (1998:46) explains, the text–reader encounter is prominent in Morley's study although not in its reception aesthetics version (that is as a process of the negotiation between text and readers), but in terms of Hall's model of the moments of encoding and decoding (see the discussion of Hall's theory in Unit 6). The *Nationwide* reception study was a combination of the analysis of how the text (the *Nationwide* programme) was constructed, and viewers' interpretation of the text.

Other early reception studies, especially romantic serials such as soaps, were conducted by Hobson (1981), Katz and Liebes (1984, reported in Liebes & Katz 1990) and Ang (1985). These groundbreaking reception studies became known as qualitative audience reception studies where the researchers more or less followed the same research procedure: they first analysed a text and then studied its reception among particular audiences by conducting in-depth or group interviews (focus groups). The exception though is the study by Ang (1985) who did not conduct interviews with viewers of the then world famous American soap opera, *Dallas*, but merely placed an advertisement in a magazine inviting viewers to write letters in which they explain why they watched *Dallas*. In this study there was never interpersonal contact between Ang (1985) and the respondents (participants) who replied to her letter. Ang (1985) analysed the letters as discourses to explain how the respondents in her study interpreted the messages in *Dallas*.

These small-scale reception studies paved the way for the ethnographic turn in audience research, or, as Alasuutari (1999:4) puts it, there was a gradual shift away from the audience reception paradigm to the new audience ethnography paradigm. Ang (1991) singles out Morley's (1980) seminal work – the *Nationwide* project – as the most important influence in the use of audience ethnography by members of the cultural studies approach.

To understand the ethnographic turn in audience studies, we must first explain the influence of classic (anthropological) ethnography on the development of audience ethnography.

7.2 CLASSIC (ANTHROPOLOGICAL) ETHNOGRAPHY

According to Spradley (1979:3), and Marcuse and Fischer (1986:18), anthropological ethnography "is the work of describing a culture ... a research process in which the anthropologist closely observes, records and engages in the daily life of another culture". The core of this form of observation is to understand the way of life from the native point of view. In other words, classic ethnography emphasises studying a phenomenon – usually an aspect of a foreign culture – in its natural environment: the researcher goes to the place where the action is happening and lives with that culture for an extended period of time. In order to really understand and grasp activities of foreign and/or subcultures, researchers should spend lengthy periods of time – at least two years and longer – among those groups. Say, for example, we want to study the communication patterns of the Khoisan (or any cultural group other than the one to which we belong) we should go and live with them for an extended period of time.

7.2.1 Assumptions of ethnography

We agree with Deacon, Pickering, Golding and Murdock (1999:250) that ethnography, as applied by audience researchers (especially those belonging to the cultural studies approach), has lost a great deal of the precision it once had. The claim to ethnographic status in studying media audiences does remind us however, of its anthropological roots. These roots are reflected in assumptions which both classic and audience ethnography share.

- Ethnographic researchers believe in the ontological assumption (shared view about the nature of social reality) that the way people interpret and interact with events, is central to social life. As researchers we want to see the world (reality) as experienced by participants (the people we observe) themselves. Put differently, we want to look at reality through the same cultural lenses as the participants do.
- Ethnographic researchers are concerned with the epistemological assumption (shared view about appropriate methods to gather knowledge about reality) that

social reality can only be revealed in natural settings – where things are happening or lived out. As researchers we must thus become part of that social reality to experience it from the native point of view, that is from the views of the cultural group(s) being studied. Applied to ethnographic research in communication, the following example:

To determine the role of the media in people's lives, we should go to the places where media use takes place (e.g. home, hostel). We then observe and talk to those people who read (magazines, newspapers) and watch (television programmes, films) to present their own points of view over a period of months. According to Deacon et al (1999:249) we can use research techniques such as in-depth or group (focus) interviews to supplement our ethnographic observation (to be discussed in section 7.4.3 in more detail).

- The above assumptions clearly explain that researchers should study cultural practices and people's appropriation of media messages in their natural surroundings and as part of the interpretive communities to which they belong. Researchers stay for extended periods of time with the culture, unit, or group of people they are studying. Applied to media studies, the text–reader engagement must be situated within an ethnographic framework which contextualises mass media – television, radio, newspapers – as part of everyday life.

7.3 EARLY AUDIENCE ETHNOGRAPHIC STUDIES

When we take a critical view of the way the first audience ethnographic studies were conducted, we see that these studies differ vastly from classic ethnography. The main reason is that many studies that claimed to be ethnographic research often simply amounted to qualitative group and in-depth interviews which did not last longer than two to three hours. As Alasuutari (1999:5) notes, these studies were not conducted in the natural context where the action occurred. (In our discussion of the assumptions above, we pointed out that to conduct proper audience ethnography, researchers must stay for extended periods of time – at least several months – in the field, or the primary site where the action is taking place.) In our earlier mention of the study conducted by Ang (1985), we noted that there was *no* interpersonal contact between the researcher and the participants – Ang did not observe and talk to the participants over a period of time.

Seiter, Borchers, Kreutzner and Warth (1991:3) explain that they are aware of the shortcomings of their seminal audience ethnographic studies. For example, considerable variations exist in terms of how the interviews were conducted, the appropriate settings for the interviews, the uses of group interviews (focus groups) and the problems of contacting television viewers willing to be studied and willing to talk about their experiences with the media. To illustrate these problems we briefly discuss two ethnographic audience studies conducted by two members of the cultural studies approach, Dorothy Hobson (1991) and John Tulloch (1991).

- *Dorothy Hobson* (1991) investigated the way television soap operas fitted into the cultural environment of the workplace (office). She conducted focus-group interviews over a period of one week with six women working in the same department and who watched the same soaps. She met with the six women at a restaurant during their lunch break and conducted focus-group interviews to determine how soaps fitted into their workplace. Hobson tape-recorded these interviews while her secretary took notes and at a later stage transcribed the tapes.
- *John Tulloch* (1991) studied a group of elderly viewers' television viewing habits and their interaction with and interpretation of the television soap opera. Tulloch conducted his research in two phases: he first analysed the letters elderly fans wrote to the fan club and to producers of soap operas. The analysis of these public discourses (fan mail) provided insight into the elderly people's feelings about an interaction with soap operas.

  The second phase of his research was to conduct interviews with the elderly in their home environment. Tulloch's uncle who lived in old age home in Bournemouth, England, arranged the interviews among 20 people he knew in the home. The first set of interviews took place in November 1985 in the flats (apartments) of the participants. During these interviews Tulloch discussed with them their television likes and dislikes, their viewing habits, daily routines and a little of their past background.

  During the second series of interviews Tulloch sat with each set of participants for a couple of hours on a Wednesday evening in November 1986, writing down their reaction to television shows (especially *Dallas*, because at the time of the investigation it was the most popular soap opera and also the focus of most reception research); their conversations; and their choices of programmes.

As we can deduce from the above examples, they are not the same as the lengthy periods of participant observation carried out by pioneers of classic ethnographic research where, for example, Malinowski lived for three years amongst the Trobriand Islanders (Moores 1993:4). Although the research of Hobson (1991) and Tulloch (1991) worked with extremely small non-random samples, and did not comply to all the requirements of "ethnography proper" research, we can deduce that both researchers attempted to deal with questions of how viewers create meaning within specific social contexts.

We must keep in mind that one of the underlying assumptions of audience ethnography, is to determine how audiences make sense of and derive pleasure from their daily interaction with their favourite media; television programmes (whether fictional or news/documentary/sports programmes) and television characters. Furthermore, audiences should be studied as part of the interpretive communities to which they belong. According to Morley (1996:321–2), the value of audience ethnographic research is to help us "to make things out" in the context where they occur. In other words, to understand the use of television and other media practices, we should go to the primary site where media use occurs.

There are, however, valid and practical reasons why researchers nowadays cannot spend lengthy periods of time in the (native) field where the action or phenomenon is happening: it is expensive, time consuming and sometimes difficult to get entry to the primary group we want to observe. We discuss these problems in section 7.6 in more detail. At this stage, suffice to say that in spite of criticism, much of the early audience research has played an important role in promoting a greater sensitivity for the potential of ethnography in audience studies.

7.4 ETHNOGRAPHY IN COMMUNICATION RESEARCH: A PRACTICAL ILLUSTRATION

We have mentioned several times in this unit, that not all researchers who conduct ethnographic research are disciples of the cultural studies approach. For example, Patricia Gillard (2000:125) feels that there is a great need to study audiences qualitatively and she recommends the ethnographic approach because it offers an excellent methodology for studying the relationships between media and audiences' interpretation. Gillard (2000) says, by "ethnographic" she does not mean the research conducted in the last 15 years by the cultural studies tradition in the United Kingdom. Instead, this author favours an ethnographic approach that involves fieldwork over a period of time, which requires that the researcher become closely involved with the group being observed. To gather data during ethnographic observation (research), Gillard (2000) recommends that researchers should employ a combination of qualitative research methods such as participant observation, focus-group interviews and in-depth interviews.

With Gillard's (2000) suggestions in mind, we provide a practical illustration of how to plan and conduct ethnographic fieldwork. We suggest the following stages, proposed by Deacon et al (1999:268–276), be followed when planning and conducting ethnographic research (fieldwork):

- Entry
- Planning
- Data collection and data analysis

7.4.1 Entry

First of all we state our topic (research problem) and define our audience to make sure that we have entry to the locations and people we need to observe.

Locations

Deacon et al (1999) distinguish the following locations:

- Open locations, which can usually be entered by the public, for example shopping malls, libraries, restaurants, cinemas, theatres, hospital out-patients departments, and so forth. We usually do not have to ask permission to enter these public venues. However, not all libraries are open to the public. For example, we know that at

University of South Africa (Unisa), both personnel and students need identity cards to enter the university library.

- Closed locations imply conditional entry because we must first ask permission to enter. For example, when a researcher outside Unisa (who is not a student or employee) wants to observe Unisa students' use of electronic media in the main library, he/she will first have to ask permission from the relevant authorities to access the library over a period of time.

  Another important closed location is the family, because we must first ask permission to enter the house for research purposes. The same rule actually applies to all media institutions, schools, and hostels. Deacon et al (1999) quite correctly observe that it is indeed ironic that the majority of the elements of mass communication (from the production of media messages to the consumption thereof by audiences) that need to be studied by means of ethnography, are closed for observation. Therefore, we must negotiate entry to these premises. Even if we want to do observations at discos and cinemas, which in principle are open to the public, an entrance fee must be paid and not all researchers – especially when there is a big age gap – can easily remain inconspicuous in a teenage disco crowd.

Roles of observers: overt and covert

When we enter premises, we must also consider the role that we, as observers, will adopt during our observation. That is, we must decide whether we will adopt an overt or covert role.

- When we adopt an *overt* (open) role, the people (participants, subjects, respondents) being observed are aware of our status as researchers and the purpose of our study.
- Alternatively we can observe under cover or as "flies on the wall" – then our roles as researchers are *covert* (our identities remain a secret) and the participants do not know that they are being observed.

We have already said that conducting research in public places does not pose any problems with regard to entrance. However, public places do not really have much use for communication researchers, because very few of the communication activities we want to investigate, are in public places. Yes, we can indeed observe peoples' nonverbal behaviour in a queue, or teenagers' behaviour at rave parties, but if we do not have a very good reason for doing so, it becomes "*so what*" research. Merely observing teenagers' behaviour will not give us enough information about the reasons why they attend rave parties, for example, or why they prefer certain music genres (e.g. hard rock, kwaito). We will thus have to combine our covert role with follow-up studies of participant observation, focus groups and in-depth interviews at the primary site where events are happening.

In brief, the most common type of ethnographic observation is where we conduct *overt research* in *closed locations*. Deacon et al (1999) say that the key to successful research work is to negotiate entry with the relevant authorities and explain

- the purpose of our research;
- what access we require and who or what we want to observe;
- the time we anticipate we will spend on location; and
- possible disturbances our research may cause.

No matter which location we need to enter, we must be honest and open about our objectives as well as the possibility of the inconvenience our research may engender.

However, we do find examples of ethnographic research (mainly in disciplines such as the social sciences) which have in the past been conducted under cover (covert research). Such instances occur because researchers have established over the years that one way to understand a "problematic" cultural sub-unit (e.g. street children, prostitutes, gays, lesbians, those involved with satanism) is to go to the places where cultural groups live, or that they frequent. One of the main problems is to gain entry to subcultural groups because if we reveal our identity as researchers, group members may become distrustful.

Furthermore, certain contexts are dangerous to enter. In such cases we can enter the premises under cover, that is conceal our roles as researchers, become a member of the group and participate actively in their daily activities. However, our physical appearance must match that of group members, for example cultural identity, age, in some cases even gender and language skills. The following is an example of an undercover observation.

- Babbie (1983:264–265) refers to a study where a researcher joined the Church of Satan to study the reasons why people become satanists, their rituals and the dynamics of interpersonal relationships in their church. Through his participation in church activities, the researcher was able to learn details of rituals and other practices that were kept secret from outsiders. The researcher regretted his decision to keep his identity and purpose concealed, and felt increasingly unethical. In the final stages of his research he went to the high priest to tell him the truth and to request permission to publish an article on his findings.
- The critical question was whether the priest felt that the researcher had been unethical in attempting deception. "Not at all" the priest smiled "it was an appropriate satanic thing to do!" (1983:265).

We must add that such a warm "priestly" acceptance is not always the case. In fact, involvement with certain street populations such as drug dealers, prostitutes, and gangsters may present real physical danger to researchers.

When we conduct a study that requires that we have to conceal our identities, we are faced with an ethical dilemma – is it ethical to deceive people we are studying? We may solve the problem by means of a debriefing interview. "Debriefing" means that we inform participants that they have been observed without their knowledge; we explain the importance of our study and ask their permission to use the data for research purposes. We should also give the participants the assurance that they are entitled to have access to the outcomes of the research project.

7.4.2 Planning

Ethnographic research, like all forms of research, needs careful and flexible planning. Without a well-constructed plan of what our research entails, we will soon drift into confusion. Deacon et al (1999:268–276) provide the following guidelines to plan ethnographic research:

- What do we wish to find out?
- What information do we need?
- Who are the people we need to observe and talk to?
- What questions should be addressed?
- What are the dynamics of social relations of the culture we want to study?

Although these guidelines may change in the course of our investigation, we must keep them in mind and constantly revise them throughout the period we spend in the field. Our questions should be based on a clear theoretical understanding of the issues raised by our research. We do not conduct ethnographic research because we want to *see what it is like in X ("so what"* research, referred to earlier), but try and answer questions arising from our literature review of the topic and the planning of our observation. We must thus familiarise ourselves with what other researchers and theorists in the literature have to say about the topic that we want to investigate.

We apply the above guidelines to the hypothetical example of students' use of electronic media in the main library of the University of South Africa (Unisa).

- *What do we wish to find out?*
  Our main aim is to establish why students use the electronic media, that is, computers and the Internet, in the Unisa library and not at home or other venues such as telecentres, Internet cafés, schools and post offices.
- *What information do we need?*
  We will not have difficulty in finding literature on the use of electronic media by First World and Third World countries. We may find that statistics in the literature reveal that the use of electronic media in Third World countries is lower than that in First World countries. As we mentioned earlier, we must also have a thorough theoretical understanding of the implications of electronic media. In the literature we find different theoretical views – or schools of thought – on electronic media. For example, one school offers a Utopian vision of the future, that is, all media users will have unlimited access to computer networks and will become part of the electronic information highway.

  On the other hand, we may find theories with a negative view of the influence of electronic media. Such theories for example, offer a Dystopian vision of the future, which means that an increase in choices of electronic media implies higher costs that will inevitably produce greater inequalities in access to electronic information between nations as well as individuals (McQueen 1998:221). In other words, the gap between the "haves and the have-nots" will increase, because only a small élite will be able to afford new electronic media.

  These theories may be used to help us to structure our research questions.

- *Who do we need to observe and talk to?*
  The main aim of our ethnographic research (our hypothetical example) is to establish why students use electronic media in the Unisa library and not at home or other venues such as telecentres, Internet cafés, schools, post offices, and so forth. We first observe and talk to student users to determine whether the Unisa library is the primary location (site) where they use electronic media. We then make arrangements with these students to talk to them and observe them over a period of time.
- *What questions should be addressed?*
  Based on our literature survey and theoretical points of departure, we may use the following questions to guide our ethnographic research:
  - Why do students use the electronic media in the library and not at home or other venues such as telecentres and Internet cafés?
  - Are the students from disadvantaged communities?
  - For which courses are the students who use the electronic media, registered?
  - What are their computer skills (how computer-literate are they)?
  - Which computer and Internet facilities do they use most often?
  - For what purposes do they use these facilities?
  - How do they perceive theories about the gap between the information rich and information poor societies?
  - How do they feel about the increasing pressure to become part of the electronic superhighway?
  - Do they have optimistic/pessimistic views of the consequences of the electronic superhighway?
  - What suggestions do they offer to make more computer facilities available to students who do not have access to computers and the Internet at home or venues near the place where they live?
- *What are the dynamics of social relations of the culture we want to study?*
  For example, do they form a social collective group with a shared group spirit? (See the case study of Lemish below.)
  - Can we identify different types of users such as leaders, followers and observers? (See the case study of Lemish below.)

During our observation we may notice that many students visiting the library, do not use the computer and Internet facilities. We may then decide to observe and talk to those students as well, and find out why they do not use these facilities. *We can now see how our initial planning may change as we observe other behaviour that we did not initially set out to study.*

As Deacon et al (1999) point out, the crux of observation is to keep a list of all the questions we need to address and alongside them we jot down the kinds of data we need to collect. Every day we have to revise the list to make sure that we have not omitted something, and then adjust our planning to supply the missing information or data.

7.4.3 Data collection

We may use a combination of research methods (techniques) such as participant observation, group discussions (focus groups) and in-depth interviews in ethnographic research.

- Participant observation requires that the researcher get actively involved in the daily activities of the group being investigated, whether the group is a community of people, or an organisation, or a crowd of people involved in a process or event (e.g. toy-toying; marching; a family watching television together). In its original form, participant observation implies that we participate fully in the group being observed, to become part of the group's inner circle (Huysamen 1994:169). The role we adopt is that of *participant-as-observer* (Wimmer & Dominick 1997). Participant observation allows us to gradually build up a relationship of trust with the participants which then enables us to obtain first-hand information about the topic being investigated.
- Nowadays, however, approaches such as the cultural studies approach, find it acceptable to merely observe activities and talk to the participants over a period of time without getting actively involved. For example, in the research conducted by Dorothy Hobson (see section 7.3 of this unit) she spoke to female soap opera viewers in a restaurant over a period of five days to determine how soaps fitted into the cultural environment of their workplace. In other words, she did not actively watch soaps with these women, neither did she go to their place of work to actively participate in the soap opera culture being created at the workplace. This type of observation is called partial observation where the researcher adopts the role of *observer-as-participant* (Wimmer & Dominick 1997). Keep in mind that because our observation is overt (open), we must inform the participants about our status as researchers and ask their permission to observe them over a period of time.

  Applied to our example, we observe what the students are doing at the computer centre in the library. For example, do they stand in rows to use the computer? Or do they have to make bookings to use the computer facilities? How much time are they allowed to work on the computer – half an hour, one hour or more? As we gradually build up a relationship of trust with the students, we may ask them if we may sit with them while they are working on the computer. In this manner we will obtain first-hand information on what computer and Internet facilities they use most often.

To supplement our ethnographic observations, we may also use the focus-group method and the in-depth interview.

- The focus-group method is used when we want to investigate a group's attitudes and meanings about a specific topic – a group is typically composed of six to 12 members. Say, for example, that during our participant observation we see that there are different opinions about the research problem being investigated. We may then use focus-group interviews where we put together those people who share the same views, and conduct an interview with them as a group.

  In our example of Unisa students' use of computers and the Internet, we may conduct focus-group interviews with users and non-users.

- The in-depth interview (one-to-one-interview) is used when we want to conduct interviews with separate participants, that is, on a one-to-one basis. Say, for example, we need additional information of a personal nature (for instance, why a person is not participating in the focus-group discussion or group activities) we may conduct an interview with that participant alone.

It is important to record our conversations with students. The most popular recording devices are *tape recorders, video cameras,* and *note taking.* We should first ask the participants' permission to use tape recorders and video cameras. We may conceal the apparatus in order not to disturb the natural flow of conversation that could be impeded by participants feeling self-conscious or embarrassed. Note taking should also be done as unobtrusively as possible because feverish note taking can be distracting.

The analysis of ethnographic data consists mainly of filing and analysing the content of our field notes and recorded interviews. Filing involves the arranging of transcriptions of interviews and our field notes in an orderly way, for example by using categories. The types of categories will depend on the research problem and the type of data we have collected. In our example of Unisa students' use of electronic media in the library, we can use the following categories based on our research questions:

- Primary users, secondary users (those students who have access to computers in other venues), and non-users
- Computer and Internet facilities used most often
- Positive/negative perception of the new electronic superhighway
- Suggestions of how to make more computers available to students
- The dynamics of social relationships

To further explain ethnography in practice, we provide an actual example of audience ethnographic research, in the following case study.

7.5 A CASE STUDY: AUDIENCE ETHNOGRAPHIC RESEARCH

We use the study by Daphna Lemish (1985) as an example of actual ethnographic research. Although Lemish refers to her study as "naturalistic", we equate "naturalistic" with "ethnographic" because her research complies with all the requirements of ethnographic research.

Case study 7.1: Soap opera viewing in college: a naturalistic enquiry (Lemish 1985)

Lemish conducted a naturalistic (ethnographic) investigation of the soap opera viewing patterns of college students at the Ohio State University in the United States of America (USA). The aim of her study was to examine a particular sub-audience (or a subcultural group) of soap viewers in specific viewing situations, namely college students who view soaps in public college locations (context of viewing). Because these locations were open to the public, Lemish had no problem entering the premises. The students were observed in two locations, the sports lounge and the recreational centre on campus, where access to these locations was free to all students. At 14h55 each afternoon these two locations were filled with students who wanted to enjoy a break from schoolwork and to watch their favourite soap, *General Hospital*. According to Lemish, viewing soaps was an established pastime for students, involving both females and males, and under-graduate and post-graduate students. The viewing of *General Hospital* thus has become a ritual.

The following research questions guided Lemish's research:

- Why do students watch soap operas?
- Which kinds of needs do soap operas satisfy?
- What role does the social context play in the viewing of soap operas?

Lemish's study was based on the following theoretical assumptions:

- Viewers actively select media content and show a definite preference for particular programmes.
- Exposure to the medium fulfils certain needs such as those of entertainment, relaxation, excitement, and so on.
- The social context of media use (e.g. television viewing) plays an important role in the lives of viewers.

This research was a longitudinal study, which means that Lemish studied the students' soap viewing patterns over a period of time of nine months. A total of 55 note-taking observation hours took place in the two locations (the sports lounge and the recreational centre on campus).

Lemish used naturalistic (ethnographic) field research methods such as participant observation, in-depth and group interviewing during the nine months that her fieldstudy lasted. The students she interviewed were aware that Lemish conducted research. She used a concealed tape recorder for the recording of spontaneous conversations. These interviews enabled Lemish to draw conclusions about students as social groups, for example to identify different types of viewers such as leaders, followers, observers and challengers:

- *Leaders* were regular viewers, well versed in the story lines and plot and always prepared to share their knowledge with enthusiasm. They were always surrounded by other viewers who, by then, had become acquaintances.
- *Followers* were identified by their attentiveness about what leaders had to say. Although followers were familiar with the story lines, they usually asked questions which were answered by the leaders. Leaders thus influenced other viewers' interpretation of soaps.
- *Observers* were often situated in a secondary viewing situation, were quiet and did not initiate conversation. Although observers did watch *General Hospital*,

they told Lemish that it was more fun to watch other viewers' reactions such as shouting and cheering in response to what occurred in soaps.

- *Challengers*. These viewers made challenging, disapproving and negative remarks and could not understand why viewers become addicted to soaps. During the interviews, however, it became clear that challengers were quite familiar with story lines and characters in *General Hospital*.

As far as the social context of soap viewing is concerned, the results indicate that student viewers did form a social collective group, as short-lived as it was, with a shared group spirit; for example viewers shared information, opinions and personal feelings with strangers. Together they laughed, giggled, clapped hands and cheered. They gathered around leaders, and passed essential information around the room. In some cases lasting friendships were formed and soap viewing served to cement their friendship.

The results thus reveal that the social context (viewing in public places) does play an important role in viewing soap operas. Many of the students admit that they do not watch with the same intensity and involvement when watching alone or at home. Lemish came to the conclusion that when watching television programmes in public places with peers, students discover a new interactive, social dimension of television viewing. The research results also provide additional information about the role that leaders play in group dynamics.

The results of the research also indicated that the following needs were satisfied by soaps: to relax; to be entertained; and to escape from daily routine or anxiety.

To test the validity of the study, Lemish conducted a series of post-research interviews with participants and informants. These interviews generally confirmed her conclusions and provided additional validity to the research results.

7.6 CRITICAL EVALUATION OF ETHNOGRAPHY IN COMMUNICATION RESEARCH

7.6.1 Advantages

- Ethnography allows us to obtain *first-hand information* on the scene or primary site where an event is taking place. For example, to assess students' motives for using computer facilities in the Unisa library, we get more information compared to when we ask students in a questionnaire how many times they use computer and Internet facilities. For instance, in the questionnaire they fill in that they use the computer and Internet in the library only once or twice a week. Reasons may be lack of reliable transport, economic factors and so on. However, we would not have been aware of these reasons if we did not observe and talk to the students. In addition, if they are delayed due to a taxi strike, for example, how does it affect their use of electronic media? If they have to make bookings in advance, they lose out. In other words, what frustrations and problems do they experience to obtain access to computer and related services? Obviously, these complex variables will be difficult to investigate by methods other than ethnographic observation that allows us to probe for additional information.

- First-hand information also implies *immediacy*. When we are at the primary site we actually witness event happenings and therefore do not have to rely on people's memories – we know how fallible our memories of events can be! Deacon et al (1999:259) provide the example of a film director who works with children. Instead of asking "how do you usually handle children?" we should rather become eyewitnesses of how members of the film crew control and manipulate unruly children.
- Ethnographic research is *flexible* because we can modify our assumptions and research questions as we continue with our observation. We have already provided an example in our discussion of our observation of Unisa students, that is, that although we initially set out to observe those students who use computer and Internet services, we realised, as the observation progressed, that non-users should also be studied. In a survey this cannot be done because researchers must keep to the pre-planned questionnaire. Thus, if crucial information has not been included, the survey questionnaire cannot be changed.
- Ethnography is one of the best ways to study the *subtle nuances* of people's attitudes and behaviours. The result is that we obtain rich and detailed information about the group that we are observing. In addition we gain this information from the perspectives of the people being observed. That is, we see and experience reality as the participants do.

7.6.2 Disadvantages

- One of the big limitations of ethnographic research is that although such research projects are based on *small samples*, researchers often interpret these results as though they were collected via large probability sampling techniques. Such practice will create problems in the long run because our decisions may be incorrect if they are based on the results obtained by means of small samples (Wimmer & Dominick 1997).
- Deacon et al (1999:262) remind us that sometimes *participation can hinder observation*. This happens when we get involved with the participants and their views to the extent that we begin to *"go natural"*. That is, we begin to think and act as the participants do. Babbie (1983:248) says that as researchers we have a dual role: one where we experience the activities of the group, and the other where we maintain enough distance to remain objective and scientific.
- We must also be careful that we do not *intrude on people's privacy*. Peering over people's shoulders, or perching on their desks asking embarrassing questions, can make participants uncomfortable. Unfortunately, there are no hard and fast rules

about how to handle such problems. The golden rule is to "read the situation" and be sensitive; to back off when we observe that people are becoming embarrassed.

- Finally, we have pointed out that few researchers have the luxury of time and money required to spend months or even years in the (native) field where the action or phenomenon is happening. This is, indeed, a real problem, as can be seen when working through the sources at the end of this unit; we notice that in most cases research examples were conducted between 1930 and 1980. (An alternative to ethnographic research is provided in the summary below.)

Summary

In this unit we discussed ethnography as one form of observation in media studies. We began by explaining that early reception research paved the way for the use of ethnography in audience research by the cultural studies approach. To understand audience ethnography, we explained classic ethnography and the assumptions that audience and classic ethnography share.

Then followed examples of pioneer studies in audience ethnography. We indicated that although the pioneer studies of Hobson (1991) and Tulloch (1991) worked with extremely small samples, and that their research did not comply with the requirements of "ethnographic proper" research, both researchers tried to deal with how viewers interpret messages within specific social and cultural contexts.

In order to create an awareness of what it entails to conduct ethnographic research, we included an illustration of the practical side of ethnography. We discussed three stages in ethnographic research, namely entry, planning, data collection and analysis – each stage was illustrated with practical examples. We further explained ethnography in practice by means of actual audience ethnographic research (the study by Daphna Lemish). In the last section of this unit we provided a critical appraisal of the use of ethnography in media studies.

In conclusion: in the literature there exists confusion about the differences between reception research and audience ethnography. For example, Scroder (1999:42) says that the contemporary ethnographic approach to studying media audiences includes both reception research and more genuinely ethnographic approaches. Unfortunately, this is an over-simplified and perhaps incorrect assumption, especially against the background of the basic requirement of ethnography that communication researchers must spend at least a few months in the field (the primary site) with the group they want to observe. Although we have discussed the "ethnographic turn" in reception research, this only applies to researchers of the cultural studies approach.

As we have repeatedly said in this unit, there are many researchers who do not have the time and/or money to conduct intensive, ethnographic research. Fortunately, however, there is another option available for qualitative researchers. The option is reception research (reception theory in practice – see Unit 6) which is very much alive and has been used by many qualitative audience researchers, for example

- Biltereyst (1995) investigated Belgium audiences' interpretation of locally produced television programmes.
- Liebes and Katz's (1990) well-known research studied foreign cultures' interpretation of the American soap opera *Dallas*.
- Pitout (1996) conducted reception research to determine how female viewers of different cultures in South Africa interpreted the portrayal of the South African realities in the locally produced soap *Egoli: Place of Gold*.

All three of the above studies used focus-group discussions to gather data about audiences' interpretation of messages. Furthermore, there are also examples of actual reception research in Dickinson, Harindranath and Linne (1998). The advantage of reception research over ethnography is that researchers do not have to stay for months at the primary site of the group that they want to investigate or observe.

Finally, when we want to collect "thick" descriptive data, and when we want to put flesh to the bones of quantitative research methods (such as survey research), we need intense procedures to collect such data. One of the logical choices then is ethnography.

Research activities

1 Explain in one paragraph, the ethnographic turn in reception research.

2 Define classic (anthropological) ethnography in your own words.

3 Which assumptions do classic and audience ethnography share? Explain each assumption in your own words and illustrate your explanation with examples related to media audiences.

4 Compare the pioneer audience ethnographic research of Hobson (1991) and Tulloch (1991). Explain the similarities and differences between these two studies in terms of the ontological and epistemological assumptions of ethnography.

5 Use the following three stages to explain how you will conduct ethnographic research: *entry, planning* and *data collection*. Select a topic that lends itself to ethnographic research. You may consider one of the following topics:

   - The television viewing patterns of a group of four families. You can, for example, concentrate on the role of family dynamics in television programme selection: Who decides what to watch? Who controls the remote? Start with observing your own family.
   - The social aspects of watching videos, soap operas, sports programmes and so on
   - The role different music genres (types) play in the lives of teenagers
   - AIDS awareness and the role of the media
   - Family planning and the role of the media
   - The influence of private computers on family relations
   - Eating disturbances related to media portrayals (role models)
   - The role of cellular (cell) phones in peoples' lives

- Media use of professional women
- Group (team) dynamics involved in writing a script for a television advertisement

6 Apply the advantages and disadvantages of ethnography to your ethnographic research topic.

7 How do you feel about concealed observation in ethnography? Make a list of five topics that you think should be studied by concealing your identities. Give reasons why you think these topics should be studied under cover.

8 After you have studied the case study by Lemish (1985), answer the following questions:
   a) Did Lemish have to ask for permission to enter the college locations?
   b) Would you describe the students' locations as open or closed?
   c) Which role did Lemish adopt – overt or covert?
   d) What was the main purpose of her study?
   e) What are the ontological and epistemological assumptions of Lemish's study?
   f) Which theory did Lemish use to formulate the theoretical assumptions of her study?
   g) Did she formulate research questions and/or hypotheses?
   h) Was the study short term or longitudinal?
   i) Which research methods (techniques) did she use to gather the data?
   j) Which data-gathering techniques did Lemish use to record the data?
   k) What were her main findings with regard to the dynamics of social group relations?

Further reading

Deacon, D, Pickering, M, Golding, P & Murdock, G (eds). 1999. *Researching communications: A practical guide to methods in media and cultural analysis.* London: Arnold.

Dickinson, R, Harindranath, R & Linne, O (eds). 1998. *Approaches to audiences: a reader.* London: Harper.

Gillard, P. 2000. Shaping audiences online: principles of audience development for cultural institutions. *Media International Australia* 94:117–137.

Morley, D. 1992. *Television, audiences and cultural studies.* London: Routledge.

Moores, S. 1993. *Interpreting audiences: the ethnography of media consumption.* London: Sage.

Seiter, E, Borchers, H, Kreutzner, G & Warth E (eds). 1991. *Remote control: television, audiences, & cultural power.* Paperback edition. London: Routledge.

Bibliography

Alasuutari, P (ed). 1999. *The media audience.* London: Sage.

Ang, I. 1991. Wanted: audiences. On the politics of empirical audience studies, in *Remote control: television, audiences, & cultural power,* edited by E Seiter, H Borchers, G Kreutzner & E Warth. Paperback edition. London: Routledge.

Babby, E. 1983. *The practice of social research.* 3rd edition. Belmont, CA: Wadsworth.
Biltereyst, D. 1995. *Hollywood in het avondland.* Brussel: Vubpress.
Brunsdon, C.1981. Crossroads: notes on soap opera. *Screen* 22(4)52–7.
Deacon, D, Pickering, M, Golding, P & Murdock, G (eds). 1999. *Researching communications: A practical guide to methods in media and cultural analysis.* London: Arnold.
Dickinson, R, Harindranath, R & Linne, O (eds). 1998. *Approaches to audiences: a reader.* London: Harper.
Fejes, F. 1984. Critical mass communication research and media effects: the problem of the disappearing audience. *Media, Culture and Society* 6(3)219–232.
Gillard, P. 2000. Shaping audiences online: principles of audience development for cultural institutions. *Media International Australia* 94:117–137.
Hall, S.1980. Encoding/decoding, in *Culture, media, language* edited by S Hall, D Hobson, A Lowe & P Willis. Birmingham: University of Birmingham.
Hobson, D. 1991. Soap operas at work, in *Remote control: television, audiences, & cultural power,* edited by E Seiter, H Borchers, G Kreutzner & E Warth. Paperback edition. London: Routledge.
Lemish, D. 1985. Soap opera viewing in college: a naturalistic enquiry. *Journal of Broadcasting & Electronic Media* 29(3):275–293.
Liebes, T & Katz, E. 1990. *The export of meaning: cross-cultural readings of Dallas.* New York: Oxford University Press.
Marcuse, GE & Fischer, MMJ. 1986. *Anthropology as cultural critique.* Chicago and London: The University of Chicago Press.
McQueen, D. 1998. *Television: a media student's guide.* London: Arnold.
Morley, D. 1980. *The nationwide audience.* London: British Film Institute.
Morley, D. 1996. The geography of television: ethnography, communications and community, in *The audience and its landscape*, edited by J Hay, L Grossberg & E Wartella. Boulder, CO: Westview, Press.
Pitout, M. 1996. Televisie en resepsiestudie: 'n analise van kykersinterpretasie van die seep-opera "Egoli: Plek van Goud". Ongepubliseerde doktorale proefskrif. Pretoria: Universiteit van Suid-Afrika.
Scroder, KM. (1999). The best of two worlds? Media audience research between rival paradigms, in *The media audience*, edited by P Alasuutari. London: Sage.
Seiter, E, Borchers, H, Kreutzner, G & Warth E (eds). 1991. *Remote control: television, audiences, & cultural power.* Paperback edition. London: Routledge.
Spradley, JP.1979. *The ethnographic interview.* New York: Holt, Rinehart & Winston.
Tulloch, J. 1991. Approaching the audience: the elderly, in *Remote control: television, audiences, & cultural power*, edited by E Seiter, H Borchers, G Kreutzner & E Warth. Paperback edition. London: Routledge.
Wimmer, RD & Dominick, JR. 1997. *Mass media research: an introduction.* 5th edition. Belmont, CA: Wadsworth.

The Social Psychology of Media Consumption

8

Magriet Pitout

Overview

When we consume mass media, there are a lot of physical and mental activities going on. For example, when we watch television, we must first decide what we want to watch, then switch on the television set and sit down with something to eat and/or to drink. If we cannot make up our minds about what to watch, we may zip and zap through channels to find the right programme. These are more or less the physical activities associated with television viewing.

The second activity deals with what is going on in our minds when we make meanings (interpretation) of the media products we consume. Therefore, we must also study the psychology of media consumption. That is, we must understand the psychological relationships between messages and consumers, with the emphasis on psychological states. However, these states are always part and parcel of our interpersonal relationships and social circumstances because there is a dialectical relationship between our minds, other people and our social and cultural circumstances.

Making sense of open texts – that is, where the same text can generate different meanings – involves both rational/cognitive and affective (emotional) dimensions. This is contrary to the psychology model, which follows a more rational approach. The latest trend in audience studies is therefore to also pay attention to the "irrational" features of sense-making which are especially operative in the case of polysemic (open) television programmes. (See Unit 6: Reception theory, for a discussion of the polysemic nature of television texts.)

In this unit we look at both the psychological and social aspects of media consumption. First we consider the views of Grossberg, Wartella and Whitney (1998) who point out that because researchers have failed to adequately describe the psychological relationship between media products and audience members, we should have a closer look at the psychological state of audiences. These "mind" states include the affective state dimensions such as emotions, moods and pleasures.

Because Grossberg et al (1998) concentrate mainly on the affective dimension of the psychology of media consumption, we also consider the contributions of Höijer (1992; 1998) who discusses the cognitive dimension in detail. Hoijer (1998) contends that although external factors such as the physical viewing environment, family interaction, and social talk do have a great influence on our interpretation of the media, we should also consider our mental experiences – that which we carry within ourselves. Therefore "mind" is a central concept which needs to be investigated. When we address "mind" or thought processes we address a missing link in reception analysis, which, according to Hoijer (1998), is the cognitive level of interpretation. "Cognitive" not only means intellectual, rational and analytical processes but also includes emotional processes. Therefore, the cognitive dimension can also be irrational, emotional and intuitive (innate). However, without cognitive processes we cannot interpret messages because it is precisely that which occurs in our minds, that determines reception.

After our discussion of the affective and cognitive dimensions of media consumption, we discuss the sociology of media consumption which includes the physical contexts where we consume messages (for example at home, with friends, and in public venues – bars, community centres, restaurants, theatres) and the influence thereof on our interaction with and interpretation of media messages.

Learning outcomes

After completing this study unit you should be able to demonstrate your knowledge and understanding of

- cognition, and the illustration thereof with examples;
- the application of the psychological dimensions to everyday media experiences; and
- the application of the sociology of media consumption to everyday media experiences.

8.1 INTRODUCTION

We have already seen that our study of audiences is based on the assumption that we are actively involved in selecting and interpreting media messages (cf. units 6 and 7). A great deal of cognitive activity goes on when we consume media. Cognition means "the act of attending to and making sense of the world; it is the application of consciousness to the world" (Grossberg et al 1998:239). Even viewers who show no physical activity (they are sometimes called "couch potatoes") are cognitively involved while watching television because their minds are engaged in an effort to make sense of what is going on, on the screen. In other words, cognition refers to mental processes we are engaged in when we try to make sense of incoming messages. Cognition includes our mental processes such as perception, memory, reasoning, judgement, imagination, thinking, understanding, interpretation and our ability to speak (Microsoft Encarta Encyclopaedia 1999).

Apart from the general socially acceptable meaning we attach to media messages, researchers agree that interpretation is also subjective and highly individual. For example, think of different ways members of the same household interpret messages – an adolescent may find the financial section of a newspaper boring, while the father reads these sections faithfully every day.

8.2 SOCIAL PSYCHOLOGY OF MEDIA CONSUMPTION: THE AFFECTIVE DIMENSION

To explain the relations between audiences and media, Grossberg et al (1998:237) suggest that we should look more directly at the psychological states of the audience, keeping in mind that such states are always part and parcel of interpersonal relationships and social circumstances of audiences. Grossberg et al (1998) concentrate specifically on the affective dimension of psychology. Affective states deal with feelings and emotions such as being angry, sad, or happy. We may over a period of a day experience these emotions at different levels of intensity, for example we can be very angry, or extremely happy, while at other times we only experience moderate feelings of happiness, irritation and anger.

We look at three affective states proposed by Grossberg et al (1998:250–257) and their relations to our media use:

- Emotional state
- Mood state
- Pleasure state

8.2.1 Emotional state

Emotions mean certain feelings or sensations caused by our interaction with media products. For example:

- Advertisements often use an emotional appeal to manipulate us to buy a product by invoking certain feelings such as "feeling good". For example, advertisements for facial creams usually promise women eternal youth and happiness. These are of course false promises because older women know from experience that facial creams do not really do the trick. But because of the emphasis in society on youthfulness, the media perpetuate the idea that being young is more desirable and acceptable than being old and wrinkly. To prevent the undesirable effects of ageing, women will time and again fall for false promises in advertisements about eternal youth. And although facial creams may have wonderful, velvet textures that make us feel good, they will not remove wrinkles. However, not only women are lured by advertisements – we can think of many examples of how men are manipulated to buy products to retain youth, for example lotions to prevent hair loss, products to increase their sexual performance, and so on.
- Audiences, in turn, also use the media to experience certain emotions. For example, we may even enjoy shedding a few tears (of happiness) when a film has a happy ending. Watching our favourite sports team can also provide us with a wide variety of emotional reactions and rewards, such as being excited and cheerful when our team beats the opposition. However, the opposite happens when our team loses!

  Research results (cf. Grossberg et al 1998:151) indicate that audiences do not seem to get tired of such emotional experiences. Below we provide examples to illustrate how viewers repeatedly watch the same film, television programme, or listen to the same music and every time they experience the same emotions:

- A female viewer watched the film – the *Titanic* – 13 times and each time she cried at the end where the hero (played by Leonardo DiCaprio) sacrifices his life for his beloved in the icy waters of the North Atlantic Ocean.
- Audience members sometimes watch the same thriller repeatedly and no matter how prepared they are for the scary scenes, they still scream at the same points, although they know what is coming. For example, one of the scariest scenes in the psychological thriller *Psycho*, is the famous shower scene where the female character is stabbed more than 50 times with a knife whilst taking a shower. And although viewers may have seen this film several times, and know the exact sequence of the murder, they have the same emotional response each time they watch the shower scene.

We can also relate to the reliving of emotional feelings when watching reruns of sport programmes, especially in tightly contested matches. Although we know the outcome of a match, we still experience the tension and excitement when our team scored the winning goal or try, or when an athlete won a race. Many South Africans may still remember the Olympic Games in Atlanta in 1996 when

- Josiah Thugwane won gold in the marathon,
- Penny Heyns received two gold medals for swimming (100-metre and 200-metre breaststroke) and
- Hezegiel Sepeng received a silver medal for second place in the 800 metres.

Almost all of us who are interested in athletics, experience the excitement and tension again when we watch these races for a second and a third time. That is, we relive the same emotions – the tension, the excitement and perhaps fighting back tears of joy and pride when these outstanding athletes win their events and their medals.

Another memorable occasion was when South Africa's rugby team beat the All Blacks (New Zealand) in 1995 to become the rugby world champions. During the 1999 world championships, the South African team was dethroned by Australia. But in spite of the fact that the South African team are no longer the rugby world champions, rugby fans are still buying (in the year 2000 – six years later) the video of the unforgettable match to experience time and again how South Africa became world champions in 1995.

8.2.2 Mood state

Perhaps we all have a vague idea of what mood means. Broadly we can define mood as a state of feeling which is closely connected to our emotions: sometimes we feel good or "on top of the world" and sometimes we feel bad or "down in the dumps". Our mood, whether good or bad, will colour just about everything that happens to us during the course of a day. We agree with Grossberg et al (1998:251) that mood is actually very complex and unstable – things that made us happy yesterday will irritate us today and vice versa. For example, when we are relaxed and at peace with the world, we enjoy a comedy and have a good laugh. However, if we are in a bad mood for whatever reason(s), we may find the humour tacky, the acting poor and switch off the television because we find the comedy irritating.

One of the most powerful means of affecting people's mood is music. Research results indicate that the omnipresence of background music has a calming effect on people (Grossberg et al 1998: 252–253). This may be one of the reasons why many students play their favourite music whilst studying. We can use music for different purposes such as to improve a bad mood, or to put us in the right mood. Because music has such a powerful effect, we associate it with certain events, for example, lullabies from our childhood, songs we were taught at school, and songs that remind us of lovers and/or loved ones. In other words, we should consider the sort of memories different types of music evoke.

In short, we can use music to manipulate our mood. When we think about the power of music in our lives, we can ask ourselves what memories – happy or sad – do certain songs bring back. These memories may be unique for each person. However, music can also construct socially shared moods, for instance the singing of a national anthem may enhance feelings of unity. In South Africa the Minister of Sport, Mr Ngconde Balfour and the previous coach of the rugby team Mr Nick Mallet, requested white spectators to partake in the singing of our national anthem with more gusto when attending international rugby matches. We can deduce that the underlying message of this request is that the singing of our national anthem may enhance the feeling of unity in South African society.

8.2.3 Pleasure state

When we ask people why they watch particular television programmes and films, tune in to particular radio stations, read newspapers/magazines, or prefer certain music genres, the majority will say "because we enjoy them". Enjoyment and pleasure are closely related because we cannot really enjoy something that is not pleasurable. (Also see Unit 8, Volume 1 for a discussion of entertainment and pleasure.)

However, Grossberg et al (1998: 253) warn that the notion of pleasure is not as simple as it appears because pleasure involves mechanisms which we know very little about. In the context of this study, pleasure in the first place involves different relationships we have with the media. Let us consider some affective (emotional) relationships we may have with the media and which give the majority of us great pleasure:

- Media consumption affords us the opportunity to escape from or forget negative situations. For example, when we have an argument with our spouse/partner or boss, or if we do not want to get involved in an argument we escape from the situation by means of one or other mass medium (reading a book, watching television). We also escape from the everyday humdrum existence because it is pleasurable to become part of a dream world where our daily problems are temporarily forgotten.

- Many of us find it pleasurable to identify with a particular character. Identification for example reinforces certain moral beliefs, values and worldviews that we share with a character(s). However, we need not always have to identify with the protagonist (the traditional hero) – many times we wish to be like the antagonist but dare not admit so publicly. And through identification with the bad guy (albeit temporarily), we fulfil socially unacceptable desires and needs which provide us with a cathartic experience. (Also see Unit 6, Reception theory for a discussion of identification.)
- Many viewers like to get involved with the personal and emotional life of television characters. Fiske (1987) calls this the pleasure of gossip. Research on soap operas indicates that soap fans love the "gossipy" nature of soaps. Because viewers see soap characters every weekday they regard these characters as friends; friends they can talk to and share in their hardship, problems and joy (Pitout 1998).

8.3 SOCIAL PSYCHOLOGY OF MEDIA CONSUMPTION: THE COGNITIVE DIMENSION

As we already explained (cf. units 6 and 7), interpretation is the core of the reception process, therefore "mind" (also called cognition in social psychology) is a central concept that needs to be addressed.

The cognitive dimension is complex and difficult to understand. To simplify matters, we base our discussion on the following concepts and mind processes identified by Hoijer (1992; 1998):

- Universal, cultural and individual experiences
- Cognitive schemas which consist of
  - mode schemas
  - perspectivising schemas
- Psycho-dynamic processes

8.3.1 Universal, cultural and individual experiences

To get a better understanding of cognitive schemas, we first pay attention to how the formation of our cognitive structures are influenced by the following experiences:

- *Universal-human experiences* are those experiences we all share because we are human beings. That is, we all have in common basic experiences such as the cycle of life and death which includes birth, childhood, adulthood, ageing, health, illness, death. And almost all of us share universal emotions such as fear, love, pain, anger and hate. Höijer (1998:591) says that when we interact with television messages, we focus on media content or themes that are "psychologically close", that is, universal human experiences that we have in common or share with others. Most of us have, to a greater or lesser degree, experienced feelings of compassion when suffering, loneliness and pain are portrayed in the mass media. A picture in a newspaper of a child dying of hunger, a news event of a person having been kidnapped or an account of a brutal murder would arouse such feelings. Over the period April 2000 to October 2000, many of us followed the news about Callie and Monique Strydom of South Africa, who were kept hostage by Philippine rebels on Jolo Island. We could to a great extent relate to the emotions they experienced: despair, hope and despondency.

These common-ground human experiences make up the universal dimension – a dimension that contributes to and explains the global success of narratives (stories) and genres. Or, as Hoijer (1998:170) says, without the universal dimension of experience, the global success of narratives and genres would probably not be possible. We may now have a better understanding why American television programmes such as *The Bold and the Beautiful* (soap opera), *Ally McBeal* and *The Cosby Show* (situation comedies), *Witness* (police and detective thriller), *ER* (hospital drama) have such universal appeal with different cultures worldwide: they all address universal human experiences such as love, broken relationships, uncertainties about identities, role relations (*Ally McBeal*), justice and the fight against crime, sickness and death.

- *Cultural experiences* are the products of a society, culture or a subculture in which we grow up. Since the day we are born, we are socialised into the norms and value systems of our society, our gender roles, religion and social class. The socialising agents are our parents and family, the schools we attend, the religion we believe in, and the mass media. Thus, together with universal interpretations and experiences, we also find variations in interpretation patterns. Variations in interpretation are due to interpretation frames or cognitive schemata (see the discussion below) that are to a large extent determined by our social and cultural history. Therefore, different cultures will use interpretation frames based on their cultural background and cultural experiences to interpret media messages.

  For example, in a study dealing with how women of different cultures interpret the messages in the multicultural South African soap *Egoli: Place of Gold*, the researcher found that this soap opera is not popular with black respondents. One of the main reasons is that both Afrikaans and English are used in *Egoli*. One black respondent is against the use of Afrikaans. She said:

  > ... there is too much Afrikaans. Basically we [the blacks] don't like Afrikaans ... because of the bad connotation of the past – it is the language of the oppressor. Afrikaans is a stigmatised language. And now we don't want to listen to a language that caused so many problems for us in the past.
  >
  > (Pitout 1996)

A possible explanation for this cultural (ideological) interpretation is that because of different social, cultural and political circumstances in South Africa, the participants have developed cultural identities and interpretation frames that could be linked to these circumstances. The black respondents' reaction against Afrikaans for instance, can be traced back to 1976 when police shot at black school children, during a demonstration against the use of Afrikaans as one of the official languages in black schools. We must point out, however, that since the African National Congress (ANC) came to power in 1994, Afrikaans is no longer one of the official languages or a compulsory subject in black schools. Therefore, such antagonistic (and ideological) interpretations may have changed. For example, six years after the ANC came to power two Afrikaans television programmes, *Maak 'n las* and *Vetkoek Paleis* are also very popular with other language and cultural groups in South Africa.

- *Private (subjective) experiences* can be described as those experiences that are unique to the individual. No two people's experiences are the same – not even members of the same household. Furthermore, we are born with different abilities and personalities and even a homogeneous culture cannot cast its members in the same mould (Daun, in Höijer 1998:170). When we apply this to our own lives, we can think of differences in media tastes between members of the same household – the husband has a keen interest in classical music while the wife may prefer romantic music.

With the above different kinds of experience briefly explained, we must, however, keep in mind that dividing experience in three dimensions is artificial and only for explanatory purposes. When we interpret media messages, we use a dynamic mixture of universal, cultural and private experiences as interpretation frames or cognitive schemas.

8.3.2 Cognitive schemas

By cognitive schemas we mean the processes whereby social reality is turned into internal mental models when we interpret and reconstruct social reality (Hoijer 1998:171). Cognitive schemas are used as frames of reference to interpret messages and contain all the information we need to interpret them. For example, members of a culture share certain practices which influence the interpretation of media messages, such as language, religious belief systems (Christianity, Judaism, Islam [one who practises Islam is a Muslim], New Age Movement, Buddhism), norms and values. For instance, when sexual promiscuity and divorce are portrayed in the media (e.g. films, television entertainment programmes), Muslim communities may be offended because their faith requires sexual fidelity (faithfulness) and proven adultery can be punished by 100 lashes. Divorce is only allowed in cases where the wife is maltreated and abused by her husband (Microsoft Encarta Encyclopaedia 1999). Western audiences, on the other hand, who believe in monogamy (custom of having only one spouse at a time), may find it hard to come to terms with the polygamous marriages (being married to more than one wife) of Islam communities. Polygamy is approved by the sacred scripture of Islam, the Koran, which allows a man to take as many as four wives. However, the Koran also states "if you fear you cannot do justice among co-wives, then marry only one wife" (Microsoft Encarta Encyclopaedia 1999).

Cognitive schemas can be subdivided into mode schemas and perspectivising schemas.

Mode schemas (organising schemas)

We can distinguish between two types of mode schemas that *organise* our experience – narrative and paradigmatic (or argumentative) schemas. We can also describe schemas as modes or ways of thinking.

- Narrative schemas refer to the way we tell stories according to a specific structure. This structure includes sequence of events – how a story unfolds, the characters in the story, their mental states and the events they (the characters) encounter. Usually such a story (narrative) has a clear beginning, middle and ending. Narrative schemas are dramatic and moral and develop early in childhood. When we tell a story or a happening, we usually take a moral or ethical stance (viewpoint) because we make value judgements. For example, we side with the antagonist (the "baddie") or the protagonist (the hero). And we use emotive words that indicate our moral judgement. For instance, when we listen to a child's version of a story, we will notice how often emotive words are used, for example "the bad, ugly wolf", and "the good, beautiful princess". And usually such a story has a happy ending: "The beautiful princess was saved by the handsome, strong prince". On this level, children learn to express the differences between moral and immoral behaviour and by implication also learn about gender roles – women are helpless and will always be saved by men who according to fairy tales are the stronger sex. As we said, the narrative schema develops early in childhood and we use it in our everyday interaction with the world.

  The narrative schema is the basic form we use to structure our stories about ourselves, things we experience and the retelling of events in the media (see the example of Callie and Monique Strydom below).

- The paradigmatic schema explains our rational, logical reasoning and the way we formulate concepts. This schema is based on propositions, arguments, facts, figures and the inferring of causal relation between events. When children enter adolescence, they start using this schema to interpret factual programmes such as news.

  The results of Hoijer's (1998) research indicate that there is a big difference in the way people understand news and fiction genres. For example, respondents' recall or retelling of a news broadcast is often brief, incomplete and fragmented and not at all as coherent and elaborated as the understanding and retelling of fiction. The reason may be that fiction is easier to interpret because it is closer to the way we use narrative schemas to interpret our everyday existence.

  We must add that when hard news becomes a human-interest story and is sensationalised by the media, our narrative schemas take over to understand and retell such an event in detail. For example, the abduction of Monique and Callie Strydom by rebels was initially hard news and we used paradigmatic schema to interpret the initial news reports about their abduction. But the prolonged efforts to set them free, and because they are South Africans, captured the imagination of the South African public and the media. In our interpretation and discussion of this event, we switched from paradigmatic to narrative schemas. For example, Callie and Monique were captured by the "baddies" (the rebels), but after months of negotiation they were saved by the heroes (the South African Government and General Gadaffi).

We must keep in mind that such events are not only given prominence in news reports: magazines and other television programmes (documentaries) also expand on these sensational events which adds to our awareness, understanding and interpretation thereof.

Perspectivising schemas

Perspectivising schemas are also called super-themes, or fundamental themes. Hoijer (1998:173) says that perspectivising schemas allow us to interpret news and daily events in

- *concise* or in *metaphoric form*. For example, people who have great admiration for Nelson Mandela's leadership qualities, may equate him with Ghandi and use a metaphor such as "Nelson Mandela and Ghandi are saints"(in this sentence the word "saints" is a metaphor for the integrity of these men). Another example would be that those people who do not believe in president Mbeki's credo of an African Renaissance will regard the renaissance dream as "pie in the sky" (metaphorical meaning is thus an impossible dream).

Furthermore, fundamental schemas also include to a large extent

- *ideological views about aspects of reality*. For example, we have certain ideological perspectives about gender, race, religion, morals and genre conventions. For instance, men and women may resort to gender perspectives to interpret messages. The example below illustrates how a female viewer uses a gender perspective to interpret a countryside lunch scene from a fiction television programme about the social structure of the late 1940s:

  Typical men of that time. I am sure it was like that then. Men had lunch and it had to be cultured and they should talk about business and serious matters. Men talk to men. Trying to butter them up with a good lunch and the like ...
  (Hoijer 1998:173)

What the above discussion boils down to, is that it explains how stereotypes are used to interpret social reality and aspects thereof. Almost all of us are familiar with perspectives (stereotypes) about gender (all women are bad drivers, all men are chauvinists) and race. Pitout (1996) in her study of viewers' interpretation of *Egoli* established that white and black participants tend to think in terms of stereotypes when they talk about the different cultural groups in South Africa. For example, one black female respondent regards Elsa (one of the Afrikaans-speaking characters in *Egoli*) as a racist because "Elsa acts like a typical Afrikaner boerevrou", while some white respondents regard "all blacks as cruel".

Because stereotypes in most cases have underlying ideological meanings, we can deduce that the participants in the above example, use to a large extent ideological interpretation frames, linked to their historical roots, to interpret the South African realities portrayed, for example, in *Egoli*.

8.3.3 Psycho-dynamic processes

Psycho-dynamic processes take place within the individual and are the result of personal experiences (such as traumas) and of cultural myths and ideologies. According to Hoijer (1998), psycho-dynamic processes include the mental room in which the never-ending tasks of building bridges between our individual identities and our social and cultural identities take place. Certain activities are especially suited for this. Hoijer (1998:176) provides examples of the developmental phases of these activities:

- Already babies start to create an intermediate area of experience where cognition about inner conditions and outer world can meet. For example, when a baby is comforted by a blanket, a doll or whatever else, this object creates the intermediate (or transitional) area where one can comfort oneself. This area then serves as the mental room where the baby can reduce the tension between the inner and outside worlds or realities.
- As the baby grows up, playing games serves as an intermediate area. Thus, play serves as the intermediate area to resolve conflict between our inner and outside worlds. For example, children play house, cowboys and crooks, television games and so on, to come to terms with the requirements of society and to prepare themselves for their roles as adults. When they become adolescents, they may listen to music or watch films/television programmes that deal with problems they experience, such as love, anger, sexual identity, and rebellion against authority. This may help them to solve their inner conflicts and traumas.
- When we enter adulthood, we still need an intermediate area of conflict resolution because we are never free from the strain of relating our outer and inner realities, and to solve the conflict between the two. Art, religion, films and fictional television programmes may all serve as examples of intermediate areas. Viewers regard fiction viewing as more relaxing than news viewing which is perceived as more demanding. Research conducted by Hoijer (1998), revealed that viewers have often told her that watching fiction helps to "relax the brain". However, this "non-demanding" quality of television fiction serves as an intermediate area of experience because it is an area that is not challenged. Thus, while we may regard fiction viewing as a "mindless" activity, it actually serves as a site to resolve the struggle between our inner and outer realities. In other words, when we struggle with a problem – for example difficult study material or a personal problem – we can watch television, a film, read a book or go for a walk. These activities distract us from the problem because they help our brains to relax. When we return to the problem at a later stage, we do so with new insight to solve the problem.

To summarise our discussion of the cognitive dimension: To understand the cognitive dimension of media consumption, we should first consider the influence of universal, cultural and individual experiences on the formation of cognitive schemas. One of the main functions of cognitive schemas is to help us to internalise (interpret and reconstruct) social reality and aspects thereof (e.g. media messages).

Two important types of cognitive schemas are *mode* and *perspectivising* schemas. *Mode schemas* can be subdivided into narrative and paradigmatic schemas that help us to organise our (media) experiences. A *narrative schema* refers to the way we tell stories according to a specific structure – a clear beginning, middle and ending. A *paradigmatic schema* explains how we develop the ability to formulate rational and logical concepts. This schema enables us to establish causal relations between events, for example, a newspaper that is the mouthpiece of a political party, will support the ideologies of that party.

Perspectivising schemas (also called foundational schemas), on the other hand, help us to interpret news (and other media events) in metaphoric form and include to a great extent ideological views about aspects of reality, for example, gender, race and religion. These ideological views are reflected in the media.

Lastly, we considered some *psycho-dynamic processes* to explain how we use a mental room to build bridges between our innate (inborn) identities and our social and cultural identities. That is, how we conform to norms of society in order to become functional inhabitants of our society and the role the media play in this process of formation and conformation.

Now let us turn to the third dimension of social psychology, namely the sociology of media consumption.

8.4 SOCIOLOGY OF MEDIA CONSUMPTION

In Unit 6 (Reception theory), we discussed the social character of television viewing with reference to concepts such as parasocial interaction, social interaction and identification. In this section we deal with the social dimension of media consumption (that is the social component of the social psychology) which includes places where we consume messages (e.g. at home, with friends, in public places – bars, community centres, restaurants, theatres), and the social relations that media consumption brings about.

8.4.1 Geography or contexts of media use

In their discussion of the geography of media use, Grossberg et al (1998:259–265) distinguish between private and public contexts of media consumption.

- *Private context (space).* The most important private space of media consumption is the home. In this environment we are first introduced to the mass media such as newspapers, magazines, radio, television, computers and video machines.

Of all the mass media, television viewing is regarded as the most important family activity. The television often serves as background where different activities take place such as talking, eating, reading, doing homework and even sleeping. Applied to our own televison viewing behaviour, it may be a useful exercise to make a list of the activities we engage in while watching television.

However, television viewing as a family activity must now compete with other electronic devices in the house such as computers, music centres, and television games. Because electronic devices are becoming increasingly cheaper, there is a tendency to buy more than one television set per household (and sometimes more than one computer) where these devices can be used in the privacy of family members' bedrooms. Thus, where we once believed that television has replaced the fireplace as gathering place for the family, television viewing is increasingly becoming a private activity – at least for middle and upper-middle class families.

- *Public context (space).* We can distinguish various public sites of media consumption where we share space with members of the public, for example in movie theatres, museums and concert venues. The following public venues have been introduced with the advent of the latest technological developments (Grossberg et al 1998:260–261):
  - Television bars where sport events are broadcast on a large screen. Those of us who are soccer, cricket and rugby supporters know that before an important international match, supporters gather in bars or shopping centres where matches are being broadcast.
  - The development of diamond vision – the use of huge television screens in arenas during concerts and sports events – has facilitated the viewing of such events by larger audiences. We can think of the use of diamond vision screens during Pavarotti concerts, soccer and rugby matches. And many of us may still remember the memorial service of Lady Diana in Westminister Abbey, London, where thousands of people outside the church could watch the ceremony on big screens.
  - Multiple television sets are used in departmental stores, not only to advertise their own products, but also to act as "babysitters" for customers' children.

From this brief discussion of the social geography of media consumption we can deduce that the media have permeated about every space of our everyday life. However, to get a better understanding of the complexity of media consumption, we should also understand the various social relations we have with the media and other media consumers.

8.4.2 Social relations of media consumption

Our media consumption includes anonymous and institutional social relations as well as social relations we have with our families and peer groups.

- *Anonymous social relations* refers to behaviour we display when we use public venues to consume media. For example, when we go to a movie, we abide by unwritten rules or etiquette: we do not talk aloud, jump up and down in our seats, run around or display any other form of socially unacceptable behaviour while watching the film. When attending an opera, we applaud after certain arias or in the case of a symphony concert, at the end of the last movement.

Daphna Lemish (1982) conducted participant observation research to determine the rules involved in watching television in public places. The following are a few rules she identified:

- *A public viewer adjusts to the setting.* Cheering the team on, and shouting out advice to the referee is acceptable in a television bar but would not be acceptable when watching the game in a departmental store. Lemish noticed that viewers adapted their behaviour from public setting to public setting.
- *A public viewer adjusts to other viewers.* By trying to fit in to the social group, viewers will talk only if other people in the group are talking. Furthermore, viewers keep a safe, social distance and thus do not invade other viewers' personal space.
- *A public viewer adheres to television-related social interaction.* One of the most consistent aspects of public viewing is that it initiates and sustains social interaction among viewers. Lemish's findings indicate that the shared social context of public viewing allowed viewers to form a social collective group, as short-lived as it was, with a shared group spirit. For example, viewers shared information, opinions and personal feelings with strangers – together they shouted comments, clapped hands and cheered on their teams. We must add that this type of social interaction is also displayed when people attend live sports events.

- *Relations with family.* As we have discussed, the family home is the primary context where we are introduced to different media. The way we are taught how to interact with the media and our media tastes are to a great extent determined by our parents or other primary socialising agents. In his research about family viewing, Morley's (1986) findings were that
  - children of parents who are well informed about public matters, are themselves better informed than their peers because they have been raised in information-rich environments (daily exposure to newspapers, literature, magazines) and modelled their parents' attitudes and values;
  - power relationships in the family, structure the social hierarchy of media use. For example, Morley has found that in a patriarchal family structure the father controls the remote control and decides what to watch, and is sometimes so rude as to switch channels while the rest of the family is trying to watch something else.

Morley's research was conducted in the early 1980s and we wonder whether the situation as far as the role of the patriarch (the father) has changed for the better in the new millennium. Applied to our own television viewing – who controls the remote and who decides what to watch?

- *Relations with peers.* When children enter adolescence, peer group pressure begins to play an increasingly important role in the way adolescents choose and select media use. Therefore, the social relations adolescents have with the media are to a greater extent influenced by their friends, rather than by their parents. The following research findings of Morley (1992) are thus to be expected: When adolescents have to choose fashions such as clothing, hairstyles, music and media in general, the advice of friends is more important than that of their parents. Based on our memories of our adolescent years, maybe we can recall the influence peer group pressure had on our behaviour, media and fashion tastes.

Summary

In this unit we have discussed one of the important perspectives – social psychology – employed by media researchers to investigate our affective experiences with the media. We cannot deny that almost all of us get some kind of pleasure and emotional rewards when we use the media. Although theoretical perspectives such as functionalism and uses and gratifications (cf. units 7 and 8 in Volume 1) also investigate the psychological functions that the media provide to their audiences, they have been seriously criticised. The main criticism stems from lack of studying the social dimensions of media use and therefore reduces media use to an individualistic psychological relationship. We have indicated in this unit that our interaction with the media has a strong social component because we seldom use media in isolation. In fact, we are often engaged with others whilst using the media.

We followed the suggestions of Grossberg et al (1998) to investigate more directly the psychological state of audiences, with the focus on the affective dimensions of audience members' psychology. Dimensions such as emotions, moods and pleasure were discussed. Also included was a discussion of the cognitive dimension of media consumption, because without cognitive activities we cannot interpret messages. (A visual summary of the psychological dimensions of media use is provided below.)

Because of the complexity of cognitive processes, we have merely concentrated on important concepts and processes such as universal, cultural and individual experiences, cognitive schemas and psycho-dynamic processes. We agree with Hoijer (1998:179) that no single theoretical perspective can account for the complexity of audience interpretation. Even working with several theories is no guarantee that we can fully grasp what should be included to get a general picture of the process of interpretation and the influence of society. In fact, many social psychological perspectives pass over macro levels with the result that society becomes subordinate in their analysis.

Hoijer (1998:179) correctly observes that concepts such as hegemonic structures, dominant ideologies, cultural reproduction or power relations are seldom part of psychology theories. A solution to the problem is to build a theoretical bridge between society and public culture, on one hand, and cognition, on the other. However, in the

Affective dimension	Cognitive dimension

Affective states
• Emotional
• Mood
• Pleasure
	Experiences influencing formation of cognition
	• Universal
	• Cultural
	• Private
	
	Cognitive schemas
	• Mode schemas
	  – Narrative
	  – Paradigmatic
	• Perspectivising schemas
	  – Metaphor
	  – Ideology
	
	Psycho-dynamic processes
	• Mental room for development phases

process of building that bridge we must keep in mind that neither society nor human thinking are coherent and ideological consistent structures. On the contrary, they are partly irrational, emotionally loaded and filled with societal dilemmas. And so are we, the media audiences.

We concluded this unit with a discussion of the social context of media use and the social relations we have with the media. We have illustrated, with practical examples, that the places where we consume media, have an influence on our interaction with and interpretation of media messages.

Research activities

1 Why is it important to investigate the psychological relationship between audiences and texts?

2 Explain in four to five lines, the concept "cognition".

3 Explain in four to five lines, the affective dimension of social psychology.

4 Name three affective states. Summarise each state in about five sentences. Then answer the following questions and illustrate your answers with examples from your own personal experience of the media:
   a) Have you ever been lured by advertisements to make you feel good? Put differently, have you bought products being advertised? Did the products work for you or not?
   b) Have you ever used the media to experience certain emotions repeatedly?

5 Conduct an interview with a friend/colleague/family member to determine whether the media sometimes appeal to his/her emotions and if he/she sometimes uses the media to experience certain emotions.

6 Do you agree with Grossberg et al (1998) that mood is complex and unstable? Illustrate your answer with examples from your personal experiences and the role that the media play in your mood states. After your own account of the role of the media in your mood state, conduct an interview with a friend/colleague/family member to find out what role the media play in his/her mood state.

7 Briefly describe pleasure state. Do you sometimes use the media to escape from certain situations, and/or identify with a character, and/or get involved with the emotional lives of characters? Write down your answers. Then repeat the same exercise by interviewing a friend/colleague/family member about the pleasures he/she derives from his/her interaction with the media.

8 Explain the cognitive dimension in four to five lines.

9 Briefly explain three experiences – universal, cultural, individual – that influence the formation of cognitive structures. After watching a television programme, or reading a book/short story/in a magazine/newspaper, or listening/watching the news or a documentary programme, apply these experiences to your own media use (write down your experiences).

10 Explain cognitive schemas in four to five lines and illustrate your explanation with your own examples.

11 Write down a fiction story that you have watched, read, or listened to over the radio. Which mode schema(s) have you used – narrative and/or paradigmatic schemas? Then ask somebody you know to retell a fictional narrative to determine the mode schema he/she has used.

12 Repeat the same exercise above, but replace the recall of fiction with the recall of a news event. Which mode schema was used? Based on the results of your application, answer the following question: *Is it possible to apply narrative and paradigmatic schemas to real life situations?*

13 Explain perspectivising schemas in five sentences. Then watch a television programme, or read a newspaper report, or listen to radio drama/news event, or read a magazine story/article and make a list of the following components of perspectivising schemas:
- Metaphors
- Ideological perspectives of gender, race, religion, genre conventions

14 Do you agree with Hoijer that psycho-dynamic processes include a "mental" room to solve conflict between our inner and cultural identities? Explain your viewpoint by using the development stages from infancy to adulthood.

15 Name two contexts of the geography of media use. Explain each one in your own words. Then answer the following question: *How do you think the introduction of*

new media technologies into private homes has reshaped (or will reshape) your domestic space and way of life?

16 Briefly discuss the different social relations we have with the media, for example anonymous social relations and relations with family and peers. Illustrate your explanation with examples from your own media experience.

Further reading

Dickinson, R, Harindranath, R & Linne, O (eds). 1998. *Approaches to audiences: a reader.* London: Arnold.

Grossberg, L, Wartella, E & Whitney, D. 1998. *Mediamaking: mass media in a popular culture.* California: Sage.

Henrich, DJ. 2000. Language dubbing and cultural comprehension: the comparative effects of Kiswahili language dubbing in Kenya. *Communicatio* 26(1):5–23.

Hoijer, B. 1992. Socio-cognitive structures and television reception. *Media, Culture & Society* 14:583–603.

Hoijer, B. 1998. Social psychological perspectives in reception analyses, in *Approaches to audiences: a reader*, edited by R Dickinson, R Harindranath & O Linne. London: Arnold.

McQuail, D. 1997. *Audience analysis.* London: Sage.

Bibliography

Dalgren, P. 1998. Critique: elusive audiences, in *Approaches to audiences: a reader*, edited by R Dickinson, R Harindranath & O Linne. London: Arnold.

Fiske, J. 1987. *Television culture.* London: Routledge.

Jensen, KB. 1998. The world in the head: world cultures look at television news, in *News of the world: audiences' uses of television news in world cultures*, edited by KB Jensen. London: Routledge.

Lemish, D. 1982. The rules of viewing television in public places. *Journal of Broadcasting* 26(4):775–781.

Morley, D. 1986. *Family television: culture power and domestic leisure.* London: Comedia.

Morley, D. 1992. *Television, audiences and cultural studies.* London: Routledge.

Pitout, M. 1996. Televisie en resepsiestudie: 'n analise van kykersinterpretasie van die seep-opera "Egoli: Plek van Goud". Ongepubliseerde doktorale proefskrif. Pretoria: Universiteit van Suid-Afrika.

Pitout, M. 1998. Reception analysis: a qualitative investigation of the parasocial and social dimensions of soap opera viewing. *Communicatio* 24(2):39–47.

Potter, WJ. 1988. Perceived reality in television effects research. *Journal of Broadcasting & Electronic Media* 32:23–41.

Shore, B. 1996. *Culture in mind. Cognition, culture and the problem of meaning.* New York: Oxford University Press.

Audience Research

9

Magriet Pitout & GM (Trudie) du Plooy

Overview

In the previous three units we dealt mainly with mass media research conducted at universities and colleges and which is theory-driven. In this unit we concentrate on audience research (also called applied research) which is pragmatic (practical) and attempts to examine specific practical issues and to solve specific problems, rather than to construct theory. Applied research is usually conducted in the private sector, for example private organisations (businesses, advertising companies), state departments and research companies such as Markinor in South Africa.

These two research settings do, however, have some common ground, for example they often share the same goal – that is, to explain and predict consumer and audience behaviour, and both settings use the same research techniques (methods) and approaches which originated from academic research.

In this unit we deal with the focus-group interview and survey research because they are two of the most popular standard research methods used to investigate mass media audiences, media workers (e.g. journalists, scriptwriters), employers and employees in organisations, and the users and buyers (audiences) of specific products.

Learning outcomes

At the end of this unit you should be able to

- plan and conduct a pilot research study in which focus-group interviews are used in order to do audience research; and
- plan and conduct a pilot research study using a survey self-administered questionnaire in order to do audience research.

9.1 INTRODUCTION

We mentioned in the overview that this unit deals with audience research, which is to a great extent practised in the private sector. Wimmer and Dominick (1997:342) explain the following differences between research in the private and academic sectors:

- Academic research is more theoretical while audience research is applied with the view to solve specific problems.
- The data used in academic research is public while much research in the private sector is based on propriety (protocol).

- Academic researchers have more freedom in selecting research topics while topics for private sector research are often determined by top management of an organisation.

Many of us have at one or other stage been involved in audience research. For example, we may have been contacted by means of a telephone call, postal, e-mail, and Internet questionnaires to

- evaluate new products (e.g. a new brand of margarine), advertisements in a magazine, or a new service provided by a company (e.g. a Telkom help-line for customers);
- determine our media usage patterns (e.g. our television programme preferences; our newspaper and magazine usage patterns);
- give our opinions about political parties, political leaders, the crime wave in South Africa, soccer/rugby/athletic coaches and so on.

In the above examples we have been involved in survey research where telephone, e-mail, Internet and postal questionnaires were used to gather the relevant data. We may however, also investigate audiences by means of focus-group interviews where there is direct (or interpersonal) contact between a group of people (members of a target audience) and a moderator who leads the discussion about a specific topic. Before discussing focus-group interviews and survey research in more detail, we first look at another way to categorise research.

9.2 CATEGORISATION OF TYPES OF RESEARCH

Another, and very useful categorisation of types of research is based on the *objective* of our investigation, of which three types of objectives can be distinguished: exploratory, descriptive, and explanatory. We provide a brief description of each of these purposes below, with reference to focus-group interviews and survey research methods as examples.

- Exploratory research is usually undertaken to gain a better understanding of a communication problem or phenomenon where little is known about our topic of interest, or when we want to develop a measuring instrument to be used at a later stage (e.g. a self-administered questionnaire). An exploratory survey is therefore *not* aimed at providing final answers to a research question or hypothesis. Research questions usually begin with "What ...?", or "Where ...?", or "Which ...", or "How ...?".

  For example:
  - Which communication channels do employees of company X prefer, to be informed about managerial decisions?
  - How many readers of our newspaper are teenagers?
- In contrast, when our objective is descriptive, we describe what exists at the moment (Wimmer & Dominick 1997). Research questions usually begin by asking "Why...?".

For example:
- Why are employees not in favour of being informed by e-mail about managerial decisions?
- Why do teenagers watch the soap opera *7de Laan* on SABC2?

- When conducting a study for explanatory purposes, we must reformulate the research question as a statement (that is a hypothesis), in which we indicate a causal relation between two or more variables. In an explanatory study the answer-statement must be formulated in such a way that at least two variables are causally related and the design would therefore enable us to verify or reject the causal assumption on which this hypothesis is based.

  For example: The publication of a new Sunday newspaper has led to the decline in our newspaper's weekly sales.

9.3 STEPS IN PLANNING AND CONDUCTING COMMUNICATION RESEARCH

When we conduct research, and this includes audience research, we must follow certain steps to plan and conduct our communication research. The following are generally guidelines of the steps involved:

1 Formulation of the research problem.
2 Statements of the research problem, subproblems, assumptions, research questions and/or hypotheses.
3 Determine the relevant research design and methodology *(this includes our selection and motivation for using either focus-groups interviews or a survey research).*
4 Collect relevant data.
5 Analyse data and interpret results.

9.3.1 Formulation of the research problem

The first step in the research process is to identify a research problem. This entails that we first reflect on the purpose (objective) of the study, the choice and explanation of a research topic and the significance of that topic. The research problem determines not only the nature and quality of the investigation but also (eventually) the research design, research method and procedures of our study. We should therefore explain our research problem clearly and motivate why it is important to investigate this problem.

9.3.2 State the research problem, subproblems/research questions and/or hypotheses

When doing research, we should write down a precise description of the problem to be investigated and the purpose(s) (objectives) of the study. We already mentioned that in audience research the objectives of our studies might be exploratory and/or descriptive, and/or explanatory. This activity (the statement of the problem) provides us with a focus for the research and can be worded as a *statement* or a general *research question*. For example:

- The purpose of this study is to determine which communication channels employees of organisation X prefer, to be informed about decisions by top management.
- Which sections of a magazine (e.g. *You* or *Huisgenoot* or *Drum* or *Reader's Digest*) are the most popular with different age groups and gender?

A clear understanding and actual formulation of the problem, or general research question, is crucial since it guides the specific issues that we as researchers should address when we gather data by means of research methods (e.g. focus-group interviews and surveys). Furthermore, we should break down the general research question/statement of the problem into specific subproblems (or research questions) and assumptions, to guide the research process.

Examples of subproblems

- Which articles do female readers of magazine E prefer?
- What are the reasons for their preferences?

Examples of assumptions

- Women's preference of articles in magazine E differ according to their demographic characteristics (e.g. age, level of education, living area, socio-economic level).
- Women prefer entertainment articles such as gossip columns (e.g. articles dealing with celebrities such as movie stars, television personalities), fiction (stories) and recipes.
- Women read these articles to be entertained, to be informed, and to escape.

When we use focus-group interviews (discussed in section 9.4), the main problem and subproblems may change as the research progresses. However, the initial problem and subproblems at least give us a starting point to organise our thoughts. This is one of the major advantages of qualitative research over many other methods (e.g. quantitative methods such as surveys). When undertaking focus-group interviews, we ought to be open and receptive to the group being studied and not enter the setting with specific hypotheses to be tested. Nevertheless, we must identify at least a few subproblems and assumptions before our research begins and refine them as the research progresses.

9.3.3 Determine the relevant research design and methodology

The research design refers to the process involved in planning the way we will collect and analyse data. The research design is essentially the blueprint for the collection of data. During this phase (step 3) we explain which research method(s) (e.g. focus groups and/or survey research) will be used to gather data.

9.4 THE FOCUS-GROUP INTERVIEW

The *focus-group interview* is

- a research method for investigating the attitudes and opinions of a group of people regarding a specific topic;
- typically composed of 6 to 12 members who are selected because they have certain characteristics in common that relate to the topic of investigation;
- not a free-flow conversation among group members – the focus group has a clear focus and agenda (therefore this method is called the *focus*-group interview);
- led by a moderator (discussion leader) who promotes interaction between members and makes sure that the discussion remains on the topic of interest (Krueger 1994; Stewart & Shamdasani 1990).

A clear statement of the problem (see 9.3.2 above) is crucial to the success of a focus-group interview. Such statements generate specific questions that we as moderators should address during the focus-group interview session. Focus groups are particularly useful when we conduct exploratory research (see 9.2 above) where little is known about our topic of interest. For example, when

- identifying problems which audience members have with existing television programme schedules, or the content of a specific radio station, or the content of a particular newspaper, or problems employees may have with communication channels;
- probing the effectiveness of advertising (or any other particular genre, such as news reportage) in a mass medium (television, newspapers, magazines), or the effectiveness of e-mail circulars to inform employees of managerial decisions, or the effectiveness of AIDS campaigns;
- determining audience members' attitudes, perceptions, frames of reference and media usage (viewing, reading, listening) patterns.

9.4.1 Guidelines on how to design a focus-group study

We use the following steps to design focus-group research.

Determine the number and composition of a focus-group interview

To compose a group, we should keep in mind that a focus group is characterised by homogeneity, but with sufficient variation among the members of the group to elicit contrasting opinions. In general, we look for homogeneity in terms of variables such as age, gender, education, family characteristics, or use of a particular mass medium. The guiding principle in the composition of a group, is the degree to which the above variables will influence participation within the group discussion. Research findings indicate that the following combinations do *not* work well and we must therefore exercise care when combining these groups (Krueger 1994:77–78; Stewart & Shamdasani 1990:51–52).

- Individuals from different lifestyles and life stages do not mix well, that is, we must try to avoid, for example, combining young working women with mature homemakers who have never been employed outside the home. However, if the topic or research problem clearly cuts across these lifestyles and life stages, then these two groups can be combined. For instance, when we want to determine views about advertisements of household products (e.g. soap powder) we may combine working women with homemakers because the majority of women use soap powder to do their washing. (Because of changing roles of gender, men may also be included to evaluate soap powder.)
- The mixing of gender in focus groups can sometimes create problems especially if the topic is experienced differently by each gender. Furthermore, there is a tendency for some men to speak more frequently and with more authority when in the company of women. This is called the *peacock effect* and can irritate the women in the group, which in turn can have a negative effect on the research.
- The combination of husband and wife in the same focus group does not work well because there is a tendency for one spouse to dominate the discussion while the remaining partner remains silent or is reluctant to comment even when such comments are solicited from the discussion leader (moderator).
- A group composed of parents and children will produce a different type of discussion than one group of parents and a separate group of children. The same applies to combining highly skilled people with novices; or technically skilled with non-technical people – the presence of skilled people may inhibit the participation of the rest of the group (Stewart & Shamdasani 1990:51).

The above discussion may create the impression that different genders, ages, occupations or family members should not be combined in a group discussion. Though these variables should always be taken into consideration, in some situations it is desirable to use a group made up of a mixture of people, such as viewers of a television channel and the programme managers of that channel, or readers and non-readers of a particular newspaper. The way we compose our focus groups will be determined by the purpose, main problem, and subproblems of our research, for example:

- To determine employees' communication channel preferences, will it be necessary to conduct separate focus groups with male and female employees?
- Should we distinguish between race and age when determining communication channel preferences?

If we are in doubt regarding the membership of a focus group, we should first conduct a pilot study and take the preliminary findings as guidelines to determine the selection and composition of focus-group members. A pilot study refers to the pre-testing or pre-study of a topic which allows us to identify mistakes and problems that can be rectified before we begin with our actual research.

We can follow the same procedure when we want to determine the opinions and feelings of people about sensitive issues such as advertisements/campaigns dealing with the prevention of AIDS. In such cases we should, for example, take cultural differences into consideration. However, to test the assumption that people of different cultural, gender and age groups differ in their perception of AIDS, we must first conduct a pilot focus-group interview consisting of one cultural group (consisting of only men or women) and ask them if they would mind taking part in a focus-group interview which will be composed of different cultural, gender and age groups. If we notice that people are hesitant to talk about sensitive issues we may then consider survey research where responses are more private (see section 9.5 below).

To summarise, the kind of questions we are faced with:

- Do we deal with men and women in separate groups?
- Do we have to take into consideration variables such as age, income, living conditions, race or differences in language preferences?

We should keep in mind that composition of groups it is not a haphazard exercise. We must therefore anticipate (or determine my means of pilot studies) the impact of the way a group is composed before recruiting participants. Furthermore, we should take care that the characteristics of members of any given focus group are consistent with the objective of the study. This implies that the objective, main problem and subproblems to be investigated must be established clearly and at a very early stage of the research project.

After the population parameters (characteristics such as age, gender) have been established for the composition of each group, the next step is to select a sample from the target population, that is, to *recruit participants*.

Recruit participants (sampling)

Because focus groups consist of a small number of participants per group (between 6–12 participants) we need to define a narrow audience for the study, keeping in mind that data gathered by means of focus groups cannot be generalised beyond the members of focus groups to a larger population. Therefore, Stewart and Shamdasani (1990:20) suggest that the sample need be only a good approximation of the population of interest, for example members of a rural community who have access only to a specific form of mass communication (e.g. the radio), or elderly people living in an old-age home who have access to one communal television set and cannot exercise a choice of programme selection.

We may choose one of the following forms of non-probability sampling to recruit participants: available sampling, volunteer sampling and purposive sampling. (We merely summarise the different forms of non-probability sampling because you have already studied this type of sampling in the second-year compulsory research module – Research in the Social Sciences.)

- Available sampling (also called convenience sampling) is used when we collect respondents among a readily accessible group of people. For example, we want to determine the viability of a new radio music programme for teenagers. We can go to a high school, which is conveniently situated near our offices, and recruit learners of that school (with permission from the relevant authorities) until our sample reaches the desired size. That is, until we have enough respondents to make up two or three focus groups (6–12 respondents per group).

- We use volunteer sampling when we ask people to participate voluntarily in a research project. For instance, we want respondents to evaluate an AIDS advertisement in newspaper X. We can place an advertisement in the newspaper and ask for volunteers who have been exposed to the campaign, to participate in our research project. We may then use the first 24 respondents and divide them in two to three focus groups.
- When using purposive sampling, we base our selection on respondents who share specific characteristics or qualities and eliminate those who do not fulfil the requirements (Bless & Higson-Smith 1995; Wimmer and Dominick 1997). Suppose we want to determine how Indians (18 to 35 years of age) in South Africa perceive advertisements dealing with the prevention of AIDS, we select only Indians (and no other cultural group) between 18 and 35 years old. Because of the reasons mentioned above (for instance the influence of gender), we should conduct separate focus groups with Indian men and women, except of course if we can establish beforehand (e.g. by means of a pilot study) whether female respondents will not be inhibited by their male counterparts.

Determine the location

The closer the location is to the potential participants' workplace or home, the more likely they are to participate. For example, we may conduct the focus groups during participants' lunch break. If one hour is not sufficient to conduct the focus-group interview, we can extend it over a two-day period. We may also consider conducting the interviews during a weekend in a community centre or any other venue that is convenient for the participants (respondents).

Prepare the study mechanisms and focus-group material

This step includes decisions regarding the type of recording apparatus to be used (e.g. video and/or audio recording) and the remuneration that participants will receive for their participation. Guidelines to help us in our planning before conducting the actual focus-group interviews, are the following:

- Decide which recording devices will be used (e.g. video cameras, tape recorders, pen and paper). (See section 9.4.3 of this unit for more information on the recording strategies for focus-group interviews.)
- Prepare a *pre-group questionnaire*. Participants are required to complete such a written questionnaire before the start of the focus-group interview.

- Prepare a *moderator (interview) guide* that contains the topics to be addressed during the focus-group interview. For example, when we want to research which communication channels employees prefer, to be informed about important decisions in their company, we can make a list consisting of all the possible channels – e-mail, departmental meetings, brochures, circulars – and ask the participants to evaluate and discuss each channel.

  The existence of a moderator guide does not mean that we cannot ask questions that are not in the guide. One advantage of focus groups is that this method allows us to deviate from the guide as groups sometimes take on lives of their own. In such instances the agendas are dictated by the natural flow of the discussions. A moderator guide is just that – a guide to address issues pertaining to the research problem. The moderator and group members should be allowed to modify the agenda if it proves desirable to resolving the initial problem (Wimmer & Dominick 1997). For example, when the moderator observes that employees are not in favour of e-mail messages, he/she can probe for further information. By means of probing, the moderator can, for instance, establish that the main reason why e-mail is not regarded as a suitable communication channel is that it is being used by colleagues and management as a vehicle to fight personal battles. Consequently, employees ignore e-mail messages and therefore miss out on important messages about managerial decisions.

9.4.2 Conducting the session

We always begin the actual focus-group interview with an explanation of the purpose of the research project. To put the participants at ease and to create a warm, friendly atmosphere we can explain that

- there are no right or wrong answers;
- they (the participants) may differ from one another in their views regarding a topic;
- the session is being recorded (and ask their permission for recording the data);
- they should regard the discussion as an informal gathering; and
- they should not hesitate to speak without being invited (Wimmer & Dominick 1997).

When we act as moderators, we should exercise self-discipline. For instance, we must withhold our personal opinions and refrain from being sarcastic towards or critical of participants. The latter is particularly important if we are faced with participant such as the

- *expert* – some people in a group consider themselves experts because they have considerable experience about the topic under discussion;
- *dominant talker* – people in a group who regard themselves as experts, with more experiences or who have a higher educational qualification and who tend to answer on behalf of other participants;
- *rambler* – participants who never get to the point and drone on and on, wasting valuable time.

For the novice moderator (which no doubt applies to the majority of us), conducting a focus group may seem a daunting task. Fortunately, interviewing improves with practice and experience. We can, for instance, practise on a group of friends, fellow students or even family members.

9.4.3 Recording, analysing and interpreting results of focus groups

Focus-group interviews produce an overwhelming (voluminous) amount of data. One single focus group could produce 10 to 15 pages of field notes combined with 30 to 60 pages of transcripts. The question is how do we analyse and interpret this data? First, however, we look at the different strategies that can be used to transcribe focus-group interviews.

- *Transcript-based strategy.* The first type of strategy is to transcribe the entire group interview. A complete transcription not only provides us with a basis for further analysis, but also establishes a permanent record of the focus-group interview that can be shared with other interested parties. The transcriptions may be edited to increase readability. For example, half-finished sentences, nonsensical thoughts or inaudible voices on the tape may be omitted. However, it is important that the character of participants' answers be maintained – even if they sound confused or use poor sentence construction and grammar. Since one of the aims of a focus group is to learn how people talk and think about a topic, too much editing of a transcript should be avoided.
- *Tape-based strategy.* This type of strategy means that we transcribe the group interview in its entirety (just like transcript-based analysis) but summarise the transcriptions for further analysis. Thus instead of using participants' own words, we summarise the main points and present the results in the form of summaries of the main themes.
- *Note-based strategy.* When we use this type of strategy, we do not tape-record the focus-group interviews but makes notes of conversations during the focus-group sessions. We should, however, ask someone (a colleague or friend) to assist with note-taking because it is sometimes difficult to make meaningful notes and to conduct or guide the interviews at the same time, especially when a group consists of more than six participants.
- *Memory-based strategy.* This strategy means that we do not tape-record or make notes of the focus-group interviews, but rely solely on our memories. After the completion of the focus-group interview, the moderator writes a summary of the main findings. However, this strategy can only be used if we have excellent memories! And we all know how fallible memories are. Therefore, this analytical strategy should not be attempted, and especially not by novice moderators.

Once the transcription of the focus-group interviews has been completed (irrespective of the strategy being used to record the data) we can analyse the data further by means of content analysis. In this way, themes addressed during the focus-group discussion may be identified. Content analysis gives us an indication of persistent patterns in the discussion; for example we can divide responses into separate themes and categories and determine whether the responses to the themes/categories are positive, neutral or negative.

According to Wimmer and Dominick (1997:100), focus-group interviews conducted in the private sector (e.g. audience research) rarely go beyond a summary of the content of focus groups. An example of the summary of focus-group interviews is the research conducted by Cardwell-Gardner and Bennett (1999). The aim of their study was to determine how children view advertisements directed at them and the formats that appealed to them. The authors (1999:53–54) summarised the girls' discussion of their favourite commercial, as follows:

> When asked to select the commercial that they like the most, all the female participants in two of the focus groups felt that they preferred the 'Scone Mix' commercial, whereas all the participants in the third focus group felt that they preferred the 'Jelly Tots' commercial. The fourth focus group also showed similar preferences, since half of the participants in that focus group felt that they also preferred the 'Scone Mix' commercial, whereas the other half of the participants chose the 'Jelly Tots' commercial as their favourite. ... When asked to select the commercial they liked least, all four of [the] focus groups agreed that they neither understood nor liked the 'Fanta' commercial ...

We may also use a nominal scale to record the frequency of occurrence. For example, we can quantify results by indicating that there is a marked difference between boys and girls: 80.1% girls prefer the Jelly Tots advertisement as opposed to boys where only 19.9% selected the Jelly Tots as their favourite commercial. (The latter is only a hypothetical example of how the above results could have been quantified.)

9.5 SURVEY RESEARCH: SELF-ADMINISTERED QUESTIONNAIRES

Survey research is probably one of the best methods available to communication scientists who are interested in collecting original data, especially in studies where the population is too large for direct observation (e.g. television viewers, radio listeners, newspaper readers).

We may conduct surveys by telephone, by mail, group administration, personal interviews, e-mail and the Internet. However, for the purpose of this unit, we focus on a self-administered questionnaire, which can be administered to a group of respondents in one location; or it could be sent to respondents by mail, as an insertion in a magazine, attached to a television licence account, or via e-mail.

We must make sure that items (questions and/or statements) disseminated by means of a self-administered postal questionnaire are easy to read and understand, because the items cannot be explained to the respondents. In a group-administered survey – where we administer a questionnaire to a group of respondents simultaneously in one venue – the items must be concise and easy to fill in. However, more complex questions can be used since we have the opportunity to clarify such questions.

9.5.1 The design of a self-administered questionnaire

When constructing a questionnaire, the items (questions and/or statements) must clearly and unambiguously communicate the desired information to the respondents. One of the aims of survey research is to provide systematic information about any large group of people (their views, opinions, attitudes, needs, expectations).

If we discover at a later stage that we need additional information, it is difficult (if not impossible) to return to the same respondents to collect that data. It is therefore crucial to plan ahead and make sure that the items in the questionnaire will provide all the relevant information that we need to address the research problem.

In self-administered questionnaires, respondents fill in the questionnaire in their own time and their participation is voluntary. We should, however, keep in mind that a self-administered questionnaire might not be suitable in cases where *respondents do not have the necessary reading and writing skills to read or fill in a questionnaire.* In such cases more suitable methods are the personal structured/unstructured interview or focus-group interviews.

When constructing a questionnaire, we must take particular note of the distinction between using items that determine

- *factual information* (e.g. gender, age, monthly income) versus
- items that require responses based on *opinion* (e.g. a respondent's motives, needs, attitudes, preferences and dislikes). Opinion questions/statements can be more problematic because the answers depend on a respondent's subjective feelings or state of mind, and because respondents may give socially desirable answers, which are more *acceptable* than *truthful.* For example, when doing a survey among elderly people in an old-age home about their preferences of television programmes, they may (because of fear) be inclined to hide the fact that they have no freedom of selecting channels and programmes.

9.5.2 Items used when constructing a questionnaire

When we use a postal questionnaire we must remember to include a letter of introduction (a covering letter) where we explain the purpose and the importance of our survey.

The following are examples of the type of items we can use in constructing a postal or a group administrative questionnaire.

Open-ended questions

In open-ended questions, respondents are required to give their own answers. No restrictions or guidelines are given – the respondents are completely free to express their answers as they wish. An open-ended question is useful if we want respondents to express their opinions or attitudes in their own words and if we are not sure of the number of different responses we may elicit (Du Plooy 1995:133).

For example:

> What do you think are two of the major advantages of a cellular phone? Write your answer in the space below.
>
> ____
>
> ____

Closed-ended questions

Closed-ended questions provide the respondent with a range of possible answers from which the respondent has to select one. For example:

> How often do you use a cellular phone? Select **one** option and make a tick in the appropriate box.
>
> ☐ Never ☐ Less than once a week ☐ Once a week ☐ Daily

Contingency questions

It sometimes happens that certain questions in a questionnaire apply only to some respondents in the whole sample. These questions are known as contingency questions. A filter question is used to identify this group of respondents. For example:

> Q1 Do you have access to e-mail at home? Please make a tick in the appropriate box.
>
> ☐ Yes ☐ No
>
> If your answer is **Yes**, answer question 2. If your answer is **No**, disregard question 2 and go to question 3.

In the above example, question 2 is a contingency question for those respondents who in fact have access to e-mail at home. The "Yes" "No" options thus "filter out" a specific subgroup in a sample. The following is an example of a question that will be filled in by those people who have access to e-mail at home.

> Q2 People have different reasons why they use e-mail at home. Please read each reason and then tick **"Yes"** if the reason applies mostly to you or **"No"** if it does not apply to you.

I use e-mail for business arrangements	Yes	No
I use e-mail to contact my family	Yes	No
I use e-mail to contact my friends	Yes	No

Ranking questions

A ranking question (a special type of closed-ended question) requires respondents to rank a set of possible options relative to the others. For example:

> Instruction: Which of the following communication channels do you regard as important to inform employees about managerial decisions? Number the channel that you regard as the most important **1**, your second choice as **2**, and so on, with the least important as **5**.
>
> ☐ Grapevine
> ☐ Circulars addressed to each employee personally
> ☐ Staff meetings
> ☐ E-mail circulars
> ☐ Circulars on the noticeboard in the secretary's office

Inventory questions

An inventory question is a type of closed-ended question that provides respondents with a list of items and they are asked to indicate on the list those items that apply to them. For example:

> For which of the following reasons do you use a cellular phone? Please tick **all** the reasons that apply.
>
> ☐ Shopping
> ☐ Appointments
> ☐ Dealing with emergencies
> ☐ Personal contact with friends
> ☐ Personal contact with family
> ☐ Business arrangements
> ☐ Other (fill in other reasons that do not appear in the list above)
>
> ____
>
> ____
>
> ____

Please note that when a list is not exhaustive, we fill in "Other" which is open-ended. This category makes the question better adapted to all situations (Bless & Higson-Smith 1995:121).

Statements

Closed-ended questions can also be asked in the form of statements. The most common scale used to measure attitudes and opinions, is the Likert scale.

A Likert scale usually consists of a series of positive and negative statements on a four- five- or seven-point scale. The respondents are then asked to indicate on the scale to what extent they agree or disagree with each statement. The scale comprises a positive and negative pole, for instance, "strongly agree" to "strongly disagree". For example:

Below are a number of statements regarding your views on the credibility of the political leader, Jan Plaatjies. Please indicate the extent to which you agree with each of the statements about him by making a circle in the appropriate box. For example, if you totally disagree with a statement, encircle 1.

	Strongly agree	Partly agree	Neutral	Partly disagree	Strongly disagree
He is trustworthy	5	4	3	2	1
He is knowledgeable	5	4	3	2	1
He is articulate	5	4	3	2	1
He is fair	5	4	3	2	1
He is honest	5	4	3	2	1
He is reliable	5	4	3	2	1

The Likert scale can also be used to evaluate a series of statements as accurate or inaccurate. In this case the scale ranges from "almost always true" (or "definitely true") to "almost never true". Or to measure amount, for example "enough", "more than average", "average", "little", "none".

Determine the necessity of questions/statements

We should keep the following issues in mind when considering whether or not an item (question or statement) ought to be included in the questionnaire:

- Is the question/statement really necessary? (Will it solve the subproblems?) Suppose we want to determine employees' choices of communication channels, will it be necessary to include questions about marital status, household income and race?

- Will the respondent be able (and willing) to give a meaningful answer or response to this item? For instance, we want to determine respondents' opinions about AIDS; will they give an honest answer to a question such as:

  Do you still have multiple sex partners? | Yes | No |

  This is also a biased question – because whether the respondent answers "Yes" or "No" the implication is that respondent has more than one sex partner.
- Does the item adequately cover the subproblem(s) that we want to investigate? (Should two or more items [questions/statements] not be formulated instead?)

9.5.3 Conduct a pilot study

To determine whether a survey has been properly planned and the questionnaire well constructed, we must conduct one or more *pilot studies* to eliminate errors and problems that might arise. As mentioned earlier, pilot studies can save a great deal of time, money and frustration because errors that can drastically influence the validity and processing of data can be traced and corrected timeously.

After conducting the necessary pilot study, we are ready to select respondents by means of sampling.

9.5.4 Sampling

Sampling is based on selecting a certain number of people (e.g. survey research) from a large population. The people included in the sample should be representative of the target population. The size of a sample depends on the degree of accuracy required; on homogeneity (where individuals display much the same characteristics, e.g. Grade 10, Northern Sotho speaking girls in Mamelodi High School), or on heterogeneity (where individuals differ greatly, e.g. people taking part in a general election); and on the sampling method used.

We cannot begin the sampling process without carefully considering the nature of the data required and without making sure that the sample can be justified both logically and statistically. Before selecting a sampling design, the characteristics of the target population as a whole also need to be analysed. The main categories of sampling are probability and non-probability sampling (discussed above).

Probability sampling

We consider probability sampling when each member of a population has an equal chance of being selected in the sample. When using one of the probability sampling methods below, the results can be generalised to the population as a whole. (We merely summarise a few of the different forms of probability sampling because you have already studied this type of sampling in the second-year compulsory research module – Research in the Social Sciences.)

- Simple random sampling. This type of sampling is based on the principle that each member of a population has an equal chance of being included in the sample. The simplest way of drawing a random sample is where we put the names of our population (e.g. the names of all the employees working for company X) in a container, shuffle them and draw a sample. Each employee then has an equal chance to be selected. A more sophisticated way to draw a simple random sample is to use a table consisting of random numbers (to be found in most books dealing with research methodology).
- Systematic or interval sampling. Simple and systematic samples are very similar, but differ in the way (procedure) in which the systematic sample is drawn – instead of relying on a random number table, we can decide to select elements using equal intervals, starting with selecting a random element on the population list. Suppose we want to draw a sample of 50 people from a population consisting of 500, the length of the intervals is determined by the ratio. A simple formula to determine the ratio is

  $$\frac{\text{population size} \quad 500}{\text{desired sample size} \quad 50} = 10$$

  Thus, every tenth person should be selected to draw a systematic sample. We randomly select a starting point, for example 5; the sample elements will then be 5, 15, 25, 35, ...485, until a sample of 50 people out of 500 has been drawn.
- Stratified sampling. Whereas a simple random sample and a systematic sample are cumbersome when we work with large populations, the stratified sample is easier to use because we divide the population into strata or subgroups. We can, for instance, use demographic variables (e.g. age, gender, area of residence) as strata.

  For example: We want to research congregation members' attitudes towards the new pastor appointed in their church. The previous pastor retired and, although kind, he was formal and had a fixed style of preaching. The new pastor is an attractive young woman with a modern dress code, has an informal manner, and is charismatic in the way she delivers sermons. We expect that age and gender will play a major role in the congregation's attitudes towards the new female parson. The composition of the adult congregation population is 5 000 (3 000 women and 2 000 men). Age can be taken as young (between 18 and 40 years) and older (above 40 years). When drawing a random stratified sample, we must make sure that the proportion of gender and age are the same as in the population.
- Cluster or multistage sampling. This type of sampling is used when we do not have a complete list of the elements (e.g. people) we want to study, for instance readers of the *Pretoria News*, a daily newspaper. We have a list of the subscribers, but we do not know how many non-subscribers read this newspaper. To identify the "unknown number" of readers, we can use cluster sampling where we start by sampling a population that is much more general than the final one. For example, we can make a list of all the census blocks (clusters) in Pretoria, and draw an initial random sample

from these. We may then draw up a list of persons living in each of the selected blocks and draw a sub-sample of people in each selected block. We continue the process of listing and sampling until we reach the population to be investigated. We can then draw a final sample from this population.

After selecting the appropriate sample, we are ready to administer or send the questionnaires to the respondents in our sample.

9.5.5 Analysis and interpretation of data

Depending on the type of data gathered, a wide choice of statistical techniques to analyse data is available. For example, descriptive statistics; data transformation; how to test hypotheses for statistical significance; and basic statistical procedures which include a discussion on the use of nonparametric statistics or parametric statistics – the t-Test, analysis of variance, Two-Way ANOVA, basic correlational statistics, and so on. (The different types of statistical methods are to be found in methodological handbooks.)

Sometimes we become so involved in the construction of questionnaires, sampling, bias, and evasion that we may lose sight of the overriding purpose of the research – the orderly and valid presentation of correctly interpreted data. Interpretation of data involves more than just presenting the information in different forms such as tables or graphs. It also means drawing conclusions from the data. The latter is done by examining the data analytically. Answers are placed in various categories, and the characteristics of each category are critically determined on the basis of the key words used in the responses. Furthermore, we must also relate the responses to the research purpose, the subproblems, the assumptions, as well as research questions and show how and to what extent the results support or reject the latter.

Summary

In this unit we first dealt with an overview of the differences between audience (applied) research and basic research. We then explained that we can categorise research based on the objective of an investigation, for example, exploratory, descriptive and explanatory. Next we considered the steps in the planning and conducting of communication research. In our discussion of the choice of the relevant research design and methodology we distinguished between two research methods (techniques) that can be used to investigate media audiences in audience research.

We first discussed the focus-group interview by explaining its characteristics and provided guidelines of how to design a focus group (determining the number and composition of focus groups; recruiting participants; preparing the study mechanisms and focus group material). We also explained how to conduct a focus-group interview and how to analyse and interpret the results of focus-groups interviews.

We concluded this unit with a discussion of survey research, explaining that the focus in on the application of a self-administered questionnaire. We provided guidelines on how to design a self-administered questionnaire such as the distinction between factual and opinion information; items that can be used in constructing a questionnaire (e.g. open-ended questions; closed-ended questions; contingency questions; ranking questions; inventory questions; statements in the form of a Likert scale). We emphasised the importance of conducting a pilot study. Furthermore, we discussed the use of sampling with specific reference to probability sampling and the different types of probability sampling. We ended with a discussion of the analysis and interpretation of data gathered by means of a questionnaire.

Throughout our discussion we provided examples of communication research problems, subproblems, research questions, assumptions and how these problems can be investigated by means of focus-group interviews and self-administered questionnaires. Practical examples were also given of how to plan and conduct focus-group interviews and survey research.

Research activities

1 Summarise how research can be categorised according to the purpose of an investigation. Distinguish between exploratory, descriptive and explanatory purposes and illustrate each with your own example.

2 Define focus-group interview.

3 Select a research topic suitable to be investigated by means of the focus-group interview. Apply the following steps:
   - Formulate the research problem, subproblems, assumptions and the purpose of the study.
   - Design a focus-group interview(s) by taking the following into consideration:
     - composition of groups
     - recruitment of participants
     - venue to conduct focus-group interview(s)
     - recording devices
   - Assemble a group consisting of 6–8 people (respondents) and conduct a pilot interview. Select respondents who could have been part of the hypothetical sample. For example, if your research problem is aimed at establishing adolescents' opinions on a new music programme on radio FM, the 10 respondents must be listeners of this channel.
   - Select a suitable strategy for recording the focus-group data.
   - Explain which categories you will use to analyse the focus-group data.

4 Design a survey on a topic of your choice using a survey self-administered questionnaire to gather the data. Include the following steps in your design:
   - Formulate the research problem, subproblems and assumptions.
   - Explain the purpose of your study (exploratory, descriptive, explanatory).
   - Develop a questionnaire consisting of 10 to 12 items, to collect the data.

- Explain the size and type of sample that you would hypothetically draw to investigate your research problem (in reality).
- Design a covering letter.
- Draw a purposive sample of 10 respondents who could have been part of the hypothetical sample and conduct a pilot study of the questionnaire. For example, if your research problem is aimed at establishing readers' opinions of the new format of an existing newspaper, then the 10 respondents must be readers of that newspaper.

Further reading

Babbie, E. 1990. *Survey research methods.* 2nd edition. Belmont, CA: Wadsworth.

Bless, C & Higson-Smith, C. 1995. *Fundamentals of social research methods: an African Perspective.* 2nd edition. Cape Town: Juta.

Cardwell-Gardner, T & Bennett, JA. 1999. Television advertising to young children: An exploratory study. *Communicare* 19 (1):44–60.

Du Plooy, GM (ed). 1995. *Introduction to communication – course book 2: communication research.* Cape Town: Juta.

Leedy, PD. 1997 (or earlier edition). *Practical research: planning and design.* 6th edition. Columbus, OH: Merrill, an imprint of Prentice Hall.

Pitout, M. 1998. Reception analysis: a qualitative investigation of the parasocial and social dimensions of soap opera viewing. *Communicatio* 24(2):39–47.

Wimmer, RD & Dominick, JR. 1994 (4th edition) or 1997 (5th edition). *Mass media research: an introduction.* Belmont, CA: Wadsworth.

Bibliography

Berger, AA. 1991. *Media analysis techniques.* Revised edition. Newbury Park, CA: Sage.

De Vos, AS (ed). 1998. *Research at grass roots: a primer for the caring professions.* Pretoria: Van Schaik.

Krueger, RA. 1994. *Focus groups: a practical guide for applied research.* 2nd edition. Thousand Oaks: Sage.

Marshall, C & Rossman, GB. 1989. *Designing qualitative research.* Newbury Park, CA: Sage.

McQuail, D. 1994. *Mass communication theory: An introduction.* 3rd edition. London: Sage.

Pitout, M. 1996. Televisie en resepsiestudie: 'n analise van kykersinterpretasie van die seep-opera "Egoli: Plek van Goud". Ongepubliseerde doktorale proefskrif. Pretoria: Universiteit van Suid-Afrika.

Stewart, DW & Shamdasani, PN. 1990. *Focus groups. Theory and practice.* Newbury Park, CA: Sage.

Media and Psychoanalysis 10

Stefan Sonderling

Overview

This unit provides an introduction to the use of psychoanalytical theory to the study of film. Psychoanalysis explains how viewing film and television programmes resembles the act of dreaming that provides a pleasurable experience for the viewer. A framework for the analysis of film and television is also described.

Learning outcomes

The purpose of this unit is to introduce you to the basic assumptions of psychoanalysis and the theories of Freud and Lacan and their application to the study of film and television.

After completing this study unit you should be able to

- describe the basic assumptions of applying psychoanalysis to the study of film and television;
- describe the psychoanalytical theories of Freud and Lacan;
- compare the film and television experience to the act of dreaming; and
- identify, describe and give examples of the viewer's experience of film and television programmes.

10.1 INTRODUCTION

The popularity of television viewing, as well as that of film, indicates that these media must somehow have a natural relationship with their audiences' frame of mind. Watching films and television programmes is both meaningful, as we follow the story line, and pleasurable, because we enjoy these stories. However, traditional film and television theories have largely ignored the spectator's experience and focused on the structure of the film or television programmes as if they were like the *text* that a viewer reads; or the theories examined the intention, personality or genius of the author/producer of the film, forgetting that films and television programmes are made for the viewer. In fact, film and television as industries and as artistic and cultural forms could not exist without the viewer!

The psychoanalytic approach to the study of film and television provides an insight into the viewer's conscious and unconscious experience of film and television *texts*.

The film or television programme as text, refers to the fact that watching a film is similar to the way we read a story written in a language that we understand; the viewer of a film may be considered as the reader or interpreter. Psychoanalysis explains the link between the pleasures and desires of the spectator for the fantasies and desires represented in film and television texts.

The application of psychoanalysis to the study of film and television is based on the assumption that film and television viewing resembles a state of dreaming. Watching film and television activates conscious and unconscious mechanisms of the viewer's mind and gratifies some repressed and hidden desires (cf. Flitterman-Lewis 1987:179).

Indeed, there is a long tradition in film theory, dating as far back as 1916 to Hugo Münsterberg's psychological study, which suggests that films, like dreams, project the spectator's imagination on the screen. Subsequent generations of critics followed the film-dream analogy and considered Hollywood, the major producer of popular feature films, the dream factory (cf. Altman 1977:264–265). Likewise, the popularity of television may be related to its dream-like quality: in its form and content, television projects the dream-life of a whole society (cf. Wood 1982) performing a *ritual condensation* – giving abstract ideas a visible material form (cf. Fiske & Hartley 1982:89–90).

Considering film and television viewing as being similar to dreaming also means that it is no longer possible to regard these media in terms of either a *window* through which we view objects in the world, or as a picture *frame* that shapes and constructs the meaning of images appearing within its space. Rather, we can consider film as if it were a *mirror* reflecting the viewer's inner mental states (cf. Altman 1977:260; Andrew 1984:134).

Psychoanalysis as a cultural theory and method of analysis contributes to the understanding of art, literature, film and television and explains how the conscious and unconscious mental processes function in the production and understanding of works of art (cf. Wright 1984:9). The application of psychoanalysis to the study of film and television may be considered as an extension of the theory of structuralism. Structuralism attempts to uncover some coherent unity that underlies and makes meaningful the surface manifestation of diverse cultural phenomena. Freud's theory of the mind is similar to the structuralist theory: the unconscious part of the mind and its link to sexuality provide the hidden structure that animates our conscious behaviour. Psychoanalytic methods involve the interpretation of dream narratives and uncovering their hidden meaning may be described as a form of structuralist textual analysis. Psychoanalysis applied to film and television is a critical discourse that explains the various levels of the viewing process and the way the viewer and text interact (cf. Wright 1984:17).

Although the application of psychoanalysis to the study of art, literature and film is by now a well-established intellectual enterprise and dates back to Freud's own work on art and literature, its application to the study of television is still a new and problematic field. Some theorists object to the direct application of psychoanalytic methods developed in film studies to television, because of differences between these media (cf. Flitterman-Lewis 1987). However, it must be remembered that similar objections, based on the formal differences between film and dreams, were raised against the application of psychoanalysis to the study of film (cf. Altman 1977:265). The objection to the application of psychoanalysis to television may be based on the *élitist* stance of scholars who still consider television as a vulgar form of popular culture and an unsuitable object of study to be included among "high culture" products such as literature and film (cf. Petro 1986).

While it must be acknowledged that film and television are two different and distinct media, they share many similarities making it possible to apply psychoanalytic methods developed in film studies to the study of television fictional programmes such as the soap operas (cf. Butler 1986; Flitterman-Lewis 1987), and to be extended to the study of news and actuality programmes (cf. Stam 1983). Television and film may be considered as two different technologies that share a single language: the language (or codes) of the cinema (cf. Hall and Metz, in Heath & Skirrow 1977:7). In contemporary society, film and television exist in a symbiotic relationship: television has taken over most of the conventions of mainstream narrative film, for example, television programmes are structured like the films we see in the theatre, and films, in turn, are influenced by the conventions of television, for example, we expect to see more fast action in films because we see such fast action in television dramas (cf. Barker 1988:50; Ellis 1984:237–239; Hilmes 1985).

In order to understand the application of the psychoanalytical method to the study of film and television we need to become familiar with the basic concepts of psychoanalysis as developed by Sigmund Freud and Jacques Lacan.

10.2 PSYCHOANALYTIC THEORY

Psychoanalysis is the name Freud gave in 1896 to a scientific theory of the human mind and personality and a therapeutic method of investigating unconscious mental processes. Freud also used psychoanalysis as a tool for the analysis of literary texts (cf. Kaplan 1990:12).

For Freud, the human personality is the product of the relationship between inner biologically determined drives or urges and the external constraints of the physical world and society. The human mind may be considered as an iceberg: beneath conscious activities lies hidden an unconscious element and any proper understanding of conscious activities must also take into account the unconscious. The human being is born with powerful sexual instincts or drives, which demand gratification. However, human existence is characterised by a harsh struggle for physical survival. In order to survive, basic needs must be provided by toil and labour undertaken in social association with other people. The basic necessity to work and cooperate with others means that human beings must repress their natural tendencies to seek pleasure and gratification. Thus, human society and culture are built on a principle of repression, and humankind finds itself in permanent conflict between the fundamental motivation to avoid pain and seek pleasure and social demands for self-control, delayed gratification and sublimation of desires towards more valued social ends.

According to Freud, happiness has no cultural value; renunciation and delay in satisfaction of desires are a prerequisite for social progress (cf. Marcuse 1973:23). Every human being must undergo repression of the *pleasure principle* by the *reality principle* to become a member of society (cf. Eagleton 1983:151). The mechanism by which the individual is socialised is the Oedipus complex. The Oedipus complex is based on the Greek myth of a son killing his father and his incestuous relationship with his mother. Freud considers the myth of Oedipus as being symbolic of the desire of the son to sexually possess his mother and kill his father, which every male-child entering social relationships must overcome. The socialisation process for the female child according to Freud is different.

In the pre-Oedipal stage, the male-child has a close relationship with his mother and depends on her for the satisfaction of his physical needs for survival. Through the satisfaction of physical needs, such as sucking the mother's breast, the child discovers that performing this essentially biological activity is also pleasurable. This is the beginning of sexuality, which develops through various stages when different parts of the infant's body become the centre of sexual pleasure.

During the development of sexuality the male-child also experiences libidinal desires for the mother. This close incestuous relationship between the child and the mother is shattered when he becomes aware of the father. The father is seen as posing a threat to the male-child's sexual desires for the mother and becomes a rival for love and affection. The threat that the child experiences is of punishment by castration. As a result of this threat and fear of castration, the child detaches himself from the mother and identifies with the father and takes on a position of a *gendered* subject in society. The father's prohibition of incest is symbolic of all other higher authority in society that the male-child will experience later in life. The male-child's forbidden sexual desires for the mother are repressed into the unconscious. The unconscious is in fact created in the process of repression. The result of this massive repression creates an individual who is split between two levels of existence: a person who has a conscious life as member of society and an unconscious life of repressed sexual desires.

The repressed sexual desires lodged in the unconscious manifest themselves in dreams, artistic and linguistic expressions (cf. Wright 1982:113). Dreams are considered as the symbolic fulfilment of unconscious wishes; these wishes manifest themselves in symbolism because direct expression of the material could be shocking and disturbing to the individual. The unconscious softens and distorts the true erotic meaning of these desires, through a process Freud terms the dream work. The dream work projects the *latent* or hidden content (such as the repressed desires) into coded and distorted *manifest* content. In order to understand the true meaning of the dream, the manifest contents needs to be interpreted. In this manner we can understand how the unconscious mind speaks its distorted messages through various processes (cf. Eagleton 1983:157; Wood 1982:519). The following is the way the unconscious mind works.

- *condensation* – by which latent elements are compressed, combined and fragmented into one single manifest image;
- *displacement* – by which a latent element is replaced by a more remote or obscure image and the meaning of one object is displaced onto another somehow associated with it;
- *inversion* – by which thought is translated into images;
- *dramatisation* – by which the latent thoughts are given some continuous dramatic forms.

The operation of the unconscious, especially through condensation and displacement can be compared with the two primary operations of language: *metaphor* – which implies condensing meaning together, and *metonymy* – which implies displacing one meaning for another.

This analogy is what motivates French psychoanalyst Jacques Lacan to claim that the unconscious is structured like language. For Lacan, the unconscious is not a biological residence for drives and instincts but a linguistic and cultural construction. Lacan points to the fact that any understanding of the unconscious demands understanding of language.

Indeed, language and the unconscious have other close similarities. Ferdinand De Saussure (1974) describes language as a system or structure (*langue*) which can be distinguished from actual speech (*parole*). Language as system is in the unconscious of every speaker of whom the speech act is only meaningful in relation to the unconscious structure (cf. Archard 1984:60). The unconscious element is also in operation in the linguistic sign – the sign divided into *signifier*, the sound-image and *signified*, the concept conjured up by the signifier (cf. Fourie 1988:29), thus the signified is always indirectly and imaginatively invoked from the unconscious.

Freud provides a theory of human development that is incomplete without consideration of language; Lacan reinterprets Freud's theory in the light of structural linguistics. Language is an important element in human development as without it no social relationship can be imagined. In fact, human life is life in a *symbolic universe* of language and meaning. In other words, we can understand what is happening around us because we interpret and translate it into words.

According to Lacan, the individual is socially constructed in two stages:

- the mirror stage at the age of six months during which the child becomes aware of its image;
- the symbolic stage at the age of eighteen months when "the child enters into society and society's language enters into the child" (Harland 1988:38–39).

According to Lacan, the early pre-Oedipal and pre-linguistic stages of the child's development process are the realm of the *imaginary*. At this stage the child cannot distinguish between itself and the outside world and exists in an amorphous and genderless state which Lacan, using a pun, calls *l'hommelette – homme-lette* meaning the *little man* or child is shapeless like an *omelette* (cf. Wright 1984:107–108). The child develops a sense of self through perceptual identification with its image in a mirror – the mirror stage. The concept of the mirror coined by Lacan should not be taken literally, as what is meant is that the child either sees an image of itself reflected in the mirror or another image, such as its mother's face, which it mistakes to be itself and with which it can identify (cf. Eagleton 1983:165). The child's identification with a mirror image (primary identification) which it takes to be a unified concept of itself is a misrecognition, as the child mistakes an image for a more perfect whole than it actually is. The misrecognised image is then projected outside itself and considered as ideal. Later this is again internalised and a desire to identify with others begins (cf. Greenberg & Gabbard 1990:100).

Freud's Oedipus complex is seen by Lacan as an entry into the symbolic order of language and culture and the acquisition of sexual identity. The figure of the father, which according to Freud signifies the threat of castration and prohibits the total unity of the child with the mother, is seen by Lacan as signifying the introduction of the child to language and the wider social order. For Lacan, the father is symbolic of the laws of the patriarchal society which repress the libidinal drives in the child and his incestuous identification with the mother. The acquisition of language occurs simultaneously with the primal repression that constitutes the unconscious (cf. Lemarie 1982:53). In order to overcome his painful separation from the mother, the child develops linguistic skills to represent the mother's absence, to represent his sexual desires and represent his identification with the role of the father (secondary identification). Not being able to express his desires directly, language becomes a symbolic substitute, always standing between desires and the objects of desires. Thus begins life in the symbolic order.

Language is a primary medium for symbolic identification as it essentially provides a point of reference for human beings to constitute themselves as subjects. Language provides *empty forms* which speakers can appropriate for themselves and relate to personal identity defining themself as "I" and the partner to discourse as "you" (cf. Benveniste in Morse 1985:2). The "I" and "you" are only understood in relation to the existing social relations in society. The concept of *self* or "individuality" is not a natural phenomenon nor is it a unified and concrete "personality" but an illusive construction through social and linguistic processes.

The entry of the individual into society and language also means that he enters into the ideological framework provided by language. Ideology is a system of representations – images, discourse, myths – which explain and make meaningful the social conditions in which people live, reflecting the meanings of these conditions as interpreted by dominant social classes. Ideology is part of the unconscious; it is the taken for granted assumptions about the way things are. Ideology is *inscribed* in discourse in the sense that it is literally written or spoken in it; it is not a separate element which exists independently in some free-floating realm of "ideas" and is subsequently embodied in words, but a way of thinking, speaking, experiencing (Belsey 1986:5).

Through the acquisition of language the human being can make sense of the self and the world. Conversely, understanding human beings and society is made possible by the scientific study of language, as is claimed by the theory of structuralism. This is so because all the practices that make up a social totality take place in language, and it becomes possible to consider language as the *place* in which the social individual is constructed (cf. Coward & Ellis 1986:1).

From a psychoanalytic perspective, an individual is the product of biologically determined sexual drives, culture and language. The concept of a human being's identity as a gendered subject has been internalised during the formative years of the Oedipal drama of infancy. Through the use of language and the media such as film and television the primal processes are reinforced.

10.3 PSYCHOANALYSIS AND THE STUDY OF TELEVISION

Television as a medium of communication and a cultural and commercial institution could not exist without its *audience*, after all, television programmes are made for the viewer, or stated differently by Godard: "television doesn't make programmes – it makes viewers" (in Flitterman 1983:95). For the viewer, watching television is a *pleasurable* and meaningful experience: no one is forced to watch television, yet large numbers of people turn on their television sets day and night and find the experience enjoyable. The pleasure of television viewing is not limited to the traditional entertainment genres such as drama, fictional feature films, or the soap opera, but also includes viewing of documentary and news broadcasts (cf. Stam 1983:23).

The pleasure of film and television viewing is found in the characteristic features of these media. Television is a highly visual medium that combines images and sound to tell stories or fictional narratives. Thus, the pleasure of the viewer is derived from a combination of looking and listening to narratives.

Television and film are *storytelling machines*; technologies utilised to tell tales and satisfy a human desire for narratives (cf. Andrew 1984:143). Thus, like the film, television can be described as a *technique of the imaginary* (cf. Metz 1982:3). This means that television consists of

- *imaginative* or fictional narratives creating a world of fantasy in their texts;
- *imagery* or iconic images telling their narratives audio-visually; and
- the *imaginary* order as described by Lacan's distinction between the *imaginary* order and the *symbolic* order.

As most films and popular television programmes are fictional narratives represented visually, they resemble dreams. Thus, viewing a film or a television programme can be compared to the act of dreaming; the audio-visual text of these media mobilises the conscious and unconscious of the viewer. The film or television text lures the viewer to enter the world of fiction, and suspend his belief or disbelief in the unreality of the text.

Wood (1982:514–516) outlines the similarities between television and dreams:

- Television and dreams have a highly visual quality;
- they are highly symbolic;

- have a high degree of wish fulfilment;
- appear to contain much that is disjointed and trivial;
- they have powerful content, most of which is readily and thoroughly forgotten; and
- both make use of material drawn from recent experience.

The viewer as a dreamer is positioned and engaged by a whole complex structure of television technology and social institutions. The television institution is not merely the industry that produces programmes, but it is also the mental machinery of the viewers accustomed to television (cf. Stam 1983:38). Together these are known as the cinema-apparatus or the television-apparatus (cf. Flitterman-Lewis 1987:181). The complex television-apparatus consists of the following elements:

- the technical base, such as the camera, film, video, lights and the projection of the images on the screen;
- the condition of viewing, in the home and familial setting;
- the television "text" itself; the way it is constructed in order to present visual continuity, illusion of space and illusion of reality;
- the mental machinery of the viewers, their conscious and unconscious mental processes.

The television-apparatus thus positions the viewer in such a way that he has an illusion of being the actual producer of and the main character in the text. Viewers consider the television text as their own fantasy designed to fulfil their desires. It is obvious that the viewer is an important and central part of the whole complex television-apparatus. The television-apparatus both invites and makes place for and positions the viewer for participation and experience. The viewer's experience and involvement may be represented as a complex process.

To help us understand and analyse the viewer's involvement with film and television, we can consider viewing film and television as a progression through different stages, which are examined in the following section.

10.4 ANALYSIS OF THE TELEVISION VIEWER'S INVOLVEMENT

The interaction between the viewer and the text in the televisual-apparatus centres on a number of elements: desire and pleasure, regression, identification and the mode of enunciation (cf. Flitterman-Lewis 1987). In other words, the viewer regresses to a dream-like state where the images on the screen are taken by him as his own dreams; in this dream-state he is able to identify with images and views presented on the screen. Regression and identification are induced by the quality of the text itself, techniques through which the text is constructed and its mode of addressing the viewer.

10.4.1 Desire and pleasure

The imaginative narrative is pleasurable in itself. Eidsvik (1978:6) suggests that all narratives, regardless of their medium invoke the viewer's imagination by initially asking the viewer or reader an implicit question "what if ...?" that can only be answered imaginatively in the narrative. The viewer's imaginary participation in narrative fantasy is cathartic and pleasurable because it relieves the pressure of frustration, both conscious and unconscious (cf. Fourie 1988:78). The pleasure and catharsis are derived from re-experience of the Oedipus complex that motivates all narratives. Because all narrative plots follow an Oedipal structure, the protagonist's desire and the text itself originate in the primordial desire for the mother and the search for the father. In a more complex sense the text may be considered as a signifier of deeper basic psychosexual structuring processes associated with the Oedipus (cf. Altman 1977:258–259). Thus the narrative is an endless return to the primal scene. Freud's Oedipus is essentially a *family romance*, re-enacted in every film or narrative of television soap opera.

The narrative itself, in its formal structure and a fantasy, is also a source of sexual pleasure. The pleasure of the narrative text is derived from its resemblance to sexual intercourse in its orgasmic rhythm of tensions and resolutions and culminating in a climax (cf. De Lauretis 1984:108).

In addition to the pleasure of narratives, the pleasure of film and television is based largely on perception. According to Lacan (cf. Metz 1982:58), the desire to see (scopophilia and voyeurism) and the desire to hear are major components of the sexual drive and thus a source of pleasure. Film and television viewing satisfy the erotic pleasure of perception itself as well as the pleasure of looking on at images of human form that are erotically stimulating.

10.4.2 Regression

Viewing a film or television entails a mental process of denial or disavowal, a double suspension of belief or disbelief – believing and not believing simultaneously – in the reality of the fiction and regression to the pleasures of the imaginary stage. Film and television construct their fictional narrative by the use of iconic images creating an illusion of reality. The power of these media is derived from their ability to convince the viewer that the unreal has been realised (cf. Metz 1974:5). Film and television and their photographic/video iconic images stage their effect with the presence of images (signifiers) which point to the absence of the original object – a play of shadow, referential illusion, or a play of signifiers that leads Metz (1982) to term the cinema as the imaginary signifier. The viewer knows that he is seeing a fictional narrative but suspends this knowledge in order to remain in the state of the illusion and the dream-like state (cf. Metz 1982:69–78). The quality of the visual image reduces the viewer's awareness of his actual distance from the real object. The viewer feels as if he were not in the presence of a signifier but that of the signified or the object itself. The image has iconic visual similarity to the world it records and is also an index of this world as it is an imprint left behind by the real object. The viewing situation and mental machinery allow the viewer to suspend belief and enter the dream-like state. The viewer has already been prepared by the primordial experience of the mirror stage. Thus the viewer in front of the screen is like the infant in front of the primordial mirror, fascinated by the images. The viewer's regression and entry into the imaginary world of the narrative have also been prepared by the knowledge and experience of other cultural forms of narrative such as art and literature (cf. August 1981:417).

The viewing situation in the cinema, for example the dark theatre, the reduced physical activity of the viewer, the comfortable seats, anonymity, the withdrawal from everyday reality, all resemble the situation of the helpless infant and are considered to induce a dream-like state. Television viewed in the privacy of the home with its domestic distraction may superficially seem to exclude regression. It is claimed that television has a quality of *immediacy*, a "live medium" bringing to the viewer the events of the world as they happen. But the "liveness" and immediacy of television is, rather, a myth.

In fact, much of what we think as television originates on film; filmed series have predominated over live television since the mid-1950s. Yet still we speak of television's immediacy, spontaneity, intimacy. These terms originated in the early 1950s in reference to truly *live*, unrecorded television; the fact that they have lived on for 30 years after its demise, points past technology to ideology (Hilmes 1985:30).

Television modes of address, especially news, documentaries and talk shows seem to address the viewer directly as if he were a partner in discourse, and shatters the voyeuristic illusion. However, television is not experienced as real by its audience. Television is a *new mode of fiction* because the viewer does not consider the television images on the screen as being truly present, or partners to a discourse, but rather as quasi-subjects. Television offers an illusion of discourse: "we know that elsewhere discourse may be *real*, but in our living room that same discourse is imaginary" (Morse 1985:3). Therefore, the viewer is able to regress to an imaginary stage and enter the fictional world of soap operas, televised films, commercials, talk shows and news programmes, and take his pleasure in them. The pleasure of television viewers' identification is derived from experience and participation as subjects in the multiple discourses that make the social reality. However, Freudian and Lacanian psychoanalytic theories' fixation with the over-determination of the Oedipal construction of the subject have neglected other discursive influences that construct the individual beyond the infantile stage.

10.4.3 Mirror identification

The experience of viewing television may be compared to Lacan's mirror stage where the child identifies itself in an image. Viewing a film or television is pleasurable to the viewer precisely because he has experience of this in infancy. In viewing, the viewer identifies with his own act of looking, and the look itself is termed primary identification. The viewer's identification with his own look, is a source of narcissistic pleasure. Primary identification in television coincides with the look of the camera, and offers the viewer an unlimited camera view and possibilities of identification (cf. Stam 1983:24). Through the primary identification, the viewer experiences secondary identifications, with the perceived human and non-human characters on the screen. Television offers endless sources of secondary identification, characters both imaginary and real with whom the viewer can identify (cf. Stam 1983:27).

The pleasure of perception and identification positions the viewer as an ideal voyeur: looking on the "private world" represented by the images and gratifying his sexual desires. The position of the voyeur also gives the viewer a sensation of power as he can look on the action and be unobserved. The pleasure of perception of film and television is theorised as that of the male viewer. According to this perspective, the traditional Hollywood film and contemporary television reflect the dominant patriarchal ideology and produce filmic/televisual texts that satisfy the male unconscious (films are made by male producers for male viewers). The dominant ideology is communicated through the use of a complex series of cinematic and televisual "looks" in which the viewer is implicated as a male subject: (1) the look of camera to the filmic event among others; (2) from the male viewer to the screen; and (3) the interplay of looks exchanged between the characters on the screen (cf. Flitterman 1981:243). The structure of the reverse shot and matching view shots increase the illusion of participation as the viewer always has a certain subjective view from the position of one of the characters with whom he may imaginatively identify. The pleasure and fascination of film and television reinforce pre-existing patterns of fascination already at work within the viewer. According to feminist theories, film and television images reveal and play on socially established sexual differences, thus the female form in most narratives becomes a centre of attraction and is displayed for the benefit of the predominantly male audience. In this way dominant cultural ideology is reflected and reinforced (cf. Mulvey 1985:307). However, the feminist view cannot explain why women viewers find film and television pleasurable. Television programmes such as sport represent both male and female bodies for display, while other fictional programmes present images of male sexuality that both men and women may identify with. For example, a male figure such as Thomas in the detective series *Magnum PI*, or the young characters in soap opera such as *The Bold and the Beautiful*, far from repressing the erotics of the gaze, the structures of fascination in looking at the male body are utilised to permit this signifying articulation (cf. Flitterman 1985:43).

10.4.4 Modes of enunciation

The regression and entry to the imaginary are helped by the modes of enunciation or the specific structure of the text and through the use of production techniques that create the illusion in the viewer that he is observing his own fantasies. The term *enunciation* is derived from structural linguistics and refers both to the said and the act of *saying*, in other words a distinction between a *story* (*historie*) which refers to the content, and *discourse* or the way the content is communicated. In film and television theory enunciation attempts to describe the way the cinematic/televisual text is organised and how this act of organisation is distinctively concealed, creating a specific form of address to the viewer constituting him as a subject.

A discourse implies the position from which the various subjects speak and address each other as "I" and "you". Each of the participants is aware of the other person and his own position. A story is experienced in a more oblique way, according to Barthes, as soon as a fact is *narrated* no longer with a view to acting directly on reality but intransitively, that is to say, finally outside of any function other than that of the very practice of the symbol itself, the voice loses its origin (Barthes 1984:143).

For the film and television text to be taken by the viewer as if it were his own dream fantasy, all the marks of construction, and the fact that it is a discourse should be eliminated. Every film and television programme has a place of enunciation from which it proceeds, or a point of view from which the representations are organised and made meaningful. This point of view is occupied by the director or author of the film/ television programme and coincides with the view of the camera recording the film/television programme.

The same point of view must be then given to the viewer who can imagine that he can see his own desires visualised on the screen (cf. Flitterman-Lewis 1987:185). Thus the experience of film and television is based on the disappearance of the producer, who leaves his place empty for the viewer to take over the production of the discourse. The position of the viewer is considered as an *empty space*, which can be filled by any viewer. The viewer can occupy this empty position as he was already prepared for it through the acquisition of language. In classical Hollywood film, the effacement of the marks of enunciation are produced by the smooth editing of various scenes and combining matching camera shots, all creating a feeling of continuity and coherence of narrative, distracting attention from the fact that a film consists of various shots and sequences that are cut and joined together. The concealment of the marks of enunciation transform the film from a *discourse* to that of a *story* as if told by no one, and is a mere fact from the viewer's own unconscious story (cf. Flitterman-Lewis 1987:186).

Television has incorporated the conventions of film to conceal its modes of enunciation (cf. Hilmes 1985). However, television also uses its own specific technique to provide unity and coherence to its text and allows the viewer to imagine that he hears his language and society speaking. Because he has internalised language and ideology, it is the viewer's own story of repressed desires which is narrated.

Television consists of diverse programmes, genres and commercials (advertising) which superficially may seem fragmentary. However, television is experienced by the viewer as a unified whole that *flows* continually (cf. Williams 1974:95). The texts of television receive their unity from the commercials that seemingly break programmes, but in fact provide the undercurrent ideology of the consumer society, performing a "condensation of values and aspirations with commodities" (cf. Flitterman 1983:95). The diverse texts on television are also united by self-referential advertising and the cross-programme references by which characters from one show appear on another, creating a metatext of the self-enclosed world of television. The unity of fictional and non-fictional programmes "brought together as parts of a larger, continuous imaginary world ... addresses the spectator-as-ideal-subject across temporal, spatial, and narrative diversity" (White 1986:62). Thus, rather than evaluating television according to its live programmes such as news and talk show, these programmes should be evaluated according to the fictional and imaginary nature of television.

The unity of television provides a general ideological framework, a *continuous story* for the viewer's perception of his society. However, the continuous story of television as a metatext is unique and characterised by its *unity of contradiction* and reflects the viewer's own complexity. Thus television may be termed a *postmodern* medium.

10.5 CRITICAL EVALUATION

Freudian and Lacanian psychoanalysis as applied to film and television is not free from criticism. Psychoanalysis is based on Freud's biological behaviourism that resembles a stimulus-response model. The overemphasis on the determinism by the Oedipus complex of the human personality during the infant years is reductionist and does not consider other important stages of human development. The importance of the Oedipus complex in Freud's theory is

> a reduction and a rewriting of the whole rich and random multiple realities of concrete everyday experience into the contained, strategically pre-limited terms of the family narrative – whether this be seen as myth, Greek tragedy, or *family romance*.
>
> (Jameson 1983:21–22)

Thus psychoanalysis attempts to interpret all human phenomena as manifestations of a single myth of the bourgeois (conventionally middle-class/capitalist) family. When this is applied to film and television, the interpretative activity is reduced to the endless search for the characters in the Oedipal drama. Criticism of poststructuralists, such as Michel Foucault, of structuralism and psychoanalysis provides the insight that the individual is not constructed merely by a single episode in infancy but is continuously constructed as a subject in and through the interplay of the numerous discourses that constitute the social totality. The subject thus gains experience of multiple forms of identification and competence to assume various positions required of him by the social discourses.

The viewer's encounter with television therefore reflects the sum of his experience as a discursive subject and his ability to assume different positions required by the various discourses of television. Thus the subject's involvement with television is not merely passive but an interactive encounter (cf. Deming 1985).

Psychoanalytic film theory acknowledges the complexity of the viewer and the importance of the pre-linguistic stage but it traditionally privileges the symbolic dimension, thus "manifest content of images as well as formal structures tend to get read as signs of a symbolic order implicit in the materiality of the images" (cf. Koch 1985:147). The analysis of film tends to be limited to the symbolic and linguistic experience. However, the symbolic is preceded by a pre-linguistic imaginary stage unmediated by language, and the experience of film is not only symbolic but also involves the re-experience of the pre-social pre-linguistic realm that is unmediated by language (cf. Koch 1985:147).

Psychoanalysis film and television theorists also do not draw the proper conclusion from the structuralist theory of enunciation. Enunciation implies the removal or *death* of the author and the birth of the reader. But psychoanalytic critics perpetuate the *auteur theory* in an attempt to discover a *real* person as the producer and source of the textual truth and meaning. However, Foucault (1981) points out that the author is merely a name and social function whose existence is of no relevance because the text does not depend on its author for existence and meaning. According to Barthes (1984:146), a text does not convey a "message" from an author but it is a multidimensional space in which a variety of writings, none of them original, blend and clash. The text is a tissue of quotations drawn from the innumerable centres of culture (Barthes 1984:146).

The unity of any text does not lie in its origin but rather in the destination or its viewer (cf. Barthes 1984:148).

The reader or viewer is highly complex and an articulated subject whose unity is imaginary. Thus the viewer's pleasure is derived from his likeness to the highly complex and articulated texts of film and television. He can enjoy the multiple identifications and contradictions offered by the text because these reflect his experience of the discursive, symbolic and pre-linguistic experience of the imaginary.

The experience of viewing film and television is gratifying because it is complex and contradictory. The images and narratives of television may be experienced as unified and mediated by the symbolic sphere and simultaneously as discontinuous dreams.

Because television is a heterogeneous system of representation, "a site of textual intersection and coexistence of varying narratives, genres, appeals and modes of address" (White 1989:161), the viewer's experience is "at once dispersed and distracted while at the same time intensely preoccupied and absorbed" (Petro 1986:18). Roland Barthes' pertinent description of the television viewer:

> Imagine someone (a kind of Monsieur Taste in reverse) who abolishes within himself all barriers, all classes, all exclusions, not by *syncretisms* but by simple discard of that old specter: *logical contradiction*; who mixes every language, even those said to be incompatible; who silently accepts every charge of illogicality, of incongruity; who remains passive in the face of Socratic irony (leading the interlocutor to the supreme disgrace: *self-contradiction*) and legal terrorism (how much penal evidence is based on psychology of consistency!). Such a man would be the mockery of our society: court, school, asylum, polite conversation would cast him out: who endures contradiction without shame? Now this anti-hero exists: he is the reader of the text at the moment he takes his pleasure.
>
> (Barthes 1986:3)

What Barthes describes is the way we can view and identify with the strangest fantasies while watching a film or the different television programmes we see during one evening.

Summary

In this unit we discussed the basic assumptions that underlie the application of psychoanalysis to the study of film and television. The theories of Freud and Lacan were discussed, the act of viewing film and television was compared to the act of dreaming and the viewer's experience was explained and analysed through a series of stages such as desire and pleasure, regression, identification and modes of enunciation.

Research activities

1 Explain the similarities between the act of dreaming and that of viewing film and television.

2 Explain the viewer's experience of film and television with reference to the following aspects:
   - regression
   - mirror identification
   - modes of enunciation

   Provide your own example to explain the different stages of the viewer's experience of film and television.

Further reading

Andrew, D. 1984. *Concepts in film theory*. New York: Oxford University Press.

Bywater, T & Sobchack, T. 1989. *Introduction to film criticism: major critical approaches to narrative film*. New York: Longman.

Eagleton, T. 1983. *Literary theory: An introduction*. Oxford: Basil Blackwell.

Ellis, J. 1984. *Visible fictions: cinema, television, video*. London: Routledge & Kegan Paul.

Flitterman-Lewis, S. 1987. Psychoanalysis, film, and television, in *Channels of discourse*, edited by RC Allen. London: Methuen.

Kaplan, EA (ed). 1990. *Psychoanalysis and cinema*. New York: Routledge/American Film Institute.

Metz, C. 1982. *The imaginary signifier: Psychoanalysis and cinema*. Bloomington: Indiana University Press.

Wright, E. 1984. *Psychoanalytic criticism: Theory in practice*. London: Methuen.

Bibliography

Altman, CF. 1977. Psychoanalysis and cinema: the imaginary discourse. *Quarterly Review of Film Studies* 2(3):257-272.

Archard, D. 1984. *Consciousness and the unconscious*. London: Hutchinson.

August, B. 1981. The lure of psychoanalysis in film theory, in *Cinematographic apparatus: selected writings*, edited by T Hak Kyunk Cha. New York: Tanam Press.

Andrew, D. 1984. *Concepts in film theory*. New York: Oxford University Press.

Barker, D. 1988. "It has been real": forms of television representation. *Critical Studies in Mass Communication* 5(1):42–56.

Barthes, R. 1984. *Image, music, text.* London: Fontana.

Barthes, R. 1986. *The pleasure of the text.* New York: Hill and Wang.

Baudry, J-L. 1975. Ideological effects of the basic cinematographic apparatus. *Film Quarterly* 28(2):39–47.

Belsey, C. 1986. *Critical practice.* London: Methuen.

Butler, JG. 1986. Notes on the soap opera apparatus: televisual style and "As the world turns". *Cinema Journal* 25(3):53–70.

Bywater, T & Sobchack, T. 1989. *Introduction to film criticism: major critical approaches to narrative film.* New York: Longman.

Coward, R & Ellis, J. 1986. *Language and materialism: developments in semiology and the theory of the subject.* London: Routledge & Kegan Paul.

De Lauretis, T. 1984. *Alice doesn't: feminism, semiotics, cinema.* London: Macmillan.

De Saussure, F. 1974. *Course in general linguistics.* London: Fontana/Collins.

Deming, RH. 1985. The television spectator-subject. *Journal of Film and Video* 37(3):48–63.

Eidsvik, C. 1978. *Cineliteracy: film among the arts.* New York: Random house.

Eagleton, T. 1983. *Literary theory: An introduction.* Oxford: Basil Blackwell.

Ellis, J. 1984. *Visible fictions: cinema, television, video.* London: Routledge & Kegan Paul.

Fiske, J & Hartley, J. 1982. *Reading television.* London: Methuen.

Flitterman, S. 1981. Women, desire, and the look: feminism and the enunciative apparatus in cinema, in *Theories of authorship: a reader*, edited by J Caughie. London: Routledge & Kegan Paul/British Film Institute.

Flitterman, S. 1983. The real soap opera: TV commercials, in *Regarding Television – critical approaches: an anthology*, edited by EA Kaplan. Frederick, MD: University publications of America.

Flitterman, S. 1985. Thighs and whiskers: The fascination of "Magnum, p.i.". *Screen* 26(2):42–58.

Flitterman-Lewis, S. 1987. Psychoanalysis, film, and television, in *Channels of discourse*, edited by RC Allen. London: Methuen.

Foucault, M. 1981. What is an author? in *Theories of authorship: a reader*, edited by J Caughie. London: Routledge & Kegan Paul/British Film Institute.

Fourie, PJ. 1988. *Aspects of film and television communication.* Cape Town: Juta.

Greenberg, HR & Gabbard, K. 1990. Reel significations: an anatomy of psychoanalytic film criticism. *Psychoanalytic Review* 77(1):89–110.

Harland, R. 1988. *Superstructuralism: the philosophy of structuralism and poststructuralism.* London: Routledge.

Heath, S & Skirrow, G. 1977. Television: a world in action. *Screen* 18(2):7–59.

Heath, S. 1981. *Questions of cinema.* London: Macmillan.

Heath, S. 1985. Jaws, ideology and film theory, in *Popular television and film*, edited by T Bennett, S Boyd-Bowman, C Mercer & J Woollacott. London: British Film Institute.

Hilmes, M. 1985. The television apparatus: direct address. *Journal of Film and Video* 37(4):27–36.

Houston, B. 1984. Viewing television: The metapsychology of endless consumption. *Quarterly Review of Film Studies* 9(3):183–195.

Jameson, F. 1983. *The political unconscious: narrative as a socially symbolic act.* London: Methuen.

Kaplan, EA (ed). 1990. *Psychoanalysis and cinema.* New York: Routledge/American Film Institute.

Koch, G. 1985. Ex-changing the gaze: re-visioning feminist film theory, *New German Critique* 34:139–153.

Laplanche, J & Pontalis, J-B. 1973. *The language of psycho-analysis.* London: The Hogarth Press.

Lemarie, A. 1982. *Jacques Lacan.* London: Routledge & Kegan Paul.

Marcuse, H. 1973. *Eros and civilization.* London: Abacus, Sphere Books.

Metz, C. 1974. *Film language: a semiotics of the cinema.* New York: Oxford University Press.
Metz, C. 1982. *The imaginary signifier: Psychoanalysis and cinema.* Bloomington: Indiana University Press.
Modleski, T. 1979. The search for tomorrow in today's soap operas. *Film Quarterly* 33(1):12–21.
Modleski, T. 1983. The rhythms of reception: daytime television and women's work, in *Regarding Television – critical approaches: an anthology*, edited by EA Kaplan. Frederick, MD: University publications of America.
Morse, M. 1985. Talk, talk, talk. *Screen* 26(2):2–15.
Mulvey, L. 1985. Visual pleasure and narrative cinema, in *Movies and methods: an anthology, volume 2*, edited by B Nichols. Berkeley: University of California Press.
Petro, P. 1986. Mass culture and the feminine: the "place" of television in film studies. *Cinema Journal* 25(3):5–21.
Singer, B. 1988. Film, photography, and fetish: the analyses of Christian Metz. *Cinema Journal* 27(4):4–22.
Stam, R. 1983. Television news and its spectator, in *Regarding Television – critical approaches: an anthology*, edited by EA Kaplan. Frederick, MD: University Publications of America.
White, M. 1986. Crossing wavelengths: the diegetic and referential imaginary of American commercial television. *Cinema Journal* 25(2):51–64.
White, M. 1987. Ideological analysis and television, in *Channels of discourse*, edited by RC Allen. London: Methuen.
Williams, R. 1974. *Television: technology and cultural form.* London: Fontana/Collins.
Wood, PH. 1982. Television as dream, in *Television: the critical view*, 3rd edition, edited by H Newcomb. New York: Oxford University Press.
Wright, E. 1982. Modern psychoanalytic criticism, in *Modern literary theory*, edited by A Jefferson & D Robey. London: Batsford.
Wright, E. 1984. *Psychoanalytic criticism: Theory in practice.* London: Methuen.

Part D

Media Production

Newspaper Production

11

Corrie Faure

Overview

In this unit we introduce you to the practice of newspaper production. The discussion is divided into four sections: a classification and definition of the newspaper; newspaper design; the newspaper organisation; and modern newspaper production.

In the first section (11.1), we define and classify print media and introduce you to the newspaper as an example of regular print media. Thereafter (section 11.2), we discuss the nature of the newspaper by touching on the development of the newspaper industry, a definition and classification of the newspaper, and the appearance of the newspaper. To explain the appearance of the newspaper, we deal with newspaper design, which covers aspects such as the different sections of a newspaper, page layout and its approach to news. The newspaper organisation is described in section 11.3. We concentrate on the newsroom as the most important department in a newspaper organisation and explain the hierarchical structure and the functions of key personnel in the newsroom; we touch on the nature of the functions of other departments. The general functions of newspaper journalists are detailed and aspects such as the news-gathering process, the interviewing process and the writing of newspaper reports – for example, the writing of a lead and the inverted pyramid writing style – are dealt with in the discussion. In section 11.4 we concentrate on modern newspaper production. We touch on changes in the production process brought about by new technological developments, and traditional and modern production techniques are contrasted. We discuss social implications for newspaper workers and reasons why the industry had to move on and respond to new technological developments and demands in a changing world.

We live in a technological era; an information society that depends to a large extent on the Internet. The Internet has a profound influence on modern newspaper production and this includes the development of what is known as the electronic newspaper (e-paper).

We deal briefly with the electronic newspaper, by explaining why it is an important development in the modern newspaper world, after which we provide a case study on the nature, scope and format of e-papers on the Internet. Finally, we discuss the importance of community journalism and media with particular reference to the community newspaper. To highlight the characteristics of community newspapers in general, we have a closer look at *Record* as an example of a community newspaper in Pretoria. In conclusion, we provide a list of the most common journalistic terms that you will come across in a newspaper office.

Learning outcomes

The overall learning outcome of this unit is that you can explain the practice of newspaper production. After completion of the unit, you should be able to

- define and classify the newspaper as an example of regular print media;
- explain newspaper design with regard to the different sections of a newspaper, page layout and a newspaper's approach to news;
- discuss the newspaper organisation in terms of happenings in the newsroom and other departments, as well as the hierarchical structure of key personnel in the newsroom, and their functions;
- contrast traditional and modern newspaper production in terms of changes in the production process brought about by new technological developments;
- define and explain the nature, scope and format of the electronic newspaper; and
- identify and explain the main characteristics of community newspapers.

11.1 INTRODUCTION

The print media are part of our everyday lives. Usually we start our day by reading a daily newspaper and we do not like to miss an issue of our favourite magazine. Newsletters, pamphlets and brochures are offered free of charge or pushed into our mailboxes, and during elections political posters are stuck on lampposts and fences. We read books for entertainment and academic purposes and we visit bookshops and libraries regularly. Therefore, the print media form part of our daily lives and lifestyles and it is difficult to imagine life without them.

The newspaper belongs to the family of print media: "all those media that communicate with printed matter: books, newspapers, magazines, newsletters, etc." (Hiebert, Ungurait & Bohn 1991:637). We can elaborate on this definition by describing print media as media that are

- manufactured by a printing process;
- characterised by their public nature; and
- produced by unique communicators – media workers such as journalists and advertisers.

Media workers create messages in specific circumstances (e.g. within the limits of a newspaper organisation or the laws of a country), and supply these messages to a target group – the readers whom a specific newspaper aims to reach. Readers understand and interpret these messages in their unique circumstances (social, cultural, political and economic).

Print media are often classified by the *frequency* with which they are published (see Figure 11.1).

Figure 11.1 A classification of print media according to frequency of publication (Faure 1996a:5)

Once-only print media, as the name indicates, are publications that usually appear once only. The nature of once-only publications depends on the different purposes for which they are used. The form of these publications therefore varies, but we should not underestimate their importance as media for conveying messages to recipients. Important once-only publications are books, posters, brochures, pamphlets and handbills. With the exception of books, these publications are often referred to as the *smaller print media* or "special publicity and promotion media" (Hiebert et al 1991:162). Although these types of print media are classified as once-only publications, they can also appear regularly. For example, a city council may distribute monthly pamphlets to urge people to pay their electricity bills.

Regular print media includes newspapers and magazines and also the so-called *smaller regular publications* such as annual reports and newsletters. Smaller regular publications are characterised by the fact that their scope for distribution is usually considerably smaller than that of other regular publications. Such a publication is normally directed at a specific target group or institution. They vary from occasional publications – in which persons concerned are informed of new developments – to public relations bulletins specifically directed at workers or the general public. These publications are usually designed to build an organisation's image and/or convey new information to interest groups.

Although all types of print media look different, they have the same aim: to inform, entertain and educate. It is, however, not within the realm of this unit to discuss all the various print media available to us (Faure 1996a:4–29). In this unit we focus on the *newspaper* as print media. The reason for selecting the newspaper is that it is a very important form of print media and historically the first true mass medium in the Western World. Despite many developments in the terrain of mass media and electronic media in general, millions of people still read newspapers on a daily basis. Also, most of the general characteristics of newspapers are applicable to other print media as well.

11.2 THE NEWSPAPER

Technological developments played a significant part in the development of the newspaper industry. Printing presses were initially operated by hand. The invention of steam power, however, made matters a good deal easier because steam was used to operate these machines. This development accelerated the printing process considerably (cf. DeFleur & Dennis 1988:46; Hiebert et al 1991:221). An even greater breakthrough was the invention of the *rotary* press. This press could print large numbers of copies in a short time. Other technological inventions such as the telegraph and telephone facilitated and considerably improved the gathering of news. Today we have the computer and the Internet. We live in the *electronic era* or the information society of the twentieth century and beyond, which changed the production of newspapers considerably.

With the exception of the electronic newspaper, the basic character of a newspaper or the way it is presented to its readers has not changed significantly since the early part of this century. Most newspapers in the world still share certain *characteristics*. A newspaper is a carrier of news and other information that (DeFleur & Dennis 1988:43; Burns 1990:339):

- appears regularly (e.g. daily, weekly, fortnightly or even monthly);
- is printed (e.g. by rotary press or Desk Top Publishing [DTP]);
- is available at a fixed price (usually quite inexpensive – newspapers rely mostly on advertisements for profits);
- is factual and covers news of common interest;
- is actual (it deals with current affairs – it reports on the here and now); and
- is easy to read for most people.

There are different kinds of newspapers. For example, we can classify newspapers according to the area of distribution, the rate of publication, language, target-population groups, political interests and circulation and/or readership figures (Faure 1996a:18–22).

A *geographical classification* would, for example, be based on the area of distribution, which could be national or limited to a particular province or region, a particular city or to certain suburbs. Some newspapers are directed only at particular rural communities.

An equally possible classification would be based on the *rate* of publication and in terms of this criterion, papers are classified as dailies, weeklies and weekend newspapers.

Daily newspapers are published either in the morning (e.g. the *Sowetan* and *Die Burger*) or late in the afternoon (e.g. *The Star, The Pretoria News* and *Cape Argus*). The morning edition usually covers news that happened the previous day, while the late afternoon edition covers events of the present day. Weeklies generally serve more specific areas than dailies and cover news specific to the readers of that area (e.g. community newspapers, such as Pretoria's *Record*, mainly cover local news). Some weeklies, such as the *Mail & Guardian*, however, interpret and analyse national and international news of the previous week by linking facts and by asking "why" events happened as they did. Weekend newspapers such as *The Sunday Times* report on the main national and international news of the previous week, but because it is a weekend paper it also includes entertainment inserts and magazines for leisure reading (Greer 1999:185).

Generally, a newspaper's rate of publication affects the nature of the news presented by the newspaper. Weeklies and weekend newspapers, for instance, concentrate more on in-depth reporting than daily newspapers do; they offer their readers the stories behind the news of the previous week.

Lastly, newspapers are usually written for anyone with Grade 9 (or equivalent) reading and comprehension ability, but they can also be aimed at more qualified readers. Newspapers are relatively cheap and are mostly published in broadsheet format (A2 size) or tabloid format (A3 size). Newspapers are produced on low quality paper because they are usually thrown away after their readers have finished with them. Newspapers vary in volume and thickness – this often depends on the "extras" and how many advertisements the newspaper contains. Most newspapers also have a distinct style and a "look" of their own – this is the topic of the next section.

11.2.1 Newspaper design

The ultimate aim of newspaper editors is to sell their product to readers and advertisers. To do this they have to consider their market and present their product as attractively as possible.

Newspaper design determines what the publication looks like. Although the content of a newspaper is very important for keeping readers as clients, the design is important in getting readers to become clients. Design can be seen as the "wrapping" in which the content is presented.

Sections

As we all know, newspapers consist of a front page, inside pages and a back page. Readers attach different meanings and importance to these pages. Some readers, for example, read their newspapers back to front or they read the sport section first. Other readers first read an important part of the inside pages – the editorial section or page. Some households divide the paper among family members, so that each member can read his or her preferred section. How people read their newspapers does not really matter, but what is important is that the front page is the first thing to attract the attention of potential buyers of newspapers.

The *front page* is the show window of all newspapers; it is the most important element of newspaper design. Because readers see the front page first, it gives them their first impression of the paper's contents. Readers cannot ignore the front page. The newspaper's name, title or masthead usually occupies a fixed position at the top of the page. The lead story, the most important news item in the paper, appears below a bold heading on the front page. Depending on the importance of the news event, this heading may be in the form of a banner headline (a headline that stretches from the one side of the page to the other side of the page) or a headline that stretches over three or more columns (sometimes stacked into various lines). According to Harriss, Leiter and Johnson (1992:526–527), multicolumn headlines as well as photographs should be used generously in front-page design.

The *inside pages* and *back page* consist of a mixture of advertisements and editorial matter. The main function of every page is to convey information. Advertisements also convey information. News items are, however, more important and advertisements are considered a sideline. Nonetheless, advertisements are essential for the survival of a newspaper. The editor does not have much control over the insertion of advertisements and has to plan editorial content around them.

Some special newspaper sections form part of the inside pages and back page, namely the editorial section, the sport section, the financial section and the entertainment section.

The *editorial section* is clearly distinguished from the rest of the newspaper as the page(s) of "opinion" and "comment". In this section subjective content is legitimate. It reflects the newspaper editor's opinion and the newspaper's policy.

The editorial section has a key position in most newspapers. Advertisements may be used, but they must not overshadow the editorial comment. The editorial page usually carries a general heading such as "opinion", "comment" or "viewpoint". The following are some major elements of the editorial section:

- An editorial column or comment
- Expert opinion
- A cartoon
- Readers' letters

"Letters to the editor" show that the paper is read and gets a response. Individual letters are usually given their own headings and are clearly distinguished as letters from readers.

The *sport section* depicts the sporting world. This world is colourful, full of action, daily conflict, heroes and heroines and human drama. The sport section should reflect this excitement by means of big headlines and action photographs (Harriss et al 1992:441). The main typographical feature of the sport page is the use of action photographs. Often these photographs form the nucleus of each page. Inevitably the content includes statistical data like match scores and schedules. This type of information is important to many readers. The needs of two kinds of readers have to be met: those who study statistical data and those who find them boring. The second category prefers a verbal description of the match and nothing else. Generally, readers will not buy a newspaper to learn the result of a match. Radio and television provide this information in direct broadcasts, but readers cannot remember everything that they saw or heard so a printed version of the event and statistical figures are a popular service rendered by newspapers.

The nature of the *financial section* is sometimes reflected in an unusual type of page layout that has more than the normal amount of blank space, with sober headlines and photographs. But more often than not the writing style has changed from a display of facts that only business people seem to understand, to interesting investigative and analytical reports (Harriss et al 1992:374). In this section, we find reports about the people involved in big business and reports on how the business world assists communities with their development programmes. Although the target group is mainly readers who are involved in business management, a large section of the financial news is of general interest (e.g. news about new job opportunities, improved transport services, electricity and petrol price hikes and tourism).

The *entertainment section* caters exclusively for readers' entertainment and diversion. It usually includes stories about film and television stars and programmes, crossword puzzles and competitions, features and comic strips. Comic strips are regarded as a major entertainment element of most newspapers and virtually all newspapers therefore have comic strips on one or two pages.

In the subsection that follows, we discuss the basic principles of the layout of a newspaper page.

Page layout

The layout of a newspaper page is part of the overall design of a newspaper. Layout gives indications about the importance of the various contents of the newspaper and it helps to establish a newspaper's identity. For example, the consistent use of the same typography and style of presentation and the placing of items such as news, sport, editorial comments and TV programmes in the same part of the paper in each issue becomes familiar to the reader. Readers identify with "their" newspaper and are able to find their way around it with ease.

Layout is made up of five basic elements: columns, text, headlines, photographs and advertisements. Words or text are the editor's verbal tools to convey meaning.

Everything else is a visual tool. To convey meaning to the reader, the editor has to select the right words and organise the facts and ideas systematically. The layout helps the reader to "hear" the editor's tone of voice (e.g. which news reports are important according to the editor) through the appearance of the text (e.g. typography – size and thickness of print) and the position of the text in the newspaper. For example, the text on the first page is more important than the text on the other pages. A reader gets to know that the main report (the lead story) appears on the first page with a big headline and that it is often illustrated with a photograph. Photographs illustrate and enhance news reports (cf. Keene 1993). According to Harris and Spark (1993:20), a photograph "needs to grasp the essence of the news". Photographs are not only used to provide information; they are also used to focus the reader's eye. When you open a newspaper you usually notice the photographs before you start scanning the headlines. When designing a newspaper layout, the layout persons know that most readers unconsciously start reading from the top left-hand corner of a page (Harriss et al 1992:524). The reader's eyes move from the top left to the bottom right and this is called the reading diagonal. But "magnets" – such as photographs, headlines, black frames, blank space and colour – also draw the eye. Generally, the eye follows an *inverted-six pattern*, moving from the top left to the bottom right to the bottom left and from there to the centre of the page.

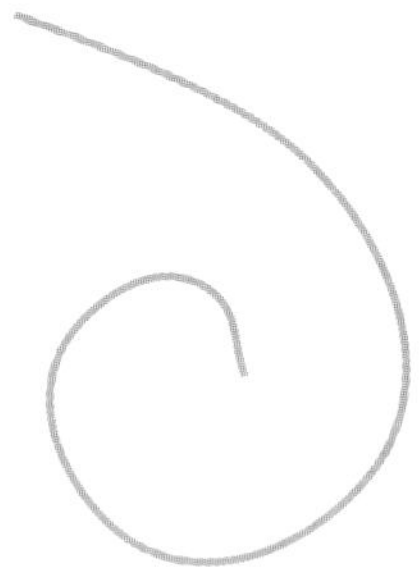

Figure 11.2 Inverted-six reading pattern

Lastly, it is important to be aware of the fact that the design of a newspaper, or its overall appearance, refers not only to what a publication looks like – the use of typography, photographs, layout and colour – but also to the way that it writes its stories – the newspaper's approach to news (how the newspaper defines news). This, together with visual aspects, gives a newspaper its identity. Amongst other things, newspapers define news in terms of their ideological orientations (strong ideas about cultural, social and political issues) (cf. Louw 1989; Louw & Tomaselli 1991; Faure 1996c:266–281). The ideological orientations of newspapers and their readers are always interdependent and reciprocal – the one influences the other. Let us explain.

Newspapers are usually born as a result of a certain need or popular demand. The newspaper responds to that need and is influenced by people's ideas about issues (e.g. political and social issues). The newspaper writes about these issues and highlights or emphasises certain aspects through the selection and placing of news, the way journalists write the news (from a specific angle), and the use of eye-catching photographs and especially viewpoints and comments in the editorial columns. In this way, a newspaper helps to shape and articulate the ideas of its readers. The newspaper's ideological orientation comes to the fore. In other words, the newspaper influences the ideological orientation of its target group, and the target group also influences the way the newspaper goes. If the newspaper deviates too much from the ideas of its readers, people will stop buying the paper and it may cease to exist. Ultimately, a newspaper's relationship with its readers and its definition of news is a reciprocal process.

You now know the reasons why a newspaper looks like it does and handles news in a certain way, but you should also know something about the workings of the newspaper as an organisation.

11.3 THE NEWSPAPER ORGANISATION

A newspaper is produced by a formal organisation that has the capital, human resources and technology to do so. The newspaper organisation consists of different departments that are necessary to produce a newspaper. The most important department, the newsroom, is where the news is actually produced. The other departments include the administration, advertising, circulation and production departments.

11.3.1 Key personnel in the newsroom

The key personnel in the newsroom operate within a hierarchical structure. This means there are various posts at different levels. Of course, the structure varies from one newspaper to another, depending on the size and specific needs of the paper. The hierarchical structure of a small daily paper could, for example, look like the diagram on the next page.

Some of the *key functions* of the various posts are the following (Harris & Spark 1993:213–216; Nel 1998:4–6; Greer 1999:7–8):

- The *editor* is appointed by the board of directors. He or she is legally accountable for everything that appears in the newspaper. In addition to formulating its overall policy, editors usually write the editorial column (commentary) in which the newspaper's point of view, opinion and/or ideological stance on a matter are reflected. Some editors also write other regular columns. Administratively they act as links between editorial staff and the board of directors.
- Depending on the size of the newspaper, editors may have assistants whose task it is to relieve the editor's workload. An assistant may be put in charge of a particular section of editorial staff (e.g. the political section). Often assistants are groomed to take over as editors eventually. Other tasks could include writing feature articles and parts of the editorial column.

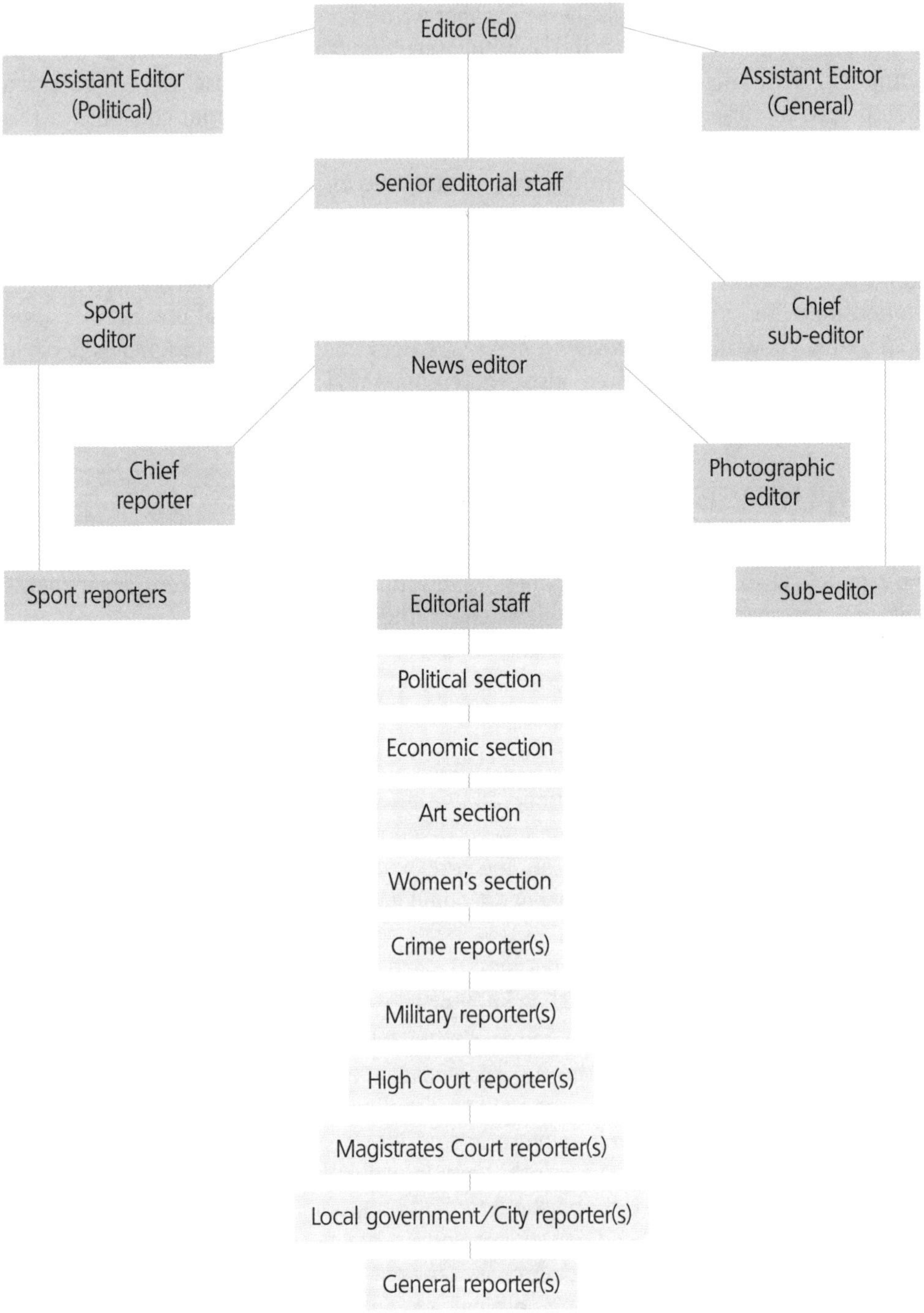

Figure 11.3 Hierarchical structure of key personnel in the newspaper organisation

- The editorial board represents the editorial élite of a newspaper. Usually members are appointed to their posts on the basis of seniority, proven journalistic expertise and loyalty to the paper. Their tasks include writing specialist articles, conducting in-depth interviews with prominent persons, and so on. They generally attend the daily news meetings with the news editor, when the strategy and planning for the next issue of the paper are worked out.
- The news editor is responsible for the news content of the paper. The advertising department usually gives the news editors a mock-up or "dummy" on a miniature page plan, showing all the advertisements that are to appear in the paper on a given day (or week). This enables them to calculate how much news can be accommodated in an issue. The news editor keeps a journal (or diary) in which newsworthy events are recorded. On the basis of the diary, journalists (sometimes with a photographer) are assigned to cover specific events. News editors also have to keep abreast of the latest news reaching the paper from news agencies. Sometimes they are assisted in this by a copy-taster who identifies and selects newsworthy events. They assign the copy received from journalists to specific pages; whereafter sub-editors attend to copy editing and layout.
- The chief sub-editor, sometimes called the layout editor, ensures that the language and layout of the paper are in order. He or she will assign specific pages to the various sub-editors in the sub office. The sub-editors will first copy edit (make corrections or clean) their page, plan its layout and provide stories with headings or headlines. Usually the chief sub-editor is responsible for the front page.
- The sport editor is responsible for the sport pages. This editor is in charge of a team of sport journalists, each of whom covers a particular type of sport, for example soccer, rugby, cricket. Often sport editors do their own layout.
- The chief reporter, as the name indicates, is the most important reporter or journalist on the newspaper. This post is often given to a journalist with a proven record of investigative journalism. Chief reporters are usually not restricted to particular beats (topics or areas of reporting).
- The photographic editor and his or her photographers have to take the photographs that are to be published in the paper. In some newspapers this editorial post is equal to that of news editor.

The rest of the editorial staff can be classified according to the areas of reporting they deal with, for example politics, economics, the courts and so on.

11.3.2 The newsroom and other departments

Like any other business, newspapers want to show a profit. For this, newspapers not only need a newsroom where news is gathered and written, but also an administration, advertising, circulation and production department. The newsroom operates relatively independently of the other departments. Some of the functions of the various departments are highlighted in the next section (Nel 1998:11–12; Greer 1999: 8–11).

- The *newsroom* represents a place where journalists, photographers and illustrators are given their assignments for the day or the week, reports are written and edited and queries and work progress are discussed. Journalists collect facts, write the stories on their computers by using a special programme such as QuarkXPress, check for accuracy and then send their stories to the news editor who edits them and if necessary suggests changes. Thereafter stories are sent to the chief sub-editor, who attends to layout, length of stories and the size of headlines. The sub-editor then takes over to check and "polish" the stories and to write headlines and captions for photographs and illustrations. The chief sub-editor does the final checking. The stories that journalists write are mostly based on information in the news editor's diary (e.g. major events, court cases, weddings, council meetings), unexpected events (e.g. accidents, strikes, robberies, natural disasters), and *tip-offs* – information from contacts in the community.
- The *administration department* caters for, amongst other things, the processing of salaries and wages, personnel, debtors and creditors, and purchases.
- The *advertising department* sells the newspaper to advertisers. Advertising revenue is a prerequisite to keep a newspaper going financially. Although some mass media can survive without advertisements (e.g. books), advertising revenue is generally viewed as the most important source of income for most mass media. Advertising revenue amounts to more or less two thirds of a newspaper's total revenue. Therefore any rise or fall in these figures affects a newspaper's income directly. Advertisements also offer a useful and valuable service to the newspaper reader. According to Bogart (1989:32), "a variety of surveys have shown that newspaper advertising is especially welcome to readers and that it is perceived as informative and useful, much as editorial content is". Advertisements come in the form of display and classified advertisements. Display advertisements are of different sizes and displayed throughout the newspaper, while classifieds are small in size and arranged in columns under various subjects in the classified section of the newspaper. A special form of advertising is the use of promotion articles (or "advertorials" or "write-ups").
- The *circulation department* distributes newspapers to the readers, but the income attributed to copy sales is not as high as the income from advertising revenue. However, the circulation figures of newspapers (the number of copies that are sold) are regarded as very important by editors because these figures determine the cost of advertising. Say for example that a newspaper sells approximately 10 000 copies each day for the first six months of a year and the cost of a single advertisement is R300. If the newspaper sells 20 000 copies in the second half of that year the cost of the advertisement will increase with another R300. Therefore, the decrease and increase of circulation figures relate directly to a newspaper's financial survival.

  Circulation figures are determined by subscriptions to the newspaper and by sales in shops or on street corners. Changes in a newspaper's circulation or readership figures (the number of people who read the newspaper) can be attributed to a variety of factors, such as

- the impact of new media (for example a new newspaper on the market);
- a change in the newspaper's content or a change in the newspaper's ideology (for example a conservative newspaper becomes liberal);
- changes in the demographic profile of the readers (factors such as age, sex, residence, education, profession and income). For example, people move to another city and are forced to change to another local newspaper as well, or people lose their job and cannot afford to buy their favourite newspaper anymore.

Advertising revenue ultimately influences the number of copies distributed, the distribution areas, the nature of the paper's readership, levels of staffing and, sometimes, the news content of the newspaper (e.g. a display advertisement of a swimming pool next to a news report about the drowning of a child in a swimming pool would be frowned upon by the advertiser).

- The *production department* is the place where the final product, the newspaper, is put together and copies are printed. More about this later in the unit.

It is not an easy task to fill a newspaper with news reports. It takes considerable planning and organisation on the part of the news editor. Let us look at the general functions of journalists working in the newsroom.

11.3.3 Functions of newspaper journalists

When journalists first start working at a newspaper organisation, they are usually assigned to the general editorial staff. They are called general reporters. They do not have a specific beat (a particular area of reporting) and very often do not know what to expect when they walk into the newsroom. They have to cover at a moment's notice, any event that has just occurred, from police affairs to country or environmental affairs. Also, issues often overlap. This means that, for example, a story on abortion may touch on social welfare, the plight of street children, court cases and unemployment. Once they have proven themselves as a general reporter, they are sometimes assigned to a specific beat.

A *beat reporter* is responsible for the covering of news in a particular area of reporting, such as police stations, the City Council (politics and politicians), the courts, schools, unions, sport or business (Nel 1998:7–8; Greer 1999:154–161; cf. Harris & Spark 1993). Beat reporters usually become experts in covering particular beats and have the opportunity to get to know important sources or contacts – people who they can approach for information on a regular basis. For reporters to become experts on specific beats (or sections of beats), is especially important. For example, reporters need to be knowledgeable about the specific sport they report on. Without a sound knowledge of, for example, soccer, the reporter will not be able to write an informed and good report about it. The same applies to, for example, political or arts reporting. Without a sound knowledge of politics or art, you cannot report on the inner workings of parliament or on specific aspects of the art world, such as opera or jazz.

Picture yourself as a *sports reporter*. You attend sporting events to describe the experience of being there. You are the outsider looking in. This is a challenge – you will need factual details about the event and you will need to highlight any news or human-interest angles (reports that evoke emotions – for example a rugby hero was hurt during a match). You are busy with eyewitness reporting, so you need to get to know your sources and to get information from them that you are allowed to quote. Remember that the experience of attending an event as an ordinary member of the public is very different from being a reporter there. You need a notebook and/or a tape recorder to record interesting facts and to do interviews. You are on the lookout for what is unusual; the newsworthy events. You need to collect a mass of detail and impressions that will go towards the creation of your report. You should guard against biased reporting: although the readers are usually fans of the game, journalists must remember that they are also writing for the players, coaches and managers so it is important to keep their goodwill and respect in mind. The above picture of you as a sport reporter could also be a picture of you on any other beat

As indicated above, journalists have specific functions, but there are also some general functions that apply to all journalists in the newspaper organisation. We concentrate on these general responsibilities in this section of the unit. But, before we do that, we must emphasise that new technological developments have influenced the way that journalists do research and the way in which a story passes from the journalist to the published page. Although there have been many changes, the basic work that a journalist has to do on a local story for example, has remained the same. Journalists still have to go out and look for news.

Broadly stated, journalists' basic responsibilities are to:

- identify and gather newsworthy information, and
- acquaint themselves with good interviewing and writing skills.

The news-gathering process

Some journalists have a nose for news (Hough 1995:34). In other words, they instinctively know where to find the news and how to collect it. Not all journalists have this ability and they must know how to develop ideas and skills to find sources, they must know how to look after their sources, and they must learn how to collect the news from those sources (Nel 1998:68–72; Greer 1999:62–69). The process of finding ideas will usually bring journalists into contact with people who can provide them with the information they need. In their line of work, they will meet interesting and powerful people. When this happens they must be alert and on the lookout for those people who are influential and knowledgeable about their environment. Most of the information that they will be using in stories will come from information that they get from personal sources or contacts. Personal sources are very valuable when journalists need to contact them for facts for stories. For example, journalists must identify and meet with leaders because they could become key contacts and introduce them to other key contacts.

Leaders are people with many responsibilities, knowledge and power and could provide journalists with information about important issues in politics, business, court, sports or general events and issues in the society or community.

It is of course good policy to focus on leaders and influential people, but journalists must not forget how valuable the "little" people may be for "inside information" and a different angle on the information that they have already obtained from an influential source (Greer 1999:52). For example, there seems to be a drug problem in one of the schools in town. The editor of the newspaper assigns a journalist to get a story on this. Of course, the journalist first tries to contact the headmaster and some of the teachers to get their views on the situation. However, the story will only be complete if people such as the cleaner and/or the gardener as well as the pupils and some of the parents of the youngsters who are involved are also interviewed. In this example the cleaner and/or the gardener and the pupils and parents are the "little" people. They are very important sources – a big story may come from them. The pupils could be the ones with real information on the drug dealers and how they use children to become drug dealers themselves.

Very often sources approach journalists themselves. Although the issue of who approaches whom is a reciprocal process (sources seek access to journalists and journalists seek access to sources), it is often the sources who take the first step. It is sometimes not easy for journalists to decide whether or not sources are reliable, or if they really have information that might be newsworthy. When sources approach journalists, the latter must ask questions such as: What are this person's motives or reasons? Why does this person want to give me information? A source may, for example, be a concerned member of a community, a dissatisfied worker in a local store, or someone who is looking for revenge. In other words, journalists must learn to *evaluate* their sources (Greer 1999:53–54). For example, the head of a school who contacts the newspaper to cover a school sports event (he or she thinks the school has a good chance of winning) is not the same kind of source as a concerned citizen who contacts a journalist about the many road accidents on a certain corner in his or her neighbourhood. The head of the school can be on an ego trip whilst the concerned citizen might feel that publication of the problem will trigger some action from the authorities. Another type of source could, for example, be a politician who sees a rival politician enter a place with a bad reputation and contacts the newspaper to give information about it. In other words, the politician might want to put the rival politician in a bad light for the purpose of gaining votes or to make him or herself look better in comparison. Sometimes a source leaks information about something such as a proposed law that will forbid people to smoke in public places. This type of source wants to get reactions from the public about the proposed law. Another type of source might feel that he or she is not getting the official attention needed to solve specific problems – to right a wrong done to him or her. For example, a doctor's negligence causes a patient to be disfigured and the information is published in a newspaper. Numerous reactions from other people who were disfigured by the same doctor can prompt official questions and might lead to corrective action.

Journalists should thus uncover as much information as possible about events or issues to get a solid foundation of facts for the story that they plan to write. Good reporting is usually backed by good research. Research will give journalists background information and sometimes a different angle on an event or issue. There are two important resources that journalists should use when they do research, namely official records and the computer. Computer-assisted reporting has a profound influence on the research possibilities for modern journalists. Computer-literate journalists have access to the most modern databases worldwide. Nowadays, all the information they may need is at their disposal even in the most remote areas of the world (Nel 1998:77–80; Greer 1999:57).

When journalists understand the nature of the assignment they received from the news editor and have done some basic research on the topic, they can approach some sources and interview them.

The interviewing process

We define the interviewing process as a special type of interpersonal communication which is purposeful and serious, involving questions and answers, with the goal of sharing information about a story-related topic as required by journalists. The main aim of the interviewing process is to gather information for publication directed at a large body of recipients. Interviewing is an important journalistic skill which journalists use more or less every day (Nel 1998:88–104; Greer 1999:82–93; Hough 1995:38).

From the start you should know that the interviewing process is not a perfect process. Journalists encounter many unexpected problems. They have control over some things, such as their own preparations – but it is sometimes impossible to control sources. Nel (1998:88) illustrates this by writing: "Successful politicians did not get to be successful politicians by being dumb enough to tell journalists the truth. Or to tell journalists much of anything." Journalists should keep this in mind when they conduct interviews with important people or even with less important people.

To prepare for a scheduled interview, journalists should find out as much as possible about the topic by, for example, visiting the newspaper's cutting library or by searching the Internet. They should also prepare some explicit questions beforehand (vague questions trigger vague answers). It is important that they keep the readers of the newspaper in mind. What would they like to know about a certain topic or a certain person? Ultimately, practice and experience help journalists to prepare adequately for an interview and to avoid problems. For example, the editor has assigned a journalist to interview the head of a police station in a certain community about weapons uncovered in the local school. The journalist plans the interview correctly, but then the right interviewee is not available. Only a young constable is available. The journalist decides to approach him for the interview and the constable agrees to it. The problem with this situation is that the young constable was not *authorised* (given permission) to give the information as he or she was not involved with the weapon issue at all and thus comments without the inside knowledge that the head of the police station has. Hence, the information gathered is not accurate and not authorised by the original source that the reporter planned to interview. In other words, journalists should not base their reports on information obtained from the wrong source.

Lastly, the interviewing process is not just about asking questions. The relationship or rapport between the journalist and the source is crucial to the outcome and success of the interview.

The relationship is sometimes relaxed and sometimes tense. Sometimes the journalist is between "the devil and the deep blue sea" – on one hand the public has a right to know and, on the other hand, nobody is really obliged or can be legally forced to speak to journalists. Therefore, to get the information a journalist needs versatility, creativity and insight into human nature. Experienced journalists instinctively know which approach to take with different interviewees. Sometimes the direct approach works well, but sometimes journalists have to be more subtle and sometimes they have to be stubborn and keep on trying to interview a reluctant source. However, it is always important before attempting to write a news report, to check if the facts are correct and accurate. If a source, for example, accuses another person of wrongdoing, journalists have to get that person's version of what happened as well. Journalists should always try to get more than one side of a story.

In the next subsection, we concentrate on the most basic skills that journalists have to master when writing and editing news reports.

The writing of a newspaper report

Writing for newspapers is different from all other forms of writing – and the ability to write newspaper reports well is one of a journalist's most important abilities (cf. Nel 1998; Greer 1999; Hough 1995; Brooks, Kennedy, Moen & Ranly 1996; Hodgson 1993). Writing for newspapers is a clear and concise ("to the point") style of writing. This style is necessary because newspaper space is limited and the time that readers have to read their daily newspaper is also limited. The space available in a newspaper for news reports is linked to the number and size of advertisements sold – for financial reasons newspapers want to publish as many advertisements as possible. Therefore journalists have to say as much as possible in the little space available. It may be necessary to shorten or *cut* some reports and this means that the most important information is usually written first, at the beginning of the story. English is the main language of mass communication in South Africa and journalists have had to find a type of English language that is acceptable to readers from all backgrounds. How do they go about it? Imagine a chat with a friend on a certain topic and write down every word you use during the conversation. You will probably have to write a few pages and some words only you and your friend would understand. A newspaper report is different – it must be concise and in generally understood English. The language should be similar to the language used in radio and television news reports.

- *Writing the lead*
  The reporter has gathered all the facts for the news report. Now he or she has to decide which of the facts and how many of the facts should appear in the lead or introduction paragraph of the news report. The lead should not confuse readers about the "what" or the topic of the news report; it should tell the reader enough to answer major questions. At least some of the who, what, where, when, why and how questions – in order of importance – should be answered in the lead. It is good policy to begin your news report with what is new and important (Nel 1998:52–54; Greer 1999:110–117; Brooks et al 1996:49). For example, you would not tell your friends a devastating story by giving them the background information first! You usually follow a direct approach by coming straight to the point.
  In general, leads should not be too crowded with detail. This may confuse readers. A lead should be a direct indication of what the reader can expect from the news report. In other words, leads should be focused and as simple as possible.
- *The inverted pyramid and other structures*
  Journalists use various writing styles to write a news report. The most common of all the writing styles is the *inverted pyramid* (Nel 1998:55–56; Greer 1999:126; Brooks et al 1996:47–70). For the beginner journalist the inverted pyramid is a good place to start. It is a simple way of learning how to organise the collected information. It is also an expected form of writing – readers expect it and editors expect it. Readers have learned to scan the story for important facts and then decide to either continue reading or turn to the next story. Editors read the story and usually start cutting it from the bottom upwards, to fit the space available on the page. Therefore, one of the advantages of this style of writing is that it is easy to edit because the story is written in the order of the importance of the information – the information becomes less and less important as the story continues. Hence, after the editing process the important facts at the top remain intact and the news report remains readable and intelligible.
  Here is an example of the structure of the inverted pyramid news report:

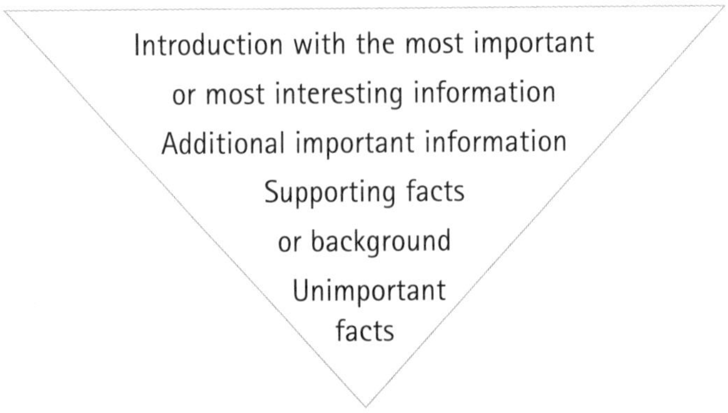

Figure 11.4 The inverted pyramid structure

Newspapers are increasingly experimenting by rearranging the traditional inverted pyramid structure. Examples of these different writing styles are the narrative, the Wall Street Journal, and the champagne glass structure (Greer 1999:126–130). Each of these styles emphasises different elements of writing a news report.

The *narrative* structure reflects the way people experience events. When journalists write in a narrative style, they explain events in a way that is similar to telling someone a story.

The *Wall Street Journal* structure is based on a structure used by many journalists but especially by journalists from the *Wall Street Journal*. In this style the focus is first on the individual and then it moves to the larger issue at stake. The story ends with a strong statement. For example, readers sometimes find it hard to relate to statistics: 80% of workers of a certain company are being retrenched. Readers can, however, relate to the plight of a certain man who works for the company and how his retrenchment affects him and his family profoundly. Therefore the news report first focuses on the plight of a specific family and then focuses on the general plight of all involved. The news report will conclude on a strong note – again it focuses on the family, who are sure to lose their home and have to move to an informal settlement.

The *champagne glass* structure is a variation of the inverted pyramid. The lead is organised in the same way as the lead of the inverted pyramid, but then the action is described in logical order (first this happened, then this, then this, and so forth). The news report closes with a kick – this requires a strong conclusion. The ending is important and should not be cut by the editor. News reports written in the champagne glass style are usually difficult to edit – if necessary, they should be cut in the middle.

Generally, journalists try to write the fewest and shortest words possible – they avoid long sentences. They also try using everyday language, but avoid slang or jargon. "Slang" refers to language that only certain groups of people will understand, for example words used by a group of street children such as "this chick is so cool". "Jargon" refers to language used in specific professions, for example, doctors use medical language and refer to a broken "femur" instead of a broken "leg". However, journalists should not confuse jargon with technical language. It is sometimes necessary to use technical language when writing for a specialist target group or discussing a special topic. They cannot change standard computer language, for example.

It is further important that journalists should try to use the active voice and avoid the passive voice in their news reports. For example, they should write "John walked his dog when ..." and not "The dog was walked by John when ...". Also, the repetition of words can make a news report boring. For example, when quoting a source they avoid something like this: John Smith said "My car is stolen, I don't know what to do ...". John Smith also said that ... (He explained or added). Lastly, journalists must give the news and not their own opinion. Journalists' own opinions are only important in the editorial column.

- *Designing headlines*
  Nel (1998:130) emphasises the importance of headlines: "The best stories in the world are worthless if no one reads them. The job of selling the story falls, in large part, to the headline." The term headline refers to the words above the news report – they are a very brief summary of the lead that follows. According to Harriss et al (1992:507), the headline should be the lead translated into "sharp, punchy, dramatic words". The headline has three functions:
  - It summarises the story for readers who are in a hurry.
  - It helps the reader to evaluate the news.
  - It helps to make the newspaper attractive to readers (it forms part of the visual pattern or layout of the page).

  There are various options for designing headlines. Generally, copy-editors choose a simple one-line heading, starting at the left side of a column. Sometimes longer headlines need to be stacked into various lines. Other variations are "kickers" and "reverse kickers". The kicker is the smaller headline above the main headline, while the reverse kicker is the smaller headline below the main headline.

  Composing a headline is a creative process (Nel 1998:130–134; Greer 1999: 142–145). Journalists have to read through the copy and try to come up with suitable wording. This is easy with some stories – as you read the copy the wording just jumps out at you, so to speak – but other stories are more difficult to describe in a few suitable words. It helps to write down some keywords and shuffle them around as in a puzzle. Sometimes half a dozen keywords come up and then they have to be arranged in the right order to give balance and meaning.

In the next section, we introduce you to some of the changes in modern newspaper production. These changes happened during the last few decades of the twentieth century and were mainly the result of the application of new computer-linked technologies. Generally, the computer has changed or revolutionised the writing of news reports, the process of editing and layout as well as the old printing craft – the traditional hot metal printing technology – into a modern high-tech working and production system.

11.4 MODERN NEWSPAPER PRODUCTION

In the electronic era, industries and organisations have to be competitive to survive economically. To do this they have to constantly adapt to new communication media as they are developed. The process of adaptation requires technological upgrading and a rethinking of old and trusted methods of production. The people who work for these industries and organisations also had to adapt socially. These workers had to reformulate their ideas about what their work involves. It seems that young people who enter the job market experience few problems because most of them already have sufficient background – they "surf" on the Internet and have had computer training at school, college or university. It is not the same for older people with years of experience in a certain work environment; they have to adapt to major changes in their work situations. All this also applies to the rapid changes in the newspaper industry.

The majority of newspapers in the Western World, South Africa included, use new technologies such as computers, the Internet and satellite links. New media constantly supply the newspaper industry with new and innovative ideas for the collection of news, storage of information and distribution of information. As in any large organisation, the degree to which the newspaper industry adapts to new technology determines competitiveness, profitability and survival of the industry. When we explain the implications of modern newspaper production and editing you will see that it is extremely important for journalists to be computer literate (Faure 1996b:256–258).

Computer technology increases the efficiency and speed with which journalists gather information. For example, laptop computers (small and portable computers) and portable fax machines increase the mobility of journalists. Journalists can work from home or in small district offices or from hotel rooms. In other words, journalists can be closer to their sources for longer periods without having to return to the main office. Therefore physical distance is no longer a major factor in the capturing and processing of data. This is also true for visual images. Images can be stored on a computer disk and sent, via telecommunication links, to the news desk. Furthermore, the electronic storage of vast amounts of information also provides the media worker with readily available data for future use. We refer to this as computer-assisted reporting (Friend 1994:63). Computer-assisted reporting is the retrieval of data to obtain background information from previously published material. This raw data can be processed, sorted and analysed by the media worker in order to reveal patterns.

The use of computer technology by media workers enhances the flexibility of the production process. For example, last-minute changes to pages, headlines, typography, layout and content are possible with the use of computer technology. The impact on the layout of pages means, for example, that there is now a wider choice of typefaces, that more economical type can be used and that copy can be measured to the millimetre. Today it is possible to set copy in almost any form – for example in a circle, or surrounding a photograph. It is no longer unusual to find a more dynamic and interesting mix of vertical and horizontal styles of layout. Also, last-minute copy changes in advertisements can be done directly from a terminal in the advertisers' own work environment to a terminal in a newspaper office. In other words, changes can be made close to the time of printing of copy without extra costs. Special editions (e.g. in the case of disasters) for an up-to-the-minute news update are also possible, because of computer technology. A further important area of development is the increasing sophistication of the use of colour in newspapers. It is no longer unusual to find more than one colour photograph on a page and to have frames in colour, because modern scanners can do a colour separation within five minutes – whereas a few years ago colour separation took much longer to do. The use of graphics is now also common in newspapers.

In the next section we highlight some features of traditional production techniques and contrast them with modern production techniques.

11.4.1 Traditional and modern production techniques

In the modern newspaper industry, type is no longer set in the laborious hot-metal process – electronic typesetting is now the norm. As a rule journalists are now also responsible for typography. Once reports were hammered out on a typewriter; today they are keyed in at a terminal (Faure 1996b:258).

The traditional production process worked in the following way:

- In the newsroom, editors and news editors selected the material for each edition from pictures and copy submitted by the journalists and received from news agencies.
- In the composing room, linotype operators typed copy received from the editorial department.
- Make-up men created a layout form and then arranged copy and pictures in a metal form.
- A plate was made from the metal layout. The plate was put on the press to print the newspaper.
- A sheet of paper ran through the press. In one hour newspaper presses could turn out as many as 60 000 64-page newspapers of standard size, or 50 000 144-page newspapers of tabloid size (only in black and white).
- After printing, a folding machine (a complex arrangement of gears, cylinders and knives) took over and cut the newspaper into pages, arranged the pages in order and folded them. Folded papers were then ready for collection and distribution.

Today, newspapers can be produced entirely by computer. Design, layout, scanning and placing of photographs, are all done by means of computer. Special computer programmes are created to make copy flow and also make it possible to retrieve past issues and stories. Therefore sub-editors now have the means as well as more time to do more ambitious design and layout. Today there is also a greater need for "stop-press" stories, to compete with the instant news available on television, radio and the Internet. Some functions of the past have become obsolete in the modern newspaper industry; for example, the composing room is now obsolete and make-up men are no longer needed to put type into metal format. Plates are still needed in a varied form but this process is now automated – the completed pages are sent electronically from the newsroom to the printing presses (which do not have to be in the same building as the newspaper) and plates run into the presses electronically.

The above shows you some of the changes in the production process of newspapers. Next, we highlight some social or "human" implications of these changes.

11.4.2 Social implications

During the 1970s and early 1980s, some newspapers were reluctant to adapt to new information technology (IT). One of the reasons for the newspaper industry's reluctance to use computers was that print workers, for example, could lose their jobs and this could cause industrial conflict. Another reason was that computers needed a huge capital investment with a long payback period and uncertain returns. Noon (1994:22) writes: "The competitive advantages of being first to innovate had to be balanced against the risk of being first along the learning curve." Computers need substantial capital investment at a time of decreasing profitability. Decreasing profitability in the newspaper industry is especially linked to the expansion of the mass media (e.g. television) and therefore a decrease in advertising revenue for newspapers.

Another problem linked to the reluctance of the newspaper industry to adapt to computer technology was the "ignorance of managers when faced with technological change" (Noon 1994:23).

Computer technology in the newspaper industry was gradually accepted during the 1980s. It was recognised that the use of computers gave media workers numerous opportunities to improve their efficiency and overall performance. The industry realised that media workers had to adapt to the increasingly sophisticated technology in order to stay in business.

According to Noon (1994:20), the newspaper industry now uses computer technology because it needs to

- survive in the changing market (an increasingly competitive environment),
- improve quality and cost reduction, and
- have greater control over the production process.

The newspaper industry needs to improve human performance and productivity and also to improve the production process itself. It is therefore extremely important for the newspaper industry to use computer technology.

To conclude this subsection, it is believed that computer technology should be used in the newspaper industry because it will

- improve the service offered to advertisers;
- improve the product (e.g. the inclusion of later news);
- develop the product (e.g. the use of colour);
- give editors greater control over the total production process; and
- make possible electronic publishing of newspapers (no paper is necessary and news can be updated immediately).

In recent times, some newspapers have become available in electronic form on the Internet as well as in printed form, and some newspapers are only published electronically. These developments have opened up new avenues and possibilities for the newspaper industry as well as for individuals and small groups of people who want to produce their own (community) newspaper or newsletter.

11.4.3 The electronic newspaper

All over the world the newspaper industry has embraced the Internet with all its possibilities. One of these possibilities is the electronic distribution of newspapers via the Internet. When you search for newspapers on the Internet you will discover that there are many South African electronic newspapers as well. Not only large newspapers, such as the Naspers digital newsgroup *News24*, and Independent Newspapers' *Independent On Line*, but also many smaller newspapers such as the *Mail & Guardian* (*eM&G*) and community newspapers as well as university or school newspapers. Examples of these smaller electronic newspapers in South Africa are *The Zoutpansberger, Die Afrikaner, al-Qualam, The Asian, Eikestad Nuus, e-Standard, Hermanus Times, The Midrand Mirror, Die Perdeby, Loslit* and *Record Online*. The number of electronic newspapers increases continuously and the sophistication of the format improves all the time.

We view electronic newspapers, amongst other things, as important for the following reasons (Faure 1998:43–51; cf. Fourie 1998):

- Millions of people all over the world can be reached by local and national newspapers – hence new markets are continuously developing. The *Dispatch Online*, for example, has regular readers as far away as New York, Perth and London, and Afrikaans newspapers such as *Beeld* publish electronically in English as well and therefore also reach the English-language population.
- The electronic newspaper gives printed newspapers a new dimension. It provides news events and issues continuously for 24 hours. Whenever news breaks, the readers of electronic newspapers are able to read about it.
- The electronic newspaper is still a newspaper – important news is illustrated with big headings and photographs and the homepage (the first page) is similar to a newspaper's front page, because it establishes the newspaper's identity.
- The electronic newspaper and the traditional newspaper supplement or complement each other. To get the total news picture it is sometimes necessary to read both the electronic and the paper editions. The electronic newspaper supplies, for example, background information to specific events for which there was no space in the paper edition.

The Internet and other technological innovations have many advantages for readers and newspapers. For example, they may increase the interaction between readers and the newspaper. Readers increasingly use e-mail to express their views on events and issues. They send letters directly to electronic newspapers as well as to traditional newspapers that have e-mail addresses – it seems more convenient and of course is quicker for readers to send letters electronically (e-mail) rather than by mail or in Internet language "snail mail".

Newspaper journalists of the future must master a variety of skills (called *multiskilling*) that were previously used by separate specialists. Journalists have to find information fast and they must master coding and graphic skills and acquire the ability to work with new technology such as digital cameras, portable computers and cellular telephones.

In the case study that follows, we give you a basic and general overview on new media and some features of electronic newspapers. The case study is partly a reproduction and translation of a published research article by Faure (1998).

Case study 11.1: New media and electronic newspapers on the Internet

The existence of new media and the availability of new technology are interrelated (Brody 1990:58). This statement means that new inventions usually lead to new developments in the field of communication, as well as developments in mass media. Technology is of course a very broad concept which includes *all* technology available to people, but it also includes technology which has changed the nature of communication and made mass media possible. For example, without the invention of electricity and batteries most forms of mass communication (e.g. radio and television) would not be possible.

We may present the relationship between media and technology in a graphic manner as illustrated in Figure 11.5.

Technology (e.g. the steam engine and the rotary press)
↓
Mass Media (e.g. the newspaper)
↓
New Technology (e.g. television cameras)
↓
Mass Media (e.g. television)
↓
New Information Technology (e.g. the microchip → the computer)
↓
New Media (e.g. the Internet – interactive)

Figure 11.5 Technologies tend to build on one another (Faure 1996b:245)

New media refers to numerous new communication developments such as cable television, high definition television, satellite distribution of information and the Internet. New media is usually interactive media, which refers to a many-to-many model of communication. Let us explain.

A new many-to-many model of communication

Traditionally mass communication technology meant big capital investments in big organisations. The mass communication model was theoretically dominated by one communicator (e.g. the owners and managers of the mass media) who used a powerful medium (e.g. newspapers, radio and television) to send messages to numerous passive recipients. Presently, modern technology such as the digital transference of text, audio and video has changed the traditional one-to-many mass communication model. Computer technology offers the traditional recipient of mass communication the opportunity to become a producer as well as a user of information. A new model of many communicators and many recipients developed towards the end of the twentieth century. Today any person with a modem, a personal computer (PC) and a telephone connection can become a publisher of information – for example, some school newspapers are offered on the Internet as electronic newspapers.

Electronic newspapers

As in the traditional newspaper, the identity of the e-paper is established on the first or primary page, the homepage of the e-paper. The name or title of most e-papers is often the same or similar to their traditional equivalents, for example, the *Mail & Guardian* and the *Electronic Mail & Guardian* (*eM&G*). As in traditional editions, photographs, graphics and advertisements appear in the e-paper and the size of headings also indicates the degree of importance attributed by journalists to the news reports. Traditional newspapers also use computers as a means to search for, assimilate, analyse and edit news and information, and layout possibilities are continuously explored (Uys 2000:12; Smuts 2000:13). Improving media technology causes traditional newspapers to be less and less dependent on manual labour.

What then are some of the *main features* of e-papers compared to their traditional counterparts? To answer this question, we have to look at the nature, the scope, format and readers of e-papers.

Nature of e-papers

With the above discussion in mind, we can safely define e-papers as

- electronic variations of traditional paperbound newspapers
- the result of the use of computers in the writing, editing, layout *and* the publishing/distribution of newspaper text, photographs, graphics and in some cases even audio and video news.

The computer delivers the *final* product to the readers. The boundaries between the newspaper and other mass media have become more vague. Audio and video is often added to e-papers' content to enhance the impact of news reports, entertainment or advertisements. Furthermore, traditional newspapers are bound in space and time while e-papers transcend space and time. In this regard, Manoim, the editor of the *Electronic Mail & Guardian* (*eM&G*) writes: "Its major virtues are speed and global reach" (Faure 1998:44), and Barry Sandland, the editor of *The Star Internet* writes: "Many of the readers are not in our print-distribution area so the fact is a large amount of appeal for the Internet is the ability to reach a wider audience" (ibid). As soon as an e-paper appears on the Internet it can be read all over the world – time and space are diminished. Other features include that readers can read today's editions as well as previous editions, with the same effort. The reading of previous issues as well as newspaper archives on the Internet offer specific advantages for purposes of research.

Scope of e-papers

There is a continuous increase in the number of e-papers on the Internet. The newspaper industry has to compete in a fast and developing technology in the world of the media. For example, statistics show a sharp increase of 750 e-papers on the Internet during 1996 – from 365 to 1 115 commercial e-papers in one year only. The following year the number of e-papers increased to 2 171 (dailies and weeklies). The next comparison includes all e-papers, also university newspapers (Outing 1996):

Electronic newspapers according to geographical location

USA	65,8%
Europe	15,8%
Canada	7,8%
Latin/South America	5,2%
Asia	3,0%
Oceanea	1,4%
Africa	0,6%
Mideast	0,5%

The daily newspaper is taking the lead in Internet/online publishing. The combination of all other types, however, is more than the total number of daily newspapers (Outing1996):

Daily newspapers	48,0%
Weekly newspapers	22,2%
University newspapers	16,4%
Speciality newspapers	7,3%
Business newspapers	3,1%
Alternative newspapers	3,0%

Although statistics about e-papers cannot be totally correct – they may differ from day to day – they can give us an idea of the scope of e-papers on the Internet. In South Africa, the weekly newspaper the *Mail & Guardian's eM&G* was the first e-paper in Africa (1994). Many followed soon after. For example, in August 1996, *The Star Internet*, the e-paper of the daily Johannesburg newspaper *The Star* was born; *Beeld*, as the biggest Afrikaans daily newspaper (cf. De Beer & Steyn 1997) entered the world of e-papers on the Internet in September 1997 with *eBeeld*; and *Dispatch Online*, the e-paper of the *Daily Dispatch* of East London, was introduced in September 1997.

Now we know that e-papers seem important to newspaper organisations. Many newspapers climbed on the bandwagon to promote their newspapers and to embrace the challenges of new competitive possibilities. Other examples of big South African newspapers or news groups which feature on the Internet are *Business Day, Cape Argus, Die Burger, Financial Mail, Independent Newspapers, Natal Newspapers, Natal Witness, Sunday Independent* and *Sunday Times* (cf. Editor & Publisher 2000).

Format of e-papers

Some of the most important distinguishable features of e-papers are

- the ease and continuity with which content can be adapted and changed;
- the use of hypertext; and
- the possibility of the nearly unrestricted length of individual reports.

Through the use of, for example, hypertext the electronic newspaper can offer the reader a more personal and interactive experience. Hypertext can be seen as the equivalent of a footnote. Gilster (1996:363) defines hypertext as "data that provides links between key elements, allowing you to move through information nonsequentially". Hypertext is usually seen in the form of a menu on the homepage and in the form of highlighted words or sentences in a given text. The menu gives the reader a choice to ignore the lead reports on the homepage and to jump in seconds to topics in his or her field of interest. Topics can vary from economics, politics, sports and the arts to weather forecasts and comic strips and can be changed or adapted at any time (e.g. daily or hourly) by the media worker. The possibilities are many and changes in format and content require only seconds. Hypertext within a report refers to the availability of more information about the topic of the specific report. However, the extra information appears only after the user has asked for it. Hypertext-links replaces the time consuming paging through of traditional newspapers. The reader is guided by his or her own need for information and so obtains the greatest possible information advantage in the shortest time possible (Gilster 1996:4). For example, hypertext leads to further topic-relevant information, background information and further explanations or statistics about a given topic. Hence, hypertext decreases the need to cut news reports due to a lack of space. Important news can be added to the e-paper the moment it breaks – it is not necessary to wait for the next edition. E-papers are updated at least once a day and often even four times or more, such as in cases of *The Star Internet* and *eM&G*'s ZA*NOW.

We are all aware of the fact that *advertisements* in newspapers are very important for the survival of newspapers. But, what about the e-paper?

Advertisements are also an important aspect of e-papers and they influence its format. As in traditional newspapers, advertising revenue is linked to the "circulation figures" of e-papers. In order to establish the circulation figures of e-papers the server log files of newspapers are audited according to the standards of the Audit Bureau of Circulations' Internet section, Abis (Audit Bureau of Internet Statistics). The Abis figures are published four times annually and they provide advertisers with page impressions, user sessions and unique hosts/visits. For example, according to Manoim, *eM&G*'s figures for March 1998 were 296 182 user sessions and 135 064 unique visits. This is a daily average of about 4 500 unique visits (Faure 1998:47). The number of page impressions or unique visits influences advertising expenditure in e-papers. The more page impressions, the more attractive for the advertiser. Advertisements are, for example, sold from a central provider and each time a reader visits a page, a new advertisement is offered on a rotating basis. According to the Abis-advertising model of payment per page read (page impressions), the advertiser pays a fixed tariff (for example 20 cents per page read on which the advertisement appears). The tariff can thus be the same for all Web publications but the number of pages read determines the ultimate cost for the advertiser (Faure1998:47). Some speciality publications ask higher tariffs than general publications, but this is still a very recent development and not widely applied. Advertisers can also request certain particulars such as specific recipients – for example, only South African or only foreign readers or only academics, and so forth. These particularities are calculated according to the IP (Internet protocol) addresses of visitors. A further characteristic of advertisements in e-papers is that how much further or deeper the visitor clicks through an advertisement (i.e. the more the reader follows the advertisement) the more attractive it becomes for advertisers.

Presently, advertisements in e-papers are mostly a secondary source of income for newspapers. For example, Manoim writes: "Our advertising sales are handled by Oracle Online Sales, an M-Net subsidiary that sells four of the biggest sites in the country as a joint 'package'. Our major source of revenue comes from Web sites developed for third parties as part of a 'package' arrangement with other sections of the *Mail & Guardian*, for example, the books publishing and TV divisions" (Faure 1998:47). *Dispatch Online* primarily depends on advertising revenue as a source of "independent" income (Faure 1998:48) and *The Star* and its electronic edition's income is interdependent (advertisements, subscriptions and daily sales of the paper newspaper) (ibid). Although advertisements do not presently play a big role in the financing of e-papers, they will probably play a more important role in future when the software for the handling of advertisements improves (ibid). In general, e-papers are carried or subsidised by their traditional counterparts or news groups. However, from the beginning, the *eM&G* was more or less independent of the *Mail & Guardian*, which only possesses a 35% share in *eM&G*. The main shareholder of *eM&G* is M-Web (one of the big Internet service providers in South Africa).

Except for the circulation figures of newspapers, *demographic profiles* of newspaper readers are also important for advertisers. They want to know if readers are financially able to buy their products. The question we try to answer is: Who are the readers of e-papers and how do they differ from the readers of traditional newspapers?

Readers of e-papers

Traditionally, newspaper readership is influenced by factors such as literacy, age, income, education, concerns and interests. Most literate people read a newspaper regularly or at least now and then (Bogart 1989:78). The continuity of the "relationship" with the newspaper, however, is dependent on other factors. Research has shown, for example, that young people read newspapers less frequently than older people (1989:89). Readership is also influenced by factors such as distribution problems, editorial policy, radio and television news and the cost of newspapers. Furthermore, reading patterns are not a constant – especially big changes in lifestyle and circumstances can influence reading patterns negatively or positively (1989:89–94). However, it is significant that in spite of differences in age, and other variances, people in a higher income group and with a higher level of education are more inclined to be regular newspaper readers. The reading of newspapers is learned behaviour and already established during a person's early years. But who are the readers of e-papers?

The readers of e-papers are, of course, users of the Internet. The Internet user is firstly computer literate and secondly he or she earns enough to afford a personal computer (PC) and an Internet connection, or has access to the Internet in the work environment. Therefore, computer literacy correlates usually with level of income and level of education. According to Verwey (Faure1998:46), 90% of people who read e-papers have had tertiary or university education.

Employers often provide computers and access to the Internet to workers with a certain level of education and rank. For those persons, access to e-papers is free. If access to the Internet is paid for personally, such costs do not only include the reading of newspapers, but also the numerous other options offered by the Internet. Newspapers also do not yet consider so-called subscription fees for access to their e-papers. The daily news will probably always be offered free of charge, but it can happen in future that experts and researchers have to pay for specific news such as economic news or archive material (Faure1998:46).

An important difference between the characteristics of traditional newspaper readers and the readers of e-papers, however, has to do with a difference in age. Older people often experience a type of technophobia; they are afraid of new technology. They are often established in their habits and become computer users because their jobs require it. On the other hand, the younger generation is more inclined to use electronic media ('n Hele geslag ... 1997:3). Lauterer (2000) writes: "Young readers, the very group that seems NOT to be reading traditional papers, EAT UP online papers".

> The younger generation who are dealing with computers through schools, technikons and universities are more likely to read the Internet version of the newspaper. As more of this generation reaches adulthood, it is likely that there will be some drop in the circulation figures of the physical *Daily Dispatch* and a corresponding increase in the figure of Internet readers.
>
> (Biberauer in Faure1998:46)

The readers' market for e-papers is a new market and in the process of developing. This is even more so in a country such as South Africa with a large Third World population. "We are not living in Europe or America. We have a phenomenally large uneducated base of population. No phone lines, costly services and a lack of running water. ISDN lines are rarities. Fibre-optics are even further away" (Sandland in Faure 1998:47).

With regard to the demographic characteristics of the readers of e-papers, only some general characteristics can be established, such as readers' geographical location. This can be deduced from the IP addresses on the IP lists. Most e-papers have a large number of foreign readers and South African people who work or study in other countries. For example, only 40% of the readers of *The Star Internet* are from South Africa and the rest live in other countries.

However, general impressions about reader profiles are gleaned from thousands of e-mails that journalists receive from readers. For example, according to Manoim, more women than men read e-papers and access to the Internet at the workplace is especially important for this; not necessarily having a PC at home. These people "do white collar work, but not necessarily at a senior level, and they read the Internet either as part of their job or during moments of boredom. Because they get news free online, they will increasingly be tempted to stop reading daily newspapers" (Manoim in Faure 1998:47).

Ultimately, the "surf" on the Internet and the possible reading of e-papers is often dependent on an attitude about change (for example the acceptance and use of new technologies) in general, as well as a curious nature and a general interest in new (media) developments (cf. Faure 1995: ch 2). However, it is probable that people who read traditional newspapers and are also users of the Internet, are likely to read the electronic equivalent of their traditional newspapers and thereafter also visit other e-papers. Traditional newspapers often advertise their own e-papers to encourage readers to visit their homepages.

Demographic profiles of readers are important, but the circulation figures of e-papers provide advertisers with more specific information, which helps them to decide whether or not to advertise in e-papers. Perhaps they will not be able to establish exactly *who* the readers of the advertisements are, but they can at least ascertain *how many times* users are exposed to their advertisements (although not necessarily different users in every case).

The last feature of e-papers that we consider, highlights a somewhat negative perspective of e-papers as "shovelware sites". Let us explain this view briefly.

Shovelware sites?

Some Web experts view e-papers on the Internet as "shovelware sites", where the content of the traditional newspaper is transferred to the Internet. The homepage is, according to these experts, only valuable when it contains unique information especially meant for the Internet.

People who feel that way, are not totally wrong. An important function of the journalists of *The Star Internet* is, for example, "to shovel from the paper to the Internet site" (Sandland in Faure 1998:49). Approximately 70% of the reports in the *Mail & Guardian* also appear in the *eM&G*, but the *eM&G* also provides a large amount of new information that is not covered in its paper edition. E-papers often offer added value by supplying different and more recent news. Also, providing new information is not necessarily the most important goal of e-papers – the archive of e-papers can be as valuable. Sandland (in Faure 1998:49) writes: "We consider the idea of electronic archiving to be essential to publication. The Internet is a way where we can both get electronic archiving and then use the information to expand our publishing parameters".

Therefore, the importance of e-papers should not be diminished by the fact that they are partly shovelware sites. Advantages, such as that millions of people can be reached by local newspapers, hence new markets are developed, and that news can be adapted and changed continuously, seem more important. Traditional newspapers are dependent on mass production – it is generally not financially worthwhile to print "extras" with breaking news. Another important advantage is that the Internet increases the opportunities for recipients' participation in the mass communication process. Thousands of e-mails received from readers contribute to debates on social and political issues and may also contribute to a more democratic society. The readers of e-papers become active creators of information: their e-mails can be read, and responded to or acted on, by people all over the world.

A further advantage, which relates to our next and final topic in the unit, is that even one individual with journalistic skills, access to the Internet and Desk Top Publishing (DTP) facilities can start his or her own community newspaper or newsletter on a small scale. The *eM&G*, for example, started with only one person.

In the following section, we introduce you to the community newspaper as an established and widespread phenomenon in South African communities.

11.4.4 The community newspaper

Imagine you live in a rural community near Johannesburg or Pretoria or any other big city in South Africa. You read a newspaper every day and obtain a lot of information about your nearest city and about what happens in South Africa. However, there is no community newspaper or community newsletter in your area and your community's specific interests are not covered in any of the big newspapers you read. You are interested in your community – the local school, church and sports events, its leading personalities, the markets, new shopping centres, and so forth. But, the national and local newspapers do not cover even the most important events in your community. You feel left out.

To find out why community newspapers are important to the members of communities, we have to know more about the nature, role and functions of these newspapers and the communities they serve.

Relevant concepts

The concept of *community* is rather vague. This may describe the public in general, or a group of people who share a certain neighbourhood, district or area. Furthermore, the concept often refers to a social group, a minority group and an interest group. We refer, for example, to the business community. It is also significant that in the information age, communities defined by common interests can be global communities. These communities are connected in cyberspace on the Internet. This means that whenever we refer to "community" we also have to keep in mind the context in which we use the concept. In the case of the "community newspaper", for example, the concept "community" refers mostly to a group of people living in the same area and who share interests that are directly related to the area in which they live and work. In other words, the common interests of these people are especially geographically determined.

The main difference between *community media* and other mass media, such as national newspapers, radio or television, is one of scale. According to Lundby (Aldridge 1996:191), "community media are small-scale media, and this scale relates to factors such as frequency of publication or broadcast, small-scale resources, small visible media outputs and small audiences". Community media address specific communication environments and serve to link members of the community with one another. Through the practice of community journalism, community media define a common identity for the members of a community and link them with their external situation or the larger society.

Community journalism is journalism at its highest level: finding and raising issues of great interest to local viewers/listeners/readers; "developing stories and other creative coverage; and providing information and a catalyst for debate" (Newsroom resources ... 2000). Community journalism should bring people together by helping them to understand their neighbours and foster a sense of community. It should orient recipients within a community of humans and not just within a system of institutions. Remember that a very important component of redefining news value in a democratic society is a renewed respect for the audience, which will in turn create opportunities for their voices to be heard. Journalists should listen to their readers.

In the practice of community journalism, the participation, rights, needs, interests and aspirations of recipients are crucial and should be central when formulating policies for community media (cf. Mullins 2000). Recipients have a right to relevant information, a right to react, and a right to a means of communication within their community, interest groups and subculture (McQuail 1989:121–123). Community journalism is about the importance of the following aspects:

- the multiplicity/diversity of media (e.g. many television and radio channels and many newspapers);
- the small-scale use of media (e.g. community newspapers/radio);
- the local nature of media (e.g. community newspapers/radio);
- the reciprocal role of communicator and recipient (e.g. communication between journalists and the recipients of community newspapers/radio);
- horizontal communication (e.g. communication between journalists and the recipients of a community newspaper/radio on the *same* level); and
- interaction and involvement (e.g. active involvement of recipients with their community newspaper/radio).

The discipline of journalism as a profession requires the mastering of three basic skills: the identification of news, the gathering of news, and the writing or the piecing together of news reports. Community journalism requires the same three skills. The only differences are that journalists who work for community media identify and gather relevant news primarily in and for the community that they serve. They concentrate on news that mostly concerns the interests of the members of the community (their readers, viewers and listeners). For example, scholars describe the *community newspaper* as primarily a newspaper of, for, and by a local community (cf. Clarke 1993; Garcia 1981). "When we talk about a community newspaper we are talking about a newspaper produced for and by the community, reflecting the life of that community, whether geographical or social" (Clarke 1993:1).

In the next section, we highlight some characteristics of the community newspaper.

The nature of community newspapers

An important aim of the editor and journalists of a community newspaper should be to create a sense of community awareness and a voice for the members of a particular community. Generally, the editor and journalists live in and are part of the community that they report on – but they must "maintain their independence while being part of the scene" (Mullins 2000). In other words, these journalists know the "ins and outs" of the community and they have usually earned the loyalty and trust of their readers.

When we apply the characteristics of newspapers in general to community newspapers, we mainly discover some differences in emphasis or degree. For example, the *type of content* covered in a community newspaper is close to that of the readers' own life world. In community newspapers, the coverage of the members of a community and their doings – their work, schools and social or political activities – are usually emphasised. According to Garcia (1981:199), "the community papers mirror on the community level what the metropolitan dailies cover on the national scale. The big difference is that the names are those of the boy next door and the neighbour across the street; people you know." This does not mean that news of national interest does not concern specific communities. The angle from which the news is presented, however, is usually community oriented (the news is presented from the perspective of the community – what is important and of interest to a specific community).

The characteristics of a community determine the type of journalism that should be practised in a specific community. Sometimes a community newspaper is designed to support political or ideological views or to counteract the establishment press – it cannot be the lapdog of establishment interests; the people's interest must come first (cf. Louw & Tomaselli 1991; Louw 1989; Mullins 2000). In general, the role and functions of the community newspaper depend on

- the nature of the geographical area (whether urban or rural) covered by the community newspaper;
- the frequency of the publication;
- the intention of the editor; and
- the type of community that it aims to reach.

The community newspaper is often *free of charge* and distributed to and available to everybody in a certain area. Franklin and Murphy (1991:79) write: "what sets free newspapers apart from their traditional paid-for equivalents, however, is their total reliance on advertising to the exclusion of all other revenues". Advertising revenue is essential to keep a free newspaper financially viable. For these newspapers to be classified as community newspapers they have to be distributed to certain geographical areas and contain news items of specific interest to the people from that area. In other words, a bombardment of advertisements and promotion articles does not make a community newspaper! The question is: Do these newspapers cover local news and serve the interests of a community?

In the next case study, we elaborate on the nature of community newspapers and the importance of advertisements for community newspapers, by illustrating some characteristics of a specific community newspaper.

Case study 11.2: *Record* – A community newspaper in Pretoria

Record is a community newspaper that is distributed weekly in Pretoria. It was started more than a decade ago when Capital Media, the owners and publishers of *Record*, first saw the need for such a newspaper in the Pretoria region. It is a member of the Community Newspaper Association and well known as a very good example of community journalism.

Seven different versions of *Record* are published every week for the seven regions of Pretoria in which it is distributed. Each of the seven different tabloid-sized *Record* newspapers focuses on the community that it serves. Not only the news and information in every issue of the newspaper centres on the specific community that it serves, but also the advertising.

According to *Record*'s manager, Mr Albert Basson, the newspaper is extremely successful. He says more than 180 000 copies of *Record* are distributed weekly and that the paper has more readers than any other newspaper in the city. It is thus not your average small community newspaper, but one that excels at what it does.

According to Basson, *Record*'s main concern is the welfare of the community that it serves. It fills a void that is not filled by other mainstream daily and weekly newspapers. *Record* focuses on informing all its readers and giving them what they ask for. Thus, matters of interest to the community such as new developments in certain areas, interesting events, school news and crime reports, are usually featured in the paper. The comprehensive television guide and information about community happenings are also firm favourites among readers. The paper does not act as mouthpiece for any political organisation. It therefore does not carry political news or opinions. *Record* fills a void that the national and provincial papers cannot fill.

Like most other community newspapers, *Record* is distributed free of charge. Advertising is therefore its only source of income. Basson says *Record* has survived over the years because it has managed to give its advertisers what they want. Since different newspapers are distributed to different geographical areas of the city, different markets can be served. Advertisers in the east of Pretoria thus feel that they are advertising for their own market when they advertise in *Record East*, while Mamelodi's businesses advertise in *Record Mamelodi*. Advertisers do not feel they are wasting money by advertising to people who would not come to their businesses or support them.

Record is not only an English newspaper, but also appears in Afrikaans. Language of publication is determined by reader preference in each of the seven areas of distribution.

According to Basson, *Record* acts as a link between its advertisers and its readers. Because advertisers see the advantages of advertising in their own area, they pay for a product which gives readers from a specific community the chance to get local news, which of course includes advertising news which is not available in other newspapers.

Basson says the management of a community newspaper must tread carefully to ensure that its expenses do not exceed its income. He says the paper's management should also know what advertisers would be able to afford to pay for advertising. If the newspaper's fees for advertisements are too high, businesses will not use it to advertise and the paper will not have enough money to survive. "Because we depend totally on advertising income, a community newspaper such as *Record* needs to pay all its bills out of the money that is made by advertising. Thus, the salaries of journalists, photographers, editors and other workers must be paid out of advertising money as well as all the other things such as the actual printing of the paper and its distribution."

Therefore a major part of every *Record* is devoted to advertising. About 67 percent of every *Record* consists of advertisements. An agency is used to obtain advertisements from national advertisers, that is big companies such as Shoprite or Dions. This gives *Record*'s own advertising representatives more time to go to local businesses for advertisements. *Record* also carries classified advertisements, which is a very good source of income for the paper.

Record's management has decided that they will not carry political news, nor will they publish any pornographic material. Because the paper is a community paper and is delivered free of charge to homes, the management must be very careful not to offend any of its readers. The newspaper thus does not carry advertisements for things such as escort agencies, adult entertainment, or erotic messages.

Record carries promotional articles for certain of its advertisers. However, the editor and journalists do not really like this practice as they feel that these articles take away some of the valuable space that could be used for community news and articles of real value.

According to Mr Gerhard Kleijn, *Record*'s editor, the journalists in a community newspaper are very industrious:

> The community journalist must be able to write on many different topics. A community newspaper usually cannot afford beat reporters; therefore any journalist must be able to cover any story. Because there is always a lack of space in a community newspaper, journalists must be able to write very well. They must keep their stories short, be able to work under pressure and be friendly at all times. They go out and work in the community which their newspaper serves; therefore they have to stay on a good footing with all the people that they meet.

Kleijn adds that the people who do the newspaper's layout must always keep a good balance between news and advertisements:

> Even though a paper such as *Record* carries more advertisements than news, readers must not feel that they are just looking at a promotional paper when they hold a copy of our paper in their hands. Readers must really feel that they want to read the paper when they see it. It must be laid out well and there must be enough stories, interesting photographs and eye-catching headlines throughout the paper.

The team responsible for the good coverage given to community news in *Record* consists of an editor, an assistant editor, a news editor, ten journalists who take their own photographs, and five sub-editors. They work closely with management and with the paper's ten advertising representatives.

Basson (the manager) says that even though *Record* is a big organisation, it will always stay a community newspaper that will never get so big that it can no longer serve the needs of its readers properly. "The content will always be relevant to the daily life of the members of the community and it will always enable them to stay in touch with events and developments in their community."

Summary

In this unit we introduced you to the practice of newspaper production, discussing and elaborating on such matters as classification and definition of the newspaper, newspaper design, the newspaper organisation, and modern newspaper production. We explained the profound influence of the Internet on modern newspaper production that led to the development of the electronic newspaper. We provided a case study on the nature, scope and format of e-papers on the Internet. Finally, we discussed the importance of community journalism and media with particular reference to the community newspaper and provided a second case study in which the characteristics of community newspapers were highlighted by using *Record* as an example.

To conclude this unit, we provide a list of the most common journalistic terms that you will come across in a newspaper office, and we present two research activities.

Newspaper terminology

ABC	Audit Bureau of Circulations, the body that authenticates and publishes newspaper circulation figures
Ad dummy	The blank set of pages of an edition with the shapes and positions of advertisements marked in
Advertising agency	An organisation that prepares and designs advertisements for clients, and buys advertising space
Back numbers	Previous issues of a newspaper
Banner	A headline stretching right across the page – also *streamer*
Bill	A newspaper poster that advertises the contents of the paper at selected sites – also *poster*
Blanket	Newspaper page proof
Blurb	Text or illustration used to draw a reader's attention to the contents of other pages
Box	A story framed with lines on all four sides – also *panel*
Broadsheet	Full size newspaper page as opposed to tabloid, half size
Byline	Name of the writer of a story – usually appears just below the heading

Caps/Upper case	Capital letters
Caption	Line(s) of type identifying or describing a picture
Characters	Letters, symbols, and so forth, used in printed matter
Circulation	The number of copies of a newspaper sold
Column	Standard vertical division of a newspaper page
Content	Newspaper material as a whole
Copy	Information in story form submitted for use in a newspaper
Copyright	Exclusive right to written or printed material
Copy-taster	Person who sorts, classifies and selects incoming copy
Coverage	The news covered in the newspaper
Cut	To reduce a story by deleting facts or words
Deadline	Latest time a story can be filed, accepted or set
Diary	The newsroom list of jobs for the day or week
Display ads	Advertisements in which large type or illustrations predominate
Dummy	A miniature page plan on which the position and size of advertisements and the available editorial space are indicated by the layout person
Edit	Checking the language (syntax, spelling, grammar) of copy
Editor	Person heading a newspaper and responsible for newspaper policy and its execution
Editorial	The newspaper's opinion on important issues, usually written by the editor and published on a specific page inside the newspaper
Embargo	A request/instruction not to publish a story before a specific time
Features	Subjective articles published in newspapers, in contrast to objective news material. They include advice, comment, opinions or evaluations published under the name of the author
Filler	Short news item of one or two paragraphs
Fold	The horizontal fold that divides a newspaper into an upper and lower half
Follow-up	A story that follows up information in a previous story in order to uncover new facts or new angles
Format	The shape and regular features of a newspaper; its regular typographical appearance and design
Freelance journalist	A reporter not employed by any newspaper who reports on events at his or her own initiative and provides stories to newspapers for payment

Graphics	Drawings used as illustrations in page design
Gutter	The margin between two pages
Hard news	Important news (as opposed to soft news) on major events based on solid facts
Head	Heading of a story
Intro	First paragraph of a story – also *lead*
Investigative journalism	A type of reporting in which news is examined in depth and wrongdoings uncovered by a team of journalists working under a leader
Knock-and-drops	Newspapers relying entirely on advertising revenue and distributed free of charge to readers – also *free sheets*
Layout	Positioning of stories, heads and photographs on the editorial part of the page, by the layout person
Lower case	Small letters as opposed to capital letters of the alphabet
Masthead	The name or title of the newspaper at the top of the front page
Nationals	Newspapers sold country-wide
News agency	Organisation that collects and edits news for distribution to newspapers
Pica	Printer's measure used to indicate the width of the columns and photographs
Readership	Total number of readers of a newspaper – not the number of copies circulated
Reporter	Person who gathers and reports the news – also *journalist*
Rotary press	Traditional press in which newspapers are printed by the letterpress method from curved metal relief plates
Scoop	Exclusive story
Section	A separately folded part or easily identified part of a newspaper
Soft news	Less important news as opposed to hard news (e.g. human interest stories)
Sub-editor	A person who checks and edits material for a newspaper to fit the available space, and writes the headlines
Subheading	Second heading of a story, usually in smaller print
Tabloid	Half-size newspaper

Research activities

1 Write a news report according to the inverted pyramid method. Base this news report on any environmental issue in your neighbourhood.
Follow these instructions:
- Gather all the necessary information you need to write a comprehensive news report.
- Explain how you gathered all the necessary information. In other words, give a step-by-step progress report of your preparation and interviewing activities – for example, particulars about your research of the topic, the interviewees and the questions you prepared and asked.
- Write the lead and the body of the news report.
- Edit the news report.
- Design a headline for the news report

2 Compile a case study, in the form of an essay, about the production of a newspaper of your choice (e.g. the local newspaper in your town) and gather information about the following:
- a brief history of the newspaper (e.g. establish when and why the newspaper was founded – the role and goals of the first editor);
- the present policy of the newspaper with regard to, among other things, its approach to or definition of news (news angle);
- the different departments of the newspaper and the functions of each department;
- the hierarchical structure and functions of the key personnel in the newsroom;
- particulars about design and the layout that the newspaper follows;
- advertising policy and the role of promotion articles;
- the printing process;
- whether the newspaper also has an electronic version and, if so, what its characteristics are.

Further reading

Greer, G. 1999. *A new introduction to journalism.* Cape Town: Juta.
Harris, G & Spark, D. 1993. *Practical newspaper reporting.* 2nd edition. London: Focal.
Hodgson, FW. 1993. *Subediting: a handbook of modern newspaper editing & production.* 2nd edition. London: Focal.
Nel, F. 1998. *Writing for the media in South Africa.* 2nd edition. Johannesburg: Thompson.

Bibliography

Aldridge, M. 1996. Information flows and community media: is empowerment possible through electronic media? *Ecquid Novi* 17(2):190–211.

Bogart, L. 1989. *Press and public: who reads what, when, where, and why in American newspapers.* 2nd edition. Hillsdale, NJ: Lawrence Erlbaum.

Brody, EW. 1990. *Communication tomorrow: new audiences, new technologies, new media.* New York: Preager.

Brooks, BS, Kennedy, G, Moen, DR & Ranly, D. (The Missouri Group) 1996. *News reporting and writing.* 5th edition. New York: St. Martin's Press.

Burns, Y. 1990. *Media Law.* Durban: Butterworths.

Clarke, A. 1993. *A focus for change: the role of community newspapers.* Community Services Group: Glasgow.

De Beer, AS & Steyn, E. 1997. "Beeld" as a mirror on the world: a qualitative study of international news flow and news selection at South Africa's biggest Afrikaans daily. *Communicatio* 23(1):16–27.

DeFleur, ML & Dennis, EE. 1988. *Understanding mass communication.* 3rd edition. Boston: Houghton Mifflin.

Faure, C. 1995. Ondersoekende joernalistiek en sosiale verandering: 'n ontleding en evaluering van die agendastellingsrol van "Vrye Weekblad" (1988–1993). DLitt et Phil-proefskrif. Universiteit van Suid-Afrika: Pretoria.

Faure, C. 1996a. Introduction to the print media, in *Introduction to communication: journalism, press and radio studies*, edited by LM Oosthuizen. Cape Town: Juta:3–29.

Faure, C. 1996b. The press and new information technology, in *Introduction to communication: journalism, press and radio studies*, edited by LM Oosthuizen. Cape Town: Juta:244–263

Faure, C. 1996c. The alternative press, in *Introduction to communication: journalism, press and radio studies*, edited by LM Oosthuizen. Cape Town: Juta:264–281.

Faure, C. 1998. Die era van papierlose koerante? *Communicatio* 24(2):43–51.

Fourie, J. 1998. A comparative study of a printed newspaper with its electronic counterpart on the Internet with specific reference to "Mail & Guardian". MA in Technology Journalism. Pretoria: Technikon.

Franklin, B & Murphy, D. 1991. *What news? The market, politics and the local press.* London: Routledge.

Friend, C. 1994. Daily newspaper use of computers to analyze data. *Newspaper Research Journal* 15(1):63–70.

Garcia, MR. 1981. *Contemporary newspaper design: a structural approach.* Englewood Cliffs, NJ: Prentice-Hall.

Gilster, P. 1996. *The mosaic navigator: the essential guide to the Internet interface.* 2nd edition. New York: John Wiley.

Greer, G. 1999. *A new introduction to journalism.* Cape Town: Juta.

Harriss, J, Leiter, K & Johnson S. 1992. *The complete reporter: fundamentals of news gathering, writing, and editing.* 6th edition. New York: Macmillan.

Harris, G & Spark, D. 1993. *Practical newspaper reporting.* 2nd edition. London: Focal.

Hiebert, RE, Ungurait, DF & Bohn, TW. 1991. *Mass media VI. An introduction to modern communication.* 6th edition. New York: Longman.

Hodgson, FW. 1993. *Subediting: a handbook of modern newspaper editing & production.* 2nd edition. London: Focal.

Hough, GA. 1995. *News writing.* 5th edition. New Jersey, Boston: Houghton Mifflin.

Keene, M. 1993. *Practical photo-journalism: a professional guide.* London: Focal.

Louw, PE. 1989. The emergence of a progressive-alternative press in South Africa with specific reference to "Grassroots". *Communicatio* 15(2):26–32.

Louw, PE & Tomaselli, K. 1991. Developments in the conventional and alternative presses, 1980–1989, in *The alternative press in South Africa*, edited by K Tomaselli & PE Louw. Bellville: Anthropos.

McQuail, D. 1989. *Mass communication theory: an introduction.* London: Sage.
Nel, F. 1998. *Writing for the media in South Africa.* 2nd edition. Johannesburg: Thompson.
Noon, M. 1994. From apathy to alacrity: managers and new technology in provincial newspapers. *Journal of Management Studies* 31(1):19–32.
Williams, F. 1987. *Technology and communication behavior.* Belmont, CA: Wadsworth.

Newspaper articles

'n Hele geslag raak verslaaf aan inligting: kinders verkies rekenaars glo bo maats. 1997. *Beeld*, 9 Desember:3.
Smuts, C. 2000. Ai die genot van torring. *Beeld*, 20 Oktober:13.
Uys, S. 2000. Los die braaivleis, jou rolpers roep! *Beeld*, 20 Oktober:12.

Internet sources

Editor & Publisher. 2000. *Newspaper sites in South Africa.*
Available: http://emedia1.mediainfo.com/emedia/resu...r&region=africa&abbreviation=southafrica
Accessed on 2000/10/23
Lauterer, J. 2000. The state of community journalism: you are here. [O].
Available: http://www.pa-newspaper.org/publications/press/july98/lauterer.htm
Accessed on 2000/12/01
Mullins, E. 2000. Community journalism JN 317. [O].
Available: http://www.ccom.ua.edu/journalism/JN317/purpose.htm
Accessed on 2000/12/01
Newsroom resources: community journalism project. 2000. [O].
Available: http://www.rtnda.org/resources/cj.html
Accessed on 2000/12/01
Outing, Steve. 1996. *Newspapers online: the latest statistics.* [O].
Available: http://www.mediainfo.com/ephome/news/newshtm/stop/stop513.htm
Accessed on 2000/10/23

Television Production 12

Stefan Sonderling

Overview

The purpose of this unit is to provide you with an understanding of the principles and techniques of television and video production. You will become familiar with the stages of television production, identify the planning activities that are undertaken during preproduction, become familiar with the roles of the people involved in television production, understand the functions of the television studio and identify the principles of the television camera, editing and distribution of video and television programmes.

Learning outcomes

After you have studied this unit you should be able to

- describe the process of television and video production;
- distinguish between broadcast and non-broadcast television production;
- identify and describe the roles of the people involved in television production;
- identify and describe the stages of preproduction, production and postproduction; and
- apply your knowledge to plan your own video production.

12.1 INTRODUCTION

Television and video production are practical activities that involve the use of expensive equipment demanding technical skills. Obviously, it is difficult to learn television and video production simply by reading a study unit and it would be useful for you to also have audio and video equipment to work with. However, if such equipment is not available, you will still gain a good understanding of the television and video production process by working through this unit. The knowledge you will acquire will be useful to you because you may be confronted with a job opportunity where such knowledge is essential. Indeed, many people in the television and video industry have found that a solid understanding of the tools and techniques of the whole production process has made a major difference to their own success and to the success of their productions. In television production, as in most of today's technologically complex mass communication industry, knowledge is power. Knowledge of the television and video production process will also provide you with a better understanding of the theoretical approaches to the study of the media that you encounter while you study Volume 1 of this book.

You should also note that although studio and field production for broadcast television will be emphasised in this unit, what is presented is also applicable to a variety of productions for smaller audio- and video-based media. For all such media, the production process is very much the same once you know the basics.

Before we proceed with the discussion we must clarify the use of two terms, "television" and "video", which are used interchangeably by most people.

Television

The word television, which means "far seeing", is used to describe both the *technology* and the *institutions* involved in the transmission of images and sound from a communicator to an audience. Television is a complex phenomenon: it is at once a technology, a cultural institution and an industry of great economic significance. As a technology, television refers to the transmission of sounds and images over great distances by means of electronic signals to an almost unlimited number of recipients. In its simple form it is a basic system consisting of a television camera connected to a television screen; the image that the camera "sees" appears on the television screen. Television becomes more complex when it involves more than one camera, sound, recording of the image on videotape, mixing of various images together, editing and the transmission of the images through a broadcasting station.

Video

The word video has three meanings, referring to:

- all the aspects of electronic picture technology as opposed to film, for example television programmes as against films in the cinema;
- the image portion of a television programme that is transmitted by the television system, for example the pictures you see on your television screen; and
- production activities that are undertaken for *non-broadcast* purposes, for example, training programmes or "home videos".

12.2 THE SOCIAL CONTEXT OF TELEVISION AND VIDEO PRODUCTION

Television and video production are complex processes through which the programmes of television are constructed. For example, visual images are recorded by a television camera and then reconstructed through a process of editing that puts these visual images and sounds together in particular sequence to form a coherent programme. What this means is that television and video production are communication processes. As you will remember from your studies, communication is a process by which a communicator gives expression to a message, encoding it in the medium of television or video. This means that in the communication process we are concerned with *content* (the "what") and *form* (the "how") of messages. Applied to television we need to look at the following:

- *Communication of content*: creating messages that are meaningful and provide significant experience to the audience for whom they are intended, for example, the stories that are presented in the soap opera programme. In other words, what the stories are about.
- *Communication technique*: refers to how the television stories are told. This requires the use of techniques of television production, the use of equipment, and so on. This also requires knowledge about the coding potential of the medium of television and its specific characteristics.

In the medium of television and video, the communicated content and the formal techniques of presentation of that content are interrelated and cannot exist independently (cf. Davis 1974:9). For example, the uses of techniques in television production

> ... have one main object: to make the camera work and editing as unnoticeable as possible ... They aim to make the camera work and the editing invisible to the beholder so that nothing may come between him and his concentration on the subject matter ... The best technique highlights that which is important, eliminates that which is unimportant and obliterates itself by its own perfection.
>
> (Davis 1974:10)

You must be aware of the self-effacing nature of television and video production techniques and be careful not to think that television and video programmes bring us images of a reality. For example, usually when you watch a television soap opera you pay attention to what is said by the actors and follow the story and you do not notice the techniques that were used in recording the programme, such as the quality of lighting, the camera angles, the way sound was recorded, and so forth. The production of television and video programmes involves a complex process of creation, selection (editing) and manipulation of images and sounds. The activity and the technology involved in the production of audio-visual signs is called a "signifying practice" – producing or manufacturing meaningful images within the ideological framework of society. You will learn more about this process in this unit.

12.3 CATEGORIES OF PRODUCTION

Television production may be classified according to its different levels of complexity and its purpose. The two main categories or types are broadcast and non-broadcast (or narrowcast) television production. We may term production for broadcast purposes as "television production" and production for non-broadcast purposes as "video production".

The differences between broadcast and non-broadcast productions involve the following:

- The manner in which programmes are transmitted to the audience: broadcasting is "public" communication and anyone who owns a television set is able to receive television broadcasts; non-broadcast is more "private" as programmes are produced for a specific and limited audience.
- Broadcast television demands higher technical quality of the image and sound (the distinction is only in terms of technical and engineering quality of the electronic recording instruments and not quality of content); programmes produced for non-broadcasting purposes may be of the same technical quality as programmes produced for broadcasting, but do not have to be.
- The institutional characteristic of broadcast television, for example a large institution such as the South African Broadcasting Corporation (SABC), as against a more flexible and diverse nature of non-broadcast productions, which may consist of a small team of people and a video camera.

12.3.1 Broadcast television production

Television broadcasting may be defined as the transmission through space, by means of radio frequencies, of signals capable of being received aurally and visually by the general public (cf. Chester, Garrison & Willis 1978:3–4). Broadcast television production involves complex operations undertaken by television studios such as the SABC, or private professional production organisations such as e.tv or M-Net. The constant demand for new programmes by major television networks and stations means that these organisations are not able to produce all of their own programmes, and outside professional organisations such as film and video studios are becoming more involved in production for television.

The aim of all television production is to create programmes for commercial transmission to a large or mass audience. Broadcast television is essentially an industry, "an electronic factory in which the production (or manufacture) of television programmes is organised on industrial lines" (Hood 1983:33). The industrial nature of television production is characterised by high levels of hierarchy and rigid division of labour that have important effects on the types of programmes produced and the procedure of production.

12.3.2 Non-broadcast (narrowcast) video production

Non-broadcast video production is a whole range of production activities that are not aimed at the traditional broadcasting media but rather at a more limited audience (narrowcast as against broadcast) which includes groups such as industry, government departments, business, churches, communities and schools. Non-broadcast video includes such diverse productions as "industrial video", "corporate video", "educational video" and "home video". These productions vary in size, professional ability of the people involved and quality of equipment they use. For example, large corporations and government departments may engage in complex production of their own programmes aimed at providing information, public relations, sales, and staff training.

Within the range of non-broadcast video production it is customary to distinguish between the following categories:

- Large format video refers to the quality of the equipment and the recorded image. Large format video may include broadcast quality (known as "High Band") as well as "industrial" video equipment (known as "Low Band") that make it possible to edit and duplicate the recorded images without loss of image and sound quality. Large format video refers to the size of the videotape such as the U-matic video cassette recorders (VCR) using $^3/_4$ inch (19 mm) tape.
- Small format video is not broadcast quality and the equipment is relatively less expensive than that for broadcast or large format video. Small format video includes the VHS (Video Home System) and Betamax equipment using a $^1/_2$ inch (12.5 mm) home videotape. The small format video is easy to operate and its use has become more widespread. Increasing use is made of digital video camera that records images like computer data files. Within the small format category we may distinguish the following usage (cf. Burrows & Wood 198:12):
  - Personal video. These include production of videos for personal use such as family events. The product is never intended to reach a large audience beyond its small circle of participants.
  - Community video. The use of small and portable video cameras and recorders enables communities to produce programmes about their social, educational and political concerns. The community video is a fast growing area of production activity and offers alternative means of communication to the government-controlled broadcasting channels. The community video has become "television for and by ordinary people" (cf. McLellan 1987:144). Community video acts as a catalyst for cooperation and interaction "giving people the confidence to take control of their lives and encourage them to see themselves as having ideas worth expressing" (Armes 1988:196).
  - Video art. This is the use of video by an artist to create artistic images for his/her own use or for use in art exhibitions that serve as a means for communicating the work of art to a larger audience.

12.4 TOOLS OF PRODUCTION

In order to produce television and video programmes we need equipment, people to operate the equipment and a place where production could take place, such as the studio or outdoor locations.

12.4.1 Basic equipment

We need equipment or tools such as cameras, video recorders, lighting, and so on, to be able to record good quality images and sound that could be used for broadcasting. The basic tools of production are (cf. Bermingham, Talbot-Smith, Symons & Angold-Stephens 1979; Zettl 1984:3):

- video cameras and a zoom lens;
- videotape recorders (VTR) used in the television studio, and video cassette recorders (VCR) used mainly with portable television cameras;
- microphones and sound recorders;
- lighting systems; and
- video and sound editing equipment.

12.4.2 Areas of production: studio and on location

Television programmes can be recorded either in the studio or on actual location outside the studio. However, most productions, even when shot on location, may also include segments that are shot in a studio. So let us become familiar with the studio.

The studio

The studio is the main centre of activity where the whole production process comes together. The studio is divided into two main sections: the front stage or set; the back stage and control rooms.

- The front stage (the *set*) is the area where the action is staged and shot by the camera. In the front stage the important elements are:
  - scenery or décor
  - lighting system
  - cameras
  - microphones
  - actors, presenters and people appearing on the show
  - camera and sound operators.

Control areas

The control room is the place from where all the production elements such as the camera, sound, video recording, crew and performers are coordinated. The control area is divided into separate compartments or sections (cf. Bermingham et al 1979:16):

- Production control, where the director and vision mixer are located.
- Vision control, where the lighting director and vision engineers are located.
- Sound control area, where sound specialists are located.

The studio also has other separate rooms where the videotape and video cassette machines are situated.

- The *audio director* arranges for the audio recording equipment, sets up and checks microphones, monitors audio quality during the production, and then disassembles and removes the audio recording equipment and accessories after the production is over.
- The *microphone boom* or *grip operator* watches rehearsals and decides on the proper microphones and their placement for each scene.
- The *videotape recorder operator* arranges video recording equipment and accessories, sets up video recordings, performs recording checks, and monitors video quality.
- In dramatic productions, the *continuity secretary* carefully makes notes on continuity details as each scene is shot to ensure that details remain consistent between takes and scenes.
- The *electronic character generator* (operator) types the opening titles, subtitles, and closing credits into a computer device that inserts the text over the picture during the production.
- *Camera operators* set up the cameras and ensure their technical quality, work with the director, lighting director, and audio technician in setting up and shooting each shot.
- Depending upon the production, there may be a *floor manager* or *stage manager* responsible for coordinating activities on the set. He or she may be assisted by one or more *floor persons*, or *stagehands* who may be assigned various responsibilities on the set.
- After shooting is completed, the *video editors* take the video recordings and blend the segments together, adding music and video and audio effects to create the final product.

12.6 THE PRODUCTION PROCESS

Television and video programmes come in different form, structure and content. The production of different programmes may vary from single to multiple camera, elaborate studio operation or outdoor location, live broadcast or recorded production. However, essentially all production is the result of proper planning. Television and video production may be divided into three main stages: the *preproduction* stage, the *production* or actual shooting stage and the *postproduction* stage.

12.6.1 Preproduction

Preproduction refers to all the activities that precede the actual shooting and recording of the video programme. Preproduction is essentially a process of planning and design through which the video programme is conceptualised and developed, and practical aspects of its creation and its eventual forms of presentation are decided on. The preproduction process is similar for all types of programmes – the basic ideas and approaches of the production are developed and set into motion. It is in this phase that the production can be set on a proper course, or messed up to such an extent that no amount of time, talent, or editing expertise can save it!

In order for the programme to be successful, the needs, interests and general background of the target audience – the audience your production is designed to reach – must be studied and kept in mind throughout each production phase. In order for your programme to have value and a lasting effect, the production must in some way affect the audience emotionally. This ends up being a major key to success. During preproduction all of the major elements are planned.

Once all the basic elements are in place, *rehearsals* can start. A complex production may require many days of rehearsal. These generally start with a reading of the script by the actors. Then there are *dress rehearsals* where the actors are "dressed" in the appropriate wardrobe and all production elements are in place.

Let us now look at the stages of the preproduction process more closely.

Ideas for programmes

All programmes begin with an idea or a concept in someone's mind. Some individual, an organisation or community may have an idea for a programme considered worthwhile producing. In broadcast television production, ideas are considered worthwhile if they can be produced according to well established and successful formulas, for example, many soap operas have similar story lines. However, before any idea can be converted into a programme, two important questions must be answered (cf. Baddeley 1981:13):

- What is the purpose of the programme?
- What type of audience it is aimed at?

Aims and objectives of the programme

Programmes are produced for specific purpose, for example, in commercial television programmes have two objectives (cf. Watts 1984:16):

- to entertain and
- to inform.

Other objectives especially applicable to non-broadcast video production, may include:

- educating
- persuading
- creating a favourable image for a corporation
- mobilising public opinion and political action
- expressing artistic vision.

At the outset it is very important to decide what the aims of the programme are and to define the actual purpose clearly. For example, stating the aim of a programme as "public relations" or "social concern" does not help much as it is too vague. The actual purpose and objectives and the specific concern must be described in detail. Selecting and specifying objectives are important for a number of reasons, amongst other that

- clear objectives will lead to realistic expectations and save money, time and effort during production;
- a video programme has a specific and limited viewing length and is not very effective for the presentation of large amounts of information, therefore a clear objective will ensure that only the essential will be presented and emphasised.

The aims and objectives of the programme must also coincide with the type of audience the programmes are aimed at. The need to know the audience is important, because it is difficult to produce a successful programme for more than one type of audience; for example, not every one likes soap operas.

Research

Research means that information is gathered about the subject or topic of the programme. The information allows the producer and scriptwriter to prepare the script and make effective production choices, such as selecting the correct costumes for actors.

Budget

All productions cost money because equipment must be bought or hired and personnel paid. The amount of money available will also influence the type and quality of production. The production budget is traditionally calculated according to "above-the-line" and "below-the-line" costs.

- *Above-the-line* refers to the cost of the creative, artistic and non-technical elements of production and includes the cost of personnel, such as the fees for the producer, the director, performers, and scriptwriter(s).
- *Below-the-line* refers to the physical elements such as the cost of production facilities, equipment, costumes, set design and the cost of technical personnel.

Options

The medium of television and video offers various techniques for communication of messages. Selecting an option means that the producer decides on the video format, choice of colour or black and white, place of production such as a studio or shooting on far-away location, live broadcast or pre-recorded programmes, and the type of presentation, for example a talk show or a drama (cf. Watts 1984:31).

Treatment

Treatment is a brief explanation of what the programme is about, or the "story" of the programme presented in a short paragraph or two containing all the things that should be included in the programme. The treatment should include a description of the programme style and mood. A treatment must also provide other information such as the style of presentation indicating whether it is a documentary, a talk show or a dramatisation; if it contains dialogue, spoken commentary and music; and a description of the scenery and place of production such as in a studio or on location (cf. Baddeley 1981:12–13).

The following is an example of a treatment for a historical documentary reconstructing the building of a railway line in Africa at the turn of the century:

> We open with a shot of the East African landscape, wild, rugged and without a sign of human habitation. We dissolve through a series of introductory scenes showing East Africa as it was, untouched by any civilizing hand – empty plains, wide expanse of bush, the Rift Valley, the rolling highlands, and then Uganda, green and fertile.
>
> The commentator begins: "East Africa at the end of the nineteenth century. A land without history. In these vast tracts of land, today was the same as yesterday. And yesterday was the same as it had been for centuries. Time stood still." The commentary continues to point out that in those days what is known as Kenya was a scarcely populated, barren region, arid in the east, rising up to a high plateau inhabited by only a few nomadic tribes. In fact, the idea that it should be settled, populated and farmed had not yet entered anyone's head. It was regarded as no more than the route to Uganda ... for Uganda was known to be green and fertile, a land with great potentialities.
>
> Then we see, coming through the bush, a slave-train. The slaves, their heads bowed down by heavy wooden halters, plod on, driven unmercifully by their captors.
>
> The commentary refers to the blot of slavery on this land – a scourge that was now condemned by the European Powers but by no means suppressed.
>
> (Baddeley 1981:14)

Script and story board

The *story board* is a rough visual plan which translates a concept from word to pictures and is an aid in planning the shooting. The story board is organised according to the main or key shots of the whole production. A script is a precise plan that combines images and sound into a programme.

Reconnaissance

Reconnaissance means a detailed inspection of the outdoor location where the video will be shot. The aim of reconnaissance is to find out what the location has to offer for production and establish the practical problems that may be experienced when shooting begins. Inspection of the actual location will determine the shooting script. It will also provide answers to some of the following questions (cf. Watts 1984:25–30; Wrench 1987:1):

- Is the location accessible for the camera equipment?
- Is the natural light from the right direction?
- Are there any noise problems which may prevent good sound recordings?
- Can the camera be placed close enough to the subject?

- Is there electricity for the cameras, recording equipment and lighting?
- Is the location accessible to vehicles?
- What local people may be of assistance?
- Is accommodation available for crew and actors?

The inspection of the location is also useful for planning camera positions, shot sequence and the whole shooting schedule.

Shooting script

The shooting script contains all the details of each shot besides the dialogue or voice-over commentary. It indicates the number of each shot, the number of people in each shot, camera positions and angles from which shots will be taken, the sound requirements and camera movements (cf. Wrench 1987:1). In multiple-camera production shot in a studio or outdoor each camera person also receives a *camera card* which shows the successive floor positions, allocated shots and camera movements (cf. Millerson 1979:327).

12.6.2 Production

Production means the actual on-camera shooting, whether live or for videotape recording, in the studio or on location. The actual shooting may be a multiple camera production where two or three cameras shoot the action continuously and the images and sounds are edited by switching between the different cameras (this is called "real-time" editing or "switching"), and the image recorded on the videotape machines in the control room. Production can also be carried out by using a single camera on location away from the studio.

The actual shooting of the video and the sound recordings usually proceed according to the shooting script. With location and pre-recorded production, scenes do not have to be visited in the same order as they appear in the script. All shots recorded from the same physical position may be recorded at once even though they are spaced out through the whole script (cf. Wrench 1987:1). The shots are put together into their proper sequence later in the postproduction editing stage. Of course, in the live production the shooting script must follow the chronological order of the master script itself.

The main elements of the actual production include *lighting*, *camera work* and *sound recording*.

Lighting

Light is the most important element in video production because the pictures that you see on the television screen are light and shadows. Video and film cameras are simply ways of capturing light; television transmitters are ways of distributing light; and the television set is a way of reproducing light (cf. Watts 1984:160). As is the case with all other techniques of production, light serves a double purpose. Light serves

- an aesthetic function – creating atmosphere in the images that you see on the screen, for example, brightly lit images create a happy atmosphere; and
- a technical function – video recordings need the correct amount of light to function properly and record a well defined image. The main practical lighting problems encountered during actual shooting are excessive lighting or insufficient light, and excessive contrast or contrast that is much too low. For example, excessive contrast is when someone in the picture wears black trousers and a white shirt. Low contrast is when a person wearing a red shirt is filmed against a red background.

Camera work

The heart of the video production is the actual shooting and recording of the visual images on videotape. The use of the camera in video production must be considered at two levels simultaneously: actual technical or mechanical manipulation of the equipment and the aesthetic effects that these technical functions fulfil. For example: a zoom-in by the camera provides more details in the picture and also provides more emphasis and importance to the subject that is filmed. A zoom-out is done in order to extend the field of view or to include more subjects in the frame, but aesthetically it serves to reduce emphasis (cf. Millerson 1979:294).

Composition

Composition refers to the arrangement of various objects within the television or video screen. Composition helps produce attractive and significant images that direct the viewers' attention and influence feelings about the subject on the screen. Composition involves deliberate arrangement of objects in front of the camera or positioning the camera in such a way as to select whatever is relevant and exclude what is irrelevant or unimportant (cf. Millerson 1979:81). "It is useful to think of the screen not as an area in which we include what we want, but as a mask with which we can exclude what we don't want" (Tyrrell 1972:58). The following are some important rules that should be observed in framing the shots by the camera (cf. Davis 1974:27–34):

- *Head room.* This is the space between the person's head and the top of the frame. The head of the subject should not touch the top of the frame and the chin should not touch the bottom of the frame. In close-up shots, both the top of the head and the chin should be cut by the frame.
- *Lead room, nose room* or *talking space.* With an individual close shot, if the subject is looking to the right, the picture should be composed with him/her slightly off-centre to the left. Similarly, if the subject is looking to the left, the picture is composed with the subject slightly off-centre to the right. If a subject is moving across the frame, he/she should be off-centre and more space should be given for the subject to move into.
- *Depth composition.* Television and video pictures are flat areas that reproduce a three-dimensional world on a two-dimensional surface. Illusion of depth is created by various means such as linear perspective, placing objects at an angle and use of

light. Linear perspective, for example, creates the illusion of parallel lines that meet at the horizon drawing the eye into the picture. Depth can be created by not placing a group of people in a straight line across the frame and placing one or two people in the foreground while others are placed further back. Depth illusion is also created by placing objects in the foreground or using a wide-angle lens. The creative use of light and shadow also creates an illusion of depth.

- *Natural cut-off lines of the human body.* Natural cut-off lines such as the neck, waist, hands or knees should not coincide with the frame. The cut-off line should be above or below these natural lines. In close-up shots, the chin should not touch the bottom of the frame nor should the top of the head touch the top of the frame.

Continuity

The video programme is a flow of images and accompanying sound. The shots must be organised and balanced and the flow of images must appear unbroken and coherent; the smooth flow of images is called continuity. Video continuity refers to the continuity in *space, time* and *motion* and is produced according to specific rules that ensure that each shot is matched with others preceding and succeeding it in the final production (cf. Glimcher & Johnson 1975:98).

- *Continuity of space.* Continuity of space is achieved through carefully matched camera shots, for example, a logical sequence of succeeding shots including the following: establishing the whole scene with a wide shot, then cutting to a close up of some particular detail in the scene (cf. Burrows & Wood 1986:302). The logical progression from an establishing wide shot followed by a cut to medium shot and then a cut to a close up, is a set formula in television news production (cf. Stone & Hinson 1974:43).
- *Continuity of relative positions of objects within the frame* is another important aspect, for example, the primary object within the frame should not jump from one position on the screen to another when the shots are changed. Matching shots are particularly important in cross cutting sequence. Cross cutting means that the camera cuts back and forth many times between the same pair of shots. Cross cutting establishes an imaginary line that is drawn through two people facing each other. The camera should be kept to the same side of the line when its position is changed. When these shots are edited together, the cross cutting between the two people in conversation will present them as looking at each other.
- *Continuity of action.* Action or motion in video production refers to
  - movement of the subjects or objects within the frame, and
  - camera movements.

Camera movements are usually motivated by the movements of the object or subject in front of the camera, for example, panning or tracking in order to keep the object within the frame. Continuity of action means that all movement of the characters and objects on the screen proceed in the same direction – if an object is shown leaving the frame at the right, in the next shot it must be seen entering the frame from the left. Continuity of action means that the various shots are matched without breaking the continuity of motion when the camera angle is changed between the various shots. For instance, if one scene ends with the actor or subject opening a door and leaving, the next shot must begin with the actor emerging from the other side of the door.

Sound recording

Sound is an integral part of the video production and care must be taken to record good sound quality during shooting. The correct microphone must be used and placed close enough to the subjects in front of the camera, but concealed from the camera view. In a documentary or news interview the microphone may be visible.

12.6.3 **Postproduction**

Postproduction refers to all the activities that take place after the actual shooting and recording of the programme (e.g. editing and distribution of the programme). Let us look at the main stages in postproduction.

Editing

Editing refers to selecting the appropriate shot from the various takes that have been recorded by the camera, on to videotape and the putting together of the selected shots to create coherent and continuous narrative.

A distinction is made between different types of editing:

"Real-time" editing

Real-time editing is an integral part of live television production, and performed during the actual shooting. It is also called "video switching" as the producer switches from one camera to the next and records only the desired images, for example, broadcasting live from a soccer game the producer or director will switch between different cameras that are placed in different positions of the field.

Off-line editing

Off-line editing is rough pre-editing done on cheaper video recording machines. Off-line editing is a useful trial for actual editing and gives an indication of how the final product will look.

On-line editing

On-line editing is the actual editing process that is done on computerised editing machines. In video editing the recorded tape is not cut physically as in film, but is an electronic process whereby the various segments are brought together from one or more original recorded tapes and electronically transferred to another tape where they are recorded in the desired sequence. Most video cameras and recorders record the image and the soundtrack on the same tape, thus keeping the vision and sound synchronous; in other words, the lip movements of the characters on the screen correspond with the sound. In practice this means that sound and vision must be edited simultaneously.

Editing involves how to change from one shot to another while maintaining picture and sound continuity.

There are four basic editing techniques:

- The cut
  The cut is the simplest, and an instantaneous transition from one shot to another. The cut is used for the following reasons:
  - To continue an action from another angle of view.
  - To reveal detail when cutting from a wide shot to close up.
  - To change the scene.
  - To change impact.
  - To cut from one person to another during a dialogue.
- The dissolve (mix or lap-dissolve)
  The dissolve is produced by fading out one image while fading in the next. The two images temporarily overlap on the screen. Dissolving or mixing between two images provides a smooth transition between the images.
- The fade
  During the fade, the image either turns gradually to black (fade-out) or appears gradually from a black screen (fade-in). The fade-in suggests a beginning and the fade-out an ending to a shot sequence.
- The wipe
  In the wipe, one picture seems to push another off the screen, so replacing it. The wipe may be termed a "special effects" device.

During the editing process, graphics, titles and various images generated by film, slide or computer animations as well as sound, commentary and music may be incorporated in the final version of the video.

Dubbing or duplicating

The product of editing is a master tape that may be used or viewed directly. However, to avoid damage to the original master tape owing to repeated viewing, duplicate copies are made for distribution.

Distribution and broadcasting

Television programmes are usually "distributed" to the audience through broadcasting, cable television or satellite transmission.

Video programmes are usually distributed on a video cassette and viewed by individuals in their homes or in communal settings such as film and video festivals, art museums, community centres or schools.

Summary

In this unit we discussed the principles and techniques of television and video production. We explained the difference between the concepts of video and televison, identified the various categories of video and television production, the role of the personnel involved in production, and the sections of the television studio. We analysed the stages of preproduction, production and postproduction and identified the role of camera work and editing.

Research activities

1 Explain the various categories of television and video production.

2 Explain the following concepts: preproduction, production and postproduction.

3 You have been asked by your community to produce a video presentation on the problems of the youth in the community. Prepare a complete plan for your video production process. Discuss your video production planning and explain what activities you will undertake during the following stages:
   - Preproduction
   - Production
   - Postproduction

4 View a video or a television programme and list the various types of editing techniques that are used.

Further reading

Armes, R. 1988. *On video.* London: Routledge.

Du Plooy, GM. 1989. *Understanding television: guidelines for visual literacy.* Cape Town: Juta.

Millerson, G. 1979. *The technique of television production.* 10th edition. London: Focal Press.

Zettl, H. 1984. *Television production handbook.* 4th edition. Belmont, CA: Wadsworth.

Bibliography

Armes, R. 1988. *On video.* London: Routledge.

Baddeley, WH. 1981. *The technique of documentary film production.* 4th edition. London: Focal Press.

Baker, D & Weisgerber, B. 1981. *Television production.* Englewood Cliffs, NJ: Educational Technology Publications.

Bermingham, A, Talbot-Smith, M, Symons, J & Angold-Stephens, K. 1979. *The small television studio.* London: Focal Press.

Bretz, R. 1976. *Handbook for producing educational and public-access programs for cable television.* Englewood Cliffs, NJ: Educational Technology Publications.
Budd, JF. 1983. *Corporate video in focus: a management guide to private TV.* Englewood Cliffs, NJ: Prentice-Hall.
Burrows, TD & Wood, DN. 1986. *Television production: disciplines and techniques.* Dubuque: Brown.
Chester, G, Garrison, GR & Willis, EE. 1978. *Television and radio.* 5th edition. Englewood Cliffs, NJ: Prentice-Hall.
Curran, J, Gurevitch, M & Woollacott, J. 1985. The study of the media: theoretical approaches, in *Culture, society and the media,* edited by M Gurevitch, T Bennett, J Curran & J Woollacott. London: Methuen.
Davis, D. 1974. *The grammar of television production.* 3rd edition. London: Barrie & Jenkins.
Du Plooy, GM. 1989. *Understanding television: guidelines for visual literacy.* Cape Town: Juta.
Elliott, P. 1973. *The making of a television series: a case study in the sociology of culture.* New York: Hastings House.
Ellis, J. 1984. *Visible fiction: cinema, television, video.* London: Routledge & Kegan Paul.
Fourie, PJ. 1988. *Aspects of film and television communication.* Cape Town: Juta.
Fourie, PJ (ed). 1991. *Critical television analyses: an introduction.* Cape Town: Juta.
Fuller, BJ, Kanaba, S & Brisch-Kanaba, J. 1982. *Single-camera video production.* Englewood Cliffs, NJ: Prentice-Hall.
Glimcher, S & Johnson, W. 1975. *Moviemaking: a guide to film production.* New York: Columbia University Press.
Hood, S. 1983. *On television.* 2nd edition. London: Pluto Press.
McLellan, I. 1987. Video and narrowcasting: TV for and by ordinary people. *Media in Education and Development* 20(4):144–149.
Millerson, G. 1979. *The technique of television production.* 10th edition. London: Focal Press.
Pateman, T. 1974. Ideological criticism of television technical manuals. *Screen Education* 12:37–45.
Stone, V & Hinson, B. 1974. *Television newsfilm techniques.* New York: Hastings House.
Watts, H. 1984. *On camera: how to produce film and video.* London: BBC.
Wrench, K. 1987. Directing a single camera video unit. *Media in Education and Development* 20(1):1–2.
Zettl, H. 1984. *Television production handbook.* 4th edition. Belmont, CA: Wadsworth.
Zettl, H. 1990. *Sight, sound, motion: applied media aesthetics.* Belmont, CA: Wadsworth.

Radio Production

13

David Wigston

Overview

Radio is often referred to as the "forgotten medium". Not only is the medium an invisible one, but it has also been overshadowed by developments in the electronic media field. Does this mean that radio is slowly disappearing from the media environment? Marilyn Matelski (1993:2) says not so; radio is really a victim of its own success. As a medium, radio has become so omnipresent that we simply take it for granted. This is due to two reasons: the dominance of television and the invention of the transistor. With its emphasis on visual images, television has achieved a critical mass that simply overwhelms the electronic media environment. In its initial years, television swept up audiences, advertisers, talent and programming genres from radio. Yet the coming of the transistor in 1954 gave radio something that television has never been able to attain with much success; portability. We can take radio with us wherever we go throughout the day. It is within this context that radio had to reinvent itself. Radio responded with the development of the format concept of programme production.

In this unit we take a closer look at how radio programmes are put together, by analysing their basic structures. To do this we place the focus on music programmes featured on commercial radio stations and consider briefly the various formats available in South Africa. However, the basic principles of programming, which is our point of departure, are applicable to all types of radio broadcasting. The way radio programmes are put together is not a random event. Much thought and planning goes in to the placement of the various sound elements that make up the programmes we hear. To this end we look at various factors that determine programme content. We also consider a set of criteria that will allow us to analyse the structure of a radio programme and determine how radio stations create a unique image. We discuss thirteen factors that can be used to improve the success rate of any radio programme. While all these factors are important, what ultimately drives radio today is the triangular relationship between programmes, the audience those programmes attract, and the potential that audience has for advertisers. The unique nature of community radio is not ignored, and the programming requirements of a community station are also considered. The unpinning mechanism that determines programme production has been, and always will be, the economic viability of the radio station. This is a point we make in our conclusion to this unit where we take a critical look at the value of the programme format to radio production.

Learning outcomes

At the end of this unit you should be able to

- describe the basic principles of radio production;
- explain the concept of programme formatting;
- describe the various elements associated with programme formatting;
- identify various radio programme formats;
- analyse the structure of a radio programme;
- compare the programme formats of different radio stations and different dayparts;
- evaluate a radio programme in terms of the various success factors;
- summarise the characteristics of community radio;
- describe the type of programming essential for the successful operation of a community radio;
- evaluate the role played by formatting in radio programming; and
- produce a short radio programme.

13.1 INTRODUCTION

Chances are good that wherever you live, you have access to several radio stations. And the chances are that you choose not to listen to some of them. Why? The reasons could be many, but the most likely reason is that you simply do not like the programmes that are on offer. Thus we can consider the programmes offered by a radio station as a marketable and consumable product, which we, as the audience, can select pretty much as we would select one brand of toothpaste over another.

Just as consumable products are tailored to specific markets, so each radio station tailors its programmes to a specific audience, and also for a specific part of the day. As a result, we can find a variety of radio programmes varying from all-talk through to all-music and an eclectic mix in between. Through market research, station managers know who we are and where we live and what radio station we are likely to listen to. So, if you are in your late teens or twenties, for example, the likelihood is that you will be listening to a radio station that plays popular music, during the course of which you will also be exposed to advertisements.

Successful radio stations offer more than just specific types of music, talk and information. They also offer a certain sense of community through their programming options. In this way, radio stations develop a unique identity and create a loyal following of listeners. Yet radio programmes are not compiled in a casual manner. Successful radio stations follow a scientific approach to the structuring of their programmes, which determines what can be aired at certain times and how the various programme elements are to be combined with one another. The nature of this scientific approach into the production of radio programmes is the topic of this study unit.

13.2 BASIC ORGANISATION OF A RADIO STATION

Before we can begin discussing radio production, it is necessary that we have some basic understanding of the organisation of a radio station. From the organogram illustrated in Figure 13.1, we can see that a radio station consists of more than just the on-air talent. We can divide the employees into four broad groups, as indicated in the organogram. Each group requires specialised training within their field of expertise, usually acquired on-the-job, after graduating with a degree. When studying this organogram, we need to remember that some radio stations use different titles for the various positions indicated. Also, the bigger the radio station, the more complex the organogram. Of all the staff involved in running a radio station, for the purposes of this unit we are mainly interested in the position of the announcer and producer, since the work that they do is most directly related to the production of radio programmes.

Figure 13.1 Generalised organogram of a typical small radio station

The working conditions of an announcer, or disc jockey, vary greatly from radio station to radio station. Only a very few disc jockeys have ideal working hours and command huge salaries. On average, announcers can expect to spend between three and four hours on the air, after which they are expected to perform a number of administrative and public relations duties. In addition, they also need to prepare for their next session on air. Usually, the smaller the station, the more varied the number of jobs announcers are expected to do. Many radio stations employ their on-air talent on a contract basis only, which means the position lacks job security and many of the benefits ("perks") that go with permanent employment, such as medical aid, housing loans, insurance coverage, and so forth. On the plus side, however, broadcasting as a career option, can be intrinsically satisfying to anyone who is naturally creative.

In the film and television industry, the producer is the person who handles the finances. In radio, the producer is described by Kaye and Popperwell (1992:89) simply as the person who has the ideas. Basically, the producer facilitates the realisation of those ideas within a given framework, which is usually limited by time and money. As such, the producer is probably the most important person working at a radio station. The producer is responsible for the scheduling and content of programmes. In other words, it is the producer who determines the "sound", or image, of the radio station. We can divide the role and function of the producer into three distinct aspects:

- *Preproduction* concerns the activities that precede the actual making of a programme. This involves a lot of research work and finding the right people in order to realise the initial idea for a programme.
- *Production* is the time spent, usually inside a studio, making the programme. Sometimes the programmes go out live; in other cases the programme is pre-recorded. Pre-recorded programmes have an advantage over live programmes in that errors can be easily corrected at a later stage before the programme is aired. In radio production, timing is of essence. It is the responsibility of the producer to ensure that the programme fits the allotted time, to the precise second.
- *Postproduction* includes the editing of a pre-recorded programme, as well as the writing of a suitable lead-in (opening phrases that introduce a programme or programme insert) and wrap (concluding statements following a programme or programme insert). Postproduction also involves the necessary paperwork concerning copyright, facilitation of payments and letters of thanks, where applicable, to those who helped make the programme.

However, in some radio stations the role of the announcer, producer and manager can be combined in to one position. Having established the roles played by the producer and announcer in a radio station, we can now begin to examine the radio programme in considerably greater detail.

13.3 RADIO AS COMMUNICATION

Radio, as a mass medium, is totally dependent on auditory codes in order to transmit messages. Hence we often refer to radio as being a blind medium. We can distinguish four distinct auditory codes that are used in radio programming, namely:

- Sound effects
- Human voice (speech)
- Music
- Silence

It is from these codes that the very essence of radio is determined.

As a result of the way in which the codes are combined, we can determine the

- genre and format of the programme
- progress of the programme (is it the beginning or the end or somewhere in between?)
- reality of the radio station and the announcers

In this unit we are not so concerned about the deeper cultural or ideological messages that are being relayed, but rather the "packaging" or format of those messages in order to attract an audience. In other words, we are looking at the way in which radio stations arrange the four basic codes in order to create a certain image through programme content, which can then be marketed to a specific audience. This arrangement is based on two basic principles of radio production, that of *consistency* and *variety*. At first glance, these two principles seem to be paradoxical. But we will explain in the next section how they, in fact, complement each other.

13.4 BASIC PRINCIPLES OF RADIO PRODUCTION

13.4.1 Consistency

Norberg (1996:4) defines consistency as successful programming which fulfils listener expectations that in turn are based on what the station has done in the past. Consistency is the uniform pattern created by the various elements used to build programmes, even to the placement of advertising, use of jingles and station identification. Norberg (1996:5) says that within the context of expectation, as far as we, the listeners, are concerned, what a radio station is doing at any given moment is actually irrelevant to the established image of that station. It is that which is coming next that is important and keeps us listening. We have a very good idea of what is coming next based simply on our previous listening experience. The argument is thus: if our expectations, as listeners, are met, we feel rewarded and will tune in more often and listen for longer periods, such as for several hours at a time. And if these expectations are not met, then we quickly tune to another station.

This is an important point for the radio station as it is much harder to regain a lost listener than to keep existent listeners. Thus our perceptions and expectations of a radio station, as listeners, are made up of a very clear idea of that station's identity and image. For example, if we tune our radio to, say 5FM, we expect to hear rock and pop music with a quick and snappy presentation aimed at the urban youth market. In other words, the station must do what it did in the past. Through the application of consistency in programming, a radio station creates frequent and loyal listeners. It is for this reason that station managers are always reluctant to make drastic changes to a programme's format. Instead, changing a format becomes a subtle and prolonged activity so as not to destroy the expectations of the existing audience (see Case study 13.1 for a discussion on the relationship between format change and audience numbers).

13.4.2 Variety

While expectancy, created through consistency, is a basic principle of programming, there is also a need for variety in that consistency. For example, on a music programme, while we become accustomed to hearing a "golden oldie" or "new release" at a certain time (consistency), variety is created by playing different artists and composers in that time slot. There is also some form of crossover between formats, and we can find various elements of talk, such as news and informational programme inserts in music formats. Through consistent placement and style of presentation and with reliable content, such diverse elements can become structural elements of programmes while providing for variety. Variety is then responsible for providing contrast within a programme.

But too much contrast can prove to be a disruptive influence on our listening as this leads to inconsistency, which in turns reduces our levels of expectation. There is a point at which too much variety results in inconsistency. According to Norberg (1996:8) it is difficult to identify this point. Much depends on the type of format being used and the nature of the target audience. For example, a mature and conservative audience will be less tolerant of high levels of variety in a programme, than a teenage audience. A general rule given by Norberg (1996:18–19) is that one may include as much variety as possible, as long as that variety is consistent with the station image. The key is to present diverse programme elements in such a way that they meet our expectations, as listeners. We should also bear in mind that, as listeners, we are never entirely predictable and from time-to-time often enjoy the element of surprise that comes from the inclusion of novelty. With the principles of consistency and variety as background, we need to move on and consider the actual content of radio programmes, which we do in the next section.

13.5 DETERMINING PROGRAMME CONTENT

Programming refers to the way broadcasters select and arrange the various elements, such as music and speech that make up a programme in a way that is considered as pleasing to us, the listeners (Smith 1990:153; O'Donnell, Benoit & Hausman 1993:289). Programming includes not only the selection of individual items, but also the sequencing of those items on either a daily, weekly or seasonal basis (Head 1985:283).

Within the context of this unit, content is the actual material that makes up the programme. If we are asked to explain the content of a programme, we can begin by listing the individual items that were used to make up that programme. In a news bulletin, for example, we would list the individual items presented in that bulletin; in a musical programme we would list the items played either by artist, composer or genre. For the purposes of this unit, we focus specifically on radio programmes that predominantly feature music. This does not mean that you have to limit your study of radio production to music programmes. The concepts discussed here are just as applicable to programming on all-talk and/or full-spectrum radio stations.

Have you given any thought to the various musical items that feature in any given radio programme? What criteria were used to determine what was, or, in some instances, wasn't played? And who determined those criteria? Radio stations today have very strict rules concerning what is played and when it can be played. The management of the radio station, together with the producer (or programme director) decides on the overall "sound" of the radio station. The producer then draws up a list detailing specifically what music is to be played on the station, and, in some cases, the order in which it is to be played. This list, which is referred to as the playlist, is then given to the announcers or disc jockeys. Very seldom are disc jockeys allowed to play any music of their own choice. If they are allowed to make a choice, this is usually from a predetermined list. The playlist is standard operating procedure at most radio stations, and is normally updated on a weekly basis. On some stations this list can be limited to as few as 40 titles, which are played over and over again – from whence the name "Top-40" was derived.

To summarise then: content is but the outer layer of the programme that is determined by the underlying structure or format. While content will change on a daily basis, the format should always remain fairly constant. In terms of the basic principles of radio programming, the content provides variety while the format maintains consistency. To take as an example, the content of a news bulletin would be the individual items that make up that bulletin. We could list these in the sequence in which they were read:

- Ex-President Mandela is expected to make an announcement tonight concerning the disruption to elections in KwaZulu-Natal.
- The South African Chamber of Business slams strike by Cosatu.
- The Truth and Reconciliation Commission meets in Cape Town tomorrow.
- The petrol price is to be increased from midnight.
- A woman was shot and killed at a taxi rank in Pietersburg.

In the case of a music programme, the content would be made up of various musical items, which we could then list as follows:

- *Caribbean Blue* by Enya
- *Wonderland* by Simply Red
- *Every Road Leads Back to You* by Bette Midler
- *Another Day in Paradise* by Phil Collins
- *Across the Night* by Danny Antill

For each programme we would produce a different list. In the next section we briefly look at how the playlist originated and the relationship of the playlist to that of the programme format.

13.6 THE CONCEPT OF RADIO FORMATS

Historically, the playlist is said to have originated with Todd Storz (Kahn 1982:181) who owned station KOWH in Omaha, Nebraska, USA. Legend has it that Storz got the idea of the playlist in 1956 from watching patrons selecting the same music over and over again from a jukebox in a bar (MacFarland 1995:37–38). From this behavioural pattern, Storz decided to repeat the more popular music on his radio station more often than the less popular tunes. From these beginnings, the concept of "hit rotation" emerged into what is today's playlist. However, the concept of the programme format is credited to Peter Steiner, an economist who studied the economics of radio station markets in relation to that of programme regulation during the 1950s (Owen 1977:308–312).

The development of the playlist and programme formatting was inevitable, but the process was speeded up considerably by the advent of television. Before television became dominant (particularly in the USA), radio programming was of a catholic nature, made up of genres such as news, sports commentaries, drama, soap operas, comedy, documentaries and various types of variety programmes that included talk mixed with music. These programmes were presented in fifteen-, thirty- or sixty-minute segments. The radio station thus provided a bit of everything to a wide and diverse audience.

With the coming of television, two significant events occurred:

- Radio stations lost listeners as they moved to the newer medium of television.
- Previously popular radio programmes, such as comedies, dramas and soap operas moved to television where the visual element added to their popularity.

To counterbalance the movement of audiences to television, radio stations gradually moved away from presenting a wide variety of programmes intended for a general audience, to generic programming using the playlist concept. The radio station simply singled out one particular segment of its audience and directed all programming at that audience. One specific programme was expanded in time, for example from thirty minutes, until that programme filled the entire broadcast day.

The reaction of radio in South Africa to the introduction of television in 1976, followed much the same pattern as elsewhere. Radio stations with diverse programming, such as Springbok Radio, had the most to loose. Springbok Radio was the SABC's first commercial service, which came on the air in May 1950 and continued to broadcast until 1985. Programming was made up of a mix of soap operas, comedy shows, quiz shows, dramas, magazine and request programmes. Not only were Springbok Radio's listeners watching television, but they also moved to the recently introduced independent stations of Radio 702 and Capital Radio with their "clean" and "fresh" images. The initial reaction by Springbok Radio was to phase out sponsored programmes so that changes could be easily made. During the first four years of television (1976–1979), Springbok Radio underwent many dramatic changes (see our discussion about making dramatic changes to programming in section 13.4.1 and 13.10 of this unit). Programme genres such as quiz shows, dramas and soap operas were dropped, as they simply could not compete with the glitz and glamour of their televised counterparts. Although audience levels did stabilise somewhat during the early 1980s, by 1985 it was clear that Springbok Radio could no longer compete in the new broadcasting environment. By the end of 1985 the SABC decided the only alternative was simply to close the station down.

Contrary to predictions of doom and gloom, radio prospered with the development of smaller radio stations specialising in either all-talk, or classical music, or jazz and so on. In most cases programming is dominated by pre-recorded music with limited amounts of news, information and advertisements. The ways in which these elements are blended together produce the format. Format is defined by O'Donnell, Benoit and Hausman (1990:297) as the radio station's strategy to attract a particular audience. Over the past four decades, programme formats have become more and more specialised. By the turn of the century, more than seventy different formats were recognised in the United States (MacFarland 1995:40). In South Africa, even with the coming of many new private and community broadcasters, radio has not yet fragmented to this degree. However, we can still clearly identify a number of distinct formats that are used, such as that of Classic *f*M, which focuses exclusively on classical music, or 5FM, which limits its playlist to that of contemporary hit radio (CHR). In the South African market, we have fewer radio stations thus we find fewer formats. Some of the formats that we can identify are briefly described below (Shane 1995:4–7; MacFarland 1995:33–35).

- *All-talk*, as the name suggests, places an emphasis on talk with a minimum of music. The format comes in many variations. The best known takes the form of the phone-in, but can also include talk in the studio with one or more hosts, sometimes with guests. Programme content includes news, business information, and discussions. The all-talk format is aimed at a slightly older market, which feels that talk-radio provides information unavailable in the print media. The all-talk format is the most expensive of all formats to maintain. Examples are Radio 702, Cape Talk and Punt Gesels Radio.
- *Contemporary Hit Radio* (CHR) is driven by the music industry, and the programmes are a mix of rock 'n' roll and popular music. Programming is aimed at the teenage market since teens and young adults spend more money on musical recordings than any other age group. CHR is a development of the original top-40 format that made use of a very limited playlist, such as we find on 5FM.
- *Adult Contemporary* (AC) eludes definition since this format is more often described by what it is not – not too hard, not too soft. The format is loosely described as one that most people feel comfortable with, even if the station is not their favourite. The AC target audience is a diverse one, with the result that the format is prone to fragmentation and can include aspects of urban contemporary or easy listening formats. Programming usually consists of long music sweeps (where three or more musical items are played with no interruptions between the items). Examples are East Coast Radio, Highveld Stereo and KFM.
- *Urban Contemporary* plays musical items primarily by contemporary black artists with a mix of jazz, blues and rock, but usually without rap or high-energy dance music. Urban contemporary shows great strength in coalescing black listeners. Examples are Radio Bop, Metro FM and Kaya-FM.
- *Golden Oldie* stations are described as the top-40 stations of yesterday. The target audience consists largely of ageing top-40 listeners indulging in nostalgia. Music from the late 1960s, 1970s and 1980s features predominantly. However, the listeners

to such formats often have high disposable incomes and thus are attractive to potential advertisers. An example is Jacaranda Stereo.

- *Beautiful Music* is a rather vague description than reveals little about the actual content, but indicates an automated format that Fornatale and Mills (1980:77) term "wall-to-wall" music or alternatively "musical wallpaper". The intention is to be unobtrusive and low-key as there are no announcements, no advertising and little, if any, on-air promotion. An example is Radio 2000.
- *Classical/Jazz* formats offer listeners highly specialised programming featuring either classical or jazz music genres, with announcers who are considered experts in those musical fields. Programmes are characterised by the inclusion of longer musical items. Stations airing either of these formats usually have a small but extremely loyal audience. Examples are Classic *f*M, Fine Music Radio and P4.
- *Full-spectrum programming* is not really considered a format, but is a term usually reserved for a diversity of programme genres such as news, sports commentaries, dramas, documentaries, variety and musical programmes. Full-spectrum programming is traditionally the domain of public service and community radio. The best example here would be Radio Sonder Grense (RSG). SAfm originally offered full-spectrum programming, but has since opted for an emphasis on news and information programming.

Today, the concept of format is of particular importance for commercial radio. These stations generate income by selling air-time to advertisers. The programme format is used to attract an audience, which is then "sold" to the advertiser. The objective for the radio station is to devise a programme format that will attract and hold an audience that will appeal to advertisers. From this perspective, the commercial survival of the radio station is highly dependent on providing a unique and specific format. Thus radio stations select a particular target audience and seek to reach only that market. An arrangement such as this is advantageous for advertisers who want to reach specific markets rather than cover a small segment within a general audience. For example, a CHR format is constructed around popular music enjoyed mostly by listeners between 15 and 25 years old. The more teens and young adults who listen to the station, the more the station can charge potential advertisers who specifically want to reach that market.

13.6.1 Scheduling

Scheduling refers to the practice of coordinating the tempo of formats to complement listeners' activities. Most radio stations schedule their programmes in an hourly rotation, creating a sequence of hourly cycles throughout the day (see section 13.8, The hot clock). As the day progresses, so the hourly pattern is changed to match listener demographics (see Figure 13.2) and activities. For example, during the morning drive-time, listener numbers tend to be at their highest. The programme tempo will also be considerably quicker than for the afternoon drive, since listeners are preparing to start their day and energy levels are usually higher than in the late afternoon (Head, Sterling & Schofield 1994).

13.6.2 Dayparts

In the past, radio stations would schedule programmes that had a distinct beginning, middle and end. The boundaries between programmes were clear-cut and often the different programme genres would be scheduled adjacent to one another. For example, we could have a book-reading followed by a request programme, followed by a quiz show. The trend today is to use seamless programming where there is no distinct boundary to any one programme. Rather, the broadcast day is divided into specific dayparts, largely determined by the activities of the listeners. We can identify five specific day parts (Hyde 1995:250, Johnson & Jones 1978:140–141):

- *06:00–10:00 The morning drive time*: This is when listeners are getting up, preparing for work or school and are in transit. The need for information is high, such as news, weather and time checks. Listenership tends to peak in this daypart as many people listen in their cars en route to work.
- *10:00–16:00 Midday*: Children are in school, and most people at work. The need for information is less important, with the emphasis now on entertainment, except around lunchtime when many use the opportunity to catch up on the news. The audience tends to be predominantly female.
- *16:00–19:00 The afternoon drive time*: Children have come home from school and workers are driving home. This daypart tends to mirror the morning drive time, but with a somewhat more relaxed pace.
- *19:00–00:00 Night-time*: The audience tends to decline after 19:00 as they migrate to television. Specialist programming tends to do better in this daypart than general programming.
- *00:00–06:00 Overnight*: Since audiences are at their lowest, many stations use an automated format until the cycle starts again at 06:00.

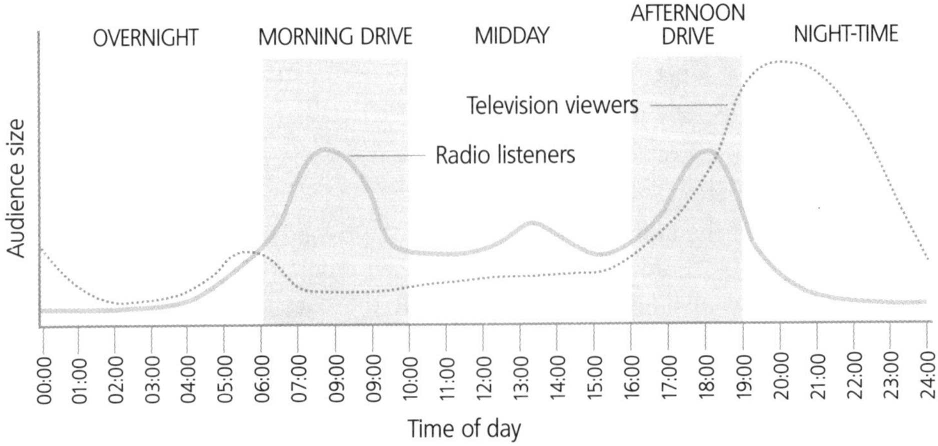

Figure 13.2 A generalised distribution of listeners during the day for radio compared with television

Although radio may make use of seamless programming, there are subtle variations to accommodate the different dayparts. We find that the midday daypart contains more music with less talk in the form of news, headlines and traffic updates, since we, as listeners, do not need this information during the early afternoon (compare Figure 13.3 with that of Figure 13.4).

13.7 ANALYSING THE PROGRAMME STRUCTURE

As producers (or programme directors) for a radio station, we need to concern ourselves with, not only the needs of our audience, but also with what competing radio stations are presenting to our audience. It is common knowledge that the listening habits of an audience are hard to break. This means that having lost a listener to the competition, it will not be easy to win that listener back again. Therefore, it is essential to present a top rated programme. It takes careful planning and knowing what the opposition is doing that keeps programmes top rated. A way to achieve this is to examine the other station's format or programme structure. This means doing some research. In this section we examine a number of aspects that we can use to analyse the structure of a radio programme.

13.7.1 Ratio of music to talk

Ratio refers to a quantitative relationship between two aspects. The two aspects we are concerned about here are music and talk by the announcer within a time frame of one hour (since that is the period of time used on the hot clock). What we intend doing is to calculate how much time is devoted to speech and how much to music. The best way we can do this is to sit with a stopwatch and time the various segments within the hour we selected to analyse. Then we simply add up how many minutes (within the hour) were spent on talk, and how many devoted to music. To be more meaningful and to allow for comparison with other hourly segments, we can convert our figures to a percentage and then express the relationship in the form of a simple graph. The question now arises: What do we do regarding advertisements featured during the hour we are analysing? As advertisements often include a mix of both talk and music, how are we to classify them? The answer is simple – advertisements do not really form part of the programme content, so we need not include them in our time calculations.

13.7.2 Style of address used by the presenter

The style of language used is an integral part of the format used by a particular radio station. The words used on air can either win or lose the target audience. For example, CHR format programmes are aimed at youth, so the patter of the DJ (disc jockey) needs to include idioms and modes of speech associated with the target audience (Shingler & Wieringa 1998:32). We need to consider the appropriateness of the style of address used by the announcer for specific programme content. For example, reading the news requires a totally different style to that used in announcing the latest top-20 hits, yet both these aspects may occur within the same hour and be presented by the same announcer. When considering the style of address used by the presenter, there is not much purpose in our saying the presentation was "casual" or "lively", unless we include a quote to illustrate what we mean by "casual" or "lively". Consider the following two examples:

Example 1: Checking out your weather for the rest of this afternoon, there is a chance of scattered thundershowers. So, if I were you, I'd snuggle up inside, lock that dial down on 99.2 FM, and stick with the station you love the best.

Example 2: We're here to enjoy the afternoon. A little bit of a grim afternoon, a little bit chilly, and a little bit of rain last night. Enough rain really, I would say. But any way, lots of music and that will keep you warm.

While both are casual, we can definitely say that the first example has considerably more pace than the second. The first example comes from a radio station with a CHR format, while the second is from a station with an AC format.

Ideally we need to discuss the presenter's style of address in measurable terms. A consequence of radio's limitation to auditory codes is the fact that speech (or spoken words) cannot be separated from the speaker. Therefore we have to take into account various aspects, such as the intonation of the speaker's voice when analysing the programme structure. Hyde (1995:58–59) refers to these aspects as speech personality. Speech personality is made up of the following seven variables:

- *Pitch* – which includes range and inflection. Pitch can be either low or high; low is considered better than high, although there should be variety.
- *Volume* – which is the degree of loudness and seldom presents a problem to professional broadcasters. Sometimes an increase in volume is used to indicate excitement.
- *Tempo* – or rate of delivery. This is determined by the number of words per minute that have to be read or spoken. We need to judge what speed is appropriate to the mood of the programme. There is no single correct tempo, although there are limits at which point articulation is sacrificed and the text becomes unintelligible.
- *Vitality* – or enthusiasm. A sense of vitality is often indicated by rapid speech, but can also be achieved when speaking slowly. Disc jockeys often make use of a low volume but attain vitality by speaking rapidly.
- *Voice quality* – which includes resonance, timbre and tone. A thin voice is usually caused by shallow weak breathing and speaking at too high a pitch.
- *Pronunciation* – which is concerned with accent or dialect.
- *Articulation* – which sometimes is referred to as diction or enunciation, that is the breaking up of speech into recognisable words.

The announcer or disc jockey's voice is shaped by the first six variables and is then rendered meaningful to the listener by the seventh. In addition to the above-mentioned variables the announcer may also show some of the following voice problems.

- *Nasality* – caused by breathing out through the nose when speaking.
- *Huskiness* – or an excessively hoarse voice is usually a result of a throat problem, or nervous tension. Sometimes huskiness in the voice can add colour.
- *Sibilance* – this is the hissing sound when pronouncing words that include the letters *s*, *sh* or *z*.

13.7.3 Characteristics of the overall "sound"

Here we need to consider the question of why a radio station needs to have a unique image or individual "sound". With the increasing choice offered to listeners, radio stations need to consider themselves as a product that needs to be treated as an integrated package, just as any other marketable commodity. To be known, it becomes vital to create a brand or image of the station that makes it stand out from the others. This identity, or "sound", is made up from a combination of the auditory codes used in radio (we discussed these earlier in section 13.3). These codes are drawn from various sources, such as advertisements, jingles, musical items, reports, announcements and so on. It is the blending of these sources, within the context of the principles of consistency and variety, that creates a specific image (or "sound") which makes one radio station different from the next, and in the process competes for the attention of the audience.

The "sound," or image, then emerges out of a combination and repetition of programme elements, such as:

- the type (or genre and/or sub-genre) of music selected;
- the style of address used by the presenter;
- the techniques used in the production of the programme and advertisements;
- the style(s) used in advertisements;
- the placement of those advertisements;
- the placement and presentation of news bulletins; and
- other special techniques and production methods used, such as jingles and stings (short attention-getter usually a few seconds in duration) to identify and promote the station.

All of these elements must fit the projected image and be appropriate for the selected format. "This means that absolutely everything broadcast should reflect, represent and re-enforce the 'image' of the station" (Hannan 1997:41). For example, a radio station that adopts a classical music format should then not feature an advertisement that uses rap music for the jingle.

Most radio stations today make use of pre-recorded music, simply because this is the easiest and cheapest way of filling time. The person who provides a commentary on the music played is usually referred to as a disc jockey (alternatively the terms jock, DJ, deejay, personality or on-air talent are used). The disc jockey is traditionally associated with popular music and can therefore make use of a wide variety of announcing styles, from rapid delivery to casual, or laid back, the characteristics of which we discussed in section 13.7.2. On the other hand, announcers on classical music stations, such as

Classic *f*M, need to be more relaxed in their presentation, but are also more limited in the range of style they may adopt.

Aspects that we can take into consideration when assessing the image provided by the content and format of a particular radio station, include the following:

- *Pace* – in the case of a CHR format, the various programme elements will come fast and furious. Some of the elements in a fast-paced format, such as a sting, can last but a few seconds in length. This means that we can identify a large number as well as a large variety of sound sources within the programme. Obviously the converse is true for a station using an easy listening format. Here we will find far fewer sound sources.
- *Content* – here the station needs to strive for a combination of continuity and variety.
- *Announcing style* – refer back to our discussion in section 13.7.2.
- *Blending of sound sources* – some stations try to combine as many different auditory codes as they possibly can. For example, traffic reports are read over a background of sound effects of traffic noise; Jacaranda Stereo sometimes uses a music bed (background of music) for certain news bulletins. We need to decide whether this strategy is always appropriate, in terms of the content, for the overall "sound" of the station.

The format and image adopted by a radio station is by no means a hit-or-miss affair. Much research and careful planning goes into determining the format a radio station will ultimately select. Obviously, if the listening public do not like what they hear, the consequence will be economic disaster for the station. As a result, radio stations develop certain strategies to relate the programme content to their intended audience. The methods used to achieve this are the topic of the next section.

13.7.4 Strategies used to relate programme content to listeners

Except for Public Broadcasting Services (PBS), such as RSG, which offers full-spectrum programming, commercial radio tends to focus on specific demographic groups or niche marketing. For example, 5FM opts for a CHR format (pop and rock music) because research has shown that this format attracts a young audience; 5FM appeals to this audience segment simply by virtue of their preference for a certain type of music.

The appeal to young listeners is further heightened by giving the disc jockeys a form of star status by naming their programmes after them. The DJ uses a variety of recurrent devices, such as jingles or stings, within his or her programme to remind the listener of the identity of the station. In this way, the identity of the radio station is mediated through the presenter of the programme, while the identity of the presenter is mediated by his or her style of presentation. We, therefore, have a double layered mediation of the radio station's identity. For example, a typical disc jockey voice for announcing musical items is hyped-up and upbeat, while conversations with listeners via the telephone could make use of an empathetic voice in order to establish an intimacy with the listener. We discussed the variables that make up the disc jockey's speech personality (or identity) in section 13.7.2.

Nevertheless, the relationship between the audience and the format adopted by a radio station is a delicate one. (We briefly discussed the role that expectancy plays in maintaining this relationship, in section 13.4.1.) Does this mean that once a radio station has decided on a particular format and image it cannot change these? From our own listening experiences we know that stations do make minor changes to their programmes as a means of introducing novelty. Yet changes are not made lightly. For example, the radio station may decide to introduce a new format or image in order to target a different audience (see Case study 13.1 later in this unit for an example). Changes to the location of the various sound sources within a programme are usually indicated by means of a graphical device known as the "hot clock".

13.8 THE HOT CLOCK

Radio is heavily dependent on time. Programmes must start and end on time, usually working around fixed points, such as news bulletins. The hot clock is a graphic representation of this dependence on time. Try and imagine the contents of a programme superimposed on to a clock face. The programme starts at the 12 position on the clock, and moves clockwise until we get back to the 12 position after a period of sixty minutes has elapsed. This means that a hot clock diagram can only represent one hour of any programme. To represent a second hour, a second clock will be required and so on.

In a radio station, the purpose of the hot clock is to indicate the rotation of musical items featured on the playlist in addition to the placement of other programme elements during a particular broadcast hour. The producer can then graphically see the balance between the various elements that make up the programme. This is useful in maintaining consistency and introducing variety. Changes to the format can then be made with a minimum of disruption to the running order of the programme. This helps the station develop a specific sound of its own (McLeish 1988:133).

For the disc jockey or announcer, the hot clock indicates exactly where certain insertions are to be made, such as advertisements, traffic reports, news and other programme elements. All these elements need to be indicated as segments on the hot clock, including the various sub-genres of music featured by the selected format. We can also use hot clocks to see the difference between programme structures from various dayparts. To illustrate this, we have selected the morning drive, illustrated in Figure 13.3 and the midday daypart, illustrated in Figure 13.4, from Kaya-FM, a Gauteng-based radio station that uses an urban contemporary format.

It is easy to see that there are far more programme elements indicated in the morning hot clock than in the midday hot clock. While the format remains the same, the pace of the programme has slowed down in the early afternoon with a greater emphasis on music over that of information for the morning drive daypart. Speech elements in the

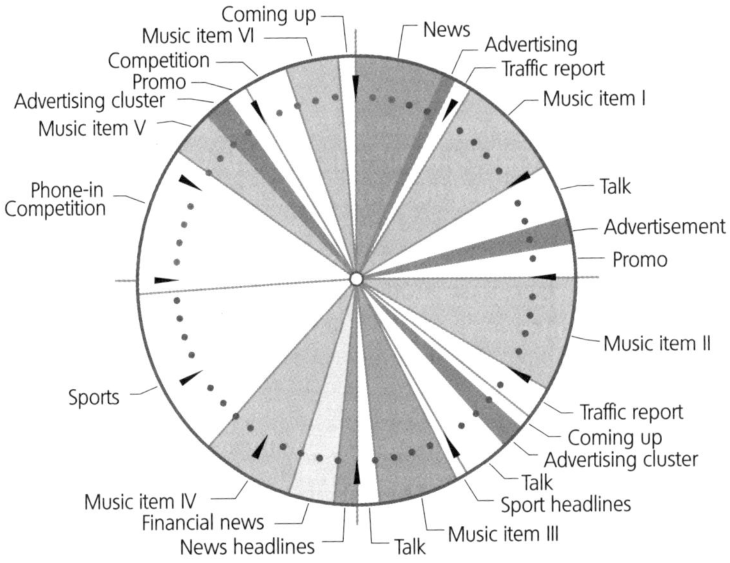

Figure 13.3 Kaya-FM hot clock, 07:00-08:00, weekdays (morning drive daypart)

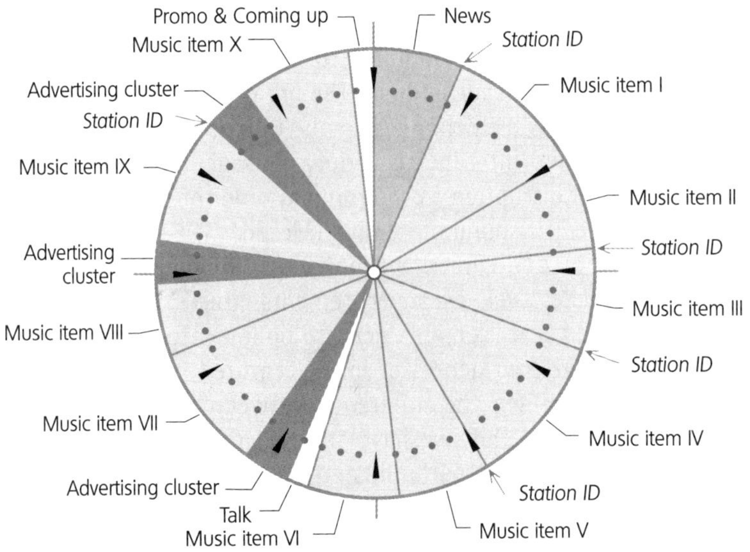

Figure 13.4 Kaya-FM hot clock, 14:00-15:00, weekdays (midday daypart)

drive-time daypart are made up of a variety of aspects such as news, information about the music played, sports and financial news, traffic reports, competitions, and promotions for forthcoming programmes. However, by contrast, there is limited talk during the midday daypart segment although the station is identified frequently. Note how the hot clock indicates the position of the station identification jingles.

We can also use the hot clock to compare the programme structure of differing radio stations. Figure 13.5 illustrates the programme structure for SAfm, which uses an all-talk format during the morning drive-time daypart. However, consistent placement of programme elements is partly accountable for the success, or lack thereof, of any programme. A number of other factors also have to be taken into account. In our next section we look at some of these.

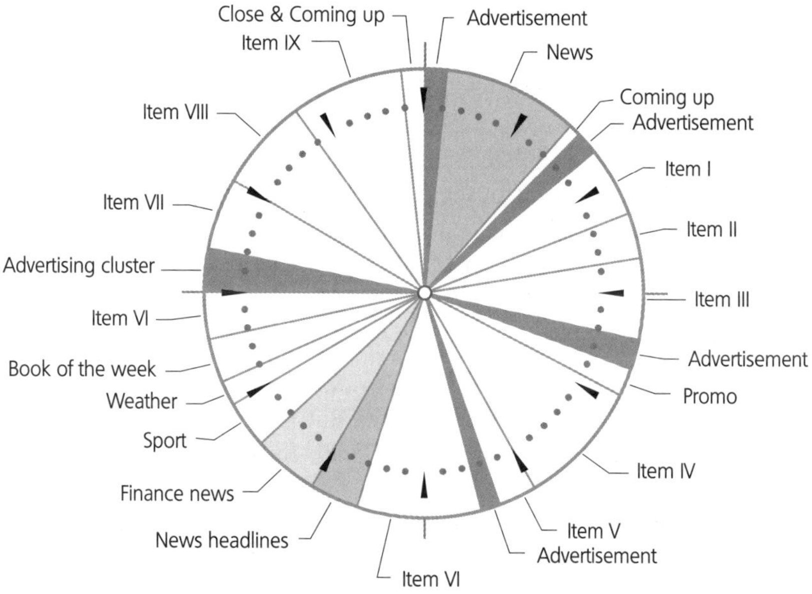

Figure 13.5 SAfm hot clock, 07:00-08:00, weekdays (morning drive daypart)

13.9 SUCCESS FACTORS IN RADIO PROGRAMMING

We need to ask what factors contribute to the success of a particular programme. The fact that a radio station continues to broadcast a particular programme does not imply that the programme is successful. While the number of listeners to a programme is an indicator of success, you need to ask how big the listenership must be for a programme to be successful. Johnson and Jones (1978:13–31) identify a number of factors that can contribute to the success of a programme by attracting more listeners.

The factors we describe below are the basic requirements for the success of any radio programme. But we also need to study programme content in order to determine what the programme consists of and what the potential and limitations of that programme are. Despite all the success factors mentioned here, programme producers must not forget their listeners. The basic criterion for a successful radio programme is whether that programme can attract and retain the listeners' attention; as producers, we must know what our listeners want to hear.

13.9.1 Economy

What is omitted from a programme is just as important as what is retained. Every element retained in a programme must fulfil a purpose. Radio programmes require long-term success, not short-term popularity. Listeners will quickly tire of a programme if certain elements, such as novelty, are overplayed. The watchword here is understatement.

13.9.2 Graciousness

A gracious programme will give listeners the impression that they could have presented that programme themselves. Graciousness is achieved by thorough preparation and skill in compiling, and presentation and technical finish which results in a smooth flowing combination of the various sound sources that make up the programme.

13.9.3 Novelty

Good programme material arises from what is new and fresh, on one hand, and surprise and escape from the over-familiar, on the other. But, at the same time, listeners like the security brought about by use of the conventional. Thus there is a need for novelty to be balanced with the familiar. This is closely related to the two basic principles of programming – consistency and variety. Novelty can also be obtained through the use of jingles and stings to identify the radio station and the specific programme.

13.9.4 The human touch

People are interested in their own doings and those of others. This interest is often reflected in personal, homely comments made on-air by announcers. However, there is a thin line between what can be considered as innocent and that which is flippant and offensive to the listener.

13.9.5 Humour

Most people enjoy laughing – but not at the expense of others or at something in poor taste. Humour relieves everyday tensions because it is possible to laugh at virtually any situation that crops up in daily life, provided that situation is presented with due

12.5 PRODUCTION PERSONNEL: WHO DOES WHAT

Production personnel refers to the people that work in television production and what roles they have in production. Television and video production involve teamwork where people work together and fulfil certain roles. Here we present an overview associated with big televison productions. However, many of the roles discussed below will be scaled down, combined, or eliminated in smaller productions.

- The person that is generally in charge of the entire production is the *producer*. He or she comes up with the programme concept, lays out the budget for the production and makes the major decisions. This person is the team leader; the person who works with the writers, decides on the key talent, hires the director, and guides the general direction of the production.
- In a large production, the producer will be responsible for hiring a *director*. This is the person in charge of working out production details; coordinating the activities of the production staff and on-camera talent; working out positions of camera and talent or actors and presenters on the set; selecting the camera shots during the production; and supervising postproduction work. In other words, the director is the frontline commander in charge of taking the script to the very end of the production process. In small productions, the director may also handle the producer's responsibilities. In this case the combined job title becomes a *producer-director*. Some productions may also have an *associate producer* who, in general, assists the producer throughout the production.
- On a large production, one of the producer's first jobs is to hire a *scriptwriter* to write a script. The script is like a written plan or blueprint for the production.
- The *talent* includes actors, reporters, hosts, guests, and off-camera narrators – anyone whose voice is heard or who appears on camera. Sometimes "talent" is broken down into three sub-categories: *actors* who portray other people in dramatic productions; *performers* who appear on camera in non-dramatic roles; and *announcers* who do not appear on camera.
- Assisting a director in the control room is typically a *technical director* who operates the video switcher. The technical director is also responsible for coordinating the technical aspects of the production.
- One or more *production assistants* may be hired to help the producer and director. During rehearsals these people keep notes on production needs and changes, notify the personnel involved about changes, and so forth.
- The *lighting director* designs the lighting plan, arranges for the lighting equipment needed, and sets up and checks the lighting.
- On some productions there will be a *set designer* who, along with the producer and director, will design the set and supervise its construction, painting and installation.
- There may be a *make-up person* who, with the aid of cosmetics and hair-spray, will ensure that the talent look their best.
- Major productions will have a *wardrobe person* who is responsible for seeing that the talent all have clothes that are appropriate to the story and script.

decorum. Different listeners prefer different types of humour and these differences provide an inexhaustible source of inspiration for programme material.

13.9.6 Participation

A programme that involves its listeners is practically assured of success. Participation may vary from singing along with a song that is being broadcast, phoning in to a competition or listening to a commentary on a cricket match. The more interaction there is between the station and the listener, the better the chances of success for the programme. There are a number of additional aspects that invite audience participation. For example, a package tour organised by the radio station is promoted during the programme and events coming up during the next programme or later in the day or during the course of the week, are highlighted. Telephone and fax numbers or e-mail addresses are given over the air so that listeners may respond to what they have heard.

13.9.7 Expectations

Anticipation is built up by giving listeners an advance indication of what is coming up and then delaying that moment. After a while the listener becomes eager to hear an interview with, for example, a popular recording artist, which has been announced repeatedly. At the beginning of a programme the announcer should provide a brief résumé of the contents of the programme.

13.9.8 Expressive speech

The first principle of writing for radio is that the text is intended for the ear. The written word can be read over and over again until the reader is sure of the meaning. But the spoken word is fleeting and therefore must be clear and unambiguous. Also, poor speaking habits are guaranteed to turn listeners away. But, on the other hand, formal speech can be inappropriate to certain radio formats, such as CHR, where a more colloquial approach will win favour with the audience. Formal speech is more suited to reading news and formal announcements.

13.9.9 Personality

Radio is a direct, intimate, personal, individual orientated medium and therefore an informal, friendly presentation is sure to be effective. The principle that the radio speaker is a guest in the listener's home (or car) must be observed at all times. A deep (in the case of male announcers), well-modulated voice is no longer a guarantee of success. Today's listeners are more interested in *what* is said than in *how* it is said, provided that the voice is pleasant to listen to and the speaker has prepared what is being said. At all times, the announcer should sound as if she or he is in a conversation with the individual listener, rather than merely reading from a script.

13.9.10 Music

Music is a dominant factor in radio programming since recorded music is inexpensive to broadcast and is popular with most listeners. Music can be very personal and evoke many different emotions. There is a correlation between a listener's musical taste and education level, experience, personality, social position, and so on. The type of music played by a radio station will determine the number and quantity of listeners. For example, pop music tends to draw a large teenage audience, while the audience for classical music tends to be, by comparison, far more mature, but also much smaller in size requiring niche marketing. However, lovers of classical music can be as passionate, if not more so, as any teenager is about his or her music genre.

13.9.11 News

Very few people can say that they have no interest in the latest news. It for this reason that the inclusion of a news bulletin in a programme is considered essential. A glance at any market research will show that news usually attracts far more listeners than any other programme. News is given as the most frequent reason why people turn on their radio.

13.9.12 Celebrities

Many successful radio stations use celebrities as an attraction. Advertisers tend to feel that their products will receive better publicity if endorsed by someone with whom the listeners can identify, rather than by, for example, an ordinary announcer. We also need to bear in mind that some announcers have achieved minor celebrity status of their own and will attract attention when making personal appearances.

13.9.13 Promotion

We can identify two types of radio promotion:

- *Listener promotion*, which takes place on the air to encourage listener participation.
- *Sales promotion*, which makes use of other media to promote the radio station.

The radio station needs to sell itself in much the same way as any consumer product. The station needs a full-time promotions team to attract new listeners as well as to satisfy the interests of existing listeners, for example by advertising in the press and on television in addition to handing out bumper stickers, t-shirts and providing photographs of radio personalities. Many stations promote themselves by arranging outside broadcasts, either at shopping malls or agricultural shows. On-air promotions include aspects such as competitions in addition to the jingles used to identify the station. There is also sales promotion aimed at advertising agencies to persuade their clients to buy advertising time on the station. An important aspect to keep in mind when canvassing advertising agencies is the ratings of the station. The better the ratings, the more likely advertisers will want to buy air-time as this means more people are listening to that station. However, we must not forget that the image of any radio station is also largely determined by the quality of its programmes and word-of-mouth recommendations, and not just a slick advertising campaign.

13.10 THE IMPORTANCE OF THE AUDIENCE IN DETERMINING FORMAT

Despite it being considered ideal, formats do not remain constant. Apart from variations during the day (see *scheduling* in section 13.6.1 and *dayparts* in section 13.6.2), formats also evolve over a period of time. Competition from other stations, and sometimes from other media, acts as a catalyst for a change in format. But any overnight change to the format is considered a desperate move with dramatic consequences. Sudden change is usually strongly resisted by listeners who often show their displeasure to the change by tuning to other stations in large numbers. A number of factors can necessitate a change in format, for example listeners' tastes are constantly changing, there may be less competition in an alternate format, or an alternative market has greater economic potential.

Most radio stations in South Africa, irrespective of their licence type, rely on the sale of advertising time to provide their income. To achieve this, the radio station then effectively markets its audience as a commodity to the advertisers in terms of certain measurable criteria, such as age, income, lifestyle, taste, and so forth. The price the radio station charges the advertiser is based on a formula which takes into account the time of day and the size of the audience, scientifically determined by market research and rating. The general rule is, the greater the number of listeners, the more the radio station can charge potential advertisers. Conversely, should listeners, for some reason, stop listening to the radio station, the amount the radio station can charge potential advertisers will drop. At the same time, advertisers are keen to reach as large an audience at any one time as they possibly can.

Economics is a key factor in sustaining a radio station. As more radio stations come on the air in South Africa, so audiences are beginning to fragment with the result that existing stations are finding it increasingly difficult to keep audience statistics high. The audience is therefore the crucial factor within the broadcasting environment that determines the viability of any radio station. Each radio station needs to make every attempt to draw as large an audience as possible from the upper income groups as it is this group of listeners that is most attractive to advertisers. And people will only listen to the radio if they enjoy or find some need for the programmes. Ultimately it is the format of the station that makes listeners remain tuned-in, and therefore the station should give their core-listeners (i.e. those in the upper-income groups) what they want to hear (Hannan 1997:40). This symbiosis between audience numbers, advertising revenue and programme format is best explained by means of a practical example, such as that given in Case study 13.1. Note also the implementation of many of the success factors we discussed above in section 13.9.

Case study 13.1: The impact of competition on format – the case of Radio 702 and 5FM

Radio 702 came on the air during June 1980 as Channel 702, promoting itself as the *Rainbow of Sound*. This original marketing concept was based on the premise that apartheid would not be enduring and that the various markets would soon integrate. While this strategy proved highly successful from the very beginning, the policy was way ahead of its time and the main focus remained on white youth in the 16-24 age group. Radio 702 made use of a slick contemporary rock format to which they added the pulling power of on-air personalities such as John Berks. From the beginning, Radio 702 encouraged audience participation and allowed listeners to express their views; a tactic not obvious on SABC radio stations of the time. Serious competition remained negligible, which meant that Radio 702 very quickly took the market share and dominated broadcasting in the Gauteng area for the next five years. However, the lack of competition led to complacency and the station started to lose its focus. And with this came a drop in listener numbers.

Also competing for teenage audiences was Radio 5, originally acquired by the SABC in the early 1970s from the Radio Club of Mozambique, following the independence of that country, where the station was known as LM Radio. By early 1985 Radio 5 had acquired a Cinderella status within the hierarchy of the SABC and was considered to have a limited future. In addition, the station was losing its audience to Radio 702, with the result that advertisers were taking their adspend (the amount of money advertisers are prepared to spend on advertising) elsewhere. To ensure the survival of the station, something had to be done to boost audience numbers. The winning format of Radio 702 was copied and quickly gained Radio 5 an increase in listeners. Programme content was improved and community involvement introduced. The concept of star status for announcers and deejays, always considered anathema at the SABC, was changed when Radio 5 enticed Radio 702 talent, such as Alex Jay and Martin Bailie, by offering them huge salaries. This strategy represented a complete break from convention at the SABC. The star status of the deejays was further enhanced by national exposure on television – a ploy denied to the personalities of Radio 702. Presenters on any of the independent radio stations were forbidden, under SABC policy of the time, to appear in any programme or advertisement screened on SABC-TV.

The consolidation and rationalisation of SABC radio stations during 1985 and 1986 was to benefit Radio 5. The closure of Springbok Radio meant that its FM frequencies were now available. On 1 September 1986 Radio 5 made a strategic move from medium wave to FM, changing its name in the process to 5FM. When programming consists largely of music, the use of FM becomes very important as the quality of the music heard improves dramatically over that on medium wave. A further enhancement for 5FM came with the phasing in of stereo broadcasts, beginning 31 August 1988 in the Gauteng area and reaching national coverage by 1 December 1988. This technological development paid handsome dividends in the form of a substantial increase in listeners (see Figure 13.6 which shows listenership figures for Radio 702 and 5FM).

A similar move was out of the question for Radio 702. For political reasons at the time, Radio 702 was required to broadcast from the so-called independent homeland of Bophuthatswana. In order to reach its target area, Radio 702 had little choice but to make use of a medium wave frequency. While FM offers superior sound quality, the signal has a limited geographic coverage (at the most about 60 kilometres) when compared to medium wave signals (which can cover up to 400 kilometres during the daytime and considerably further at night).

By 1986 Radio 702 was losing listeners – change was vital for the station to survive. This led to the first of several major changes over the next few years. The name was changed from Channel 702 to Radio 702 and the *Rainbow of Sound* image was dropped for that of *702Land.* This unique marketing concept would ultimately generate a close association with an already loyal audience. But it was felt that the involvement of the audience needed to become more physical and tangible. To this end, sponsorship of a crisis centre and various help lines were introduced.

The increased listenership which resulted from the head-on-head competition between Radio 702 and 5FM in the Gauteng area resulted in a marked increase in

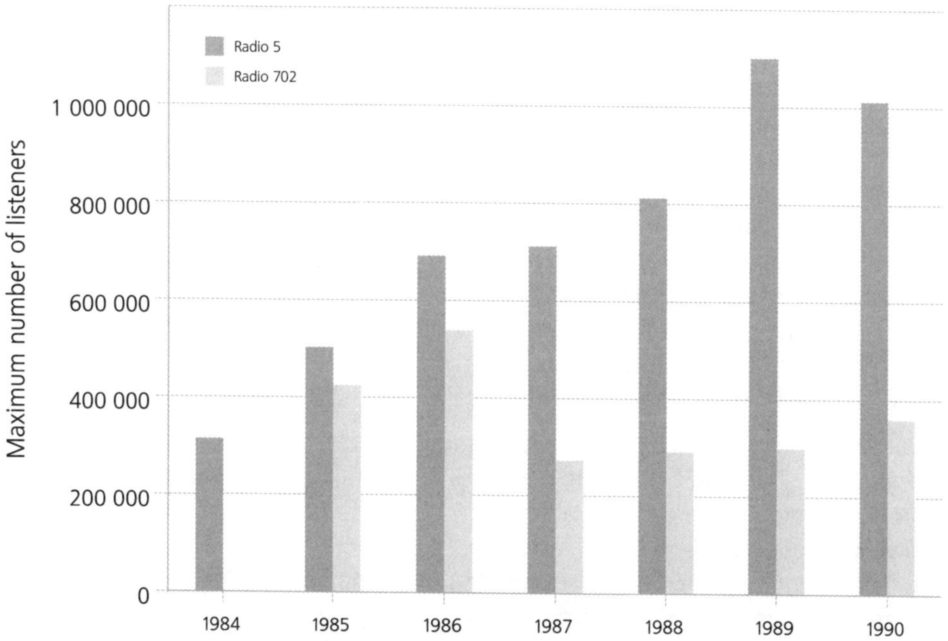

Figure 13.6 Changes in maximum listener figures for Radio 702 and 5FM for the period 1984–1990

adspend from R14 million in 1986 to R26 million in 1987. Revenue earned from advertising on 5FM doubled from R6 million in 1986 to the same amount within the first six months of 1987. By 1988, 5FM made more money in one month that any other radio station in the history of the SABC. Radio 702, on the other hand, hardly showed any increase in advertising revenue over the same period. 5FM, which by 1985 had lost half of its listeners to Radio 702, showed a staggering 300% increase in listenership by 1988. The station gained the majority share of the 16–24 age market, scooping 22% of the total Gauteng radio audience, where seven stations were competing for listeners.

By July 1988, after two further years of lacklustre audience statistics, Radio 702 felt another major change had become necessary. It was proving particularly difficult to compete against 5FM. Despite extensive promotional and marketing efforts, the odds were always in the favour of 5FM – it broadcast nationally on FM in stereo. It was clearly obvious that to continue head-on-head competition with 5FM would, in the end, be self-defeating. The only solution lay in targeting a different audience and that required a complete revision of Radio 702's current format.

Thus, in June 1988 Radio 702 was re-launched as a full-service adult radio station, with the focus now on the 25–49 year-old age group as opposed to the 16–24 year-old age group. An emphasis was placed on information, which is considered important to this particular age group. This resulted in more talk and less music. The shift in target audience also meant a change in the type of music played, with a concentration on the hits of the sixties; music familiar to the target audience when they were teenagers. This format change had a positive spin-off for the advertising industry, as the change in target audience would mean a change in the advertising line-up. Radio 702 was now seen as once again having growth potential in the Gauteng area.

An 18% increase in listeners during 1988 confirmed the success of the format change. The 50-year-old plus audience doubled while the 16–24 year-old audience remained unchanged initially, and then began to decline. The drive by Radio 702 for adult listeners required further adjustments to the format. On 5 June 1989, Radio 702 increased the content of news and comment to reinforce the inroads the station had made into the upper-income adult market. Commenting on the change, Stan Katz, then general manager of the station, said:

> Our move last year (1988) into the adult market has once again been vindicated. The adult listeners we seek have taken with relish to our programming and we are now able to offer our advertisers more purchasing power per adspend rand than ever before.
>
> We're not a kiddies' radio station and we're not competing with slam-bang rock 'n' roll. We're here to entertain and inform, not pound into oblivion with the bass drum.
>
> (Gray 1989:10)

On the change in format, Katz later added that:

> Our adjusted programme format has been enormously successful ... We see ourselves as a force which brings listener and advertiser together. 702 constantly delivers fresh prospects to both, through innovative ways of marketing its airtime. We continually assess ways in which to improve our service to the advertiser.
>
> We believe that market forces should dictate the programme format. Success depends on how you interpret the needs and demands of the market.
>
> (And now we are ten ... 1990:53)

While the marketing of a radio station is not any different from that of any other product or service, the image (or brand character) is made up of all the different impressions received by the listener. Radio 702 was now in competition with Radio South Africa (now SAfm), Highveld Stereo and Jacaranda Stereo. The new music format appealed to the more mature audience and included what could not be heard elsewhere. Since shedding its youth image and becoming talk orientated, the question of using MW frequencies ceased to be a problem and the revised format steadily attracted listeners. The successful repositioning of Radio 702 from a popular music format to an all-talk format, was a lengthy process. The amount of talk was gradually increased over a period of several years. This meant Radio 702 lost their traditional youthful audience, but gained an upper-income adult audience. The key deciding factor that facilitated the change in format was Radio 702's inability to compete with 5FM once the latter began broadcasting on FM.

13.11 THE COMMUNITY RADIO STATION

13.11.1 What is community radio?

Community radio, being of neither a public service nor commercial nature, makes up the third tier of the traditional broadcasting triad. Yet it is difficult to provide an exact definition of community radio, because there are so many variations that we can find in the model. Moving from country to country, it is possible to find a vast range of differences, dependent on how community radio is integrated into a nation's broadcasting environment. The concept is also known by a variety of terms, such as local radio in Britain, *radio priveé* in France, *radio libre* in Belgium, *nærradio* (or near radio) in Scandinavia, *radio di informazione* in Italy, *lokalradio* in Switzerland, *emisora municipale* (municipal radio) in Spain and until recently, public radio in Australia (Kleinsteuber & Sonnenberg 1990:92; Thompson 1999:23). Despite the differences, we can still identify some common elements. Two key elements are the reduced scale, or local nature of operation, where the listeners are actively involved in the broadcasting process.

But merely localising radio does not make the medium any different from that of commercial and public broadcasting. A reduction in scale does not automatically make a radio station community orientated. That radio is presented on a local level does not imply it is an alternative to commercial and public broadcasting. A local radio station can be purely commercial in operation. However, being local in scale does present radio with a certain potential through the reduction of distance between broadcasters and listeners. The level of local recognition in programme content can be increased whereby issues relevant to the community, such as unemployment, levels of crime, and the environment, are discussed (Drijvers 1992:197). Localisation can bring about a demassification of radio, but only if there is an active integration with the community in which the station operates. The operation of the station must contribute to the development of the community in terms of favourable social change, the purpose being to serve the interests and aspirations of the community by helping the community to "diagnose their problems and clarify their objectives so that they may be able to make wiser decisions" (Libiero 1993:218). Only when these criteria are successfully fulfilled can a radio station style itself as community radio. The major differences between the mainstream media, which is made up of commercial and public broadcasting, and community radio are set out in Table 13.1.

Table 13.1 The differences between mainstream broadcasting and community radio (adapted from Bhatia 1992:51)

Mainstream broadcasting	Community radio
• Programme content determined by producers and experts	• Programme content based on formative research and audience needs
• Broadcasters work independently in producing a programme	• Programmes produced by a team involving experts, broadcasters and the community
• One directional – top down	• Two directional
• Broadcasting to a general audience	• Narrowcasting to a specific audience
• Programme content is general with a wide scope	• Programme content has specific outcomes
• Information and entertainment orientated	• Participatory and action orientated
• Programme topics sequencing ad hoc	• Serial approach with continuity of topics
• Sporadic evaluation	• Continuous evaluation

13.11.2 Common characteristics of community radio

The broad concept of community radio evidences a number of common characteristics. We briefly look at some of these, keeping in mind there are many variations to be found.

- *Relationship with political authorities.* There is a need for both passive and active involvement. Local and national governments need to exercise restraint from political interference, but because of the economic vulnerability of community radio, certain protective measures need to be put into place (Drijvers 1992:199). In other words, community stations need to be guaranteed autonomy as part of national broadcasting policy.
- *Licences.* The community station operates with a licence issued by a regulatory authority. In South Africa, this is the Independent Communications Authority of South Africa (ICASA) who issue two types of community licence. One is a for a four-year term, the other is a short-term licence for a maximum of thirty days to cover special events such as Deepavali or the Grahamstown National Arts Festival (Independent Broadcasting Authority 1999:15).
- *Finance.* While community stations can get financial support from a variety of sources, the key is that they are non-profit entities. This means that any profit the station makes cannot be distributed amongst owners, employees or shareholders, but has to be returned to the community in some or other way. Fundraising is an important issue to the continued wellbeing of a community radio station. In South Africa, community stations can generate income through the sale of advertising time on air, but this is barred in some countries like Switzerland, Sweden and Finland (Kleinsteuber & Sonnenberg 1990:101). Even so, many community stations find it difficult to attract advertisers as the audiences are often considered as unsuitable markets because of their low income. It is also a major challenge to attract potential advertisers without compromising the purpose of community broadcasting. The audience maximising techniques of commercial radio are not always readily compatible with the concept of community radio (Thompson 1999:26). Other ways of obtaining finance are through grants and donations. Most community radio stations operate on shoestring budgets, particularly those in developing environments. This means that if the economy moves into a downturn, the station can easily be plunged into a financial crisis as there will be fewer donations and adspend is usually cut back dramatically. This could result in the closure of the station (Halper 1991a:53). The viability of a community radio station is then closely linked to the issue of autonomy, where we need to ask if a particular community is in a position to support a radio station (Libiero 1993:222).
- *Coverage.* The power of the transmitters is usually very low, which means that the signals can only be heard within a reasonably small geographic area.
- *Access and participation.* The station is open to the community with varying degrees of control. Full involvement of the community is essential in planning, producing and evaluating programmes. This ensures that programme content is relevant to

community needs and increases awareness, understanding and possibilities for change to occur (Fisher 1990:23). Participation gives people a sense of belonging, importance and achievement. Listeners must feel they are an important part of the process (Libiero 1993:219).

- *Staff.* There are usually only a few paid staff members, the majority of workers being volunteers from the community. Kleinsteuber and Sonnenberg (1990:101) write that the logic behind this is that radio provides such "fun and fulfilment that people are highly motivated to produce radio without any financial compensation". Paid staff is usually limited to those in management and technology with no programming responsibilities. However, that volunteer staff is used does not mean that a community radio station can get away with amateurish and shoddy programming. Volunteer staff needs to be adequately trained in order to present quality programmes. There are seldom clear-cut roles for staff in a community radio, and it is possible that job descriptions need to be extended to cover various roles. For example, announcers are expected to cover and report on community meetings when a journalist is unable to do so. Interaction between the staff and the community is also essential. Interest and participation by the community is directly related to the degree by which staff identifies with the audience (Fisher 1990:23).
- *Research.* Formative evaluation is necessary to determine the needs, interests and potential of the community. Continuing research is essential to keep programme content effective and relevant to the community. Stations that cannot afford to pay for the services of a professional market research company can easily design a questionnaire of their own and make use of local students to survey the community. But, says Halper (1991a:63), the easiest way to gather information is simply to talk to the community on an individual basis and ask them what their interests are and what they like and want.
- *Local content.* The nature of community radio is such that local content should be considerably higher than in any other type of radio, as the topics included in the programmes are determined by issues relevant to the community (Kleinsteuber & Sonnenberg 1990:103). In South African, the music selected for programmes is subject to ICASA regulations, where a minimum of twenty percent local content is required between the hours of 05:00 and 23:00 daily. As seen from Figure 13.7 most community stations comply with this requirement. Afrikaans and African language community stations tend to show higher percentages of local content where music by local artists reflects community interests, such as kwaito, mbaqanga and choral music.

13.11.3 The role of community radio

Within a developing environment, community radio has the potential to bring about *social change* and *conflict resolution*, and is seen as an essential element in the process of democratisation. It represents an affordable way of reaching large numbers of

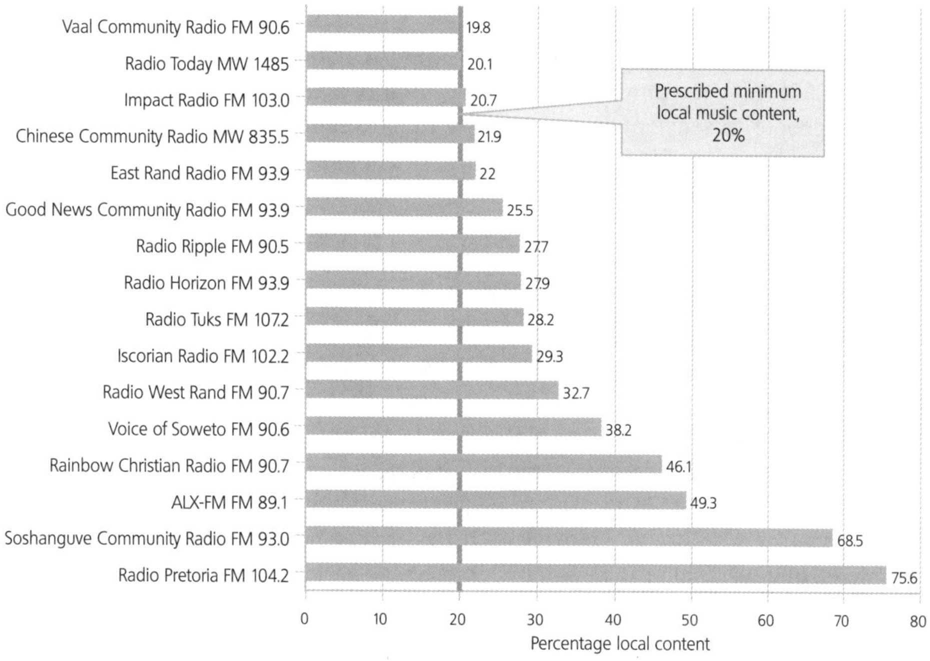

Figure 13.7 Percentage of local music content for selected community radio stations operating in the Gauteng area for the period 1999–2000
(Independent Communications Authority of South Africa 2000:51–52)

illiterate or semi-literate people. However, in developed environments, community radio fulfils the specific needs of groups by providing a means of *self-expression* not available through the mainstream media. In environments with autocratic or dictatorial governments, community radio becomes a tool for resistance by offering a voice for the opposition. These three particular positions embody certain common principles, such as the right to participation and management of communication in which a group can reproduce their cultural identity. Community radio is then seen, in broad terms, as part of the struggle to access the media (Radio Netherlands [sa]). The types of communities that can benefit from a community radio station include (Community Radio Association 1987:6):

- ethnic minorities, often the most disadvantaged and discriminated against groups in society, such as the Chinese, Greek, Portuguese and Italian communities of South Africa;
- geographic communities in rural areas, often seriously under-served by the media;
- urban groups under-represented by existing services, such as women, gays, the disabled, senior citizens, the youth, and so on;
- special interest groups such as those focusing on high arts.

13.11.4 The concept "community"

At this point we need to pause briefly to consider the concept "community". Lewis and Booth (1989:90) refer to community "as something of a weasel word used to mean all things to all people". A sense of community is a form of solidarity generated by historical contexts. A war, for example, generates a sense of community, where a common enemy tends to bind various divisions within a society. Lewis and Booth (1989:91) sum up the concept in the simple terms of insider versus the outsider where a sense of belonging derives from the principal aims of the group rather than from geographic nearness. However, the concept has become anchored in the notion of locality. This artificial association came about through the work of British sociologists, whose post World War II studies were geographically restricted, the result of which the concept "community" became associated with locality despite the fact that these studies revealed clear divisions within identified groups. Outside of sociological circles, this distinction between locality and a sense of community has gone largely unquestioned (Lewis & Booth 1989:91–92). In the South African context, the concept "community" is politically loaded; being traditionally associated with the so-called historically disadvantaged communities who were subject to forced removals as part of the separate development policies of Apartheid. The emphasis on locality within this situation has strengthened the connotative link between community and place – community radio is seen as a liberating mechanism and part of the process of democratisation of such historically disadvantaged communities. However, it is a false assumption to say that because a group of people is defined in terms of specific social boundaries, that they share common interests (Stevens [sa]). We also need to remember that within the framework of this discussion, we can find clear examples of developed and developing communities in South Africa.

13.11.5 Types of community radio

Because of the distinction between locality and interest in the concept "community", we find two types of community radio in the South African broadcasting environment. These are (Open Society Foundation 1999; Independent Broadcasting Authority 1999: 31–32; Independent Communications Authority of South African 2000:43):

- Stations serving a geographic community, for example Radio Winterveld in North-West Province.
- Stations serving a community of interests, where we can further distinguish three sub-sections, namely:
  - Institutional communities, such as universities (as evidenced by campus radio, such as Radio Turf from the University of the North) and large organisations such as Iscorian Radio for the employees of Iscor in the Vaal Triangle.
  - Religious communities such as Radio Kingfisher for Christian listeners in the Eastern Cape and Radio Islam for Muslim listeners in Gauteng.
  - Cultural communities such as Radio Today for senior citizens and Comunidade Portuguesa for the Portuguese community living in Gauteng. This category would

also include a radio station like Fine Music Radio of Cape Town, which broadcasts classical music and jazz.

13.11.6 Serving the community

For a community radio station to serve its designated community, the station must have a high visibility in that community. Visibility is determined by means of the effective use of the three Ps, namely:

- programming
- personality
- promotion.

These three elements do not operate in isolation, but are fully integrated with each other. The one is dependent on the other in order to function efficiently in making the station visible in the community. This makes it rather difficult for us to separate them out, even artificially, so that we can discuss them. Should one, or more, of these elements be absent, then the visibility of the station in the community is diminished accordingly. We discuss each element in turn.

Programming

What types of programmes should be broadcast on community radio? The answer to this question depends on several factors, such as how long the station is on the air each day, but is largely determined by the community served by the station. A radio station serving a community of interests can adopt a more homogeneous approach to its programming, as the listeners are a far more cohesive group by virtue of their common interests. Therefore, programming can follow a more formatted approach and need not be diverse. For example, a campus radio station would schedule music genres popular with students throughout their programmes, using a CHR format. From this point of view, we need to question whether a service like a campus radio station qualifies for status as a community service (Stevens [sa]). This also implies that local content quotas are likely to be lower than for radio stations serving a geographic community (see Figure 13.7). Complying with local music requirements is problematic for certain radio stations such as New PanHellenic Voice for the Greek community in Johannesburg and Chinese Community Radio for the Chinese community in Gauteng. There is very little or no South African music that is relevant to these communities (Independent Communications Authority of South Africa 2000:27).

But to serve a geographic community adequately, the radio station needs to have a clear understanding of the social stratification of the community that it serves. Stations serving a geographic community need to cater for all the various interest groups and members of the designated community, from the children to the elderly (Ibrahim 1999:15). Apart from age differences, local communities are also made up of different social classes, ethnic and religious groups, each of which needs access to the radio station. "Being 'local' does not of it own accord dispel the mythical notions of the public that are so common among public service broadcasters" (Drijvers 1992:199). To provide coverage of important issues for a diverse community requires diverse programming. This in turn requires that the station be innovative and provide programming different from that available on commercial and public radio stations. Unlike public service broadcasters, who are under constant pressure of market forces to compete with commercial radio stations, the community broadcaster does not have to contend with the threat of ratings that results in the tight programming structures we discussed in section 13.6.

The best programming option that provides for variety and diversity must surely be that of a full-spectrum service. In this way a community radio station can offer news, sport, talk, religion, health, education and music to the community. An example of just how diverse full-spectrum programming can be is illustrated in Table 13.2 where the programme schedule of Radio Zibonele is given. In this programme schedule, we can see that Radio Zibonele adequately covers the information, education and entertainment functions of radio, and in so doing provides for the diverse needs of the community in which it operates. In offering a full-spectrum service, the diverse elements are held together by a strong local focus "and the commitment to being a lot more to the community than just a jukebox" (Halper 1991a:39). Worthwhile programming comes from knowing exactly what is important for members of the community, while a willingness on the part of the station to reach out to individuals in the community makes community radio so different (Halper 1991a:57).

A full-spectrum service can succeed in a market of any size, but needs time and patience to become established in the community. Simply because a community has the privilege of having a community radio station does not automatically engender loyalty to that station. Even for a community station, an audience is not an automatic given. Stations need to win over their audience slowly. It is also a well-established fact in broadcasting that listeners are resistant to change, and this is particularly more so with a mature audience (Halper 1991a:42). Listeners only become loyal listeners if they perceive the station as being credible and this requires the station to create and maintain a favourable impression, over a period of time, in the community. From research into reasons why people listen to the radio, we can divide the audience for full-spectrum programming into four broad groups (Halper 1991a:60, 62).

- The *information seekers* are the most serious of the four groups, as they listen to the radio in order to be stimulated and to learn. They look for in-depth coverage of events in their community from news and phone-in programmes and are not particularly interested in hearing much music. This group makes up about 33 percent of all listeners.
- The *involved music fans* love everything about radio. They enjoy the companionship provided by radio, particularly the variety offered by a full-spectrum service, such as the contests, sports, phone-in programmes and music. This group makes us about 31 percent of all listeners.

Table 13.2 Programme schedules for Radio Zibonele, community stations broadcasting to the community of Khayelitsha in Cape Town (Open Society Foundation 1999)

Weekdays		Saturday	
05h00–08h00	*Itshayile*, Let's go to work	05h00–07h00	*Sivuka kunye*, We wake together
		07h00–08h00	*Abantwana*, Children's programme
08h00–09h00	*Abantwana*, Children's programme	08h00–09h00	*Amagqabantshintshi*, Sports update
09h00–09h15	*Inkonzo*, Devotion	09h00–09h15	*Inkonzo*, Devotion
09h15–10h15	*Impilo*, Health	09h15–10h15	*Impilo*, Health
10h15–12h00	*Oomama*, Women's programme	10h15–11h15	Coca-Cola Full Blast
		11h15–12h00	*Amakhosikazi*, Women's programme
12h00–14h00	*Celingoma*, Request programme	12h00–13h00	*Isingqi sasekhaya*, African beat
		13h00–15h00	*Ezoluntu*, Cultural programme Older people talk show
14h00–16h00	*Indalo*, Environment	15h00–16h00	*Izaziso*, Announcements
16h00–17h00	*Ikhondo Iwam*, Careers	16h00–18h00	*Ulutsha*, Youth
17h00–18h00	*Impilo yakho*, Your health		
18h00–19h00	*Indaba/Imidlalo*, News/Sport	18h00–19h00	*Indaba/Imidlalo*, News/Sport
19h00–21h00	*Abahlali*, Community affairs	19h00–20h00	*Siyabafisa*, Birthdays
		20h00–21h00	*Ezangaphandle*, International Top 20
21h00–00h00	*Imfundo*, Education talk show	21h00–00h00	*Ulonwabo*, Party Time

- The *sports fans* seek mainly entertainment and companionship, but with lots of sport, some music and minimal news. This group makes up about 26 percent of all listeners.
- The *habit-bound tuned-outs* are the least involved, listening superficially. They are not interested in lengthy discussions, being of the opinion that announcers talk too much. They want their information to be supplied as briefly as possible with lots of music and few, if any, feature programmes. This group makes up about 10 percent of all listeners.

Of course, this grouping of listeners to a full-spectrum service represents a generalisation. Much of the format of any community station depends on being topical and knowing what matters to their specific audience (Halper 1991a:63). By knowing the audience, the station can adjust its style and programme mix; being more in-depth at times and having a faster pace at others.

While having a strong signal and using the local vernacular helps, nothing can save a community radio station if it is out of touch with its community. This includes knowing what is socially acceptable in order to determine what topics can and cannot be included in programmes. Tackling taboo subjects head-on, as some of the more revolutionary commercial radio stations are inclined to do, can result in a rejection of the station by the community. This means that efforts must be made to avoid using questionable language or shock-jock (disc jockey that uses foul language and discusses offensive topics on air) techniques. As the community station needs to offer a wide variety of programming, the image of the station should reflect a family orientation in its content. At the same time, the station must promise "to keep the listeners informed, but it doesn't shout at the audience or insult its intelligence" (Halper 1991a:42). From Rosario-Baird's (1989:68–69) advantages of community radio we can establish five criteria that should be found in the programmes broadcast by community radio stations. The programmes should:

- have strong indigenous links;
- contain content that is non-commercial and local in flavour;
- have content with little, if any, colonial influences;
- make appropriate use of indigenous material and resources; and
- depict the community's actual reality.

Although community radio differs from commercial and public radio in purpose and organisation, the two principles of radio production that we discussed in section 13.4, that is consistency and variety, apply. The programming structure needs to be fluid so that it can meet the changing needs of the community. At the same time, the station needs to avoid making dramatic changes to programming.

Personality

Despite offering quality programming, the announcers contribute significantly to the radio station's image in the community through their personality. Although offering news, sports and community service may make the station popular, the announcers provide for the station's uniqueness. Their style needs to be warm and friendly without the high-paced and rapid style associated with CHR. The tempo needs to be conversational, treating the listener as a close friend. It is important that announcers and journalists know the community and also be known by the community. In this way staff of the station can keep up with local events and issues and be able to discuss them. This approach needs a long-term commitment on the part of announcers who need to show an honest respect for the audience, irrespective of whom they are. This means the announcers must be capable of more than playing music. Not only do they need to be actively involved in the community, but ideally they should also be members of the community; then the staff should have a feel for the aspirations and problems of the community (Libiero 1993:219). Becoming a successful announcer on a community radio station takes time and is a lot of hard work (Halper 1991a:85).

Promotion

Let us now turn to the value of promotion in maintaining a high visibility of a radio station in the community. Promotion of a community station is not limited to just what is broadcast by the station, but must include getting out in to the community. In addition to the aspects we discussed in section 13.9.13, the purpose of promotion in a community radio station is to create the impression that the station is everywhere in the community. Promotion is more that a matter of offering large and valuable prizes for competitions and having the station's logo and slogan plastered on billboards. The station needs to use promotions to create a high profile image that ultimately leads to, and maintains, the station's credibility and reliability in the community. This requires on-going public contact. Even stations with limited promotional budgets can enhance their image simply by being physically seen in the community, such as having staff attend council meetings, school debates, sports meetings, bazaars, church socials and services. In this way the station staff makes friends with people in the community (Halper 1991a:75). However, each community station needs to establish its own unique way of serving its listeners. This can be as simple as announcers handing out cups of coffee to early morning commuters at a local bus stop, and sponsoring concerts and sporting events. Such activities lead to a high visibility of the station within the community.

Running competitions and offering prizes to listeners is generally regarded as a way of promoting the station. Since most community radio stations operate on limited budgets, this could be problematic. This is not necessarily so, says Halper (1991a:77). Large and expensive prizes, such as overseas holidays, cars and jewellery are not what every listener wants to win. It is better to offer a number of smaller, but worthwhile prizes than an occasional big prize. Is this way, more listeners can participate. Prizes should relate to listeners' lifestyles with the intention of making their lives easier, such as a week's supply of groceries, a course of sewing lessons, or can even be as simple as tickets to local sporting events or concerts.

13.11.7 Some problems experienced in community radio

To conclude this section on community radio we need to look at some of the factors that can impede the effectiveness of community radio. Drijvers (1992:199–200) warns of the dangers of becoming too parochial. Zaïre, for example, requires a one hundred percent local content. Community radios need to urge their listeners to look beyond the local in order to avoid provincialism and ethnocentrism. An outward orientation to programme content encourages listeners to feel part of a larger culture and polity, which, says Drijvers (ibid), is essential for establishing any notion of citizenship or national identity.

Except possibly for rural areas, community radio has to function in areas where other media can also be found. As a result of the choices offered, a community station cannot risk giving its listeners bad radio. Because community radio operates on a small scale, it does not imply that the service has to be unprofessional. This extends beyond programming to include aspects as simple as how station staff and announcers dress when seen in public, and whether the building housing the station is clean, neat and pleasant looking (Halper 1991a:69). Community radio is all about making people in the community feel good and making the listener feel important. In this context, community radio stations become competitors to the mainstream commercial and public broadcasters, particularly in developed areas where there is stiff competition for a marketable audience. This could pressure a community service operating in such an environment to copy the formats used by commercial radio. It is very easy for a community station to slide into a commercially driven format, becoming nothing more than a jukebox (Ibrahim1999:15) where the station is local in distribution, but not in form nor in content. Playing hit records is simply not enough to generate community involvement. It means that the station cannot satisfy the needs of the local community and therefore no longer qualifies to be called a community radio station (Drijvers 1992:198). We can identify two factors that compound this situation. Commercial radio stations are perceived to be *money-spinners*, while staff, both volunteers and paid members, lack the necessary *training and skills* to develop suitable community-orientated programming. Often staff simply do not fully comprehend the differences between public, commercial and community broadcasting. This lack of training and understanding has become a major stumbling block in developing the potential of community radio in South Africa.

13.12 A CRITICAL EVALUATION OF THE CONCEPT OF RADIO FORMATS

We need to consider the value of radio formats. This we will do from three perspectives, that of the listener, communication scholars and then the broadcaster.

For the listener, radio formats function simply as a pointing device to clearly distinguish one radio station from another. Formats also provide us, through our expectations as listeners, with a good idea of what we are likely to hear when we turn on the radio, be it information, education or entertainment.

For the scholar of communication, the most important point of commercial broadcasting is simply to make money. This does not mean that the people working in radio have no love for music or the medium. It is just simply that the purpose of the organisation is a commercial one. The relationship between listeners, programme content and the sale of air-time to advertisers is a well established fact. As a result, the making of money becomes extrinsic to communication. Rothenbuhler (1996:132) says the "message purpose" of communication becomes subordinate to the "money purpose". Thus, from our point of view as communication scholars, commercial radio is problematic.

The very nature of the medium is such that radio stations cannot know their audience as individuals. Instead, they rely on typifications (generalisations) produced by market research. As a result, the audience is identified in terms of its distribution, demographics and statistics. Two results follow from this reliance on a typified audience:

- Formatting leads to stereotypical programmes because broadcasters think all listeners are more or less alike.
- The composition of the audience is ephemeral because no one on radio is talking to them as individuals, but as classes and types.

By having to rely on market research, the radio-listening audience becomes nothing but a distribution of probabilities (Rothenbuhler 1996:134). Any real understanding of the audience is limited because people are seen within the context of broad groups, for example, black women between ages 25 and 34, who earn R2 000 a month, live in urban areas, and don't like to listen to heavy metal music.

For the broadcaster, what is the value of having a format-driven programme structure? Most radio stations operate 24 hours a day, and this time needs to be filled meaningfully with messages. The amount of information that needs to be processed to fulfil this need is quite monumental. It means that someone has to make a decision literally every minute or so throughout the day regarding who may be listening, what information should be given, and how it should be presented to them. Thus, formatting is essentially a compromise as it provides broadcasters with rules, or conventions, for this decision-making process, based on the typification of listeners. Rothenbuhler (1996:137–138) identifies five advantages of using formats in radio from a business point of view. They are as follows:

- Formats reduce the number of programming decisions that need to be made. Items are only included in programmes if they fit the format.
- Formatting restrains the choices of announcers or deejays, thus reducing their autonomy and making the on-air talent more manageable.
- Formatting allows a station to achieve a more consistent sound and allows the audience to hear familiar content.
- Formatting provides less variable ratings, which can then be used as a management tool in assessing on-air talent. Since the type of music played on a radio station is

similar throughout the day, rating can be used as an indicator of the performance of on-air personnel.
- Formatted programmes produce more consistent ratings and reduce variability which sales and marketing staff need to use. If the format used throughout the day remains consistent, then this makes the sale of advertising time that much easier as sales staff can use the same pitch to all potential advertisers.

Using formats to produce radio programmes then makes life simple and arbitrary for the broadcaster. Simple, because the format and structure tells the broadcaster what needs to be said at what point in time. Arbitrary, because they can now really say anything. To broadcast without a format would consume an immense amount of time, money, energy and talent.

To conclude, Rothenbuhler (1996:137) sums up the context of radio production by saying: "The instrumental orientation of the businessperson has replaced the normative orientation of the communicator; efficiency rather than expression becomes the governing value". Think about this when you next listen to the radio.

Summary

In this unit we discussed radio from the point of view of programme production, where radio is seen as a commercial venture based on the triangular relationship between listeners, the programme structure and the sale of air-time to advertisers. We discovered that the basic principles of radio production, consistency and variety, are designed to keep us tuned to our radio for as long as possible, by depending on our expectations to hear what we heard before. However, the content and structure of a radio programme is by no means a random event. The radio station makes use of certain devices, such as the format, the playlist and scheduling to structure their programmes. These devices are linked to the activities of listeners, which are broadly defined according to the part of the day in which those activities take place.

We discussed a set of criteria that can be used to analyse the structure of a radio programme. These include:

- the ratio of music to speech;
- the style of address used by the presenter;
- characteristics of the overall "sound" of the station; and
- strategies used to relate programme content to listeners.

The hot clock is a useful graphic representation of the structure of an hour of air-time. We can see at a glance where the various programme elements have been placed and how often they have been repeated. It is a useful analytic tool that allows us to easily compare the programme structures from various dayparts or between different stations. For the broadcaster, the hot clock is a tool to maintain consistency and add variety, as it indicates what can be said and done, and when. However, the hot clock alone is not sufficient to guarantee a successful radio programme. Johnson and Jones (1978:13–31) identify thirteen success factors that need to be considered in terms of the content of the programme.

From the point of view of providing for consistency and expectation, formats should not be altered drastically. However, minor changes occur regularly to provide for the element of variety. A radical change in format is usually only advocated when a radio station is losing listeners in large numbers. In Case study 13.1 we considered just such a situation when Radio 702 changed from a CHR format to all-talk.

In our discussion of community radio we briefly considered the difficulty in defining the concept because of the many differences that are found. However, two common elements are the local nature of operation and emphasis on community participation. The success of a community radio station is dependent on having a high visibility within the community and this can be achieved through the three Ps, programming, personality and promotion, each of which was discussed. We concluded this unit by critically evaluating the value of formatting in commercial broadcasting from three perspectives, that of the listener, the communication scholar and the broadcaster.

Research activities

1 Explain how Case study 13.1 illustrates the basic principles of radio programming, that is, consistency and variety. Under what circumstances would these principles work against the success of a radio station?

2 Describe how the target audience, to large degree, determines the success of any particular format used by a radio station.

3 Locate a list of schedules for radio stations in either a magazine or a newspaper or from the radio station's Web site. Analyse these schedules in order to determine the format offered by those radio stations, and identify the possible target audience.

4 Evaluate any radio programme of your choice in terms of the various success factors identified in this unit. Offer some suggestions as to how the programme could be improved.

5 Analyse the structure of similar dayparts offered by two different radio stations competing for a similar market, for example Radio Bop and Metro FM. What similarities and differences can be noted? Account for any differences you observe.

6 You are the producer for a local community radio station. As part of the station's in-house training programme you need to instruct new announcers on the basic principles of programming. How will you explain these basic principles and what examples will you use to illustrate your seminar?

7 You are the station manager at Radio E•A•S•I which targets a mature upper-income market in a large metropolitan area, with an easy-listening format. It has come to your attention, via office gossip, that your staff considers you disloyal to the station as you listen to the programmes of competing radio stations. As this is causing some

tension and unhappiness among your staff, which is beginning to reflect in programme content, you decide to address the matter at the next staff meeting. How are you going to explain and justify your listening behaviour to your staff?

8 "Format change is a process of evolution rather than drastic revolution." Discuss what is meant by this statement.

9 Select one of the formats discussed in this unit. Briefly identify your target audience and then produce a half-hour radio programme, for that particular audience, on an audio-cassette, in which you demonstrate the various techniques of radio production.

Further reading

Adams, MH & Massey, KK. 1995. *Introduction to radio – production and programming.* Madison, WI: Brown & Benchmark.

Crisell, A. 1986. *Understanding radio.* London: Methuen.

Halper, DL. 1991a. *Full-service radio: programming for the community.* Boston: Focal.

Halper, DL. 1991b. *Radio music directing.* Boston: Focal.

Keith, MC. 1987. *Radio programming: consultancy and formatics.* Boston: Focal.

Keith, MC. 1997. *The radio station.* 4th edition. Boston: Focal.

MacFarland, DT. 1990. *Contemporary radio programming strategies.* Hillsdale, NJ: Erlbaum.

McLeish, R. 1994. *Radio production: a manual for broadcasters.* 3rd edition. Oxford: Butterworth-Heinemann.

Norberg, EG. 1996. *Radio programming: tactics and strategy.* Boston: Focal.

O'Donnell, LB, Benoit, P & Hausman, C. 1990. *Modern radio production.* 2nd edition. Belmont, CA: Wadsworth.

Shingler, M & Wieringa, C. 1998. *On air: methods and meanings of radio.* London: Arnold.

Bibliography

Adams, MH & Massey, KK. 1995. *Introduction to radio: production and programming.* Madison, WI: Brown & Benchmark.

And now we are ten ... 1990. *Marketing Mix* 8(9):53–54.

Bhatia, BS. 1992. Development broadcasting. *Media Asia* 19(1):49–53.

Bittner, JR. 1991. *Broadcasting and telecommunication: an introduction.* 3rd edition. Englewood Cliffs, NJ: Prentice Hall.

Brown, A. 1991. Talk radio is talkback democracy. *Vrye Weekblad*, 2–8 August:10.

Burton, L. 1995. Getting started with radio and sound. *Metro Education* 3:43–48.

Community Radio Association. 1987. *Community radio: an open door to media access.* 2nd edition. Bristol.

Crisell, A. 1986. *Understanding radio.* London: Methuen.

Denisoff, RS. 1973. The evolution of pop music broadcasting: 1920–1972. *Popular Music & Society* 2(3):202–226.

Drijvers, J. 1992. Community broadcasting: a manifesto for media policy of small European countries. *Media, Culture and Society* 14(2):193–201.

Evans, E. 1977. *Radio: a guide to broadcasting techniques.* London: Barrie & Jenkins.
Fisher, HA. 1990. Community radio as a tool for development. *Media Development* 37(4):19–24.
Fiske, J. 1982. *An introduction to communication studies.* London: Methuen.
Fornatale, P & Mills, JE. 1980. *Radio in the television age.* Woodstock, NY: Overlook.
Foster, ES. 1982. *Understanding broadcasting.* 2nd edition. Reading, MA: Addison-Wesley.
Girard, B. 1992. *A passion for radio: radio waves and community.* Montréal: Black Rose.
Goldman, D. 1998. South Africa: a new TV model for emerging markets? *InterMedia* 26(2):3–36.
Gray, I. 1989. More changes as adult listeners tune into 702. *The Sunday Star*, 7 May:10.
Halper, DL. 1991a. *Full-service radio: programming for the community.* Boston: Focal.
Halper, DL. 1991b. *Radio music directing.* Boston: Focal.
Hannan, K. 1997. Bye-bye personality ... hello stationality! *Screen Africa* 9(3):40–41.
Hannan, K. 1998. Radio promotions: making them work for the station both on and off the air. *Screen Africa* 10(2):28–29.
Head, SW, Sterling, CH & Schofield, LB. 1994. *Broadcasting in America: a survey of electronic media.* Boston: Houghton Mifflin.
Head, SW. 1985. *World broadcasting systems: a comparative analysis.* Belmont, CA: Wadsworth.
Hesbacher, P. 1974. Sound exposure in radio: the misleading nature of the station playlist. *Popular Music & Society* 3(3):189–202.
Hochheimer, JL. 1993. Organizing democratic radio: issues in praxis. *Media, Culture and Society* 15: 473–486.
Hochheimer, JL. 1999. Organizing community radio: issues in planning. *Communications: the European Journal of Communication Research* 24(9):443–455.
Hyde, SW. 1995. *Television and radio announcing.* 7th edition. Geneva, Ill: Houghton Mifflin.
Ibrahim, Z. 1999. Reality check: what does "community" mean for community radio. *Rhodes Journalism Review* December:15.
Independent Broadcasting Authority. 1999. *Annual report.* Sandton.
Independent Communications Authority of South Africa. 2000. *Discussion Paper on the review of local content quotas.* [O].
Available: http://www.iba.org.za
Accessed on 2001/02/26
Johnson, JS & Jones, KL. 1978. *Medium radio station practices.* 2nd edition. Belmont, CA: Wadsworth.
Kahn, FJ. 1982. Radio: regulating format diversity. *Journal of Communication* 32(1):181–191.
Karunanayake, N. 1986. The Mahaweli Community Radio in Sri Lanka: a promising experiment. *Media Asia* 13(4):209–214.
Kaye, M & Popperwell, A. 1992. *Making radio: a guide to basic broadcasting production and techniques.* London: Broadside.
Keith, MC. 1987. *Radio programming: consultancy and formatics.* Boston: Focal.
Keith, MC. 1997. *The radio station.* 4th edition. Boston: Focal.
Kleinsteuber, HJ & Sonnenberg, U. 1990. Beyond public service and private profit: international experience with non-commercial local radio. *European Journal of Communication* 5(1):87–106.
Leurdijk, A. 1997. Common sense versus political discourse: debating racism and multicultural society in Dutch talk shows. *European Journal of Communication* 12(2):147–168.
Lewis, PM & Booth, J. 1989. *The invisible medium.* Houndsmill: Macmillan.
Libiero, F. 1993. Community radio: An alternative for broadcasting. *Media Asia* 20(4):218–223.
Lin, CA. 1995. Network prime-time programming strategies in the 1980s. *Journal of Broadcasting and Electronic Media* 39(4):482–495.
Lloyd, L, Maluleke, J, Mngadi, J, Ngubeni, D & Zikhali, S. [Sa]. *Towards a democratic radio broadcast media in South Africa.* Montréal: AMARC World Association of Community Radio Broadcasters.

Lynch, JR & Gillispie, G. 1998. *Process and practice of radio programming*. Lanham, MD: University of America.
MacFarland, DT. 1979. *The development of the Top 40 radio format*. New York: Arno.
MacFarland, DT. 1990. *Contemporary radio programming strategies*. Hillsdale, NJ: Erlbaum.
MacFarland, DT. 1995. Rethinking the hits: why Top 40 is no longer the dominant radio music format. *Journal of Radio Studies* 3:32–40.
Matelski, MJ. 1993. Resilient radio. *Media Studies Journal* 7(3):1–13.
McLeish, R. 1988. *The technique of radio production: a manual for broadcasters*. London: Focal.
McLeish, R. 1994. *Radio production: a manual for broadcasters*. 3rd edition. Oxford: Butterworth-Heinemann.
Modoux, A (ed). 1997. *World communication report: the media and the challenge of the new technologies*. Paris: United National Educational, Scientific and Cultural Organisation.
Mueller, W. 1994. *Understanding today's youth culture*. Wheaton, Ill: Tyndale House.
Norberg, EG. 1996. *Radio programming: tactics and strategy*. Boston: Focal.
O'Donnell, LB, Benoit, P & Hausman, C. 1990. *Modern radio production*. 2nd edition. Belmont, CA: Wadsworth.
O'Donnell, LB, Benoit, P & Hausman, C. 1993. *Modern radio production*. 3rd edition. Belmont, CA: Wadsworth.
O'Donnell, LB, Hausman, C & Benoit, P. 1996. *Announcing: broadcast communicating today*. 3rd edition. Belmont, CA: Wadsworth.
Open Society Foundation. 1999. *Community radio manual*. [O]. Available:
http://www.osf.org.za/About%20CRM
Accessed on 2000/09/04
Orlik, PB. 1988. *Critiquing radio and television content*. Boston: Allyn & Bacon.
Owen, BM. 1977. Regulating diversity: the case of radio formats. *Journal of Broadcasting* 21:305–319.
Peterson, RA & Berger, DG. 1975. Cycles in symbol production: the case of popular music. *American Sociological Review* 40:158–173.
Priest, SH.1996. *Doing media research: an introduction*. Thousand Oaks, CA: Sage.
Radio Joint Audience Research Limited. 1997. *The nature of radio relationships: how listeners use their repertoire of stations*. [O]. Available:
http://www.rab.co.uk/publications/insights/rajins1.htm
Accessed on 1998/11/09
Radio Netherlands. [Sa]. *Community radio*. [O]. Available:
http://www.rnw.nl/realradio/community/html/definition.html
Accessed on 1999/03/02
Rosario-Baird, F. 1989. Communication and the community. *Solidarity* (123):66–71.
Rothernbuhler, EW & McCourt, T. 1992. Commercial radio and popular music: processes of selection and factors of influence, in *Popular music and communication*, 2nd edition, edited by J Lull. Newbury Park, CA: Sage:101–115.
Rothernbuhler, EW. 1985. Programming decision making in popular music radio. *Communication Research* 12(2):209–232.
Rothernbuhler, EW. 1996. Commercial radio as communication. *Journal of Communication* 46(1):125–143.
Schultze, F. 1997. Community radio broadcasters: are you the one having sleepless nights? *Screen Africa* 9(1):86.
Servaes, J & Arnst, R. 1993. First things first: participatory communication for change. *Media Development* 40(2):44–47.
Shane, E. 1995. Modern radio formats: trends and possibilities. *Journal of Radio Studies* 3:3–9.

Shane, E. 1998. The state of the industry: radio's shifting paradigm. *Journal of Radio Studies* 5(2):1–7.

Shingler, M & Wieringa, C. 1998. *On air: methods and meanings of radio.* London: Arnold.

Shoemaker, PJ & Reese, SD. 1996. *Mediating the message: theories on mass media content.* 2nd edition. New York: Longman.

Smith, FL. 1990. *Perspectives on radio and television: telecommunications in the United States.* 3rd edition. New York: Harper & Row.

Steiner PO. 1952. Program patterns and preferences, and the workability of competition in radio broadcasting. *Quarterly Journal of Economics* 66(2):194–223.

Stevens, J. [Sa]. *Unbundling the word community.* [O]. Available:
http://journ.ru.ac.za/radio/theory4.htm
Accessed on 1999/02/25

Strauss, N (ed). 1993. *Radiotext(e)*. New York: Semiotext(e).

Taub, E. 1998. Radio flyer. *Emmy* 20(5):24–25.

Thompson, M. 1999. Some issues for community radio at the turn of the century. *Media International Australia* (91):23–31.

Van der Merwe, C. 1995. *Electronic media manager.* Johannesburg: Africa Growth Network.

Wigston, DJ. 1996. Radio genres and programming, in *Introduction to communication – course book 5: journalism, press and radio studies*, edited by LM Oosthuizen. Kenwyn: Juta:359–390.

Windschuttle, K. 1985. *The media: a new analysis of the press, television, radio and advertising in Australia.* Ringwood, Victoria: Penguin.

Film Production

14

Beschara Karam

Overview

In this unit we outline the six fundamentals of film production, namely, production, form, style, cinematographic properties, editing and sound. While the purpose of this unit is not to equip you to produce a film, it will enable you to become aware of some of the basic concepts in film production. Films, by their very nature, are open texts that invite an infinitude of meaning and this unit will introduce you to the concepts that will allow you to watch films critically.

It is important to note that this unit is based predominantly on the following seminal works in film studies: David Bordwell and Kristin Thompson's *Film art: an introduction* (1993), and Louis Giannetti's *Understanding movies* (1996).

Learning outcomes

At the end of this unit you should be able to

- describe the social factors in film production;
- describe the most technical and aesthetic developments of film;
- conduct research on the production of a film;
- list the four non-narrative forms of film;
- give a description of film form;
- describe the concept of *mise-en-scène*;
- describe the concept of film noir;
- look critically at the fundamentals of film sound;
- discuss the four ways in which the dimension of sound relates to the other aspects of film; and
- explain what is meant by film editing.

14.1 INTRODUCTION

Film is an important medium of popular culture because it has an enormous effect on people's attitudes. Understanding film's effect on the media includes understanding the varied technical aspects of film, such as the use of editing, sound and film style.

14.2 FILM PRODUCTION

14.2.1 Technical factors in film production

Film differs from other art forms in that it presents us with the illusion of motion. How is this illusion created? When a film is made, the film camera does not actually film movement. Instead, it takes a huge number of photographs in very quick succession – *twenty-four pictures per second*. These pictures are taken on a single continuous strip of film, made from a material known as *celluloid*. Different filmstrips come in different widths (or *gauges*). Standard international gauges are super 8 mm, 16 mm, 35 mm, and 70 mm. Generally speaking, the bigger the gauge the better the quality of the film; the standard gauge for commercial films is 35 mm. Amateur filmmakers and experimental filmmakers usually use video cameras – *Leaving Las Vegas* (1996) and *The Blair Witch Project* (1999) – which gives the film a grainy, gritty authenticity.

When the film is projected on to the screen, it also shows twenty-four pictures per second. This is so fast that we cannot see the gaps between the pictures, and we think that we are seeing actual movements. Film is therefore about fooling the human eye and the human brain in order to create the illusion of motion. Three machines are used to bring a film to the screen:

- The *camera*, which takes the pictures.
- The *printer*, which prints or develops the film (just as photographs are developed).
- The *projector*, which displays the developed film on the screen (Bordwell & Thompson 1993; Wyver 1989).

Films do not exist in a human vacuum: they are conceived, produced, distributed and consumed within specific economic and social contexts (Kochberg 1999:14).

14.2.2 Social factors in film production

Social factors refers to the human side of film production – that is, what people have to do to make a film. Most films go through three phases – preproduction, production and postproduction. This is especially true of films made by *studios*. Studios are commercial film companies such as those in Hollywood. The industrial system in operation today is called the "package-unit" system. Under this system, the self-contained studio and long-term contract studio employee of the studio era have been replaced by rentable studio space and short-term contract employment (Kochberg 1999:32).

Preproduction – the producer and the writer

Preproduction refers to the planning and preparation of a film. The two most important people in this process are the *producer* and the *writer*. The producer raises the money for the film and makes the arrangements for hiring the people who will work on the film. They are responsible for bringing together all the components of a film's production – finance, the "property", equipment, studio space – on a short-term film-by-film basis (Kochberg 1999: 32). Examples of producers include Kevin Spacey: *The Big Kahuna* (2000); Jerry

Bruckheimer: *Gone in Sixty Seconds* (2000), *Enemy of The State* (1998), *Armageddon* (1998), *Con Air* (1997), and *The Rock* (1996); Bob and Harvey Weinstein: *Reservoir Dogs* (1992), *Scream 3* (2000), *Reindeer Games* (2000), *The Cider House Rules* (1999), *Music of The Heart* (1999), *The English Patient* (1996), *Shakespeare in Love* (1998); and Steven Spielberg: *The Peacemaker* (1997), *Deep Impact* (1998), *The Mask of Zorro* (1998), *American Beauty* (1999), *Jurassic Park 3* (2001), *The Flintstones* (1994), and *Men in Black* (1997).

The writer, on the other hand, prepares the script. Well-known scriptwriters include David Mamet: *Hannibal* (2001), *Wag the Dog* (1997), *Ronin* (1998), *The Untouchables* (1987); Quentin Tarantino: *Natural Born Killers* (1994), *True Romance* (1993), *The Rock* (1996), *From Dusk till Dawn* (1996); and Woody Allen: *Sweet and Lowdown* (1999), *Celebrity* (1998), *Deconstructing Harry* (1997), *Everyone Says I Love You* (1996), and *Mighty Aphrodite* (1995).

Production – the director

The process of physically making the film is known as production (also called *shooting*). The most important person in this phase is the *director*, who decides what the film should actually look like. Famous directors include Steven Spielberg: *Schindler's List* (1990) and *The Colour Purple* (1985) and more recently, *Saving Private Ryan* (1998); Quentin Tarantino: *Reservoir Dogs* (1992), *Jackie Brown* (1997), *Pulp Fiction* (1994) and *Four Rooms* (1995); Brian de Palma: *M. Butterfly* (1993), *Snake Eyes* (1998); Martin Scorcese: *The Age of Innocence* (1993), *Casino* (1995), *GoodFellas* (1990), *Taxi Driver* (1976) and *Kundun* (1997); Oliver Stone: *Platoon*, (1986), *Born on the Fourth of July* (1989) and *Natural Born Killers* (1994); Stanley Kubrick: *2001: Space Odyssey* (1968), *Barry Lyndon* (1975), *Full Metal Jacket* (1987), *Eyes Wide Shut* (1999); Paul Verhoeven: *The 4th Man* (1984), *Starship Troopers* (1997), *Total Recall* (1990); James Cameron: *Terminator I* (1991) and *Terminator 2: Judgment Day* (1991), *Titanic* (1997); and Ridley Scott: *Alien* (1979), *Bladerunner* (1982), and *Gladiator* (2000).

There are a huge number of people who work behind the scenes to help the director. This group of people is known as the *crew*, which includes camera operators and assistants. The group of actors appearing in the film is known as the cast (Bordwell & Thompson 1993). A star's association with a film project affects the ease with which it could be made. A star's appearance in the film is also held to be an important factor in a film's box-office performance (Kochberg 1999:33). For example, the Wachowski brothers, Andy and Larry, could not raise any finance to make a futuristic action film, *The Matrix* (1999). However, once big star Keanu Reeves committed to starring in the film, many studios were prepared to invest in it. As a result, *The Matrix* was made and its success at the box-office is partly attributed to Reeves' presence in the film.

Postproduction – the editor

Postproduction is the process of putting the film into its final form – that is, as it will be shown in cinemas. The most important person in this process is the *editor*. Only a small fraction of all the film that is shot will actually be used in the final version. It is the editor's job to decide what will be used, and this process starts while the film is being shot. The editor is also in charge of how the film should sound. Well-known editors who introduced different editing techniques include Russian filmmakers Sergei Eisenstein and VI Pudovkin. Contemporary editors include Kevin Smith, Woody Allen, Brian de Palma and Steven Spielberg.

Some films are made on small budgets outside of the big studios. These are known as *independent films*. Independent films are often made in a simpler way. *Individual* film production is when one filmmaker takes on the major roles in all phases of film production – that is, he or she functions as producer, director and editor, for instance when Woody Allen wrote, produced, directed, and even acted in *Deconstructing Harry* (1997). *Collective* (or major) film production is when several filmmakers share all roles equally, and have an equal say in the film and big stars even forgo a pay-check for a cut of the profits (Bordwell & Thompson 1993; Kochberg 1991; Wyver 1989). For example, Jack Nicholson was not paid a salary for *Batman* (1989) but he did receive a percentage of the gross merchandising, which resulted in him being paid out a whopping R350 million. Similarly, two-time Oscar winner Tom Hanks was not paid a fee for his part in *Saving Private Ryan* (1998), but he received a percentage of the gross receipts resulting in him being paid out R350 million.

14.2.3 After production: distribution and exhibition

While distribution refers to the process where films are sent from the filmmaker to the cinema, exhibition refers to the cinemas and other places where films are shown (Bordwell & Thompson 1993). Throughout the studio era and before, the most powerful sector of the film industry was exhibition. In today's film economy, however, distribution is the dominant sector (Kochberg 1999).

There are three major types of film exhibition:

- commercial cinemas – showing mainly commercial films, such as big blockbusters *Batman* (1989), *Snake eyes* (1998), *Armageddon* (1998), *Titanic* (1997) and *The Perfect Storm* (2000);
- "art house" cinemas – showing independent films, such as Robert Rodriguez's *El Mariachi* (1992), and Quentin Tarantino's *Reservoir Dogs* (1992); and
- secialised exhibitions showing experimental films, such as director David Lynch's *Eraserhead* (1978).

There are also commercial, "art house" and experimental distribution companies catering for each of these three kinds of exhibition.

It is worth noting that there are a variety of different types of cinema-run in operation today. A run can be exclusive (where a film is only screened in one movie theatre); multiple (where a film is shown simultaneously at a number of screens); or saturation (where a film is shown simultaneously at an enormous number of screens – usually a minimum of 1 000 screens in the American and Canadian market – accompanied by heavy media promotion) (Kochberg 1999:29). An example of an exclusive run would be the Australian film *The Interview* (1998), with unknown actor Hugo Weaving, which was screened at only one theatre and as is usual with exclusive runs it was a film of low budget with no stars. An example of a multiple run would be the medium-budget film *The Crying Game* (1992) which was distributed into cinemas across the United Kingdom upon its release; and an example of a saturation run, with much media publicity, would be the major film production *Mission Impossible: 2* (2000) with superstar Tom Cruise.

Apart from cinemas, a very important form of film exhibition is the video format, which includes television and home video. In some countries such as the United States, films make more money from video than from cinema exhibition. In fact, many films are now specially made for television and home video, without ever being shown in cinemas. Video does not have the same picture quality as cinema film, but the situation is improving with laser disc and now with DVD (Digital Versatile Disc) (Bordwell & Thompson 1993; Webster 1999; Wyver 1989).

14.2.4 Implications of different modes of film production

The way in which a film is produced is important for reasons of classification, social factors and authorship.

Classification

We tend to classify films according to the way they are made. In *fictional* films, there is a great deal of control over every aspect of the filmmaking process. With *documentaries* (such as *The making of Steven Spielberg's Jaws* [1995]), the filmmaker has control over the shooting, but not over the script or the people appearing in front of the cameras. With *compilation* films, the filmmaker does not even have control over the shooting, but puts the film together from extant film images. With *animation*, the characters in the film are not filmed, but drawn. Animated films include *Aladdin* (1992), *Beauty and The Beast* (1991), *El Dorado* (2000), and *The Lion King* (1994). There is also computer-generated imagery (CGI), for example *Jurassic Park* (1993), *Toy Story I* and *Toy Story II* (1995 and 1999), and *Small Soldiers* (1998). Tim Burton's *Mars Attacks!* (1996), a film about the Earth being invaded by Martians with irresistible weapons and a cruel sense of humour, is, on the other hand, a prime example of the use of special effects. At one point or another it makes use of every kind of special effect used in Hollywood today. *Mars Attacks!* is predominantly computer-generated, with the synthesis of CGI, live-action, in-camera effects and computer animation (Webster 1999:77–79).

Social factors

Methods of film production are affected by the level of technology and degree of industrialisation in a society.

Authorship

The way in which a film is made determines who we see as the "author" or creator of the film. In most forms of cinema, the director is regarded as the author, because he or she has overall control of the shooting process. With independent films, authorship may be more collective; often pieced together by the producers, directors, writers and stars (Bordwell & Thompson 1993; Giannetti 1996; Wyver 1989). Even prestigious filmmakers such as Federico Fellini and Akira Kurosawa preferred collaborating with others in creating the events of a story (Giannetti 1996:322).

With regard to *auteur theory*, which was popularised in the French periodical *Cahiers du Cinema* in the mid-1950s, this is a view that emphasises the dominance of the director. The other collaborators (writers, cinematographers, actors, editors, and so on) are simply the director's technical assistants. Francois Truffaut and Jean-Luc Godard proposed that the greatest movies of our time are dominated by the personal vision of the director, and as such, the director's "signature" can be perceived through an examination of the director's total output, which is characterised by a unity of theme and style. The *auteur* theory works best with those film artists who control all the major creative decisions – both in terms of subject matter and execution. The impressive Ingmar Bergman, for example, is indisputably an *auteur* director. His films are semi-autobiographical, like *Fanny and Alexander* (1983), one of his many outstanding pieces of work (Giannetti 1996:291–292, 445–450, 498). Other *auteur* directors include Alfred Hitchcock: *Psycho* (1960), *North by Northwest* (1959), *Vertigo* (1958); Pedro Almodovar: *Woman on the Verge of a Nervous Breakdown* (1988), *Tie me Up! Tie me Down* (1990); Francis Ford Coppola: *Apocalypse Now* (1979), the *Godfather* trilogy (1992); and even Kevin Smith: *Dogma* (1999), *Chasing Amy* (1997), *Clerks* (1994) and *Mall Rats* (1995). South African *auteur* directors are Katinka Heyns: *Paljas* (1997), *Fiela se Kind* (1987), *Die Storie van Klara Viljee* (1991); Darrell Roodt: *Cry the Beloved Country* (1995), *Sarafina!* (1992), *Place of Weeping* (1987), *The Stick* (1987), and *Jobman* (1990); and Jyoti Mistry: *Yoni* (1997), *B.E.D* (1998), *Paw-paw* (1998), and *anOther ny story* (2000).

We are now going to look at two case studies – *Jaws* (1975) and *The Crying Game* (1992) – from their conception to their distribution and exhibition, adapted from Kochberg 1999. These two films were selected because they represent different concepts, for example *Jaws* is a big budget major American production, whilst *The Crying Game* is a medium-budget British production.

Case study 14.1: *Jaws* (1975): a big budget major American production

Synopsis

Jaws is about a peaceful summer resort town on Amity Island. The community has become victim to series of attacks by a man-eating great white shark. Because it is the Fourth of July (American Day of Independence) week-end, the officials hesitate to warn the people about the shark, as they are wary of the possibility of losing business during their busiest time of the year. Martin Brody, the chief of police, takes it upon himself to kill the shark, aided by Matt Hooper, a young marine biologist and Quint an eccentric shark expert.

Script development and preproduction

The property, *Jaws*, started life as a novel by Peter Benchley. In July 1973, months before the book was published, Doubleday (the American publishers) opened the bidding for the film rights to the book. Richard Zanuck and David Brown, independent producers working out of Universal Pictures, acquired the screen rights for approximately US$200 000. Under the terms of the deal, Peter Benchley was to produce the screenplay for the film. The director for the project was selected by the producers after the completion of the first draft of the screenplay. Steven Spielberg joined the package-unit production just as the producers and Benchley started on a second draft of the script. As is typical with mainstream production, several drafts of the script were produced.

During preproduction, the budget was set at US$4 million, with a two-month shooting schedule. Universal Pictures was the financier-cum-distributor of the film. Meanwhile, during the period before shooting had begun, the success of sales of the hardback edition of *Jaws* was continuously increasing the value of the film property.

Cast

Included in the cast were well-known actors Roy Schneider (Chief Martin Brody) and Robert Shaw (Quint), as well as academy nominee Richard Dreyfus (Matt Hooper).

Production and postproduction

The production stage commenced in April 1974. There were many well-publicised difficulties of location, resulting in the extension of the Martha's Vineyard shoot (an Island off the East coast of the USA) from two months to five and a half months. Costs increased accordingly, from an original budget of US$4 million to US$8 million. During location shooting on Martha's Vineyard, Universal did not miss the opportunity to promote the film.

In October 1974, filming shifted to Los Angeles for the last remaining scenes, including the final confrontation with the shark, which had yet to be filmed. The final underwater footage was shot in "the waters of the Pacific off Catalina island, and in one or two studio tanks, where lighting could be carefully controlled" (Kochberg 1999:36).

Editing had commenced long before the completion of principal photography. The film's editor, Verna Shields, assembled a rough-cut as the sequences were being shot. At the end of the production phase, only the rough-cut of the last third of the film was to be done. Spielberg worked closely with the editor Shields, to deliver the first print. In March 1975 the film was handed over to Universal Pictures for audience test-previews and distribution. Universal Pictures retained the authority over the final cut of the film. But in response to the excellent audience previews, only small changes were made by director Steven Spielberg and editor Verna Shields. The date of the opening of *Jaws*, set by universal Pictures, was 20 June 1975.

Distribution and exhibition

For the film's distribution and exhibition, Universal Pictures designed and coordinated a highly ingenious plan. Universal Pictures and the paperback's publishers, Bantam, had designed a logo which would appear on the paperback and on all film advertising – an "open-mouthed shark rising toward a lone female swimmer" (Kochberg 1999:36). Both publisher and distributor recognised the mutual benefits that a joint promotion strategy would bring. Such was the cooperation between the two parties that producers Zanuck and Brown "embarked on a 6-city tour sponsored by Bantam books" (Kochberg 1999: 36). This tour was to promote the publication of the paperback and also the upcoming release of the film.

At the end of April 1975, Universal Pictures invited blind bids from the United States and Canadian exhibitors. Because of the enormous success of the paperback and the film's excellent "sneak" previews, Universal Pictures was able to command very stiff financial terms from exhibitors.

June 1975 marked a new era in the promotion and distribution of major film releases. For the first time, the exploitation of a movie incorporated saturation booking technique with simultaneous nationwide media promotion on a worldwide scale. The idea behind this strategy was to create maximum exposure of the film as quickly as possible, so as to recoup production costs also as quickly as possible.

Coinciding with the nationwide opening of *Jaws* in the United States was a media blitz that included approximately twenty-five 30-second adverts per night on American prime-time network television, for three days preceding the opening of *Jaws*. By December 1977 the worldwide box-office gross for Jaws was over US$250 million (cf. Kochberg 1999:34–37).

The case study of *Jaws* can be compared to that of the case of *The Crying Game* (1992).

Case study 14.2: *The Crying Game* (1992): a medium-budget British production

Synopsis

An unlikely kind of friendship develops between Fergus, an Irish Republican Army volunteer, and Jody, a kidnapped British soldier lured into an IRA trap by Jude, another IRA member. When the hostage-taking ends up going horribly wrong, Fergus escapes and heads for London, where he seeks out Jody's lover, a hairdresser named Dil. Fergus adopts the name "Jimmy" and gets a job as a day labourer. He also starts seeing Dil, who knows nothing about Fergus' IRA background. But there are some things about Dil that Fergus doesn't know.

The Crying Game was conceived, written and directed by filmmaker Neil Jordan.

Script development and preproduction

In 1982, Neil Jordan produced an outline and partial script for a project called *The Soldier's Wife*. The project was turned down by Channel Four, a new television channel offered on British television.

Nearly ten years later, in 1991, the project was set in motion again, to be directed by Neil Jordan and produced by Stephen Woolley of Palace Productions. Despite many potential backers (including Miramax) being put off by what were perceived as "difficult" themes – race, transgressive sexuality and Northern Ireland politics, a "pack-of-cards" finance package was arranged through the summer and autumn of 1991. The participants included British Screen, Eurotrustees (a pan-European distribution alliance, one that included Palace Pictures), Channel Four and Nippon Development and Finance (a Japanese distribution company). Financing was very tight – a modest US$4.7 million budget – and hard won, with the producer literally begging Channel Four for financing (Kochberg 1999:38).

Cast

Stephen Rea (Fergus), Miranda Richardson (Jude), Forest Whitaker (Jody) and Jaye Davidson (Dil).

Production and postproduction

Despite the fact that the financing of the picture was not fully completed until 10 November 1991, shooting of the film commenced a week earlier, on location in Ireland. As the film went into production, Palace Pictures – of which Palace Productions was a part – was in serious financial trouble. Despite Palace's problems, however, the production proceeded.

After less than a week's shooting in Ireland, the production shifted to London. Location work occurred in central London (in, for example, Eaton Square and Fournier Street – Spitafields). The rest of the film was shot at Shepperton Studios. Shooting ended just before Christmas 1991.

By the end of January 1992, a rough-cut had been completed. Subsequently a new ending was shot at extra cost. By April 1992, the film was completed in its entirety and had acquired the title, *The Crying Game*.

Initial United Kingdom distribution and exhibition

The film opened in the United Kingdom at the end of October 1992, having failed to secure a Cannes première, but having been seen at the Venice Film Festival that autumn. Films with low budgets and no stars tend to have extended exclusive cinema runs upon release, to give the film a chance to build an audience through word of mouth. This was not the case with *The Crying Game*, however. Mayfair, the United Kingdom distributors decided to book the film into cinemas across the country after only a few weeks' "platform" exhibition in London. Anecdotal evidence suggests that the unfortunate coincidence of the film's release with an Irish Republican Army bombing campaign on the British mainland, on top of the poor marketing, severely hampered its success. For, despite generally favourable reviews, the film's initial box-office performance was weak.

United States distribution and exhibition

In the spring of 1992, the partners in the film struck a distribution deal with Miramax, for US$1.5 million. Miramax in the early 1990s was an independent distribution company, now owned by Disney, with a reputation for handling non-Hollywood products.

After screening the film at the Telluride, Toronto and New York Film Festivals, *The Crying Game* was released in the United States at the end of November 1992. Miramax demonstrated its agility in non-blockbuster distribution with its careful marketing strategy. On its United Kingdom release, those marketing the film had requested that the press not reveal the film's "secret" in their reviews. Miramax picked up on that idea as a promotional tool, and enlisted not only the media, but the audience as well, in a conspiracy of silence. The film was "sold" to the public as an action thriller/film noir with a secret (the transsexual and Irish Republican Army themes were played down). An inspired advertising slogan – "The movie everyone is talking about, but no one is giving away its secret" – certainly helped to fire the imagination of the cinema-going public. Meanwhile, Miramax also built a steady Oscar-nomination campaign for the film through late 1992 and early 1993.

The promotional campaign was supported by a carefully orchestrated theatrical release pattern. The film debuted on only six screens in the United States at the end of November 1992. By early February 1993, when the Oscar nominations were announced, the film was booked into 500 screens. The film received six nominations (best film, best director, best screenplay, best actor, best supporting actor, best editing), and on the weekend following the announcement of the nominations, it grossed US$5.2 million at the box office: a "400 per cent increase over the previous week" (Kochberg 1999:39). By the eve of the Academy Awards – 29 March 1993 – the number of screens had been increased to saturation level; 1 093 in total.

On Oscar night, the film only won one Academy Award, for best screenplay. Nevertheless, Miramax's effective handling of the film assured it continued box-office success. If United States grosses for 1992 were a healthy US$4.5 million, grosses for 1993 were outstanding: at around US$59.3 million. By 1997, the gross figure for the United States was estimated at around US$68 million. Miramax's handling of the film in the United States proved to be a classic example of how to build an audience successfully for a relatively low-budget, non-United States feature film (cf. Kochberg 1999:37–39).

14.3 FILM FORM

14.3.1 The concept of form in film

Form refers to the total system of a film, as perceived by the viewer. The importance of form in film lies in the fact that as human beings we tend to look for order and structure in the world around us. We do the same thing with the artworks we create, including film. Given that form refers to the total system of a film, it follows that this term refers to subject matter as well as overall structure. No attempt will therefore be made to distinguish between "form" and "content" (Bordwell & Thompson 1993).

Our understanding of the form of a film can be based on several different criteria:

- real-life experience of situations similar to those depicted in the film;
- knowledge of other films;
- knowledge of *genres*, or different types of films, and the typical form of each genre;
- the types of emotions depicted in the film, and our own response to these emotions;
- our *interpretation* of a film – that is, what we think is the meaning or message or moral of a film, for example, *The Thin Red Line* (1998) is an anti-war film. The story is set in World War II, centred on the outcome of the battle of Guadalcanal, which will strongly influence the Japanese's advance into the Pacific. A group of young soldiers is brought in as a relief for the battle-weary Marine units. The exhausting fight for a key-positioned airfield that allows control over a 1 000-mile radius puts the men of the Army Rifle Company C-for-Charlie through hell. The horrors of war form the soldiers into a tight-knit group; their emotions develop into bonds of love and even family. The reasons for this war get further away as the world for the men gets smaller and smaller until their fighting is simply for survival. *The Thin Red Line's* message highlights the atrocities of World War II;
- our *evaluation* of a film – that is, our opinion as to the quality or artistic merit of a film.

14.3.2 Principles of film form

There are five general principles that can be used to understand the form of a particular film: function, similarity and repetition, difference and variation, development, and unity/disunity.

Function

Every film has many different *elements* – namely, many different aspects such as characters, style of filming, actions, and so forth. We need to consider the *function* of each element of the film, that is, its purpose within the film as a whole.

Similarity and repetition

This is when two or more similar elements appear in a film, or when the same element appears several times. Such an element is known as a motif (as a distinctive feature or dominant idea/subject or recurring theme).

Difference and variation

Variation refers to the way in which repeated elements in a film usually differ slightly. Difference refers to the way in which some elements are quite different from each other, sometimes to the point of being exact opposites.

Development

This refers to the narrative structure of the film, and how the story develops. It refers to the way in which the story is broken up into different parts, and how the situation at the beginning of the film has changed at the end.

Unity/disunity

Unity occurs in a film when all the different elements are tightly connected. Disunity is when they are not connected, which may be unintentional, or it may be deliberate in which case it is known as formal disunity. In *Pulp Fiction* (1994), for example, three different stories are linked through various characters, but are seemingly unconnected. The stories of two mob hit men, a boxer and a pair of diner bandits intertwine in three tales of violence and redemption. The film initiates with two small-time thieves, Honey Bunny and Pumpkin, who spontaneously decide to hold up a restaurant. The film then shifts to the story of Jules and Vincent, hit men for the well-known and feared Marcellus Wallace who is caught up in a "deal gone wrong" with struggling boxer Butch Coolidge.

14.3.3 Narrative as a formal system: principles of narrative construction

Narrative films are those which tell a story. A film narrative can be described in two ways:

- the *plot*, which consists of all the events we see on screen;
- the *story*, which consists of all the events of a film, both those we see on screen and those which take place offscreen (i.e. we hear about them but we don't see them).

A narrative can be summarised as a set of events connected by cause and effect, time and space.

Cause and effect

This refers to the way in which there is usually a reason for everything that happens in the film – that is, there is a *cause*, and what happens is an *effect*. Usually it is the characters that cause things to happen. The important characters in a film have distinct personal qualities (habits, likes and dislikes, strengths and weaknesses). These qualities are known as *traits*, and it is these traits that serve as causes, and make the events of the story happen.

Time

Time is important in three ways:

- *Temporal order* – the order in which events happen over time. Even if events are presented out of sequence, we (the audience) can rearrange them to give us the correct order.
- *Temporal duration* – the length of time it takes for the events of the narrative to occur. This can refer to the length of the plot, the length of the story, or the length of the actual film.
- *Temporal frequency* – the number of times a particular action is repeated in a film. A single action can be shown more than once, or a very repetitive action may be shown only a few times.

Space

This refers to the *setting*, that is the place or places where the events of the film occur. It can mean the setting of the plot, for instance those places we see on screen, or the setting of the story, which can include places we never actually see.

It is also important to notice patterns of development in a narrative – how the plot is structured, and in particular how the story begins and ends. It is important to remember that nothing in a film is meant to be there by chance – everything that happens is there for a purpose.

14.3.4 Narration: the flow of story information

Films are constructed so that information is given to the viewer in a very controlled way. In other words, the *story* of the film is gradually revealed to the viewer as the *plot* progresses. This process is known as narration, and is controlled by the range and depth of story information, and the narrator.

Range of story information

This refers to the amount of information that is given to the viewer throughout the film. It can be *unrestricted* – that is, more information is received by the viewer than is available to the characters in the film. In *The Truman Show* (1998), for example, we as an audience know that the principal actor's world is a large studio set, complete with actors. Truman (Jim Carrey) only finds out at the end of the film that his world is fictitious. The amount of information could be *restricted* – that is, the viewer receives only the information that is available to one character. Information can also be *mixed* – that is, somewhere between the two.

Depth of story information

This refers to how deeply the narrative goes into the minds of the characters. If we only see what characters say and do, then this is *objective* narration. If we see what they are thinking, then this is *subjective* narration. In *Buffalo 66* (1998), for instance, director-star Vincent Gallo plays Billy Brown, a convict, just released from prison, who kidnaps a teenage girl (Christina Ricci) and demands that she pose as his wife to impress his parents. Their evolving relationship makes up the bulk of this film. Gallo, whose directing debut this is, also co-wrote the screenplay and composed the music. In this film, the audience is shown what the principal actor (Gallo) is thinking, by a series of still frames. These two forms of narration, subjective and objective, can be mixed or alternated.

The narrator

Some films use a *narrator*; a person who tells us the story of the film. The narrator can be a *character* narrator, which is a principal character in the film, such as Alabama (Patricia Arquette) who narrates the story in *True Romance* (1993). Alternatively, a *non-character* narrator can be used. This is an unknown person and usually an anonymous voice. *The Big Lebowski* (1998), for example, is narrated by a character that has no part in the story. The presence of a narrator does not necessarily mean that we will gain more information; it is simply a way of controlling the flow of information.

14.3.5 Narrative conventions

There are two common ways of looking at narrative conventions:

Genres

This refers to different types of films. Films that belong to the same genre have certain typical features in common. These features may relate to the subject matter, the setting, or even the style of performance. The audience will therefore have certain expectations about a film according to its genre.

The classical Hollywood cinema

This tends to be the dominant form of cinema narrative, even in many countries outside the United States. It is based on the idea that individual characters make the story happen, that is they provide the *causes* that set the *effects* of the narrative into motion.

The film tends to focus very strongly on this process of character-based cause and effect. Classical Hollywood cinema usually involves a central character with a strong *desire* to achieve a certain goal. Normally there is another character that tries to prevent the central character from achieving his/her goal. Narration tends to be *objective and unrestricted*. At the end of the film, all problems are resolved, and all mysteries explained.

14.3.6 Non-narrative formal systems: types of non-narrative form

Non-narrative films are those which do not tell a story. Bordwell & Thompson (1993) identify four broad types of non-narrative form: *categorical* form; *rhetorical* form; *abstract* form; and *associational* form.

Categorical formal systems

When the subject matter of a film is divided into parts, then we refer to these parts as *categories*. These categories might be logical and scientific, or they might be based upon popular beliefs and perceptions. Because there are different ways to divide things into categories, any one thing can belong to many different categories. Categorical films normally have a very simple structure, being based on repetition with slight variation, and with simple patterns of development.

Rhetorical formal systems

A film is rhetorical when it tries to present a persuasive argument. Some people might refer to such films as propaganda. There are four basic characteristics of rhetorical film:

- It openly tries to convince the viewer to accept a particular set of opinions or beliefs.
- The subject of the film will usually be a matter of opinion, not a matter of fact.
- The film will often appeal to the viewer's emotions.
- The film will often try to persuade the viewer to make a choice that will affect his or her everyday life.

There are three main types of argument used in rhetorical films:

Arguments from source

Here the film will try to create the impression that it is a reliable source of information. In other words, because it is reliable, viewers should accept what it says without question.

Subject-centred arguments

Here the film tries to "prove" that its point of view is correct. The arguments that it uses will usually not be entirely logical, but will use various tricks to create the impression of logic (e.g. presenting things in a misleading way and appealing to popular beliefs) (cf. Bordwell & Thompson 1993).

Viewer-centred arguments

These are arguments that appeal to the emotions of the viewers, so that they will not examine the reasoning too closely.

Abstract formal systems

An abstract film is based around physical images; that is, it focuses on things like colour and shape. All films put some emphasis on this, but with an abstract film, images are the main focus. The things that are filmed are not linked by subject matter, as in other formal systems, but by their physical appearance. The film is structured according to the way in which it presents different types of images.

Associational formal systems

Associational films try to create a mood or express an attitude. They do this by using images that suggest particular emotions. Images that suggest the same kind of emotions will be grouped together, even if their subject matter is not connected.

14.4 FILM STYLE

Film style refers to the particular combination of cinematic techniques used in a particular film.

14.4.1 The shot: *mise-en-scène*

Mise-en-scène is a French expression that refers to the way in which the director controls what we see in each *shot.* A *shot* is a continuously filmed piece of action (Bordwell & Thompson 1993). *Mise-en-scène* is a complicated blend of visual conventions. In the movies it resembles the art of painting, in that an image of formal patterns and shapes is presented on a flat surface and is enclosed within a frame. Added to that, cinematic *mise-en-scène* is also fluid choreographing of visual elements that correspond to an idea or a complex set of ideas (Giannetti, 1996:40).

14.4.2 Realism

Viewers often judge a particular shot according to whether or not it is "realistic". We must remember, however, that different people and cultures have different ideas of what is realistic. We must also remember that realism is not appropriate in some films, and should instead focus on the *functions* of *mise-en-scène*. In other words, why has the shot been made in this way, and how does it contribute to the film as a whole (Bordwell & Thompson 1993).

14.4.3 The power of *mise-en-scène*

Because the director is able to control what appears in each shot, he or she has the power to create special effects, and to show things that are not possible in daily life.

14.4.4 Aspects of *mise-en-scène*

The four basic aspects of a shot that can be controlled by a director are the setting, costume and make-up, lighting, figure expression and movement.

Setting

This can either be in a studio, or *on location* – that is, in a place that already exists, either outdoors or in a building. Usually a studio gives a director more control over a shot. In a studio, a director can decide whether the scenery, buildings and so forth should be realistic or less realistic. By using sets, models, paintings and computer graphics, the director can create almost any kind of setting. The director can also use *props*. A prop is an object that is of central importance in a particular shot, or even in several shots (in which case it becomes a motif) (Bordwell & Thompson 1993).

Giannetti (1996) points out that filming on location is less expensive than building sets. Location shooting gives the film undeniable authenticity: it is after all, the real thing. On the other hand, the main allure of shooting on studio sets is usually their lack of realism, which then gives the director an opportunity to create real worlds for fantasy settings. Studio sets allow the filmmaker to create a magical, fantastical, ethereal environment, one where all the elements of nature are under the complete control of the director – where nothing is left to chance. For example, the director Federico Fellini, director of films such as *Amarcord* (1974), who started his career as a realist filmmaker, discovered that the studio was a place to create magic: "[t]o me and other directors like me, the cinema is a way of interpreting and remaking reality through fantasy and imagination. The use of the studio is an indispensable part of what we are doing" (Giannetti 1996: 305).

Costume and make-up

Costumes can be either realistic or *stylised* (deliberately unrealistic). Stylised costumes are used for their physical appearance, and they help to give the shot a particular visual style. They can also help to lend a certain atmosphere to a shot (Bordwell & Thompson 1993). In most films, costumes are not simply frills incorporated to enhance an illusion, but are in fact aspects of character and theme. Depending on the cut, texture and bulk, certain costumes can suggest refinement, respect and agitation (Giannetti 1996:310). "Clothing is a wonderful doorway that most easily leads you to the heart of an individual" author Tom Wolfe notes; "[i]t's how characters reveal themselves" (Giannetti 1996:316). The costumes in *Titanic*, for example, not only indicate a specific time period, that of the early 1900s, but also indicate the differences in class. For instance, while socialite Rose (Kate Winslet) dresses in rich, opulent textures and bright colours, representing her wealth and upper-class status, the free-spirited Jack (Leo di Caprio) dresses in muted browns and beige, with roughly textured fabrics, clearly representing his working-class background. Possibly the most famous costume in film history is Charlie Chaplin's tramp outfit. The costume represents both class and character, indicating a blend of vanity and dash that makes Chaplin so entrancing. His moustache, derby hat and cane represent the "dandy" (Giannetti 1996:311). The baggy trousers, many sizes too large, however, along with his oversized shoes and tightly fitting jacket represent his insignificance and highlight his poverty.

The same approach can be followed with make-up, and elaborate "special effects" make-up can be used to completely change the appearance of an actor (Bordwell & Thompson 1993). *Batman* (1989) and *Batman Returns* (1992) featured Jack Nicholson as the Joker and Danny de Vito as the Penguin – characters completely transformed through the use of make-up and prosthetics. Make-up for cinema is by far subtler than it is for theatre; even the slightest change in make-up can be noted onscreen. Giannetti (1996:315) gives the example of Mia Farrow in *Rosemary's Baby* (1968), whose "pale green face" was used to highlight the "corruption of her body while pregnant with the devil's child". In *Greystoke: The Legend of Tarzan, Lord of the Apes* (1984), audiences were amazed at the animation and expression of the apes in this film. The apes were perceived as being human as their expressions imitated human emotions so superbly. This is particularly notable because the apes were played by actors wearing amazing make-up and costumes.

Lighting

Lighting in cinema refers to the artificial lights shining on to the shot. These lights are not just there in order to help us see the shot clearly, but also to change the appearance of a shot. This is done in several ways:

- *Creating shadows and highlights* – highlights are patches of brightness.
- *Focusing light on one area* – if one area of the screen is brighter than the others, it will emphasise whatever is in that area.
- *Using light to change shape and texture* – the physical appearance of particular objects in the shot can be changed according to the way that lighting is used.
- *Using "hard" or "soft" lighting* – hard lighting is intense and creates clear shadows; soft lighting is gentle and makes it more difficult to distinguish between light and shade.
- *Changing the direction of lighting* – lights can be shone on the shot from many different angles to create many different effects.
- *Using lighting as a motif* – different kinds of lighting can be used for different kinds of shots.
- *Using various colours of lighting* – apart from the conventional white and yellow lights, other colours can be used as well (Bordwell & Thompson 1993).

Film noir (literally, "black cinema" [Giannetti 1996:18]) for example, is a style defined primarily in terms of light, or the lack of light. *Film noir* is typical of a variety of American genres in the 1940s and early 1950s. "*Noir* is a world of night and shadows." Its style is almost "exclusively urban". *Film noir* abounds in images of dark streets, cigarette smoke and fog in dimly lit cocktail lounges and bars, with symbols of "fragility", for instance "windowpanes, sheer clothing, glasses and mirrors". Motifs of entrapment are evident: alleyways, tunnels, subways, elevators, and train cars. Often the settings are locations of "transience, like grubby rented rooms, piers, bus terminals and railroad yards. The images are rich in sensuous textures, like neon-lit streets, windshields streaked with mud, and shafts of light streaming through windows of lonely rooms. Characters are imprisoned behind ornate lattices, grillwork, drifting fog and smoke. Visual designs emphasise harsh lighting contrasts, jagged shapes, and violated surfaces" (Giannetti 1996:18). The tone of *film noir* is "fatalistic" and schizophrenic. The films are awash with "pessimism, emphasising the darker aspects of the human condition". The themes typically focus on "violence, lust, greed, betrayal and depravity" (ibid). *Double Indemnity* (1944), directed by Billy Wilder is film noir (Giannetti 1996:18). Although the *Batman* quartet (late 80s, early 90s), *Blade Runner* (1982) and *The Matrix* (1999) are recent films, filmed predominantly in colour, they do have a *film noir* quality about them. The *Batman* quartet, for instance, is a story based in the fictitious Gotham City, a city that is part comic-book, part *film-noir* creation. The city's towering skyscrapers strain upward, poking through the polluted and sullied skies. Sinister alleyways and dark, cave-like nooks depict heinous crimes against humanity. *Blade Runner* is set in Los Angeles in the year 2019. "Nature has gone berserk"; the city is deluged with rain. Smoke, fog and steam add to the congestion. It is a dark city, seemingly only night, interrupted by "neon signs in day-glow colours, cheap Orientalised billboards and a profusion of advertising come-ons" (Giannetti 1996:309). Discarded, rusted machinery fills the streets. The soundtrack combines unearthly sounds with echoes and the noises of flying vehicles shuttling through the polluted sky (ibid).

Figure expression and movement

Figure refers to the important people, animals, or objects on the screen. The director controls the movements of the figures, and their positions when they are not moving. In the case of films that use actors, the director also controls their performances – their style of acting. This includes their appearance, movements, gestures, facial expressions, and the sounds they make.

Realism is often used as a criterion for judging good acting, but ideas of realistic acting have changed over time, and not all film genres suit realistic acting. The important question is whether or not the performance of a particular actor in a film is appropriate for the *context* of that film. *Context* refers to the general situation of the film, composed of its genre, narrative, and overall *mise-en-scène*.

We also need to compare the acting performance to other aspects of the film such as the setting and lighting and camera angles. Does the performance fit in well with these things? It must also be remembered that the actor's performance can be edited in different ways. In other words, various shots of the actor can be combined in different ways to create different effects.

14.4.5 *Mise-en-scène* in space and time

A film is essentially about *change*, both in space and time.

Space

Each shot is shown on the cinema screen, which is a flat surface. But usually the action depicted in the film is three-dimensional. It is the *mise-en-scène* of the film that enables us to believe that we are seeing something three-dimensional. The director manipulates space in the following ways in order to achieve this:

- *Movement of objects and scenery.* This attracts our attention.
- *Colour contrast.* Different colours or types of colour are used to make a distinction between different objects and scenery.
- *Balance of distinct components.* This refers to the size and importance of objects and scenery in different parts of the screen. Sometimes this will be *symmetrical* (equally balanced), and sometimes less symmetrical or even *asymmetrical* (deliberately unbalanced). The way in which balance is achieved is known as *composition.*
- *Variations in size.* Different objects on screen will be of different sizes. Human vision will tend to register the larger objects first.
- *Depth cues.* Some objects will be filmed further away from the camera than others. The viewers will see these objects as being further away, and this will help to create the illusion of three-dimensional space (Bordwell & Thompson 1993).

Time

With some shots, things seem to be happening slowly, that is time seems to be moving slowly, and with other shots the opposite is true. This is known as the *rhythm* of time, and is similar to the rhythm of music. The director controls this rhythm by controlling the number and speed of the different movements on the screen.

14.4.6 Narrative functions of *mise-en-scène*

Mise-en-scène is important in both narrative and non-narrative films. In narrative films, the specific shape and content of shots helps to give story information to the audience. This includes direct information, visual clues that give hints about information, and repeated motifs. In the early stages of a film, what we see on screen gives us clues as to what will happen later, thereby raising our expectations.

14.5 THE SHOT: CINEMATOGRAPHIC PROPERTIES

Cinematographic qualities refers to *how* a shot is filmed, in terms of its technological aspects.

14.5.1 Photographic image

The image on the screen can be physically manipulated in three ways:

The range of tonalities

This refers to the range of colours, or the range of shades of black and white, that we see on screen. This in turn depends on the type of *film stock* used. Film stock means a particular kind of celluloid film with particular chemical qualities. Even after the shot has been completed, the film image can be further manipulated by the way in which it is developed in the laboratory.

Speed of motion

When filming a shot, the rate at which the camera takes pictures can be decreased or increased from 24 images per second. The fewer the images per second, the faster the motion shown on screen, and vice versa. These effects are known as *fast motion* and *slow motion*. Extreme fast motion is known as *time-lapse*, and extreme slow motion is known as *high-speed* (because it allows us to see very high speed events). As with the range of tonalities, the shot can be further manipulated in the laboratory (Bordwell & Thompson 1993).

Perspective relations

Perspective refers to the fact that objects appear smaller and smaller the further away they get from us. By manipulating the camera lens, and using special lenses, the filmmaker can manipulate the way perspective is presented on screen. Perspective can be altered to increase or decrease *depth* (i.e. how far away the image reaches). Objects on the screen can also be distorted and made to lean in various directions, or made to look bigger or smaller than they really are. The *focus* of the camera can be altered to make images look sharper or softer. Perspective can also be manipulated to achieve special effects (Bordwell & Thompson 1993).

14.5.2 Framing

The frame of a shot refers to the borders of the image. It is important because the filmmaker consciously chooses it, for the position of the camera determines the position of the frame (Bordwell & Thompson 1993). Each movie image is enclosed by the frame of the screen, which defines the world of film, separating it from the actual world of the darkened auditorium. Unlike a painter or still photographer, the filmmaker does not conceive of the framed compositions as self-sufficient statements. Film is a temporal as well as spatial art, and consequently the visuals are constantly in flux (Giannetti 1996: 40–41). Framing affects the image in the following ways:

Frame dimensions and shape

The frame is almost always in the shape of a rectangle. The exact type of rectangle is measured in terms of *aspect ratio*. This refers to the ratio of the width of the frame, as compared to the height of the frame. Since the early 1960s, *widescreen ratios* (i.e. high width to height ratio) have become dominant, although television and video use a narrower ratio. Widescreen shots are created with special lenses, by manipulating an ordinary lens, or by manipulating the film in the laboratory.

Widescreen images allow for more objects in the shot, and for more complex composition of a shot. Filmmakers have to bear in mind that their films may eventually be shown on television or video, and try to shoot the film in such away that it can be successfully converted (Bordwell & Thompson 1993). The widescreen is particularly suited to capturing the vastness of a locale. For example, in Stanley Kubrick's *2001: A Space Odyssey*, the widescreen is used to reflect the limitlessness of space, and in *Waterworld* (1995) the widescreen is used to indicate the endlessness of the ocean.

Onscreen and offscreen space

Onscreen space is what we can see on the screen. *Offscreen* space is space that we cannot see on the screen, but which is part of the story. The filmmaker can take advantage of this to conceal and reveal various figures and objects and the information that goes with them (Bordwell & Thompson 1993).

Angle, level, height and distance of framing

All these terms refer to the position from which the audience views each shot:

- *Angle*: the angle at which we look on the shot
- *Level:* whether or not the frame is parallel to the horizon
- *Height*: the height above the ground from which we look at the shot
- *Distance*: how far away the shot appears to be (Bordwell & Thompson 1993)

There are five basic angles used in film: the bird's-eye-view; the high angle; the eye-level shot; the low angle; and the oblique angle (Giannetti 1996:12–13).

- The *bird's-eye-view* is "perhaps the most disorienting angle of all, for it involves photographing a scene from directly overhead" (Giannetti 1996:14). The subject matter of such shots often seems "unrecognisable and abstract" (ibid), and filmmakers tend to avoid this type of set-up. However, in certain contexts this angle can be "highly expressive. In effect, bird's-eye-view shots permit us to hover above the scene like all-powerful gods. The people photographed appear ant-like and insignificant" (ibid).

- Ordinary *high-angle shots* are not as extreme as the bird's-eye-view shot, and therefore are not so disorientating. High angles give a viewer a sense of general overview, but not necessarily one "implying destiny or fate. High angles reduce the height of the objects photographed and usually include the ground or floor as background. High angles reduce the importance of a subject ... [a] person seems harmless and insignificant photographed from above" (Giannetti 1996:15). This angle is also effective for conveying a character's self-contempt.
- *Eye-level shots* tend to be the norm, used by all directors at some time during filming. This shot is used to avoid extreme angles; shot from approximately five to six feet off the ground, normally the way in which an actual subject would survey a scene. This is very often used to "capture the clearest view of an object" (Giannetti 1996:12)
- *Low angles* have the opposite effect of high angles. They increase height and thus are useful for suggesting "verticality" (ibid). More practically they increase a short actor's height. Motion is speeded up, and in scenes of violence especially, low angles capture a "sense of confusion. Environment is usually minimised in low angles, and often the sky or ceiling is the only background. Psychologically, low angles heighten the importance of a subject. The figure looms threateningly over the spectator, who is made to feel insecure and dominated. A person photographed from below inspires fear, awe and respect. For this reason, low angles are often used in propaganda films or in scenes depicting heroism. When an extreme low angle is combined with a perspective-distorting wide-angle lens, a character can seem threatening, for he or she looms above the camera (and us) like a towering giant" (Giannetti 1996:15–16).
- An *oblique angle* involves a "lateral tilt of the camera. When the image is projected, the horizon is skewed. A man photographed at an oblique angle will look as though he is about to fall to one side. This angle is sometimes used for point-of-view shots – to suggest the imbalance of a drunk, for example. Psychologically, oblique angles suggest tension, transition and impending movement. The natural horizontal and vertical lines of a scene are converted into unstable diagonals" (Giannetti 1996:14–16). Oblique angles are not used often, for they can disorient a viewer. In scenes depicting violence, however, they can be effective is capturing precisely this sense of visual anxiety (ibid).

Some filmmakers avoid angles because they are too manipulative and judgemental. In avoiding the use of angles, some filmmakers believe that the camera is then neutral and dispassionate, allowing viewers to make up their own minds about what kind of people are being presented.

Once again, when studying framing positions, we need to ask ourselves what the function is of each position in a film, and whether or not it is appropriate. There are no "good" or "bad" framing positions.

The mobile frame

Because cinema depicts motion, the frame is able to move, and thereby to change framing position whilst the shot is still taking place. This is achieved by moving the camera in various ways. The most common of these are:

- *Pan shot*: The camera is stationary and rotates on a vertical axis. Pans in extreme long shots are especially effective in epic films where an audience can experience the vastness of a locale. The pan shot is also an effective way of preserving the cause-effect relationship between the two subjects and of emphasising the solidarity and connectedness of people.
- *Tilt*: The camera is stationary and rotates on a horizontal axis. Tilt shots can be used to keep subjects within frame, to "emphasise spatial and psychological interrelationships, to suggest simultaneity and to emphasis cause-effect relationships" (Giannetti 1996:109).
- *Tracking or dolly shot*: The camera travels in any direction along the ground. These shots are usually taken from a moving vehicle (dolly). The dolly actually moves in or out or alongside a moving subject/object which is photographed in motion. Occasionally tracks (similar to railway tracks) are laid on the set allowing for fluid movement (which gives this shot its name – tracking shot). Today cameras are even mounted on trains, cars, motorbikes and bicycles (Giannetti 1996:110).
- *Crane shot*: The camera moves above ground level (Bordwell & Thompson 1993). Crane shots are "essentially airborne dolly shots" (Giannetti 1996:116). In many respects the crane resembles those used by a telephone company to repair lines. It can move up, down, diagonally, in or out or any combination of these. "Because of its flexibility, a crane shot can suggest a number of complex ideas. It can move from high, long distances to low, close ones" (ibid).

Not only do camera movements provide a greater variety of framing perspectives, but they also strengthen the illusion that we are watching real events, often from the perspective of one of the characters. There are also technical reasons for mobile framing:

- *The mobile frame and space.* The frame can move to areas that were previously offscreen, and can accommodate the movements of figures and characters, which includes following particular movements in new directions.
- *The mobile frame and time.* The camera movements can be fast or slow, and last a short or a long time.
- *Patterns of mobile framing.* Repeated framing patterns can be used to create motifs (Bordwell & Thompson 1996).
- *Slow motion.* This prolongs time (Giannetti 1996:124).

14.5.3 Duration of the image: the long take

The *long take* is a shot of far greater than average length. It can be an alternative to a conventional series of shorter shots, and can even be used to present an entire scene in the film. Long takes often use mobile framing.

14.6 THE RELATIONSHIP OF SHOT TO SHOT: EDITING

14.6.1 What editing is

Editing refers to the way in which each shot is joined to the next. The ways in which this is done are known as *joins*. Through editing, we can use many shots to depict a single scene, or even jump back and forth between scenes. Traditionally, this has been done in the laboratory by physically cutting up and rejoining the celluloid film (using special glue or adhesive tape). Editing on video has also been done in the last few years, and editing on computer is the trend of the future (Bordwell & Thompson 1993).

Some common types of *joins* are:

- *Fade-out and fade-in*: The fade-out gradually darkens the old shot to black, and the fade-in lightens the new shot from black until you can see it.
- *Dissolve*: This briefly puts the beginning of the new shot on top of the old shot, mixing them together.
- *Wipe*: We briefly see both shots together on the screen, but separated by a line. The line moves across the screen, and the new shot replaces the old one.

14.6.2 Dimensions of film editing

When editing, the filmmaker needs to consider how each shot is related to the next. There are four ways of looking at this:

- Graphic relations between Shot A and Shot B
  This is when the focus is on the *visual* aspects of the two shots. In other words, the filmmaker is concerned with the way in which each shot looks similar or different to the next one. If the two shots are similar in terms of the use of colours, shapes, lighting and so on, then this is called a *graphic match*. If the two shots are dissimilar, this is known as a *graphic conflict*.
- Rhythmic relations between Shot A and Shot B
  This refers to the length of each shot in relation to the next. Short shots create a feeling of speed, whilst lengthy shots slow things down. The combination of shots of different and similar lengths results in a rhythm similar to that of music.
- Spatial relations between Shot A and Shot B
  The point in space shown in one shot, as it relates to the point in space shown in the next, is what is known as spatial relations between the two shots. Shots can show the full space occupied by a particular scene in a film, or they can show parts of that space. Furthermore, shots can be filmed in totally different places, but put together in such a way that they look as if they belong to the same place.
- Temporal relations between Shot A and Shot B
  As we have already seen, time is an important aspect of the construction of a film narrative in terms of the *order* of events, the *duration* of events, and the *frequency* of events. Editing can be used to emphasise all of these things by manipulation of

the *order, duration* and *frequency* of different shots, and different kinds of shots, in the film (Bordwell & Thompson 1993).

14.6.3 Continuity editing

Editing can be very disruptive to the viewer, as it shifts from one shot to the next. *Continuity editing* is one approach that seeks to keep this to a minimum. The editing is planned in such a way that it tells the story of the film in a smooth and continuous manner. This is the major form of editing for narrative filmmaking. The two most important aspects of continuity editing are *space* and *time*:

- Spatial continuity: the 180° system
  This is a system of filming where all the action is planned along a straight line. All camera placement is in a semicircle on one side of that line. This system ensures that each shot of the action shows some of the same space as the previous shot. It also means that all of the shots show things happening in the same direction, which determines that the shots flow smoothly into one another.
- Temporal continuity: order, frequency, duration
  These three aspects of time in a film are handled in the following way:
  - *Order*: Usually events are presented in the actual order in which they happen in a film. The most common exception is the flashback.
  - *Frequency*: An event that happens once in the story is usually only shown once in the film.
  - *Duration*: The length of the film is usually less than the length of the story. It is sometimes equal, but almost never greater (Bordwell & Thompson 1993).

14.6.4 Alternatives to continuity editing

Whereas continuity editing focuses on space and time, other approaches might focus on the graphic and rhythmic aspects of editing. This is particularly the case with non-narrative films, but it happens with narrative films as well. Other narrative films may focus on space and time, but may deliberately emphasise *discontinuity*. In other words, they may deliberately use editing that tells the story in a way that is not smooth or continuous, and may even be confusing. This does not mean that they are bad films. Discontinuity is simply a different way of telling a story, and may be very appropriate for a particular film (Bordwell & Thompson 1993).

14.7 SOUND IN THE CINEMA

14.7.1 The power of sound

Although sound is recorded during shooting, it is also added later, and even dialogue can be re-dubbed over the original. The sound of a film is therefore created separately from the images, and can be manipulated and edited to suit the purposes of a film. Its importance also lies in the fact that it appeals to the sense of hearing, whereas the images appeal to the sense of sight. Sound therefore makes a film far deeper and more complex. Sound works together with images in the following ways:

- An image can be combined with a sound that "fits" it, to express a particular idea or emotion more strongly.
- Sound can direct our attention to a particular figure or object on the screen.
- It can include offscreen noises, which give us clues as to what we will see next.
- It can cause viewers to form expectations, and can increase tension.
- Sound makes the occasional use of silence very effective (Bordwell & Thompson 1993).

Silence can be more powerful than sound in certain cases. In the poetic fantasy, *Wings of Desire* (1988), a film about an angel who longs to become mortal, the angel often sits on a statue high above the city of Berlin, encompassed by silence. The discordant clash of modern life far below is softened by the soothing distance (Giannetti 1996:202).

Absolute silence in a sound film tends to call attention to itself. Any stretch of silence creates a vacuum – a sense of something impending, about to erupt. Arthur Penn exploited this phenomenon in the conclusion of *Bonnie and Clyde* (1967). "The lovers stop on a country road to help a friend (actually an informer) with his truck, which has presumably broken down. Clumsily, the friend scrambles under the truck. There is a long moment of silence while the two lovers exchange puzzled, then anxious, glances. Suddenly, the sound track roars with the noise of machine guns as the lovers are brutally cut down by policemen hiding in the bushes" (Giannetti 1996:209). Silence in a sound film is often used to symbolise "death, because we tend to associate sound with the presence of ongoing life" (Giannetti 1996:210).

In several scenes of Alfred Hitchcock's *Psycho* (1960; remake by Gus van Sant 1998), Bernard Hermann's score – consisting entirely of strings – replicates shrill bird noises. This motif is used as a form of characterisation. A shy and appealing young man (Anthony Perkins) is associated with birds early on in the film. He stuffs birds as a hobby, and his own features are intense and rather hawk-like. During the brutal shower scene murder sequence, the sound track throbs with screeching bird music. The audience assumes the murderer is the boy's mother, but birds have been associated with him, not her. "One of Hitchcock's recurrent themes is the transference of guilt. In this film, the transfer is rather complex. The youth has dug up his long-dead mother's body and literally stuffed it. Often he dresses himself up in her clothing. Although we think we see the mother killing two victims, we have in fact seen the schizophrenic youth as his other self – his mother. The bird music offers an early clue to this psychological transfer" (Giannetti 1996:206).

To illustrate the use of dialogue, Giannetti (1996) gives the example of *Dick Tracy* (1990), with Glenne Headly and Al Pacino. The blowhard villain, Big Boy Caprice (Pacino) is always in the loud range. His grating voice is magnified and reverberates throughout the film. Dialogue is shouted rather than spoken. Our ears are assaulted by a "barrage of relentless threats, delivered at a furious pace. Dick Tracy's girlfriend Tess Truehart (Headly) is, of course, intimidated" (Giannetti 1996:209). In *Never Cry Wolf* (1983), the hero of this movie, based on the actual Canadian author Farley Mowat, spends much of his time alone in the Arctic to study the "behaviour of wolves". Whether we hear the melancholy whine of the wind, the crunch of snow underfoot, or the plaintive howl of distant wolves, the sound effects are masterfully mixed, often "producing a haunting, poetic effect" (Giannetti 1996:208).

The gangster films, *Reservoir Dogs* (1992) and *Pulp Fiction* (1994) feature an almost steady torrent of foul language, as violent as the lives of the characters. In fact, eventually the swearing becomes grotesquely comical, adding to the movies' bizarre tone, which blends violence, cruelty and pathos with black comedy. "In cases like these, sanitised dialogue would be a form of aesthetic dishonesty, totally at odds with the movies' nasty edge of realism" (Giannetti 1996:232).

14.7.2 Fundamentals of film sound

Acoustic properties

- *Loudness*. The volume of the sound in a film will be deliberately turned up or down at different times, according to the needs of the film at that moment.
- *Pitch*. This refers to how "high" or "deep" a sound is. Different sounds in a film can be told apart according to their different pitches. Pitch can also be manipulated to serve specific purposes in a film.
- *Timbre*. As the "flavour" of a particular sound, it helps us to tell different sounds apart, especially with the *soundtrack* (the background music) to a film. Timbre can also be changed according to the needs of the film (Bordwell & Thompson 1993).

The enormous popularity of George Lucas's (director) *Star Wars* quartet revived the tradition of large-scale symphonic accompaniments to heighten the dramatic impact of the scenes. "John Williams's score is brassy, powerful and richly orchestrated, very much in the manner of the lushly romantic and full-bodied scores of Hollywood's golden age" (Giannetti 1996:214). Critic Frank Spotnitz noted that "the score is like a second screenplay, commenting on and enriching the first" (ibid).

Sound effects can also express internal emotions. In Robert Redford's *Ordinary People* (1980), for example, an "uptight mother (Mary Tyler Moore) has prepared French toast for her emotionally unstable son. Though it is his favourite breakfast food, the young man is too tense to eat: his ambivalent attitude toward his mother is one of his main problems. Irritated by his 'selfish' indifference to her gesture of maternal concern, she swoops up his plate and carries it to the sink, where she stuffs the French toast into the garbage disposal, its grinding roar a symbolic embodiment of her anger and agitation" (Giannetti 1996:208).

Selection, alteration and combination

There are three types of sound in film: *speech, music* and *noise* (otherwise known as *sound effects*). Sound editing involves

- *Selection* – a choice is made from all three types of sound
- *Alteration* – electronic equipment is used to change the sounds as desired
- *Combination* – different sounds are placed together, and are played simultaneously.

Usually dialogue is the most important type of sound, with music and sound effects in the background. There are times when this changes, however. The three types of sound are designed to work together and complement each other (Bordwell & Thompson 1993).

In *Apocalypse Now* (1979), the sound-mixing in Francis Ford Coppola's surrealistic Vietnam epic is masterful, suffused with grotesque ironies. In one sequence, American helicopters hover and "swirl like huge mechanised gods, dropping napalm bombs on a jungle village to the music of Wagner's inexorable 'Ride of the Valkyries,' which thunders on the soundtrack. As the scared Vietnamese farmers run for shelter, American soldiers go surfing in the poisonous napalm fumes" (Giannetti 1996:210).

14.7.3 Dimensions of film sound

Sound relates to other aspects of a film in four ways:

Rhythm

Apart from music, speech and sound effects also have rhythm. Usually the filmmaker will edit the sounds in the film so that their rhythm matches the visual rhythm of the images. Sometimes the sound will be edited so that the two rhythms will not match. This will have a specific function in the film.

Fidelity

This refers to whether or not a sound matches the figure or object on screen that is supposed to be making that sound. If it does not, this will usually be for a specific purpose.

Space

Sound in film is generally geared to space. When a severe discrepancy exists, the effect can be disorienting and even frightening. In *The Exorcist* (1973, re-release 2000), the devil has possessed a young girl (Linda Blair). "The sounds emanating from her tiny body echo loudly, creating a cavernous effect as if the girl's slight figure has been spiritually expanded thousands of times to accommodate the demons that possess her" (Giannetti 1996:207).

Some sounds in a film are connected to figures and objects that are *diegetic* (part of the story), whether onscreen or offscreen. Other sounds such as the soundtrack, or a non-character narrator, are *nondiegetic*. *Diegetic* sound can also be *internal* – that is, a character's thoughts represented by spoken words. *Sound perspective* is also important.

This refers to the amount of distance suggested by a sound; how near or far away a sound seems to be.

Time

In most films, the sounds are *synchronised* with the objects and figures that are supposed to be causing them; that is, there is a realistic match. Sound that does not match the image is called *asynchronous*, and is sometimes used for specific purposes. In a similar way, every event in the story of a film has sounds associated with it. Usually the sound is played simultaneously with the image depicting the event. Occasionally, for specific purposes, the sound will be played earlier or later than the image.

Summary

This unit looked at some of the basic concepts of film production, namely, technical and social factors in film production; distribution and exhibition; film form; narrative construction; non-narrative form; film style – *mise-en-scène*; cinematographic properties; editing and sound. The unit provided you with many examples to illustrate the various concepts found in film production. Two case studies were included: one dealing with the film *Jaws* and the other with the film *The Crying Game*.

Research activities

1 List all the concepts found in film production

2 Conduct research on the production of a film/video of your choice:
- Select a film/video of your choice.
- Give a brief synopsis of the film/video (briefly describe the film/video).
- State which studio released the film/video.
- State which country released the film/video.
- State the year of the film/video's release.
- List the central characters' names and the actors that portray them.

All of this information is recorded on the film/video at either the beginning or the end, when the credits appear.

3 After you have read the two case studies provided, stipulate the differences between the film *Jaws* and the film *The Crying Game* in terms of their respective production, distribution and exhibition.

4 Select a film or video of your choice and provide a detailed account of both the plot and the story as you understand it.

5 Select a film/video of your choice. Comment on the following three concepts therein: music, dialogue and special effects. For instance, stipulate whether or not you think that the dialogue is a realistic portrayal of the time period or whether the dialogue used is relevant to the film/video. For example, the film *Boyz N the Hood*

(1991) uses dialogue that realistically depicts life in American ghettos. The film *New Jack City* (1991), on the other hand, uses dialogue that is used by actual drug dealers. While *Shakespeare in love* (1998) and *Elizabeth* (1998) use sixteenth-century dialogue to realistically portray that era. An example of the absence of any dialogue is the film *Evita* (1998) by British director Alan Parker; communication takes place through the use of song.

6 Select a film/video of your choice and state whether or not the film is narrated by voice-over narration. If the film is narrated by voice-over narration, state whether or not the character that narrates the film/video is central to the film/video, and if so, why.

7 Select a film of your choice and give a description of that particular film's form.
   - Go to the video store and take out a video of a film that interests you, OR go to the cinema to view a film that you want to see.
   - Watch the film/video closely.
   - Provide a short description of the film/video you have viewed.
   - At the end of viewing the film/video, comment on the following: the film/video's message; the content and subject matter; detail the characters and their personalities; and state why you think that the film/video has any artistic merit based on your idea of what constitutes an artistic view of film.
   - Substantiate your views by providing examples from the film/video, thereby motivating your interpretation.
   - Keep in mind that this is *your* interpretation of the film/video and as such there are no right or wrong answers.

8 Select a film/video of your choice and analyse the use of costumes and make-up. State whether or not the costumes are realistic or stylised.

9 Demonstrate an understanding of film noir cinema by listing all of the concepts related to film noir style of cinema.

10 Describe the five basic angles used in film.

11 Describe the concept of continuity editing.

Further reading

Bernstein, S. 1994. *Film production.* Boston: Focal Press.

Bordwell, D. 1989. *Making meaning: inference and rhetoric in the interpretation of cinema.* Cambridge, MA: Harvard University Press.

Glimcher, S. 1975. *Movie making: a guide to film production.* New York: Simon & Schuster.

Goodell, G. 1998. *Independent feature film production: a complete guide from concept through distribution.* New York: St. Martin's Griffin.

Horwin, M. 1990. *Careers in film and video making.* Boston: Focal Press.

Malkmus, L. 1990. *Arab and African film making.* London: Zed Books.

McLeod, MK. 1990. *The effects of visual training, film making and photography on aesthetic visual perception.* Ann Arbor, MI: University Microfilm International.

Tomaselli, KG. 1990. *Making sense of film: how to read films about Southern Africa.* Durban: Media Resource Centre, University of Natal.

Bibliography

Bordwell, D & Thompson, K. 1993. *Film art: an introduction.* New York: McGraw-Hill.

Fourie, PJ (ed). 1997. *Introduction to communication – course book 6: film and television studies.* Kenwyn: Juta.

Giannetti, L. 1996. *Understanding movies.* 7th edition. Englewood Cliffs, NJ: Prentice-Hall.

Kochberg, S. 1999. Cinema as an institution, in *An introduction to film studies*, 2nd edition, edited by J Nelmes. London: Routledge.

Lapsley, R & Westlake, M. 1988. *Film theory: an introduction.* Manchester: Manchester University Press.

Nelmes, J (ed). 1999. *An introduction to film studies.* 2nd edition. London: Routledge.

Webster, C. 1999. Film and technology, in *An introduction to film studies*, 2nd edition, edited by J Nelmes. London: Routledge.

Wyver, J. 1985. *An introduction to moving pictures.* London: Routledge.

Educational Media: Television

15

Beschara Karam

Overview

In this unit we commence the discussion of educational television (ETV) and development by describing and defining content key terms that are used repeatedly throughout the unit, and which – if used in different contexts – could convey different meanings. Approaches to mediated teaching and learning are then investigated by considering different learning theories and approaches.

A development perspective of teaching/learning follows, which deals with suggested goals or aims; learners; different types of interaction; criteria that ought to be considered when determining the scope and sequence of what is taught/learned; the importance of formulating aims and objectives; and an application of the Pareto principle.

It is important to note that while drastic changes have taken place since 1996 in terms of outcome-based education and South African Qualifications Authority (SAQA), such as the recognition of prior learning; the definition of lifelong learning; and the distinction among foundational, practical and reflexive competencies, and although these changes are of the utmost importance, it is not the focus of this unit to address these changes.

Following the application of the Pareto principle, the adaptability of television as a communication medium is investigated with the focus on four issues, namely the means of distributing ETV; the educational implications of the means of distribution, and of the encoding (medium) characteristics; and the importance of television-mediated experiences. A distinction is drawn between formative and summative evaluation of ETV, with the emphasis on the purpose and value of formative evaluation in particular. The unit ends with a discussion of the planning, implementing and evaluating of educational television as a continuous cycle. This unit is based predominantly on: Du Plooy, T. 1997. Educational television and development, in *Introduction to communication – course book 6: film and television studies*, edited by PJ Fourie. Kenwyn: Juta.

Learning outcomes

At the end of this unit you should be able to demonstrate a critical understanding of

- the different theories/approaches to teaching/learning, by describing their respective assumptions;

- the significance of modelling and play for children and adults as learners, by describing the main assumptions surrounding these issues;
- the main assumptions on which a development perspective of teaching/learning can be based, by describing them in detail;
- teaching aims and learning objectives, by describing actual examples;
- the Pareto principle, by applying the principle in the analysis of a skill or task that has to be taught;
- the adaptability of television as a communication medium for the purposes of education and development, by explaining the central assumptions surrounding these issues;
- the application of formative evaluation during the planning and preproduction stages of designing an ETV programme, by writing short notes on the application of formative evaluation and applying formative evaluation to the planning and preproduction stages of designing an ETV programme that you have selected; and
- the difference between formative and summative evaluation, by applying summative evaluation to an actual ETV programme.

15.1 INTRODUCTION

The focus in this unit is on television as a medium of communication, used for the purposes of education and development. The reason why we concentrate on *television* is mainly due to its encoding characteristics – such as movement – and therefore its ability to simulate reality. Despite the emphasis on television, many of the assumptions, arguments and guidelines discussed below can be applied to other educational media, such as photographs, slides, tape-slide presentations, overhead projections and computers.

This unit is written with four general assumptions in mind, the first of which is that as we begin the new millennium, we find ourselves in a world that is characterised by an increasing *pace* of change. Technological innovations are one of the forces that contribute to the increasing rate of human obsolescence, which is evident in fields such as health care and organisational settings. For example, managers of relatively stable organisations of a decade ago are no longer effective in managing volatile organisations of the present. In order to deal with transformation, the second assumption is that current educational goals ought to be innovative and adaptive, if learners are to engage in continuous change (Botkin, Elmandjara & Malitza 1979; Faure, Herrern, Kaddoura, Lopes, Petrousky, Rahmerna & Ward 1972). This brings us to the third assumption, namely that in order to cope with change and instability, our whole education system needs to be structured around the concept of lifelong learning. If this assumption were accepted, then learning resources must be made accessible to learners at their convenience, which is a challenging requirement. Fourthly, humanity needs to be developed to become proficient in taking autonomous responsibility – including responsibility for their own learning (Toffler 1980).

If our aim is to develop social consensus among members of a future generation and when focusing specifically on the education and development of children, then at least three assumptions can be added to the four mentioned above.

These assumptions are as follows:

- Children need certain skills to survive in future decades.
- Children need an understanding of the natural and social sciences, including communication skills and the ability to communicate in more than one language.
- Learning has to be extended to the real world (and kept in contact with changes in this world).

15.2 DESCRIPTION AND DEFINITION OF CONTENT KEY TERMS

Certain terms that may denote different meanings to different readers are repeatedly used in this unit. In order to avoid misunderstanding, and in an attempt to demarcate the parameters within which the terms are used, they are defined and described in this section.

Teacher: It is important to realise that the term *teacher* as used in this unit is *not* limited to its traditional connotation of formal education as provided by schools, colleges, universities or other institutions. Instead, *teacher* as used in this unit refers to a variety of people, from communication practitioners, researchers, health professionals, planners, and facilitators to farmers. In fact, even an illiterate parent can in certain situations be regarded as a *teacher*. Nevertheless, the term *teacher* is used in this unit to refer to someone who knows the content of the subject or requirements of a particular skill being taught/learned.

Learner: Reference to *learner* is intended to be interpreted in the widest possible sense, to include preschool children, pupils at school level, students at tertiary level of education, trainees who may already be employed, as well as adults who may be unemployed, illiterate and even retired.

Target destination: The term *target destination* is frequently used in this unit, to denote those learners for whom the messages are specifically intended. Although both *learners* and *target destination* are somewhat vague abstractions (like *television audiences*), they are intended to refer to *individual* persons.

Content: Is used in this unit in the broadest of connotations and can therefore refer to actual subject curricula and any other form of lifelong learning, at any age, including experiences beyond the school walls.

Education: A distinction is made between *formal* education, *nonformal* education and *informal* education:

- *Formal education* is traditionally represented by and characteristically manifested in the physical, educational and managerial structures found in schools, colleges, technikons, universities and similar educational institutions, whatever their source of finance or legal status. When educational television forms part of the educational technological services of these formal educational institutions, it fulfils mainly a supporting service. In this type of education, educational television is particularly dependent on specialised personnel, the training and positive attitude from teachers in the use of the medium, and the provision of funding and an infrastructure which is integrated with the education system of an institution and/or education department on regional, provincial and/or national levels.

- *Informal education* begins in the family and, as a child grows older, informal education continues as the child is exposed to people and situations beyond the family circle, such as relatives, friends, the church, and the mass media such as television. Learning takes place while children and adults watch everyday television programmes that are aimed mainly at entertainment, such as sport, soap operas and sitcoms. Social and moral values may be learned informally through exposure to advertising, violence, sex, pornography and/or stereotypical discriminations.
- *Nonformal education* is mainly (but not exclusively) provided by television as a mass medium, and differs from informal education in that programmes are planned to fulfil specific educational needs. Examples of such needs are: to improve the level of literacy; health education; induction programmes; in-service training; industrial training programmes in commerce and industry; and other ad hoc needs.

  Nonformal educational programmes aimed at preschool children, usually deal with cognitive processes (e.g. the enhancement of perceptual discrimination, classification and ordering); the child's physical environment (e.g. plants and animals); and the social environment (e.g. the self and social roles), with the aim of improving the child's readiness for formal education in school.

  Nonformal education, aimed at adults, is often aimed to meet the functional needs of adults, such as helping people to adapt to new stages in their life cycle, bringing up children, caring for and looking after the elderly, dealing with retirement, or dealing with social and other changes in society. The latter are examples of subject areas in which non-degree courses have been offered by formal distance-education institutions, such as Open University as part of its Community Education Programme, since the 1980s.

Development has historically had serious definitional problems, depending on whether the context in which it is used relates to individual, institutional, national or even international changes. Even its continued use, instead of terms such as *transformation, beneficial change, liberation, revolution* and *social mobilisation*, is being questioned (Crocker 1993:62; Nyirenda 1995:58–81). Nevertheless, from a communication perspective we continue to use the term *development* and to view it in a more holistic manner, by defining it (for the purpose of this discussion) as a process that enables all people to improve their quality of life. By defining it as a *process*, the emphasis is on continual change and continued improvement on a lifelong basis. *Quality of life*, as used here, includes an increase in knowledge and skills to increase productivity and the use of resources, with the intent that each individual will enjoy personal, material and social advancement (Ngugi 1995:6). Development is therefore *not* used here only in the historical sense of providing for the improvement of the marginalised, poor, underprivileged, illiterate or alienated people.

On the basis of the above two descriptions, it is important to realise that (as used in this unit) education signifies a wider sphere of development at all stages of life, such as fostering intellectual development, the formation of character, widening an individual's horizons, stimulating aesthetic needs, imagination and creativity. Education is accordingly ultimately aimed at the transmission of knowledge to promote socialisation and integration and to facilitate cultural promotion. Development (as used in this unit) can, on the other hand, in certain instances, be regarded as synonymous with training, such as the acquisition of specific skills.

Education and *development* are used interchangeably in this unit because we argue that by acquiring a particular skill, the learner will have access to employment opportunities, which can stimulate personal aspirations and ultimately fulfil the educational aims of a particular culture and society.

Development communication: Keeping the above definition of *development* in mind, *development communication*, as used here, refers to communication in interpersonal, small-group and mass-communication settings, in which the content and form of messages are planned with well-defined objectives in mind (e.g. to inform, to motivate and train in particular skills), or with specific learning outcomes in mind.

Educational television (ETV) can connate different meanings, depending on the target destination, the aims and the means of distributing programmes. (See sections 15.4 and 15.5 below for a discussion of the relevance of these three and other variables and their implications for the planning/production and reception of ETV programmes.) For introductory purposes, ETV is defined as the use of television as a medium of communication for educational and development purposes.

Effective teaching/learning is used to mean a qualitative change in the way in which a learner understands and deals with reality.

ETV designer is used as a collective term in this unit to denote the individual (or, in the majority of instances, a team of specialists) that is responsible for all the stages from planning to disseminating an ETV programme. The ETV designer should have creative, administrative and organisational abilities. In a team context, the designer must be represented by a teacher (content expert), medium expert, researcher and any other members required for specialised tasks, such as a graphic designer.

15.3 THEORETICAL APPROACHES TO MEDIATED TEACHING AND LEARNING

The explosion of knowledge related to education not only guides different views of teaching and learning, but also influences approaches to the use of ETV. Prior to the 1950s, educationists and psychologists focused their research on the teaching of children and the youth. Consequently, our education systems were guided by concepts found in pedagogy (i.e. the art and science of teaching children). Since then, research has also focused on the art and science of adult learning (andragogy). Although this unit cannot deal with either the pedagogical or andragogical models in detail, certain characteristics that must be taken into account for effective learning are noted and discussed.

Of central concern in this unit is: in what ways can human communication (when mediated by means of television) be regarded as an *educational* activity?

15.3.1 Learning theories

A *learning theory* consists of the formulation of laws (and/or conditions) of learning, which consists of principles (or generalisations) which formulate (or attempt to formulate) those conditions under which learning occurs.

Learning theories can be grouped into two families, namely the so-called *behaviourist* theories and the *Gestalt* theories.

Behaviourist (also called *connectionist*) theories regard learners' behaviour to be a reaction or a direct *response* to a stimulus (or stimuli). In other words, behaviourists (Skinner 1953; 1974) focus on that (behaviour) which can be empirically observed as so-called responses. In the case of ETV, the codes of content (e.g. the presenter) and the codes of form (e.g. the paradigmatic camera shot selected) are – according to these theories – examples of stimuli. Forms of individualised learning, such as programmed instruction are based on this stimulus-response assumption. The content keywords in behaviourism (O'Sullivan, Hartley, Saunders, Montgomery & Fiske 1994:28) are *shaping* or *moulding*, whereby someone (e.g. a teacher) moulds or shapes someone else's behaviour by rewarding *right* behaviour and punishing *wrong* behaviour. From a research point of view, behaviourists rely mainly on experimental research methods and criticise the importance of thoughts, emotions or cognitive processes in teaching/learning as being subjective and biased.

According to Chaplin (1968:201), the main exponents of the Gestalt school (also called *field, organismic*, or *cognitive* theories) were Max Wertheimer, Wolfgang Köhler and Kurt Koffka. Gestalt theories assume that cognitive processes – which include our insight, intelligence and organisational abilities – are the basic characteristics of human behaviour. The best known Gestalt contributions are in the field of perception, such as the figure-ground concept; laws that govern our perceptual organisation (such as proximity, contrast, similarity and contiguity) and psychological closure. The work of educational psychologist Jean Piaget (1964), for example, suggests that elements (e.g. visual codes) that make up a scene are perceived by humans as elements, but together with the symbolic meanings conveyed by such elements. His work also emphasises the importance of learned behaviour in a child's development and growth.

The position taken in this unit is an eclectic one according to which we argue (1) that ETV programmes must be carefully planned and evaluated in order to function as clear, relevant and effective inputs or stimuli; and (2) that the learners' cognitive processes must be stimulated through activities that promote participation and practice.

15.3.2 Modelling and play

Teaching and learning are special types of communication, because they take place when "communication is accompanied by heightened levels of consciousness among teachers and learners" (Hamilton 1990:16). In other words, teaching and learning as forms of communication are influenced by the intentions, needs and values of both teachers and learners, and are shaped – or even constrained – by social circumstances. These circumstances include cultural norms, conventions and codes that are characteristic of the situations in which teachers and learners find themselves.

Young children learn appropriate behaviour by means of nonverbal communication (i.e. watching adults who serve as models, or watching and imitating television characters). For example, preschool children are most likely to select as their imaginary playmates those television characters who are physically attractive, who wear costumes and use props, and have distinguishing and easy-to-imitate nonverbal and/or verbal behaviour (James 1981:204). The relevance of modelling is well illustrated by a black (American) child's exclamation: "Look! He looks like me and he knows the answers!" (Lesser 1974:86).

Learning that is based on *showing how*, is, however, not restricted to young children, but is a feature of teaching and learning that takes place within an employment situation, such as apprentices learning certain crafts and trades. Modelling (or teaching through showing) is therefore implicit or indirect, and a process that can be repeated until the desired aims have been fulfilled.

According to various investigators (Secord & Backman 1964:532), the following principles account for a learner's actual choice of a model (and could by implication influence a child's socialisation process):

- *Secondary reinforcement* – A learner chooses a person as a model because the latter often rewards the learner.
- *Maintenance of approval* – A learner chooses a person as a model for fear of losing the model's affection, attention or approval.
- *Avoidance of punishment* – A learner chooses a person as a model for fear of being punished or injured.
- *Envy* – A person is chosen as a model because he or she is envied (e.g. for wealth, status or importance).
- *Power* – A person is chosen as a model because he or she has the potential power (e.g. due to a social position) to reward the learner – irrespective of whether or not such rewards materialise.

- *Similarity* – A learner perceives another person to have characteristics or traits that are similar to his or her own and chooses that person as a model because of these perceived traits.

One of the most important forms of learning (and teaching) takes place *off stage* or in *simulated* conditions, where *rehearsal* and *play* enable learners to acquire experiences for later life. Whereas the real world represents frustrations and painful emotions, in the play world "these real-world fears and hurts are transmuted into humor, pleasure, and delightful wish-fulfilment" (Stephenson 1967:200). Make-believe play is commonly associated with good feelings, and researchers have suggested that this is so because play is a kind of "power transformation by which the child ... reconstitutes a miniature world which follows his or her rules" (Palmer 1986:113).

By means of simulated rehearsals, both children and adults can gain in confidence and competence in specific tasks, without the exposure to the demands, safety risks or expenses that are involved in real-world circumstances. The use of simulation in the training of future aircraft pilots is one example where this form of teaching/learning is valuable.

According to Meehan (1995:17–28), play theory enables a teacher to explain to a learner why a competent performance can be evaluated as being competent and why an error can be treated as an error. The assumption is that, by learning a set of criteria and having opportunities for questioning, confirmation and rebuttal, a learner will develop the ability to apply knowledge to other areas (beyond the scope of a particular subject or content).

Two elements often overlooked or minimised by curriculum designers and media specialists are *ethical values* and *interpersonal relations*. When considering these two elements, we are forced to reconsider the following contextual variables:

- Values are necessary reference points when we have to make decisions, yet values are not necessarily synonymous with facts.
- Certain forces bind our values to other cultures (or even subcultures).
- Certain instructional practices contain values of a hidden curriculum – of which teachers ought to be (made) aware.
- Values that change (or that are perceived as changing) ought to be frequently re-examined.
- The need for a shift in emphasis from material values to respect for human values ought to be recognised.

When considering the above variables, the educational and cultural importance of play has two further implications for teaching and learning. Sport as a form of organised play is taken as an example to illustrate that *play* can cultivate values and lifestyles (in addition to acquiring specific skills). The emphasis which South African schools (in the past) placed on boys playing competitive games, such as rugby, can be interpreted as a form of play to inculcate values such as hard work, team identity, fair play, sportsmanship and manliness. In other words, through play (which in this example is organised sport) children learn *how* to do things, but simultaneously acquire the cultural and social values related to such activities. Secondly, because play is a surrogate for the real world and therefore contains elements of daydreaming and fantasising (e.g. being a nurse or being the chief fire-fighter), it has to be applied in such a manner that the learner can bridge the gap between the play world and the real world.

Teachers, administrators, curriculum researchers and ETV designers make diverse contributions regarding the scope and sequence of learning experiences when designing and developing an ETV programme. A variety of viewpoints exists regarding aspects such as relationships between different subjects; how learning takes place; how learning should be paced; and/or what constitutes the "best" type of schooling system. Despite these differences, the following three aspects are singled out as being central to curriculum development (Shane & Tabler 1981:87–88) and are adapted for the purpose of this discussion:

- an educational philosophy that determines whether a subject-centred or a learner-centred approach ought to be followed;
- specifying general goals and aims that the curriculum is designed to teach (and objectives that learners learn to achieve);
- guidance for instructional practices that are based on assumptions on which the fields of human development and learning theory are based.

The discussion that follows in this unit considers these aspects in greater detail and with the purpose of answering this question: How do these aspects influence educational television and development in a southern African context?

15.3.3 Subject-centred versus learner-centred approach

The debate as to whether learning experiences ought to concentrate on the subject matter (or content) or whether the focus ought to be on the development of the learner, dates back to the nineteenth century. The following is a brief overview of the arguments on which these two approaches are based.

Subject-centred approach

A subject-centred approach specifies for teachers which skills and knowledge they are responsible for developing. This implies that teachers experience a sense of security and that learners' exposure to knowledge and development of skills occurs in an orderly manner. By demarcating the scope and sequence of learning experiences, this approach also facilitates group planning by teachers. Based on the assumption that knowledge is the only outcome of learning experiences that can be measured, learners' progress can be evaluated in a methodological manner. Furthermore, the overlapping between grades or levels, or the repetition of similar subject content in formal education is reduced.

However, in a discussion of the barriers that inhibit effective learning, especially open learning, Strang (1987:26) warns that where the subject material or teachers are the source of knowledge, physical or external barriers (such as time, place and pace) and psychological barriers between learner and teacher may hinder learning.

Despite the fact that many ETV productions follow the subject-centred approach, it has some flaws (Zettl 1976:380–381). As the subject specialist selects the content, the criteria to be used when evaluating the programme are mainly determined by the prior selected content and not the input of the ETV designer or the encoding capabilities of the medium. The emphasis on the content can also increase the division that may already exist between the subject specialist and the medium expert. Lastly, according to this approach, television is treated merely as a distribution mechanism rather than a communication medium. In other words, this approach denies the fact that television can influence the way in which the content is conveyed and received.

Learner-centred approach

A learner-centred approach does not prescribe the scope or sequence of learning experiences that teachers have to follow. Instructional styles are varied and adjusted according to the needs of individual learners. The latter can have a positive influence on both the teacher and the learner. The individual teacher is permitted more latitude for modifying teaching according to learners' development changes and individual differences, and for selecting content regarded as suitable for a group of learners. This approach enables a teacher to consider aspects such as the development levels, personal interests, home and sociocultural environments, and home languages of young learners as individuals. The implication is that the subject content is more likely to be relevant to individual learners, and this in turn can have a positive influence on their learning experiences.

As attention, according to this approach, is focused on the learner's performance, it is acknowledged that a learner-centred approach or orientation to teaching/learning can create barriers to effective learning. This explains the movement towards study-skills training, which was further promoted by distance education, and in which learners are taught reading, writing and study skills (Dansereau, Collins, McDonald, Holley, Garland, Diekhoff & Evans 1979; Brown, Campione & Day 1981). Nevertheless, it is acknowledged that study-skills training alone does not automatically result in effective learning taking place. By focusing attention on the learner, we should acknowledge that *qualities*, such as a learner's attitude, intentions and decisions (Rogers 1983) contribute to or function as a barrier to effective teaching/learning.

Buckingham (1990:215) regards the distinction between the subject-centred approach and the learner-centred approach as being problematic. Firstly, because the emphasis on either the one or the other suggests that we should treat them as being mutually exclusive; secondly, because the emphasis on the distinction between content and learner is distant from what actually occurs in practice.

The emphasis – according to the subject-centred approach – on selecting *what* should be communicated, with little or no attention given to *how* the content will be *encoded, disseminated* or *received* by learners, gave rise to Zettl's (1976:381–387) *effect-to-cause approach*. This approach emphasises the following four aspects:

- a need for an assessment of the television audiences, including the general public and community leaders;
- viewers' involvement during and after watching the programme;
- the audiovisual medium characteristics;
- feedback and programme evaluation tests.

From the above discussion it becomes clear that one cannot settle for a linear view of ETV, or decide on an approach which focuses only on one of two components of the communication process. Consequently, it is worthwhile to consider an adaptation of the general systems theory as a viable alternative.

15.3.4 General systems approach – an application

The general systems approach developed out of the work of mathematicians and scientists in the field of cybernetics, and is accredited to Ludwig Von Bertalanffy (1956). This approach emphasises the functional structure of a system (especially the interdependence and relations among parts thereof), and it determines the significance of parts of a system in terms of their relation to the balance or equilibrium of the system as a whole.

When ETV is treated as a *system*, it means that balance or equilibrium can only be acquired if some form of control is applied to the *inputs* that are processed to become *outputs*. As a control mechanism, two elements are required, namely *feedforward* and *feedback*. Feedforward refers to the target, specifications or standard (usually stated as aims, objectives or learning outcomes) against which the feedback is measured. Feedback refers (in this instance) to the measurement of interaction or final output by means of formative and summative evaluations.

A good example of the application of a systems approach to communication activities is found in Fourie's (1976) model, *Communication by objectives (CBO)*. Fourie (1976) divides the communication process into four stages (planning, encoding, delivery and feedback) and, when applying this approach to ETV productions, the following two points are worth noting:

- A control or self-regulating system is based on the assumption that an ETV designer must always evaluate decisions against the answers provided by previous decisions.
- Irrespective of the sequence which an ETV designer follows during the initial planning or subsequent encoding stages, the main directive force at each stage are the objectives, or learning outcomes which are to be realised.

The importance placed on the interrelatedness and consequential functions fulfilled by the parts of a system (to maintaining a balanced state of equilibrium of a system) has the implication that a distinction must be made between a *dysfunctional* and a *nonfunctional* part (Merton 1968; Jansen 1989). A part that fulfils a nonfunction is redundant and ought to be removed, whereas a part that fulfils a dysfunction does not make a positive contribution to the maintenance of a system. In the latter case the part concerned has to be adapted, or an alternative part can take over its functions. According to this approach, the communicator and recipient(s) are regarded as functional (or, in some instances, dysfunctional) parts of the system and consideration of their intentions or needs is not important (except when they contribute to the maintenance of the system).

The distinction made between a part fulfilling a dysfunction and a nonfunction is of particular relevance to ETV, because of the following: very often the repetition of a message component represents redundancy and on a manifest level represents a nonfunctional part of the message system. However, on the latent (or covert level) it does *not* fulfil a nonfunction because it can reinforce previously introduced *new* information.

When reconsidering the above brief introductions to a number of approaches to ETV (which are by no means exhaustive), it becomes clear that the emphasis is placed on either the message, the recipient (target destination) of the message, the effects (objectives) to be achieved, or the equilibrium of the system as a process. Taken collectively, the elements that are emphasised in these approaches do not deviate from current theoretical models of communication. Yet, if components such as the communicator (and the communicator's intentions), the actual medium of communication, or the communication setting were to be given equal attention – as they ought to be – it seems a worthwhile exercise to consider what is called a *social marketing approach*. This approach is not traditionally associated with ETV, nor usually mentioned in literature that deals with teaching/learning or development by means of ETV.

15.3.5 Social marketing approach – an application

A social marketing approach to ETV can be defined as the planning, design and dissemination of programmes with the intentional aim of increasing the acceptability of behavioural practices, an idea, a service or a commodity, by the target destination of learners. According to Bagui (1995:47), the use of advertising and marketing communication principles "represents the state-of-art in public health communication education practice today". The application of formative evaluation during every phase of the planning and production stages corresponds with this approach, because through consultations and pretesting, the feedback from the user-destination or consumer-destination is monitored on a continuous basis. In so doing (i.e. by means of formative evaluation), attitudes, perceptions and beliefs of the destination can be identified, in addition to their sociographic and demographic characteristics and needs.

The four Ps

Terms such as the right *product/service, price, place* and *promotion* (the four Ps) are traditionally the core of social marketing (Wilcox, Ault & Agee 1992:15). When applied to educational television (as is done in this unit), the four Ps give a more comprehensive overview of the use of ETV, without ignoring the destination:

- *Product* can refer to opinions, beliefs, values, an idea, an attitude, forms of behaviour, knowledge or skills, which the learner will benefit from when receiving and acting on the ETV programme.
- *Price* does not only refer to the financial costs involved in producing, disseminating and/or being able to afford/receive ETV programmes. For the learner, costs may include any one or all of the following: having less time for leisure and other activities, expending physical and mental energy, and undergoing a change in lifestyle – especially when considering adult learners who work full-time and study part-time.
- *Place*, when applied to ETV, refers literally to the actual setting in which the programme is viewed, and refers in addition to the communication medium (or combination of media) by means of which messages are conveyed. (As discussed in section 15.5, educational television/video can be viewed in a number of settings, such as in a classroom or at home, and can be combined with various other media, such as audiotapes, printed workbooks and also face-to-face interaction with a teacher and/or with peers.)
- *Promotion* refers to the use and/or application of the product. If, for example, the product of an ETV programme is *attitude change*, then we enter the debate as to whether television can effectively change attitudes to the extent that it will result in changes in learners' social behaviour (e.g. to start using condoms to prevent the spreading of AIDS, as part of health education).

Marketing communication strategies

Marketing communication usually ranges (in five progressive steps) from unawareness (e.g. of a product) on the part of a recipient of the message, to awareness, comprehension, conviction and eventually action. Marketing, as such, is almost exclusively aimed at or concerned with sales. When adapted and applied to teaching/learning, the teaching aims that are basic to these five steps are therefore to have new ideas adopted or new products accepted.

The awareness of learners' needs and progress, and the introduction of new experiences is a prerequisite for learning to take place effectively and very often requires of the teacher to be innovative. According to South Africa's Green Paper on Science and Technology (SA 1995:Appendix-C), innovation is "the transformation of an idea into a new or improved saleable product or operational process of a new approach in environmental or social science". According to this definition, it is clear that the innovation processes facing South Africa include not only education and development in general, but more specifically, investigating the application of marketing communication strategies to teaching and learning.

Learners are traditionally analysed in terms of demographics, such as age, gender, level of formal education, and home language. Applying marketing communication measures, and specifically lifestyle measures, in combination with demographics, offers the ETV designer a more comprehensive profile of learners (as target destination). Lifestyle measures are also called "AIO measures" (Russell & Verrill 1986:64), which is an acronym that refers to people's activities (e.g. community involvement), interests (e.g. family orientations) and opinions (e.g. views on social issues). AIO measures are typically interested in finding answers to the following questions:

- How do respondents spend their time at work and during leisure time (activities)?
- What is important to respondents in their surroundings (interests)?
- How do respondents feel about themselves, their community, and the larger world (opinions)?

Having given a brief overview of some of the theories/approaches to teaching/learning in this section, the next section deals with the same topic, but with greater emphasis on development. Section 15.4 must therefore be read with cognisance of the position taken in section 15.2 regarding the intended meaning of the terms *development* and *development communication*. The term "*revisited*" is aimed specifically at South Africa in the twenty-first century, and as we find ourselves in a world that is characterised by an increasing *pace* of change.

15.4 TEACHING/LEARNING – DEVELOPMENT REVISITED

Different assumptions about the nature of learning/teaching appear to be based on different assumptions about the nature of knowledge. According to Boot and Hodgson (1987:5–15), a *dissemination orientation* regards knowledge as a commodity that can be stored and transmitted and which exists independently of human beings. In contrast, a *development orientation* to knowledge (or knowing) is regarded as a process of involvement and attributing meaning to and making sense of oneself and the world. It is from the latter orientation that we consider the nature of learning/teaching, with the purpose of education being the development of the individual as a whole. Meehan (1995:21), for example, argues that, if the maintenance and/or improvement of conditions of life for each individual is the overall purpose served by acquiring knowledge, then four second-order purposes need to be satisfied (in order to fulfil the overall purpose). These purposes are aimed at the learner's ability to describe, predict, control and make choices.

15.4.1 Teaching/learning and development goals

Against the background of educational and development issues that challenge South Africa (as reflected in Figure 15.1), we position teaching/learning *by means of ETV* from a development perspective by demarcating the following ten goals (or aims):

1 *To acquire and develop basic skills* – to acquire information and interpret meaning through observation, listening and reading; to express information and share meaning with others through speaking, writing and nonverbal communication; to manipulate symbols and use mathematical reasoning.

Changes in education

Political parties disagree on direction of education bill

More exciting syllabus changes

Your culture is safe, and the earth's flat

'Government should help with literacy'

A brighter future in store for pupils

A proper education means more than getting a matric

Reaping the costs of a liberal education

New threat from the race school parents

Getting along in the land of eleven tongues

Poverty affects many South African children

How do you contribute to the Reconstruction and Development Programme (RDP)?

Ministry launches literacy campaign

Student Code of Conduct

Figure 15.1 News headlines illustrate some educational and development issues that challenge South Africa

2 *To develop a self-concept* – to distinguish among different concepts of self in varying roles and social situations, whilst recognising that self-concept is acquired and developed while in interaction with others.
3 *To understand other people* – to appreciate that although people are similar in certain ways, individuals differ; to appreciate that attitudes, behaviour and lifestyles must be interpreted in terms of the value system and context of the society in which they are accepted and learned; to communicate with others who share similar characteristics and/or who differ in sociographic characteristics (social level, religion, race and other attributes); to understand that our values and behaviour are derived from and influenced by our local and national cultures, as well as subcultures which are closely linked in communal organisations and affinities (e.g. kinship and clanship groups, religious affiliations and trade unions).
4 *To understand the world* – to apply accumulated knowledge of basic principles and concepts related to the sciences, arts and humanities to understand personal experiences and to understand and evaluate public issues; to participate in society's problems and processes.
5 *To promote wellbeing* – to promote and participate in healthy leisure-time activities; to secure basic services, as well as environmental and other facilities that contribute to physical and mental wellbeing; to change and improve any constraints to such wellbeing.
6 *To participate in the economic world* – to create an awareness and acquire knowledge of the economic world of production and consumption (such as career opportunities and making informed consumer decisions). (In order to deal effectively with a competitive market, learners have to develop creativity, entrepreneurship and flexibility. For managers who have no professional background, specialist subject areas would have to be identified, such as finance, economics and communication.)
7 *To be a responsible member of society* – to understand and respect the resources of the environment; to behave according to the norms, values, rules and roles related to group living; to appreciate the ethical principles of impartiality, integrity, honesty and empathy.
8 *To promote creativity* – to give expression to our own, and value the expressions of others' imaginations.
9 *To adjust to change* – to tolerate perceptions and views that are new or different; to learn to appreciate the value of adaptability; to recognise alternatives when circumstances change.
10 *To continue learning* – to understand the necessity to continue lifelong learning because life is characterised by transitions and change. (In institutional or organisational settings, this would, for example, require employers to have the knowledge of and become skilled in strategic communication, marketing and management methods and styles.)

When reconsidering the ten goals described above, they can be summarised in two overall goal statements, namely

- to meet the learning needs of individuals, from infancy to death; and
- to make learning materials, resources, learning opportunities and support available to as wide a range of the population as possible.

The position taken regarding the use of ETV for development communication purposes, as reflected by the above goals, is a definite move away from using the media for the (top-down) transfer of information and persuasive messages (Varghese 1995:145). Instead, the application of ETV for purposes of development is regarded as a medium to be used for horizontal and bottom-up flows of communication to meet community needs and to develop "self".

Central to each of these goals is the very complex phenomenon of comprehension, a detailed discussion of which is beyond the scope of this book. Nevertheless, one of the characteristics of comprehension is that it occurs on several levels and that it may be fragmentary, global, detailed and/or critical. *Fragmentary comprehension* means that a learner has the ability to recognise, or identify, segments of the content learned. *Global comprehension* refers to a learner's ability to build a larger *picture* by structuring and restructuring smaller parts; for example, to be able to construct a topic outline, based on content keywords. *Detailed comprehension* relates to a learner's ability to differentiate between fact and fiction, to reconstruct information by generalising details, to describe the structure key ideas and the content key ideas communicated by means of written and audiovisual texts. *Critical comprehension* refers to a learner's ability to identify the main purpose of a message, to evaluate the content and intentions of a communicator, and, in certain instances, the covert meanings of messages.

In fields such as health education, it has, for example, become imperative to shift the aims from *knowledge* or *attitudes* to actual *changes in behaviour*. Bagui (1995:44) working as a specialist in health information, media work and research in Rwanda, argues that health communication education can be realised "through a strategic design that draws from principles and methods of social marketing, behavior analysis techniques and anthropological methods". For example, in a study of the relationship between watching ETV programmes in the promotion of health and nutrition, and consequent behavioural changes (in a southern state of India), Saibaba, Mohanram, Kumar Dube and Prasanna Krishna (1995:173) found a strong correlation between "meaningful and need-oriented educational programmes" and desired behavioural change.

The construction of a young child's identity and eventually his or her idea of society occurs through interaction with others – parents, siblings, friends, other reference groups, including television as a mass medium. In informal education, the relevance of the (family) viewing situation as a codeterminant of how a young child experiences television therefore cannot be underestimated. Television represents an immediacy not found in print media (e.g. colouring-in books or comic books). It is therefore understandable that television is an enjoyable companion and – in the absence of peer and family relationships – may become the child's substitute for real-life experiences. Furthermore, because this companion makes no demands on the child (or any viewer), it can in many homes substitute interpersonal family communication.

A former president of the National Broadcasting Company (USA) made the following statement almost 50 years ago: "It is the breaking down of barriers between groups and between nations which is the noblest function of television" (Wolseley & Campbell 1957:228). For the purpose of the discussion in this section, we argue that television should and can be used by teachers to break the barriers between the child and the real social world *out there*.

But what of adult learners? How is their learning directed? What motivates them to learn? Adult learners should not be approached or treated in the same manner as we would approach children as learners; the reasons for this viewpoint are found in the following characteristics:

- *Adults need to be self-directing*. This implies that, if an adult has been conditioned to regard *education* as something that is taught, they may not be able to take responsibility for their own continuing education. Education programmes must, therefore, contain strategies that facilitate a transition from having been dependent learners to becoming self-directing learners. Towards this end, learning resources must be available to adult learners at a time, place and pace of their own choosing.
- *Adult learners represent individuals* with different life experiences. Programmes must therefore not only provide for individualisation, but also for the use of other resources, such as peers.
- *Readiness to learn*, amongst adults, is often *linked to their life tasks and life problems*. In other words, adults' orientation to learning centres round life, specific tasks and problems, rather than centring round a specific subject. ETV programmes must therefore be guided by the knowledge and skills required by adults, to become more effective in fulfilling, for example, their parental roles or their roles in specific work-related situations. Life situations (and not compartments of subjects or learning programmes) must therefore form the core of learning experiences.
- *Intrinsic motivators*, such as increased self-esteem, improving ways in which self-expression can find outlets, dealing successfully with more difficult responsibilities *are more important* motivating forces for adults learners, than extrinsic motivators, such as marks received in a test (or other forms of reward or punishment).

15.4.2 Interactionary processes

In an attempt to conceptualise a development communication model of learning, the approach would be neither subject-centred, nor learner-centred. Such a model would regard learning as an interactionary process, which involves mutual exchange between teacher and learner and which is based on negotiation and reciprocity (Mortensen 1979; Burton & Dimbleby 1988; Du Plooy 1989).

When considering the process of interaction, we can distinguish between social interaction and symbolic interaction. Social interaction refers to the exchange and negotiation of meanings that take place between teacher and learner, or between learner and peers, within a social context. Role-playing, group membership, motivation, prejudice, perception and nonverbal communication are some of the criteria that are important during such interaction.

However, when a learner reads a book or watches an ETV programme, the interaction is more of a symbolic nature because it lacks the reciprocal exchange found in social interaction. In view of the absence of the above social criteria, we argue that the meanings which learners gain from messages (verbal speech, printed texts or ETV) ought to be guided by the objectives or learning outcomes they aim to achieve whilst interpreting (listening, reading, watching) the message. In other words, although many objectives require learners to interpret the meaning that was intended by a communicator (speaker, author), we argue that a text – including an ETV programme – can have many meanings.

The discussion above may initially read as a contradiction, but it represents a move away from a positivist (or dominant paradigmatic) view of ETV to that of a current postmodern view. In the 1960s and 1970s the importance of using television as a mass medium for educational and development purposes was based on its ability to multiply messages. In positivist terms this means that the following variables were *not* regarded to be significant: the learners' individual differences, differences between cultures and regions, the active involvement of the learner as viewer, and that the programme as text can have many meanings. For example, an agriculture programme broadcast nationally in South Africa, would be interpreted differently (and would very likely be ineffective) due to differences in learners' languages, in soil and climatic conditions, rainfall patterns, irrigation systems and differences in the availability of water.

When regarding ETV in current postmodern terms (O'Sullivan et al 1994:234–235), then two characteristics can be isolated to be of particular relevance, namely *intertextuality* and the relevance of *play* (section 15.3).

Any learning situation that involves ETV (whether in a traditional classroom, or any other formal or nonformal learning situation), involves four basic interactions:

- between learner and teacher
- between learner and learner
- between learner and ETV
- between teacher and ETV.

Figure 15.2 contains a graphic illustration of these interactions as they apply to a classroom (or face-to-face) interaction between learner and ETV, involving the presence of a teacher; whereas Figure 15.3 represents interactions between learners, and between learners and ETV, where the teacher's physical presence is not required in the teaching/learning setting.

The interaction between learner and medium can only be regarded as a learning experience if the immediate application of that which has been learned occurs, or if subsequent physical or mental revision occurs, so that reinforcement of that which is learned takes place. We therefore argue that although some knowledge, for example, may be acquired whilst watching ETV, no reinforcement for the retention of knowledge will occur unless some form of application and/or revision takes place.

We argued above that teachers ought to use television to break the barriers between the child and the real social world *out there*. Even in the case of broadcast television (informal education broadcast by means of entertainment programmes), the teacher can break such barriers by means of role-playing, drawings and guided conversation. Although a preschool child is not familiar with conventions found in dramatised television programmes, such as consistency and plausibility of characters' actions, or

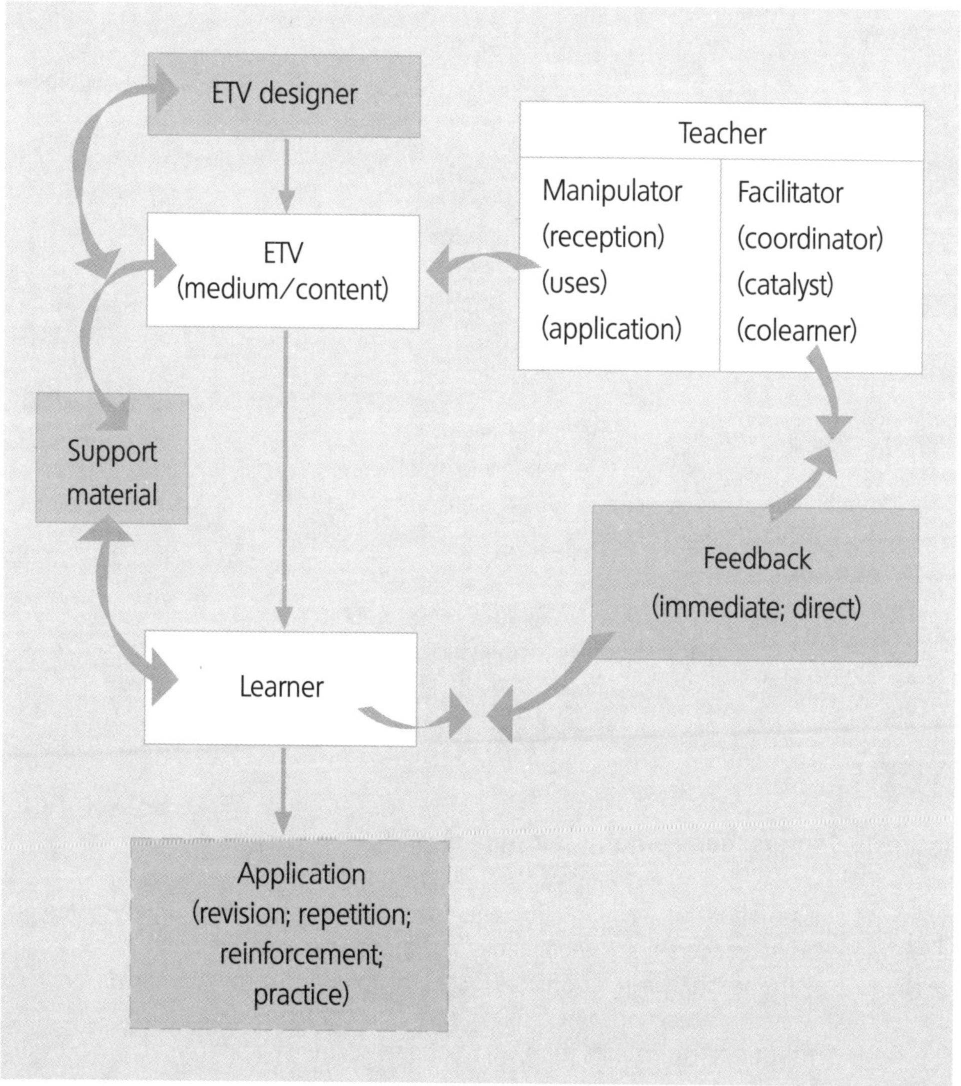

Figure 15.2 Interactions among learner, teacher and ETV

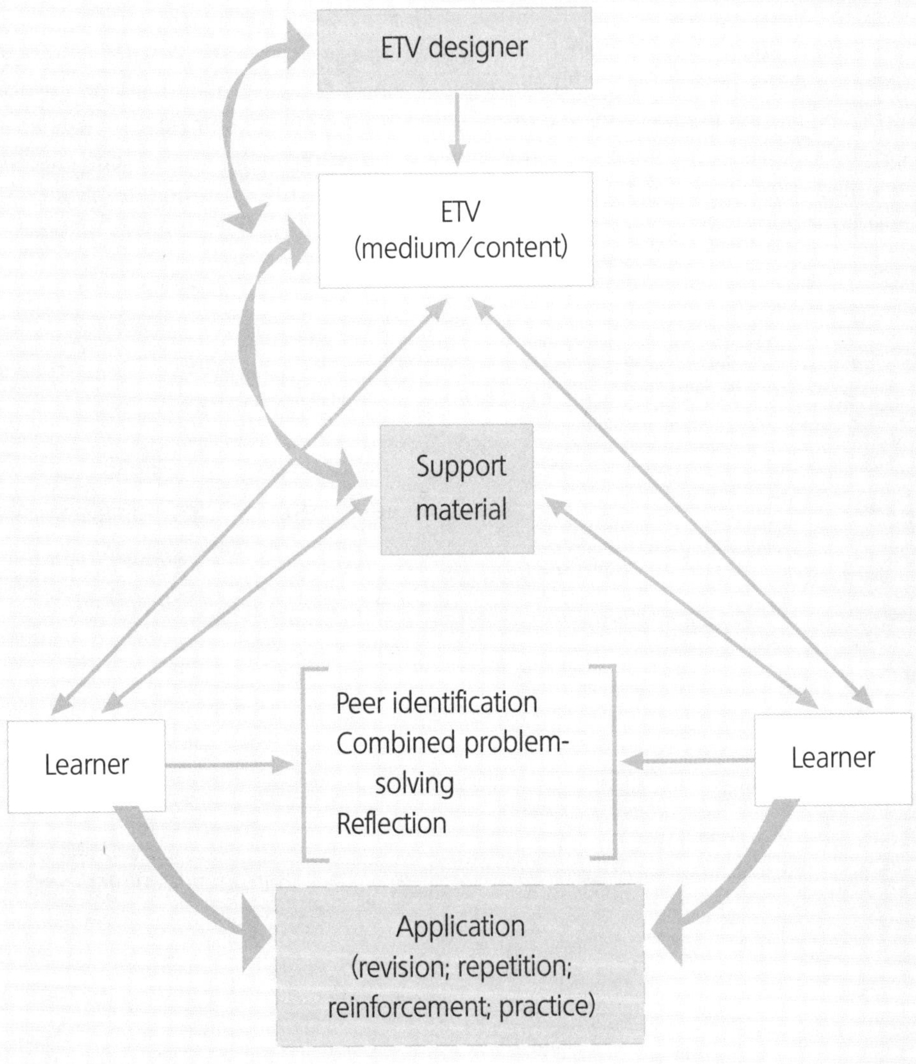

Figure 15.3 Interactions among learners and ETV

aware of a distinction between reality and fantasy, these genre characteristics and conventions offer teachers a knowledgeable background to interact with learners.

The role of the teacher in relation to ETV and in relation to the learner *differs* from that of a conventional teacher. When using an ETV programme as a teaching/learning aid, the presentation of the information, instructions, sequence and format, are provided by the programme. (In the absence of ETV, a conventional teacher has to select and structure what is taught and how it is presented. This can obviously vary, depending on the teacher's ability, mood, interest or lack of interest.) When using an ETV programme, communication occurs by means of audiovisual codes, where the presence of iconographic codes is of particular significance. (In the absence of ETV, the conventional teacher usually relies on words and written materials or notes.) With the presence and use of ETV, the teacher's role changes to that of a catalyst and facilitator, and the teacher is able to fulfil other equally important educational functions (e.g. giving individual attention to specific learners).

Interaction between learner and learner (peer interaction) is regarded as valuable for the following reasons (Gravett 1995:35; Champagne & Bunce 1991:31):

- Being criticised by or making mistakes in the company of a peer member is less threatening for a learner.
- Interaction and combined problem-solving promote reflection on what is learned and complex problems become more manageable.
- Because the learner's understanding is arguably closer to that of peer members than to that of a teacher, a learner is in a better position to identify a peer member's misconceptions.

When reconsidering the aim to *educate for life*, the ability of a medium (such as television) to teach norms and values is, however, questioned (Yule 1990:6–7). Nevertheless, the extent to which television can deal with this *affective domain* of education and development is determined by the programme and the inputs of the ETV designers as a team. That is, although the learners interact with a *medium*, they are still being taught by *people*.

The value of differentiating these four relations becomes clear only if they are used as criteria for research and evaluation purposes. In other words, while planning an ETV programme, the following questions need to be asked repeatedly: *Are the four basic educational interactions being promoted?* (and) *If not, what changes (e.g. content, codes, format) can be made to facilitate these interactions?* (The ways in which interaction between learners and their environment can be accommodated by means of television is further discussed and illustrated in section 15.5.)

15.4.3 What should be taught/learned?

Willard Olson (1949), Erik H Erikson (1963), Abraham H Maslow (1962) and Robert J Havighurst (1950) are historically regarded to be the better-known human development specialists. Maslow's view of a person's striving toward self-actualisation (theory of hierarchical needs) is probably the best known; an idea which he describes as "an episode ... in which the powers of the person come together in a particularly efficient and intensely enjoyable way" (Maslow 1962:23).

Drawing on the above works, two criteria that ought to be considered when determining the scope and sequence of what is taught/learned, are singled out for the purpose of this discussion. Firstly, development tasks change with age; and secondly, each person grows at his/her own pace. We elaborate on these two criteria below.

Development tasks change with age

The physical, psychological and social development tasks that confront a learner, change with age. During *infancy* and *early childhood*, for example, these tasks include learning to walk, to talk, to relate emotionally to parents, family members and others; to differentiate between right and wrong; and to form concepts that are relevant in a physical and social reality. During *middle childhood* such tasks include, for example, learning to read, write and calculate; developing physical skills that are applied in games, developing attitudes towards oneself, as well as towards peers, social groups and institutions outside of the home environment; developing values and morality. During *adolescence*, these tasks include, for example, becoming emotionally and economically independent (from parents and teachers), developing intellectual skills, building relationships with peers of both genders, and preparing for an occupation.

During *early adulthood*, in addition to managing a home, marriage and rearing children, such tasks include, for example, starting an occupation and taking on civic and social responsibilities. During *middle age* the nature of the tasks focuses less on *learning* and more on *maintaining* and *adjusting*. For example, to maintain social and adult civic responsibilities, as well as an accepted standard of living; to support and assist children and/or grandchildren and ageing parents; and to adjust to personal physiological changes and other aspects, such as leisure-time activities.

Tasks that face the learner during *late maturity* are mainly those of *adjustment*. During this stage of life, the kind of adjustments that are required, relate to poor health, less strength, reduced income, retirement from an occupation, death of friends and/or a spouse, and different living conditions. Despite the emphasis on *adjustment*, civic and social responsibilities must still be met and affiliation with peer-group members and younger generations in the family have to be maintained or re-established. For example, in the South African context the older generation may, in coming years, have to adjust continually to members from a younger generation who no longer show the same interest in and/or respect for folklore, traditional leaders, or their ancestors.

Each person grows at their own pace

Each person grows mentally and physically at varying rates. This criterion has at least three implications for teaching/learning and development: to recognise that individual needs differ; to make provision for adjustments in the scope and level of content taught; and to adjust teaching (instructional) methods to suit individual needs. The unfortunate reality of the degree of poverty in southern Africa emphasises the importance of this criterion. It is, for example, estimated (*Rekord Moot* 1996:5) that more that 70 percent of black children live in poverty-stricken conditions, and the implications (not only for them as individuals, but also for the country's future) become significant when considering that approximately 38 percent of the population are children under the age of 16.

From a development perspective, a renewed call is made for education not only to transmit knowledge, but also to instil appropriate attitudes towards that knowledge as a means of developing awareness (e.g. of moral, spiritual and aesthetic values). Although education cannot stand separate from the rapid developments in the fields of science and technology (e.g. telecommunications, nuclear energy, lasers and biotechnology), it can – and should – keep learners in touch with the sources of their culture. In South Africa this is already taking the form of rethinking the traditions and history of the country, of linking formal schools with the community, of promoting a greater awareness of African art and films, and acknowledging the use of local and regional languages as a medium of communication.

When compared with other countries, this renewed emphasis on our traditional and cultural heritage in South Africa is not new. According to Rassekh and Vaideanu (1987:90–93), even those countries that are the leaders in scientific progress, such as Japan, have subjects such as *music* figuring prominently in their school curricula.

15.4.4 Teaching aims and learning objectives

The importance of teaching aims and learning objectives receives mention throughout the above discussion. In this section we concentrate on the importance of formulating objectives as guidance for (1) the planning and implementation of ETV and (2) for purposes of evaluation and assessment.

It is claimed that up to 90 percent (Case-Grant 1973:5) of what a child learns is perceived by means of sight, that is, through seeing. In this regard, some teachers in South Africa may be criticised for concentrating mainly (sometimes exclusively) on verbal (spoken and written) language as a means of communicating with and evaluating learners.

This dilemma provides a point of departure for the formulation of a cardinal aim for the use of ETV (in addition to the aims that are relevant to the subject/content). This aim is to develop learners' nonlinear thinking abilities, since most learners are taught in an education system geared to linear thought, and to broaden their language experience beyond the basic ones of reading and writing. Other aims (which may be regarded as long-term aims) can include any of the following: to increase learners' self-confidence; to promote perceptiveness or powers of observation; to promote awareness, sensitivity, insight and appreciation; to improve the quality of interpersonal communication; and to develop problem-solving abilities.

Three domains in a taxonomy of learning objectives

Objectives may be divided into three categories or areas of behaviour, namely the *psychomotor*, the *affective* and the *cognitive* domains (Bloom, Engelhart, Furst, Hill & Krathwohl 1956). The psychomotor domain includes physical skills like writing, drawing, handling a tool or operating equipment. The affective domain is concerned with those objectives and learning outcomes associated with feeling and emotion, such as attitudes, appreciation, interests and adjustment. The cognitive domain describes intellectual skills and behaviour such as knowing, understanding, analysing, distinguishing, synthesising, integrating and evaluating.

The cognitive domain, according to Bloom et al (1956), may be divided into the following six major categories, which form a hierarchy from simple to complex: knowledge, comprehension, application, analysis, synthesis and evaluation. This hierarchy determines the progressive order in which activities can be structured and applies also to the teaching/learning of particular skills.

- *Knowledge:* The learner has to recall information previously learned. The learner is therefore not required to explain why, how, when or under what circumstances data may differ, alter or be contradicted.
- *Comprehension:* The learner is required to show some form of understanding beyond the basic recall level. Comprehension may be tested through such questions as *How would the outcome of this process differ if this element (specified) is left out by accident?*
- *Application:* Application includes elements of construction, demonstration and problem solving. It may be regarded as a higher level of understanding, because the learner is required to apply information previously learned in a novel (and/or practical) situation; for example, to demonstrate how a specific dish is prepared, having previously learned only the theoretical requirements and descriptions of the ingredients involved and having viewed a demonstration in an ETV programme.
- *Analysis:* The learner – through processes of recognition and differentiation – is required to distinguish between parts by breaking down previously learned information into smaller components. Having learned why and under which normal conditions one would use certain options or follow particular procedures, the learner's analytical ability may be tested by having to analyse a number of television sequences that demonstrate different procedures: for example, to service a motorcar's engine, and having to describe which procedures are used; why they are used; and how they differ from one another.
- *Synthesis:* As a logical continuation of analysis, the learner is now required to create a new whole from the various parts by constructing his or her own problem-solving solutions. Synthesis therefore represents an integration of the previous categories.
- *Evaluation:* At the highest cognitive level, the learner has to judge the value of a construct, variables, processes and procedures according to specific criteria.

By using this hierarchy, the typical pattern in the teaching/learning of any content is as follows:

- Know the theoretical principles (knowledge).
- Understand the principles (know-how).
- Apply the principles to a novel situation.
- Design/construct a new message using these principles.
- Judge when and why the principles either apply or do not apply (attitudes and skills).

Functions and values of objectives

Briggs (1970) distinguishes more than twenty functions of clearly formulated objectives as an essential basis for any teaching/learning strategy. With reference to assessment, and for illustrative purposes, the following three are isolated:

- to inform learners of the purpose of the learning activity and simultaneously to guide them in their learning efforts and self-evaluation of progress;
- to assist the learner to understand the criteria for evaluation;
- to provide criteria to determine when a learner fails in a task (indicating a need to re-evaluate objective[s], methods and materials and/or give further assistance, guidance or remedial treatment).

In the words of John Dewey (1916/1987:69), *educational aims* means "acceptance of responsibility for the observations, anticipations, and arrangements required in carrying on a function – whether farming or educating". This view of an educational aim points to the importance of acknowledging the needs of a given individual learner, and that teaching aims and learning objectives should be translatable into the activities and capacities of the learner.

Formal education traditionally gives precedence to the learner's acquisition of knowledge – with assessments based on an evaluation of the quantity (and very often the conformity) of knowledge acquired. From the above discussion it is clear that traditional learning objectives, in order of importance are:

1 Knowledge
2 Know-how
3 Attitudes and skills

Rassekh and Vaideanu (1987:144) present a reversal of these traditional objectives and in so doing change the priority of objectives to:

1 Attitudes and skills
2 Know-how
3 Knowledge

One of the assumptions on which they base this reversal of priorities is that a person who "knows how ... is best prepared to receive and renew his [her] cultural and occupational training" (Rassekh & Vaideanu 1987:145).

Although this reversal of traditional educational objectives is a simplification of teaching/learning, which is a complicated and diversified process, it does shift the emphasis to the identification, selection and organisation of content that will develop attitudes and skills.

This brings us to an application of what is known as the *Pareto principle* – which is based on a systems approach to the components of a teaching/learning system.

Application of the Pareto principle

According to the Pareto principle, which is accredited (amongst others) to Vilfredo Pareto and his theses presented at Lausanne University, Switzerland (1897–1916), *in any activity, 20 percent of its elements tend to occur 80 percent of the time* (Jordan 1978). Whether applied to the marketing activities of an organisation, or skills required for a specific job, the relevance of the Pareto principle appears to be valid in a variety of teaching/learning situations.

For example:

- Twenty percent of an organisation's customers contribute 80 percent of the organisation's revenue.
- Twenty percent of a company's range of products tends to turn over 80 percent of the finance.
- Twenty percent of all the activities which a dentist is capable of performing, occupy 80 percent of the dentist's working life.
- Twenty percent of the activities which a motorcar mechanic has been trained to do, are carried out 80 percent of the time

The Pareto principle represents a number of assumptions and implications that are worth considering when designing training courses (or designing ETV programmes) for specific occupations. Although the following discussion is adapted for the purposes of discussing what should be taught/learned, full credit is given to Jordan (1978), with whose permission this adaptation is published.

ASSUMPTION 1

In each occupation, certain elements, activities or events occur with very high frequency over a period of a few years, whereas others occur infrequently. The assumption is that because these activities occur or are performed frequently, they will be learned quickly.

The implication of this assumption is threefold. The ETV designer can

1. isolate those (e.g. 20%) elements or activities of an occupation that repeat themselves with high frequency (e.g. 80% of the time);
2. study the content of this 20 percent; and
3. teach the activities/elements with the aim of obtaining a high degree of skill.

ASSUMPTION 2

Based on the last-mentioned implication (i.e. to teach the activities/elements with the aim of obtaining a high degree of skill), the assumption is that a learner trained with this aim in mind should be highly competent 80 percent of the time in the particular occupation.

ASSUMPTION 3

In each occupation, certain elements, activities or events occur at a low frequency and therefore a much longer period of time is required for learning to take place (i.e. sufficient time has to pass so that these low frequency events can occur).

The implication of this assumption is also threefold. The ETV designer can

1 isolate those elements or activities of an occupation that repeat themselves with low frequency (e.g. 10%), but which are critical to survival and safety, such as health occupations or those which affect cost or quality in industry;
2 analyse the content of these elements, activities or events in detail; and
3 devise an ETV programme (or series of programmes) that contains simulators or other methods of recreating the elements, activities or events to provide the necessary experience of these events during training.

Based on the three assumptions and their related implications described above, the overall (or eventual) course of action which an ETV designer can follow is:

- to base a series of programmes (as part of a training programme) on the above 30 percent of an occupation's elements (i.e. the 20% of elements, activities or events which are assumed to occur with high frequency and the 10% which are assumed to occur with low frequency, but which are critical); and
- to cater for (plan and elaborate) this 30 percent so that it takes up 90 percent of the actual time allocated for the series of programmes.

In concluding this brief discussion of the Pareto principle, we can isolate two implications for this course of action. Firstly, with reference to the (70%) noncritical elements, activities or events that occur infrequently in an occupation, it means that only 10 percent of a programme series needs to deal with such content; and that problems (if and when they occur) can be dealt with by consulting co-workers who, by virtue of many years of experience, can assist. Secondly, and most importantly, the high frequency and critical elements (30% of an occupation) can be thoroughly learned (by spending 90% of the time on such elements and activities).

Having considered teaching/learning from a development perspective, with suggested goals (or aims) and objectives, as well as criteria that ought to be considered when determining the scope and sequence of the content, we concentrate in the next section on the adaptable nature of television as a medium of communication.

15.5 TELEVISION: AN ADAPTABLE COMMUNICATION MEDIUM

Television requires electricity, technology and experts who can operate and see to the maintenance of the equipment.

This is a simplistic view because the use of broadcast television obviously requires *infrastructures* that rely on policies, managerial styles and finances. In addition, networks (consisting of an infrastructure of transmitters and listening/viewing points), programming (a daily, weekly or monthly periodicity of output at specified hours), and staffing and crews at national and regional points throughout the country are inherent in any public broadcasting enterprise.

Nevertheless, we commence this section with this simplistic view for the purpose of drawing attention to the need for electricity, technology and maintenance of equipment because without these, *television* cannot be considered for any communication purposes – let alone for purposes of education or development.

At the time of writing, South African education policies and departments, the South African Broadcasting Corporation's (SABC) three television channels, are all in a state of debate, transition and nonfinality. Although it is anticipated that satellite access to television would be extended in the coming years, proposals to actually equip schools throughout South Africa with satellite facilities in the near future, is currently impracticable. There have been many changes in the role of the SABC as a public broadcasting service (e.g. provided for in the Broadcasting Act, no 4 of 1999); although this bears mentioning in passing, it is not the aim of this study to focus on these changes.

Transition is characterised by change. The *change* in the South African context involves not only education or educational television but, at the same time, the promotion of democracy, increased participation in public life, the government's need for a credible information service, the expansion of technological facilities, and especially funding and the much-needed generation of revenue.

A norm which is (or ought to be) central to these changes is found in movement away from so-called *state television broadcasting* to that of *public television broadcasting*. In developed countries, such as Britain, Canada and the United States of America (USA), public television broadcasting was not originally introduced with educational purposes in mind, such as to combat illiteracy. The functions of public broadcasting are traditionally held to be threefold, namely to inform, to entertain and to educate.

The cornerstone of public broadcasting (as opposed to state broadcasting) is found in the principles on which broadcasting practices in countries such as the USA are based. One such principle is the USA's *fairness clause* "which guarantees equitable time to opposition parties within any political debate" (Powell 1996:4).

The above recommendations are supported by the positions taken in this unit, namely the distinction between formal and nonformal education; that learning is a lifelong process; that the responsibility of ETV by means of broadcast television ought not to be shouldered by one or two television institutions, but should involve governmental and nongovernmental stakeholders; and lastly, that a clear distinction must be made between the child as a learner and the adult learner.

15.5.1 Means of distributing ETV

The most familiar means of distributing ETV programmes is by means of *broadcast* television, and videotape viewing by means of *video-playback facilities*. Between these two so-called *extremes*, the variety of means of distribution that are possible is briefly described below. The introduction of interactive computer technology such as the Internet has opened up new possibilities for ETV distribution.

Broadcast television

A public (or commercial) television station transmits signals that are received in the signal area by anyone (as a group or individually) who has access to a television receiving set which is connected to an antenna (usually roof-mounted) that picks up the audio and video signals. The audio signal is sent via FM radio, whereas the video signal is carried on either the UHF (ultra-high frequency) or VHF (very-high frequency) on the electromagnetic spectrum.

ITFS

ITFS is an acronym for *Instructional Television Fixed Service* which, as in the case of broadcast television, transmits television signals over the air, on a point-to-point basis. It differs from broadcast transmission in the sense that special equipment is installed at the receiving points to enable large numbers of people to watch.

Although an ITFS is essentially one-way communication, it does provide for a two-way response system whereby a learner at one of the receiving points presses a button and can talk back either to a central studio or to other receiving sites connected to the circuit. (The first of these services was introduced in America in 1963 and, by using four channels, other than those used for regular noncommercial ETV, enabled educational institutions to receive different ETV programmes at the same time.)

ITFS is also applied as a Multi-point Distribution Service (MDS) whereby users hire service time on the system, to be used on an occasional basis, for the purposes of personally orientated or intraorganisational ETV communication. For example, at the time of writing, an insurance company in South Africa announced the launch of a R6,5 million project, called *PowerMatric*. It involves distance teaching by means of satellites and television in eleven subjects to 7 000 learners at 300 centres. These transmissions will use the transmitters of MultiChoice at a cost to learners of R300 per subject.

Satellite broadcasting

Geosynchronous satellites orbit the earth at the same speed at which the earth rotates. This means that the satellites remain over the same spot above the earth and function as a relay point between two points on earth. In South Africa the Electronic Media Network (M-NET) beams its programmes off a satellite called *Intelsat VI* and then retransmits these programmes terrestrially, on designated frequencies. The service is, however, only available to those who can and want to subscribe. In 1995 the Pan-Am-Sat 4 (PAS 4), which beams a footprint that includes South Africa, was launched. (A *footprint* is the area on earth that is covered by the satellite beam.) Both the SABC and MultiChoice Limited have leased transponder capacity and in time to come coverage of a bigger audience and delivery from various sources are expected to increase (Independent Broadcasting Authority 1995b:57).

CATV

CATV is an acronym for *Community Antenna Television* or *Cable Television*. The distribution system consists of a distribution centre, from where – via a master antenna television – signals are either originated or fed forward to television receiving sets in specific buildings via a cable (which involves copper telephone wire, coaxial cables and fibre optic cable). Sets connected to the cable system receive the signals.

Due to the absence of atmospheric and other external interferences, and because a master antenna for such a system is of a higher quality than the average home antenna, the visuals transmitted are of a better quality and the antenna can cope with more channels.

CCTV

Closed-circuit television (CCTV) is similar to the transmission means of CATV (i.e. signals are transmitted by a cable and received by any set connected to the circuit). However, CCTV differs from CATV in a number of ways. Firstly, unlike CATV, a CCTV system is not licensed. Secondly, the educational uses of CCTV can be adapted to local conditions and needs. For example, in formal educational institutions (e.g. teachers' training colleges), classrooms, lecture halls, dormitories and other strategic points can be connected. Such a system can cater for a multichannel approach, which means that different ETV programmes can be transmitted from a central transmission centre simultaneously to meet different needs concurrently. Thirdly, flexibility is enhanced because programmes can be repeated and transmission times adapted to meet different schedules and/or to be integrated with individual lessons.

If connected to two-way cables, CCTV enables a learner to respond to material received, and such immediate and direct feedback has the obvious potential of increasing the efficiency of communication.

VCR&M

VCR&M is an acronym for *video cassette recorder and monitor* and the emphasis is not only on recording off-air signals, but also the use of a VCR as a playback machine. Providing that a teacher has access to a source of electricity, the combination of a video-playback machine with a television monitor, enables that teacher (or learner) to view a videotape in the remotest rural sites of any country. In addition to electricity, the one other requirement is compatibility between the tape (e.g. a VHS cassette tape) and the playback machine.

15.5.2 Teaching/learning implications of the means of distribution

The teaching/learning implications of the means of distribution are fourfold, namely being able (or not being able) to:

- identify the target destination of learners;
- formulate specific teaching aims, learning objectives or learning outcomes;

- structure the content, sequencing and format with a destination and objectives/ outcomes in mind; and
- manipulate or control the reception, use and application of an ETV programme.

The ability to identify or demarcate the learners as a target destination in broadcast television is virtually impossible, because of the large, multilingual and demographically diverse nature of its mass audience. Instances where the channel and programme are labelled as *education*, the programme content can be structured according to specific teaching aims, but due to continuous broadcasting, the format cannot contain temporal *paragraphs* or breaks. Instances where individual programmes or series of programmes are aimed at the general public, such programmes are (due to the above reasons) guided by general aims and the purposes of nonformal education, and/or as supplemental material and curricular segments in formal education.

Broadcast schedules are in the hands of broadcasting authorities and, unless consulted, education authorities or even the individual teacher, have no control over the times or dates when programmes are broadcast.

In contrast to broadcast television, CCTV and other means of distribution, such as by VCR&M, enable teachers and ETV designers to manipulate the encoding possibilities with particular teaching aims in mind.

The following are four examples to illustrate the latter statement:

- The content can be structured to meet the learners' needs, interests, abilities and levels of achievement.
- The format of the programme can be paragraphed into sections and the viewer-as-learner instructed to stop the videotape at predetermined points to undertake another activity. In so doing, participation or practical application can be encouraged.
- Two soundtracks, such as English and isiZulu, can be added to a videotape, which facilitates a wider use of the programme by learners with different first language preferences.
- Reinforcement can be accommodated through repetition and variation.

The reception, use and/or application of the above means of distribution (e.g. VCR&M) also represent the following *differences*, when compared with broadcasting as a means of distribution:

- Information can be stored and retrieved at a later stage.
- Time and personpower can be saved, in that the teacher need not repeat the same explanations or demonstrations.
- When linked to a camera, this means of distribution can be used for self-evaluation in a variety of educational fields, such as sporting activities, coaching, teacher training, primary health education, farming methods or industrial training.
- Immediate and direct feedback (from learner to teacher) is possible.

- The learners have control over when and at what pace they watch a particular programme, and whether they want to rewind and revise certain sections for a second or a third time.

Technological designs, combined with interactive video (IV), give learners access to information and support not found in the traditional classroom, namely:

- through telecommunication links, a learner can have access to library collections and on-line data bases;
- computerised dictionaries and visual collections become accessible; and
- visual, auditory or written feedback from peers or teachers can be obtained directly.

However, Vivian (1991:191) points out that, with new and future services such as pay-per-view (PPV), low-power television (LPTV), direct broadcast satellite (DBS) and subscriber television (STV), these means of dissemination increase the fragmentation of audiences into more and smaller segments.

15.5.3 Educational implications of encoding (medium) characteristics

Communicationists often find themselves sandwiched between two *worlds*. On one hand, traditional teachers criticise those who advocate the use of educational media as having gone overboard with technology, and on the other hand the technologists criticise communicationists for not having enough technical training or technological know-how.

The advantages, which means that teachers have more time for research through being relieved of the need to continuously teach, are not generally accepted as being important. Therefore, attempts to introduce different methods of instruction are also frequently met with a lack of enthusiasm and are therefore introduced with great difficulty. Yet, by using ETV, the teacher can spend more time and focus on remedial teaching of those learners who need such attention. However, traditionally, especially in formal education where teaching time is scheduled into fixed periods, films and videotapes have been used to fill time, not to save time.

The use of television for educational and development purposes has also not occurred without criticism (Wigren 1967:148–184), the main one being that television conveys mediated (or second-hand) experience. Despite this criticism, research findings (e.g. in the case of *Sesame Street* disseminated by means of broadcast television) do support the value and effectiveness of ETV compressing, elongating, structuring and reinforcing first-hand experience (Noble 1983; Schramm, Lyle & Parker 1961).

Despite the above criticism, the encoding (medium) characteristics of television in general, and more specifically ETV, enable ETV designers to use it to fulfil a number of educational functions (Zettl 1976; Goldenberg 1979; Kemp 1980; Masterman 1980; Du Plooy 1989). Examples of some of the educational uses are as follows:

- Invisible forces can be visualised (e.g. the nature of chemical reactions or gases by means of graphics).

- Abstract relationships and processes can be visualised (e.g. cause-and-effect relations between medication and the organs of the human body).
- Processes, ideas and technical structures can be simplified (e.g. the functions of the digital and analogue computer; or the effects of pollution on the ecology).
- Sensitive subjects, such as sexual intercourse, can be desensitised (e.g. by using animation).
- The past can be recreated and the future projected in the present (e.g. the political power structures in South Africa).
- Elements that are related can be progressively introduced (or progressively subtracted) at a pace and level of complexity suited to the content, objectives and destination (e.g. a motorcar engine built stage-by-stage, starting with the crankshaft).
- Visual codes, such as colour, shades of light and dark, vectors, movements and close-up shots can indicate differences, similarities, keep the viewer's attention, and direct attention by showing detail or through emphasis.

Television also provides instantaneousness, such as monitory and diagnosis in health settings; as well as functioning as a link among separate educational units and thereby exchanging teacher-and-learner feedback.

15.5.4 The importance of television-mediated experiences

It is accepted that verbal ability (the ability to speak, read and write a language) remains one of South Africa's primary educational goals – for children and adults alike. A position taken in this unit is that teaching/learning by means of ETV can promote the development of perceptual skills in addition to that of reading and writing skills.

Table 15.1 contains a summary of how two visual codes, namely lighting and colour, can be manipulated in ETV to fulfil specific communication functions and, at the same time, promote the achievement of learning objectives (e.g. to comprehend, analyse, compare and evaluate). These learning objectives belong to the cognitive, affective and psychomotor domains.

Each medium of communication (e.g. film, radio, print media) is limited to the use of particular encoding characteristics. In the case of television, these codes include iconographic codes (e.g. colour, lighting, vectors, balance, camera shots, camera movements and editing) and auditory codes (i.e. music, sound effects and the human voice). When applying a medium of communication mainly for educational purposes, the encoding characteristics of the selected medium would need to meet certain criteria if it were to fulfil educational functions effectively. Ten essential criteria are distinguished and briefly dealt with below in terms of the extent to which they can be met by means of ETV.

Table 15.1 Two visual codes – manipulated to fulfil communication functions and learning objectives

LEARNING OBJECTIVE(S): to comprehend, analyse, compare and evaluate the aesthetic and production codes in terms of the communicative functions fulfilled in a particular context in a television programme.

Examples of communicative functions	Examples of visual codes that may be manipulated
to clarify spatial, tactile, temporal and seasonal orientations	control of light; use attached or cast shadows
to make a sense look realistic	use chiaroscuro lighting; colour combination
to illuminate specific important areas on the screen	use Rembrandt lighting
to focus viewers' attention on a performer	use cameo lighting
to emphasise contour rather than volume	use silhouette lighting
to create visual harmony	combine colours with hues that, for example, lie opposite each other on the colour circle
to manipulate visual reality and create plausible visual illusions	use a medium yellow filter, such as when changing a light blue sky to dark gray; chroma-key matting; record a daylight scene with a special dark red filter to create a moonlight image
to express an essential quality of an event, object or condition	use a combination of colours or desaturated colours to express, for example, softness
to emphasise certain screen areas and de-emphasise others	use a low-energy colour scheme in larger set areas with high-energy coloured props
to make the foreground appear more vivid	surround the foreground colour with its exact complementary colour
to create a feeling of anticipation	use predictive lighting
to emphasise an object (such as a product in an advertisement) and de-emphasise the environment	use limbo lighting

☞

Examples of communicative functions	Examples of visual codes that may be manipulated
to create legibility of subtitles (on both colour and black-and-white television)	use letters that contrast sufficiently in hue and brightness with the background
to change the appearance of an object or the internal structure of an event	reverse the polarity
to effect a structural disintegration of the image	reduce the intensity of the electron beam
to create adequate illumination (without drama or emotion)	use Notan lighting
to intensify the scene physically/ psychologically	use a light shining into the lens; above-key or below-key light positions
to establish a mood or an atmosphere	use low-key and high-key lighting; colour such as warm, highly saturated colours, to create a happy, energetic mood/event; chiaroscuro lighting
to draw attention to the theme or story and intensify the inner emotion/ orientation	use cameo lighting; use warm, bright colours; omit colour
to influence the viewers' perception and judgement of temperature	flood the scene with warm, red light to emphasise, for example, the heat of fire
to influence the viewers' perception and judgement of size or space	use blue, cold colours to emphasise, for example, confined space
to create structural changes for dramatic or emotional effects	use video feedback
to produce variety	use a variety of colours or colour combinations through internal manipulation of the primary colours – red, green and blue
to intensify a lifelike rhythm	use lighting for continuous action by lighting overlapping action areas
to bring the pictorial elements into a compositional balance	use chiaroscuro lighting

Mass education and development

Messages must be distributed simultaneously over great distances to a large (quantitative) and unlimited number of learners simultaneously. Broadcast television meets this criterion to the greatest extent, rather than CATV or Pay-TV, because of greater accessibility to signals broadcast.

Individualised education and development

It is difficult to individualise ETV programmes in order to cater for individual learning and development needs, because of the production costs involved.

Through continuous monitoring of learners' needs and progress, the changing or introducing of different experiences becomes not only relevant, but is important for learning to take place. The immediacy required to adapt to the support needs experienced by learners can be provided for by pre-recorded ETV. However, to a limited and qualified degree, this requirement can be accommodated if the ETV system is interactive and makes provision for two-way communication between learner and teacher.

Catering for different levels

Once a series of programmes has been planned and produced to suit different levels of educational advancement, individual programmes can be sequenced to cater for progress from one level to the next. Distribution systems, such as CCTV and VCR&M are the best suited to meet this criterion. An individual programme can clearly not be adapted (once produced) to meet this criterion.

Presenting visual detail

In subjects where the perception of visual details is important to the learning process, those details must be clear and distinct. The ability to focus on and/or emphasise detail is one of the main encoding characteristics of television. This is accomplished through camera-lens movement (e.g. to zoom in); editing and especially the selection of shots (e.g. to cut from a medium shot to a big close-up shot), lighting techniques (e.g. cameo lighting), the use of colours to distinguish between smaller parts in a whole (e.g. motorcar engine); and by shot composition (e.g. a split-screen image).

Additive and subtractive progression

Certain learning situations (and objectives) require that events be structured to progress through a series of stages, some of which have to be investigated in greater detail than others. For example, individual instances can be observed separately and structured in an ETV programme on a continuum to infer a general law or principle by means of inductive reasoning.

In an *additive progression* an event requires a progression from a base, by adding elements as they become appropriate (e.g. presenting the growth of a plant). In the case of *subtractive progression*, elements are progressively removed from a *whole* event. For example, the disassembly of a machine into its parts or dividing a word into syllables.

Television is ideal for the application of either additive or subtractive progression; for example, by means of dissolves (between a number of shots) an additive progression can be presented and, although a lapse of time is signified, visual continuity is maintained simultaneously.

Using more than one sense

Television uses both auditory and visual codes (which include dimensions such as time, depth, colour and movement). Redundancy (i.e. the repetition of the same message in both visual and auditory codes) can contribute to reinforcing the message. However, if not carefully considered, the combination of these codes may not have the desired effect. The following are some of the criteria which determine whether either the auditory or the visual codes ought to be dominant (Marsh 1983:95–102). The visual codes ought to dominate when the message is long, complex, and its arrangement complicated, and when reality is to be reproduced. The auditory codes (including sound effects and music) ought to dominate when immediate attention from the viewer is required; when exact spatial discrimination is not important, and when a sequential presentation is appropriate.

The communicative functions that are fulfilled by sound include (amongst others) the creation of an atmosphere, the bridging of two or more visual scenes, and special effects. For the purpose of fulfilling informational and especially educational functions, auditory codes (especially sound effects) can be used to provide additional information that is not portrayed visually, and to emphasise information which does appear on the screen.

Control over exposure

Some learners and some learning situations require different exposure times, whereby the teacher/learner has to be able to hold, revise or proceed with a particular segment of the work.

A learner's control over the timing, frequency and duration of a specific learning situation can enhance commitment and self-motivated learning. In addition, learners can progress at their own pace and need not feel threatened by more rapid learners. Television can meet this requirement, depending on the means of distribution used, for example VCR&M.

ETV as independent education

A series of television programmes (*lessons*) can be designed to present the content of a particular subject and to meet the minimum requirements of a particular course or learning programme. Programmes can be broadcast, viewed and reviewed independently of the presence of a teacher. Such ETV lessons are usually accompanied by audio or printed texts, such as learners' workbooks, which accompany the programmes. Additional texts can be integrated with the programmes (i.e. paragraphing the ETV programme with instructions, such as "stop the tape, refer to the workbook and complete the next activity, before you continue watching the tape"). Or, instead of such an integration of support material (also referred to as wrap-around presentations), audiotapes, photographs, graphic models, graphic mind-maps and/or other printed texts can be used separately from the ETV programme, containing activities which learners complete as summative self-evaluation tests, or for the purposes of giving an overview or summary of key issues.

ETV as a form of independent education, is particularly useful when large numbers of learners must be reached simultaneously. Such programmes can be repeated and used by learners either in small-group settings or on an individual basis, and are especially useful in subject areas which are characterised by a shortage of qualified teachers. In the South African context, where the norms and standards of formal education are in the process of being standardised, ETV as a form of independent education can in addition contribute towards fulfilling this need. All learners who view the programmes receive the same content, sequenced in the same order and presented in the same manner. Although such fixed sequencing does not cater for individual needs and differences, it does contribute to the standardisation of curriculum content.

This type of programming is also relevant in nonformal education for children and adults. In South Africa, the Film Resource Unit, established in 1986, has since 1992 made films and videotapes related to southern Africa available to educational institutions, community and service organisations, Aid agencies, government bodies, schools and individuals. Their 1995 video catalogue categorises more than two hundred cleared programmes and includes (amongst others) these categories: music and culture (e.g. *Songololo: Voices of Change*); cultural history (e.g. *Robben Island: Our University*); environment and development (e.g. *South Africa the Wasted Land*); reconstruction and reconciliation (e.g. *Cry of Reason: Beyers Naudé*); education (e.g. *Colouring in our Classrooms*); women and gender (e.g. *Phambili: Working Women in South Africa*); health and AIDS (e.g. *Challenges in AIDS Counselling*); labour and economy (e.g. *Gomomo – Working for the Workers*); and land and shelter (e.g. *Crossroads*). More recent examples of education-oriented television programmes include *Yizo Yizo, Soul City, Khululeka* and *Soul Buddyz. Yizo Yizo*, for instance, deals with contemporary problems facing teachers and their students, such as rape, school safety, corruption, although it also focuses on positive issues, such as leadership, reading and technology. The year 2001 saw the introduction of *Yizo Yizo 2*, and with its very controversial issues, the producers hope to encourage dialogue about important ongoing social issues/problems facing South Africa's youth, for instance, one episode dealt with the reality of being in jail, which included scenes of gang rape. *Soul City*, produced by Soul City Institute for Health and Development Education and licensed to the South African Broadcasting Corporation, deals with health issues such as HIV/Aids, sexually transmitted diseases and domestic violence, and does so in a very entertaining manner. In the 2000 *Khululeka* series, an important landmark year for South Africans with the election of the new South African president, Mr Thabo Mbeki, this series included voter education, provincial government elections and the importance of voting. *Khululeka* generally deals with human rights issues and how they impact on the youth of today. *Soul Buddyz* is a heart-warming story following a group of young friends and their trials and tribulations growing up – their different cultures and races transcended as they embrace life to the fullest, with their optimistic and exciting motto: "Tomorrow is ours" (Oliphant 2001:6).

ETV as segments of courses, subjects or programmes

ETV can be used to present certain segments or courses or programmes, subjects or programmes on a regular basis. The use of television in this manner is of particular value when the subject content deals with personalities, events, situations or materials that are *not* easily available to the teacher. Examples of such unique or special contents are historical events recorded on filmed footage, art exhibitions in foreign countries, or demonstrations of scientific experiments.

The teacher plays a prominent role in the use of ETV in teaching segments of a subject. This role relates not only to the manner in which these types of ETV programmes are integrated in lesson structures, but relates also to aspects such as the prior preparation of learners, and to the application of what is learned during follow-up activities and tasks.

ETV as supplemental enrichment material

The terms *supplemental* and *enrichment* refer to the use of ETV programmes that are not planned or designed to meet either specific curriculum requirements or teaching aims. Instead they are produced to meet general needs shared by different groups of learners, such as related to environmental matters (e.g. water pollution), guidance (e.g. the development of a positive self-concept) or health (e.g. how to obtain a balanced diet).

From the above discussion and examples it becomes clear that the use of communication media, especially television, for educational purposes requires two key *ingredients*, namely interaction and what media specialists are inclined to call high-tech/high-touch. The latter ingredient means that a human touch has to be integrated with the programme.

In reply to the question (section 15.4.3 above): *What should be taught/learned?* we argue that not enough consideration is given to the role of the human element in the selection of communication media, or to the training and skills of teachers and ETV designers, or to their knowledge of the sociocultural, political and especially economic milieu of the target destination of their messages. Soola (1995:28) refers to the crucial role of this human element as "operational communication" as opposed to sophisticated modern communication technological hardware. In other words, an effort ought to be made to promote closer interaction among the people involved in planning and producing educational programmes – the need of which is supported by the research findings of Saibaba et al (1995:173) regarding health-educational programmes broadcast on television in India.

Interaction between learners and their environment can be accommodated by means of television in two ways.

- Firstly, the design (format or structure) of the programme can be such that it promotes (or restricts) interaction.

  An ETV programme that follows a linear design, produces reactive interaction from learners. This means of communication is essentially *reactive* instead of *interactive*. The ways in which a learner reacts to programme content are predetermined by the ETV design team. These designs usually require learners to answer questions or follow directions to do other tasks or activities. By drawing a distinction between linear programmes and branching programmes (discussed below) we are not suggesting an either-or choice. In fact, certain learners may benefit more from prescriptive or linear structuring of learning materials, which allow learners little option of following different branches or routes. Reactions from learners to a linear design are therefore programme-directed and feedback is programme-controlled.

  The term *branching* as used here refers to the options – routes or pathways – built into a programme which learners have to follow as they progress. *Linear branching* is nonconditional. In other words, the format of the programme directs learners in a specific sequence, irrespective of the responses which learners may or may not make. In contrast, *conditional branching* directs learners through a programme in sequences, depending on the responses they make. Three variables that govern branching and the nature of programme-controlled feedback are (1) the type of response (e.g. whether it is correct or incorrect), (2) the number of responses required and (3) the amount of time required to respond. Learning outcomes (responses or learner feedback) have to be anticipated and built into the programme design. The overt educational aim of branching designs is therefore to produce proactive and coactive interaction, with the covert aim of encouraging the learner to be more self-directing.

  Designs aimed at promoting the following, can make fruitful use of advance organisers (e.g. informing learners in advance of the content and learning objectives of each section) and in-text questions:

  - proactive or coactive interaction,
  - providing the learner with more freedom to control the pace of presentations,
  - the type of feedback required, and
  - the actual occasion and opportunity for feedback.

  Quite apart from the distinction between linear and branching designs, a question which is of particular significance to South Africa, is whether or not the actual content presented is of greater significance to promote learners' involvement and indirectly interaction (irrespective of the design used). For example, popular theatre techniques (folk drama) are rooted in traditional forms of communication, such as dance sequences, songs, chants, narration and masquerades. Because televised (or video) recordings of community theatre include the theatre-audience members' reactions they can (1) contribute to identifying problems and finding possible solutions; (2) ensure that the traditional roots of a particular culture are honoured; and (3) relay these messages in an entertaining manner, characterised by theatre.

The fact that we cannot offer final answers in this regard (especially not within the context of change in South Africa) further reiterates the need for formative evaluation of ETV material during the planning stages.

- Secondly, interaction between the learners and their environment can be accommodated by means of television through interaction between two or more learners in a small-group setting; and/or between teacher and learner; as well as their interaction with the programme.

By way of a summary we therefore argue that the ideal is that both the design and content of an ETV programme ought to be tailored to promote (1) optimal control by the learner; and (2) interpersonal communication among viewers (as peers and in teacher-learner relations).

15.6 FORMATIVE VERSUS SUMMATIVE EVALUATION OF ETV

There is no universally agreed-upon model to implement the planning and design of an ETV programme. However, for the purpose of this unit, two criteria can be singled out, namely that the process must be cyclical and the approach collaborative, involving as many of the stakeholders as possible. The meanings of both these criteria become clear when reading the sections that follow.

Someone once said: *If there's no listening, there's no communication!* The term listening in this section refers not to listening as in an interpersonal setting, but instead to listening to the ETV viewers' feedback with the sole purpose of evaluating the programme, or segments thereof.

The distinction between formative evaluation and summative evaluation was first made by Scriven (1980:56) who illustrates it with reference to this analogy: "When the cook tastes the soup, that's formative; when the guest tastes the soup, that's summative". The need for formative evaluation applies throughout all the planning stages, but is of particular importance during the initial planning stage, especially as any conflicts of interest can delay the planning and subsequent processes.

The research methods that can be used for the purposes of formative evaluation consist of ethnographic observations, focus-group discussions, in-depth interviews, self-administered questionnaires, and in the case of printed support material, readability tests and content analyses of essays written by young learners. One of the methods that originated (in America in 1978) because of the need to investigate the *appeal* of segments, sequences and scenes (e.g. at 10-second intervals), involves the use of a *Program Evaluation Analysis Computer (PEAC)* (Mielke & Chen 1983:42–43). Each respondent (in groups as large as 40) uses a hand-held microprocessor to key in responses whilst watching an ETV segment. The following are examples of measurement scales from which a respondent selects whilst watching the programme. These examples were used by the Human Sciences Research Council's evaluation of ETV programmes produced in South Africa (Van Vuuren & Herselman 1987:308–312).

—	Too slow
—	Just right
—	Too fast

—	Clear
—	Uncertain
—	Not clear

—	Interesting
—	Don't know
—	Not interesting

As a measuring instrument, the PEAC system represents a number of advantages. It is convenient and can cater for group testing. The respondents' reactions can be monitored from moment to moment, the feedback is immediate and the individual respondent remains anonymous. From a research point of view, a major advantage is that data collected by means of a PEAC system have high internal validity.

Formative research therefore refers to proactive evaluation that is aimed at decision making, development and improvement of an ETV programme (Duby 1987:171–221). The importance of formative evaluation during the planning and development stages of an ETV programme is particularly important when considering that, as learners continue to obtain access to learning via the mass media, teachers will to an increasing extent find themselves in the anomalous position of knowing less and less about their learners.

Such research can be guided by answers to these two questions:

- *Whose* evaluative inputs will be the most valuable at each stage? For example, would it be that of a subject specialist, an experienced teacher, a communication scientist, a psychologist, or a media specialist? The conception of a profession adviser as an *expert* is especially justified in certain fields, such as the pure sciences, medicine and engineering.
- *Which criteria* will have the most meaningful effect as an input at each stage? The significance of the ETV design team investigating and agreeing on the criteria

according to which each stage is to be evaluated, is evident if we remember the aim of formative research. This position is supported by Bagui (1995:49) who states that the "purpose of pretesting [formative evaluation] ... is to have materials that are understandable, relevant, culturally sensitive, and credible, as well as attractive and acceptable to the target audience".

As already pointed out above, no ready-to-use formula can be given for the phases, stages, procedures or sequences to be used when planning or evaluating ETV. Nevertheless, when using summative evaluation, the main purpose is to determine the effectiveness of the final programme as a whole. Summative evaluation is therefore retroactive. A distinction can be made between the *immediate outcome evaluation* of the programmes (e.g. whether knowledge has been acquired, whether attitudes have changed and/or whether intentions by the learners to change future behaviour have been stimulated), versus *longitudinal impact evaluation*. In the latter instance it becomes extremely difficult to establish a causal relation between ETV and attitudinal or behavioural change, because many factors (not related to ETV) can contribute to a learner's knowledge, attitude, values or behavioural continuation or actual changes over a period of time. Examples of such factors include the learners and their peers and family members, the cultural context and even stress caused by trauma and violence, in which their daily living takes place.

15.7 PLANNING, IMPLEMENTING AND EVALUATING ETV: A CONTINUOUS CYCLE

From the outset it needs to be acknowledged that the design and development of an ETV programme (or series of programmes) is a time-consuming process. When considering the stages discussed below – which are divided into five stages for the purposes of discussion only – it becomes clear that one particular stage (e.g. *scripting and preproduction*) may take several weeks. Each stage differentiated below also represents at least one checkpoint at which the ETV designer ought to apply formative evaluation according to previously agreed upon criteria.

15.7.1 Stage 1: Need assessment

Constituting an ETV design team

During the initial meeting(s), agreement has to be reached as to who ought to be represented on the design team and the work procedures to be followed (e.g. keeping minutes of meetings). The roles and responsibilities of members of the ETV design team need to be defined, and the functions and responsibilities of the various individuals or stakeholders represented and involved in the production, need to be discussed and clarified. For example, some specialists have yet to acquire an appreciation for the requirements of effective teaching, as well as for the technological quality of the end product.

At these planning meetings it may also be necessary to identify the need for specific functions and roles that have to be fulfilled during a later stage, such as that of the scriptwriter, producer, production secretary, person designated to be responsible for scenic services (administration and design), cost control and décor construction.

During this stage, a rationale to describe the reasons why energy, time and/or money ought to be expended to plan/produce the ETV programme also has to be formulated. For example, by conducting focus-group discussions with learners who represent the actual learners as research population, such a rationale incorporates learners' needs, views and experiences. The involvement of present or potential learners will more than likely also promote their acceptance of the challenge and motivation to learn, and can increase the appropriateness, versatility and applicability of the programme.

Why ETV?

All constraints represented by the medium and its means of anticipated distribution must be identified. The central question to be asked during this stage is whether television (or video) is the most appropriate medium for educational and development purposes. In order to answer this question, we need to seek answers to three further questions, namely: (1) What does the programme aim to achieve? (2) What is the nature of the subject content? and (3) Who is the target destination?

After establishing that television/video as a *medium* is appropriate and affordable, the teaching methods that are applicable to the subject content and teaching/reception situation need to be decided, whilst keeping in mind whether the programme is intended for nonformal or formal education.

Analysis of the target destination

The target destination has to be researched and demarcated with reference to variables, namely past experience, psychographic characteristics, sociographic characteristics, present level of formal education, level of literacy, language preferences, and any other variables (such as their AIOs – section 15.3 above) which the ETV design team deems necessary.

Teaching aims and learning objectives

The teaching aim(s) must be formulated and learning objectives clarified, because they assist in establishing relationships, syntheses, generalisations and structuring evaluations.

If, for example, the teaching aim of the programme is mainly informational, then a linear format should suffice. If, in contrast, learners have to understand procedures and master mechanical skills, then an interactive format is advisable. In the latter instance, the programme format must be planned so that learners are given the opportunity to demonstrate their understanding of the procedures and skills. In cases where the aim of the content is to persuade and to change learners' attitudes, an interactive format should also be considered, together with follow-up face-to-face discussions between teacher and learner.

Defining objectives for a course or an ETV programme may prove to be more time-consuming than anticipated. This may be partly due to teachers sometimes being unclear as to exactly what behavioural and skill outcomes the programmes aims to achieve, partly because media specialists have different ways of formulating and interpreting such objectives, and partly due to the audiovisual encoding characteristics of the medium itself. Nevertheless, the specification of learning objectives should include the actions; conditions of performance and practice; and the standards of successful performance. (*Standards*, in this instance, identify the levels of quality and quantity at which the learner has to perform to be regarded as successful.)

Content

The content of the programme (concepts, principles and skills) needs to be demarcated and described, with cognisance of factors such as the target destination, the subject, level of development, the ETV means of distribution, the role of the teacher and other support material. If possible, criterion checks at strategic points need to be designed as early as this stage, to provide the teacher (and learner) with the means of diagnosing learners' progress and successes, or points of difficulty or breakdown.

Before proceeding to the next stage, the selection of particular teaching aims and learning objectives need to be evaluated in terms of the content, and according to criteria previously agreed on by the ETV designer (team).

15.7.2 **Stage 2: Scripting and preproduction**

This stage is essentially concerned with the writing, development, editing and supervision of the content, the story board and the television/video script.

Formulating a teaching/learning strategy

The teaching/learning strategy has to be decided upon, with due consideration to the means of dissemination, the anticipated format, the aim of the programme, the nature of the message (e.g. sensitive), and especially the budget and availability of expert personnel.

The integration of activities with the format of an ETV programme should be guided by the teaching aims, the subject content, the level of difficulty and the target destination. The following are some examples of the types of activities that can be considered, as well as the communication (and thus teaching) functions they fulfil:

- learning and revising the meanings of terminology
- analysis of practical examples
- self-assessment (e.g. writing content outlines or content summaries)
- try-to-do-it-yourself tasks
- questions to promote reaction from learners

- questions to stimulate meaningful discussion among learners as peers and/or between learners and teacher
- an integration between content and action (to combine knowledge, application and synthesis).

Activities can expose learners to experiences that are not usually found in their life-worlds, such as addressing cultural issues. And although other examples can be added to the seven activities listed above, the purpose of using activities is essentially threefold: (1) to learn, (2) to evaluate, and (3) to enrich.

As the selection of a teaching/learning strategy has a direct influence on the scripting and preproduction planning, it is worth considering the following guidelines when preparing an ETV script that is learner-centred:

1 Identify and include only information which is essential.
2 Use terminology in the dialogue or commentary (on-camera or voice-over) which the target destination will understand.
3 Relate the content to the target destination's (anticipated learners') milieu (which is influenced by numerous variables such as age, level of formal education or work requirements).
4 Use clear graphics (in terms of contrast, colours and actual conceptual content).
5 Use analogies and especially examples (which promote understanding because they enable learners to relate abstract knowledge to their real world).
6 Commence with what is known and progress to the unknown.
7 Be gender sensitive by referring to both men and women.
8 Do a reliability check on both the verbal and visual content.

Promoting active involvement of the learners, and actual interaction with the programme, requires creative planning on the part of the ETV design team. For example, allowance could be made for variety in the format, such as the use of games and simulations. In the American preschool children's series, *Sesame Street,* producers for example, use the following as *attention grabbers*: puppets, animation, visual movement, lively music, rhyming, repetition of words, special sound effects, changing vignettes, fast pacing and quick resolution of problems (Lesser 1972:108–165). In other words, the format must be appropriate for the target destination. Interestingly, in *Takalani Sesame*, introduced in 2000 and broadcast by the South African Broadcasting Corporation, the four central puppet characters were created especially for the South African audience, a combination of *Sesame Street* and radio (apparently a world first) which works together with an outreach programme, initially targeted for KwaZulu-Natal, Eastern Cape, Northern Province and Northern Cape.

In addition, the use of different questioning techniques must also be considered and where possible linked to branching, which offers the learner more than one option to follow in order to proceed during a learning activity.

A visual overview in the form of a graphic flowchart (combined with mind-maps where applicable) could also be useful to enable all the members of the ETV design team to understand how the various elements (such as visual content, voice-over commentary or graphics) interrelate with objectives and branching options offered by the activities integrated in the programme format.

Support material

Support material can consist of any one or all of the following media: audiotapes, other television programmes, self-study guides, instructional guides with visuals, workbooks and/or test cards. At this stage it is important that the ETV design team agrees on which support materials (media) will be integrated with the programme; and with which teaching aims in mind (the discussion of support material above, in section 15.5).

These support media can fulfil three functions, namely to supplement ETV, to reinforce the message, and as a medium of self-evaluation. Because self-evaluation tests (to test retention, learning and understanding) ought to be an integral part of the sequencing and flow of an ETV programme, they need to be formulated during one of these initial planning stages.

Scripting and other preproduction requirements

During this stage the story board and script have to be planned, their progress evaluated (with reference to variables such as the duration, format, style and use of repetitions) and finalised.

In the event of the actual production involving other institutions (e.g. external production companies), the following specifications need to be spelled out at the outset: the scope of the content; the difficulty level; the technical standards of both visual and auditory quality; licensing requirements and, where applicable, the marketing strategy; cost estimates and from which fund payments are to be secured; and a time schedule. (It may, for example be necessary to secure a sponsor, whose approval of content and objectives may also be required.) It may during this stage also be necessary (or a wise option) to economise the production by obtaining quotations from outside designers or suppliers. For example, the use of a single communication code, namely *mood music*, requires payment of copyright and licence fees prior to its inclusion in a production (SARRAL 1995).

During the scripting and preproduction stage, a number of other aspects related to planning and production need to be decided and finalised. These could include some or all of the following: booking of scenic designers; booking of studios; plans for décor construction; finalising graphics and even make-up; clothing designer, costumier or property buyer; submitting costing and financial estimates; and having the budget approved. In addition to artwork and the design of costumes, the provision of scenic facilities may involve model-builders (e.g. involved in the construction of miniature sets and props) as well as electrical designers involved in designing and building moving models, marionettes and puppets. The presence of lighting and sound technicians may also prove valuable, prior to finalising the script.

Before commencing with the actual production, formative evaluation of the story boards and script needs to be undertaken, for example, by using focus groups that represent the target destination. The emphasis in these evaluations would be on the appropriateness of using the following in relation to the ETV team's intentions: the auditory codes (types of presentation, use of active and passive voice, repetitions, sound effects and music – especially when used as a cue to stop the programme and undertake an activity), visual codes of content (décor, colour, lighting, dress, studio, the presenter's gender, age and eye contact with the viewers) and visual codes of form (camera shots, camera movements and editing techniques).

15.7.3 Stage 3: Production

Once the actual recording and production commences, more technical and procedural aspects, which differ from one production house to another, are involved. For example, writing the scenario (from which detailed information, related to camera cards and instructions for the vision mixer, sound mixer, film editor, titles, and so forth, are compiled) as well as finalising texts, the floorplan and inputs from other production personnel.

The ideal would be to record and produce certain selective sequences so that formative evaluation of style, content, format, activities, support material, and so on, can be undertaken. However, such formative evaluations will have had to be preplanned and scheduled, because of the costs involved once actual full production commences.

15.7.4 Stage 4: Postproduction

Depending on the extent to which continuous editing took place during production, the essence during this stage is to view the final edit and do quality control. The ETV design team may also be required – depending on the institution and stakeholders concerned – to prepare special instructions for transmission and/or distribution, and to prepare promotional material or a synopsis that accompanies the programme, for example for press coverage.

15.7.5 Stage 5: Distribution

Even prior to the actual distribution (or broadcast) of a programme, the ETV design team ought to begin the summative evaluation. (In other words, the ideal would be to start the summative evaluation of the completed programme once the postproduction stage has been completed.)

As discussed above (section 15.6) summative evaluation is retroactive and aimed at determining the relevance, applicability and approval of a programme and ultimately its selection for actual use. The latter can be guided by determining (evaluating) the extent to which the teaching aims and learning objectives are realised by a particular programme; and by judging the worth or merit of the content and form of the programme. The assessment of the effectiveness or improvement of ETV cannot therefore be based solely on a learner's performance by itself; the assumption being that a bright learner will improve despite ETV and despite the teacher. Validation needs to be related to the objectives that were initially defined with precision. In other words, one of the main concerns of the summative evaluation is whether a learner (for whom the programme was designed) performs as described by the standards of performance.

Figure 15.4 provides a graphic summary to illustrate the cyclical nature of the stages involved in formative and summative evaluation.

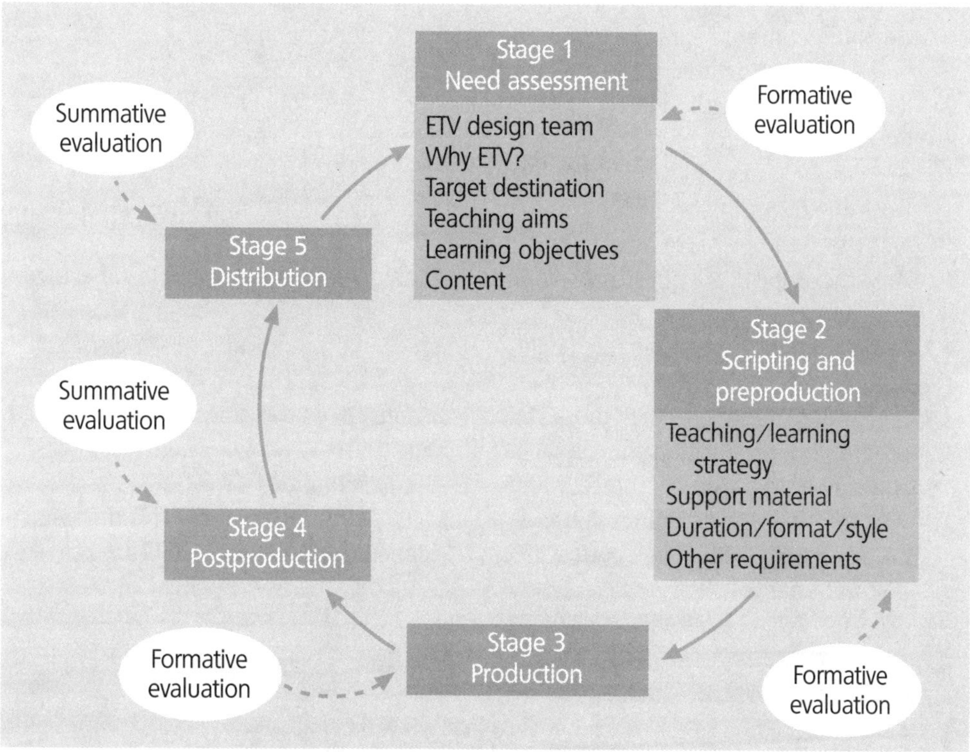

Figure 15.4 Evaluating ETV: a cyclical process

We end this section with four checklists that can be applied during any of the formative evaluation stages and/or for the purpose of summative evaluation. They contain examples of questions that the ETV design team has to investigate, discuss and research as part of formative evaluation and/or summative evaluation.

Checklist 1 – Teaching/learning variables

1 Are the teaching aims clear from the programme?
2 Are the learning objectives clear from the programme?
3 Are the learning objectives related to actions; conditions of performance and practice; and standards of successful performance?
4 Does the content reflect cognisance of the target destination's demographics and AIOs?
5 Is the subject content correct?
6 Does the content represent components of knowledge and skills?
7 Is the content divided into smaller manageable sections?
8 Does the sequence in which the content is presented follow logically?
9 Is the visualisation of the message(s) appropriate to the content?
10 Are practical examples included in the programme?
11 Does the introduction of the programme (and subsections) motivate learners to want to find out more about the subject?
12 Are the types of questions varied (e.g. open-ended versus closed-ended questions)?
13 Are summaries used at the end of each section and at the end of the programme?
14 Is the duration of the programme suitable (for the target destination, programme format and the subject content)?
15 Has a human touch been integrated with the programme?
16 Are the four basic educational interactions being promoted? If not, what changes (e.g. content, codes, format) can be made to facilitate these interactions?

Checklist 2 – Visual codes

1 How are the codes of content arranged in the screen space?
2 Is the lettering (size, font and contrast) of words on the screen legible?
3 Does the use of colour fulfil an information function?
4 Are keywords used on the screen?
5 If icons are used, what functions do they fulfil?
6 Is a visual time-code used?
7 Does the understanding of keywords require prior knowledge of the content?
8 How are summaries visualised?
9 Is the audiovisual combination (with the emphasis on visual codes) appropriate for the content; and for the teaching aim?
10 How credible is the presenter's nonverbal behaviour?

Checklist 3 – Auditory codes

1 Does the verbal speech correlate with the visuals?
2 Are verbal explanations, directions or instructions easy to understand?
3 Is the language appropriate to the educational level of the target group?
4 Which of verbal speech, music and sound effects are used to summarise subsections and the programme as whole?
5 Which communicative functions are fulfilled by the sound effects?
6 Which communication functions are fulfilled by the music?
7 Is the audiovisual combination (with the emphasis on auditory codes) appropriate for the content; and for the teaching aim?
8 Does the type of address (direct address, dialogue and/or voice-over commentary) contribute to coactive interaction?

Checklist 4 – Integration with support material

1 Is the programme structured with predetermined breaks?
2 What kind of activities are used to promote learners' active involvement?
3 Is appropriate feedback given after each activity?
4 Is feedback given in the programme, in support material or in both?
5 Are previous sections or examples reviewed?
6 Are the stop-start directions easy to follow?
7 Is a visual time-code used to facilitate interaction with support material and to facilitate references to previous sections of the programme?
8 Do the nature and content of the feedback guide learners to undertake self-evaluation?
9 Does feedback provide actual answers to problems or criteria which learners can use in assessing their own answers?
10 Does the feedback cater for different levels and abilities among learners?
11 Which of the following skills are addressed in activities: reading, writing, study, reflection, problem-solving, analytical and/or critical?
12 Are the four basic educational interactions being promoted? If not, how can support material be used to contribute to these interactions?

One ingredient which planning-and-implementation models (schemes or checklists) normally overlooks and which is omitted on purpose from the outline above, is *political* goodwill (McKee 1992). *Political* is used as an umbrella term to include the wider social, cultural, political and especially economic context in which ETV is to be applied. This includes coordination among different stakeholders, such as broadcasting institution(s), education departments, financial resources, nongovernmental organisations, teachers, parents, learners, and social priorities, such as the RDP.

The selection, orientation and organisation of individuals who plan, implement and evaluate each phase of the process is of cardinal importance, as well as the ETV designer (as individual) who has to direct, manage, facilitate and coordinate the variety of activities. When dealing with conflict of interests, these may vary depending on whether they deal with administrative, didactic, technological, policy, financial matters or decision-making procedures.

The relevance of the above supportive goodwill and effective coordination is anticipated to increase as the trend in Africa, and especially in South Africa, towards decentralisation of educational matters, increased privatisation, and a greater focus of nongovernmental organisations on provincial and local levels, continues.

When reconsidering *effective teaching/learning* (as defined above in section 15.2), the necessity to develop standards (or criteria) for the evaluation of ETV programmes *and* to define the extent and content of such standards, is crucial. Yet, this is by no means an easy task.

Summary

The position taken throughout this unit is that ETV can be applied for the purposes of education and development within and beyond the parameters of school-walls learning.

We commenced the discussion of educational television (ETV) and development by describing and defining nine content key terms that were repeatedly used throughout the unit. An overview of the theories/approaches to, and a development perspective of, teaching/learning followed. Thereafter the adaptability of television as a communication medium was investigated with the focus on four issues, namely the means of distributing ETV; the educational implications of the means of distribution, and of the encoding (medium) characteristics; and the importance of television-mediated experiences. A distinction was drawn between formative and summative evaluation of ETV, and the unit ended with a discussion of the planning, implementing and evaluating of educational television as a continuous cycle. The checklist (that can be used for formative and/or summative evaluations) functions as a *summary* of this unit and is included with the acknowledgement that it cannot cater for or do justice to all the complexities involved in teaching, learning and development.

If ETV or other forms of mediated teaching/learning were to be effective in South Africa then at least two issues remain. First, the problem of accessibility and especially the lack thereof which leaves the majority of learners confined to alienation and exclusion. Second, a redefinition of the conception of expertise seems to be required – especially in South Africa. It has become necessary to shift the emphasis of the teacher-as-expert to the teacher as adviser (facilitator, coordinator) and colearner. More importantly, if teaching/learning is to be an interactive process, then the wealth of knowledge and experience which non-specialists or so-called lay people can contribute to education and development need to be acknowledged and their active involvement sought.

Despite the realities of South Africa where millions of people are in need of housing, accessible water supplies and rural electrification, and where learners in the formal education sector lack basics such as desks, chairs, books ... and much more ... we end this unit on a positive note by concluding that in time to come, communication media – such as television – will facilitate mass education and, at the same time, cater for individual development needs.

Research activities

1 Describe, in the form of short notes, the basic assumptions of the theories/approaches to teaching/learning. Compare these assumptions by determining which of the following components of the communication process are emphasised (or regarded to be more important than the others): communicator (teacher); recipient(s) (learners); messages (signs and codes, encoding and decoding, meaning, interpretation); medium and channel; feedback; and context.

2 Consider your personal needs, as well as those of your family members, friends and fellow workers. Imagine also that you are invited to participate in the formulation of policy guidelines for the planning and production of future ETV programmes to be broadcast on national television in South Africa, or in the country where you reside.

In terms of the needs that you have identified:

- Elaborate on one or more of the ten goals listed in section 15.4. For example, when considering the tenth goal – *to continue learning* – how would you redefine and elaborate this goal in terms of the needs that you have identified?
- Formulate other goals that come to mind (and which are not specified in section 15.4) and motivate their inclusion with reference to your needs as an individual and/or the social needs of your community.

3 The promotion of a culture of learning in South African schools and a national literacy campaign are two of the key projects of the RDP (Reconstruction and Development Programme) in South Africa.

Select one of these projects. Assume that you are involved in the planning of an ETV programme to be shown in your community. Describe the following:

- The general teaching aim(s) of the programme.
- The characteristics of your target destination.
- The learning objectives of this programme.

4 Explain in writing (a short paragraph), in your own words, why you think teaching aims and learning objectives have to be formulated as an integral part of the initial planning stages for an ETV programme. Illustrate the explanation with reference to actual examples.

5 Test the validity of the Pareto principle in terms of your personal experience, by doing the following:

- Keep a diary of your activities (e.g. in your work situation) during one or two months and determine whether certain tasks, such as answering the telephone, constitute one-fifth (20%) of your activities. Differentiate between routine activities that you perform daily (e.g. to clock in and out of work), versus routine activities that occur on a weekly basis, and keep a record of the frequency of these activities.
- Calculate whether these activities are repeated 80 percent of the time during the period you selected.

6 Select one of the means of ETV distributions described in section 15.5.1. Compare this means of distribution, together with the implications of its encoding (medium) characteristics, with other means of distribution, by using *branching* and *learner control* as criteria. For example, you could select and compare broadcast television with that of the VCR&M.

7 Discuss the application of formative evaluation during the planning and preproduction stages of designing an ETV programme of your own choice and/or specifically related to the project that you selected from point 3 above. That is, either an ETV programme on the promotion of learning in South African schools or an ETV programme on a national literacy campaign.

8 Select an ETV programme to which you have easy access. (This unit mentions some of the more popular ETV programmes, such as *Yizo Yizo 2* and *Soul City*, amongst others, and it is preferable to select a programme with which you are familiar or of which you have video copies.) Undertake a formative or a summative evaluation of the programme by applying checklists listed in section 15.7. That is, check the teaching/learning variables; visual codes; auditory codes; and the integration of support material. Include a short description of the ETV programme that you have selected and mention some of the central educational issues that the programme deals with, giving examples from the programme you have selected. For instance, the series *Khululeka* deals with social and human rights issues and applied these issues to, for example, the South African elections.

   Whilst doing the evaluation, make notes of other criteria and considerations discussed in this unit (but not necessarily listed in the checklist) that guided your evaluation and which were relevant to the programme being evaluated.

Further reading

Buckingham, D. 1990. Towards a theory of media learning, in *Watching media learning. Making sense of media education*, edited by D Buckingham. London: Falmer.

Champagne, AB & Bunce, DM. 1991. Learning theory-based science teaching, in *The psychology of learning science*, edited by SM Glynn, RH Yeany & BK Britton. Hillsdale, NJ: Lawrence Erlbaum.

Crocker, AD. 1993. Toward an ethic for development. *The Courier* 137:62.
Hamilton, D. 1990. *Learning about education. An unfinished curriculum.* Milton Keynes: Open University Press.
Lester, PM. 1995. *Visual communication: images with messages.* Belmont, CA: Wadsworth.
McKee, N. 1992. *Social mobilization and social marketing in developing communities: lessons for communicators.* Penang Malaysia: Southbound.
Rowntree, D. 1990. *Teaching through self-instruction. How to develop open learning materials.* Revised edition. London: Kogan Page.
Rowntree, D. 1992. *Exploring open and distance learning.* London: Kogan Page.

Bibliography

Baggaley, J, Duby, A & Lewy, A. 1987. *Evaluation of educational television.* Johannesburg: South African Broadcasting Corporation.
Bagui, GJ. 1995. The substance of health communication education. *Africa Media Review* 9(2):38–57.
Barnes, L & McDuling, A. 1995. The future of Portuguese in South Africa: maintenance and shift factors. *Language Matters. Studies in the Languages of Southern Africa* 26:147–162.
Bloom, BS, Engelhart, MD, Furst, EJ, Hill, WH & Krathwohl, DR (eds). 1956. *Taxonomy of educational objectives; the classification of educational goals: handbook I, cognitive domain.* London: Longmans.
Boot, RL & Hodgson, VE. 1987. Open learning: meaning and experience, in *Beyond distance teaching – towards open learning*, edited by VE Hodgson, SJ Mann & R Snell. Milton Keynes: Open University Press.
Botkin, JW, Elmandjara, M & Malitza, M. 1979. *No limits to learning.* Oxford: Pergamon.
Briggs, LJ. 1970. *Handbook for procedures for design of instruction.* Pittsburgh: American Institute for Research.
Brown, AL, Campione, JC & Day, JD. 1981. Learning to learn. On training students to learn from texts. *Educational Researcher* 10(2):14–21.
Bryant, J & Anderson, DR (eds). 1983. *Children's understanding of television. Research on attention and comprehension.* New York: Academic.
Buckingham, D. 1990. Towards a theory of media learning, in *Watching media learning. Making sense of media education*, edited by D. Buckingham. London: Falmer.
Burton, G & Dimbleby, R. 1988. *Between ourselves: an introduction to interpersonal communication.* London: Edward Arnold.
Case-Grant, A. 1973. *Visual literacy: an exciting environmental adventure.* Richmond, VA: Richmond Public Schools.
Champagne, AB & Bunce, DM. 1991. Learning theory-based science teaching, in *The psychology of learning science*, edited by SM Glynn, RH Yeany & BK Britton. Hillsdale, NJ: Lawrence Erlbaum.
Chaplin, JP (ed). 1968. *Dictionary of psychology.* New York, NY: Dell.
Crocker, AD. 1993. Toward an ethic for development. *The Courier* 137:62.
Dansereau, DF, Collins, KW, McDonald, BA, Holley, CD, Garland, T, Diekhoff, G & Evans, SH. 1979. Development and evaluation of a learning strategy training programme. *Journal of Educational Psychology* 7(1):64–73.
Dewey, J. 1916/1987. Aims in education, in *Value theory and education*, edited by PF Carbone. Malabar, Fl: Robert E Krieger.

Duby, A. 1987. Formative evaluation of ETV in the early stages of programme development, in *Evaluation of educational television*, edited by J Baggaley, A Duby & A Lewy. Johannesburg: South African Broadcasting Corporation.
Du Plooy, GM. 1989. *Understanding television: guidelines for visual literacy*. Cape Town: Juta.
Du Plooy, T. 1997. Educational television and development, in *Introduction to communication – course book 6: Film and television studies*, edited by PJ Fourie. Kenwyn: Juta.
Erikson, EH. 1963. *Childhood and society*. 2nd edition. New York: Norton.
Faure, E, Herrern, F, Kaddoura, A-R, Lopes, H, Petrousky, AV, Rahmerna, M & Ward, FC. 1972. *Learning to be*. Paris: United Nations Educational, Scientific and Cultural Organization.
Film Resource Unit. 1995. *Films from Southern Africa – video catalogue*. Johannesburg: Film Resource Unit.
Fourie, HP. 1976. *Communication by objectives*. Isando: McGraw-Hill.
Fourie, PJ (ed). 1997. *Introduction to communication – course book 6: film and television studies*. Kenwyn: Juta.
Goldenberg, EP. 1979. *Special technology for special children*. Baltimore: University Park Press.
Gravett, S. 1995. The creation of a context conducive to student learning. *South African Journal of Higher Education/Suid-Afrikaanse Tydskrif vir Hoër Onderwys* 9(2):33–36.
Hamilton, D. 1990. *Learning about education. An unfinished curriculum*. Milton Keynes: Open University Press.
Havighurst, RJ. 1950. *Developmental tasks and education*. New York: Longmans & Green.
Hodgson, VE, Mann, SJ & Snell, RS. 1987. *Beyond distance teaching towards open learning*. Milton Keynes: Open University Press.
Howe, MJA (ed). 1983. *Learning from television. Psychological and educational research*. London: Academic.
Independent Broadcasting Authority (IBA). 1995a. *Issues paper: South African content on television and radio (inquiry in terms of section 28(8) of the IBA Act, 1993)*. Johannesburg: Independent Broadcasting Authority.
Independent Broadcasting Authority (IBA). 1995b. *Triple inquiry report. The protection & viability of public broadcasting services. Cross media control of broadcasting services. Local television content & South African music*. Johannesburg: Independent Broadcasting Authority.
James, NC. 1981. Television games children play: children's communicative uses of television, *PhD dissertation*. Ohio State University, Ohio.
Jansen, N. 1989. *Philosophy of mass communication research*. Cape Town: Juta.
Jordan, Y. 1978. *Training officer's operating manual. Industrial Training Unit*. Durban: Technikon Natal.
Kapoor, S, Mathur, P & DiMiceli, D. 1991. Indian television at crossroads. *World Communication* 20(2):79–90.
Kemp, JE. 1980. *Planning and producing audiovisual materials*. 4th edition. London: Harper & Row.
Lesser, GS. 1972. Assumptions behind the production and writing methods of *Sesame Street*, in *Quality instructional television*, edited by W. Schramm. Honolulu: University Hawaii Press.
Lesser, GS. 1974. *Children and television: lessons from "Sesame Street"*. New York: Vintage.
Lester, PM. 1995. *Visual communication: images with messages*. Belmont, CA: Wadsworth.
Lombaard, S. 1996. Securing our children's rights. *SA Now. A View on Our Country* 1(1):29–36.
Marsh, PO. 1983. *Messages that work. A guide to communication design*. Englewood Cliffs, NJ: Educational Technological Publications.
Maslow, AH. 1962. *Toward a psychology of being*. New York: Litton Educational Publishing.
Masterman, L. 1980. *Teaching about television*. London: Macmillan.
McKee, N. 1992. *Social mobilization and social marketing in developing communities: lessons for communicators*. Penang Malaysia: Southbound.

Meehan, EJ. 1995. An essential addendum to existing education. *South African Journal of Higher Education/Suid-Afrikaanse Tydskrif vir Hoër Onderwys* 9(2):17–28.

Merton, RK. 1968. *Social theory and social structure*. New York: Free.

Mielke, KW & Chen, M. 1983. Formative research for "3-2-1 Contact": methods and insights, in *Learning from television. Psychological and educational research*, edited by MJA Howe. London: Academic.

Mortensen, CD (ed). 1979. *Basic readings in communication theory*. 2nd edition. New York: Harper & Row.

Nevo, D. 1987. The meaning of evaluation and its practice, in *Evaluation of educational television*, edited by J Baggaley, A Duby & A Lewy. Johannesburg: South African Broadcasting Corporation.

Nguni, M. 1995. Development communication: a clarification of constructs. *Africa Media Review* 9(2):1–15.

Noble, G. 1983. Social learning from everyday television, in *Learning from television. Psychological and educational research*, edited by MJA Howe. London: Academic.

Nyirenda, JE. 1995. Social mobilisation for adult literacy in Botswana. *Africa Media Review* 9(2):58–81.

Oliphant, L. 2001. TV sugars the learning pill. *Saturday Star*, 17 February:6.

Olson, W. 1949. *Child development*. Boston: Heath.

O'Sullivan, T, Hartley, J, Saunders, D, Montgomery, M & Fiske, J. 1994. *Key concepts in communication and cultural studies*. 2nd edition. London: Routledge.

Palmer, P. 1986. *The lively audience. A study of children around the TV set*. Sydney: Allen & Unwin.

Piaget, J. 1964. *Judgment and reasoning in the child*, translated by M. Warden. Paterson, NJ: Littlefield, Adams.

Poverty affects many South African children. 1996. *Rekord Moot* 9 February:5.

Powell, I. 1996. Plan to beam politics live into lounges. *Sunday Times*,14 January:4.

Rassekh, S & Vaideanu, G. 1987. *The contents of education. A worldwide view of their development from the present to the year 2000*. Paris: United Nations Educational, Scientific and Cultural Organization.

Rensburg, RS (ed). 1996. *Introduction to communication – course book 4: communication planning and management*. Cape Town: Juta.

Reynolds, JM. 1996. Formative evaluation and production of a videotape for UNISA communication students. Unpublished BA (Hons) Project. University of South Africa, Pretoria.

Rogers, C. 1983. *Freedom to learn. For the '80s*. 2nd edition. Colombus, OH: Charles E Merrill.

Rowntree, D. 1974. *Educational technology in curriculum development*. London: Harper & Row.

Rowntree, D. 1990. *Teaching through self-instruction. How to develop open learning materials*. Revised edition. London: Kogan Page.

Rowntree, D. 1992. *Exploring open and distance learning*. London: Kogan Page.

Russell, T & Verill, G. 1986. *Otto Kleppner's advertising procedure*. 9th edition. Englewood Cliffs, NJ: Prentice-Hall.

Saibaba, A, Mohanram, M, Kumar Dube, A & Prasanna Krishna, T. 1995. Television as a health pedagogue in India. *Media Asia* 22(3):169–173.

SARRAL (South African Recording Rights Association Limited). 1995. Schedule of minimum rates for the licensing of our members' mood music, library works and recordings in films, T.V., radio and video productions. Braamfontein: SARRAL.

Schramm, W, Lyle, J & Parker, E. 1961. *Television in the lives of our children*. Stanford: Stanford University Press.

Schwalbe, H. 1987. Education for staff training in Germany, in *Beyond distance teaching – towards open learning*, edited by VE Hodgson, SJ Mann & R Snell. Milton Keynes: Open University Press.

Scriven, M. 1980. *Evaluation thesaurus.* 2nd edition. Inverness, CA: Edgepress.
Secord, PF & Backman, CW. 1964. *Social pshychology.* New York: McGraw-Hill.
Shane, HG. & Tabler, MB. 1981. *Educating for a new millennium: views of 132 international scholars.* Bloomington, IN: Phi Delta Kappa Educational Foundation.
Skinner, BF. 1953. *Science and human behaviour.* New York: Free.
Skinner, BF. 1974. *About behaviourism.* New York: Knopf.
Soola, EO. 1995. De-mystifying the development process: the role of communication in community participation for sustainable development. *Africa Media Review* 9(2):16–37.
South Africa. 1995. *South Africa's Green Paper on Science and Technology: preparing for the 21st century.* Pretoria: National Science and Technology Forum (28 November).
Stephenson, W. 1967. *The play theory of mass communication.* Chicago: University of Chicago Press.
Stevenson, RL. 1988. *Communication, development and the Third World: the global politics of information.* New York: Longman.
Strang, A. 1987. The hidden barriers, in *Beyond distance teaching – towards open learning,* edited by VE Hodgson, SJ Mann & R Snell. Milton Keynes: Open University Press.
Toffler, A. 1980. *The third wave.* New York: Bantom.
Van Vuuren, DP & Herselman, C. 1987. The evaluation of ETV-programmes in South Africa: some HSRC initiatives, in *Evaluation of educational television,* edited by J Baggaley, A Duby & A Lewy. Johannesburg: South African Broadcasting Corporation.
Varghese, K. 1995. Rethinking mass media's potential in participative development: the relevance of access. *Media Asia* 22(3):144–149.
Vivian, J. 1991. *The media of mass communication.* Boston: Allyn & Bacon.
Von Bertalanffy, L. 1956. General systems theory, in *Yearbook of the Society for General Systems Theory* 1:1–10.
Wigren, HE. 1967. The process of change in educational television, in *Perspectives on educational change,* edited by RI Miller, New York: Appleton-Century-Crofts.
Wilcox, DL, Ault, PH & Agee, WK. 1992. *Public relations. Strategies and tactics.* 3rd edition. New York, NY: Harper Collins.
Wolseley, RE & Campbell, LR. 1957. *Exploring journalism: with emphasis on its social and professional aspects.* 3rd edition. Englewood Cliffs, NJ: Prentice-Hall.
Yule, RM. 1990. Educational technology 90's. *Informedia. Journal of the National Film Library* 37(2):6–7.
Zettl, H. 1976. *Television production handbook.* 3rd edition. Belmont, CA: Wadsworth.
Zettl, H. 1990. *Sight, sound, motion: applied media aesthetics.* 2nd edition. Belmont, CA: Wadsworth.

Educational Media: Radio 16

David Wigston

Overview

Before we can begin our study of education by radio, we need to establish the varying forces that impact on it and in so doing shape the final broadcast product. The context in which education by radio takes place is described in terms of seven factors that interact with each other in varying ways. Having established these factors as variables that can influence education by radio, we turn our attention to education as one of three primary functions of radio; the other two being information and entertainment. However, there is no clear-cut demarcation between these three functions. This leads to some uncertainty concerning what aspects are actually covered within the educational function. To try and resolve this problem we consider a definition of educational broadcasting. Here we make a distinction between the concepts "educational" and "educative" and apply these to radio programming. In addition, we distinguish between formal, informal and nonformal education, with each type making use of a particular strategy. Within nonformal education by radio we can consider using two broad strategies to present programmes: that of open broadcasting versus the use of radio listening groups. It is the latter to which we give most of our attention because of its potential in a developing context. To this end we discuss the procedures to be followed in organising an educational campaign that makes use of radio listening groups as a strategy. A brief discussion follows on the declining role of public service broadcasting in the provision of educational programmes. We conclude this unit with a consideration of the effectiveness of radio as a medium for education by comparing its limitations with the advantages.

Learning outcomes

At the end of this unit you should be able to

- discuss the context in which education by radio takes place;
- describe the various forms of education by radio;
- compare and evaluate the various strategies that broadcasters can use in educational programmes;
- design a nonformal educational campaign using radio listening groups as a strategy;
- evaluate the role of public service broadcasting in the provision of educational programmes; and
- discuss and compare the advantages and limitations of radio as a provider of education.

16.1 INTRODUCTION

From the very beginnings of radio, the potential of the medium for use in education has always been upheld. Early developers were strongly motivated by what radio could offer in order to improve the standard of education. This notion was based on current thinking of the day, which considered the media to have enormous powers in influencing behaviour (White & Thomas 1988/89:1). However, the results proved to be uniformly disappointing. Findings from research indicated that there was no significant difference achieved between formal face-to-face instruction in a classroom when compared to that provided via radio (Jamison & McAnany 1978:12). Hopes that radio would provide the long sought-after breakthrough in education proved disappointing. But two policy implications emerge from this First World situation that are of particular relevance to a developing country. Firstly, if radio is of equal effectiveness to that of formal face-to-face classroom teaching, then radio could possibly have the edge when it comes to matters of *cost effectiveness.* This is an important point for developing countries that have large demands to provide education. Secondly, radio can *supplement education* in areas where existing teachers are untrained or below standard.

Jamison and McAnany (1978:15) question the validity of research findings that suggest radio is a mere equal to the formal classroom situation. These findings, they say, are a result of the demands of the research process, where, in order "to be scientifically adequate a comparison of radio with traditional instruction ... should hold everything constant except the medium, i.e. one should have the same lecturer lecturing in the same way to the same sort of students in the same environment. Under these circumstances it should cause little surprise to find no difference in outcomes." There is evidence that properly structured programmes can stimulate thought and provide insight (White & Thomas 1988/89:1). Radio can teach, but how successfully ultimately depends on how the medium is put to use.

We can identify three basic aims for providing education by radio (White & Thomas 1988/89:2):

- To improve the quality of existing education by providing information or experiences that teachers or textbooks cannot.
- To equalise or spread educational opportunities more widely by improving access to people living in remote areas or whose circumstances preclude further formal education.
- To reduce the cost of learning through a scale of economies where a central expert team can reach thousands of learners.

How successfully these aims can be met depends largely on the context in which radio is used for providing education.

16.2 THE CONTEXT OF EDUCATION BY RADIO

Education by radio is claimed to exist in almost every country in which there is radio. However, the extent of such broadcasting and the nature of the programmes offered

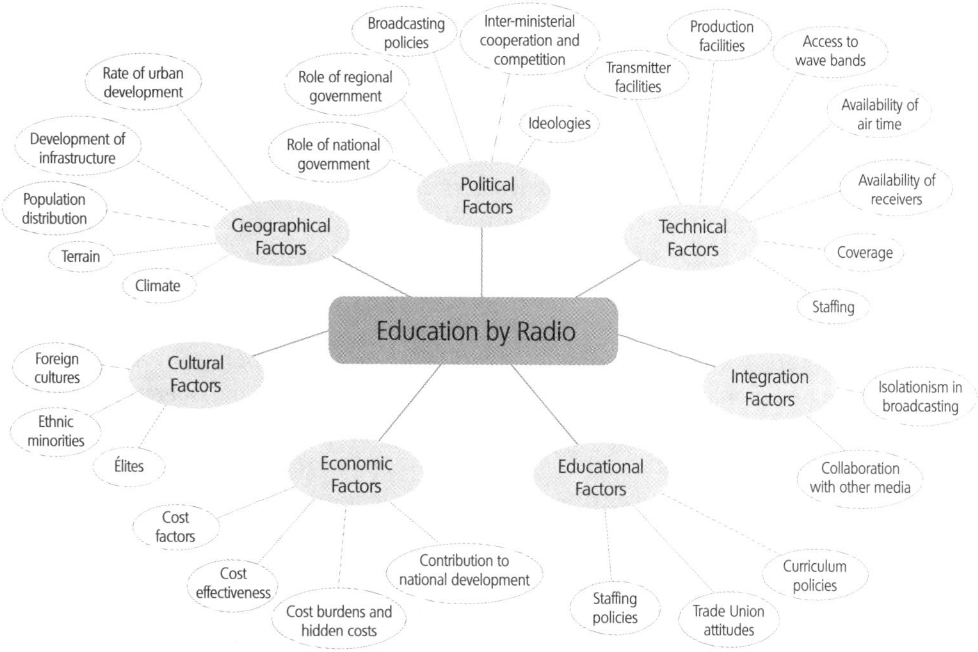

Figure 16.1 A map showing the context of education by radio (adapted from Hawkridge & Robinson 1982:31)

vary considerably. Attempts to try and categorise these differences by means of a cohesive taxonomy have so far proved fruitless, simply because of the vast number of differences that exist. The current global trend towards the deregulation and democratisation of broadcasting also compounds this issue. Hawkridge and Robinson (1982:30) are of the opinion that a taxonomy is of little value in any event, since it only indicates the variations that exist, without revealing why these variations occur. The reasons for differences are to be found in the context of each broadcasting situation, and this is why we need to give consideration to the context.

Neither broadcasting nor education occurs in a vacuum and we need to be very aware of the context in which radio and education operates (Seibert 1972:150). Although education by radio is but a small part of broadcasting, the fact that radio is used as a means of dissemination for educational purposes places any study of it firmly within the framework of the mass media. This means the use of radio for education needs to be seen within the broader perspective of the broadcasting environment. This further implies that any study of education by radio must also be within the particular sociopolitical context in which it occurs. Hawkridge and Robinson (1982:30–44) describe seven factors we should consider when establishing this context. Figure 16.1 illustrates a map that shows some of the variable components that make up these factors, each of which is briefly discussed below.

- *Geographic factors:* The physical lie of the land and distances to be covered are often limiting factors in the distribution of radio signals. For example, mountainous terrain, or high buildings in an urban area, can block out signals. FM signals can only cover a radius of about 60 kilometres from the transmitter site and therefore provide coverage of a limited geographic area. Because of the high cost of building and maintaining radio transmitters, broadcasters like to place them in areas with the densest population settlements. If our intended audience lives in an area where it is difficult to receive radio signals, then all efforts at education by radio will be for naught. A lack of infrastructure could also hamper the distribution of support material to some, particularly in the rural areas.
- *Political factors:* National ideologies exert a powerful influence in shaping the broadcasting environment. Decisions regarding the installation and operation of radio stations and their coverage are political ones, as licences to broadcast are issued by various government departments or government appointed agencies. The degree of control exercised by the government varies considerably from country to country. Control is not just limited to government control in the form of regulations and censorship, amongst others, but can also come in the form of boards of directors, commissioners and management, who can control aspects such as funding and scheduling of educational projects. Education by radio usually falls in the domain of public broadcasting services (PBS), with the result that it is extremely vulnerable to the number of variables that constitute control. We return to the problems associated with public broadcasting and the role it plays in providing education later in this unit. The important point to bear in mind here is that control, whether liberal or authoritarian in nature, is always exercised in an exclusive manner. With the democratisation of South Africa in 1994, there followed major changes to the broadcasting environment, with a number of new radio stations coming on air, but mostly in the major urban areas.
- *Cultural factors:* The role of the élite within a society is important. Their influence is usually strong, and they employ the mass media, often in subtle ways, in order to enhance their own situation. In this way, education by radio may, in fact, be widening the cultural gap rather than narrowing it, as the élites tend to benefit more than other groups by virtue of their position in society. The basis of the élite group can vary, being either political, racial, economic, religious or a mix of these elements. This perspective has grave implications for the value of education as a means of bringing about social change. Education by radio may also introduce a foreign culture, and in the process cause conflict to develop. For example, using a national language in order to provide an educational programme to remote rural communities in place of using a local language, can be seen as being representative of former colonial powers. If staff receive training in another country, such as the United States or Britain, as is often the case of Africa, then programmes produced by such trainees can show British or American cultural influences.
- *Educational factors:* Government policies in education obviously have a great impact on education by radio. National admission policies determine who should receive

training. For example, an emphasis can be placed on primary education to the exclusion of secondary or tertiary levels, even though the demand for the latter may exist. Curriculum policies determine what is to be taught, and this can in turn be influenced by cultural factors. In the informal and nonformal sectors this is not such a problem as decisions about content are usually a matter of deliberation amongst interested parties. Staffing policies may require that lesser qualified teachers use broadcast material, where the teacher acts more in a supervisory role. We also need to take into account the view of teachers' unions, where a union may block government efforts to supplement teachers with broadcast material.

- *Economic factors:* During the middle of the twentieth century, an assumption was made that economic growth was linked to education. Thus, more education meant a greater growth to the economy. This view was based on the premise that educated individuals earn more than lesser-educated ones. In addition to social reasons, therefore, there was an economic justification in promoting education. Within this context, education by radio could then be promoted as being a highly cost-effective way of providing education for large numbers of people. However, this link between economic growth and levels of education is now considered a more tenuous one as developing countries that devoted large proportions of their national budgets to education have not shown corresponding increases in their economies. There is also doubt that education by radio can still be justified simply on the grounds of being cost effective. However, this does not mean that the effects of costs are to be ignored when making a judgement about education by radio. More important is the decision regarding who is to pay the costs of using radio for education. Very rarely does the broadcaster actually foot the bill. In South Africa, it is the government who pays the South African Broadcasting Corporation (SABC) to produce and transmit educational material. In reality, economic factors are proving to be an increasing restraint on using radio for education. For example, while the cost of electronic equipment is becoming cheaper, the need to constantly upgrade technology can have the reverse effect on costs. This can pose a serious problem for developing countries where a lack of foreign currency and exorbitant exchange rates and taxes can simply preclude the purchase of new equipment.
- *Technical factors:* With the democratisation of broadcasting in Africa and Europe, the resultant growth in the number of radio stations has meant space on the frequency spectrum is at a premium. Air-time (time allotted for a broadcast), particular during prime time (time when audience numbers are at their highest) has also become scarce. Producers are then pressured to schedule educational programmes at other times that are often inconvenient for the listener, in order to free up prime-time slots for programme content that draws a larger and more lucrative general audience. Technical solutions do exist to alleviate these problems, such as recording programmes to facilitate delayed listening. The issue at stake here then changes from being a technical one to an economic one, since the learner now has to incur additional costs in the purchase of suitable recording equipment. To present an

educational programme on a national level also presents technical problems, as few radio stations in South Africa cover all the major urban areas; even fewer broadcast on a truly national level whereby they include coverage of the rural areas. The ability, or inability, to reach potential learners can impact negatively on the effectiveness of education by radio. Entire projects can be scuppered, simply because a portion of the target audience cannot be reached. Another technical issue is the control of the supply of studio facilities and maintenance of production and transmission facilities, such as studio equipment and transmitters, which rests with staff that have little to do with education. Such technical staff are likely to be strongly influenced in their decisions by the demands of general broadcasting. The transmission system used by the radio station to distribute its signal has implications on the efficacy (ability to produce a desired effect) of programmes. Each system has its advantages and disadvantages. For example, while direct broadcast satellites can cover vast areas with one beam, up to as much as half the continent of Africa, receiving equipment is expensive, power-hungry, and technically advanced to operate. Other transmission systems include FM, medium wave, short wave, encrypted signals, cable networks, digital broadcasting (DBS) and the Internet. The availability of receivers is a crucial link in the provision of education by radio and here control lies outside the sphere of both broadcasters and educators. In rural areas and squatter settlements, the lack of a power supply may mean that learners have to rely on battery powered equipment. However, for many people living in these areas, even the mere cost of batteries represents a large proportion of their income. Again, an economic factor dominates. Control here rests in the hands of the listeners who need to be persuaded rather than coerced into acquiring receivers. Finally, a major problem in Africa is the shortage of skilled technical staff to operate and maintain the broadcasting equipment.

- *Integration with other media:* For educational broadcasting to have maximum impact, it is necessary to integrate programme content with material provided via another medium, such as print in the form of textbooks or workbooks for the learners. Other media can include posters, broadsheets, pamphlets, compact discs, audio- or video-cassettes, newspapers and magazines. It is also easy for broadcasters to become isolationist and ignore what the listener does with the programme. However, the degree of integration does depend on the type of programme and intended effect desired. The highest level of integration should be found in programmes intended for formal education, and the least, if any, for informal education. Integration can also be problematic, where it can drain off large amounts of money from a limited budget, leaving little finance available for other activities. Other problems may occur if the programme and supporting material are too tightly integrated. If for some reason the learner cannot hear the programme, the support material then becomes useless. As the programme is under the control of the broadcaster, so support material should be under the control of the learner.

Within the various contexts we discussed here, we need to establish some assumptions (for the purpose of argument, taken as true) regarding the relationship of the media to their sociopolitical context, before we can continue with our investigation of education by radio (Silverstone 1999:145–146). The following five assumptions then form our point of departure when discussing education by radio in this unit.

- The media are embedded within a particular society, where the media appear as material and symbolic objects and as instruments for action through the efforts of individuals and institutions. These actions are political in that they involve a struggle for meaning and control.
- The media, as a cultural force, are subject to conflict concerning access, representation and participation. The consequences of this conflict are seemingly contradictory, in that the media simultaneously connect and separate by offering freedom of expression yet claiming surveillance and control, while eliminating old equalities as they create new ones.
- The media are a crucial part of the social process through the dissemination of information, which is essential for effective government and management of a country.
- The media are constantly changing in their relationship to the society in which they are embedded. At the same time that society is also evolving and changing.
- The society in which the media are embedded is a plural one, which results in the constant presence of difference.

16.3 WHAT IS EDUCATION BY RADIO?

Before we begin discussing education by radio, we need to take a brief look at the concept "education". For the purposes of this unit we can consider education to mean any form of socially accepted change in behaviour, attitudes and/or values that occur as a result of the acquisition of knowledge, information and/or skills over a period of time. This is a rather broad definition, but it does illustrate the vast area and possibilities that make up the field of education. Within this definition we can identify three specific issues that may clarify the concept for us. These are (Legge 1982:2):

- The type of subject, that is *what* are we teaching?
- The meaning of learner, that is *who* are we teaching?
- The type of activity, that is *how* are we teaching it?

Figure 16.2 provides us with an idea of the diverse number of subjects and types of learners that we can include in the concept "education" in order to answer the first two questions asked above. A wide range of subjects, both vocationally and non-vocationally orientated, fall under the umbrella of education. These subjects fulfil the personal and social needs of an equally large variety and type of people. To move on to the third question, the context of this unit provides us with an answer; that is, educational programming within the framework of radio broadcasting (Skidmore, Harrop & Woodcock 1996:35).

The British Broadcasting Corporation (BBC) makes a distinction between *educative* and *educational* programmes. Skidmore et al (1996:36–38) indicate there are two aspects that we can use to differentiate between these two types of programmes: these are what the audience does with the content versus the intent of the producer.

Firstly, we look at what the listener does with the contents of the programme. Educative programmes are aimed at a general audience "whose contents are retained as a general impression rather than a body of knowledge or expertise" (Crisell 1986:107). On the other hand, educational programmes contribute in an organised way to the growth of knowledge in the listener by drawing an active disciplined response, such as making notes from the programme. Such programmes can vary from a formal university lecture to a do-it-yourself programme. Therefore, whether we see a programme as educative, or educational, depends on how the listener reacts to the content. Let us consider a radio dramatisation of a Shakespeare play. For a Grade 12 learner who requires to study the work for examination purposes, the broadcast will be educational. For that learner the programme is located within an educational context that requires greater concentration in the form of a disciplined response. The learning process is an active one. But, for the casual listener, there is little extended literary knowledge because there is no retention of information in any systematic or disciplined manner. Because the learning process is a passive one, the play merely becomes an educative experience for the casual listener. From this particular point of view, it would seem as if any radio programme, such as the news, travel, documentary, drama, classical music concerts, and so forth, can simultaneously have an educational and educative function. The implication here is that the distinction between educational and educative is really an artificial one, as we cannot always easily maintain a clear distinction between educational and educative programmes. This is where we need to consider the second aspect, that is, the intention of the programme producer.

According to Crisell (1986:107–108), despite the fact that listeners can use programme content in a variety of ways, the format (style in which the programme is presented) of a programme selected by the producer clearly indicates an intent for the programme to draw, either an educational response or an educative one. The basic distinction used here is that educational programmes have, as their main outcome, some form of structured learning with the implication that the listener will do something as a result of the programme. Structured learning is then the key to educational programming (Skidmore et al 1996:37).

With these two aspects in mind we can then establish a continuum with informational programming at one end, represented by news bulletins and educational programmes at the other, with current affairs, documentaries and educative programmes in between, as illustrated in Table 16.1.

The value of having a continuum enables us to place any radio programme on the scale in order to analyse the potential of that programme for educating the listening audience. To sum up, we can quote Skidmore et al (1996:38) when they say, "the greater the 'educational intent' and the more 'definite' the subsequent 'activity', the greater the likelihood that the programme could be seen as 'educational' rather than 'educative'."

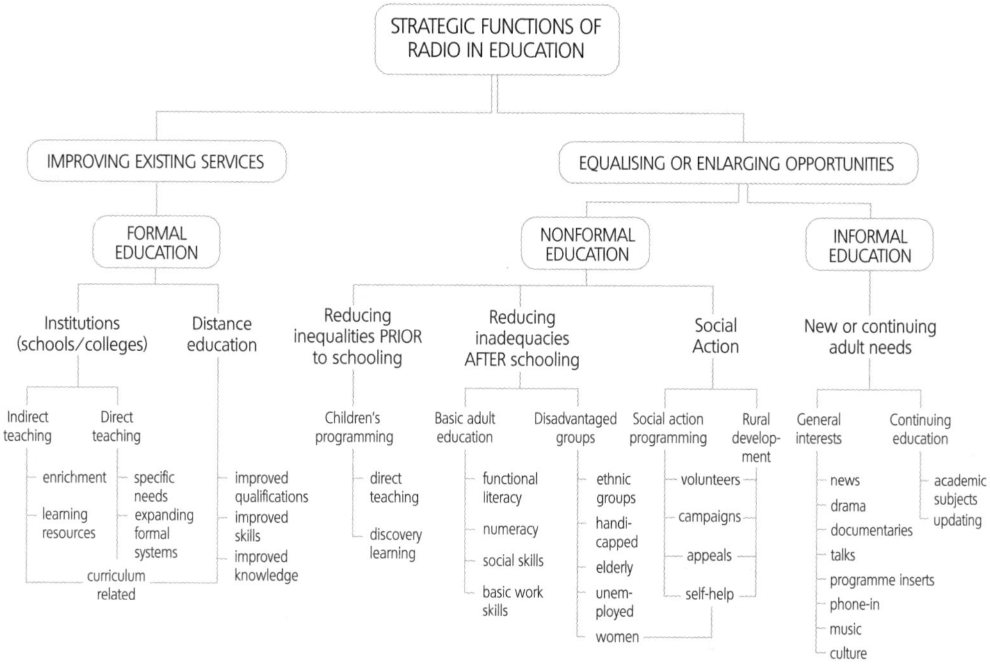

Figure 16.2 The strategic functions of radio in education (adapted from Bates 1984:9)

In addition to making a distinction between educational and educative programmes, we can, at another level, distinguish between three categories within the field of education, depending on the purpose of the programme – formal, nonformal, informal.

Table 16.1 Continuum of educational broadcasting (adapted from Skidmore, Harrop & Woodcock 1996:38)

	Educational	Educative	Informational
Intent	• specific skills	• objective for specific group	• inform/motivate
Outcome	• support material • group discussion • further study	• encourage further learning	• action
Type of programme	• talk • lecture	• current affairs • documentaries	• news • weather reports • stock exchange prices

- *Formal education* is linked to a set syllabus and usually leads to a formal qualification. The aim here is to use broadcasting to improve the quality of existing formal education and is directed at those already in formal education (Bates 1984:15).
- *Nonformal education* refers to radio programmes and campaigns that are not part of any formal educational syllabus, with the purpose of equalising or spreading more widely educational opportunities (Bates 1984:15).
- *Informal education* is an ongoing process affecting almost everyone and is gained from almost all radio programmes. The focus here is placed on a wider access to broadcasting, which in turn allows for extensive community use of the medium.

A summary of the differing categories of education by radio is summarised in Figure 16.2. To go back to our earlier example of a radio dramatisation of a Shakespeare play, for the Grade 12 learner this would represent formal education, while for the casual listener it would be nonformal. However, if we learn something in passing from listening to a news bulletin, this would be informal. We discuss each category in greater detail.

16.4 FORMAL EDUCATION

The use of radio for formal education has existed almost as long as radio broadcasting itself. The use of radio for formal education purposes started as an experiment in Britain by the BBC in 1924. By 1935, one out of every four schools in Britain was making use of radio broadcasts for schools. According to White and Thomas (1988/89:2), we can distinguish two kinds of formal educational broadcasting. These are:

- *Schools broadcasting*, which aims at providing educational material for the teacher at primary, secondary and tertiary levels. The purpose is to enrich or supplement existing learning materials being used by the teacher.
- *Distance education (DE)*, which provides for learning materials outside conventional classrooms in order to provide flexibility to the time-schedules, life-situations and needs of learners.

In South Africa, the Nguni and Sotho services of the SABC started a school's radio service in the early 1960s (South African Broadcasting Corporation 1981:87). The objective of this service was to remove some of the difficulties encountered by teachers and learners in the learning process, and it proved valuable in rural areas for developing basic skills. The other large-scale use of radio for formal education in South Africa were the Radio Unisa programmes broadcast on Radio 2000. Begun as a pilot project in 1989 with less than a dozen programmes, the project grew to enormous proportions. The content of these programmes was specifically related to undergraduate university courses offered by University of South Africa (Unisa), the programmes being prepared and presented by the lecturers concerned. Although aimed at a very limited target audience, that is, students of distance education who register for a specific course such as Economics 1, the programmes proved to be popular with the general radio audience. The scheduling of programmes during the early evening and on Saturday and Sunday morning could account in part for the popularity, as the programmes were readily accessible. Radio Unisa programmes were suspended in 1995 pending the restructuring of broadcasting in South Africa.

From the above, we can identify three major challenges to using radio for DE (White & Thomas 1988/89:7). These are:

- An enormous amount of time is needed to cover all the specialised courses that are currently available.
- DE programmes compete with pure entertainment programmes for prime-time slots in order to make the content available to learners.
- The production of programmes is subject to the internal demands and professional ideals of the broadcaster and educational institution.

Despite these challenges, White and Thomas (1988/89:7–8) say radio offers a number of pluses for DE. Such radio programmes:

- make the learning process more personalised by creating a sense of belonging in the learner – achieved through an identification of and with the course designers and the creation of a feeling that the teaching institution is personally interested in the learner;
- reduce the time required by learners to master course contents to less than they would spend by reading alone;
- help to attract potential learners either to the institution or to a specific course or to the subject matter;
- establish academic credibility of the institution and course to the outside world.

The success of any radio programme designed for formal education is dependent on cooperation between the broadcasting and educational authorities. This cooperation helps the programme series gain material that is meaningful and curriculum related. Formal education by radio is limited unless backed up by supportive material, such as charts, workbooks, and so forth. These have to be distributed to participants well in advance of the broadcast, which requires a good deal of logistical administration and organisation. We can increase the success of formal broadcasts considerably if we give attention to adequate advance preparation, active participation and follow-up. By the 1980s most broadcasters had abandoned formal educational broadcasts, as they had become increasingly more costly and time-consuming to organise and operate (British Broadcasting Corporation 1981:21).

16.5 INFORMAL EDUCATION

Informal education lies in the domain of general broadcasting. Bates (1984:119) puts forward the argument that much of the content, especially news, current affairs, music and drama programmes, is educative since it improves our knowledge of the world, raises cultural standards and provides a stimulation for further education. For example, radio news keeps us up-to-date with political and economic events, while current affairs and magazine programmes help us to stay informed about economic, technological and consumer matters. The use of a more popular format than that found in formal and nonformal programmes means listeners are often unaware they are adding to their general or specific knowledge since the content is presented in the guise of entertainment. Many such programmes have proved very popular, such as the BBC's *Twenty Questions* or *My Music*, which have been exported across the English-speaking world.

This approach is based on the perception, generally held by broadcasters, that all good broadcasting also provides good education. This view that general broadcasting has a strong educational role to play is based on one of the tenets of public broadcasting services (Bates 1984:119–120). Programme content is not linked to any specific syllabus and therefore can have a more philosophic approach, be broader in nature; and thus is more popular. In order to stimulate listener interest, elements of entertainment must be present in the programme.

However, there is no conclusive proof that general broadcasting has any direct effect on learning. For example, research by Findahl and Höijer (1975) indicates that we can recall only a few items from a radio news bulletin, even when quizzed directly after transmission. Such poor recall is due to the format of radio news, where a number of short unrelated items are packaged together without relevant background or interpretation. This, says Bates (1984:120), points to a conflict between the roles of entertainment and information in a programme, which we discuss later in this unit. Thus, while news attracts listeners, it does not educate them adequately. Despite such findings, news is still regarded by the broadcasting industry as being of prime importance in the schedule of any radio station.

16.6 NONFORMAL EDUCATION

Radio in *nonformal education* refers to those programmes that are not part of the formal education system, being primarily designed for those who are educationally and socially disadvantaged, in order to help such people have better lives by enabling them to make use of existing social and economic facilities (Kaye 1982:11). Nonformal educational broadcasts do not presuppose any prior educational preparation on the part of the listener as with formal education. We can divide the needs for nonformal education into three broad groups, as illustrated in Figure 16.2, namely:

- pre-school
- post-school
- social action

The purpose of nonformal education in each of these groups is to reduce an inadequacy of some or other sort. Nonformal programming is widespread and may be the only access that many people have to ongoing education. As a result, nonformal education by radio is ideal in a developing context, and it is for this reason that we concentrate on nonformal education in this unit. We must remember, however, that nonformal education by radio is not restricted to a developing environment and can be used in a variety of situations. Kaye (1982:9–10) indicates some disciplines that make up nonformal education. These are:

- *Functional literacy and numeracy skills* which are related to everyday practical needs such as reading a newspaper, completing forms, following instructions and so on.
- *Social coping skills* which are needed to cope with the complexities of modern society, such as seeking employment, social services, basic health care, legal rights and so forth
- *Parental and family education* aimed at parents in the education and development of their children.
- *Consumer education and domestic economy* aimed at providing diverse aspects – from balancing a housekeeping budget to carrying out basic repairs and maintenance of the home.
- *Community education* to provide information that enables members of a community to take action as a group in order to improve their lives through the provision of improved health, educational facilities and provision of employment.
- *Vocational and professional training* to provide people with new skills in order to return to gainful employment, or to change to different employment, or to upgrade existing skills, but without leading to a formal qualification.

To provide nonformal education in these disciplines by means of radio programmes, we can make use of two broad strategies. These are:

- open broadcasting, and
- radio listening groups (RLGs).

16.6.1 Open broadcasting

Open broadcasting refers to the planning, production and broadcasting of educational programmes without organising the listener or dispatch of support material. Open broadcasting relies entirely on the programme to carry the message (Bates 1984:83). The open broadcasting strategy is based on three assumptions, namely:

- Those people who have radios (such as people at home and drivers in cars) will be listening to their radios most of the time.
- A person within hearing distance of a radio will listen to whatever is broadcast.
- If we hear, we learn.

Open broadcasting is the most widespread strategy for the following reasons:

- Programme production is much less expensive than for radio listening groups.
- No effort is required to organise the listeners into groups.
- Formats associated with popular radio can be used with little adaptation, for example spot announcements use the same format and technique as radio advertising (Bates 1984:83).

Nonformal education can be used in any situation. For example, radio stations that feature music often include short programme inserts (a short self-contained programme inside another programme) into their scheduling which can then serve a nonformal educational function. A programme insert is a short, self-contained mini programme lasting a few minutes at the most, and is usually inserted between musical items. These inserts deal with a variety of matters such as family relationships, finance, driving, gardening, health and so on. Broadcasters feature these inserts at regular intervals throughout the day.

Other formats that can be used in open broadcasting include drama (for a single programme) or a soap opera (for a longer running series) which, through the use of a popular format, can skilfully present messages relating to a variety of topics to a mass audience. More overtly didactic (meant to instruct) formats include current affairs and magazine programmes that can give in-depth reports on selected news events. A less common format that can be used in open broadcasting is the quiz show, where information is provided through a series of questions and answers (Bates 1984:83–84).

Ultimately, open broadcasting has to succeed on the strength of the programme alone. This, in turn, is heavily dependent on the skills and talent of the producer. Little, if any, attention is paid to how the listener receives the programme. This represents a weakness of open broadcasting, namely that providing people with information is not enough to bring about the changes which are expected as part of the educational process.

An evaluation of open broadcasting

To begin, we first need to establish some criteria for evaluating the two strategies we consider in this unit. To this end Moemeka (1983:519) provides us with some goals that radio programmes should fulfil in nonformal education. These are:

- introducing people to *action* geared towards desirable states and standards of living;
- providing people with *general information* for action;
- teaching *skills*, such as in the areas of agriculture and health;
- eliciting the type of *behaviour* which is considered beneficial for the social, economic, cultural and political wellbeing of the individual and the community.

We can then evaluate the strategy used in terms of these specific goals. Open broadcasting is usually aimed at a national audience without any attempt to organise those listeners. Thus, the possibility of success is very much left to chance. From this point of view, authorities justify continued use of open broadcasting as a strategy by the belief that less learning on the part of more listeners represents a better allocation of resources than a strategy that produces more learning on the part of fewer listeners. The strategy of open broadcasting, in realising the above-mentioned goals, is based on the maxim that half a loaf of bread is better than none (Moemeka 1983:519).

With open broadcasting it is unknown whether people are listening actively or passively. Nor is it known whether those who do listen actually learn anything. This criticism is based on the assumption that listening to the radio neither means acceptance of the message nor the incorporation of the message content into the listener's life. Although open broadcasting ensures wide coverage, the strategy lacks the following aspects:

- an encompassing planned structure;
- guaranteed participation by the listeners; and
- message acceptance.

16.6.2 Radio listening groups

The radio listening group (RLG) strategy is made up of a combination of radio programmes and support material which is presented to an organised group who subsequently discuss the content or share some common learning experiences. RLGs function on the assumption that for learning to occur, dialogue must take place, not only between the fieldworker (or group leader) and members of the group, but also among the members of the group (Hall 1972:1). The idea is that such group activity results in a collective decision or a common action as a direct consequence of the discussion. The fieldworker is given training to stimulate and coordinate discussion, but is not considered an authority on the subject of the campaign. In this way the emphasis is shifted from that of the teacher (represented here in the form of the fieldworker) to that of the participants in the listening groups. This arrangement is generally considered to be more pedagogically sound that the subject-centred approach used by open broadcasting. Historically, the radio listening group strategy is derived from the concept of the radio school and the radio forum. Let us briefly consider the contribution made by each of these concepts.

The radio school

The radio school was a form of organised listening that originated in Columbia in 1947 when a Catholic priest, Father Salcedo, began to use radio broadcasts to reach his parishioners. The geographic area is mountainous and it was not easy for parishioners to get to the church regularly. Programme content contained both religious and educational messages. Gradually Father Salcedo began to send out written material and to train fieldworkers, who were selected from opinion leaders in the community, to answer questions and act as a source of feedback from the group to the central organisation. Although radio schools are strictly within the domain of formal education, we include them here because the concept provided some of the principles on which radio listening groups, as a strategy for nonformal education, are based today.

The radio forum

While radio schools are usually *learning groups*, radio forums are more *discussion groups* geared to a group action. Historically, radio forums began in 1939 in rural Canada, where they were known as farm forums (agricultural radio programmes for group listening by farmers). These farm forums were a joint effort between the Canadian Broadcasting Corporation (CBC) and the Canadian Federation of Agriculture with the purpose of organising groups of farmers who met regularly in order to receive special broadcasts. Following the broadcast, the farmers would discuss certain problems and then decide on a particular course of action. As farm forums, these lasted for twenty years in Canada. All India Radio (AIR) adopted the idea in 1949, where it obtained measurable achievements in improving farming practice. The strategy was first introduced to Africa by Ghana in 1961 (Lewis & Booth 1989:167–168).

The structure of a radio listening group

Lewis and Booth (1989:173) provide us with a list of seven basic elements that make up radio listening groups. These are:

- a central team of *administrators*, who design the course and train community leaders to act as fieldworkers or group leaders, including the coordinating committee and broadcasters;
- *fieldworkers*, who are drawn from within the targeted community;
- a *multimedia* approach, with radio as the primary source complemented by additional material such as charts and workbooks;
- a *radio station* which has a programme schedule intended for a general audience in addition to those programmes intended for the radio listening forum – the intention is to make optimum use of radio's ability to cover a wide geographic area;
- the formation of *local level agencies*, such as farmers' cooperatives, women's organisations and self-help projects to facilitate projects at grass-root level;
- *cooperation* with existing development agencies;
- *feedback* in the form of reports and questions based on each programme in the series.

We illustrate the complex nature of the interaction between these various elements in Figure 16.3. We need to note that while there is only one broadcaster, we can have many, even thousands as indicated in Case study 16.1, of listening groups.

Organising a nonformal educational campaign

We can identify a number of stages through which the organisation of a nonformal educational campaign, which makes use of radio listening groups as a strategy, must move. Designing the campaign needs to start at least a year to a year-and-a-half before the actual campaign takes place. Planning is vital to the success of any nonformal educational radio campaign. As indicated in the discussion that follows, much work needs to be done before the actual programmes can be aired. It is the role of the coordinating committee to work out a timetable of everything that needs to be done. We illustrate an example of such a hypothetical (supposed, but not necessary real) timetable in Figure 16.4

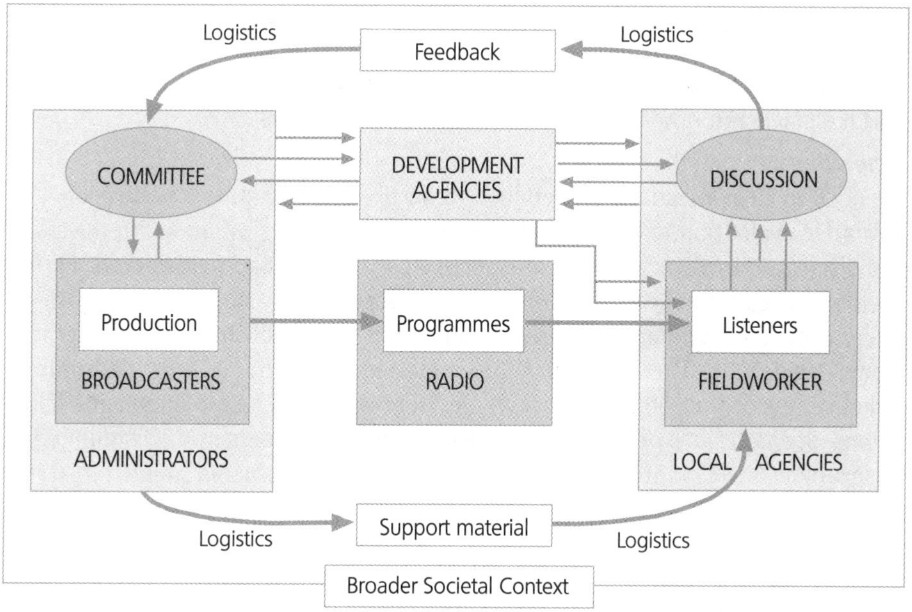

Figure 16.3 The structure and organisation of elements found in a radio listening group (adapted from Wigston 1996:344)

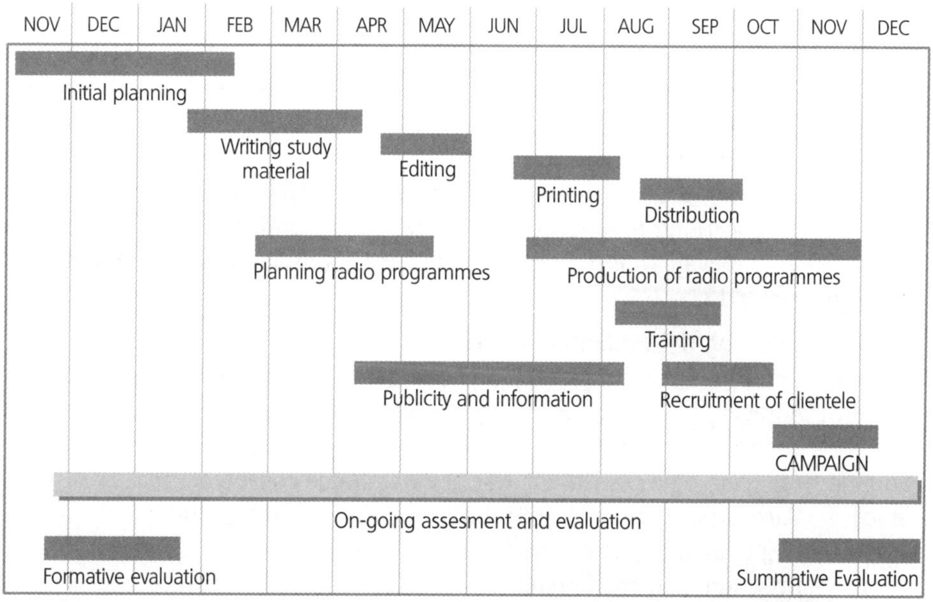

Figure 16.4 A hypothetical timetable showing activities and deadlines required in the planning of a nonformal educational radio campaign (adapted from Hall 1972:6)

Some of the actions required by the organising committee are briefly discussed below. We need to read these in conjunction with the flow chart illustrated in Figure 16.3 and the hypothetical timetable in Figure 16.4, so that we get an idea of when these activities are to take place and how long each activity is likely to take.

- *Evaluation*

  We need to clearly distinguish between formative and summative evaluation. We use formative evaluation to establish the needs of the listeners by analysing the situation and discussing those needs with prospective participants and fieldworkers. Formative evaluation can consist of ethnographic observation, focus groups, in-depth interviews, questionnaires and readability tests to establish levels of literacy (Du Plooy 1997:380). The purpose of summative evaluation is to determine the effectiveness of the campaign as a whole. Here we would test if knowledge has been gained, or if attitudes or behaviour have changed in members of the listening groups. For example, if we want to test an increase in knowledge, then a simple ten-item test can be given to a sample of groups both before and after the campaign, and the results compared. Procedures for monitoring the progress of listeners in order to maximise participation and to determine dropout rates, also need to be agreed upon beforehand. For example, it is possible to combine the forms necessary for everyday administration of the campaign with those to be used for evaluation. Demographic data can easily be included in registration forms (Hall 1972:19). Table 16.2 summarises some of the evaluation undertaken and the methods used in an actual campaign.

  Campaign evaluation should not be limited to just formative and summative evaluation, but should rather be part of a constant process of evaluation that continues for the duration of the campaign. In this way the organising committee can avoid problems which can result in delays in the planning process. Also, the authority that initiated, or who is paying for the campaign, usually wants informed judgements concerning progress of the campaign in fulfilling its objectives. In the broad sense, the evaluation process usually consists of seven stages (Hawkridge & Robinson 1982:113):

  Stage 1: Selecting the evaluation team
  Stage 2: Agreeing on the objectives and general design of the evaluation
  Stage 3: Agreeing on the instruments to be used, such as a questionnaire, and collection of the data
  Stage 4: Agreeing on a plan to analyse the data once collected
  Stage 5: Carrying out the data collection, analysis and interpretation
  Stage 6: Preparing a report on the findings
  Stage 7: Disseminating the findings

  It is seldom that the evaluation process follows these stages neatly in the sequence indicated here. Some stages can occur simultaneously, and it might also prove necessary to revise some of the original plans. For instance, during data

Table 16.2 Design and methods of evaluation used in the *Wakati Wa Furaha* radio listeners' campaign (adapted from Hall 1972:18)

Evaluation outcomes	Methods
1 Campaign costs per participant	Accounting procedures
2 Description of the operation of training seminars	Training reports from staff
3 Participant's reaction to training seminars	Participant reaction forms
4 Demographic data of listeners • sex of listener • age of listener • occupation of listener • education of listener	Registration forms
5 Rate of attendance (dropout rate)	Class registration forms
6 Geographic distribution of groups	Group registration forms
7 Amount of knowledge gained during campaign	Cognitive knowledge test
8 Obstacles to organising group study	Evaluation seminars Fieldworker questionnaires

interpretation (Stage 5) it might become clear that the selected measuring instrument (Stage 3) is inadequate and needs to be replaced. An important part of evaluation is that objectives be set out in well-defined terms so that everyone understands the purpose of the campaign and the evaluation. For example, there is no value in stating that the objective of educational broadcasting is to increase educational opportunity (Hawkridge & Robinson 1982:122–123). What, exactly does this mean and by what criteria are we to measure any increase in educational opportunity? A wide range of research methods is available for evaluation, but the appropriateness of each method should be thoroughly considered in terms of the anticipated findings. For example, if the attitudes of learners towards the educational broadcast need to be assessed, this can be done through the use of a combination of interviews, questionnaires and cognitive tests. Changes in behaviour and practice need to be evaluated through observation over a specific period of time (Hawkridge & Robinson 1982:132).

Jamison and McAnany (1978:130) identify two constraints on the effective evaluation of a nonformal educational campaign. These are:

- Creating an effective feedback system to provide for evaluation is expensive.

- Production units and administration can be slow to respond when changes or amendments are required, even when there is clear evidence there are problems in the system.

Effective evaluation is closely linked to the feedback mechanism set in place, which we briefly consider in the next point.

- *Feedback*
Procedures for obtaining regular feedback from listeners and fieldworkers on the quality and effectiveness of programme content and support material need to be incorporated into the campaign design. Burke (1976:109) suggests that the most efficient method in getting information back to the organisers is delivery in person. The fieldworker can then spend some time talking to organisers about the campaign, programmes, research and evaluation, and so provide valuable insight through personal contact. However, in most cases this simply is not practical because of distance. Depending on available funding, the next best options include the services of a courier company or the post office to deliver evaluation forms to the organising committee. We have to keep in mind that we are often dealing with groups who do not have access to new media technologies such as fax machines or e-mail because they live in remote areas of the country without the necessary infrastructure, or they cannot financially afford to use the technology should it be available, or they simply lack the necessary know-how to use the equipment.
- *Organising the listeners*
The purpose of organising a campaign is that it should create conditions which encourage the listeners to help themselves. To achieve this, various activities need to be planned for the listeners to do, either during or following the broadcast. These can take various forms, either as an individual or group activity. Meetings do not need to take place in a formal venue such as a classroom, but can take place in any convenient location, such as peoples' homes, community centres and so forth. Meeting in a group is considered to be of greater motivational importance than educational value (Kaye 1982:17). Ideally, the size of any group should be between 10 and 15 members. Using organised groups does have a drawback as it is limited by the time and place of the meeting and any hierarchy that exists between members of the group.
- *Planning the programmes and setting the outcomes*
Once the general direction of the campaign has been determined, only then can some specific learning outcomes be established. Here we need to ask ourselves what knowledge, skills and attitudes we want our learners to acquire and what our learners should be able to do as a result of their newly acquired knowledge, skills and attitudes. Only once the outcomes have been established and agreed upon, can the programmes be planned (Burke 1976:36). It goes without saying that the programmes should always be of immediate relevance to the listeners in terms of learning outcomes and format. The programmes have to provide the information,

knowledge and skills necessary to bring about concrete changes in the listeners. This means the programmes need to be designed in terms of real-life situations, such as finding employment or balancing the household budget, rather than in terms of associated disciplines such as literacy or numeracy. These are matters that need early decisions, along with the actual number of programmes in the campaign, as well as the content and duration of each programme. A synopsis of the programmes needs to be provided at the planning stage. For example, a synopsis for a literacy project at a beginner's level could look something like that illustrated in Table 16.3.

Table 16.3 An example of a programme synopsis for a literacy campaign for beginners living in a rural area (Burke 1976:37–38)

First week	
Programme 1	• Orientation for the new learner – what to expect from the radio programmes • Why it is important to read and write • Details about the schedule of programme • What materials will be needed • Relating of literacy to the theme that learning of any kind enhances human dignity
Programme 2	• Introduction of the concept that language has certain sounds, combinations or families of sounds • These sounds can be represented by visual symbols • Establishment of the idea of literacy
Programme 3	• Introduction to two basic sounds and two basic words which make use of these sounds, such as the open 'a' vowel sound • Sentences using these words introduce some basic concepts in family development
Second week	
Programme 1	• The learner can only recognise and interpret the visual symbols studied thus far • Later in the course, the learner will be able to draw graphic representations which will enable the learner to communicate ideas with others • Guidelines and specific instructions for drawing the correct symbols • The learners need to practise drawing the symbols after the programme by drawing at least thirty of each symbol ☞

Programme 2	• Two more basic sounds and their symbols are introduced • Repetition and reinforcement of material learned in the previous week • Introduction of the word *milk*, and link with the concept of milk as an important part of the daily diet • Construction of sentences using the word *milk*
Programme 3	• More work of sound combinations, with the same sound in different positions within certain words • Learners asked to think of their own examples, the fieldworker to send these in to be read out during the next week's programmes • Review of what has been learned during the first two weeks • Preview of what is to come during the next week

While Table 16.3 only illustrates two weeks of the campaign, we would need to prepare an outline for the entire series of programmes that make up our campaign. The purpose of the synopsis is to enable us to see, with reasonable accuracy, the themes that we are dealing with, the emphasis that is being placed on those themes and whether these will achieve our intended outcomes in the learners. Not only should the synopsis clarify the sequence of the programmes, but also the sequence of the learning experience for the learners. This initial planning process is the same, irrespective of the topic: the outcomes are decided upon, the content is chosen and the sequence of learning experiences established. If we follow this process, we can then avoid the problem of merely using radio as a means of reaching the learner, but rather as part of the learning process (Jamison & McAnany 1978:125).

- *Support material*

  To optimise learning by means of radio, some support material must accompany the broadcasts. This can take the form of leaflets, charts, supplements to newspapers or magazines or study-guides. This material should contain background ideas and suggestions for practical activities in order to test the listeners' newly acquired knowledge. Care needs to be taken that the application of that knowledge is always relevant to the listeners' personal context. The limitations of using print-based support material with preschool, basic adult education and some disadvantaged groups is that such material requires both a reading habit and a certain level of literacy. Support materials need to be piloted with representatives from listening groups before being finalised in order to establish whether they are within the comprehension levels of the target audience. Support material needs to be designed in such a way that it can also be used independently of the radio broadcasts. There must be a clear indication of what listeners must do during and after each programme, such as, for example, summing up the theme of the programme and a few points for discussion by the group (Hall 1972:11). Obviously, the content of the radio programmes needs to be decided on before support material can be produced. As we note from Figure 16.4, the production of support material requires a lengthy lead-time (time between beginning and concluding a project).

- *Distribution of support material*
  A decision needs to be made if support materials are to be supplied free-of-charge to listeners. If not, then a mechanism needs to be put in place to collect funds, for example in the form of a registration fee. The physical distribution of support material needs to be considered carefully. The modes available for distribution include post, air, courier, road or dissemination via fieldworkers at seminars. The committee needs to keep in mind that infrastructure in rural areas can be a seriously limiting factor in the timely distribution of support material.
- *Recruitment and training*
  Besides being supplied with sufficient copies of the support material, fieldworkers need additional guidelines and advice on what to tell listeners in their groups, and how to tell it (Hall 1972:14). This, and other information, is usually provided in a training seminar for the fieldworkers, such as the following:
  - the duties of a fieldworker
  - study group leadership
  - conducting meetings
  - how to provide feedback to the organising committee
  - where and how to obtain additional support material.

  The training of fieldworkers is a key factor in the success of any campaign, for it is the fieldworker who is responsible for the establishment and functioning of the various listening groups (Hall 1972:20). This training is usually provided in regional seminars by education officers appointed by the organising committee. A number of practical problems need the attention of the organising committee, such as providing transport for fieldworkers from their homes to the venue where seminars are to take place. Because of the rural location of many of the fieldworkers, physical contact with them can be difficult, if not totally impossible, in order to confirm attendance or change in venues, and so on.
- *Coordination*
  The organising committee needs to meet on a weekly basis in order to review the work done during the previous week, and to allocate new tasks. Progress charts and checklists are needed to keep track of progress. From a logistical point of view, if all the members of the organising committee do not have a working knowledge of the language selected for the campaign, then arrangements need to be made for translation, which could add to costs and slow down the production of material.
- *Publicity*
  Continuous information needs to be provided about the campaign through press and radio coverage. Posters advertising the campaign can be put up in public places such as schools and post offices. However, there is no point in publicising the campaign too early as potential participants could loose interest and not attend the group discussions.

  Nonformal educational campaigns tend to be more successful in a developing context. We can ascribe this to the fact that within a First World environment, listeners are far more discriminating as regards what the radio presents to them. Programmes need to be presented in a far more skilful manner in order to attract and sustain attention. In a developing environment, where there are many difficulties in the successful application of broadcasting as a development tool, the radio listening group does provide a workable strategy. Within a developing context, campaigns need to be oriented towards concrete action on the part of the listener, with short-term quantifiable outcomes (White & Thomas 1988/89:10). A number of fairly successful campaigns have been run in a number of African countries and one of the most widely cited was carried out in Tanzania (Hall, 1973; Díaz Bordenave 1977:60–66; Jamison & McAnany 1978:72–77; Byram & Kuate 1980:84–87; Bates 1984:95; Lewis & Booth 1989:169–170; Kiwanuka-Tondo 1990:53). In Case study 16.1 we outline this campaign.

Case study 16.1: National radio study campaign for civic education in Tanzania

Genesis, background and reasons for the project

Tanzania closely links activities in adult education to social, economic and political policies – especially socialism and rural development, with an emphasis on self-reliance. Radio listening groups were first formed in 1967 by the Cooperative Education Centre (CEC) in Moshi, and the Institute of Adult Education (IAE) in Dar es Salaam. Results of activities were made available to other institutions. A workshop held by the Adult Education Advisory Committee to Radio Tanzania did much to encourage the concept of radio listening groups. Radio courses were run as part of the Five-year Development Plan initiated in 1969. Experience in these campaigns was used in the design of two nationwide pilot studies (*Uchaguzi ni wako – The Choice is Yours* which dealt with the purpose and conduct of elections, and *Wakati wa furaha – Time for Rejoicing* which related to the country's tenth anniversary of independence). The pilot studies were followed by a large-scale campaign (*Mtu ni afya – Man is Health*) on health education and sanitation.

Sponsorship

A foreign government financed the campaign in part (the Swedish International Development Authority); the balance was funded by a nongovernmental organisation (the Institute of Adult Education), several government ministries (Health, Social Welfare and Education), a political party (TANU) and the Rural Development Division of the Prime Minister's office.

Audience (clientele) and agents

The radio programmes were aimed at adults countrywide, particularly in rural areas. At the time, adult literacy in Tanzania was estimated at more than 70 percent countrywide, with a higher figure for rural areas.

For the campaign, some 75 000 fieldworkers were trained over a period of five months. Regional literacy training teams were enlarged to include officers of the

Ministry of Health and were given orientations on the group study method in seven regional seminars. These teams went to districts where they held about seventy seminars for district training teams, which included district adult educational officers, TANU officials, district medical officers, agricultural officers and people from voluntary agencies. The district teams held about 2 000 seminars of two days each to train fieldworkers.

Scope

The campaign was nationwide in scope, designed for one million people, three-quarters of whom lived in cooperative villages and one-quarter in six districts. The campaign reached nearly two million Tanzanians. The radio campaign received top priority in Tanzania and was the subject of two national speeches made by the Prime Minister who stressed the importance of participation.

Objectives

The campaign had three objectives, namely to:

- provide information about the symptoms and prevention of specific diseases;
- increase awareness of measures that can be taken to improve health through improved sanitation; and
- encourage the use of newly acquired reading skills by providing follow-up written material to participants in the national literacy campaign.

These objectives were based on the assumption that if learning was to occur, there had to be dialogue not only between the fieldworker and group members but also among group members. The role of the fieldworker was to stimulate and coordinate study, not to direct it.

The campaign placed an emphasis on action resulting from discussion. Group members were encouraged to engage in activities that resulted in improved health for the community.

Campaign design

Tanzania selected the campaign approach rather than making the forums a continuing institution, with a separate theme for each campaign. This approach required close cooperation amongst all participants and careful planning before the commencement of each campaign. To facilitate cooperation, a coordinating committee was formed. This committee planned activities and organised the production of media material. The committee was made up of representatives from the institutions and organisations involved. Planning began eighteen months before the first broadcast of the campaign.

The media

The main medium for the campaign was radio, supplemented by printed materials and publicity. The campaign was conducted in Swahili and involved twelve radio programmes of half-an-hour each, once a week, repeated twice. Other material included a large-print (for newly literate people) textbook, a study-guide and a fieldworker's manual. Publicity material included two national speeches by the Prime Minister and a cloth printed with designs emphasising the campaign.

Application

It is impossible to determine exactly how many Tanzanians listened to the broadcasts on their own initiative without joining a registered group. The radio audience in Tanzania is estimated at 8 million out of a population of 13 million. However, the campaign was based on the principle of learning through group discussion.

The campaign was planned for one million adults, but ultimately involved two million. Half of the study group never used the radio programmes because they lacked a radio or experienced poor reception and relied only on the printed material. A second problem encountered in the campaign was group size – groups were too large to allow participation by all, while printed material was sometimes in short supply.

The campaign resulted in the construction of hundreds of thousands of latrines, the provision of safe water, and the diagnosis, control and prevention of malaria and tuberculosis.

Research and evaluation

Evaluation was complex. The campaign used interim evaluation reports based on tours and local supervisor reports after visits to 2 131 groups. Group leaders administered orally a pre- and post-campaign multiple-choice test of 13 items. The average gain in health knowledge was 20 percent. It was impossible to find a control group whose members had been isolated from the campaign. A pre- and post-campaign survey of eleven observable health practices was made in eight villages. There was a 15 percent gain after the campaign. The largest change involved the construction of latrines and clearing vegetation from around houses.

From this campaign and the two pilot studies it is clear that radio is an effective way of reaching rural adults not reached by traditional school or adult education. Radio is a valuable way of involving rural people in development through an increase in understanding and a change in attitudes and behaviour. Although radio listening groups represent a flexible and cost-effective strategy in nonformal education, two major problems emerged:

- *Distribution of material* – this necessitates intensive planning and preparation long before the beginning of a campaign and also requires considerable cooperation between the clientele and agents to ensure that participants receive the material before broadcasts begin.
- *Feedback and follow-up* – planning did not take into account questions from participants or the supply of additional information.

This case study is but one example of how a campaign can be undertaken using radio listening groups as a strategy in order to develop rural areas.

An evaluation of radio listening groups

We can best evaluate radio listening groups by comparing the strategy with that of open broadcasting. Figure 16.5 summarises the differences between the two strategies while the complexity of each strategy is summed up in Table 16.4. Despite the widespread use

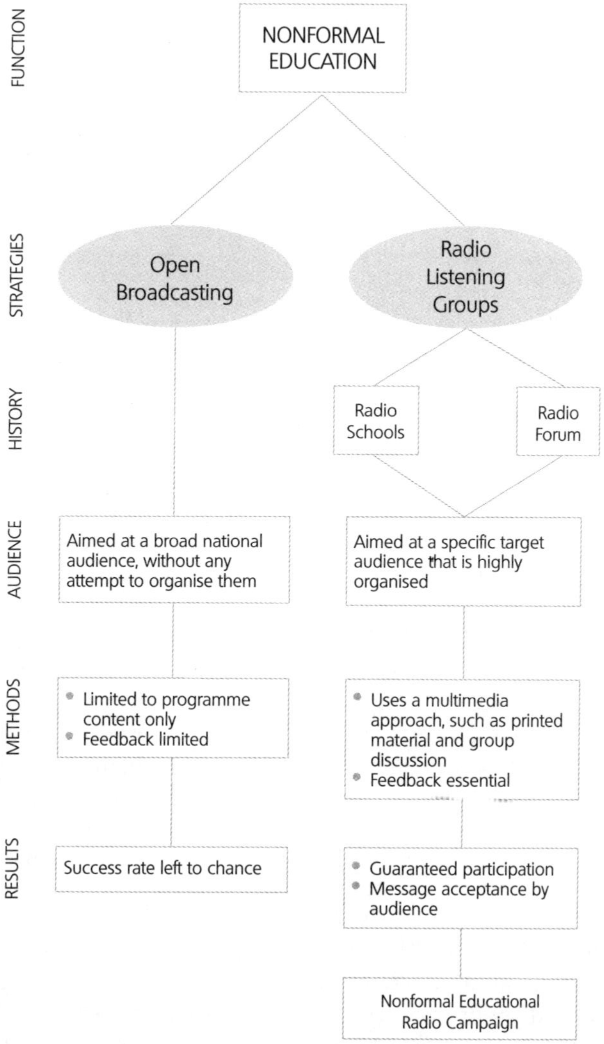

Figure 16.5 The differences between open broadcasting and radio listening groups as strategies for nonformal education

of open broadcasting for nonformal education, research indicates that the group listening strategy has far greater potential for positive effects. In some circumstances, nonformal education can make use of both strategies simultaneously. For example, if we have a campaign making use of listening groups, for those who hear the broadcast but who are not part of any organised group, the programme becomes an open one. Unlike open broadcasting, radio listening groups place strong emphasis on group discussion concerning the issues raised in the radio broadcast. Feedback from the many groups forms an important element of this strategy. The questions and decisions raised by the various groups can be used to formulate subsequent programmes. This is the strength of the radio listening group since it ensures commitment to certain actions and, as a result, social change. Membership of listening groups ensures exposure of the participants to information and decisions of importance to the community.

Table 16.4 The complexity of radio listening groups compared with open broadcasting as a strategy for use in providing nonformal education

	Open broadcasting	Radio listening groups
Time constraints	• relatively quick • ± six weeks to prepare one programme	• relatively lengthy • ± one year to prepare for a single campaign
Structure	• top-down • driven by what the broadcaster thinks the listeners need • subject-centred	• grass-roots • driven by audience needs determined by formative evaluation • learner-centred
Organisation	• relatively simple to organise • small number of people involved, limited to staff of the broadcasting organisation	• relatively complex to organise • large number of people involved, extending over a number of agencies, NGOs, government departments, as well as the broadcasting organisation

The combination of radio as a mass medium together with interpersonal discussion results in characteristics that make for desirable change to take place in social, economic, cultural and political situations. However, Moemeka (1983:520) and Quarmyne (1985:3–4) consider the successes achieved by using radio listening groups to be concentrated in small pockets throughout Africa. Moemeka suggests the following factors may bring about this limited success:

- In Africa, radio is too *formalised* to be used successfully for nonformal educational purposes. Radio listening groups tend to attract only those who can contribute intelligently and who have authority within the community. These people are invariably considered the local élite and the people who are really in need are frightened away by the attention paid to the élite.
- A *lack in cooperation* among the various agencies involved in nonformal educational projects produces a do-it-alone tendency. This results in a waste of energy and resources and can lead to conflicting projects. For example, one project can promote the use of manure to produce better crops while another discourages using manure because of a sanitation problem. This can confuse the local community, which in turn leads to apathy.
- The message content tends to be of a *generalised nature*. Local communities in Africa are many and varied and so are their problems. As a result, issues addressed in a programme are not always specific to any particular community's needs. Having to make use of a centralised radio station, which broadcasts to the whole nation, rather than a local radio station, often complicates the issue.

According to Moemeka (1983:525), one way of resolving these problems is to localise radio broadcasting. A local radio station knows and can serve the particular needs of the people living in its reception area. Educational programmes are then produced within the community that receives the broadcast, under local conditions, with local people taking part in the production. This approach helps to eliminate the three factors discussed above that limit the success of radio listening groups.

With the liberalisation of broadcasting policies throughout Africa, there has been a dramatic growth in the number of alternative radio stations coming on air. However, what role these stations would play in providing nonformal education remains a moot point. Most of these stations have opted for a commercial format rather than adopt a participatory orientation. Those that have are usually shoestring operations and the lack of funds is always a serious limiting factor.

16.7 THE ROLE OF PUBLIC RADIO IN EDUCATION

The concept of a public broadcasting service (broadcasting which emphasises quality programming) (PBS) is credited to Lord Reith (1889–1971), and even today, is strongly associated with that of the BBC. Reith, first director-general of the BBC, with his strongly Calvinistic background, had distinct views regarding the function of radio in the early days of broadcasting. He was of the firm opinion that radio should set out to give the public not what it wanted, but what it needed. Reith argued that few listeners knew what they wanted; even fewer knew what they needed. Today, such a paternalistic attitude is unacceptable as it is considered arrogant and élitist. It was Reith who identified the three basic functions of broadcasting, namely to inform, educate and to entertain, with a strong emphasis on the first two items. So, while the concept of a public broadcasting service has changed over the years, the tradition remains. It is this contradiction which has precipitated a number of problems for public service broadcasters.

Before we continue with the problems facing PBS, we need to briefly consider the two strands that make up the PBS tradition. The one is providing a public service; the other is responsibility. Within the concept of public service, such radio stations are expected to provide programming for minority groups, but also programmes with a broad popular appeal encompassing high cultural and intellectual standards in production. Where responsibility is concerned, PBS stations are under an obligation to ensure that listeners are not misled or exploited, by applying standards of objectivity and fairness to programmes such as in the news, current affairs and documentaries.

From its inception, up until the 1970s, PBS dominated the broadcasting environment, with the United States being an exception. But, since the 1970s the public broadcaster has found itself in a position such that it can only proceed and survive by changing itself (Tracey 1998:39). PBS has subsequently been engaged in a perpetual re-examination of its purpose, nature and mission. This has been brought about by two forces – the phenomenal growth of multichannelled commercial services and a change in the ideology that nurtured the original PBS concept. As a result of these forces, the way listeners are perceived by broadcasters has shifted from that of citizens of the nation to consumers in a marketplace (Tracey 1998:40–41, 49). These two forces manifest themselves though the erosion of PBS audiences. Given the relationship that exists between financing the broadcasting organisation and the audience size, public broadcasters have come under increasing pressure to abandon their public service tradition and provide programming with audience appeal. While educational programmes are still considered an important aspect of PBS, the economic realities are that audiences to such programmes are limited. Despite the pressures and changes, PBS continues to offer education by radio, even if in a very limited form (as indicated by the graph in Figure 16.6), as part of the PBS commitment still remains the provision of educational programming at all levels.

The SABC has not been immune to these forces, pressures and changes. The SABC is under an obligation, by virtue of its charter, contained in the Broadcasting Act of 1999, to provide "significant amounts of educational programming" as part of its public broadcasting service (South Africa 1999). Yet if we look at Figure 16.6 it is clear to see that some PBS radio stations are not adequately fulfilling this function. SAfm, long considered the flagship station of the SABC, has moved away from full-spectrum programming, having opted for a news and information format in an attempt to increase audience numbers. As a result, SAfm features no educational programming at all. Yet, looking at the graph, we can see that several commercial radio stations, notably Metro FM and CKI FM, are providing educational programmes on levels comparable to, and even greater than, some PBS stations. Such developments help to provide a new level of respectability for commercial services but also increase the pressures on the public broadcasters by having to compete for listeners (Tracey 1998:30). In terms of the political economic model, on which most broadcasting organisations are based, educational broadcasting enjoys little attention. This is evidenced by the fact that the SABC has only one full-time educational producer for each of the eleven public broadcasting radio stations (South African Broadcasting Corporation 2000).

The SABC provides educational programming in the following seven general areas:

- *Civic education programmes* focus on human rights, justice, gender issues, adult basic education and the disabled. A drama format was used to provide voter education before the 1999 general election in an attempt to reduce voter apathy.
- *Educator development programmes* place the focus on establishing a culture of learning and training in order to resolve problems in education. This is achieved by means of panel discussions and debates.
- *Curriculum support programmes* focus on study skills, examination preparation, career guidance and Grade 12 support. Programmes on health use a talk-show format.
- *Early childhood development programmes* focus on child rearing, parenting and development. These programmes are used by educators as an aid to mothers and grandmothers taking care of young children.
- *Science and technology programmes* include programmes on environmental and agricultural matters.

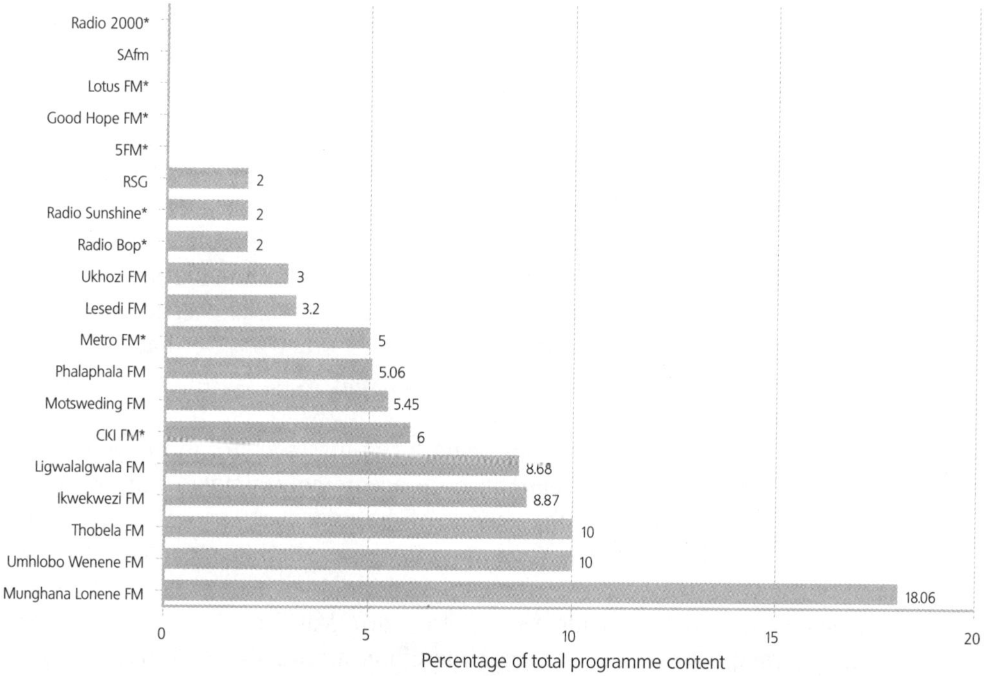

Figure 16.6 Educational programming presented by SABC-operated radio stations during 1999/2000 as a percentage of all programme content Stations indicated with an asterisk fall into the SABC's commercial portfolio
(South African Broadcasting Corporation 2000)

- *Youth and culture programmes* introduce cultural issues to young people.
- *Commerce and financial programmes* deal with issues such as taxation, consumer rights and basic banking and are usually presented in a current affairs or magazine-style format.

The number of educational programmes made by the SABC is limited by the procurement of funding. This could explain why we see such low percentages of educational programmes, as illustrated in Figure 16.6. To date, all educational programmes are funded by a government grant through the Department of Communications or as projects negotiated with individual government departments. A grant of R1.2 million was received from the MOTT Foundation in the United States for voter education in the run-up to the 1999 general election (South African Broadcasting Corporation 2000).

16.8 THE EFFECTIVENESS OF RADIO IN EDUCATION

As a conclusion to this unit we briefly evaluate the effectiveness of radio as a medium for education. In order to come to a decision in this matter we need to weigh up the limitations of radio against its advantages. In this discussion we need to keep in mind the distinction between educational and educative programmes on one hand, and formal, nonformal and informal education on the other.

16.8.1 The limitations of radio in education

Both Bates (1984:233) and Crisell (1986:113) are of the opinion that radio is not the most effective medium for educational programmes. This, they argue, is largely due to the auditory nature of the codes used in radio, which work against effective retention of the programme content. (See Unit 13 for an explanation of the various codes used in radio.) Radio codes (sound effects, speech, music, silence) exist in time rather than space and it is this aspect which makes the medium difficult for the listener to control. For instance, we simply cannot pause a radio programme in order to refer back to a point that was made earlier in the programme, in the way that we could flip back a page or two in a book. However, we can overcome this problem if we record the programme on an audio-cassette (the copyright issue not being taken into account in this argument), which then allows us to adjust the learning pace accordingly, simply by stopping and rewinding the tape. But in terms of the volume of material that can be presented and the ease of access to that material, radio programmes (whether recorded on audio-cassettes or not) just do not have the efficiency of printed material.

This means it is often difficult for us to learn skills or to develop a deep understanding through broadcasting alone. Therefore, argues Bates (1984:139), print remains the dominant medium because of its visual and stable nature. As a result, the role of radio is usually limited to revision or the reinforcement of knowledge or skills originally acquired through other media. Even so, to be most effective, an educational programme on the radio requires additional support material, usually in a printed form.

It is also true that some topics cannot be easily presented in a programme because of the auditory nature of radio's codes. Evans (1977:17) suggests, as an example, that it is almost impossible to teach anyone to tie a knot without making use of visual codes. In this case, television would be a much more appropriate medium to use. Similarly, certain topics, such as mathematics and chemistry, which rely heavily on the use of diagrams and equations, cannot be effectively taught by means of radio. However, Evans qualifies his assertion by saying: "nine times out of ten the trouble lies not with the subject but with the speaker, and his lack of imagination". This matter of attitude and approach brings us to another important aspect that limits the educational use of radio.

Bates (1984:233) writes that radio's potential for meeting educational needs remains largely unexploited simply because many broadcasters are not experts in the field of education and vice versa. Although broadcasters and educators share common aims, they have differing perspectives and therefore use differing criteria for judging the effectiveness of programmes. These differences arise largely out of the working environment. The values and criteria used to judge programmes are largely determined by the ideology of the organisational and professional demands on broadcasters on one hand, and educators on the other (Bates 1984:10). For example, broadcasters talk about programmes in terms of quality while educators talk in terms of effectiveness (Schramm 1972). The broadcaster's concern for quality implies that programmes need to be judged against standards developed in the broadcasting industry over a long period of time. Value is seen in the actual programme itself. Not only that, but for the broadcaster, the programme occupies a central position. For educators, effectiveness lies beyond the programme, decided by a predetermined set of criteria, such as the objectives and learning outcomes of the programme. Value is seen in observable changes in the target audience. For the educator, the radio programme is seen as a small part of the much broader learning context (Bates 1984:234). These differing points of view represent the divergent philosophies of broadcasters and educators. While neither the broadcaster's, nor the educator's points of view are necessarily wrong, this dichotomy works against the effective use of radio in education as quality and effectiveness are not mutually exclusive concepts. While we can say that programme quality may be a necessity for programmes to be effective, the important point we are making here is that the criteria for the evaluation of those programmes are different for educators and broadcasters and we can see this as a limitation in the use of radio for education.

The way in which the content is presented in a programme can also have a limiting effect. Crisell (1986:114–115) expresses a concern that, even when a programme is educational in its intent, we tend to treat that programme as educative, simply because we regard radio more as an entertaining medium than we do printed material such as books and newspapers. Therefore, we do not always respond in a disciplined way to the contents of the programme. Bates (1984:176) refers to this effect as the Warm Bath theory of realism. The Warm Bath theory holds that realism in, for example, a documentary programme makes it difficult for listeners to adopt an analytical approach to the content of that programme. Realism, argues Bates, brings about a state of relaxation because of its familiarity, much like a warm bath. There follows an acceptance of the programme's content rather than analytical questioning. Learning does not take place unless there is associated mental effort. This factor makes broadcasting a weak medium for use in education.

It would seem from our discussion here that the potential of radio in education would be rather limited. However, Crisell (1986:108–109) says that while these limitations are real, they are over-estimated. After all, radio makes use of the same oral mode that is used in any teaching or training situation. Let us now look at the advantages radio has to offer.

16.8.2 The advantages of radio in education

Despite its apparent limited potential, there are two obvious advantages that radio has over other media. Radio can easily span long distances while at the same time reaching a large number of listeners, more so than could be easily accommodated in a classroom. However, these advantages represent a simplistic point of view and do not offer any counter-argument against the limitations we discussed above.

From an educative point of view, radio transcends other media, particular print media, in that radio can offer listeners a direct impression within a natural domain. In this way, radio provides primary source material and, as such, access to knowledge and information in a direct and concrete form (Bates 1984:20). For example, resource material can take the form of interviews with, and speeches by national leaders and people in authority, or commentaries on significant events. We have to concede, says Crisell (1986:116), that while radio provides us with experiences beyond that of the print media, radio cannot do so to the extent of visual media, like television. But, this can also be an advantage in certain circumstances, such as when learning a foreign language or music, where the visual element would be a distraction.

Radio's major contribution to education lies in its seemingly contradictory ability to present reality, yet because of the lack of visual codes, this reality needs to be imagined on the part of the listener. The combination of these two aspects, reality and imagination, are considered to motivate learning indirectly. Through stimulation of the imagination, a reality is constructed inside the mind of the listener that may then differ from the original reality. Radio's relative inefficiency as an educational medium means that we should treat educational programmes as educative. This relegates radio to being a secondary, rather than a primary teaching medium. If radio lacks credibility as an educational medium, it is radio's ability to present us with reality that makes it is important as an educative medium. Radio functions best when used as a source of enrichment rather than as a direct teaching tool.

16.8.3 Enhancing the effectiveness of radio in education

When thinking about using radio for educational purposes, we need to give some thought about using a format that elicits a disciplined response from listeners. The kind of programme that allows for learning to take place is different from those intended for general audiences. Crisell (1986:108, 115) identifies three such formats:

- direct instructions to perform certain actions, such as in cooking
- the lecture or talk
- music recitals, drama and actuality programmes.

The first two formats simply describe a situation or tell the listener to do various things, whereas the third differs by providing a form of experience for the listener.

Crisell (1986:108–109) is of the notion that, in educational programmes, the quality of production is not of paramount importance. Here Crisell argues that the nature of the content is such that the structuring of the programme does not require the variety typically associated with general programming (see Unit 13 for a discussion of variety as a principle of radio production). This argument is based on the assumption that listeners to educational programmes are more motivated than are listeners to educative or general programmes. If this is the case, then the standard of presentation and language in educational programmes becomes less important. Bates (1984:199–201) does not fully agree with this sentiment. He is of the opinion that if educational programmes are perceived as having lower standards than general programming, this will result in audience resistance. If this is so, then the converse also applies. Professionally produced educational programmes provide added value by attracting audiences. However, professionalism on its own is not enough and can, in certain circumstances, be counter-productive, such as that indicated by the Warm Bath theory we discussed earlier. Great care is needed to ensure that production techniques do not offset educational aims that require the listener to stop and think. The rules of good teaching, such as having an objective and learning outcomes, are as essential as good production for effective learning to take place (Bates 1984:187).

Bates (1984:187–189) discusses several aspects of programming associated with audience appeal in educational and educative programmes:

- *Ambition* is associated with large budgets that allow for the use of all aspects identified with quality programming. Through great effort and care, material which would otherwise be inaccessible for the listener can be presented. For example, we can hear leading statesmen talk or professional actors interpreting dramatic works. However, we need to be cautious, as ambition can also result in the inclusion of irrelevant material – having gone to enormous lengths to obtain particular material it has to be used irrespectively. As Bates (1984:187) so aptly says, it is very easy to "get carried away by the sheer glamour of the process".
- The *development of characters* and their relationships with other characters in programmes can become immensely popular and in this manner draw an audience to that programme. Through identification with the characters, the listener can experience a wide range of emotions. Character development is best associated with soap operas and drama, but can also be used successfully in documentaries.

- *Controversy* of any sort in programme content requires cautious handling. The code of conduct for South African broadcasters, contained in the Independent Broadcasting Authority Act of 1993, requires that controversial issues be handled in a balanced way. The broadcaster is required, by law, to present significant points of view either in the same programme or in a subsequent programme. Thus, the appearance of a bias towards one side or the other is avoided. In an educational programme such a neutral approach can weaken the very purpose of the programme. In many cases there are more than two points of view and some ideas need lengthy treatment such as, for example, the claim that HIV does not cause AIDS. Educationally, it is easier to remember a single coherent argument than two contradictory arguments. For educational purposes a programme can, therefore, be polemic (i.e. contain controversial discussion). This does not mean the content is biased or that alternative views need to be presented at a later stage. However, because of legal requirements this is simply not practicable.
- The *use of personalities* or people currently in the news, such as sports stars, to present educational programmes can be counted upon to increase audience appeal. However, the use of personalities can also be a distraction when the listener tends to concentrate on the personality rather than the content of the programme.

All these aspects work towards creating a whole experience. But, ultimately what really counts are the principles of good writing, good topics and good performances. By emphasising these principles, we also tend to emphasise the value of entertainment. The entertainment factor has now become the prime element in drawing an audience and increasing the effectiveness of programmes, particularly in the nonformal sphere. This emphasis on entertainment has resulted in a crossover between education and entertainment, which has produced a function known as edutainment (a combination of education and entertainment), which we illustrate in Figure 16.7. An implication is that nonformal education programmes should be broadcast on general channels and not on special education channels and at times when the listener is seeking entertainment (White & Thomas 1988/89:9–10). The very time at which educational programmes are broadcast is important in enhancing their effectiveness (Bates 1984:234). Within the context of our discussion on the role of public service broadcasting, most broadcasters schedule educational programmes at unsociable hours simply because such programming does not generate the huge audiences that entertainment-based programmes do.

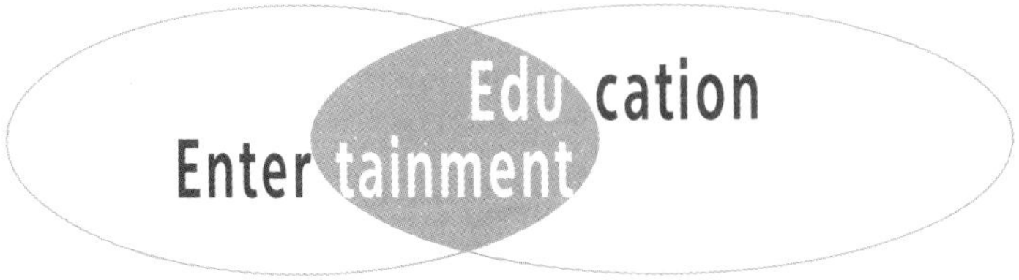

Figure 16.7 The creation of the *edutainment* function from education and entertainment elements in a programme (Wigston 1996:341)

To achieve, or better, the standards and quality of general programming, educational and educative programming need to be well-financed in order to attract top production talent. Experience has shown that programmes produced by teachers, technocrats or ministerial bureaucrats result in "heavy, boring, didactic and authoritarian style" programmes (White & Thomas 1988/89:11). This aspect points back to the differences between educators and broadcasters we discussed earlier in this section. Despite the heavy emphasis on entertainment, Crisell (1986:110) suggests three points be kept in mind when preparing educational programmes so that they can be more comprehensible for the listener. These are:

- Limit the number of main points to be made during the programme.
- Reinforce those points through repetition.
- Provide concrete illustrations when referring to abstract principles.

The volume of material required to fill a broadcasting day, together with the requirement that programmes be presented in an attractive way, often force a producer to rely on standard conventions (customary practice) of production which have been tried and tested for audience appeal. In many instances these conventions are used without question, to establish the type of programme and the role of people within that programme. The aim of the producer is to provide an apparent natural smoothness to the programme with the listener being unaware of the construction of that programme. When used to encourage the listener to construct relationships between various aspects, using the conventions of radio can be extremely valuable.

But when unrelated to the educational purpose of the programme, such conventions can become distractions. For example, let us look at the magazine and phone-in format. These are popular formats made up of a mix of short items, seldom longer than five minutes, which are unrelated or at least loosely connected. These short duration packages of information have become known as the sound bite (short piece of audio said to sum up a point of view; able to stand alone). Neither format can deal adequately with complex issues in the space of a few minutes. The results are a set of assertions rather than any meaningful argument. Explanations are never adequately given nor discussed fully and there is no real chance of understanding what the issues are about. The conventions used in these formats are based on the assumption, albeit a false assumption, that the listener has a short span of attention. It is this assumption that has led to the fragmented nature of such programmes, which in turn works against successful learning. But, such programmes do have some educational value in updating those already well-informed, and providing new sources of information (Bates 1984:186).

Summary

Education by radio can be considered the Cinderella of the broadcasting industry. It is often ignored, complex in structure and organisation, and forms but one small aspect of a large broadcasting organisation. The context in which the educative process takes place ultimately determines the potential for success of any efforts at providing education by radio. We identified seven factors that we need to consider when assessing the context of education by radio. We also need to take into account the relationship between radio, as a mass-medium, and the political and social environment in which it occurs. To this end we identified five assumptions on which our study of education by radio was based.

Next, we considered what is understood by the concepts "education" and "education by radio". We can divide education by radio into two broad groups; that is educational or educative. The key in determining whether a programme is educational or educative lies in what the listener does with the content of that programme. The determining factor which makes a programme educational is the retention of information presented in that programme through a disciplined action on the part of the listener. We can then further categorise the programme content as formal if it is linked to a set syllabus that leads to a formal qualification, or nonformal if the content is educational in nature but not linked to any syllabus, while educative programming tends to be informal as it is part of the ongoing process of daily listening to the radio.

While almost every programme format that is presented on radio can have some educational qualities, there are two distinct strategies that we can use in nonformal education, that is open broadcasting or the radio listening group. The key distinction between these two strategies lies in the organisation of the listener or lack thereof in the case of open broadcasting. Both strategies have distinct advantages and disadvantages which need to be taken into consideration when determining the outcomes of an educational campaign that makes use of radio. We looked in greater detail at the structure and organisation of an educational campaign that makes use of radio listening groups as a strategy, including a case study from a successful campaign undertaken in Tanzania on civic education. The number of successful campaigns in Africa is limited, and we considered some reasons for this situation.

Education by radio has traditionally been the domain of public broadcasting. But with the global change in the broadcasting environment, public broadcasters have come under enormous pressure from commercial services, with the result that efforts at providing educational and educative programming has shrunk or even disappeared altogether. We concluded our study of education by radio, by comparing the limitations of the medium with the advantages. Out of this discussion we described some aspects that can be used to enhance the effectiveness of using radio in education.

Research activities

1 Analyse the campaign described in Case study 16.1 and describe what we can learn from this campaign for the improvement of present and future campaigns using radio listening groups as a strategy.

2 Draw up a plan for a nonformal educational campaign using a multimedia approach but with radio as the primary medium in order to promote one of the following aspects of development:

- basic health care
- awareness of how national, provincial and/or local government operates
- basic literacy skills
- self-determination
- improved nutrition
- improved food production through advanced agricultural techniques

3 Explain how radio schools and farm forums contributed to the strategy of radio listening groups.

4 Keep a log for a period of one week of everything you hear during your normal course of listening to the radio. Indicate which programmes are educative and which are educational. Assign what you heard to formal, nonformal and informal categories. What do your findings indicate regarding the attention the radio station(s) you listen to gives to the three categories of education by radio?

5 You are the programme manager at a community radio station. You have commissioned several third-year journalism students to write a series of four-minute radio talks on improving the skills of the unemployed when attending a job interview. How would you explain to these students the distinction between educational and educative programming so that they can position their talks as educational? What additional advice would you give to the students so as to help them structure their talk in order to maximise success?

6 Discuss the role played by entertainment in educational and educative radio programmes.

7 You are the station manager at a radio station with a public broadcasting mandate and have recently presented your annual report to the Board. The Board has taken note, with some concern, that educational programmes comprised only two percent of the programme schedule. They have asked you to explain why so little air-time has been devoted to educational programmes. How are you going to justify this low figure to the Board?

8 You are the chairperson of the organising committee for an educational campaign using radio listening groups with the projected outcome of reducing dietary risk factors in cardiovascular disease among low-income groups located in a major urban area. Prepare an outline for the formative, summative and ongoing evaluation of your campaign that you can present to your committee. You are particularly interested in assessing the knowledge change and behaviour change among your target audience.

Further reading

Bates, A. 1984. *Broadcasting in education: an evaluation.* London: Constable.
Crisell, A. 1986. *Understanding radio.* Methuen: London.
Hawkridge, D & Robinson J. 1982. *Organizing educational broadcasting.* London: Croom Helm.
Jamison, DT & McAnany, EG. 1978. *Radio for education and development.* . Beverly Hills, CA: Sage.

Russell, DD. 1992. *Learning to listen, listening to learn: experience from a South African radio forums research and development project.* Johannesburg: University of Witwatersrand Centre for Continuing Education.

Skidmore, P, Harrop, S & Woodcock, G. 1996. *A sound education? Local radio and the education of adults.* Liverpool: Liverpool University Press.

Welsh, BWW. 1973. *A handbook for scriptwriters of adult education broadcasts.* 2nd revised edition. Bonn-Bad Godesberg: Friedrich-Ebert-Stiftung.

Bibliography

Anders, D. 1983. 50 Years of educational broadcasting. *Pivot: A Journal of South Australian Education* 10(3):13–16.

Anderson, D. 1974. Educative broadcasting. *Adult education* 46:307–313.

Ball, JCH. 1974. School radio: the future. Part 1: radiovision and tape recorder. *Educational Broadcasting International* 7:28–31.

Bates, A. 1984. *Broadcasting in education: an evaluation.* London: Constable.

British Broadcasting Corporation, 1981. *BBC annual report and handbook 1982: incorporating the annual report and accounts* 1980–81. London.

Byram, ML & Kuate, CB. 1980. Radio campaigns: learning from the experiences of others. *Educational Broadcasting International* 13:84–87.

Checkland, M. 1991. Educational broadcasting: an essential element. *Combroad* (90):5–13.

Crisell, A. 1986. *Understanding radio.* Methuen: London.

Díaz Bordenave, JE. 1977. *Communication and rural development.* Paris: United Nations Educational, Scientific and Cultural Organization.

Du Plooy, GM. 1997. Educational television and development, in *Introduction to communication – course book 6: film and television studies.* Kenwyn: Juta:342–392.

Erasmus, PY. 1970. *Die radio as masskommunikasiemedium met spesiale verwysing na die situasie in Suid-Afrika.* Pretoria: Human Sciences Research Council.

Evan, E. 1977. *Radio: a guide to broadcasting techniques.* London: Barrie & Jenkins.

Findahl, O & Höijer, B. 1975. Effect of additional verbal information on retention of a radio news program. *Journalism Quarterly* 52(3):493–498.

Garcia, AP. 1980. The role of non-formal education in rural development: a 10-year case study of the Cauca River Valley, Columbia. *Educational Broadcasting International* 13(4):179–182.

Ginsburg, MB & Arias-Godínez, B. 1984. Nonformal education and social reproduction/transformation: educational radio in Mexico. *Comparative Education Review* 28(1):116–127.

Greig, A & Jackson, K. 1981. Educating Sydney with informality: an Australian public radio station. *Educational Broadcasting International* 14(2):57–60.

Hall, BL. 1973. *Wakati Wa Furaha: an evaluation of a radio study group campaign.* Uppsala: Scandinavian Institute of African Studies. (Research report No. 13.)

Halloran, JD. 1981. Media research: an overview. *Educational Broadcasting International* 14(3):98.

Hawkridge, D & Robinson, J. 1982. *Organising educational broadcasting.* London: Croom Helm.

Hezel, RT. 1980. Public broadcasting: can it teach? *Journal of Communication* 30:173–178.

Humphries, C. 1986. All change: education and the role of media. *Media in Education and Development* 19(4):141–144.

Independent Broadcasting Authority. 1995. *Report on the protection and viability of public broadcasting services, cross media control of broadcasting services, local television content and South African music (Triple inquiry report).* Johannesburg.

Jamison, DT & McAnany, EG. 1978. *Radio for education and development.* Beverly Hills, CA: Sage.
Jochum, M. 1989. Radio and education in Western Europe. *Radio and Television* 39(6):3–6.
Legge, D. 1982. *The education of adults in Britain.* Milton Keynes: Open University Press.
Kaye, A. 1982. Using the media for adult basic education, in *Using the media for adult basic education,* edited by A Kaye & K Harry. London: Croom Helm:9–29.
Kearns, K. 1985. The forgotten medium - are we too visually dependent? *NASSP Bulletin* 69(480):45–49.
Kimmel, H. 1989. Armageddon, or the last battle. The future of educational broadcasting. *EBU Review. Programmes, Administration, Law* 60(5):33–37.
Kiwanuka-Tondo, J. 1990. Educational broadcasting in Africa: the case of Uganda. *Africa Media Review* 4(2):48–63.
Lewis, PM & Booth, J. 1989. *The invisible medium: public, commercial and community radio.* London: Macmillan.
Lungwangwa, G. 1989. The rationale for basic education in developing countries: a critique of the ideology in reform in education. *Critical Arts* 4/5(1):11–22.
McLeish, R. 1994. *Radio production: a manual for broadcasters.* 3rd edition. Oxford: Focal.
Moemeka, AA. 1983. Radio's role in non-formal education. *Prospects, Quarterly Review of Education* 13(4):517–527.
Nyirenda, JE. 1981. Research in developing countries. *Educational Broadcasting International* 14(3):101–104.
Quarmyne, AT. 1985. Radio and the educational needs of Africa. *Development Community Report* (50):3–4.
Schramm, W. 1977. *Quality in instructional television.* Honolulu: University Press of Hawaii.
Seibert, WF. 1972. Broadcasting and education: ERIC/EBR annual review paper. *Educational Broadcasting Review* 6(3):139–150.
Silverstone, R. 1999. *Why study the media?* London: Sage.
Skidmore, P, Harrop, S & Woodcock, G. 1996. *A sound education? Local radio and the education of adults.* Liverpool: Liverpool University Press.
South Africa. 1999. *Broadcasting Act, no 4, 1999.* [O].
Available: http://www.polity.org.za/govdocs/legislation/1999/act99-004.html
Accessed on 1999/09/03
South African Broadcasting Corporation. 1981. *Annual report.* Johannesburg.
South African Broadcasting Corporation. 1999. *Annual report and financial statements, 1998/99.* Johannesburg.
South African Broadcasting Corporation. 2000. *Annual report and financial statements, 1999/2000.* [O.]
Available: http://www.sabc.co.za/annual_report/education.html
Accessed on 2000/11/10
Speyer, AM. 1983. Educational radio: the Brazilian experience. *Media in Education and Development* 16(1)4–9.
Sumner, H. 1991. BBC education: the effectiveness and evaluation of educational broadcasting. *Journal of Educational Television* 17(3):159–172.
Tracey, M. 1998. *The decline and fall of public service broadcasting.* Oxford: Oxford University Press.
Ward, P. 1985. The BBC help-yourself approach to learning. *Media in Education and Development* 18(4):161–165.
White, RA & Thomas, P (eds). 1988/89. Educational broadcasting. *Communication Research Trends* 9(4):1–16.
Wigston, DJ. 1996. The role and functions of radio, in *Introduction to communication – course book 6: journalism, press and radio studies,* edited by LM Oosthuizen. Kenwyn: Juta: 327–358.

Index

D

E

F

G

H

I

J

K

L

M

Q

R

S

T

The ARCHITECTURE *of* ROMAN TEMPLES

The Republic to the Middle Empire

JOHN W. STAMPER

University of Notre Dame

CAMBRIDGE
UNIVERSITY PRESS

PUBLISHED BY THE PRESS SYNDICATE OF THE UNIVERSITY OF CAMBRIDGE
The Pitt Building, Trumpington Street, Cambridge, United Kingdom

CAMBRIDGE UNIVERSITY PRESS
The Edinburgh Building, Cambridge CB2 2RU, UK
40 West 20th Street, New York, NY 10011-4211, USA
477 Williamstown Road, Port Melbourne, VIC 3207, Australia
Ruiz de Alarcón 13, 28014 Madrid, Spain
Dock House, The Waterfront, Cape Town 8001, South Africa

http://www.cambridge.org

First published 2005

Printed in the United Kingdom at the University Press, Cambridge

Typefaces Bembo 11/14 pt., Weiss, Trajan, and Janson *System* LaTeX 2ε [TB]

A catalog record for this book is available from the British Library.

Library of Congress Cataloging in Publication Data

Stamper, John W.
The architecture of Roman temples : the republic to the middle empire / John W. Stamper.
p. cm.
Includes bibliographical references and index.
ISBN 0-521-81068-X
1. Temples, Roman – Italy – Rome. 2. Temple of Jupiter Capitolinus (Rome, Italy)
3. Architecture, Roman – Italy – Rome – Influence. 4. Rome (Italy) – Buildings,
structures, etc. I. Title.
NA323.S73 2004
726′.1207′09376 – dc22 2004045666

ISBN 0 521 81068 X hardback
ISBN 0 521 72371X

CONTENTS

ILLUSTRATIONS

PREFACE

The temple architecture of ancient Rome has served as a model for architectural design for more than two millennia. Beginning with the Temple of Jupiter Optimus Maximus on the Capitoline Hill and proceeding through the buildings of the Republic and the Empire, generations of architects have copied Roman architecture directly or have been influenced by its principles and building vocabulary. Even the most abstract modern buildings often have links to ancient Rome. It has been the standard against which all other architecture and urban design is measured, and even today, nearly two thousand years after the construction of Rome's major buildings and urban spaces, hundreds, if not thousands, of architects and city planners across the United States and Europe use Rome's architecture as a vital design source.

The inventive transformations of architects such as Charles Moore, Michael Graves, and Robert Venturi or the literal interpretations of Leon Krier, Robert Adam, and Thomas Gordon Smith reveal the profound and persistent influence of Roman temple design. Even those who rail against its influence, who point out its representation of political oppression or of pagan sacrifice, or who dislike the orders in general, still marvel at the beauty of its proportions and the technical expertise of its buildings. Whatever our bias may be – traditional, modern, or something in between – the buildings of Rome provide a rich manifestation of precedent-based architectural design. Representing the power of ancient Roman culture, they commemorate its largely anonymous designers and builders.

Beyond their meaning for today's architects, the temples of ancient Rome tell us much about the city's political, social, and religious history. They played an important role in mediating between the efforts of the ruling class to legitimize its power and the needs and desires of the general populace to have a safe and secure existence. An analysis of the temples reveals much about the relationship between politics and religion on one hand and the signs, symbols, and rituals embedded in architecture and ceremony on the other. The image Roman citizens had of the temples resulted from the interplay between physical appearance and mental construct. Like all cities, ancient Rome was a composite of the manifest and the imagined, and any reading of its buildings and urban spaces must see them both as physical forms and as ancient political and religious symbols.

The purpose of this study is thus to describe the architecture and the political and religious context of the most significant sacred shrines in ancient Rome, from the Temple of Jupiter Capitolinus at the beginning of the Republic to Hadrian's Pantheon and Temple of Venus and Rome in the middle of the second century A.D. It does so in terms of both the archaeological and the literary evidence that allows reconstruction of their forms and architectural details. It describes aspects of their structural and spatial types, formal vocabulary, topographical and urban orientation, ceremonial function, and symbolic meaning. In terms of their social context, it analyzes their symbolic role as places for public ceremony and the display of political and religious authority.

This book is not intended to be an all-encompassing guide to Roman architecture. Building types other than temples – basilicas, curias, theaters, and housing, for instance – are not part of this study. Only those temples that are fairly well documented are included, and only those found in central Rome. Some examples from the Roman provinces are included, but

only for reasons of comparison. This is not an archaeological study, although it obviously draws on the work of archaeologists both past and present. Nor is it a treatise on ancient Roman religions and their mythological figures. Rather, it is a study in architectural history that focuses on the forms of the Roman temples, their urban settings, and their cultural and political contexts. It places more emphasis on reconstructions and architectural character than on the physical remains of foundations and fragments of building materials. It analyzes changes to the buildings over time and relates those changes to broader political and religious events. Finally, it considers the temples in a comparative way, not as isolated examples on a tourist's itinerary, but in relation to other temples of their time and to the urban context in which they were built.

The thousands of visitors who go to Rome each year, especially to its ancient sites and monuments – the Forum Romanum, Forum Boarium, the imperial fora, and the Campus Martius – are invariably impressed by the grandeur and dignity of what they see. They cannot, however, easily visualize the original appearance of the temples, the technical methods used in their construction, nor their role in the ancient city's social, political, and religious life. The fragments of the buildings that remain only suggest their original character; it is the task of archaeologists and architectural historians to make those images more vivid and tangible in both form and meaning (Fig. 1).

This book's purpose is to provide visitors to Rome – architects, planners, historians, and students – with a more comprehensive description of its ancient temples than exists to date. It also proposes a new reconstruction of the Temple of Jupiter Capitolinus and emphasizes both the crucial role it played as a precedent for later temple design and the basis for its political and religious authority. It reviews the principal temple and forum complexes of the Etruscan and early Republican periods, then focuses on the projects of Rome's most famous consuls, dictators, and emperors from Pompey the Great and Julius Caesar to Augustus and Hadrian – those who contributed most to the city's civic and religious architecture. It sheds new light on the form and chronological development of Roman architecture, and interprets the work of archaeologists through the eyes of an architectural historian. Discussing the authority of precedent as the basis for design and symbolic connotations, it proposes a new unity in the history of Roman temple architecture.

The illustrations include a large number of new drawings of the temples in plan and elevation that I or architecture students under my direction have produced. The classical focus of the School of Architecture at the University of Notre Dame provides these students with an excellent grounding in drawing the orders. They are highly proficient and accurate in drawing reconstructions of classical buildings. They have been further aided in this expertise by their experience of a junior year abroad at Notre Dame's Rome Studies Center, where I was director from 1990 to 1999. I have credited individual students in the illustration captions and have indicated the primary source or sources for each drawing. In most cases, several sources and data from firsthand site visits were used, including articles on recent archaeological findings from the 1990s.

I want to thank especially those students who participated in my classes in ancient and early Christian architecture from 1991 to 1995. Professionals who have been of great assistance in their recommendations and encouragement include James Packer, Tadeusz Mazurek, Margaret Miles, Mark Wilson Jones, Tom Butler, Celeste Guichard, Fikret Yegül, Thomas Noble Howe, Thomas Gordon Smith, Dennis Doordan, Michael Lykoudis, Carol Krinsky, Lynne Lancaster, Branko Mitrović, and Jeff Burden.

Financial assistance for travel and purchase of archival photographs has been made possible by Anthony K. Hyder and the Graduate School of the University of Notre Dame and by Carroll William Westfall of the Notre Dame School of Architecture.

I would like to thank the staff librarians and archivists of the Hertziana Library, the Library of the American Academy of Rome, the Deutsches Archäologisches Institut in Rome, the Istituto Centrale per il Catalogo e la Documentazione in Rome, the Regenstein Library of the University of Chicago, the Sawyer Library of Williams College, and the University of Notre Dame Libraries.

I also wish to thank those who have assisted with editing, typing, and other technical matters: Romana De Ferrari, Rogelio Carrasco. Elizabeth Norian, Gayle Rottinghaus, Molly Denver, Paula Garvey, John Mellor, Michael Shveima, Kevin Curran, Hoa Vu,

1. Perspective view of west end of Forum Romanum as it appeared in ca. A.D. 300. Drawing by E. Becchelli, 1983. Photo: Deutsches Archäologisches Institut, Rome, 74.2700.

Chad Carnahan, Marc Bailly, Amra Spahic, and Joann Sporleder. Special thanks go to Beatrice Rehl, Senior Editor, Arts and Classics, at Cambridge University Press, plus her staff members Sarah Wood and Alan Gold, and Eleanor Umali and the production staff of TechBooks.

Finally, I wish to thank my wife, Erika Pistorius Stamper, for her help with proofreading and for her patience during my many visits to Roman sites and libraries. Our daughter, Alessandra, has shown equal patience and tolerance with my travel and extensive work schedule. George and Marie Pistorius have graciously lent their expertise by helping with German translations, bibliographic questions, and proofreading.

All photographs are by the author unless otherwise indicated.

INTRODUCTION: THE AUTHORITY OF PRECEDENT

> It is my contention . . . that authority has vanished from the modern world, and that if we raise the question of what authority is, we can no longer fall back upon authentic and undisputable experiences common to all. The very term has become clouded by controversy and confusion.
>
> – Hannah Arendt, "What Was Authority?"

The design of sacred architecture, whether we consider temples, synagogues, churches, or mosques, inherently involves the concept of authority. It is present in the interpretation of a building's form – that is, we say a building has dignity, unity, conviction, or authority because of the skills of its designer and the quality of its composition. Such authority, *auctoritas,* lends itself readily to symbolic connotations related to the building's use and the person, institution, city, or state for whom it was built. Vitruvius, for instance, emphasized the link between public buildings and the authority of the state in his *Ten Books of Architecture,* which he addressed to Augustus in the mid-20s B.C.:

> when I saw that you were giving your attention not only to the welfare of society in general and to the establishment of public order, but also to the providing of public buildings intended for utilitarian purposes, so that not only should the State have been enriched with provinces by your means, but that the greatness of its power might likewise be attended with distinguished authority in its public buildings, I thought that I ought to take the first opportunity to lay before you my writings on this theme.[1]

Vitruvius's primary concern was that public buildings in Rome should possess the necessary dignity and authority appropriate for Augustus to express his power. The statement reveals the motivation behind the many large-scale public building projects in Rome: the display of power in costly, elegant structures. There was an obvious link in this sense between authority in architecture and authority in political leadership.

At yet another level, architecture operates in terms of the authority of precedents. Certain buildings, because of the quality of their forms or the reason for their construction, become paradigms, or primary models for later buildings. The first and most important Roman example that influenced many later religious buildings was the Temple of Jupiter Optimus Maximus on the Capitoline Hill. Because of its associations with the triad Jupiter, Juno, and Minerva and with the founding of Rome and the Republic, it possessed unparalleled associations with authority. Here again we cross the boundary into politics, for as the philosopher Hannah Arendt writes, Roman politics was based on the sacral character of foundation: "once

something has been founded it remains binding for all future generations."[2] Anyone engaged in Roman politics was expected to preserve the memory and the act of the foundation of the state. Similarly, in architecture, builders often sought to recall the character of the Republic's most important early monuments.

Building on the accomplishments of their ancestors – the tradition and memory of those who came before them, those who had laid the foundations – was an important way in which rulers obtained their *auctoritas,* a word derived from *augere,* "to increase."[3] Those with political authority in both republican and imperial Rome – the elders, senators, consuls, dictators, and emperors – commemorated the city's foundation through their actions; those engaged in architecture honored the important precedent set by the Temple of Jupiter Capitolinus by emulating it. This book shows that certain details of later buildings, for instance, the Temple of Mars Ultor and the Pantheon, were in part references to the Temple of Jupiter Capitolinus.

Precedents in architecture form the basis of a continuous evolution of style and building practice. One architect described precedent as "a form which has been accepted as the proper expression of good logic, fitness and beauty, proven by the test of time and accepted as a standard upon which new expression can be modeled and with which it may be compared."[4] Architects in the Roman world operated much more in terms of precedent than most architects are accustomed to today. As Arendt states, the notion of authority has virtually vanished from the modern world. In the culture of self-expression that typifies the contemporary West, where any overt use of an architectural model is often considered derivative and retrograde, it is hard to imagine the necessity for, or the authority of, precedent as it existed in the Roman world. Building types evolved over a long period of time, changing slowly according to new uses and outside influences. Features such as fitness, beauty, or political connotation captured the imagination of later architects and patrons and manifested themselves in subsequent buildings. Through these later generations of builders, the paradigms they followed were modified into new designs that met new conditions.[5] There were certain periods of high achievement – periods of perfection – and others of decline or decadence. By political and cultural necessity, however, the authority of the models remained constant. Certainly, the authority of the Temple of Jupiter Capitolinus was evident throughout the Republic and Empire until at least the second century A.D.

This study examines how Roman designers based the plans of their temples on earlier precedents and how, by such a progressive emulation, members of the Roman ruling class established and maintained their political control. The ancient Romans clearly understood that impressive architectural settings and elaborate public ceremonies were acknowledged modes of demonstrating power or establishing *auctoritas.* The spectacle of a triumphal procession amid glorious marble-clad buildings served as an important form of propaganda for the emperor, meant to impress and mediate between the ruler and the people.

While most books on ancient Roman architecture are organized on the basis of either topography or typology, this one is organized chronologically. There is a great deal to learn by studying the temples at different stages of their development, to see how they evolved over time through successive reconstructions and political regimes. For instance, discussion of the Temple of Castor and Pollux in the Forum Romanum occurs in three of the book's chapters because it – like most other temples in Rome – was built and rebuilt in three or more distinct periods of time. These periods in turn reflect different attitudes toward precedent, authority, and architectural design. This temple is first mentioned in the section on Etrusco-Roman temples; it is cited again in the discussion of the assimilation of the Corinthian Order; and, finally, its last reconstruction is analyzed in the chapters on Augustus. Each discussion corresponds to a major reconstruction and is addressed within its respective social and political context. Likewise, the all-important Temple of Jupiter Capitolinus is discussed in three chapters that take up its construction by the Etruscans and its reconstructions by Sulla and then the Flavians. This book attempts to link developments in building practice and theory to specific historical events and modes of authority.

The first chapter, "Building the Temple of Jupiter Capitolinus," introduces Rome's first, largest, and symbolically most important religious structure. It describes its site on the Capitoline Hill, reviews historical accounts of its construction, and situates it within the

political and religious context of Rome in the sixth century B.C. It then recounts how the building was "lost" for several centuries, how it was rediscovered in the nineteenth century, and how our present understanding of its architectural character evolved.

The second chapter, "A New Reconstruction of the Temple," is more technically oriented than the rest, but it is crucial to understanding the book's principal theme. It challenges the currently accepted reconstruction of the Temple of Jupiter Capitolinus, focusing especially on the version published in the late 1950s by the Swedish archaeologist Einar Gjerstad. His proposed dimensions of the temple, that is, its width, length, height, and interaxial spacings, are, in my opinion, far too large for the technology of Roman builders in the sixth century B.C. The temple as Gjerstad reconstructs it is such an anomaly in Roman architectural history that it is impossible to relate it to later Roman building practices and styles.

This book proposes a reconstruction that is based on a different interpretation of the building's physical and written evidence and one that takes into account a comparative study of both contemporary and later temple architecture in Rome. It proposes a building with dimensions that are more in keeping with the capabilities of sixth-century B.C. building techniques and one that is more compatible with later temples. The Temple of Jupiter Capitolinus presented here, in fact, would have been a paradigmatic building, one that had a major influence on the designs of many later temple structures and iconographic programs, especially during the early and middle Empire.

Chapter 3, "Etrusco-Roman Temples of the Early Republic," provides a comparative study of the Temple of Jupiter Capitolinus and the Roman temples that were built after the fall of the Etruscans. Among these are the earliest Etrusco-Roman temples of the Forum Romanum, Forum Holitorium, and the Largo Argentina, as well as examples in colonies such as Paestum and Cosa. In the latter, it was especially important for builders to emulate the Temple of Jupiter Capitolinus as a way of appeasing Rome and appealing to its political leaders. Although most of these temples from the early Republic were built at a scale about half the size of the Temple of Jupiter Capitolinus, they owe much to it in terms of their plans, architectural forms, and symbolism.

The fourth chapter, "Assimilation of Hellenistic Architecture after the Punic Wars," analyzes Roman temple architecture in the third and second centuries B.C., an important period of transition from the Etrusco-Roman tradition to the Hellenistic style, especially the Ionic Order. As Rome systematically conquered more territory in the eastern Mediterranean, it increasingly absorbed the architectural forms of Hellenistic Athens, Priene, and Pergamon. This chapter examines temple architecture from this period in the Porticus Metelli, the Forum Romanum, Forum Holitorium, and Forum Boarium. It traces the introduction into Rome of the Ionic Order as it gradually appealed to and was accepted by Roman builders and the public alike as a replacement for the Tuscan-Doric Order.

This chapter also introduces the writings of Vitruvius. Although he wrote his *Ten Books of Architecture* much later, in the first century B.C., his theories most directly apply to the Ionic Order as it developed in the previous two centuries. The Temple of Portunus in the Forum Boarium, for instance, closely corresponds to his theories of architectural beauty. Discussion of Vitruvius's theories is also important for understanding his systems of categorization according to plan and façade types. These categories apply to most temple architecture from the Republic to the Empire.

The fifth chapter, "The Corinthian Order in the First Century B.C.," describes the introduction of the Corinthian Order as another aspect of the Hellenistic influence in Rome. Examples of the new style include the Round Temple by the Tiber, the Temple of Vesta at Tivoli, Temple B in Largo Argentina, and the Temple of Vesta in the Forum Romanum. At the time these temples were being constructed, the dictator Sulla ordered the use of Corinthian columns in his rebuilding of the Temple of Jupiter Capitolinus after its destruction by fire. He brought to Rome pieces of marble Corinthian columns from the Temple of Olympian Zeus in Athens that were used in part in the Capitoline Temple's reconstruction. The use of at least the capitals, thus giving it a semblance of the Corinthian style, coincided with the Capitoline Temple's renewed political importance and served to reassert its role as a significant architectural precedent for many decades to come.

Chapter 6, "Architecture and Ceremony in the Time of Pompey and Julius Caesar," analyzes Roman

temple architecture in a changing political climate dominated by civil unrest and the emergence of the dictatorship. The assimilation of Hellenistic architecture into Roman building practices that had characterized the second century B.C. began to change at this time. Roman builders and architects continued to be influenced by eastern styles and building techniques, especially those of Asia Minor, but now they also began to exert their own influence on other regions, including Athens. This chapter discusses the theater and temple complex built by Pompey the Great, then focuses on the city's architecture and urban development under Julius Caesar, his transformation of the Forum Romanum, and the building of the Temple of Venus Genetrix in his Forum Julium. Integral to this discussion is an analysis of the role of both temples in the tradition of processions and ceremonies of the late Republic.

The seventh chapter, "Rebuilding Rome in the Time of Augustus," discusses the origins of the Empire after Caesar's assassination, the role played by the second triumvirate in making yet another transformation of Rome's political landscape, and the ascent of Augustus as emperor. Architecturally, it focuses on Augustus's construction projects on the Palatine Hill and in the Forum Romanum, as well as developments in the Campus Martius. In his *Res Gestae,* Augustus noted that he restored eighty-two temples in Rome, an achievement that dramatically changed the city's architectural character. This chapter discusses the temples on the Palatine, in the Campus Martius, and in the Forum Romanum that were built or rebuilt during the first half of Augustus's reign.

Continuing the previous discussion, Chapter 8, "Augustus and the Temple of Mars Ultor," focuses on the emperor's most important building in Rome, constructed in 37–2 B.C. A comparison with the Temple of Jupiter Capitolinus as reconstructed in this study reveals dimensional similarities that suggest a direct architectural link. It is a clear indication that Augustus and his architects looked at the Capitoline Temple as a reference point with renewed interest. They saw it as a building to emulate or recall as an important part of Augustus's efforts to establish and maintain the legitimacy of his rule. At the same time, this comparison provides a good review of the substantial differences between the Etrusco-Roman style of the early Republic and the classicism of Augustus. The architectural forms of temples had changed greatly during the 500-year period between the Etruscans and the early Empire. This comparison demonstrates the precise nature of both the differences and the similarities.

Chapter 9, "Temples and Fora of the Flavian Emperors," provides an analysis of the architecture of the Flavian dynasty from the second half of the first century A.D. The Flavians built a temple in the Forum Romanum and two imperial fora, and they rebuilt the Capitoline Temple not once but twice, both times after its destruction by fire. They also constructed the Arch of Titus, which had an important urban relationship with the Capitoline Temple because it was placed on the axis of the Via Sacra at a point where it precisely framed a view of the temple across the Forum Romanum. It was the Flavians' way of honoring the memory of Jupiter and associating their name with the temple's long history as the symbol of Rome's founding.

Chapter 10, "The Forum Traiani," discusses one of Rome's largest building complexes, built by one of its most prodigious builders. It focuses on the Temple of Divus Traianus, a giant temple begun by Trajan and finished by Hadrian. As with the Temple of Mars Ultor, it points out similarities in the dimensions that may have existed between this temple and those of the Capitoline Temple. Trajan responded to the city's most important architectural precedent, continuing the revival of interest in its history and exploiting its compelling power to sustain the legitimacy of his rule.

Chapter 11, "Hadrian's Pantheon," focuses on the most important Roman building constructed by Hadrian, an emperor who associated himself with both Zeus and Jupiter. It discusses his link to the deities and his emulation of certain aspects of the Capitoline Temple in his design of the Pantheon. Numerous architectural issues are brought up, including the form of the original Pantheon built by Agrippa, the debate over the height of the Hadrianic building's pronaos columns, the question of whether it was a temple or an audience hall, an analysis of its interior architectural features, and its iconographic meaning.

The final chapter, "Hadrian and the Antonines," analyzes Hadrian's Temple of Venus and Rome and two temples built by his successor, Antoninus Pius. It considers Hadrian's link to Zeus in Athens and the

influence of the precedent of the Temple of Olympian Zeus. It concludes with the work of Antoninus Pius and the transformations his architects made in the Hadrianic style.

In summary, this book seeks to draw attention to the authority of precedent in the design of Rome's temple architecture from the early Republic to the time of Hadrian and the Antonines. Crucial to this thesis is the new reconstruction of the Temple of Jupiter Capitolinus, which allows us to recognize its central role as a paradigm in Rome's architectural development. Possessing the political status of its association with the founding of the Republic and its religious authority as the temple dedicated to Jupiter, Juno, and Minerva, it was by inference the most important architectural model for generations of temple builders. The site of Rome derived its authority from the history of its founding, and the Temple of Jupiter Capitolinus symbolized the legitimate access to and the maintenance of political power. Underlying all authority in Rome, this foundation bound every act, including the construction of sacred buildings, honoring the beginning of Roman history and the original authority of its first ruler.

1

BUILDING THE TEMPLE OF JUPITER CAPITOLINUS

Temple architecture in early Rome from the sixth to the fifth centuries B.C. was dominated by a combination of Etruscan and Latin influences. By the beginning of the Republic in 509 B.C., however, it had a grandiosity of scale and opulence that set it apart from neighboring Etruscan and Latin cities. This was especially the case with the Temple of Jupiter Optimus Maximus (Fig. 2), built from ca. 525 to 509 B.C. It was more lavish in its decoration and larger in both plan and elevation than any other structure in the region. It was a building constantly cited by ancient writers with admiration and praise. Livy, for instance, called it a temple "so magnificent that it should be worthy of the king of gods and men, the Roman Empire, and the majesty of the site itself."[1]

The Capitoline Temple was a unique building in many ways. Commissioned by a succession of Etruscan kings, constructed by a combination of Etruscan and Roman builders, and dedicated by the founders of the Republic, it represented a city that was attempting to distinguish itself militarily, economically, and politically from its neighbors. As the earthly residence of the city's most important deity, located on its most prominent hill, and of an architectural style and form deemed paradigmatic in the Etrusco-Roman world, the Temple of Jupiter Capitolinus had a far greater influence on subsequent political, social, and architectural events in Rome than virtually any other building.

The temple stood majestically in a large, walled precinct on the southern summit of the Capitoline Hill and faced southeast across the Tiber valley and the Aventine Hill (Fig. 3). Its south front and east flank could be seen from both the Forum Romanum and the Tiber River, while its north wall was prominently visible from many points in the Campus Martius. Dominating the top of the hill, it stood out as the destination point for those traveling to Rome in much the same way as the Parthenon still does in present-day Athens. Although its style differed substantially from the Parthenon, its image as a temple on an acropolis, an elevated sacred site, or *templum,* represented an important parallel to the Greek world and accounts in large measure for its long-standing role in establishing and maintaining the authority and legitimacy of Roman leadership.

The Capitoline Hill already had religious shrines before the Temple of Jupiter Capitolinus was begun. For instance, there was the small shrine dedicated to Jupiter Feretrius, reportedly built by Romulus and used by him to consecrate the spoils of war from his victory over King Acron.[2] There may have been a small shrine dedicated to the triad Jupiter, Juno, and Minerva as early as the late seventh century B.C.[3] There were also some shrines that had been vowed by the Sabine King Tatius, who had temporarily occupied a stronghold on the Capitoline Hill after a battle against Romulus.[4] All of these earlier structures reflect a long and complicated history that extended back over 200 years before the Temple of Jupiter Capitolinus was constructed.

The Kings of Early Rome

Rome's early history, including its first temple structures, would form an essential link to the access and maintenance of political power for several centuries. The date of Rome's founding is generally ascribed to the year 753 B.C.[5] Its population from the earliest times

2. Rome, Temple of Jupiter Capitolinus, ca. 580–509 B.C., model of reconstruction according to Einar Gjerstad. Photo: Deutsches Archäologisches Institut, Rome. 73.1159.

was a combination of Etruscan, Latin, and Sabine. Every Roman citizen shared the belief in the sacral character of the site of Rome. The political culture of the Romans from the very beginning was rooted in the soil, the word *patria,* fatherland, which derived its full meaning from Roman history.[6]

The extent of Roman territory at the time of the city's founding was about 115 square miles, with an estimated 10,000 free inhabitants, mostly farmers, builders, and merchants. The first bridge over the Tiber River, the Pons Sublicius, became the most important link between the regions of Latium on the south and Etruria on the north.[7] Roads leading eastward connected to the Sabine territory, which extended into the Apennine Mountains. The earliest settlement of Rome, perhaps located on the Palatine Hill, was known as *Roma Quadrata* because of its roughly quadrangular form.[8] In the first century B.C., Dionysius of Halicarnassus recorded the legend of its foundation:

> Romulus first offered sacrifice to the gods, then watched for omens, which were favorable. He then commanded fires to be lit in front of the tents, commanded the people to come out and leap over the flames in order to expiate their guilt. He then led the people to a spot on the Palatine Hill, and proceeded to describe a quadrangular plan for the defensive wall by leading a plough drawn by a bull and a cow around the edges of the summit. Afterward, he sacrificed the bull and the cow as a further gesture toward the gods, and then ordered the people to begin work. The day of

the founding, the *parilia,* is still celebrated on April 21st.[9]

Included within the sacred boundary, *pomerium,* of *Roma Quadrata* were primitive houses, a building for religious and assembly purposes, the meeting house of the *Curia Saliorum* in which the sacred shields of Mars were preserved, and the *Lupercal,* or Sanctuary of the Wolves. The southwest corner of the Palatine was also the legendary site of the straw-covered house of Romulus and the sacred fig tree toward which the cradle bearing the twins Romulus and Remus had floated.[10]

The founding of Rome and the creation of its *pomerium* were connected to the legendary story of the tragic death of Romulus's twin brother Remus. Ovid recounts that after Romulus marked out the city's boundary, he instructed a guard, Celer, to stop and kill anyone who stepped over the furrow whether intentionally or by accident. Unaware of the ban, Remus walked across the furrow and was immediately killed by Celer.[11] The festival of the *parilia* and the founding of Rome thus possessed not only a sense of authority but also a tragic aspect that it retained throughout the Republic and Empire.

It was also largely a fiction. The story was derived from two traditions, the first by the accounts of ancient Roman authors who attributed Rome's founding to Romulus in 753 B.C., the second, by Greek authors who attributed it to Aeneas, who arrived in Rome after the fall of Troy in 1184 B.C. When Greek writers confronted the tradition of Romulus and Remus, the twins reared by a she-wolf, they invented the idea that they were descendants of Aeneas. Then, to fill the time gap between the fall of Troy and the time of Romulus and Remus, the Romans invented a succession of thirteen kings who reigned at Alba Longa between the time of Aeneas and that of Romulus.[12] After Romulus, there was a second series of kings, some of them equally legendary, and others, like Numa Pompilius and Ancus Marcius, representing a measure of historical truth.[13]

The record becomes more certain by the sixth century B.C., which corresponds to the reign of the city's three Etruscan kings. The first was Tarquinius Priscus, an immigrant to Rome from the Etruscan city of Tarquinii, who ruled from 616 to 579 B.C. The second was his adopted son Servius Tullius, who reigned from 578 to 535 B.C. The third was Tarquinius Superbus, who ruled from 534 to 509 B.C. He was either the son or grandson of Tarquinius Priscus.[14]

The principal structures erected in Rome as it expanded beyond the initial boundary of the *Roma Quadrata* – the city walls, streets, and other public amenities that extended into the lowlands between the Palatine and Capitoline Hills – date primarily from the time of these three kings. The Tarquins carried out the great projects of urban improvement, including the Temple of Jupiter Capitolinus, the Circus Maximus, the Cloaca Maxima, and the early shops around the Forum Romanum.[15] It was Servius Tullius who enlarged the city and built the first stretches of its expanded defensive wall circuit.[16] He was also responsible for constructing a large shrine dedicated to Diana on the Aventine Hill, which became an important Latin cult center.[17]

The architecture of the three kings embodied Etruscan and Latin building traditions, but they were adapted to suit both Rome's topography and its growing political aspirations. Construction demanded manpower, a need that was met by combining the skills of Etruscan technicians and workmen with the strength and numbers of the Roman labor force.[18] The Etruscans developed the tradition of temples with high, square podia, widely spaced columns, broadly overhanging roofs, strongly emphasized front façades, and elaborate terra-cotta ornamentation and statuary. With many variations in details of plan and elevation, these features became common in Roman temple architecture by the end of the sixth century B.C.

The Etruscans also affected other aspects of Roman culture. Theirs, for instance, was the concept of the *imperium,* the absolute supreme power entrusted to a person approved by the gods who governed in accordance with their wishes.[19] Additionally, the Etruscans influenced the procedures for divination, the organization and equipment of the military, the calendar, the legal system, the alphabet, social relationships between patrons and clients, public games, and religion.[20] In particular, they introduced the cult of Jupiter, Juno, and Minerva (Tinia, Uni, and Menerva), which became the focus of the state religion of the early Roman Republic.[21]

The fundamental elements of authority in Etruscan Rome were found in the family, *familia*: father

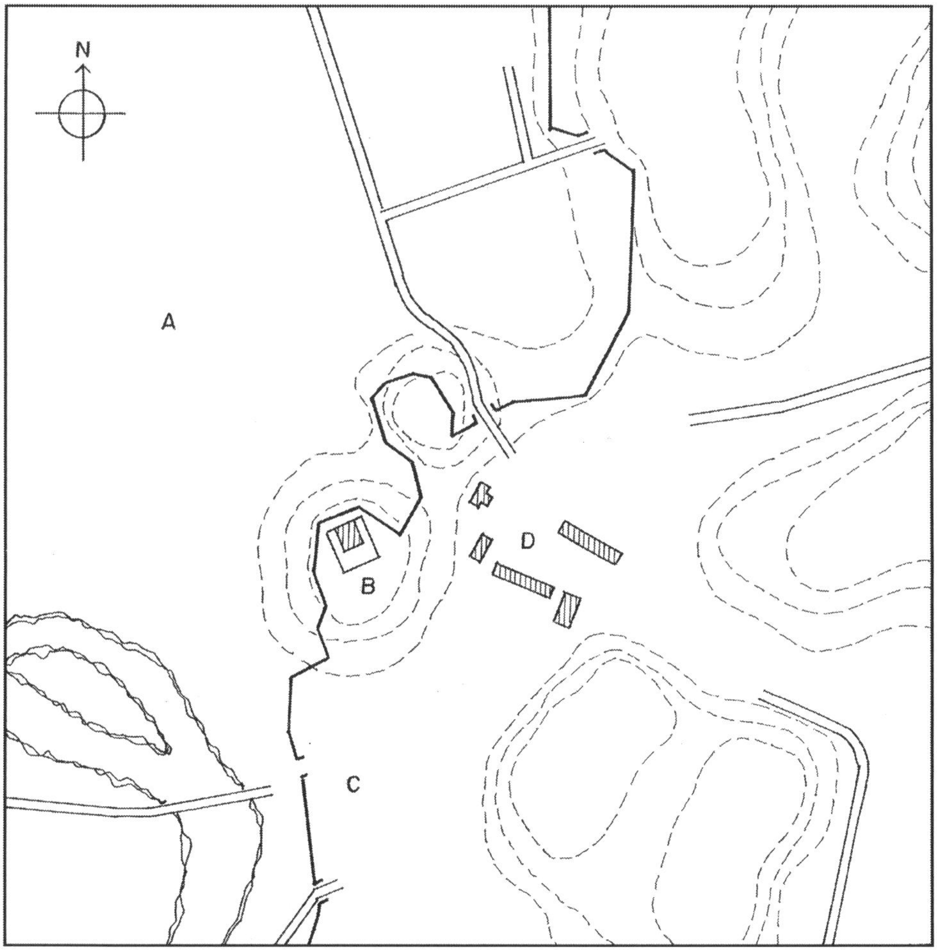

3. Rome, Capitoline Hill in ca. 509 B.C., plan: (A) Campus Martius, (B) Temple of Jupiter Capitolinus, (C) Forum Boarium, (D) Forum Romanum. Drawing: John W. Stamper.

and mother, sons and daughters, home and homestead, servants and chattels. The inherent social structure of the family, with the father as the authority figure, the paterfamilias, had important implications for the structure of Roman society as a whole. The absolute master of his household, the father maintained the strictest discipline, with the right and duty to exercise judicial authority over family members.[22] Clans headed by fathers made up much of Roman society. In this larger association, sons and clients gained a greater legal standing and could themselves participate in worship and rituals. The state was thus made up largely of principals (the *patres*) and their dependents – a patron-client relationship.[23]

As the clans and their constituent families composed the state, so the form of the government was modeled after that of the family. The power of the earliest kings over the community mirrored that of the household father over his family, and like the household father, they ruled for life. The king nominated all priests and priestesses; he concluded treaties; and he controlled the public treasury. The king's authority, or command, was all powerful in both peace and war. When he appeared in public, the guards, or lictors, who carried axes and rods before him symbolized his authority. Like the paterfamilias, he had the right to exercise discipline on those within his jurisdiction and could inflict penalties on those who broke the law.[24]

The king also built temples and carried out religious ceremonies. He communicated with the gods, consulting and appeasing them by observing the auspices, *auspicia,* objects or events (animal entrails or flights of birds) that revealed divine approval or disapproval of an act.[25] Like the founding of Rome, the authority of the auspices traces its origins back to Romulus who, according to legend, refused to accept the title of king until he had received a favorable omen

from heaven. Taking a stand under the open sky in a clear space, a *templum,* he offered a sacrifice and prayed to Jupiter to sanctify his monarchy by a favorable sign.[26] Interpreting the lightning or birds as a positive omen, Romulus established it as a custom – an authoritative observance to be followed by all of his successors – that none should accept the office of king or any other public office until heaven had given its sanction.[27]

The Latin word *templum* did not originally refer to the temple building that sheltered a god's image. The word for that was *aedes,* or house. A *templum* was a space either in the sky or on the earth marked out by an augur for the purpose of taking auspices.[28] On earth, a *templum* was a place set aside and limited by certain formulaic words for the taking of the auspices. Trees often served as boundaries, marking the space to be viewed by the augur's eye. As such, this was a special, permanently inaugurated place, so designated by an *augurium.*[29]

In the sky, following the model of Romulus, the priest marked out a portion of the sky and then watched for omens from the gods. In this sense, wherever the eye gazed was the *templum.*[30] The augur's gaze, the *conspicio,* was the equivalent of contemplation. When the augur defined a *templum,* his *conspicio* delimited a view. Looking attentively, he hoped to perceive and identify an omen.[31]

The Romans distinguished between a *templum* for observing flashes of lightning and a *templum* for observing the flight of the birds, each of which had its own orientation. The celestial *templum* for the observation of flashes of lightning was oriented from the point of view of the gods who sat in their northern abode and gazed southward.[32] Birds, in contrast, were watched in a setting in which the auspicant looked eastward. If a bird appeared in the southeastern part of the *templum,* it was a right-hand sign for the auspicant.[33]

The essential elements of a temple complex were thus the viewing space, the *aedes,* the boundary, and an altar. Such ritualization of space is perhaps the most characteristically Roman feature of temple architecture and urban design in the Roman world. This accounts for the tendency to enclose open spaces, impose human demands on the limitless forces of nature, control earth and sky to practical ends, and bargain with the gods on human terms.[34]

The Romans regarded their divinities as all-powerful beings that dominated everyday activities and set restrictions on daily existence. It was the religious duty of the rulers and their attendant priests to interpret the deity's rules or wishes and to conform to them through adherence to prescribed norms, ceremonies, and sacrifices.[35] As auspices were traced back to the great sign given to Romulus, so all authority in Rome derived from his act of foundation, binding each action to the sacred beginning of Rome and the original divine authority of its first ruler.[36]

Construction and Dedication

The influences and transformations inherent in Rome's early political, social, and religious life – and the authority of its mythological beginnings – were all expressed in the architecture of the Temple of Jupiter Capitolinus. Built during the reigns of Tarquinius Priscus and Tarquinius Superbus, its planning fulfilled a vow Tarquinius Priscus made to the gods during a battle against the Sabines. Preparation of its site was begun in the 580s B.C., but the temple's actual construction was carried out by Tarquinius Superbus from ca. 525 to 509 B.C.[37] There was a political upheaval in 509 B.C. which resulted in the Etruscan king being driven from Rome and the Republic established. The temple was thus dedicated not by the Tarquins but by the first rulers of the Republic.[38]

Just as the Capitoline Temple's size and prominent location were crucial to the efforts of the Etruscans to maintain their authority in Rome, so, too, was it important in the attempts of the Republicans to establish their legitimacy after the Etruscans' defeat. As successive rulers and emperors used the Capitoline Temple on countless occasions as a setting for ritual and sacrifice and as a precedent for the design of other Roman temples, its role in establishing and maintaining political authority continued through the Republic and into the Empire. In every case, these successive generations of rulers recalled its link both to the events and personalities associated with the origins of the city and to the divine presence of Jupiter.

When Tarquinius Priscus selected the Capitoline Hill as the site for his new temple dedicated to Jupiter,

he called the augurs together and ordered them to consult the auspices concerning the site's appropriateness. It was up to them to decide whether a site was suitable to be consecrated and would be acceptable to the gods themselves.[39] After the augurs consented that the Capitoline Hill, which "commands the Forum," was acceptable to the gods, Tarquinius ordered that it be cleared of the existing shrines. He was especially concerned with those built by King Tatius. Livy writes that Tarquinius wanted to

> build a temple of Jupiter on the Tarpeian Mount [the southern half of the Capitoline Hill] to stand as a memorial of his reign and of his name . . . and that the site might be free of all other religious claims, and belong wholly to Jupiter and his temple, which was being built there, he determined to annul the consecration of several fanes and shrines which had been first vowed at the crisis of the battle against Romulus, and had afterwards been consecrated and inaugurated.[40]

Tarquinius Priscus's destruction of the Sabine king's shrines aimed not only to establish his own authority but also to reestablish the authority of Romulus and the city's original founding in the eighth century B.C.

In the end, not all of the older shrines were removed from the site. The Temple of Jupiter Feretrius was kept, and the priests of the cults of Terminus and Juventas steadfastly refused to give up their places. This refusal caused great consternation among the augurs, but finally, Attus Navius, the highest ranking of the augurs, incorporated these god's altars into the temple precinct. With this, they came to be seen as important sacred elements related to the authority of Rome's founding.[41]

Attus Navius may also have been the one who actually marked out the area for the Temple of Jupiter Capitolinus. He possessed an innate skill of divination and was conceded to have been the most favored by the gods. At one point, he was challenged by Tarquinius, but his abilities turned out to be more powerful than the king's. From that point on, augurs and the augural priesthood were held in such high esteem that almost every official event, from popular assemblies and musterings of the army to acts of supreme importance, was preceded by a consultation of the auspices.[42]

In response to the incident of Attus Navius and the cults of Terminus and Juventas, the augurs concluded that "no occasion would ever cause the removal of the boundaries of the Romans' city or impair its vigor."[43] Livy confirmed that this incident was an omen suggesting Rome's permanence: "the whole kingdom would be firm and steadfast," he wrote, and from this moment on, the authority of Rome's founding and its future greatness could not be challenged.[44]

Given the steeply sloped, rocky outcropping of the Capitoline site, it required a great deal of preparation before the new temple could be built. In the last four years of his reign, from 582 to 579 B.C., Tarquinius Priscus ordered the construction of retaining walls, landfill, and a leveling off of the peak. The work was so extensive, however, that the king died before the temple's foundations could be built.[45] It was left to Tarquinus Superbus some forty years later to build the foundations and erect the greater part of the temple.[46]

A second omen appeared shortly after Tarquinius Superbus resumed construction of the temple. A workman digging on the site found the head of a man, recently slain, the blood still flowing from his veins. Tarquinius ordered the work to be stopped and the auspices consulted. After several attempts, the oldest and wisest of a group of augurs from Tyrrhenia confirmed earlier omens by stating, "It is ordained by fate that the place in which you found the head shall be the head of all Italy."[47] As Livy wrote, "This appearance plainly foreshadowed that here was to be the citadel of the empire and the head of the world."[48] Thus, the site was not only sacred to Rome's survival; it was to be the *caput mundi,* a phrase which gave Jupiter his surname and was applied to the hill itself.[49] Although this is admittedly a fanciful etymology, it nevertheless held sway in Roman imagination throughout the Republic and Empire.

Tarquinius Superbus summoned workmen from every quarter of Etruria to build the new temple. Etruscan designers, master masons, and terra-cotta artisans played the dominant roles of supervision and artistic direction, while the majority of the hard labor was done by the local Roman population.[50] According to

Livy, the work was difficult, but "the plebians felt less abused at having to build with their own hands the temples of the gods [rather than the Cloaca Maxima or the Circus Maximus]."[51]

The funds to pay for the temple's construction came from a tenth part of the spoils from the conquest of Suessa, an Etruscan town Tarquinius conquered in one of Rome's first military exploits in 530 B.C.[52] As construction progressed and more money was needed, Tarquinius added additional funds from spoils taken from the town of Pometia.[53] From the beginning, conquest of rival cities thus went hand in hand with the construction of major buildings in Rome. Devoting a portion of the spoils of war to the erection of a structure like the Capitoline Temple, was, on one hand, to treat it as a sort of trophy, a commemoration of Rome's ability to defeat and subdue its enemies. On the other hand, it was also evidence of the strong desire of the Tarquins to supercede in importance the Latin confederation's center of political and religious life in the Alban Hills and the old Temple of Jupiter Latiaris. Their goal was to make Rome and the new temple on the Capitoline Hill the unrivaled capital of the region.[54]

Although Tarquinius Superbus was the temple's most important sponsor, he did not remain in power long enough to dedicate it.[55] After his monarchy ended in the aristocratic coup of 509 B.C. and he was expelled from Rome, according to Livy,

> The Temple of Jupiter on the Capitoline had not yet been dedicated. Valerius and Horatius the consuls drew lots to determine which should do it. Horatius received the lot. . . . With more bitterness than was reasonable, the friends of Valerius resented that the dedication of so famous a temple should be given to Horatius. They tried in all sorts of ways to hinder it, but their schemes came to naught. Finally, when the consul's hand was on the door-post and he was in the midst of his prayers to the goddess, they broke in upon the ceremony with the evil tidings that his son was dead, assuming that while the shadow of death was over his house he could not dedicate a temple. Whether he did not believe the news to be true, or possessed great fortitude, we are not informed with certainty, nor is it easy to decide. Without permitting himself to be diverted from his purposes by the message, further than to order that the body should be buried, he kept his hand on the door-post, finished his prayer, and dedicated the temple.[56]

The fact that such great significance was attached to the temple's dedication demonstrates the importance of its symbolic role in Roman life from the moment of its construction. Although it was begun by one political regime and finished by another, its purpose remained fundamentally the same. Its dedication survived, and Jupiter, its god, came to embody the Roman Republic.

The Capitoline Temple and Its Deities

The temple's construction was the official acknowledgment of Jupiter Optimus Maximus, along with Juno and Minerva, as Rome's principal cult deities (Fig. 4). The link between Jupiter and the founding of Rome was enshrined in Roman religious doctrine by the *augustum augurium,* the auspices by which Jupiter empowered Romulus to found the city. Ennius reports that Romulus and Remus, both augurs, took auspices that established the pact between Rome and Jupiter.[57] By sending Romulus a positive sign to found the city, Jupiter not only blessed the founding, but also promised to protect it. In return for the security of the Roman state, he was entitled to the sacrifices and offerings of the official cult.[58]

Jupiter was above all a victory god who presided over the expanding Roman world, and as Rome's power grew, so, too, did his importance. He was naturally associated with the mission of power and conquest.[59] He guaranteed that treaties would be honored, and he oversaw international relations through the mediation of the college of priests.[60] He was also associated with light and anything related to the sky: the sun, the full moon, lightning, even rain and snow.[61] He was usually worshipped on the summit of a hill. Here, where nothing could intervene between heaven and earth, his activities could be most easily observed. Associated further with solemn oaths and treaties, he was a deity who invoked moral conscience and a sense of obligation.[62] He played a role as witness,

4. Capitoline Triad, Archaeological Museum, Palestrina. Photo: Ministero per i Beni e le Attività Culturali, Soprintendenza Archeologica per il Lazio.

guarantor, and avenger of oaths and pacts in both private and public life.[63]

Although essential to his identity, Juno and Minerva remained subordinate. Jupiter's association with Juno and Minerva was again the result of Etruscan influence. Juno was Rome's most important goddess, representing women and female principles of life. Associated with childbirth, she was the goddess of female slaves, the savior of women in their perils, even a savior of the state.[64] She played an important part in the ritual of marriage. On the Capitoline, she was Juno Regina, Queen Juno, the queen of heaven, the most important of all female deities.[65]

The goddess Minerva presided over handicrafts, inventions, arts, and sciences. In Roman households, she was the patron of women's weaving and spinning. On the other hand, she was also a goddess of war, the bestower of victory, whose feast days often included gladiatorial games.[66] She would later become a principal deity of the emperor Domitian, and additional temples dedicated to her would be built in the imperial fora and on the Aventine and Caelian Hills.

A statue of Jupiter was placed inside the middle cella room. Made of terra-cotta by Vulca of Veii, it was clothed with a tunic adorned with palms, an embroidered toga, a crown, and a laurel wreath.[67] A statue of Juno was placed in the room to the left; one of Minerva in the room to the right.[68] A terra-cotta quadriga bearing Jupiter, made in several pieces, was placed on the ridge of the roof. It was replaced by a new one made of bronze in 295 B.C.[69]

Devotion to the Capitoline cult remained strong throughout the history of the Roman state, from its founding by Romulus to the Empire. Generations of rulers and priests would painstakingly observe the rituals associated with Jupiter, Juno, and Minerva to ensure their correct relationship with the deities. When a victory or a good harvest favored Rome, it was proof that Jupiter and the other gods were pleased with the way the Capitoline cult was administered. When the Romans failed, it was assumed that Jupiter was displeased. He then demanded appeasement and modification of some part of the cult ritual.[70]

For the Etruscans, the temple had represented a link between the king and the gods in much the same way as eastern kings were given cult status. Such divinity had long been used to establish the binding authority of the king's power.[71] The Etruscan kings wore the same robe and had the same emblems as those on the statue of Jupiter inside the temple.[72] The kings were identified with Jupiter just as the legendary Greek kings were associated with Zeus.[73]

After the Etruscan king was banished from Rome in 509 B.C., the temple and the accessories of Jupiter it contained were not abandoned. The temple continued to be used; the robe and other emblems were

worn by the consuls and triumphant generals of the Republic.[74] The Romans' uninterrupted embrace of Jupiter is an important manifestation of the sacredness of foundation in Roman politics: once something had been founded, it bound all future generations. The temple transcended the question of rule by monarchy or by representation. Its construction and dedication to Jupiter made it distinctly Roman rather than Etruscan or monarchical.[75]

Jupiter's feast day, September 13, became the day the Republic's consuls took their oaths of office. The great ceremony featured the newly elected consuls, with magistrates, priests, and members of the Senate leading a procession up the east slope of the Capitoline Hill. They made a sacrifice on the altar, then followed it with a great banquet and the first meeting of the Senate (Fig. 5).[76] Whether on the occasion of Jupiter's feast day or in the celebration of a military victory, the manuals of the *pontifices* prescribed that sacrifice to Jupiter had to be made on a stone altar in front of the temple. They also prescribed that a young white steer was required as the sacrificial animal. Male animals were offered to gods, female to goddesses.[77]

The sacrificed animal was dismembered and its internal organs removed for examination. If they proved to be in perfect order – a good omen – they were cut into small pieces and put on the altar for the gods to consume. The rest of the carcass was prepared in a kitchen in the vicinity of the temple, and the banquet was held either in a temporary dining tent or in a dining hall near the temple. As with all other Roman rituals, the procedure for animal sacrifice in front of the Capitoline Temple was detailed and carefully performed. Any mistake was considered a dangerous omen and resulted in repetition of the ritual in its entirety.[78] During the ceremony, the doors of the temple's cella were opened wide so the statues of the deities could be observed and their presence made tangible and immediate.[79]

Triumphal processions, led by a victorious general, with official sanction by the Senate, were perhaps the most celebratory and magnificent events to involve the Temple of Jupiter Capitolinus and to manifest the relationship between the god and the Roman people. Marching from the Campus Martius, through the Circus Flaminius, up the Via Triumphalis and the Via Sacra, across the Forum Romanum, the procession came to its glorious conclusion in front of the Capitoline Temple. The victors carried their triumphal crown and consecrated their ritual sacrifices.[80] Such ceremonies were in a sense a temporary deification, the triumphant Roman impersonating the god, sometimes even painting his face like that of the Jupiter statue.[81]

The temple had several functions in addition to its role in ritual ceremonies. It was used as a place for advertising state acts, deeds, and documents. This was one of the principal means of informing the public of what was going on in the government, the military, and other official organizations.[82] The temple also housed the city's official records and guarded the bronze tablets of laws and treaties displayed in its precinct. It housed the Sibylline Books, a Greek collection of Cumaean oracles said to have been acquired by the Etruscan kings. These oracles included prophecies regarding the history of Rome, and in some cases, they ordered the introduction of Greek cults and rites into the Roman religion.[83] According to Pliny, these oracles, acquired by Tarquinius Superbus, were kept in a stone chest in the temple's basement guarded by ten men.[84]

In general, priests and high government officials were the only ones to enter the temple's cella rooms. They were sparsely furnished, housing only the cult statues and small altars for burning incense. When a Roman entered one of the rooms to make a vow, he typically attached wax tablets to the statue and then prayed while stretching out his arms toward it.[85]

As a place for personal vows, public ceremony, advertising state acts, and housing official records, the Capitoline Temple was preeminent. It had no rivals, at least until the time of Augustus. The temple stood for more than 400 years before being destroyed by fire in 83 B.C. It was reconstructed by the dictator Sulla and his successor, Quintus Lutatius Catulus. Sulla used marble Corinthian capitals imported from Athens, transforming it in part from the Tuscan Doric to a quasi-Hellenistic style.[86]

The temple was damaged twice more by fire, first in A.D. 69 during a battle between Vitellius and Vespasian, second in a great fire during the reign of Titus in A.D. 80. In each case, according to ancient historians, it was rebuilt on the same foundations, with the same plan, again using Corinthian columns from Athens, but this time in their entirety.[87]

5. Relief depicting sacrifice in front of the Temple of Jupiter Capitolinus in Rome. Photo: Fototeca Unione, American Academy in Rome, FU 13211.

In June of A.D. 455, the temple met its final destruction at the hands of the Vandals under Genseric. They plundered the sanctuary and carried off its statues and gilt bronze roof tiles to adorn Genseric's African residence. From then on, the site was used as a stone quarry and lime-kiln until all but the temple's foundations were destroyed.[88]

The Lost Site and Its Rediscovery

In the years after the Capitoline Temple's destruction by Genseric, numerous structures were built over its foundations, and for that matter, across the entire Capitoline Hill. It was only during the Renaissance that historians and authors of Roman guidebooks exhibited a renewed interest in the building and began to study its archaeological remains. There were some visible foundations of the temple in the gardens of the Palazzo Caffarelli, behind the present-day Capitoline Museum, and there were fragments of several marble columns and capitals that were found in 1545 by Giovanni Pietro Caffarelli.[89]

None of the columns or capitals exist today in their original form, although some were reportedly sketched and measured by Antonio da Sangallo the Younger. The sculptor Flaminio Vacca described the capitals as being so large that he was able to carve out a great lion from one of them. The rest of the marbles were used by Vincenzo de Rossi to carve the prophets and other statues for the Chapel of Federico Cesi in Santa Maria della Pace. No terra-cotta fragments of the entablature were found on the site, although some were reportedly discovered during the eighteenth and nineteenth

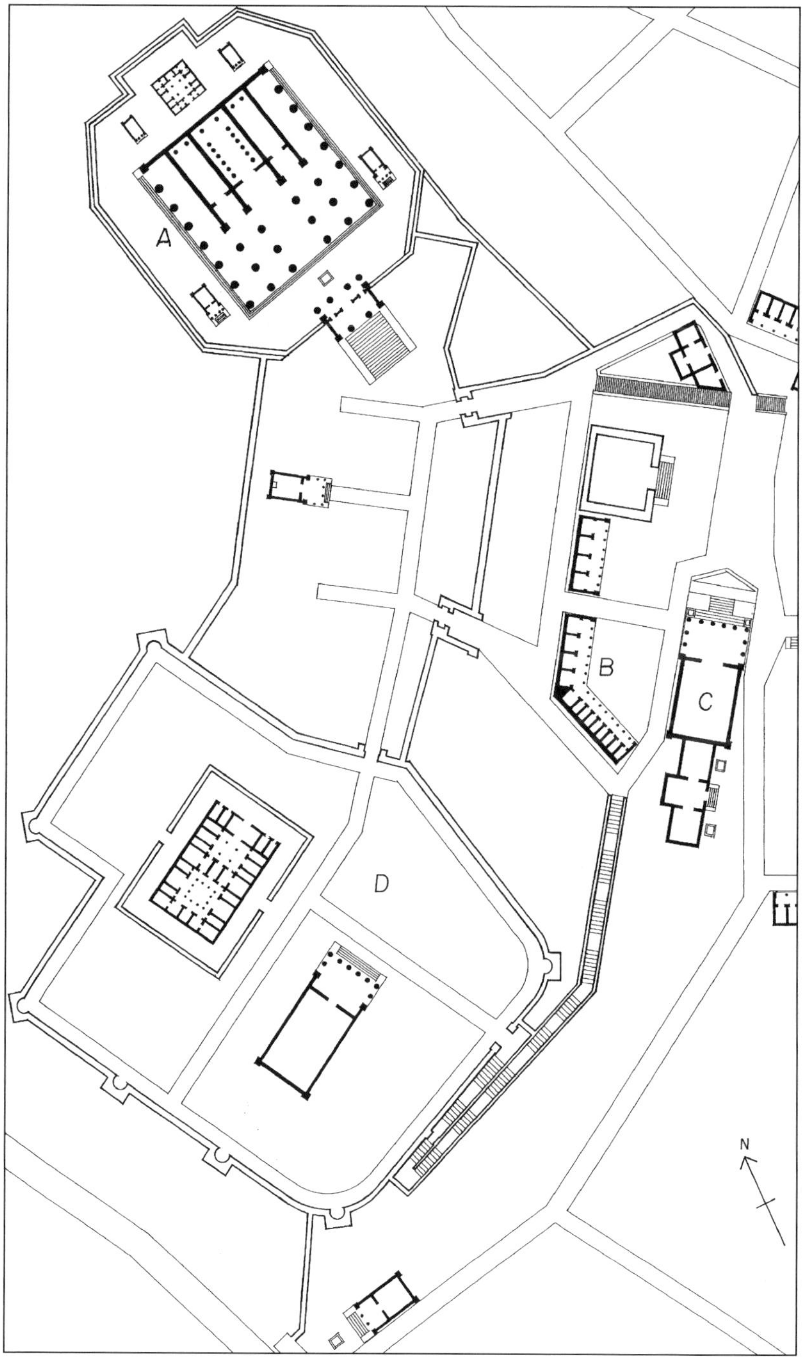

6. Plan of Capitoline Hill according to Luigi Canina, 1854. The Temple of Jupiter Capitolinus is shown on the north rather than the south summit: (A) Temple of Jupiter Capitolinus, (B) Portico Deorem Consentium, (C) Temple of Saturn, (D) Southern summit of the Capitoline Hill. Drawing: Achieng Opondo after Luigi Canina, *Esposizione storica e topografica del Foro Romano e sue adiacenze* (1973), pl. 4.A.

centuries beneath the basements of houses below the Capitoline Hill, suggesting their final resting place after the temple's destruction.[90]

Guidebooks to Rome written in the sixteenth and seventeenth centuries reveal some confusion about the Capitoline Temple concerning both its location and its appearance. Three sixteenth-century writers, Lucio Fauno, Giovanni Bartolomeo Marliano, and Bernardo Gamucci, accurately described the temple's site, referring to it as the Tarpeian Rock, overlooking the Forum Holitorium and the Piazza Montonara from the hill's southern summit.[91] In *Delle antichità della città di Roma* (1548), Fauno referred to the account of the ancient author Varro, who suggested that the hill had been called the Tarpeian because of the Vestal Virgin Tarpeia, who was killed and buried there by the Sabines.[92] Marliano,

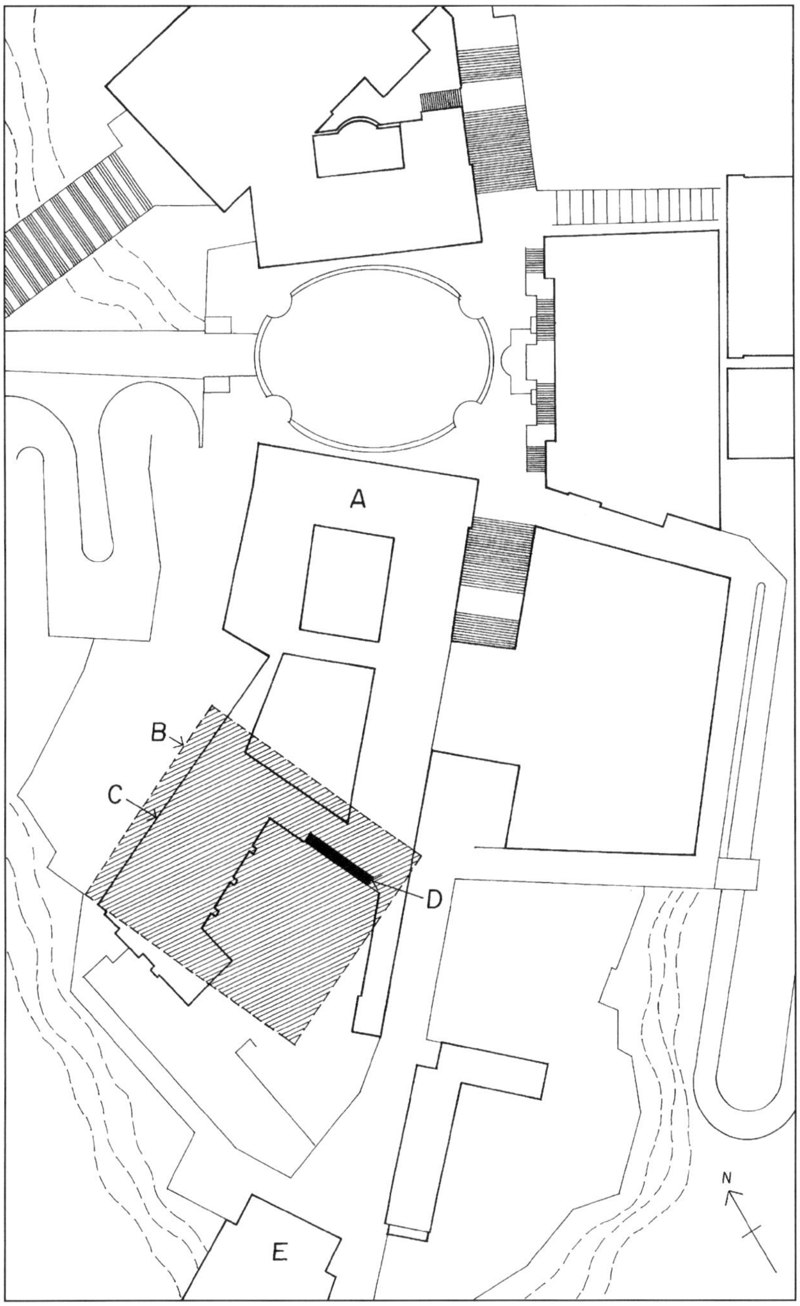

7. Plan of the Capitoline Hill with foundations of Capitoline Temple as discovered by Lanciani in the late 1890s: (A) Palazzo dei Conservatori, (B) Foundations of the Capitoline Temple, (C) Palazzo Caffarelli, (D) Ancient wall in Palazzo dei Conservatori, (E) Residence of the German Ambassador. Drawing: John W. Stamper based on Rodolfo Lanciani, *Pagan and Christian Rome* (1895), p. 86.

although agreeing in *Urbis Romae topographia Italiano* (1548) that the temple was on the southern summit, pointed out that there was, in fact, confusion over the identification of the various parts of the hill: exactly which locations should be referred to as the Capitoline, Tarpeian Rock, Rocca, or Arx.[93]

The issue became more confused about a century later when writers suddenly shifted the argument to suggest that the temple was not located on the southern summit at all, but rather on the northern one, under the Church of the Aracoeli.[94] They suggested that some of the temple's columns were used as *spolia* in the Christian structure. Faminio Nardini, for instance, in *Roma antica* (1666), based this theory on his reading of the life of Romulus provided by the ancient authors. Inverting the previous conception of the site, he insisted that the Tarpeian Rock and the Capitoline Temple were on the northern summit and that the

Rocca was on the southern summit.[95] This argument may, in fact, have been supported by contemporary readings of the ancient authors, or it may have had a political intent aimed at lending more legitimacy to the Church of the Aracoeli and its patrons. It was certainly not based on any new archaeological discoveries. There was nothing more known about the archaeology of the site in the seventeenth century than there had been in the sixteenth. The "evidence" was purely based on a change in the way the ancient authors were read and interpreted.

There was a renewed interest in the Capitoline Temple in the early nineteenth century, although most of the writers at this time again preferred the site of the Church of the Aracoeli on the northern summit. In the Roman guidebook *L'antiquario* (1804), Angelo Dalmazzoni reiterated the arguments for this location and suggested that the approach up the west side of the hill, opposite the Forum Romanum, was the route followed by triumphant Roman generals.[96] A similar line of reasoning was stated by Antonio Nibby in *Del Foro Romano* (1819), Carlo Fea in *Descrizione di Roma e suoi contorni* (1824), and Luigi Canina (Fig. 6) in *Esposizione storica e topografica del Foro Romano e sue adiacenze* (1845).[97] In each case, the author believed the temple was located on the northern summit, even though there was no archaeological evidence to support their claim.

It was not until 1875 that Rodolfo Lanciani rediscovered the true site when he pieced together several disparate elements of the temple's foundations on the Capitoline's southern summit (Fig. 7). An excavation was under way in the garden of the Palazzo dei Conservatori of the Capitoline Museum to prepare for the construction of a residence for the German ambassador. Workers uncovered a previously unknown edge of the podium, which Lanciani attributed to the period of the Tarquins and the Capitoline Temple. Along with the podium, he identified a fragment of a fluted column shaft of Pentelic marble that had also been discovered. He suggested it was from the Capitoline Temple's final version. Borings were systematically made around the site in 1876, which allowed archaeologists to trace out three sides of the podium and estimate its dimensions.[98]

Only now could proposed reconstructions of the temple be based directly on the archaeological evidence of the site. Numerous studies followed by both Italian and German archaeologists, each publishing their own interpretations of the evidence with drawings of their proposed reconstructions.

Because the Capitoline Temple was one of the largest and most influential buildings on the Italian peninsula for more than 900 years, it is unfortunate that it does not figure more prominently in historical surveys of Greek and Roman architecture. Although general surveys include the giant structures at Ephesus, Samos, Akragas, Selinus, and Athens, many studies overlook the Temple of Jupiter Capitolinus. This is true primarily because so little evidence for it exists. Based on literary descriptions and the fragmentary remains of its foundation buried under the Capitoline Museum, it was without question the largest Etruscan temple on mainland Italy and therefore deserves more study with respect to both its architectural form and to its place in the history of Roman architecture.

There is a question, however, of just how large it really was. It has long been assumed that the dimensions of the temple itself corresponded to the size of the podium, which, according to recent archaeological studies, was 53.50 meters wide by 62 meters long.[99] This would have been a colossal temple indeed, with interaxial dimensions of as much as 12 meters, or 40 Roman feet. It would have been far larger than the Parthenon in Athens and proportionally even more gigantic than any other Etruscan temple of the period. Was it really possible to build and maintain such a temple with the available technology in sixth-century B.C. Rome? Chapter 2 provides a close examination of the archaeological evidence of the building and proposes a new reconstruction, one that is smaller in size and more in keeping with the character of both its contemporaries and with later temples from the Empire.

2

A NEW RECONSTRUCTION OF THE TEMPLE

Most reconstruction drawings and models of the Temple of Jupiter Capitolinus have closely corresponded to a proposal made in the 1840s by Luigi Canina in *Esposizione storica e topografica del Foro Romano e sue adiacenze*. Subsequent scholars modified and refined its plan and changed its site as new archaeological evidence came to light during the late nineteenth and early twentieth centuries. The temple's size, however, and its basic layout have remained consistent with Canina's plan. The most detailed reconstruction, following the original outline by Canina, is that published by the Swedish archaeologist Einar Gjerstad in *Early Rome* in 1960.[1]

The issue raised in this study is simply stated. The Capitoline Temple, as it has been reconstructed by writers and scholars from Canina to the present day, is too large. The size of the temple structure in these proposals is so grand, the spans of its wooden lintels so wide, that its construction seems hardly possible in Rome in the sixth century B.C.[2] A reinterpretation of the evidence based on the foundation walls, the size of the columns, and on a comparison with contemporary temples, suggests the Capitoline Temple's size was about two-thirds that of the accepted reconstruction. In this proposal, its columns were more closely spaced by at least 4 meters, and its podium was not a large flat cubical block, but a terraced platform with successive flights of stairs connecting each level.[3]

The temple's reduced dimensions as proposed in this book are significant not only because they are more reasonable in terms of the technological means available in ancient Rome but also because they compare closely with those of later structures such as the Temple of Mars Ultor and the Pantheon. The builders of these imperial temples sought to symbolically link them to Jupiter, Romulus, and the founding of Rome. The Temple of Jupiter Capitolinus was consciously emulated and referred to as an architectural precedent by countless rulers, architects, and builders in subsequent centuries. This emulation, in several significant cases, included copying the width of its pronaos as if it was a standard for temple design. As such, the Capitoline Temple was integral to the maintaining of political authority and leadership in Rome throughout the Republic and Empire.

All previous historical accounts of the Temple of Jupiter Capitolinus have portrayed it as an isolated monument in the development of Roman temple architecture. Its presumed size was thought to be so great that it could not be compared with anything else in the city (with the possible exception of the much later Temple of Sol begun by Aurelian on the Quirinal Hill).[4] Because the authority of precedent was so strong in the history of ancient Roman architecture – as it was in politics, religion, and social relations – it should be obvious that the Capitoline Temple, dedicated to the city's most important deity, arguably had a significant influence on what followed.

The Reconstructions

Much of our knowledge of the design of Etruscan temples is derived from Vitruvius's *Ten Books on Architecture* (Fig. 8). Although the Temple of Jupiter Capitolinus did not match Vitruvius's description in all of its details, his book has been essential to archaeologists and architectural historians in interpreting the temple's

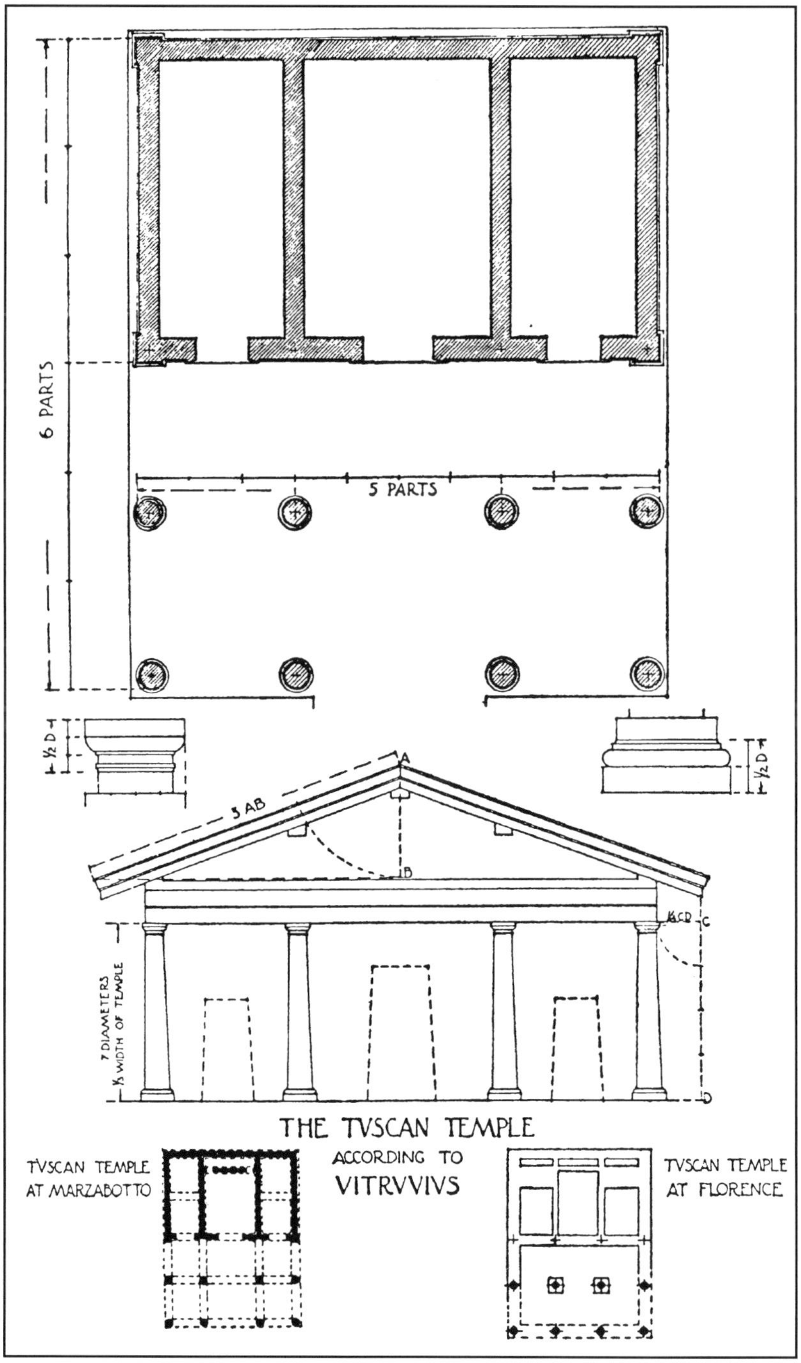

8. Etruscan Temple according to Vitruvius: plan, elevation, and details. Drawing: Herbert Langford Warren, reproduced from Vitruvius, *Ten Books of Architecture*, Ed. Morris Hickey Morgan (1960), p. 121, courtesy of Dover Publications.

remaining physical evidence and literary descriptions. Vitruvius suggested that the plan of an Etruscan temple should be slightly longer than it is wide, a ratio of 6 to 5, and that the length should be divided in half, the front being occupied by an open pronaos, the rear by an enclosed cella. He divided the cella itself into three separate rooms, the center one being wider than the flanking two.[5] He aligned the columns of the pronaos with the walls of the cella, thus creating a spatial and structural correspondence between the two.[6]

For the columns themselves, the Tuscan-Doric Order, Vitruvius suggested that the height, including the capital and base, should be seven times the lower

9. View of Capitoline Temple foundation wall located inside the Capitoline Museum. Photo: Fototeca Unione, American Academy in Rome, FU 960.

diameter, and that this height should in turn be equal to one-third of the temple's overall width. The columns were spaced far apart, their intercolumnial dimensions being over three times their diameter, a composition Vitruvius called *araeostyle* and which he criticized as being "clumsy-roofed, low, broad."[7] Finally, the roof structure was usually composed of wooden beams and posts fastened together by dowels and tenons, with the pitch of the gable having a ratio of 1 to 3.[8] The fasciae were decorated with terra-cotta revetments painted in elaborate foliate, meander, and figurative patterns, and the rooftops were decorated with standing figures and acroteria.[9]

Vitruvius's description of the Etruscan temple as a building type was essential to the reconstruction of the Temple of Jupiter Capitolinus, although in this case, we are dealing with a larger structure than he described, one that had six rather than the usual four columns on the front. Besides Vitruvius's model, the known archaeological evidence, as it was uncovered in the late nineteenth century by Lanciani and others, included a few pieces of terra-cotta frieze, portions of fluted marble columns, and the large sections of the foundation walls under the Palazzo dei Conservatori of the Capitoline Museum.[10] One of the best-preserved parts of the foundation is a wall of large squared blocks located near the platform's southeast corner. It is visible today in the corridor connecting the Palazzo dei Conservatori with the Museo Nuovo (Fig. 9) and also from the enclosed garden behind the museum. Other portions of the foundation, along its north and northwest sides, have recently been excavated and are visible in the courtyard and in the basement of the southwest wing of the Palazzo dei Conservatori.[11]

In addition to the physical evidence, there is a written account by Dionysius of Halicarnassus that provides

significant information about the temple's podium and the plan of its pronaos and cella:

> It stood upon a high base and was 800 [Roman] feet in circuit, each side measuring close to two hundred feet; indeed, one would find the excess of the length over the width to be but slight, in fact, not a full fifteen feet . . . [and it had] three rows of columns on the front, facing the south, and a single row on each side. The temple consists of three parallel shrines, separated by party walls; the middle shrine is dedicated to Jupiter, while on one side stands that of Juno and on the other that of Minerva, all three being under one pediment and one roof.[12]

Studies and measurements by archaeologists show that the dimensions of the huge substructure were 53.50 meters wide by 62 meters long.[13] This corresponds to the base described by Dionysius, whose dimensions were given in a measurement equivalent to the Roman foot (.296 meters), which in this case would be 180 by 210 Roman feet.[14]

As with early theories about the temple's site, there have been numerous reconstructions of the temple proposed since the sixteenth century. Some of them followed closely the description by Dionysius of Halicarnassus; others were way off the mark. It is clear that most early authors and illustrators worked from little more than pure speculation. An illustration in Nardini's *Roma antica*, for instance, shows a plan of the temple with eight columns across the front, three rows deep, and a double peristyle down the sides with thirteen columns each.[15] It was something of a cross between the Etruscan temple type and the Ionic temple of Artemis at Ephesus. Another common representation is found in the 1689 version of Marliano's *Ritratto di Roma antica*, which shows in elevation an enclosed church-like structure with engaged columns and a dome, a building that looks more like Palladio's San Giorgio Maggiore in Venice than any known Etruscan temple.[16]

The 1845 plan by Canina, as published in *Esposizione storica e topografica del Foro Romano e sue adiacenze*, was the first to effectively combine the Etruscan temple

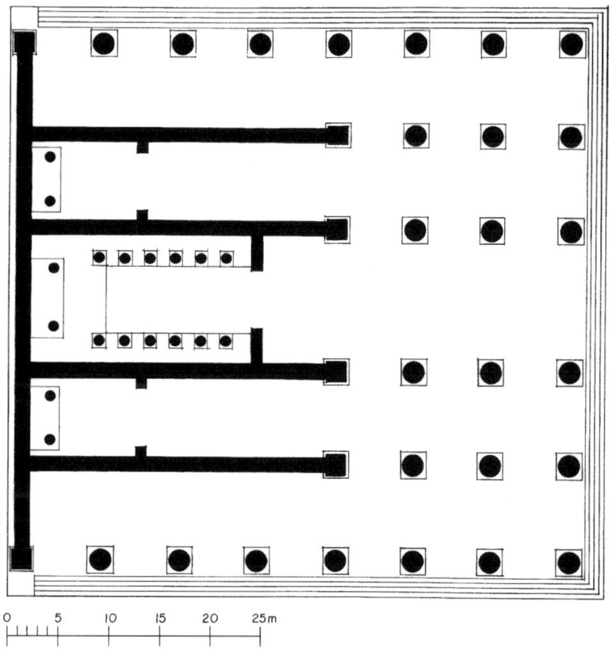

10. Plan of the Temple of Jupiter Capitolinus by Canina that formed the basis for later plan reconstructions. Drawing: John W. Stamper after Luigi Canina, *Esposizione storica e topografica del Foro Romano e sue adiacenze* (1973), pl. 4.A.

description of Vitruvius with the information provided by Dionysius of Halicarnassus (Fig. 10). Even though Canina placed the temple in the wrong location, much of the rest of his reconstruction has been accepted up to the present day: a flat, cubical podium; six columns across the front and three rows deep; a single row down each side; three cella rooms; and a continuous back wall closing off the side aisles (*peripteros sine postico*).[17]

It was only after the excavation of the temple's foundation in the 1870s that proposed reconstructions could be correlated with tangible archaeological evidence. As more sections of the foundations were excavated and measured, archaeologists from different countries pieced together the various parts of the podium. Because some of its northern boundaries were as yet unidentified, there was still disagreement about the podium's exact dimensions. In 1875, Lanciani published an article suggesting its width was 56.40 meters and its length 58.60 meters. He proposed that its interaxial dimensions would have been 9 meters and the column diameters 2 meters. He compared the column diameters with those of the Temple of Mars Ultor and the Pantheon.[18]

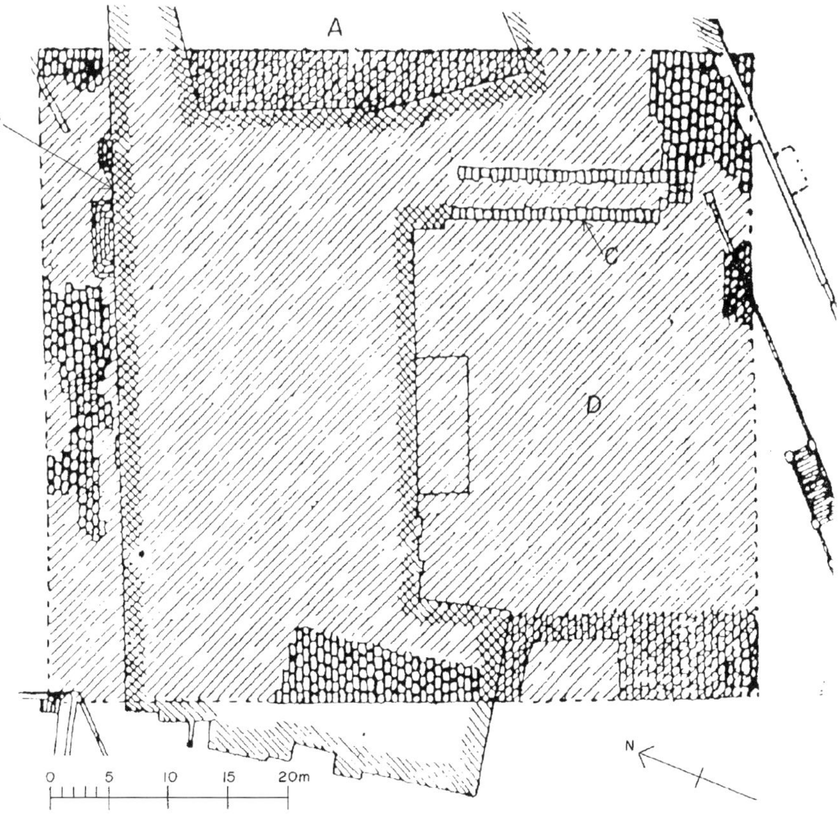

11. Temple of Jupiter Capitolinus, plan of archaeological remains discovered as of 1921 showing stones of perimeter foundation and (A) garden of the Palazzo dei Conservatori, (B) Palazzo Caffarelli, (C) wall near the temple's southeast corner visible in the Palazzo dei Conservatori, (D) garden of the Palazzo Caffarelli. Illustration: Roberto Paribeni and E. Gatti in *NSc* (1921), p. 45.

In 1895, Lanciani provided an in-depth summary of the archaeological findings and further descriptions of the temple in the book *Pagan and Christian Rome*. He described the structure as having a high platform built of squared blocks of *capellaccio*, which he compared with those found in portions of the Servian walls. In this case, he suggested its overall dimensions were 53.90 meters wide by 61 meters long, a revision of his 1875 article but still slightly wider and shorter than the actual figures would prove to be. As in Canina's reconstruction, Lanciani's had an Etruscan-style pronaos with columns three rows deep, aisles down the sides, and with interaxial spans of at least 9 meters. He made a point of stating that "the intercolumniations were so wide as to require architraves of timber," stressing the fact that marble or travertine lintels would not have worked. He also pointed out that the area and height of the podium were reduced by about one-third when the Caffarelli's built their palace in 1680.[19]

Henri Jordan, Christian Hülsen, and Ludwig Otto Richter all published articles in response to the findings of Lanciani in which they reviewed their own archaeological studies of the site, their measurements, and their speculations about the temple's form. They each had their own interpretation of the podium's overall size, their proposals differing by as much as 2 or 3 meters, and each with a different suggestion for the interaxial spacing of the columns.[20] Richter proposed the most inventive plan in which the column spacing alternated between wider and narrower interaxial dimensions.[21]

A later and more accurate archaeological study was published by Roberto Paribeni in 1921 (Fig. 11). Stating that the podium was 53.50 meters wide by 62 meters long (182 by 210 Roman feet), he was the first to properly identify its north boundary and thus confirm the description given by Dionysius of Halicarnassus that the overall perimeter was about 800 Roman feet and that the excess of the length over the width was about 15 Roman feet.[22] In the 1950s, Einar Gjerstad followed Paribeni's findings, proposing the most detailed reconstruction yet.[23]

Although Gjerstad did not invent the accepted reconstruction as we know it, he is responsible for making the most convincing proposal for its dimensions and

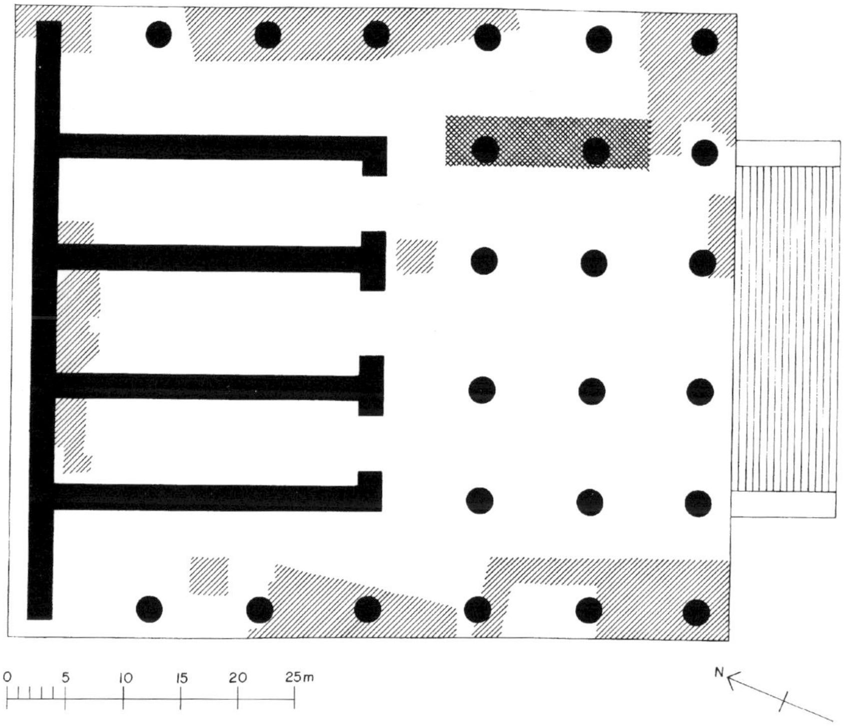

12. Temple of Jupiter Capitolinus according to Gjerstad. Drawing: John W. Stamper after Einar Gjerstad and Roberto Paribeni, in *Etruscan Culture: Land and People* (1962), pl. 12.

form (Fig. 12). Like Canina and Lanciani, he divided the podium's width into five bays, with three cella rooms, an outer aisle on each side, and a pronaos three bays deep, all contained under one roof and pediment (Fig. 13).[24] He suggested that the columns had a diameter of 2.35 meters (8 Roman feet) and a height of 16.6 meters (56 Roman feet).[25] The aisles and the lateral cella rooms were 9.5 meters wide and the central one 12 meters (32 and 40 Roman feet, respectively). These dimensions would have been the same for the interaxial spacing of the pronaos columns, one row of which would have aligned with the well-preserved wall visible in the corridor of the Palazzo dei Conservatori.[26] Every aspect of Gjerstad's reconstruction was given with precision and apparent logic, all of it based on a careful synthesis of the archaeological evidence, previous reconstructions, and the written descriptions of Dionysius of Halicarnassus and Vitruvius.

It is curious that Gjerstad and nearly every other expert who has worked on the subject of the Capitoline Temple has left unchallenged the assumption on which all previous reconstructions were based – namely, that Dionysius of Halicarnassus was referring to the dimensions of the temple structure itself rather than its base or podium. It is possible that the temple structure was smaller than the podium. It is also possible that the podium was not a single rectangular block as suggested by Gjerstad, but rather, a stepped or terraced platform like that found in many later temples from both the Republic and the Empire.[27] On close examination, it is difficult to believe that the temple's outer columns were actually aligned with the platform's outer walls, 180 Roman feet from side to side and 210 feet deep. It is even more difficult to believe that its interaxial spans were 32 and 40 Roman feet. The ability of builders in sixth-century Rome to construct such spans with wooden lintels is highly unlikely. A span of 40 Roman feet is not just large; it is unfathomable when contemplating the post and lintel structure necessary to make it stand.

If the dimensions of the accepted version are compared with those of other contemporary temples, as indicated in Tables 2.1 and 3.1, we find that the dimensions of the Capitoline Temple's facade would have been wider than the colossal Temple G in Selinus or the Temple of Zeus in Akragas, over 21 meters wider and 9 meters taller than the much more famous Parthenon in Athens (Fig. 14), and at least twice as large as any other known temple in Italy from the Etruscan period.

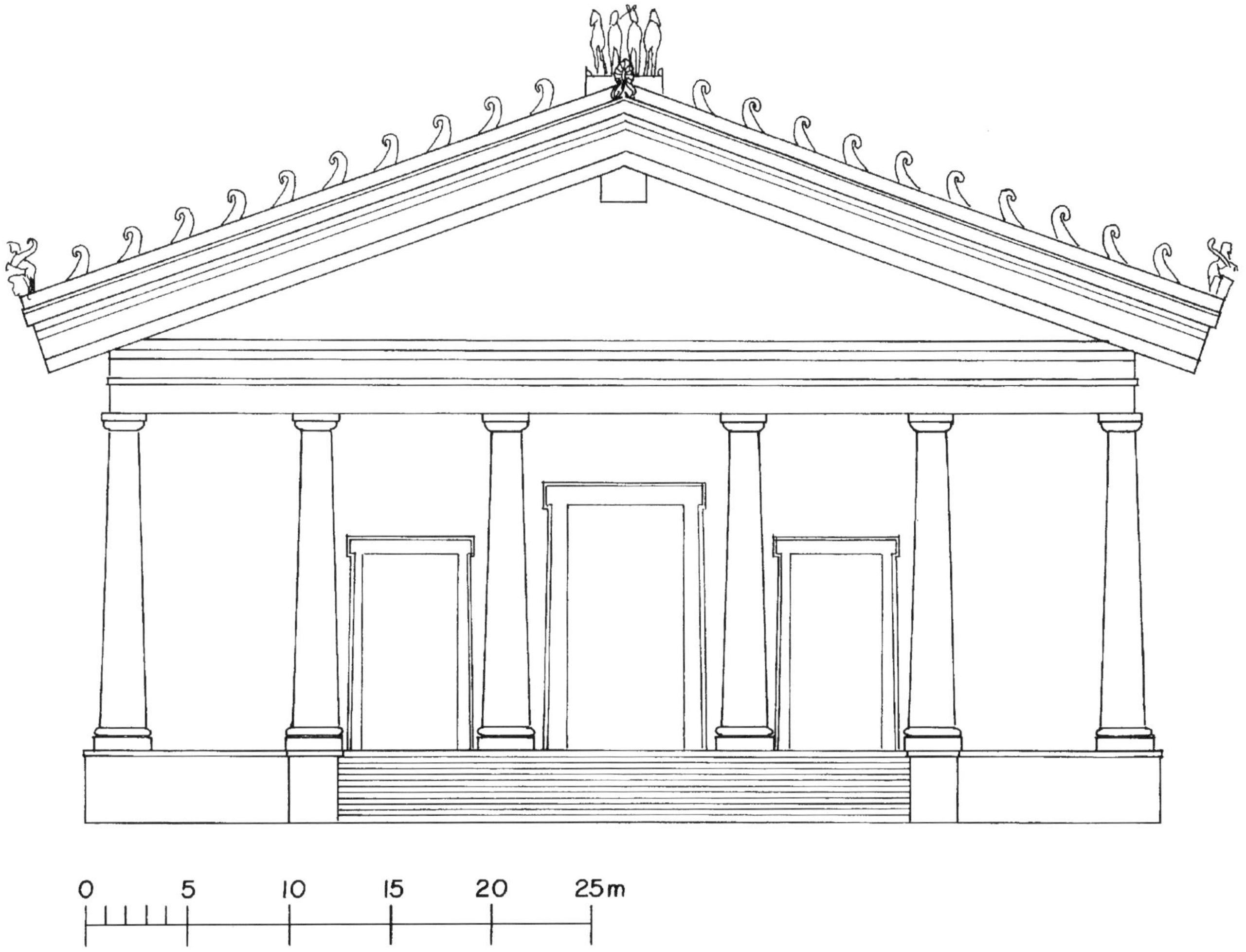

13. Temple of Jupiter Capitolinus, elevation according to Gjerstad. Drawing: John W. Stamper after Einar Gjerstad, in *Etruscan Culture: Land and People* (1962), pl. 13.

More telling is the fact that the temple's interaxial spans of 12 meters for the central bay and 9.50 meters for the rest (even with wooden lintels) is inconceivable if we compare them to 6.50 meters in Temple G, 4.30 meters in the Parthenon, and 4.50 to 6 meters as an average for most other known Etruscan temples. A central bay 12 meters wide by 16.6 meters high, spanned by timber beams that also carried several tons of roof structure, fictile revetments, and clay roofing tiles, would not have been possible without substantial instability and deflection in the center, especially because the original temple stood for 426 years. There were no elaborately formed roof trusses used by the Etruscans, only post-and-lintel construction, with maximum spans of about 7.50 to 8 meters.[28] Even then, the timber members had to be hewn from extremely large trees of a very hard and durable nature and would have been difficult to supply.[29] The assumption that the Capitoline Temple measured 180 by 210 Roman feet with spans as great as 40 Roman feet lacks essential elements of technical practicality, spatial believability, and functional efficacy. There must be an alternative.

The Evidence Reconsidered

The reconstruction as Gjerstad defined it has been accepted as fact by most authors on the subject of Etruscan and Roman temples, all of whom reproduce his plan in one form or another in their publications.[30] In every case, these authors concur with Gjerstad's plan

Table 2.1. Comparative Sizes of Colossal Temples of the Sixth to the Fifth Centuries B.C. (Podium Size, Column Diameter, and Interaxial Dimension)

		Podium		*Columns*	
City	*Temple*	*Width (m)*	*Length (m)*	*Diameter (m)*	*Interaxial (m)*
Ephesus	Temple of Artemis	55.10	115.14	1.51	8.62
Samos	Temple of Hera	59.70	115.80	1.86	8.40
Selinus	Temple G	50.07	110.12	2.97	6.50
Akragus	Temple of Zeus	52.74	110.09	4.05	8.04
Athens	Parthenon	30.88	69.50	1.90	4.30
Athens	Temple Olympian Zeus	41.11	107.89	1.90	5.49
Rome	Cap. Jup. (Gjerstad)	53.50	62.20	2.35	9.50 12.00 center
	" (Stamper)	34.0	38.30	1.47	5.90 7.40 center

Source: William Bell Dinsmoor, *The Architecture of Ancient Greece* (New York: Norton, 1975), tables, 337–340.

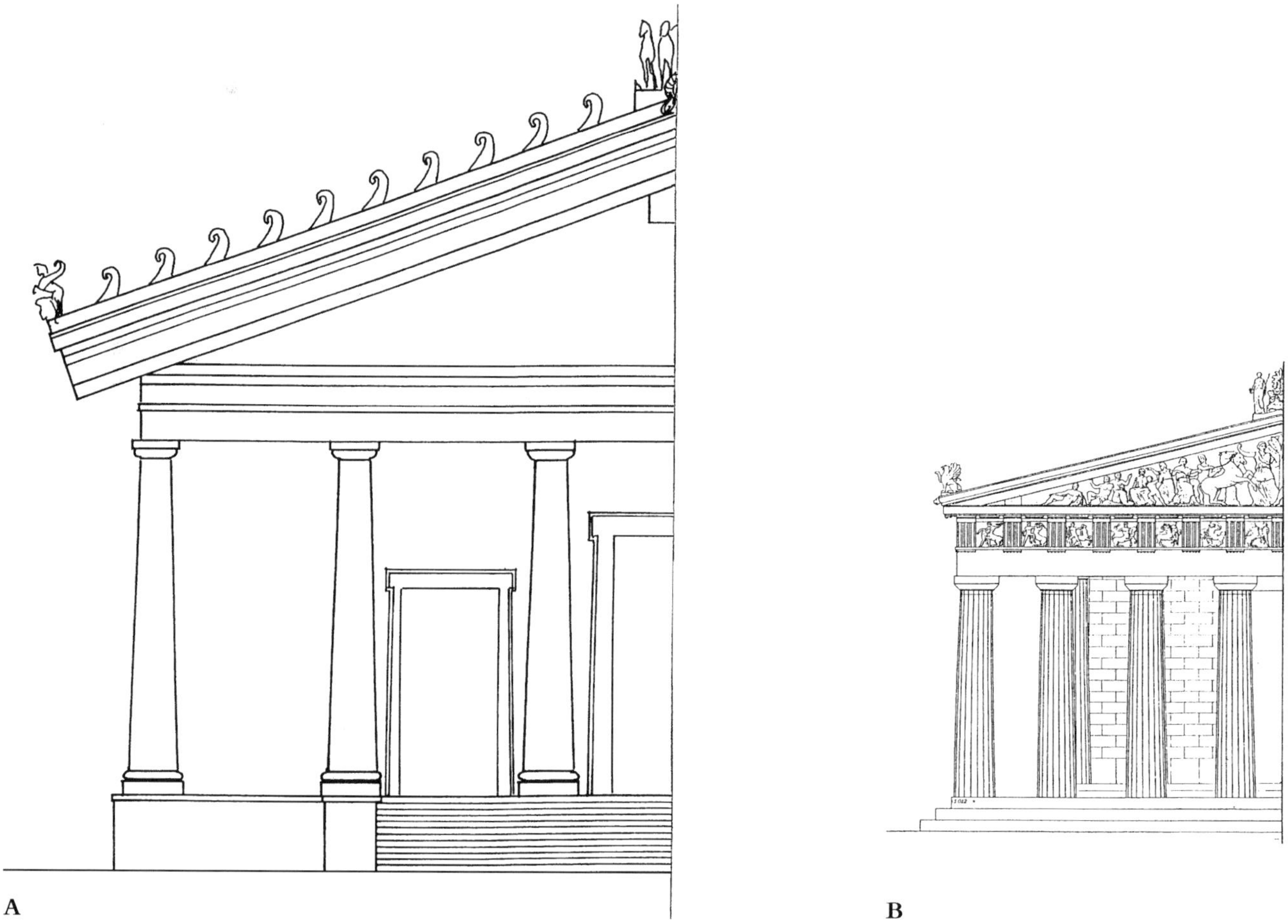

A B

14. Temple of Jupiter Capitolinus (A) compared with the Parthenon, Athens (B). Both drawings are done at the same scale. Drawing of Capitoline Temple: John W. Stamper after Einar Gjerstad, in *Etruscan Culture: Land and People* (1962), pl. 13; Parthenon drawing: Georges Gromort, *Choix d'éléments empruntés à l'architecture classique*, vol. 1 (1927), pl. 2.

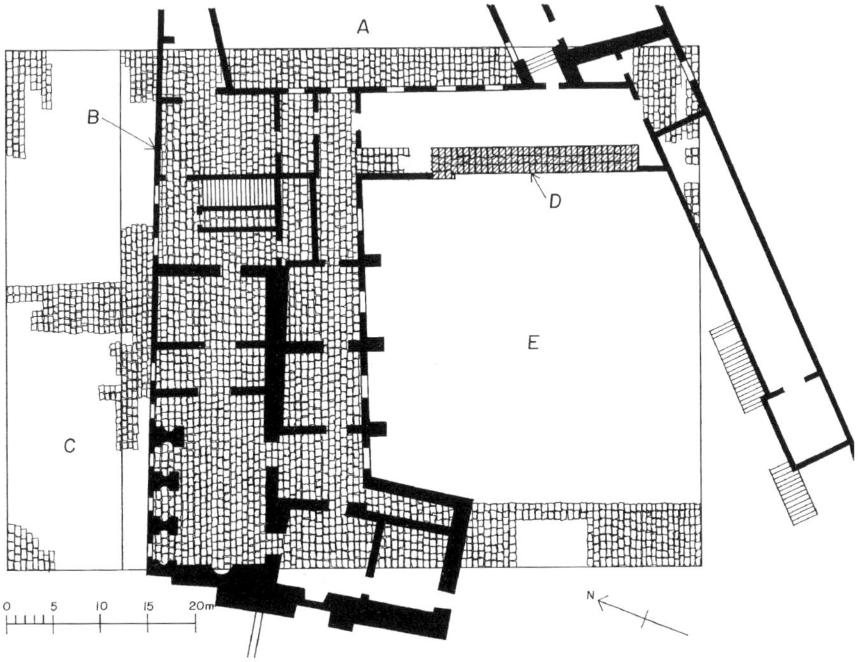

15. Temple of Jupiter Capitolinus, plan of archaeological remains discovered as of 2000 showing foundation platform and (A) garden of the Palazzo dei Conservatori, (B) Palazzo Caffarelli, (C) platform behind temple, (D) wall near the temple's southeast corner visible in the Palazzo dei Conservatori, (E) garden of the Palazzo Caffarelli. Drawing: John W. Stamper.

reconstruction and dimensions. Apparently none of them have taken a critical look at the way he or his predecessors interpreted the evidence, nor have they done a comparative study to analyze it in relation to other temples of the period.

Those archaeologists who have questioned the temple's size have been concerned primarily with the dimensions of the columns. Wooden columns 16.6 meters high and 2.35 meters in diameter would have been impossible, unless several trunks were bound together.[31] Even if they were composed of stone blocks, the erection of such tall structural supports would have been unmanageable in Rome in the 520s B.C.

The reconstruction presented here suggests that the temple's dimensions were, in fact, less than those stated by Gjerstad, his predecessors, and his followers. This alternative reconstruction continues to depend on the evidence of the foundation walls and on the written accounts of ancient authors, but it interprets them in a different way. Most notably, it suggests that the temple structure was not placed on a level, cubical podium, but on top of a series of terraced platforms.

Excavations on the site, begun in the 1990s in the basement level of the Palazzo dei Conservatori and in its garden have brought to light an enormous area of the blocks of *cappellacio* that once formed the lower portion of the temple's platform structure (Fig. 15). They have also revealed a northward extension of the foundation walls that were part of a retaining wall at the edge of the Capitoline Hill and may have been part of the temple itself.[32]

The exact configuration of the terraced platform in this proposed reconstruction cannot be fully determined from the existing archaeological evidence. A hypothetical reconstruction can be made, however, based on the location of the wall visible in the hallway and garden of the Palazzo dei Conservatori and on a comparison with other ancient temples that are known to have had terraced platforms (Figs. 16 and 17).

In this reconstruction, the width of the uppermost terrace and the temple structure itself are based on the position of the wall visible in the Palazzo dei Conservatori hallway and the garden. This wall, about 5 meters taller than any of the surrounding foundation blocks, was part of a large gridded foundation structure that stood on the lowest platform and supported the temple proper. There was a similar wall on the platform's opposite side, symmetrically placed about the central axis. The podium floor supported by this gridded foundation would have measured about 34 meters wide by 38.30 meters long, or 115 by 130 Roman feet.[33] The podium width of 115 Roman feet was an important dimension that links this building to later temples,

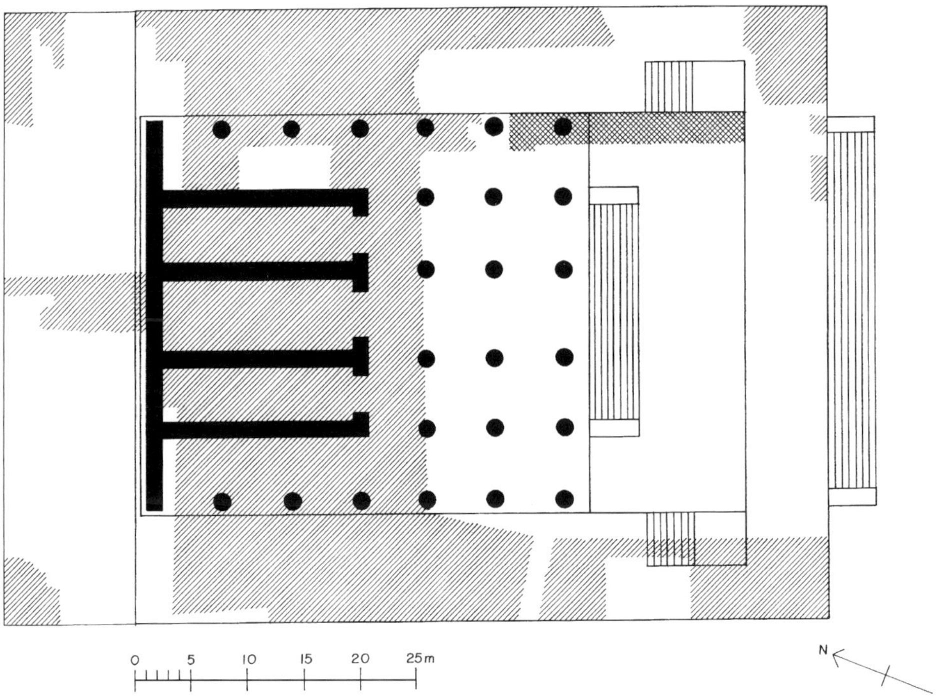

16. Proposed new plan of Temple of Jupiter Capitolinus with indication of excavated foundations and wall at southeast corner. Drawing: John W. Stamper.

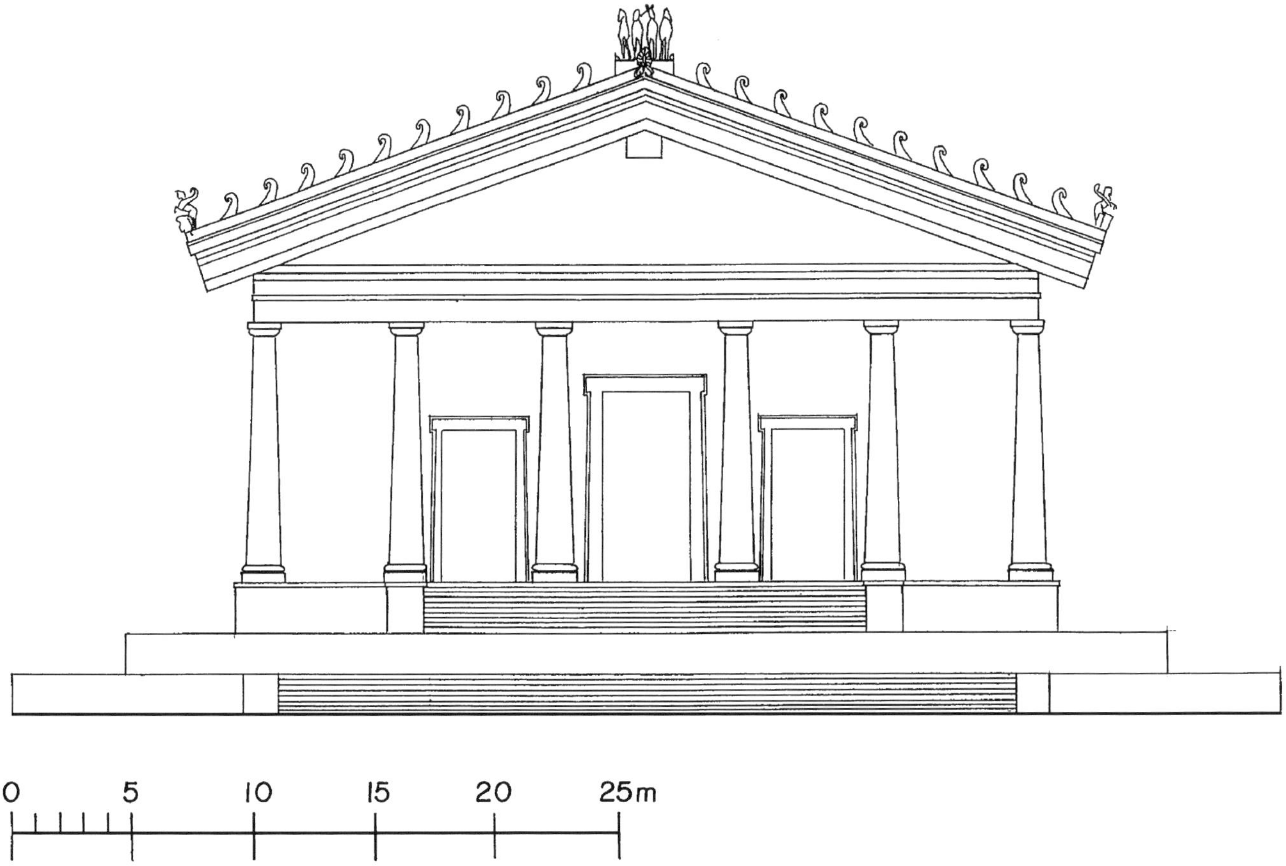

17. Temple of Jupiter Capitolinus, elevation of proposed reconstruction. Drawing: John W. Stamper.

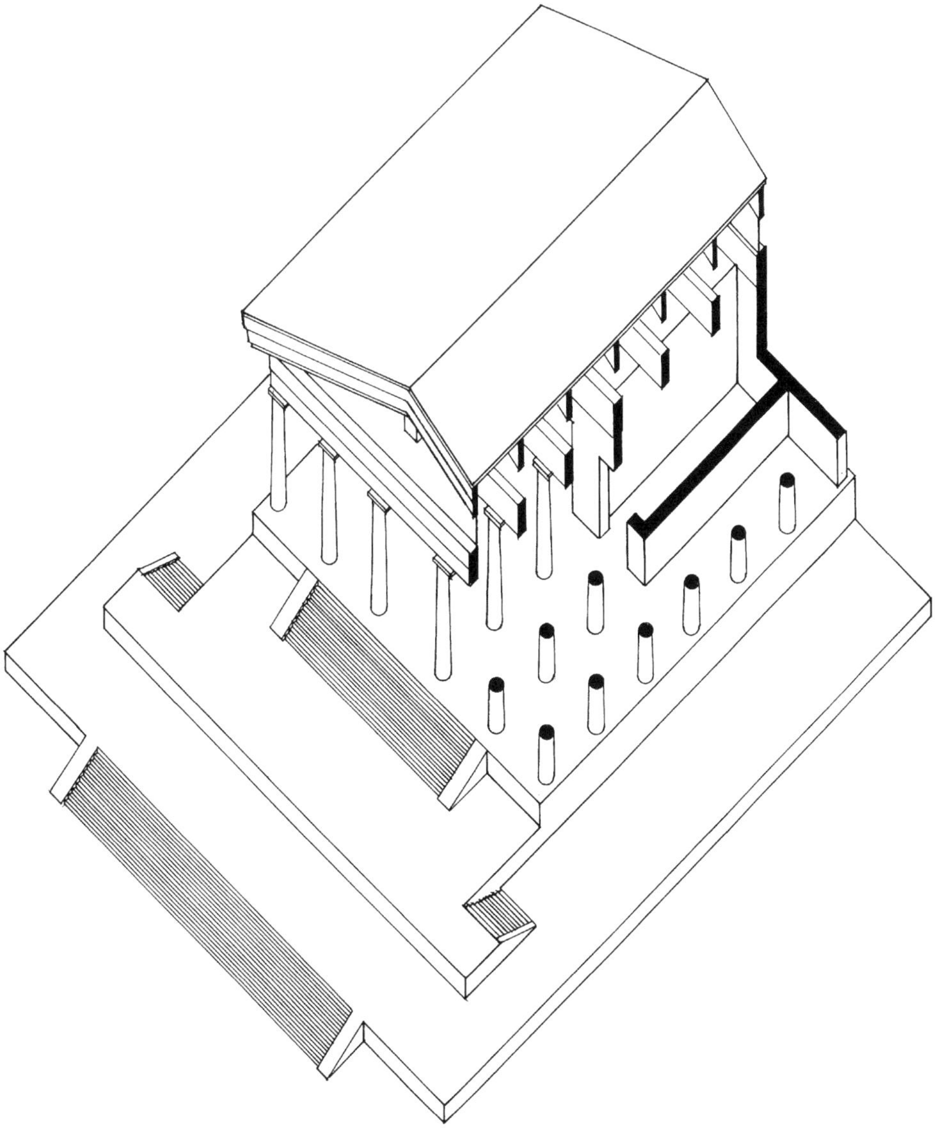

18. Temple of Jupiter Capitolinus, axonometric view of proposed reconstruction. Drawing: John W. Stamper.

including the Temple of Mars Ultor, the Templum Pacis, and the Pantheon, for instance, all of which were approximately 115 Roman feet wide.[34]

A broad flight of axially aligned stairs would have led from the podium floor down to an intermediate level, which would have served as a speakers' platform. From there, an arrangement of lateral stairs, perhaps like those of the later Temple of Venus Genetrix or the Temple of Divus Julius, would have led to the lowermost level, which alone would have corresponded to the 180 by 210 Roman feet described by Dionysius of Halicarnassus. Finally, there would have been a third flight of steps in the center of the lower platform leading to the ground level (Fig. 18).

The concept of a temple built on a large, terraced platform has many known examples from the Republic and Empire. It is enough to suggest a comparison to the Temple of Jupiter Anxur at Terracina from the first century B.C., the Temple of Hercules Victor at Tivoli (89–82 B.C.), or in Rome, the Temple of Claudius on the Caelian Hill (ca. 40–60 A.D.).[35] The overall platform in these cases would have corresponded to the *templum*, the sacred area for observing the auspices.[36] The temple itself was smaller and located at the rear of the sacred area.

The interaxial dimensions of the Capitoline Temple according to this reconstruction would have been 5.90 meters for the side bays and 7.40 meters for the

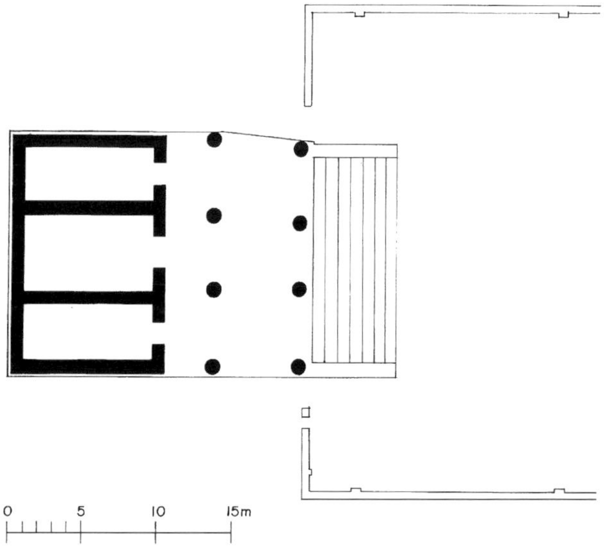

19. Orvieto, Belvedere Temple, 400s B.C., plan. Drawing: John W. Stamper after Sheila Gibson in Axel Boëthius, *Etruscan and Early Roman Architecture* (1978), p. 45, pl. 33.

center bay (20 and 25 Roman feet, respectively). Following Vitruvius's prescription, the columns would have been 1.47 meters (5 Roman feet) in diameter and 11.30 meters (38 Roman feet) high.

In this reconstruction, the Capitoline Temple still would have been the largest such building in the Etruscan world, and certainly the most important in political and religious terms. It would have been more within the realm of possibility at the time, however, for stone and post-and-lintel timber construction. It would have been in keeping with later Roman temples from the Republican period, and it would have corresponded almost exactly to several important temples from the imperial period, whose builders had ample reason to emulate it.

This reconstruction does not suggest a significant change to Gjerstad's temple plan itself. As he pointed out, the plan's exact details will never be known.[37] As such, there is no reason to suggest that his basic derivation of the plan is incorrect, only that it was smaller than he suggested. It represents well the influence of both Etruscan and Latin sources and traditions, especially the deep pronaos, three-room cella, lateral extensions of the rear wall, and terra-cotta decoration, all of which became highly influential for later temples in the Roman world.

The deep pronaos was a typical feature of most Etruscan temples, as seen, for instance, in the Belvedere Temple in Orvieto (Fig. 19), built in the early fifth century B.C. and rebuilt in the early fourth. Its podium, which is still visible, was divided evenly between a deep pronaos and three cella rooms and measured 16.93 meters wide by 21.91 meters deep, almost exactly half the size of the Temple of Jupiter Capitolinus as reconstructed here.[38] Axial symmetry was implied by the arrangement of a *templum* enclosed by walls in front of the building, a layout foreshadowing the imperial Roman fora.[39] Such a building represented the standard shape and size of most temples in the Etruscan world and is the type on which Vitruvius based his description.

The rear wall of the Capitoline Temple, which extended laterally beyond the corners of the cella in a *peripteros sine postico* fashion, was imitated by Roman builders until well into the Republic, as seen in Temple C in Largo Argentina and the Temple of Peace in Paestum, to name just two.[40] Variations of it are found in the Temples of Venus Genetrix and Mars Ultor. It is often assumed to have been common in Etruscan building practice; however, it is an arrangement that was found more predominantly in Latin temple structures like those in Ariccia, Satricum, Cascia, and Gabii.[41] Its earliest use was in the Temple of Mater Matuta I at Satricum (Fig. 20), which dates from around

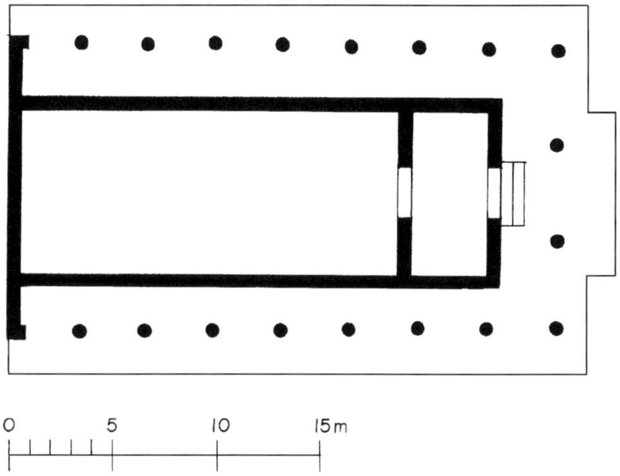

20. Satricum, Temple of Mater Matuta I, ca. 550 B.C., plan. Drawing: John W. Stamper based on Jos. A. DeWaele in *ArchLaz* 4 (1981), p. 313, fig. 3.

21. Figural frieze with processional scene, measuring about 1 Roman foot in length, sixth century B.C., terra-cotta, Palazzo Conservatori, Rome. Photo: Deutsches Archäologisches Institut, Rome, 10.993.

550 B.C., and may have been a model for the Capitoline Temple.[42]

A recent reconstruction of the Capitoline Temple, based on the excavations of the 1990s, suggests the temple's podium extended about 12 meters further to the northwest than previously believed and that there were two rooms immediately behind the cella. They would have been entered by access doors at the end of each side aisle.[43] Such an extension of the temple toward the northwest would have placed it precariously over the edge of the hill, however, and its dimensions would not have corresponded at all to the description provided by Dionysius of Halicarnassus. Also, there are no precedents or subsequent examples in Roman architecture of a temple plan type with five cella rooms.

The roof of the Capitoline Temple is typically represented in drawings and models as a gable roof with a pediment at the front and rear. Some scholars suggest it may have had a pediment only on the front, with a hipped roof at the back.[44] Some argue such a system was more appropriate to a *peripteros sine postico* plan.[45] It could have been either in the original building, although it no doubt had gables at both ends in its final reconstruction in the first century A.D.

The decoration of the Capitoline Temple included fictile revetments on the pediment, standing figures and acroteria on the roof, and a four-horse chariot at the peak of the gable. Gjerstad's reconstruction suggested that figural friezes on the horizontal and raking cornices were composed of repetitive scenes of soldiers and horse-drawn chariots.[46] Those in the horizontal cornices were shown walking, and those in the raking cornices were shown running (Figs. 21 and 22). An analysis of Gjerstad's reconstruction of this decoration reveals a further problem with his dimensions of the overall plan, however. He suggested that the individual panels of these revetments measured 6 to 7 Roman feet wide, but this is again something that was technologically impossible at the time. In fact, all of the existing fragments that can be used as comparative examples measure only 1 to 1.5 Roman feet (Fig. 23). There is no evidence whatsoever of terra-cotta panels 6 Roman feet long on this or any other Etruscan temple.[47] We have to consider also the size of the four-horse chariot on top of the temple, which in Gjerstad's reconstruction would have been about 3.6 meters high, a size virtually inconceivable in terra-cotta. At most, it would have been about half this size.

In summary, the reconstruction of the Temple of Jupiter Capitolinus proposed here differs from the previously accepted version in two important ways: its size and the character of its podium. The dimensions of the temple structure – which should be understood

22. Figural frieze with racing chariots as on the raking cornices of the Temple of Jupiter Capitolinus, sixth century B.C., terra-cotta, Antiquarium, Rome. Photo: Deutsches Archäologisches Institut, Rome, 941.

as a shrine on top of a terraced podium – were about 34 meters wide by 38.30 meters long. The dimensions of 53.50 by 62 meters, identified by Lanciani and Paribeni, were those of the lowest terrace level alone. Although the overall form of the temple in this reconstruction is similar to Gjerstad's, it is about one-third smaller in size, with interaxial dimensions of 5.90 and 7.40 meters rather than 9.50 and 12 meters. The module of its ornamental revetments was 1 to 1.5 Roman feet compared with Gjerstad's 6 to 7 Roman feet. Most importantly, the configuration of the platform is different, this one proposing a three-stepped composition with several sets of connecting stairs, a strong contrast to Gjerstad's single-level, quadrangular form.

Architecture, Politics, and Precedent

This proposed reconstruction, although diminishing the size of the Temple of Jupiter Capitolinus, is not intended to lessen its importance in the history of Rome's architectural development or social and religious life. Rather, it is to make it more apparent. A temple of smaller dimensions, comparable to the tradition of temple architecture that developed in the following centuries, makes it a far more convincing precedent or source of influence for that tradition. The authority of its deities was paralleled by the authority of the temple structure as a source for later architectural design.

Its importance was also derived from the superb nature of its setting. As the principal focus of a significant urban ensemble, the Temple of Jupiter Capitolinus was in many ways equal to the Parthenon in Athens. Like the Greek temple, the final version of which was built more than fifty years later, the Capitoline Temple was prominently placed on a rocky plateau in the center of the city; it loomed over its main commercial spaces – the Forum Romanum, Forum Holitorium, and Forum Boarium – and it served as the final destination of triumphal processions that wound their way along the Via Sacra, Rome's equivalent of the Panathenaic Way.

Power and its association with religious and mythic symbols permeate virtually every society.[48] Visual symbols, whether on currency, art, or architecture, often combine religion and the historical and mythic past to bolster the power and prestige of a given regime and to elicit powerful responses within the community it rules. The power of a symbol becomes especially significant when its normal status or traditional connotation is threatened with change, something that was especially true in republican and imperial Rome when regimes changed or religious belief was transformed.[49]

23. Temple of Jupiter Capitolinus, partial reconstruction of elevation with terra-cotta revetments shown in 18-inch modules. Drawing: John W. Stamper adapted from Einar Gjerstad, *Early Rome: Fortification, Domestic Architecture, Sanctuaries, Stratigraphic Excavations*, vol. 3 (1960), fig. 118.

As such, the power of the Temple of Jupiter Capitolinus as a symbol became especially significant in periods of change in Rome's political scene.

A society is held together by its internal agreement about the sacredness of certain fundamental symbols, of which the Capitoline Temple was among the most important. In an inchoate, dimly perceived manner, the central authority of a society is acknowledged to be the avenue of communication with the realm of sacred values.[50] Within Roman society, in its transition from an Etruscan monarchy to a republic, the Temple of Jupiter Capitolinus enjoyed almost universal recognition as the embodiment of cultural values, religious ceremony, and political authority. It heightened the moral and civic sensibility of Roman society, providing it with a symbol permeated with those values, ceremony, and authority. Successive rituals and ceremonies would repeatedly bring Roman society or sectors of it into contact with this sacred vessel of cultural and religious values, and its recalling of the city's founding.[51]

Because of its size, prominent location, political symbolism, and dedication to the important deities Jupiter, Juno, and Minerva, it is clear that the Temple of Jupiter Optimus Maximus had a significant influence on the design of subsequent temples in Rome and its surroundings during both the republican and imperial periods.[52] This fact lends to the study of Roman architecture a certain degree of unity that it has never before possessed. Rather than the city's earliest and most important temple being thought of as an isolated giant with no direct formal relationship to what came after, it should instead be considered in relation to the design of subsequent temples. Rather than being three times as large as all other known Etruscan temples, the reconstruction presented here suggests it was only twice as large; rather than being almost twice the size of the Temple of Mars Ultor or the Pantheon, it was virtually the same size. It was a building later architects directly emulated, transforming it from six columns across to eight, from *araeostyle* to *pycnostyle*, and from three cella rooms to one. It was the temple that possessed the most authority, the one most directly related to the city's founding. Its importance cannot be underestimated as a symbol of Rome's political and religious aspirations, its vision of grandeur and power.

3

ETRUSCO-ROMAN TEMPLES OF THE EARLY REPUBLIC

Temple construction in the early Republic was influenced by the architecture of the Capitoline Temple, although its great size and prominent location set it apart as a unique monument. All of the temple structures of the early Republic had a related plan type, but there was a great deal of experimentation and invention on the part of architects and builders as they sought to develop an identity that was unique to the Republic and its evolving set of social, political, and religious conditions. Nevertheless, there was a discernable style, quality of construction, and sense of proportion that linked the temple architecture of the early Republic to the Temple of Jupiter Capitolinus.

The characteristic features of the Capitoline Temple had been influenced by both the Etruscan and the Latin traditions. Its high podium, widely spaced columns, deep pronaos, and extensive terra-cotta decoration represented a synthesis of the two cultures. These features were all consistently repeated in the early years of the Republic, but they were tempered, adapted, and otherwise transformed by the Romans' changing needs, tastes, and building techniques. Successive generations of Etruscan and Latin craftsmen in Rome maintained their leading role of design and supervision in the building trades. Temples were built in variants of the Etruscan style, as were civic and market buildings, houses, and other service and domestic structures. Because it would be nearly two centuries before the dominant influence of Hellenistic architecture would make itself felt in Rome, the period of the early Republic – from about 509 B.C. until the start of the Punic Wars in the third century B.C. – can best be described as Etrusco-Roman in terms of both architectural production and character.

The Forum Romanum

At the moment Tarquinius Superbus was driven into exile in 509 B.C., Rome initiated a Republican form of government that was to last for the next five centuries, until the time of Julius Caesar and Augustus. The deposing of Tarquinius was also the city's first step in gaining independence from the Etruscan world, a move that began its long march to the conquest of all of central and southern Italy. As Rome grew and prospered, its increasingly adept military forces expanded their control over vast new territories, which eventually extended from Spain to the Middle East, and England to northern Africa.

The center of Rome's development at the beginning of the Republic was the Forum Romanum, sited in a valley between the Capitoline Hill, the Palatine, and the Velia.[1] The newly established Republic had inherited a small number of buildings and infrastructure in the Forum Romanum from the Etruscan monarchy, including early versions of the Regia, Temple of Vesta, Curia, and Comitium.[2] At the beginning of the Republic, the city encompassed an area that included the Capitoline, Palatine, and Quirinal hills, with the low-lying Forum Romanum at the center. Until then, the forum had been little more that a marshy crossroads with wooden market buildings and primitive houses dotting its irregular perimeter.[3]

The forum's usable area had been expanded and permanently secured with the construction of the Cloaca Maxima, a giant sewer, to carry water away from its lowest portions. This early drainage system was built by the Etruscan kings in the sixth century B.C., at about the same time as the erection of the Temple

of Jupiter Capitolinus.[4] The forum was probably paved for the first time in the 570s, also by the Etruscan kings, marking the beginning of a definable and unified area in the valley between the hilltop settlements.[5]

The Regia and the Temple of Vesta were located at the forum's east end, at the foot of the Palatine Hill. Their earliest history is linked to the original Latin and Sabine settlements on the Palatine and Quirinal Hills, serving as a sort of mediating point between the two. The Regia, or House of the Two Kings (although it was a temple, not a residence), was built by Numa Pompilius in ca. 700 B.C. and rebuilt several times thereafter, including at the end of the sixth century B.C., in the first years of the Republic.[6] It was built on a triangular site where the Via Sacra bifurcates as it enters the forum. It was at first linked to the cult of Vesta, but during the Republic it became the official headquarters of the *pontifex maximus*, and it contained the sacred spears and shields that the Salii carried in their processions. It also held the archives of the *pontifices*, and the tablets from which the *Annales Maximi* were compiled.[7] Its primary function was to house important religious rites, especially the Rex Sacrorum.[8]

The plan of the Regia was an irregular polygon, roughly triangular in outline. It consisted of two parts: a southern trapezoidal roofed area and a northern polygonal area open to the sky. The enclosed portion was divided into three rooms: the first with a raised circular hearth, the sacrum Martis, then a vestibule, and finally, a small chamber, the sacrarium Opis Consivae.[9] It underwent innumerable changes and rebuildings as required by successive regimes.

The small circular temple dedicated to the cult of Vesta, the goddess of the sacred fire, was first built in about 575 B.C. as a primitive wooden structure with a thatched roof.[10] It was destroyed and rebuilt in 390 B.C., probably in the Etrusco-Roman manner, with Tuscan columns and decorative terra-cotta revetments.[11] It was destroyed and rebuilt again several times between the third century B.C. and the early Empire.[12] There is evidence it was damaged and rebuilt after the fire of A.D. 64 and that Trajan rebuilt it early in the second century A.D. as part of his extensive public works projects.[13] It served as an urban focal point when approached from either the Palatine or Quirinal Hills or from the east on the Via Sacra.

The reconstructed portion of the temple that stands today in the forum is made up of fragments from a late imperial version of the building which were found on the site during excavations in 1877. Their placement in the rebuilt structure was based on images found on medals and bas-reliefs. We can be sure that from the very beginning the temple had a circular form.[14] The use of Corinthian columns and a domed roof in its later version represents a specific Hellenistic influence that did not appear until at least the second century A.D., however.[15]

The sacred fire housed inside the Temple of Vesta was traditionally rekindled once every year on the first day of March by rubbing two sticks together and placing the flame in a bronze sieve. A small enclosure within the sanctuary held sacred elements used in rituals, and it is reported to have held the statue of the goddess Pallas Athena that Aeneas had brought from Troy. The statue and other sacred objects were rescued and preserved each time the temple was rebuilt.[16]

The spirit of fire, Vesta, was thought by the Romans to dwell in the hearth; thus, it was an essential part of every household. There was a direct link between Vesta, the hearth of the city, and the hearths of individual families.[17] During the chief meal each day, a piece of sacred salted cake was thrown into the fire from a small sacrificial dish.[18] Vesta never became a fully personified goddess like other Roman deities, for there was no statue of Vesta in the building.[19] More important was her goodwill, which was needed because of the complication of rekindling the fire on those occasions when it went out. The Temple of Vesta was traditionally opened (only to women) from June 7 to 15, religious days when it was considered wrong to engage in any unnecessary labor.[20]

At the forum's opposite end, just below the Capitoline, stood the Curia Hostilia (Fig. 24), the first meeting house of the Senate.[21] It was built in ca. 600 B.C., for there was a Senate of sorts even during the Etruscan monarchy, and it had to establish an identity for itself as representing the people of Rome.[22] The building acted as a meeting place for discussion, religious rituals, and banquets.[23] It occupied a somewhat different site than the later Curia Julia, which still stands. It was several meters to the west of the Curia Julia, corresponding to the location of the Church of

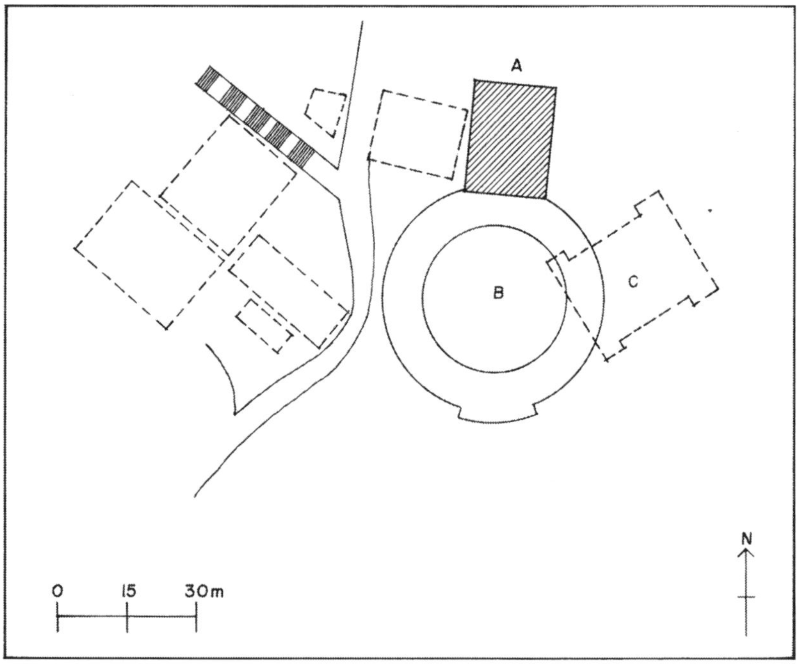

24. Rome, Curia Hostilia and Comitium, site plan, ca. 600 B.C.: (A) Curia Hostilia, (B) Comitium, (C) future location of Curia Julia. Drawing: John W. Stamper based on Filippo Coarelli, *Il Foro Romano*, vol. 1 (1983), p. 23, fig. 5.

SS. Luca and Martina. Large enough to hold 300 senators, it was rectangular in plan and topped by a gabled roof, in the Etrusco-Roman style. In front of it was the comitium, a series of steps, either circular or square in plan, where assemblies could gather to hear speeches and announcements, as well as to vote.[24]

The two earliest Etrusco-Roman temples in the forum were constructed at the beginning of the fifth century, within ten to twenty years of the dedication of the Temple of Jupiter Capitolinus. The Temple of Saturn, built in 501–498 B.C., was located at the forum's southwest corner, the Temple of Castor and Pollux, built in 484 B.C., at its southeast corner. Their construction in the forum suggests the extent to which it now played a significant role in the commercial, civic, and religious life of the Roman populace, becoming identified early on as the Republic's urban center and in need of its own cult temples distinct from those on the Capitoline and Palatine Hills.[25]

The Temple of Saturn, referring to the agricultural god of sowing and corn, a staple in Rome's food production, was initiated by Tarquinius Superbus, but like the Temple of Capitoline Jupiter, its dedication occurred only in the early Republic. The name of the dictator at the time, T. Larcius, may have been inscribed on the building.[26]

The temple faced northeast and was situated between the Clivus Capitolinus and the Vicus Jugarius on the east.[27] In its earliest form, it may have been based on the Temple of Jupiter Capitolinus, but at a smaller scale (Fig. 25). Although its exact dimensions at that time are not known, it must have ranged between 15 to 20 meters wide. It had a characteristic deep portico, a

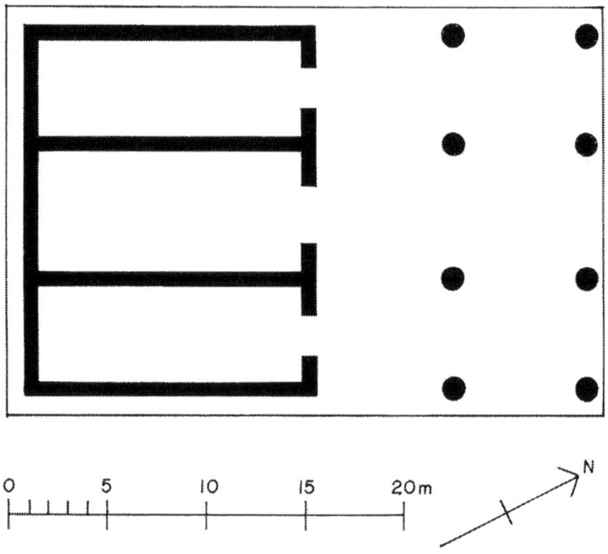

25. Rome, Temple of Saturn, 498 B.C., plan. Drawing: John W. Stamper.

cella divided into three rooms, a gabled roof with wide overhangs, and a long flight of stairs in front.[28] It also contained the city's treasury in well-protected rooms within its high podium. Here were kept the treasures and archives of the state, as well as the balance used for the weighing of precious metals.[29]

Because Rome's economy was based on agricultural production, such a temple dedicated to the cycle of the seasons and the growing and harvesting of crops was important. The notion of divine embodiment in the seasonal death and rebirth was essential to the agrarian culture, a tradition that related to Demeter in the Greek world, the primary divinity associated with crops.[30] A statue of Saturn that stood inside the cella was wrapped with woolen bonds which were undone on the day of the feast, December 17, an event that included a ceremonial sacrifice, with senators and knights dressed in togas, and a banquet that ended with the chant "Io Saturnalia." Like the feast day of Jupiter, it was a day of festive gaiety, with shops, schools, and lawcourts closed, an event that became a yearly holiday.[31] Ceremony, festivity, honor, and gaiety all became distinguishing features of the events surrounding the cult temples. Although none matched the importance of the events associated with the cult of Jupiter, they nevertheless imitated their style and intensity of spirit, becoming a defining characteristic of Roman culture.

Like the Temple of Saturn, that of Castor and Pollux faced northward onto the Via Sacra, in this case, very near the Temple of Vesta. It was begun by Aulus Postumius Albinus shortly after 496 B.C. and completed by his son in 484 B.C.[32] The twin gods Castor and Pollux, the Greek Dioscuri and sons of Zeus and Leda, were horsemen who were believed to have helped the Romans magically in the victorious battle at Lake Regillus in 496 B.C.[33] They were thought to have lived half of their time on earth and half in heaven and had been worshipped in Tusculum since early times.[34] After Rome defeated Tusculum, it adopted Castor and Pollux as the patrons of its cavalry, or the knights of Rome. They were often depicted with their horses, riding from Regillus to Rome with news of the battle. Called simply *Castores* and their temple the *aedes Castoris*, they came to be widely worshipped in Italy as savior gods.[35] Their adoption by the Romans was typical of the borrowing characteristic of their religious practice, transferring to themselves the power

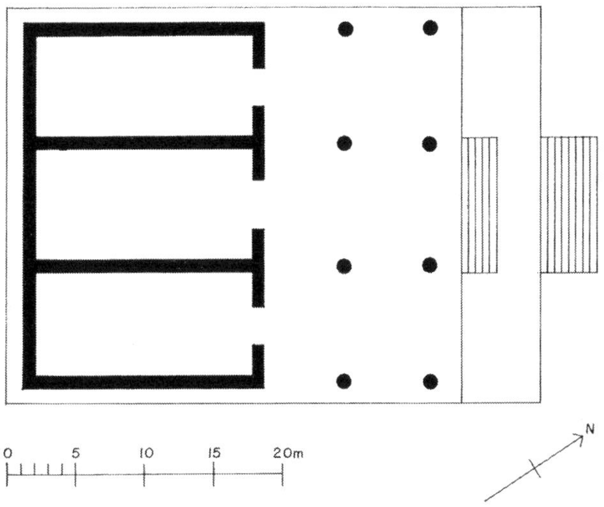

26. Rome, Temple of Castor and Pollux, 484 B.C., plan. Drawing: John W. Stamper adapted from Tenney Frank, in *MAAR* 5 (1925), fig. 2.

and the following of the divinities of defeated cities or states.[36]

The original Temple of Castor and Pollux was again in the Etrusco-Roman style with similarities to the Temple of Jupiter Capitolinus, but it certainly was not a copy. Its pronaos had four columns across and it probably had a three-room cella.[37] There have been several reconstructions proposed for the first Temple of Castor and Pollux, most of them suggesting a relatively small building measuring 16.20 meters wide by about 21.60 meters long (55 by 73 Roman feet), about half the size of the Capitoline Temple.[38]

In contrast, recent excavations of the building's perimeter foundation walls prove the original temple was much larger, its dimensions nearly corresponding to the final version from the time of Augustus and Tiberius, which is represented by the three great Corinthian columns visible on the site today.[39] Now it is believed the first temple was 27.50 meters wide by about 37 meters long (93 by 125 Roman feet), about two-thirds the size of the Capitoline Temple as it is reconstructed in this book.[40]

The earliest foundation walls were laid out in a grid, which allowed for a temple plan of four columns across the front, and the cella divided into three rooms (Fig. 26). The interaxial spans of the pronaos columns would have been about 7.50 meters, just slightly larger than the central span of the Temple of Jupiter

Capitolinus as reconstructed in this study. The pronaos was either three or two bays deep. The front row of columns either stood near the edge of the podium or back one bay from the front. In the latter case, the podium would have extended out from the facade, possibly at a lower level, providing a terraced effect similar to that of the Temple of Jupiter Capitolinus.[41] With some repairs and modifications, this temple stood until it was rebuilt in 117 B.C.[42]

Because the Temple of Castor and Pollux was prominently located and was large enough to hold a gathering of people, it was used for both religious and political purposes. The two consuls made it their headquarters, convening some assemblies and conducting official business on its podium facing the forum.[43] The feast day of Castor and Pollux occurred on July 15, a day in which the temple was the main focus of a ceremonial parade of the *equites*, commemorating the battle at Lake Regillus. Roman knights, crowned with olive branches and wearing purple robes with stripes of scarlet, began their procession from a temple outside the city that was dedicated to Mars. They passed through the Forum Romanum and up to the temple's podium where they were reviewed by the censors. As each man advanced individually, he was either approved to continue service or discharged. After a lapse in tradition during the time of Sulla, the ceremony was revived by Augustus and continued to be celebrated throughout the course of the Empire.[44] The temple would assume further functions as time went on, especially by the second century B.C., when it would accommodate meetings of the Senate and its podium would serve as a voting site of the *comitia*.[45]

Now the site of two Etrusco-Roman cult temples, plus the Temple of Vesta, the Regia, curia, and several commercial structures, the forum was a discernable city center, a focal point for trade, politics, and religion. The many buildings around it provided boundaries and the points of access took on topographical importance.[46] Its architectural setting foreshadowed its future importance as the center of an ever-expanding world.

The Politics and Authority of Building

The construction of temples during the early Republic went hand in hand with the expansion of Rome's sphere of influence. The development of Rome's broad-ranging empire began on a small scale with a series of battles against its immediate neighbors, both Etruscan and Latin, then gradually expanded across the entire Italian peninsula.[47] The first was the battle fought at Lake Regillus in 496 B.C., in which Rome's infantry quelled a Latin uprising. Other skirmishes followed in the middle and late fifth century B.C., first against the Aequi, then the Volsci, the Sabines, and the nearby city of Veii, the latter being captured in 396 B.C. by the Roman general M. Furius Camillus.[48] His military success secured new territory for the Romans and gave them control of the Tiber north of the city, which increased their economic security and defensive position. He also repelled an invasion of Gauls, who marched down the Italian peninsula in 390–89 B.C. and killed up to 15,000 Roman soldiers while burning many of Rome's houses and temples before being stopped.[49]

While Rome recovered, the psychological impact of the invasion on its inhabitants was great and explains in part the reason for Rome's increased militarization, warfare with its neighbors, and general expansionist tendencies.[50] A new defensive wall was built around the city in 378 B.C. to protect it against future invasions.[51] During the period of rebuilding and increased security, Rome's population and economic activity expanded greatly, and new colonies were established in the regions north and south of the city, to provide both military garrisons and sites for the resettlement of its growing population.

From the beginning of the Republic, political control of Rome was in the hands of a pair of consuls who served as the chief civil and military officers, presiding over the Senate and leading the armies in war.[52] The Senate, or council of elders, was composed of 100 members, mostly from aristocratic families. Its members were called *patres*, fathers, who were generally the heads of clans or *gentes*.[53] In addition, there was the Popular Assembly, the *comitia centuriata*, which was responsible for enacting laws, electing consuls and praetors, declaring war, and conducting trials.[54] By the end of the third century B.C., some of the responsibility for legislative proposals was transferred to a series of tribal assemblies, the *comitia tributa* and the *concilium plebis*.[55]

Control of Rome's urban development was shifted from the kings to the censors, who were members of the Senate charged with the responsibility of maintaining the city's finances and deciding on state contracts for building and public works projects. Although

the censors' primary job was the taking of the census and determining who was eligible to be a member of the Senate, they were also involved with many of the city's day-to-day operations, and they controlled the treasury.[56] They assumed the responsibility for signing leases for public land, granting water rights, and constructing and maintaining public buildings, roads, and sewers.[57]

Throughout the Republic, all public building projects, including most temples, were contracted out by censors or other magistrates. It was the responsibility of the censor or magistrate to see that the work on a building was done in a satisfactory way. They made down payments for the cost of the work to be done, and the contractor (*redemptore*) had to provide assurance and securities to guarantee the fulfillment of his obligations. Small temples could be constructed by a single contractor, whereas larger temples were usually the work of several.[58]

The money to build the temples came primarily from the senators, aristocrats, and generals whose wealth was tied not just to land ownership and agriculture, but to military conquest. The standing of the landed class in society was based on both the military prowess of the household heads and on their contribution to the city's civic well-being. The political ethos and value system of the Roman aristocracy was focused entirely on achievement in political and military leadership – *gloria* and *dignitas* – which could only be attained through distinguished public service, especially leading armies in war. As rival leaders sought to prove themselves and establish their authority, they often sought out opportunities for war, risky adventures, and exploitation of foreign lands. Among the middle and lower classes, there was, if not outright support for their authority, certainly no strong resistance to such policies for attaining it.[59]

The accumulation of wealth made it possible for members of the aristocracy to undertake substantial building projects in Rome. Working with and through the censors, the household heads carried out innumerable *munia* as part of their general responsibility to the state for furnishing contributions and rendering service. They paid for their *munia* through a combination of spoils of war, port duties, pasture tribute, and quotas of produce from their farms.[60]

Whereas ultimate control over the building and dedicating of temples was in the hands of censors, generals, and magistrates, the administrative authority of Rome's religious system was in the hands of the priests and their organizations, the "colleges." During the early Republic, there were several colleges: the pontifs (*pontifices*), the augurs (*augures*), and the men for sacred action (the *duoviri*), later increased to ten (the *decemviri*). To these can be added a fourth, the fetials (*fetiales*). Members of these colleges, who typically held office for life, were drawn from the ranks of the ruling oligarchy. They were regularly consulted as experts by the consuls and the Senate. The *pontifices* had a recognized leader, the *pontifex maximus*, at first appointed by his colleagues but, after the third century B.C., elected publicly.[61]

As described in relation to the Temple of Jupiter Capitolinus, the augurs were called on at important times to interpret the will of the gods. The most common of their techniques was the observation of natural phenomena such as the flight of birds, thunder and lightning, and the behavior of certain animals.[62] The actual observation was done by a consul, general, or a senator. It was the augur's job to interpret what he saw. Observations were made in the context of the *templum*, whose left, right, front, and back sides were defined in relation to a rectangular viewing area in the heavens. The priest or augur would stand facing south and note the qualities of the thunder and lightning, the type and number of birds, the direction of their flight, and their position in the sky.[63] The expertise of the augurs involved both the interpretation of signs and the demarcation of religious space and its boundaries.[64]

Every official public action vested with religious authority took place within a particular space and was held according to prescribed rituals that were ruled on by the augurs. The situating of temples, as well as the passing of laws, the holding of elections, and meetings of the Senate and the assemblies, all occurred in spaces that were ritually analyzed by the augurs.[65] Before the meeting of an assembly, for instance, the presiding officer typically went to the site of the assembly between midnight and dawn, carefully taking the auspices along the way.[66] The meeting would be held the next day only if all of the signs were positive.

Although there was an extensive system of priestly organizations and no significant public act or event could occur without the aid of the priests, the actual initiative and control of religious events was held by the consuls and the senators. These leaders consulted

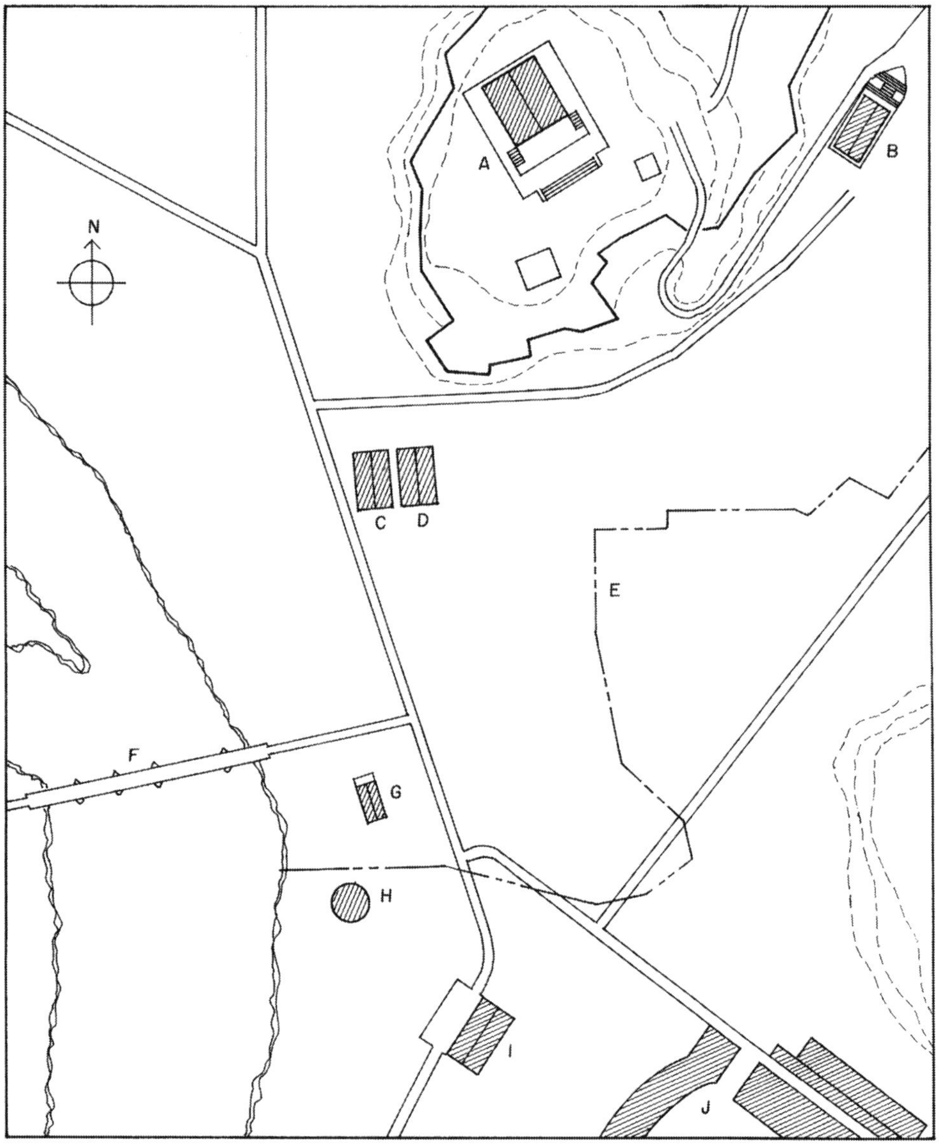

27. Rome, Forum Boarium, plan, ca. 350 B.C.: (A) Temple of Jupiter Capitolinus, (B) Temple of Saturn, (C) Temple of Fortuna, (D) Temple of Mater Matuta, (E) Cloaca Maxima, (F) Ponte Aemilius, (G) Temple of Portunus, (H) Round Temple by the Tiber, (I) Statio Annonae, (J) Circus Maximus. Drawing: John W. Stamper after Rodolfo Lanciani, *Forma Urbis Romae* (1990), pl. 28.

the gods, dedicated temples, made vows, and presided over sacrifices, but they always did so in conjunction with the counsel of priests and the augurs. It was the priests' responsibility to dictate or prescribe the prayers and formulas, to advise on the interpretation of the auspices, and to comment on procedures. Although they lacked power of action, they were nevertheless accepted as supreme authorities on sacred law.[67]

Temples of Fortuna and Mater Matuta in the Forum Boarium

Other areas of the city in addition to the Forum Romanum were developed during the early Republic, especially the Forum Boarium and the Largo Argentina. Since the founding of Rome, the Forum Boarium, which lay southwest of the Capitoline Hill in the low-lying area between the Forum Romanum and the Tiber River (Fig. 27), provided access to the river and served as the bridgehead for the Pons Sublicius and the Pons Aemilius.[68] Rome's main river port, it had the function of a market for the trade of agricultural goods and livestock. It also served as a gateway to the city, or port of entry, for outside visitors and immigrants.

Like the Forum Romanum, the Forum Boarium had sacred zones interspersed within its market area. Most notable was the precinct of the twin temples of Fortuna and Mater Matuta, located at the foot of the Capitoline Hill, adjacent to the present-day Church

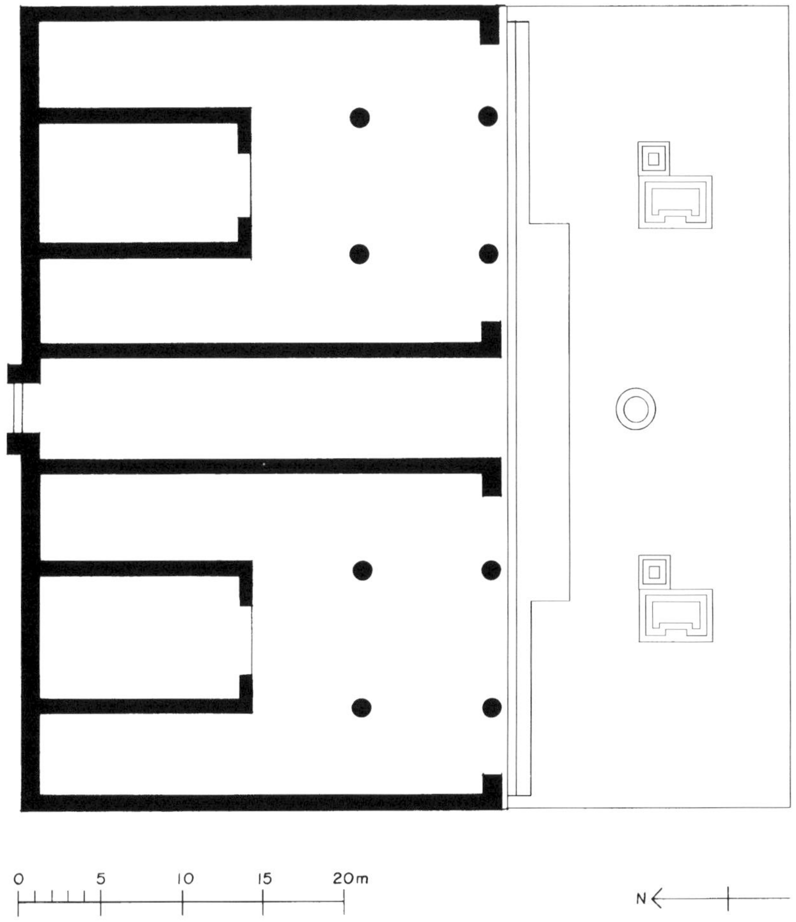

28. Rome, Temples of Mater Matuta (top) and Fortuna (bottom), ca. 396 B.C., elevation and plan. Drawing of elevation: John W. Stamper after Giovanni Ioppolo in *RendPontAcc* 44 (1971–1972): fig. 9; Drawing of plan: John W. Stamper after Giovanni Ioppolo in Filippo Coarelli, *Il Foro Boario: dalle origini alla fine della Repubblica* (1992), fig. 32.

of Sant' Omobono.[69] According to legend, both temples were established by King Servius Tullius in the sixth century B.C.[70] The remains of only one temple from this earliest period have been found, however, probably that of Mater Matuta. Located southeast of Sant' Omobono, it was a small square structure, measuring 10.60 meters on a side. Its original construction may date from as early as 580 B.C., well before Servius Tullius.[71] In the 530s B.C., corresponding to Servius's reign, it was rebuilt on a larger plan.[72] Its podium was enlarged and extended toward the south such that it now measured 11.20 by 13.20 meters. It was richly decorated with terra-cotta ornamentation, including images of Hercules, Athena, Eos, and Keflos.[73] The temple was destroyed by fire at the end of the sixth century B.C., about the time the Tarquins were driven out of Rome.[74]

The remains of the fire-damaged temple, including some of its terra-cotta revetments, were dismantled and scattered around the site in preparation for a new construction phase.[75] Earth and rubble were added to the site to raise it about 5 meters above the original

building. A new podium of peperino in *opus quadratum* was built with much larger dimensions, 47 meters on the sides, and oriented in a more southerly direction. Two identical temples were built on the podium – one dedicated to Mater Matuta on the east, the other, on the west, to Fortuna (Fig. 28). Some ascribe this initial construction of the twin temples to the 490s B.C., at the beginning of the Republic; others suggest they were built in 396 B.C. by M. Furius Camillus after his seige of Veii.[76]

Each temple was raised above the podium on a cubical base, each had a three-bay composition, and each had a deep pronaos enclosed by side walls that framed two columns in antis.[77] Each temple measured about 21 meters wide by 30 meters long (71 by 102 Roman feet) and had an interaxial dimension in the center bay of about 7.50 meters (25 Roman feet), the maximum possible at the time.

Such a plan arrangement, different from that of the Temple of Jupiter Capitolinus because of its enclosing side walls, can be compared with a reconstruction of the Portonaccio Temple at Veii (Fig. 29), built originally in ca. 530 B.C. and then rebuilt after the Roman takeover by M. Furius Camillus.[78] Measuring 18.6 meters square, its cella was divided into three rooms and its pronaos had two columns in antis, the side walls again extending from front to back.[79] The entire structure was covered by a low-pitched wooden roof sheathed with terra-cotta tiles, and its ridge was ornamented with terra-cotta statues of gods and goddesses, which are now housed in the Villa Giulia Museum in Rome.[80] This plan type can be further traced to Greek *in antis* temples and treasuries such as the Athenian Treasury in Delphi and others found at Paestum, Olympia, and Selinus. The *in antis* plan type was, in fact, so common in the Greek world that the Etruscans and Romans must have been aware of it and adapted it in their temple design.[81]

Of the two temples in the Forum Boarium, the Temple of Fortuna is thought to have contained an archaic statue of gilded wood draped by two togas that survived another fire in 213 B.C.[82] Some have identified it as a statue of Servius Tullius because the robes had belonged to him, and he was himself a legendary child of Fortuna. Pliny and Varro, however, suggest it was a statue of Fortuna, the goddess of the happy outcome.[83] Fortuna was someone frequently represented holding

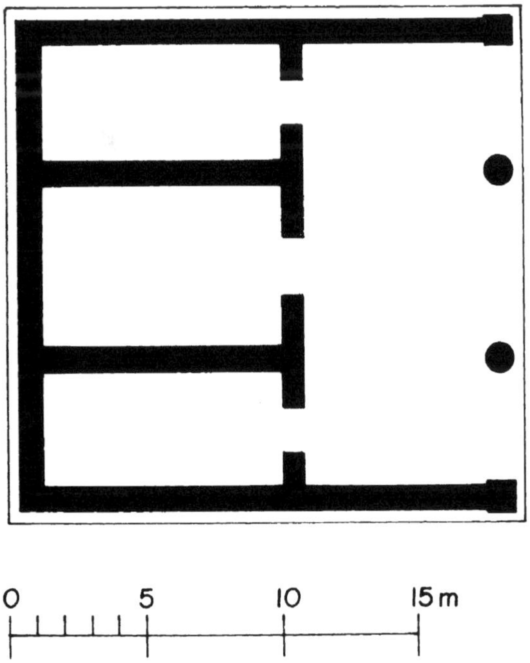

29. Veii, Portonaccio Temple, elevation and plan, 400s B.C. Drawing: John W. Stamper adapted from Arvid Andrén, *Architectural Terracottas from Etrusco-Italic Temples*, vol. 1 (1940), fig. 76; and Michael Rowe, *Etruscan Temples: A Study of the Structural Remains, Origins and Developments* (1989), fig. 14.

babies and children, and she was revered by mothers as granting numerous offspring. Craftsmen and traders paid honor to her in hope of success in their trade or business.[84]

The Temple of Mater Matuta represented the goddess of Dawn, who protected children as they grew to

Table 3.1. Comparative Sizes of Etrusco-Roman Temples of the Sixth to the Third Centuries B.C. (Podium Size, Column Diameter, and Interaxial Dimension)

		Podium		*Columns*	
City	*Temple*	*Width (m)*	*Length (m)*	*Diameter (m)*	*Interaxial (m)*
Rome	Cap. Jup. (Gjerstad)	53.50	62.20	2.35	9.50 12.00 center
	" (Stamper)	34.0	38.30	1.47	5.90 7.40 center
Rome	Saturn	[15–20]	–	–	–
Rome	Castor and Pollux I	27.50	37.0	–	7.50
Rome	Mater Matuta	21.0	30.0	–	7.50
Rome	Fortuna	21.0	30.0	–	7.50
Rome	Temple C, Largo Argentina	17.10	30.50	.70	4.45
Veii	Portonaccio	18.60	18.60	.88	5.30 6.19 center
Orvieto	Belvedere	16.93	21.88	.97	6.19
Paestum	Peace	21.20	30.0	1.80	6.20 front
Cosa	Jupiter	23.0	41.50	1.50	6.50

Source: For the dimensions of Etruscan temples, see Inge Nielsen and Birte Poulsen, *The Temple of Castor and Pollux I* (Rome: Edizione de Luca, 1992); and Patrick Michael Rowe, *Etruscan Temples: A Study of the Structural Remains, Origins, and Development* (Ph.D. diss., Florida State University, 1989).

Note: All podium dimensions of the Roman temples indicated in this book are for the top of the podium as opposed to the base or ground level. Cap. Jup. = Jupiter Capitolinus.

maturity. Her feast day, the Matralia, was celebrated each year on June 11, by Roman wives at the temple, where prayers were recited for growing children. The goddess also received toasted cakes, and on her feast day a slave woman was ceremoniously led into the temple and then driven out again, recounting the legend that the deity's Greek counterpart, Ino, had a slave who was having an affair with her husband, Athamas. The slave accused Ino of distributing toasted seed-corn to the people so that the seeds would not grow. Mater Matuta thus hated slave women, and the ritual reenactment of driving the slave from the temple was an appeasement of her prejudice.[85]

The two temples were reconstructed immediately after the fire of 213 B.C., the project directed by a special commission of three magistrates. The base of the sanctuary was restored with Grotto Oscura blocks, and its pavement was of Montiverdi tufa. The temples' walls were made of Fidense tufa. In 196 B.C., L. Stertinius built in front of the temples two arches adorned with gilded statues.[86]

The site of the Temples of Fortuna and Mater Matuta is visible today in the large, open archaeological zone south of Sant' Omobono. The foundations of the Temple of Fortuna are visible, whereas those of the Temple of Mater Matuta are incorporated into the basement walls of Sant' Omobono. Although the history of the site goes back to the time of Servius Tullius, just before the construction of the Temple of Jupiter Capitolinus, the principal temples for which it is known date primarily from the time of M. Furius Camillus in the fourth century B.C. They were identifiably Etruscan and Latin in inspiration, but their enclosed pronaos, a plan feature that also may have characterized the first Temple of Mater Matuta from 580 B.C., suggests there were special requirements of the priests for the cult ceremonies. This plan type did not necessarily become a dominant trend, only an alternative type for temple design.

As for their size, the temples' width of 21 meters made them about two-thirds the size of the Capitoline Temple as it is reconstructed in this study. This was

large in comparison with other Etrusco-Roman temples, and the 7.50-meter interaxial dimension of their central spans was the maximum possible for the available means of construction. As indicated in Table 3.1, many Etrusco-Roman temples were less than 20 meters wide, about 17 meters being the average. This is significant because 17 meters is exactly half the width of the Capitoline Temple. A general rule can be suggested, therefore, that many of the Etrusco-Roman temples of the early Republic were about one-half the size of the Temple of Jupiter Capitolinus, as it is reconstructed in this book. Those that were larger, as in the case of the temples of Fortuna and Mater Matuta, were about two-thirds the size.

The Rectangular Temples of Largo Argentina

The sacred area known as the Largo Argentina (Fig. 30) evolved into a religious complex beginning in the third century B.C. This site was located away from the main forum areas, west of the Capitoline Hill in the southern part of the Campus Martius. The significance of this site in the history of Rome's early development lies in the fact that it demonstrates the way new places for cult worship were established in various areas around the city as complements to the principal sites on the Capitoline Hill and Forum Romanum. The Largo Argentina may have marked the beginning of many triumphal processions, the temples' construction being the result of offerings from successful generals.[87]

When the first temples were built, the site was little more than an open field. By the beginning of the Empire, however, the area around it had become heavily built up with the Baths of Agrippa on the north, buildings around the Circus Flaminius on the south, the Theater of Pompey and its portico on the west, and the colonnaded Portico Minucia Frumentaria on the east.

For many years after their discovery, the four Republican temples did not have any proven attribution. They were named by archaeologists Temples A, B, C, and D from north to south, respectively. More recently, however, attributions have been proposed for each temple: Temple A, Juturna; Temple B; Fortuna Huiusce Diei; Temple C, Feronia; Temple D, Lares Permarini.

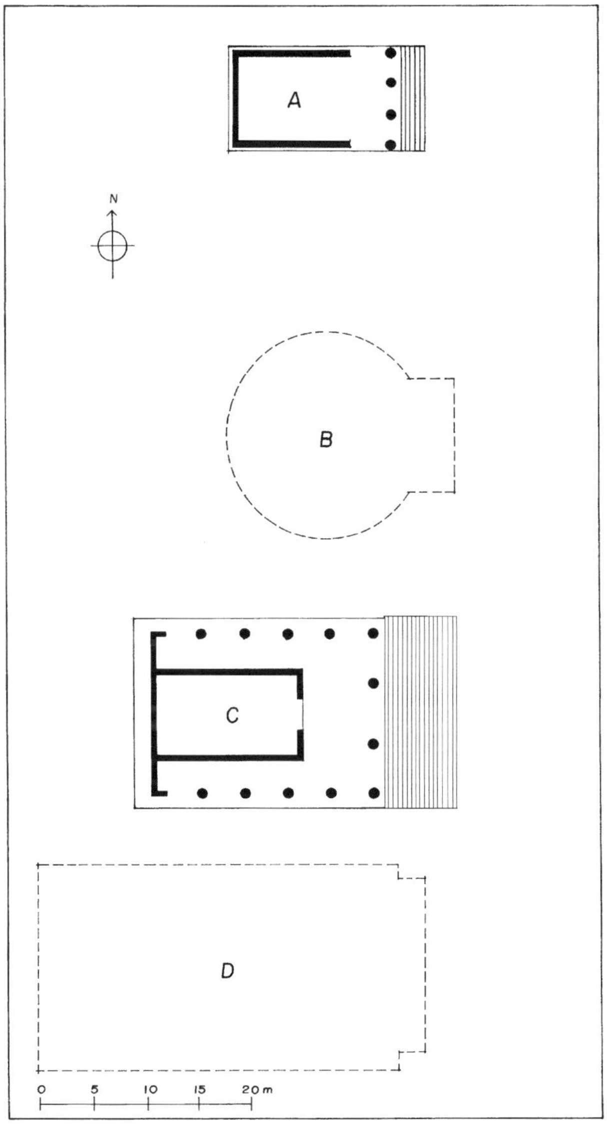

30. Rome, Largo Argentina, in the third century B.C., site plan with Temples A and C. Drawing: John W. Stamper based on G. Marchetti-Longhi, in *BullCom* 82 (1970–1971), pl. 1.

The oldest of the four is Temple C, Feronia, the second from the left when facing the site (Fig. 31). The first version of this temple is thought to have been built in ca. 290 B.C. by Manius Curius Dentatus after a victory over the Sabines.[88] Curius Dentatus was also responsible for building Rome's second aqueduct, the Anio Vetus, which was four times longer than the earlier Aqua Appia and carried twice as much water.[89] The conquest of the Sabines and the opening of the aqueduct would be consistent with the introduction of Feronia, which originated among the Sabines, and which was a divinity of agriculture. It is also significant

31. Largo Argentina, Temple C, view of podium. Photo: John W. Stamper.

that there are a number of fountains near the temple, suggesting the connection to the source of water. There were, in fact, at least five temples in the Campus Martius related to divinities associated with water.[90]

The Temple of Feronia stood on a high podium of Grotta Oscura, Fidene, and Aniene tufa in *opus quadratum*. It measured 17.10 by 30.50 meters (58 by 104 Roman feet) and was *peripteros sine postico* with four columns on the front and five on the sides. The intercolumniations on the sides were 3.16 meters, and those on the front were 3.75 meters.[91] The columns supported a pediment and gable roof covered with fictile revetments of terra-cotta.

The podium was originally 4.25 meters high, but the pavement around it was raised in about 100 B.C., dramatically changing its proportions. It had moldings at the top and bottom, and it was faced with stucco to give it the finished appearance of marble. On the front was a broad flight of stairs, giving emphasis to the building's facade and the axiality of approach. An altar, which is still visible today, was located in the center of the platform, both in its original version and in a later rebuilding.[92]

The original columns were Tuscan Doric, whereas the final ones were Corinthian. The Aniene tufa shafts are from the original columns, but in a restoration by Domitian in A.D. 80, they were fitted with new bases and capitals. Three of the bases remain, two on the south side and one on the north. Further evidence of Domitian's remodeling include a mosaic floor and the remains of the cella walls.[93]

The first version of Temple A, Juturna, the northernmost of the four, was built by Lutatius Catulus in 242–41 B.C.[94] Like the Temple of Feronia, the divinity of this temple was related to water. There was a naval triumph celebrated by Gaius in 242 B.C., and it is known that during the Republic the Campus Martius was the place from which the Roman navy departed for battle. The temple also constituted the central sanctuary of the office of Rome's water officials, the *Statio aquarum*. There was a strong connection beween the office and the divinity, and it was appropriate that the office and the temple should be near each other.[95] The foundations of a rectangular building between Temples A and B can probably be identified with the *Statio aquarum*.[96]

The first version of the Temple of Juturna was a small shrine, again on a high platform of squared Grotta Oscura blocks. This temple had a shallow pronaos, with four columns across, and a single cella, rectangular in plan, measuring 9.50 by 16 meters (32 by 54 Roman feet). Like Temple C, it would have been decorated with fictile revetments on a low-pitched gable roof with widely overhanging eaves. A long flight of stairs, with possibly as many as eighteen steps, extended across

its width and connected it to a low platform with an altar in the center.[97]

The temple was altered sometime in the mid–second century B.C. by the addition of a top layer of tufa blocks to its podium, along with base and crown moldings. Later still, probably in the first century B.C., it was transformed by the addition of a peristyle of Aniene tufa columns with Corinthian capitals, six on the front and nine on the sides.[98]

The third temple constructed on the site was Temple D, Lares Permarini. It was voted by the praetor Lucius Aemilius Regillus in the course of a naval battle against Antiochus III in 190 B.C. and was dedicated by the censor Marcus Aemilius Lepidus in 179 B.C. The Lares Permarini were divinities that protected mariners.[99] Today, the temple is partially buried under Via Florida at the site's southern end.

As indicated in these brief descriptions, the Largo Argentina was a site that was under almost constant construction, repair, and rebuilding. Its location in the Campus Martius certainly lent it a military association as a place for worship and sacrifice for generations of military leaders, praying for victory and offering thanks for their success. It would take on its final form in the first century B.C. with the construction of the circular Temple B, Fortuna Huiusce Diei.[100]

Rome's Conquest of the Italian Peninsula

By the end of the fourth century B.C., Rome was developed in many of its most important aspects – its commercial centers, religious zones, residential quarters, service areas, harbors, and warehouses. It was a working-class city, although the number and size of its Etrusco-Roman cult temples – especially the Temple of Jupiter Capitolinus – lent it an air of monumentality that distinguished it from its neighbors and suggested its aspirations of power and economic superiority. As explicit signs and symbols, these temples were integrally linked to the authority and legitimacy of Rome's governing class – first the Etruscans and then the magistrates of the Republic. Like every triumphal procession, public speech, and spectacle, they greatly contributed to the government's authority, making it more visible and understandable to the Roman population and, in each case, recalling the sacredness of the city's foundation.

The period of the mid-Republic – the third and second centuries B.C. – was a time when Rome's territorial control was extended throughout the Italian peninsula and into Greek Sicily as well as the Greek mainland. Beginning in the 330s B.C., Rome sent out troops against the Samnites of central and southern Italy, fighting a series of battles that allowed it to extend its control southward along the coast. Within thirty years, the Romans dominated the Campania, including Naples, although remnants of the Samnite civilization continued to fight against them for several decades. These pockets of resistance formed a loosely allied federation with tribes of Gauls, Umbrians, and Etruscans scattered around northern and central Italy, and although they attempted several attacks, the Romans successfully subdued them by the 290s B.C.[101]

Continuing southward, the Romans took Paestum in 273 B.C., and they moved into the regions of Puglia and Calabria.[102] The long history of fighting for land and booty, which was evident among nearly all city-states, did not always lead to large-scale expansion and imperialism. In the case of Rome, however, especially in the period of expansion from the Samnite to the Punic Wars, it clearly did.[103] Rome's particular brand of imperialism engaged in near continuous warfare and territorial expansion with the purpose of subjecting the defeated populations permanently to its rule or will. This is the very definition of empire-building and exploitation.[104]

The political organism in Rome supporting the expansionist effort remained the same throughout most of the process: rule by an aristocracy controlling the Senate and assemblies. Also during much of this period, the power of the city-state was based on a system of alliances that it manipulated autocratically.[105] Typically, these alliances were established after a military victory. The enemy's unconditional surrender was demanded, and the terms of peace were dictated. Although Rome granted varying degrees of autonomy to the defeated, it frequently annexed a substantial part of its newly acquired territory and used it to establish colonies of Roman and Latin citizens.[106]

With the conquest of the Greek settlements of southern Italy in the 270s B.C., Rome's generals and soldiers occupied cities with fully formed Greek temples,

agoras, and gridded plans for the first time. This occupation accelerated Greek influence from southern Italy – then called Magna Graecia – on Roman culture, but most of this influence was confined to sculpture, art, and literature. Architecture in Rome exhibited little direct influence. The Greek temples of Paestum – the two temples dedicated to Hera, the third to Athena – did not seem to impress the Romans. Their archaic and classical styles, with heavy, ponderous columns and exaggerated capitals, appeared too foreign to Roman taste. There is no evidence, for instance, of any temple structures being built in the manner of the Temple of Hera II in Rome during the second half of the third century B.C. There is no suggestion, either in written references or in archaeological finds, of a peristyle temple with a four-sided stylobate, fluted Doric columns, bulbuous capitals, and Doric entablatures with triglyphs and metopes. Any influences that may have occurred were substantially transformed by the Romans and adapted to their traditional Etrusco-Roman plan type.

Roman architecture from this period remained in distinct contrast to the Greek temples of southern Italy. Probably owing to the conservative nature of religion and the traditional character of Roman rites, there was an outright rejection of Greek temple architecture as a precedent for design in Rome, the form and connotations of the Etruscans and Latins remaining dominant. The experimentation and innovation of Roman builders still resulted in transformed plan compositions that were based loosely on the Temple of Jupiter Capitolinus. An adherence to the *araeostyle* type, and the distinctive Etruscan tradition of terra-cotta decoration remained the dominant features of Roman temple architecture until the second century B.C.

Perhaps of more significance is the reverse influence of Rome on its newly acquired territories as it sought to expand its authority and legitimacy in an ever wider area. In Paestum, for instance, the Romans constructed a number of new buildings – a bath structure, the Temple of Peace, an amphitheater, and, most important, a new forum in the middle of the city covering over what may have been the original Greek agora. The Temple of Peace was begun shortly after 273 B.C. and dedicated originally to the Capitoline triad of Jupiter, Juno, and Minerva. It contained three inner sanctuaries and had a pronaos with six closely spaced columns

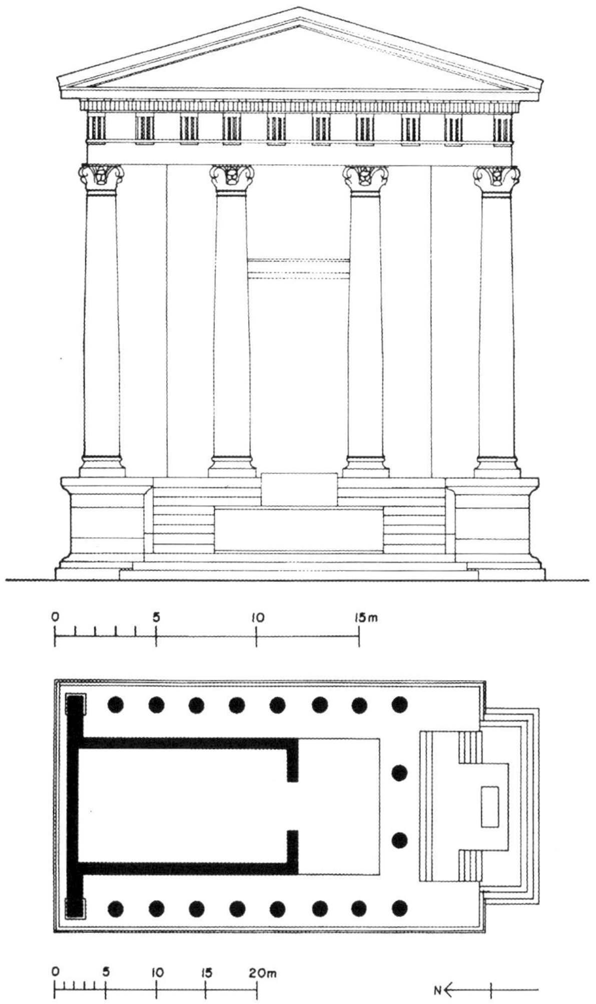

32. Paestum, Temple of Peace, 273 B.C., rebuilt ca. 80 B.C., plan. Drawing: Marianne Cusato after Emanuele Greco, *Magna Grecia: Guide Archeologiche Laterza* (1981), p. 29.

across the front. It was transformed in about 80 B.C., however, with a change to a single cella room and a pronaos of four columns (Fig. 32). Unlike Paestum's Greek temples, it was oriented to the south for the best exposure of the auspices in the Roman tradition, and it stood on a high podium with stairs only on the front. Its fluted columns had Composite capitals and supported an entablature with a Doric frieze of triglyphs and sculpted metopes. It was an unusual combination, one that reflected both the local Greek tradition and the influence of the conquering Romans.[107] The temple, like countless other urban interventions in Italy's conquered cities, represents Rome's political motive of imposing its rule and its own Capitoline cult not only as a complement to the original city and its traditional

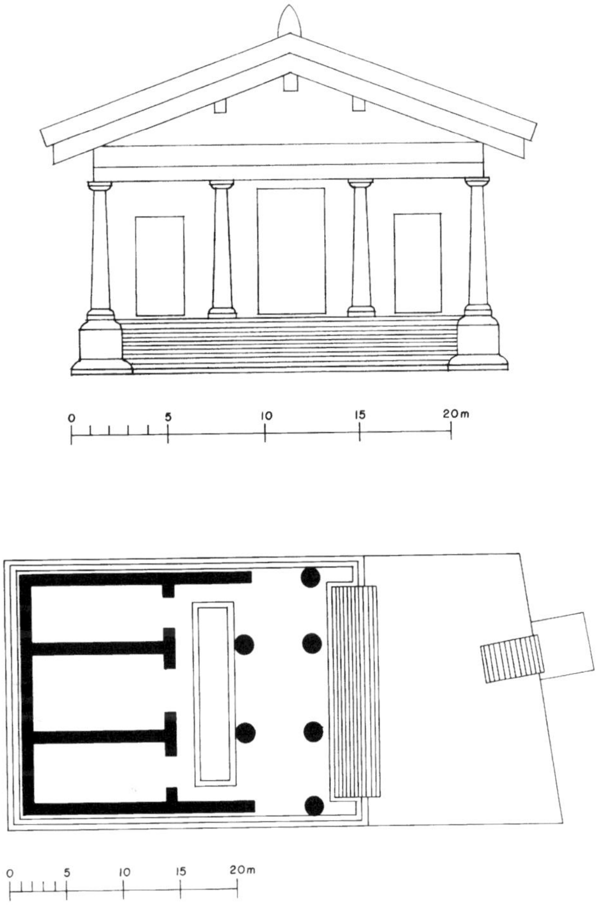

33. Cosa, Temple of Jupiter Capitolinus, 150 B.C., plan and elevation. Drawing: Rogelio Carrasco after Sheila Gibson in Axel Boëthius, *Etruscan and Early Roman Architecture* (1978), p. 131, fig. 127.

Greek deities, but also as a way of superseding them with a distinctly Roman imprint. At the same time, it adapted local building traditions in creating a new synthesis of architectural form.

In the case of its northern conquests, in the region of Etruria, Rome followed the Etruscan style in a more literal way. At the town of Cosa, the Romans built the Temple of Jupiter in 241 B.C. in a purely Etruscan style. Located high on a rocky cliff, facing northeast across the city and with a dramatic view of the coastline at its back, it was one of the most beautifully sited and grandly built Etruscan-style temples of the Roman world (Fig. 33). The original building was demolished and replaced by a larger temple, again dedicated to Jupiter, in about 150 B.C., a building that was the city's crowning achievement and its most important temple structure. It was composed of three sanctuaries side by side, preceded by a deep, half-enclosed pronaos with four columns across the front and two columns *in antis* in the middle.[108] The Etruscan style of the region was here more fittingly expressed in relation to the influence of Rome's Capitoline temple.

The Etrusco-Roman tradition of temple architecture during the early and mid-Republic thus took on many variations, although always remaining identified with its roots in sixth-century B.C. Etruscan and Latin precedents and its first great achievement, the Temple of Jupiter Capitolinus. The defining features of the "Tuscan" style – a high podium, sometimes terraced, a deep pronaos, widely spaced columns, and terra-cotta decoration – in fact held sway for a period of at least 250 years, if not more. The Temple of Jupiter Capitolinus remained a dominant reference stylistically and symbolically, although none of the temples from this period, in Rome or its colonies, approached its size, not even that of its corrected version as presented in this book. Only in the second century B.C. did Roman temple architecture begin to show a loosening of the Etrusco-Roman tradition and the acceptance of a new source of influence from the outside.

4

ASSIMILATION OF HELLENISTIC ARCHITECTURE AFTER THE PUNIC WARS

The new influence on Roman architects, builders, and patrons in the second century B.C. was not the Greek temples of Sicily and southern Italy, but the Hellenistic architecture of mainland Greece and Asia Minor. This occurred only after a time of intensive and protracted warfare – a serious threat to Rome's very existence – known as the Punic Wars. After the defeat of the Samnites, there appeared an even more dangerous enemy: the northern African city of Carthage. In all, the Roman's fought three wars against the Carthegenians: the first Punic War from 264 to 238 B.C., the second from 218 to 202 B.C., the third from 149 to 146 B.C.[1] In the latter, the Roman's invaded northern Africa and laid siege to Carthage. They eventually destroyed the city and declared north-central Africa a province.[2]

During the second century B.C., Rome was also engaged in battles in the East, as they conquered and added Macedonia, Greece, and Syria to their list of provinces.[3] All significant resistance to Rome in both the eastern and western Mediterranean was now eliminated. In Italy itself, Rome solidified its control over the peninsula by establishing dozens of new colonies from the Campania to the Alps, and by settling thousands of military veterans and extending its system of laws and taxation.[4]

The taking of Greece, one region or city-state at a time, from the 190s to 140s B.C. gave the Romans access to all of the important Greek temple complexes – Athens, Delphi, Corinth, Aegina, Epidaurus, Sounion, Olympia – and fostered the first important wave of direct Greek influence on Rome's architecture and art. As Roman military personnel returned to Italy and Greek craftsmen were brought to Rome and given commissions to build monuments equal to those of their home country, buildings such as the Erechtheum and Temple of Athena Nike in Athens (Fig. 34), the Tholos and Temple of Apollo in Delphi, and the Tholos and Theater at Epidaurus began to exert an influence on Roman architecture. As a result, Roman architecture of the late second century B.C. was gradually transformed by the influence of Hellenistic models from Greece.

The ensuing transition to a new Hellenized style is especially evident in the temple structures in and around the Forum Romanum, the Circus Flaminius, Forum Holitorium, and the Forum Boarium. Although there were innumerable other temples scattered around the city, it was these four areas – concentrated on either side of the Capitoline Hill and along the Tiber River – that experienced the most extensive development during the late Republic and displayed the most direct foreign influence from the newly conquered lands in the East.

These innovations went hand in hand with an increasing grandiosity in public ceremonies such as triumphal processions. Plutarch's description of the triumphal march of Aemilius Paullus after his defeat of King Perseus of Macedon in 167 B.C. provides some idea of the sense of spectacle associated with such events:

> The people put up platforms in the horse-racing stadia and around the Forum, and they took up position in other parts of the city that gave a good view of the procession; then, dressed up in clean white clothes, they watched the spectacle. Every temple was open and filled with garland and incense; and numerous officials and *lictores* held the people

> back from streaming together into a disorderly crowd and rushing about in all directions – and so kept the streets free and clear. The procession was divided over three days. The first was scarcely long enough for the display of the captured statues, paintings and colossal figures, transported on two hundred and fifty chariots. On the next day, the finest and most valuable of the Macedonian weapons were carried along in numerous carts. . . . On the third day . . . 110 stall-fed oxen, with gilded horns, were driven past, decked with ribbons and wreaths. Leading the animals in their procession to sacrifice were young men wearing aprons with fine purple borders, and boys carrying silver and gold offering cups.[5]

The incredible parade of the spoils of war was followed by the family and attendants of King Perseus, then 400 wreaths sent by Roman cities to honor Aemilius's victory. Then came the general himself:

> riding on a chariot magnificently adorned, a man worthy of admiration, quite apart from such pomp. He was dressed in purple robe shot with gold, and he held a spray of laurel in his right hand. His whole army also carried laurel, following the general's chariot in their ranks and divisions.[6]

The celebration of victory, public spectacle, and magnificent buildings were all employed with exuberant ceremony to mark the conquest of Rome's enemies. The assimilation of Hellenistic architecture is inseparable from Rome's military expansion and occupation of foreign lands.

Vitruvius's Classifications of the Republican Temples

A theoretical and historical discussion of this transformation of Roman architecture brought about by Hellensitic influences is found in part in the pages of Vitruvius's *Ten Books on Architecture*. Although Vitruvius did not complete and dedicate the *Ten Books* until the time of Augustus, probably about 25 B.C., it is instructive to outline his classifications of temple plans and to discuss his descriptions of the orders at this juncture. They are essential to an understanding of the assimilation of Hellenistic architecture into Roman building practices.[7] Such a review is appropriate here because the *Ten Books* provides for us examples and principles of design.that can be readily compared with some of the actual buildings constructed between the Punic Wars and the time Vitruvius wrote his treatise. The *Ten Books* essentially gives us a summary of the assimilation process along with his own interpretation of what path should have been followed.

We see in Vitruvius a conservative approach to temple architecture. He was critical of both the Etrusco-Roman and the Greek Doric traditions, and at the same time, he disapproved of the radical changes taking place in Rome.[8] He embraced instead Hellenistic theories and building practices, especially the buildings and theories of Hermogenes of Priene (active ca. 220–190 B.C.) and Hermodorus of Salamis (active 150 to 130 B.C.), which had formed the basis of his education as a young man in the 60s and 50s B.C.[9]

Vitruvius synthesized these into a codified system of building that he hoped would have an influence in Rome at the beginning of the Empire. His classification system was based, in its broadest sense, on the orders, beginning with the Ionic, which was the most predominant mode used in new temple construction during the second and early first centuries B.C. He followed this with a discussion of the Corinthian Order, which ultimately replaced the Ionic, and he reviewed the Doric and Tuscan Doric Orders, which he viewed as styles of the past. In each case, he gave rules for design, speculations about the orders' origins and descriptions or critiques of relevant examples.

Within his discussion of the Ionic Order, he provided two means of classifying Hellenistic and Roman temples, the first according to their elementary forms and plan arrangements, the second according to the composition of their elevations. Although he applied these classifications primarily to temples in the Ionic Order, they were equally relevant to the Corinthian. A review of his classifications can serve as a guide to better understanding the temples of the mid- to late Republic. It is important to keep in mind, however, that the relationship between his descriptions and the way the temples were actually built was often checkered with exceptions. His theoretical prescriptions did not

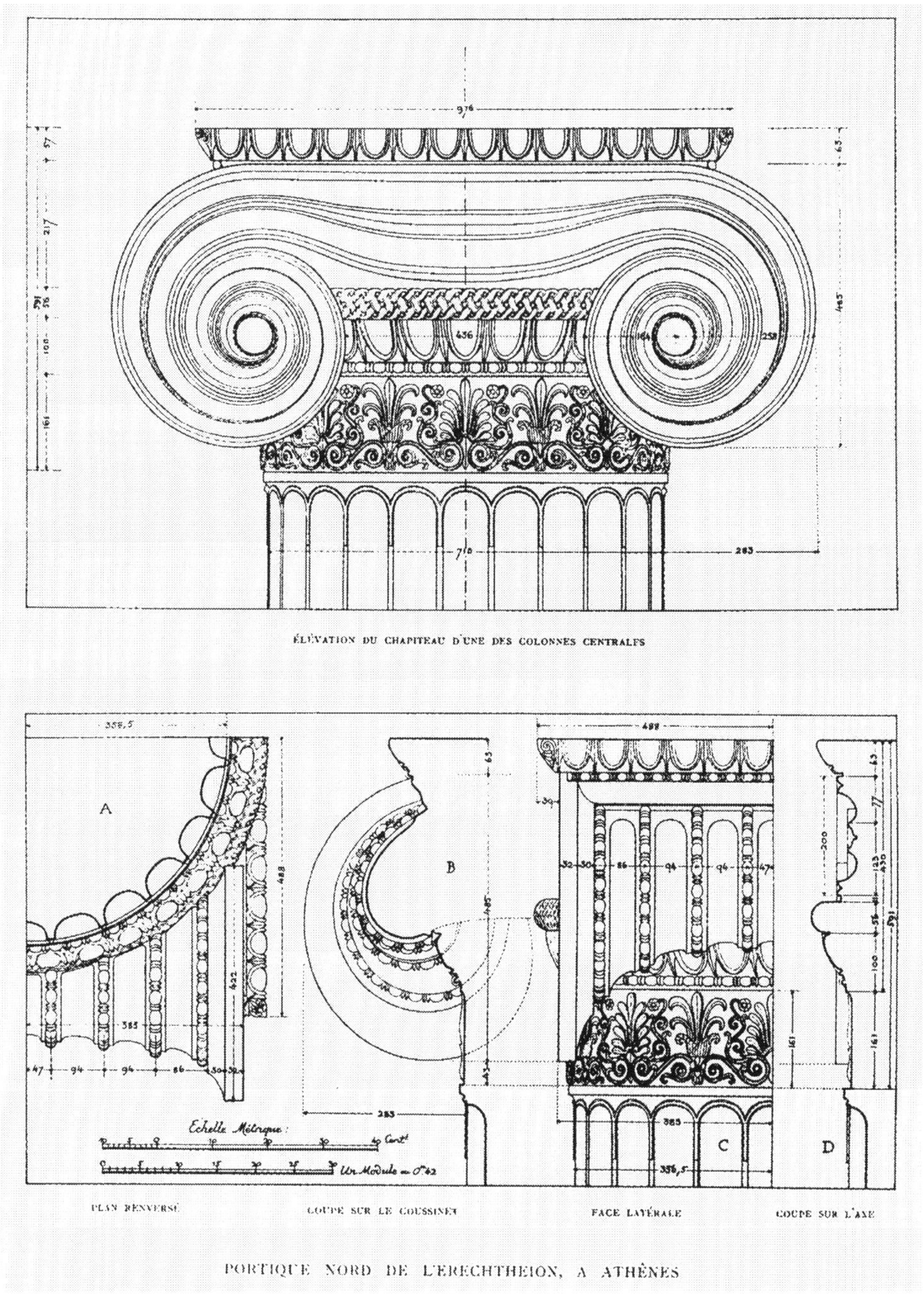

34. Athens, Erechtheum, Ionic capital from north portico, 421–405 B.C. Illustration: Georges Gromort, *Choix d'éléments empruntés à l'architecture classique,* (1927), vol. 1, pl. 6.

necessarily result in simple relationships or in simple dimensions. More often than not, architects and builders combined theory with pragmatic decisions based on factors other than canonical correctness.[10]

Vitruvius provided seven plan categories for elementary temple forms and plan arrangements. These are not italicized in this book as they have a common usage: in antis, prostyle, amphiprostyle, peripteral, dipteral, pseudodipteral, and hypaethral. The plans represented primarily Hellenistic types, which were, in fact, distinct from those commonly found in Rome through much of the Republic and the early Empire.[11] For instance, Vitruvius considered as an exception the plan type used by the Etruscans, with its deep pronaos, widely spaced columns, and frontal approach. He judged this building type as native or old-fashioned.[12]

He also considered as an exception the unique Roman synthesis he called pseudoperipteral, as found

Table 4.1. Temple Types According to Vitruvius Based on Intercolumniations and Column Sizes

Temple Type	*Diameter/ Intercolumniation*	*Diameter/ Height*	*Examples*
Pycnostyle	$1 : 1\frac{1}{2}$	$1 : 10$	Deified Julius, Forum Romanum Venus Genetrix, Forum of Julius
Systyle	$1 : 2$	$1 : 9\frac{1}{2}$	Equestrian Fortune, near Theater of Pompey
Eustyle	$1 : 2\frac{1}{4}$	$1 : 9\frac{1}{2}$	Dionysius, Teos
Diastyle	$1 : 3$	$1 : 8\frac{1}{2}$	Apollo and Diana, Palatine Hill
Araeostyle	$1 : 3\frac{1}{2}+$	$1 : 8$	Ceres, Circus Maximus Hercules Pompeianus, Circus Maximus, Capitoline Jupiter

Source: Vitruvius, *The Ten Books of Architecture*, trans. Morris Hickey Morgan (New York: Dover Publications, 1960), 75–86.

in the Temple of Portunus, later versions of the Temple of Saturn, and numerous other examples. He wrote that some builders greatly increased the size of a temple's cella by eliminating the pteroma and filling in the spaces between the columns. While leaving the design of the orders in the same symmetrical proportions, he wrote, they "appear to have produced a new kind of plan with the new name pseudoperipteral."[13]

A third Roman plan type he described as an exception, seen in the temples of Spes and Juno Sospita in the Forum Holitorium, is one that has a deep pronaos with two inner rows of columns aligned with the cella walls. Where there were projecting *antae* in the pronaos, the builders set up two columns in a line with each of the cella walls. Such an arrangement – a combination of Tuscan and Greek influences – took the plan of the Tuscan order and applied it to buildings in the Corinthian and Ionic modes.[14]

He made the scantest mention of a fourth plan type used with great frequency by the Romans – the Temple of Jupiter Capitolinus being the principal model – the temple with a three-sided peristyle and a plain back wall with lateral extensions, or in the *peripteros sine postico* manner. It was used at the time of Vitruvius in such prominent buildings as the Temple of Venus Genetrix in the Forum Julium, and the Temple of Mars Ultor in the Forum Augustum; it is curious that he did not describe either in terms of their plan.[15]

In contrast to his categories of plan types, Vitruvius's descriptions of temples according to the composition of their elevations was more consistent with Roman practice. He identified five classes, or elevations, based on column proportions and their spacings, some of which we have already encountered: *pycnostyle, systyle, diastyle, araeostyle*, and *eustyle*. He worked out a series of ideal proportions in which the height and diameter of the columns varied inversely with their intercolumniations.[16] In his ideal, as the distance between the columns was increased, the thickness of the shafts had to be enlarged and the height of the columns reduced in proportion to the increase.[17] On one hand, thick, short columns spaced closely together, as in a *pycnostyle* plan, resulted in the shafts looking swollen and ungraceful; a *pycnostyle* composition required tall, slender columns. On the other hand, tall, thin columns widely spaced, as in an *araeostyle* temple, often looked too thin, with the air appearing to "eat away and diminish the thickness" of the shafts.[18] An *araeostyle* composition required short, squat columns (see Table 4.1).

In Vitruvius's judgment, the *eustyle* was the most ideal because it was based on principles developed with a view to "convenience, beauty and strength."[19] The intercolumniations of the *eustyle* are two-and-one-quarter times the column diameter. In some cases, a wider center bay was three times the column diameter. With this arrangement, Vitruvius argued, there is no obstruction at the entrance, and the walk around the cella is dignified. As an example, he noted the Ionic temple dedicated to Dionysius in Teos by Hermogenes from ca. 220–205 B.C. (Fig. 35), and to this we can add

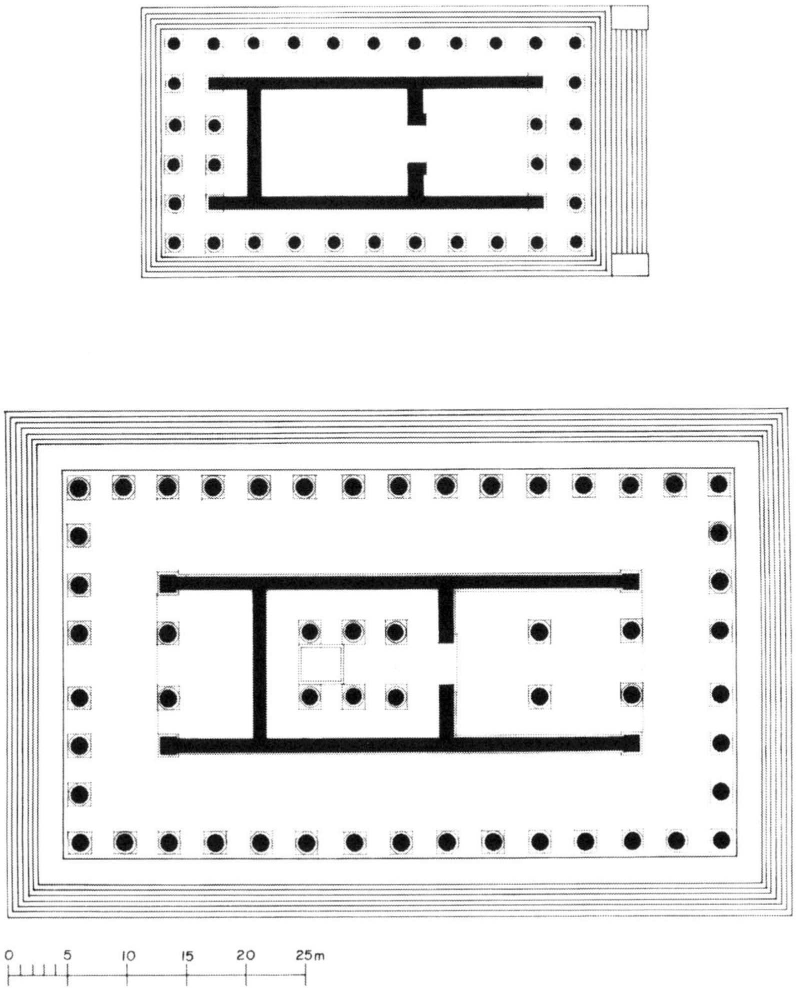

35. Teos, Temple of Dionysius (top), Hermogenes, ca. 220–205 B.C.; Magnesia, Temple of Artemis Leukophryene (bottom), Hermogenes, ca. 205–190 B.C. Drawings: John W. Stamper after Herbert Langford Warren, in Vitruvius, *Ten Books of Architecture* (1960), p. 121; and D. S. Robertson, *A Handbook of Greek and Roman Architecture* (1954), p. 155, fig. 67.

the Temple of Artemis Leukophryene at Magnesia from 205–190 B.C., also Ionic.[20]

In general, Vitruvius's intention was to promote the adoption of Hellenistic architecture, but faced with the great diversity of plan types he found in Rome, he grudgingly acknowledged their existence as exceptions to the rule. He surely did not foresee the dramatic way in which they would in fact continue to take precedence over most of the purely Hellenistic examples he preferred.

The Temples of Juno Regina and Jupiter Stator in the Porticus Metelli (Octaviae)

The temples of Juno Regina and Jupiter Stator (Fig. 36) were among the earliest in Rome to exhibit the direct influence of the Hellenistic architecture so admired by Vitruvius. One of them, the Temple of Jupiter Stator, is famous for being the first temple in Rome built of marble. Both temples were located on the north side of the Circus Flaminius, near its eastern end in the Porticus Metelli, the present-day Porticus Octaviae.[21] Both were destroyed during the Middle Ages; however, reference to their site is provided by the ancient entrance portico in front of the Church of S. Angelo in Pescheria, and one of the columns of the Temple of Juno Regina is built into a nearby medieval house.

The area of the Circus Flaminius was located directly west of the Capitoline Hill in a low-lying area of the southernmost part of the Campus Martius. It was first laid out in the second half of the fourth century B.C. and was reconstructed in the 220s B.C., possibly by the censor C. Flaminius.[22] The space was a large field-like area with a main axis that extended from the

southeast to the northwest. It was used for games, the *ludi Taurii*, equestrian events, and markets, and it was a staging ground for triumphal marches.[23] The Theater of Marcellus was built at its eastern end in the first century B.C.[24]

The first temple in the Porticus Metelli, devoted to Juno Regina, was vowed during the Ligurian wars in 187 B.C. and completed in 179 B.C. by M. Aemilius Lepidus.[25] Its plan had six columns across the front and a pronaos three bays deep, with the cella walls extending forward an additional bay as *antae*. Its original columns were probably Ionic, with tall, fluted shafts standing on Attic bases. Later rebuildings were done at the time of Augustus and again during the time of Septimius Severus.[26]

The Temple of Jupiter Stator was built by Caecilius Metellus Macedonicus in 143 B.C., just after the Third Punic War ended and northern Africa and Greece were made colonies. It was dedicated in 131 B.C., the year Metellus was censor.[27] He commissioned one of Vitruvius's most favored Greek architects, Hermodorus of Salamis, to design the temple.[28]

Vitruvius described the Temple of Jupiter Stator as the first temple in Rome to be built of marble, including both its columns and cella wall.[29] He described it as having six columns on the front and rear and eleven on the flanks, using it as an example of a peripteral temple. He stated, "Let the columns be so placed as to leave a space, the width of an intercolumniation, all round between the walls and the rows of columns on the outside, thus forming a walk around the cella of the temple."[30] The way the temple appears in the Marble Plan it is *peripteros sine postico*, but this represented a later reconstruction, possibly in the time of Augustus.[31]

The original temple also corresponded to Vitruvius's prescription that the columns should be placed so that there were twice as many columnar bays on the sides as there were on the front, the building's length being twice its breadth. He warned that those who make the number of columns rather than intercolumniations double "seem to be in error, because then the length seems to be one intercolumniation longer than it ought to be."[32] The cella was long and narrow, also a Hellenistic Greek influence, and its pronaos was deep with the cella walls projecting as *antae*. An interior column was aligned with the *antae* walls on each side.

A cult statue of Jupiter Stator inside the cella was reportedly done by Polycles and Dionysius, sons of Timarchides. Other works inside the building included "Olympus Struggling with Pan" by Heliodorus, "Venus Bathing" by Diodalsas, and "Standing Venus" by Polycharmus.[33] Two tympanum statues found on the site and probably belonging to this temple represent Jupiter and an unidentified female figure.[34]

When he built the Temple of Jupiter Stator, Metellus Macedonicus also repaired the Temple of Juno Regina and surrounded both of them with a portico, the Porticus Metelli.[35] It was a large, nearly square enclosure with a double portico on all four sides. It faced southwest onto the Circus Flaminius. Initially, it did not have the central entrance propylon as seen on the site today.[36] It was simply a continuous colonnade across the front. This, combined with the two adjacent portico enclosures extending to the northwest toward the Theater of Pompey – the Porticus Philippi and the Porticus Octavia – provided a nearly uninterrupted walkway along the entire northern side of the Circus Flaminius.[37]

After Metellus Macedonicus built the porticus, he installed twenty-four equestrian statues by Lysippus, which he had brought as part of the spoils of his war in Macedonia. They had been commissioned by Alexander to commemorate those of his men who had fallen in the battle of Granicus.[38] This complex thus became one of the earliest examples in Rome of a forum and temple precinct enclosed by porticos and also filled with monumental Greek statuary. The complex, along with the nearby Porticus Octavia, were considered luxurious by the ancient writer Velleius Paterculus.[39] Such a commemorative civic space would have a great influence on the urban design of later dictators and emperors, from Julius Caesar and Augustus on. Its importance was reaffirmed in the 20s B.C., when it was rebuilt and dedicated by Augustus in honor of his sister Octavia with a new gate and a *schola*, or *curia octaviae*, behind the temples.[40]

Temples of Apollo Medicus (Sosianus) and Bellona

Yet another temple complex was developed in the vicinity of the Circus Flaminius in the second century

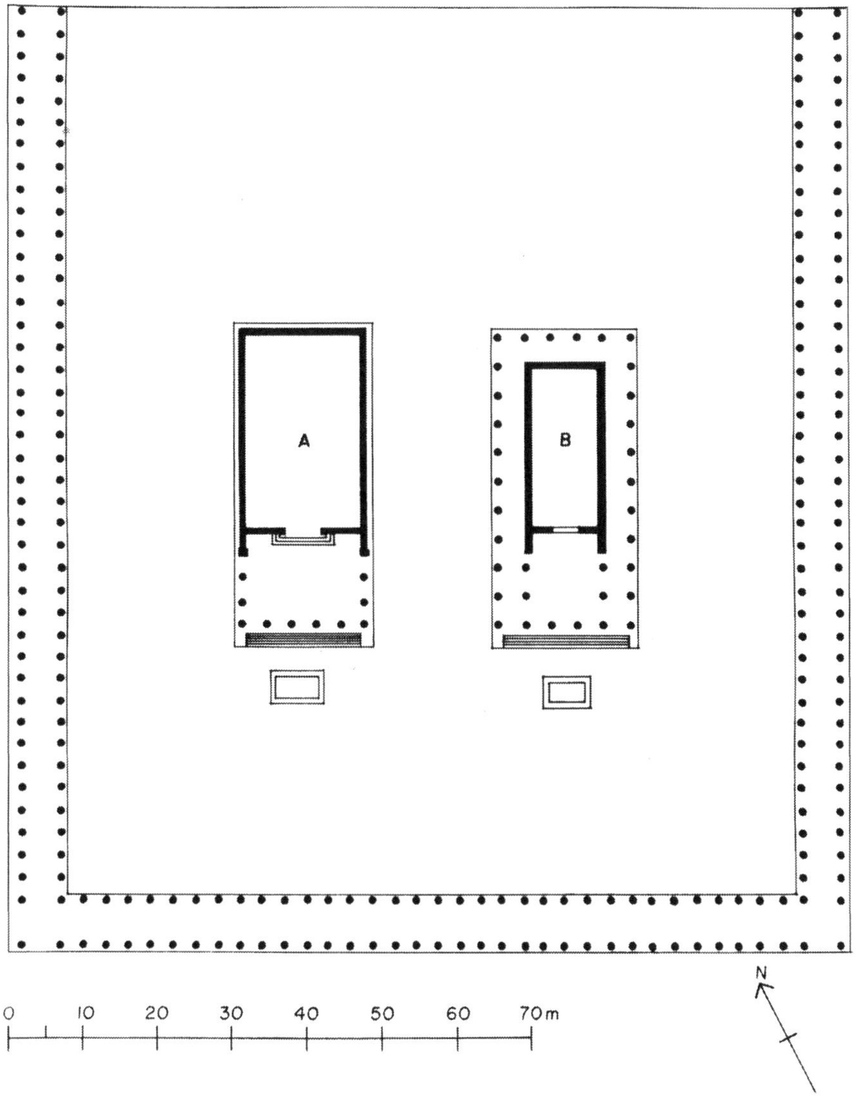

36. Porticus Metelli (Octaviae): (A) Temple of Juno Regina, 187–179 B.C., (B) Temple of Jupiter Stator, 143–131 B.C. Drawing: John W. Stamper based on Rodolfo Lanciani, *Forma Urbis Romae*, (1990), pls. 21 and 28.

B.C., in this case immediately to the east of the Porticus Metelli. The Temple of Apollo Medicus and the Temple of Bellona, constructed side by side, faced not directly onto the Circus Flaminius, like those of the Porticus Metelli, but were oriented directly southward. They formed an urban transition to the Forum Holitorium, which extended to the south along the river. There was also an early theater built in front of the temples, the area forming a sort of theatrical zone long before the construction of the Theater of Marcellus.

The site of the Temple of Apollo Medicus was associated with the cult of Apollo as early as the sixth century B.C. An Etrusco-Roman temple was built on the site in 433–431 B.C., dedicated by Cn. Julius after a pestilence. It was one of the first to be built outside the walls. The presence of the Temple of Apollo near the Circus Flaminius had an important relationship in regard to triumphal processions, which typically passed through the Circus. The laurel wreath, a symbol of Roman victory, was fundamental to the cult worship of Apollo.[41]

The temple was restored in 353 B.C. after being damaged by fire. It was rebuilt entirely in 179 B.C. by Fulvius Nobilior, a project that was done in conjunction with the construction of a theater with a stage located in front of the temple, a site that was slightly to the north and west of the Theater of Marcellus.[42] It is possible that the steps of the Temple of Apollo and the Temple of Bellona formed part of the cavea of the early theater.[43] The linking of a theater with a temple was common in Italian architecture in the first and second centuries B.C., as seen, for instance, in the

Temple of Fortuna Primigenia at Palestrina and the Temple of Hercules at Tivoli.[44] An excavation under the podium of the Temple of Apollo suggests Fulvius Nobilior's structure had a pronaos with four columns on the front and two deep, with a single cella. Vitruvius categorized it as *diastyle*.[45]

Pliny reports that several sculptures produced at this time were intended for this temple, including a colossal statue of Apollo by Timarchides, an Apollo statue by Philoskos of Rhodes, and a group of Niobids by Praxiteles or Skopas.[46]

The Temple of Bellona was built immediately to the east of the Temple of Apollo Medicus beginning in 296 B.C.[47] It was commissioned by Appius Claudius Caecus, following a victory against the Etruscans, and it was to be used as a meeting place for the Senate *extra pomerium*, especially for deliberations about granting triumphs.[48] It was also used for the leave-taking of governors and pro-consuls departing for their provinces. Finally, it was used by the Senate to meet with the ambassadors of countries against which Rome was waging war.[49] Bellona was a deity of Italian origins that was related to war, and it was appropriate that the temple was in proximity to the Circus Flaminius, the staging ground of many triumphal marches.

Temples of Concordia and Castor and Pollux in the Forum Romanum

At least one new temple structure was erected and another rebuilt in the Forum Romanum just after the Punic Wars.[50] The Temple of Concordia was built on the Forum's west side in 121 B.C., whereas the Temple of Castor and Pollux was rebuilt at its southeast corner in 117 B.C. Both were done in the Ionic Order, thus being the first structures in the Forum Romanum to represent the Hellenistic influence of the time.

The Temple of Concordia was located on a prominent site at the foot of the Capitoline Hill, between the Temple of Saturn and the Curia Hostilia.[51] An older monument had stood on the site, the Aedicule Concordiae, built in 304 B.C. and removed in 121 B.C.[52] The senator L. Opimius ordered the construction of the new temple following the death of Gaius Gracchus and the end of an effort at social reform that had been initiated in the 130s B.C.[53]

The attempted social reform had come about in reaction to the ever-expanding circle of imperial dominance resulting from the military exploits and conquests by Rome's aristocratic families. A crisis had developed in the capital city as the concentration of power and property in the hands of the relatively small number of aristocrats began to be challenged by the middle and lower classes.[54] Reform measures were initiated in the Senate and in a tribal assembly by Tiberius Gracchus and later by his brother Gaius Gracchus. They not only pushed forward with land reform but also with procedural changes that transferred power – at least for a short period of time – from the Senate to the assemblies and the equestrians.[55]

These reforms were opposed by conservative members of the Senate, and both Gracchus brothers were eventually killed by supporters of the aristocracy, thus bringing to an end much of the impetus toward reform.[56] The Temple of Concordia was the Senate's official symbol of victory over the social reformers and was meant to evoke the honor of peace and stability within the traditional hierarchy of aristocratic authority and plebeian acquiescence.[57]

A later version of the Temple of Concordia, built in the first century A.D., had an unusual plan with the long dimension of its cella placed perpendicular to the pronaos. The structure of L. Opimius, however, may have had a traditional rectangular plan with columns on three sides and a back wall in the *peripteros sine postico* form.[58] Details of the temple's decoration are conjectural, but it may have employed Ionic columns in a manner similar to the Temple of Juno Regina and the Temple of Portunus in the Forum Boarium. Its dedication to commemorate the Senate's victory over Gaius Gracchus made it a symbol of the victorious nobility, a reaffirmation of its authority and control.[59] It became an alternative meeting place for the Senate, especially when there was a question of civic discord to be discussed, and its podium served as a speaker's platform for such orators as Cicero and Julius Caesar.[60] The temple would be remodeled again in A.D. 7 by Augustus and Tiberius, with details inspired by the Erechtheum in Athens.[61]

The Temple of Castor and Pollux, originally built in 484 B.C., was altered in about 200 B.C. and again in 117 B.C. by the Senate and Caecilius Metellus Delmaticus.[62] The new structure was erected over

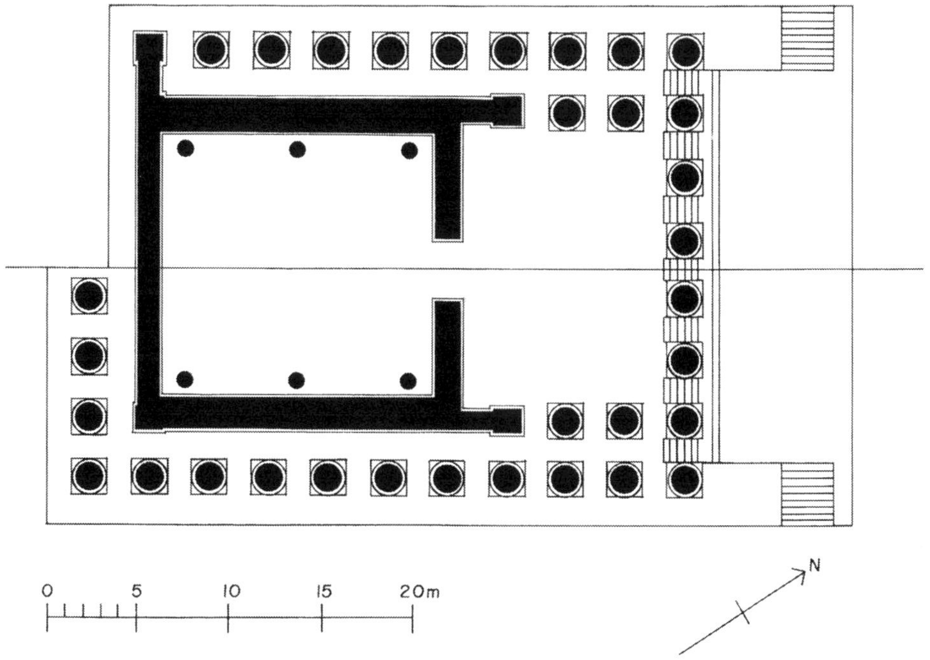

37. Rome, Temple of Castor and Pollux, plan at time of rebuilding in 117 B.C., showing two options as peripteral or *peripteros sine postico*. Drawing: John W. Stamper based on Inge Nielsen and Birte Poulsen, eds., *The Temple of Castor and Pollux I: The Pre-Augustan Temple Phases with Related Decorative Elements* (1992), pp. 108–9, figs. 100–1.

the original foundations with some modifications (Fig. 37). The new podium measured 27.50 meters wide by 40 to 44 meters long (93 by 136–150 Roman feet), and was 6 meters high, about twice that of the previous version.[63] Manifesting the Hellenistic influence of the period, it rejected the widely spaced intercolumniations of the earlier versions, as well as the paradigm of the Temple of Jupiter Capitolinus. It was now composed of eight columns across the front and nine along the flanks. It was either *peripteros sine postico* or peripteral with columns on the back. Evidence on the site indicates that it was certainly peripteral in its last rebuilding, done in 7 B.C. to A.D. 6 by Augustus and Tiberius (see Chapter 8).[64]

The temple's column arrangement was *pycnostyle*, or closely spaced, with the intercolumniations being 3.20 meters, less than 1.5 times the column diameters. Like the Temple of Concordia, its columns were probably Ionic at this stage, suggesting the influence of Athenian buildings such as the Erechtheum. It was changed to the Corinthian Order during its rebuilding in the following century by Augustus and Tiberius.

Although the temple's column spacing and Ionic Order were very different from that of the earlier two buildings on the site, it maintained the Etrusco-Roman features of a deep pronaos and high podium that, like the Temple of Jupiter Capitolinus, was terraced in front to provide a large speakers' platform. Two lateral stairs provided access to the platform level, and from there a broad flight of steps led axially up to the portico, possibly penetrating through the line of columns.[65]

By the time of its rebuilding in 117 B.C., use of the temple for public oratory and gathering had increased substantially. These included meetings of the general assemblies, the Senate, public voting, and possibly public trials.[66] At this time, still well before the construction of the Temple of Divus Julius and the Arch of Augustus to the north and east of the temple, there was ample room in front for large gatherings of people. The lateral stairs at the front of the podium would have served the logistics of public voting well because participants would have ascended one side of the podium, deposited their ballot in an urn, and descended by the opposite stair.[67]

A law was passed designating this podium as the spot on which magistrates took their oaths.[68] It housed the standard weights and measures of the marketplace, it was used as an office for the presiding consuls, military victories were announced from its platform, and aristocratic funeral rights were observed there.[69] There are more references in ancient literature to the use of this temple's platform than to any other in the Forum Romanum. It served as a major stage for Roman events during the next several decades.[70]

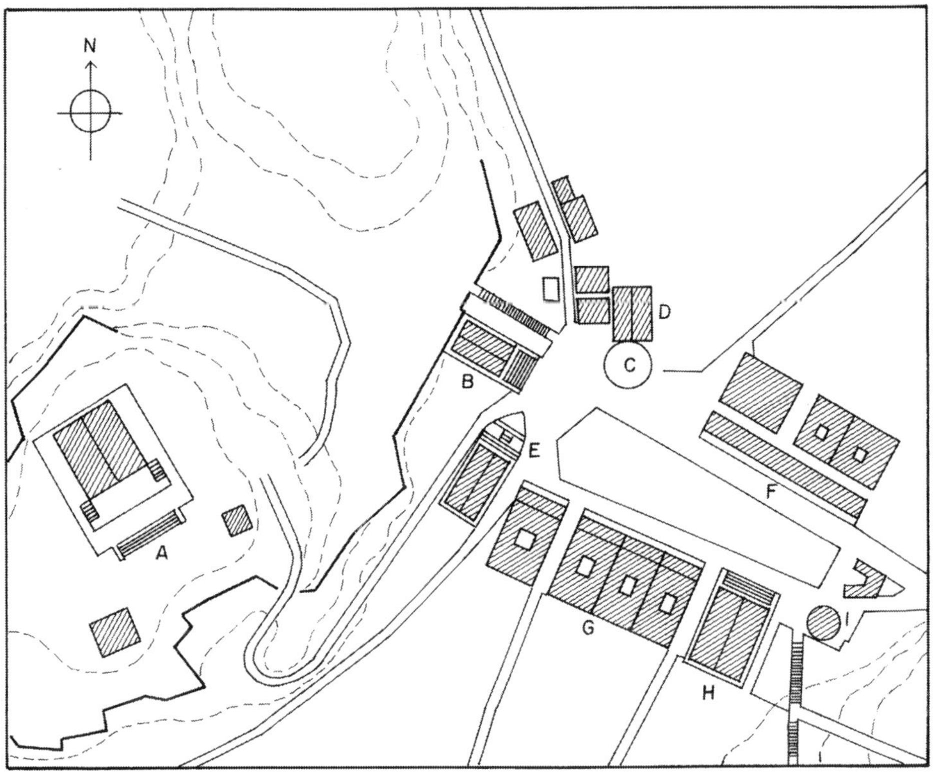

38. Rome, Forum Romanum, plan, ca. 200 B.C.: (A) Temple of Jupiter Capitolinus, (B) Temple of Concord, (C) Comitium, (D) Curia Hostilia, (E) Temple of Saturn, (F) Tabernae Novae, (G) Tabernae Veteres, (H) Temple of Castor and Pollux, (I) Temple of Vesta. Drawing: John W. Stamper.

A raised platform, whether used for reviewing processions or for speeches, became an increasingly important component of the forum. In addition to the temple podiums, a separate speakers' platform, the rostra (plural in Latin) were built at the forum's west end. The first were built in 338 B.C., located near the comitium. This was the tribunal most often used for public meetings conducted by the magistrate or a consul. The name of the rostra, the Beaks, was derived from its adornment with beaks of ships captured at Antium by the admiral and censor Gaius Maenius.[71] From the rostra people were informed of the activities of the curia, warned of danger, and admonished against wrongful practices. Cicero, for instance, delivered from the rostra two orations against Cataline, warning people of a real and present danger.[72]

Signs of authority did not only identify those in authority; they frequently helped to bridge the gap between the office and the person.[73] A consul, Senate member, or military general standing on a temple podium like that of Castor and Pollux was set off physically as someone special. The setting indicated the person's special standing within society and commanded respect, even if, in another setting – a house, for instance – he would not have commanded such respect. The leader's setting, combined with his regal clothing and supporting entourage, all added dignity to the Forum Romanum and marked the leader as important in the context. Symbols of authority come to be associated with positions of authority, and they make it easier psychologically for those who are in subordinate positions to accept the authority of the ruler. The symbols of authority were tangibly and physically present in a way that the office was not.[74] The temple building as a symbol predisposed many in Rome to accept the authority of the rulers. It developed a history and a tradition of great symbolic importance that was passed down from one generation to the next.

Such projects as the Temples of Concordia and Castor and Pollux all represented *munia*, the necessary tasks of aristocratic household heads. The names L. Opimius, Caecillius Metellus Macedonicus, Aemilius Lapidus, and Fulvius Nobilior represent leading members of the aristocracy, men who carried out their obligations to the state, their general responsibility for furnishing contributions and rendering service. Whether

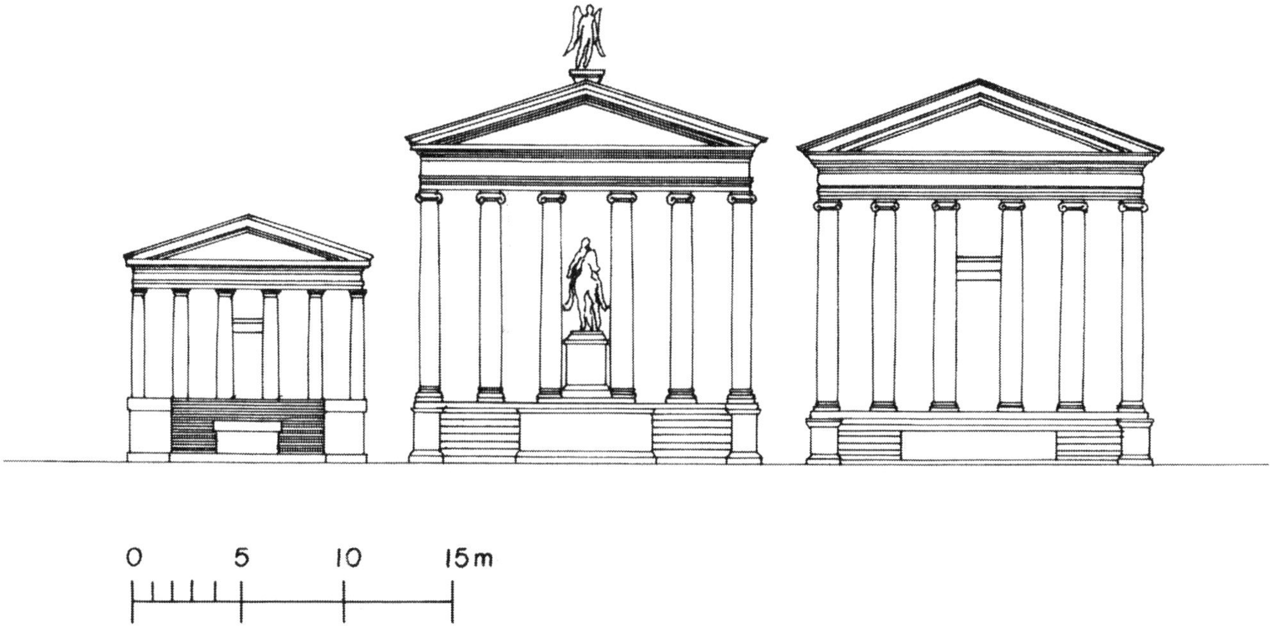

39. Rome, Forum Holitorium, third to first centuries B.C., elevation. Drawing: Karen Parolek based on Hector Lefuel in *Roma Antiqua: Grandi Edifici Pubblici* (1992), p. 213, pl. 118.

their money came from spoils of war or profits from their agricultural lands, the fact that they fulfilled their responsibility for public service is a mark of their interest in improving the city and their desire for public recognition through their built works. These were distinctly buildings of the aristocratic class: a temple built in honor of the Senate's victory over the plebeians and a temple dedicated to the Roman equestrians. Just as the political ethos and value system of the Roman aristocracy was focused on political and military achievement, so, too, was the aristocracy's architectural program a way of proving its authority and power, its need to build magnificent architectural ensembles reflecting its role as the primary arbiter of urban development and architectural excellence.

With the construction of these temples, the Forum Romanum (Fig. 38) was in a sense rejuvenated.[75] Rome's survival of the Punic Wars, its near defeat and comeback to victory, was a major turning point. The conquest and reconquest of territories, the importation of new ideas, craftsmen, and laborers, led not only to new building activity but also to a new expression in architectural design. Hellenistic architecture, especially as the Romans experienced it in Greece and Asia Minor, now took on great importance as an influence for design.

Temples of the Forum Holitorium

The Forum Holitorium, Rome's ancient vegetable market, located between the southwest edge of the Capitoline Hill and the northern border of the Forum Boarium, encompassed several buildings within a sacred area, both temples and porticos (Figs. 39 and 40).[76] Its main focus was three temples arranged in a line along its west side, portions of which are now incorporated into the Church of S. Nicola in Carcere.[77] The northernmost shrine has been identified as the Temple of Janus; the middle, the Temple of Juno Sospita; and the southernmost, the Temple of Spes. Opposite the temples, on the sacred area's east side, are the remains of a late republican-era market arcade with engaged Tuscan Doric half-columns and plain frieze, a motif that prefigured the Colosseum and is related to the Tabularium and the forum buildings at Palestrina.[78]

The Temple of Janus, the northernmost of the three, was built by C. Duilius in ca. 260 B.C. during the first Punic War. It commemorated the Roman's first naval victory over the Carthagenians. It was rebuilt during the first century B.C., and later restorations were done during the early Empire.[79] It is notable for its Ionic columns, some of which are visible on the north side of the complex and which probably date

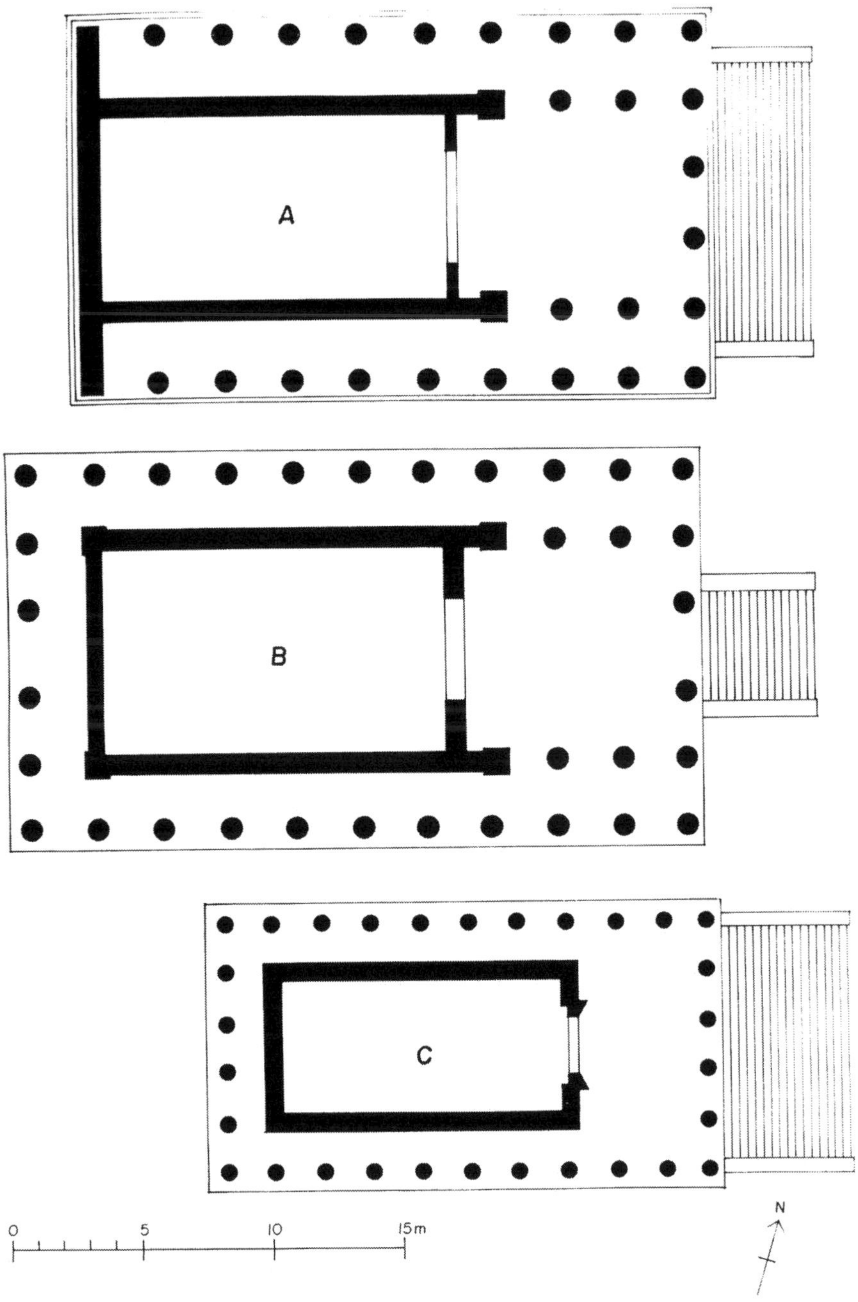

40. Forum Holitorium, plan of temples, (A) Temple of Janus, (B) Temple of Juno Sospita, and (C) Temple of Spes. Drawing: John W. Stamper based on L. Cozzoli Aite in Filippo Coarelli, "Forum Holitorium," *LTUR*, vol. 2, p. 466, fig. 127.

from the rebuilt version in the first century B.C. They were arranged with six across the front and nine on the sides and had tall, slender, monolithic shafts with Attic bases. There was a single cella with lateral extensions of its rear wall and *antae* extending one bay into the pronaos. The columns and the entablature of the cella were peperino, and the entablature of the pronaos was travertine.[80] The difference in materials was concealed by stucco in which details of ornamentation were executed.

Janus was one of the oldest gods in the Roman pantheon, represented on coins with two heads back-to-back. According to Roman legend, he ruled on the Janiculum Hill, where he founded a city and is said to have civilized the first inhabitants of Latium. One legend suggests that he received Saturn when he was driven from Greece by Jupiter. The mythical reign of Janus is said to have been a golden age when men were perfectly honest and there was peace and prosperity. He may have invented the use of money, and, indeed, the

41. Forum Holitorium, columns remaining from the Temple of Spes. Photo: Fototeca Unione, American Academy in Rome, FU 929.

oldest bronze Roman coins had the effigy of Janus on one side and the prow of a boat on the other. Because of his legendary role in the war between Rome and the Sabines, it was decided that in the time of war, the door of the Temple of Janus should always be left open so that the god could come to the aid of the Romans. It was only closed when Rome was at peace.[81]

The Temple of Spes, the goddess of hope, was also built during the period of the First Punic War, in 258 B.C. Its builder, A. Atilius Calatinus, wanted to build a temple that in essence continued the work of C. Duilius, who built the Temple of Janus just two years earlier.[82] It was struck by lightning and burned in 218 B.C. and was damaged by fire again in 213 B.C. and immediately rebuilt.[83] In 31 B.C., it was again damaged by a fire that also burned part of the Circus Maximus and other nearby temples.[84] It was rebuilt yet again and restored by Tiberius in A.D. 17. Its last rebuilding took place under Antoninus Pius in the second century A.D.[85]

The southernmost of the three temples, its remaining columns are visible on the south side of S. Nicola in Carcere (Fig. 41).[86] Of the three temples, it was unusual for its time because it had six by eleven columns in a peripteral arrangement. Yet its order was Tuscan, not Greek Doric, the echinus of the capitals having a slightly rounded profile while the abacus was quite small.[87] The travertine column shafts were unfluted, and although they diminished in size near the top, there was no entasis.

The Temple of Juno Sospita, built in the space between the first two, is directly embedded in S. Nicola. It was first constructed in 197–194 B.C. after being vowed by C. Cornelius Cethegus, the Roman consul during a battle against the Insubrians along the Po River. It was restored in 90 B.C.[88] Like the Temple of Spes, it was peripteral with six columns across the front and back and eleven on the sides.[89] Its Ionic columns and cella walls were of peperino tufa, and the entablature was travertine.[90]

Arranging these temples together, so closely spaced as to create a portico-like front to a common sacred area, was a new architectural development during this period, an even more dense grouping than found in the Largo Argentina. The intention was to provide a backdrop to the sacred area and market, making it more monumental by means of horizontal extension and repetition of the columnar facades.[91] The columns of the various temples appeared to march in a unified line, while their pediments emphasized their vertical dimension and the individuality of each structure.[92] All three temples represented a synthesis of Etruscan, Roman, and Hellenistic practice, combining Etrusco-Roman features like the high podium, frontal approach, and

Table 4.2. Comparative Sizes of the Psuedoperipteral Temples of the Mid-Republic (Podium Size, Column Diameter, and Interaxial Dimension)

		Podium		*Columns*	
City	*Temple*	*Width (m)*	*Length (m)*	*Diam. (m)*	*Interaxial (m)*
Rome	Juno Regina	18.50	42.50	–	–
	Jupiter Stator	19.70	41.50	–	–
	Castor and Pollux	27.50	40	1.60	3.20 sides 3.50 front
	Janus, Forum Holit.	14.50	24.50	.80	2.50
	Spes, Forum Holit.	10.97	19.70	.60	1.88
	Juno, Forum Holit.	14.99	26.70	.87	2.52
	Portunus	10.50	19.0	.90	2.70
Tivoli	Sybil	9.10	15.90	.76	2.87
Cori	Hercules	8.30	17.65	.65	2.26

Source: For dimensions of the temples in Largo Argentina, Forum Holitorium, Temple of Portunus, and Temple of Castor and Pollux, see Inge Nielsen and Berte Poulsen, *The Temple of Castor and Pollux I* (Rome: Edizione de Luca, 1992); and Filippo Coarelli, "Topografia e storia" in *L'Area Sacra di Largo Argentina* (Rome, 1981); for Temple of Sybil, Tivoli, see Mark Wilson Jones, "Designing the Roman Corinthian Order," *JRA* 2 (1989).

deep pronaos with the Hellenistic use of stone construction, closely spaced columns, and, in the case of two of them, the use of the Ionic Order.[93]

Relative to Vitruvius, they were typical of the Roman builders' tendency to develop and refine indigenous plan types that adhered to Etruscan and Latin traditions while allowing, or experimenting with, certain Hellenistic ideas. Especially influential, however, was the Hellenistic imprint on the order, the Ionic becoming clearly the dominant mode. The result was a new synthesis that combined Hellenistic canons with long-standing Etruscan and Latin practices (see Table 4.2).

Temple of Portunus in the Forum Boarium

As the Forum Boarium developed during the Republic, a second sacred area was built south of the Etrusco-Roman temple complex of Fortuna and Mater Matuta. Located directly on the bank of the Tiber, this new zone also consisted of two temples, in this case, one rectangular, the other circular (Fig. 42). With the exception of the Pantheon, no other ancient temples in Rome are so well preserved and thus tell so complete a story about the city's architectural development as this pair. The first was commonly known as the Temple of Fortuna Virilis but is now accepted by many as being dedicated to Portunus.[94] The second has long been referred to as the Round Temple by the Tiber, although there are two proposed attributions, one, the Temple of Hercules Victor, and the other, the Temple of Hercules Olivarius.[95]

Both temples were built on the foundations of earlier buildings; however, the final versions both date from the late Republic, between 120 and 80 B.C.[96] The Temple of Portunus is sited parallel to the Tiber, facing north toward the street that led to the Pons Aemilius. It was originally enclosed on two sides by porticos.[97] The Round Temple, curiously, is behind it, with its door facing to the east. Although they were constructed at about the same time, and in close proximity to each other, they actually occupied separate sacred zones.

The attribution of the rectangular temple to Portunus is based on a statement in Varro, which speaks of such a temple standing on the bank of the Tiber near the Forum Boarium.[98] Portunus was represented on sculptural reliefs as youthful, with long hair and attributes of an anchor and serpent. He was equated

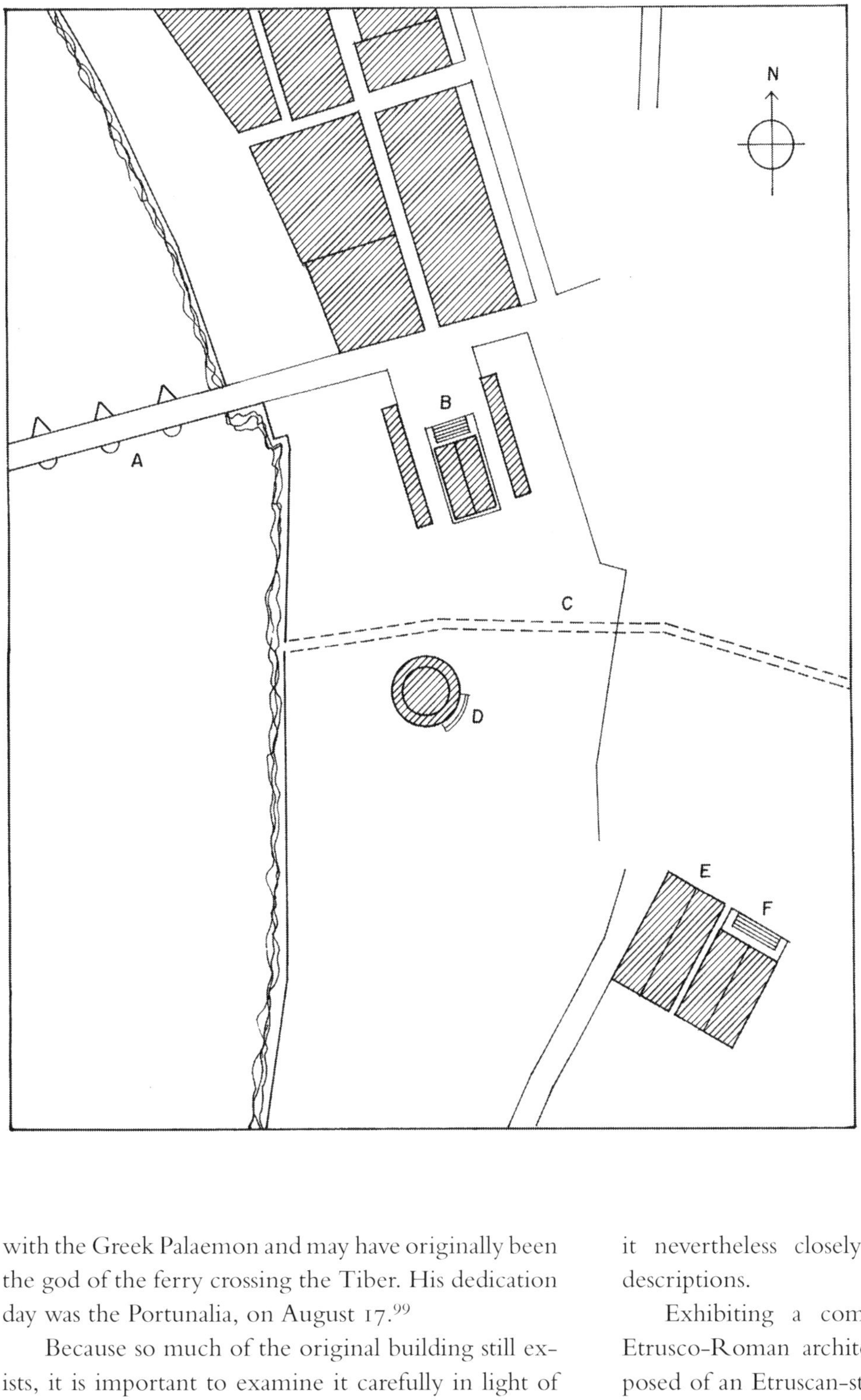

42. Rome, Forum Boarium, plan: (A) Ponte Aemilius, (B) Temple of Portunus, (C) Cloaca Maxima, (D) Round Temple by the Tiber, (E) Statio Annonae, (F) Temple of Hercules Invictus (?). Drawing: John W. Stamper based on Filippo Coarelli, *Il Foro Boario* (1992), pp. 104–5, fig. 20.

with the Greek Palaemon and may have originally been the god of the ferry crossing the Tiber. His dedication day was the Portunalia, on August 17.[99]

Because so much of the original building still exists, it is important to examine it carefully in light of what it reveals about temple architecture in the late second century B.C. (Fig. 43).[100] It is especially revealing to analyze it according to Vitruvius's descriptions of both the Ionic Order and the *eustyle* plan type. While Vitruvius made no mention of this particular temple in his many references to Roman buildings, it nevertheless closely compares to his canonical descriptions.

Exhibiting a combination of Hellenistic and Etrusco-Roman architectural influences, it is composed of an Etruscan-style podium with a frontal approach and a deep pronaos. Its Ionic columns, pilasters, and entablature are Hellenistic, and its pseudoperipteral composition is what Vitruvius described as a unique Roman synthesis of temple categories in which the builders remove the temple walls, transferring them to the intercolumniations.[101] For a temple of such small

43. Rome, Temple of Portunus, ca. 120 B.C. Photo: Istituto Centrale per il Catalogo e la Documentazione, F.17379.

size, a peripteral arrangement would have left no room at all for a cella.

Smaller than the Ionic temples of the Forum Romanum and Forum Holitorium, the pronaos of the Temple of Portunus has just four columns across and

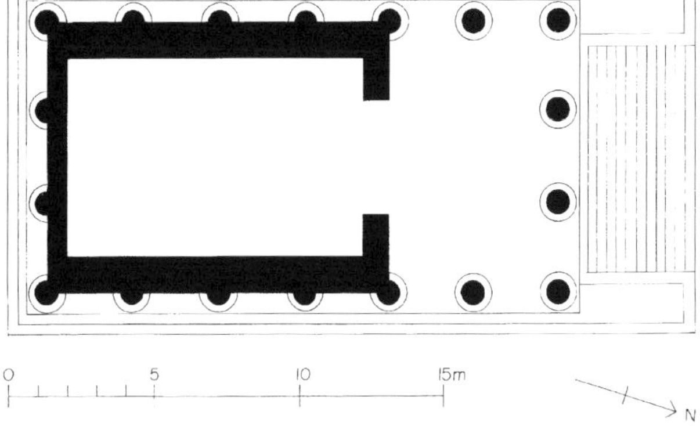

44. Temple of Portunus, plan. Drawing: John W. Stamper after Ernst R. Fiechter, in *RömMitt* 21 (1906), pl. 6.

two deep (Fig. 44). The cella is lined with five engaged half-columns on the sides and four on the back. The dimensions of the podium are 10.50 meters wide by 19.30 meters long (36 by 62 Roman feet).[102] It is an elongated plan, with the pronaos occupying about one-third and the cella two-thirds of the stylobate.[103]

The columns have a lower diameter of .85 meters and a height of 8.20 meters, a proportional height of 9.5 times the diameter. The intercolumniations are a little over two times the diameter, 1 to 2.15 on the long sides and 1 to 2.20 on the short sides, which corresponds to Vitruvius's *eustyle*.[104]

The temple had its counterpart at Tivoli, whose Temple of Sybil, dating from ca. 150–125 B.C., was also pseudoperipteral, with four Ionic columns across the front and six along the flanks – five of them engaged to the cella walls (Fig. 45). Its pronaos was two bays deep, although the cella walls projected as *antae* the length of one bay.[105] The engaged quarter-columns of the cella walls, which are still visible, clearly suggest the

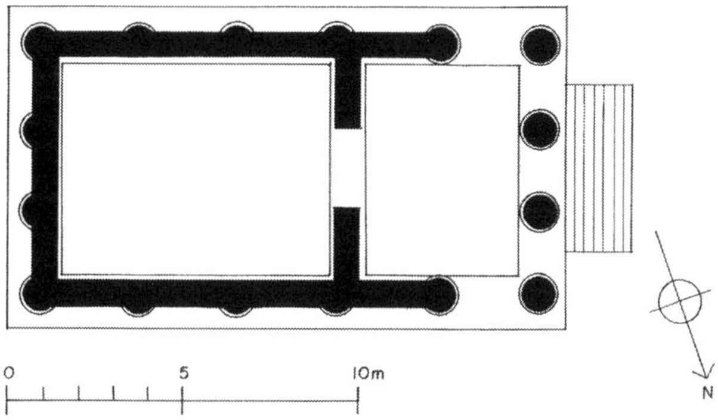

45. Tivoli, Temple of Sybil, ca. 150–125 B.C., plan. Drawing: Nora Martin after Richard Delbrueck, *Hellenistiche Bauten in Latium* (1907), vol. 2, p. 12, fig. 13.

building's proportion, scale, and articulation in its original state and link it closely to the Temple of Portunus.

As a further example, we can add the Temple of Hercules at Cori (Fig. 46), built in the first century B.C. A pseudoperipteral temple with four columns across the front and nine on the sides – six of them engaged as pilasters on the cella walls – it represents a unique synthesis, in this case, with the Doric Order, the peripteral appearance, and the Roman plan type with a deep pronaos.[106]

Since the Temple of Portunus was built before marble became widely accepted as a construction material in Rome, it represents a continuation of older Roman building practices, with locally quarried tufa and travertine. Its podium is *opus caementicium* faced with Anio tufa and travertine. Its pronaos columns and the two engaged corner columns on the southeast side are travertine. The rest of the half-columns, plus the walls of the cella and the frieze and cornice, are tufa. The architrave, column bases, and capitals are travertine. The entire structure was covered with a thin coat of stucco at the time of its initial construction. Somewhat later, elements of decoration were added to the walls, columns, and the entablature, most of which have now disappeared. Portions of the frieze decorations that do remain represent garlands hanging between putti, candelabra, and bucranian heads (Fig. 47).[107]

The Temple of Portunus is significant to the history of Roman temple architecture not only because it is so well preserved, but also because it is a near canonical example of the use of the Ionic Order as described by Vitruvius.[108] Beginning with the temple's column bases, which are Attic style, there is a correspondence with Vitruvius's rules. He prescribed that the height of an Attic base, excluding the plinth, should equal one-third the thickness of the column shaft. The height should be divided into four parts, one-fourth constituting the upper torus and the other three divided equally, one part composing the lower torus and the other the scotia with its fillets.[109]

For the Ionic capital, Vitruvius prescribed that the width of the abacus should be slightly larger than the lower column diameter.[110] The capital's height, including the volutes, should be one-half of the lower diameter. Because Ionic column capitals normally have two parallel faces and two parallel side scrolls, the problem of directionality was solved in the Temple of Portunus, as it was, for instance, in the Erechtheum or the Temple of Athena Nike, by allowing the adjacent faces to meet at a 45-degree angle. They also compared directly to the Temple of Dionysius at Teos and

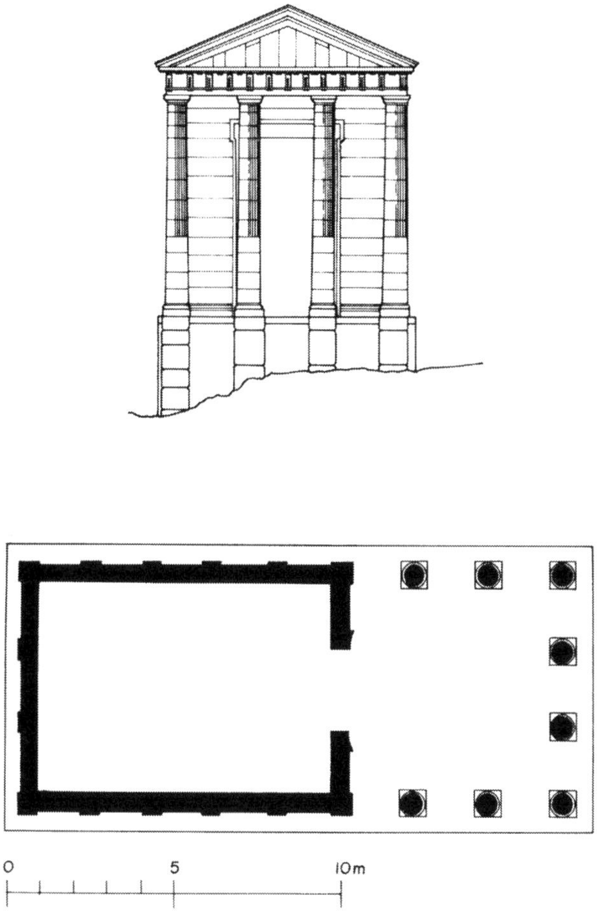

46. Cori, Temple of Hercules, first century B.C., elevation and plan. Drawing: Rogelio Carrasco after Richard Delbrueck, *Hellenistiche Bauten in Latium*, (1907), vol. 2, pl. 15.

the Temple of Artemis Leukophryene at Magnesia by Hermogenes.[111]

The proportions of the temple's architrave, as prescribed by Vitruvius, were based on an overall height of one-twelfth the column height. The cymatium is one-seventh of the height of the architrave. The fascias of the architrave are divided into twelfths, the lower one three-twelfths, the second four-twelfths, and the third five-twelfths. The frieze is three-fourths the height of the architrave and so on until the top of the corona is reached.[112]

In all, the Temple of Portunus is one of the most elegant combinations of Italic and Greek taste from the period.[113] As Greek architects were brought to Rome, they carried with them their Hellenistic style, which they adapted to Roman buildings like this one. Its pseudoperipteral form gives it the appearance of a Greek peripteral temple, and its Ionic columns and two-sided capitals with corner volutes at a forty-five-degree angle are purely Greek in style. Its Ionic Order is in fact a near canonical example as it was described by Vitruvius, thus making this temple one of the best we have to demonstrate the way Hellenistic influences were adopted and transformed in Rome in the second-century B.C.

Stress must be given to the phrase "near canonical," for as with most Roman temples, it was, in fact, a pragmatic combination of theoretical principles and adjustments made in response to local site conditions, building traditions and materials, not to mention individual taste. As Vitruvius himself pointed out, many other factors besides the desire for dimensional harmony were important in building design.[114]

In terms of the ideal, Vitruvius suggested that proportion (*eurythmia*) and symmetry (*symmetria*) are the beauty and fitness that result from adjustments of the order's individual elements. This is attained when the details of the work are of a height suitable to their breadth and of a breadth suitable to their length. Proportion consists of using a fixed module, both for the parts of the building and for the whole. Symmetry, arising from proportion, is specifically the relation of individual elements and the overall composition. Symmetry is a concept that relates numbers, measures, and proportions to artistic and philosophical questions. Suggesting a commensurability of parts, it involves measure, ratio, number, and shape.[115]

What often happened, however, was either an adherence to ratios that did not produce simple dimensions or else a use of modules that did not necessarily result in simple relationships.[116] Architects typically followed canonical principles to a point, then made minor adjustments to suit their artistic judgment.

The Temple of Portunus represents the extent to which Hellenistic influence in the form of the Ionic Order was predominant in Rome during much of the second century B.C. It had become gradually more appealing and acceptable to Roman builders and the public alike, although in some cases it was used in conjunction with traditional Etruscan plans or adapted to fit distinctly Roman cult needs or site conditions. As Ionic temples of the Ionian coast and mainland Greece became accessible as both models and sources of building material, their style of architecture became common in Roman practice. It was typically the use of the order more than plan types that was borrowed most directly from Hellenistic models. This trend continued until about the end of the second century B.C., when the pure Corinthian style came to dominate most Roman temple architecture and Roman architects and builders began to develop their own interpretations.

During much of the Republic, Rome had been a city of contrasts: a Latin population with a substantial Etruscan minority; largely Etruscan-influenced architectural, religious, and political traditions; and a sizable and aggressive army that gave it a measure of security and autonomy from its neighboring cities. As Rome's internal political changes and conquests revolutionized its economy, the Roman and Etruscan cultures diverged. Its new contacts with other civilizations led to an increasing tendency to absorb new populations, religions, and cultural influences into its own sphere, all of which gave it a progressive and cosmopolitan air. The Romans were by no means ashamed of such borrowings; on the contrary, they made a positive virtue of the fact that they owed most of their institutions and customs to other people.[117] It was a great source of pride for them, especially because they had achieved superiority over their Etruscan masters, and it helped chart a course for the future as they came to absorb and transform the culture of the Hellenistic Greeks, an expropriation of artistic and architectural traditions that revolutionized the city's urban character and building practices.[118]

For the Romans, temple architecture based on Hellenistic precedents was an important vehicle for

47. Temple of Portunus, elevation and details of cornice and column capitals. Illustration: Andrea Palladio, *Four Books of Architecture* (1965), vol. 4, pl. 32. Courtesy of Dover Publications.

culturally appropriating Rome's imperial conquests. The power to represent what was beyond Rome's own borders derived from the power of an imperial society, and that power took the form of a reshaping or reordering into the local conventions of Roman building practice.[119] Roman builders represented what they saw beyond their borders, yet they felt no need to copy Hellenistic buildings in their entirety. They felt free to change them as they desired to suit their own traditions, materials, and functional needs.

5

THE CORINTHIAN ORDER IN THE FIRST CENTURY B.C.

Rome was at war both abroad and at home throughout much of the first century B.C. In the mid-80s B.C., Rome's first dictator, Lucius Cornelius Sulla, led a military expedition against Mithradates VI in Asia Minor.[1] The conflict soon expanded into a civil war between Sulla and Caius Marius and his son Marius the Younger.[2] Although Sulla was victorious against both Mithradates VI and the Mariuses, much of Rome, including the Temple of Jupiter Capitolinus, was destroyed during the fighting. A state of unrest continued in the second half of the century as Pompey, Julius Caesar, Marcus Anthony, and, finally, Octavian waged one battle after another in pursuit of power and hegemony over Italy and its colonies.

Architecture during this period continued to be transformed by the influence of the Hellenistic style, but now it involved a gradual change from the Ionic to the Corinthian Order. By the middle of the century, the Corinthian Order, with its elegant, stylized acanthus-leaf capitals, came to dominate temple construction.[3] Examples that clearly manifest this change in the first half of the century include the Round Temple by the Tiber and the temples of the Largo Argentina.

In keeping with this trend, Sulla ordered the rebuilding of the Temple of Jupiter Capitolinus after its destruction in 83 B.C. by using Corinthian capitals taken as *spolia* from the Temple of Olympian Zeus in Athens. In so doing, he transformed it in part from its original Etrusco-Roman style to the Hellenistic style. Even though it is probable only the capitals and not the whole columns were used, this transformation had the effect of modernizing the Capitoline Temple, bringing it up-to-date with the latest fashion, and thus reaffirming its influence on subsequent Roman architects and patrons alike.

The Round Temple in the Forum Boarium

The Round Temple by the Tiber is the best-preserved Corinthian temple in Rome from the first century B.C.[4] Today it stands in a small park between the Lungotevere and the Via del Teatro di Marcello. Its marble Corinthian columns rise boldly against an earth embankment that separates the park from the river. Rather than an entablature and domical roof, the columns support a makeshift wooden roof, giving it the appearance of a primitive hut. Despite its present appearance, the refinement of its details, the magnificence of its materials, and the drama of its original site are readily apparent.

The Round Temple is one of the many examples of *munia*, constructed by an unknown member of the aristocracy, possibly a victor in a recent military campaign. This particular builder had an obvious passion for the Corinthian Order, and Hellenism in general, and he wanted to build in Rome a distinctive monument that would transcend the dominant Ionic style (Fig. 48). This temple unquestionably played an important role in the introduction and development of the Corinthian Order in Roman temple architecture.

The identification of the temple's cult deity has been much debated. It was once thought to have been dedicated to Vesta, but Rome's Temple of Vesta was clearly the circular temple located in the Forum Romanum.[5] Some archaeologists gave an attribution to Mater Matuta, although the site of that temple

48. Rome, Round Temple by the Tiber, ca. 100–90 B.C. Photo: Istituto Centrale per il Catalogo e la Documentazione, E.636.

has been definitively identified as the Etrusco-Roman temple group adjacent to Sant' Omobono.[6] Many authors refer to it simply as the Round Temple by the Tiber.[7] At present, there are two theories about its dedication, the first to Hercules Victor *ad portam Trigeminam*, the second to Hercules Olivarius. Neither has been definitively substantiated, however, because the question of both its dedication and the date of its construction remains open to debate.

In the first case, reference to the temple is made in an inscription on a slab of peperino found in the eighteenth century on the Caelian Hill. The inscription states that a temple of Hercules Victor was dedicated from war booty by L. Mummius Archaicus.[8] Having conquered the Aachaeans and destroyed Corinth while he was consul in 146 B.C., he returned to Rome the following year and celebrated a triumph. He dedicated both the temple and a statue of Hercules Victor.[9] The location *ad portam Trigeminam* refers to an area of the Forum Boarium on which the Round Temple is located that was just outside the Servian wall. Running parallel to the Tiber, this strip of land ranged from 60 to 100 meters wide.[10]

In the second case, the Round Temple's dedication is attributed to Hercules Olivarius, the god of olive oil production. An inscription on a cult statue found near the temple makes reference to Hercules Olivarius, and it is known that the sculptor was Scopas the Younger, who was active in the last decades of the second century B.C.[11]

The surname Olivarius suggests the temple's founder was engaged in olive oil trade. The ancient writers Servius and Macrobius provide the name of this seafaring merchant as M. Octavius Herrenus and state

that he dedicated a tenth of his profits to Hercules. Later on, while fighting off pirates, he had a vision of Hercules, who saved him. He requested land from the magistrates to build a temple to Hercules Victor.[12] Servius states further that shrines dedicated to Hercules are usually round, a statement that is corroborated by Livy, who writes of a round Temple of Hercules in the Forum Boarium.[13]

The temple's relationship to Hercules Olivarius is further confirmed, according to this theory, by a relief on the Arch of Trajan in Beneventum, in which the emperor is shown arriving at the *Portus Tiberinus*. At his left and right are images of Apollo, Hercules, and Portunus, which correspond to three temples located here: the image of Apollo Caelispex near the Circus Maximus, the Temple of Hercules Olivarius, and the Temple of Portunus.[14]

There are numerous objections, however, to both of these theories. In the case of L. Mummius Archaicus and the Temple of Hercules Victor *ad portam Trigeminam*, scholars argue that the finding place of the inscription on the Caelian Hill means it referred to a temple or a small shrine in that location rather than one in the Forum Boarium.[15] In the case of M. Octavius Herrenus and the Temple of Hercules Olivarius, some argue that he could not have been in a position to build and dedicate a marble temple in Rome. He was not a general and did not have sufficient financial resources. Also, the statue by Skopas was not the cult statue of Hercules that would have been inside the temple. Rather, it was a statue that stood in the sacred precinct outside the temple along with several others.[16]

As yet, the temple's attribution remains an open question. It seems certain that it belonged to the prestigious cult of Hercules, but because a more specific identification remains undetermined, it will continue to be referred to here as the Round Temple by the Tiber.[17]

Just as the temple's proper name remains in question, so, too, is the date of its construction. If it was the Temple of Hercules Victor *ad portam Trigeminam* built by L. Mummius, it would have been constructed as early as the 140s B.C., just after the first marble temple of Jupiter Stator in the Porticus Metelli. Both L. Mummius and Caecilius Metellus Macedonicus, each of whom took an enormous amount of war booty, would have commemorated their victories by founding temples. They were rival generals, both of whom fought against the Achaeans, and both would have desired distinctive architectural monuments.[18]

If it was the Temple of Hercules Olivarius built by M. Octavius Herrenus, then its construction would have occurred in ca. 80–70 B.C. Literary evidence suggests Octavius Herrenus was born around 120–110 B.C., which would mean his victory over the pirates must have occurred sometime after 80 B.C.[19] According to the passage in Macrobius, the name Hercules Victor was a reference to both the past triumphs of Hercules and to the recent victory of Octavius Herrenus, who may have been responsible for the introduction of the cult of Hercules into Rome.[20]

Again, there are objections to both theories. On one hand, a date as early as the 140s B.C., if built by Mummius Archaicus, would not have been possible because stylistically the temple relates to buildings of a later period.[21] On the other hand, a date of 80 to 70 B.C. for a temple built by Octavius Herrenus is too late based on the temple's material, the stylistic qualities of its capitals, and the conditions of the Tiber River harbor at the time.[22] The most widely accepted date at the time of this writing, and the one preferred here, is between 100 and 90 B.C., shortly after the Temple of Portunus.[23]

The Round Temple's circular form was derived from the Greek tholos, such as those at Delphi, Epidaurus, and Olympia, all from the fourth century B.C. Although these structures combined in various ways the Doric, Ionic, and Corinthian Orders, in each case the Corinthian Order was confined to columns or piers inside the cella as opposed to the outer colonnade.[24] With the Round Temple in Rome, Corinthian columns were used exclusively, and only on the exterior.

The temple's circular stylobate (Fig. 49) has a diameter of 16.50 meters (56 Roman feet).[25] Its twenty freestanding, fluted columns (one column is missing) are spaced according to the *pycnostyle* composition.[26] Eleven of its columns, on the north and west quadrants (that is, on the right and back when facing the temple), were replaced after a fire in the imperial period. They were done in imitation of the originals, with slight differences in the manner of carving.[27] They are of Lunense marble, however, whereas the originals are of Pentelic marble.[28]

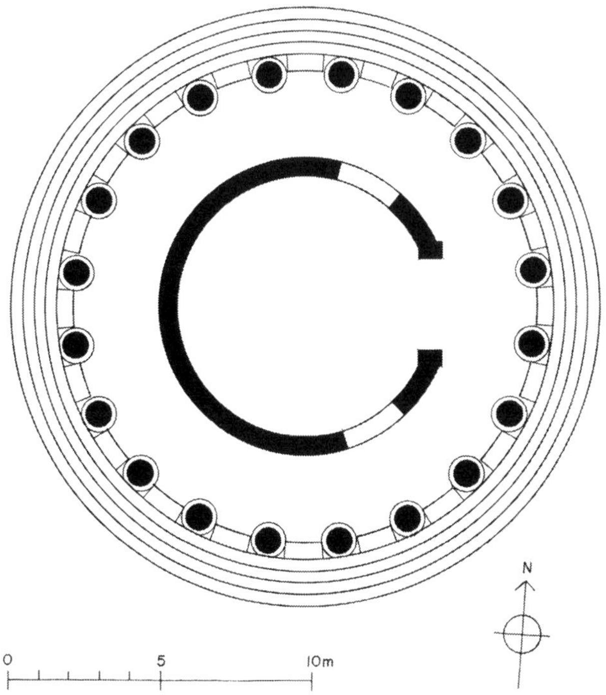

49. Round Temple by the Tiber, plan. Drawing: John W. Stamper after Friedrich Rakob and Wolf-Dieter Heilmeyer, *Der Rundtempel am Tiber in Rom* (1973), pl. 1.

The temple's plan dimensions correspond to Vitruvius's prescription for circular shrines: "let two steps and then the stylobate be constructed below. Next, let the cella wall be set up, recessed within the stylobate about one fifth of the breadth thereof, and let a place for folding doors be left in the middle to afford entrance."[29]

With an outer dimension of 16.50 and an external cella diameter of 9.91 meters (34 Roman feet), the cella is, in fact, recessed within the stylobate one-fifth the overall diameter. From this standpoint, it corresponded to a convention that Vitruvius considered appropriate.[30]

Curiously, however, the height of the temple's columns were not in accordance with Vitruvius's standard, for they were notably taller than he deemed suitable. He described a proportional relationship for round temples such that the height of a column should be equal to the interior dimension of the cella's diameter.[31] With a column height of 10.60 meters and an interior cella dimension of 8.53 meters, however, the columns in this case are more than 2 meters taller than they should have been according to Vitruvius (Fig. 50).

A similar discrepancy is found in the proportion of the columns' height to their lower diameter, 10.60 meters to .96 meters, a ratio of 11.15 to 1. This did not correspond to Vitruvius's standard ratio of 10 to 1, which was, in fact, found in most other Corinthian temples. Although the columns do have a 6 to 5 ratio between their overall height and the height of their shaft, which was also standard for later Corinthian temples, they were very much attenuated in comparison with the standard that Vitruvius preferred.[32] If Vitruvius knew about this temple, assuming a construction date at the beginning of the first century B.C., it is apparent that he did not consider its columns to be representative for such a temple type.

Despite the Round Temple's proportional anomalies, the quality of design and craftsmanship exhibited in its details is spellbinding. To begin with the columns, their bases, all of Pentelic marble, are typical of the Attic Corinthian tradition with two tori separated by a scotia. Their plinths are unusual in that they follow the temple's radial lines, the blocks being carved wider at the front and narrower toward the back.[33]

The temple's original capitals (Fig. 51), those of its south and east quadrants (on the left and front as one faces the temple), have broad divisions of the lobes, widely spread points, and rounded fleshy ribs.[34] The

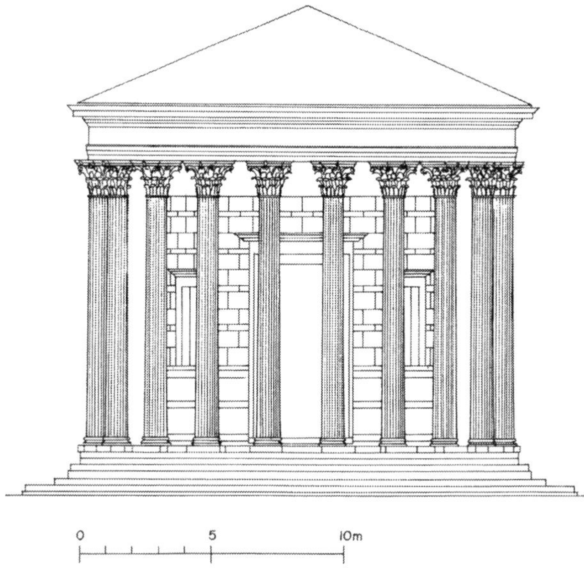

50. Round Temple by the Tiber, elevation. Drawing: John W. Stamper after Friedrich Rakob and Wolf-Dieter Heilmeyer, *Der Rundtempel am Tiber in Rom* (1973), pl. 23.

51. Round Temple by the Tiber, detail of the original column capital, typical of south and east quadrant. Photo: Deutsches Archäologisches Institut, Rome, 63.1556.

bells are fully elaborated with two rows of acanthus leaves plus eight cauliculi with outstretched leaves supporting the volutes. They are made in two halves, and all of their elements are sharply delineated and sculpted in rich three-dimensionality with the tops of the leaves curving outward and downward.[35] They represent a Hellenistic style with origins in buildings like the Hekateion in Lagina in southwest Asia Minor.[36] The high point of this style in the East was reached in the time of Antiochus IV, in 175–164 B.C., and is represented by such influential examples as the propylon of the Bouleterion in Miletus and the Temple of Olympian Zeus in Athens.[37]

The later capitals have several features that distinguish them from the earlier group (Fig. 52).[38] For instance, on the acanthus leaves, the upper point of one lobe overlaps the point of the lobe above so as to leave a narrow, wedge-shaped hollow. Also, typical features of the post-Augustan period are a flat midrib of the acanthus leaf, drill holes used to make the lobe divisions, and rough carving of the cauliculi. These characteristics became common after the time of Augustus and were almost universal by the time of the Flavians in the 70s and 80s A.D.[39] For this reason, the replacement capitals are dated to ca. A.D. 20. One theory proposes that the original columns may have been destroyed in a catastrophic flood of the Tiber River, which occurred in A.D. 15 during the reign of Tiberius.[40]

The temple's entablature was removed during the Middle Ages, leaving its exact form open to speculation. Palladio reconstructed it as a standard Corinthian entablature with a pulvinated frieze, although we have no way of knowing how accurate he was (Fig. 53).[41] There are extant fragments of coffering that were used in the peristyle ceiling, which are characterized by recessed panels framed by ovolo and cyma reversa moldings and decorated with a rosette composed of acanthus leaves.[42] The origin of this type of coffering was again Greek, as seen in the Erechtheum in Athens and the Tholos at Epidauros. It was adapted by Roman architects with relatively few changes, the motif appearing in numerous examples including the Temple of Mars Ultor.[43]

52. Round Temple by the Tiber, detail of a replacement capital from the first century A.D., typical of north quadrant. Photo: Deutsches Archäologisches Institut, Rome, 63.1595.

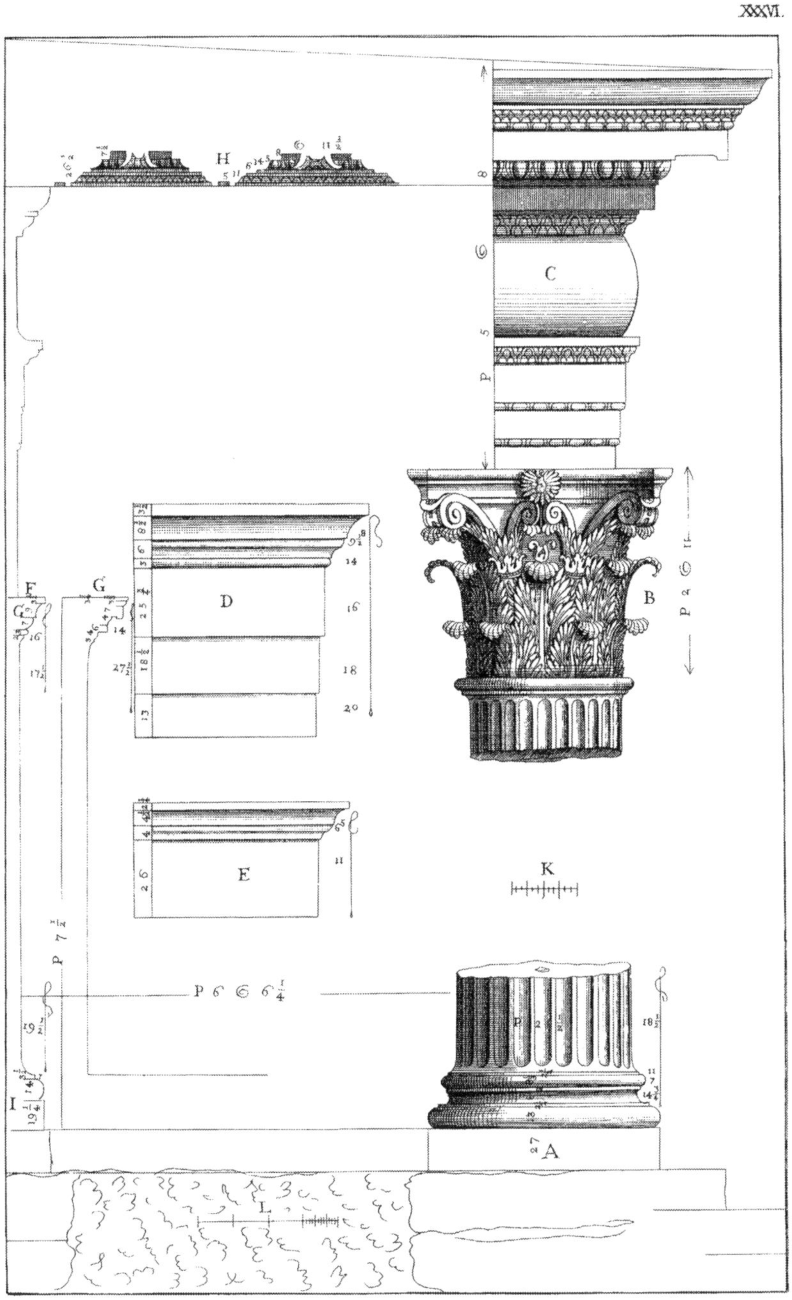

53. Round Temple by the Tiber, detail of column. Illustration: Andrea Palladio, *Four Books of Architecture* (1965), vol. 4, pl. 36. Courtesy of Dover Publications.

As for the roof, Vitruvius prescribed that there should be a domed cella and that the "proportions of the roof in the center should be such that the height of the rotunda, excluding the finial, is equivalent to one-half the diameter of the whole work."[44] Palladio assumed it had a dome much like the Pantheon's, with a drum created by the upward extension of the cella. Others reconstruct it with a conical roof, some as a single element spanning the building's entire width, some with it split in two parts with a shed roof over the columns and a conical roof only over the cella.[45]

The temple's cella walls are composed of Pentelic marble revetments on a travertine core.[46] There are no columns or pilasters inside as there were in the Greek tholoi.[47] Its single door faces east and is flanked on each side by a window. The wall is scored to indicate rustication, the pattern divided into two levels: the lower one with large blocks, the upper one emphasizing smaller

54. Tivoli, Temple of Vesta, first century B.C. Photo: Istituto Centrale per il Catalogo e la Documentazione, C.5021.

individual blocks in alternating tall and short courses.[48] Such coursing and the manner of indicating joints is similar to the work of Hermogenes in the second century B.C., especially the Temple of Artemis at Magnesia. Hermogenes was not the originator of this finely drafted masonry technique, but his adoption of it was an important factor in establishing its use in Rome. The most outstanding example of the technique is seen in the Temple of Mars Ultor.[49]

The Round Temple represents the purity of Hermogenes in its use of Pentelic marble, the Attic bases, and the Corinthian capitals.[50] In general, the strong evidence of Greek influence is congruent with the first half of the first century B.C., but in this case, it is not so much a Roman transformation as it is a pure product of Greek hands. Not so straightforward, however, are the proportional relationships of its columns and plan dimensions. Vitruvius did not mention this temple in his discussion of the circular building type, nor did he include its columns as examples of the Corinthian Order, even though their craftsmanship was remarkable by Roman building standards. Although he surely saw

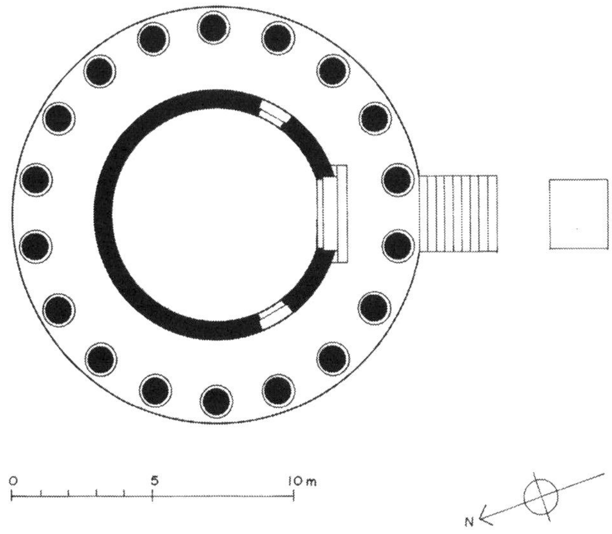

55. Tivoli, Temple of Vesta, plan. Drawing: John W. Stamper after Richard Delbrueck, *Hellenistische Bauten in Latium* (1907), vol. 2, p. 12, fig. 13.

the Round Temple while he was writing his book, he must have found it wanting in terms of its proportions, the columns being too tall relative to both their lower diameter and in relation to the cella diameter.

Vitruvius's description of a round temple was more in keeping with the Temple of Vesta at Tivoli (Figs. 54 and 55), which also dates from early in the first century B.C.[51] This temple has a column height of 7.10 meters (24 Roman feet) compared with the inner cella diameter of 7.10 meters. This corresponds directly to Vitruvius's principle that the column height should be equal to the inner cella diameter.[52] The temple's overall diameter is 14.20 meters (48 Roman feet), however, which means the cella is recessed within the stylobate one-fourth the overall diameter, not the one-fifth ratio prescribed by Vitruvius. As in other cases, Vitruvius made his proportional recommendations for the round temple based on a combination of firsthand observation and on what he considered idealized proportions, excluding some temples, basing his standards directly on others.

Other features of the Temple of Vesta manifest an adherence to prescribed principles and at the same time the use of compromise when necessary. This temple is a good example of *symmetria* in some of its aspects, while it represents compromise in others. In terms of purely numerical ratios, there is both a rational aspect to the building and one that is purely subjective. The interior diameter of the cella and the height of the columns are both half the overall diameter. The height of the podium and the width of the door opening are one-sixth the overall diameter, the width of the window opening is one-twelfth, and the height of the complete façade is about three-fourths, all simple geometric ratios. The height of the entablature breaks with the progression of simple ratios, however, in that it is a few inches higher than the ideal. The architect wanted to avoid what he feared would be a visually unsatisfactory proportion. He compromised between the ideals of *symmetria* and the actual appearance to a viewer standing on the ground next to the temple.[53]

Stylistically, the Temple of Vesta is an example of an Italian transformation of the Corinthian style that is distinct from its Hellenistic sources.[54] The temple is composed of eighteen fluted Corinthian columns, ten of which survive, and a Hellenistic entablature with a frieze decorated with ox heads, garlands, rosettes, and *paterae*. The capitals (Fig. 56) differ markedly from those of the Round Temple by the Tiber in that their lower and middle rows of acanthus leaves are tightly grouped, and their outer and inner spirals rise parallel and independent from them. The outer spirals have an odd flat shape and a corkscrew projection. Between them is a large flower standing out from the upper part of the bell.[55]

The columns have typical Attic bases with two tori and a scotia, but they are further distinguished from those of the Round Temple in that their flutes are cut square at the top. This motif was typical in Tivoli, Palestrina, and Pompeii in the final years of the second century B.C., representing a unique characteristic of a regional variation of the Corinthian Order.

It is also instructive to compare the Round Temple by the Tiber with the circular Temple B, Fortuna Huiusce Diei, in Largo Argentina.[56] It was a similar building type, but like the Temple of Vesta in Tivoli, it represented a distinctly different quality of craftsmanship and materials.[57] Constructed in ca. 90 B.C., Temple B had Corinthian columns, eighteen in this case, with tufa shafts and travertine bases, capitals, and cornice (Figs. 57 and 58).[58] The fluting of the column shafts was rounded off at the top as in the Round Temple by the Tiber. Its indigenous travertine capitals, showing Greek and Asiatic influence, were hewn in two

56. Tivoli, Temple of Vesta, detail of column, capital, and entablature. Illustration: Georges Gromort, *Choix d'éléments empruntés à l'architecture classique* (1927), vol. 1, pl. 37.

57. Rome, Temple B, Largo Argentina, ca. 90–80 B.C. Photo: Deutsches Archäologisches Institut, Rome, 76.1928.

pieces.[59] Stylistically, they represent the late phase of the Hellenistic period, which lasted until the time of Julius Caesar.[60] Little is known about the form of the entablature, although, it was probably of travertine with a carved frieze of Pentelic marble. Its cornice may have been ornamented with carved lions' heads.[61]

Like the Round Temple by the Tiber, this temple's columns are too tall according to Vitruvius's standard. Their total height is 11 meters, and their lower diameter is 1.10 meters, representing a slenderness ratio of just less than 11 to 1, compared with Vitruvius's standard of 10 to 1. Likewise, their overall height of 11 meters is greater than the cella's internal diameter of 9.54 meters (32 Roman feet).[62] The diameter of the podium is 19.20 meters (65 Roman feet), and its cella, according to Vitruvius's convention, was recessed three-fifths the overall diameter (Fig. 59).[63]

Later in the century, perhaps at the time of Pompey or Octavian, the temple underwent significant alterations. The first was the removal of the cella wall

58. Rome, Temple B, detail of capital. Photo: Deutsches Archäologisches Institut, Rome, 68.1863.

and the filling in of the intercolumniations. The columns now appeared as half-columns in a pseudoperipteral arrangement. The cult statue was moved to the back of the enlarged cella, and the perimeter of the podium was enlarged with an additional ring of peperino.[64] At the same time, a pronaos with four columns across may have been added to the front.[65] Two lateral walls projecting from the podium on either side of the stairs were probably used as bases for statues.[66] Finally, perhaps at the time of Domitian, an outer brick wall was added to the cella, in this case, hiding entirely the original columns.[67]

A comparison can also be made with the Temple of Vesta in the Forum Romanum, which was rebuilt after a fire in 14 B.C.[68] It was restored again at the time of Nero and again under Trajan before its final reconstruction by Julia Domna (Fig. 60).[69] As it is represented on a relief in the Uffizi in Florence, which probably corresponds to its appearance at the time of Augustus, it stood on a high podium with projecting plinths under each column. The columns were fluted and had, in this case, either Composite or Ionic capitals.[70] There were twenty columns in all, and they had a diameter of .51 meters and a height of 5.61 meters. They supported an entablature with a plain frieze and a low-pitched conical roof. The podium was 14 meters (48 Roman feet) in diameter (Fig. 61), but the diameter of its cella, at least of the earlier versions, is unknown.[71] As it was rebuilt in the early third century B.C., it was recessed in from the ring of columns by only about one-sixth the overall diameter.

The comparison of these four temples (Table 5.1) reveals the diversity evident in the circular temple as a building type and in the design of the Corinthian Order in Roman architecture during the first century B.C. There was a wide range of proportional relationships and coexisting stylistic details such as column flutes

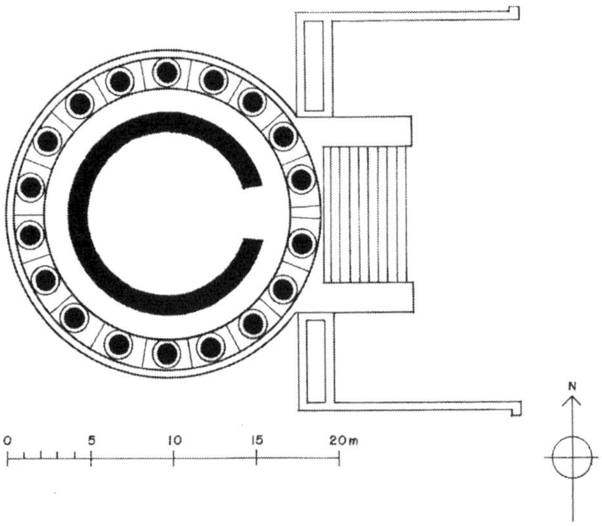

59. Rome, Temple B, plan. Drawing: John W. Stamper after G. Marchetti-Longhi in *BullCom* 76 (1956–1958), pl. 2.

60. Rome, Temple of Vesta, Forum Romanum, as built by Septimius Severus and Julia Domna in ca. A.D. 200. Photo: Istituto Centrale per il Catalogo e la Documentazione, D.6143.

that were rounded at the top in contrast to those cut square at the top, or small flowers in front of the abacus in contrast to large flowers in front of the bell. In general, the former represents a direct Hellenistic transplant, the latter a more distinct Roman transformation of the Corinthian Order designed and executed by local builders. The buildings represent a diverse range of varied solutions to the same problem, as well as the presence of competing stylistic trends, each with its roots in Hellenistic architecture, but each a different interpretation and combined or adapted in a different way.

The Rectangular Temples of Largo Argentina

In addition to the construction of the circular Temple B, a number of transformations of the three rectangular temples took place in the Largo Argentina during the

Table 5.1. Comparative Sizes of the Circular Temples of Hellenistic Greece and the Mid-Republic in Rome (Podium Size, Column Diameter, and Interaxial Dimension)

	Podium		*Columns*	
Temple	*Diameter (m)*	*Cella Diameter (m)*	*Diameter (m)*	*Interaxial (m)*
Delphi, Tholos	14.93	8.53	–	–
Epidaurus, Tholos	20.12	13.10	–	–
Rome, Round Temple by Tiber	16.50	8.44	.96	2.40
Rome, B, Largo Argentina	18.95	9.50	1.10	2.70
Tivoli, Vesta	14.23	7.16	.76	2.50
Rome, Vesta, Forum Romanum	14.0	9.58	.51	1.95

Source: Cella diameters are given as interior dimensions. The columns heights are indicated inclusive of base and capital. For the Round Temple by the Tiber and Temple of Vesta in Tivoli, see Mark Wilson Jones, "Designing the Roman Corinthian Order," *JRA* 2 (1989): 35–69, and "Principles of Design in Roman Architecture: The Setting Out of Centralized Buildings," *PBSR* (1989): 106–51.

first century B.C. (Fig. 62). A reconstruction of Temple A resulted in a building with a higher podium, a new plan, and Corinthian rather than Tuscan columns. The new podium of concrete and rubble, *opus caementicium*, faced with tufa blocks, was built over the original podium.[72] It had larger dimensions, 15 meters wide by 27.5 meters long (51 by 93 Roman feet), and it was

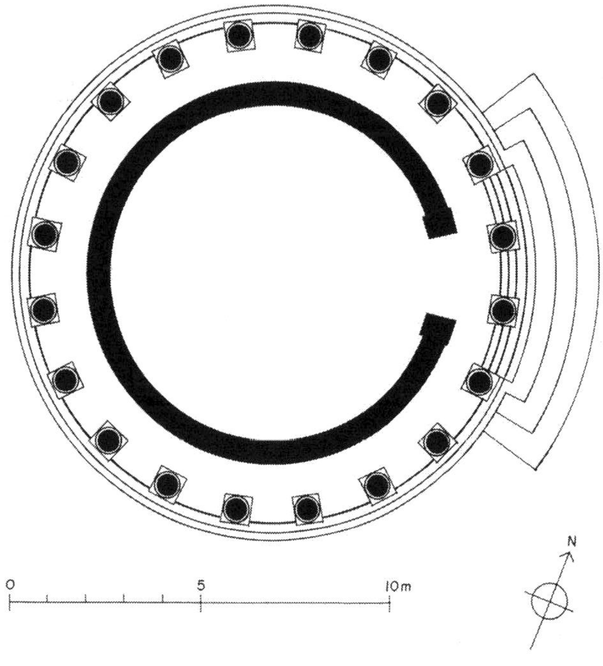

61. Temple of Vesta, Forum Romanum, plan. Drawing by Achieng Opondo after Hans Auer, *Der Tempel des Vesta und das Haus der Vestalinnen am Forum Romanum* (1888), pl. 6.

peripteral, with six columns on the front and rear and nine on the sides. The cella walls and columns of this version were of tufa, and the Corinthian capitals were travertine.[73] It now had the character of a Hellenistic building, a sort of small-scale version of the temples Vitruvius admired at Teos and Magnesia.[74]

In their origins, none of the temples of the Largo Argentina were built at the same grade level. The oldest, Temple C, was built on the original level of the Campus Martius, and the later temples were built at alternately higher levels. This remained the case until around 111 B.C., when the entire sacred area was raised about 1.40 meters. This reduced by half the height of the podia of the temples, making them seem more Hellensitic as opposed to Etrusco-Roman in appearance.[75]

The complex was given its final form sometime after A.D. 80, when the pavement level was again raised, this time with travertine paving stones. The access stairs to all of the temples were rebuilt, and a new portico was built around the entire area. This portico extended along the northern side of the temple zone and was connected to other porticos on the north and east.[76] There were also significant changes made to some of the buildings, Temple A, for instance, receiving its new travertine columns and Temple C receiving a new mosaic floor pavement.

The transformations of the temples of the Largo Argentina are representative of the increasing influence of Hellenistic architecture in Rome. The first versions of Temples C and A from the first half of the third

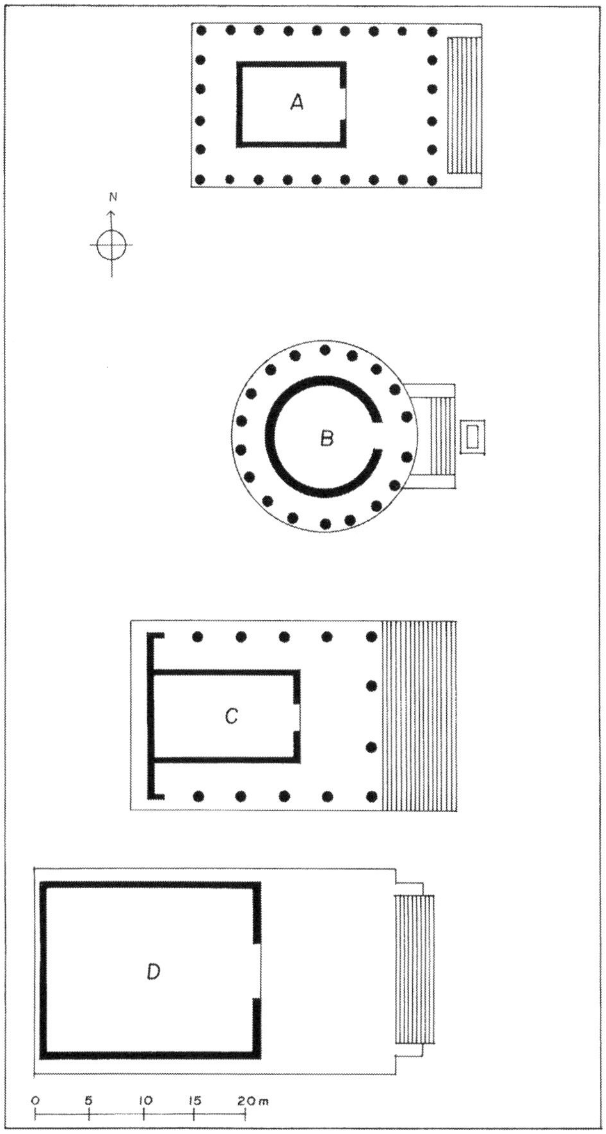

62. Rome, Largo Argentina, Temples A, B, C, and D, first century B.C. Drawing: John W. Stamper based on G. Marchetti-Longhi in *BullCom* 82 (1970–1971), pl. 1.

century B.C. were primarily Etrusco-Roman structures, although relatively small, with only a single cella and an abbreviated pronaos. When they were rebuilt in the first century B.C. and the first century A.D., they were changed radically, becoming decidedly Hellenistic. Temple C was rebuilt more or less on its original plan, whereas Temple A was altered completely. The addition of temples D and B completed the complex, now with four temples, all of them Corinthian.

The complex typifies two additional features of late republican architecture and urban design in Rome. One was the tendency to group several temples in a row with their front columns more or less on the same plane, creating a more monumental facade than was possible with a single temple. The other feature was the presence of the portico enclosure, which borrowed from Hellenistic architecture and became especially popular in the second and first centuries B.C. In the Roman context, such porticoes would tend to be used in a more symmetrical manner, emphasizing the axiality of the temples, a plan motif that became the model for the later imperial fora.

By the beginning of the first century B.C., the influence in Rome of the Corinthian Order from the Hellenistic East had become predominant. It had become gradually more appealing and acceptable to Roman builders and the public alike, although in some cases it continued to be used alongside near-traditional Etruscan plans or adapted to fit distinctly Roman cult needs or site conditions. As Corinthian temples from the East became accessible as models, the style of architecture became common in Roman practice. It was typically the use of the order more than plan types that was borrowed most directly from Hellenistic models. This trend continued through the end of the first century B.C. and into the early years of the Empire, until finally, the pure Corinthian style became the standard in all Roman temple architecture.

Sulla's Capitoline

It was at this critical time of transition to the Corinthian Order in Roman temple architecture that the Temple of Jupiter Capitolinus was destroyed by fire. Its destruction coincided with Sulla's return to Italy in 83 B.C. after his war in Greece. As he and his troops marched to Rome from the port at Brundisium, the Capitoline Temple mysteriously caught fire and burned to the ground.[77] Its rebuilding became one of the most important construction projects of Sulla's reign.

When he arrived in Rome, Sulla went to the Capitoline Hill in a magnificent triumphal procession to give thanks to the gods for his success in Greece. He was hailed as *imperator* by his troops, who saw him as the only legitimate defender of Rome.[78] In his speech in front of the burned temple, he enumerated his achievements and good fortune, and he concluded

with an order that he should be called Felix, "the Fortunate."[79]

On a later occasion, he paraded treasures that had been stolen by the younger Marius from Roman temples, and he restored them to their original owners. In November of 81 B.C., he initiated annual games, the *ludi victoriae Sullae*, as a way of further legitimizing his power and striving for public acceptance.[80] He knew well the value of celebrations, games, and parades for attracting the attention and following of the general population.

Sulla began his reconstruction of the Capitoline Temple in 83 B.C., and it was continued by Quintus Lutatius Catulus.[81] He dedicated it in 69 B.C., and included on it an inscription with his name.[82] Catulus also built the Tabularium on the edge of the Capitoline Hill, where it overlooked the Forum Romanum (Fig. 63).[83]

The project to reconstruct the Capitoline Temple was for both Sulla and Catulus an integral part of their program to legitimize their authoritarian rule.[84] To rebuild the temple was to recall the founding of the city, the Republic, and the establishment of Jupiter as the city's most important deity.[85] Such symbolic value would continue to make this Rome's most important temple throughout the imperial period.

Pliny writes that Sulla took columns from the unfinished Temple of Olympian Zeus in Athens to be used for temples on the Capitoline.[86] This has been interpreted by some scholars as meaning he used them specifically for the Temple of Jupiter Capitolinus.[87] They suggest further that crews of Greek artisans were brought to carry out the reconstruction, and either full columns or, more likely, just the capitals from the Temple of Olympian Zeus were used.[88]

Although its original plan and proportions were adhered to, the podium was raised about 2 Roman feet by the addition of several courses of *cappellaccio* tufa.[89] Catulus had wanted to lower the level of the Capitoline Hill around the podium in order to lift the temple and make the podium – whether it was terraced or flat – better proportioned to its roof. He was prevented from doing so because of the presence of *favissae*, underground chambers like cisterns, which were filled with rubble and broken building material.[90]

Although this would not have been the first example of the use of the Hellenistic Corinthian Order in Rome, its appearance in such a prominent building would have greatly added to the appeal of the order. If both the Athenian column shafts and capitals were used, the new columns would have been taller and more slender than the originals. Vitruvius wrote later, however, that the Sulla-Catulus version was still *araeostyle* and that it, like other Etruscan temples, appeared "clumsy-roofed, low, broad."[91] This would suggest the Temple's overall proportions were not changed, only that its details were altered.[92]

It is certain that better materials were used in the rebuilt version. Dionysius of Halicarnassus wrote, "For the temple that was built in the time of our fathers after the burning of this one was erected upon the same foundations, and differed from the ancient structure in nothing but the costliness of the materials."[93] Pliny reported that its roof tiles were gilt bronze.[94] Also, there is this statement Cicero made to Catulus:

> By grace of the Senate and people of Rome, your own glory is being hallowed within that temple; and together with that temple, the memory of your own name is being made sacred for all time. It is you who must concern yourself, and you who must exert yourself, to ensure that as the Capitol has been rebuilt with greater splendor, so it shall be adorned with greater richness than before; let us feel that conflagration to have been the will of heaven, and its purpose not to destroy the Temple of Almighty Jupiter, but to require us one more splendid and magnificent.[95]

The Capitoline Temple was thus rebuilt by Sulla and Catulus on the same plan as the original and with the same proportions in terms of column height and spacing. Only its materials and details were changed, and most importantly, its capitals were probably changed to the Corinthian Order, making it more lavish in appearance and in step with the current trend.

Because the oracles housed in the temple had also been destroyed in the fire, Sulla ordered its guardians to reconstruct the collection by scouring the Roman world for Sibylline prophecies. He demanded that they be alert to forgeries to ensure that the Roman world would receive only trustworthy messages from the gods.[96] Some of the new oracles came from

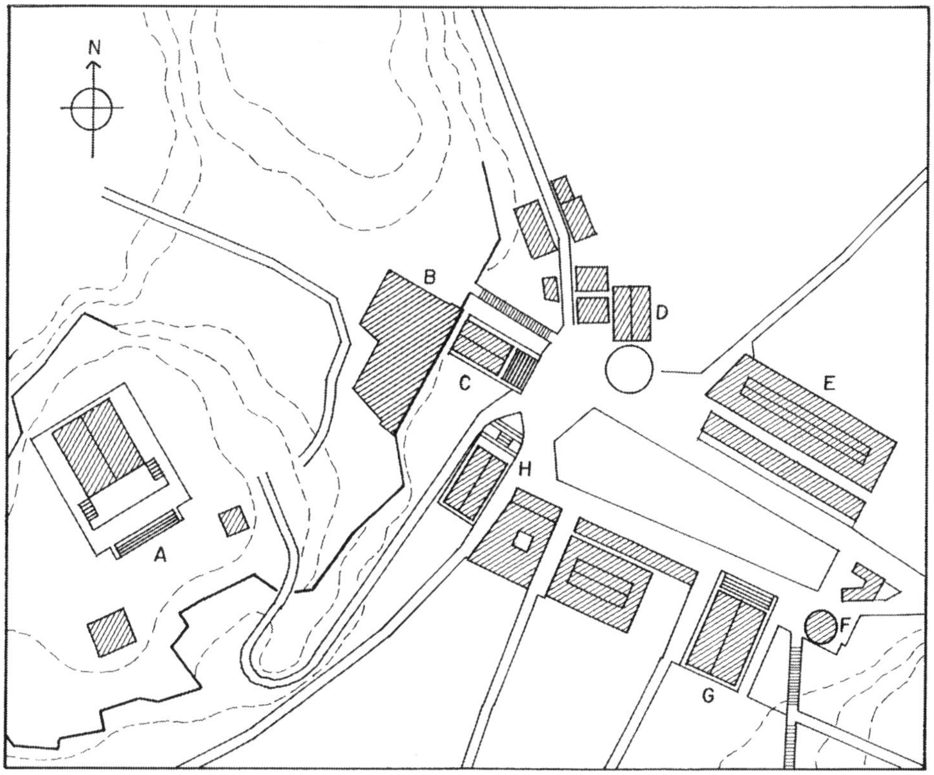

63. Rome, Plan of the Capitoline Hill and Forum Romanum at the time of Sulla: (A) Temple of Jupiter Capitolinus, (B) Tabularium, (C) Temple of Concordia, (D) Curia Hostilia, (E) Basilica Aemilia, (F) Temple of Vesta, (G) Temple of Castor and Pollux, (H) Temple of Saturn. Drawing: John W. Stamper.

Italy; others came in the form of copies from Asia Minor. Some were interpolations of the original Sibylline oracles.[97] The cult statues of Jupiter, Juno, and Minerva were also destroyed and new statues had to be made. The new statue of Jupiter depicted him seated in imitation of contemporary statues of Olympian Zeus.[98]

Thus, the temple was rebuilt, its oracles and cult statues replaced, and its position as Rome's most important cult temple was reestablished. An inscription recognizing Quintus Lutatius Catulus as the one who built the new temple remained until the first century A.D.[99] In 62 B.C., Julius Caesar attempted to substitute his name for that of Catulus but without success.[100]

It is evident that the Temple of Jupiter Capitolinus continued to embody the very notion of the Roman state itself. Roman society was held together by its internal agreement about the sacredness of the temple as a fundamental symbol. The central authority of the society was the avenue of communication with the realm of sacred values.[101] The Temple of Jupiter Capitolinus enjoyed almost universal recognition as the embodiment of cultural values, religious ceremony, and political authority. It heightened the moral and civic sensibility of Roman society, providing it with an important symbol. Successive rituals and ceremonies repeatedly brought Roman society into contact with this sacred vessel of cultural and religious values.

6

ARCHITECTURE AND CEREMONY IN THE TIME OF POMPEY AND JULIUS CAESAR

Rome's architectural and urban development at the end of the Republic was related directly to the lives of Pompey the Great and Julius Caesar. Aristocratic landowners and military generals, their political careers were established during the dictatorship of Sulla in the 80s B.C.[1] Both men came to maturity after a series of successful military exploits and political maneuvers in the following two decades. During the 60s B.C., in an effort to expand and maintain Rome's control over its vast domain, Pompey engaged in battles, skirmishes, and wars in virtually every part of the Empire, from Spain to the Middle East. His exploits were rivaled only by Julius Casear, who engaged in a protracted war in Gaul, then a civil war in Macedonia against Pompey himself, and finally, wars in Spain and Africa.

During the time of Pompey and Julius Caesar, Rome's temple and forum architecture became increasingly more monumental, the use of marble as a building material and the Corinthian Order lending a new quality and grandeur to urban development. New settings were devised for cult temples to make them appear even more grandiose. In one case, the temple was placed at the top of the *cavea* of a theater; in another, it was framed by two long porticos. The temples were made larger than their Etrusco-Roman counterparts, their height was attenuated, and their building materials were more beautiful.[2]

At the same time, the use and connotations of authority began to change as some of the temples were built to represent both a traditional deity and a person – the general, dictator, *princeps* – who took on a public role similar to that of the gods.[3] Architects, artists, and sculptors were paid well to glorify these men through their work.[4] The added magnificence in temple design was thus paralleled by a change in use that allowed the dictator to be seen as and compared with the gods very much in the style of the Hellenistic East.

Pompey the Great and the Temple of Venus Victrix

The military career of Pompey the Great (Fig. 64) was well established by the mid-60s B.C., after being granted extraordinary powers by the Senate to clear the Mediterranean of Greek pirates that had been threatening Rome's maritime interests.[5] As Pompey's navy fanned out across the Mediterranean, it not only cleared the shipping lanes of pirates, but also initiated dozens of skirmishes in coastal cities from Spain to Greece, as well as the Middle East, Asia Minor, and Africa, all in an attempt to reassert the rule of Rome over increasingly independence-minded local officials. Pompey established new cities in those regions he attacked, thus further consolidating the influence of Rome and adding new wealth to its treasuries.[6] In 63 B.C., he and his army conquered Jerusalem, and in the following year, with the death of Mithridates VI, he gained control of important transportation routes across Asia to India.[7]

When the adventurous general returned to Rome in 62 B.C. after conquering Jerusalem, he was awarded one of the largest and most magnificent triumphal processions in the city's history.[8] Plutarch writes that his triumph had such a magnitude that, even though it was distributed over two days, there was not enough time to include everything that had been prepared. There was enough to dignify and adorn yet another

64. Sculpture portrait of Pompey the Great, Museo Archaologica, Venice. Photo: Deutsches Archäologisches Institut, Rome, 82.686.

triumphal procession. Plutarch also enumerates a long list of Pompey's conquests:

> Pontus, Armenia, Cappadocia, Paphlagonia, Media, Colchis, Iberia, Albania, Syria, Cilicia, Mesopotamia, Phoenicia and Palestine, Judaea, Arabia, and all the power of the pirates by sea and land which had been overthrown. Among these people no less than a thousand strongholds had been captured, according to the inscriptions, and cities not much under nine hundred in number, besides eight hundred piratical ships, while thirty-nine cities had been founded.... But that which most enhanced his glory and had never been the lot of any Roman before, was that he celebrated his third triumph over the third continent. For others before him had celebrated three triumphs; but he celebrated his first over Lybia, his second over Europe, and his last over Asia, so that he seemed in a way to have included the whole world in his three triumphs.[9]

Great pageantry and ritual to mark the occasion of his conquests were critically important opportunities for the victorious general, a chance to project a powerful authoritative image to the public. Ritual and ceremony were modes of exercising power, the spectacle a way of explaining, justifying, impressing, and mediating.

Pompey's most ambitious architectural undertaking in Rome for the purpose of providing an appropriate setting for this kind of ceremony, was the giant complex in the Campus Martius that included the Theater of Pompey (Fig. 65), the Temple of Venus Victrix, and the giant Porticus Pompeiana, which enclosed a formal garden. Known collectively as the *opera Pompeiana*, the complex was begun in 61 B.C. – just after his most important foreign conquests – and dedicated with a series of spectacles in 55 B.C.[10] Pompey provided musical and gymnastic contests, and in the Circus Maximus he sponsored a horse race and the slaughter of wild animals. Cassius Dio reports that 500 lions were killed in five days and that men in heavy armor fought against eighteen elephants.[11]

The theater had a semicircular plan measuring 162 meters in diameter. The circular steps of the *cavea* had a capacity of approximately 12,000.[12] The temple shrine of Venus Victrix was located on the theater's main axis at its uppermost level (Fig. 66).[13] Smaller shrines were dedicated to four other deities: Honos, Virtus, Felicitas, and Victoria.[14] Fourteen statues set up around the top of the *cavea* represented the fourteen nations conquered by Pompey.[15] A statue of the goddess Venus Victrix housed in the temple stood fully draped, holding a victory figure in her outstretched right hand and supporting a long scepter with her left.[16]

The theater was the first to be built in Rome entirely of masonry and concrete. Its curved outer façade was composed of a multilevel pier-and-arch structure with engaged half columns. It may have employed the orders in an ascending arrangement – Doric, Ionic, and Corinthian – a motif that would influence the later Theater of Marcellus and the Colosseum.[17]

The complex, with a theater and temple combined, can be compared with three sanctuaries located outside of Rome, built only a few years earlier. The

65. Rome, Porticus Pompeiana with Theater, Temple of Venus Victrix, Porticus, and temples of Largo Argentina, 62–55 B.C., site plan. Drawing: John W. Stamper after Rodolfo Lanciani *Forma Urbis Romae* (1990), pl. 21; and Kathryn L. Gleason in *JGH* 14 (January–March 1994): p. 18, fig. 5.

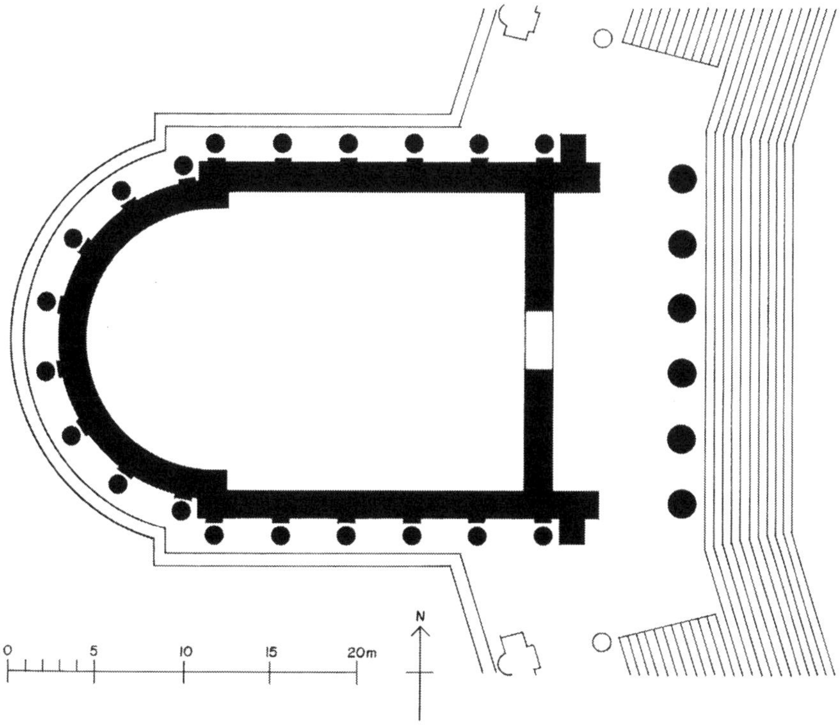

66. Rome, Temple of Venus Victrix, 62–55 B.C., plan at top of *cavea* of the Theater of Pompey. Drawing: John W. Stamper based on Rodolfo Lanciani, *Forma Urbis Romae* (1990), pl. 21.

first was the temple precinct of Fortuna Primigenia at Palestrina (Fig. 67), which is attributed to the first half of the first century B.C.[18] The upper part of the complex, once one of the most impressive sanctuaries for processional rituals in the Roman world, was composed of a series of ramps and terraces that stepped up the side of a hill and culminated with a theater and circular temple at the top. The large uppermost terrace, measuring 118 meters wide, was framed on three sides by porticos.[19] Although arranged in a different sequence than Pompey's complex, it shared with its Roman counterpart similar elements: theater, temple, and colonnaded enclosure.

A second comparison can be made with the Sanctuary of Hercules Victor at Tivoli built in 89–82 B.C. In this case, the temple was placed at the back of a large built-up platform that measured 152 meters wide by 119 meters deep.[20] Again, the platform was surrounded on three sides by porticos, and at the open front was a semicircular theater, aligned with the temple's axis. A similar arrangement is found in the older sanctuary and theater complex at Gabii. The temple precinct was surrounded on three sides by colonnades, shops, and *tabernae*, and in front of the temple was a semicircular theater that measured 60 meters across.[21] All three of these sites were easily accessible to the Romans and were certainly known by Roman architects. The design of Pompey's complex was a synthesis of the elements found in these complexes, but the theater was larger and it had an external façade masking angled vaults that supported the *cavea*.

Before the time of Pompey, theaters in Rome had been built of wood. Typically, they were built for one man for a single show and afterward were dismantled. Personal glory as expressed by such buildings was a transitory event. Pompey's construction of a permanent theater structure and his inclusion of a temple in the *cavea* was a way of ensuring that the complex would not be destroyed by the Senate, in its effort to erase past political allegiances, after his death. In this sense, the Temple of Venus Victrix was considered as important as the theater itself, the central wedge of seats of the *cavea* forming a sort of monumental staircase leading up to the temple, the deity of which presided over all the events held on the stage and orchestra below. It was under the protection of Venus Victrix that Pompey had triumphed over many of Rome's Mediterranean enemies, and it was her protection that would ensure the memory of Pompey through the great theater's maintenance and sustained use.[22]

In addition to the theater and the temple, there was a porticus surrounding a large rectangular garden that was attached to the back of the stage building and extended eastward as far as the Largo Argentina. This enclosure, the first public park in Rome, was highly influential in subsequent urban design, especially for the imperial fora.[23] Vitruvius describes the functions of a porticus: "Colonnades must be constructed behind the *scaena*, so that when sudden showers interrupt plays, the people may have somewhere to retire from the theater, and so that there may be room for the preparation of all the outfit of the stage. Such places, for instance, are the colonnades of Pompey."[24]

Porticos were designed to provide sheltered walkways, protecting people from wind, rain, heat, and cold. As with the Porticus Metelli, they housed collections of sculptures and exhibitions of paintings that had been captured in military conquests. They also provided localized urban unity, conveying a sense of orderliness, while creating a well-defined space within the crowded cityscape.[25]

Vitruvius went on to describe the design and construction of the porticos, a composition which was derived from the Greek stoa. He suggested that they should have two aisles, with Doric columns on the outside, and that their architraves and ornaments should be finished according to the law of modular proportion. The width of each aisle should be equal to the height of the outer columns. The inner row of columns, he suggested, should be one-fifth higher than the outer row and should be designed in the Ionic or Corinthian style.[26]

The origins of the stoa as a building type date to the late seventh century B.C. in cities such as Didyma, Smyrna, Samos, and Argos.[27] From the beginning, they were planned as freestanding buildings with long, narrow plans and had both an inner and outer colonnade. The long back wall was often divided into individual rooms corresponding in width to the column bays.[28] They were used as market buildings and, in some cases, as public buildings to display the spoils of war.

Rare marbles were often used in their construction, sometimes the column capitals being gilt with gold, their floor pavements inlaid with jasper and porphyry. The spaces they enclosed were laid out in formal gardens with box, myrtle, laurel, arbutus, and pine trees shading reflective pools and fountains. Each of them had a special character and attraction that gave them a particular identity and meaning.[29]

According to the *Forma Urbis Romae*, Pompey's formal garden was organized with two double groves in elongated rectangles that were laid out symmetrically about the main axis. This axis extended eastward 287 meters (975 Roman feet) from the Temple of Venus Victrix to a point tangent to the Temple of Fortuna Huiusce Diei in the Largo Argentina. The space was surrounded by colonnades on all four sides. In addition, on the north was a long basilican structure called the Hecastylon, on the east was a curia, and on the south, shops and perhaps a house Pompey constructed for his own use.[30]

The placement of the sacred groves inside the space was an appropriate gesture to Venus because one of her functions was the protectress of gardens. The grove probably consisted of plane trees, while other plants and shrubbery, including myrtle and laurel, provided low ground cover. Fountains helped to both cool the air and provide a soothing background sound.[31] As suggested by Vitruvius in his description of colonnaded squares,

> The space in the middle, between the colonnades and open to the sky, ought to be embellished with green things; for walking in the open air is very healthy, particularly for the eyes, since the refined and rarefied air that comes from green things, finding its way in because of the physical exercise, give a clean-cut image, and, by clearing away the gross humours from the eyes, leaves the sight keen and the image distinct.[32]

He goes on to suggest that by walking in open spaces, the human body is freed of bad air. It leaves the lungs and is drawn upward in the air:

> That this is so may be seen from the fact that misty vapors never arise from springs of water which are under cover, not even from watery marshes which are underground; but in uncovered places which are open to the sky, when the rising sun begins to act upon the world with its heat, it brings out the vapors from damp and watery spots, and it rolls it in masses upwards. Therefore, if it appears that in

67. Palestrina, Sanctuary of Fortuna Primigenia, perspective view of model, first half of first century B.C. Photo: Istituto Centrale per il Catalogo e la Documentazione, E.37230.

> places open to the sky the more noxious humors are sucked out of the body by the air, as they obviously are from the earth in the form of mists, I think there is no doubt that cities should be provided with the roomiest and most ornamented walks, laid out under the free and open sky.[33]

Was Vitruvius writing in response to his experiences of the Porticus Pompeiana? Was he describing a new type of urban space in Rome, one aimed at improving the health of Rome's citizens? It is very possible he viewed the Porticus Pompeiana as much for its benefits of health and its aesthetic appearance as he did its political intent.

The central axis led the viewer's eye toward the garden's western end where, at the time of Pompey, the Temple of Venus Victrix may have been visible across the top of a low, temporary stage house. The *Forma Urbis Romae* also suggests the presence of an arch or a victory monument just east of the stage house. The porticus, theater, and temple were thus intended to be experienced as a unified whole all for the greater glory of Pompey. Later, in 32 B.C., Octavian built a larger stage structure that would have blocked the view between the theater and garden. Not only did he desire a monumental stage for the theater, he also wanted to separate the garden from the theater as a way of diminishing Pompey's legacy.[34]

Pompey filled the porticus with works of art – Greek statuary and paintings – much of it collected and arranged by Atticus, a friend of Cicero, and Demetrius, Pompey's secretary. Included in the collection were Nicias's portrait of Alexander and a famous work by the Greek painter Polygnotus of Thasos. All were spoils of war from the East. Such an exhibition was a means of illustrating and glorifying Pompey's victories in the eastern Mediterranean, done so to add *dignitas* and *auctoritas* to his name.[35] Julius Caesar would emulate this type of image-building in his design of the Forum Julium, and it would be repeated by numerous emperors afterward.

With Pompey we see the overt use of temple architecture – not for a purely religious purpose, but as a political victory monument, built by a private individual on his own property. Pompey inherited from Sulla and others before him the concept of public works as a means of political propaganda and personal glorification. Bringing religious concepts into close association with personal political ambitions, the ritual and ceremony associated with the theater and temple complex were aimed at projecting an authoritative image to the public.[36] The fight for political

power became also a fight for control over the gods. Whether the ruler's intentions were sincere or his devotion to the gods a sham, he could use religion to obtain and maintain his domination. To keep control, the ruler had to maintain a firm grip on both society and the gods.[37] With Pompey, we see a powerful and victorious general indulging in self-promotion in the Hellenistic manner while still making a votive offering to a pagan deity.[38] It was a monument in which the dictator's personal intentions and the public purpose were combined.[39]

Pompey's personal intentions included not just his promotion as a military hero or his connection to Venus Victrix. His motives may have included his actual elevation to the status of a god. Such personality worship was a new aspect of Roman politics and religion, primarily influenced by practice in the eastern Mediterranean. Pompey received numerous honors in the East which served to demonstrate that certain groups there praised him as a god. A cult was named after him on the island of Delos, a month was renamed after him at Mytilene, and it is probable that cult temples were built in his honor.[40]

Such worship was becoming increasingly common as Roman generals and governors moved into leadership positions in eastern cities. They came to be treated in the same way as Hellenistic rulers, especially as Alexander the Great had been.[41] As time went on, they became used to such honors and promoted the building of monuments and the staging of festivals and games in their honor. In Rome, officers and soldiers who came back from the East told of the divinity of rulers and the cults of Roma.[42] Pompey came the closest to instituting this tradition in Rome, and Julius Caesar furthered its cause. Some would say he in fact made it an official part of Roman religion.

Despite his godlike status, Pompey's theater and temple complex was barely completed when his political fortunes began to turn. Jealousy and political rivalry unraveled his power in a far shorter period of time than it had taken to build it. He had a long-standing problem with the Senate and the consuls, and eventually, in a display of intransigence, they blocked his efforts to reward his troops returning from battle with grants of land. At the same time, they blocked an attempt by his friend Marcus Licinius Crassus to pass a law related to his financial interests.[43]

Julius Caesar, too, had difficulties with the Senate. Preparing to run for election as consul for the year 59 B.C., he was denied by the Senate the opportunity to run in absentia as he waited to be granted a triumph for battles he had won in Spain. In a mood of isolationism, the Senate opposed and offended within one year Pompey, Crassus, and Caesar just when they and their armies, in the name of Rome, had taken control of virtually the entire Mediterranean world.[44]

As a result, the three formed what has been called the first triumvirate, a clandestine coalition, its intent being to attack and weaken the Senate in revenge for its shortsightedness and lack of support for their military victories. Many historians acknowledge this moment as the beginning of the end for the Republic. Although consuls continued to be elected yearly, the Senate never again wielded the sort of influence and power it had enjoyed throughout the Republic's previous history.[45] The position of generals with personal armies became preeminent.

Julius Caesar

The first triumvirate was most significant for the development of the power base of Julius Caesar (Fig. 68).[46] Despite the Senate's attempt to stop him in 59 B.C., he succeeded in being elected to a consulship, after which he was appointed governor of Gaul.[47] Remaining there for the next nine years, he embarked on a renewed expansionist military campaign, one that eventually gave Rome control of nearly all of northern Europe, a complement to its holdings around the Mediterranean basin that had been secured by Pompey.[48]

Between 54 and 48 B.C., the first triumvirate disintegrated with the death of Crassus and the outbreak of a civil war between Pompey and Caesar. At Pharsalus, in Macedonia, Julius Caesar emerged as the victor and claimed control of the entire Empire.[49] He fought more battles in Egypt and Spain before returning to Rome and being elected as dictator in 46 B.C.[50] He celebrated four triumphs in honor of his victories over Gaul, Egypt, Africa, and Juba, each of them accompanied by extravagant ceremonies, games, and banquets that rivaled those of Pompey fourteen years earlier.[51] He ordered combats of foot soldiers, cavalry fights, a combat of elephants, and a mock sea battle staged on

68. Portrait bust of Julius Caesar, Museo Torlonia, Rome. Photo: Deutsches Archäologisches Institut, Rome, 1933.55.

an artificial lake.[52] Paintings depicting the deaths of the conquered enemies were produced and carried in the processions.[53] As had been the case with Pompey, such ritual and ceremony were objective modes of exercising power. Royal pageantry, pomp, and spectacle were a vivid way of explaining, justifying, impressing, and mediating between the ruling class and the masses. They were important opportunities for the dictator and his supporters to project an authoritative image to the public.

Caesar's political and military ascendance meant power and prestige for both himself and those around him.[54] For the bureaucrats and the officers who made up his court, an expansion of power meant more office positions, more patronage, and better opportunities for promotion. Power-oriented prestige for Caesar's own political bureaucracy had a strong dynamic, replacing what had been the cohesive aristocratic social fabric that was not only competitive but also disciplined and united. From this point on, Caesar rose above the rest, maintaining dictatorial control.

Despite Caesar's inherent role as dictator and the increasing animosity it caused among the nobility and the Senate, Rome had, after years of warfare, a stable course under a known leader. Even though it was evident that he had an interest in essentially reestablishing a monarchy, the system of government that the Romans had effectively banished more than four hundred years earlier, his popularity remained strong among the people and the all-important legions. After his magnificent triumphal celebrations, much of the Roman populace became almost idolatrous.[55] Despite his mistrust of the Senate, his political objectives gained its members' implicit support. It granted him symbolic powers like the right of sitting on a curule chair between the consuls at meetings and of speaking first on all questions brought before the assembly. He acquired control over morals, a power that had previously belonged to the censors; the right to give the signal at all games; and the right to replace the name of Catulus by his own on the Temple of Jupiter Capitolinus. A triumphal chariot with a statue of Caesar, a globe at his feet, was installed inside the temple.[56]

Although Caesar made outward gestures to deny any interest in kingship, he continued to accept titles and decrees that suggested otherwise. He was granted the title of imperator as a hereditary name, and was given authority to appear at all official occasions in triumphal clothing and to wear a laurel wreath. The anniversaries of his military victories were to be celebrated with annual sacrifices, and the entire management of the army and finance were put in his hands alone. A decree was issued that his ivory statue on its special litter should be carried with the images of other gods in the procession in the Circus Maximus.[57] It was through such events that the notion of the ruler cult, seen earlier with Pompey the Great, gained more acceptance in Roman life. With Julius Caesar, the very foundation of Rome's civil and religious discourse was decisively changed.[58]

There has long been a debate over whether Julius Caesar actually became a god before his death.[59] Some scholars argue that although many gestures were made to link him to the deities, he was not as yet officially elevated to their status. There was an accepted tradition that Rome had been founded by Romulus, who was

a descendant of Mars, and who was later himself elevated to the gods. Throughout the Roman Republic, however, there had never been a mortal man, living or dead, added to the realm of the gods. Romans had given honors and tributes to its men of distinction, but they nevertheless avoided direct identification of a hero as a deity.[60] A transformation of this long-held tradition was clearly under way at the time of Pompey and Julius Caesar.

The Temple of Venus Genetrix and the Forum Julium

In 54 B.C., Julius Caesar began planning a new forum in Rome that he would dedicate in his own name.[61] Its intended purpose was to provide additional space for the activities of the Forum Romanum, especially the law courts.[62] Caesar also anticipated creating a spectacular architectural setting where he could deliver speeches and preside in a regal manner over public ceremonies.

The forum was located in a long, narrow space northwest of the Forum Romanum. Cicero reports that while Caesar was engaged in a war in Gaul, he acted as the general's agent to purchase the land. It contained a number of houses and apartment blocks built in the second and first centuries B.C.[63] At the time of its purchase, the ground sloped upward at the northwest side to a ridge that once connected the Capitoline and Quirinal Hills. An important street, the Via Argentarius, which led from the Campus Martius, passed along the site's southwest side and continued into the Forum Romanum.[64]

Caesar ordered the existing buildings on the site to be destroyed in 54 or 53 B.C. and began construction of the new forum complex, which included both a temple and porticos to enclose the forum space.[65] It took several building campaigns by Caesar, and after him Octavian, to bring it to completion.[66] Caesar's plans for the project may have changed in 52 B.C. when the Curia Hostilia, which was immediately adjacent to his forum, burned down.[67] Desiring to keep the focus of Rome's civic functions within the realm of the Forum Romanum while at the same time allowing them to expand into his new forum complex, he initiated plans to incorporate a new curia into his forum.[68] He was at first unsuccessful, however, as the curia was reconstructed on its original site by Faustus Sulla, the son of the former dictator. It was not until 44 B.C. that the Senate granted Caesar the necessary decree allowing him to build a new curia on a new location at the southeast corner of his forum (Fig. 69).[69]

Another change in the program occurred in 48 B.C., during the battle against Pompey at Pharsalus. Caesar vowed that if victorious, he would build a temple dedicated to Venus Victrix.[70] When he returned to Rome, he decided to apply this vow to the temple he had already started in his forum. Thus, he gave the project the twofold purpose of adding to Rome's civic and judicial center while creating a monument to honor him and his victory over Pompey. By the time of its dedication, however, he changed its name because Pompey had already dedicated his temple in the Theater of Pompey to Venus Victrix after his victory at Jerusalem. Caesar changed his dedication to Venus Genetrix, a new epithet never before given to Venus or any other deity.[71]

Caesar had claimed to be a descendant of Venus at least since the late 50s B.C.[72] During the civil war, Pompey was obsessed with worry over Caesar's appropriation of his goddess.[73] Plutarch reports that he had a dream the night before the battle at Pharsalus: "That night Pompey dreamed that as he entered his theater the people clapped their hands, and that he decorated the temple of Venus Victrix with many spoils. On some accounts he was encouraged, but on others depressed by the dream; he feared lest the race of Caesar, which went back to Venus, was to receive glory and splendor through him."[74]

On the same night, Caesar had his own vision and he made his vow, as related by Appian:

> He offered sacrifice at midnight and invoked Mars and his own ancestress, Venus (for it was believed that from Aeneas and his son, Iulus, was descended the Julian race, with a slight change of name), and he vowed that he would build a temple in Rome as a thank offering to her as the bringer of Victory if everything went well. Thereupon a flame from heaven flew through the air from Caesar's camp to Pompey's where it was extinguished. Pompey's men said it exemplified a brilliant victory for them over their enemies, but Caesar

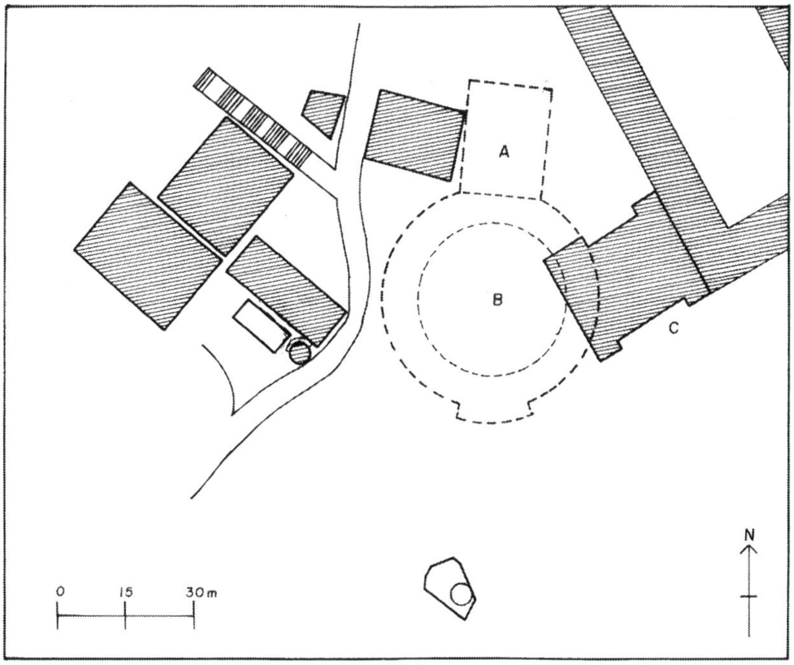

69. Rome, Curia Julia, 44–29 B.C. site plan: (A) site of Curia Hostilia, (B) site of Comitium, (C) Curia Julia. Drawing: Rogelio Carrasco based on Filippo Coarelli, *Il Foro Romano* (1983), p. 139, pl. 39.

interpreted it as a meaning that he should fall upon and extinguish the power of Pompey.[75]

In eventually changing his temple's dedication from Venus Victrix to Venus Genetrix, Caesar did not mean to exclude connotations of Victory but instead to include them with other benefits of the goddess while emphasizing his family ties to her.[76] The temple was now meant to serve as Caesar's "gift" to his divine ancestress. Venus, Aphrodite to the Greeks, was the goddess of love and beauty, the daughter of Zeus and Dione in the *Iliad*. Alternately, as in Botticelli's famous painting, she was thought to have sprung from the foam of the sea. This birth at sea took place near the Greek city of Cythera, from where she was taken to Cyprus.[77] Besides being known for her beauty, as we have seen with the Porticus Pompeiana, she also denoted growth in nature, especially in gardens, as she was the protectress of cultivation and human toil.

As part of the celebration of his four triumphs in 46 B.C., Caesar dedicated the forum and its temple even though they were only partially completed.[78] A celebration of games in honor of Julius, the *ludi victoriae Caesaris*, took place in conjunction with the dedication, an event that was repeated by Octavian in later years, normally in the month of July.[79]

The Curia Julia, under construction on its new site, was interrupted at the time of Caesar's death in 44 B.C. but was resumed two years later by order of the Senate.[80] Octavian continued construction of the forum and the Temple of Venus Genetrix and rededicated them along with the curia in 29 B.C.[81] He also constructed a chalcidicum, although its location – whether it was behind or in front of the curia – remains an open question.[82]

The forum complex underwent a number of changes in later years. During the reign of Domitian, in the A.D. 80s, the curia was rebuilt, and the forum's southeast end was altered in conjunction with the Forum Transitorium.[83] From A.D. 98 to 106 Trajan rebuilt the Temple of Venus Genetrix, dedicating it in A.D. 113. In fact, the three columns and the entablature fragments visible on the site today are from the Trajanic reconstruction.[84] In A.D. 283, the curia and the forum were damaged by fire and were restored by Diocletian.[85]

The Temple

The temple stood on a high podium that was made of *opus caementicium*, squared tufa blocks, and marble

70. Rome, Forum Julium with Temple of Venus Genetrix, 54–29 B.C., rebuilt A.D. 98–106 by Trajan, perspective view by Olindo Grossi in Homer F. Rebert and Henri Marceau, *The Temple of Concord in the Forum Romanum* (1925). Photo: Fototeca Unione, American Academy in Rome, 13225.F.

revetments. It measured 23 meters wide by 33 meters long (78 by 112 Roman feet).[86] This excluded the speakers' platform, which was added by Octavian and increased the podium size to 29.50 meters wide by 39 meters long (100 by 132 Roman feet).[87]

The temple's plan had eight columns on the front and eight deep, with the cella's rear wall projecting at the sides and turning ninety degrees to align with the columns in a modified *peripteros sine postico* manner (Figs. 70 and 71). The use of small intercolumniations corresponded to Vitruvius's description of the *pycnostyle* arrangement, a ratio of column diameter to the intercolumnial spaces of 1 to 1.5.[88] This was not a plan type Vitruvius favored, for he was adamant in his criticism against it and even named the Temple of Venus Genetrix as an example of its worst qualities:

> When the matrons mount the steps for public prayer or thanksgiving, they cannot pass through the intercolumniations with their arms about one another, but must form a single file; then again, the effect of the folding doors is thrust out of sight by the crowding of the columns, and likewise the statues are thrown into shadow; the narrow space interferes also with walks round the temple.[89]

It is a telling remark on his part for it is another example, as with his criticisms of the Temple of Jupiter Capitolinus, in which he put himself at odds with actual Roman building practices. Although he related well to Rome's adaptation of Hellenistic architecture to its building needs, he did not adequately respond to the particular transformations of it that Roman builders carried out.

The temple's design may have been influenced by the Temple of Castor and Pollux the way it was rebuilt in 117 B.C. by Caecilius Metellus Delmaticus, having

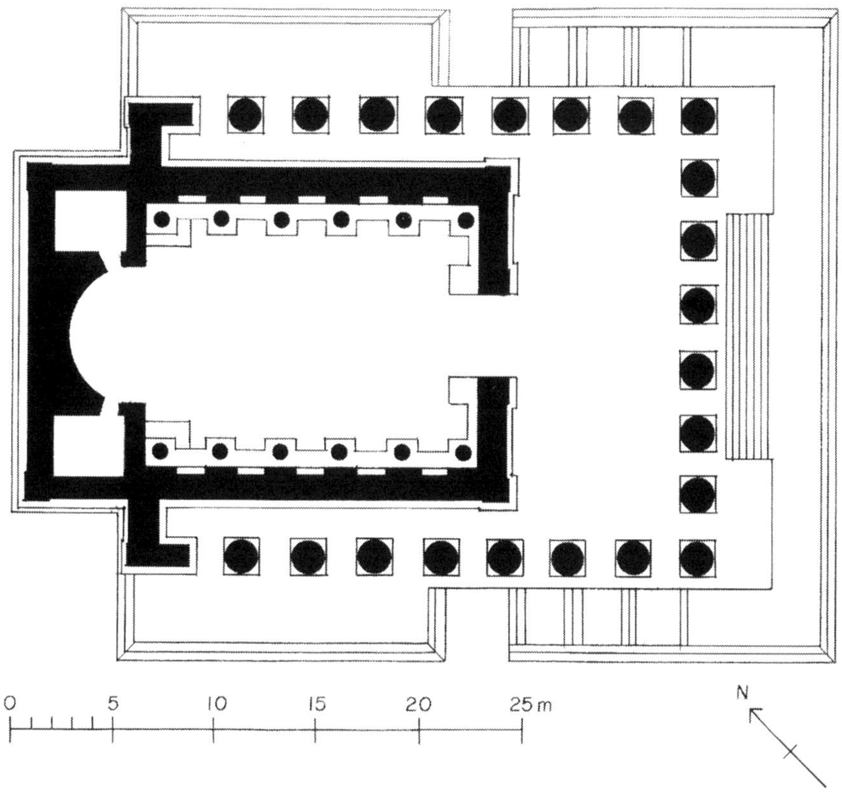

71. Temple of Venus Genetrix, plan. Drawing: John W. Stamper after Carla Amici, *Il Foro di Cesare* (1991), p. 96, pl. 160.

nearly the same dimensions and the same number of columns. The use of a terraced podium with a main stair combined with two lateral stairs may also suggest the influence of the Temple of Jupiter Capitolinus as reconstructed in this book.

Other features that would become common in temple design include the presence of a two-story row of Corinthian columns along the inside walls of the naos and an apse in the back wall housing the deity's cult statue. The rear wall of the naos was originally formed by a simple arched opening that led to the apse. During the rebuilding at the time of Domitian, two small rooms were added to either side of the apse, and two massive ante walls with decorative pilasters were added to frame the apse opening.[90] A simple niche for the cult statue was thus transformed into a more complex and articulated composition.[91]

The materials used in the temple were expensive and exotic, its columns, entablature, and cella walls being of travertine and Carrara marble quarried from the region northwest of Florence.[92] Elaboration of detail and stately magnificence would become typical features of temple design with the new availability of marble.

Because most of the architectural fragments on the site today date from a rebuilding at the time of Trajan, we can only make assumptions about the details of the temple's original Corinthian style. They could perhaps be most closely compared to the cornice and modillion details found on the site of the Regia: simple, blocky, and with shallow carving.

The existing architectural details are richly and beautifully detailed with spiraling acanthus plants, dentils, modillions, and double cyma moldings with carved dolphins, seashells, and tridents, which refer to Venus and the sea (Fig. 72).[93] Also significant is the presence of small interconnected circles between the dentils of the cornice, a characteristic feature of Domitian's principal architect, Rabirius.[94]

The columns, three of which were re-erected in 1933, have Ionic bases, fluted marble shafts, and Corinthian capitals (Fig. 73). The front pediment had an angle of inclination of twenty degrees, which was common for temples in central Italy. The rear pediment, which was smaller, covering just the apse and the flanking rooms, had a higher inclination of twenty-eight degrees.[95]

72. Temple of Venus Genetrix, partial elevation. Drawing: Marcello Reyna and Amy Propes based on Andrea Palladio, *The Four Books of Architecture* (1965), vol. 4, pl. 96.

The Forum

The plan of the forum space in front of the temple (Fig. 74) was laid out to focus effectively and dramatically on the temple's pronaos as a sort of theater stage. It was a long, narrow rectangle, its interior dimensions extending 103 meters in length by 30 meters wide (350 by 102 Roman feet), a ratio of 3.4 to 1. By contrast, the main axis of the Theater of Pompey and the Porticus Pompeiana extended 287 meters, nearly three times as long. Even so, this was a grandiose setting given the length of the space relative to its width, the repetitive rhythm of the flanking colonnades, and the tall podium on which the temple stood.

73. Temple of Venus Genetrix, reconstruction of three of the temple's columns and entablature from the rebuilding by Trajan. Photo: Istituto Centrale per il Catalogo e la Documentazione, G.4211.

The ratio of the forum's plan dimensions of 3.4 to 1 did not correspond to Vitruvius's preference for a more square-like forum space:

> The size of a forum should be proportionate to the number of inhabitants, so that it may not be too small a space to be useful, nor look like a desert waste for lack of population. To determine its breadth, divide its length into three parts and assign two of them to the breadth. Its shape will then be oblong, and its ground plan conveniently suited to the conditions of the shows.[96]

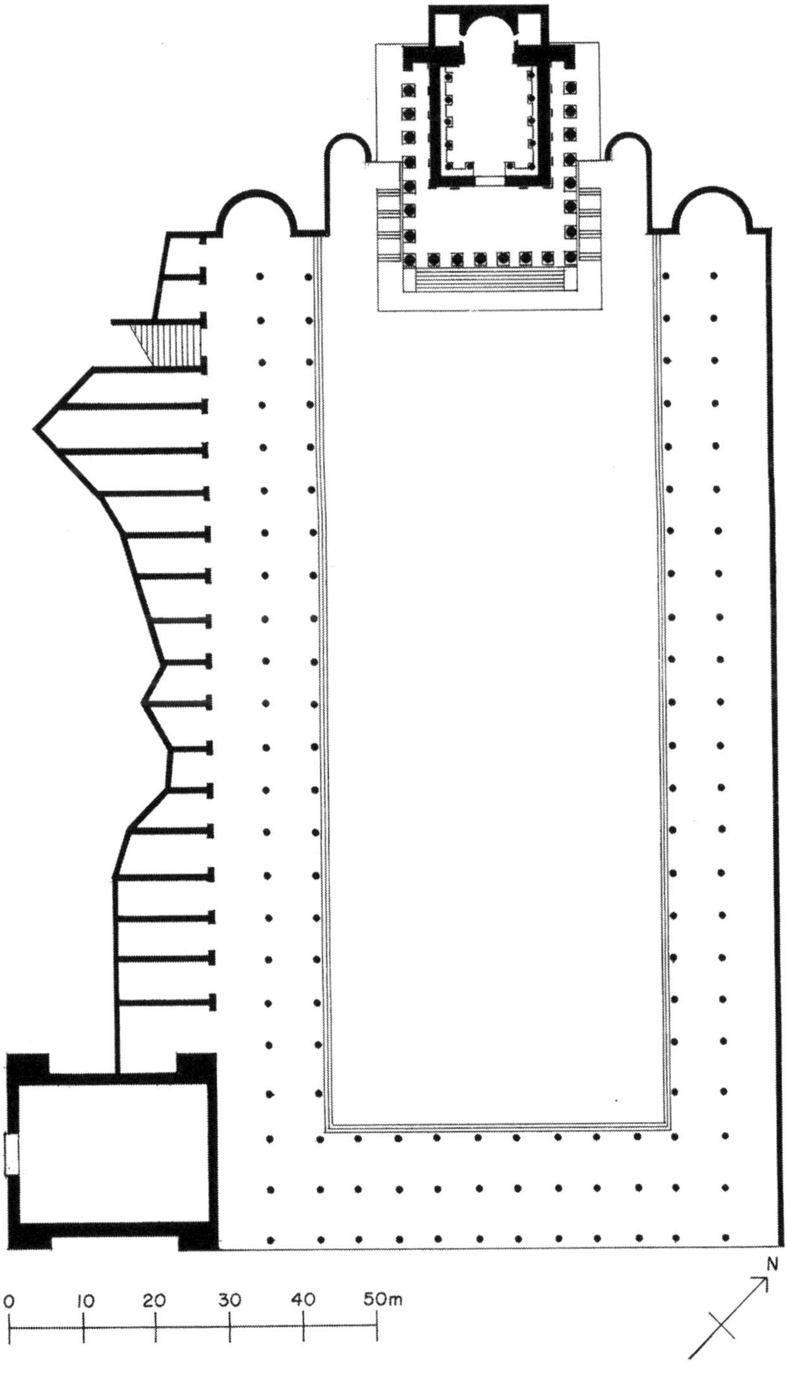

74. Forum Julium, plan of forum. Drawing: John W. Stamper based on Carla Amici, *Il Foro di Cesare* (1991), p. 96, pl. 160; and P. von Celsing, Fototeca Unione, American Academy in Rome, FU 13772.

The long, narrow space of Caesar's forum, which was the result of the site's particular topography and of the limited amount of land Caesar was able to buy, created a space in which greater emphasis was given to the temple's façade by the framing colonnades.[97] A similar emphasis would be found in the later Forum Augustum and Forum Transitorium.

Comparisons can be made also to the fora of innumerable colonial cities throughout Italy, many of which were under construction at about the same time. The forum at Paestum, for instance, was begun when Rome conquered the city in 273 B.C. and completed with the addition of a surrounding Doric colonnade at about the time of Julius Caesar. It measured 150

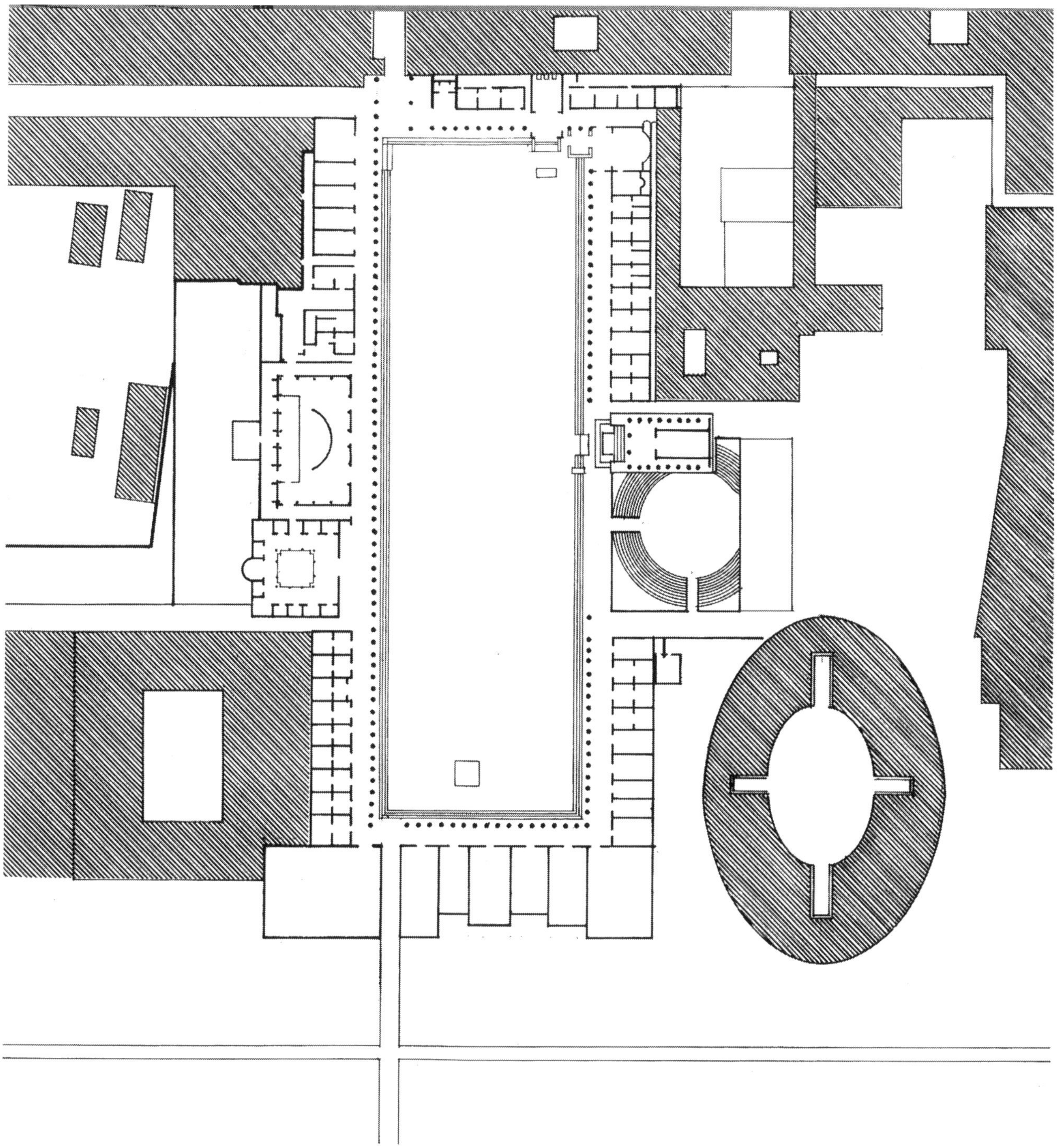

75. Paestum, Roman Forum, ca. 273–50 B.C. Drawing: Joseph Smith based on A. C. Carpiceci and L. Pennino, *Paestum and Velia Today and 2500* (1989), p. 51.

by 55 meters, the length being 2.7 times the width (Fig. 75).[98] The forum at Pompeii was even more elongated with dimensions of 146 by 32 meters, the length being 4.5 times the width (Fig. 76).[99] This forum's arrangement of colonnades on three sides and a temple prominently placed at one end can be directly compared to the Forum Julium. Many earlier examples are found among Hellenistic shrine complexes such as those at Priene and Miletus, which likewise had temples with spaces framed by colonnades or stoas.

The ultimate influence may have been Persian market squares.[100]

Vitruvius also writes about the need to adapt the design of fora to their use and changes in their use from one country to another:

> The Greeks lay out their forums in the form of a square surrounded by very spacious double colonnades, adorn them with columns set rather closely together, and with entablatures of stone or marble, and construct walks above in the upper story. But in the cities of Italy the same method cannot be followed, for the reason that it is a custom handed down from our ancestors that gladiatorial shows should be given in the forum.[101]

For this reason, he specifies that the intercolumniations in the colonnade of a Roman forum should be wide, equivalent to an *aerostyle* temple, that behind the colonnades could be located bankers' offices, and that in the balconies above should be shop spaces to bring in public revenue.[102]

In the case of the Forum Julium, the colonnades on the two long sides were composed of two parallel rows of widely spaced marble Corinthian columns standing on a raised platform, with three steps descending to the forum pavement. The granite and marble columns visible on the site today date from the rebuilding by Diocletian after A.D. 283.[103] They are smaller and more closely spaced than the originals, and they stand on plinths. They created, therefore, a different scale and rhythm than would have been evident at the time of Caesar.[104]

In the initial construction an outer perimeter wall was erected to enclose the forum on its two long sides. During the time of Octavian, this wall, at least on the southwest side, was removed and a series of *tabernae* constructed to link the forum to the Via Argentarius.[105] These tabernae served as supplemental offices, archives, and storage rooms. The dividing walls were made of tufa blocks, good for fireproof construction and able to support multiple levels. An upper story communicated with the Via Argentaria with shops opening onto the street. A secondary cross axis, aligning directly with the front wall of the temple's podium, is suggested by the presence of a stairway that descended through the portico from the Via Argentarius.[106]

There are two hypotheses about the forum's short southeast side, which adjoins the Argiletum. One suggests that at the time of Julius Caesar, this portico had two rows of columns. A third row was added during the construction phase of Octavian.[107] The other hypothesis suggests a double nave was built entirely at the time of Caesar.[108] In either case, this end of the forum was altered between A.D. 85 and 98 when Domitian built the Forum Transitorium. His architect filled in the intercolumniations of the outer row of columns as part of his perimeter wall.[109]

The series of piers and arches visible at the forum's southwest corner, referred to as the Basilica Argentaria, was constructed at the time of Domitian and Trajan. In the original plan, this corner of the portico ended in an open apse built up against the ridge that had connected the Capitoline and the Esquiline Hills. A second, smaller apse, also built against the ridge, terminated the space between the colonnade and the temple's left flank.[110]

In the late 80s A.D., Domitian ordered the excavation of the ridge, clearing out a passage around the back of the temple. He may have begun construction of the Basilica Argentaria, but it was completed by Trajan in the first decade of the second century A.D.[111] It continues the southwest colonnade, although the floor is raised nine steps higher. Composed of massive rusticated piers of travertine and peperino, it had concrete vaults and projecting balconies.[112]

The main axis of the forum and temple complex was defined by an altar, two fountains, or water basins, and an equestrian statue of Julius Caesar.[113] Historical descriptions also point out that a number of additional statues along with paintings were displayed throughout the forum and its colonnades just as in the Porticus Pompeiana.

Inside the temple a giant statue of Venus Genetrix by the sculptor Arcesilaus was placed in the apse.[114] It was flanked on one side by a statue of Julius Caesar and on the other by a gilt bronze statue of his lover Cleopatra.[115] He had begun having an affair with her in 47 B.C., shortly after his defeat of Pompey. The pair had plotted to kill her half-brother, Ptolemy XIII. They eventually succeeded in overthrowing him in a civil war, and Cleopatra was declared queen of Egypt and

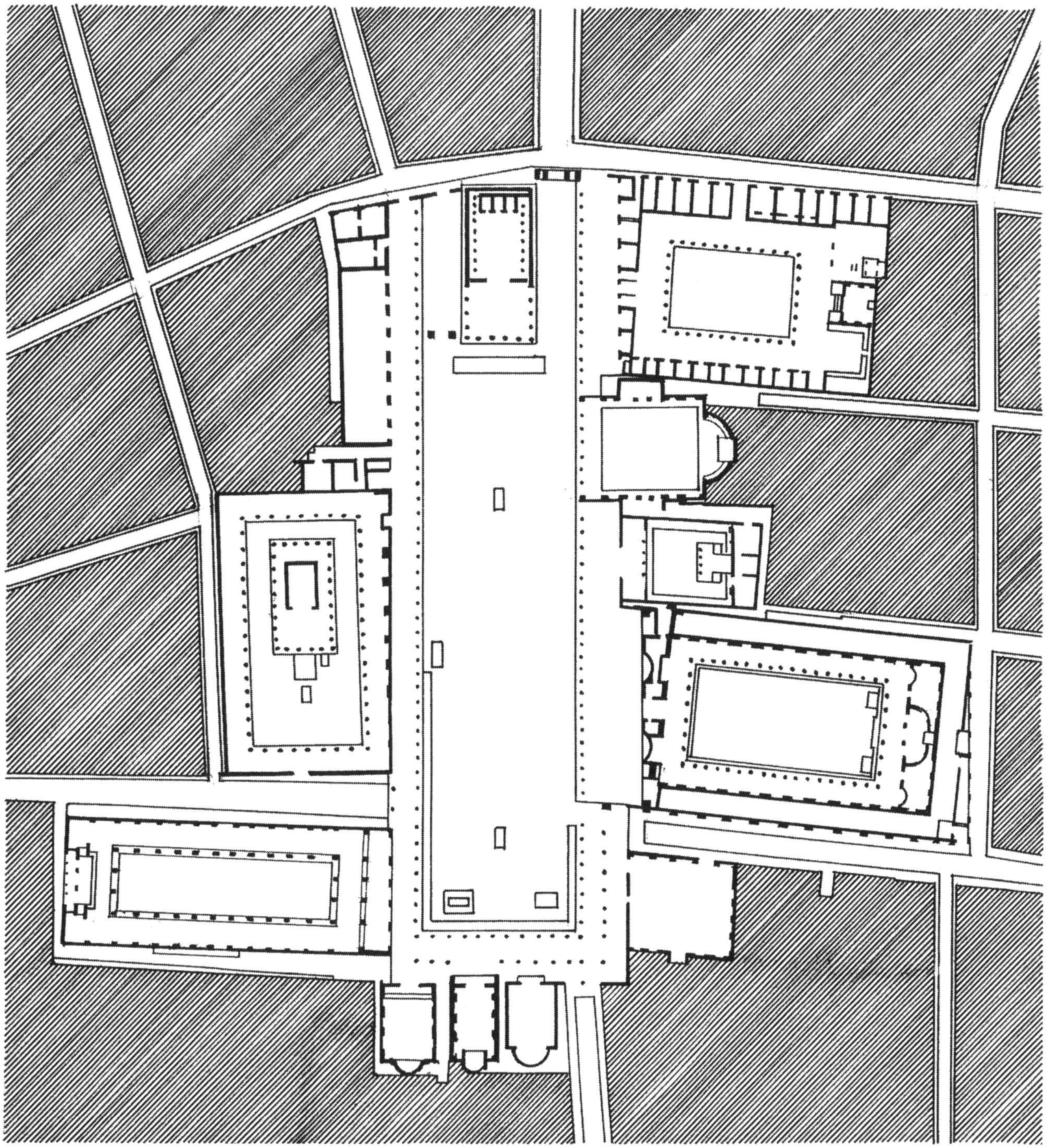

76. Pompeii, Roman Forum, ca. 80 B.C.–A.D. 79. Drawing: Elizabeth Butler Janney after Roberto Marta, *Architettura Romana* (1985), fig. 208.

a client of Rome.[116] This conquest proved to be the most profitable of all for Caesar, because Egypt's treasury was the richest in the world, with vast stores of gold, silver, and jewelry. Access to this immense wealth, together with the spoils from his previous wars, made it possible for Caesar to return to Rome and carry out the construction of his forum and other projects.

It was an unprecedented honor for the queen of Egypt to have her statue set up in an important temple in Rome and to be a part of the imperial cult that was

developing around the Julian house.[117] The statue also provided an allusion to Cleopatra's divine status as the reincarnation of Isis, who was identified with Venus.[118] With the inclusion of the three statues of Venus Genetrix, Cleopatra, and himself, Caesar transformed the iconographic program of the Roman temple. He introduced into Rome the Egyptian and Hellenistic custom of placing statues of kings and queens in shrines as divine companions to the gods.

In the East, such ruler portraits had long been used to commemorate the power and prestige of individual Hellenistic kings. The tradition of public statuary during the Roman Republic had until now been restricted to the use of togate statues in which the ruling figure – a consul, praetor, or augur – was characterized by attributes appropriate to his political or religious title. There was nothing godlike about these statues; rather, they represented an egalitarian style that matched the political system in which leaders served on a rotating yearly basis. Superhuman attributes and privileges reserved only to the gods had never been conferred on republican rulers until now.[119]

By filling his forum and temple with displays of public art, Caesar manifested the appearance of civic responsibility. There were laws against the personal use of war booty, the spoils of war being considered distinctly public artifacts, not for personal use. The value of captured art for public purpose and national interest explains the display of such objects in a great space like Caesar's forum. The application of art to public purposes became a standard feature of Roman civic life.[120] At least by the first century B.C., everything done by those who aspired to higher office seemingly had a civic purpose in mind. However, by making public displays of the great statues and artworks brought from Greece and other conquered territories, political leaders also served their own purposes of establishing dignity and authority.

With the construction of his own forum and temple, Julius Caesar now had a place separate from that of the Senate, a place where he could assemble veterans and ordinary citizens alike and deliver speeches in adequate splendor.[121] It is recorded that earlier, in 62 and 59 B.C., he had presided over civic functions from the podium of the Temple of Castor and Pollux. Now he had his own setting, associated with his power and historical legacy, which he linked to Venus and Cleopatra. It was here that he now presided over ceremonies, seated in a throne, watching processions of senators and military figures passing before him.[122]

Like the Porticus Pompeiana, the forum and temple were used here for public purposes, while at the same time honoring the dictator. As on the podium of the Temple of Castor and Pollux, or the rostra, the ruler was set off physically as someone important. The setting indicated his special standing within society and commanded respect. Combined with his regal clothing and supporting entourage, the setting of the forum and temple created a sense of dignity. As such a symbol of dignity and authority came to be more and more associated with positions of power, they made it psychologically easier for those who were in subordinate positions to accept the ruler's authority.

The building of a new forum was related to the desire for prestige. Caesar's power had a specific internal dynamic, and on the basis of this power, he yearned for a special prestige, which could reflect itself equally in his architecture and the external conduct of his power. The building of the forum was important in enhancing the prestige of his imperial authority because he appeared to be doing something of enormous importance. The sentiment of prestige was able to strengthen the ardent belief in the existence of his own might.[123]

Although not finished until the 20s B.C. by Augustus, the forum became an important space in Roman civic life.[124] Being the first of the imperial fora, the Forum Julium set a new standard for urban design, one with a formal, symmetrical plan, Hellenistic architecture, and with a symbolic focus on the dictator that would be imitated by all subsequent imperial fora. The forum is significant not just because it was the first imperial forum to be constructed outside the Forum Romanum but also because it marks the beginning of a transformation in Roman urban design. We have already seen the use of colonnades surrounding a public space or group of temples, as in the Porticus Metelli and the Porticus Pompeiana. However, this is the first time in Rome that a forum complex was composed in just this way, with a single temple placed on axis, at one end of the space, dominating it hierarchically and relating to it as a unifed urban composition.

Forum Romanum in the Time of Caesar

Although the Forum Romanum was overcrowded with buildings, its importance was not completely circumscribed by the Forum Julium. A significant amount of construction was in fact carried out in the Forum Romanum during Julius Caesar's lifetime. In addition to the construction of the Curia Julia at the forum's northwest corner, both large basilicas on its north and south sides were rebuilt at a larger scale and in a more decorative way.

Throughout the forum's history, much of its perimeter area was occupied by shops, *tabernae*, which stood in front of private houses. In the early second century B.C., shortly after the Second Punic War, the *tabernae* on the north side were rebuilt in brick and timber frame construction.[125] In 179 B.C., the first Basilica Aemilia was erected behind them by the censors M. Aemilius Lepidus and M. Fulvius Nobilior.[126] This basilica was rebuilt and expanded by Lucius Aemilius Paullus and his son in 55–34 B.C., but it was paid for by Julius Caesar from the spoils of the Gallic Wars.[127] It included a new façade on the forum featuring Doric half-columns and a frieze with triglyphs and metopes.[128] It was rebuilt yet again during the reigns of Augustus and Tiberius between 14 B.C. and A.D. 22, in which the interior decorative elements, which are still evident on the site, were added.[129] These included columns of africano and cipollino with white marble bases and Corinthian capitals.

Julius Caesar and Lucius Aemilius Paullus also began a reconstruction of the Basilica Sempronia on the forum's south side, renaming it the Basilica Julia in honor of Caesar's daughter.[130] Begun in 54 B.C., the year she died, it was again paid for by the spoils of the Gallic Wars. It was dedicated in 46 B.C. by Octavian while still unfinished.[131] It was soon destroyed by fire and rebuilt on an enlarged plan; it was dedicated in 12 B.C., this time in the names of Gaius and Lucius Caesar.[132]

The basilica was constructed to contain banking and other business, and later it housed the Centumviral court, a panel of 180 jurors, which heard cases on inheritance.[133] With dimensions of 100 meters long by 50 meters wide, its long side faced the forum, and its back wall, lined with *tabernae*, was embedded in a hillside. Its principal façades on the north and east sides were two stories in height, and each bay was framed by half-columns and an entablature, Tuscan on the ground story and Ionic above.[134]

With the completion of these two basilicas during the time of Augustus, along with the construction of the Temple of Divus Julius at the forum's southeast end, its final shape and organization were established. Many of the forum's other buildings, like the Temple of Castor and Pollux and the Temple of Saturn, would be rebuilt in Augustus's unprecedented building campaigns, but the forum's essential formal qualities were fixed by the late 40s B.C.

In the final years of Caesar's life, he continued to receive honors from the Senate in recognition of his role as dictator and cult ruler. He was granted the title of *pater patriae*, his birthday was declared a public holiday, and he was given permission to wear triumphal garb and to use the curule chair at any time or place he considered appropriate. The month of his birth, Quinctilis, was changed to the name of Julius, and his son or adopted son was to be designated *pontifex maximus*, a veiled recognition of hereditary monarchy.[135]

In spite of all the honors and privileges Julius received, his attempt to turn his rule into a monarchy, however guarded it was, inevitably caused growing opposition within the Senate. Eventually, fearing an outright revolt, he forbade his supporters in the Senate from initiating a move to grant him the title of king.[136]

In the midst of Julius Caesar's extensive development of Rome and of his de facto seizure of complete control of the Roman bureaucracy, he began formulating plans for future military campaigns in the East and in Dacia, in central Europe. He has been called the new Alexander the Great, someone who aspired to be the founder of a military absolutism of the eastern type, which would justify itself by military success and worldwide imperialism. Although he did not live to carry out his goal, he at least began it by raising an enormous army of sixteen legions, as large as Alexander's, adequate enough to ensure him a victory in a comprehensive eastern campaign. A marriage with Cleopatra would have allowed for the annexation of Egypt, and then only Germany and the Danube remained to be conquered for him to complete his empire.[137]

As hostility toward Caesar grew and the day of his departure neared, a conspiracy involving as many as sixty Senators arose, led by Cassius and Marcus Brutus. In March of 44 B.C., they stabbed him to death in the curia of the Theater of Pompey, an act of vengeance that would dramatically alter the course of the Roman world.

Pompey and Caesar had been bitter military rivals from the beginning, then cooperated as triumvirs, then competed in a different way by carrying out large building projects in Rome that both glorified their military exploits and memorialized their godlike standing within the Roman Republic. Pompey built his great theater and garden complex with a temple dedicated to Venus Victrix. The temple was located at the top of the theater's *cavea*, set off against the great tree-lined garden with its magnificent perspectival view from the far end. Julius Caesar sought to rival Pompey's ambitious complex, but he built his immediately adjacent to the Forum Romanum, with the new Curia Julia as the principal transitional element. He sought to consolidate his power by maintaining the judicial and market functions of the Forum Romanum while allowing them to expand into his new forum. Similar building projects would be carried out by Octavian, but with even more intensity and on a much vaster scale.

7

REBUILDING ROME IN THE TIME OF AUGUSTUS

Rome's urban development and temple building increased dramatically during the time of Augustus. In his capacity as triumvir and then as emperor from 27 B.C. to A.D. 14, Augustus restored many of Rome's existing civic and religious buildings and built countless new ones. According to his biography, the *Res Gestae*, he "restored eighty-two temples of the gods within the city, neglecting none that then stood in need of repair."[1] Using huge quantities of marble from Carrara and northern Africa, he commissioned new temples and rebuilt old ones, constructed new theaters, porticos, triumphal arches, altars, streets, and a huge mausoleum.[2] Such a mobilization of the building industry was an effective way of demonstrating his power to the Roman populace. He took the opportunity to use these monuments as forms of propaganda to great advantage.[3]

Some of Augustus's public works, especially those begun during the period of the second triumvirate, when he shared power with Marcus Antony and Marcus Lepidus, were carried out in the names of relatives or friends: the Theater of Marcellus in the name of his son-in-law, for instance, or the Porticus Octaviae in the name of his sister.[4] Others were carried out by partisans of Antony, and still others by Agrippa, a brilliant military general who had been a friend of Augustus since childhood. Later, Augustus's adoptive son, Tiberius, would carry out several rebuilding projects in the Forum Romanum and the Campus Martius.[5] In the end, however, it was Augustus himself who took the credit: "I found Rome built of bricks; I leave her clothed in marble."[6]

Buildings of the Augustan era were, in fact, characterized primarily by the use of marble. It had been employed earlier in palaces and villas of the aristocracy as a luxury item. It was only during the time of Pompey and Julius Caesar, however, that freshly quarried marble started to become the staple of new construction in temple architecture.[7] It was imported from quarries in Greece and northern Africa and soon was available in large quantities from Luni in the Carrara region, a town that had the closest thing to the white marble of Greece.[8] Lunense marble was used, for instance, in the Temple of Apollo Sosianus, the Temple of Apollo Palatinus, and in structures such as the Ara Pacis and the rebuilding of the Temple of Concordia.[9] Above all, the Corinthian Order became the most widely used mode as stonecarvers gained experience and the quality of the work improved markedly. The new language of architectural ornament that was developed in Rome set a new standard for the rest of the Empire.[10]

In general, the architecture of the Augustan period represented an important transformation characterized at first by experimentation and diversity. It eventually developed into a fully orthodox Corinthian style.[11] Augustan architecture possessed qualities of dynamic tension between formal variety and unified conceptualization.[12] No two temple structures were exactly alike, although many of them shared common features.

By this time in Rome's architectural development, we are not speaking so much about direct influences from Athens as we are about a similarity of developments taking place in both Athens and Rome. We are speaking of a vocabulary with Greek origins, but with a definite Roman interpretation. We will not find in Roman architecture from this period direct quotations from Athens, but, more importantly, we must consider the relationship between Roman temples themselves, how one influenced the next – how certain temples

were more experimental, others more canonical.[13] The Corinthian capitals made for new buildings in Athens – for example, the Odeion of Agrippa – were modeled more on Roman examples than they were on Hellenistic ones.[14] Most important for this study is the distinct Roman character of these stylistic features and the relationship between one Roman temple and another, especially between Augustus's early temples and his most grandiose Roman monument, the Temple of Mars Ultor in the Forum Augustum.[15]

Augustus's Rise to Power

Born Gaius Octavius in 63 B.C., the future emperor distinguished himself early at the Battle of Pharsalus when his great uncle Caesar defeated Pompey.[16] Referred to in his early years as Octavian, the young man was granted special favors by Caesar. While still a boy, he was elected to the college of the *pontifices*, assuring him the dignity of priesthood for life, and in 47 B.C., he was made prefect of Rome. He participated in the celebration of Caesar's great triumph and games in 46 B.C. He was only nineteen years old at the time of Caesar's death.[17]

When Octavian made a claim of inheritance as Caesar's adoptive son, he was challenged by Marcus Antony and Marcus Lepidus, both of whom had been Caesar's closest deputies. Octavian emerged as a credible rival, however, and his hereditary position was further amplified in 42 B.C., when the deifed Julius was admitted into the state cult and his worship was accepted in Rome and the Empire. This gave Octavian the advantage of being *divi filius*, the son of the deified Caesar.[18]

In 43 B.C., Octavian entered into an agreement with Antony and Lepidus to form the second triumvirate, which acted essentially as a three-man dictatorship.[19] Its power eclipsed that of the Roman consuls and Senate, just as Caesar's triumvirate had done sixteen years earlier. They divided up control of the Roman territories and spheres of influence, Anthony claiming the East, Octavian the West, and Lepidus the Italian peninsula and northern Africa. In 42 B.C., the triumvirs avenged Caesar's death by tracking down his assassins, Brutus and Cassius, and defeating them in a battle at Philippi in Macedonia.[20]

The triumvirs remained in power through most of the decade of the 30s B.C.; however, as animosity between the political partners grew, Octavian took the initiative to force Antony and Lepidus out of power and assume control of the entire Empire himself. In 36 B.C., he successfully challenged Lepidus in Sicily after a battle against Sextus Pompey.[21] In 31–30 B.C., he defeated Antony and Cleopatra in a naval battle at Actium, thus forcefully bringing an end to the second triumvirate.[22] Octavian claimed control of Antony's eastern half of the Empire, annexing Egypt in the process. He retained personal control of Egypt's immense treasury and its agricultural production, and went on to use this windfall to pay for the development of cities across the Empire, generous compensation of his veterans, and, most important, rebuilding Rome.[23]

When Octavian returned to Rome, he was honored by the Senate with the pledge of a triumphal arch to be erected in the Forum Romanum. In the following year, 29 B.C., he celebrated a triple triumph commemorating his conquest of Illyrium and Egypt, plus his victory at Actium. Celebrations were held on three consecutive days, with grand festive events that were meant to both provide a demonstration of his military power and to legitimize his political control over the Roman state.[24] Above all, they honored the fact that he had succeeded in bringing peace to the Roman world, an end to the countless wars and military adventures of the last one hundred years. It was a time of reconciliation and an opportunity for social stabilization.[25]

He received a further honor in 27 B.C. when he was officially granted his title of Augustus (thus changing his name from Octavian) in return for restoring – at least in appearance – the government of Rome to the Senate and people.[26] The change of his name was an important symbolic act that elevated him to the role of emperor and head of an empire rather than a republic (Fig. 77).[27]

In the *Res Gestae*, he stated, "I excelled all in *auctoritas*, although I possessed no more official power than others who were my colleagues in the several magistracies."[28] He, in fact, had no institutionalized authoritarian power, no perpetual dictatorship as had been voted for Julius Caesar.[29] The distinction he made between power and authority is significant, for the

77. Statue of Augustus from Prima Porta, Vatican Museums, Braccio Nuovo. Photo: Thomas Gordon Smith.

former implied the amount of legal control over his subjects, whereas the latter was more suggestive, demanding participation, interpretation, and response. Far from being confining, his concept of authority had clear intentions that encouraged creative response and interpretation, whether in art, architecture, literature, or theater. There was a dynamic relationship between authoritarian intent and the latitude of response that accounts for much of the vitality of Augustan culture.[30]

It was about the time Octavian was granted the name Augustus that Vitruvius presented him with a copy of his writings urging him to design his public buildings with dignity and authority consistent with the Hellenistic East. He encouraged the emperor to consider as part of his attention to the welfare of society and the establishment of public order that his projects for new public buildings should enrich the state by its "distinguished authority."[31] He felt the best way to achieve this goal was to follow the principles and practices of skilled architects such as Hermogenes of Priene and Hermodoris of Salamis.

As we have seen in the context of Rome in the first century B.C., Vitruvius took a conservative approach to temple architecture. He was critical of the Etrusco-Roman and the Greek Doric traditions, and he was likewise critical of the many innovations that had appeared in Roman temple architecture in recent decades. We have seen that he considered as anomalies to canonical practice the Etruscan plan type, the pseudoperipteral plan type, temples whose pronaos had antae and inner rows of columns, and the *peripteros sine postico* arrangement for the back wall of a cella. He only grudgingly acknowledged the existence of these building practices as he attempted to promote in their place the adoption of a more purely Hellenistic approach to design.

He synthesized the Hellenistic tradition of Hermogenes and Hermodorus into a codified system of building that he hoped would have an influence on Roman architecture. His rules for the orders, for proportions, column spacings, and plan types did have an influence, but they were in nearly every case tempered or transformed by particular builders not only for functional reasons but also for purely visual refinement. Canonical proportions were more often than not adjusted or altered as the builders deemed necessary for the most effective design.

Hermogenes had the most influence on Vitruvius and other architects of his time because he had reacted against transitions that were taking place in Hellenistic architecture, changes like the development of the pilaster and the pier-and-arch motif that tended to dilute the purity of the orders. Hermogenes had returned to the careful sections of his classical predecessors and formulated a series of proportions closer to the classical Greek than to the work of his contemporaries. At the same time, he accepted certain changes, which he saw as contributing to the cause of a better definition and refinement of the orders. For instance, he combined the continuous frieze with dentils in the design of entablatures, and he refined the Ionic capital and chose the Attic base as being the most appropriate for the Ionic column.[32] Vitruvius credited him with developing the pseudodipteral and *eustyle* temples, which

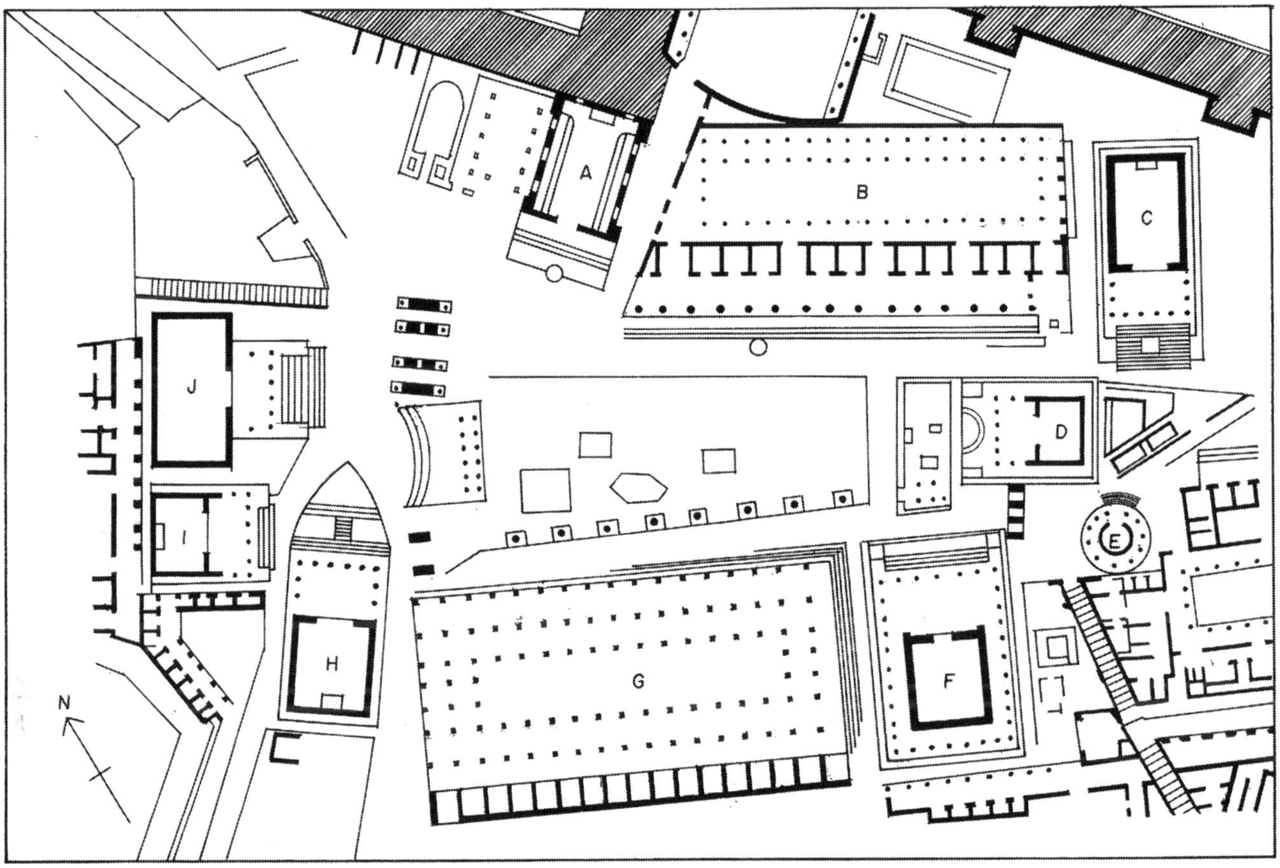

78. Rome, Forum Romanum, plan as existed by the middle Empire: (A) Curia Julia, (B) Basilica Aemilia, (C) Temple of Antoninus and Faustina, (D) Temple of Divus Julius, (E) Temple of Vesta, (F) Temple of Castor and Pollux, (G) Basilica Julia, (H) Temple of Saturn, (I) Temple of Vespasian, (J) Temple of Concordia. Drawing: John W. Stamper after Giuseppi Lugli, *Roma Antica: Il Centro Monumentale* (1946), pl. 4.

saved expense and labor while improving function and enhancing the temple's overall appearance.[33]

Whether Hermogenes invented these details or was simply the first to write about them we will never know, but he certainly contributed the most to making them popular.[34] His classical standards of design in the Greek East gradually began to be applied in Rome and became more widely held after being embraced by Vitruvius. It was during the reign of Augustus that the standards of Hermogenes and Vitruvius together noticeably transformed provincial Italic versions of the Ionic and Corinthian Orders.[35] Even so, as we look at buildings from the Republic and early Empire, we will find that Vitruvius's descriptions of the Ionic and Corinthian Orders only partially corresponded to what was actually built. There was a clear tendency on the part of Roman builders to develop and refine distinctly indigenous plan types that adhered more directly to Etruscan and Latin traditions, with various transformations being made relative to the needs of the cult sacrifices or conditions of the site. Likewise, they often did not follow Vitruvius's preference for basing proportions on the lower diameter of the column shafts. To this was added the authority of the Temple of Capitoline Jupiter and its political and religious significance, which would reappear as an influence at various points along the way. The resulting synthesis, although approaching a canonical adherence, first to the Ionic, then to the Corinthian Order, transformed and readapted long-standing Roman traditions in light of Hellenistic precedents. It is this process of synthesis that characterized Roman inventiveness and creativity and distinguished it from other architecture in the Mediterranean world.

79. Temple of Divus Julius, 42–29 B.C., elevation. Drawing: Achieng Opondo after Otto Richter in *JDAI* 4 (1889), p. 157.

Temples of Divus Julius and Saturn in the Forum Romanum

Octavian was responsible for dramatically transforming the Forum Romanum. In fact, virtually the entire Forum Romanum was a construction zone during his reign as he and his political favorites built or rebuilt nearly all of its buildings in an attempt to restore its role as the principal civic and religious center of Rome and the Roman world (Fig. 78). When we consider Augustus's statement "I found Rome built of bricks; I leave her clothed in marble," we are especially drawn to images of the forum.

From the early years of his reign, two forum temples in particular must be considered: the Temple of Divus Julius and the Temple of Saturn. The first was built beginning in 42 B.C. and completed and dedicated in 29 B.C. It was located at the forum's eastern end, directly in front of the Regia and north of the Temple of Castor and Pollux (Fig. 79).[36] An earlier effort had been made to commemorate Julius Caesar on this site, the spot where his body was cremated after his assassination. A group of freedmen and followers who had been present at the burning of his body erected an altar and a column. They made preparations to consecrate the site and to establish sacrifices to Caesar like those afforded other gods.[37] As reported by Suetonius: "[The people] placed in the Forum a column of Numidian marble, some twenty feet high, with the inscription 'To the Father of His Country.' "[38] It was taken down in less than a year, however, by the consul Dolabella, who had opposed Caesar's deification.[39] This did not deter Caesar's supporters, who continued to view the site as sacred to the memory of Caesar, and, when he was officially deified in 42 B.C. and plans were begun for the construction of a temple, this site was without question the most appropriate for the purpose.

The building was placed on a high podium of *opus caementicium* that was faced with travertine blocks and marble revetments (Fig. 80).[40] It measured 26.97 meters wide by 30 meters long (91 by 102 Roman feet); however, it was larger than the cella and pronaos

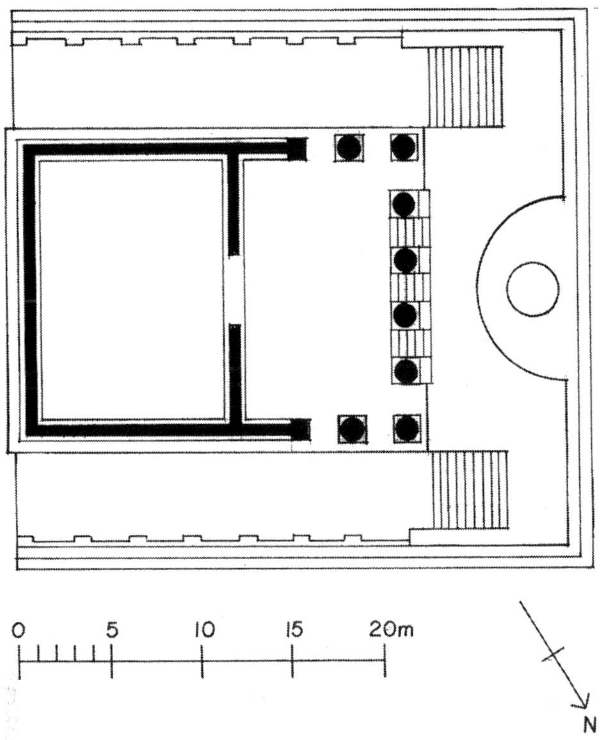

80. Rome, Temple of Divus Julius, plan. Drawing: John W. Stamper based on Otto Richter in *JDAI* 4 (1889), p. 157.

because it had steps at the sides similar to those of the Temple of Venus Genetrix, and its front wall projected out well beyond the façade columns.[41] It was made unique, however, by the presence of a semicircular niche in the center of its front wall. An altar was placed there to mark the spot where the earlier altar and column described by Suetonius had been located.[42] Later, probably in 14 B.C., the altar was removed and the niche filled in.[43]

It was long believed that the podium served as a speaker's platform and that the prows of ships taken at Actium were attached to its face at the time of its dedication.[44] This would seem improbable, however, given the presence of the circular niche and the altar. Recent studies suggest that the rostra in this area of the forum referred to by ancient writers was not the podium of Caesar's temple but was instead a separate platform built west of it in alignment with the older rostra on the forum's opposite end.[45] The two rostra served to formalize the forum's spatial definition, and they were linked symbolically by the presence of the ships' prows, the older one with those from the victory at Antium in 338 B.C., the newer one with those from Actium.[46]

Like the nearby Temple of Castor and Pollux, the Temple of Divus Julius had a *pycnostyle* composition. It had six closely spaced columns on the front, with blank walls on the sides and rear. Only the corners of the cella were highlighted by pilasters.[47] Representations of the temple on coins seem to suggest the columns were either Ionic or Composite, and that is how it has been depicted in most reconstruction drawings.[48] Because of fragments of Corinthian pilaster capitals found on the site, some scholars have suggested it combined an Ionic pronaos with Corinthian pilasters on the cella walls (Fig. 81). It is more likely, however, that the coin images show badly rendered Corinthian capitals and that it was, in fact, Corinthian throughout.[49]

The cella walls were made of travertine, while the entablature and columns were marble.[50] The frieze was decorated with a repetitive scroll pattern with intermittent female heads, gorgons, and winged figures, one of the first such examples from the early Augustan period. The carving techniques evident on the frieze panels from the front and sides were markedly better than those panels from the rear wall, suggesting the presence of two teams of stonemasons.[51]

The cornice had dentils and one of the earliest uses of modillions in Roman temple architecture. Straight across the front and flat on the bottom, they suggested the idea of support for the cornice, like small projecting beams (Figs. 82 and 83). They were crowned by a cyma reversa, and their undersides were decorated with narrow rectangular panels.[52] Derived from Greek precedents, they became common in temple architecture during the Augustan period, both in exterior applications and in interior decoration and fresco painting.[53]

The cella contained a statue of Caesar, which had a star placed on its head to commemorate an event in 44 B.C. when a comet was visible in the sky for seven days. This was a sign, according to Octavian, of Caesar's apotheosis.[54] Pliny suggests that Octavian inwardly rejoiced in the sign of the star, because it was something to which he would eventually hope to ascend himself. It soon began to appear on other statues of Caesar, and eventually on Octavian's own helmet, as well as on coins, rings, and seals, all symbols of his *auctoritas* as the son of a god.[55] Also in the cella was a

81. Temple of Divus Julius, Corinthian capital. Photo: John W. Stamper.

famous painting by Apelles of Venus Anadyomene, a reference to the ancestry of the Julian family.[56]

Three other buildings in the immediate vicinity of the Temple of Divus Julius were built or rebuilt at about the same time. The Regia, directly behind the temple, was destroyed by a fire in 36 B.C. and was rebuilt by Domitius Calvinus.[57] Immediately to the south of the temple was the Arch of Augustus, built in 19 B.C. to commemorate the emperor's diplomatic exploit of recovering the Roman field standards that had been lost to the Parthians by Marcus Crassus.[58] Finally, the circular Temple of Vesta was rebuilt after a fire in 14 B.C.[59]

The forum's western end was also altered during the early years of Octavian's reign by a project to reconstruct the Temple of Saturn (Fig. 84). The original Etrusco-Roman temple was replaced by a new one in the Hellenistic mode. It was begun in 42 B.C. by the

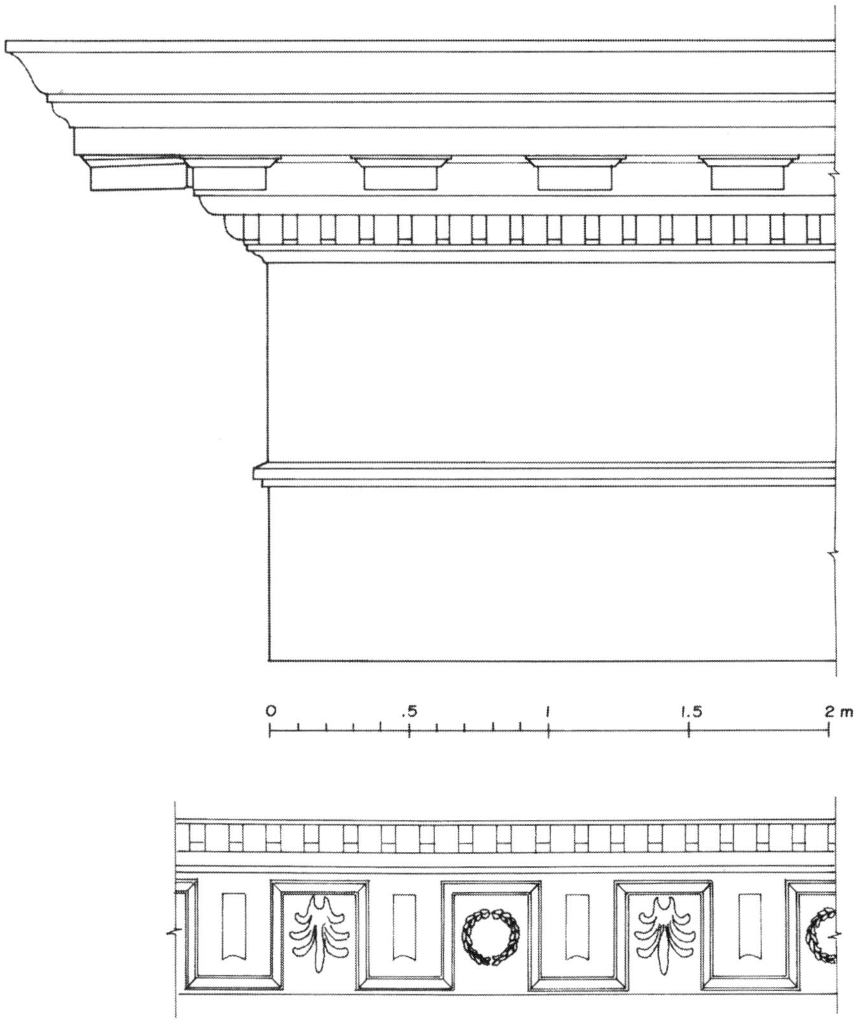

82. Temple of Divus Julius, cornice details. Drawing: John W. Stamper after Fritz Töebelmann, *Römische gebälke* (1923), p. 8, fig. 7.

83. Temple of Divus Julius, cornice details. Photo: John W. Stamper.

84. Rome, Temple of Saturn, Forum Romanum, rebuilt 42–30 B.C. Photo: John W. Stamper.

consul Lucius Munatius Plancus, who paid for the project with the spoils from a war against Rieti. Construction was completed near the end of the 30s B.C.[60] The temple would be rebuilt again in the second half of the fourth century A.D.[61]

The temple faced north, with the Via Sacra passing directly in front of its pronaos and turning along its west side, where it became the Clivus Capitolinus. From the center of the forum, the temple could be seen in perspective view and in relation to the Temple of Jupiter Capitolinus on the hill above. In contrast, a visitor entering the forum's northwest corner from the Clivus Argentarius saw the temple directly and dramatically on axis as he passed by the small prison structure, the *carcere*. From this direction, the full scope of the temple's front elevation could be perceived.

The temple served the function of a public treasury, *aerarium*, because when Saturn lived in Italy,

85. Rome, Temple of Saturn, elevation. Drawing: John W. Stamper based on G. Foglia and G. Ioppolo in Patrizio Pensabene, *Tempio di Saturno: architettura e decorazione* (1984), folio 1.

according to legend, no theft was ever committed. Also, under Saturn, private property did not exist, thus, whatever was contained in the temple was considered common to all. In 49 B.C., however, in the midst of a civil war, Julius Caesar is reported to have helped himself to the public funds stored there, spoils that had come from the Punic Wars, from Persia, Gaul, Crete, Cyprus, and Greece. Among Caesar's loot was reportedly 15,000 bars of gold and 30,000 of silver; for the first time, in the words of Lucan, "was Rome poorer than Caesar."[62] Shortly afterward, the treasury and the archives were transferred to a separate building located near the temple.[63]

Most of the temple's podium visible today dates from the reconstruction of Lucius Munatius Plancus in 42 B.C. The side facing the forum is 11 meters high (Fig. 85), and the opposite side is less because of the steep rise of the adjacent Clivus Capitolinus. In plan the podium measures 24 meters wide by 33 meters long (71 by 112 Roman feet). It was built of *opus caementicium* and blocks of travertine with a marble facing.[64] It was pseudoperipteral, with six columns across and three deep in the pronaos (Fig. 86). Its cella walls were articulated with engaged pilasters.[65]

The fourth-century columns and capitals of the pronaos standing today are the result of a rebuilding after a fire. A patchwork of *spolia* the columns on the front are grey granite, those at the sides are red granite. Their height, including the base and shaft, is about 13 meters. Their shafts measure about 11.65 meters high with lower diameters averaging 1.35 meters.[66] They are monolithic shafts, although some are pieced together from different columns. Similar to the granite shafts used in the second century A.D. by Trajan and Hadrian, they were imported from the Mons Claudianus in Egypt and may have originally been used in the Forum Traiani.[67] The Ionic capitals, with proto-Byzantine influences, are typical of the late Empire and early Christian eras. They are composed of four faces with volutes placed diagonally at the corners, and they have as a base a *hypotrachelion*, a rope-like convex molding.[68] In contrast to most capitals from the

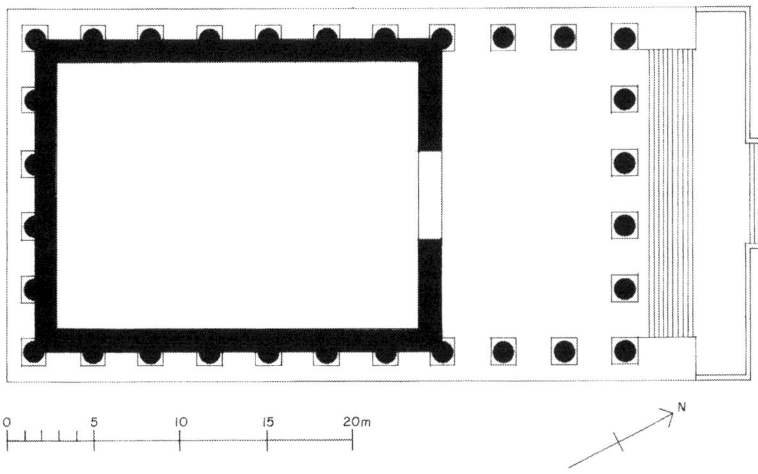

86. Rome, Temple of Saturn, plan. Drawing: John Stamper based on Luigi Canina in Patrizio Pensabene, *Tempio di Saturno: architettura e decorazione* (1984), p. 169, fig. 105.

Augustan period, they are a badly rendered form of Ionic, ill-proportioned and crudely carved.

About half of the entablature is from the Augustan building; however, the architrave and frieze were reversed when it was rebuilt in the fourth century so an inscription could be carved on its outer face. The original architrave and the carved surface of the frieze are visible today on the inside of the pronaos. While about half of these are from the Augustan building, the other half was carved in poor imitation at the time of the fourth-century reconstruction. The frieze is composed of carved acanthus plants with spiraling shoots alternating with palm leaves that are tied at their base with ribbons.[69] The cornice was supported by modillions and there were rosettes in the intermediate spaces (Fig. 87). The form of the modillions is different from that of the Temple of Divus Julius and the Regia in that it has a straight front but an S-curved underside.[70]

Of greatest interest is whether the Augustan building was Ionic or Corinthian. There are several interpretations, one theory suggesting that it was Corinthian and that the surviving Ionic capitals represent a change made only in the fourth-century restoration.[71] Another theory, related to that proposed for the Temple of Divus Julius, suggests that the Augustan building was a combination of Ionic columns in the pronaos and Corinthian pilasters on the cella walls.[72] Fragments of a Corinthian capital found near the site have been attributed to the cella pilasters of the Augustan version.[73]

It is more likely, however, that the fragments of the Corinthian capitals were not from the Temple of Saturn and that it was instead a purely Ionic temple from the time of its reconstruction in 42–30 B.C. One of two marble parapets dating from the late Empire and now exhibited in the curia, the *Anaglypha Traiani/Hadriani*, depicts the Temple of Saturn alongside the later Temple of Vespasian. The temples serve as a backdrop to a scene of porters carrying books of public debtors to be burned in front of the rostra. The Temple of Vespasian is shown as a Corinthian structure while the Temple of Saturn, in a clear contrast, is rendered with Ionic columns.[74] This must be a true representation of the temple's appearance in the second century A.D., and it would mean the reconstruction in fourth century A.D. was done in imitation of the Augustan-era temple.

With this and other building projects carried out during the reign of Augustus, the Forum Romanum took on a new sense of organization. Although it retained the trapezoidal plan it had from the beginning, there was now a near axial alignment of the Temple of Divus Julius and the rostra at the opposite end.[75] There was a new formality to its plan that made it more consistent with the Forum Julium and the fora of Pompeii and Paestum. This formality was further achieved by the rebuilding of the two basilicas on its north and south sides, projects that were initiated by Julius Caesar and finished by Octavian.

Augustan Temples on the Palatine Hill

The southwest corner of the Palatine Hill had important historical associations with much of Rome's

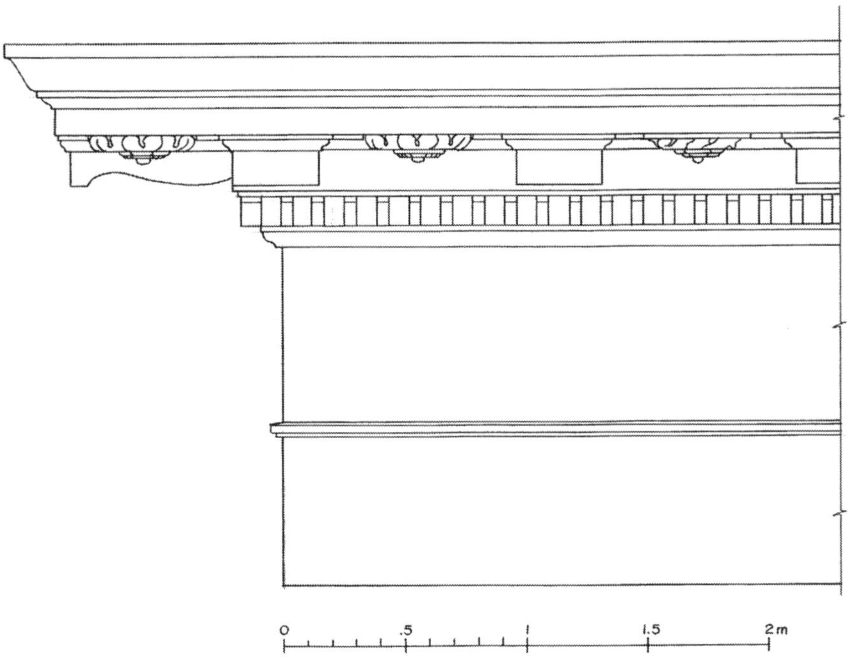

87. Temple of Saturn, detail of entablature and cornice. Drawing: John W. Stamper after Fritz Töebelmann, *Römische gebälke* (1923), p. 7, fig. 6.

ancient past: the *Roma Quadrata*, the Lupercal, and the House of Romulus. It was here that Augustus built his own house and where he also built and restored two temples.[76] To the southeast of his house he built the Temple of Apollo Palatinus; to the northwest he rebuilt the Temple of Magna Mater.[77]

The Temple of Apollo Palatinus (Fig. 88) was begun in 36 B.C. and dedicated in 28 B.C. for the purpose of commemorating a victory Octavian achieved several years earlier over Sextus Pompey, the son of Pompey the Great.[78] At the time of its construction, Octavian considered himself to be under the special protection of Apollo. Although Roman worship of Apollo had been adopted from the Greeks, possibly as early as the sixth century B.C., with Octavian the god became a more significant figure within the Roman world.[79]

Octavian consecrated the temple's site after it was struck by lightning, an event that he thought was an important omen related to the deity.[80] To this is added the fact that his victory over Antony and Cleopatra at Actium occurred in the vicinity of a well-known sanctuary of Apollo. Proclaiming his belief that Apollo helped him achieve his victory, he rebuilt the temple at Actium and founded games in Apollo's honor.[81]

Apollo had certain parallels to Jupiter. Like Jupiter, he was identified with the sun (Sol or Helios), which was an important factor in his acceptance by the Roman people. In the writings of many philosophers at the time, the sun was also described as the ruler of other heavenly bodies, the King of Heaven. The sun was a visible symbol of the supreme deity, thought by some to be the deity itself.[82] Octavian's embrace of Apollo thus provided him with a new image of a sun god, distinct from traditional belief in Jupiter yet equally as potent as a cult figure. As the sun shone unchallenged in the sky, so Octavian stood unchallenged at the head of the Roman state.

The Temple of Apollo Palatinus stood at the northeast edge of a large platform and was approached by a broad flight of steps which was divided into several sections. Its pronaos had six Corinthian columns on the front and three deep, and there were possibly seven engaged pilasters along the sides, making it pseudoperipteral. Its podium measured 22.40 meters wide (76 Roman feet), making it about two-thirds the size of the Temple of Jupiter Capitolinus.[83] Fragments of architectural decoration discovered on the site confirm that the temple was built of Carrara marble. Based on the size of the temple's capitals, the height of the columns was 14 meters (48 Roman feet). Their intercolumniations equaled three times the lower diameter, making it *diastyle* rather than *pycnostyle*.[84]

The platform in front of the temple sloped down toward the south by as much as 9 meters, necessitating

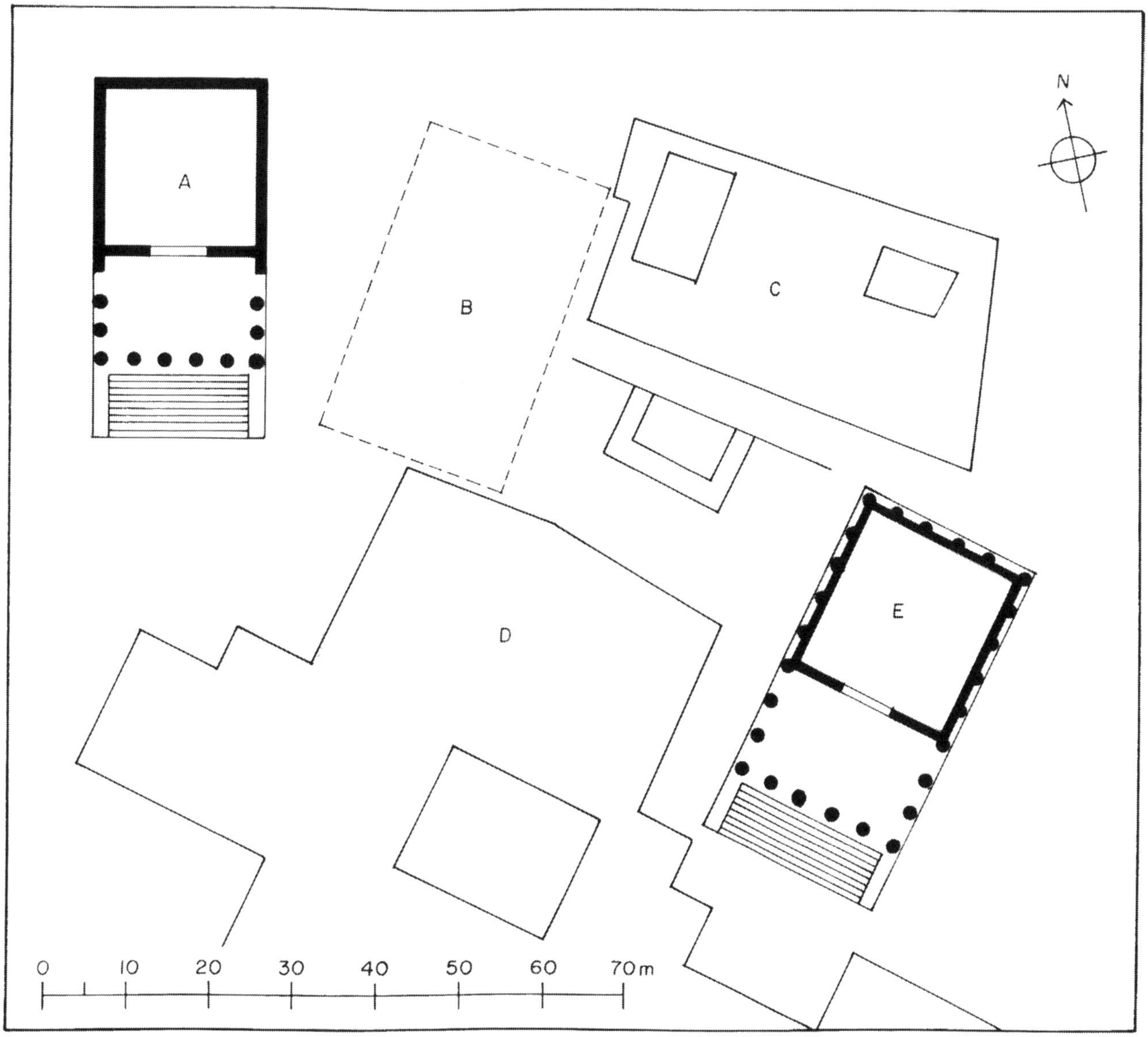

88. Rome, Temple of Apollo Palatinus, 36–28 B.C.: (A) Temple of Magna Mater, (B) Temple of Victoria, (C) Domus of Livia, (D) Domus of Augustus, (E) Temple of Apollo Palatinus. Drawing: John W. Stamper based on Elizabeth Riorden in John Stambaugh, *The Ancient Roman City* (1989), p. 60, fig. 5.

several terraced levels. At its southwestern edge, there was a series of ramps and stairs that connected it to the adjacent house of Augustus.[85] This platform was also related to a portico of Numidian marble columns located southwest of the house. Octavian used the portico to house statues of Danaus and his fifty daughters, the Danaids.[86] He used the platform space to receive guests on official business, meet foreign ambassadors, and perhaps even call meetings of the Roman Senate.[87] Two libraries for Greek and Latin collections were located on the opposite side of the platform, to the southeast.[88] Each had an exedra at the back and faced toward the northwest.[89]

The temple was decorated with a wealth of sculptural ornamentation and famous works of Greek art. Ivory carvings on the cella door represented in one scene the killing of Niobe's children by Apollo and his sister Diana, and in another the expulsion of the Gauls from Delphi.[90] Inside the cella there were at least three cult statues, Apollo by Scopas, Diana by Timotheus,

and Latona by Cephisodotus.[91] Its roof was topped by a chariot of the sun and other sculptures.[92]

Twenty terra-cotta panels found on the temple's site depict Greek-inspired mythological scenes that were characteristic of the religious and political time of Octavian. They include the battle for a tripod between Apollo and Hercules, scenes of adoration of sacred objects, and scenes with scroll patterns and flying victory figures.[93] The display of such Greek images from the archaic and classical periods made the composition in essence an homage to Greek culture.[94]

To emphasize further the importance of the Temple of Apollo Palatinus Octavian had the Sybilline Books moved here from the Temple of Jupiter Capitolinus. He also ordered that the games held in his honor, which concluded the past and solemnly introduced a new and better age, should culminate in a ceremony in front of this temple. Octavian gave the deity a special role in his birth of a new age. Presenting himself as the restorer of a golden age, the man divinely assigned to transform the world, he acknowledged Apollo's regular assistance.[95]

A second temple site was located adjacent to the house of Augustus, this one on its northwest side, and in this case with a pair of older temples: Victoria and Magna Mater.[96] Neither of these structures ranked high in Augustus's view of Rome's historical deities, but given their proximity to his Palatine Hill house, he had no choice but to maintain them.

The Temple of Victoria had been constructed by L. Postumius Megillus, consul for the year 294 B.C.[97] It measured 19.35 meters wide by 33.40 meters long (76 by 113 Roman feet), with a podium built of *opus quadratum*. It had a stairs leading to the front of the podium, and its plan was *peripteros sine postico*, with six columns on the front and nine on the sides. The composition was similar to that of Temple C in Largo Argentina and the Temple of Janus in the Forum Holitorium.[98] A temple of this type dedicated to this cult was appropriate to the period at the beginning of the third century B.C. immediately following an important victory over the Samnites and the influence of analogous cults in Greece.[99]

The adjacent Temple of Magna Mater was rebuilt by Augustus in 3 B.C. It was originally constructed in 204–191 B.C. by the censors M. Livius and C. Claudius.[100] Destroyed by a fire in 111 B.C., it was rebuilt by Caecilius Metellus Numidius.[101] Its purpose was to house a black stone that represented the goddess, which was brought to Rome from Pessinus in Phrygia in 204 B.C.[102] While the temple was under construction, the statue was housed temporarily in the Temple of Victoria.[103] On the day of the temple's dedication, the *ludi Megalenses* were instituted and a celebration was held on a platform in front.[104]

The columns at the time of rebuilding in 111 B.C. were Corinthian, with capitals of peperino tufa, some fragments of which have been found around the temple's base. Their upper portion was carved with helices and volutes, and the rest of their surface was left smooth, a technical and stylistic parallel to those of the Temple of Jupiter in Pompeii.[105]

The temple was oriented toward the southeast, making it slightly skewed relative to the neighboring Temple of Victoria. It had a massive podium, which measured 17.10 by 33.18 meters (78 by 113 Roman feet) and was built of concrete and faced with blocks of peperino. Its pronaos had six columns on the front and four deep, and the walls of its cella were lined on the inside with columns, possibly in two stories.[106]

When Augustus rebuilt the temple in 3 B.C., its existing columns and capitals were incorporated into the new building.[107] The cult of Magna Mater was an exotic one, with celebrations featuring ecstatic dances and long-haired priests.[108] Although it played a secondary role in Augustus's pantheon of the gods, during his reign, certain aspects of the goddess were nevertheless increasingly emphasized. The Phrygian homeland, for instance, was linked to Rome's Trojan origins when Aeneas fled from Troy to Latium.[109] In Virgil's *Aeneid*, Magna Mater was portrayed as a protectoress of Aeneas on his journeys.[110]

Together, these three temples, Apollo Palatinus, Victoria, and Magna Mater, were linked to Octavian's construction of his house on the southwestern corner of the hill, near the legendary site of the house of Romulus. They added to the dignity of the house and represented the emperor's religious virtue through his ties to important deities. The presence of the temples, the manner in which they framed the house on either side, and the prominence of the complex on the edge

of the hill, lent it an air of nobility and respectability worthy of the emperor.[111]

Temples of the Circus Flaminius

A third area of development during Octavian's reign was the Circus Flaminius, where many of the temples originally built in the third and second centuries B.C. were reconstructed.[112] The circus itself was transformed by the construction of the Theater of Marcellus at its eastern end. Although it was begun by Julius Caesar in 46 B.C., most of its construction was carried out in a second building campaign between 11 B.C. and A.D. 3.[113] It was intended to rival the already existing theater and temple complex of Pompey the Great.

Directly north of the Theater of Marcellus was the Temple of Apollo Medicus, which was built in 433–431 B.C. and rebuilt in 179 B.C. It was reconstructed a second time by the Roman general C. Sosius from 34 to 20 B.C. in honor of a triumph over Judea. Sosius, one-time governor of Syria and consul in 32 B.C., was an ally of Marcus Antony.[114] It is probable that Sosius ordered the temple's reconstruction immediately after his triumph and that it was intended as a counterpoint to Octavian's Temple of Apollo Palatinus. He used his position as consul for active opposition to Octavian, and in 31 B.C. he commanded a post in Antony's fleet at Actium. He was arrested shortly after the battle at Actium and condemned to death. He soon gained Octavian's favor, however, was freed, and became one of his allies.[115]

With the two men's reconciliation, work on the temple, known today as the Temple of Apollo Sosianus, or Apollo in Circo, was continued. Its dedication and iconographic program, however, were changed on behalf of Octavian.[116] Rather than depicting a victory over Judea as originally planned, its finished sculpted reliefs represented Octavian's Illyrian triumph of 29 B.C.[117]

The original temple constructed by Fulvius Nobilior in the second century B.C. had a pronaos with four columns on the front and two on the sides. The new structure was pseudoperipteral with six Corinthian columns across the front and ten columns and half-columns on the sides (Fig. 89).[118] Its dimensions were 21.32 meters wide by 40 meters long (72.5 by 136 Roman feet), which were almost identical to those of the Temple of Apollo Palatinus.[119]

Its columns were closely spaced in the *pycnostyle* manner (Fig. 90) like those of the Temple of Divus Julius and others of the period. They were 18 meters high, the shafts 12.5 meters. Their lower diameter was 1.47 meters, with a ratio of height to diameter of 10 to 1, the standard for Roman temple design.[120]

Although the temple's plan and system of proportions were fairly standard, its details overtly contradicted the classical canon.[121] Its columns, three of which were reerected on the site, had richly decorated bases with two tori whose surfaces were carved with a rope motif. All of the moldings were lined with small, pearl-like spheres. The column shafts were carved alternately with wide and narrow flutes.[122] Those of the pronaos, including the half-columns at the corners of the cella, were all Lunense marble. The walls of the cella were constructed of Aneine tufa in *opus quadratum* and were decorated with stucco mixed with travertine particles. The shafts of the engaged columns on the side walls of the cella were made of stucco-coated brick.[123]

The column capitals, carved in two blocks, featured shoots of laurel which held up the corner volutes. In the center there was a floral cluster and a richly decorated abacus. The lower rows of abacus leaves were interrupted by a cauliculus from which emerged a shoot of acanthus and a single small leaf.[124]

The entablature, like the columns, was very much out of the ordinary for Roman Corinthian architecture (Fig. 91). A mixture of materials, it was composed of a travertine core that was faced with thin marble panels on the sides and bottom. Most unusual was the use of four fascias on the architrave rather than three. Carving on the frieze depicted branches of laurel hanging between bucrania and tied in the middle to a *thymiaterion* used for burning incense during a sacrifice.[125] The cornice was supported by S-curved modillions faced with acanthus leaves, and in the soffits recessed coffers were divided up into small panels decorated with rosettes.[126]

Archaeological evidence suggests the interior of the temple's cella was elaborately finished with rows of freestanding columns down the sides and back, two

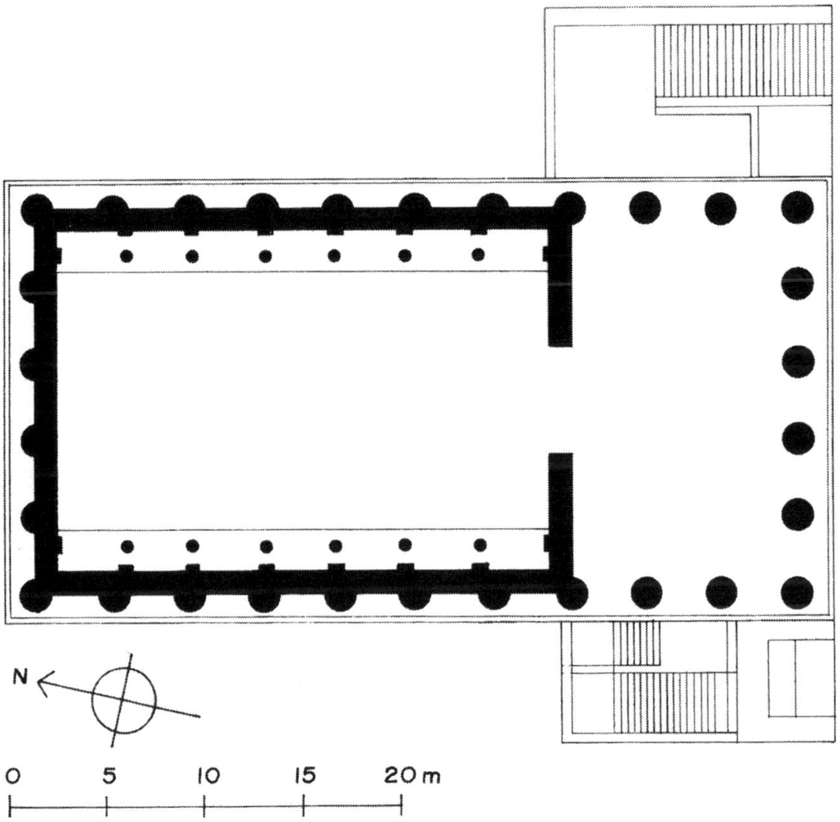

89. Temple of Apollo Sosianus, 34–20 B.C., plan. Drawing: Brian Kane after Antonio M. Colini, in *BullArchGov* 68 (1940), p. 33, fig. 25.

stories high. Framed between the columns in each bay were aedicules with alternating segmental and triangular pediments.[127] Like the columns of the pronaos, the surfaces of the column and pilaster bases were richly decorated with carved laurel leaves, egg-and-dart, and bead-and-reel motifs. The columns were of africano marble, with white marble bases and capitals.[128] The lower half of the capitals was ornamented with double spirals of acanthus leaves; while on the upper half, rather than helices and a flower in front of the abacus, there was a tripod surmounted by a woman's head inscribed in a corolla. This tripod was flanked by two serpents taking the place of the acanthus volutes.[129]

The entablature was equally decorative with a two-step architrave, the upper fascia of which was lined with acanthus leaves and the frieze was composed of sculpted figures depicting scenes of battle and triumph. One of the processional scenes may have represented the triple triumph Octavian celebrated in 29 B.C.[130]

It remains to be explained what exactly was the reason for the unique vocabulary of decorative elements used in this building's design. Such details as the alternating wide and narrow flutes of the column shafts, the richly decorated bases, and the four-stepped architrave were not often used in other buildings and thus were not assimilated into the Augustan-era Corinthian Order. This was an unusual interpretation of the order that was more episodic than evolutionary.[131]

During the time the Temple of Apollo Sosianus was under construction, the adjacent Temple of Bellona came to be considered a sort of memorial to the *gens Claudius*, a tomb of which was located nearby on the slope of the Capitoline Hill. The temple's reconstruction may have been ordered in 33 B.C. by Appius Claudius Pulcher, who claimed a victory in Spain. Unlike Sosius, who changed his allegiance from Marcus Antony to Octavian, Appius Claudius Pulcher had been a strong friend of Octavian from the beginning. Even more important was the fact that he was a relative of Octavian's wife, Livia. Thus, a temple erected to the *gens Claudius* adjacent to the Temple of Apollo Sosianus was an important addition to Octavian's transformation of the Circus Flaminius into an urban center symbolic of his dynasty.[132]

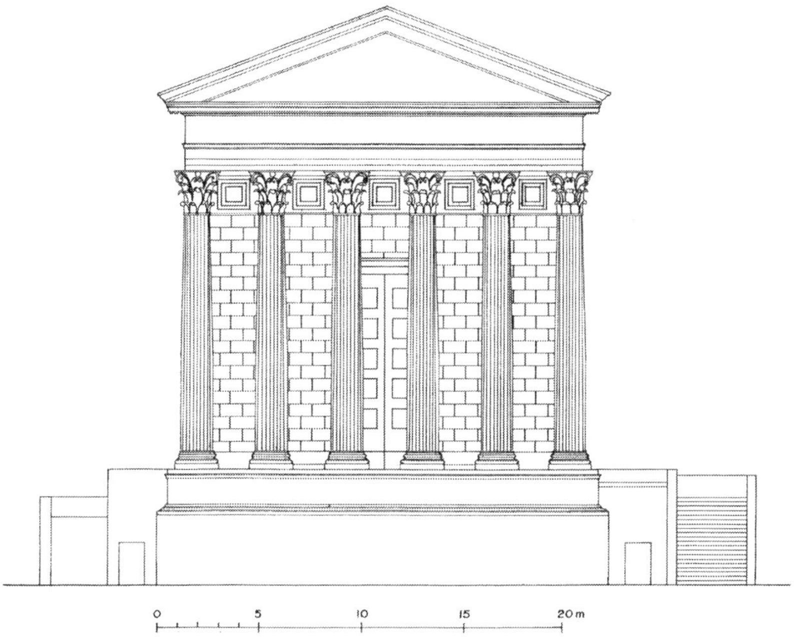

90. Rome, Temple of Apollo Sosianus, elevation. Drawing: Rogelio Carrasco after Antonio M. Colini, in *BullArchGov* 68 (1940), p. 33, fig. 25.

Although only a portion of the podium of the Temple of Bellona has been documented, it is known from the *Forma Urbis Romae* that its plan was peripteral, with six columns on the front and nine on the sides. Column and frieze fragments found on the site suggest it was in the Corinthian Order and that it combined Lunense marble and travertine. Some of its decoration was coarsely carved, probably by local craftsmen, whereas certain elements were more refined, suggesting the work of a different group of carvers.[133]

A total of three temple precincts were located directly northwest of the Temples of Apollo Sosianus and Bellona (Fig. 92). Each was enclosed by a porticus and each faced onto the Circus Flaminius. The first, the farthest to the northwest, was the Porticus Octavia, built in 167–66 B.C. by Gnaeus Octavius as a monument to his naval victory over Perseus of Macedonia.[134] Velleius Paterculus called it one of the most beautiful structures in Rome.[135] Pliny stated that it had double porticos and that it was referred to as "Corinthia" because of its bronze capitals.[136] Augustus stated in the *Res Gestae* that he restored the porticus and preserved the name of the original donor.[137] He also placed in it the standards of Gabinius, which he recovered from the Illyrians in 33 B.C.[138]

The second precinct was the Porticus Philippi, built in 33–29 B.C. by L. Marcius Philippus, Octavian's stepfather. He constructed it to enclose the temple of Hercules Musarum, which had originally been constructed by M. Fulvius Nobilior in 187 B.C.[139] Ovid reports that the porticus was adorned with paintings by Zeuxis, Antipilus, and Theorus.[140]

The third precinct, the closest to the Temple of Apollo Sosianus, was the Porticus Metelli, built by Caecilius Metellus Macedonicus in 143–131 B.C. It contained the two second-century temples dedicated to Juno Regina and Jupiter Stator.[141] Its reconstruction was begun by Claudius Marcellus in 33 B.C., but it was paid for largely by Octavian and it was dedicated and renamed the Porticus Octaviae by his sister Octavia in 23 B.C.[142] This porticus with its temples of Juno Regina and Jupiter Stator should not be mistaken for the Porticus Octavia, which was built by Gnaeus Octavius.[143]

When Marcellus, Octavian, and Octavia built the new portico, they carried out a substantial restoration of the two temples (Fig. 93), including changing the Temple of Jupiter Stator from a peripteral temple to *peripteros sine postico*.[144] They also replaced the northeast portico of the original complex with a new one located about 10 to 15 meters further to the northeast. The overall size of the new enclosure was about 115 meters wide by 135 meters long. In the space between the temples and the new portico, they added a *schola*, or *curia octaviae*, and a library that had both Greek and

91. Temple of Apollo Sosianus, detail of columns and entablature. Photo: Deutsches Archäologisches Institut, Rome, 59.744.

Latin sections.[145] The *schola* was on some occasions used for meetings of the Senate.[146]

Also added to the complex was an entrance propylon on the southwest side, facing the Circus Flaminius (Fig. 94). In the original structure, the front colonnade was continuous across the front. The foundations of the propylon visible on the site today date from the time of Augustus. According to the *Forma Urbis Romae*, it had six columns in two rows. The composition with four columns framed by piers is the result of alterations by Domitian and later by Septimius Severus.[147] The pediment was rebuilt with *spolia* after a fire at the time of Septimius Severus and Caracalla, and their names were added to the inscription on the frieze.[148] Each of the flanking colonnades on the north and south contained two parallel rows of Corinthian columns.[149] All of the visible granite columns with white marble capitals and bases are from the Domitianic or Severan reconstructions.[150]

Following the example of these three enclosed temple precincts, and taking into account the Porticus Pompeiana, such complexes had obviously become popular during the decades of the 30s and 20s B.C. Not only did the porticos provide a formal setting for a temple or group of temples, they also served as covered walkways, especially when interlinked, for pedestrians

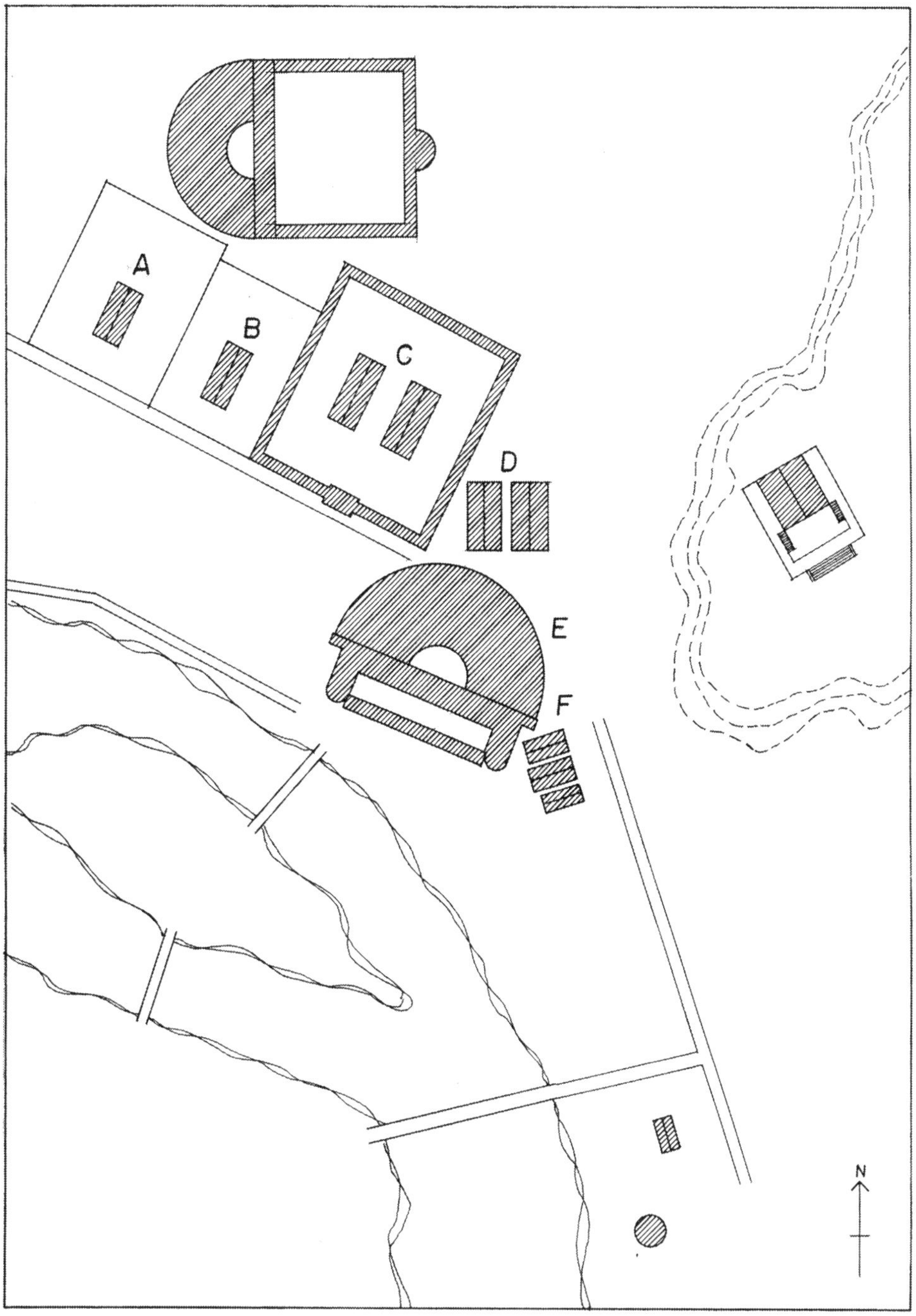

92. Rome, plan of area around Circus Flaminius. (A) Porticus Octavia, (B) Porticus Philippi, (C) Porticus Octaviae, (D) Temples of Apollo Sosianus and Bellona, (E) Theater of Marcellus, (F) Forum Holitorium. Drawing: John W. Stamper based on Rodolfo Lanciani, *Forma Urbis Romae* (1990), pls. 21 and 28, and Filippo Coarelli, *Il Campo Marzio: dalle origini alla fine della Repubblica* (1997).

to go easily from one part of the city to another. Much of the area west of the Capitoline Hill was eventually divided up into precincts of various sizes and shapes by a vast quantity of similar portico enclosures, most of them interconnected to form an extensive network of covered streets.[151] Toward the end of the Empire, according to Lanciani, it was possible to walk from the Capitoline as far as St. Peter's almost entirely under the cover of porticos.[152]

The temple architecture commissioned by Octavian as well as his supporters and his detractors in the decades following the death of Julius Caesar possessed a discernable style. If we consider together buildings like the Temple of Divus Julius, voted in 42 B.C. and dedicated in 29 B.C.; the Temple of Saturn, begun in 42 B.C. and finished after the battle at Actium; the Temple of Apollo Palatinus, voted in 36 B.C. and dedicated in 28 B.C.; and the Temple of Apollo Sosianus, from 34 to

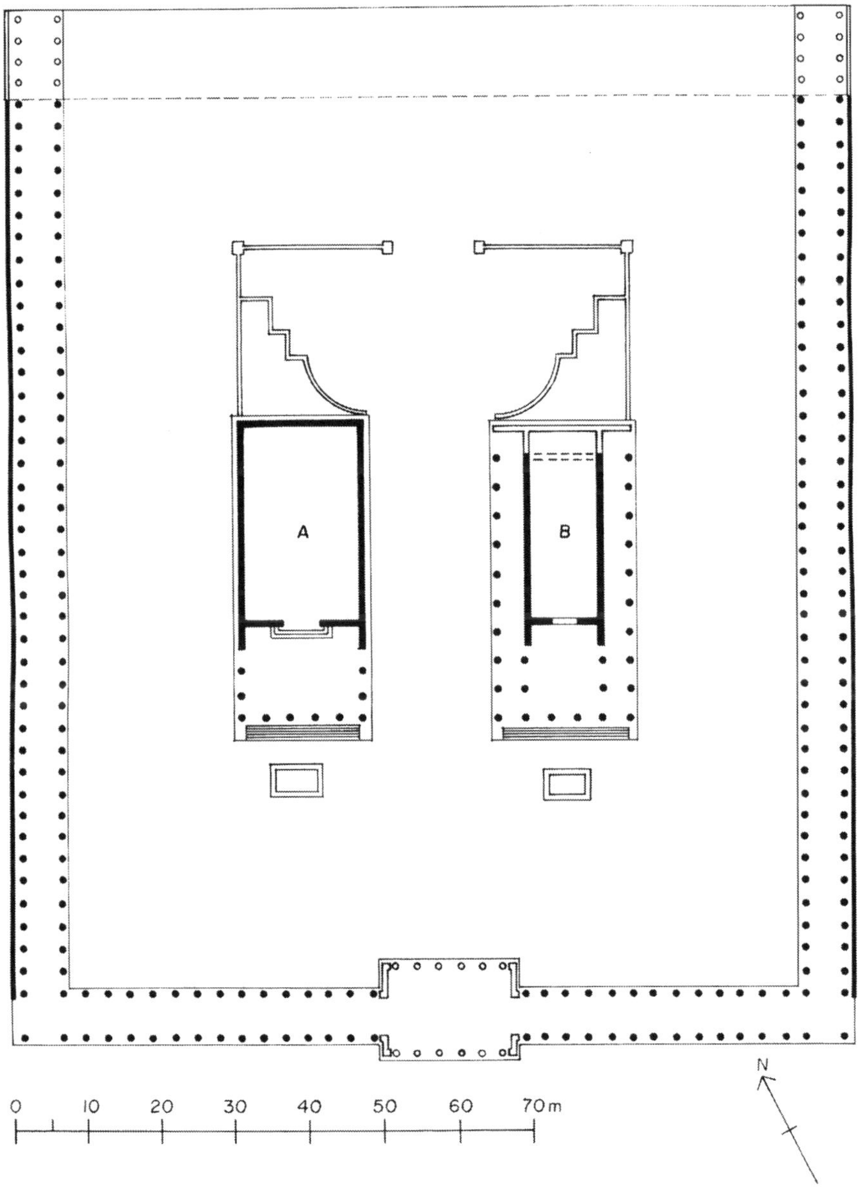

93. Rome, Porticus Octaviae (Metelli) showing addition of entrance pavilion and *scola* or *curia octaviae*, 33–23 B.C.: (A) Temple of Juno Regina, (B) Temple of Jupiter Stator with new *peripteros sine postico* plan. Drawing: John W. Stamper based on Rodolfo Lanciani, *Forma Urbis Romae* (1990), pl. 21.

20 B.C., we see a certain continuity that was unique to Rome. Most of these temples had marble Corinthian capitals with precise formal and technical characteristics that showed a clear influence of Hellenistic sources but with a particular Roman refinement. In the zones of shadow, for instance, the closely spaced lobes of the acanthus leaves assumed the character of a triangle and a waterdrop. Analogously, the space between the helices and the volutes was almost always occupied by a shoot with a rosette. These characteristic features were derived not so much from Athenian examples, but were particular to the Roman interpretation of the Corinthian Order.[153]

By this time in Rome's architectural development, it was not so much the direct influences from Athens we are concerned about, but, rather, a similarity of developments taking place in both Athens and Rome. The vocabulary had Greek origins, but it had a definite Roman interpretation.[154] There were no direct quotations from Athens, but more importantly, we find a relationship between Roman temples themselves – how one influenced another, how certain temples

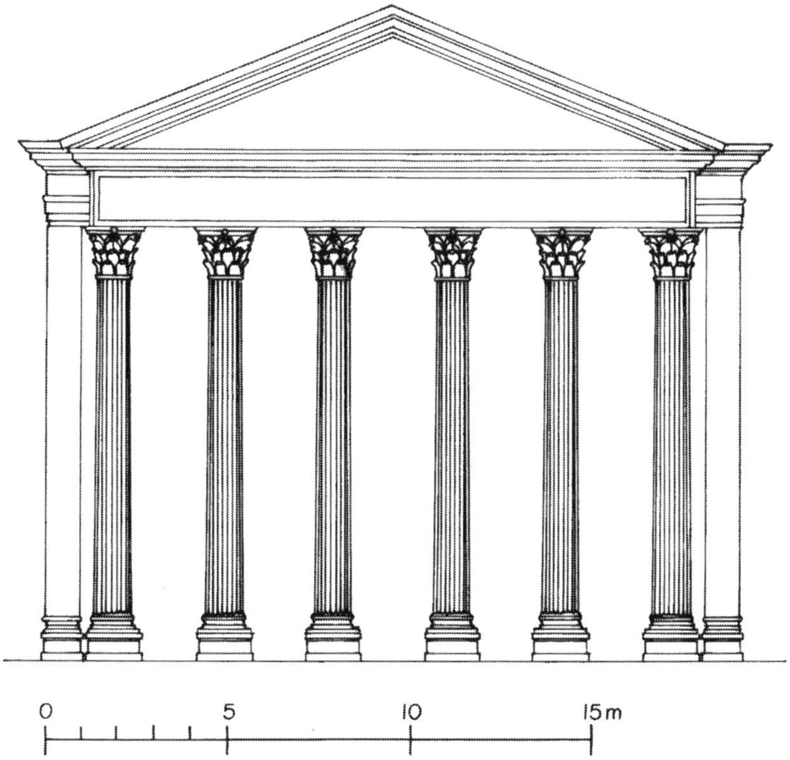

94. Porticus Octaviae (Metelli), entrance pavilion at the time of Augustus, 33–23 B.C. Drawing: John W. Stamper adapted from Georges Gromort, *Choix d'éléments empruntés à l'architecture classique* (1927), vol. 1, pl. 38.

were more experimental, others more canonical.[155] Most important for this study is the distinct Roman character of these stylistic features, the relationship between one Roman temple and another, and, ultimately, the influence these immediate precedents had on the design of the Temple of Mars Ultor in the Forum Augustum.[156]

In terms of the plan types, if we consider the same four temples – Divus Julius, Saturn, Apollo Palatinus, and Apollo Sosianus – we see a distinctly Roman tradition prevailing over the Hellenistic plans preferred by Vitruvius (see Table 7.1). All were prostyle with six columns on the front. The pronaos of all but the temple of Divus Julius was three columns deep (Fig. 95); in the case of the Divus Julius, the pronaos was the same depth, but its cella walls extended one bay as *antae*. All but the Temple of Divus Julius were pseudoperipteral with engaged columns or pilasters. The Divus Julius Temple had pilasters engaged only at the corners of the cella. Finally, their dimensions were very similar, their podia measuring between 21 and 27 meters wide and 30 to 40 meters long. The plan types were not derived from Athens or Asia Minor, but were a distinctly Roman derivation, one that Vitruvius considered an exception to the canonical rules.

Capitoline Hill

Jupiter and the Capitoline Hill also figured prominently in Octavian's Roman building campaigns. In 32–30 B.C., he reconstructed the Temple of Jupiter Feretrius, the first temple built on the Capitoline Hill by Romulus and now long neglected.[157] It was a small temple, measuring only about 4 meters long. It did not contain a cult statue but was used as a repository for the ritual implements, the sceptre and knife of the *fetiales*, and the armor of the King of Veii, Lars Tolumnius.[158]

Octavian ordered necessary restoration work on the Temple of Jupiter Capitolinus itself and he built a third temple on the Capitoline Hill, this one dedicated to Jupiter Tonans, the Thunderer.[159] Claiming to have had dreams sent by Jupiter, he related how he had been miraculously saved from a flash of lightning during the war he fought in Spain against the Cantabrians in 26 B.C. A slave, who was walking torch

Table 7.1. Temples Built in the First Century B.C. (Podium Size, Column Diameter, and Interaxial Dimension)

	Podium		Columns	
Temple	*Width (m)*	*Length (m)*	*Diameter (m)*	*Interaxial (m)*
Capitoline Jupiter	34.0	38.30	1.47	5.0
				7.40 center
Venus Genetrix	29.47	38.92	1.25	2.95 front
				3.04 sides
Divus Julius (podium)	26.97	30.0	1.16	2.92
Saturn	24.0	33.0	1.35	4.50
Castor and Pollux	27.50	40.0		3.20 and 3.50
Apollo, Palatine	22.40	38.92	–	–
Magna Mater	17.10	33.18	–	–
Apollo Sosianus	21.32	40.0	1.47	3.63

Source: Inge Nielsen and Birte Poulsen, *The Temple of Castor and Pollux I* (Rome: Edizioni de Luca, 1992).

in hand in front of Octavian's litter, was killed while he was spared. He therefore ordered this new temple of Jupiter Tonans. Located near the entrance to the sacred precinct of the Capitoline Temple, this structure, according to Pliny, had solid marble walls and contained a cult statue by Leochares.[160] In a later dream, Jupiter appeared to Octavian to protest that this new temple was taking worshippers away from his principal temple. Cassius Dio writes:

> The people . . . approached Jupiter who is called Tonans and did reverence to him, partly because of the novelty of his name and of the form of his statue, and partly because the statue had been set up by Augustus, but chiefly because it was the first they encountered as they ascended the Capitol; and thereupon the Jupiter in the great temple was angry because he was now reduced to second place as compared with the other.[161]

Augustus replied that Jupiter Tonans was only the gatekeeper of the Capitoline Jupiter and could not possibly be thought of as a competitor: "Augustus said to Jupiter Capitolinus, 'You have Tonans as your sentinel:' and when it was day, he attached a bell to the statue as confirmation of the vision. For those who guard communities at night carry a bell in order to be able to signal to the inhabitants whenever they need to do so."[162]

The temple was represented on a coin of Octavian with six Corinthian columns across the front. Jupiter was shown in the center bay with a sceptre and a thunderbolt.[163]

The Capitoline Hill was thus an important site in Octavian's building programs in the 30s and 20s B.C. Although he devoted much attention to other sites in the city, especially the Palatine Hill and the Circus Maximus, the Capitoline Hill continued to play a dominant role in the politics of religious authority.

The Agrippan Pantheon and the Campus Martius

A further aspect of the role of political and religious authority in the time of Octavian is seen in the construction of the first Pantheon in the center of the Campus Martius. It was constructed by Octavian's trusted general Marcus Agrippa in 29–25 B.C., one of several buildings he erected in the area.[164] It was one of three structures aligned on a north-south axis, with the Pantheon on the north, then the Basilica of Neptune, and finally the Baths of Agrippa, which extended almost as far south as the Largo Argentina.[165] Adjacent to these buildings, on the east, was the *Saepta Julia*, a

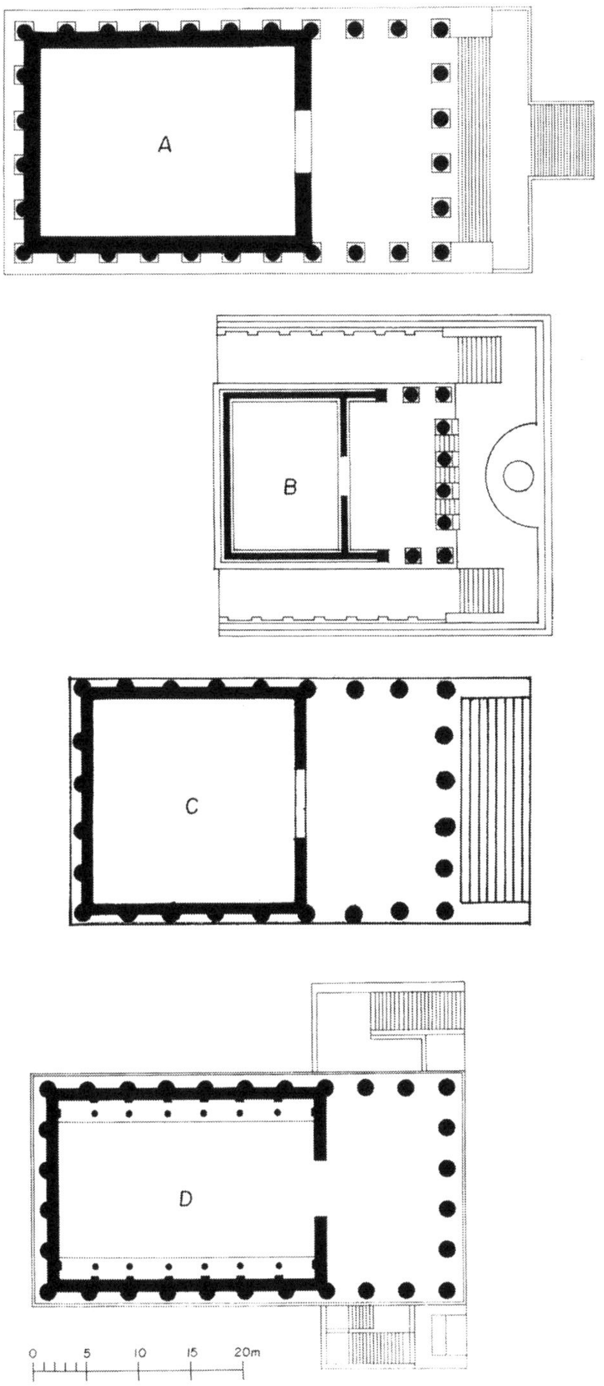

95. Comparison of temple plans built in Rome between 42 and 34 B.C., all plans at the same scale. (A) Temple of Saturn, (B) Temple of Divus Julius, (C) Temple of Apollo Palatinus, (D) Temple of Apollo Sosianus. Drawing: John W. Stamper.

voting hall that was begun by Julius Caesar and finished by Agrippa in 26 B.C.[166] In addition to these, the Aqua Virgo was under construction, as were the Porticus Argonautarum, the Diribitorium, and the Porticus Vipsania. These buildings together, most of which were initiated after the grand triumph of 29 B.C., suggest a large-scale project, one with an almost completely unprecedented scope and range of building types.[167]

In writing of Agrippa's Pantheon, Cassius Dio stated, "he completed the so-called Pantheon. It has this name perhaps because it received the images of many gods and among them the statues of Mars and Venus; but my own opinion is that the name is due to its round shape, like the sky."[168]

Because Cassius Dio wrote *Roman History* in the third century A.D., he was looking at Hadrian's later Pantheon constructed in A.D. 118–128. He assumed the original building by Agrippa had a similar circular shape.[169] It is significant that he referred to two of the deity statues it housed, Mars and Venus, proof of a symbolic link to both Augustus and Caesar.

There are numerous debates about the original building's orientation, architectural form, and iconographic meaning. Archaeologists have long believed Agrippa's temple was not oriented northward as is Hadrian's later building, but rather to the south. Excavations carried out in the 1890s revealed that the original temple's foundation blocks were located directly under the present pronaos. Initial interpretations of these foundations by Lanciani suggested that the original temple was T-shaped in plan and that its pronaos was oriented to the south.[170] It would have corresponded to the entrance passage and main doorway in the present building's intermediate block, while the rectangular cella would have corresponded to the existing pronaos, its back wall aligned with its northernmost row of columns.[171] The space occupied by the present rotunda was thought to have been a paved area, circular in plan, surrounded by a wall, and open to the sky.[172]

An alternative interpretation suggests that the original structure under the present pronaos was an open propylon rather than a cella and that it provided access to the open circular space.[173] The latter would have corresponded to a *templum*, the sacred ground for the augur to take bearings in the sky and to pronounce the inauguration of the site. The seriousness of the boundaries so demarcated by the augur was paramount: the *templum* was fixed immutably, and no later restoration could change it.[174] Just like the *templum* of the Capitoline Jupiter, once it was established, it was intended

to last forever. When Hadrian rebuilt the structure in the second century A.D., according to this theory, he built over the sacred *templum*, thus honoring both the history of the site and the memory of Augustus.

New excavations carried out in 1996–1997, however, have revealed a different understanding of the Agrippan Pantheon. An access stairs was discovered that led to the original pronaos on the building's north side, directly under the stairs of Hadrian's building. This discovery proves that Agrippa's Pantheon was oriented northward, identical to the existing building.[175] The original pronaos was in the same location as the existing one, and the original cella would have been circular, possibly covered with a wooden roof structure.[176]

Although the original pronaos occupied the same position as Hadrian's, the evidence suggests it was wider, 43.80 meters as opposed to 34.20 meters, and that it could have had ten columns across the front rather than eight.[177]

Other details of Agrippa's building are provided by the ancient authors. Pliny wrote: "The Pantheon was embellished for Agrippa by Diogenes of Athens; and among the supporting members of this temple there are caryatids that are among a class of their own, and the same is true of the figures of the pediment, which are, however, not so well known because of their lofty position."[178] Archaeologists have assumed that the caryatids were visible in the building's pronaos. It was also furnished with bronze capitals from Syracuse.[179]

The excavations of 1996–1997 also clarified details of the original podium's front wall showing that the stairs did not go all the way across. Rather, there were two small stairs near the podium's east and west ends, with a speakers' platform in the middle.[180] This use of lateral stairs would have been a variant on the theme seen in numerous temples from the late Republic, including the temples of Divus Julius, Castor and Pollux, and Venus Genetrix, not to mention the Temple of Jupiter Capitolinus as it is reconstructed in this study.

Agrippa's selection of the site for the Pantheon was significant in its relation to both the founding of Rome and to the Augustan family.[181] The original building faced across a vast marshy area of the Campus Martius that had not yet been developed.[182] Several Augustan structures, however, were being built or were already completed at its northern and northeastern edges. Most notably, there was the great circular Mausoleum of Augustus, an imperial tomb and symbol of the Julian family built in 28–23 B.C.[183] It was located about 800 meters north of the Pantheon, exactly on axis with its front door.[184]

Nearby was the Ara Pacis, the principal entrance of which faced toward the center of the Campus Martius. Its sculpted panels represented scenes of Romulus and Remus at the Lupercal and Aeneas sacrificing a white sow to the Penates, the two images celebrating the birth of Rome and the Julian family.[185] Finally, the Horologium Solare, erected in 13–10 B.C., was a large sundial whose marble floor covered an area about 160 meters wide by 75 meters deep. Its gnomon was a red granite obelisk brought from Heliopolis, which stood 100 Roman feet high.[186]

Agrippa may have lined the space between the Pantheon and the Mausoleum with trees to form a grand royal park. The sightline connecting the two monuments would have served to link Augustus and the Pantheon of the gods.[187] Cassius Dio wrote further:

> Agrippa desired to place Augustus also there [in the Pantheon] and to take the designation of the structure from his title. But, as his master would not accept either honor, he placed in the temple itself a statue of the former Caesar and in the anteroom representations of Augustus and himself. This was done not from any rivalry and ambition on Agrippa's part to make himself equal to Augustus, but from his superabundant devotion to him.[188]

We thus know that both the original building and Hadrian's replacement contained statues of numerous gods, including Mars, the father of Romulus, Venus, the divine ancestor of the Caesars, and, finally, the deified Julius Caesar. In its pronaos were statues of Augustus and Agrippa.[189] The combination of these clearly made it a sanctuary to the dynasty of the *gens Julia*.[190] Although the initial project was intended to be a true Augusteum, that is, a temple dedicated to the living sovereign, its actual dedication was to the previous deified ruler, Julius Caesar. At the same time, it forecast the deification of Augustus, and perhaps of Agrippa.[191]

A final consideration is a link between the Pantheon and the founding of Rome. It is no coincidence that Augustus built his house on the Palatine

Hill near the legendary site of the House of Romulus and the *Roma Quadrata*. It is no coincidence either that the Pantheon was located not only 800 meters from the Mausoleum of Augustus, but also 800 meters from the Temple of Jupiter Capitolinus.[192] It was located an equal distance from both monuments to suggest a political connection to both.

There were many references to Romulus and the founding of Rome in Augustan propaganda. Especially telling are the parallel stories of the twelve vultures. When Romulus looked for omens to assure him of the appropriateness of the Palatine Hill as the location for the *Roma Quadrata*, twelve vultures appeared in the sky.[193] Likewise, Suetonius wrote: "In Augustus' first consulship, when he was taking the auspices, twelve vultures appeared, as they had to Romulus, and, when he slaughtered the victims, all their livers were found to be doubled inwards underneath; all the experts agreed in interpreting this as an omen portending a good and great future."[194]

This obsession with Romulus was especially prominent in the years from 29 to 27 B.C. When the Senate voted to give Octavian the name Augustus, Romulus had been considered but in the end was rejected only because of the connotation of the Etruscan kingship.[195] Those who suggested the name Romulus did so on the grounds that Octavian, too, was a "founder of the city." Munatius Plancus argued successfully, however, that he should take the name Augustus because it was both new and grander. Holy places that had been consecrated by augural rights were termed *augustus* from the term for an increase in dignity, *auctus*.[196] Just as an "august" place was one that had been consecrated by the augurs as especially holy, so, too, would an "august" man be filled with the genius of authority. From 27 B.C. on, the rank of "Augustus" was always reserved for those in supreme authority.[197]

The Agrippan Pantheon thus played an important role in making a link between Augustus and Romulus and the founding of Rome. Its location midway between the Mausoleum of Augustus and the Temple of Jupiter on the Capitoline Hill suggested that it was intended as a new *umbilicus Romae*, a central shrine tying together the old dynasty with the new.[198]

8

AUGUSTUS AND THE TEMPLE OF MARS ULTOR

The Temple of Mars Ultor in the Forum Augustum (Fig. 96) was Augustus's most ambitious architectural undertaking. It was a new forum and temple complex located north and east of the Forum Julium, extending in the direction of the Subura.[1] It was begun in the mid-30s B.C., the result of a pledge he made after the deaths of Brutus and Cassius in 42 B.C.[2] Its construction continued for three decades, and although it was not yet completed, it was dedicated in 2 B.C.[3] By the time of its dedication, it had gained a symbolic nature that surpassed even the original aims of Augustus's military youth. Becoming an integral part of his imperial program, the temple was a political entity aimed at magnifying the significance of his role in avenging Caesar's murder. It was built as a monument to elevate the status of the event and to further legitimize Augustus's unprecedented rule.

The forum complex was a monument in which Augustus's personal intentions and the public purpose converged. It also fulfilled Vitruvius's aim that public buildings should enhance the ruler's *auctoritas*.[4] It did so through the breadth of the architectural influences it embraced and through the level of invention within the classical vocabulary. To this was added an extensive sculptural program that reflected a multiplicity of historical associations, links to both mortal men and deities, and a relation to foreign policy and conquest.

Architecturally, there is evidence that the Temple of Mars Ultor was influenced by certain aspects of the Temple of Jupiter Capitolinus, especially the dimensions of its pronaos. Because its width is nearly the same as that of the Capitoline Temple as reconstructed in this study, it is likely that Augustus's architects studied and perhaps emulated the older building. It was important for Augustus to make a link to Rome's founding and to the cult of its oldest deity. A significant aspect of the authority of the Roman emperor was derived from the precedent of Rome's founding, and gestures that recalled the importance of the Capitoline Temple were essential in establishing this authority.

The Emperor and the Cults

During the period of construction of the Temple of Mars Ultor, Roman society was permeated by religious reform. One manifestation of this spiritual fervor is reflected in the Senate's commission in 29 B.C. for Octavian to revive several old priesthoods that had fallen into neglect. He reconstituted countless forgotten cults and restored their statues, rituals, priestly garb, and chants. Among his most important appointments was the priest of Jupiter, a position that had stood vacant since 87 B.C. owing not only to the complicated taboos associated with the position but also to the decades of republican disarray that preceded Octavian's rule.[5]

The bad state of repair of most religious buildings at the beginning of Octavian's reign involved more than just architectural aesthetics. Although Roman religion was not an actively moral religion like Christianity would later become, the sight of sacred buildings and rituals nevertheless functioned in part as an inducement to moral behavior. Because Romans believed that the gods protected the Roman state, the survival of the state before the gods depended on proper moral comportment. The dilapidation of the buildings devoted to the gods and the disregard of their sacrificial rights could only reflect a weakened moral resolve in Roman society.[6] Horace wrote in 28–27 B.C.,

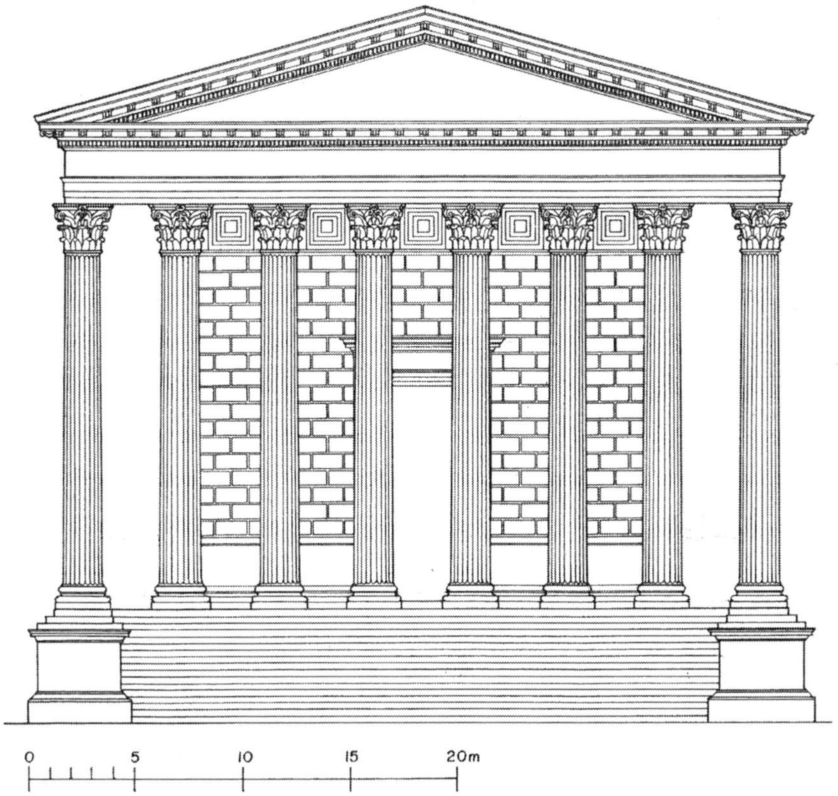

96. Forum Augustum, Temple of Mars Ultor, 37–2 B.C., elevation. Drawing: Rogelio Carrasco after Fritz Toebelmann, *Römische Gebälke* (1923), pl. 39.

"You will continue to pay for the sins of your fathers, Roman, though innocent yourself, until you restore the crumbling temples and shrines of the gods and their statues filthy with black smoke."[7] The Romans' suffering could not be reversed until the neglect of the gods had been corrected.[8]

In 12 B.C., Augustus was named *pontifex maximus*, the most important position of the priesthood and therefore the head of the entire state clergy.[9] His election to this position was an occasion for an impressive demonstration of popular support, and his formal title as head of state religion suited well his extensive campaign to revise the cults and their religious observances and to restore their temples.[10]

Although Augustus promoted himself as the son of a god, the deified Julius Caesar, his own deification did not occur until his death. Even so, many thought of him as a god, and the cult of his guardian spirit became established in many cities of the western Mediterranean region, with the building of temples dedicated to Rome and Augustus and oaths being taken in his name.[11] In Rome, at least, there was adulation without official deification.

In the eastern Mediterranean, his status was different. The concept of the divinization of the emperor was influenced by long-standing practices in Egypt and Greece.[12] For centuries, ruling figures in the East were directly linked to religious rites. The king played a central role, for instance, at the festival of the new year, which dramatized the return, or rebirth, of the god responsible for the renewed fertility of the land. In Egypt, Mesopotamia, and Palestine, the king frequently assumed the role of the deity in such ceremonies. By the time of the Hellenistic period, when Alexander the Great and his successors adapted themselves to the eastern conception of a ruler as a divine world-master, all these oriental and Greek festivals celebrating the appearance of a god were well established, and popular ceremonies were readily transformed into a royal epiphany. In the Hellenistic epiphany the king's appearance at the gate of the city resembled or, in fact, was the epiphany of a god.[13]

Although the republican tradition of forbidding citizens to worship a king directly was still strong in Rome, in the East, the tradition of a direct connection between the kingship and divine authority was now

having a strong impact. It was in the East that Julius Caesar was, in fact, first given his divine honors. After centuries of opposition, such status now slowly came to be accepted in Rome itself, especially after Augustus conferred honors on the dead Caesar.[14]

The Roman triumph was a Latin adaptation of the royal Hellenistic rite in which the triumphant ruler was received as the image of a god, the ruler of heaven, whom the populace joyously welcomed.[15] The perception of the emperor as an equal to the gods engendered feelings of omnipotent power, and nowhere was Augustus's omnipotence more directly and forcefully expressed than in the Temple of Mars Ultor and the Forum Augustum.

The Temple of Mars Ultor

Augustus dedicated the temple in his new forum to Mars Ultor, but it also held numerous representations of the *princeps* himself and the *gens Julia*. Augustus was obviously looking closely at Caesar's forum and temple complex. He wanted to create a monumental architectural setting, one that was focused on a temple adorned with statues of the emperor, his family, and appropriate deities. The forum complex was important in enhancing the prestige of his imperial authority, and its proximity to the Forum Julium served to further link Augustus to his deified father.[16] It had the functional purpose, according to Suetonius, of providing new space for law courts, where jury selection and criminal prosecutions could take place.[17] Its primary aim, however, was the symbolic expression of Augustus's authority and power.

Although the complex was begun in ca. 37 B.C., long delays plagued the project.[18] The work of clearing the site and of laying the foundations was probably carried out in the decade of the 20s B.C. Most of the actual temple construction dates from about 10 B.C.[19] It thus represents primarily the later phase of Augustan architectural production, in which the use of the Corinthian Order reached a new level of invention and refinement.[20]

The architects of the Temple of Mars Ultor synthesized the components of the Corinthian Order – the carving of the capitals, the use of moldings, and the use of modillions – creating a new expression of Roman classicism that distinguished itself by transcending the influences of Hellensistic architecture of Greece and Asia Minor. It was one of the most perfectly designed and crafted temple structures of the period, employing the Corinthian Order in an orthodox way in terms of proportions, dimensions, and motifs, yet embellishing it with new types of ornamentation that was unique to Roman builders.[21] It was the definitive statement of the Corinthian Order in the first century B.C.[22]

To suggest that the design of the temple had dimensional similarities to the Temple of Jupiter Capitolinus is to indicate a direct link to the authority of Rome's oldest temple and the long history that it represented. The width of the podium is 36 meters, its length 50 meters.[23] Compared with the Capitoline Temple's width of 34 meters as reconstructed in this study, the architects' imitative strategy is clearly revealed. Faced with building one of the largest temples in Rome in 500 years, they may well have taken their cues from the precedent set by the temple most closely associated with the city's founding.[24]

This was only one influence, however, for the architectural details of the Temple of Mars Ultor were an innovative synthesis of many Greek and Roman architectural and planning elements. Its axiality and symmetry were traditional to Roman architecture and urban design, and its high podium went back to Etruscan precedents. Its Corinthian Order was influenced by Hellensitic examples, but it was enriched through a distinctly Roman interpretation.

The podium, which remains substantially intact, was a combination of Roman concrete with tufa and travertine blocks in *opus quadratum* and faced with a veneer of Carrara marble. It was reached by a flight of seventeen marble steps, which had a large rectangular altar in the middle.[25]

Although the width of the pronaos may have corresponded to that of Capitoline Jupiter, it had eight columns on the front rather than six (Fig. 97).[26] The pronaos was three bays deep, and there was a second row of columns on each side of the main axis, aligned with the cella walls. There were eight columns on the sides, with the aisles ending in a rear wall in a manner similar to a *peripteros sine postico* composition.[27]

Like the Temple of Venus Genetrix and the Temple of Castor and Pollux, the Temple of Mars Ultor

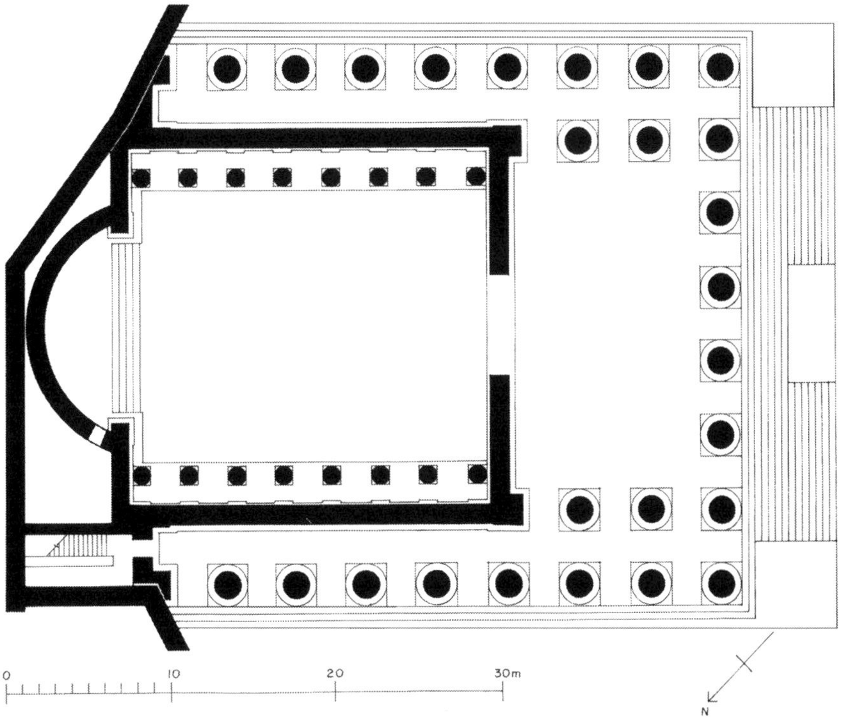

97. Temple of Mars Ultor, plan. Drawing: John W. Stamper after Joachim Ganzert, *Der Mars-Ultor-Tempel auf dem Augustusforum in Rom beiheft Erläuterungen* (1996), vol. 2, pl. 47.

had a *pycnostyle* arrangement, its columns being closely spaced in a 1 to 1.5 ratio of diameter to intercolumniation. The columns' fluted shafts were made of Lunense marble, and they had Corinthian capitals that were hewn in two blocks, similar to those of the Round Temple by the Tiber (Figs. 98 and 99). The proportions of the capitals, typical of Augustan-era classicism, reflected the fact that they were carved in two blocks in that the leaf ranges took up about half their total height, and the abacus appeared tall relative to the rest of the capital. The ample height of the upper zone allowed for a prominent central stem, which was an important design feature. In later temples, constructed in the first century A.D., the leaf ranges were made taller and the volutes flatter.[28]

Also typical of Augustan-era capitals were the acanthus leaves, in which both ranges were divided into three or four main lobes, and a deep, pear-shaped recess was formed at the junctions of the lobes. The *caliculi* were vertically fluted and were topped by a rim that was horizontaly fluted. The top of each stem flute was decorated with a small, semicircular leaf that curled over.[29]

With their base and capital, the columns were 17.76 meters high (60 Roman feet), and they had a lower diameter of 1.77 meters (6 Roman feet), a ratio of 10 to 1.[30] This was the same ratio used in the Temple of Apollo Sosianus, and it would become the standard in a rebuilt version of the Temple of Castor and Pollux, the later Temple of Vespasian, and the Temple of Divus Hadrianus. The diameter of the column shafts in all of these examples was of primary concern to their designers. They treated the diameter as an integral dimension, which they related in a direct way to other parts of the column and entablature.[31]

The ratio of the columns' total height (60 Roman feet) to the height of their shafts (50 Roman feet) was 6 to 5, also a common ratio.[32] One of the qualities of the 6-to-5 rule was that it could remain fixed as the essential reference point for design and yet permit great variety in specific details. Any variation of the slenderness of the column, for instance, the slenderness of the capital, or the relative height of the entablature resulted in a fairly strong visual impact.[33]

The temple's entablature reflected an orthodox classicism, composed of a three-stepped architrave and a plain frieze topped by an astragal, ovuli, dentils, and a cornice with modillions. The corona along the sides featured carved lion's heads and antefixes with palmettes and acanthus leaves. The motif was similar to

98. Temple of Mars Ultor, view of columns. Photo: John W. Stamper.

that found in the contemporary reconstruction of the Erechtheum in Athens, which was also commissioned by Augustus.[34]

The treatment of the modillions combined elements from classical scroll brackets like those of the north door of the Erechtheum and from traditional Roman modillions found on buildings like the Regia or the Temple of Divus Julius. They were decorated with a scroll at their forward edge, and on the sides they were decorated by means of a scrolling fillet that followed the lower edge. A half-palmette springing from a leaf-calyx filled the space between the fillet and the top of the modillion. Their underside featured a band of guilloche flanked by fluting.[35] The soffit spaces between the modillions were decorated with recessed coffers that were framed by a decorated molding and

99. Temple of Mars Ultor, detail of column capital and entablature. Illustration: Andrea Palladio, *The Four Books of Architecture* (1965), vol. 4, pl. 9. Courtesy of Dover Publications.

contained a single rosette in high relief. Such a design was a synthesis of traditional Roman forms and influences from Hellenistic Athens and was much more classical than Augustus's earlier temples on the Palatine and in the Forum Romanum.[36]

The cella walls were scored in a manner similar to that of the Round Temple by the Tiber, following closely the canon established for such work by Hermogenes.[37] They were marked along the top by engaged Corinthian capitals aligned with the columns. The spaces between the capitals were articulated with coffers, and above, as with the building's main external entablature, there was a three-step architrave and a plain frieze topped by astragal and ovulo moldings

and dentils. The ceiling above the side aisles was also decorated with coffers, which were embellished with rosettes.[38]

Inside the cella, the refined classicism characteristic of the exterior was substituted for a more innovative decorative program, similar in part to the interior of the Temple of Apollo Sosianus.[39] The pavement featured a lively play of rectangles alternating in africano and pavonazzetto.[40] Ledges ran along the two side walls and extended into the apse as a raised platform. They supported a row of freestanding columns, six on each side on two levels, with corresponding pilasters against the walls.[41]

Indicative of the cella's innovative decorative features were the bases of the columns, which were composed of a plinth, two tori, the lower one decorated with a vertical tongue pattern, the upper one with intertwined strands and palmettes. The tori were separated by two scotias, which were divided in the middle by two astragals decorated with rope motifs symmetrically disposed.[42] The capitals were a unique transformation of the Corinthian Order in which the corner volutes were replaced by the heads and forelegs of horses representing Pegasus. The lower register of acanthus leaves were fairly canonical, and those above were represented with vigorous swirls from which the Pegasus figures emerged.[43] Such stylization of the leaves may have been influenced by the capitals in the cella of the Temple of Apollo Sosianus.[44]

Considered together, the exterior and interior orders of the Temple of Mars Ultor represented a new synthesis and creativity in the Corinthian style. Whereas the exterior columns and entablatures were rather orthodox, with similarities to Attic models, especially in terms of their proportions and profiles, the interior diverged markedly from this orthodoxy. It reflected a great deal of experimentation with richly decorated surfaces and innovative capital types. In this respect, it was similar to the slightly earlier Temple of Apollo Sosianus, reflecting a new interpretation of the order that was unique to Roman builders.

The Temple and Its Forum

As with the Temple of Venus Genetrix, the Temple of Mars Ultor was located within a colonnaded forum, rectangular in plan and dominated at one end by the temple (Fig. 100). Augustus's forum, however, was not as long and narrow as its predecessor.[45] Its interior dimensions were 54 meters wide by approximately 70 meters long, its shape conforming closely to Vitruvius's prescription that a forum's width should equal two-thirds its length.[46]

The forum's exact length remains open to question because its southwest end remains buried under the Via Fori Imperiali, and the nature of its connection to the Forum Julium has not been determined. The overall length of the complex, from the Forum Julium to the rear of the apse of the Temple of Mars Ultor, was about 125 meters. It was 85 meters wide, including the colonnades.[47]

The most imposing portion of its enclosure, which still remains, is a massive firewall immediately behind the Temple of Mars Ultor, directly adjacent to the back of the apse. Constructed of peperino and Gabine blocks in *opus quadratum* and highlighted by courses of travertine, it is 35 meters high. Much taller than the temple itself, it was used both as a firewall and as a definitive separation from the working-class residential district to the north.[48]

The forum space was planned to be symmetrical from within, although an irregularity in its northeast corner required its back wall to follow the angled line of a street that bordered the site. This compromise in the plan's composition was carefully concealed in the forum space itself by the porticos that flanked the temple. Suetonius explains that Augustus was unable to purchase all the land he wanted to lay out the forum, and thus his architect was required to work around the intrusion while still making the composition appear symmetrical.[49] In the forum's northwest corner, where there was more room available, the architect placed the Hall of the Colossus, a tall, square space that held a colossal statue of Augustus, rendered either as Mars or as the *genius Augusti*.[50]

The stoalike porticos framing the sides of the forum space were 14.90 meters wide, each with a facade of Corinthian columns of giallo antico, 9.50 meters high, and a rear wall of peperino and Gabine stone in *opus quadratum*. It had long been assumed the porticos were covered with a flat wooden roof structure; however, it has been recently argued that a barrel vault made of plaster was suspended from triangular wooden roof

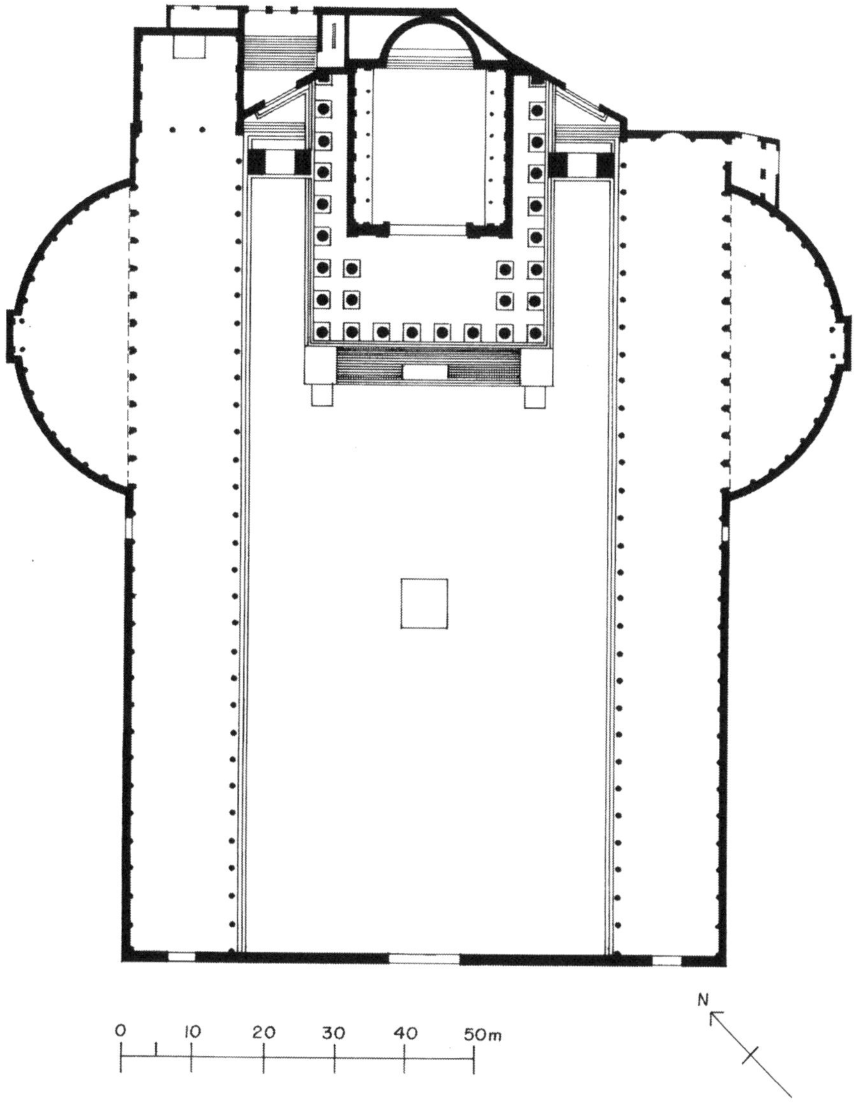

100. Forum Augustum, Temple of Mars Ultor, site plan. Drawing: John W. Stamper after Valentin Kockel and Heinrich Bauer in *LTUR*, vol. 2, p. 454, fig. 117.

trusses. This barrel vault was shielded from view by an entablature and a tall attic zone that was articulated with caryatids and large sculpted panels with shields and the heads of divinities in high relief (Fig. 101).[51] The top of the attic was crowned with statues and trophies.[52]

The caryatids in the attic zone were an especially interesting feature in that they were derived at a reduced scale from those of the Erechtheum in Athens. They had the same characteristics of clothing and way of representing hair as their Greek models.[53] Their capitals were richly decorated with an echinus of ovuli and lancets, and they were topped by a plain abacus. The entablature, in a *cyma reversa* profile and decorated with lotus leaves, projected out above each caryatid.[54] Standing in the attic zone as they did, they served to accentuate vertical alignments that reinforced the rhythm of the lateral portico columns.[55]

Visitors must have marveled at the forum's magnificence, which was achieved in terms of scale, refinement of details, and in the brilliance of materials. The pavement of the forum space was white marble, as was the temple's gleaming pronaos. This was contrasted with the giallo antico columns of the porticos lining the space on either side. The attic zones with their caryatids were again white marble. The floors of the temple and porticos were colorful combinations of giallo antico, africano, pavonazzetto, and bardiglio.[56]

One of the many planning innovations evident in the forum was the presence of a pair of large semicircular rooms, or hemicycles, located behind the flanking

101. Forum Augustum, caryatid order of the flanking colonnades. Photo: Deutsches Archäologisches Institut, Rome, 61.1659.

colonnades. Their walls were made of peperino in *opus quadratum* like the forum's back wall, and they were topped by a wooden roof structure.[57] They were derived from Greek exedrae and from smaller curved niches for the display of sculpture like those found in many Roman houses.[58] With an outer diameter of 45.40 meters, they were certainly influential in the later design of the Forum Traiani and possibly the Pantheon.[59]

The curved walls of the hemicycles as well as the back walls of the porticos were articulated with engaged half-columns. They framed a series of rectangular niches that held over 100 portrait busts intended to represent Augustus's dual ancestry.[60] To the left of the temple was a collection of busts of members of the Julian family, including Aeneas, the descendant of Venus, and the fourteen kings of Alba Longa, the home of the Julian family. On the right were busts of heroes of Rome's past, legendary figures like Romulus and the kings of Rome, with inscriptions of their military heroics. Both series culminated in large statues of the *princeps*. The entire cycle was meant to illuminate Augustus's family lineage and to exalt his divine authority by making it a part of the new national myth.[61]

The temple's pediment contained a statue of Mars flanked by Venus, Fortuna, Romulus, and Roma, and Augustus's name appeared on the entablature below.[62] On top of the pediment was a quadriga bearing Augustus and flanked on one side by Aeneas and on the other by Romulus. Ovid describes the composition:

> Mars strong in armor looks upon the temple pediment and rejoices that unvanquished gods occupy the places of honor. At the entranceways he sees arms of all sorts from all the lands conquered by his soldier [Augustus]. On one side he sees Aeneas with his precious burden and about him the many ancestors of the Julian house; on the other Romulus, son of Ilia, with the arms of the enemy chief he conquered with his own hand and statues of distinguished Romans with the names of their great deeds. He gazes upon the temple and reads the name Augustus.[63]

A second bronze quadriga carrying the emperor was located in the center of the forum space. On its base was inscribed *Pater Patriae*. Finally, four statues inside the cella represented Augustus in the company of Mars Ultor, Venus Genetrix, and the deified Julius.[64]

The play between Aeneas and Romulus, represented in the two hemicycles and above the temple's pediment, was an integral aspect of Augustan culture, meant to personify both civic and military virtues.

There was a balance represented by the two. On one hand, Aeneas, leading his son and carrying his father and the *penates* to Latium, was the incarnation of *pietas*, or social responsibility. On the other hand, Romulus bears a military trophy representing his virtue. Augustus, in the center of the two, was their honorable descendant who strove to carry on what they had started.[65]

Hellenism, Classicism, and the Emperor's Authority

Within the context of Roman temple and forum architecture as a whole, the Temple of Mars Ultor and the Forum Augustum represent one of the largest and most refined examples of a typology that began with the Porticus Metelli, the theater complex of Pompey the Great, and the Forum Julium, and continued through the rebuilt temples in the Forum Romanum, the Temple of Apollo Sosianus, and the Temple of Apollo Palatinus. The use of white marble Corinthian columns, entablatures, pavements, and wall veneers throughout the complex was influenced by Greek and Hellenistic models, but the interpretation of the design vocabulary was distinctly Roman.[66] The architects who designed and decorated Rome's most important temples since the time of Julius Caesar created an individual style that showed the influence of Greece and Asia Minor while being uniquely Roman.[67] Although Athens, Pergamon, and Didyma were important sources of influence for Augustan architecture, Rome in the last two decades of the first century B.C. was far more prodigious in its building programs. At the same time, it was defining its own distinct version of the Corinthian Order, as well as temple plan types and means of construction. Considering buildings such as the Temple of Rome and Augustus on the Acropolis and the Odeion of Agrippa in the Agora, if anything, Rome was proving to have more influence on Greek architecture than vice versa.[68]

The plan of Augustus's temple and forum complex was particularly Roman in character: the temple sat on a high podium, a *peripteros sine postico* rear wall, the rigid axiality, and a defined forum space in front, representing an enlarged and formalized *templum*. The Roman tradition of a temple in a forum was evident not only by the twin enclosing porticos, but also by the large fire wall behind the temple.[69]

102. Statue of Mars Ultor, Museo Capitolino. Photo: Deutsches Archäologisches Institut, Rome, 3149.

Numerous activities took place in the Forum Augustum, including the reception of foreign dignitaries, the administering of oathes of obedience, deliberations over war plans, the sending of governors to their provinces, the display of military trophies, the celebration of festivals, and, for young Romans, the assuming of the toga of manhood. It essentially functioned as the official reception room of the city and Empire, integrating the traditions of the Julian family with those of the Republic.[70] The forum space conveyed a tightly controlled regularity appropriate for the new world order.[71] Cassius Dio writes that Augustus dedicated the temple:

> to Mars, and that he himself and his grandsons should go there as often as they wished, while those who were passing from the class of boys and were being enrolled among the youths of military age should invariably do so; that those who were sent out to commands abroad should make that their starting point; that the Senate should take its votes there in regard to the granting of triumphs, and that the victors after celebrating them should dedicate to this Mars their sceptre and their crown; that such victors and all others who received triumphal honors should have their statues in bronze erected in the Forum; that in case military standards captured by the enemy were ever recovered they should be placed in the temple; that a festival should be celebrated beside the steps of the temple by the cavalry commanders of each year; that a nail should be driven into it by the censors at the close of their terms; and that even senators should have the right of contracting to supply the horses that were to compete in the Circensian games, and also to take general charge of the temple, just as had been provided by law in the case of the temples of Apollo and of Jupiter Capitolinus.[72]

Mars Ultor (Fig. 102), or the Avenger, was one of the most authentically Roman of all the gods, patron of agriculture and war and the father of Romulus and Remus.[73] In Rome, Mars had especially been known as the god of war, protecting the state during a time of battle and so making him the most important god after Jupiter.

Before Augustus's founding of the temple, sanctuaries of Mars typically served as a kind of sentinel, not necessarily in the city, but rather at the edge of the wilderness where dangers lurked, where armed enemies hid.[74] The Regia had contained the sacred spears of Mars. The consul was supposed to shake them if a war broke out and shout, "Mars, wake up!" In a war, his only association was with combat itself. Anything that preceded hostilities depended on Jupiter, and after a victory, generals typically took great liberties in selecting other gods to honor.[75]

When Augustus dedicated his temple to Mars Ultor, the avenger of Caesar's murder, he gave new meaning to the worship of Mars. The temple took on a double meaning after the victory over the Parthians in 20 B.C., commemorating the revenge on the Parthians for earlier Roman defeats.[76] The standards that were returned to the Romans were moved, along with Julius Caesar's sword, into the temple after being temporarily displayed on the Capitoline Hill, at first in the Temple of Jupiter Feretrius, then in a small circular shrine, a *sacellum*, set up next to it.[77]

The dedication of the Forum Augustum took place on August 21 B.C., which was the anniversary of Augustus's conquest of Alexandria. There was a link to Alexander the Great suggested in the forum by the presence of a colossus of Alexander, as well as paintings of him by Apelles, and two tents from his camp in Alexandria.[78] Augustus portrayed himself as the new Alexander, who was able to conquer and at the same time rule peacefully.[79]

A series of spectacular events marked the temple's dedication. Augusutus held a circus in which 260 lions were reportedly killed. He also staged the Trojan games in the Forum Romanum, gladiatorial games in the Saepta, and a hunt for crocodiles in the Circus Flaminius. He built a large *naumachia* along the banks of the Tiber, and with thirty large ships staged a reenactment of the Battle of Salamis between the Athenians and the Persians as a commemoration of his naval battle at Actium.[80]

The Forum Augustum represented imperial imagery at its highest manifestation.[81] In the words of one scholar, Augustus managed to combine in one grand public monument "everything of peace and war, of politics and traditional society, of religion and patriotism, and to link them directly with his name and deeds and with those of his family: he had avenged Julius's death, and he had brought his peace to war-weary nations."[82] Drawing inspiration from eastern sanctuaries dedicated to Hellenistic rulers, as well as from the near-at-hand Forum Julium, Augustus's architects created a "monumental exhibition of the allied religious and dynastic foundations claimed for the new world monarchy."[83]

Like the temples of Castor and Pollux and Venus Genetrix, the setting of the temple and its forum provided a stage that set the leader off physically as someone important. The setting was symbolic of the emperor's special standing within society, and as such it

commanded respect. The leader's elaborate dress, the surrounding dignitaries and court officials, combined with the magnificent column-lined space and the elevated podium with the pedimented facade behind it, created the image of *dignitas* and *auctoritas*. The architectural symbol of authority connected directly to the position of authority, making it easier for those who were in subordinate positions to accept the emperor's rule.

In one sense, authority is the recognition that differences exist. The consuls, emperors, and gods were in the temples or sacrificing at their altars, while the common people inhabited the forum spaces at their base. In another, more complicated sense, however, society had to take into account the needs and desires of the weak as well as the strong, once those differences were acknowledged.[84] A process of mutual recognition characterized the social dynamic of the fora and temples, the point where the plebeians and the aristocracy met and defined their relationship to each other.

Architecturally, the Temple of Mars Ultor represented the standard for the Corinthian Order in Rome during the early Empire. The proportional ratios, the treatment of the entablature and cornice, the fluting of the columns were the canon for temple design from the late Augustan to the Flavian period. Trajan would introduce a more decorative treatment of the order, and Hadrian would delve into more experimental details and building forms, representing signs of a renewed attempt at innovation and originality. The exterior of the Temple of Mars Ultor represented the orthodoxy of the Corinthian canon, synthesizing what had come before and setting the standard for what followed. Its interior was more decorative and inventive, following the richly ornamented cellas of buildings like the Temple of Apollo Sosianus.

The Forum Romanum at the End of Augustus's Reign

Two temples in the Forum Romanum are further indicative of the classical Corinthian style of Augustus's final years: the rebuilt versions of the Temple of Concordia and the Temple of Castor and Pollux. Both projects were begun in 7 B.C. by Tiberius, who had just been elected consul for the second time and who had returned from a successful military campaign on the northern frontier.[85] Tiberius married Augustus's daughter Julia and later, in A.D. 4, became Augustus's adopted son. From this point on, he collaborated closely in the governing of the Empire, including participation in a number of military campaigns during the last years of Augustus's reign. In A.D. 13, he effectively became coruler, and he became emperor when Augustus died the following year.[86]

Tiberius initiated the project to rebuild the Temple of Concordia (Fig. 103) to commemorate his military campaign in the north and to forge a link between himself and the Senate's official symbol of victory over the social reformers of the second century B.C. It was meant to evoke the honor of peace and stability within the traditional hierarchy of aristocratic authority. Tiberius was awarded a triumph, and early in 7 B.C. he convened the Senate to request permission to rebuild the temple, which had been destroyed in a fire two years earlier.[87] In return, he asked that the names of both he and his brother Nero Drusus, who had died during a military campaign in the Rhine delta, be inscribed on it.[88]

During the Augustan era, the concord of the state and the concord of the imperial family had become linked, manifested in this case by the fact that Tiberius vowed the Temple of Concordia on January 1 in the Porticus Octaviae, which had been rebuilt by Augustus's sister. On the same day, Tiberius and his mother, Livia, dedicated the Porticus Liviae, which also contained a shrine to Concordia that Livia had presented to Augustus. Finally, Tiberius dedicated the Temple of Concordia on January 16, A.D. 10, the anniversary of the day Augustus assumed his new name.[89]

Tiberius's building replaced the original Ionic temple of 121 B.C. with a new Hellenized building on an enlarged plan in which the cella was placed at a ninety-degree angle to the portico (Fig. 104). The cella measured 43.50 meters wide by 22.70 meters deep (148 by 77 Roman feet). Its pronaos, which measured 25.60 meters wide by 14.80 meters deep (87 by 50 Roman feet), had six Corinthian columns on the front and three on the sides.[90] They had a diameter of 1.68 meters and an intercolumniation of 2.65 meters in the *pycnostyle* manner. Because of the high podium and the limited space in front of the temple, the steps may have penetrated between the columns as in the Temple of Venus Genetrix.[91]

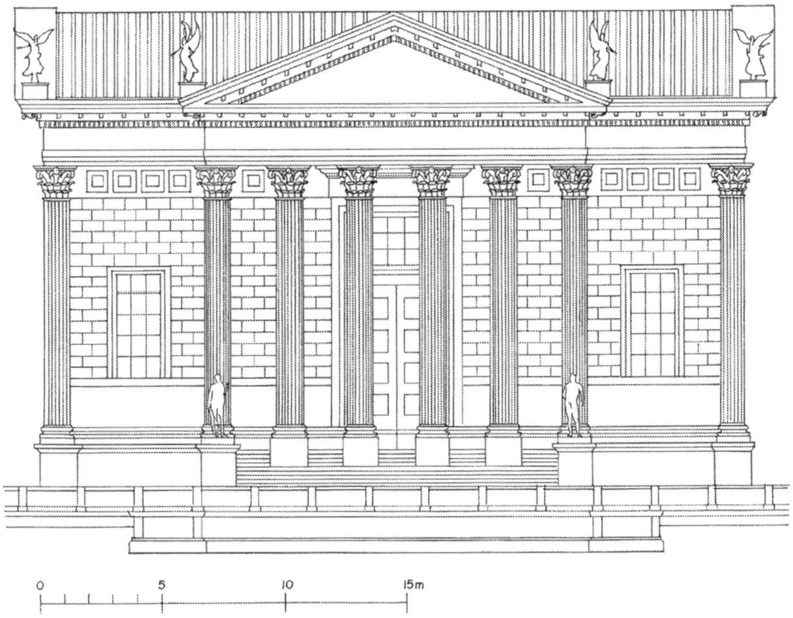

103. Rome, Temple of Concordia, rebuilt 7 B.C.–A.D. 10, elevation. Drawing. John W. Stamper after Homer F. Rebert and Henri Marceau in *MAAR* 5 (1925), pl. 51.

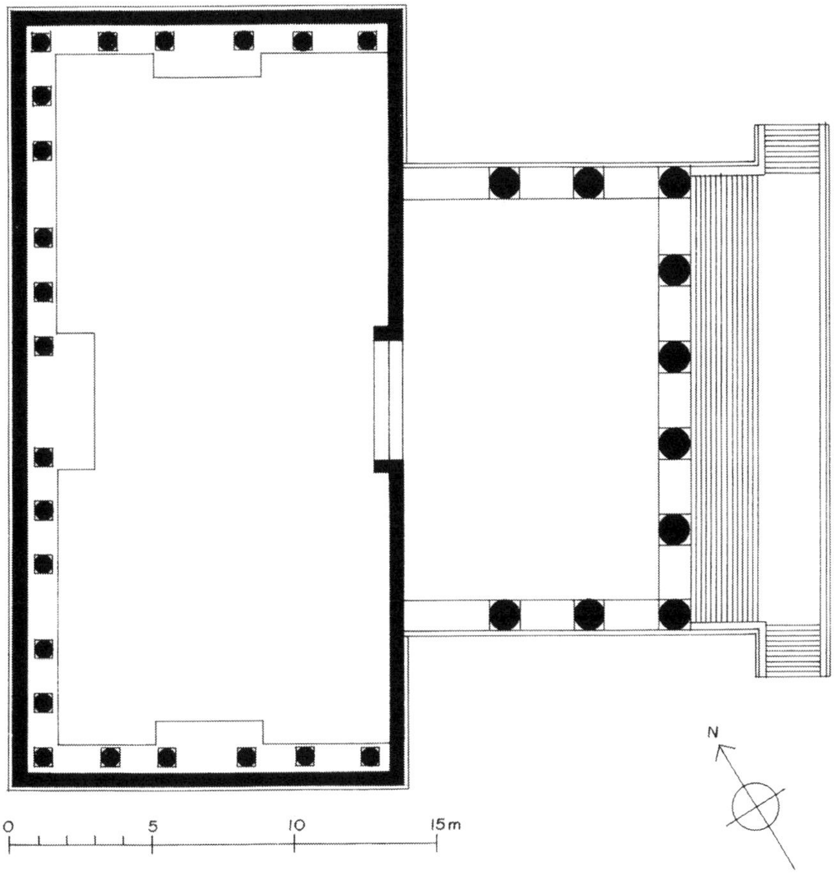

104. Temple of Concordia, plan. Drawing John W. Stamper after Carlo Gasparri, *Aedes Concordiae Augustae* (1979), pl. 24.

105. Temple of Concordia, detail of cornice. Museo Capitolino. Photo: Joann Sporleder.

A portion of the building's marble cornice, preserved in the Tabularium today, reveals a highly decorative design with dentilwork, egg-and-dart motifs, ornamented modillions, and acanthus leaves (Fig. 105). The entablature's design owes its general character, especially its basic profile to that of the Temple of Mars Ultor, but it is much more richly decorated, with surface reliefs on nearly every molding. The modillions were more elaborate than those of the Temple of Mars Ultor, more closely related to the brackets of the Erechtheum in Athens.[92]

Representations on coins show the pediment was decorated with a sculpted group of female figures, probably Concordia, Peace, and Salus, flanked by two statues of Tiberius and Drusus. Acroteria as Victory figures recalled Tiberius's military campaign in the north. Two female figures were located on the sides of the cella, and on the stairs were figures of Mercury and Hercules as custodians of the sanctuary.[93]

Inside the cella, exotic multicolored marble revetments were used. There was a central niche in the

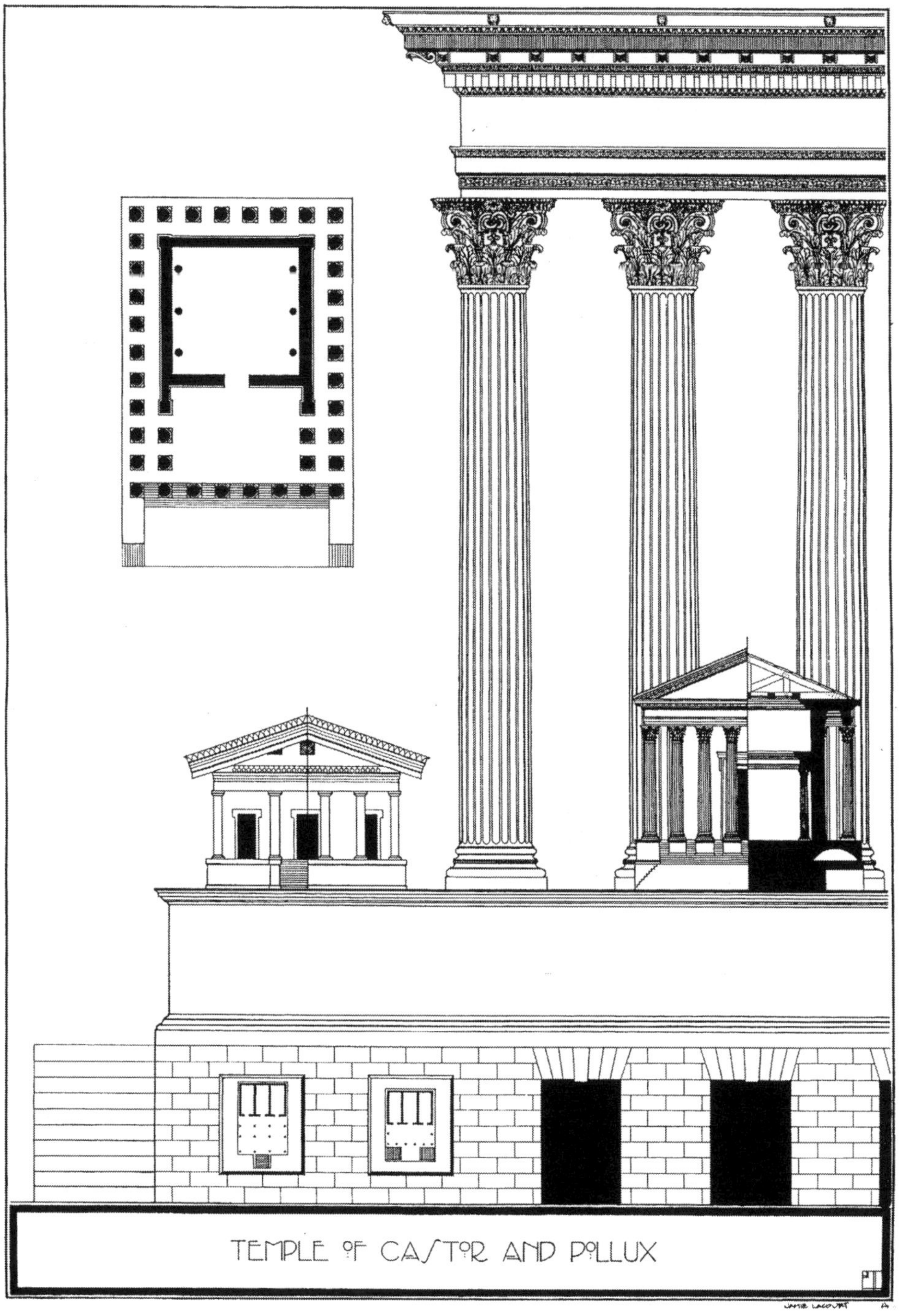

106. Rome, Temple of Castor and Pollux, rebuilt 7 B.C.–A.D. 6, analytique showing temple in its different phases. Drawing: Jamie Lacourt, plan after Inge Nielsen and Birte Poulsen, *The Temple of Castor and Pollux I* (1992), vol. 1, p. 108, fig. 100.

back flanked by ten side niches, each of which contained allegorical statues, including Apollo and Hera, Latona Nursing Apollo and Diana, Asklepios and Hygieia, Ares and Hermes, Zeus, Athena, Demeter, and Hestia.[94] Columns surrounding the space had highly unusual Corinthian capitals with pairs of rams at the four corners in place of volutes.[95]

At every level, the Temple of Concordia was meant to evoke the link between members of the Augustan family and peace within the Roman Empire. The venerable site of the earlier Aedicula Concordiae and then the Temple of L. Opimius was transformed into an Augustan entity. It reaffirmed the past, celebrated the present, and affirmed Tiberius as the rightful heir to the Augustan legacy.[96]

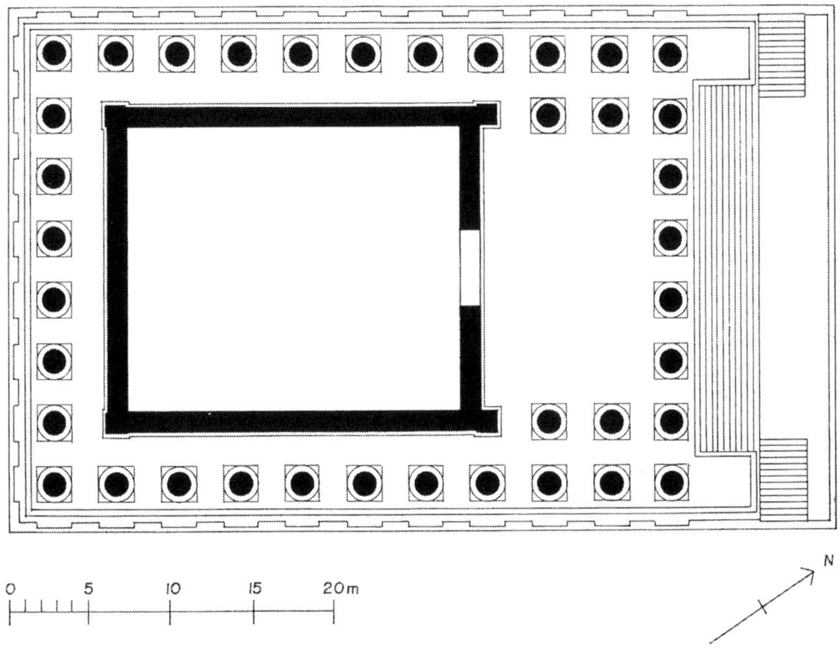

107. Temple of Castor and Pollux, plan at the time of Augustus. Drawing: John W. Stamper after Otto Ludwig Richter, in *JDAI* 13 (1898), fig. 8.

The rebuilding of the Temple of Castor and Pollux (Fig. 106) was undertaken to replace the Hellenistic version that had been constructed in 117 B.C. by Caecilius Metellus Delmaticus. The new temple was dedicated in A.D. 6 in the names of Tiberius and Drusus.[97] The three columns and entablature visible today, along with several capital fragments scattered along its northwest side, date from this reconstruction.[98]

Built on nearly the same plan as the Metellan version, it had eight columns across the front and eleven along the flanks (Fig. 107).[99] In this case, it was certainly peripteral. Much larger than the nearby Temple of Divus Julius, it stood on a higher podium, had taller and more elaborate columns, and had a deeper pronaos. The podium, now measuring 32.10 meters by 49.50 meters (109 by 168 Roman feet), was built with a tufa, brick, rubble, and concrete core and was faced with large ornamental marble slabs that projected as pedestals beneath the columns.[100] To serve as a speaker's platform, it was straight across the front and was approached from the sides by lateral stairs.

The Lunense marble columns were 18.55 meters high (50 Roman feet) and supported an entablature with a three-step architrave and a plain frieze (Figs. 108 and 109).[101] These columns, like those of Apollo Sosianus, deviated somewhat from the 6 to 5 ratio of column height to shaft height. Here it was 50 Roman feet to 42 Roman feet, a ratio of 6 to 4.80, the architects preferring a column with dimensions in whole feet rather than following a canonical ratio.[102]

As a further example of the variety in temple design during the Augustan era, the architrave's middle fascia was ornamented with a carved acanthus motif. This was combined with the more standard use of an ornamented *cyma reversa* molding between the upper fascia and the frieze, as seen in the Temple of Concordia and the Temple of Mars Ultor.

The cornice was supported by modillions framing deeply recessed rosettes (Fig. 110). The modillions had a scroll at the forward edge and had the same scrolling fillet on the sides as in those of the Temple of Mars Ultor. Here the design of the scroll and the use of acanthus leaf decoration on the underside was more like those from buildings of the early Augustan period.[103]

Combining a Roman taste for rich decoration with classical profiling and proportions, this design, like the Temple of Mars Ultor, would become highly influential in Rome's subsequent temple architecture. Little would be changed in the Corinthian Order during the post-Augustan Empire, except for occasional added decorative motifs and different means of carving.[104]

With the completion of these projects, the final shape and organization of the Forum Romanum was

108. Rome, Temple of Castor and Pollux, view of columns. Photo: Istituto Centrale per il Catalogo e la Documentazione, F.18635.

established. Its length measured 102 meters, and its width varied from 45 meters at the west end to 36 meters at the east (Fig. 111).[105] Its entire perimeter was defined by new, marble-clad buildings: the curia and the Basilica Aemilia on the north, the Temple of Divus Julius and Arch of Augustus on the east, the Basilica Julia and the Temple of Castor and Pollux on the south, and the rostra, the Temple of Saturn, and the Temple of Concordia on the west. Behind these, on the side of the Capitoline Hill, was the Tabularium, a great hall of records built by Sulla and Quintus Lutatius Catalus.[106] Beyond that was the Temple of Jupiter Capitolinus. Only the Temple of Vespasian and the Arch of Septimius Severus had yet to be built.

109. Temple of Castor and Pollux, detail of columns and entablature. Photo: John W. Stamper.

Not only was the forum's appearance transformed in a formal sense, but also in terms of its symbolic or propogandistic intent. In every direction, the visitor saw images connoting victory. The pediment of the Temple of Saturn was ornamented with Tritons blowing trumpets in reference to Octavian's naval victory at Actium. The triumphal arch at the forum's east end, the ships' beaks on the two rostra, and a Victory figure above the pediment of the new curia all served to remind the Roman populace of Octavian's important military achievements.

How do we judge the architecture of Augustus? Imperial? Hellenistic? International? It was all of these. It retained much of its Etruscan, Latin, and Roman traditions while embracing influences of the Hellenistic style, its materials, its elegance, and its grandeur as a means of establishing the emperor's *auctoritas*. Augustus promoted a civic image that was both new and yet reminiscent of a golden past.[107] The tall, slender Corinthian columns of the Temple of Mars Ultor or the rebuilt Temple of Concordia or the Temple of Castor and Pollux were, if anything, magnificent in stature in that their fluted marble surfaces reflected the gleaming sun and retreated in dark shadows. Each building was a creative and individual response to the needs of the Augustan building program.

Tiberius to Nero

Augustus died in A.D. 14 in the town of Nola, near Naples.[108] The Empire as he left it was more or less maintained during the successive principates of Tiberius, Gaius, and Claudius, but then nearly disintegrated at the hands of Nero. Tiberius collaborated with the Senate to develop and consolidate the institutions Augustus had established: the government bureaucracy, financial systems, and organization of the provinces. As we have seen, he was prodigious in his execution of public works, rebuilding the Temple of Concordia and the Temple of Castor and Pollux. In addition to these, he built a temple dedicated to Divus Augustus at the southeast corner of the Forum Romanum, plus a new

110. Temple of Castor and Pollux, detail of columns and entablature. Illustration: Andrea Palladio, *The Four Books of Architecture* (1965), vol. 4, pl. 48. Courtesy of Dover Publications.

stage for Pompey's Theater, the Arch of Tiberius, and a huge palace on the Palatine Hill.[109]

Tiberius was succeeded in A.D. 37 by Gaius Germanicus, nicknamed Caligula, the footgear of soldiers. In the first year of his reign, he held a celebration and a festival to mark both his birthday and the death of Augustus.[110] He dedicated the Temple of Divus Augustus that had been started by Tiberius, and he persuaded the Senate to erect a temple dedicated to him, possibly on the Capitoline Hill.[111] On the Forum Romanum, he used the Temple of Castor and Pollux as part of a vestibule leading to the Palatine

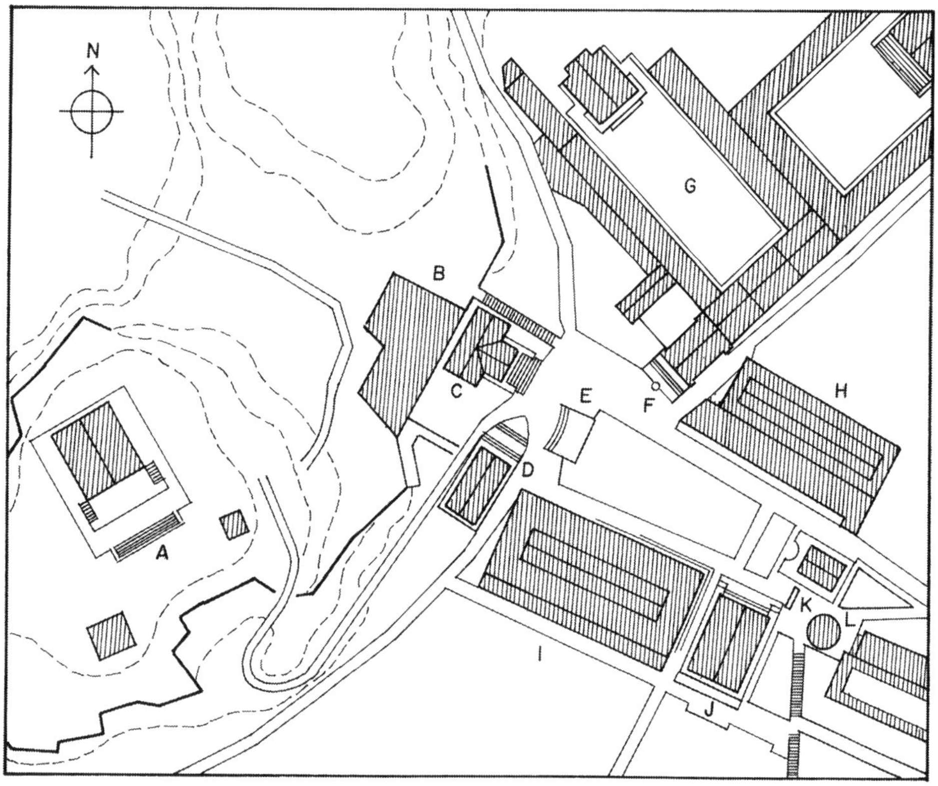

111. Rome, Forum Romanum at the time of Augustus, ca. A.D. 10: (A) Temple of Jupiter Capitolinus, (B) Tabularium, (C) Temple of Concordia, (D) Temple of Saturn, (E) Rostra, (F) Curia Julia, (G) Forum Julium, (H) Basilica Aemilia, (I) Basilica Julia, (J) Temple of Castor and Pollux, (K) Temple of Divus Julius, (L) Temple of Vesta. Drawing: John W. Stamper.

Hill. There are reports that he often stood between the statues of Castor and Pollux so he could be worshipped by visitors. He also joined the Palatine and the Capitoline Hills by a bridge so that he could proceed more quickly to conversations with Jupiter.[112]

Caligula proved to be driven by such an exaggerated ambition for divinity, taking the notion of eastern ruler-worship even further than Augustus or Tiberius deemed appropriate. He was soon feared and held in contempt, and by the time of his assassination, the stability of the Empire was threatened.[113]

Tiberius Claudius succeeded Caligula in A.D. 41. He was often at odds with the Senate and is generally regarded as an impetuous, though capable administrator.[114] After Claudius died in A.D. 54, he was deified by the Senate, and a temple dedicated to him was begun on the Caelian Hill by his widow Agrippina.[115] It was located at the northern edge of the hill, situated on a huge platform overlooking the future site of the Colosseum. It measured 195 meters wide by 165 meters deep and ranged in height from 20 to 30 meters, depending on the terrain of the hill. The platform was arranged as a formal garden with planters and rows of trees, and its edges were lined with porticos. The eastern wall was articulated with exedrae and niches, which may have served as fountains at their base.[116]

The temple was located near the middle of the platform. In the *Forma Urbis Romae* it is shown with five columns across the front, but it probably had six. It measured 29 meters wide by 46 meters long (98 by 156 Roman feet), with interaxial dimensions of about 5 meters (17 Roman feet).[117]

This project was eventually abandoned by Claudius's successor, Nero, who gave up the worship of his deified father.[118] The partially completed temple was transformed into a giant nympheum as part of a new palace complex. It was completed and dedicated as a temple by Vespasian in the late A.D. 70s.[119]

As emperor, Nero spent lavishly on building his giant palace, the Domus Transitorium. After a fire in A.D. 64, he rebuilt it as the Domus Aurea on an even larger scale. Located east of the Forum Romanum,

its site extended from the Esquiline to the Palatine and included a lake on the future site of the Colosseum. The palace was composed of a series of buildings and pavilions all interconnected by porticos. At its entrance Nero placed a colossal statue of himself, one that Hadrian would later move and rededicate as a sun god. The complex made extensive use of gardens, fields, and pastures, and the buildings were all decorated with stucco work, paint, and gilt.[120]

The fire of A.D. 64, according to Tacitus, also destroyed a great deal of the Palatine Hill and the Forum Romanum. Much of the city's population took refuge in the Campus Martius, many in Agrippa's public buildings. Of Rome's fourteen districts, only four remained untouched by the fire. Three were totally destroyed, the other seven only partially. In the four worst-hit areas, entire houses, palaces, and temples were destroyed, along with spoils from wars and Greek artistic masterpieces, hundreds if not thousands of irreplaceable objects.[121]

The last years of Nero's reign were fraught with social unrest, high taxes, and an increasingly degraded public display on the part of the emperor.[122] He committed suicide in A.D. 68 as the Roman armies of Spain, in open revolt, proclaimed their governor, Galba, to be the new emperor.[123] Rome was overcome by chaos, and when Galba was assassinated after only seven months, his place was taken by Otho, and then by Vitellius.[124] The latter marched into Rome from Gaul in A.D. 69, and his troops occupied the city, took over houses, and drove out residents.[125] Even he was not destined to remain in power for long, as troops loyal to general Vespasian, at war in Egypt and Palestine, set in motion a process that crushed Vitellius and installed the Flavians as the Roman Empire's next significant dynasty.[126]

9

TEMPLES AND FORA OF THE FLAVIAN EMPERORS

A major function of the Roman temples was to combine religion and the historical and mythic past to bolster the power and prestige of a particular emperor or general. As such, they elicited powerful responses within the city. The image of a temple as a symbol was even more significant when its normal status or traditional connotation was threatened with change, something especially true in republican and imperial Rome when regimes changed or religious belief was transformed.[1] There was a significant change in political leadership between the reign of Tiberius and that of the Flavian emperor Vespasian (Fig. 112), who came to power in A.D. 70. During this thirty-three-year period, numerous buildings in Rome, especially the Temple of Jupiter Capitolinus, represented important aspects of continuity in the Empire's religion, culture, and politics.

Vespasian and his two sons, Titus and Domitian, had much work to do to bring the Empire under political control after the fall of Vitellius. Vespasian restored the treasury, which had been plundered by the excesses of Nero and the civil war with Vitellius, using not only the spoils of war from Palestine, which his son Titus was bringing back by the shiploads, but also by reorganizing the collection of taxes.[2] At the same time, the Flavians proved more successful at developing Rome's civic architecture than any emperors since Caesar and Augustus. The Colosseum alone represents one of the most famous legacies of civic building on a grand scale, one that has left a vivid imprint on the city's character and architectural heritage. The Flavians, however, built much more that contributed directly to the city's temple architecture: the final rebuilding of the Temple of Jupiter Capitolinus, the construction of the Templum Pacis, Temple of Vespasian, and Temple of Minerva, as well as the construction of the Arch of Titus, which had an important urban relationship with the Temple of Jupiter Capitolinus. All of these served as important symbols of the Flavian dynasty.

In the face of the troubles engendered by the abrupt change from the Julio-Claudian line to the Flavians, the continuity of religious symbols played a cohesive role. They supplied potent images that ennabled the new emperor to gain adherents and to expand his power and prestige. They bolstered his supporters, defended him against detractors, and suggested a tangible idea of the force behind the world: the divine power of the emperor.[3] There was a great deal of continuity between the regimes, even with the decisive change in political leadership. Although Vespasian denounced the image and memory of Nero, he stressed ways in which he could continue what had come before. Ongoing building projects were completed, but with new patronage credits. New dedications were added to existing buildings and complexes. Cult sanctuaries continued to function as before, but they were now linked to the new emperor, their symbolic connotations reframed according to inherent changes in imperial rule.[4]

The Flavian Rebuilding of the Capitoline Temple

One of the reasons for the Flavians' prodigious building campaigns was the need to rebuild the city still ravaged from Nero's fire of A.D. 64.[5] Much of the Palatine Hill and the Forum Romanum had yet to be rebuilt when Vespasian came to power.[6] The situation had been made worse by a civil war that erupted as Vespasian attempted to claim the throne from Vitellius.

112. Portrait bust of Vespasian, Uffizi, Florence. Photo: Deutsches Archäologisches Institut, Rome, 77.347.

An ensuing battle destroyed even more of the city, including the Temple of Jupiter on the Capitoline Hill.

It is not entirely clear from the historical accounts which side was responsible for setting the Capitoline Temple on fire. There was a standoff between the supporters of Vitellius and those of Vespasian, the latter, including the young Domitian, occupying the Capitoline Hill.[7] When Vitellius's troops stormed the Capitoline, the Flavians pelted them with stones and tiles from the roof of the Porticus Deorem Consentium between the Temple of Saturn and the base of the hill. The Vitellians attacked all of the entrances to the hill and finally succeeded in advancing from the north and northeast sides by coming through a range of apartment buildings that hugged the side of the hill.[8] They came out onto the roofs of the buildings but were met with stiff resistance by the Flavians, who hurled firebrands at the houses and set them ablaze. As the intensity of the fire grew, flames lept to the wooden roof structure of the Capitoline Temple and quickly engulfed it. Within hours, the entire structure burned to the ground, taking with it the archives of Roman history recorded on more than three thousand bronze tablets, which contained the texts of Senatorial decrees and laws going back to Rome's earliest days.[9] Many of the Flavian supporters died or were taken prisoner. Domitian escaped with the help of one of the temple attendants.[10]

Although the Capitoline Temple had been destroyed before, in the time of Sulla, this fire of the Vitellians and Flavians was, according to Tacitus, "the saddest and most shameful crime that the Roman state had ever suffered since its foundation. Rome had no foreign foe; the gods were ready to be propitious if our characters had allowed; and yet the home of Jupiter Optimus Maximus . . . this was the shrine that the mad fury of emperors destroyed!"[11] Calling this the worst crime against the Roman state since its founding was a clear indication of the high esteem in which many Roman citizens still held the Capitoline Temple. They correlated this building with the city's founding, seeing it as a symbol of Rome's strength and greatness. Tacitus went on to admonish the Romans for sacrificing the Capitoline Temple to a civil war: "The Capitol had indeed been burned before in civil war [83 B.C.], but the crime was that of private individuals. Now it was openly beseiged, openly burned – and what were the causes that led to arms? What was the price paid for this great disaster? This temple stood intact so long as we fought for our country."[12] A Roman army had itself brought on this destruction of Rome's most sacred shrine, an act that represented disgrace to all Romans.

Vespasian began the temple's reconstruction soon after taking power. According to Suetonius, he was "the first to lend a hand in clearing away the debris, and carried some of it off in his own hand."[13] Again, there was great importance attached to being the first: just as Horatius had been the first republican consul to dedicate it, now Vespasian was the first emperor to begin its reconstruction after a fire. It was also significant that this was the first major building project in Rome since the death of Nero. It gave Vespasian the opportunity to show that his policy toward financing and planning such projects would be modeled after that of his predecessors.[14] Vespasian recognized the temple as a visual symbol capable of bolstering his power and prestige within the community he ruled. The fact that the temple's very existence had been threatened greatly increased its significance as a symbol. Vespasian rescued it, and by extension, he rescued the Empire itself.

113. View of Temple of Jupiter Capitolinus with Corinthian columns as rebuilt by Vespasian, A.D. 70–79. Photo: Fototeca Unione, American Academy, Rome, FU.13570.

Vespasian also ordered a thorough search for copies of the many bronze tablets that had been stored inside the temple. They were the Empire's most ancient and priceless records, containing decrees of the Senate and acts regarding everything from alliances and treaties to special privileges granted to individuals almost from the time of the city's foundation.[15]

The temple's actual construction was carried out by L. Julius Vestinus, a member of the equestrian order, and its architect may have been one of the Flavians' principal architects, Rabirius.[16] Vestinus was directed by the haruspices to carry away to the marshes the ruins of the old temple and to construct the new one on the same site. Tacitus states, "the gods were unwilling to have the old plan changed," and thus it was rebuilt with the same number of columns and the traditional three-room cella (Fig. 113).[17]

The official beginning of the temple's reconstruction was marked by a great ceremony appropriate to Rome's most historic monument:'

> On the twenty-first of June under a cloudless sky, the area that was dedicated to the temple was surrounded with fillets and garlands; soldiers, who had auspicious names, entered the enclosure carrying boughs of good omen; then the Vestals, accompanied by boys and girls whose fathers and mothers were living, sprinkled the area with water drawn from fountains and streams. Next Helvidius Priscus, the praetor, guided by the *pontifex* Plautius Aelianus, purified the area with the sacrifice of the bull, and placed the vitals of the victim on an altar of turf; and then, after he had prayed to Jupiter,

> Juno, and Minerva . . . he touched the fillets with which the foundation stone was wound and the ropes entwined; at the same time the rest of the magistrates, the priests, the senators, knights, and a great part of the people, putting forth their strength together in one enthusiastic and joyful effort, dragged the huge stone to its place. A shower of gold and silver and of virgin ores, never smelted in any furnace, but in their natural state, was thrown everywhere into the foundations: the haruspices had warned against the profanation of the work by the use of stone or gold intended for any other purpose.[18]

Although the temple was rebuilt on the same plan as the original, images on coins from the Flavian period show clearly that Corinthian columns and capitals were used (Fig. 114).[19] Plutarch states that they were Pentelic marble brought from Athens.[20] We can assume they were taken from the Temple of Olympian Zeus, just as Sulla had taken its capitals in 83 B.C. Plutarch went on to criticize the way they were adapted to the Capitoline Temple, however: "their thickness was once most happily proportional to their length; for we saw them at Athens. But when they were recut and scraped

114. Coin with image of Temple of Jupiter Capitolinus from Flavian period. Photo: Istituto Centrale per il Catalogo e la Documentazione, FU. 13219.

at Rome, they did not gain as much as they lost in symmetry and beauty, and they now look too slender and thin."[21]

They may, in fact, have been cut improperly, but the visual disproportion was more likely due to the fact that they were spaced so far apart in the temple's *aerostyle* composition. It was a strong contrast to the closely spaced *pycnostyle* or *eustyle* arrangement in which Corinthian columns were most commonly used.

The exact size of the new columns can only be surmised. According to Tacitus, "The temple was given greater height than the old; this was the only change that religious scruples allowed, and the only feature that was thought wanting in the magnificence of the old structure."[22] They could have been as tall as 16 or 17 meters as in the case of the the Temple of Mars Ultor or the Temple of Olympian Zeus (Fig. 115). If they had the standard slenderness ratio for Corinthian columns of 10.5 times the diameter, then their lower diameter would have been approximately 1.9 meters.[23] Again, these dimensions can only be estimated, but they are given to suggest a basic idea of the temple's transformation to the Corinthian Order.

This third reconstruction was barely completed when the temple was again destroyed by fire. In this case, it was the fire of Titus of A.D. 80, which engulfed not only the Capitoline Hill but also much of the Campus Martius. Titus initiated the fourth reconstruction, although it was completed and dedicated by his brother Domitian, again using columns of Pentelic marble from the Temple of Olympian Zeus in Athens.[24] Dedicated in A.D. 82 by Domitian, this final version of the temple (Figs. 116 and 117), according to Plutarch, surpassed its predecessors in magnificence.[25] Zosimus reports that not only were the roof tiles gilded bronze, the front doors were plated with gold.[26]

Images on coins also show an elaborate program of sculptural reliefs in the pediment with marble statues representing the Capitoline triad enthroned and an eagle with widely spread wings.[27] Statues crowning the roof included a quadriga at the apex, standing figures of Mars and Venus, and lateral acroteria in the form of *bigae* driven by Victories.[28] Suetonius stated that Domitian put the inscription of his own name on the building, not that of the original builder.[29]

115. Athens, Corinthian columns of the Temple of Olympian Zeus. Photo: Deutsches Archäologisches Institut, Rome, 80.4178.

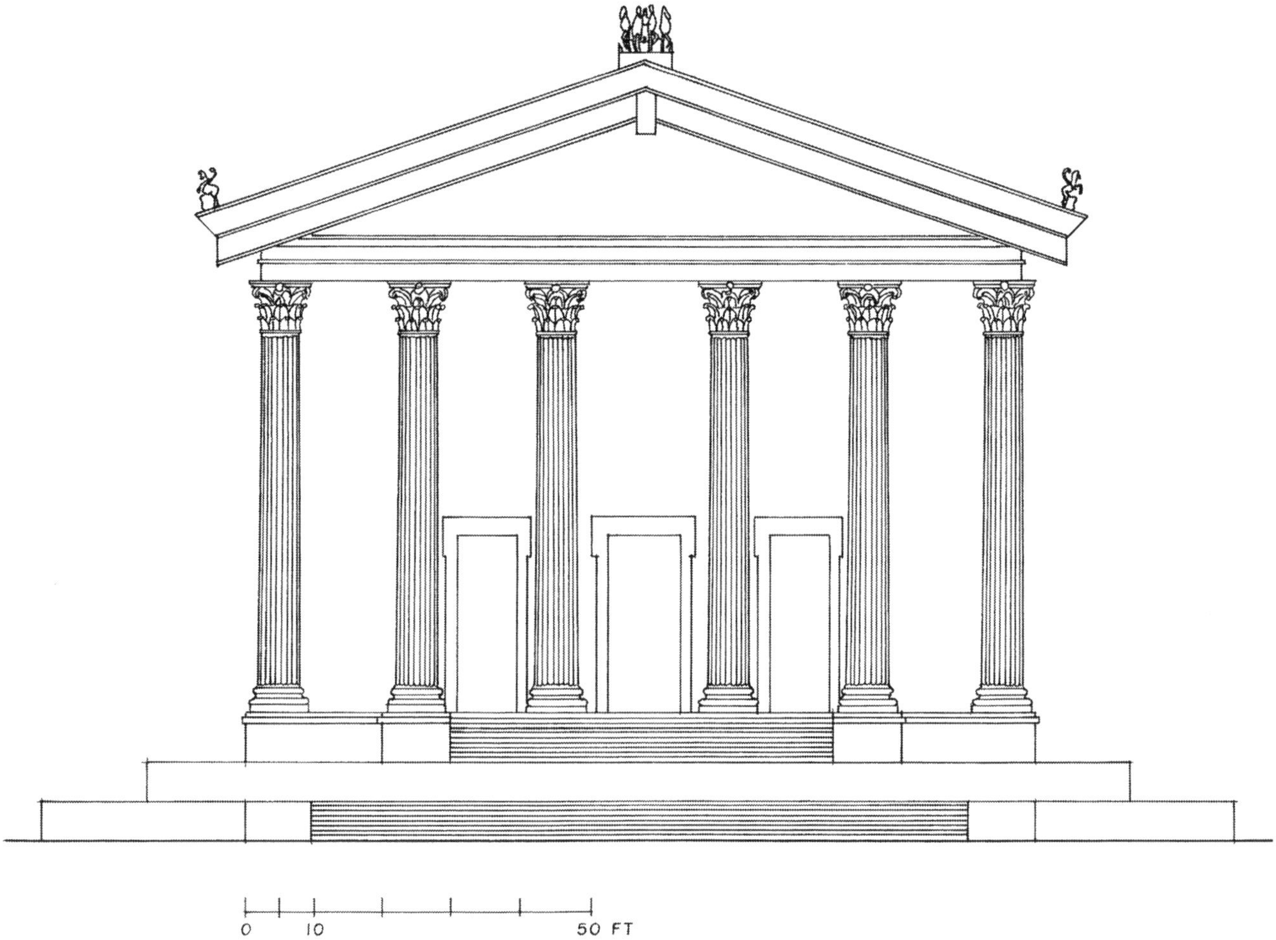

116. Temple of Jupiter Capitolinus after reconstruction by Vespasian. Drawing: John W. Stamper.

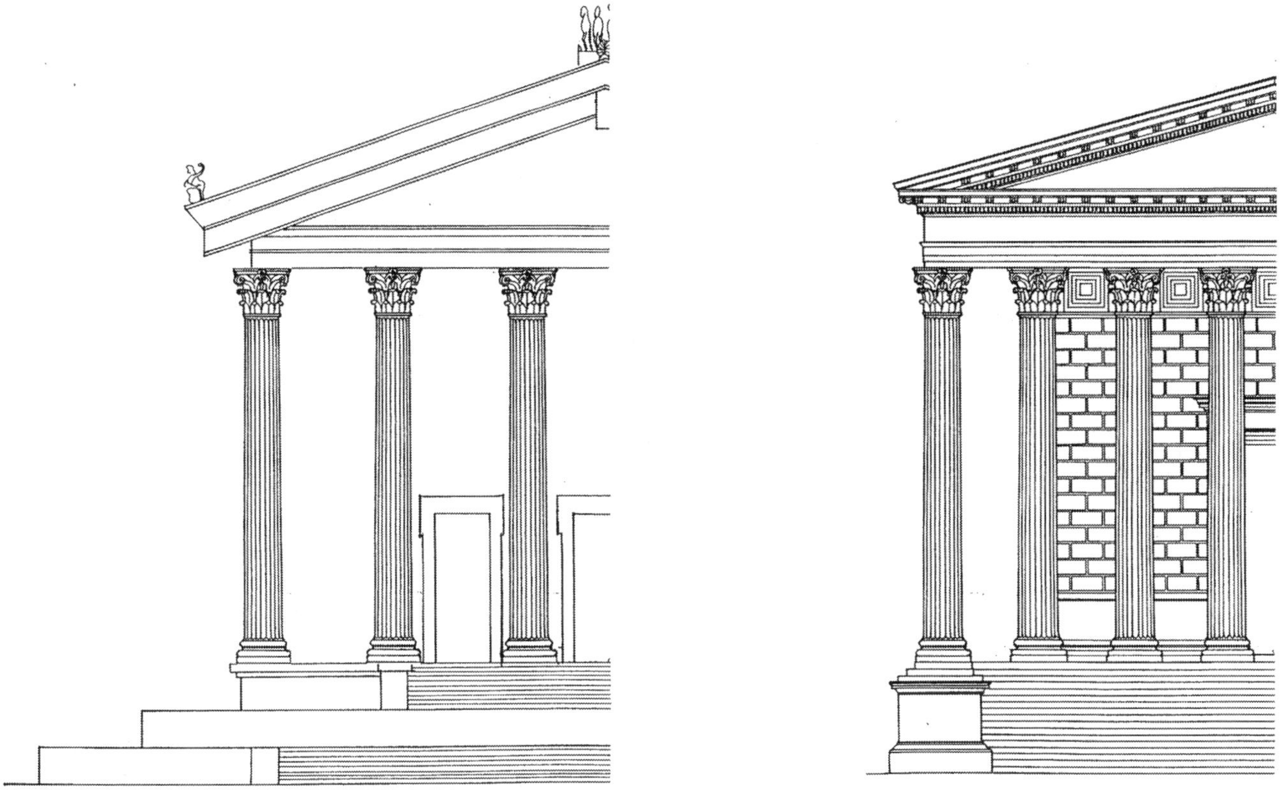

117. Temple of Jupiter Capitolinus, elevation compared with the Temple of Mars Ultor. Both drawings at the same scale. Drawing: John W. Stamper and Rogelio Carrasco.

Domitian also constructed a smaller temple dedicated to Jupiter Conservator on the site of the house of the custodian who had concealed him during the fire that destroyed the temple in A.D. 69. He later enlarged this shrine and rededicated it to Jupiter Custos.[30] Inside was a statue of the god bearing Domitian in his arms.[31] His construction of this temple represented a declaration of gratitude for his survival of the battle between Vespasian and Vitellius. It also represented a warning statement that the emperor was fully aware he did not have the support of all his subjects, but that his opponents should remember that if they took his life, they would be murdering the supreme god himself.[32]

The Temple of Jupiter Capitolinus survived in its final form until A.D. 455, when it was plundered by Geneseric and the Vandals. Its gilt roof tiles and statues were hauled away, and, over time, its walls and columns were dismantled and used as *spolia* in new structures or burned in lime kilns.[33] While it stood, however, it continued to have a great influence on temple architecture in the middle and late Empire.

The Templum Pacis

While Vespasian's reconstruction of the Capitoline Temple was underway, he also initiated a project to build the Templum Pacis (Fig. 118), which was carried out from A.D. 71 to 75. It was located east of the Forum Augustum, on the opposite side of the Via Argelitum, a road that connected the Forum Romanum to the Subura. Its purpose was to commemorate the victory over the Jews in Palestine by Vespasian and Titus and to identify the new dynasty with peace after a long period of civil war.[34] Although the complex included a large forum space, it was referred to as the Templum Pacis until at least the fourth century A.D., some 300 years after its construction.[35]

Pliny considered the Templum Pacis to be one of the most beautiful structures in Rome.[36] Its great square space was originally lined on all four sides with porticos and the temple itself was embedded in the forum's southeast side, at the edge of the Velia, the hill on which the Basilica of Maxentius and Constantine was

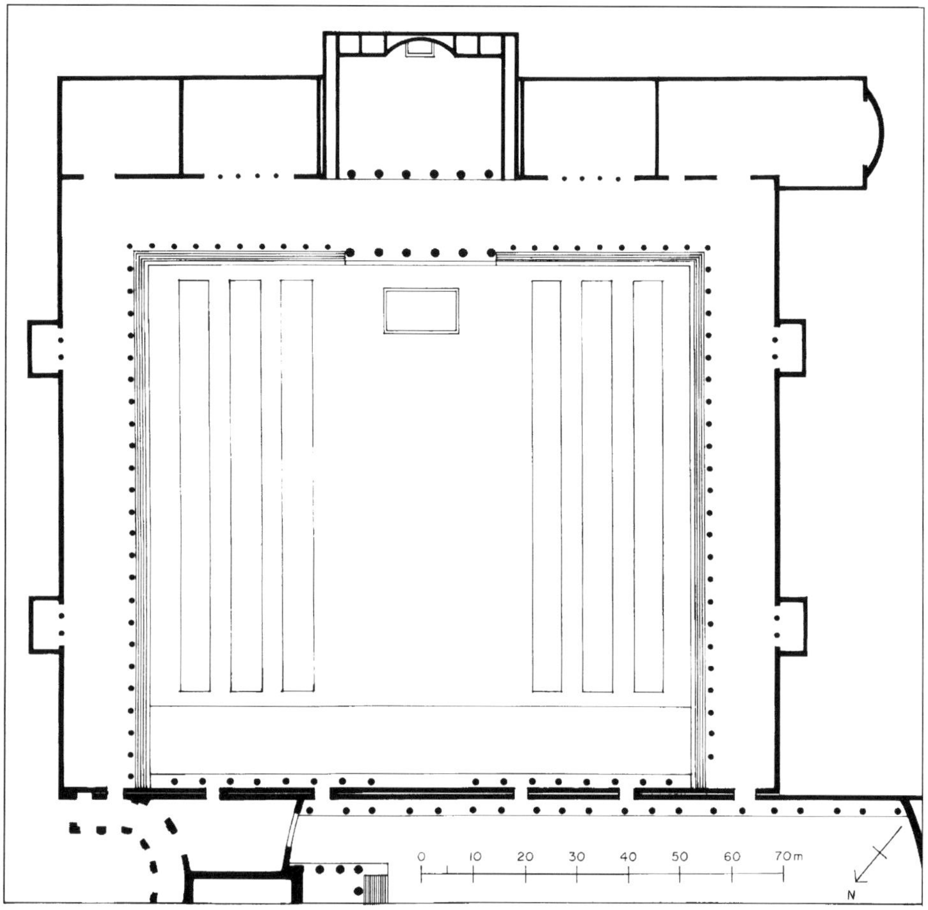

118. Rome, Templum Pacis, A.D. 71–75, plan. Drawing: John W. Stamper based on Silvana Rizzo in *Crypta Balbi – Fori Imperiale: Archeologia urbana a Roma e interventi di restauro nell'anno del Grande Giubileo* (2000), pl. 53.

later built.[37] Because the space was nearly square in plan rather than long and narrow like the Forum Julium or the Forum Augustum, the temple's façade was flanked by porticos that extended laterally on either side. The temple itself was emphasized by six columns at slightly wider intervals.[38]

The main forum space had inside measurements of 137 meters wide by 134 meters long (465 by 456 Roman feet). Including the surrounding porticos and temple, it measured 150 meters by 140 metters (509 by 475 Roman feet). It was built on the site of a former market, the Macellum, which had served Rome throughout the Republic but was destroyed in the fire of Nero in A.D. 64.[39] Vespasian's architect followed much of the Macellum's plan and reused its foundations.[40]

The porticos flanking either side of the temple and those on the northeast and southwest sides were 12.50 meters deep and lined with red granite columns on the front and a perimeter wall at the back of tufa and peperino in *opus quadratum*. Two small rectangular exedrae opened out from each of the side walls.[41]

The forum's southeast side originally had a portico similar to those of the northeast and southwest sides. A row of *tabernae* may have faced out onto the Argiletum.[42] This portico and row of shops were altered when Domitian built the Forum Transitorium beginning in the late A.D. 80s.[43] The *tabernae* were replaced by a wall that was articulated on the exterior by spur walls and columns at widely spaced intervals.[44] The portico inside the forum space was replaced by a brick platform with a grid of small square holes that served as drains to catch rainwater.[45]

The plan of the temple itself was composed of a large apsidal hall, 34 meters wide by 22 meters deep (115 by 75 Roman feet). Again, a relationship to the Temple of Jupiter Capitolinus is evident. Even though the temple structure was flanked by colonnades, its actual width was the same as the Temple of Jupiter Capitolinus as it is reconstructed in this study.

A cult statue would have stood on a rectangular base in the apse of the main hall. The main hall was flanked on either side by a long, narrow room, each with an apsidal rear wall.[46] The temple was unlike most others both in the way its façade appeared to be extended laterally by the adjacent porticos and because its podium was very low.[47]

The Templum Pacis was used in large part to house the spoils of war from Jerusalem, including the treasures from the Jewish temple: silver trumpets, golden vessels, and the seven-branched menorah, which are represented in a sculpted relief on the Arch of Titus. There was also a great deal of Greek art, part of it from Nero's Domus Aurea, which Vespasian took over and relocated. He thus made what had once been the private collection of a tyrant part of the public patrimony. His connection to the artworks and their historical links to ancient Greece served to elevate his authority in the eyes of the Romans.[48]

Like the porticus of the Theater of Pompey, the forum's open space was filled with long planters, three on each side of the main axis. They served as flowerbeds or planters for trees and were supplied with water from the platform of drains along the forum's northwest side.[49] They served an important functional purpose, as we have seen described by Vitruvius, for providing space to walk in the open air, freshened and cleared by the vegetation, a space good for the eyes and the lungs.[50] Also like the porticus of the Forum of Pompey, the planters framed a perspective view of the temple proper located at the southeast end of the axis. Vespasian followed the model set by Pompey and Vitruvius in building an urban space that was aimed at both improving the health of Rome's citizens and providing an exalted perspective view of his temple structure.

Both the plan and the architectural details of the Templum Pacis proved influential to the architects working for Trajan in the A.D. 100s, and Hadrian in the A.D. 120s. The Forum Traiani would have many similarities (see Chapter 10), and Hadrian's large building project in Athens, Hadrian's Library, built in A.D. 121–132, followed it closely in both plan and detail.[51]

The history of the Templum Pacis is also notable for the fact that it housed the famous Marble Plan of Rome, the *Forma Urbis Romae*. This plan was housed in a rectangular room located at the forum's southeast corner, between the temple and the nearby Via Sacra.[52] Vespasian may have ordered the original map in A.D. 77.[53] This part of the complex, however, along with the Temple of Vesta and the House of the Vestals, was destroyed by fire during the reign of Commodus in A.D. 191.[54] The surviving fragments of the map date from a reconstruction of the complex by Septimius Severus in A.D. 203–211.[55] The building itself was restored and decorated in *opus sectile* and dedicated as the *Templum Sacrae Urbis*.[56]

After the restoration by Septimius Severus, the room with the Marble Plan probably served as a record office for the real estate and property evaluations of the city. It would have been controlled by the city's urban prefect, who was closely associated with the imperial fora. The Marble Plan itself was not used for official record keeping, but was a symbol of the office.[57]

The Templum Pacis was in many ways different from the imperial fora of Julius Caesar and Augustus. It was a type of forum in which the cult temple was almost an appendix to the forum as a whole rather than

119. Portrait bust of Titus, Museo Nazionale, Naples. Photo: Deutsches Archäologisches Institut, Rome, 76.1135.

its main focal point. Its function was not limited solely to the worship of the cult.[58] Not only did its long planters provide a parklike atmosphere, but it may also have been used for commercial purposes, a continuation of the former Macellum on the site. To this was added its function of commemorating the victory over Jerusalem and its accommodation of the Marble Plan of Rome and the records office. It was very much an architectural hybrid that continued a building tradition going back to the Porticus Pompeiana but which became more diverse in its function and iconography over time.[59]

Titus and Domitian

When Vespasian died in A.D. 79, his oldest son, Titus (Fig. 119), sought to continue his governmental reforms. He became ill in the summer of A.D. 81, however, and died at the age of forty-two.[60] His brother Domitian, the youngest of the Flavian sons, had held the office of consul several times during the reigns of his father and Titus. When Titus died, Domitian (Fig. 120) was recognized by the praetorian guards and voted by the Senate as the next emperor. He was fortunate to inherit a political system that worked relatively well, a stable economy, and peace in the Empire.[61]

Domitian initiated and carried on a number of important public works projects, financed at this point not by the booty of lucrative military campaigns – because he did not have any – but by the revenues of taxes, most of which had been levied by Vespasian. In the early A.D. 80s, he completed the final restoration of the Temple of Jupiter Capitolinus and the construction of the Temple of Vespasian in the Forum Romanum. He also began remodeling projects of the Temple of Castor and Pollux, the Temple of Divus Augustus, and the House of the Vestals. In the Campus Martius, he initiated restoration work of the Porticus Octaviae and Agrippa's Pantheon, and he built a circus on the site of the present-day Piazza Navona. In the narrow space between the Forum Augustum and the Templum Pacis, traversed by the Via Argiletum, he began construction of what is known as the Forum Transitorium with its Temple of Minerva, and he completed the Colosseum and the adjacent Baths of Titus.[62] On the Palatine Hill he restored Augustus's Temple of Apollo Palatinus and its adjacent libraries, along with the Palace of Tiberius. Finally, he continued construction of his own palace on the Palatine, which was designed by the architect Rabirius and which, because of its great size and magnificent architecture, became an official imperial residence.

120. Portrait bust of Domitian, Vatican Museum. Photo: Deutsches Archäologisches Institut, Rome, 40.591.

The Temple of Vespasian

The Temple of Vespasian was built by Titus and Domitian between A.D. 79 and 87 in honor of their deified father.[63] It was located just below the Capitoline Hill at the southwest corner of the Forum Romanum in a space between the Temple of Concordia and Porticus Deorem Consentium (Portico of the Twelve Gods) (Fig. 121).[64] The Clivus Capitolinus passed directly in front of it, and the Temple of Saturn was directly across the clivus, to the southeast.[65]

121. Rome, Temple of Vespasian, A.D. 79–87, elevation. Drawing: Rogelio Carrasco after Stefano De Angeli, *Templum Divi Vespasiani* (1992), fig. 144.

The temple was laid out in a small pseudoperipteral plan (Fig. 122) measuring 21 meters wide by 27.75 meters long (71 by 94 Roman feet).[66] Its pronaos had six columns across and two deep, with the uppermost steps of the front stairway penetrating between the columns. The cella walls were travertine, faced with marble slabs. Inside the cella was a cult statue of Vespasian, the base of which is still visible against the back wall.[67]

The fluted Corinthian columns, three of which were restored by Valadier and Camporese in the early nineteenth century (Fig. 123), measured 14.14 meters with a shaft height of 11.79 meters (48 and 40 Roman feet), a ratio of 6 to 5. The slenderness ratio of the column height to its diameter, 1.40 meters ($4\frac{3}{4}$ Roman feet), is 10 to 1. The architect chose to follow the 10 to 1 slenderness ratio even though it meant that the column diameter would not be a whole number.[68]

The columns supported one of the most beautiful entablatures of the high classical period. It was composed of a three-step architrave adorned with bead-and-reel and inverted acanthus leaf moldings (Fig. 124), above which is a sculpted frieze and a cornice with dentils, egg-and-dart moldings, and modillions.[69] On the sides, the frieze is decorated with sculpted instruments of sacrifice and priestly attributes – the *albogalerus, aspergillus, urceus*, knife, *patera*, and axe – spaced alternately with bucranian heads.[70] The presence of these sacrificial instruments and priestly attributes were meant to connote the high dignity of the imperial cult.[71]

The symbolic relationship between the emperor and the instruments of sacrifice had been evident since the late Republic and early Empire, especially on coins minted for Julius Caesar and Augustus.[72] They appeared again on the coins of Vespasian and Titus.[73] In each case, the reference of sacrifice and priestly symbols were meant to relate directly to the dictator or emperor. They were meant to suggest his profound

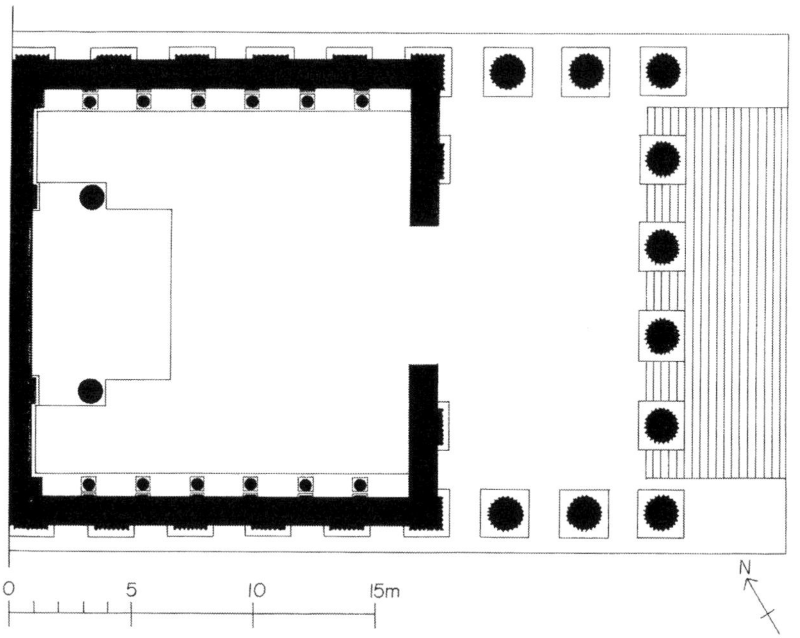

122. Temple of Vespasian, plan. Drawing: Rogelio Carrasco after Stefano De Angeli, *Templum Divi Vespasiani* (1992), fig. 143.

religiosity, his *pietas*, and thus one of the most important values of Roman politics and public life.

In the cornice are tiny interposed rings between the dentils, a detail typical of Domitian and Rabirius and found on other monuments by Domitian including the Flavian Palace and Forum Transitorium.[74] On the front of the entablature was a flat panel that extended the entire width of the portico and carried an inscription referring to the deified Vespasian, the Senate, and the Roman people, as well as to a restoration done by Septimius Severus and Caracalla.[75]

By placing the temple dedicated to their father between those of Concordia and Saturn, Titus and Domitian sought to affirm the legitimacy of their dynasty as a successor to the Julio-Claudians. The site would have a similar appeal later to Septimius Severus, who also sought to symbolize his imperial dynasty with the Arch of Septimius Severus, recalling the importance of the succession from the father to son – Vespasian to Titus, and Septimius Severus to Caracalla.[76]

Architecturally the Temple of Vespasian was one of the highest achievements of imperial Rome, representing a level of refinement and grace that exceeded that of the Augustan period. The extreme delicacy of the carving of the capitals, the gracefulness of the column shafts, the skillfulness of the carving, and the details of the emblematic program of the frieze are all characteristic of the architecture of the Flavians. They represent the superb accomplishment of their architects' design and the craftsmanship of their workers, all reflecting their authority in the world of both art and politics.

Temple of Minerva and the Forum Transitorium

The columns and entablature standing in the Forum Transitorium, or Forum of Nerva, suggest a level of elegance and sophistication that was similar to that of the Temple of Vespasian. Begun by Domitian in A.D. 85 or 86, it was completed and dedicated by his successor Marcus Cocceius Nerva in A.D. 98.[77] The forum and its Temple of Minerva were built on the Via Argiletum, a long, narrow space between Vespasian's Templum Pacis and the Forum Augustum (Fig. 125).[78] This space had served as one of the main streets leading into the Forum Romanum from the Subura neighborhood on the north. It had long served as a market area, with stalls for cobblers and booksellers, among others.[79] During the Republic, the Argiletum may have referred to the entire area north of the Forum Romanum, extending eastward to the Velia, and westward to the ridge between the Esquiline and Capitoline Hills.[80] The area to

123. Temple of Vespasian, view of columns with Temple of Saturn in the background. Photo: Deutsches Archäologisches Institut, Rome, 96.1947.

the east was primarily markets, including the *piscarium*, Forum Coquinum, and the Macellum; the area to the west was primarily apartment blocks.[81]

In Vespasian's original design of the Templum Pacis, the outer face of its northwest wall was lined with *tabernae*. Portions of the opposite side of the Argiletum were lined with colonnades, especially at its southwest corner where it met the Forum Julium.[82] When Domitian began construction of his new forum and the Temple of Minerva, in order to obtain sufficient space, he demolished the row of *tabernae* and filled in the intercolumniations of the colonnade at the southwest corner.[83]

The new forum was as much a street as it was a forum, a space that provided a more ceremonial entrance into the Forum Romanum. Measuring 45 meters wide by 131 meters long (153 by 445 Roman feet), its northern and southern ends were both shaped in the form

124. Temple of Vespasian, entablature and cornice. Photo: Joann Sporleder.

of a crescent. The temple dedicated to Minerva was embedded into the northern crescent (Fig. 126).[84] An arched gateway in the wall to the right of the temple marked the north entrance to the forum itself and led to a secondary space to the north. This space, U-shaped in plan, surrounded by a double colonnade, served as a vestibule or transition between the forum and the Subura neighborhood.[85] The south entrance was also marked by an arched opening, this one leading to a narrow space between the Basilica Aemilia and the Curia Julia before opening onto the Forum Romanum.

Somewhere near the south end of the space, there may have been a shrine of Janus Quadrifons, possibly a small arch structure with openings on each of its four sides.[86] Two possible locations have been suggested, one in the center of the forum, the other at

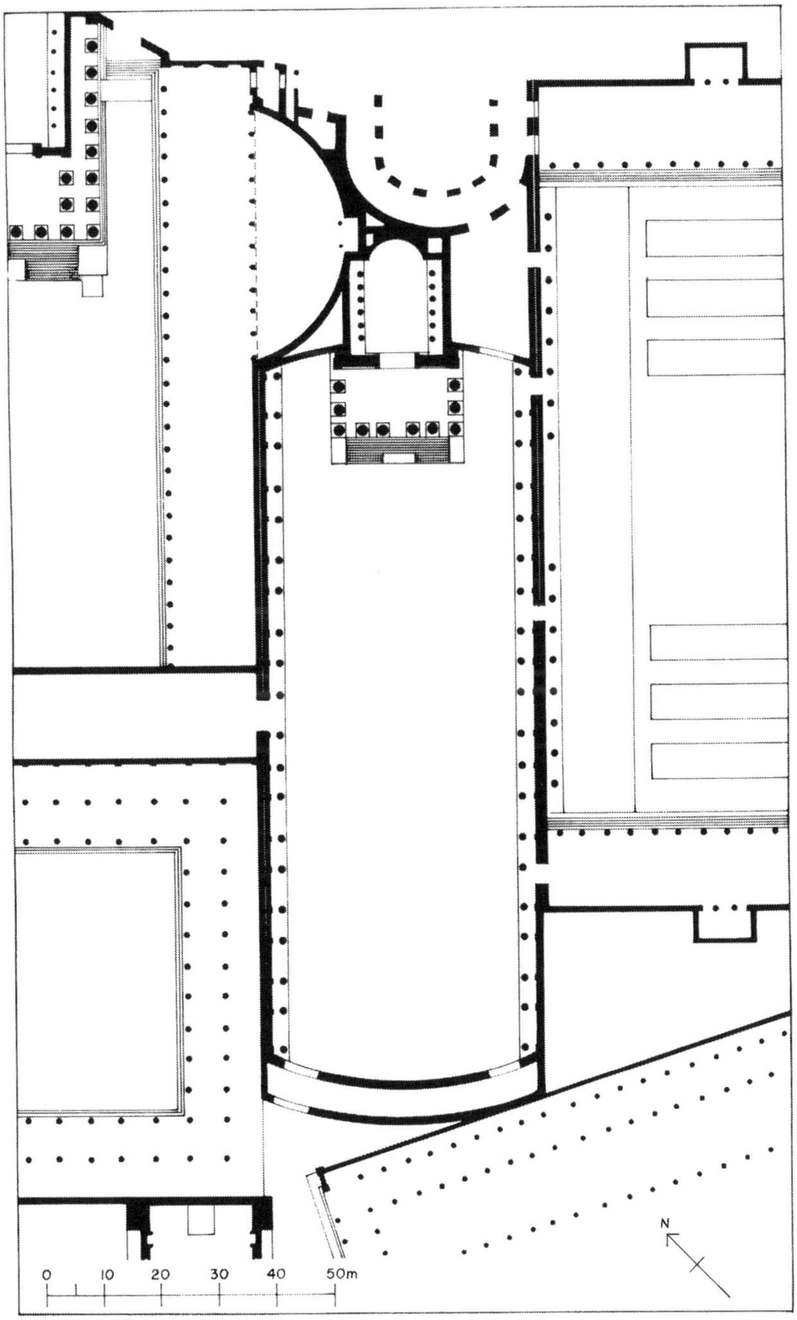

125. Rome, Forum Transitorium, A.D. 85/86–98, site plan. Drawing: John W. Stamper after Heinrich Bauer in *RendPontAcc* 49 (1976–1977), fig. D.

the southwest corner near the entrance to the Forum Romanum.[87] A four-sided statue of the god brought from Falerii was set up inside it and consecrated as a templum.[88] Its importance was related to the crossing of the underground Cloaca Maxima, which ran the length of the forum.[89] The forum was constructed around Janus, who was not only a witness to changes in the area, but also preserved the memory of the Argiletum as a crossroads and a water crossing.[90]

The enclosing walls of the forum, which already existed in part along the Forum Augustum, were built of peperino with marble revetments. To make a decorative effect for the side walls, Domitian's architect devised a system of freestanding, fluted Corinthian columns that carried a decorative entablature and parapet (Fig. 127).[91] The columns had alternate spacings of 4.50 meters and 6.86 meters center to center. Their centerline was set 2.05 meters from the wall.

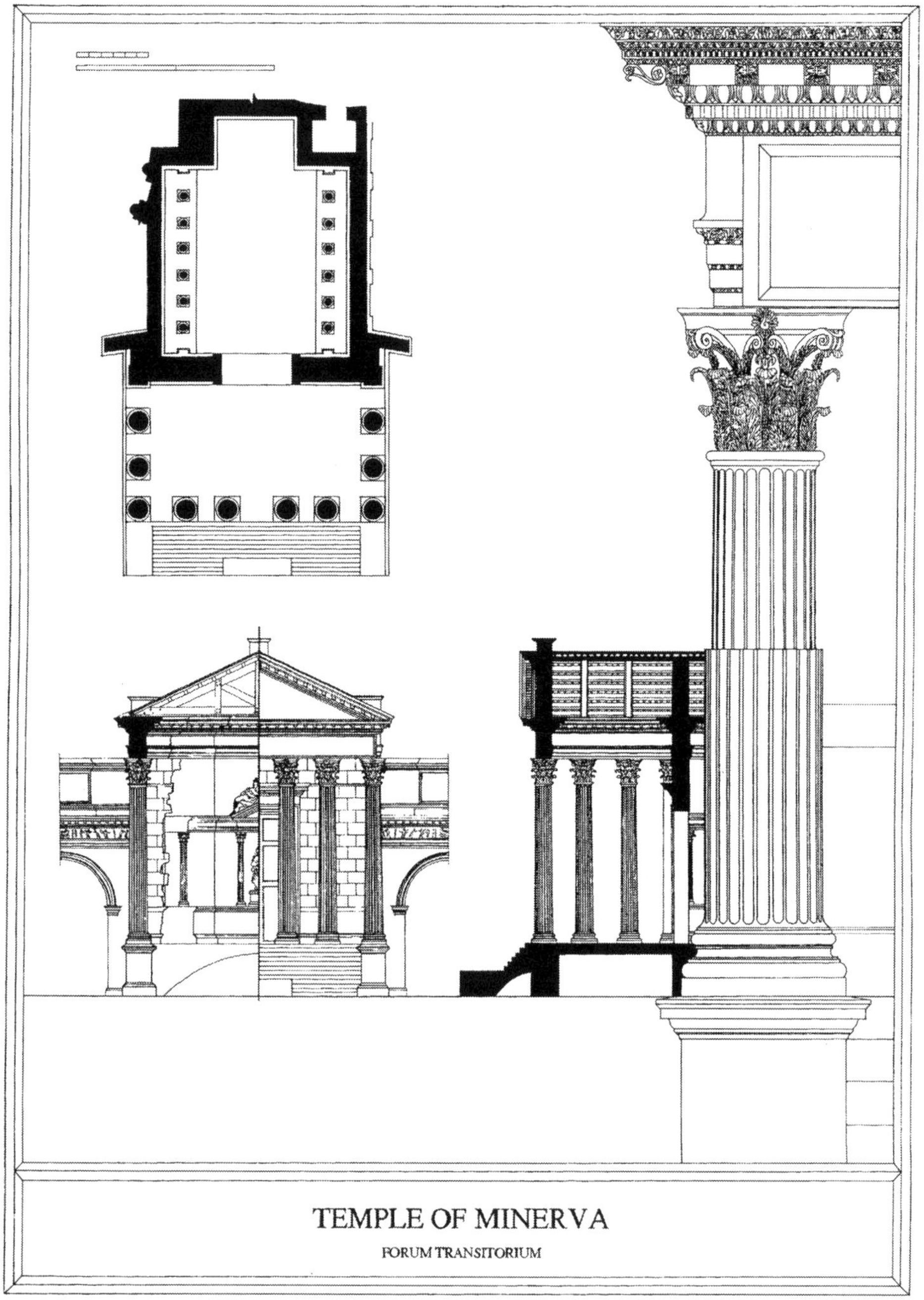

126. Forum Transitorium, Temple of Minerva, analytique. Drawing: James Leslie based on Andrea Palladio, *The Four Books of Architecture*, vol. 4, pls. 11, 12, 15; and Heinrich Bauer in *LTUR*, vol. 2, fig. 147.

A flat pilaster corresponded to each column along the walls.[92] Segments of the entablature and attic projected out from the wall over each column. The entablature, one bay of which remains, is composed of a three-step architrave with bead-and-reel moldings between each step, a sculpted frieze, dentils with interconnected rings, an egg-and-dart molding, and modillions supporting the cornice.[93] The richness of the carving and the presence of the double rings between the dentils suggests the work of Domitian's architect, Rabirius.[94]

The remains of the carved frieze show vivid images of women engaged in the female arts.[95] They depict Minerva teaching the arts of sewing and weaving, along with the myth of Arachne and other female scenes and stories.[96] A larger statue of Minerva, an example of which is on the parapet above, was presumably repeated in each bay.[97] The Arachne myth tells the

127. Forum Transitorium, detail of columns along sidewall of forum. Photo: Istituto Centrale per il Catalogo e la Documentazione, D.6160.

story of a defiant young woman with an exceptional talent for weaving, so much so, that she thought she could challenge Minerva. The two engage in a contest, after which Minerva destroy's Arachne's cloth in a fit of jealousy. She strikes Arachne, then turns her into a spider, thereby affirming her supremacy.[98]

Further scenes, to the left and right of the Arachne scene, show other female figures of various ages, involved in all aspects of weaving. Several looms are shown, a vertical type with upper and lower beams, which allowed the weaver to sit while she worked.[99] A matron's skill at the loom represented the sanctioned ideals of womanhood, especially a selfless dedication to the duties of the household.[100]

The Temple of Minerva was still standing in the early sixteenth century, and it was recorded by both Baldasarre Peruzzi and Palladio.[101] In plan, its pronaos had six columns across and three deep. Its rectangular cella may have been lined with rows of columns on the inside, and it ended in an apse for the placement

128. Arch of Titus, A.D. 70–81 or 82–90, view through the arch toward Capitoline Hill. Photo: John W. Stamper.

of the cult statue.[102] Given the constraints of the forum space, there were no exterior columns along the temple's flanks. An unusual feature about the plan is the fact that the pronaos was slightly wider than the cella.[103] The temple's architrave bore a dedicatory inscription, and the cornice and raking cornice featured modillions and dentils.[104] The pediment's raking cornice had an angle of forty-five degrees, which was tall compared with other Roman temples.[105]

Together, the temple and the forum created a setting that monumentalized the street which led from the Forum Romanum to the Subura district to the north.[106] It reminds us that the fora were often more than just enclosed squares, but accommodated circulation paths as well. They had numerous points of access and could be traversed from one end to the other as a visitor moved between one part of the city to another. The Forum Transitorium was the most overt of all, however, in its directional circulation, resembling a wide boulevard. The axial placement of the Temple of Minerva served to formalize and monumentalize it in conjunction with the columns lining its walls, which provided architectural unity and definition.[107] Thus was created one of the most grandiose urban spaces in Rome, flamboyantly representing the legacy of Domitian and the Flavian dynasty.

Just as Julius Caesar claimed to have been a descendent of Venus, Domitian claimed to have descended from Minerva, member of the Capitoline triad, associate of Jupiter. His adherence to Minerva was sincere and profound, declared unequivocally on his coinage, in the Temple of Minerva, and in the festivals he arranged in her honor. Through Minerva, he was able

to derive a relation to Jupiter, which he believed to be a necessary part of statesmanship.[108] The two worked together as his protectors. There was no theological dichotomy between his private devotion to Minerva and his public appearance as Jupiter's representative on earth.[109] By linking himself to both, he was seeking absolute control, for which purpose power was indispensible.[110] The way to convey the worth and stability of the dynasty was through the building of a temple to the goddess who protected the Flavian family.[111]

Public display was also essential for Domitian in establishing and maintaining his power. He celebrated a regimen of games, the *quinquatria* in honor of Minerva. Held at his villa in the Alban Hills, these annual games included contests in oratory and poetry along with shows of wild beasts and stage plays.[112] According to Cassius Dio, all was done at a magnificent scale.[113] He also established a *quinquennial* contest in honor of Capitoline Jupiter, one with three parts – music, riding, and gymnastics – and with far more prizes awarded than had been the custom.[114] He staged competitions in Greek and Latin prose declamation, musical competitions for lyre players and choruses, and races in the Circus Maximus. He presided over the competitions in half-boots, clad in a purple toga and wearing a golden crown with figures of Jupiter, Juno, and Minerva. At his side sat the priest of Jupiter and the college of the *flaviales*, dressed in similar clothes but with crowns including the additional figure of Domitian himself.[115]

The Arch of Titus and the Capitoline

The Arch of Titus (Fig. 128), located on the Via Sacra, on a low ridge connecting the Velia and the Palatine Hill, marked the eastern entrance to the Forum Romanum. It was on the highest point of the Via Sacra on this side of the forum and was thus prominently visible from both the Colosseum and from inside the forum itself. It was, in fact, high enough that for visitors approaching the forum, it framed the view ahead, a view that extended across the rooftops of the forum's temples and basilicas to the Capitoline Hill and its Temple of Jupiter. The primary purpose for its construction on this particular site was unquestionably to provide this framed perspective view of the Capitoline Temple.

The exact date of the arch's construction is not known, nor is it certain whether it was built as a commemorative or a triumphal arch. If it was the former, it would have been built just after Titus's death, that is, from A.D. 82 to 90. If it was a triumphal arch, it would have been started before his death, perhaps in A.D. 70, by the Roman Senate and completed or possibly rededicated in A.D. 81 by Domitian.[116] Domitian would have dedicated it with the intention of glorifying the Flavian family, and for his personal gain in that he would be perceived as the brother of a deified emperor.[117]

Although triumphal arches are not the subject of this book, it is essential to include this one because of its relationship with the Temple of Jupiter Capitolinus and the long tradition of triumphal processions passing through the forum and culminating on the Capitoline Hill. The Arch of Titus is a single-bay arch, with a barrel-vaulted opening framed by wide piers and topped by an attic. The piers are articulated at their corners with engaged three-quarter columns with Composite capitals. All of the original columns were fluted, although those of the outer corners, restored in the early nineteenth century, were left unfluted and executed in travertine (not the marble of the original structure) to distinguish them from the originals. The lower half of the arch is of Pentellic marble, the attic of Lunense marble, and the restored portions are of travertine.[118]

The engaged columns stand on high pedestals and carry an elaborate entablature and cornice with a three-step architrave, sculpted frieze, and modillions and dentils.[119] The frieze represents a procession with soldiers bearing the god of the river Jordan on a litter, accompanied by animals for sacrifice and soldiers bearing booty. The attic zone contains a large panel on both sides dedicated to the deified Titus (Fig. 129).[120]

The spandrels above the archway are adorned with sculpted winged victory figures carrying trophies of war, and in the middle, on a vertically placed console applied to the face of the keystone, is a statue of Roma on one side, and perhaps that of Fortuna on the other.[121] Two sculpted panels inside the archway represent Titus's triumphal return after the battle against

129. Arch of Titus, detail of attic inscription. Photo: John W. Stamper.

the Jews in Palestine. In one his army carries the spoils of Jerusalem, including the seven-branched candlestick and silver trumpets that were put on display in the Templum Pacis. In the other, Titus is seen in a four-horse chariot with the goddess Roma leading the horses and Victory crowning the emperor with a laurel wreath. In the center of the coffered ceiling is a square relief panel depicting the apotheosis of Titus, who is carried to heaven by an eagle.[122]

Roman arches were richly symbolic and commemorated a wide range of events: a military victory, a triumphal procession, deeds of the emperor, his deification, and his authority as ruler. As a symbol of the emperor, an arch remained vividly in the memory of the people, immortalizing him and his family long after his earthly death. That the emperor regarded the arch as an important symbol of his royal power, heavenly abode, and seat of authority is confirmed in the image of the Arch of Titus on the near contemporary Tomb of the Haterii. Here the emperor appears within the archway, recalling the portal where god-images made their seasonal entrance, the appearance and triumphal reception of the divine ruler, and the archway where the emperor sat in judgment. As such, the beautifully decorated arch acquired royal, divine, and celestial values.[123]

The divine connotation of the arch equated it with an advent or epiphany, the manifestation or appearance of a superhuman being. This dual function as a symbol of victory and advent was associated with the Greek epiphany, or "Appearance." At first this was a purely religious event pertaining to the anniversary and seasonal coming of a god, which in turn was derived from older religions of the ancient East where at the beginning of the new year, or on the occasion of a seasonal festival, the populace met at the city gate their

god-image, often in the person of the king.[124] The lasting symbolic ideas associated with the gateway and the ritual of ruler-worship were derived from elaborate ceremonies with which the cities of the Hellenistic and Roman East welcomed their rulers at the gateway as a resplendent sun god and universal "Master of Heaven and Earth" and a "Savior" destined, it was hoped, to bring peace, prosperity, and happiness to their adoring subjects.[125]

Roman triumphal processions, with which such arches were associated, originated, it is widely thought, with Romulus celebrating his victory over King Acron. Dionysius of Halicarnassus reports that after a series of battles against neighboring towns, Romulus

> led his army home, carrying with him the spoils of those who had been slain in battle and the choicest part of the booty as an offering to the gods; and he offered many sacrifices besides. Romulus himself came last in the procession, clad in a purple robe and wearing a crown of laurel upon his head, and, that he might maintain the royal dignity, he rode in a chariot drawn by four horses. The rest of the army, both foot and horse, followed, ranged in their several divisions, praising the gods in songs of their country and extolling their general in improvised verses. They were met by the citizens with their wives and children, who, ranging themselves on each side of the road, congratulated them upon their victory and expressed their welcome in every other way. . . . Such was the victorious procession, marked by the carrying of trophies and concluding with a sacrifice, which the Romans call a triumph, as it was first instituted by Romulus.[126]

From that time until the reign of Titus, there were nearly 130 triumphs, a number so large that the Romans passed laws requiring that no official triumph should be allowed unless 5,000 of the enemy were slain in one battle, the victory was verified on oath by the general, it was approved by the Senate, and, finally, an official resolution was passed by the magistrates of the city. In addition, a procession could not be granted unless the conqueror was a dictator, consul, or praetor.[127]

While the returning general and his soldiers waited for such a decree to be issued, they remained encamped outside Rome near the Porta Capena, in what is today the plain below the Janiculum Hill between the Vatican and the Castle Sant'Angelo, or in the Campus Martius. As soon as the permission was conceded, sacrifices were offered to Mars, Juno, Jupiter, and others depending on the circumstance. The conqueror then robed himself in his triumphal habit and assumed the laurel crown. With a palm-branch in his hand, he distributed honors to his soldiers and set out in a solemn march toward the forum.[128] Roman citizens lined the streets along the way, and those participating in the procession arranged themselves in accordance with the community's political organization: members of the Senate, civil authorities, soldiers, priests and priestesses, children, citizens proper, women, and finally slaves, freedmen, and visitors. White garments and wreaths were prescribed to all participants, and many were designated to carry torches, burn incense, pour aromatic oils, or strew flowers. There were official chants of welcome, and the conqueror was hailed as "benefactor and savior."

As the procession began, all the temples were opened, and porticos, theaters, forums, and other public buildings were hung with festoons and all sorts of ornaments; the houses and palaces were decorated with hangings and tapestries, and everything was arranged to contribute to the festival's splendor. With the emperor riding in a chariot, the procession passed by the Theater of Marcellus, through the Forum Boarium, and across the Circus Maximus. It reached the Via Appia and turned onto the Via Sacra, went through the Arch of Titus, then proceeded into the Forum Romanum. Finally, it ascended the Capitoline Hill to the Temple of Jupiter. This circuitous route was adopted to afford to the greatest number of people the opportunity of witnessing the magnificent cortege.[129] These processions and honors, evolving from a tradition bestowed originally only to the gods, had, therefore, a divine meaning, a meaning that manifested itself in the triumphal arch.

The building of the Arch of Titus was significant in the urban development of the Forum Romanum because it served as a framing element for views of the Temple of Jupiter Capitolinus during such processions. The arch was precisely located at the highest elevation

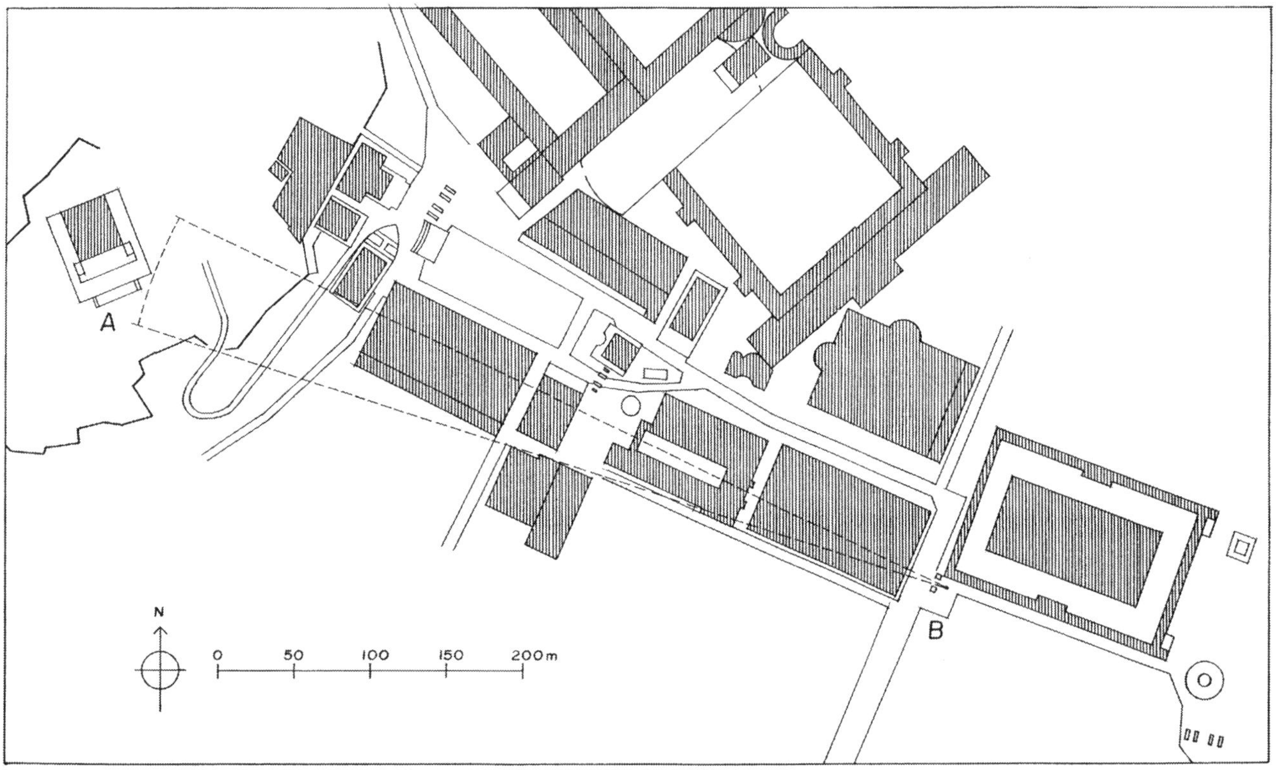

130. Arch of Titus, plan of Forum Romanum with indication of view from the Arch of Titus to the Temple of Jupiter Capitolinus. Drawing: John W. Stamper.

of the Via Sacra as it enters the Forum Romanum from the east and directly in alignment with the Temple of Jupiter Capitolinus (Fig. 130). The arch provided both an entrance to the forum as well as a view to the destination of the processional route. The goal of a visitor, or the triumphant emperor, as he made his way through the forum was evident, and thus an object of anticipation. In addition to its usual role of commemorating a triumph or the emperor's life, the arch in this case was an ordering element of its urban setting. It was an object to be seen in its own right, as well as a framing device to view the city's most important temple. It thus had both a primary and a secondary role within its urban context.[130] It was part of a grand urban scheme, a master plan devised to create an implied order for the city, complex as it was. In so doing, it manifested the authority of the Flavian dynasty, its link to Jupiter, and its ability to reshape the city in its own image.

The Flavians were clearly prodigious temple builders. They inherited a city in A.D. 70 that had been largely destroyed by fire. Even the great Temple of Jupiter Capitolinus lay in ruins after its destruction in the civil war between Vespasian and Vitellius. Its reconstruction by Vespasian resulted in a dramatic transformation because he succeeded in using Corinthian columns brought from Athens, a proposal that had originally been made by Sulla more than 140 years earlier. The temple was now consistent with the current architectural style, even though it was still only *araeostyle* with six columns on the front. It was now definitely more modern and elegant, although it was a compromise, a synthesis of the Etrusco-Roman tradition and the classicism of Athens.

Vespasian's other major temple project, the Templum Pacis, was also a compromise between two traditions: the nearly square portico enclosure and the standard Roman temple with eight columns across the front and a width of 34 meters (115 Roman feet). The design of the porticos, with an elaborate garden in which to display the spoils of war from Jerusalem, combined with the temple front that was the same size as the Temple of Mars Ultor and perhaps the Temple of Jupiter Capitolinus, represented a significant attempt on Vespasian's part to make reference to the city's

principal cults, Romulus and Augustus. He wanted to base his authority on the gods, on the founder of the city, and on the founder of the Empire.

There were two significant features of the temple architecture of Titus and Domitian, as seen in the Temple of Vespasian, Temple of Minerva, and the Arch of Titus. First was their planning on an urban scale, whether in filling in a densely packed setting or in relating monuments across vast distances. Second was the refined sense of proportion and the incredible craftsmanship of the masons working under the direction of Rabirius. The legacy of the Flavians would set a high standard for what followed during the reigns of Trajan and Hadrian.

10

THE FORUM TRAIANI

The many large-scale building projects of the Flavian emperors did much to expand and develop the areas near the Forum Romanum. The construction of the monumental Colosseum to the east added a new focus to that district of the city, changing traffic circulation, pedestrian paths, and significantly altering the approach to the Forum Romanum. The development of the Templum Pacis and the Forum Transitorium nearly doubled the area of the imperial fora, and it is probable that Domitian had even greater aspirations given the fact that he began clearing the vast area to the northwest of the Forum Augustum the future site of the largest imperial forum: the Forum Traiani.[1]

This chapter and the next mark a culmination to this book's principal theme that the Temple of Jupiter Capitolinus had a more direct and significant influence on imperial temple architecture in Rome than has previously been recognized. In the case of the Temple of Divus Traianus, the majority of the reconstructions proposed by archaeologists since the 1890s suggest its design may have corresponded in size to the Temple of Jupiter Capitolinus as reconstructed in this study. In nearly every case, the Temple of Divus Traianus is shown with a pronaos width of 34 to 36 meters, virtually identical to that of the Capitoline Temple and, likewise, similar in dimension to the Temple of Mars and the Templum Pacis. It is likely that Trajan instructed his architect to base his design at least in part on the precedent of the Capitoline Temple, especially in its general plan, the width of its podium, and the use of the Corinthian Order.

Trajan in Dacia

Marcus Ulpius Traianus was adopted as Nerva's son in a formal ceremony in the Temple of Jupiter Capitolinus in A.D. 91.[2] When Nerva died in A.D. 98, Trajan (Fig. 131) was leading a military campaign in Dacia, in the Empire's northeastern frontier between the Danube and the Rhine. It was an area in which he would spend much of his career, returning again to do battle in A.D. 101 and 104.[3] During his final campaign, his military architect, Apollodorus of Damascus, built a daring bridge across the Danube by which he could move troops and huge amounts of supplies.[4] Trajan claimed victory the following year when the Dacian ruler Decebalus took his own life and his troops surrendered. The victory resulted in the annexation of Dacia as a Roman province, which Trajan settled with citizens from other parts of the Empire in dozens of newly established colonial towns.[5]

When he returned to Rome in A.D. 107, heavily laden with war booty, Trajan made a triumphal entry and initiated a series of celebrations, including games that lasted four months. As many as 11,000 animals and 5,000 gladiators, many of them captured Dacian soldiers, were reportedly killed in the Colosseum.[6] In A.D. 109, he inaugurated a naumachia for mock sea battles. For six days, pairs of gladiators battled each other on boats, a protracted event that effectively completed the celebrations for his conquest of Dacia.[7]

During the years of peace that followed, Trajan used the spoils of war to embellish Rome and several provincial cities with a series of public works. He developed a strong reputation as a restorer of Rome's

131. Portrait bust of Trajan, Villa Albani, Rome. Photo: Deutsches Archäologisches Institut, Rome, 1937.1519,

public buildings, as well as a builder of new ones, many of them designed by Apollodorus. He initiated numerous construction projects, both as a way of self-aggrandizement and for the practical purpose of rebuilding parts of the city that had been destroyed by fires in A.D. 64 and 80. While the Flavian emperors had done much to reconstruct Rome and many of its public monuments and religious shrines, much work remained to be done.[8]

Among the building projects Trajan initiated or completed, including several that were started by Domitian, were his imperial forum and market complex, improvements to the riverfront, the building of drainage channels to prevent flooding, and improvements of the harbor facilities at the Forum Boarium and downstream at the Porticus Aemelia. He also built a large bath complex on the Esquiline Hill overlooking the Colosseum, modeling its plan after earlier, smaller bath complexes of Titus and Agrippa. Finally, he carried out restoration projects for the Colosseum, the Circus Maximus, and the Temple of Venus Genetrix in the Forum Julium.[9]

Building the Forum Traiani

The Forum Traiani, with its Basilica Ulpia, commemorative column, libraries, and temple dedicated to the deified Trajan, was begun by Trajan in A.D. 106–107 and completed by Hadrian in A.D. 128. Both emperors should be rightly credited for their involvement in the project, although Trajan's architect, Apollodorus of Damascus, was probably responsible for the complete design. The forum complex (Fig. 132) was located north of the Forum Julium and northwest of the Forum Augustum. It extended northwestward in the direction of the Campus Martius between the Capitoline and Quirinal Hills. It was a vast, irregular area that was enlarged even more by cutting back the slopes of the two hills.[10]

Overshadowed today by the Monument to Victor Emmanuel II, the site lies some 15 feet below the Via Fori Imperiali, which traverses its southern half. Rows of granite columns from the Basilica Ulpia mark the location of its great nave and side aisles. The well-preserved Column of Trajan is the most visible sign of the forum's original monumentality. The pavement and steps of the forum's north portico, with a large hemicycle extending behind it, lines the edge of a second archaeological zone that includes Trajan's Markets. The eastern half of the forum space was recently excavated, although extensive remains of the foundations of medieval apartment buildings were left in place to allow for a broad-based historical interpretation.

The earliest work on the site was done before Trajan, probably by Domitian, who began clearing it with ambitious plans to complement the Templum Pacis and the Forum Transitorium with a third Flavian monument. His project of clearing and leveling the area would have been started in the early A.D. 90s but it was abandoned after his death in A.D. 96.[11] Trajan began his work on the complex in A.D. 106–107, and he held a dedication ceremony in A.D. 112.[12] His initial six-year building campaign resulted in the construction of the forum and its colonnades, the basilica, and the

132. Rome, aerial view of imperial fora with Forum Traiani in the foreground, A.D. 106/07–128. Museo Civico, EUR. Photo: Deutsches Archäologisches Institut, Rome, 73.1088.

two libraries.[13] The Column of Trajan was begun in A.D. 107–108 and dedicated in A.D. 113.[14] The temple, probably begun early in Hadrian's reign, possibly in A.D. 118, was finished in A.D. 128.[15]

The principal designer of the complex, Apollodorus of Damascus, was Trajan's chief architect and military advisor. He distinguished himself as an engineer and bridge builder during the Dacian wars with his design and construction of the bridge over the Danube. Extending an unprecedented 1,135 meters long, it is shown in one of the reliefs of Trajan's Column as a wooden structure on masonry piers.[16] In Rome, Apollodorus built, in addition to the Forum Traiani, the Baths of Trajan, an odeum, and probably Trajan's Markets.[17]

The Forum Traiani was sanctioned by the Roman Senate as a commemoration of Trajan's victories over Dacia in A.D. 98, 101, and 104.[18] It also had the practical purpose, as had been the case with the fora of Julius Caesar, Augustus, and the Flavians, to provide more open space in the center of the city to serve the needs of the Romans for public administration and judicial activities.[19] It was the most formal example yet in Rome of the Greek-inspired agora, where commercial and financial business, political events, and trials could be transacted in the open air or in the adjacent basilica.[20]

As seen in its sculpted reliefs, it also had an important propagandistic function related to Trajan's military success. The commemoration of Trajan's victories in the Dacian wars was the first and foremost symbolic role in his projects for Rome's urban development. Statues of captured Dacians, an equestrian statue of the emperor and the sculpted reliefs of Trajan's Column,

both its base and its shaft, represent vivid images of Trajan's military campaign, the battles, and the defeated enemies.[21]

In terms of its architectural form and stylistic details, it was meant to symbolize the idea of continuity in the Empire. Its grandeur and magnificent scale were meant to be understood as a newly achieved perfection in imperial architecture and political symbolism.[22] Through its decoration and iconographic program, it had the ultimate function of serving as a means of propaganda for the emperor. It was a way of glorifying his reign and of establishing his authority as emperor.[23]

Apollodorus of Damascus was perhaps influenced by the earlier vision of Domitian, the forum serving urbanistically to unify the design of the previous imperial fora, a final climax in the series.[24] The plan of its principal space was essentially a mirror image of the Templum Pacis on the opposite side of the Forum Augustum and the Forum Transitorium. It had similar dimensions, a similar colonnaded enclosure, and similar statuary and trees.[25]

The complex was laid out symmetrically with a progression of buildings and spaces totaling 310 meters in length.[26] Today, Trajan's Column is the best-preserved monument in the complex, and much of the Basilica Ulpia has been excavated, with several of its granite columns reerected. The forum colonnades and the libraries have been documented through several decades of archaeological work, and the foundations of one of the colonnades are largely visible. In contrast, little physical evidence has been found of the Temple of Divus Traianus, and none has been located of the triumphal arch. Both were represented on coins from the period of Trajan's reign, but archaeologists still debate their location and exact form.[27]

The Forum

The main forum space was 118 meters long and 89 meters wide (400 by 300 Roman feet).[28] It was framed on its two long sides by colonnades with covered passages 12 meters wide. The columns were composed of pavonazzetto, with white marble Corinthian capitals and bases. The attic zone, reminiscent of the Forum Augustum, included a marble statue of a Dacian soldier above each column, standing on a pedestal and supporting a cornice. The panels between were ornamented with carved heads of historical figures set within circular frames.[29]

Details of the architectural decoration were, in general, more closely related to those found in the Forum Augustum than to any buildings of the Flavians. One scholar suggests the Forum Traiani represented an "Augustan Revival" based on the manner of detailing the architraves, fasciae, and cornices. For instance, the elaborate anthemia in acanthus foliage typical of Flavian architraves was abandoned in favor of a more severe cymation; a bead-and-reel motif rather than a cymation was used to divide the first and second fasciae; and a recessed bar was used to connect the dentils of the cornice rather than the arch-and-rings motif characteristic of the Flavians.[30] This return by Trajan's architects to the more severe style of Augustus produced some of the most refined architecture in the history of the Empire.

A crossing axis in the forum's plan was marked by two large hemicycles that extended out from the back wall of each passage. They were entered through a screen of square piers that was aligned with the back wall of the passages. These hemicycles, similar to those in the Forum Augustum, were taller than the adjoining passage walls. They were presumably roofed, and their walls were lined with niches to hold statues of important figures in the family line of Trajan and in the history of Rome.[31] The niches had white marble frames and entablatures with modillions and cornices. The main axis of each hemicycle was marked by a rectangular recess framed by grey granite columns and topped by a small barrel vault. Presumably they both contained a colossal statue.

The forum space itself was paved with blocks of white marble set in parallel rows. Its broad expanse was interrupted by four avenues of trees that ran in parallel rows in line with two side porches of the basilica.[32] A bronze statue of Trajan mounted on a horse stood prominently in the forum.[33] It was not located on the crossing axis of the exedrae as long supposed, but nearer the forum's southeast wall.[34]

Most reconstructions of the forum complex indicate the southeast wall as a high enclosing wall lined with freestanding columns on the forum side similar to those of the Templum Pacis. Scholars have long believed there was a triumphal arch entrance in the center, on the forum's main axis, and that there were two

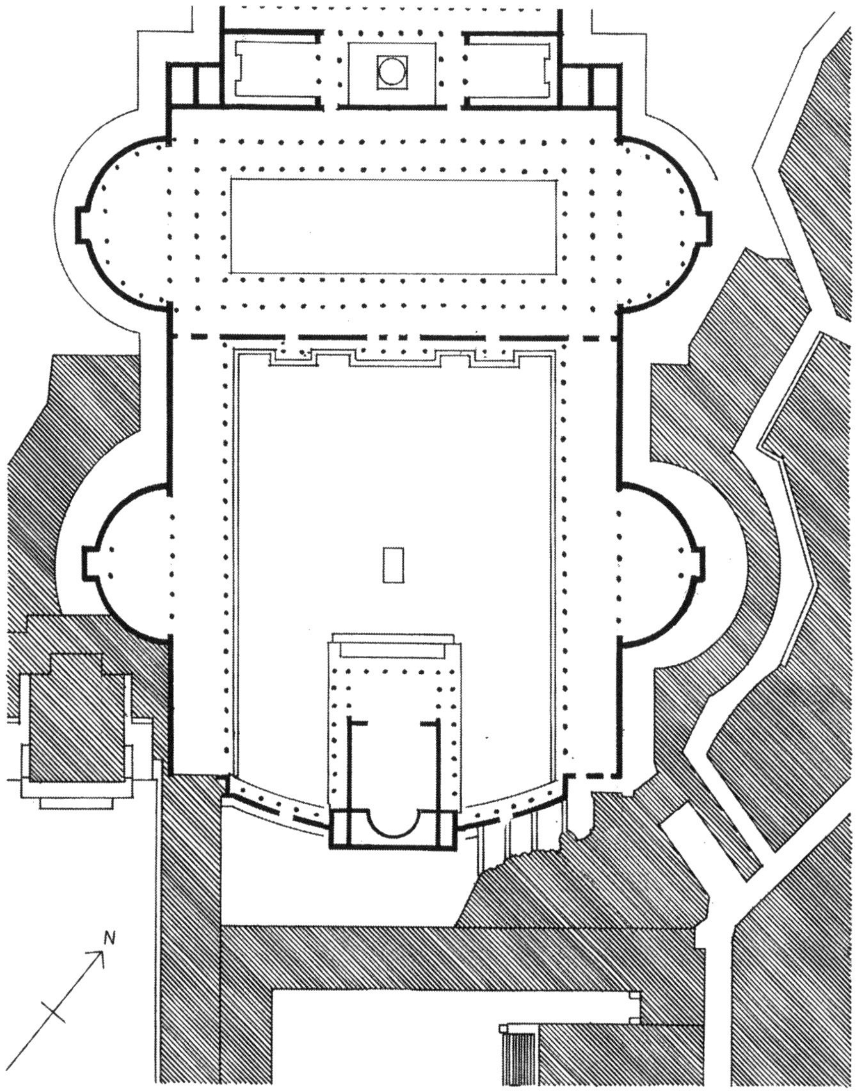

133. Forum Traiani, proposed plan with Temple of Divus Traianus at southeast end of the forum. Drawing: John W. Stamper based on Roberto Meneghini in *RömMitt* 105 (1998), p. 145, pl. 14.

smaller entrance gates on either side, marking two secondary axes.[35] However, in the 1990s, a challenge to this hypothesis was made by Italian archaeologists who proposed that the forum's southeast end was enclosed not by a triumphal arch but was instead the location of the Temple of Divus Traianus (Fig. 133). According to this hypothesis, the temple's pronaos would have faced across the space to the basilica, and its back wall would have stood against the forum's southeastern enclosing wall. This reconstruction would have represented a more direct link to the Forum Augustum as a precedent given the relationship between the temple and the flanking colonnades with their hemicycles.[36] It also would have followed a long line of tripartite forum complexes found in other Roman cities in which a basilica and a temple were placed at opposite ends of the forum space.[37] Finally, it would have resolved the problem inherent in previous reconstructions of the unusually cramped space between the temple and Trajan's Column.[38]

Curiously, excavations carried out in 1998–2000 did not reveal evidence of either a triumphal arch or the Temple of Divus Traianus. Instead, they suggest the presence of a square vestibule space outside the enclosure wall, connecting it to the northwest wall of the Forum Augustum (Fig. 134). This vestibule contained a colonnade on three sides and a wall with a niche on the fourth.[39] On the forum side, there may have been something like a temple front in the center, with eight columns supporting a pediment.[40] Even these latest

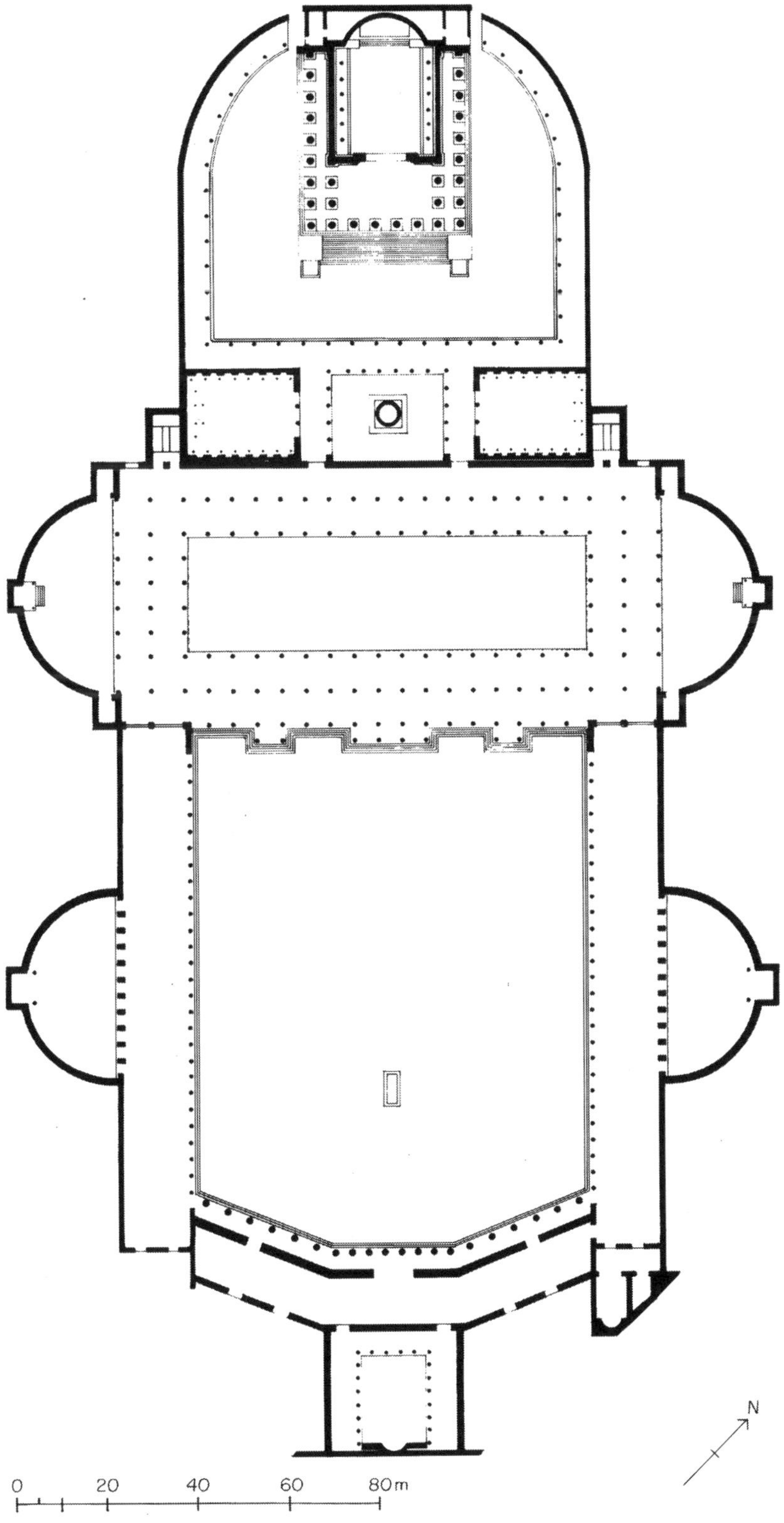

134. Forum Traiani, proposed plan with Temple of Divus Traianus at northwest end of complex. Drawing: John W. Stamper based on Studio Groma in James Packer, *The Forum of Trajan in Rome* (1996), vol. 1, p. 262, pl. 149; and Silvana Rizzo in *Crypta Balbi – Fori Imperiale: Archeologia urbana a Roma e interventi di restauro nell'anno del Grande Giubileo* (2000), pl. 62.

135. Rome, Forum Traiani, archaeological remains of Basilica Ulpia. Photo: Istituto Centrale per il Catalogo e la Documentazione, E.41211.

interpretations remain open to debate, leaving the issue of the forum's southeast enclosure unresolved, not to mention the question of what would have been the actual location of the temple and the Trajanic arch whose presence is indicated by their repeated images on coins from Trajan's reign.[41]

Basilica Ulpia

The forum's northwest end was defined by the Basilica Ulpia (Fig. 135), which Trajan used to receive visiting dignitaries and preside over trials and ceremonies. Set perpendicular to the forum's main axis, it completely closed off the forum's northwest end and provided a noble backdrop for the forum's imperial activities. The inspiration for designing the forum with a focus on a basilica rather than a temple may have come from the tradition of planning for military camps, many of which at the time of Trajan had a basilica closing off one side of a large open area.[42] Typically, behind the basilica there were rooms for storage of military archives, and between these was the sanctuary for the legion's standards and an image of the emperor. It is possible that Apollodorus of Damascus, with his background in military architecture, may have wanted to commemorate Trajan's military glory by evoking such associations in the forum's plan.[43] The military camp and the Roman forum were thus synthesized into a new plan type. The focus on the basilica combined with the portico enclosures created a forum space that both incorporated and transcended the urban typology of the imperial Roman forum.

The basilica was a five-aisled structure, measuring 117.50 meters long by 58.80 meters wide (400 by 200 Roman feet).[44] Its central nave measured 24.97

by 88.14 meters (85 by 300 Roman feet).[45] At its ends were large apses approximately the same size as the exedrae behind the forum colonnades.[46] The interior columns, some of which are visible today, had unfluted shafts of Egyptian granite and marble Corinthian capitals.[47]

Reconstruction drawings have long suggested that the Basilica Ulpia was a walled structure with a central entrance porch and two flanking porches facing southwest onto the forum.[48] A recent study has proposed that its forum façade was defined not by a wall but by a row of columns.[49] This is how it appears in representations on coins, and fragments of the columns found on the site support the presence of a colonnade rather than a wall.[50] If this were the case, it would have been more directly open to the forum in a manner similar to the earlier Basilica Julia in the Forum Romanum.

The façade columns in the new reconstruction would have been composed of pavonazzetto shafts with marble Corinthian capitals and bases like those of the forum colonnades. The three porches had similar columns, but with shafts of giallo antico.[51] A continuous entablature above the façade columns and the porches was enriched by an elaborately decorated frieze with repeated florid S-spirals of acanthus with rosettes flanking a central vase and framed by winged cupids. Again, Dacian soldiers were located in the attic zone, one above each column, and supporting a second cornice.[52] Numismatic evidence suggests that a bronze quadriga carrying Trajan with a raised right arm stood on top of the central porch, while a biga, or two-horse chariot, was placed above each side porch.[53]

Most previous reconstructions of the basilica suggest its façade was three stories high, two floor levels plus a clerestory zone.[54] The same study that proposed it had a columnar façade argues it was only two stories high and that the second level was enclosed not by a wall but again by an open colonnade. This colonnade would have been set back from the main façade, enclosing only the space above the main nave.[55] These second-floor columns were Ionic with unfluted cipollino shafts.[56]

Evidence is strong for the open colonnade of the main façade and the second-level clerestory; however, there remain unresolved problems with this reconstruction because of a lack of lateral support, especially with the freestanding colonnades of the upper levels. In virtually every other colonnaded structure of the Roman world, colonnades were built in conjunction with a bearing wall standing within 10 to 15 meters. These bearing walls served to stabilize the colonnades through their connection to the roof structure. Typically, these walls were composed of tufa blocks in *opus quadratum* and were strong enough to withstand lateral forces, both for themselves and for the colonnades to which they were linked. The two worked together as a structural unit and could resist moderate earthquake forces. All of the porticos in the imperial fora, for instance, worked precisely in this way.

A grand and noble building, the Basilica Ulpia was the centerpiece of the forum and of Trajan's building program in general. It was the largest single structure in the complex, the most lavishly decorated, and the most directly linked to the day-to-day projection of the emperor's authority and power. The place where he regularly sat in state, receiving delegations or presiding over a court, it was, with all its splendor, the appropriate imperial setting for Rome's leading citizen.

Trajan's Column

Trajan's Column, standing immediately behind the basilica, was the most overt symbol of the emperor's military genius. It was the first such column to employ a continuous narrative frieze that winds around its shaft and depicts the trials and victories of the Dacian wars.[57] According to a dedicatory inscription on its base, it was erected by the Senate and the people of Rome to honor Trajan and his career as emperor and military leader.[58] It was thought that it had the secondary purpose of showing how high the portion of the Esquiline Hill had been before it was excavated for the forum's construction, but this legend was unlikely the case.[59] As an honorific architectural object, the column was a synthesis of various traditions: the freestanding column like several others erected in the Forum Romanum, the stair tower or belvedere like the lighthouse of Alexandria, and the obelisk, the history of which is also linked to ancient Egypt.[60]

The column's pedestal contains a vestibule that gives access to a small L-shaped suite of rooms and the landing of a spiral staircase that rises to the

summit, where a visitor had an excellent view of ancient Rome.[61] One of the pedestal rooms contained Trajan's ashes, which were deposited here after his death in A.D. 117.[62] Ancient writings refer to his ashes being contained in a golden cinerary urn and deposited in the forum "under the column."[63] One of the pedestal rooms may have also housed select spoils from the war in Dacia, especially because the entire exterior of the pedestal was decorated in carved relief with Dacian arms and armor, garlands held by eagles, and a giant victor's laurel wreath in the form of a torus base for the column.[64]

The column stood 44.07 meters high (150 Roman feet) to the top of the bronze statue of Trajan. It was made of twenty-nine blocks of Lunense marble, which were roughly cut in the quarry and erected on the site ready for the finished carving.[65] The column shaft itself rises 29.60 meters (100 Roman feet), from the torus to the top of the capital, which serves as a balcony with a railing.[66] The capital is of the Tuscan-Doric Order: a square abacus, with the echinus below ornamented with egg-and-dart, the astragal, with bead-and-reel. Above the capital is a cylindrical block capped with a segmental sphere that originally supported the statue of Trajan, who was depicted with a spear in one hand and a globe in the other.[67] (The existing statue of Saint Peter was installed on the order of Pope Sixtus V in 1587.[68])

The reliefs carved on the shaft emphasized the dominant role of the emperor.[69] As imperial military propaganda, they manifested the desired official image of the emperor relative to the military, the Senate, and the people.[70] Throughout, the emperor is shown with great frequency, and always in a position of dominance. It would appear from the reliefs that Trajan oversaw practically every aspect of the military campaign, supervising the beginning and the final victory of each battle, reviewing the day-to-day activities of the troops, as well as negotiating with foreign envoys and receiving leaders of the defeated enemies, carrying out religious sacrifices, and meeting with local community leaders.[71] In each case, he is presented either in full military uniform or in a short tunic and is always accompanied by senior officers of his army. The general theme is the portrayal of the emperor laboring with his soldiers to protect, preserve, and enhance the civilized life of the Empire.[72]

The column was surrounded on three sides by a peristyle with Corinthian columns supporting an entablature and a coffered timber ceiling. The frieze was embellished on its outside face with griffons and candelabra and on its inside face with sphinxes and candelabra. Archaeological evidence suggests the peristyle went through two building phases. In the first, the northwest side was composed of eight columns and an enclosing wall with a door on the main axis. Shortly after its construction, it was altered by the removal of both the columns and the wall to open onto the temenos of the Temple of Divus Traianus.[73]

Flanking the column and peristyle on either side were two library buildings, one for Greek collections, the other for Roman collections. Each was a rectangular hall measuring 20.10 meters wide by 27.10 meters long, with a balcony level and a vaulted roof structure. The walls contained niches on both levels for storing books and scrolls.[74]

Temple of Divus Traianus

The Temple of Divus Traianus may have been planned by Apollodorus of Damascus, but its construction was largely the responsibility of Hadrian.[75] Inscriptions indicate that it was a family shrine, dedicated jointly to Trajan and to his wife Plotina, who died in A.D. 123 and was also given divine honors.[76] The *Historia Augusta* indicates that this is the only temple on which Hadrian included his own name.[77]

After the results of the excavations in the forum in 1998–2000, it must be assumed, as previously believed, that the temple was, in fact, located in a secondary forum of its own, northwest of Trajan's Column.[78] Colonnades flanking the space on the southwest and northeast sides curved inward toward the cella of the temple.[79] Coin images indicate the temple was on a tall podium similar to that of the Temple of Mars Ultor.[80] Archaeological evidence suggests it would have been 4.37 meters high.[81]

Fragments of the temple's granite column shafts have been found.[82] One of the shafts and a capital are lying near the base of Trajan's Column, a few yards from the temple's presumed site.[83] This shaft measured 14.80 meters high and was 17.70 meters (60 Roman feet) with its marble Corinthian capitals and bases. Its

lower diameter was 1.858 meters.[84] This corresponds to those of the Temple of Mars Ultor and to the final version of the Temple of Jupiter Capitolinus. In plan, the temple probably had eight columns across the front and was pseudodipteral. The width of the façade was about 36 meters (124 Roman feet), slightly larger than the temples of Mars Ultor and Jupiter Capitolinus, but certainly within close approximation.[85]

Inside the cella there were two superimposed rows of columns that divided the space into a nave and two narrow side aisles. It can be assumed the interior walls were faced with exotic marbles, highly refined decoration similar to the temples of Concordia and Vespasian. As with the Temple of Mars Ultor, there was an apse at the back to hold the cult statue, depicting Trajan.[86] Images on coins depict the statue between the two center façade columns. His right arm is raised, and his left rests in his lap. His upper torso is bare, while his waist and legs are draped. His right hand may have held a sceptre, his left a winged victory statue.[87]

The temple's architrave had three fasciae, like that of the Temple of Mars Ultor, and the frieze would have included carved figures. Images on coins show, in addition to the seated figure in the central bay, a seated central figure in the pediment, flanked by two reclining river gods, possibly the Danube and the Tigris or the Euphrates. The pediment's apex was surmounted by a standing figure, and its corners were adorned with winged victories.[88] Based on comparisons with the Temple of Mars Ultor, the statues in the pronaos, the pediment, and on top of the pediment were probably all of Trajan.[89]

The influence of the Forum Augustum was pervasive throughout Trajan's giant forum complex. The Augustan revival Apollodorus of Damascus pursued was manifest in planning details, the forum's colonnades with their attic zones and rear hemicycles and in the design of the architraves, fasciae, and cornices. This Augustan revival marked a distinct break with the florid decoration of the Flavians, and it went on to influence the early architectural projects of Hadrian, especially the Pantheon.[90]

The Forum and the Emperor's Authority

Multiple images of the emperor confronted the visitor in every part of the forum complex: chariot groups over the three entrances to the basilica, an equestrian statue in the middle of the forum space, statues on the pedestals of the colonnade and basilica attic zones, the reliefs that spiraled around the Column of Trajan, and the pediment of the temple. In all of these, Trajan was portrayed as an omnipotent victor. In the hemicycles and tribunals of the basilica he was the wise administrator and *pontifex maximus*, in the reliefs of the column the victorious general, in the statue on the top the deceased hero, and inside the temple the deified god. The entire forum was meant to represent a biography in stone that successfully revealed the various stages in the emperor's life as he progressed from mortality to deification.[91]

There has to be a certain degree of consensus for a governmental entity to retain its authority. For an emperor like Trajan to remain in power, there had to be a degree of consensus among those participating in each process of interaction and within the society as a whole. For the mutually beneficial and successful interaction between the emperor and the inhabitants of Rome and the Empire, it was necessary to have some mutual understanding and agreement, whether tacit or implicit. While a certain amount of coercion was necessary at times, no emperor could maintain an unpopular regime through force for very long. The necessary mutual understanding and agreement in Roman society was the manifestation of the common possession of and attachment to buildings and places like the Forum Traiani and the ceremonies that occurred in them, which served as both symbols of authority and cosmic belief. The symbols that regulate a particular interaction of people in communication with each other are part of a wider cosmos of symbols which many persons share in that society to varying degrees and in various situations of interaction.[92]

The kind of ceremonies that took place in the forum projected certain correct or authoritative notions of what was important and beneficial to the interests of the Empire. Such ceremonies and rituals were in essence stereotyped, symbolically concentrated expressions of beliefs and sentiments regarding ultimate realities. An elaborate etiquette had much in common with ritual in its rigidly stereotyped structure, in its specification of actions, and in its symbolization of differing appreciation of the charismatic qualities embodied in great authority, power, and eminence. However, etiquette was at the periphery of

the relation to sacred things, whereas ritual was at the center.[93]

Remaining first and foremost a military leader, Trajan embarked on yet another military campaign in A.D. 113 in Parthia (present-day Armenia). In the midst of battle, he had to deal with a rebellion in Palestine, which spread to Cyprus, Cyrene, and Egypt. After thousands of Romans living in these regions were killed, the survivors retaliated with massacres of their own.[94] The insurrections were eventually brought under control by Trajan's troops, but in A.D. 117 the emperor became seriously ill and began a retreat to Italy.[95] Cassius Dio reports that

> the people in Rome were preparing for him a triumphal arch besides many other tributes in his own forum and were getting ready to go forth an unusual distance to meet him on his return. But he was destined never to reach Rome again nor to accomplish anything comparable to his previous exploits, and furthermore to lose even those earlier acquisitions.[96]

His ship took him as far as Cilicia, on the coast of present-day Turkey, where he died in August of A.D. 117. The Senate granted him a triumphal celebration after his death, and when he was deified, he retained the title Parthicus, which he had given himself in battle.[97]

As a builder, Trajan left a significant legacy of imperial architecture in Rome. His forum, with its basilica, commemorative column, libraries, and temple, along with Trajan's Markets, the Baths of Trajan, improvements to the riverfront, and countless projects for reconstructing existing buildings, all helped further the transformation of the city that had been so impressively started by the Flavians. Hadrian would continue the record of large imperial projects, although he would not add directly to the five imperial fora north of the Forum Romanum. He would concentrate his efforts instead in the Campus Martius and on the east end of the Forum Romanum with his construction of two of the greatest monuments of the second century A.D. after the Forum Traiani: the Pantheon and the Temple of Venus and Rome.

11

HADRIAN'S PANTHEON

The Pantheon stands today in the heart of Rome, the best-preserved and most revered ancient building in the city. It is visited by thousands of tourists a year, is the site of weekly Catholic masses and countless concerts and recitals, and houses the tombs of Italian monarchs and artists alike. Walking into its rotunda space, whether for the first time or the hundredth, the experience is truly awe-inspiring. The richness of its materials, perfection of its proportions, refinement of its orders, and the vastness of its space all combine to form one of the most significant works of architecture in the history of the Roman world.

Although the Pantheon itself has survived over 1,800 years, its urban setting has changed dramatically. The street and piazza level around it has been raised 10 to 15 feet, medieval and Renaissance buildings have been constructed over half of its original forum space, and the ancient buildings that once framed it on the east, south, and west have all but disappeared. It is no longer used by emperors, dignitaries, and pagan priests; rather, it is filled with admirers from the modern world who cannot help but marvel at its architectural and structural brilliance.

Like other temples before it, the Pantheon had significant links to earlier precedents, including the Temple of Jupiter Capitolinus and the Temple of Mars Ultor. At the same time, it transcended these influences to a greater extent than we have previously seen, its architect achieving a new synthesis of innovation within the classical language and a redefinition of the temple as a building type. Rather than a temple dedicated to a single cult, or even two or three, it was a sanctuary of all the Roman gods, directly indicative of the Greek origin of its name, *Pantheia*.[1]

In architectural terms, the Pantheon combines the traditional temple pronaos with a cella that was circular in plan and topped by a great hemispherical dome. Its symbolic connotations were both religious and political, for as with previous emperors, there was a significant political side to Hadrian's all-encompassing religious devotion. The sphere, the most perfect geometric figure, represented both the unity and the universal character of the religious and political life of the Roman Empire. Hadrian's far-reaching interests led him to embrace both a Hellenic identity based on the city of Athens and the cult of Zeus and the Latin culture focused on Rome and the Capitoline triad Jupiter, Juno, and Minerva. The Pantheon served as a unique manifestation of this religious and political synthesis across cultural borders, its architecture reflecting both tradition and innovation.

Hadrian: Emperor and God

Publius Aelius Hadrian was born in Rome in A.D. 76 (Fig. 136). As a young man, he was placed under the guardianship of Trajan, who later appointed him to his first governmental post and gave him his first military command.[2] In A.D. 100, the relationship between the two men was further sealed when Hadrian married the emperor's grand-niece Sabina.[3] Hadrian held a number of government posts, including quaestor, tribune, and praetor, and he also served with Trajan in two of his military campaigns in Dacia. From A.D. 107 until 117 he served in military and governmental positions in Greece and the Middle East.[4] Hadrian was serving as governor of Antioch in A.D. 117 when he was informed

136. Portrait bust of Hadrian, Uffizi, Florence. Photo: Deutsches Archäologisches Institut, Rome, 1937.713.

of Trajan's death and of his official adoption as the emperor's son.[5]

Hadrian arrived in Rome in July of A.D. 118, eleven months after his elevation to emperor. He requested divine honors for Trajan, but in contrast to his adoptive father, he refused a triumph the Senate offered him and declined all other honors they attempted to bestow on him. He made it clear that the triumph over Dacia should be granted to Trajan, and thus refused to indulge in the kind of victory celebrations his father had initiated.[6] Deference to his predecessors would mark Hadrian's rule until the end. Whether it was out of genuine self-effacement or as a subtle way of tying his legitimacy and his authority to the memory of those who came before him, he made a great effort to honor others besides himself.

Throughout his reign, Hadrian traveled extensively, taking lengthy journeys from province to province, visiting cities, towns, and countryside. In the decade of the 120s A.D., he traveled on more than one occasion to Gaul, Britain, Spain, northern Africa, the Middle East, Asia Minor, and Greece.[7] He initiated building projects in nearly every major city he visited, although perhaps nowhere did he devote so much attention as Athens. There he started several building projects, including a library, gymnasium, a Temple of Hera, and the sanctuary of the Panhellenion, which served to strengthen the political and cultural union of the scattered city-states of Greece.[8] Perhaps even more significant was his completion in A.D. 131–132 of the Temple of Olympian Zeus, which had been left unfinished and partly dismantled.[9] After more travel in the Middle East, he returned to Rome in A.D. 134 where he spent most of his remaining time divided between the city and his villa at Tivoli.[10]

In all of his travels, Hadrian was accompanied by an extensive retinue of architects, engineers, draftsmen, and builders who surveyed, documented and proposed designs for new buildings, bridges, aqueducts, harbors, and roads. Wherever he went, the frontiers were studied, defenses improved, legions exercised, and client kings and rulers consulted.[11] New cities bearing his name were constructed, and temples to the gods were built or restored.[12] New priesthoods and endowments were granted and cults, both current and past, flourished again, as they had done under Augustus.

As in the period of Julius Caesar and Augustus, many in the East responded to the Roman emperor as a god arrived on earth, giving him extravagant titles such as "savior, protector, nourisher of Hellas."[13] In A.D. 129, he accepted in the East the title of Olympios and propagated his cult, not only through the completion of the Temple of Olympian Zeus, but also through the consecration of dozens of altars and other temples.[14] By the end of his reign, at least ninety altars had been dedicated to him as Zeus Olympios in Asia Minor alone. He was honored throughout the eastern half of the Empire in inscriptions, dedications, statues, temples, and festivals as the earthly representative of Zeus, a supreme and generous god.[15]

Hadrian kindled in his subjects an enthusiastic awareness of religious community, of devotion to the gods, and in Rome especially to Jupiter. The worship of Hadrian-Jupiter in Rome was the equivalent to the worship of Hadrian-Zeus in the East. Thus, an

essentially new divinity brought the whole empire, East and West, together at its religious apex, the Pantheon being its spiritual center.[16]

An analysis of Hadrian's most important temple project in Rome demonstrates an inventiveness within a strong classical tradition. The Pantheon's design was based on the use of the Corinthian Order, but there was much experimentation in the treatment of the columns, entablatures, and cornices just as there was in the shape of the plan. His architect, as had been the case with Rabirius and the Flavians, was especially creative in the formation of space – not just in terms of how one building related to another, but in the design of interior space. Experimentation within a traditional language was the norm in all of his architectural production, just as it was in his cultural and intellectual endeavors. He relied on precedents while at the same time looking to the future.

The Pantheon: Introduction

Built between A.D. 118 and 128, the Pantheon is one of the most unique buildings in the history of Roman architecture (Fig. 137).[17] It is one of the great architectural creations of all time: original, bold, and rich in associations and meaning.[18] Architecturally it was an innovative synthesis of several trends of the day. First was the creation of geometrically inventive interior space – in this case, the circle and the hemisphere. Second was the development of vaulted concrete construction, here, the largest concrete dome in history. Third was the innovation in the use of the classical vocabulary, taking the Corinthian Order to new levels of refinement and scale juxtaposition.[19] It was related to the precedent of the Temple of Jupiter Capitolinus as reconstructed in this study, both architecturally and symbolically. The width of its pronaos was 115 Roman feet, the same as the Temple of Jupiter Capitolinus, and the deity Jupiter Optimus Maximus was among those honored in its circular cella. It was a fitting culmination, a synthesis of influences, traditions, and beliefs about the gods and the role of the emperor.

Hadrian did not dedicate the building in his own name; rather, he included on the pediment frieze the inscription: "Marcus Agrippa, son of Lucius, made this in his third consulship."[20] This was a reference to the fact that his building replaced the earlier one on the site that had been constructed by Agrippa between 29 and 19 B.C.[21] Because of this inscription, however, it was long believed the existing building was Agrippa's original structure.[22] It was only in the nineteenth century, after an analysis of brick stamps in both the rotunda and the intermediate block, that it was proved the existing building was constructed in its entirety during the time of Hadrian.[23]

Recent excavations in the piazza in front of the Pantheon have proven that the earlier building on the site had the same northward orientation as the present structure and that they had a similar pronaos and cella, with only minor differences.[24] The pronaos of the Agrippan and the Domitianic buildings was wider by about 10 meters, and the rotunda was covered not by a concrete dome, but by a wooden roof structure, probably conical in shape.[25]

As discussed in Chapter 7, the original building of Agrippa was one of three civic and religious structures he erected in this area of the Campus Martius. All three were aligned on a north-south axis, with the Pantheon on the north, then the basilica of Neptune, and finally, the Baths of Agrippa, extending southward to the Largo Argentina.[26] Agrippa's Pantheon fronted onto a vast expanse of the Campus Martius that was being developed at the time by Augustus with buildings at its north and northeast edges: the Mausoleum of Augustus, the Ara Pacis, and the Horologium. The space between the Pantheon and the Mausoleum may have been lined with trees planted by Agrippa to form a formal royal park with the sightline connecting the two monuments. Such an urban plan would have served to link Augustus and the Pantheon of all the gods.[27]

It is probable that the original temple contained statues of the deified Julius, Mars, and Venus, the all-important deities of the *principate* of Augustus, as well as Jupiter, Juno, and Minerva.[28] Agrippa's construction of the original Pantheon was intended as a larger scheme for honoring Augustus and his reign as emperor. Agrippa at first wanted to name the building after Augustus and to place a statue of Augustus inside. When Augustus refused the honor, Agrippa changed his plan to include a statue of Julius Caesar inside while putting statues of himself and Augustus in niches at the back of the pronaos.[29]

137. Rome, Pantheon, A.D. 118–128. Photo: Deutsches Archäologisches Institute, Rome, 72.3098.

Agrippa's building stood until A.D. 80, when it was damaged in the fire of Titus. It was restored shortly afterward by Domitian.[30] During the reign of Trajan, it was struck by lightning and burned a second time. The reconstruction by Hadrian resulted in an entirely new building but on nearly the same plan as the original.[31]

Hadrian formalized a new forum space in front of the rebuilt temple, on its north side, by building two porticos and closing off the end with a monumental gate (Fig. 138). This space was as wide as the Forum Augustum, but it was at least twice its length, about 60 by 150 meters.[32] The porticos framing the space on either side were 4.6 to 6 meters deep and were raised on a platform 1.8 meters above the pavement of the forum itself. Their columns were smaller versions of those of the pronaos, with similar granite shafts and marble capitals and bases.[33] The portico on the west side separated the forum from the Baths of Nero, and that on the east adjoined the Saepta Julia, a large enclosed voting space that had been built by Julius Caesar (Fig. 139). In the middle of the forum space, on axis with the Pantheon's front door, was the Arcus Pietatis, a structure that resembled a triumphal arch with reliefs depicting the emperor as the country's generous benefactor.[34]

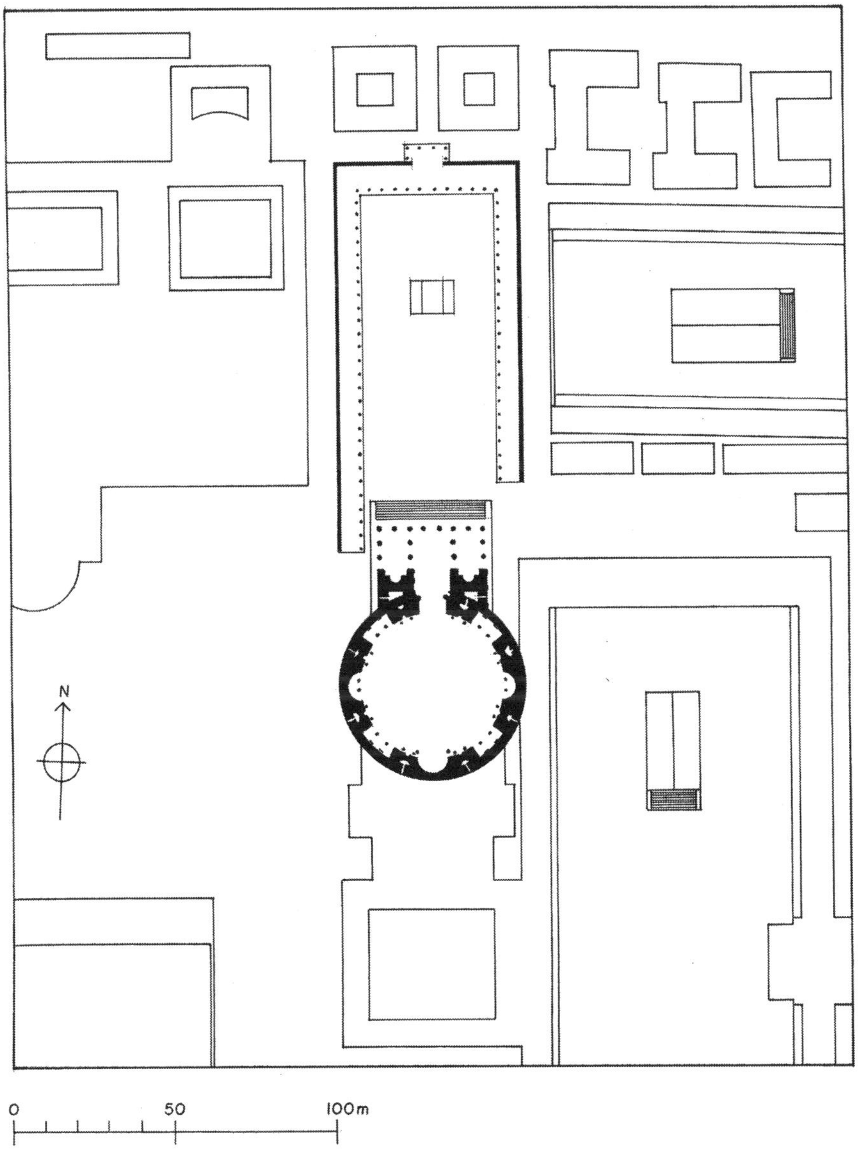

138. Pantheon, site plan with forum. Drawing: John W. Stamper based on Rodolfo Lanciani, *Forma Urbis Romae* (1990), pl. 15.

Hadrian's Pantheon is composed of three elements: the pronaos, an intermediate block, and the domed rotunda (Fig. 140). These elements were themselves derived from long-standing Roman building types but were here transformed into a new synthesis of plan and volumetric composition. The Corinthian pronaos and the intermediate block were based on the traditional Roman temple, with specific references to the Temple of Jupiter Capitolinus and the Temple of Mars Ultor. The circular cella was derived from buildings like the Round Temple by the Tiber, the octagonal hall in Nero's Domus Aurea, and the hemicycles behind the colonnades of the Fora of Augustus and Trajan.[35] These precedents were significant to the building's design; however, it was not directly imitative. Instead, the Pantheon represented innovation and creativity, each element being a significant transformation of its precedents, both in form and detail.

The Pronaos and Intermediate Block

As it was rebuilt by Hadrian, the pronaos is composed of eight columns across and three deep. Its width is 34.20 meters (115 Roman feet), nearly the same as the Temple of Mars Ultor and the Temple of Jupiter Capitolinus as reconstructed in this study. Its depth from the front row of columns to the wall of the intermediate

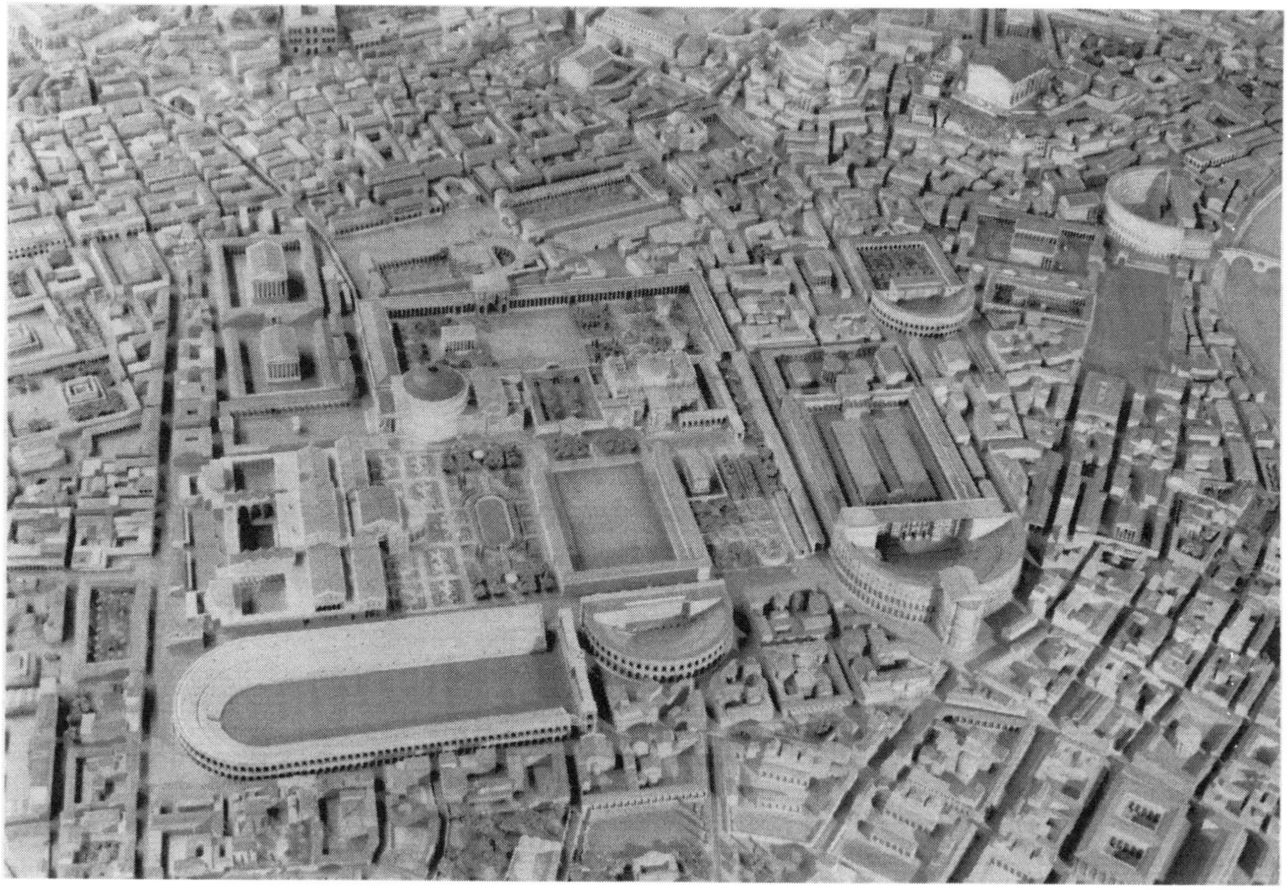

139. Aerial view of Campus Martius with Pantheon, Museo Civico, EUR. Photo: John W. Stamper.

block is 15.62 meters (53 Roman feet).[36] Compared with most Roman temples, the Pantheon's podium as it was built by Hadrian was relatively low, 1.32 meters, with seven steps across the front leading from the level of the forum to its summit. By comparison, the original podium of Agrippa's temple was about 2.45 meters high and required eleven steps.[37] Today it is impossible for a visitor to the Piazza della Rotonda to discern the podium's original height because the ground level has been built up over the centuries. It is actually lower than the level of the existing piazza, creating a completely distorted picture of the building's front elevation.

The podium extends forward as a terrace 4.6 meters beyond the line of columns. The stairs are framed at each end by extensions of the podium that presumably served as bases for statues. At the foot of the pedestals there are remains of rectangular fountains edged by low curbs.[38]

The temple's Corinthian columns are similar to those of the Temple of Mars Ultor, but their shafts are smooth-faced and monolithic rather than fluted, and made of several independent drums. Those along the front are grey granite from Mons Claudianus, and the rest are red granite from the Aswan quarries in Egypt. Their bases and capitals are white Pentelic marble.[39] The bases are composed of a square plinth and three tori, the middle one divided into two small convex moldings (Fig. 141), and the column shafts are 11.8 meters (about 40 Roman feet). The total height of the columns with their base and capital is 14.2 meters (48 Roman feet), a ratio of 6 to 5, as in the Temple of Mars Ultor.[40]

The architrave has a traditional three-step composition, and the plain frieze is separated from it by a *cyma reversa* with a fillet (Fig. 142). As was typical in the post-Augustan period, the lower two steps together are equal in height to the upper step and its molding.[41] Again, it is almost identical to that of the Temple of Mars Ultor, except more simplified, lacking the articulation of dentils or lesbian motifs.

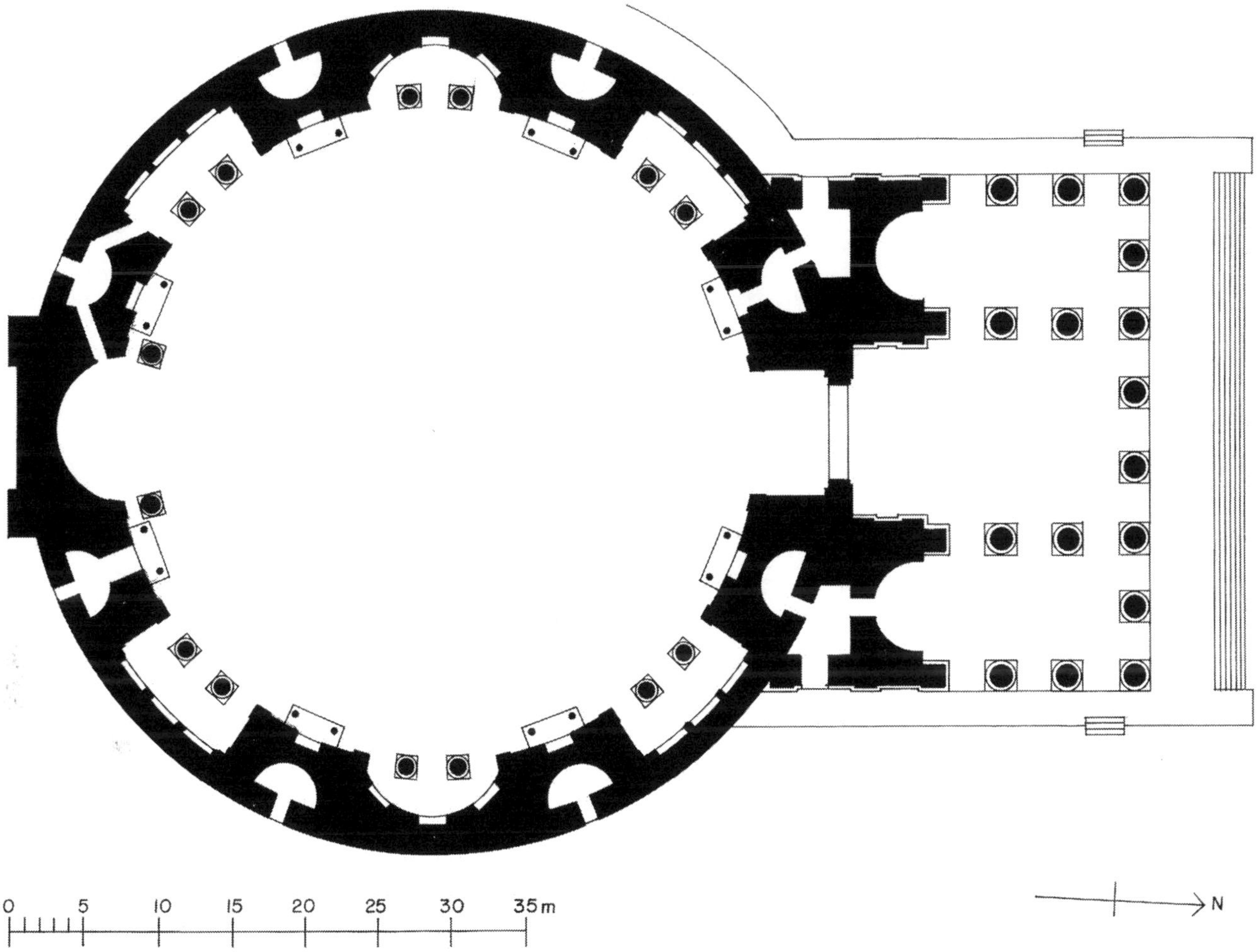

140. Pantheon, plan. Drawing: John W. Stamper based on Kjeld de Fine Licht, *The Rotunda in Rome* (1968), 91, fig. 98.

The cornice is composed of an egg-and-dart molding and volute consoles, and the underside of the corona is decorated with coffers and rosettes (Fig. 143). The Pantheon's architect experimented with optical corrections by slightly distorting the rosettes and slanting the front edge of the coffers outward. Such corrections, although slight and not easy to recognize, provide a more dynamic appearance to the cornice, and they relate to a similar treatment of the dome's coffers inside the rotunda. They show a sensitivity to the distinction between the actual shape of an object and the way it is perceived by the human eye.[42] This technique went back to the influence of Greek builders and the many optical refinements found in buildings such as the Parthenon in Athens.[43]

One aspect of the Pantheon's design diverged from the Temple of Mars Ultor and other predecessors, although this divergence was perhaps not intended. It may have been the result of a change in the original design. A recent study suggests the columns should have been taller and larger in diameter, 60 Roman feet high rather than 48.[44] There has been much criticism of the building over the years because of the awkward way in which the pronaos and intermediate block relate to the rotunda. Nothing lines up, as the pronaos cornice falls between two intermediate cornices of the rotunda.[45] It is arguable that good design practices would have required a more unified appearance with a consistent cornice height.

The building's architect may have originally intended to produce a more harmonious alignment of the building's horizontal components by employing columns that would have been taller and wider in diameter than those actually used (Fig. 144).[46] There may

141. Pantheon, right side of pronaos showing column base and portion of corner pilaster. Photo: John W. Stamper.

have been a sudden change in plans during construction, perhaps because of a lack of supply of the longer column shafts. Such monolithic columns were, after all, difficult to come by in second-century Rome. They had to be shipped across the Mediterranean, and sometimes such loads ended up at the bottom of the sea.[47]

If 60-foot columns had been used, like those of the Temple of Mars Ultor or the Temple of Divus Traianus, the increased height would have allowed for an alignment of the pronaos cornice with the intermediate cornice of the rotunda.[48] Also, the ratio between the columns' lower diameter and the dimension of their intercolumniations would have been more in keeping with the *pycnostyle* composition, as it appeared in the Temples of Mars Ultor, Castor and Pollux, Vespasian, and others. The spaces between the Pantheon's columns are an average of 3 meters ($10\frac{1}{4}$ Roman feet), and the column diameters are 1.5 meters (5 Roman feet), a ratio of about 2 to 1, which is wider than the usual ratio of 1.5 to 1 for *pycnostyle* temples.[49]

Not only is there the problem with the misaligned cornices and the divergence from the *pycnostyle*

142. Pantheon, right side of pronaos showing detail of entablature. Photo: John W. Stamper.

composition, there is also a problem with pilaster-faced piers attached to the pronaos' back wall and aligned with its columns. The side of these piers that face the pronaos niches are about a half a foot wider than the opposite sides. In contrast, the capitals of all three faces are the same size. The capital face over the wider side is thus aligned asymmetrically with the pilaster shaft, and there is a redundant strip of uncarved marble between it and the wall.[50] This suggests the pilasters, like the columns, were originally intended to be wider, but then their dimension was changed during construction.

To the well-trained eye, the columns look too slender and too far apart, the pediment too large and top-heavy. It is possible that Hadrian's architect was experimenting with a new look, but there are too many factors pointing to a change in the design during construction. The pediment appears ungainly not just because of the column spacing, but also because its raking cornices are set at a 23-degree angle. An average of 15 to 18 degrees was standard.[51] It was probably made taller in this instance to relate more effectively to the intermediate block behind it, and it had the added benefit of providing a larger area on which to put ornamentation.

It was recently discovered that the full-size templates for the Pantheon's pediment and pronaos entablature are inscribed in the travertine pavement in front of the Mausoleum of Augustus. These drawings, which can still be seen today, show the slope of the raking cornice, the consoles of both cornices, the height of the frieze, and the spacing of the columns, all of which correspond to the Pantheon as it was built. It is probable that the marble used to construct the Pantheon was unloaded from ships at a port adjacent to the Mausoleum, cut to size according to the template, and then carted to the construction site, some 800 meters away.[52]

This template corresponded to the Pantheon as it was constructed, and it also would have corresponded if taller columns had been used. The size of the

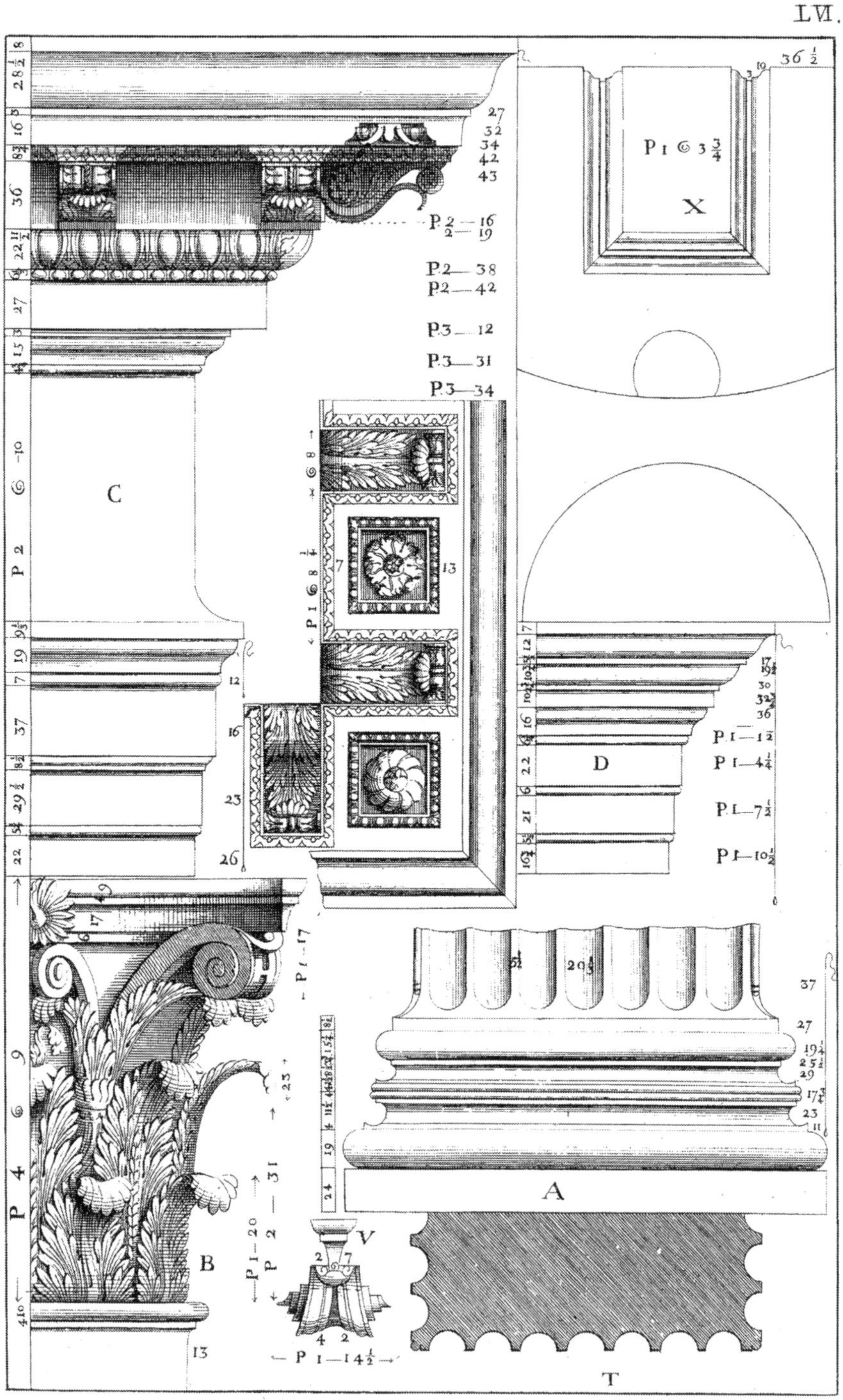

143. Pantheon, details of pronaos column and entablature. Illustration: Andrea Palladio, *The Four Books of Architecture* (1965), vol. 4, pl. 55. Courtesy of Dover Publications.

entablature and pediment would have remained the same, as would the columns' axial spacing. Because only the column centerline locations are indicated on the template, not their actual diameter, their size could easily have been altered at any moment during the construction. As further evidence for taller columns, the template of a single capital included at the Mausoleum site does not correspond to those used in the Pantheon, but is instead larger, corresponding to a column 60 Roman feet high rather than 48.[53]

The pediments of both the original Pantheon of Agrippa and that of Hadrian may have been ornamented with a giant eagle inside a wreath of oak leaves (Fig. 145). This referred to the fact that when Augustus

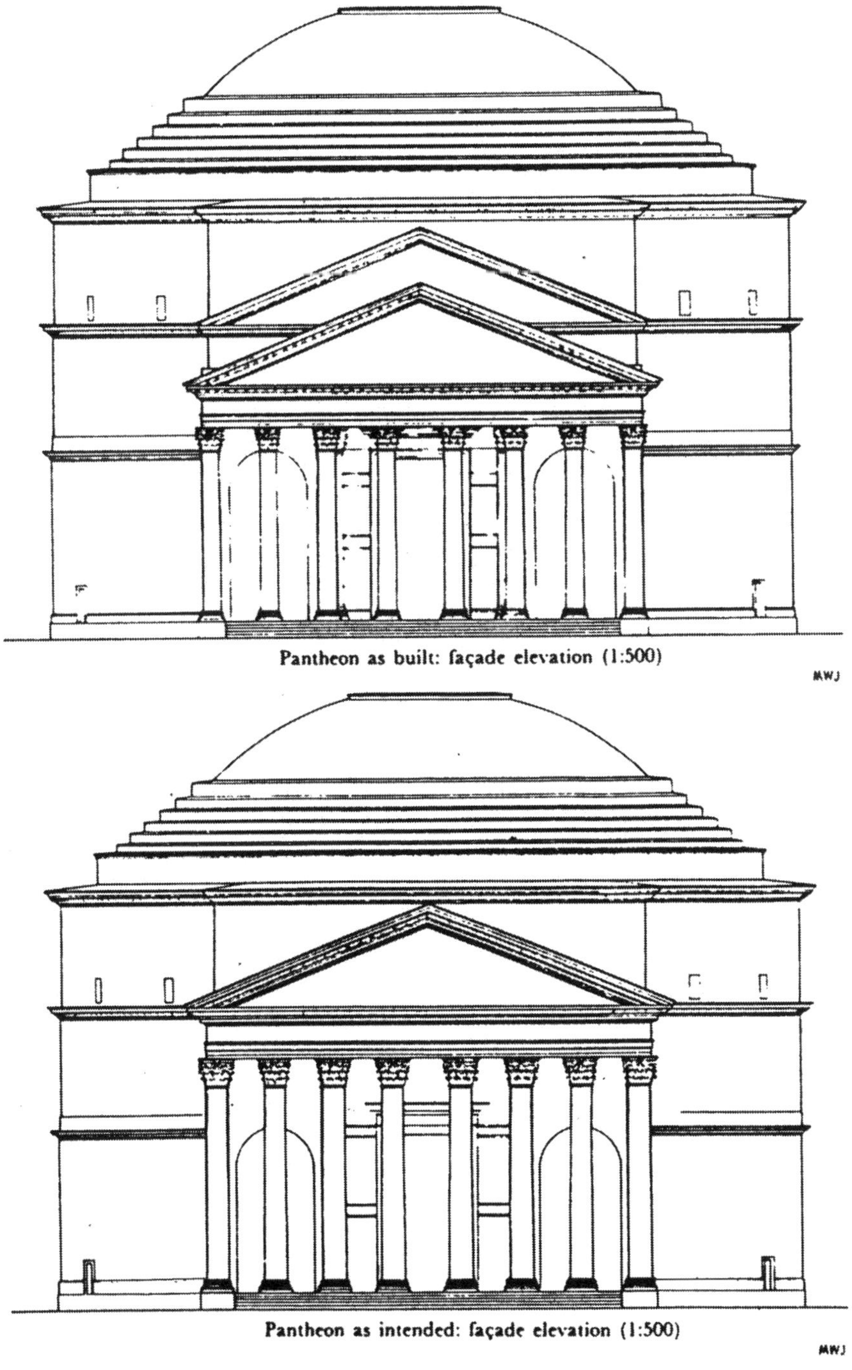

144. Pantheon, elevation as built (top); hypothetical elevation with taller columns (bottom). Drawing: Paul Davies, David Hemsoll, and Mark Wilson Jones in Art History 10 (June 1987), p. 139, figs. 4 and 5.

changed his name from Octavian in 27 B.C. and was made emperor by the Senate, a wreath of oak leaves was hung over the entrance to his house on the Palatine.[54] Coins from the period of Augustus sometimes depicted an eagle or a wreath of oak leaves.[55] This symbol came into common usage in the first and second centuries A.D., appearing on countless public buildings, coins, and other imperial objects.

The presence of an eagle and an oak wreath on Hadrian's Pantheon contributed to the building's symbolism as the center of the Julian household gods and the family of Augustus, one of the references Hadrian often referred to as the basis of his authority.[56] He enthusiastically took up the imperial role of Augustus, promoting his policies as the continuation of those of the early Empire and stressing their traditional

145. Pantheon, hypothetical reconstruction of pediment with eagle in a laurel wreath. Drawing: Achieng Opondo.

elements. In A.D. 123, to commemorate the establishment of the Empire and to further identify himself with its revered founder, Hadrian ordered a radical change of imperial coinage, replacing the previous portrait and cluttered background with one of classical simplicity and with the noble title of Hadrian Augustus.[57]

The image of the dignity of the imperial cult is further expressed by a series of carved friezes on the side walls of the intermediate block and the passage leading to the main door. The sections of walls between the pilasters are demarcated horizontally by two friezes ornamented with sculptural reliefs.[58] Included among the images are sacrificial utensils and garlands with fruits and flowers tied to decorated candelabra by wide, fluttering ribbons.[59] The utensils portrayed were well-known decorative motifs, some of which we have seen on the Temple of Vespasian: a metal bowl, *patera*, long-necked flask, *guttus*, woollen cap, *apex*, sprinkler, *aspergillum*, pitcher, *urceus*, incense box, *acerra*, and an augur's ward, *lituus*. These objects served to link the emperor and the building to the sacrificial nature of the pantheon of religious cults. They were found on numerous other Roman temples and their origins go back to the Augustan period and structures like the Ara Pacis.[60] Their presence was meant to connote the religious virtue of the emperor and to equate the cult of the emperor with the traditional deities.[61]

Finally, of great historical interest is the pronaos ceiling. There is a well-known story that in the 1620s Bernini and Urban VIII removed the original bronze ceiling elements, melted them down, and used it either to build the Baldachino in the Vatican or to make canons and ammunition.[62] Today, the visitor sees an open ceiling with exposed timber trusses. Drawings by Renaissance architects suggest the beams themselves were bronze, the different elements being held together by pins.[63] Because ancient bronze had little compressive strength, however, it is likely the trusses were made of wood and covered with bronze sheathing.[64] The central bay is higher than the two outer bays and was in the form of a barrel vault. In drawings done by Palladio before the bronze structure was removed, the center aisle is shown with a combination of small trusses, struts, and arches framing the vault, whereas the side aisles had smaller trusses for a flat ceiling.[65]

In all, the Pantheon's pronaos is the one aspect of the building that was most like traditional Roman temples. With eight columns on the front and three deep, it can be compared directly to the pronaos of the Temple of Mars Ultor, and it shared numerous similarities in the detailing of the column bases and capitals and of the entablature. Because of a compromise made during construction, its columns were shorter (48 Roman feet as opposed to 60) and their intercolumniations were wider, resulting in a divergence from the *pycnostyle* composition. They had monolithic granite shafts, marking a radical departure from the use of fluted marble shafts. Elements of decoration in the pediment and

146. Pantheon, interior view. Photo: Istituto Centrale per il Catalogo e la Documentazione, E.56965.

in the frieze panels on the sides and in the entranceway provided important iconographical elements that served to link Hadrian to Augustus and the Julian family and to display his religious ties to the cults of the older deities.

The Rotunda

Although the Pantheon's pronaos and rotunda, when taken together, appear to lack design resolution, the domed interior reflects a remarkably unified geometry (Fig. 146). The visitor is struck by its perfect circular shape and the way the hemispherical dome seems to hover effortlessly overhead. The interior diameter is 43.80 meters (148 Roman feet), and the space is nearly the same dimension in height, 43.44 meters.[66] The walls of the cylinder and the arc of the dome each rise 21.72 meters. A full circle can be inscribed in the space (Fig. 147).[67]

The structural mastery of the rotunda represents one of the most impressive achievements of Roman architectural technology. A concrete aggregate with travertine fragments was used in its foundation ring, and brick and concrete were used in the main walls. The foundation ring is 7.30 meters thick, and the main walls are 6.20 meters. The walls are filled with cavities, chambers, staircases, and large exedrae that open to the inside.[68] These exedrae effectively divide the rotunda wall into eight massive piers connected at their upper level by a system of vaults and relieving arches.[69]

In the dome, a lighter pumice mixture was used in the upper level and its tapering shell. It is 5.90 meters thick at its lowest ring and 1.50 meters thick at

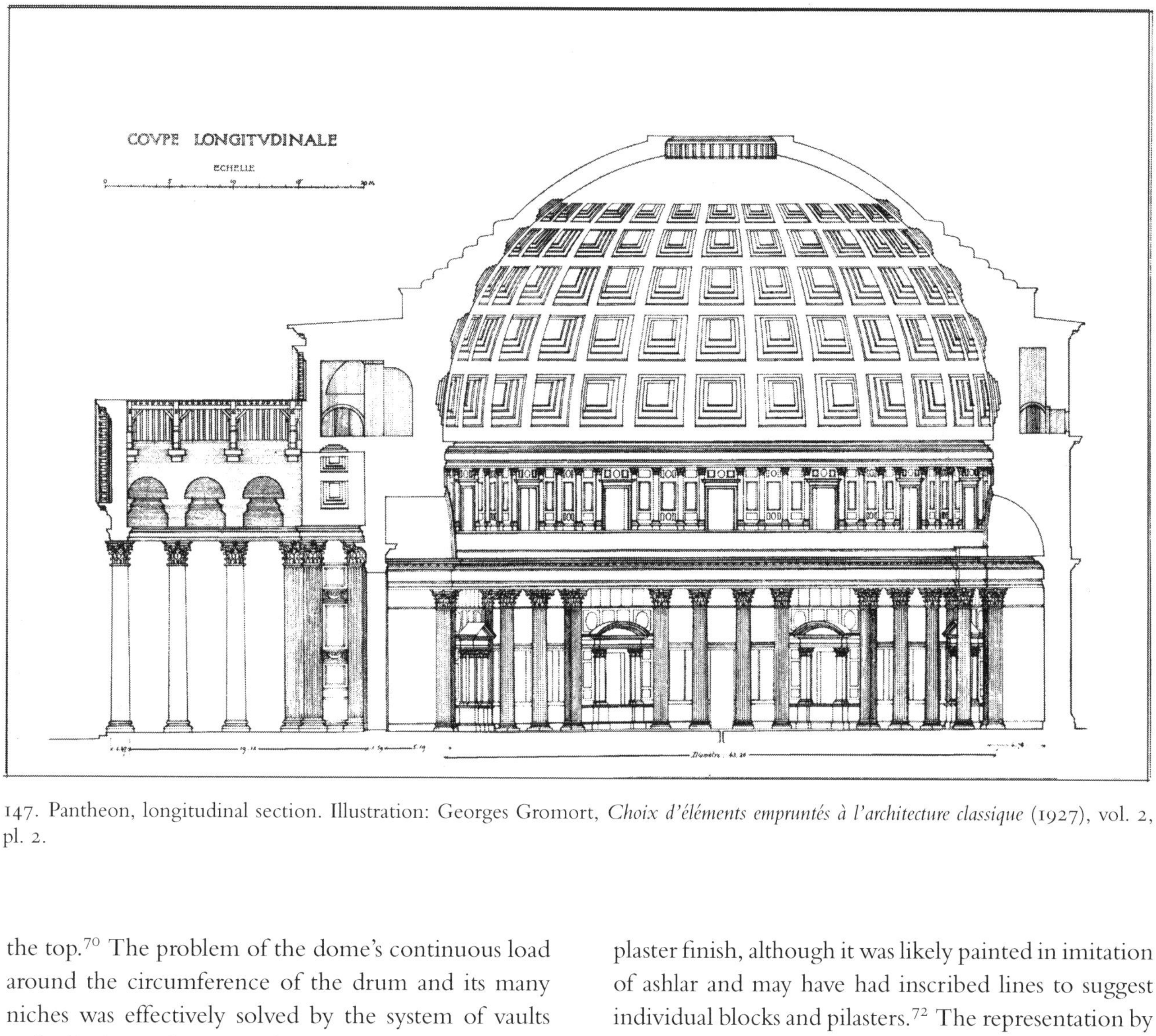

147. Pantheon, longitudinal section. Illustration: Georges Gromort, *Choix d'éléments empruntés à l'architecture classique* (1927), vol. 2, pl. 2.

the top.[70] The problem of the dome's continuous load around the circumference of the drum and its many niches was effectively solved by the system of vaults and relieving arches, a combination that distributes the weight of the dome to the eight massive supporting piers. In a structural sense, their principal connecting vaults were conceived in exactly the same way as a Roman bridge or aqueduct, with each vault providing a counteracting force to the lateral thrust of the adjacent vaults.

It is possible to identify today the supporting piers and relieving arches on the rotunda's exposed exterior walls. In Hadrian's time, however, such a noble imperial temple would have required a more dignified outer appearance. The surface of the brick wall was probably covered by a layer of plaster or stucco. Traces of the original plaster surface are evident in several places near the cornices and along ledges and window frames.[71] It is impossible to know the exact appearance of this plaster finish, although it was likely painted in imitation of ashlar and may have had inscribed lines to suggest individual blocks and pilasters.[72] The representation by Palladio, for instance, indicates Corinthian pilasters on the rotunda's upper two tiers.[73]

Architecturally, the rotunda's interior was one of the most elegant and refined of all Roman imperial buildings. It is beautifully proportioned and detailed with yellow, white, red, grey, and veined white marble cladding. It is highlighted by the exedrae and by aediculae attached to the piers, and it is topped by the magnificent coffered dome.[74] The juxtapositions of color and geometric forms are equally evident on both the walls and the floor. The latter is composed in a geometrical pattern of alternating circles and squares of porphyry, yellow marble, and grey granite. These circles and squares are inscribed in larger squares defined by a grid of pavonazetto bands that run parallel to the cardinal axes.[75] It is the largest and best surviving

example of an inlaid marble floor from ancient Rome.

It is immediately evident to the visitor that the floor is not flat, but rather slightly convex in profile. It is a very dramatic effect that contributes to the rotunda's dynamic quality. It originally served to carry away water when it rained through the oculus, although the original convex profile was flattened slightly in the center and several drain holes were added in a later restoration.[76]

The rotunda's perimeter wall is divided horizontally into two zones, the lower one with piers and the openings to the exedrae, the upper one articulated with panels and windows. The three exedrae on the cardinal axes are apsidal in plan; the four on the diagonal axes are trapezoidal. The opening to each exedra is framed by pilasters and divided into three bays by columns. Although their overall height is smaller (10.57 meters or 36 Roman feet), these columns have the same proportions as those of the pronaos.[77] Their marble capitals are detailed in exactly the same way; however, their shafts are giallo antico and are fluted, with cabling in the lower portion. Those framing the main exedra opposite the rotunda's entrance door are of pavonazetto.[78]

The wall surfaces between the exedrae are decorated with geometric square and rectangular panels of pavonazetto, verde antico, giallo antico, and bigio africano.[79] An aedicule in the center of each pier is composed of a high base and two Corinthian columns supporting a pediment. The columns of the aediculae on either side of the main axis are fluted giallo antico and support a triangular pediment. Those flanking the crossing axis are of granite or red porphyry and support a segmental pediment.[80] The use of such aediculae with alternating pediments may have been influenced by the cella of the Temple of Apollo Sosianus.[81]

The primary columns and pilasters support a beautifully carved entablature composed of a tripartite marble architrave, a plain frieze of red porphyry, and a marble cornice supported by acanthus consoles. Its proportions are similar to those of the pronaos, although its details are more refined.[82] This entablature is the rotunda's single most important unifying feature, establishing a horizontally continuous element encircling and defining the space. It is interrupted only at the main exedra, which is topped by a coffered half-dome. The coffering and crosses evident in this exedra are from a later restoration.[83]

During the time of Hadrian, the attic zone was very different from how it appears today. It was originally articulated with sixty-four porphyry pilasters, arranged in groups of four and alternating with windows. The composition was altered in 1747 by Benedict XIV and his architect Paolo Posi, who removed the original marble veneer, pilasters, and windows and added large rectangular panels and larger windows with pediments.[84] These alterations were made to create a more severe, classical image in keeping with contemporary taste.[85] One bay was later restored to its original condition based on drawings by Palladio and the famous painting of the Pantheon by Giovanni Paolo Pannini (Fig. 148).[86]

The presence of an attic zone was related to the well-established tradition found in the colonnades of the Forum Augustum and the Forum Traiani, in which a parapet wall carried by the columns masked the barrel vaults of the colonnades. It can also be compared with those found in the hemicycles of the terraced temple structure at Palestrina, where a parapet wall rose above a columnar order to mask annular vaults. The height of these attic walls corresponded to the radius of the vault they concealed. The wall in both cases was decorated with colonettes above the main columns, a motif comparable with that of the caryatids that articulated the attic above the colonnades of the Forum Augustum.[87]

The attic zone played a crucial role as a visual transition between the rotunda wall and the coffered dome. Its original multicolored decoration of small pilasters and rectangular windows, however, was not necessarily meant to suggest a formal system of load and support for the massive dome overhead. It was purely architectonic, giving no suggestion of a connection to the building's structural system, and connoted a painter's illusion of a gallery or a miniature colonnade as found in Third Style Pompeian fresco painting.[88] It was common in Pompeian frescos to represent sky seen through an upper-level colonnade. In the Pantheon, the decorative colonnade provided a light ambiance, the suggestion of looking at the sky through a screen of columns at the top of a circular wall.[89]

The articulation of the dome's hemispherical surface consists of vertical rows of coffers, five in each row, twenty-eight rows in all (Fig. 149). They diminish in

148. Pantheon, interior view showing reconstruction of original attic zone. Photo: Fototeca Unione, American Academy, Rome, FU.11019.

size toward the top; those of the lower four courses contain four steps, and those of the uppermost course contain three.[90] They are each enhanced for perspectival reasons by having wider steps on the bottom than on the top, an effect that makes the dome's overall appearance seem lighter and less static than it would otherwise be.[91] At the top of the dome is, of course, the oculus, completely open to the sky, 8.92 meters (30 Roman feet) in diameter.[92] In Hadrian's time, the dome and its coffers were decorated with painted stucco and bronze ornaments. The coffers may have had gilded stars or rosettes on a sky-blue ground.[93]

There is a unique dynamic quality to the dome that stems from the architect's use of twenty-eight rows of coffers. Each quadrant has seven coffers, an odd rather than even number. This results in different alignments between the coffers and the exedrae on the cardinal and diagonal axes of the rotunda's wall. The exedrae on the

main north-south and east-west axes each correspond to a row of coffers; those on the diagonal axes correspond to a rib. Each pier is left with a compromised alignment of a rib and half a coffer.[94] This shift creates a sense of tension, the coffers having their own rhythm independent of the piers.[95] The smaller-scale rhythm of the pilasters of the original attic story, although not expressing direct lines of load and support, would have mediated these differential alignments more effectively than is presently the case.

The composition of the cella wall and the coffered dome take on a further dynamic aspect when considered in relation to the rays of sunlight penetrating the oculus. The sun disk falls on the building's interior at different points depending on the time of day and year. At noon, for instance, the vertical axis of the sun disk coincides with the northward-facing entrance door. It shines on the surface of the dome above the door on the winter solstice, December 21, when the sun is low on the horizon. In contrast, the noon light shines entirely on the floor in front of the door on the summer solstice, June 21, when the sun is highest in the sky.[96] During the fall and spring, the times of the vernal and autumnal equinoxes, the sun disk shines midway between the floor and the dome, directly on the attic zone.

Symbolic Meaning

Hadrian's intentions for the building's symbolic and iconographic meaning are impossible to determine in their entirety given the lack of written and physical evidence. For instance, it has not been possible to establish the identity of all of the cult statues that occupied the rotunda's eight aediculae and seven larger exedrae.[97] There are numerous theories, however. The first suggests that the planetary deities were represented – namely, the Sun, the Moon, Mars, Mercury, Jupiter, Venus, and Saturn – and that they would have been displayed in the seven major exedrae, including the apse. The dome was a symbol of the heavens, the place where the gods resided, ruled over by Jupiter, the most supreme of all.[98]

A second theory proposes a slightly different list, one based not on the seven planetary deities, but on those associated with the family of Augustus, which would have been found in the original building erected by Agrippa. It is known from Cassius Dio that Agrippa had wanted to dedicate the temple to the cult of Augustus but that he had refused.[99] In spite of this refusal, the sculptural program may, in fact, have followed the lines of an Augusteum as found in other parts of Italy and the provinces. The deities represented in this case would have included Jupiter, Juno, and Minerva as the triad in the central niche, Venus and Mars, because they were the principal protecting families of the Julian family, then Apollo, Diana, Neptune, and Mercury.[100]

This theory is related to the path of the sun disk inside the rotunda. For instance, the rising sun on April 1 aligns with the building's transverse axis. This is significant because April 1 is the Veneralia, the day dedicated to the goddess Venus from whom Julius Caesar claimed descent and another of the deities to which Hadrian himself wanted to be related.[101] If the cult statue of Venus had been located in the exedra on the building's west side, the rays of the morning sun rising in the east would have fallen on the dome above it. By the same reasoning, the statue of Mars would have been placed in the exedra opposite, on the building's east side. The remaining four exedrae on the diagonal axes would have been assigned to the other four gods, Apollo, Diana, Neptune, and Mercury.[102]

A third theory of the rotunda's symbolism is based on the relation to the moon and the monthly calendar. Why did the architect use twenty-eight as opposed to some other number of coffers and ribs in the dome – thirty or thirty-two, for instance?[103] There may have been a relationship to the number of days for the moon to orbit the earth. Ancient astronomers knew that it takes twenty-seven and one-third days to complete its orbit, or simply that its orbit is completed early on the twenty-eighth day. Furthermore, the quadrants can be linked to the four phases of the moon – new moon, first quarter, half moon, last quarter – which were related to the four axial positions on its orbit. Thus, twenty-eight coffers in the Pantheon's dome divided into four quadrants could have been intended to relate to the moon's orbit.[104]

Some recent scholars have argued on the contrary that there was no iconographic program intended in

149. Pantheon, interior view showing dome. Photo: Istituto Centrale per il Catalogo e la Documentazione, E.56964.

the Pantheon, that any religious or cosmic interpretation is widely off the mark.[105] They prefer the explanation that the building was simply an exercise in perfect geometric forms, noting that the main spatial relationship between the cylinder and the cupola is a demonstration of the *symmetria* between a sphere and a cylinder of equal diameter. Archimedes' theories on the subject were well-known to architects and builders.[106]

Related to this, scholars have noted that a sixteen-sided figure can be inscribed in the rotunda and that the division of the rotunda's wall into eight solid sections and eight open sections may have been the basis for the building's design module.[107] Finally, there is the point that the twenty-eight rows of coffers represent a perfect number and that the use of this rare perfect number coincided with arithmetical perfection as defined by Euclid and Pythagoras.[108]

Such theories are sometimes used to support the argument that the Pantheon was not a temple, but an audience hall.[109] The fact that it was used on occasion by the Senate, for instance, must preclude its use as a temple. Cassius Dio writes: "He (Hadrian) transacted with the aid of the Senate all the important and most urgent business and he held court with the assistance of the foremost men, now in the palace, now in the Forum, or the Pantheon or various other places, always being seated on a tribunal, so that whatever was done was made public."[110] There is nothing unusual, however, about a temple building serving multiple purposes, including meetings of the Senate. The Curia Julia itself was a *templum*. For a meeting of the Senate to be

lawful, it was required that it be convened in a *templum*. The fact that the Senate met in the Pantheon supports its status as a temple. Other temples were used on numerous occasions by the Senate, including the Temples of Concordia, Castor and Pollux, Jupiter Stator, Apollo Palatinus, Apollo Sosianus, and Bellona, to name just a few.[111] Hadrian's use of the building equally as a temple and an audience hall represented the diverse uses to which sacred buildings were commonly used.

Numerous scholars believe beyond a shadow of a doubt that the Pantheon was a temple. In whatever way it may have been used in a larger functional or secular context, its sacred aspects are unmistakable.[112] Literary evidence is found in the *Historiae Augustae*, and a religious iconography is represented by the sacral instruments portrayed in the marble reliefs in the entrance passage and on the side walls of the intermediate block.[113] These are similar to those found in the frieze of the Temple of Vespasian and have the same connotations of the high dignity of the imperial cult. Evidence also includes the fact that in A.D. 59 the Arvales, who normally gathered in the Temple of Apollo Palatinus or in the Temple of Concordia, met in the Agrippan Pantheon.[114]

Hadrian was fascinated by the occult and religion. He dabbled in mysteries, explored temples throughout the Empire, and carried on long discussions with priests, oracles, and magicians. He had a great devotion to the gods of both Greece and Rome, which reflected the two sides of his interest. On one hand, he had an antiquarian's enthusiasm and insatiable curiosity in places and things from the historical past. On the other hand, he sought a communion with the absolute, an anticipation of the felicity beyond death, which he hoped would engender a state of inner peace. As with previous emperors, there was a strong political side to his religious devotion, for he knew how to manipulate religious feeling for political ends.[115] In this sense, the sphere, the most perfect geometric shape, symbolized the hoped-for unity and perfection of the Empire.[116] He encouraged the growth of a Hellenic identity focused on Athens and Zeus, as he did a Latin one focused on Rome and Jupiter.[117]

It is important to reiterate Hadrian's standing in the East, where he was worshipped as Zeus. In Rome, he associated himself with Jupiter, which was the equivalent of Zeus of the Greeks, and the emperor's special protector. This would support the presence of the Capitoline triad in the Pantheon's main niche.[118] By assuming divine status, Hadrian kindled in his subjects an enthusiastic awareness of religious community, of devotion to the gods, and especially to Jupiter. The worship of Hadrian-Zeus in the East was the equivalent of worshipping Jupiter and the Roman emperor in Rome. This all-encompassing divinity brought the whole Empire, East and West, together at its religious apex, with the Pantheon at its spiritual center.[119]

Hadrian's restoration and transformation of Agrippa's *templum* was a significant event that referred back to the reign of Augustus and the founding of the Empire. Agrippa had prescribed the sacred space through augural ritual. Hadrian as a restorer could change the appearance of the sacred space or building, but he would have had difficulty changing its location or plan, just as those who rebuilt the Temple of Jupiter Capitolinus after its destruction by fire were expected to maintain its original site and plan. Hadrian restored Agrippa's temple precinct in such a way that it retained its topographical and religious link with the imperial family of Augustus and his role in the early days of the Empire. The Pantheon continued to face onto the Campus Martius and the buildings that had been developed by Augustus: the Mausoleum of Augustus, the Ara Pacis, and the Horologium (Fig. 150). There is also the fact that it was located 800 meters from the Mausoleum of Augustus and 800 meters from the Temple of Jupiter Capitolinus.[120] Hadrian intended to encourage and support the idea that his reign was a continuation of that of Augustus and that its history had a direct link to the city's founding.[121] The Pantheon combined the functions of sacred temple and imperial audience hall, a place where the emperor could be in direct association with the protecting gods of the imperial family, with Romulus, and with the founding figures of imperial Rome – Caesar and Augustus.[122] The Pantheon provided the perfect place for Hadrian's efforts toward spiritual and political unity.[123]

By replacing Agrippa's original building with a domed rotunda, Hadrian added a new level of symbolism to the original cult building – that of the cosmos. The sphere, which according to Aristotle was the

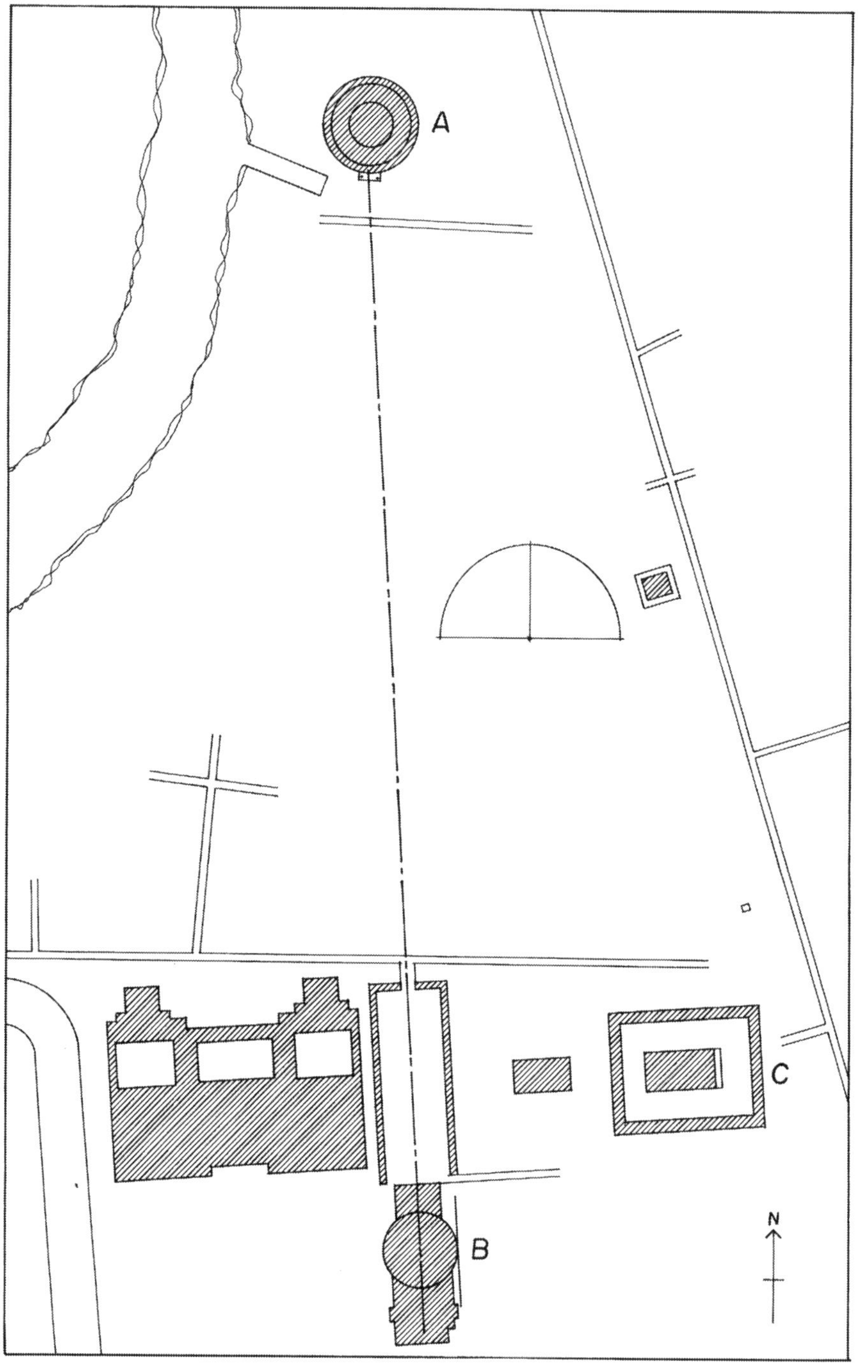

150. Plan of the northern Campus Martius showing (A) Mausoleum of Augustus, (B) Pantheon, (C) Temple of Divus Hadrianus. Drawing: John W. Stamper.

most ideal and perfect form, represented the shape of the universe. It is likely that the Pantheon, in Hadrian's time, was one of Rome's most important temples for the worship of the institution of the emperor as Zeus and Jupiter within the context of the cosmos and several other important deities, especially Venus and Mars.[124] Universality and unity were expressed throughout in the Pantheon, thus strengthening the cult of the emperor. It brought together all of the gods in a space built to symbolize the community of heaven under its prodigious and daring dome.[125] It was the symbol of an equal fraternity of provinces and nations harmoniously linked by tradition and administration around the person of the emperor.[126]

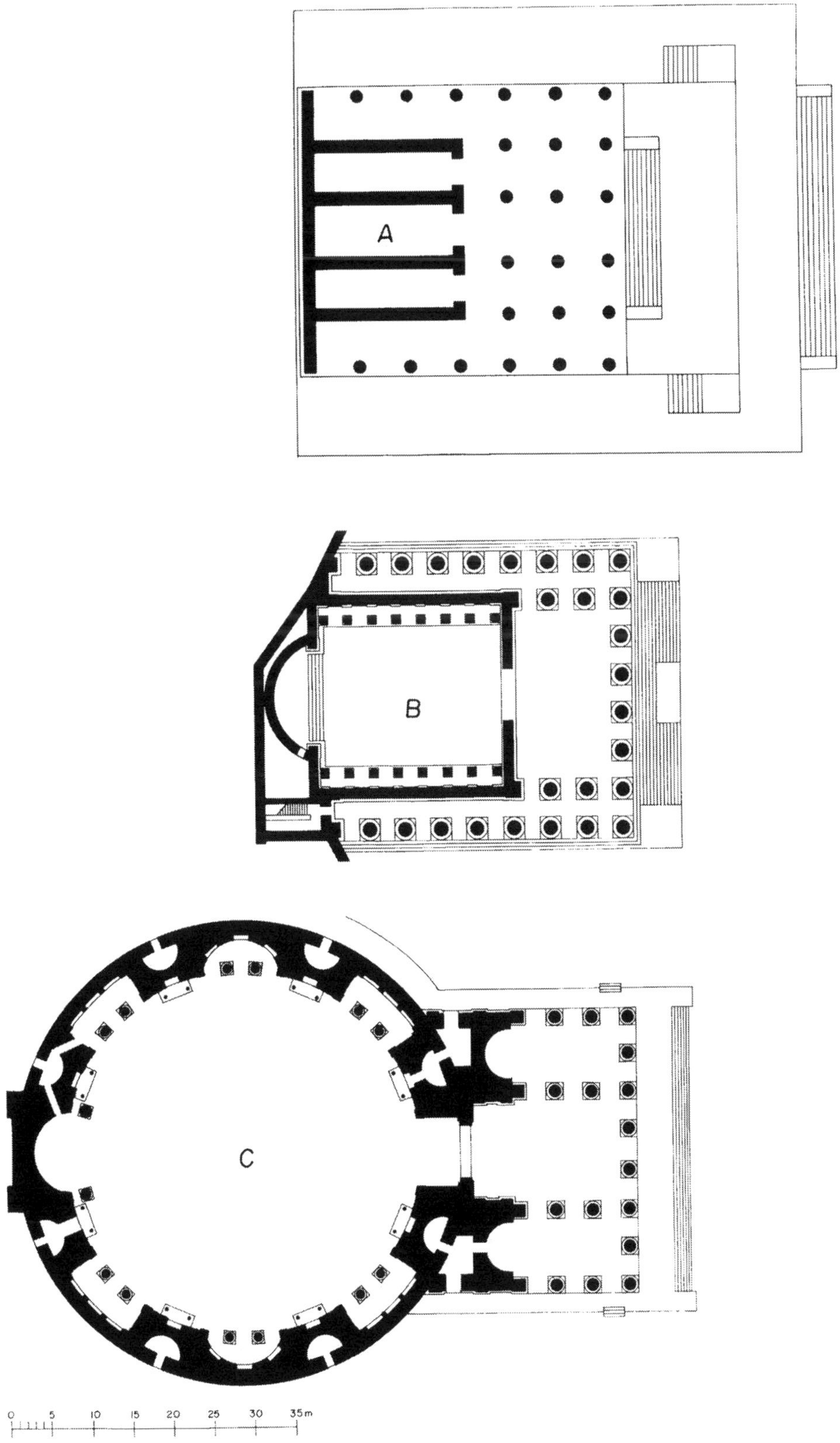

151. Comparison of (A) Temple of Jupiter Capitolinus, (B) Temple of Mars Ultor, (C) Pantheon. All plans are at the same scale. Drawing: John W. Stamper.

Table 11.1. Comparative Sizes of the Imperial Roman Temples Based on the Model of the Temple of Jupiter Capitolinus (Podium Size, Column Diameter, and Interaxial Dimension)

	Podium		*Columns*	
Temple	*Width (m)*	*Length (m)*	*Diameter (m)*	*Interaxial (m)*
Capitoline Jupiter	34.0	38.30	1.47	5.90 7.40 center
Mars Ultor	36.0	50	1.80	4.46
Templum Pacis	34.0	22	–	–
Divus Traianus	36.0	50	1.86	–
Pantheon	34.20	–	1.48	4.50

Source: For the Pantheon, see Mark Wilson Jones, "Designing the Corinthian Order," *JRA* 2(1989); for Mars Ultor, see Valentin Kockel, "Forum Augustum," *LTUR*, vol. 2; for Divus Traianus, see James E. Packer, *The Forum of Trajan in Rome: A Study of the Monuments*, vol. 1 (Berkeley and Los Angeles: University of California Press, 1996).

As with the Temple of Mars Ultor, the Templum Pacis, and the Temple of Divus Traianus, the Pantheon's pronaos had dimensional similarities to that of the Temple of Jupiter Capitolinus as it is reconstructed in this study, specifically, the width of 115 Roman feet (see Table 11.1). Reminding us of the authority of the precedent set by Rome's oldest and most important temple, there may have been a conscious line of continuity over time, the paradigmatic influence of the Capitoline remaining strong even after 600 years. The Capitoline Temple would have been the primary precedent. The architects of the Temple of Mars Ultor, the Templum Pacis, the Temple of Divus Traianus, and finally, the Pantheon may have sought to emulate it, make reference to it, recall its memory by repeating the dimensions of its pronaos (Fig. 151). In this sense, the building of the Pantheon reflects Hadrian's association with Jupiter, the founding of Rome, Augustus and the Julian family, and the founding of the Empire.

The Pantheon's bold originality and formal beauty, coupled with its exceptional state of preservation, encouraged its imitation not only by the Romans, but also by subsequent cultures throughout the Western world. This far-reaching influence is seen in buildings such as the Baptistery in Florence and St. Peter's in Rome, in designs by Palladio and his followers, and at Thomas Jefferson's University of Virginia campus. If history is any indication, its power over the architectural world will continue indefinitely into the future, its prototypical form going on to inspire countless architects to come.

12

HADRIAN AND THE ANTONINES

Construction of the Pantheon was well under way when Hadrian began planning another, even larger structure, the Temple of Venus and Rome. It was to be located on the Velian Hill, between the Forum Romanum and the Colosseum, along the north side of the Via Sacra (Fig. 152). The site had been occupied by late republican-era houses and, at its eastern end, the vestibule of Nero's Domus Aurea. At its southwest corner stands the Arch of Titus with its reliefs that memorialize the sack of Jerusalem.[1] The hill had also been the site of the cult dedicated to *Romae Aeternae*, which remained as one of the temple's two dedications.[2] The temple's stylobate is occupied today by the Church of San Francesca Romana, which stands directly over the west room of the temple's two-room cella.

Throughout his reign, Hadrian associated himself with both Jupiter and Zeus, and he made these associations explicit in the architectural design and iconographic programs of his temples.[3] An analysis of the Temple of Venus and Rome reveals the extent to which second-century temple architecture in Rome continued to be dependent on earlier precedents for design. It also shows how such temples continued to express the emperor's relationship with the deities. It demonstrates the continuing need for consensus in the interaction between the emperor and his subjects. There was a common language between them, a shared understanding of the relationship between the emperor, the deities, and the Roman people. This building, like the Pantheon, was a vivid symbolic statement about the role official imperial architecture played in maintaining that relationship.

Temple of Venus and Rome

The massive foundations of the expansive platform beneath the Temple of Venus and Rome stands along the side of the Via Sacra where it ascends to the Arch of Titus. Granite columns mark the location of a portico that surrounded the perimeter of the platform and formed an enclosure for the temple precinct. While half of the temple's site is occupied by the Church of San Francesca Romana, the other half is an open field, with a portion of the cella clearly visible in the rear wall of the church complex.

The Temple of Venus and Rome was very different from the Pantheon, in both its architecture and its iconography. In this case, Hadrian's interest in Greek architecture – both his antiquarian enthusiasms and his interest in basing the design of a new temple on earlier precedents – was overtly expressed. In A.D. 124, just before construction of the new temple was begun, he visited Athens, then made a brief excursion to the Peleponnesus – Megara, Argos, Mantinea, and Olympia. In each of these cities, he saw temples that may have had a degree of influence on the Temple of Venus and Rome. The most important of these, however, was the Athenian Temple of Olympian Zeus.[4]

Although he used the Olympian Zeus Temple as a model, he transformed it into a new plan and temple type, one that was appropriate to Rome and its specific setting (Fig. 153). Hadrian's use of this building as a precedent is not surprising given that he had ordered the completion of the Athenian building according to its original design.[5] It was a temple he viewed as the summit of the Greek pantheon, olympian in its

152. Rome, Temple of Venus and Rome, A.D. 125/126–140/145, aerial view showing its location between the Colosseum and the Forum Romanum. Photo: Deutsches Archäologisches Institut, Rome, 73.1084.

superhuman scale, a temple that symbolized the drawing together of the entire Greek world, its gods, and its culture.[6] He wanted to create the same kind of building in Rome, his intent being to draw together the whole Roman world, its gods, its culture, and its art, East and West.

Hadrian consecrated the site of the Temple of Venus and Rome in A.D. 121 in conjunction with the festival of the Parilia, which had been transformed into the Romaia.[7] Coins issued in A.D. 121 refer to the initiation of the games of the Parilia, celebrated on April 21, while some refer to the temple with the words *Romae Aeternae, Veneris Felicis*.[8] Actual construction of the building did not commence until A.D. 125 or 126.[9] Most of its construction was carried on in the late A.D. 120s and 130s, and it was dedicated, still unfinished,

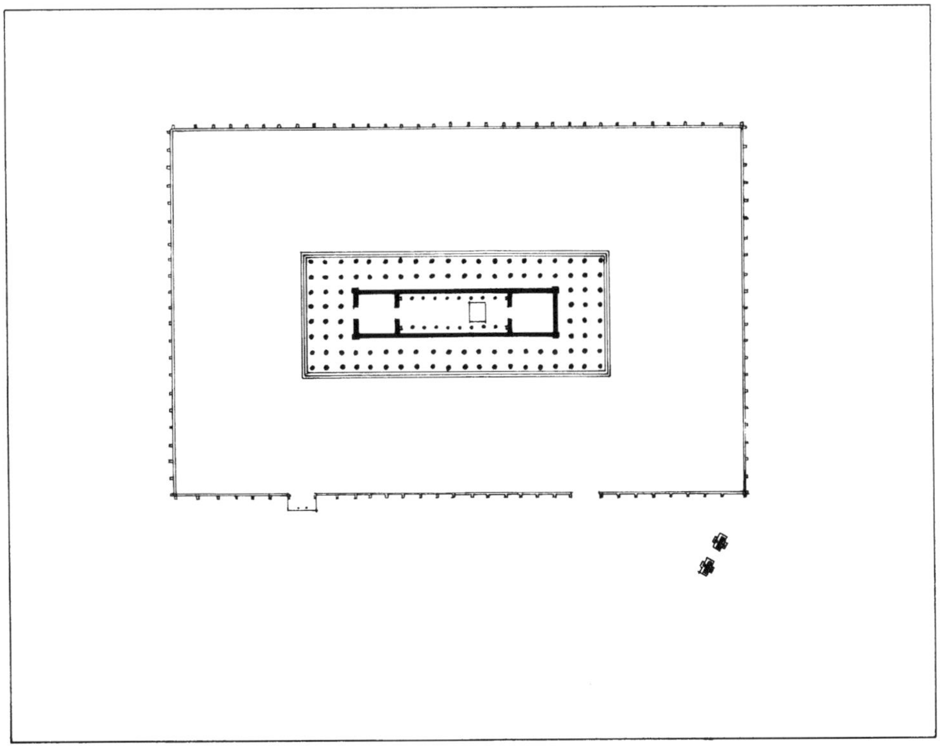

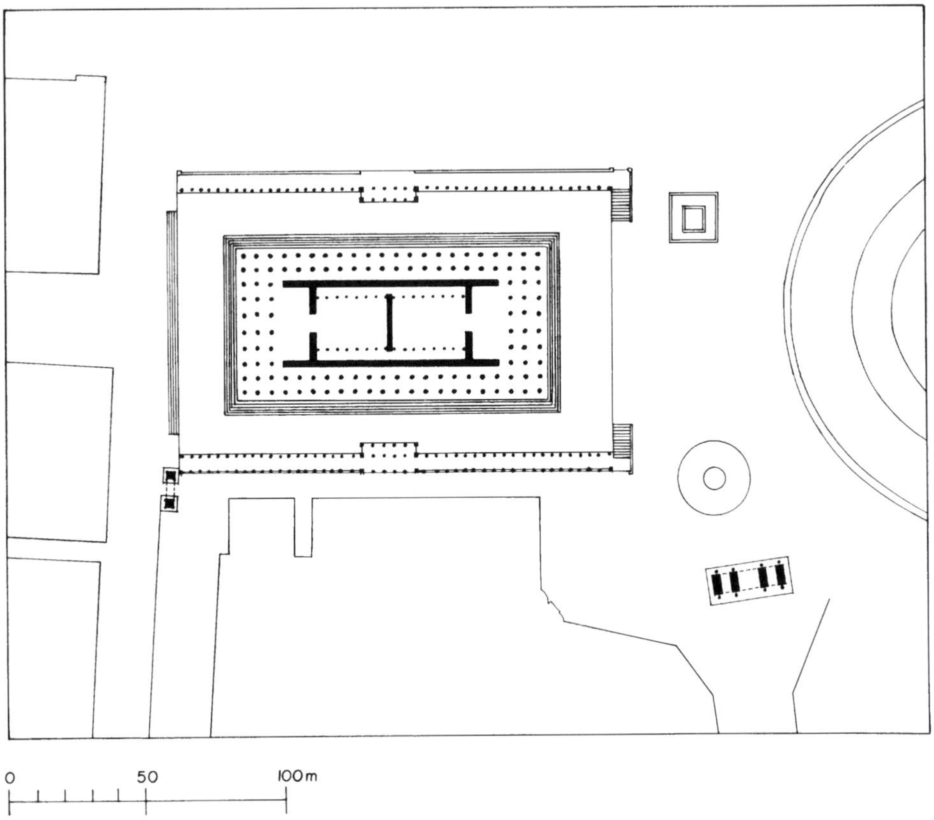

153. Athens, Temple of Olympian Zeus, view of temple with Hadrian's Gate (top); Temple of Venus and Rome (bottom). Drawing: John W. Stamper.

154. Rome, Temple of Venus and Rome, elevation with the statue of the sun god, Sol Invictus. Photo: Deutsches Archäologisches Institut, Rome, 34.194.

in A.D. 136–137. Hadrian's successor, Antoninus Pius, completed it in A.D. 140–145.[10]

During the time of Nero, the vestibule that led to his Domus Aurea complex was surrounded by colonnades and had in its center a 100-foot-high bronze statue, the Neronian Colossus.[11] When originally cast in Rome by Zenodorus, the statue represented Nero, but after his death, Vespasian altered its head to represent the sun god, Sol Invictus. The statue remained in its place overlooking the Forum Romanum until A.D. 121. When Hadrian chose the Velia as the site for the construction of the Temple of Venus and Rome, he ordered the statue moved to the temple's east side, situating it in the space between the temple and the Colosseum (Fig. 154). Ancient sources report that twenty-four elephants were used to slide it from its original spot to the new one, all the while having it upright within a strong scaffolding of wood. It was placed on a pedestal that was built of concrete with brick facing and sheathed with marble revetments.[12] It was still standing on this site at the time of Constantine, when it formed an axial focus for the central passage of the Arch of Constantine.

The large platform on which the temple stood was formed by natural tufa rock on the west and built-up concrete piers and vaults on the east.[13] It was faced in its entirety with peperino in *opus quadratum*.[14] A series of rooms formed by the vaulted structure provided service spaces for the Colosseum, a suggestion that may have been made by Apollodorus of Damascus early in the building's planning stage.[15] The platform's summit was reached on the west end from the Forum Romanum by a broad flight of steps. On the east end, it was reached by two smaller flights of steps placed at each corner (Fig. 155). The columnar porticos that framed its two long sides were built of red and grey Egyptian granite, with Corinthian capitals of white marble.[16] The northern portico was 5.90 meters deep and was enclosed by a wall; the southern portico, 7.60 meters deep, was composed of two rows of columns, thus screening the view of the temple from the Via Sacra.[17]

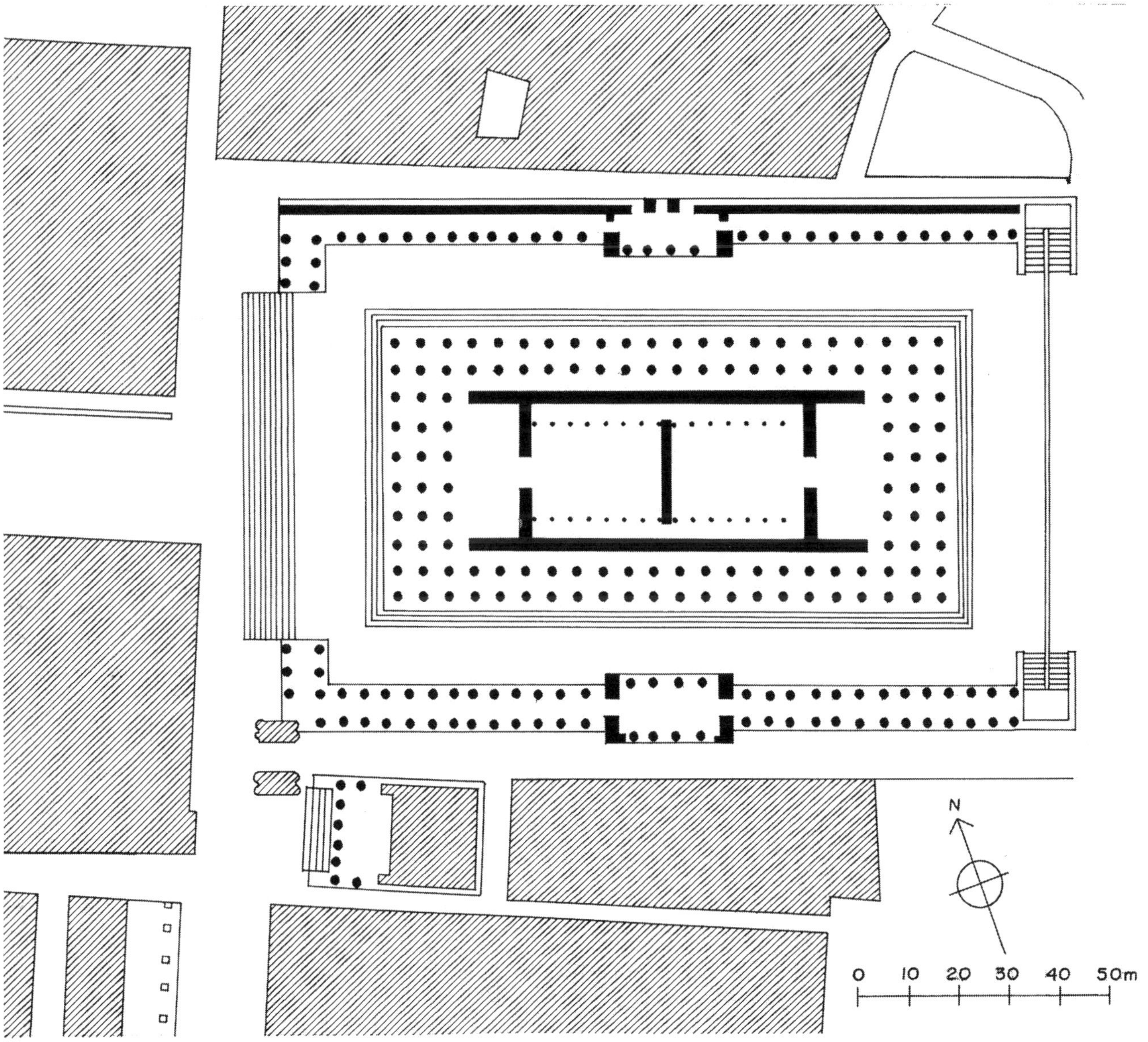

155. Temple of Venus and Rome, site plan. Drawing: Ming Hu based on Alessandro Cassatella and Stefania Pensabene in *ArchLaz* 10 (1990): p. 54, fig. 2.

The central bays of each portico were marked by a pavilion, or propylaeum, which projected into the temenos. They were each five bays wide, and their columns were distinguished by the use of cipollino. They marked a crossing axis at the temple's midpoint, although neither actually provided access from outside the temple zone. In plan they recalled the entrance portico of the Porticus Octaviae as it was built at the time of Augustus.[18]

The temple itself was almost purely Greek, its four-sided peristyle relating directly to the Temple of Olympian Zeus. It was raised above the platform by seven steps, which ran continuous on all four sides. With ten by twenty columns, and measuring 54 meters wide by 111.50 meters long (183 by 379 Roman feet) at the top of the stylobate, it exceeded in size its Athenian model, which had eight by twenty columns and measured 41.11 meters wide by 107.89 meters long (140 by 366 Roman feet).[19]

Some published plans of the temple suggest that its peristyle was composed of a single row of columns; however, recent investigations have revealed that it was

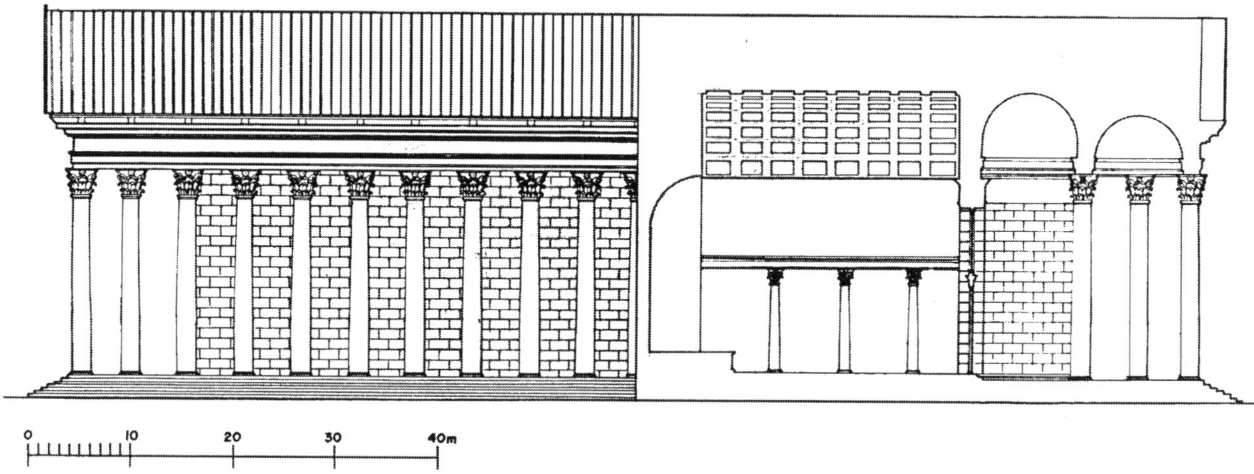

156. Temple of Venus and Rome, elevation and section. Drawing: Susan Bridgewater based on Leon Vaudoyer in *Roma Antiqua* (1985), pp. 249–52, figs. 120–2.

dipteral, with two rows on the sides and three at the ends, exactly like the Temple of Olympian Zeus.[20] The columns, of Proconnesian marble, may have been the same size as those of the Temple of Olympian Zeus, about 16.90 meters high (57 Roman feet) with diameters of about 1.90 meters.[21] The columns on the east and west ends were arranged so that the central bay was widest and there was a progressive reduction of the bay widths toward the corners. The interaxial width of the central bay was approximately 6 meters (20 Roman feet), and that of the two outer bays was 5.035 meters (17 Roman feet). The latter dimension was used consistently on the long sides.[22]

The entablature, of Lunense and Proconnesian marble, was composed of a two-step architrave topped by three moldings, cavetto, ovolo, and astragal. The two-step architrave marked a significant change from the Pantheon and most other temple architecture from the first century A.D. in which the architrave typically had three fasciae.[23] Precedent for the architrave crown's three moldings can be found in the work of Hermogenes in both the Temple of Artemis at Magnesia and the Temple of Dionysius at Teos. This composition was widely adopted in the East, but did not become a dominant motif in Rome.[24]

Above the architrave and its crown was a plain frieze and a cornice ornamented with consoles, palmettes, and lions' heads.[25] Coins from the time of Hadrian show a standing figure of Roma in the center of the pediment, holding a sceptre, and flanked by additional standing figures.[26] The roof was covered with gold-plated bronze tiles.[27] Some of the ornamentation is attributed to a rebuilding campaign initiated by Maxentius after a fire in A.D. 306.[28]

The cella was unusual in that it was divided into two rooms, with the statues of the two deities Venus and Roma placed one in each room, back to back (Fig. 156). That of Venus was in the east room, facing the Colosseum, while Roma was in the west room facing the Forum Romanum.[29] The cella walls were made of brick-faced concrete, lined inside and out with marble revetments. It is almost certain that the semicircular apses with coffered half-domes, which are still visible behind the Church of San Francesca Romana, were part of the Maxentius rebuilding project.[30] In Hadrian's original design, the two rooms were rectangular in plan and were lined with a row of eight columns on either side. The floor of the side aisles was raised 20 centimeters above that of the central nave.[31] A single wall separated the two rooms in the middle while allowing passage from one room to the other by means of two doors.

The influence of Greek architecture on this building was important, but it was not the exclusive source for its design. The peripteral plan, four-sided stylobate, and size were directly influenced by the Temple of Olympian Zeus; the profiles of the capitals and moldings and their manner of carving were influenced by the Hellenistic architecture of Asia Minor. Similarities between the entablatures of this building and the

Trajaneum at Pergamon suggest that Hadrian may have employed a Pergamene architect and that he brought with him a group of craftsmen.[32] Although some of the minor decorative details were the work of local Roman workers, the main order was surely the responsibility of Greeks from Asia Minor.[33] This was an important example of a temple design in Rome that broke away from the Augustan-era Corinthian Order that had predominated in Roman temple architecture for nearly a century.[34] It established a new precedent for Roman architecture, going on to influence the design of the Temple of Divus Hadrianus built near the Pantheon after the emperor's death. In many ways, it was a Greek building in a Roman city.

Although the deity Roma had long been worshipped in the Greek East as an act of political homage to the capital city, her worship in Rome itself was a relatively new phenomenon. Roma had often been represented in relation to the *princeps*, especially during the reign of Augustus, but it had not been common to worship her as such.[35] She was seen with increasing frequency on coins and sculptural reliefs during the Flavian period, and for Hadrian she represented a further link to Augustus and his authority as a member of the Julio-Claudian family.

The cult of Venus was an entirely different matter. There had been shrines erected in Rome to Venus as early as the third century B.C. Pompey the Great and Julius Caesar both did much to exalt the deity by making her their ancestor and protectoress and constructing the temples of Venus Victrix and Venus Genetrix.[36] Hadrian referred to the deity as Venus Felix, the goddess of fecundity and prosperity. Images of her and Roma together appeared on coins, with both figures sitting in thrones or chairs, and wearing long robes. Venus Felix is shown holding a spear and a winged Amor; Roma is shown with a spear and Palladium, the symbol of the eternal city. Through these two deities, the temple's placement along the Via Sacra stressed the association of Roman triumphs with the divine origins of the city.[37]

Urbanistically the Temple of Venus and Rome played an important mediating role between the Forum Romanum and the Colosseum. It was placed on the same axis as the amphitheater and the Via Sacra in the Forum Romanum, and although it effectively closed off the view between the two, it gave emphasis to their axial correspondence. Equally significant was Hadrian's placement of the Colossus statue between the temple and the Colosseum, on axis with the Via Triumphalis. It served as a focal point for those passing along the Via Triumphalis and marked the spot where a visitor or a processional entourage turned westard onto the Via Sacra. There was another link to Athens in its site with its location across the Forum Romanum from the Temple of Jupiter on the Capitoline Hill, compared with the relationship of the Temple of Olympian Zeus and the Acropolis in Athens.[38]

When the building was dedicated in A.D. 136–137, official valedictory coins were issued that praised Hadrian for having achieved peace, stability, prosperity, and unity. One such coin, with an image of Herakles, proclaimed that the whole earth was abundantly fruitful and comfortably stable thanks to the efforts of this emperor so much like Herakles, "the great adventurer, traveler and friend of men."[39]

Hadrian and Antoninus

Hadrian died in the city of Baia, on the coast of Naples, in A.D. 138, after serving nearly twenty-one years as emperor.[40] His adopted son and successor, Antoninus, accompanied his body to the nearby town of Pozzuoli, where a temple was commissioned to be built on the grounds of what had once been Cicero's villa. After a short time, Antoninus continued on to Rome with the body, where he interred it in the great Mausoleum still under construction on the north side of the Tiber.[41]

Antoninus faced a hostile Senate that wanted to annul the acts of Hadrian and refuse him deification. The emperor's long absences from Rome had so alienated him from the city's ruling aristocracy that he had fallen completely out of favor by the end of his reign. But a persistent Antoninus took charge of the situation and succeeded in swaying the reluctant senators to his wishes. Hadrian was deified, and Antoninus established a quinquennial contest in his honor and appointed priests and fraternities to venerate his memory. Finally, he commissioned a temple to be dedicated to Hadrian, located in the Campus Martius, east of the Pantheon and the Temple of Matidia, which Hadrian had commissioned in A.D. 119 in honor of his mother-in-law.[42] Together, the two temples formed a

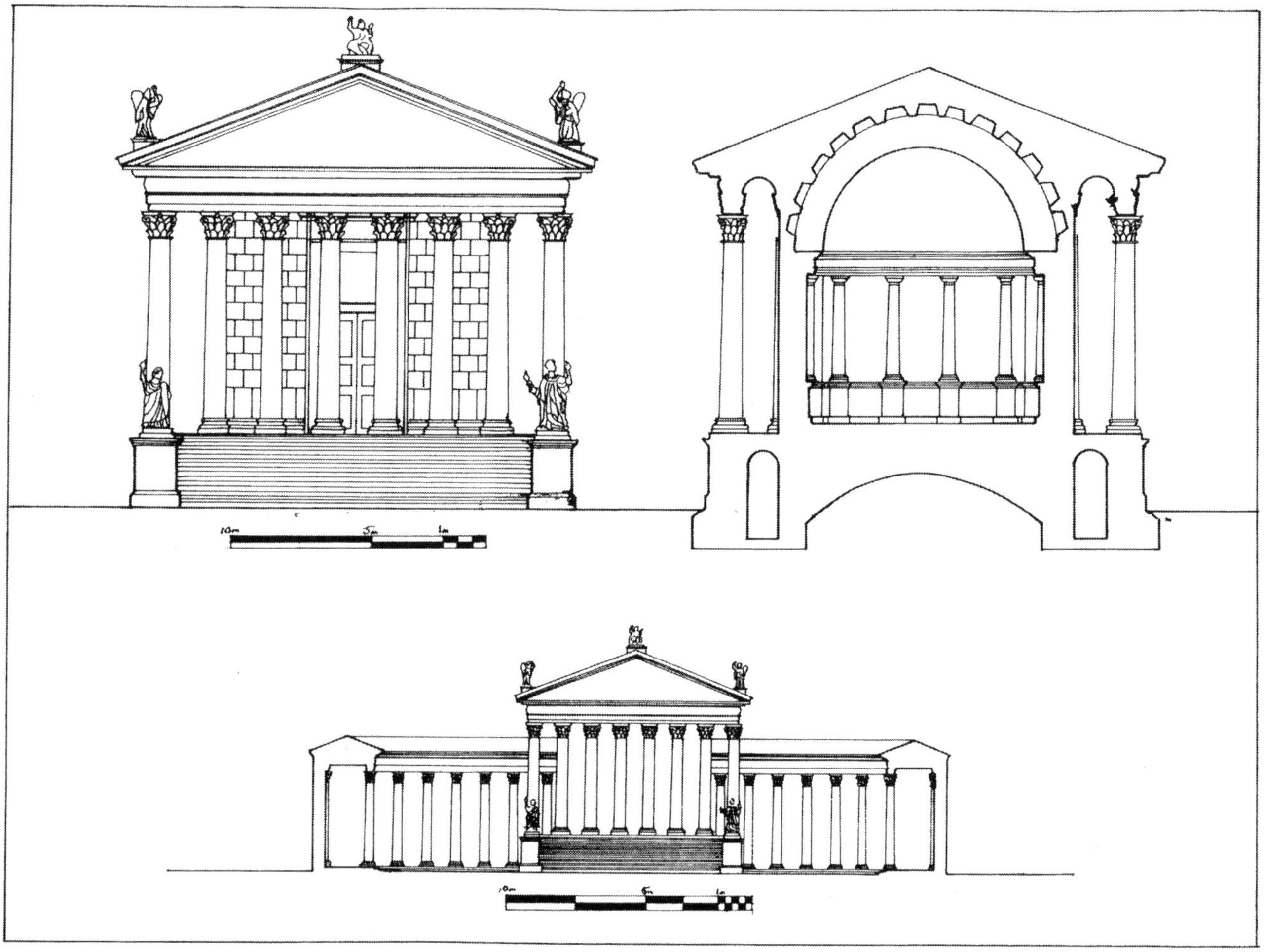

157. Rome, Temple of Divus Hadrianus, A.D. 139–145, section and elevation. Drawing: Matt Fitzgerald based on V. Passarelli in *Atti CongStArchit* (1938): p. 123.

monumental funerary complex in the middle of the Campus Martius.[43]

The Temple of Divus Hadrianus (Fig. 157) was begun in A.D. 139 and dedicated by Antoninus Pius in A.D. 145.[44] Antoninus may have employed some of the same craftsmen and architects Hadrian had used in building the Temple of Venus and Rome. Materials used in the building were peperino, travertine, and Proconnesian marble.[45] Like the Temple of Venus and Rome, the Temple of Divus Hadrianus was peripteral in plan, although smaller (Fig. 158). Composed of eight by thirteen columns, its podium measured 27 meters wide by 45 meters long (92 by 153 Roman feet). The fluted columns, eleven of which remain today in the façade of the Roman Stock Exchange, measure 14.80 meters (50 Roman feet) in height, including the base and capital. In typical Greek fashion, their shafts were made of drums, rather than being monolithic as in the Pantheon.[46] The height of their shaft is 12.30 meters (42 Roman feet), a ratio of column height to column shaft of 6 to 5.[47] The closest comparison can be made to the temples of Apollo in Circo and Castor and Pollux. Like them also, its columns have a slenderness ratio of 10 to 1, based on the height of 50 Roman feet and a diameter of 5 Roman feet.[48]

The entablature was similar to that of the Temple of Venus and Rome in that its architrave was divided into two fasciae and crowned by three moldings, a cavetto, ovolo, and astragal.[49] Its frieze was pulvinated and had a deeply projecting cornice with modillions. Lions' heads and palmettes were carved on the corona (Fig. 159).[50] The entablature visible today is heavily restored in stucco, and only the central part of the cornice resembles the original.[51]

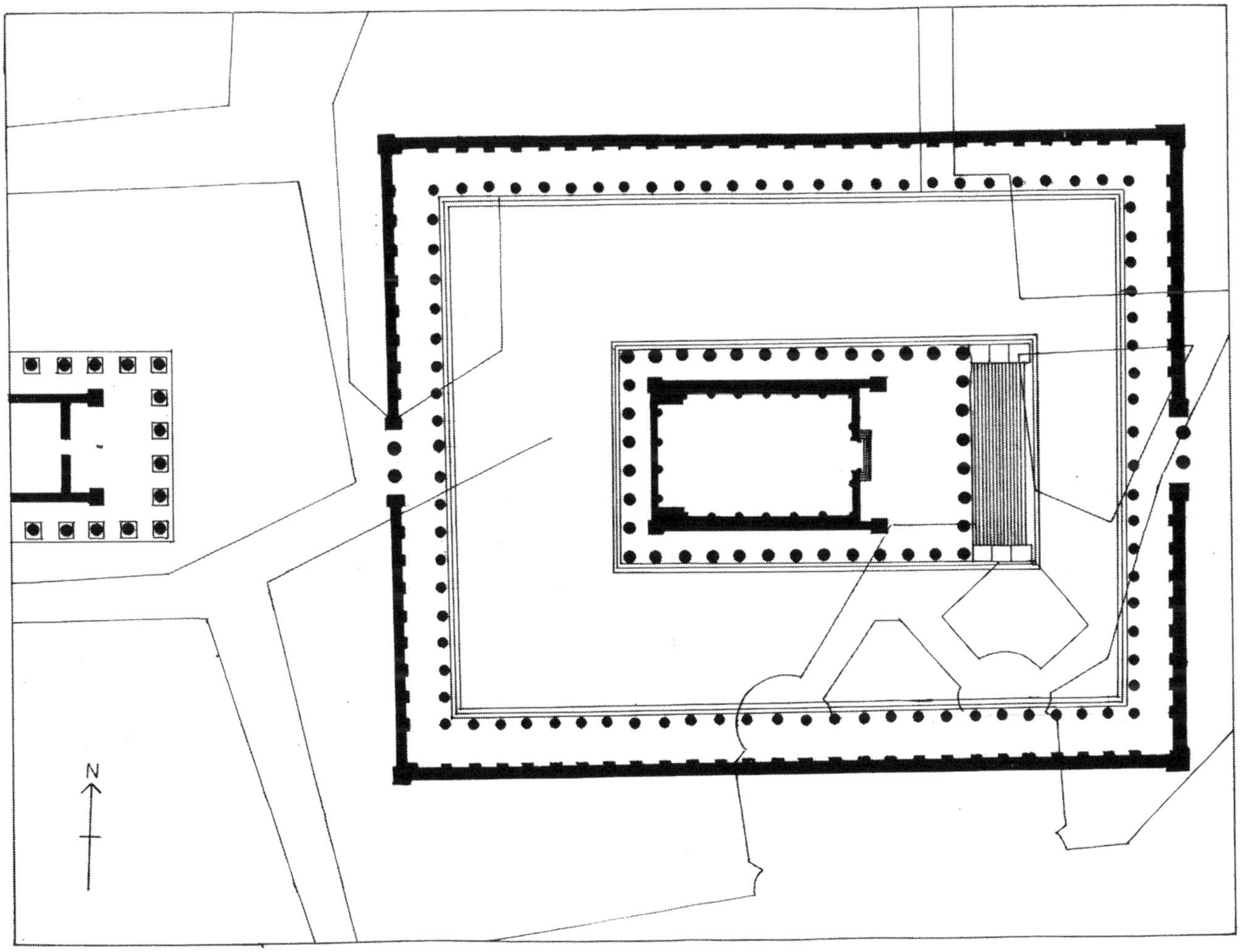

158. Temple of Divus Hadrianus, plan. Drawing: Matt Fitzgerald based on Rodolfo Lanciani, *Forma Urbis Romae* (1990), pl. 15.

The peristyle had a vaulted ceiling with coffers on all four sides, and the cella walls had pilasters corresponding to the columns. The interior of the cella was likewise vaulted and coffered. The interior was lined with columns on each side, and the west end had a squared-off apse. A richly decorated entablature carried around the top of the interior walls, its convex frieze sculpted with spirals of acanthus and candelabra.[52]

Marble panels lining the podium may have contained relief sculptures representing the Roman provinces that Hadrian served and indicative of Hadrian's benevolence to the provinces.[53] Surviving fragments of these are displayed in the courtyard of the Capitoline Museum and in other museums in Rome and Naples.

The temple was placed in the middle of a rectangular forum space, surrounded on all sides by a colonnade. Entrance gates were placed on the main axis on the east and west sides.[54] It was an unusual arrangement in that the temple was in the middle of the space rather than at one end as was typical of the imperial fora. As in the case of the Temple of Venus and Rome, it was a response to the importance of both approaches, the Via Flaminia from the east, the Pantheon and the Temple of Matidia from the west.

Antoninus was also active as a builder in the Forum Romanum, constructing there the Temple of Antoninus and Faustina (Fig. 160). It was begun by a decree of the Senate after the death of the Empress Faustina in A.D. 141.[55] When Antoninus died in A.D. 161, it was rededicated in his name.[56] Today, it is the most intact

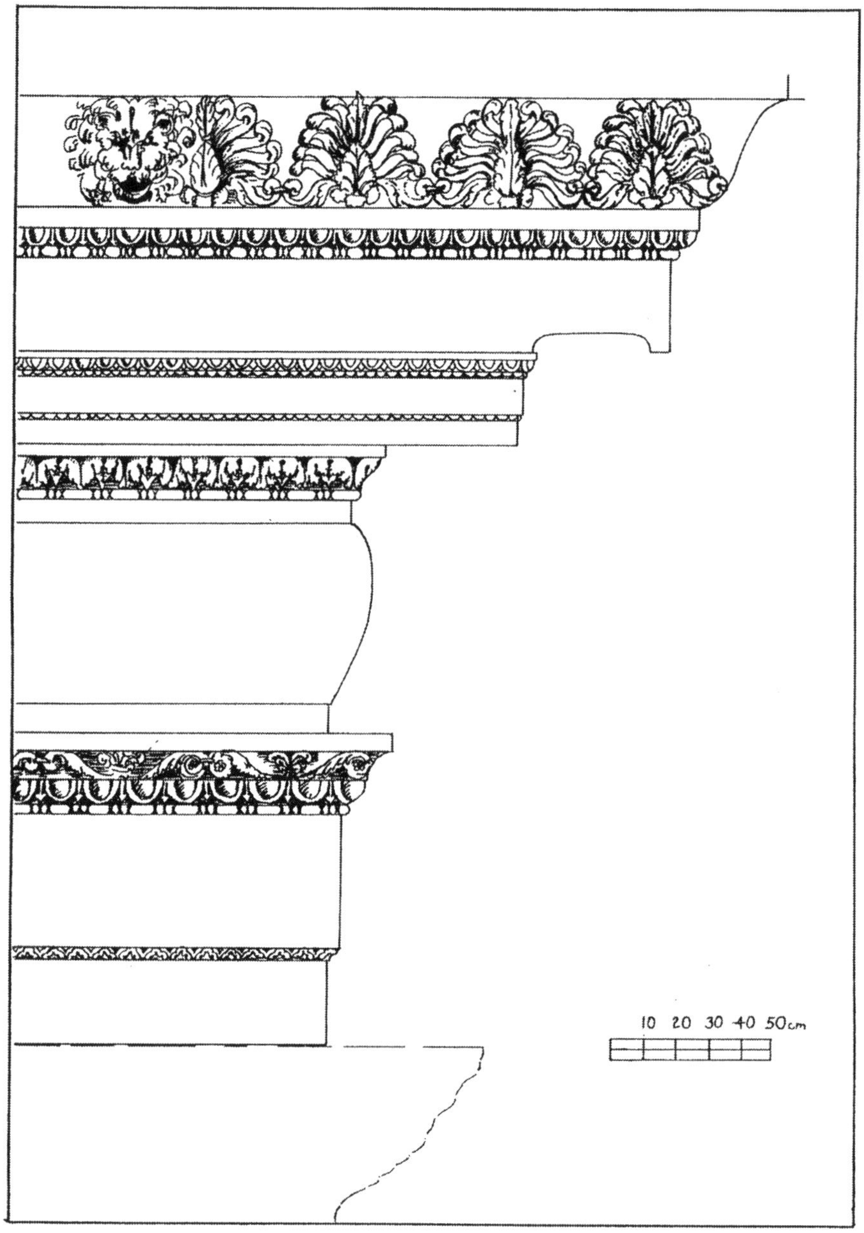

159. Temple of Divus Hadrianus, entablature and cornice detail. Drawing: Cheryl Thompson after Antonio da Sangallo the Elder in Lucos Cozza, *Tempio di Adriano* (1982), p. 20, fig. 19.

of all the temples on the Forum Romanum thanks to its conversion into a church in the seventh century A.D. It was later made the Church of San Lorenzo in Miranda, and in 1536, the Renaissance façade seen today was added.[57]

The building has a high podium of peperino in *opus quadratum*, with twenty-one steps leading to the pronaos (Fig. 161). An altar was located in the middle of the stairs, and images on coins indicate a balustrade-like fence across the front.[58] The cella walls, like the podium, are peperino. They were originally covered with marble revetments, but these were removed at the time the Renaissance façade was added.[59] With six columns on the front and three deep, the pronaos followed the well-established model of buildings such as the Temple of Saturn and the Temple of Apollo Sosianus, among others.[60] The overall measurements are 22 meters wide by 38 meters long (75 by 129 Roman feet), making it almost identical in size to the Temple of Apollo Palatinus.

160. Rome, Temple of Antoninus and Faustina, A.D. 141–161. Photo: John W. Stamper.

As with the Pantheon, the column shafts are monolithic cipollino, with white marble Corinthian capitals. Also like the Pantheon is the columns' overall height of 14 meters (48 Roman feet). Their shafts are 11.80 meters (40 Roman feet), a ratio of 6 to 5. The ratio of column height to their diameter is 9.60 to 1.[61]

The entablature of the Temple of Antoninus and Faustina, like that of the Temple of Venus and Rome, had only a two-step architrave. It is ornamented on the temple's flanks with sculpted griffons, acanthus scrolls, candelabra, and sacrificial vessels (Fig. 162).[62] On the front, the architrave has the inscription "DIVAE FAVSTINAE EX S C," and the frieze is inscribed with "DIVO ANTONINO ET."[63]

In all, the later temple architecture of Hadrian and that of Antoninus Pius exhibited both a continuation

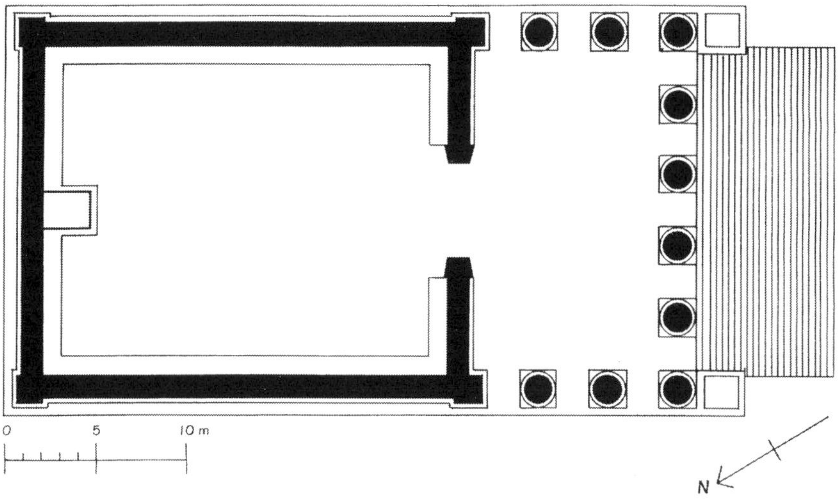

161. Temple of Antoninus and Faustina, plan. Drawing: Andrew Bucci after F. Bianchi and A. Bartoli in *MonLinc* 23 (1914): pl. 1.

162. Temple of Antoninus and Faustina, detail of entablature. Photo: Istituto Centrale per il Catalogo e la Documentazione, E. 8678.

of the Augustan classical style and a divergence away from it based on influences from Athens and Asia Minor. The Temple of Venus and Rome was a synthesis of Athenian influences with those of Asia Minor. Its plan and its columns were modeled after those of the Temple of Zeus, but the details of its entablature were more related to Pergamon. The Temple of Divus Hadrianus had many similarities to the Temple of Venus and Rome, only at a smaller scale. It was influenced by sources from both Pergamon and Athens, with adaptations to its Roman context. The Temple of Antonius and Faustina was a synthesis of Augustan-era temples for its plan, the Pantheon for its columns, and the Temple of Venus and Rome for its architrave. As with much of Rome's temple architecture, tradition, innovation, and transformation all served to produce a noble structure that represented the emperor, his links to the past, and his visions of the future.

EPILOGUE

This study's primary intention has been to analyze the architectural, religious, and political importance of the Temple of Jupiter Capitolinus in Rome from the time of its dedication at the beginning of the Republic to the middle Empire. The Capitoline Temple exerted a powerful influence on Roman society for centuries, serving as the focal point of the city's religious and political culture. From its location on top of the Capitoline Hill, the temple dominated the city around it just as the Parthenon came to dominate Athens after its construction in the mid–fifth century B.C. The Capitoline Temple was a timeless beacon guarding over the city, evoking memories of Rome's founding, its greatest leaders, and its long tradition of celebratory events.

Throughout the Republic, no other temple in Rome rivaled the Capitoline Temple in size or religious and political importance. Most other temples were barely half its size, and none commanded such an imposing site. It was only in the time of Augustus, with the construction of the Temple of Mars Ultor, that it was rivaled in scale and prominence. The width of this temple's pronaos was, in fact, nearly equal to that of the Temple of Jupiter Capitolinus as it is reconstructed in this study, suggesting that Augustus's architects looked to the ancient building as a precedent. The Capitoline Temple may have been the model in a similar manner for Vespasian's architect in building the Templum Pacis and again for the builders of the Temple of Divus Traianus and the Pantheon.

This study's second intention was to analyze Rome's temple architecture as it changed over time. It has taken into account the fact that many of the temples, whether in the Forum Romanum, the Forum Boarium, the Largo Argentina, or around the Circus Flaminia, were built, destroyed, and then rebuilt again. In some cases, this was a cycle that was repeated two or three times. The Temple of Jupiter Capitolinus was built and rebuilt four times between 525–507 B.C. and A.D. 82. With each of these rebuildings, certain features of the temple's plan or stylistic details were altered to reflect the changing political and religious context and the effects of new stylistic influences.

This book began with a challenge to the currently accepted reconstruction of the Temple of Jupiter Capitolinus, arguing that its width, length, height, and interaxial spacings are far too large for the technology of Roman builders in the sixth century B.C. Because of its exaggerated size, it has been viewed by most architectural historians as an anomaly in the history of Roman architecture. This exaggerated size has always made it difficult to relate the Capitoline Temple to any other temples, whether Etruscan, republican, or imperial.

The new reconstruction proposed here is based on a different interpretation of the building's physical evidence and written accounts by ancient authors. It also takes into account a comparative study of later temple architecture in Rome to which it was indubitably linked. It proposes a building whose dimensions are more compatible with both contemporary and later temples, and thus more within the capabilities of builders in the sixth century B.C. The Temple of Jupiter Capitolinus presented here is seen not as an anomaly, but as a paradigmatic building that had a major influence on the designs of many later temple structures and their iconographic programs, at least until the middle of the second century A.D.

The review of Etrusco-Roman temples from the fifth and fourth centuries B.C. revealed a period of experimentation in plan type yet a continuing use of

characteristic Etruscan and Latin features, for instance, the tall podium, widely spaced columns in a deep pronaos, and terra-cotta decorative details. Temples from this period owed much to the Temple of Jupiter Capitolinus in terms of their plans, architectural forms, and symbolism, yet they were all built at a scale about half its size as it is reconstructed in this study. This in itself is a significant difference, but not nearly so if we consider the fact that they would have been only about one-third the size of the previously accepted reconstruction.

The analysis of Roman temple architecture in the third and second centuries B.C. covered an important period of transition from the Etrusco-Roman tradition to an adaptation of the Hellenistic style, especially the introduction of the Ionic Order. As Rome systematically conquered more territory in the eastern Mediterranean, it increasingly absorbed the architectural forms of Hellenistic Athens, Priene, and Pergamon initially in the form of the Ionic Order, and then in the Corinthian.

The writings of Vitruvius were also introduced in this context. Although he wrote his *Ten Books of Architecture* much later, in the first century B.C., his theories on temple architecture most directly applied to the Ionic Order, which was introduced into Rome two centuries earlier. The Temple of Portunus in the Forum Boarium, for instance, closely corresponded to his theories of architectural beauty and illustrates the way builders typically followed the proportional canons Vitruvius described, while altering them when they felt it necessary for visual refinement. Discussion of Vitruvius's theories early in the study also provided an outline of his systems of categorization according to plan and façade types so that they could be used as a reference throughout the study.

The introduction of the Corinthian Order was then described as a further aspect of Hellenistic influence on Roman architecture. Early examples of the new order included the Round Temple by the Tiber, the Temple of Vesta at Tivoli, and Temple B in Largo Argentina. Contemporary with these was the partial transformation of the Capitoline Temple by the dictator Sulla, who used elements of Corinthian columns from the Temple of Olympian Zeus in Athens as he rebuilt the structure after a fire. The introduction of the Corinthian Order into Rome continued with projects like Pompey's Temple of Venus Victrix and Caesar's Forum Julium. Integral to this discussion was an analysis of the role of temple architecture in the processions and ceremonies of the late Republic.

The assimilation of Hellenistic architecture into Roman building practices began to change at the time of the second triumvirate – Octavian, Antony, and Lapidus – in the late first century B.C. Roman builders and architects continued to be influenced by eastern styles and building techniques, especially those of Asia Minor, but at the same time they made their own distinct interpretations. They also began to exert an influence on other regions, including Athens. Their distinctly Roman interpretations of the Corinthian Order were evident, for instance, in the Temple of Divus Julius, Temple of Saturn, Temple of Apollo Palatinus, and the Temple of Apollo Sosianus. We see in these buildings a certain continuity that was unique to Rome. Most of them had marble Corinthian capitals with precise formal and technical characteristics that showed a clear influence of Hellenistic sources but with Roman refinements.

Discussion then focused on the Temple of Mars Ultor, Augustus's most important building in Rome, constructed in 37–2 B.C. A comparison between this building and the Temple of Jupiter Capitolinus revealed dimensional similarities in the width of its pronaos, which suggest a direct architectural link. It was an indication that Augustus and his architects may have looked at the Capitoline Temple with renewed interest as a reference point for their own imperial architecture. They saw it as a building to emulate or recall as an important part of Augustus's efforts to establish and maintain the legitimacy of his rule. At the same time, this comparison provided a review of the differences between the Etrusco-Roman style of the early Republic and the classicism of Augustus.

The architecture of the Flavian dynasty from the second half of the first century A.D. represented the work of an especially prodigious group of builders who achieved a new level of refinement and perfection in temple architecture. They constructed the Temple of Vespasian, Templum Pacis, and Forum Transitorium, and they rebuilt the Capitoline Temple twice, making it a more characteristically Corinthian structure while maintaining its original plan. They also constructed the Arch of Titus, which was placed on the axis of the Via

Sacra at a point where it framed a view of the Temple across the Forum Romanum. It was the Flavians' way of politically honoring the memory of Jupiter and associating their name with the temple's symbolic reference to Rome's founding.

Discussion of the Temple of Divus Trajanus, the giant temple begun by Trajan and finished by Hadrian, again pointed out similarities in dimensions that may have existed between this temple and those of the Capitoline Temple. Like Augustus, Trajan responded to the city's most important architectural precedent, continuing the revival of interest in its historical significance and exploiting its compelling power to maintain the legitimacy of his rule.

This dimensional unity in temple architecture in imperial Rome culminated with Hadrian's Pantheon, which had the same 115-foot width as the Temple of Jupiter Capitolinus as it is reconstructed in this study. Maintaining a long association with the East, Hadrian associated himself with both Zeus and Jupiter. His link to the deities and his emulation of certain aspects of the Capitoline Temple in his design of the Pantheon, plus its equidistant location between the Capitoline Temple and the Mausoleum of Augustus, were discussed as a representation of both the unity and the universal character of the religious and political life of the Roman Empire. Hadrian's far-reaching interests led him to embrace on one hand a Hellenistic identity based on the city of Athens and the cult of Zeus and, on the other hand, the Latin culture focused on Rome and the Capitoline triad Jupiter, Juno, and Minerva. The Pantheon served as a unique manifestation of this religious and political synthesis across cultural borders, its architecture reflecting both tradition and innovation.

The analysis of Hadrian's Temple of Venus and Rome and the two temples built by his successor, Antoninus Pius, further considered his link to Zeus in Athens and the influence of the precedent of the Temple of Olympian Zeus. It concluded with the work of Antoninus Pius and the transformations his architects made to the Hadrianic style in the middle of the second century A.D.[1] These temples of Hadrian and Antoninus Pius were not the last constructed in Rome, but they were the last to represent a discernable unity in temple design with a lineage going back to the Capitoline Temple and the Roman adaptation of the Hellenistic orders.

In summary, this book has sought to draw attention to the authority of precedent in the design of Rome's temple architecture from the early Republic to the time of Hadrian and the Antonines. Crucial to this thesis is the proposed reconstruction of the Temple of Jupiter Capitolinus, which allows us to recognize its central role as a paradigm in Rome's architectural development. Possessing the political status of its association with the founding of the Republic and its religious authority as the temple dedicated to Jupiter, Juno, and Minerva, it was the most important architectural model for generations of temple builders. The site of Rome derived its authority from the history of its founding, and the Temple of Jupiter Capitolinus symbolized the legitimate access to and maintenance of political power.

Political and religious symbols permeated imperial Rome, from visual displays and honorific inscriptions on public monuments to coins and literary texts. Emperors had many political and religious symbols to use in acquiring and consolidating their power. The republican consuls and dictators and imperial rulers alike drew on architecture and ceremony to foster power and legitimacy in Rome and the rest of the Empire.[2] How they did so is revealed most vividly in the temple and forum complexes on which they lavished much of their energy and money and which remain so striking for us to observe today in Rome's ageless topography.

The establishment and maintenance of political and religious *auctoritas* through architecture and ceremony was a part of Rome's development from its founding in the eighth century B.C. to the end of the Empire. We cannot, in fact, fully understand its architecture unless we understand the relationship between architecture and the political and religious intentions behind its production. Architecture and its urban settings, combined with the ritual ceremonies that took place within them, were the very essence of Roman society and culture.[3] While symbolizing the apparent presence of an overriding political authority, the public buildings and urban spaces of ancient Rome also represent a social balance, a mutually held belief in the value of urban settings and ritual ceremonies, an acceptance and, in many cases, a powerful visual expression of the overt presence of state authority.

As stated in the Introduction, precedents in architecture form the basis of a continuous evolution

of style and building practice, one architect describing it as "form which has been accepted as the proper expression of good logic, fitness and beauty, proven by the test of time and accepted as a standard upon which new expression can be modeled and with which it may be compared."[4] Architects in the Roman world operated much more in terms of precedent than most architects today are accustomed to.

This study examined how the design of temple structures typically made reference to earlier precedents, and how this process of both imitation and innovation was essential to members of the Roman ruling class in establishing and maintaining their political control. It was also essential to the general population – the plebeians and the middle class – in demonstrating their support for or disagreement with certain causes, their admiration for particular rulers, or their dissatisfaction with their political status. Impressive architectural settings and elaborate public ceremonies were all acknowledged modes of exercising power or establishing *auctoritas*, a concept the ancient Romans understood well. The pomp and spectacle of a triumphal procession amid monumental marble-clad buildings became a way of explaining, impressing, and mediating between the rulers and the people.

Although much of Rome's early architecture was derived from Etruscan and Latin traditions and practices, Roman architects, engineers, and planners developed their own identifiable system of planning and building adapted to specific topographical conditions and constructional capabilities. Along with other cities of central and southern Italy, Rome was especially rich in multicultural influences because it was there that the Romans, Etruscans, Latins, and Sabines, and later the Hellenistic Greeks, met one another. The Egyptians and the Greeks had been the first to build columnar temples and to organize cities on a formal grid. The Romans expanded on these concepts at a time when their military conquests and increasing wealth allowed them to build new temple and forum complexes in Rome and its colonies. Thus, they promulgated newly codified planning and building modes.

The Roman architectural community made this new expressive language its own, if not always out of agreement with its principles, then because its aesthetic results fulfilled a deeply felt need for elegance and monumentality in architecture. As temples became taller, columns more slender and attenuated, forum spaces grander and more clearly and formally articulated, basilicas more solid, and triumphal arches more refined, Romans felt a great satisfaction with their artistic production. There was an assurance in their decision making. This movement toward internationalism was already well under way in the late Republic, but reached its maturity in the time of the Flavians and Hadrian.

In looking at the temples of ancient Rome, this book has provided an analysis of this cross-cultural assimilation and transformation of early architectural traditions. It has described both the foreign sources of Roman architecture and its distinctly regional elements. It has identified the factors that allowed Roman architecture to transcend its precedents, to leap from a purely local or regional phenomenon to one of international importance. In part, it is the interplay of the localized and the universal that confers on the architecture of ancient Rome its authority, its appropriateness as a transformable and compelling language for other cultures. A universal style of architecture without some local characteristics can be lifeless and sterile, while a regional style without outside influences can appear to be provincial. Like any great architecture, that of the Romans, as this book has shown, possessed a unique combination of both the universal and the regional.

NOTES

INTRODUCTION

1 Vitr. Pref. 1.2.
2 Hannah Arendt, "What Was Authority?" in *Authority*, ed. Carl J. Friedrich (Cambridge: Harvard University Press, 1958), 98.
3 Ibid., 100.
4 William A. Boring, "What Is Precedent Doing to American Architecture?" *JAIA* 12 (June 9, 1924): 260–3.
5 Ibid.

1: BUILDING THE TEMPLE OF JUPITER CAPITOLINUS

1 Liv. 1.53.2–3.
2 For information on the Temple of Jupiter Feretrius, see Filippo Coarelli, "Iuppiter Feretrius, Aedes," *LTUR*, vol. 3, 135–6; Liv. 1.10.5–7, 1.33.9, 4.20.3–11, 4.32.4; Prop. *Eleg.* 4.10.1–51; Dion. Hal. *Rom. Ant.* 2.34.4; Flor. *Rom. Hist.* 1.1; Richardson, *Dictionary*, 219; Robert M. Ogilvie, *Early Rome and the Etruscans* (Hassocks, England: Harvester Press, 1976), 37–8; Anna Maria Sommella, "Le recenti scoperte sul Campidoglio e la fondazione del tempio di Giove Capitolino," *RendPontAcc* 70 (1997–1998): 70–1; Pierre Grimal, *The Dictionary of Classical Mythology*, trans. A. R. Maxwell-Hyslop (Oxford: Blackwell, 1996), 244.
3 For discussion of an earlier, smaller temple, or *sacellum*, dedicated to Jupiter, Juno, and Minerva and used already in the late seventh century B.C. as a destination for triumphal marches, see Jorge Martínez-Pinna, "Evidenza di un tempio di Giove Capitolino a Roma all'inizio del VI sec. A.D." *ArchLaz* 4 (1981): 249–52.
4 Dion. Hal. *Rom. Ant.* 3.69.3–4; Liv. 1.12.6.
5 For a discussion of the mythology of Rome's founding, see H. Stuart Jones, "The Sources for the Tradition of Early Roman History," *CAH*, vol. 7, 322; Howard H. Scullard, *A History of the Roman World from 753 to 146 B.C.* (London: Methuen, 1980), 46–8.
6 Arendt, "What Was Authority?" 98.
7 For information on the Pons Sublicius, see Liv. 1.33.6; Dion. Hal. *Rom. Ant.* 3.45.2; Plut. *Numa* 9; Filippo Coarelli, "Pons Sublicius," *LTUR*, vol. 4, 112–13; Richardson, *Dictionary*, 299; Scullard, *History of the Roman World*, 53. The original bridge was built of wood. It probably dated to the time of Ancus Marcius.
8 The walls and gates of the Palatine settlement remained visible down to the Empire. For a discussion of *Roma Quadrata*, see Filippo Coarelli, "Roma Quadrata," *LTUR*, vol. 4, 207–9; Dion. Hal. *Rom. Ant.* 1.88.2, 2.65.3; Plut. *Rom.* 9; Tac. *Ann.* 12.24; Theodor Mommsen, *The History of Rome*, trans. William Purdie Dickenson (New York: Charles Scribner's Sons, 1898), 63–5.
9 Dion. Hal. *Rom. Ant.* 1.88.2, 89.1; J. J. Pollitt, *The Art of Rome, c.753 B.C.–A.D. 337; Sources and Documents* (New York: Cambridge University Press, 1983), 50.
10 Coarelli states the size of *Roma Quadrata* was approximately 600 meters on average for each side. A second settlement was located on the Quirinal Hill, which also had a large cluster of houses, and a shrine dedicated to Jupiter, Juno, and Minerva, a counterpart to the later temple on the Capitoline Hill. In addition, it had a shrine dedicated to the goddess of Fidelity, and its own version of the shields of Mars. Between the Palatine and Quirinal Hills, and extending westward to the Capitoline Hill, was the low-lying Subura district. See Coarelli, "Roma Quadrata," 207–9; and Mary Beard, John North, and Simon Price, *Religions of Rome: A History*, vol. 1 (Cambridge: Cambridge University Press, 1999), 1.
11 Ov. *Fast.* 4.833–48; Liv. 1.6.3; Quoted in Beard, North, and Price, *Religions of Rome*, vol. 1, 175–6; Paul Zoch, *Ancient Rome: An Introductory History* (Norman: University of Oklahoma Press, 1998), 11.
12 For explanations of the legendary founding of Rome by Romulus see Hugh Last, "The Founding of Rome," *CAH*, vol. 7, 365–71; Scullard, *History of the Roman World*, 46–50; Ogilvie, *Early Rome*, 35–7; and Marcel Le Glay et al., *A History of Rome*, trans. Antonia Nevill (Malden, MA: Blackwell, 2001), 19–24.
13 Scullard, *History of the Roman World*, 51–3.
14 For information on the three Etruscan kings, see Scullard, *History of the Roman World*, 54–5; Hugh Last, "The Kings of Rome," *CAH*, vol. 7, 387–95; Ogilvie, *Early Rome*, 62–78.
15 For discussion of the legacy of the Tarquins, see Dion. Hal. *Rom. Ant.* 3.67.5; Liv. 1.38.1–6; Scullard, *History of the Roman World*, 54–6; Ogilvie, *Early Rome*, 71–2.
16 For the legacy of Servius Tullius, see Jacques Heurgon, *The Rise of Rome to 264 B.C.*, trans. James Willis (Berkeley and Los Angeles: University of California Press, 1973), 142–3; Scullard, *History of the Roman World*, 54–6.

17 Diana Bowder, ed., *Who Was Who in the Roman World* (New York: Washington Square Press), 490. For information on the Temple of Diana on the Aventine Hill, see Laura Vendittelli, "Diana Aventina, Aedes," *LTUR*, vol. 2, 11–13; Ogilvie, *Early Rome*, 65–8.

18 Heurgon, *The Rise of Rome to 264* B.C., 139.

19 Ogilvie, *Early Rome*, 52.

20 Andreas Alföldi, *Early Rome and the Latins* (Ann Arbor: University of Michigan Press, 1963), 201–2; Ogilvie, *Early Rome*, 49.

21 For information on the Etruscans' religion, see, for instance, Graeme Barker and Tom Rasmussen, *The Etruscans* (Malden, MA: Blackwell, 1998), 93.

22 H. Stuart Jones, "The Primitive Institutions of Rome," *CAH*, vol. 7, 414; Scullard, *History of the Roman World*, 62–3; Ogilvie, *Early Rome*, 60; Mommsen, *The History of Rome*, 72–7.

23 Jones, "The Primitive Institutions of Rome," 420; Mommsen, *The History of Rome*, 80–1.

24 Jones, "The Primitive Institutions of Rome," 425–6; Mommsen, *The History of Rome*, 81–2; Alan Watson, *Rome and the XII Tables: Persons and Property* (Princeton: Princeton University Press, 1975), 98–110.

25 For discussion of the auspices and the kings, see Jerzy Linderski, "Cicero and Roman Divination," in *Roman Questions*, 462; and Arendt, "What Was Authority?" 101.

26 Var. *Lat. Lang.* 7.8; Linderski, "Cicero and Roman Divination," 462.

27 Dion. Hal. *Rom. Ant.* 2.5.5–6.2; Jones, "The Primitive Institutions of Rome," 429–30.

28 John Stambaugh, *The Ancient Roman City* (Baltimore: Johns Hopkins University Press, 1988), 214–15; John Stambaugh, "The Functions of Roman Temples," in *ANRW*, vol. 2, 555–6; Palmira Cipriano, *Templum* (Rome: Università La Sapienza, 1983), 121–38.

29 Jerzy Linderski, "Watching the Birds: Cicero the Augur and the Augural *Templa*," in *Roman Questions*, 485–95.

30 This concept of a *templum* is implicit in Ennius's, "O great temples of the gods, united with the shining stars," or his "Trembled the mighty temple of Jove who thunders in heaven." Quoted in Var. *Lat. Lang.* 7.6–7.

31 Ibid., 7.8–9.

32 As explained in Varro, of the four quarters of the sky, the left quarter was to the east. The right quarter to the west, the front quarter to the south, the back quarter to the north. A flash of lightning that darted across the sky from left to right was significant because any sign from the left, or eastern quarter of the heavens, had a more honorable nature than anything observed on the right, or western quarter of the sky. It is from the east that the sun and the moon rise as well as the planets and fixed stars. Var. *Lat. Lang.* 7.8; Linderski, "Cicero and Roman Divination," 462; and Linderski, "Watching the Birds," 492–4.

33 The eastward orientation of an *auspicium* of birds was deduced by archaeological evidence discovered at Bantia in southern Italy. See Linderski, "Watching the Birds," 493–5.

34 Stambaugh, *The Ancient Roman City*, 215.

35 Sybille Haynes, *Etruscan Civilization: A Cultural History* (Los Angeles: J. Paul Getty Museum, 2000), 29; Jones, "The Primitive Institutions of Rome," 426–7.

36 Arendt, "What Was Authority?", 101.

37 For discussion of the role of the two Tarquin kings in the construction of the Temple of Capitoline Jupiter, see Cic. *Rep.* 2.20.36; Liv. 1.38.7, 55.2; Dion. Hal. *Rom. Ant.* 3.69.1, 4.59.1; Plut. *Publ.* 14.1; Tac. *Hist.* 3.72; Raymond Bloch, *The Origins of Ancient Rome*, New York: Frederick A. Praeger, 1960), 21; Gianluca Tagliamonte, "Iuppiter Optimus Maximus Capitolinus, Aedes, Templum (fino all'a 83 A.C.)," *LTUR*, vol 3, 146–7; Sommella, "Le recenti scoperte sul Campidoglio," 69–79; Anna Mura Sommella, "'La grande Roma dei Tarquini:' Alterne vicende di una felice intuizione," *BullCom* 101 (2000): 21–6.

38 For information about the fall of the Etruscan monarchy, see Scullard, *History of the Roman World*, 74–7; Last, "The Kings of Rome," 394–6; and Haynes, *Etruscan Civilization*, 267; Tac. *Hist.* 3.72; Tagliamonte, "Iuppiter Optimus," 144–5; Stefano De Angeli, "Iuppiter Optimus Maximus Capitolinus, aedes (fasi tardo-repubblicane e di età imperiale)," *LTUR*, vol. 3, 148–53; Stambaugh, *The Ancient Roman City*, 12; Richardson, *Dictionary*, 222.

39 Dion. Hal. *Rom. Ant.* 3.69.3–4; Flor. *Rom. Hist.* 1.1.

40 Liv. 1.60.1–6; Dion. Hal. *Rom. Ant.* 3.69.1–4; Flor. *Rom. Hist.* 1.1.

41 Tagliamonte, "Iuppiter Optimus," 144–5; Richardson, *Dictionary*, 222; Bloch, *Origins of Ancient Rome*, 59; Sommella, "Le recenti scoperti sul Campidoglio," 70.

42 Dion. Hal. *Rom. Ant.* 3.70.1–3; Liv. 1.36.4, 1.55.1–6; Linderski, "Cicero and Roman Divination," 473.

43 Dion. Hal. *Rom. Ant.* 3.69.4–6.

44 Liv. 1.55.1–6.

45 Dionysius of Halicarnassus writes in another passage of the site preparation and speaks of multiple temples, "being desirous of performing the vows made by his grandfather, devoted himself to the building of the sanctuaries. For the Elder Tarquinius, while he was engaged in an action during his last war with the Sabines, had made a vow to build temples to Jupiter, Juno and Minerva if he should gain the victory; and he had finished off the peak on which he proposed to erect the temples of these gods by means of retaining walls and high banks of earth . . . but he did not live long enough to complete the building of the temples." Dion. Hal. *Rom. Ant.* 4.59.3, 3.69.1–2; Liv. 1.38.1–6; Sommella, "Le recenti scoperti sul Campidoglio," 69–70.

46 Dion. Hal. *Rom. Ant.* 4.59.3, 3.69.1–2; Liv. 1.53.1–3; Sommella, "Le recenti scoperti sul Campidoglio," 71.

47 Dion. Hal. *Rom. Ant.* 4.61.1–4.

48 Liv. 1.55.1–6.

49 Var. *Lat. Lang.* 5.40–43; Richardson, *Dictionary*, 69.

50 Agnes Kirsopp Lake, "The Archaeological Evidence for the 'Tuscan Temple,'" *MAAR* 12 (1935): 102; Liv. 1.65; Plin. *Nat. Hist.* 35.157; Plut. *Popli.* 13.

51 Liv. 1.56.3–61.1; Sommella, "Le recenti scoperti sul Campidoglio," 69–70: Sommella, "'La grande Roma dei Tarquini,'" 26.

52 Dion. Hal. *Rom. Ant.* 4.59.3; Liv. 1.53.4.

53 The discovery of the human head, according to Livy, made the king even more willing to devote funds to the project. Liv. 1.55.6–7; Ogilvie, *Early Rome*, 75.

54 For information on the Temple of Jupiter Latiaris, see Paola Finocchi, "Il 'Templum' di Iuppiter Latiaris sul Mons

Albanus," *ArchLaz* 4 (1980): 156–8; Filippo Coarelli, "Latiaris Collis," *LTUR*, vol. 3, 177; Last, "The Founding of Rome," 349; Last, "The Kings of Rome," 405; Tagliamonte, "Iuppiter Optimus, 145.

55 Tagliamonte, "Iuppiter Optimus, 145; Georges Dumézil, *Archaic Roman Religion*, trans. Philip Krapp (Chicago: University of Chicago Press, 1970), 284.

56 Liv. 2.8.5–8, 7.3.8. The dedication occurred on September 13, 509 B.C. by the consul M. Horatius Pulvillus. See also Polyb. *Hist.* 3.22.1; Dion. Hal. *Rom. Ant.* 5.35.3; Cic. *Dom. Sua* 54.139; Tac. *Hist.* 3.72; Richardson, *Dictionary*, 222; Rodolfo Lanciani, *Pagan and Christian Rome* (London: Macmillan, 1985), 86; Dumézil, *Archaic Roman Religion*, 284.

57 Jerzy Linderski, "Roman Religion in Livy," in *Roman Questions*, 610; Enn. *Ann.* 1.72–91 in the edition of O. Skutsch, *The Annals of Q. Ennius* (Oxford: Oxford University Press, 1985), 76–7.

58 Linderski, "Roman Religion in Livy," 610–11.

59 Dumézil, *Archaic Roman Religion*, 191.

60 Grimal, *Dictionary of Classical Mythology*, 245.

61 Plut. *Mor.* 282.77; Var. *Lat. Lang.* 5.66; Sabine G. Oswalt, *Concise Encyclopedia of Greek and Roman Mythology* (Glasgow and Chicago: William Collins Sons and Follett, 1965), 161–3.

62 Var. *Lat. Lang.* 5.66; Oswalt, *Concise Encyclopedia of Greek and Roman Mythology*, 161–3.

63 Dumézil, *Archaic Roman Religion*, 178–80.

64 Var. *Lat. Lang.* 5.67; Dumézil, *Archaic Roman Religion*, 291.

65 Oswalt, *Concise Encyclopedia*, 160–3; Var. *Lat. Lang.* 5.69.

66 Einar Gjerstad, "The Etruscans and Rome in Archaic Times," in *Etruscan Culture: Land and People*, trans. Nils G. Sahlin (New York: Columbia University Press; Malmö, Sweden: Alhem, 1962), 188.

67 For references to the statue of Jupiter, see Tagliamonte, "Iuppiter Optimus," 145; Liv. 10.7.10, 30.15.11–12; Plin. *Nat. Hist.* 35.45.157; Richardson, *Dictionary*, 222.

68 Tagliamonte, "Iuppiter Optimus, 146; Liv. 7.3.5.

69 Livy reports that in 295 B.C., the aediles Gnaeus and Quintus Ogulnius brought several usurers to trial and confiscated their property. With their procedes, they put new doors on the Capitoline Temple, bought silver vessels for the three tables in the shrine of Jupiter, and placed on the roof a new statue of the god in a four-horse chariot. Liv. 10.23.12; Tagliamonte, "Iuppiter Optimus," 145–6.

70 Linderski, "Roman Religion in Livy," 609.

71 Lily Ross Taylor, *The Divinity of the Roman Emperor* (Philadelphia: Porcupine Press, 1975), 35, 44.

72 Serv. *Com. Verg. Ecol.* 10.27; Liv. 10.7.10.

73 Taylor, *The Divinity of the Roman Emperor*, 35, 44.

74 Ibid., 45.

75 Beard, North, and Price write that what had been thought of as royal ceremonial was now perceived by the Romans as Roman, not something imposed on them; see *Religions of Rome*, vol. 1, 59–61.

76 Liv. 9.8.1, 22.1.6; Pollitt, *The Art of Rome*, 10; Tagliamonte, "Iuppiter Optimus," 146; Dumézil, *Archaic Roman Religion*, 287; Robert M. Ogilvie, *The Romans and Their Gods in the Age of Augustus* (New York: Norton, 1970), 48–51.

77 White animals were necessary in sacrifices to Jupiter, Juno, Minerva, and other deities of the upper world. Black animals were prescribed for gods of the underworld. Ogilvie, *The Romans and Their Gods*, 43; Cic. *Laws* 2.19.

78 For a detailed description of the details of animal sacrifice, see Ogilvie, *The Romans and Their Gods*, 48–51.

79 Richardson, *Dictionary*, 223–4. Pliny reports that the bronze statue of Jupiter in the cella was made in Delos, which was noted for its bronze foundries; *Nat. Hist.* 34.3.7–5.10.

80 Dumézil, *Archaic Roman Religion*, 288; Grimal, *Dictionary of Classical Mythology*, 245.

81 Dumézil, *Archaic Roman Religion*, 288; Taylor, *The Divinity of the Roman Emperor*, 38; Pollitt, *The Art of Rome*, 10; Serv. *Com. Virg., Ecol.* 10.27; Plin. *Nat. Hist.* 33.36.111; Plut. *Aem. Paul.* 32–4.

82 This is known, Lanciani explains, by a clause appended to imperial letters-patent by which veterans were honorably discharged from the army or navy and privileges bestowed on them in recognition of their services. These deeds, *diplomata honesta missionis*, were engraved on bronze tablets shaped like the cover of a book, the originals of which were hung inside the temple and copies taken by the veterans to their homes. Lanciani, *Pagan and Christian Rome*, 91; Tagliamonte, "Iuppiter Optimus," 146.

83 Gjerstad, "The Etruscans and Rome,"158.

84 Pliny describes the acquisition of the Sibylline oracles during the time of Tarquinius as a wonderful piece of good luck. It was, he says, conferred on the Roman state by some beneficent deity, and it was a good fortune that lasted throughout the existence of the state, saving it often from great calamities; *Nat. Hist.* 4.62.4–6. For a discussion of how Tarquinius came to acquire the oracles, see Dion. Hal. *Rom. Ant.* 4.62.1–4; Cic. *Cat.* 3.4.9.

85 Ogilvie, *The Romans and Their Gods*, 44–5.

86 Tagliamonte, "Iuppiter Optimus," 146–7. The reconstruction by Sulla is discussed in Chapter 5.

87 Cass. Dio, *Rom. Hist.* 66.24; De Angeli, "Iuppiter Optimus," 150–3; Richardson, *Dictionary*, 223. The reconstructions by Vespasian and Domitian are discussed in Chapter 9.

88 Lanciani, *Pagan and Christian Rome*, 90; Rodolfo Lanciani, *The Ruins and Excavations of Ancient Rome* (New York: Bell, 1979), 300.

89 Rodolfo Lanciani, "Il Tempio di Giove Ottimo Massimo," *BullCom* 3 (October–December 1875): 165–203; Hans Riemann, "Beiträge zur Römischen Topographie," *RömMitt* 76 (1969): 110.

90 Lanciani, *The Ruins and Excavations*, 299; Lanciani, *Pagan and Christian Rome*, 85–6, 89–90; Christian Hülsen, "Osservazioni sull'architettura del Tempio di Giove Capitolino," *RömMitt* (1888): 150–1.

91 For sixteenth-century writers on Rome who discuss the Capitoline Temple, see Lucio Fauno, *De antiquitatibus urbis Romae* (*Delle antichità della città di Roma*) (Venice: Michele Tramezzino, 1548); Giovanni Bartolomeo Marliano, *Urbis Romae topographia Italiano*, trans. M. Hercole Barbarasa da Terni (Rome: Antonio Blado, 1548); and Bernardo Gamucci, *Le antichità della città di Roma: raccolte sotto brevità da diversi antichi e moderni scrittori* (Venice: Appresso Giovanni Varisco, 1569).

92 Previous to that, according to Varro, it was called the Saturnian Hill and was once occupied by the Latin town of Saturnia. He noted that the Temple of Saturn is placed by the road just

at its base. Fauno, *De antiquitatibus urbis Romae*, 36; Var. *Lat. Lang.* 5.40–43.

93 Marliano, *Urbis Romae topographia Italiano*; Gamucci, *Le antichità della città di Roma*. In reference to the Arx, Richardson points out that although it is often used as a reference for the northern summit, it is in fact a common noun and should apply to everything within the Capitoline's system of fortifications. Richardson, *Dictionary*, 69.

94 Lake, "Archaelogical Evidence," 103.

95 Nardini, a seventeenth-century writer, cites Tacitus, Virgil, Propertius, Plutarch, and Ovid. See Faminio Nardini, *Roma antica* (Rome: Falco, 1666), 297–301. The issue was summarized in 1689 with the publication of a new version of Marliano's book, *Ritratto di Roma antica*, which incorporated the views of Nardini but which offered no definitive resolution. See Giovanni Bartolomeo Marliano, *Ritratto di Roma antica, formato nuovamente con la autorità di Bartolomeo Marliano, Alessandro Donati, e Faminio Nardini* (Rome: M. A. Rossi, 1689), 26–7; 76–81.

96 Angelo Dalmazzoni, *L'antiquario o sia la guida de forestieri* (Rome: Angelo Dalmazzoni, 1804), 34–5.

97 Antonio Nibby, *Del Foro Romano, della via Sacra, dell'anfiteatro Flavio e de' luoghi adjacenti* (Rome: Presso V. Poggioli, 1819), 59; Carlo Fea, *Descrizione di Roma e suoi contorni abbellita della pianta e delle vedute le più interessanti della medesima* (Rome: Crispino Puccinnelli, 1824), vol. 1, 257–8; and Luigi Canina, *Esposizione storica e topografica del Foro Romano e sue adiacenze* (Rome: Canina, 1845); Luigi Canina, *Esposizione storica e topografica del Foro Romano e sue adiacenze* (Bologna: Arnaldo Forni, 1973), 86–7.

98 Much of Lanciani's information was based on archaeological work done by Jordan and Schupmann. Lanciani, "Il Tempio di Giove Ottimo Massimo," 176–80; and Lanciani, *Ruins and Excavations*, 299; Lake, "Archaeological Evidence," 102–3; Riemann, "Beiträge zur Römischen Topographie," 111.

99 A complete discussion of the temple's dimensions is found in Chapter 2.

2: A NEW RECONSTRUCTION OF THE TEMPLE

1 Einar Gjerstad, *Early Rome: Fortifications, Domestic Architecture, Sanctuaries, Stratigraphic Excavations*, vol. 3 (Lund, Sweden: C. W. K. Gleerup, 1960), 168–89. The reconstruction was published again in later volumes of *Early Rome: Synthesis and Archaeological Evidence*, vol. 4 (Lund: C. W. K. Gleerup, 1966), 390; *Early Rome: Historical Survey*, vol. 6 (Lund: Berlingska Boktryckeriet, 1973), 106.

2 The question of whether the size of the Temple of Jupiter Capitolinus was too great for the available technology in the sixth century B.C. was raised by Ferdinando Castagnoli, "Il tempio romano: Questioni di terminologia e di tipologia," *PBSR* 52 (1984): 7–9; and Cairoli F. Giuliani, "Architettura e tecnica edilizia," *Roma repubblicana fra il 509 e il 270 A.C.*, ed. Patrizio Pensabene (Rome: Edizioni Quasar, 1982), 29–31.

3 John W. Stamper, "The Temple of Capitoline Jupiter, A New Reconstruction," *Hephaistos* 16/17 (1998–1999): 107–38.

4 For information on the Temple of Sol by Aurelian, see Richardson, *Dictionary*, 163–4; Jaqueline Calzini Gysens and Filippo Coarelli, "Sol, Templum," *LTUR*, vol. 4, 331–3.

5 Vitruvius divides the width into ten equal parts in which he distributes the three rooms of the cella, the middle room being four divisions wide, the flanking two being three each; Vitr. 4.7.2; Lake, "Archaeological Evidence," 90–2.

6 Gjerstad, *Early Rome*, vol. 3, 180; Vitr. 4.7.2.

7 Vitr. 3.3.5.

8 Ibid., 4.7.5.

9 Ibid., 3.3.5.

10 The foundations were laid out in a grid plan and the cavities in between filled in with earth and rubble. Further excavations are currently under way.

11 Sommella, "Le recenti scoperte sul Campidoglio," 60–8; and "La grande Roma dei Tarquini," 20–1, figs. 17, 18, and 23.

12 Dion. Hal. *Rom. Ant.* 4.61.2–4. Importantly, Vitruvius and Dionysius of Halicarnassus observed the building in the first century B.C., some years after the original structure was damaged in a fire and rebuilt by Sulla.

13 Gjerstad's dimensions were taken from the site and correspond, with some minor differences, to those taken by Roberto Paribeni and E. Gatti in the nineteenth century. See Roberto Paribeni, "Saggi di scavi nell'area del Tempio di Giove Ottimo Massimo sul Campidoglio," *NSc* (1921): 38–49. The actual dimensions of the podium were 180 Greco-Roman feet plus 22 centimeters in width, and 210 feet plus 9 centimeters long. The few additional centimeters were due to settlement and expansion of the block structure over the centuries. See Gjerstad, *Early Rome*, vol. 3, 178–80; Tagliamonte, "Iuppiter Optimus,"147; Sommella, "Le recenti scoperte sul Campidoglio," 62.

14 Gjerstad translates his dimensions into what he calls the Greco-Roman foot, because he speculates this is what would have been used by the building's architects for laying out its plan. The term used here is the Roman foot. One Roman foot equals .296 meters or 11 $\frac{5}{8}$ inches. Gjerstad, *Early Rome*, vol. 3, 178–80.

15 Nardini, *Roma antica*, 282.

16 Marliano, *Ritratto di Roma antica*, 76.

17 Although the plans of Canina and Gjerstad have many similarities, some differences include seven columns down the sides in Canina's plan, six in Gjerstad's, a more elaborate rendering of the cella rooms by Canina, and Canina's proposal of steps on three sides of the podium, treating it more like a stylobate, as opposed to a true podium with steps on the front alone as shown by Gjerstad. See Canina, *Esposizione storica e topografica* (1973), pl. 4A; Tagliamonte, "Iuppiter Optimus," 147.

18 Lanciani, "Il Tempio di Giove,"165–89.

19 Lanciani, *Pagan and Christian Rome*, 86–7. According to Lanciani, a sketch made at that time by Fabretti and published in his volume "De Columna Trajana" shows that fourteen tiers of stone have disappeared.

20 Jordan includes in his article the excavation report of architect L. Schupmann. He describes the podium as being 51 meters wide by 55.62 meters long, and that the columns had interaxial dimensions of 9.20 meters and diameters of 1.90 meters. See Henri Jordan, "Osservazioni sul Tempio di Giove Capitolino," *Annali dell'Istituto di Corrispondenza Archeologica*

(1876): 145–72. Lanciani published a second article himself in 1876 in which he reported on the measurements done by architect William Henzen. Lanciani suggested that the podium had a width of 192 Roman feet (56.60 meters) and interaxial dimensions of 11.04 meters. Rodolfo Lanciani, "Ara di Vermino," *BullCom* 4 (January–March 1876): 31–6. See also Hülsen, "Osservazioni sull'architettura del Tempio di Giove Capitolino," 150–5.

21 Richter provided the most detailed reconstruction drawing in1901, which was based on the plan by Canina but with alternating bay widths, the interaxial dimensions measuring 11 meters (38 Roman feet) and 8.90 meters (30 Roman feet), respectively. See Otto Ludwig Richter, *Topographie der Stadt Rom*, vol. 3 (Munich: C. H. Beck, 1901), 122–3.

22 Gjerstad points out that there is a discrepancy between Paribeni's description in the text indicating dimensions of 55 by 60 meters and the drawing in the article prepared by E. Gatti, which indicates dimensions of 53.50 by 62 meters. Gjerstad agrees with the latter. Paribeni, "Saggi di scavi," 38–49; Gjerstad, *Early Rome*, vol. 3, 178; and Riemann, "Beiträge zur Römischen Topographie," 112.

23 Paribeni, "Saggi di scavi," 38–49; Gjerstad, *Early Rome*, vol. 3, 177.

24 The height of the foundation walls, at least initially, was about 4 meters, though there is evidence that they were raised twice in later rebuildings. Gjerstad, *Early Rome*, vol. 3, 176.

25 If the base diameter was one-seventh of the column's height, then the diameter in this case would have been 2.3 meters, or 8 Roman feet. Gjerstad suggests that this was, in fact, the modulus for the entire building, many of the temple's principal dimensions being multiples of eight. He assumes that the heights of the capitals and column bases of the Capitoline Jupiter Temple also followed Vitruvian dimensions, that is, half of the base diameter of the column shaft, or 4 Roman feet each. If this were true, each column would have been composed of a 4-foot-high base, a 48-foot shaft, and a 4-foot capital. Vitr. 4.7.1–5; Gjerstad, *Early Rome*, vol. 3, 178–80.

26 The total interaxial width across the front would have been 168 Roman feet.

27 The question of whether the archaeological remains of the temple should be considered foundation or the temple podium itself is raised in Giuliani, "Architettura e tecnica edilizia," 29–31; and Castagnoli, "Il tempio romano," 7–9. It is reviewed but dismissed in Sommella, "Le recenti scoperte sul Campidoglio," 67.

28 In the case of ancient roof trusses of large spans, the bottom chord was typically composed of two or more pieces of timber that were spliced together at the points of intersection with vertical and diagonal chords. There is no evidence of such splicing being used by Etruscan builders in simple post-and-lintel construction in the sixth century B.C.

29 See Trevor A. Hodge, *The Woodwork of Greek Roofs* (Cambridge: Cambridge University Press, 1960) for comparisons.

30 See, for instance, Axel Boëthius, *Etruscan and Early Roman Architecture* (Baltimore: Penguin Books, 1978), 46–8; Amanda Claridge, *Oxford Archaeological Guides: Rome* (New York: Oxford University Press, 1998), 237; and Frank Sear, *Roman Architecture* (Ithaca, NY: Cornell University Press, 1982), 10–12.

31 Boëthius states that he is unwilling to accept a height of 16.6 meters for the columns, not for an archaic Etruscan temple; *Etruscan and Early Roman Architecture*, 49. See also Giuliani, "Architettura e tecnica edilizia," 31; Castagnoli, "Il tempio romano," 7–9; R. Mambella, "Contributi alla problematica del tempio etrusco-italico," *RendPontAcc* 6 (1982): 35–42. Giuliani points out that the columns would have been much larger than those of the Pantheon; "Architettura e tecnica edilizia," 31.

32 For descriptions of the site excavations carried out in the 1990s, see Sommella, "Le recenti scoperte sul Campidoglio," 57ff, figs. 5 and 6; Sommella, "La grande Roma dei Tarquini,"18ff, figs. 25 and 26. The illustrations in both of these articles suggest neat breaks in the cappellacio blocks that seem to define foundation walls corresponding to those proposed by Gjerstad. My observation in 1999 of the newly exposed foundation blocks in the basement of the southwest wing of the Capitoline Museum gave a different impression, one of a more or less contiguous surface of the cappellacio blocks extending through several of the palace's rooms. It was not broken up in the way these drawings suggest, nor were there higher foundation walls projecting vertically as suggested in the plan reconstructions of these articles.

33 Whereas Gjerstad believed that the well-preserved wall segment located near the platform's southeast corner was an inner foundation wall of the temple, corresponding to its second row of pronaos columns, the reconstruction proposed here suggests that it corresponded to the temple's perimeter columns themselves.

34 See Chapters 8–11 for the dimensions of these imperial temples. This group may have included the Temple of Divus Traianus as well.

35 For information on the Temples of Jupiter Anxur at Terracina and Hercules Victor at Tivoli, see Filippo Coarelli, *Lazio: Guide archeologiche Laterza* (Rome: Laterza, 1984), 77–80, 308–32. For the Temple of Claudius, see Chapter 8.

36 Castagnoli, "Il tempio romano," 7–12.

37 Gjerstad, *Early Rome*, vol. 3, 177.

38 The diameter of the columns of the Belvedere Temple was about .90 meters, which would mean their height would have been 6.4 meters; Inge Nielsen and Birte Poulsen, *The Temple of Castor and Pollux I* (Rome: Edizioni de Luca, 1992), 131; and Enrico Stefani, "Orvieto: Osservazioni intorno alla struttura del tempio," *NSc*, (1925): 158–61.

39 William L. MacDonald, *The Pantheon* (Cambridge: Harvard University Press, 1976), 46.

40 Patrick Michael Rowe, *Etruscan Temples: A Study of the Structural Remains, Origins and Development* (Ph.D. diss., Florida State University, 1989), 144–5.

41 Stambaugh, *The Ancient Roman City*, 119; Roger B. Ulrich, "Julius Caesar and the Creation of the Forum Iulium," *AJA* 97 (1993): 49–80.

42 Rowe, *Etruscan Temples*, 132; and Jos A. DeWaele, "Satricum nel VI e V secolo A.C.: L'architettura templare," *ArchLaz* 4 (1981): 310–16.

43 Sommella, "Le recenti scoperte sul Campidoglio," 67, figs. 5 and 6; Sommella, "'La grande Roma dei Tarquini,'" 20–21, figs. 25 and 26. The proposal for two additional rooms at the temple's northwest end was made on the basis of an analysis

of a retaining wall on the Capitoline Hill's western face that dates from the period of the Tarquins. It is more likely that this wall was built as part of the leveling process by Tarquinius Priscus from 582 to 579 B.C. and that it supported part of a terraced area at the back of the temple.

44 Tagliamonte, "Iuppiter Optimus," 147; Giovanni Colonna, "Etruria e Lazio nell'età dei Tarquini," in *Etruria e Lazio arcaico* (1987), 64–6.

45 Tagliamonte, "Iuppiter Optimus," 147.

46 Gjerstad uses as evidence fragments of terra-cotta revetments that were found both near the Capitoline site and from other temples in Rome dating from the same period; Gjerstad, *Early Rome*, vol. 3, 185–7, and vol. 6, 105–6.

47 Gjerstad suggests that these panels measured 6 and 7 Roman feet wide and, given the right combinations, would have corresponded exactly to his column spacings of 31 and 39 Roman feet. This author's analysis of the evidence of surviving terracotta revetments, both from the Capitoline site and others from Rome and neighboring Etruscan sites, reveals that there are no such frieze panels with anywhere near the dimension of 6 or 7 Roman feet wide. Gjerstad, *Early Rome* vol. 3, 185–7, and vol. 6, 105–6.

Most known examples were about 1 Roman foot wide, as, for instance, those in the Ny Carlsberg Glyptotek in Copenhagen, the Museum antiker Kleinkunst in Munich, Museo Nazionale in Tarquinia, and the Antiquarium in Berlin. See Arvid Andrén, *Architectural Terracottas from Etrusco-Italic Temples*, vols. 1 and 2 (Lund: Haran Ohlsson, 1940).

48 Douglas Edwards, *Religion and Power: Pagans, Jews, and Christians in the Greek East* (New York and Oxford: Oxford University Press, 1996), 3.

49 Ibid., 3.

50 Edward Shils, *Center and Periphery: Essays in Macrosociology* (Chicago: University of Chicago Press, 1975), 151.

51 Ibid.

52 Gjerstad himself makes the point on several occasions; see Gjerstad, *Early Rome*, vol. 4, 390, and vol. 6, 106.

3: ETRUSCO-ROMAN TEMPLES OF THE EARLY REPUBLIC

1 Gianluca Tagliamonte, "Forum Romanum (fino alla prima età repubblicana)," *LTUR*, vol. 2, 314.

2 Romulus, the first king of Rome, reigned, according to tradition, from 753–710 B.C., Numa, from 710–670 B.C. Stambaugh, *The Ancient Roman City*, 12; Pietro Romanelli, *The Roman Forum* (Rome: Istituto Poligrafico dello Stato, 1975), 6–7.

3 For information on the early history of the Forum Romanum, see Tagliamonte, "Forum Romanum," 313–25; Filippo Coarelli, *Il Foro Romano*, vol. 1 (Rome: Quasar, 1983), passim; Cairoli F. Giuliani and Patrizia Verduchi, *L'area centrale del Foro Romano* (Florence: n.p., 1987), passim; Roberto Luciani and Leandro Sperduti, *Foro Romano* (Rome: Alma Venus, 1992), 13–27; Albert J. Ammerman, "On the Origins of the Forum Romanum," *AJA* 94 (October 1990): 627–45.

4 Liv. 1.56.2, 1.38.6; Dion. Hal. *Rom. Ant.* 3.67.5; Plin. *Nat. Hist.* 36.24; Tagliamonte, "Forum Romanum," 316; Stambaugh, *The Ancient Roman City*, 12–13.

5 The first paving and leveling of the Forum Romanum at the time of the Tarquins was done with gravel and cappellacio pebbles. Ammerman estimates the total amount of fill was nearly 10,000 cubic meters; see Ammerman, "On the Origins," 641–2; and Stambaugh, *The Ancient Roman City*, 12–13.

6 For a discussion of the history of the Regia, see Russell T. Scott, "Regia," *LTUR*, vol. 4, 189–92; Filippo Coarelli, "Il Foro in età arcaica," *ArchLaz* 4 (1981): 241–8; and Coarelli, *Il Foro Romano*, vol. 2, 190–9; Ogilvie, *Early Rome*, 85.

7 T. J. Cornell, *The Beginnings of Rome: Italy and Rome from the Bronze Age to the Punic Wars (c. 1000–264 B.C.)* (London and New York: Routledge, 1995), 94; Alföldi, *Early Rome and the Latins*, 196–7; Frederick W. Shipley, "Chronology of the Building Operations in Rome from the Death of Caesar to the Death of Augustus," *MAAR* 9 (1931): 22–3.

8 Ogilvie, *Early Rome*, 85

9 Ibid.; Frank E. Brown, "The Regia," *MAAR* 12 (1935): 67; Russell T. Scott, "Regia-Vesta," *ArchLaz* 9 (1988): 18–26.

10 For discussion of the Temple of Vesta, see Cass. Dio, *Rom. Hist.* 1.6.2; Tac. *Ann.* 15.41; Plut. *Num.* 14.1; Dion. Hal. *Rom. Ant.* 2.64.5–66.1; Ov. *Fast.* 6.247–94; *Trist.* 3.1.30; Tagliamonte, "Forum Romanum," 316; Russell T. Scott, "Vesta, Aedes," *LTUR*, vol. 5, 125–6.

11 The Temple of Vesta was rebuilt again in 241 B.C., and during the times of Augustus and Nero. Finally, it was destroyed in a fire in A.D. 191 and rebuilt for the last time during the period of Septimius Severus. The temple served as an urban focal point when approached from either the Palatine or Quirinal Hills, or from the east on the Via Sacra. Richardson, *Dictionary*, 412–13.

12 The Temple of Vesta was destroyed and rebuilt in 241 B.C., 210 B.C., and sometime in the early first century B.C. Dion. Hal. *Rom. Ant.* 2.66.1–6; Ov. *Fast.* 6.437–54; Plin. *Nat. Hist.* 7.43.141; Val. Max. 1.4.5; Liv. 26.27; Cass. Dio, 54.24.2; Scott, "Vesta, Aedes," 125–6; Richardson, *Dictionary*, 412.

13 Tac. *Ann.* 15.41; Scott, "Vesta, Aedes," 126. The temple was represented on coins at the time of Nero. See, for instance, *BMCREmp*, vol. 1, 213, nos. 104–6, pl. 40, 12–13.

14 Ovid (*Fast.* 6.247–97) writes of the reasons for the temple's circular shape and the fact that it was covered by a dome.

15 The Temple of Vesta had remained standing until 1549, when it was demolished to be burned into lime for the Fabbrica di San Pietro. Only thirty-four marble pieces of the building were found in the excavations. See Scott, "Vesta, Aedes," 127–8; and Lanciani, *The Ruins and Excavations*, 223–4.

16 As portrayed in Virgil's *Aeneid*, Aeneas brought with him the statue of Pallas Athena as well as the household god Penates, of his native land, when he fled the destruction of Troy. He first went to Lavinium and Alba Longa. Later, the statue of Pallas Athena was moved to the Temple of Vesta in the Forum Romanum. Virg. *Aen.* 8.306–58; Dion. Hal. *Rom Ant.* 2.66.5–6; Beard, North, and Price, *Religions of Rome*, vol. 1, 2–3; Scott, "Vesta, Aedes," 127–8; Richardson, *Dictionary*, 412.

17 Ov. *Fast.* 6.263–70; Beard, North, and Price, *Religions of Rome*, vol. 1, 52.

18 Ov. *Fast.* 6.304–20.

19 Ov. *Fast.* 6.285–300.

20 Howard H. Scullard, *Festivals and Ceremonies of the Roman Republic* (London: Thames and Hudson, 1981), 17, 46.

21 For discussion of the Curia Hostilia, see Var. *Lat. Lang.* 5.155; Liv. 1.30.2; Cic. *Rep.* 2.17.31; Tagliamonte, "Forum Romanum," 316; and Filippo Coarelli, "Curia Hostilia," *LTUR*, vol. 1, 331–2.

22 Cornell, *The Beginnings of Rome*, 94; Ogilvie, *Early Rome*, 51–2.

23 Ogilvie, Early Rome, 51.

24 Var. *Lat. Lang.* 5.155; Stambaugh, *The Ancient Roman City*, 109.

25 Romanelli, *The Roman Forum*, 6–7.

26 For discussion of the Temple of Saturn, see Dion. Hal. *Rom. Ant.* 6.1.4; Macr. *Sat.* 1.8.1; Liv. 2.21.2. Coarelli argues that the temple was dedicated in 501 B.C. as opposed to 498 B.C. as commonly believed. See Filippo Coarelli, "Saturnus, Aedes," *LTUR*, vol. 4, 234–5; Patrizio Pensabene, *Tempio di Saturno: Architettura e decorazione* (Rome: De Luca Editore, 1984), 7–11, passim.

27 The temple's location was referred to as *sub clivus Capitolinus* in Serv. *Aen.* 8.319 and in Dion. Hal. *Rom. Ant.* 6.1.4. It was referred to as *ante clivum Capitolinum* in Serv. *Aen.* 2.116; and as *in forum Romanum* in Liv. 41.21.12. See Coarelli, "Saturnus, Aedes," 235; Tagliamonte, "Forum Romanum," 316; Pensabene, *Tempio di Saturno*, 9–11; Lawrence Richardson, Jr., "The Approach to the Temple of Saturn in Rome," *AJA* 84 (January 1980): 53.

28 Richardson, "The Approach," 53.

29 Macr. *Sat.* 1–8; App. *Civ. Wars* 1.31; Luc. *Phars.* 3.154; Plut. *Ti. Gracch.* 10.6; Varr. *Lat. Lang.* 5.183; Coarelli, "Saturnus, Aedes," 234.

30 John Ward-Perkins and Amanda Claridge, *Pompeii AD 79: Exhibition. Royal Academy of Arts, Piccadilly, London* (London: Imperial Tobacco Limited, 1976), 57.

31 Scullard, *Festivals and Ceremonies*, 205–6.

32 For discussion of the Temple of Castor and Pollux, see Dion. Hal. *Rom. Ant.* 6.13.2; Ov. *Fast.* 1.706; Liv. 2.20.12, 2.42.5; Inge Nielsen, "Castor, Aedes, Templum," *LTUR*, vol. 1, 242–5; Ogilvie, *Early Rome*, 47.

33 Dion. Hal. *Rom. Ant.* 6.13.2; Ov. *Fast.* 1.706; Ogilvie, *Early Rome*, 47.

34 Oswalt, *Concise Encyclopedia of Greek and Roman Mythology*, 83–4.

35 Suet. *Caes.* 10; Cic. *Ses.* 85; Liv. 2.20.12, 2.42.5, 8.11.16. Pliny refers to it as the aedes Castorum. See *Nat. Hist.* 10.121, 34.23; and Tagliamonte, "Forum Romanum," 316.

36 Michael Grant, *History of Rome* (New York: Charles Scribner's Sons, 1978), 43; Scullard, *Festivals and Ceremonies*, 65–8; Ogilvie, *Early Rome*, 47.

37 Even though the temple was dedicated to two deities, it was common for Etruscan temples to have three cella rooms. Nielsen, "Castor, Aedes, Templum," 243.

38 Tenney Frank proposed this reconstruction in 1925. Its interaxial column spaces would have been 5.40 meters for the central bay and 4.90 meters for the side bays. Following Vitruvius's standard, Frank suggests that the columns would have been 5.40 meters high and .77 meters in diameter. Tenney Frank, "The First and Second Temples of Castor at Rome," *MAAR* 5 (1925), 82–5.

39 Nielsen and Poulsen, *The Temple of Castor and Pollux I*, 80–4.

40 Ibid., 75–8.

41 Nielsen and Poulsen argue that the pronaos was three bays deep. See Ibid., 75–8. However, there is no evidence of columns in the northern foundation wall of the first temple. Furthermore, it would have been unusual to have a pronaos three columns deep for a temple this size, especially considering that the pronaos would have been considerably larger than the cella. According to Vitruvius, they should have been about equal. Vitr. 4.7.2; Roger B. Ulrich, *The Roman Orator and the Sacred Stage: The Roman Templum Rostratum* (Brussells: Latomus, 1994), 85–7.

42 Nielsen, "Castor, Aedes, Templum," 242; Richardson, *Dictionary*, 74–5.

43 Frank, "The First and Second Temples of Castor," 79; Nielsen, "Castor, Aedes, Templum," 243.

44 Liv. 8.11.16, 9.46.15; Val. Max. *Mem.* 2.2.9; Scullard, *Festivals and Ceremonies*, 164–5.

45 At least from 160 B.C. the temple often served as a meeting place of the Senate. Cic. *Verr.* 2.1.129; Plut. *Sull.* 8.3; Ulrich, *Roman Orator and the Sacred Stage*, 83; Nielsen, "Castor, Aedes, Templum," 242.

46 Nicholas Purcell, "Forum Romanum (the Republican Period)," *LTUR*, vol. 2, 326.

47 For a discussion of Rome's early battles against its immediate neighbor, see Ogilvie, *Early Rome*, 92–110.

48 Located only twelve miles north of Rome, Veii controlled a strategic position on a tributary of the upper Tiber River. In the 440s B.C., having concluded that a war against Veii was at hand, the Romans suspended their consular form of government in favor of military rule. Roman soldiers moved northward in a series of attacks in the late 430s B.C., although it was not until 396 B.C. that the Roman general M. Furius Camillus proved victorious as the Romans entered the city, destroyed many of its ramparts, and claimed its territory. Grant, *History of Rome*, 47–51; Scullard, *A History of the Roman World*, 73–74; Ogilvie, *Early Rome*, 148–58.

49 Ogilvie, *Early Rome*, 150–71.

50 Kurt A. Raaflaub, "Born to Be Wolves? Origins of Roman Imperialism," in *Transitions to Empire: Essays in Greco-Roman History, 360–146 B.C., in Honor of E. Badian*, ed. Robert W. Wallace and Edward M. Harris (Norman: University of Oklahoma Press, 1996), 273–4.

51 T. J. Cornell, "The City of Rome in the Middle Republic," in *Ancient Rome*, 42–5. The new defensive wall is commonly referred to as the Servian Wall, but it was not, in fact, built by Servius Tullius. See Maddalena Andreussi, "Murus Servii Tullii: Mura repubblicane," *LTUR*, vol. 3, 319–24.

52 Stambaugh, *The Ancient Roman City*, 102.

53 Ogilvie, *Early Rome*, 55.

54 The *comitia centuriata* was an assembly of both soldiers and the wealthy upper-middle class. After the fall of the Etruscans, it became the dominant assembly for both legislative and electoral purposes. See Ogilvie, *Early Rome*, 53; Grant, *History of*

Rome, 68–9; Lily Ross Taylor, *Roman Voting Assemblies: From the Hannibalic War to the Dictatorship of Caesar* (Ann Arbor: University of Michigan Press, 1990), 85.

55 Taylor, *Roman Voting Assemblies*, 5–6.

56 The position of censor was established in 443 B.C. Previous to that, the census had been made by the consuls. The taking of the census, was done periodically to register and classify Rome's population according to gender, age, and ownership of property. It took place on the Campus Martius, with only the male heads of families participating. The population was organized according to tribes, centuries, and classes. Each man was called out according to his tribe and gave the censors information about his household and property. At first it was a minor, routine event, but as time went on, the censors exercised more power by punishing in various ways those whose mode of life or position in society they disapproved of. See Herbert Hill, *The Roman Middle Class in the Republican Period* (Oxford: Basil Blackwell, 1952), 32; Cornell, "Rome in the Middle Republic," 50; Polyb. 6.17.2–7. A detailed discussion of the role of the censors in the second and first centuries B.C., with lists of their building activity, is provided in Filippo Coarelli, "Public Building in Rome between the Second Punic War and Sulla," *PBSR* 45 (1977): 1–23.

57 Stambaugh, *The Ancient Roman City*, 102–3.

58 P. A. Brunt, *The Fall of the Roman Republic and Related Essays* (Oxford: Clarendon Press, 1988), 85.

59 Raaflaub, "Born to Be Wolves?" 278.

60 Mommsen, *History of Rome*, vol. 1, 91–2.

61 Ibid., 18–19; Scullard, *History of the Roman World*, 65–6; Jones, "The Primitive Institutions of Rome," 425–31; J. A. North, "Conservatism and Change in Roman Religion," *PBSR* 44 (1976): 1–12.

62 Beard, North, and Price, *Religions of Rome*, vol. 1, 23–4; J. H. W. G. Liebeschuetz, *Continuity and Change in Roman Religion* (Oxford: Clarendon Press, 1979), 7–8.

63 Ellen MacNamara, *The Etruscans* (Cambridge: Harvard University Press, 1991), 62; Jones, "The Primitive Institutions of Rome," 430.

64 Beard, North, and Price, *Religions of Rome*, vol. 1, 21–3.

65 Ibid., 21–23; Scullard, *History of the Roman World*, 66.

66 Taylor, *Roman Voting Assemblies*, 7.

67 Beard, North, and Price, *Religions of Rome*, vol. 1, 29–30; Liebeschuetz, *Continuity and Change*, 7–10.

68 Richardson, *Dictionary*, 163.

69 For discussion of the Temple of Fortuna and Magna Mater, see Filippo Coarelli, *Il Foro Boario dalle origini alla fine della Repubblica* (Rome: Edizioni Quasar, 1992), 206–23; Giuseppina Pisani Sartorio, "Fortuna et Mater Matuta, Aedes," *LTUR*, vol. 2, 281–5. Boëthius refers to the rectangular temple as the Temple of Fortuna Virilis; *Etruscan and Early Roman Architecture*, 138–9; 159.

70 Dion. Hal. *Rom. Ant.* 4.27.7, 4.40.7; Liv. 5.19.6; Ov. *Fast.* 6.569–72, 613–26; Coarelli, *Il Foro Boario*, 206–23; Pisani Sartorio, "Fortuna et Mater Matuta," 281–5.

71 Pisani Sartorio, "Fortuna et Mater Matuta," 282; Antonio M. Colini et al. "Area Sacra di S. Omobono," in *Lazio arcaico e mondo greco* (Rome: n.p., 1977), 9–61.

72 Coarelli, *Il Foro Boario*, 206–23; Pisani Sartorio, "Fortuna et Mater Matuta," 281–5. Many scholars believed the first temple or temples were, in fact, built by Servius Tullius. See, for instance, Gjerstad, *Early Rome*, vol. 4, 399ff.

73 Pisani Sartorio, "Fortuna et Mater Matuta," 283; Coarelli, *Il Foro Boario*, 233; Richardson, *Dictionary*, 246.

74 Pisani Sartorio, "Fortuna et Mater Matuta," 283.

75 Richardson, *Dictionary*, 246; Coarelli, *Il Foro Boario*, 210.

76 Pisani Sartorio suggests the two temples were built in ca. 490 B.C. and that they were rebuilt by Camillus after the Gallic invasion. Coarelli argues they were initially built by Camillus in 396 B.C. See Pisani Sartorio, "Fortuna et Mater Matuta," 283; Coarelli, *Il Foro Boario*, 205–10; Cornell, "City of Rome," 44; Liv. 5.19.6, 5.23.7; Plut. *Cam.* 5.

77 The reconstruction is based on that of G. Colonna and G. Ioppolo in the 1960s. See Coarelli, *Il Foro Boario*, 206.

78 Luisa Banti, *Etruscan Cities and Their Culture*, trans. Erika Bizzarri (Berkeley and Los Angeles: University of California Press, 1973), 53–4: Boëthius, *Etruscan and Early Roman Architecture*, 44; Haynes, *Etruscan Civilization*, 205–10.

79 Boëthius, *Etruscan and Early Roman Architecture*, 41.

80 Ibid., 41.

81 Rowe, *Etruscan Temples*, 124–6.

82 Liv. 24.47.15–16, 25.7.5–6; Pisani Sartorio, "Fortuna et Mater Matuta," 284.

83 Plin. *Nat. Hist.* 8.194–97, 36.163; Dion. Hal. *Rom. Ant.* 4.40.7; Ov. *Fast.* 6.569–72, 579–80, 613–26; Val. Max. 1.8.11; Cass. Dio, *Rom. Hist.* 58.7.2; Pisani Sartorio, "Fortuna et Mater Matuta," 281; Coarelli, *Il Foro Boario*, 253–363; Richardson, *Dictionary*, 154.

84 Her origins may have been Praeneste, located just east of Rome, and she is thought to have been introduced into Rome by Servius Tullius. Pisani Sartorio, "Fortuna et Mater Matuta," 281.

85 The legendary story of Ino continues, for later, Juno struck her into madness because she was angry that Ino had nursed Bacchus, the son of Jupiter and Semele. This caused Ino to kill her own son Melicertes and then jump into the sea with the dead child in her arms. Jupiter turned her into a sea goddess, Leucothea, and her son into the sea god Palaemon. Leucothea then came to the Italian town of Carmenta, whose residents gave her toasted cakes to eat – hence the offering of toasted cakes in the Roman ritual – and she announced that in Italy she would be known as Mater Matuta and her son would be the sea god Portunus. Ov. Fast. 6.475, 6.559, 6.561; Dumézil, *Archaic Roman Religion*, 50–8. Oswalt, *Concise Encyclopedia of Greek and Roman Mythology*, 181.

86 Pisani Sartorio, "Fortuna et Mater Matuta," 284; Coarelli, *Il Foro Boario*, 210; Richardson, *Dictionary*, 246.

87 Richardson, *Dictionary*, 33.

88 For discussion of Temple C, see Filippo Coarelli et al., *L'Area Sacra di Largo Argentina I* (Rome: X Ripartizione antichità belle arti e problemi di cultura, 1981), 40–2; Ferdinando Castagnoli, "Il Campo Marzio nell'antichità," *MemLinc* 8 (1948): 174ff.

89 Coarelli et al., *L'Area Sacra*, 41; Rodolfo Lanciani, *I commentarii di Frontino intorno le acque e gli acquedotti* (Rome, 1880), 255ff.

90 Coarelli et al., *L'Area Sacra*, 41–2; Coarelli, *Il Foro Boario*, 197–209; Robert E. A. Palmer, *Roman Religion and Roman Empire* (Philadelphia: University of Pennsylvania Press, 1974),

7ff. The first major public aqueduct, the Acqua Appia, was built in 312 B.C. by the order of the censor Appius Claudius Caesus. The Anio Vetus was built in 272 B.C. by Manius Curius Dentatus. Cornell, "Rome in the Middle Republic," 47.

91 The lower column diameter was .75 meters. Coarelli et al., *L'Area Sacra*, 14–15.

92 There are actually four levels of the altar platform. The oldest altar stands on the second pavement, installed by A. Postumius Albinus. Richardson, *Dictionary*, 33–4.

93 Coarelli et al., *L'Area Sacra*, 14–15; Nielsen and Poulsen, *The Temple of Castor and Pollux I*, 121.

94 Coarelli et al., *L'Area Sacra*, 44–5; G. Marchetti-Longhi, "Gli scavi del Largo Argentina: Tempio A," *BullCom* 64 (1936): 86–97.

95 Ov. *Fast.* 1.463–64; Front. *De Aq.* 4.2; Coarelli et al., *L'Area Sacra*, 45; Coarelli, *Il Foro Boario*, 243–50.

96 Coarelli, *Il Foro Boario*, 249.

97 Coarelli et al., *L'Area Sacra*, 16; Richardson, *Dictionary*, 33; Marchetti-Longhi, "Tempio A," 88–101.

98 Richardson, *Dictionary*, 33; Marchetti-Longhi, "Tempio A," 101–37.

99 Liv. 40.52.4–7; Coarelli et al., *L'Area Sacra*, 38; Filippo Coarelli, *Il Campo Marzio dalle origini alla fine della Repubblica* (Rome: Quasar, 1997), 258–68.

100 For discussion of the Temple of Fortuna Huiusce Diei, see Chapter 5.

101 Donald R. Dudley, *The Civilization of Rome* (New York and Toronto: New American Library, 1962), 30–2.

102 The remaining autonomous Greeks of southern Italy, now concentrated in the coastal settlement of Tarentum, appealed to King Pyrrhus of Epirus, a Greek mercenary, who brought 20,000 troops to fight against the advancing Romans. He withdrew within a year's time, however, and Rome's control of the southern half of the peninsula was complete. Ibid., 32–3.

103 Raaflaub, "Born to Be Wolves?" 273–4.

104 Ernst Badian, *Roman Imperialism in the Late Republic* (Pretoria: University of South Africa, 1967), 1.

105 Raaflaub, "Born to Be Wolves?" 277.

106 Ibid., 288–9.

107 Perhaps the most peculiar aspect of the Temple of Peace, however, is the fact that to have it symmetrically sited within the forum, the Romans superimposed it directly on the walls and circular stone seats of a former bouleterion. Possibly the oldest building in the forum, the bouleterion was a large, circular, theater-like structure on the forum's north side. Dating from the Greek period, it originally formed a complete circle inscribed within a square and had tiers of seats interrupted by four entrances oriented on the cardinal axes. Sestieri says the circular structure is Greek in origin and suggests it was either the bouleterion or an ekklesiasterion. Pedley argues unconvincingly that it was built by the Romans contemporary with the temple to be used as a comitium. Pellegrino Claudio Sestieri, *Paestum: The City, the Prehistoric Necropolis* (Rome: La Libreria dello Stato, 1953), 22; John Griffiths Pedley, *Paestum: Greeks and Romans in Southern Italy* (London: Thames and Hudson, 1990), 118.

108 The northeastern orientation of the Capitoline Temple at Cosa gave it a slightly skewed formal alignment with the city's main street leading from the forum, and because it could not be oriented exactly on the axis, its architects made subtle refinements to satisfy the expectation of axiality, such as the shifting off axis of the stairs between the forecourt and pronaos. Frank E. Brown, *The Making of a Roman Town* (Ann Arbor: University of Michigan Press, 1980), 51–2.

4: ASSIMILATION OF HELLENISTIC ARCHITECTURE AFTER THE PUNIC WARS

1 For information on the Punic Wars, see Adrian Goldsworthy, *The Punic Wars* (London: Cassell, 2000), 76–127, 167–243, 331–86; Brian Craven, *The Punic Wars* (London: Weidenfeld and Nicolson, 1980), 22–72, 98–248, 273–94; J. F. Lazenby, *Hannibal's War: A Military History of the Second Punic War* (Warminster, England: Aris and Phillips, 1978), passim; Arthur M. Eckstein, *Senate and General: Individual Decision Making and Roman Foreign Relations, 264–194 B.C.* (Berkeley: University of California Press, 1987), 102–55, 187–232, 233–67.

2 Dudley, *The Civilization of Rome*, 60–1; Goldsworthy, *The Punic Wars*, 340–56; Craven, *The Punic Wars*, 284–94.

3 Pollitt, *The Art of Rome*, 31–2; Goldsworthy, *The Punic Wars*, 245–68; Cornell, "Rome in the Middle Republic," 46.

4 Michael Crawford, *The Roman Republic* (Cambridge: Harvard University Press, 1993), 68, 101–6.

5 Plut. *Aem. Paul.* 32–4; Erich S. Gruen, *The Hellenistic World and the Coming of Rome*, vol. 2 (Berkeley: University of California Press, 1984), 399–528; Crawford, *The Roman Republic*, 57–79; Andrew Lintott, *'Imperium Romanum:' Politics and Administration* (New York: Routledge, 1993), 6–15.

6 Plut. *Aem. Paul.* 32–4.

7 For historical information about Vitruvius's background, see Vitruvius, *Ten Books on Architecture*, trans. Ingrid Rowland (Cambridge: Cambridge University Press, 1999), 1–19; Mark Wilson Jones, *Principles of Roman Architecture* (New Haven: Yale University Press, 2000), 34–8; Eugene Dwyer, "Vitruvius," *DA*, vol. 32, 632–6.

8 R. J. A. Wilson, "Roman Art and Architecture," *OHCW*, 773.

9 Vitruvius may have based parts of his text on an earlier treatise written by Hermogenes, the most important architect of the late third century and the early second century B.C. He had codified the rules for the Ionic Order, which through the later writings of Vitruvius had an influence on Rome's Ionic buildings. Hermogenes had also built in ca. 220–205 B.C. the Temple of Dionysius at Teos and in 205–190 B.C. the Temple of Artemis at Magnesia, which were notable in their openness, widening of columns and broader peristyle in the pseudodipteral form. Frank Brown, "Vitruvius," *MEA*, vol. 4, 335; and J. J. Coulton, "Hermogenes of Priene," *MEA*, vol. 2, 359–61. See also D. S. Robertson, who cautions against a belief that Vitruvius relied solely on Hermogenes for his theories, *A Handbook of Greek and Roman Architecture* (Cambridge: Cambridge University Press, 1954), 153–7. Wilson Jones points out that in Book 7 Vitruvius lists no fewer than forty Greek treatises he consulted. See *Principles of Roman Architecture*, 38.

10 Mark Wilson Jones, "Designing the Roman Corinthian Order," *JRA* 2 (1989): 60; J. J. Coulton, "Towards Understanding Greek Temple Design: General Considerations," *Annual of the British School of Archaeology at Athens* 70 (1975): 66–74.

11 Vitr. 3.3.1.

12 Rowe, *Etruscan Temples*, 139.

13 Vitr. 4.8.6.

14 Ibid., 4.8.5.

15 Vitruvius (3.2.5) mentions the plan type with lateral extensions of the back wall only in reference to the Temple of Honor and Virtue by Mucius, near the Monument of Marius.

16 William Bell Dinsmoor, *The Architecture of Ancient Greece* (New York: Norton, 1975), 273.

17 Vitr. 3.3.11.

18 Ibid., 3.3.1.

19 Ibid., 3.3.6.

20 Ibid., 3.3.6; Dinsmoor, *The Architecture of Ancient Greece*, 82. Robertson suggests that *eustyle* is a question-begging term, presumably coined by Hermogenes to describe what was perhaps a modification of an earlier academic classification of column spacings, which bears little relationship to ancient Greek practice. Robertson, *Greek and Roman Architecture*, 153–7.

21 For information on the Porticus Metelli, see Alessandro Viscogliosi, "Porticus Metelli," *LTUR*, vol. 4, 130–1; M. J. Boyd, "The Porticoes of Metellus and Octavia and Their Two Temples," *PBSR* 21 (1953): 152–9; M. Gwyn Morgan, "The Portico of Metellus: A Reconsideration," *Hermes* 99 (1971): 480–505. Richardson argues that the Temple of Jupiter Stator was built not in the Porticus Metelli, but further to the northwest in the Campus Martius near the Largo Argentina. Richardson, *Dictionary*, 221; Lawrence Richardson, Jr., "The Evolution of the Porticus Octaviae," *AJA* 80 (1976): 57–64. This theory is disputed by Alessandro Viscogliosi in "Iuppiter Stator, Aedes ad Circum," *LTUR*, vol. 3, 157–9.

22 The area of the Circus Flaminius was used for numerous events and games as early as the sixth century B.C. There is disagreement as to the involvement of C. Flaminius in its development. Liv. 3.54.15; 3.63.7; *Epit.* 20; Var. *Lat. Lang.* 5.154; Coarelli, *Il Campo Marzio*, 363–74; Alessandro Viscogliosi, "Circus Flaminius," *LTUR*, vol. 1, 269–72; Ferdinando Castagnoli, "Campo Marzio," *Capitolium* 35.7 (1960): 93–113; T. P. Wiseman, "The Circus Flaminius," *PBSR* 42 (1974): 3–26; Ferdinando Castagnoli, "Porticus Philippi," in *Città e architettura*, 93–118; Richardson, *Dictionary*, 83.

23 Var. *Lat. Lang.* 5.154; Coarelli, *Il Campo Marzio*, 363–75: Alessandro Viscogliosi, "Circus Maximus," *LTUR*, vol. 1, 275.

24 Coarelli, *Il Campo Marzio*, 365–6; 586–8.

25 M. Aemilius Lepidus vowed and dedicated two temples simultaneously, that of Juno Regina and one to Diana. The latter may have been located, according to Coarelli, in the vicinity of the Theater of Marcellus and the Porticus Octaviae. See Coarelli, *Il Campo Marzio*, 364, fig. 74, 485–7; Liv. 39.2.11; Alessandro Viscogliosi, "Iuno Regina, Aedes in Campo, ad Circum Flaminium," *LTUR*, vol. 3, 126–8; Alessandro Viscogliosi, "Porticus Metelli," *LTUR*, vol. 4, 131; Boyd, "The Porticoes of Metellus and Octavia," 154–5.

26 Viscogliosi, "Iuno Regina," 127; Richardson, *Dictionary*, 216–17.

27 For discussion of the Temple of Jupiter Stator, see Viscogliosi, "Iuppiter Stator," 157, and "Porticus Metelli," 131; References to the temple are found in Plin. *Nat. Hist.* 36.4.40; Vitr. 3.2.5; Macrob. *Sat.* 3.4.2; Vell. Pat. *Res Ges.* 1.11.5. Boyd argues the Temple of Jupiter Stator was built earlier than 143 B.C. and by someone other than Metellus Macedonicus. See Boyd, "The Porticoes of Metellus and Octavia," 152–4. Viscogliosi prefers the date of 143 B.C.

28 Hermodorus of Salamis may have also rebuilt the Temple of Juno Regina at the same time. In 133 B.C., he built the Temple of Mars in Circo for Junius Brutus Callaicus, also near the Circus Flaminius. Coarelli, *Il Campo Marzio*, 492–6; Fausto Zevi, "Mars in Circo," *LTUR*, vol. 3, 226–7; Marion Elizabeth Blake, *Roman Construction in Italy from Nerva through the Antonines*, ed. Doris Taylor Bishop (Philadelphia: American Philosophical Society, 1973), 52 and 131; Viscogliosi, "Porticus Metelli," 131; Viscogliosi, "Iuppiter Stator," 157–8; Morgan, "Portico of Metellus," 499ff; Vitr. 3.2.5.

29 Vitr. 3.2.5; Ian M. Barton, "Religious Buildings," in *Roman Public Buildings*, ed. Ian M. Barton (Exeter: University of Exeter Press, 1995), 70. Boyd argues the temple was built of marble only in the Augustan reconstruction in the first century B.C.; see "The Porticoes of Metellus and Octavia," 157–8.

30 Vitr. 3.2.5. The building was later altered by the removal of the rear columns and their replacement by a plain back wall.

31 See *FUR*, pl. 31; Ferdinando Castagnoli, "Peripteros sine postico," *RömMitt* 62 (1955): 139–43; Viscogliosi, "Iuppiter Stator," 158; Pierre Gros, "Hermodorus et Vitruve," *MEFRA* 85 (1973): 137–61; Coarelli, *Il Foro Boario*, 536–7.

32 Vitr. 3.4.3.

33 Viscogliosi, "Porticus Metelli," 131; Viscogliosi, "Iuppiter Stator," 158; Plin. *Nat. Hist.* 36.4.35–37.

34 Viscogliosi, "Iuppiter Stator," 158; Antonio M. Colini, "Scoperte presso Piazza Campitelli," *Capitolium* 16 (1941): 385–93.

35 The Temple of Juno Regina may have been damaged in a fire in 158 B.C. Viscogliosi, "Iuno Regina," 127; Coarelli, *Il Campo Marzio*, 487.

36 Alessandro Viscogliosi, "Porticus Octaviae," *LTUR*, vol. 4, 141–3.

37 The Porticus Philippi, containing the Temple of Hercules Musarum, was built by M. Fulvius Nobilior in 179 B.C. The Porticus Octavia was built by Gnaeus Octavius in 167–166 B.C. as a monument to his naval victory over Perseus of Macedonia. See Chapter 7 for a more detailed discussion of these two sites. See also Plin. *Nat. Hist.* 34.6.13; Coarelli, *Il Foro Boario*, 515–28; Alessandro Viscogliosi, "Porticus Octavia," *LTUR*, vol. 4, 139–40; Viscogliosi, "Porticus Metelli, 131.

38 Liv. *Perioch.* 52; Vell. Pat. 1.11.2–5; Viscogliosi, "Porticus Metelli," 132; Richardson, *Dictionary*, 225; Boyd, "The Porticoes of Metellus and Octavia," 155.

39 Vell. Pat. 2.1.2. For information on the Porticus Octavia as distinguished from the Porticus Octaviae, see Plin. *Nat. Hist.* 34.7.13; Viscogliosi, "Porticus Octavia," 139–41; Coarelli, *Il Campo Marzio*, 515–28.

40 For those changes made at the time of Augustus, see Chapter 7.

41 For discussion of the Temple of Apollo Medicus, see Alessandro Viscogliosi, *Il Tempio di Apollo 'in Circo' e la formazione*

del linguaggio architettonico Augusteo (Rome: 'L'Erma' di Bretschneider, 1996), 1–2; Viscogliosi, "Apollo, Aedes in Circo," *LTUR*, vol. 1, 49–50; Liv. 4.25.3; 40.51.5.

42 The theater in front of the Temple of Apollo Medicus was commissioned initially by the censor and *pontifex maximus* M. Aemilius Lepidus; see Liv. 7.20.9, 40.51.3–6; Viscogliosi, *Il Tempio di Apollo 'in Circo,'* 2; P. Ciancio Rossetto, "Theatrum Marcelli," *LTUR*, vol. 5, 31–5.

43 Liv. 40.51.3; Viscogliosi, *Il Tempio di Apollo 'in Circo,'* 3.

44 John A. Hanson, *Roman Theater Temples* (Westport, CT: Greenwood Press, 1978), 18ff; Filippo Coarelli, *Lazio: Guide archeologiche Laterza* (Rome: Laterza, 1984), 77–82, 137–46.

45 Vitruvius refers to this temple as the Temple of Apollo and Diana; see Vitr. 3.3.4; Viscogliosi, "Apollo, Aedes in Circo," 50.

46 For Timarchides, see Plin. *Nat. Hist.* 35.99; Vitr. 10.2.13. For Philoskos of Rhodes, see Plin. *Nat. Hist.* 36.34. See also Viscogliosi, "Apollo, Aedes in Circo," 49–50.

47 For discussion of the Temple of Bellona, see Ov. *Fast.* 5.205; Ziolkowski, *Temples of Mid-Republican Rome*, 18–19; Coarelli, *Il Campo Marzio*, 391; Viscogliosi, "Bellona, Aedes in Circo," *LTUR*, vol. 1, 190–2.

48 Coarelli, *Il Campo Marzio*, 392; Filippo Coarelli, "Il Tempio di Bellona," *BullCom* 80 (1968): 58; Viscogliosi, "Bellona, Aedes in Circo," 190–2; Liv. 10.19.17; Ov. *Fast.* 6.201ff. For examples of the Senate's meetings in the Temple of Bellona, see Liv. 26.21.1, 28.9.5, 28.38.2, 31.47.6.

49 Liv. 30.21.12, 30.40.1, 33.24.5, 42.36.2; Cic. *Verr.* 5.41; Viscogliosi, "Bellona, Aedes in Circo," 191.

50 Stambaugh, *The Ancient Roman City*, 19–20; Grant, *History of Rome*, 52–4.

51 For discussion of the Temple of Concordia, see Liv. 39.56.6, 40.19.2; Angela Maria Ferroni, "Concordia, Aedes," *LTUR*, vol. 1, 316–17; Richardson, *Dictionary*, 99.

52 An even earlier Temple of Concordia was vowed in 367 B.C. by M. Furius Camillus during troubles connected with the passage of the Licinian laws. The people of Rome voted to build the temple for him, although it was apparently not constructed. See Ferroni, "Concordia, Aedes," 316–17; Plut. *Cam.* 42.3–4; Ov. *Fast.* 1.641–4; Richardson, *Dictionary*, 99; Cornell, "Rome in the Middle Republic," 44; Ulrich, *Roman Orator and Sacred Stage*, 96–7.

53 App. *Civ. Wars*, 1.3.26; Plut. *G. Gracch.* 17.6; Ferroni, "Concordia, Aedes," 317; Richardson, *Dictionary*, 99.

54 M. Rostovtzeff, *Rome*, trans. J. D. Duff (London: Oxford University Press, 1960), 95; Matthias Gelzer, *Caesar: Politician and Statesman*, trans. Peter Needham (Oxford: Basil Blackwell, 1968), 11.

55 Rostovtzeff, *Rome*, 95; Howard H. Scullard, *From the Gracchi to Nero: A History of Rome from 133 B.C. to A.D. 68* (New York: Methuen, 1982), 22–38, 42–3; David Stockton, *The Gracchi* (Oxford: Clarendon Press, 1979), 40–60, 114–61.

56 One of the lasting consequences of the reform movement was the institution of grain distribution at low prices to the poor, a popular measure that remained in force until the end of the Empire. Dudley, *The Civilization of Rome*, 71–5; Scullard, *Gracchi to Nero*, 32–3.

57 Plut. *G. Gracch.* 17.6–9; Ferroni, "Concordia, Aedes," 317; Richardson, *Dictionary*, 99.

58 The argument for the temple of L. Opimius having not been T-shaped in plan is based on archaeological work done on the site in 1983. It contradicts the long-held hypothesis that the plan of L. Opimius and that of Tiberius were the same. See Ferroni, "Concordia, Aedes," 319–20, figs. 187–8. I agree with Ferroni on the location of the temple's north column face and cella wall; however, the placement of the south column face and cella wall is incorrect. The Temple of L. Opimius was more likely about 21 meters wide with six columns across rather than 25 meters and eight columns across as shown by Ferroni in fig. 188.

59 Richardson, *Dictionary*, 99–100.

60 Homer F. Rebert and Henri Marceau, "The Temple of Concord in the Forum Romanum," *MAAR* 5 (1925): 53–5.

61 Ibid., 53–77; Richardson, *Dictionary*, 99.

62 For discussion of the Temple of Castor and Pollux, see Ulrich, *Roman Orator and the Sacred Stage*, 89; Nielsen and Poulsen, *The Temple of Castor and Pollux I*, 55–6; Nielsen, "Castor, Aedes, Templum," 242–3. Ulrich suggests that sometime in the early second century B.C., the pronaos and podium were changed to provide a larger speakers' platform across the front and to replace the original four-column-wide pronaos to six. Nielsen and Poulsen suggest this could have been carried by the censor Aemilius Paullus in 164 B.C.

63 Nielsen and Poulsen, *The Temple of Castor and Pollux I*, 80; Ulrich, *Roman Orator and the Sacred Stage*, 94–5.

64 Inge Nielsen and Birte Poulsen, who have directed the most recent archaeological investigations of the building, conclude that it is impossible to tell if the Metellan version was peripteral or three-sided. The argument for a three-sided peristyle is strong, however, because two major temples that followed soon after and that clearly imitated its *pycnostyle* form – the temples of Venus Genetrix and Mars Ultor – had three-sided peristyles. Nielsen and Poulsen, *The Temple of Castor and Pollux I*, 114; Nielsen, "Castor, Aedes, Templum," 244.

65 Ulrich, *Roman Orator and Sacred Stage*, 11; Nielsen, "Castor, Aedes, Templum," 244; Nielsen and Poulsen, *Temple of Castor and Pollux I*, 87–94, 105–6.

66 Ulrich, *Roman Orator and Sacred Stage*, 91–3; Coarelli, *Il Foro Romano*, vol. 2, 156–66; Nielsen, "Castor, Aedes, Templum," 242; Cir. *Verr.* 2.1.129; Plut. *Sull.* 8.3.

67 Ulrich, *Roman Orator and Sacred Stage*, 91–2; Taylor, *Roman Voting Assemblies*, 41.

68 Taylor, *Roman Voting Assemblies*, 29.

69 Ulrich, *Roman Orator and Sacred Stage*, 83.

70 Ibid., 98–106; Fest. 362L; Plut. *Sull.* 8.3; Cic. *Sest.* 34, 79, and 85; *Pis.* 11, 23; *Mil.* 18, 91; *Vatin.* 31–32; Nielsen, "Castor, Aedes, Templum," 242–3.

71 Filippo Coarelli, "Rostra (età repubblicana)," *LTUR*, vol. 4, 212–13; Liv. 8.14.12; Var. *Lat. Lang.* 5.155–6; Plin. *Nat. Hist.* 34.20; Ulrich, *Roman Orator and the Sacred Stage*, 10; Richardson, *Dictionary*, 335; Cornell, "Rome in the Middle Republic," 47.

72 Taylor, *Roman Voting Assemblies*, 16.

73 Richard T. De George, *The Nature and Limits of Authority* (Lawrence: University of Kansas Press, 1985), 102.

74 Ibid., 102; Nicholas Purcell, "Forum Romanum (the Republican Period)," *LTUR*, vol. 2, 328.

75 For a general discussion of the Forum Romanum during the Republican period, see Nicholas Purcell, "Rediscovering the Roman Forum," *JRA* 2 (1989): 156–66.

76 For general discussion of the Forum Holitorium, see Filippo Coarelli, "Forum Holitorium," *LTUR*, vol. 2, 299; Filippo Coarelli, *Roma: Guide archeologiche Laterza* (Rome: Laterza 1988), 318–20. For discussion of porticos and other buildings around the temples, see Rodolfo Lanciani, "I portici dei Foro Olitorio e il tesseramento delle derrate nell'antica Roma," *BullCom* 45 (1918): 168–92.

77 In area the Forum Holitorium measured approximately 125 meters by 50 meters. Wade C. Meade, *Ruins of Rome: A Guide to the Classical Antiquities* (Ruston, LA: Palatine, 1980), 96.

78 Blake, *Ancient Roman Construction*, 38; Coarelli, "Forum Holitorium," 299.

79 For discussion of the Temple of Janus, see Tac. *Ann.* 2.49; Coarelli, "Ianus, Aedes (Apud Forum Holitorium, ad Theatrum Marcelli)," *LTUR*, vol. 3, 90–1.

80 Nielsen and Poulsen, *The Temple of Castor and Pollux I*, 122.

81 Pierre Grimal, *Dictionary of Classical Mythology*, 241.

82 For discussion of the Temple of Spes, see Tac. *Ann.* 2.49; Coarelli, "Spes, Aedes," *LTUR*, vol. 4, 336–7; Richardson, *Dictionary*, 365.

83 Liv. 21.62.4, 25.7.6.

84 Cass. Dio 50.10.3.

85 Tac. *Ann.* 2.49; Coarelli, "Spes, Aedes," 337.

86 There is a disagreement about which of the three temples was dedicated to Spes. Lanciani, Delbrück, Coarelli, and Crozzoli Aite agree it was the southernmost temple. See Coarelli, "Spes, Aedes," 337.

87 Nielsen and Poulsen, *The Temple of Castor and Pollux I*, 122.

88 For discussion of the Temple of Juno Sospita, see Liv. 32.30.10. In a later passage, Livy refers to the Temple of Juno Matuta in the Forum Holitorium, but this is probably a mistake. Liv. 34.53.3. See Filippo Coarelli, "Iuno Sospita (in Foro Holitorio), Aedes," *LTUR*, vol. 3, 128. The consul L. Julius Caesar restored it in 90 B.C. following a dream of Caecilia Metella. Richardson, *Dictionary*, 217.

89 Richardson points out that the Temple of Juno Sospita is often shown in plan with nine columns on the sides, but this is incorrect because the footings of the first two are cut in a single block of travertine for greater strength and stability and make this clearly the termination. Richardson, *Dictionary*, 217.

90 Ibid.; Coarelli, "Iuno Sospita," 128.

91 Stambaugh, *The Ancient Roman City*, 25–32.

92 Diane Favro, *The Urban Image of Augustan Rome* (New York: Cambridge University Press, 1996), 169.

93 Boëthius, *Etruscan and Early Roman Architecture*, 158.

94 Regarding the name of the rectangular temple in the Forum Boarium, Boethius, for instance, refers to it as the Temple of Fortuna Virilis. Boëthius, *Etruscan and Early Roman Architecture*, 138–9; 159. Stambaugh refers to it as that of Portunus, but with a question mark. Stambaugh, *The Ancient Roman City*, 30–1. Wilson Jones refers to it as the Temple of Portunus; *Principles of Roman Architecture*, 64–5.

95 For discussion of the Round Temple by the Tiber, see Chapter 5.

96 An earlier temple, built in ca. 300 B.C., existed on the site of the Temple of Portunus, its foundations built of blocks of grotta oscura. Its dimensions were approximately 11 by 32 meters, making it longer than the existing temple. See Carlo Buzzetti, "Portunus, Aedes," *LTUR* vol. 5, 153–4; and Isabella Ruggiero, "Ricerche sul Tempio di Portuno nel Foro Boario: per una rilettura del monumento," *BullCom* 94 (1991–2): 253–66. Buzzetti and Ruggiero date the Ionic temple to 90–80 B.C.

97 For discussion of the sacred space around the Temple of Portunus, see Antonio M. Colini and Carlo Buzzetti, "Aedes Portuni in Portu Tiberino," *BullCom* 91 (1986): 7–30; Ruggiero, "Ricerche sul Tempio di Portuno," 276–82; and Richardson, *Dictionary*, 320.

98 For discussion of the attribution to Portunus, see Var. *Lat. Lang.* 6.19; Buzzetti, "Portunus, Aedes," 153–4; G. Marchetti-Longhi, "Il tempio Ionico di Ponte Rotto: Tempio di Fortuna o di Portuno?" *RömMitt* 40 (1925): 319–50; Coarelli, *Il Foro Boario*, 113–27; Robert E. A. Palmer, "The 'Vici Luccei' in the 'Forum Boarium' and some Lucceii in Rome," *BullCom* 85 (1976–7), 143.

99 Richardson, *Dictionary*, 320; L. A. Holland, "Janus and the Bridge," *PAAR* 21 (1961): 141–78; Coarelli, *Il Foro Boario*, 114–16.

100 The temple survived because it was converted into a church in 872 and later, under Pius V, was given to the Armenian congregation and rededicated as Santa Maria Egiziaca. It eventually became part of a larger church complex as additions were made to the north and east and the intercolumniations of the pronaos were filled in to make the nave longer. It was cleared of the additions and restored to its original appearance in the early twentieth century. See Colini and Buzzetti, "Aedes Portuni," 7–30; Richardson, *Dictionary*, 320.

101 Vitr. 4.8.6. Wilson Jones points out that the all-embracing colonnade of the Greek peripteral temple had little place in Roman liturgy; and therefore, the pseudoperipteral layout was for the Romans very practical; see *Principles of Roman Architecture*, 65.

102 Richardson, *Dictionary*, 320. Detailed descriptions of the Temple of Portunus are provided in Ernst R. Fiechter, "Der Ionische Tempel am Ponte Rotto in Rom," *RömMitt* 21 (1906): 220–79; Jean-Pierre Adam, *Le Temple du Portunus au Forum Boarium* (Rome: École Française, 1994), passim; Colini and Buzzetti, "Aedes Portuni," 7–30; Ruggiero, "Ricerche sul Tempio di Portuno," 265–86. The dimensions at the base of the podium are 11.87 meters by about 25.60 meters.

103 Ruggiero, "Ricerche sul Tempio di Portuno," 272. The pronaos is 5.85 meters deep, and the cella is 11.91 meters including the thickness of the walls.

104 Vitr. 3.3.7. The dimensions used here are from Ruggiero, "Ricerche sul Tempio di Portuno," 268. Wilson Jones refers to it as *systyle*, assuming the ratio is 1 to 2; see *Principles of Roman Architecture*, 58.

105 For information on the Temple of Sybil in Tivoli, see Coarelli, *Lazio: Guide archeologische Laterza*, 90–2; and Richardson, *Dictionary*, 158–9. Ruggiero also discusses the relationship between the Temples of Portunus and Sybil; see "Ricerche sul Tempio di Portuno," 272–3.

106 For information on the Temple of Hercules at Cori, see Coarelli, *Lazio: Guide archeologische Laterza*, 262–4; and Ruggiero, "Ricerche sul Tempio di Portuno," 273.

107 Ruggiero, "Ricerche sul Tempio di Portuno," 266, 272–5; Nielsen and Poulsen, *The Temple of Castor and Pollux I*, 121; Richardson, *Dictionary*, 320.
108 A similar analysis of a near-canonical temple, the Maison Carrée, is made by Mark Wilson Jones in *Principles of Roman Architecture*, 66–8.
109 For Vitruvius's discussion of the design of Ionic columns, see Vitruvius's Third Book.
110 The width of the abacus, according to Vitruvius (3.3.5), should be one-eighteenth larger than the column's lower diameter.
111 Ruggiero states that these capitals are in fact the closest example in Rome to those of Hermogenes' temples. She also compares it to the Didymaion in Miletus from the end of the second century B.C. See "Ricerche sul Tempio di Portuno," 274.
112 Vitr. 3.5.8–13.
113 Boëthius, *Etruscan and Early Roman*, 159.
114 This point is made in Wilson Jones, "Designing the Roman Corinthian Order," 60–2.
115 Ibid., 59–60, 40–5, 83–4.
116 Ibid., 43–4; 83–4.
117 Cornell, *The Beginnings of Rome*, 170.
118 *Ibid.*
119 Edward Said discusses the reshaping or reordering of information from France's imperial colonies in northern Egypt; see *Culture and Imperialism* (New York: Knopf, 1993), 99.

5: THE CORINTHIAN ORDER IN THE FIRST CENTURY B.C.

1 Mithradates VI, king of Pontus, had expanded his control of Greece and the Black Sea, and in 88 B.C., he invaded Asia Minor, which had a large Roman population. He reportedly massacred thousands of Romans and Italians in Asia Minor and robbed the royal treasury of the Roman provincial capital, acts that galvanized Rome to launch a counteroffensive. Sulla laid seige to Athens, the standoff lasting for several months in the winter of 87–86 B.C. See Arthur Keaveney, *Sulla: The Last Republican* (London: Croom Helm, 1982), 78–80; 86–90; Scullard, *Gracchi to Nero*, 72–6.
2 Pollitt, *The Art of Rome*, 60–1; Arthur E. R. Boak, *A History of Rome to 565 A.D.* (New York: Macmillan, 1943), 184–200; Erich S. Gruen, *The Last Generation of the Roman Republic* (Berkeley: University of California Press, 1974), 48–9.
3 For a discussion of the origins of the Corinthian Order, see Wilson Jones, *Principles of Roman Architecture*, 136–8; J. B. Onians, *Bearers of Meaning: The Classicial Orders in Antiquity, the Middle Ages, and the Renaissance* (Princeton: Princeton University Press, 1988), 41–58.
4 During the Middle Ages, the building was converted into a church known as Santo Stefano della Carrozze. In 1560, its name was changed to the Church of Santa Maria del Sole.
5 Boëthius refers to the Round Temple as the Temple of Vesta but acknowledges that attribution is without foundation. Boëthius, *Etruscan and Early Roman Architecture*, 138–9, 159. Palladio and Guido Caraffa called it the Temple of Vesta; see Palladio, *The Four Books of Architecture*, vol. 4 (New York: Dover, 1965), 94–5, pls. 34–6; and Guido Caraffa, *Il Tempio detto di Vesta nel Foro Boario* (Rome: V. Ferri Editore, 1948), 5–13.
6 See Chapter 3 for discussion of the Temples of Mater Matuta and Fortuna.
7 Stambaugh and Strong and Ward-Perkins refer to the building by its shape, the Round Temple; Stambaugh, *The Ancient Roman City*, 30–1; Donald Strong and J. B. Ward-Perkins, "The Round Temple in the Forum Boarium," *PBRS* 28 (1960): 7–8.
8 The attribution to L. Mummius Archaicus is made by Adam Ziolkowski in "Mummius' Temple of Hercules Victor and the Round Temple on the Tiber," *Phoenix* 42 (Winter 1988): 309, 316–17. See also Friedrich Rakob and Wolf-Dieter Heilmeyer, *Der Rundtempel am Tiber in Rom* (Mainz-am-Rhein: Philipp von Zabern, 1973), 29, 37; Robert E. A. Palmer, "Cults of Hercules, Apollo Caelispex and Fortuna in and around the Roman Cattle Market," review of Coarelli, *Il Foro Boario dalle origini alle fine della Repubblica* in *JRA* 3 (1990): 234–44; Antonio M. Colini, "Storia e topografia del Celio nell'antichità," *MemPontAcc* 7 (1944): 41–2; Domenico Palumbi, "Hercules Victor, Aedes et Signam," *LTUR*, vol. 3, 23–5.
9 Ziolkowski, "Mummius' Temple," 316, 327–30; Palumbi, "Hercules Victor," 23; L. Pietilä-Castren, "Some Aspects of the Life of Lucius Mummius Archaicus," *Arctos* 12 (1978): 115–23.
10 Ziolkowski, "Mummius' Temple," 310–11, fig. 1; Coarelli, *Il Foro Boario*, 13–59, figs. 1, 2, and 20; Coarelli, *Roma* 16, 313–14, 321.
11 The attribution to Hercules Olivarius is made by Coarelli in "Hercules Olivarius," *LTUR*, vol. 3, 20; Coarelli, *Il Foro Boario*, 92–103, 180–204; G. Cressedi, "Il Foro Boario e il Velabro," *BullCom*, 89 (1984): 265–8, fig. 10; Rakob and Heilmeyer, *Der Rundtempel*, 37; Richardson, *Dictionary*, 187.
12 Coarelli, *Il Foro Boario*, 182–9; Servius, *Ad Aen.* 8.353; Macr. *Sat.* 3.6.10; Ziolkowski, "Mummius' Temple," 320–4.
13 Serv. *Ad Aen.* 9.409; Liv. 10.23.3; Ziolkowski, "Mummius' Temple," 312. Also, the Notitia Regionum notes in the Regio XI, in this area, a monument to Hercules Olivarius. See A. Nordh, "Libellus de Regionibus Urbis Romae," *Scrifter utgivna av Svenska Institut Rom* 3 (1949): 91.
14 Coarelli, *Il Foro Boario*, 96–7, 197–8, fig. 16; E. T. Merrill, "Some Observations on the Arch of Trajan at Beneventum," *TAPA* 32 (1901): 43–63; Palmer, "Cults of Hercules," 234–40.
15 The argument against the attribution to L. Mummius Archaicus is made by Filippo Coarelli in "Hercules Victor, Aedes (ad Portam Trigeminam)," *LTUR*, vol. 3, 22–3. He argues that the finding place of the inscription means it referred to a building on the Caelian hill and not to the Round Temple. See also Coarelli, *Il Foro Boario*, 86; Palumbi, "Hercules Victor," 24; Pietilä-Castren, "Lucius Mummius Archaicus," 139ff; Palmer, "Cults of Hercules," 235. Ziolkowski states that the discovery of this artifact on the Caelian Hill indicates it was not from the temple itself but from one of several small monuments Mummius built in various locations in Rome. It was a fragment of a series of inscriptions that listed his buildings, the Temple

of Hercules included. See Ziolkowski, "Mummius' Temple," 330.

16 The argument against the attribution to Hercules Olivarius is made by Ziolkowski in "Mummius' Temple," 320–4. See also Palmer, "Cults of Hercules," 237–8.

17 Palumbi, "Hercules Victor," 25.

18 Ziolkowski, "Mummius' Temple," 316–17, 328; Palumbi, "Hercules Victor," 25.

19 Ziolkowski, "Mummius' Temple," 320; Macr. *Sat.* 3.12.7.

20 Coarelli, *Il Foro Borio*, 98; Ziolkowski, "Mummius' Temple," 319; Serv. *Ad Aen.* 8.362–3; Macr. *Sat.* 3.6.10.

21 Ziolkowski, "Mummius' Temple," 321, 330–1.

22 There is some confusion over the attribution to Octavius Herrenus. Coarelli attributes the temple's construction to Octavius Herrenus, but prefers a date of 110 to 90 B.C. Ziolkowski points out that Octavius Herrenus could not have won his victory until 80 to 70 B.C.; therefore, he could not have built the temple before that. See Coarelli, *Il Foro Boario*, 98; Ziolkowski, "Mummius' Temple," 331. Other dates have also been suggested, including ca. 130 B.C., and even as late as 35 to 15 B.C. Ward-Perkins sums it up by stating that the Corinthian columns with their Attic bases, the capitals, fragments of coffering, the cornice, and the elegant plinth indicate the temple was a "Hellenistic intruder upon the Roman scene." See Strong and Ward-Perkins, "The Round Temple," 18–19; Lars Fagerlind, "The Transformations of the Corinthian Capital in Rome and Pompeii during the Later Republican Period," *Corolla archaeologica principi hereditario regni sueciae Gustavo Adolpho* (Lund: C. W. K. Gleerup, 1932), 120–2.

23 Rakob and Heilmeyer, *Der Rundtempel*, 36–9, n. 17; Boëthius and Frank argue likewise for the early first century B.C.; see Boëthius, *Etruscan and Early Roman Architecture*, 138–9, 159; Tenney Frank, "Roman Buildings of the Republic: An Attempt to Date Them," *MAAR* 3 (1924): 136.

24 The Tholos at Delphi, designed by Theodorus of Phocaea in ca. 390 B.C., had twenty Doric columns in the exterior ring and ten Corinthian ones inside. The Tholos at Epidaurus, designed by Polyclitus the Younger in ca. 360 B.C., had an external Doric peristyle composed of twenty-six columns and an internal Corinthian ring of fourteen. Finally, the Philippeum at Olympia, built in 339 B.C., had a circular cella surrounded by a peristyle of eighteen Ionic columns and an inner ring of semidetached Corinthian columns. Dinsmoor, *Architecture of Ancient Greece*, 235–6.

25 Rakob and Heilmeyer, *Der Rundtempel*, 3, 16; Cressedi, "Il Foro Boario," 270; Mark Wilson Jones, "Principles of Design in Roman Architecture: The Setting Out of Centralized Buildings," *PBSR* 57 (1989): 114–17.

26 Caraffa, *Il Tempio detto di Vesta*, 6.

27 Rakob and Heilmeyer, *Der Rundtempel*, 6–9; Strong and Ward-Perkins, "The Round Temple," 20–27; Boëthius, *Etruscan and Early Roman Architecture*, 139.

28 If the first column to the left of the door is labeled no. 1, and you move clockwise around the perimeter, columns 1 through 8 and 19 and 20 are original. Columns 9 through 18 are the new ones. Of the original columns, nos. 5 and 8 have replacement capitals of Lunense marble. Rakob and Heilmeyer, *Der Rundtempel*, 8, pl. 14; Strong and Ward-Perkins, "The Round Temple," 20–4, fig. 2.

29 Vitr. 4.8.2.

30 Rakob and Heilmeyer, *Der Rundtempel*, 17; Caraffa, *Il Tempio detto di Vesta*, 6.

31 Vitr. 4.8.2.

32 The dimension of the column height in the case of the Round Temple by the Tiber includes the top step of the stylobate as if it were a continuous plinth. Wilson Jones, "Designing the Roman Corinthian Order," 38–9; Wilson Jones, *Principles of Roman Architecture*, 73.

33 Although some scholars suggest the plinths were incorporated into the stylobate's upper step, I believe there was a step between each plinth and that these steps were filled in later when the intercolumniations were walled in. See Rakob and Heilmeyer, *Der Rundtempel*, 6–8, pl. 14; Strong and Ward-Perkins, "The Round Temple," 9; Donald Strong and J. B. Ward-Perkins, "The Temple of Castor in the Forum Romanum," *PBSR* 30 (1962): 5–7, fig. 1.

34 Referring to endnote 28, the original capitals would include nos. 1–4, 6–7, and 19–20. Rakob and Heilmeyer, *Der Rundtempel*, 8, pl. 14; Strong and Ward-Perkins, "The Round Temple," 21, fig. 2.

35 Strong and Ward-Perkins, "The Round Temple," 22.

36 Rakob and Heilmeyer, *Der Rundtempel*, 19–21, 23.

37 Ibid.

38 Referring to endnote 28, the later capitals would include nos. 5, 8–18. Rakob and Heilmeyer, *Der Rundtempel*, 8, pl. 14; Strong and Ward-Perkins, "The Round Temple," 21, fig. 2.

39 Rakob and Heilmeyer, *Der Rundtempel*, 21–23; Strong and Ward-Perkins, "The Round Temples," 22.

40 Rakob and Heilmeyer, *Der Rundtempel*, 23; Cass. Dio *Rom. Hist.* 57.14; Tac. *Ann.* 1.76.

41 Palladio, *Four Books*, vol. 4, pls. 35–6.

42 Valadier published a reconstruction drawing of the entablature in Giuseppe Valadier, "Tempio detto di Vesta in Roma," in *Raccolta della più insigni fabbriche di Roma antica*, vol. 3 (Rome: n.p., 1813), pl. 5. Fragments of the entablature and coffering are preserved in the Vatican Museum. Strong and Ward-Perkins, "The Round Temple," 24–5; Rakob and Heilmeyer, *Der Rundtempel*, 9–11.

43 Strong and Ward-Perkins, "The Round Temple," 24–7.

44 Vitr. 4.7.3.

45 For reconstruction drawings with various roof forms see, for instance, J.-A. Coussin, "Le Temple di Vesta nel Foro Boario," in *Restaurations des monuments antiques* (Paris: n.p., 1879), pl. 3; M.-E. Isabelle, *Les édifices circulaires et les domes* (Paris: n.p., 1855), pl. 21; and Rakob and Heilmeyer, *Der Rundtempel*, pls. 49 and 50.

46 Rakob and Heilmeyer, *Der Rundtempel*, 11–12, 16.

47 Robertson, *Greek and Roman Architecture*, 211; Strong and Ward-Perkins, "The Round Temple," 9–13.

48 Rakob and Heilmeyer, *Der Rundtempel*, 11–12; Strong and Ward-Perkins, "The Round Temple," 9–12.

49 Strong and Ward-Perkins, "The Round Temple," 12–17; 24–5.

50 Hugh Plommer, *Ancient and Classical Architecture: Simpson's History of Architectural Development, I* (London and New York: Longmans, Green, 1956), 264–5.

51 For discussion of the Temple of Vesta in Tivoli, see Boëthius, *Etruscan and Early Roman Architecture*, 163.

52 The cella of the Temple of Vesta at Tivoli is composed of concrete with an *opus incertum* facing. Presumably, this was covered with stucco in imitation of ashlar masonry. The door and window frames are of travertine, as is the ceiling of the peristyle, which is composed of panels articulated with two rings of coffers. Rosettes carved in the coffers are similar to those of the Round Temple by the Tiber. See Boëthius, *Etruscan and Early Roman Architecture*, 163; Strong and Ward-Perkins, "The Round Temple," 26–7.

53 Wilson Jones, *Principles of Roman Architecture*, 103–6; Wilson Jones, "Centralised Buildings," 117.

54 Rakob and Heilmeyer, *Der Rundtempel*, 30.

55 Robertson, *Greek and Roman Architecture*, 210.

56 Part of a colossal marble statue representing a Greek female divinity identified as Fortuna Huiusce Diei was recently found on the site between Temples B and C. Now located in the Capitoline Museum, its head and neck measure 4 feet, 8 inches tall. Coarelli et al., *L'Area Sacra*, pl. 7.

57 Rakob and Heilmeyer, *Der Rundtempel*, 29–30.

58 William L. MacDonald, *The Pantheon: Design, Meaning and Progeny* (Cambridge: Harvard University Press, 1976), 68. The podium's structure was built of tufa blocks with rubble and concrete in its core. Its original height was about 2.50 meters. Its base and cornice were in the form of a *cyma reversa* molding. Coarelli et al., *L'Area Sacra*, 19–21; G. Marchetti-Longhi, "Gli scavi del Largo Argentina: Il Tempio B," *BullCom*, 76 (1956–58): 45–118.

59 Fagerlind compares the capitals of Temple B stylistically to those of the Temple of Jupiter in Pompeii, again being cut in two sections, with acanthus leaves on the lower half. The contoured leaves appear soft and plastically modeled, and were cut with six to eight teeth that spread themselves almost flat on the capital's surface. The upper part had volutes and helices, with the spaces in between being painted with acanthus leaves, representing a somewhat earlier practice than that of the Round Temple by the Tiber. Fagerlind dates Temple B to ca. 90 B.C. based on the technical and stylistic qualities of the capitals. Some other archaeologists date the temple to ca. 120 B.C. See Fagerlind, "Transformations of the Corinthian Capital," 121.

60 Rakob and Heilmeyer, *Der Rundtempel*, 28.

61 Coarelli et al., *L'Area Sacra*, 19–20.

62 Wilson Jones, "Centralised Buildings," 117; Coarelli et al., *L'Area Sacra*, 19.

63 Coarelli et al., *L'Area Sacra*, 19; G. Marchetti-Longhi, "Gli scavi del Largo Argentina: Il Tempio B," 45–118.

64 Coarelli et al., *L'Area Scara*, 20–1; G. Marchetti-Longhi, "Gli scavi del Largo Argentina: Evoluzione e transformazione dell'area e dei templi dall'età imperiale all'inizio del Medioevo," *BullCom* 82 (1970): 20–4.

65 MacDonald, *The Pantheon*, 68.

66 The podium, likewise of tufa, was built at a level corresponding to that of the Pompey-era Temple A; Coarelli et al., *L'Area Sacra*, 14–15.

67 Ibid., 21.

68 Cass. Dio *Rom. Hist.* 54.24.2; Jane M. Cody, "New Evidence for the Republican 'Aedes Vestae,'" *AJA* 77 (1973): 43; Richardson, *Dictionary*, 412.

69 Tac. *Ann.* 15.41; Richardson, *Dictionary*, 412.

70 Coin representations of L. Cassius Longinus from 55 B.C. show the republican temple, also with an Ionic Order. See Russell T. Scott, "Lavori e ricerche nell'Area Sacra di Vesta 1990–1991," *ArchLaz* 11 (1993): 11–17. It is possible the coin images show a badly rendered Corinthian Order, but Scott argues that it was Ionic; see also Cody, "New Evidence," 48.

71 Richardson, *Dictionary*, 412.

72 Coarelli et al., *L'Area Sacra*, 16–20; MacDonald, *The Pantheon*, 68; Marchetti-Longhi, "Gli scavi dell'Area Sacra," 101–37.

73 Coarelli et al., *L'Area Sacra*, 16–17; Blake, *Ancient Roman Construction*, 136.

74 Nielsen and Poulsen, *The Temple of Castor and Pollux I*, 121. In the Middle Ages, a church was built into the ruins of Temple A, and dedicated to San Nicolò. In the eighteenth century, another church was built over the previous one at the same level as the present-day street. All that remains today are the tufa columns, the stylobate, and two apses from the church. The original plan of Temple A can be seen in fragment XVI.IIO of the *Forma Urbis Romae*. The church of San Nicolò ai Cesarini was built over it. Lanciani, *The Ruins and Excavations*, 455.

75 Coarelli et al., *L'Area Sacra*, 16; Paul MacKendrick, *The Mute Stones Speak: The Story of Archaeology in Italy* (New York: Norton, 1983), 110.

76 Coarelli et al., *L'Area Sacra*, 12–14; 21–2. Adjacent porticos included the Porticus Minucia Vitus and the Porticus Minucia Frumentaria, constructed in 107 B.C. by the Consul M. Minuco Rufo, on the east side of the site.

77 A burning of the Capitoline Temple had been foretold during Sulla's return march. The fire may have been started by the carelessness of the Temple's guards. Plut. *Sul.* 27.11; Dion. Hal. *Rom. Ant.* 4.62.5; Vel. Pat. *Rom. Hist.* 2.24–29; Cic. *Cat.* 3.9; Tac. *Hist.* 3.72; Ann. 6.12; Scullard, *Gracchi to Nero*, 77–80; Keaveney, *Sulla*, 130–1.

78 Keaveney, *Sulla*, 118–19.

79 Plut. *Sul.* 33–36, *Mor.* 318.4.

80 Keaveney, *Sulla*, 190.

81 Gruen, *Last Generation*, 12, 122.

82 For the role of Lulatius Catulus see Plut. *Publi.* 15.1–4; Plin. *Nat. Hist.* 7.43.137–141; De Angeli, "Iuppiter Optimus Maximus," 149.

83 For information on the Tabularium, see Anna Maria Sommella, "Tabularium," *LTUR*, vol. 5, 21–2.

84 Tac. *Hist.* 3.72.3; Plut. *Publi.* 15.1–4; Plin. *Nat. Hist.* 7.43.137–141; De Angeli, "Iuppiter Optimus," 149.

85 Even though he rebuilt the Temple of Jupiter Capitolinus for political reasons, the priesthood, *flamen Dialis*, of the Capitoline Temple was vacant. Sulla's rival Marius had assigned it to the young Julius Caesar after the death of Lucius Cornelius Merula in 87 or 86 B.C. Before Caesar could be formally inaugurated into the office, Sulla came to power and immediately cancelled all appointments that had been made by his enemy, Caesar's priesthood among them. For whatever reason, Sulla did not designate a new *flamen Dialis*, and the position would remain vacant until the time of Augustus. Public rituals, however, continued to be performed in the temple by the *pontifices* without interruption. Beard, North, and Price, vol. 1, *Religions of Rome*, 130–1; Tac. *Ann.* 3.58.

86 Plin. *Nat. Hist.* 36.4.45. The Temple of Olympian Zeus had been built in the 170s B.C. by Antiochus IV Epiphanes and the

Roman architect Cossutius. Constructed on the foundations of an earlier Doric structure, its measurements were immense, 41 by 108 meters, with two rows of columns on either side of the cella and three at the front and rear. Almost nothing is known of Cossutius, the designer of the Temple of Olympian Zeus, other than Vitruvius's mention that he was Roman. Whether he designed the capitals himself or whether they were designed by Greek craftsmen is unknown. Furthermore, it is not known whether Cossutius executed similar columns and capitals in Rome in the 170s B.C. As Brown explains, during the second and first centuries B.C., it was not only Greek architects from the Hellenistic East, such as Hermodores of Cyprus, who were invited to immigrate to Rome to embellish its growing civic and commercial center, but also Italian architects, who were similarly being commissioned by Hellenistic monarchs. As Brown suggests, the reciprocal coming and going of architects was both frequent and fruitful. Dinsmoor, *The Architecture of Ancient Greece*, 280; Plommer, *Ancient and Classical Architecture*, 264.

87 Axel Boëthius, "Veteris capitoli humilia tecta," *ActaAArtH* 1 (1962): 27–33; Einer Gjerstad, "A proposito della ricostruzione del tempio arcaico di Giove Capitolino in Roma. Risposta ad Axel Boëthius," *ActaAArtH* 1 (1962): 35–40.

88 Some archaeologists suggest that they used only the capitals from the Athenian temple, placing them on traditional Tuscan column shafts. Lake, "The Archaeological Evidence," 102–3.

89 Gjerstad, "The Etruscans and Rome in Archaic Times," 174–7; Gjerstad, *Early Rome*, vol. 3, 176f.

90 Richardson, *Dictionary*, 223; Gjerstad, *Early Rome*, vol. 3, 176ff.

91 Vitr. 3.3.5.

92 Some scholars argue that the Temple was not rebuilt with Corinthian columns or capitals, but rather in the Tuscan Doric style, like the original. They point to coins from 87 B.C. and 43 B.C. that seem to show the rebuilt temple with Tuscan Doric capitals. See De Angeli, "Iuppiter Optimus," 149; Lake, "Archaeological Evidence," 102–3; *RRC*, vols. 1–2, 385.1, pl. 49.3, 487.1–2, pl. 58.6–7. These images are so small and abstract, however, with the capitals appearing as small blotches, not clearly defined capitals. Use of the Corinthian Order was still a relatively new phenomenon in Rome, and coin makers did not as yet distinguish between it and the Doric and Ionic styles as they would during the Empire.

93 Dion. Hal. *Rom. Ant.* 4.61.4; quoted in Nielsen and Poulsen, *The Temple of Castor and Pollux I*, 118–19.

94 Plin. *Nat. Hist.* 33.19.57.

95 Cic. *Ver.* 2.4.31.

96 De Angeli, "Iuppiter Optimus," 149; Keaveney, *Sulla*, 178; Dion. Hal., *Rom. Ant.* 4.62.4–6; Tac. *Ann.* 6.12.

97 Dion. Hal., *Rom. An.* 4.62.6–63.

98 De Angeli, "Iuppiter, Optimus," 149–50.

99 Tac. *Hist.* 3.72.3.

100 Julius Caesar had long wanted to remove Catalus's name from the Capitoline Temple. He had Catalus charged with embezzelment and encouraged Pompey to take over the responsibility for work on the temple. His intent was to let Pompey to become embroiled in scandal and face the same fate as Catalus, but his plan backfired. Catalus's inscription remained on the temple until it was destroyed again in a fire in 69 A.D. Cass. Dio *Rom. Hist.* 37.44.1–2; Suet. *Jul.* 15; Tac. *Hist.* 3.72.3; De Angeli, "Iuppiter Optimus," 150.

101 Edward Shils, *Center and Periphery: Essays in Macrosociology* (Chicago: University of Chicago Press, 1975), 151.

6: ARCHITECTURE AND CEREMONY IN THE TIME OF POMPEY AND JULIUS CAESAR

1 For Pompey, see Gruen, *Last Generation*, 126; For Caesar, see Matthias Gelzer, *Caesar*, 20–6.

2 Pierre Gros, *L'architecture romaine du début du IIIème siècle av. J.-C. à la fin du Haut-Empire 1: Les monuments publics* (Paris: Picard, 1996), 140–4.

3 Gruen, *Last Generation*, 6–7.

4 Ulrich, *Roman Orator and the Sacred Stage*, 114–15.

5 For information on Pompey the Great's early military career, see Peter Greenhalgh, *Pompey: The Republican Prince* (London: Weidenfeld and Nicolson, 1981), 1–53; Robin Seager, *Pompey: A Political Biography* (Berkeley: University of California Press, 1979), 28–43; John Leach, *Pompey the Great* (London: Croom Helm, 1978), 55–77; Scullard, *Gracchi to Nero*, 96–8.

6 Cass. Dio 37.1–8; Scullard, *Gracchi to Nero*, 103–4; Seager, *Pompey*, 38–39; Leach, *Pompey the Great*, 73.

7 Cass. Dio 37.7–8, 10–14; Zoch, *Ancient Rome: An Introductory History*, 167–8; Leach, *Pompey the Great*, 78–101; Seager, *Pompey*, 44–55.

8 Cass. Dio 37.21; Seager, *Pompey*, 77–8.

9 Plut. *Pomp.* 45.

10 Although the theater and the Temple of Venus Victrix were dedicated in 55 B.C., they were not completed until 52 B.C.; see John Arthur Hanson, *Roman Theater Temples* (Westport, CT: Greenwood Press, 1959), 43; Pierre Gros, "Theatrum Pompei," *LTUR*, vol. 5, 35–8; Richardson, *Dictionary*, 411; Kathryn L. Gleason, "'Porticus Pompeiana:' A New Perspective on the First Public Park of Ancient Rome," *JGH* 14 (January–March 1994): 13.

11 Cass. Dio 24.38.1–4.

12 Pliny states the seating capacity was 40,000, but this is clearly exaggerated. Plin. *Nat. Hist.* 36.113–115. The third-century A.D. regionary catalogue, the *Notitia Urbis Romae*, lists 17,580 loci, which is equivalent to about 12,000 spectators. See Nordh, "Libellus de Regionibus Urbis Romae," 87; Giuseppe Lugli, *Itinerario di Roma antica* (Milan, 1970), 429; Favro, *The Urban Image*, 295, n. 69.

13 Tert. *De Spect.* 10.

14 Suet. *Claud.* 21.1.

15 For the statuary, see G. Marchetti-Longhi, "Theatrum Lapideum," *Capitolium: rassegna mensile di attività municipale* 2 (December 1926): 531–44.

16 In some images, Venus Victrix is shown with a shield by her side, and in others she is seated by a throne. Hanson, *Roman Theater Temples*, 44, 52–3.

17 Greenhalgh, *Pompey*, 54.

18 In 82 B.C., after Sulla's conquest and plundering of the city and its sanctuary, he is thought to have initiated the construction of the present upper forum and temple complex as well as a reconstruction of the lower forum with its basilica, temples, curia, treasury, and caves. The town was one of the largest of

Sulla's many colonies built to resettle his military veterans. The construction of the temple complex, which must have taken ten to twenty years to complete, was carried on after Sulla's death, possibly up to the time of Caesar. MacKendrick, *The Mute Stones Speak*, 141–2; Hanson, *Roman Theater Temples*, 29–36; Gleason, "'Porticus Pompeiana,'" 21.

19 Coarelli, *Lazio: Guide archeologische*, 140–1; Hanson, *Roman Theater Temples*, 33–5.

20 Gros, *L'architecture romaine*, 135–7; Hanson, *Roman Theater Temples*, 31–2.

21 The theater-temple complex at Gabii is thought to have been built in ca. 200 B.C. Hanson, *Roman Theater Temples*, 29–30; G. Pinza, "Gabii ed i suoi monumenti," *BullCom* 31 (1903): 330–43.

22 Greenhalgh, *Pompey*, 57.

23 See Hanson, *Roman Theater Temples*, 53–5, for a discussion of the origins of the porticus.

24 Vitr. 5.9.1; Filippo Coarelli, "Il Campo Marzio occidentale. Storia e topografia," *Mélanges de l'École Française de Rome* 89 (1977): 807–46.

25 Favro, *The Urban Image*, 170; Lanciani, *Ruins and Excavations*, 444–5; Antonio Corso, "Vitruvius and Attic Monuments," *The Annual of the British School in Athens* 92 (1997): 389–91.

26 Vitr. 5.9.2.

27 For a history of the stoa as a building type, see J. J. Coulton, *The Architectural Development of the Greek Stoa* (Oxford: Clarendon Press, 1976), 6–10 and passim.

28 Vitr. 1.18.26.

29 Lanciani, *Ruins and Excavations*, 446.

30 Gleason, "'Porticus Pompeiana,'" 14–17; *FUR*, pl. 21.

31 Gleason, "'Porticus Pompeiana,'" 19.

32 Vitr. 5.9.5.

33 Ibid., 5.9.6.

34 Gleason, "'Porticus Pompeiana,'" 24; Suet. *Aug.* 31. Stage structures at the time of Pompey were typically temporary and not very large. Only at the time of Octavian near the end of the century did they take on a monumental character.

35 Greenhalgh, *Pompey*, 55–6; Gleason, "'Porticus Pompeiana,'" 19.

36 Hanson, *Roman Theater Temples*, 47.

37 Linderski, "Cicero and Roman Divination," 482–3.

38 Paul Zanker, *The Power of Images in the Age of Augustus*, trans. Alan Shapiro (Ann Arbor: University of Michigan Press, 1990), 20–1.

39 Karl Galinsky, *Augustan Culture: An Interpretive Introduction*, (Princeton: Princeton University Press, 1996), 198.

40 Beard, North, and Price, *Religions of Rome*, vol. 1, 146–7.

41 Taylor, *The Divinity of the Roman Emperor*, 38.

42 Ibid., 35–6.

43 Cass. Dio 37.50–51; Gruen, *Last Generation*, 85–7, 96–7, 105–7, 130–1.

44 Cass. Dio 37.52–58; Suet. *Caes.* 17–22, 26–30; Grant, *History of Rome*, 208–9; Seager, *Pompey*, 80; Scullard, *Gracchi to Nero*, 112–13; Christian Meier, *Caesar: A Biography*, trans. David McLintock (New York: Basic Books, 1982), 226–32; Gruen, *Last Generation*, 90–102.

45 On the first triumvirate, see Plut. *Crass.* 14.1–3; *Caes.* 13.1–2; *Pomp.* 47–1–3; Cic. *Ad Att.* 2.3.3; Gruen, *Last Generation*, 88–92; Grant, *History of Rome*, 208–9; Scullard, *Gracchi to Nero*, 112–14.

46 Grant, *History of Rome*, 208–9.

47 Suet. *Caes.* 22–24; Gruen, *Last Generation*, 141; Scullard, *Gracchi to Nero*, 114–16.

48 Julius Caesar began in Germany and Belgium, then invaded the northern coastal regions of Brittany and crossed the Rhine to penetrate further into Germany than had ever been done by a Roman general. Afterward, he twice invaded Britain across the English Channel. When he returned to the mainland, he engaged in a number of continued battles in Gaul until the entire territory, an area of about 640,000 square miles, was reduced to subject status. Tributes were assessed and provinces established, all under the direct control of Rome. Grant, *History of Rome*, 222–5; Suet. *Caes.* 25; Cass. Dio 39.1–5, 47–49, 50–53; 40.1–11, 31–44; Gruen, *Last Generation*, 112ff; Gelzer, *Caesar: Politician and Statesman*, 154–69.

49 For the Battle at Pharsalus, see Cass. Dio 41.52–63; Suet. *Caes.* 35.

50 Suet. *Caes.* 35; Gruen, *Last Generation*, 494; Gelzer, *Caesar: Politician and Statesman*, 235–71.

51 For discussion of Caesar's triumphs, see Suet. *Caes.* 37; Cass. Dio, 43.19–22; App. *Civ. Wars* 2.15.102; Chiara Morselli, "Forum Iulium," *LTUR*, vol. 2, 299–306; Stefan Weinstock, *Divus Julius* (Oxford: Clarendon Press, 1971), 76–9.

52 Suet. *Caes.* 39; Cass. Dio 43.23; App. *Civ. Wars* 2.102.

53 Michael Grant, *Cleopatra* (London: Weidenfeld and Nicolson, 1972), 85.

54 Max Weber, *Economy and Society: An Outline of Interpretive Sociology, II*, ed. Guenther Roth and Claus Wittich (New York: Badminton Press, 1968), 911.

55 Cass. Dio 43.20; Bowder, *Who Was Who in the Roman World*, 82.

56 Cass. Dio 43.14; Suet. *Caes.* 76.1; Gelzer, *Caesar*, 278.

57 Val. Max. 1.1.16; Cic. *Verr.* 2.1.154; Weinstock, *Divus Julius*, 281–6.

58 Cass. Dio 43.42–44; Suet. *Caes.* 45.2; 76.1; App. *Civ. Wars* 2.440–43; Gelzer, *Caesar*, 307.

59 For a discussion of the debate about Julius Caesar's status as a god, see Beard, North, and Price, *Religions of Rome*, vol. 1, 140–9.

60 Taylor, *Divinity of the Roman Emperor*, 45–6.

61 Morselli, "Forum Iulium," 299–300; Cic. *Ad Att.* 4.16.8.

62 App. *Civ. Wars* 2.102–424; Plin. *Nat. Hist.* 3.10.3.35; Weinstock, *Divus Julius*, 80–81; Caesar had already begun construction of similar forum complexes in cities in Spain and Gaul.

63 Cic. *Let.* 4.17.7; Morselli, "Forum Iulium," 299–306; Edoardo Tortorici, "Curia Julia," *LTUR*, vol. 1, 332.

64 Tagliamonte, "Forum Romanum," 315.

65 Carla Maria Amici, *Il Foro di Cesare* (Florence: Leo S. Olschki Editore, 1991), 29; Cic. *Ad Att.* 17.7; Suet. *Caes.* 26.2; Plin. *Nat. Hist.* 36.25–103.

66 Ulrich suggests that the initial podium construction was intended for a much smaller temple, or even something like a triumphal arch, but then changed after Caesar's victory at Pharsalus in 48 B.C. Another possibility Ulrich suggests, because of the presence of lateral walls in the core of the podium, was the intention of building a temple with a long axis

perpendicular to that of the forum's main axis, something in the manner of the Temple of Concord, which was also built on the ridge of a hill. Ulrich, "Julius Caesar," 62–6. Amici argues that Caesar planned the temple more or less as it was built from the beginning. Amici, *Il Foro di Cesare*, 35.

67 Cass. Dio 40.49.2, 50.2–3; Tortorici, "Curia Julia," 332.

68 Immediately after the destruction of the Curia Hostilia, the Senate made do by meeting in Pompey's curia and in various temples in the Forum Romanum. Ulrich, "Julius Caesar," 54, 72.

69 Cass. Dio 44.5.2; Tortorici, "Curia Julia," 332; Morselli. "Forum Iulium," 300.

70 App. *Civ. Wars* 2.68, 2.102.

71 App. *Civ. Wars* 2.102; Cass. Dio 43.22.2; James C. Anderson, Jr., *The Historical Topography of the Imperial Fora* (Brussels: Latomus, 1984), 43; Weinstock, *Divus Julius*, 84.

72 Weinstock, *Divus Julius*, 83.

73 Hanson, *Roman Theater Temples*, 51.

74 Plut. *Pomp.* 68.6.

75 App. *Civ. Wars* 2.10.68.

76 Hanson, *Roman Theater Temples*, 51.

77 Edith Hamilton, *Mythology* (New York: New American Library, 1964), 32–3.

78 Cass. Dio 43.22; App. *Civ. Wars* 2.15.102; Amici, *Il Foro di Cesare*, 31; Ulrich, "Julius Caesar," 49–51.

79 Cass. Dio 43.22.2–23; 45.6.4; Plin. *Nat. Hist.* 2.23.93–94; Suet. *Caes.* 39.2; Anderson, *Imperial Fora*, 44; Weinstock, *Divus Julius*, 88–89; Scullard, *Festivals and Ceremonies*, 167.

80 Morselli, "Forum Iulium," 300; Chiara Morselli and Edoardo Tortorici, "B. Sintesi storico-topografica," in *CFIFT*, 218–22.

81 On the forum's dedication by Augustus, see Aug. *Res Gest.* 4.20.3; Cass. Dio 45.6.4; Morselli, "Forum Iulium," 300; Morselli and Tortorici, "B. Sintesi storico-topografica," 218–22; Amici, *Il Foro di Cesare*, 61–64; Nicholas Purcell, "Forum Romanum (the Imperial Period)," *LTUR*, vol. 2, 337.

82 Amici, *Il Foro di Cesare*, 64. Zevi argues that it was built as a portico in front of the curia. F. Zevi, "Il calcidico della Curia Iulia," *RAL* 26 (1971): 237–51.

83 Amici, *Il Foro di Cesare*, 67, 146.

84 It is possible that the same team of skilled workers who built Domitian's Temple of Minerva in the Forum Transitorium from A.D. 85 to 98, then worked on the Forum Julium from A.D. 98 to 106, and finally, worked on the Forum of Trajan after that. See Amici, *Il Foro di Cesare*, 74; Morselli, "Forum Iulium," 304; C. F. Leon, *Die Bauornamentik des Trajansforum* (Vienna: Böhlaus, 1971), 67, 97, 104–13. Images of Trajan's rebuilt Temple of Venus Genetrix are found on numerous coins. See, for instance, *BMCREmp*, vol. 3, 79, no. 354, pl. 15.5. See also Morselli, "Forum Iulium," 301; Tortorici, "Curia Julia," 333; Amici, *Il Foro di Cesare*, 31, 77–97; Ulrich, "Julius Caesar," 49–51; Robin Haydon Darwall-Smith, *Emperors and Architecture: A Study of Flavian Rome* (Brussels: Latomus, 1996), 243–4.

85 Morselli, "Forum Iulium," 301; Morselli and Tortorici, "B. Sintesi storico-topografica," 253.

86 Amici, *Il Foro di Cesare*, 31; Ulrich, "Julius Caesar," 70.

87 Amici, *Il Foro di Cesare*, 35, 51; Olindo Grossi, "The Forum of Julius Caesar and the Temple of Venus Genetrix," *MAAR* 13 (1936), 217. Archaeological evidence suggests that the front of the podium was extended further in the building campaign of Augustus. At its base was a row of statuary and a fountain, identified by Ulrich as the Appiades Fountain. See Ulrich, "Julius Caesar," 77; Nielsen and Poulsen, *The Temple of Castor and Pollux I*, 120.

88 Vitruvius (3.1.2.) writes, according to the Morgan translation, "The *pycnostyle* is a temple in an intercolumniation of which the thickness of a column and a half can be inserted: for example, the Temple of Divine Caesar, that of Venus in Caesar's forum, and others constructed like them."

89 Vitr. 3.3.3.

90 Amici, *Il Foro di Cesare*, 35, 95–6; Morselli, "Forum Iulium," 305.

91 Amici, *Il Foro di Cesare*, 84–100, fig. 124.

92 Ibid., 70–88.

93 For detailed descriptions of the architectural fragments, see Henri von Blanckenhagen, *Flavische Architektur und ihre Dekoration, untersucht am Nervaforum*, (Berlin: Verlag Gebr. Mann, 1940), 77–9; Antonio M. Colini, "Scavi dei Fori Imperiale," *BullCom* 61 (1933): 262–4; Grossi, "The Forum of Julius Caesar," 218; Morselli, "Forum Iulium," 304; Amici, *Il Foro di Cesare*, 77.

94 Amici, *Il Foro di Cesare*, 74.

95 Ibid., 77–80, 85–7.

96 Vitr. 5.1.2.

97 Vitr. 5.1.1–2.

98 For information about the Forum at Paestum, see Carpiceci and Pennino, *Paestum and Velia*.

99 Anderson, *Imperial Fora*, 45. The most important periods of construction of the forum at Pompeii were from 200 to 80 B.C. by the Samnites and then by the Romans beginning in 80 B.C. The forum had begun to take on its rectangular shape in the late third and early second centuries B.C. under Samnite control. After the earthquake in A.D. 62, much of the forum was rebuilt, with many changes being made in the reconstruction, just before the eruption of Mount Vesuvius in A.D. 79. Lawrence Richardson, Jr., *Pompeii: An Architectural History* (Baltimore and London: Johns Hopkins University Press, 1988), 138; Paul Zanker, *Pompeii: Public and Private Life*, trans. Deborah Lucas Schneider (Cambridge: Harvard University Press, 2000), 78–106.

100 App. *Civ. Wars* 2.102.424; Einar Gjerstad, "Die Ursprüngsgeschichte der römischen Kaiserfora," *OpArch* 3 (1944): 40–72; Weinstock, *Divus Julius*, 82.

101 Vitr. 5.1.1.

102 Ibid.

103 Prosp. *Tiron.* 417; Morselli, "Forum Iulium," 305; Amici, *Il Foro di Cesare*, 39, 145–6.

104 The original columns of the portico, from the time of Julius Caesar, had diameters of 1.30 meters. Those of Diocletian were .90 meters. Amici, *Il Foro di Cesare*, 37–9, 146–7.

105 Morselli, "Forum Iulium," 302; Amici, *Il Foro di Cesare*, 37–40.

106 A second lateral access point probably corresponded to this axis on the forum's northeast side, although no evidence of it has been found because of the location of the Via dei Fori Imperiali.

107 Morselli, "Forum Iulium," 302; Morselli and Tortorici, "B. Sintesi storico-topografica," 222–37.

108 Amici, *Il Foro di Cesare*, 35; Morselli, "Forum Iulium," 302.
109 Amici, *Il Foro di Cesare*, 39, 67, 146.
110 For information on the Basilica Argentaria, see Anderson, *Imperial Fora*, 58–9, 61–3, 148–9; Amici, *Il Foro di Cesare*, 43–6; Morselli, "Forum Iulium," 305.
111 Anderson, *Imperial Fora*, 59; Carla Maria Amici, *Foro di Traiano: Basilica Ulpia e Biblioteche* (Rome: X Ripartizione antichità belle arti e problemi di cultura, 1982), 67–8, 43–6; Cairoli F. Giuliani, "Mercati e Foro Traiano: un fatto di attribuzione," *QuadIstStArch* 10 (1987): 25–8; Colini, "Scavi dei Fori Imperiale," 262–4; Richardson, *Dictionary*, 167.
112 Amici, *Il Foro di Cesare*, 101–16; Richardson, *Dictionary*, 167.
113 For information on the fountains, see Amici, *Il Foro di Cesare*, 35–6, 97–100; Roger B. Ulrich, "The Appiades Fountain of the Forum Iulium," *RömMitt* 93 (1986): 405–23. For reference to the equestrian statue of Caesar, see Plin. *Nat. Hist.* 8.154s; Suet. *Jul.* 61.1; Stat. *Silv.* 1.1.84–85; Weinstock, *Divus Julius*, 85–87. The statue was modeled after an equestrian statue of Alexander.
114 Weinstock, *Divus Julius*, 85–6; Richardson, *Dictionary*, 166; Plin. *Nat. Hist.* 35.156.
115 Richardson, *Dictionary*, 167; Cass. Dio 51.22.3; Meier, *Caesar*, 446.
116 Suet. *Caes.* 52.1; App. *Civ. Wars* 2.379; Grant, *History of Rome*, 232; Meier, *Caesar*, 408–11; Gelzer, *Caesar*, 255–6.
117 Although Cleopatra lived in Rome in Caesar's palace during the mid-40s B.C., there was no suggestion that he was going to marry her, for he was already married to Calpurnia and Roman law did not allow bigamy; Meier, *Caesar*, 446.
118 Grant, *Cleopatra*, 87.
119 Zanker, *The Power of Images*, 5.
120 Gruen, *Culture and National Identity*, 111.
121 Ulrich, "Julius Caesar," 75; Cass. Dio 3.38:6.
122 Ulrich, "Julius Caesar," 77.
123 Weber, *Economy and Society*, 910–11.
124 Trajan, while building his forum 150 years later, took the task of also renovating Caesar's forum. In A.D. 283, a fire destroyed much of the space. One of the first things rebuilt by Diocletian was Caesar's Forum. See Ulrich, "Julius Caesar," 77.
125 Excavations reveal that the structure of the first Basilica Aemilia had tufa walls with a timber-framed roof and that its plan measured 90 by 27 meters. Boëthius, *Etruscan and Early Roman Architecture*, 51, 108; Pollitt, *The Art of Rome*, 50; Liv. 40.51.2–6.
126 Margarita Steinby, "Basilica Aemilia," *LTUR*, vol. 1, 167–8; Richardson, *Dictionary*, 55–6. There is some question about the identity and location of the Basilica Aemilia. Steinby suggests it was located at the forum's southeast end, the site of the later Temple of Divus Julius and Arch of Augustus. Richardson believes the basilica was in fact located on the Forum's north side, but that it was referred to as the Basilica Paulli after 54 B.C.
127 Cic. *Ad Att.* 4.16.8; Plin. *Nat. Hist.* 35.13; Plut. *Caes.* 29; Richardson, *Dictionary*, 55; Steinby, "Basilica Aemilia," 167.
128 This Doric composition is indicated in a drawing by Giuliano da Sangallo (Cod. Vat. Barb. Lat. 4424, fol. 26). Richardson, *Dictionary*, 56.
129 Boëthius, *Etruscan and Early Roman Architecture*, 51, 108; Cass. Dio 54.24.3.
130 The original Basilica Sempronia was built in 170 B.C. by the censor Ti. Sempronius Gracchus. Liv. 44.16.10; Richardson, *Dictionary*, 56; Irene Iacopi, "Basilica Sempronia," *LTUR*, vol. 1, 187–8.
131 Aug. *Res Gest.* 20; Richardson, *Dictionary*, 52–3; Cairoli F. Giuliani and Patrizia Verduchi, "Basilica Iulia," *LTUR*, vol. 1, 177–8.
132 Aug. *Res Gest.* 20; Cass. Dio 56.27.5; Suet. *Aug.* 29.4; Richardson, *Dictionary*, 52–3; Giuliani and Verduchi, "Basilica Iulia," 177.
133 Richardson, *Dictionary*, 55; Luciani and Sperduti, *Foro Romano*, 53–4.
134 Richardson, *Dictionary*, 53; Giuliani and Verduchi, "Basilica Iulia," 177.
135 Cass. Dio 44.4–5; Suet. *Caes.* 76; App. *Civ. Wars* 2.440–43; Gelzer, *Caesar*, 315; Weinstock, *Divus Julius*, 282–85; Serv. *Aen.* 1.276.
136 Cass. Dio 44.9; App. Civ. Wars 2.444; Gelzer, *Caesar*, 317.
137 Frank, *Roman Imperialism*, 343.

7: REBUILDING ROME IN THE TIME OF AUGUSTUS

1 Aug. *Res ges.* 4.20; Donald R. Dudley, *Urbs Roma: A Source Book of Classical Texts on the City and Its Monuments* (London: Phaidon Press, 1967), 15.
2 Favro, *The Urban Image*, 183–6; Henner von Hesburg, "Die Veränderung des Erscheinungsbildes der Stadt Rom unter Augustus," in *Kaiser Augustus*, 93–7.
3 R. J. A. Wilson, "Roman Art and Architecture," *OHCW*, 771.
4 Favro argues that by promoting his family in these dedications, he was really promoting himself; Favro, *The Urban Image*, 107–8.
5 Shipley, "Chronology," 9.
6 Suet. *Aug.* 1.2.28.
7 Fagerlind, "The Transformations of the Corinthian Capital," 128.
8 The Romans may have established a colony at Luni in 177 B.C. The marble was carried down the coast by ship, then up the Tiber River, where special wharves were built to unload shipments. Blake, *Ancient Roman Construction*, 53.
9 L. Lazzarini et al., "Determination of the Provenance of Marbles Used in Some Ancient Monuments in Rome," in *Classical Marble*, 402.
10 Wilson, "Roman Art and Architecture," 173.
11 Wilson, *Principles of Roman Architecture*, 139; Donald Strong, "Some Observations on Early Roman Corinthian," *JRS* 53 (1963): 75–6.
12 Galinsky, *Augustan Culture*, 142.
13 Viscogliosi, *Il Tempio di Apollo 'in Circo,'* 131.
14 Ibid., 132; Wilson, "Roman Art and Architecture," 173.
15 Gros argues against this thesis, preferring the influence of Hellenistic sources as most important for understanding the architecture of this period. Pierre Gros, "Aurea Templa: recherches sur l'architecture religieuse de Rome à l'époque d'Auguste," *BEFAR* 231 (1976): 226.

16 For biographical information on Octavian's early years, see Zanker, *The Power of Images*, 33–100; Galinsky, *Augustan Culture*, 42–79; Pat Southern, *Augustus* (New York: Routledge, 1998), 1–44.
17 Octavian was in the town of Apollonia in Illyricum when Caesar was assassinated. He was preparing with the Roman army for a Parthian expedition. Suet. *Aug.* 8; Southern, *Augustus*, 14, 22.
18 Zanker, *The Power of Images*, 35; Southern, *Augustus*, 61–3.
19 Suet. *Aug.* 13; Galinsky, *Augustan Culture*, 11–12; Southern, *Augustus*, 45–55; David Stockton, "The Founding of the Empire," *OHCW*, 532.
20 Suet. *Aug.* 9; Cass. Dio 47.45–49; Southern, *Augustus*, 64–5.
21 After Octavian's battle against Sextus Pompeius, Lepidus attempted to challenge his right to rule Sicily. Octavian challenged him, and he retreated to Rome, his military ambitions forever abandoned. Southern, *Augustus*, 83–4; Favro, *The Urban Image*, 105; Suet. *Aug.* 16.
22 Suet. *Aug.* 17; Favro, *The Urban Image*, 98–9, 105; Southern, *Augustus*, 83–6, 96–9.
23 The Egyptian booty included the palace treasury, which had accumulated for 300 years, and a large amount of real estate. Augustus established for his veterans as many as seventy-five colonies on the Italian peninsula during the course of the next forty years. Tenney Frank, *Rome and Italy of the Empire*, vol. 5, (Baltimore: Johns Hopkins University Press, 1940): 18, n. 32; Suet. *Aug.* 41; Favro, *The Urban Image*, 91–2; Grant, *History of Rome*, 242–5.
24 Campbell, *Emperor and the Roman Army*, 139; Zanker, *The Power of Images*, 79; Suet. *Aug.* 22; Cass. Dio 51.21; Favro, *The Urban Image*, 92, 103–4; W. K. Lacey, *Augustus and the Principate: The Evolution of the System* (Leeds: Francis Cairns, 1996), 17–56.
25 George Philip Baker, *Augustus: The Golden Age of Rome* (London: Grayson and Grayson, 1937), 259.
26 Suet. *Aug.* 7; Cass. Dio, 53.16; Favro, *The Urban Image*, 104; Southern, *Augustus*, 113–14.
27 Shipley, "Chronology," 48–9.
28 Galinsky, *Augustan Culture*, 11–12.
29 Stockton, "Founding of the Empire," 532.
30 Galinsky, *Augustan Culture*, 12.
31 Vitr. *Pref.* 1.2.
32 Plommer, *Ancient and Classical Architecture*, 264–5.
33 Vitr. 3.3.8.
34 Coulton, "Hermogenes," 361.
35 Plommer, *Ancient and Classical Architecture*, 264–5.
36 The Temple of Divus Julius was vowed by the Second Triumvirate in 42 B.C. For discussion of the building, see Cass. Dio *Rom. Hist.* 47.18.4; Pierre Gros, "Iulius, Divus, Aedes," *LTUR*, vol. 3, 116–17; Nielsen and Poulsen, *Temple of Castor and Pollux I*, 121; Favro, *The Urban Image*, 95–6.
37 The effort to locate the first altar and column at the site of the cremation of Caesar's body was led by Herophilus, a Greek orator who claimed to have been the grandson of the great Marius and a cousin of Caesar. Liv. *Perioch.* 116.9; Plut. *Caes.* 68; Gros, "Iulius, Divus, Aedes," 116; Coarelli, *Il Foro Romano*, vol. 2, 231; Taylor, *The Divinity of the Roman Emperor*, 83–4.
38 Suet. *Caes.* 85; Gros, "Iulius, Divus, Aedes," 116.
39 Dolabella ordered the removal of the altar and the column and, at the same time, seized the slaves and the freedmen who had put them up. He crucified the slaves and had the freedmen thrown down the Tarpeian rock. Cic. *Att.* 14.15–17; Cass. Dio 44.52.2; Coarelli, *Il Foro Romano*, vol. 2, 231; Taylor, *The Divinity of the Roman Emperor*, 88.
40 Gros, "Iulius, Divus, Aedes," 118.
41 As with the Temple of Castor and Pollux, the lateral stairs were used for the purpose of voting. Taylor, *Roman Voting Assemblies*, 41.
42 Gros,"Iulius, Divus, Aedes," 118; Coarelli, *Roma: Guide archeologiche*, 75; Coarelli, *Il Foro Romano*, vol. 2, 308–23.
43 The enclosure of the niche corresponded to the installation of a new pavement in the Forum Romanum. Coarelli, *Il Foro Romano*, 232. Gros argues that the altar was removed and the niche filled in because, by 14 B.C., Augustus no longer depended on his link to Julius Caesar. See Gros, "Iulius, Divus, Aedes," 118; Montagna Pasquinucci, "L'altare del tempio del Divo Giulio," *Athenaeum Pavia* 52 (1974), 144–55. This seems at odds, however, with the fact that at the same time Augustus was paying homage to Caesar in an even grander way by including a statue of both Venus Genetrix and the deified Julius in the cella of the Temple of Mars Ultor (see Chapter 8).
44 Cass. Dio *Rom. Hist.* 51.19.2; Suet. *Aug.* 100; Frontin. *Aq.* 29; Richardson, *Dictionary*, 213–14; Coarelli, *Il Foro Romano*, vol. 2, 308–12 Zanker, *The Power of Images*, 80.
45 For a discussion of the Rostra Aedes Divi Juli as a structure independent of the Temple of Divus Julius, see Coarelli, *Il Foro Romano*, vol. 2, 308–24.
46 Zanker, *The Power of Images*, 81.
47 Fagerlind, "Transformations of the Corinthian Capitals," 120–2; Gros, "Iulius, Divus, Aedes," 117; Vitr. 3.3.2. The arrangement of the plan can be compared to that of the Temple of Minerva at Assisi, built in 28–15 B.C. Both had a single cella with walls framed by corner pilasters and that extended as *antae* into the first bay of the pronaos. Both had six columns across the front, although the pronaos of the Temple of Minerva was shallower, two bays instead of three. Both had a high podium with lateral stairs, and, in both cases, stairs leading to the pronaos penetrated through the intercolumniations. The Temple of Minerva was, in all likelihood, an imitation of the Temple of Divus Julius, the latter being an important paradigm for numerous Augustan temples from this period. See Marcello Gaggiotti et al., *Umbria, Marche: Guide archeologiche Laterza* (Rome and Bari: Giuseppe Laterza, 1980), 159–63.
48 See, for instance, the reconstruction drawing of Otto Ludwig Richter of 1898, reproduced in Favro, *The Urban Image*, 132, fig. 57. Original image is from *JDAI* 4 (1889): 157.
49 For a discussion of the theory that the Ionic and Corinthian Orders were combined on the same building, see J. B. Ward-Perkins, "An Early Augustan Capital in the Roman Forum," *PBSR*, 35 (1967): 28. Gros and Coarelli reject this theory and argue the Corinthian Order was used in both the pronaos and the cella. See Gros, "Iulius, Divus, Aedes," 119; Coarelli, *Roma: Guide archeologiche*, 75; Richardson, *Dictionary*, 213–14.
50 Nielsen and Poulsen, *Temple of Castor and Pollux I*, 121.
51 About a dozen fragments of the frieze were discovered on the site and are preserved in the Antiquarium Forense. Gros, "Iulius, Divus, Aedes," 118–19.

52 Strong, "Early Roman Corinthian," 74–5.
53 Ward-Perkins, "An Early Augustan Capital," 28.
54 Gros, "Iulius, Divus, Aedes," 117; Ov. *Met.* 15.843–51; Cass. Dio 45.7.1.
55 Zanker, *The Power of Images*, 35; Plin. *Nat. Hist.* 2.93–94 Richardson, *Dictionary*, 214.
56 Plin. *Nat. Hist.* 35.91; Gros, "Iulius, Divus, Aedes," 117; Zanker, *The Power of Images*, 80.
57 Russell T. Scott, "Regia-Vesta," *ArchLaz* 9 (1988): 18–26; Shipley, "Chronology," 22–3.
58 Cass. Dio 54.8.3; Ward-Perkins, "An Early Augustan Capital," 28; An arch honoring Augustus was first built on this site in 29 B.C. to celebrate his victory over Marcus Antony and Cleopatra at Actium. It was built initially as a single-bay structure. Zanker, *The Power of Images*, 81; Richardson, *Dictionary*, 23.
59 Cass. Dio 54.24.2; Richardson, *Dictionary*, 412.
60 For discussion of the Temple of Saturn, see Suet. *Aug.* 29.5; Filippo Coarelli, "Saturnus, Aedes," *LTUR*, vol. 4, 234; Pensabene, *Tempio di Saturno*, 48; Richardson, *Dictionary*, 343.
61 Coarelli, "Saturnus, Aedes," 235; Richardson, *Dictionary*, 343–4.
62 Dudley, *Urbs Roma*, 80–81; Luc. *Phars.* 3.154–68.
63 The exact location of the new treasury is not known. Coarelli suggests it was part of the Temple of Juno Moneta built on the northern end of the Capitoline Hill, or Arx, in the last decades of the first century B.C. Coarelli, "Saturnus, Aedes," 235; Filippo Coarelli, "Moneta in Arce," *LTUR*, vol. 3, 279–80.
64 Coarelli, "Saturnus, Aedes," 235; Pensabene, *Il Tempio di Saturno*, 17–25; Richardson, "The Approach," 56.
65 In plan it can be compared to the Maison Carrée in Nîmes, France, built in A.D. 1–10. Both shared the three-bay-deep pronaos and the engaged pilasters or columns on the cella walls. It is probable that the architects of the Maison Carrée knew about the rebuilt version of the Temple of Saturn, and used its plan as one of their models.
66 Pensabene, *Il Tempio di Saturno*, pl. 3.
67 Ibid., 73.
68 Ibid., 64–70.
69 Of the eleven existing elements of the frieze, six are original. They are of Proconesian marble, and their carving is crisp and precise. The rest are Lunense marble, and their carving is more sketchy, suggesting they were done rapidly at the time of the fourth-century restoration. Pensabene, *Il Tempio di Saturno*, 49–51.
70 Ibid., 47; Strong, "Early Roman Corinthian," 75.
71 Strong, "Early Roman Corinthian," 75.
72 Ward-Perkins, "An Early Augustan Capital," 23–5.
73 The capital fragments are of white Carrara marble, carved from two blocks, an upper and a lower half. The inner volutes reach up to touch the lower edge of the abacus, and all the volutes display a continuous acanthus-leaf motif along their whole length. Between the volutes was a tendril with a rosette with four petals. Ward-Perkins suggests that this capital was from the north-east *antae* of the temple's pronaos. Ward-Perkins, "An Early Augustan Capital," 23–5.
74 For a discussion of the *Anaglypha Traiani/Hadriani*, see Mary Taliaferro Boatwright, *Hadrian and the City of Rome* (Princeton: Princeton University Press, 1987), 182–6; Mario Torelli, *Typology and Structure of Roman Historical Reliefs*, Jerome Lectures, ser. 14 (Ann Arbor: University of Michigan Press, 1982), chap. 4; Ann L. Kuttner, *Dynasty and Empire in the Age of Augustus: The Case of the Boscoreale Cups* (Berkeley: University of California Press, 1995), 44–51.
75 Stambaugh, *The Ancient Roman City*, 118–19.
76 For information on the House of Augustus, see Suet. *Aug.* 72.1; 29.3; 72.2; 57.2; Richardson, *Dictionary*, 117–18; Gianfilippo Carettoni, "Die Bauten des Augustus," in *Kaiser Augustus*, 265; Gianfilippo Carettoni, "Roma – le costruzioni di Augusto e il Tempio di Apollo sul Palatino," *ArchLaz* 1 (1978): 72.
77 For a discussion of the relationship between Augustus's house and the Temple of Apollo Palatinus, see Paul Zanker, "Der Apollontempel auf dem Palatin 'Ausstattung und politische Sinnbezüge' nach der Schlacht von Actium," *Città e architettura*, 21–7; Carettoni, "Roma – le costruzioni di Augusto," 72; and Susan Walker, "The Moral Museum: Augustus and the City of Rome," in *Ancient Rome*, 61–3.
78 For discussion of the Temple of Apollo Palatinus, see Pierre Gros, "Apollo Palatinus," *LTUR*, vol. 1, 54; Carettoni, "Rome – le costruzioni di Augusto," 72–4; Richardson, *Dictionary*, 14; Vell. Pat. 2.81.3; Cass. Dio 49.15.5, 53.1.3; Pensabene, *Il Tempio di Saturno*, 56; J. B. Ward-Perkins, *Roman Imperial Architecture* (New York: Penguin Books, 1985), 36–7.
79 Ogilvie, *The Romans and Their Gods*, 114.
80 It was a site he had purchased to build his own house, but after beginning construction of the temple instead, the people of Rome, according to Cassius Dio, resolved to build a house for him at public expense. Liebeschuetz, *Continuity and Change*, 82–3; Walker, "The Moral Museum," 62; Shipley, "Chronology," 47; Suet. *Aug.* 29.3; Cass. Dio *Rom. Hist.* 49.15.5.
81 Liebeschuetz, *Continuity and Change*, 82–3; Suet. *Aug.* 18.
82 Liebeschuetz, *Continuity and Change*, 85.
83 The podium's structure was tufa and travertine in *opus quadratum*. Gros, "Apollo Palatinus," 56; Vitr. 3.3.4.
84 For a discussion of the building's capitals, see Heinrich Bauer, "Das Kapitel des Apollo Palatinus-Tempels," *RömMitt* 76 (1969): 183–204; Ward-Perkins, *Roman Imperial Architecture*, 36–7.
85 Gros, "Apollo Palatinus," 56; Zanker, "Der Apollontempel," 22–3; and O. L. Richmond, "The Augustan Palatium," *JRS* 4 (1914), 203–4.
86 Beard, North, and Price, *Religions of Rome*, vol. 1, 198; Gros, "Apollo Palatinus," 54–7; Richmond, "Augustan Palatium," 200–1, 205–6.
87 Walker, "The Moral Museum," 62; Andrew Wallace-Hadrill, *Augustan Rome* (London: Bristol Classical, 1993), 28.
88 Carettoni, "Il Tempio di Apollo sul Palatino," 73–4. The location of the two libraries at the eastern edge of the platform, opposite the House of Augustus, served to frame the view to the Temple of Appollo Palatinus for visitors approaching the city by boat. See discussion in Favro, *The Urban Image*, 210.
89 Gros, "Apollo Palatinus," 55; Richmond, "Augustan Palatium," 201. The libraries were rebuilt at the time of Domitian in conjunction with his Palace. After the fire of Nero, the entire lower level of the House of Augustus had been

abandoned, and the terrace around the Temple of Apollo and the libraries was enlarged and raised by Domitian. Carettoni, "Il Tempio di Apollo sul Palatino," 73–4.

90 Beard, North, and Price, *Religions of Rome*, vol. 1, 198; Gros, "Apollo Palatinus," 54–7; Zanker, "Der Apollontempel," 27–31.

91 Plin. *Nat. Hist.* 36.25, 36.32, 36.24; Richardson, *Dictionary*, 14.

92 Plin. *Nat. Hist.*, 36.24–32; Gros, "Apollo Palatinus," 54.

93 In addition to the twenty terra-cotta panels, forty others of smaller dimensions and with more primitive representations were found. Gros, "Apollo Palatinus," 56; Zanker, "Der Apollontempel," 33–6.

94 Zanker, *The Power of Images*, 89.

95 Liebeschuetz, *Continuity and Change*, 84–5; Gros, "Apollo Palatinus," 54–57.

96 For a discussion of the area around the two temples, see Patrizio Pensabene, "La zona sud-occidentale del Palatino," *Arch Laz* 3 (1980): 65–81.

97 For discussion of the Temple of Victoria, see Liv. 10.33.9; Patrizio Pensabene, "Victoria, Aedes," *LTUR*, vol. 5, 149–50; Patrizio Pensabene, "Scavi nell'area del Tempio della Vittoria e del Santuario della Magna Mater sul Palatino," *ArchLaz* 9 (1988): 54; Paul Rehak, "The Ionic Temple Relief in the Capitoline: The Temple of Victory on the Palatine?" *JRA* 3 (1990): 172–86; Richardson, *Dictionary*, 420.

98 Pensabene, "Victoria, Aedes," 149; Pensabene, "Scavi nell'area del Tempio della Vittoria," 54.

99 Pensabene, "Victoria, Aedes," 149.

100 The Temple of Magna Mater was dedicated by the praetor M. Junius Brutus. See Patrizio Pensabene, "Magna Mater, Aedes," *LTUR*, vol. 3, 206–8; Richardson, *Dictionary*, 242; Liv. 29.10.4–11.8; Erich S. Gruen, *Studies in Greek Culture and Roman Policy: Cincinnati Classical Studies*, vol. 7 (Leiden: n.p., 1990): 5–33; Torsten Mattern, "Der Magna-Mater-Tempel und die augusteische Architektur in Rom," *RömMitt* 107 (2000): 141–53.

101 Val. Max. 1.8.11; Ov. *Fast.* 4.348; Pensabene, "Magna Mater, Aedes," 206.

102 Pensabene, "Magna Mater, Aedes," 206–8; Richardson, *Dictionary*, 242; Liv. 29.10.4–11.8.

103 Liv. 29.37.2; 36.36; Serv. *Aen.* 7.188; Juv. *Sat.* 3.138ff; Pensabene, "Magna Mater, Aedes," 206.

104 Liv. 36.36.4–5; Cic. *Har. Resp.* 24; Richardson, *Dictionary*, 242.

105 Zanker, *The Power of Images*, 109; Richardson, *Dictionary*, 242.

106 Pensabene, "Magna Mater, Aedes," 206–7; Richardson, *Dictionary*, 242; Richmond, "The Augustan Palatium,"193–226.

107 Aug. *R. Ges.* 19; Cass. Dio 55.12.4; Suet. *Aug.* 57; Pensabene, "Magna Mater, Aedes," 206.

108 Fagerlind, "The Transformations of the Corinthian Capital," 122.

109 Ov. *Fast.* 4.251–254, 4.272; Pensabene, "Magna Mater, Aedes," 206.

110 Virg. *Aen.* 2.693–697; 9.77–79; 10.252–255; Beard, North, and Price, *Religions of Rome*, vol. 1, 198.

111 Stambaugh, *The Ancient Roman City*, 60; Richardson, *Dictionary*, 117–18.

112 For a discussion of the boundaries of and the buildings around the Circus Flaminius, see Wiseman, "The Circus Flaminius," 3–26; T. P. Wiseman, "Two Questions on the Circus Flaminius," *PBSR* 44 (1976): 44–7; Viscogliosi, "Circus Flaminius," 269–72.

113 The theater was dedicated to Marcellus, Augustus's nephew, and son of Octavia. He had died in 22 B.C. at the age of nineteen. Paolo Fidenzoni, *Il Teatro di Marcello* (Rome: Edizioni Liber, ca. 1960), 25; Paola Ciancio Rossetto, "Theatrum Marcelli," *LTUR*, vol. 5, 31.

114 For discussion of the Temple of Apollo Sosianus, see Viscogliosi, "Apollo, Aedes in Circo," 50; Viscogliosi, *Il Tempio di Apollo 'in Circo,'* 4; Shipley, "Chronology," 26; Eugenio La Rocca, *Amazzonomachia: Le sculture frontonali del Tempio di Apollo Sosiano* (Rome: De Luca Editore, 1985), 16–18.

115 Viscogliosi, *Il Tempio di Apollo 'in Circo,'* 4.

116 Viscogliosi, "Apollo, Aedes in Circo," 50; Viscogliosi, *Il Tempio di Apollo 'in Circo,'* 4; Shipley, "Chronology," 26.

117 Favro, *The Urban Image*, 91; Plin. *Nat. Hist.* 36.28; Viscogliosi, "Apollo, Aedes in Circo," 50; Viscogliosi, *Il Tempio di Apollo 'in Circo,'* 4.

118 Viscogliosi, "Apollo, Aedes, in Circo," 52; Viscogliosi, *Il Tempio di Apollo 'in Circo,'* 43.

119 Its podium was built of Aniene tufa in *opus quadratum* combined with *opus caementicium*. Viscogliosi, *Il Tempio di Apollo 'in Circo,'* 52.

120 Wilson Jones, "Designing the Roman Corinthian Order," 39, 66.

121 Strong, "Early Roman Corinthian," 81.

122 Viscogliosi, "Apollo, Aedes, in Circo," 52–3; Viscogliosi, *Il Tempio di Apollo 'in Circo,'* 43–5; Richardson, *Dictionary*, 13.

123 Viscogliosi, "Apollo, Aedes, in Circo," 53; Strong, "Early Roman Corinthian," 81.

124 Viscogliosi, *Il Tempio di Apollo 'in Circo,'* 45–7.

125 Ibid., 46–9. A *thymiaterion* is a small vase with a cover that has holes, used when offering a sacrifice to a god.

126 Strong, "Early Roman Corinthian," 81.

127 Viscogliosi, *Il Tempio di Apollo 'in Circo,'* 45–7, 92–112, 160–6, figs. 187, 188, and 193; Alessandro Viscogliosi, "Die Architektur-Dekoration der Cella des Apollo-Sosianus-Tempels," in *Kaiser Augustus*, 136–48. La Rocca interprets the evidence differently than Viscogliosi, arguing that the cella interior had only one set of columns rising the full height of the space. See La Rocca, *Amazzonomachia*, 83–102; Eugenio La Rocca, "Der Apollo-Sosianus-Tempel," in *Kaiser Augustus*, 121–9.

128 Viscogliosi, *Il Tempio di Apollo 'in Circo,'* 57–77, 92–112, fig. 193.

129 Ibid., 63, fig. 64.

130 Ibid., 75–76; La Rocca, *Amazzonomachia*, 95.

131 Viscogliosi, *Il Tempio di Apollo 'in Circo,'* 50; Strong, "Early Roman Corinthian," 81; Pierre Gros, "Aurea Templa: 221–6.

132 For discussion of the Temple of Bellona, see Viscogliosi, "Bellona, Aedes in Circo," 191; Coarelli, *Il Campo Marzio*, 393–5.

133 Viscogliosi, "Bellona, Aedes in Circo," 192. For discussion of architectural fragments, including a capital from the site, see Matilde de Nuccio, "Tempio di Bellona: Studi Preliminari," *ArchLaz* 12.1 (1995): 71–7.

134 For discussion of the Porticus Octavia, see Plin. *Nat. Hist.* 34.7.13; Viscogliosi, "Porticus Octavia, 139–40; Richardson, *Dictionary*, 317; Lawrence Richardson, Jr., "The Evolution of the Porticus Octaviae," *AJA* 80 (1976): 59–60; Coarelli, *Il Campo Marzio*, 517–20.

135 Vell. Pat. 2.1.2; Viscogliosi, "Porticus Octavia," 139–40.

136 Plin. *Nat. Hist.* 34.6.13; Coarelli, *Il Foro Boario*, 515–28; Richardson, "Evolution of the Porticus Octaviae," 57–64; Viscogliosi, "Porticus Octavia," 139–40.

137 Aug. *Res. Ges.* 4.19; Cass. Dio, *Rom. Hist.* 49.43; Richardson, "Evolution of the Porticus Octaviae," 60; Coarelli, *Il Foro Boario*, 524.

138 App. *Civ. Wars*, 2.28; Viscogliosi, "Porticus Octavia," 140; Richardson, *Dictionary*, 317; Richardson, "Evolution of the Porticus Octaviae," 60–1.

139 For discussion of the Porticus Philippi, see Alessandro Viscogliosi, "Porticus Philippi, *LTUR*, vol. 3, 146–7; Viscogliosi, "Porticus Metelli," 132; Coarelli, *Il Foro Boario*, 452–84; Richardson, *Dictionary*, 187; Lawrence Richardson, "Hercules Musarum and the 'Porticus Philippi' in Rome," *AJA* 81 (1977): 355–61.

140 Ov. *Ars Am.* 3.165–8; Viscogliosi, "Porticus Philippi," 146–7.

141 Viscogliosi, "Porticus Metelli," 130–2; Viscogliosi, "Porticus Octaviae," 141–5; Coarelli, *Il Foro Boario*, 529–37; Richardson, "Evolution of the Porticus Octaviae," 61–2.

142 Richardson points out that the only reason the temple's reconstruction is thought to have been paid for by Augustus is because of a remark in Suetonius that Augustus put up buildings in the names of his family members. Richardson argues that Octavia was rich enough herself to have paid for the project. Suet. *Aug.* 29; Liv. *Epit.* 138; Richardson, "Evolution of the Porticus Octaviae," 57–64; Richardson, *Dictionary*, 317–18; Viscogliosi, "Porticus Octaviae,"141–5.

143 Festus (188L) states there were, in fact, two porticus complexes with the name Octavia, one nearer the Theater of Marcellus, the other nearer the Theater of Pompey. The descriptions of the locations provided by him have caused a substantial debate about both complexes, however. See Richardson, "Evolution of the Porticus Octaviae," 56–64; Viscogliosi, "Iuppiter Stator," 157; Coarelli, *Il Campo Marzio*, 517–28.

144 Pliny suggests the two temples were also rebuilt at the time of Augustus by two architects from Sparta, Sauras and Batrachos. Plin. *Nat. Hist.* 36.42–43; Gros, "Hermodorus et Vitruve," 143; Coarelli, "Il Tempio di Bellona," 58, n. 103; Viscogliosi, "Porticus Octaviae," 141–5; Richardson, *Dictionary*, 317. The Temple of Juno Regina was later destroyed by fire in A.D. 80 and again in 203. Septimius Severus and Caracalla restored it, three marble composite capitals of which remain. Richardson, *Dictionary*, 216–7, 225–6.

145 Viscogliosi, "Iuppiter Stator," 158; Coarelli, *Il Foro Boario*, 536–7, figs. 132–3; Richardson, *Dictionary*, 317.

146 Richardson, *Dictionary*, 317; Richardson, "Evolution of the Porticus Octaviae," 63–4; Plin. *Nat. Hist.* 35.114, 36.22; Coarelli, *Il Foro Boario*, 536.

147 In A.D. 80, the Porticus and its enclosed buildings were severely damaged by a fire. It was rebuilt by Domitian, then restored a second time by Septimius Severus and Caracalla in A.D. 203. Shortly after its second restoration, it began to be used as a fish market. In the Middle Ages, two convents and the Church of San Angelo in Pescheria were built behind the main entrance. An arch was added reusing existing blocks, thus destroying the structure's classical character and symmetry. Viscogliosi, "Porticus Octaviae," 143–4; Richardson, *Dictionary*, 317.

148 Claridge, *Rome*, 222.

149 Richardson, "Evolution of the Porticus Octaviae," 63.

150 Richardson, *Dictionary*, 317; Viscogliosi, "Porticus Octaviae," 143–4.

151 Balbus added a crypt and portico to his theater, Marcius Philippus surrounded the Temple of Hercules Musareum with a portico (located just west of the Portico of Octaviae), and Agrippa built the Portico Vipsania, Portico Argonautarum, and the Portico Eventus Boni.

152 Lanciani, *Ruins and Excavations*, 445–6.

153 Viscogliosi, *Il Tempio di Apollo 'in Circo,'* 118–20.

154 Ibid., 131.

155 Ibid., 132.

156 Ibid. Gros argues against this thesis, preferring the influence of Hellenistic sources as most important for understanding the architecture of this period. Gros, "Aurea Templa," 226.

157 Coarelli, "Iuppiter Feretrius," 135–6; Favro, *The Urban Image*, 92; Dion. Hal. *Rom. Ant.* 2.34; Liv. 4.20.

158 The exact location of the Temple of Jupiter Feretrius has not been identified. Coarelli, "Iuppiter Feretrius," 136; Liv. 4.20.7; Richardson, *Dictionary*, 219.

159 In the *Res Gestae* Octavian stated, "I restored the Capitolium and the Theater of Pompey, both at great expense without inscribing my own name on the altar." Aug. *Res. Gest.* 4.20; Favro, *The Urban Image*, 109. For discussion of Jupiter Tonans, see Aug. *Res. Gest.* 4.19; Suet. *Aug.* 1.2.29.1; Cass. Dio 54.4.2–4; Pierre Gros, "Iuppiter Tonans, Aedes," *LTUR*, vol. 3, 159–60; Richardson, *Dictionary*, 226–7.

160 Plin. *Nat. Hist.* 34.7.5, 36.19.79. There is a debate about the location of the Temple of Jupiter Tonans. Gros states its remains have not been discovered. Richardson says it was under the Via di Monte Tarpeio, remains, which are commonly identified with the Temple of Jupiter Custos. Gros. "Iuppiter Tonans," 160; Richardson, *Dictionary*, 227.

161 Cass. Dio 54.4.2–4; Gros, "Iuppiter Tonans," 159; Favro, *The Urban Image*, 201.

162 Cass. Dio 54.

163 For image of Jupiter Tonans see *RIC*, vol. 1, 46, nos. 59 and 63, pl. 2, and 83, no. 240; Gros, "Iuppiter Tonans," 159.

164 For Agrippa's construction of the Pantheon, see Cass. Dio 53.27.2–3; Adam Ziolkowski, "Pantheon," *LTUR* vol. 4, 54–5; Richardson, *Dictionary*, 283; Filippo Coarelli, "Il Pantheon, l'apoteosi di Augusto e l'apoteosi di Romolo," *CARI*, 41–6. For information on Agrippa, see Southern, *Augustus*, 72–3; J. M. Roddaz, *Marcus Agrippa* (Paris and Rome: École française de Rome, 1984), passim; Lacey, *Augustus and the Principate*, 117–31.

165 Cass. Dio 53.27.1–2; Roddaz, *Marcus Agrippa*, 261–5; Ziolkowski, "Pantheon," 55.

166 Cass. Dio 53.23.1; Emanuele Gatti, "Saepta Julia," *LTUR*, vol. 4, 228–9; Lacey, *Augustus and the Principate*, 119–20.

167 Coarelli, "Il Pantheon," 44; Lacey, *Augustus and the Principate*, 119–20.

168 Cass. Dio 53.27.2.

169 Paola Virgili and Paola Battistelli, "Indagini in Piazza della Rotonda e sulla fronte del Pantheon," *BullCom* 100 (1999): 146–7.

170 Rodolfo Lanciani, "La Controversia sul Pantheon," *BullCom* 20 (1892): 150–9; Rodolfo Lanciani, "La controversia sul Pantheon," *JRIBA* 2 (1895): 175–82; Edmund Thomas, "The Architectural History of the Pantheon in Rome from Agrippa to Septimius Severus via Hadrian," *Hephaistos* 15 (1997): 166–70; Ziolkowski, "Pantheon," 54–6; Kjeld de Fine Licht, *The Rotunda in Rome: A Study of Hadrian's Pantheon* (Copenhagen: Jutland Archeological Society, 1968), 172–9; MacDonald, *The Pantheon*, 60; Roddaz, *Marcus Agrippa*, 262–8; Ziolkowski, "Pantheon," 54–6; Coarelli, "Il Pantheon," 41–6.

171 Thomas, "The Architectural History of the Pantheon," 163–86; Lanciani, "La controversia" (1895): 175–82; Paul Godfrey and David Hemsoll, "The Pantheon, Temple or Rotunda?" in *Pagan Gods and Shrines of the Roman Empire*, ed. Martin Henig and Anthony King (Oxford: Oxford University Press, 1986), 196–7; de Fine Licht, *The Rotunda*, 172–9, 195.

172 Thomas, "The Architectural History of the Pantheon," 169–70; Lanciani, "La controversia" (1892): 150–9; Ziolkowski, "Pantheon," 54–5.

173 Thomas, "The Architectural History of the Pantheon," 170–5.

174 Ibid. 171. For alternative views, see William Loerke, "Georges Chédanne and the Pantheon: A Beaux-Arts Contribution to the History of Roman Architecture," *Modulus* 4 (1982): 40–55; Wilson Jones, *Principles of Roman Architecture*, 180–2.

175 For a complete description of the findings from the 1996–1997 excavations see Virgili and Battistelli, "Indagini in Piazza della Rotonda," 137–54; Wilson Jones, *Principles of Roman Architecture*, 180–2.

176 Virgili and Battistelli, "Indagini in Piazza della Rotonda," 142–8.

177 The larger width of the pronaos was first discovered in the 1890s. Lanciani, "La controversia," (1892): 150–9; Virgili and Battistelli, "Indagini in Piazza della Rotonda," 148, n. 45; Ziolkowski, "Pantheon," 54.

178 Plin. *Nat. Hist.* 36.38; quoted in de Fine Licht, *The Rotunda*, 195.

179 De Fine Licht, *The Rotunda*, 185; Blake, *Ancient Roman Construction I*, 63–4; Donald E. Strong, *Roman Imperial Sculpture* (Baltimore: Penguin Books, 1961), pl. 40.

180 Virgili and Battistelli, "Indagini in Piazza della Rotonda," 141–3, fig. 2.

181 Ibid., 140–1.

182 Thomas, "The Architectural History of the Pantheon," 174.

183 Cass. Dio 53.30.5, 54.28.5. For descriptions of the Mausoleum of Augustus, see Henner von Hesburg, "Mausoleum Augusti: Das Monument," *LTUR*, vol. 3, 234–7; Maria Macciocca, "Mausoleum Augusti: Le Sepolture," *LTUR*, vol. 3, 237–8; Paola Virgili, "A proposito del Mausoleo di Augusto: B. Peruzzi aveva ragione," *ArchLaz* 6 (1984): 209–11.

184 Gert Sperling, *Das Pantheon in Rom: Abbild und Mass des Kosmos* (Berlin: Ars Una, 1999) 332; Vincent Jolivet, "Les cendres d'Auguste: Note sur la topographie monumentale du Champs de Mars septentrional," *ArchLaz* 9 (1988): 90–6. Thomas states the Mausoleum was c. 740 meters to the north. Thomas, "The Architectural History of the Pantheon," 174.

185 The Ara Pacis was built in 13–9 B.C. See Mario Torelli, "Pax Augusta, Ara," *LTUR*, vol 4, 70–4; Virgili and Battistelli, "Indagini in Piazza della Rotunda," 141; Zanker, *The Power of Images*, 126–30, 177–81, 206ff; Richardson, *Dictionary*, 287–9; Eugenio La Rocca, *Ara Pacis Augustae: in occasione del restauro della fronte orientale* (Rome: 'L'Erma' di Bretschneider, 1983), 55ff; Edmund Buchner, "Solarium Augusti und Ara Pacis," *RömMitt* 83 (1976): 319–65.

186 For information on the Horologium Solare, see Edmund Buchner, *Die Sonnenuhr des Augustus: Nachdruck aus RM 1976 und 1980 und Nachtrag über die Ausgrabung 1980/1981* (Mainz-am-Rhein: Philipp von Zabern, 1982), 78, 321–65, and passim; Buchner, "Horologium Augusti," *LTUR*, vol. 3, 35–7; Richardson, *Dictionary*, 190–1; Lanciani, *Ruins and Excavations*, 464–6.

187 Thomas, "The Architectural History of the Pantheon," 170–1; Virgili and Battistelli, "Indagini in Piazza della Rotonda," 141; Loerke, "Georges Chédanne," 51; Wilson Jones, *Principles of Roman Architecture*, 180.

188 Cass. Dio 53.27.4–6.

189 Lacey, *Augustus and the Principate*, 120.

190 Coarelli, "Il Pantheon," 42.

191 Ibid., 44.

192 Sperling, *Das Pantheon*, 331–3.

193 Dion. Hal. *Rom. Ant.* 1.86.3.

194 Suet. *Aug.* 95.

195 Coarelli, "Il Pantheon," 45; Suet. *Aug.* 7; Southern, *Augustus*, 113–14.

196 Suet. *Aug.* 7.

197 Campbell, *The Emperor and the Roman Army*, 5.

198 Sperling, *Das Pantheon*, 331; Coarelli, "Il Pantheon," 45.

8: AUGUSTUS AND THE TEMPLE OF MARS ULTOR

1 The site of the forum was a commercial district when it was purchased by Augustus. Anderson, *Imperial Fora*, 65–6; Valentin Kockel, "Forum Augustum," *LTUR*, vol. 2, 290; Joachim Ganzert, *Der Mars-Ultor-Tempel auf dem Augustusforum in Rom* (Mainz-am-Rhein: Philipp von Zabern, 1996), 74–8; Richardson, *Dictionary*, 160.

2 Plin. *Nat. Hist.* 36. 24; Ov. *Fast.* 5.545–98; Suet. *Aug.* 29.2.

3 Vell. Pat. 2.100.3; Cass. Dio, *Rom. Hist.* 55.10.1, 6–10; Suet. *Aug.* 29.1; Anderson, *Imperial Fora*, 66; Lucrezia Ungaro, *Il Foro di Augusto* (Rome: Fratelli Palombi Editori, 1997), 7–9.

4 Galinsky, *Augustan Culture*, 197–9; Vitr. Pref. 1.2.

5 Galinsky, *Augustan Culture*, 289; Beard, North, and Price, *Roman Religions*, vol. 1, 131; Liebeschuetz, *Continuity and Change*, 62–5.

6 Galinsky, *Augustan Culture*, 290.

7 Hor. *Odes* 1.1.25–30.

8 Liebeschuetz, *Continuity and Change*, 56.

9 M. Rostovtzeff, *Rome*, trans. J. D. Duff (London: Oxford University Press, 1960), 183–92; Liebeschuetz, *Continuity and Change*, 56, 70.

10 Stockton, "The Founding of the Empire," 543.

11 Liebeschuetz, *Continuity and Change*, 66.

12 Earl Baldwin Smith, *Architectural Symbolism of Imperial Rome and the Middle Ages* (Princeton: Princeton University Press,

1956), 21; Ogilvie, *The Romans and Their Gods*, 53–69; Taylor, *The Divinity of the Roman Emperor*, 1–26, 38–42.

13 Smith, *Architectural Symbolism*, 21; Ogilvie, *The Romans and Their Gods*, 53–69; Taylor, *The Divinity of the Roman Emperor*, 1–26, 38–42; Liebeschuetz, *Continuity and Change*, 67.

14 Ward-Perkins and Claridge, *Pompeii*, 61; Liebeschuetz, *Continuity and Change*, 65–6.

15 Smith, *Architectural Symbolism*, 22.

16 Favro, *The Urban Image*, 97.

17 Suet. *Aug.* 29.1–10; Anderson, *Imperial Fora*, 65–6.

18 Plin. *Nat. Hist.* 36.15, 36.24; Ov. *Fast.* 5.545–598; Suet. *Aug.* 29.2; Kockel, "Forum Augustum," 289.

19 Renewed attention was given to the construction of the Temple of Mars Ultor after the return of the military standards lost by Marcus Crassus to the Parthians. Cass. Dio, *Rom. Hist.* 54.8.3; Anderson, *Imperial Fora*, 67; Ungaro, *Il Foro di Augusto*, 8–9; Kockel, "Forum Augustum," 289.

20 Strong, "Early Roman Corinthian," 81.

21 Ganzert, *Der Mars-Ultor-Tempel*, 222–3.

22 Mark Wilson Jones, "Designing the Roman Corinthian Order," 57.

23 Kockel, "Forum Augustum," 291.

24 See Mark Wilson Jones's discussion of the role of dimension in imitation as it is seen in circular structures; *Principles of Roman Architecture*, 76–84.

25 Anderson, *Imperial Fora*, 72; Ganzert, *Der Mars-Ultor-Tempel*, 86–112; Ungaro, *Il Foro di Augusto*, 16–17.

26 Ganzert and Kockel indicate eight columns on the front and eight on the sides; Joachim Ganzert and Valentin Kockel, "Augustusforum und Mars-Ultor-Tempel," in *Kaiser Augustus*, 150, fig. 51; Ganzert, *Der Mars-Ultor-Tempel*, vol. 2, pls. 5 and 47. Ungaro mistakenly states there were seven columns on the sides. Ungaro, *Il Foro di Augusto*, 17.

27 Ungaro, *Il Foro di Augusto*, 17; Anderson, *Imperial Fora*, 70.

28 Strong and Ward-Perkins, "The Temple of Castor," 13.

29 Ibid., 15–16.

30 Wilson Jones, "Designing the Roman Corinthian Order," 66.

31 Ibid., 39.

32 Wilson Jones points out that in most cases, this ratio of 6 to 5 was accompanied by other dimensions that were multiples of 6 feet for the complete columns and 5 feet for their shafts. This, Wilson Jones states, was a fundamental principle of design for the Roman Corinthian Order. Ibid., 38; Wilson Jones, *Principles of Roman Architecture*, 147–148.

33 Wilson Jones, "Designing the Roman Corinthian Order," 53.

34 Ungaro, *Il Foro di Augusto*, 17; Strong, "Early Roman Corinthian," 81.

35 Strong, "Early Roman Corinthian," 81–2.

36 Ungaro, *Il Foro di Augusto*, 17; Strong, "Early Roman Corinthian," 81–2.

37 Strong and Ward-Perkins, "The Round Temple," 17.

38 Ungaro, *Il Foro di Augusto*, 17–18.

39 Ibid., 18; Ganzert, *Der Mars-Ultor-Tempel*, 134–46, 229–31.

40 Drawings of the cella floor plan and column details were made by Antonio da Sangallo the Younger, Baldasarre Peruzzi, and others. Ungaro, *Il Foro di Augusto*, 18; Ganzert, *Der Mars-Ultor-Tempel*, 134–46, 229–31.

41 Ungaro, *Il Foro di Augusto*, 18; Ganzert, *Der Mars-Ultor-Tempel*, 236–8.

42 Ungaro, *Il Foro di Augusto*, 18; Ganzert, *Der Mars-Ultor-Tempel*, 200–1, pls. 84, 85; Ganzert and Kockel, "Augustusforum und Mars-Ultor-Tempel," 172–4.

43 Ungaro, *Il Foro di Augusto*, 18; Ganzert, *Der Mars-Ultor-Tempel*, 203–4, pls. 86, 87; Ganzert and Kockel, "Augustusforum und Mars-Ultor-Tempel," 174.

44 Viscogliosi, *Il Tempio di Apollo 'in Circo,'* 136.

45 Anderson, *Imperial Fora*, 72–3. Detailed archaeological information on the Forum Augustum is provided in Ganzert, *Der Mars-Ultor-Tempel*, 78–81.

46 Vitr. 5.1.3.

47 Anderson, *Imperial Fora*, 73–4; Filippo Coarelli, *Guida archeologica di Roma*, 108; Corrado Ricci, "Scavi dei Fori Imperiali," *Capitolium* 6 (1930): 157.

48 Stambaugh, *The Ancient Roman City*, 54–5; Favro, *The Urban Image*, 175, 221.

49 Suet. *Aug.* 56; Kockel, "Forum Augustum," 290; Ungaro, *Il Foro di Augusto*, 12; Zanker, *The Power of Images*, 155–6; Ward-Perkins, *Roman Imperial Architecture*, 32; Favro, *The Urban Image*, 110. Anderson argues it is more likely the irregular back wall had to follow the line of the street, the Vicus Longus. Anderson, *Imperial Fora*, 66.

50 Ungaro, *Il Foro di Augusto*, 55–7.

51 Heinrich Bauer, "Augustusforum, Hallen und Exedren," in *Kaiser Augustus*, 184–98. Whereas the portico of the Forum of Julius had a double row of columns, which required roof spans of about 7 meters, here there was no central row of columns. Thus, the roof structure, either gabled or arched, spanned the full 14.90 meters from the outer colonnade to the back wall. Italo Gismondi had used a flat roof in a model he made of the forum in 1937–8. Bauer proposed the plaster barrel vault on the basis of his study of remaining portions of the perimeter wall. Ungaro, *Il Foro di Augusto*, 14–15.

52 Zanker, *The Power of Images*, 13–14; Anderson, *Imperial Fora*, 77; Bauer, "Augustusforum, Hallen und Exedren," 184–9; Ungaro, *Il Foro di Augusto*, 19.

53 The caryatids from the inner propylaea at Eleusis are also similar. Ungaro suggests the caryatids represented the tradition of sacred dancers of Artemus of Karyai, thus a positive symbol of harmony and equilibrium in a sanctuary dedicated to the national memory. Ungaro, *Il Foro di Augusto*, 20.

54 Ward-Perkins, *Roman Imperial Architecture*, 33; Strong, "Early Roman Corinthian," 81; Donald Strong, "Late Hadrianic Architectural Ornament in Rome," *PBRS* 21 (1953): 129.

55 Favro, *The Urban Image*, 191.

56 Galinsky, *Augustan Culture*, 202–3.

57 Gismondi portrayed the roofs of the exedrae as half-cones with their peak at the top of the portico's back wall. Bauer suggests the slope was in the opposite direction, with a downward slope toward the middle. Like the porticos themselves, they would have supported suspended vaults of plaster. See Bauer, "Augustusforum, Hallen und Exedren," 163–4; Ungaro, *Il Foro di Augusto*, 15.

58 There were columnar screens in front of these exedrae which mimicked the colonnades in residential peristyles. Favro, *The Urban Image*, 126; Andrew Wallace-Hadrill, "The Social Structure of the Roman House," *PBRS* 61 (1988): 43–97.

59 The inner diameter of the exedrae was 42.67 meters, while that of the Pantheon was 43.28 meters. The dimensions are

derived from Greg Wightman, "The Imperial Fora of Rome: Some Design Considerations," *JSAH* 56 (1997): 86, table A.1, and 88, table A.5; see also Heinrich Bauer, "Il Foro Transitorio e il Tempio di Giano," *RendPontAcc* 49 (1976–77): 117–48.

60 The niches on the first level were 3.50 meters high, those of the second were 3.00 meters. Ungaro, *Il Foro di Augusto*, 15.

61 For descriptions of the statues in the niches see Ov. *Fast.* 5.563–8; MacDonald, *The Pantheon*, 78–82, 84–6; Favro, *The Urban Image*, 97, 126; Zanker, *The Power of Images*, 194–6, 201–2, 210–15; Beard, North, and Price, *Religions of Rome*, vol. 1, 200; Galinsky, *Roman Culture*, 203–4; Ungaro, *Il Foro di Augusto*, 22–3; T. J. Luce, "Livy, Augustus, and the Forum Augustum," in Kurt A. Raaflaub and Mark Toher, eds., *Between Republic and Empire: Interpretations of Augustus and His Principate* (Berkeley: University of California Press, 1990), 125.

62 Ov. *Fast.* 5.567–568; Luce, "Livy, Augustus," 125; MacDonald, *The Pantheon*, 78–86; Zanker, *The Power of Images*, 196.

63 Ov. *Fast.* 5.533 ff; quoted in Zanker, *The Power of Images*, 113.

64 Ov. *Trist.* 2.295; MacDonald, *The Pantheon*, 78–82, 84–6; Favro, *The Urban Image*, 97; Zanker, *The Power of Images*, 196; Galinsky, *Roman Culture*, 204; Luce, "Forum Augustum," 125; Anderson, *Imperial Fora*, 70.

65 Galinsky, *Augustan Culture*, 204–6.

66 Viscogliosi, *Temple of Apollo 'in Circo,'* 131–2.

67 Strong, "Late Hadrianic Architectural Ornament," 129.

68 Viscogliosi, *Temple of Apollo 'in Circo,'* 131–2. For information on the Temple of Rome and Augustus see Jeffrey M. Hurwit, *The Athenian Acropolis: History, Mythology, and Archaeology from the Neolithic Era to the Present* (New York: Cambridge University Press, 2001), 279–82. For the Odeum of Agrippa, see John M. Camp, *The Archaeology of Athens* (New Haven: Yale University Press, 2001), 188–9.

69 Ward-Perkins, *Roman Imperial Architecture*, 30–2.

70 Stambaugh, *The Ancient Roman City*, 55.

71 Favro, *The Urban Image*, 175.

72 Cass. Dio 55.10.

73 Stambaugh, *The Ancient Roman City* 55; Ogilvie, *Romans and Their Gods*, 115.

74 Dumézil, *Archaic Roman Religion*, 207.

75 Ibid., 208–9.

76 Anderson, *Imperial Fora*, 67; Kockel, "Forum Augustum," 289; Liebeschuetz, *Continuity and Change*, 86–7.

77 Anderson, *Imperial Fora*, 67; Cass. Dio *Rom. Hist.*, 54.8.3; Liebeschuetz, *Continuity and Change*, 86; Galinsky, *Augustan Rome*, 199; Beard, North, and Price, *Religions of Rome*, vol. 1, 199.

78 Quoted in Galinsky, *Roman Culture*, 208; Plin. *Nat. Hist.* 34.48; Cass. Dio 60.5.3.

79 Galinsky, *Roman Culture*, 208.

80 Vell. Pat. 2.100.2; Zanker, *The Power of Images*,148–9.

81 Zanker, *The Power of Images*, 192–223.

82 MacDonald, *The Pantheon*, 82.

83 Ibid.

84 Ibid.

85 Gregorio Maranón, *Tiberius: The Resentful Caesar* (New York: Duell, Sloan and Pearce, 1956), 65–6; Barbara Levick, *Tiberius the Politician* (New York: Thames and Hudson, 1976), 36–7.

86 Levick, *Tiberius the Politician*, 69–81; Albino Garzetti, *From Tiberius to the Antonines: A History of the Roman Empire AD 14–192*, trans. J. R. Forster (London: Methuen, 1974), 7–9.

87 For information on Tiberius's reconstruction of the Temple of Concordia, see Cass. Dio, *Rom. Hist.* 55.1.1; Ferroni, "Concordia Aedes," 317; Richardson, *Dictionary*, 99; Rebert and Marceau, "The Temple of Concord in the Roman Forum," 53–77.

88 Suet. *Tib.* 20; Cass. Dio *Rom. Hist.* 56.25.1; Ov. *Fast.* 1.637ff; Ferroni, "Concordia, Aedes," 317; Shipley, "Chronology," 39–41; Favro, *The Urban Image*, 133.

89 B. A. Kellum, "The City Adorned: Programmatic Display at the 'Aedes Concordiae Augustae'," in Kurt A. Raaflaub and Mark Toher, eds., *Between Republic and Empire: Interpretations of Augustus and His Principate* (Berkeley: University of California Press, 1990), 277–8.

90 Ferroni, "Concordia, Aedes," 317–18; G. Maetzke, "Regione VIII: area nord-occidentale del Foro Romano," *BullCom* 91 (1986): 372–80. For images on coins, see *BMCREmp*, vol. 1, 137ff, no. 116, 132f; vol. 6, 144, no. 307.

91 Rebert and Marceau, "The Temple of Concord," 53–77.

92 Strong, "Early Roman Corinthian," 82.

93 Ferroni, "Concordia, Aedes," 318; *BMCREmp*, vol. 6, 144, no. 307; Zanker, *The Power of Images*, 111.

94 Lanciani, *Ruins and Excavations*, 286–7.

95 Ferroni, "Concordia, Aedes," 318–19; Kellum, "The City Adorned," 280–3; Lanciani, *Ruins and Excavations*, 286–7.

96 Kellum, "The City Adorned," 295–6.

97 For information on Tiberius's reconstruction of the Temple of Castor and Pollux, see Nielsen and Poulsen, *The Temple of Castor and Pollux I*, 57; Nielsen, "Castor, Aedes, Templum," 242–3; Suet. *Tib.* 20; Cass. Dio 55.27.4; Ov. *Fast.* 1.705–8; Shipley, "Chronology," 40–1.

98 There were suggestions, based on the stylistic details of the columns and capitals, that they dated from a later rebuilding, possibly at the time of the Flavians or Trajan. Strong and Ward-Perkins convincingly refute this argument in "The Temple of Castor," 1–30.

99 For a complete discussion of the Augustan-era version of the Temple of Castor and Pollux, see Strong and Ward-Perkins, "The Temple of Castor," 1–30; Nielsen, "Castor, Aedes, Templum," 244–5.

100 Nielsen states the final width of the Temple of Castor and Pollux was 32.10 meters, but this dimension corresponds to the base of the podium, not its top. To be consistent with all other temples in this book, the measurement at the top of the podium is indicated. Nielsen's dimension for the temple's length does correspond to the top of the podium. See Nielsen "Castor, Aedes, Templum," 244. For a discussion of the changes made to the Metellan podium when the new temple was built by Tiberius, see Frank, "The First and Second Temples of Castor," 101–2.

101 Ward-Perkins, *Roman Imperial Architecture*, 39.

102 Wilson Jones, "Designing the Roman Corinthian Order," 38.

103 Strong, "Early Roman Corinthian," 83–4.

104 Ibid.

105 For a detailed description of the Forum Romanum at the time of Augustus, see Favro, *The Urban Image*, 197–200;

Tagliamonte, "Forum Romanum," 313–25; and Lanciani, *Ruins and Excavations*, 252.

106 For information on the Tabularium, see Anna Mura Sommella, "Tabularium," *LTUR*, vol. 5, 17–20; Sommella, "Il Tabularium: Progetto di consolidamento e restauro," *ArchLaz* 4 (1981): 126–31.

107 Wilson Jones, *Principles of Roman Architecture*, 139.

108 Suet. *Aug.* 98–9; Southern, *Augustus*, 190.

109 For information on the Temple of Divus Augustus built in A.D. 14–37, see Mario Torelli, "Augustus, Divus, Templum (Novum), Aedes," *LTUR*, vol. 1, 145–6. See also Levick, *Tiberius the Politician*, 118, 123.

110 For information on Caligula, see J. P. V. D. Baldson, *The Emperor Gaius (Caligula)* (Oxford: Clarendon Press, 1964), 24–57; Anthony A. Barrett, *Caligula: The Corruption of Power* (New Haven: Yale University Press, 1989), passim.

111 Torelli, "Augustus Divus, Templum," 145; Baldson, *Emperor Gaius*, 171, 173; Barrett, *Caligula*, 206–12; Garzetti, *From Tiberius*, 83.

112 Suet. *Cal.* 22; Baldson, *Emperor Gaius*, 174; Ronald Mellor, ed., *From Augustus to Nero: The First Dynasty of Imperial Rome* (East Lansing: Michigan State University Press, 1990), 267; Torelli, "Augustus Divus, Templum" 146.

113 Bowder, *Who Was Who in the Roman World*, 211–13.

114 For information on Claudius, see Barbara Levick, *Claudius* (New Haven: Yale University Press, 1990), 1–93; Bowder, *Who Was Who in the Roman World*, 119–22.

115 Robin Haydon Darwall-Smith, *Emperors and Architecture: A Study of Flavian Rome* (Brussels: Latomus, 1996), 48–9.

116 Mart. *Epigr.* 2.9–10; Carlo Buzzetti, "Claudius, Divus, Templum (Reg. 11)," *LTUR*, vol. 1, 277–8.

117 Buzzetti, "Claudius, Divus, Templum," 277–8; Darwall-Smith, *Emperors and Architecture*, 50–1.

118 Nero was the adopted son of Claudius, the son of his wife Agrippina by an earlier marriage. The young Nero was educated by Seneca, and at the age of fourteen, he received the *toga virilis*. When Claudius died, Agrippina campaigned to have Nero inherit the throne. Although the city of Rome would eventually suffer terribly from the reign of Nero, his principate started off in an optimistic way in 54. For information on the early career of Nero, see Miriam T. Griffin, *Nero: The End of a Dynasty* (New Haven: Yale University Press, 1984), 37–82; Michael Grant, *Nero: Emperor in Revolt* (New Haven: American Heritage Press, 1970), 6–41; Albino Garzetti, *From Tiberius to the Antonines: A History of the Roman Empire AD 14–192* (London: Methuen, 1974), 146–7; Darwall-Smith, *Emperors and Architecture*, 48–9.

119 Suet. *Vesp.* 9; Buzzetti, "Claudius, Templum, Divus," 277–8; Garzetti, *From Tiberius*, 144.

120 Suet. *Ner.* 31. For information on the architecture of the Domus Aurea of Nero, see Axel Boëthius, *The Golden House of Nero* (Ann Arbor: University of Michigan Press, 1960), 94–128.

121 Tac. *Ann.* 15.38–42; Mellor, *From Augustus to Nero*, 357.

122 Griffin, *Nero*, 100–18.

123 For information on Galba see Kenneth Wellesley, *The Year of the Four Emperors* (New York: Routledge, 2000), 15–33; Suet. *Gal.* 1–12.

124 For information on Otho, see Wellesley, *Four Emperors*, 56–89; Suet. Otho 1–12. For Vitellius, see Wellesley, *Four Emperors*, 90–107; Suet. *Vit.* 1–18.

125 Suet. *Vit.* 11–13.

126 For discussion of the Flavians' takeover from Vitellius, see Suet. *Vit.* 16–18; Cass. Dio 65.19–22; Tac. *Hist.* 4.3; 4.51; Pat Southern, *Domitian: Tragic Tyrant* (London: Routledge, 1997), 19–20; Wellesley, *Four Emperors*, 198–209.

9: TEMPLES AND FORA OF THE FLAVIAN EMPERORS

1 Edwards, *Religion and Power*, 3.

2 Rostovtzeff, *Rome*, 206; Albino Garzetti, *From Tiberius to the Antonines*, 240–3; Barbara Levick, *Vespasian* (New York: Routledge, 1999), 184–209; Brian W. Jones, *The Emperor Titus* (London: Croom Helm; New York St. Martin's Press, 1984), 34–76.

3 Edwards, *Religion and Power*, 17.

4 Ibid., 19.

5 Tac. *Ann.* 15.38–42; Mellor, *From Augustus*, 357.

6 Vespasian had served in the Roman army since the reign of Tiberius, first in Thrace, then as a quaestor in Crete and Cyrene. In the 40s, during the reign of Claudius, he served in Germany and Britain. In 63, he was sent as governor to Africa, and later he served as a general in Greece and Judaea. Bowder, *Who Was Who in the Roman World*, 571–2.

7 Tac. *Hist.* 3.64–69; Pat Southern, *Domitian*, 17; Wellesley, *Four Emperors*, 190.

8 Tac. *Hist.* 3.70–75; Wellesley, *Four Emperors*, 193.

9 For the burning of the Capitoline Temple, see Cass. Dio, 64.17; Suet. *Vit.* 15; Wellesley, *Four Emperors*, 193.

10 Suet. *Dom.* 1; Cass. Dio, 64.17; Tac. *Hist.* 3.74; Southern, *Domitian*, 17; Wellesley, *Four Emperors*, 193, 203.

11 Tac. *Rom. Hist.* 3.71–72.

12 Ibid.

13 For discussion of the reconstruction of the Capitoline Temple by Vespasian, see Suet. *Vesp.* 8.8. Tac., *Rom. Hist.* 4.4.2, 4.9.2, 4.53.1–4; Cass. Dio 66.10.2. Suetonius and Tacitus suggest that Vespasian began the temple's reconstruction in A.D. 70. Some other writers suggest it was not started until A.D. 73. See De Angeli, "Iuppiter Optimus," 151.

14 Darwall-Smith, *Emperors and Architecture*, 47.

15 Suet. *Vesp.* 8.8.

16 For information on Rabirius, see William MacDonald, *The Architecture of the Roman Empire: An Introductory Study*, vol. 1 (New Haven: Yale University Press, 1982), 127–8; William MacDonald, "Rabirius," in *MEA*, vol. 3, 509–11; Janet DeLaine, "Rabirius," *DA*, vol. 25, 835.

17 Tac. *Rom. Hist.* 4.53.10–36; De Angeli, "Iuppiter Optimus," 151.

18 Tac. *Rom. Hist.* 4.53.10–36.

19 See De Angeli, "Iuppiter Optimus," 223; Lake, "Archaeological Evidence," appendix 1, 138–43; Richardson, *Dictionary*, 223; *BMCREmp*, vol. 2, 133, no. 614, pl. 23.14; 168, nos. 721–2, pl. 29.5–6; *RIC*, vol. 2, 74, no. 496, pl. 2.34; 144, no. 647, pl. 25.10; 82, no. 577, pl. 3.37; 210, no. 850, pl. 41.4; 216, no. 877, pl. 42.8.

20 Plut. *Publ.* 15.4; Lake, *Archaeological Evidence*," 104–5; De Angeli, "Iuppiter Optimus," 151.

21 Plut. *Publ.* 15.4.

22 Tac. *Rom. Hist.* 4.53.40–43.

23 Fagerlind, "The Transformations of the Corinthian Capital," 125; Wilson Jones, "Designing the Roman Corinthian Order," 57.

24 Cass. Dio 66.24.1–2; Suet. *Dom.* 5.1; Plut. *Publ.* 15.3; De Angeli, "Iuppiter Optimus," 151; Lake, "Archaeological Evidence," 104.

25 Plut. *Publ.* 15.4; Southern, *Domitian*, 37.

26 Zos. 5.38.5; Plut. *Publ.* 15.4; Richardson, *Dictionary*, 223.

27 See note 19 for images on coins.

28 Richardson, *Dictionary*, 33.

29 Suet. *Dom.* 4–5; De Angeli, "Iuppiter Optimus," 151.

30 Suet. *Dom.* 1.2; 5.6–7; Tac. *Rom. Hist.* 3.74; Darwell-Smith, *Emperors and Architecture*, 110–12; Southern, *Domitian*, 18, 37.

31 Tac. *Hist.* 3.74.

32 Southern, *Domitian*, 18–19.

33 De Angeli, "Iuppiter Optimus," 152.

34 Anderson, *Imperial Fora*, 101; Jos. *Bel.Iud.* 7.158; Cass. Dio 65.15.1; Filippo Coarelli, "Pax, Templum," *LTUR* vol. 4, 67; Suet. *Vesp.* 9; Antonio M. Colini, "Forum Pacis," *BullCom* 65 (1937): 8; Stambaugh, *The Ancient Roman City*, 121; Ward-Perkins, *Roman Imperial Architecture*, 66–7.

35 The complex is referred to as a *templum*, for instance, in Plin. *Nat. Hist.* 36.24.102, and Suet. *Vesp.* 9.1. The first reference to the Templum Pacis appears in Ammianus Marcellinus 16.10.14. See also Colini, "Forum Pacis," 10; Anderson, *Imperial Fora*, 110–11.

36 Plin. *Nat. Hist.* 36.24.102; Colini "Forum Pacis," 9–10.

37 Dion. Hal. *Rom. Ant.* 1.68, 5.19; Liv. 2.7.6; Anderson, *Imperial Fora*, 102–3; James C. Anderson, "Domitian, the Argiletum and the Temple of Peace," *AJA* 86 (1982): 101–18.

38 Anderson, *Imperial Fora*, 108.

39 Tac. *Ann.* 15.38–44; Colini, "Forum Pacis," 9.

40 Coarelli, "Pax, Templum," 68; Wrightman, "The Imperial Fora of Rome," 87, table A.3.

41 The walls of one of these exedrae is conserved in the basement of the Torre dei Conti. Coarelli, "Pax, Templum," 68; Anderson, *Imperial Fora*, 108; Antonio M. Colini, "Scavo del Foro Transitorio," *BullCom* 62 (1934): 165–6; Colini, "Forum Pacis," 22–7.

42 Anderson argues that marble slabs lying parallel to the northwest wall of the Temple of Peace are remains of a colonnade that was previously in front of the *tabernae*. Anderson, "Domitian," 108–9; Anderson, *Imperial Fora*, 127.

43 It is correct to say the Templum Pacis was completed by Domitian. Stat. *Silv.* 4.3.17; Anderson, *Imperial Fora*, 110.

44 Anderson, "Domitian," 104–8; Anderson, *Imperial Fora*, 109–14.

45 Silvana Rizzo, "I cantieri di scavo dei Fori Imperiale," in *ArchGiub*, 202.

46 Anderson, *Imperial Fora*, 109–11; Coarelli, "Pax, Templum," 69.

47 Anderson, *Imperial Fora*, 109–11.

48 Dudley, *Urbs Roma*, 130–1; and Plin. *Nat. Hist.* 34.19.84–87; Coarelli, "Pax, Templum," 67; Colini, "Forum Pacis," 7, 10, n. 14; Darwell-Smith, *Emperors and Architecture*, 58–67.

49 Anderson, *Imperial Fora*, 108; Anderson, "Domitian," 105; Rizzo "Fori Imperiali," 202; Richardson, *Dictionary*, 33. Coarelli suggests they were fountains. See Coarelli, "Pax, Templum," 68–9.

50 Vitr. 5.9.5–6.

51 The similarity of the two plans is pointed out by Ward-Perkins. See *Roman Imperial Architecture*, 269. The Library of Hadrian was a huge rectangle 400 feet long by nearly 270 feet wide, with walls of Poros. The long northern and southern walls had three large apses, the middle one rectangular, like those of the Templum Pacis, the others semicircular. Near the main west façade was a colonnade of fourteen unfluted Corinthian columns filling the spaces between the antae at the ends of the prolonged side walls and the central propylum. These columns, seven of which remain, were of Carytian marble, or cipollino, with capitals of Pentelic marble. Possibly, they once bore statues.

The propylum in the middle of the west façade was fronted by four fluted Corinthian columns, only one of which remains. The eastern façade was plain, but with buttresses at the middle. At the east end are the foundations of several rooms, the middle one of which may have been used for the storage of books. The corner rooms were covered with barrel vaults and may have been reading or lecture rooms. Around the central area was a portico 24 feet wide, with columns of Phrygian marble. See Charles Heald Weller, *Athens and Its Monuments* (New York: Macmillan, 1924), 146–7; W. Sisson, "The Stoa of Hadrian at Athens," *PBSR* 11 (1929): 50–72; and Boatwright, *Hadrian and the Cities of the Roman Empire*, 154–7.

52 Anderson, *Imperial Fora*, 113–14; Ferdinando Castagnoli and Lucos Cozza, "L'angelo meridionale del Foro della Pace," *BullCom* 76 (1956–58): 119–42.

53 Evidence for an earlier plan by Vespasian is tenuous. It is known that he remeasured the city in A.D. 77, and he may have commissioned a plan at that time. See Plin. *Nat. Hist.* 3.5.66; Ferdinando Castagnoli, "Il Tempio dei Penati e la Velia," *RivFil* 74 (1946): 157–66; Anderson, *Imperial Fora*, 115–17; Lanciani, *Ruins and Excavations*, 96; 212.

54 Cass. Dio 73.24.1; Anderson, *Imperial Fora*, 113; Coarelli, "Pax, Templum," 68.

55 The scale of the Septimius Severus map was approximately 1:240, and its overall size was 18 meters long by 13 meters high. It was mounted on the wall separating this room from the temple. Some remaining fragments of the Marble Plan are exhibited today in the top floor of the Palazzo Braschi. For a description of the Marble Plan, see Gianfilippo Carettoni et al., *La Pianta Marmorea di Roma antica*, (Rome: M. Danesi, 1960), vol. 1, 177–94, 206–7; H. Riemann, "Pacis Forum," in *RE* 18 (1942): 2107–22; Anderson, *Imperial Fora*, 113–18; Janet DeLaine, "Building the Eternal City: The Construction Industry of Imperial Rome," *Ancient Rome*, 123.

56 For an account of the later history of the Marble Plan, see Anderson, *Imperial Fora*, 114; and Lanciani, *Ruins and Excavations*, 94–8; 211–14.

57 Anderson, *Imperial Fora*, 116–17; Carettoni et al., *Pianta Marmorea*, 213–18.

58 Coarelli, "Pax, Templum," 69; Darwell-Smith, *Emperors and Architecture*, 65–8.

59 Coarelli, "Pax, Templum," 69–70; Anderson, *Imperial Fora*, 112.

60 To make Titus's situation worse, there were a series of natural disasters of unprecedented scale that strained both the imperial psyche and its finances. In the first year of Titus's reign, Mount Vesuvius erupted, raining down lava, ash, and pumice on Pompeii, Herculaneum, and Stabia, killing thousands, including Pliny the Elder, the prefect of the Roman navy at Misenum. In Rome, a fire destroyed a portion of the Campus Martius, including the Agrippan Pantheon and once again damaging the Temple of Jupiter on the Capitoline Hill. Titus was forced to devote enormous financial resources to the reconstruction and resettlement in the Campania region while simultaneously rebuilding much of Rome's central district. Jones, *The Emperor Titus*, 114–80; Grant, *History of Rome*, 291; Suet. *Tit.* 6–9.

61 For information on Domitian's ascension to emperor, see Southern, *Domitian*, 32–7; Brian W. Jones, *The Emperor Domitian* (New York: Routledge, 1992), 18–33.

62 Garzetti, *From Tiberius*, 282–3.

63 Stefano De Angeli, *Templum Divi Vespasiani* (Rome: De Luca Edizioni D'Arte, 1992), 131–2.

64 Cassiod. *Chron.* 140.727M; Stefano De Angeli, "Vespasianus, Divus, Templum," *LTUR*, vol. 5, 124; De Angeli, *Templum Divi Vespasiani*, 131–8; Richardson, *Dictionary*, 412; Cassiod. *Chron.* 140.727M.

65 De Angeli, "Vespasianus, Divus, Templum." 124.

66 Ibid. The podium was 4.20 meters high, constructed of *opus caementicium*, and faced with marble.

67 Ibid., 125.

68 Wilson Jones, "Designing the Roman Corinthian Order," 39–43.

69 Von Blanckenhagen, *Flavische Architektur*, 60–2.

70 Wilson Jones, "Designing the Roman Corinthian Order," 39–43; De Angeli, "Vespasianus, Divus, Templum," 125.

71 De Angeli, *Templum Divi Vespasiani*, 139–48.

72 For coins of Julius Casear and Augustus, see *RRC*, 461, no. 443/1, pl. 52, 22; 471, no. 456, pl. 54, 8; 536–7, nos. 537/1 and 538/1, pl. 64, 2.4–5; De Angeli, *Templum Divi Vespasiani*, 139.

73 For coins of Vespasian and Titus, see *BMCREmp*, vol 2, 8–9, nos. 48–53, pl. 1, 17–18; 26, no. 144, pl. 4, 8; De Angeli, *Templum Divi Vespasiani*, 140.

74 Wilson Jones, "Designing the Roman Corinthian Order," 39–43

75 The complete inscription, known from the so-called Anonymous of Einsiedeln: "DIVO VESPASIANO AUGUSTO S.P.Q.R. IMP. CAES. SERVERUS ET ANTONINUS PI FELICES AUG. RESTITUER." Luciani and Sperduti, *Foro Romano*, 86–7; De Angeli, "Vespasianus, Divus, Templum," 124.

76 Académie de France à Rome et al., *Roma Antiqua: 'Envois' des architects français (1788–1924), Forum, Colisée, Palatin* (Rome: Académie de France à Rome, École française de Rome, École nationale supérieure des Beaux-Arts, 1985), 76–81.

77 The elderly Nerva had served twice as the Eastern consul in Byzantium, first with Vespasian in A.D. 71 and again with Domitian in A.D. 90. For discussion of the Forum Transitorium, see Suet. *Dom.* 5.7–8; Southern, *Domitian*, 128; Heinrich Bauer and Chiara Morselli, "Forum Nervae," *LTUR*, vol. 2, 307–11; Roberto Meneghini and Lucrezia Ungaro, *The Imperial Forums and Trajan's Market* (Rome: Fratelli Palombi Editori, 1993), 18–21; Roberto Meneghini, *Il Foro di Nerva* (Rome: Fratelli Palombi Editori, 1991), 8–12; Morselli and Tortorici, "B. Sintesi storico-topografica," 242; von Blanckenhagen, *Flavische Architektur*, 10–12.

78 Bauer and Morselli, "Forum Nervae," 307–8; Southern, *Domitian*, 128.

79 Mart. *Epig.* 1.2.7–8, 1.3.1–2; Anderson, *Imperial Fora*, 120–1; Bauer and Morselli, "Forum Nervae," 308.

80 Cic. *Att.* 1.14.7, 12.32.3; Edoardo Tortorici, "Argiletum," in *CFIFT*, 44–5.

81 Edoardo Tortorici, "Argiletum," *LTUR*, vol. 1, 125–6.

82 Anderson argues that there was an early colonnade along the entire northwestern side of the Argiletum and that space was available for it because the Curia Julia built by Julius Caesar and Augustus was located to the west of the curia as rebuilt by Diocletian and stands today. See Anderson, "Domitian," 104, 108–9, ill. 3. Recent excavations prove that the curia is on its original site as established by Julius Caesar. The only certain location of a colonnade on the Argiletum's northwest side is at the end of the Forum of Julius. See Tortorici, "Curia Julia," 333; Morselli and Tortorici, "B. Sintesi storico-topografica," 253.

83 B. Morselli and Tortorici, "B. Sintesi storico-topografica," 243; Anderson, "Domitian," 109.

84 The dimensions are based on Heinrich Bauer, "Il Foro Transitorio e il Tempio di Giano," *RendPontAcc* 49 (1976–1977): 136 and Fig. 19; and Wightman, "The Imperial Fora of Rome," 86, table A.2; Lanciani, *The Ruins and Excavations*, 307–8.

85 The U-shaped portico offered limited access to the forum through a confined and indirect corridor along the temple's flank. Bauer, "Porticus Absidata," 111–84, tav. A–H; Eve D'Ambra, *Private Lives, Imperial Virtues: The Frieze of the Forum Transitorium in Rome* (Princeton: Princeton University Press, 1993), 30–1; Anderson, *Imperial Fora*, 133–4; von Blanckenhagen, *Flavische Architektur*, 43–4.

86 Mart. *Epig.* 10.28.3–6; Stat. *Silv.* 4.1.12–13, 4.3.9; D'Ambra, *Private Lives*, 27–8; Edoardo Tortorici, "Tempio di Giano," in *CFIFT*, 50–1.

87 For discussion of the shrine's placement in the center of the forum, see von Blanckenhagen, *Flavische Architektur*, 45–6; For the alternative location, see Lawrence Richardson, Jr., "Curia Julia and Janus Geminus," *RömMitt* 85 (1978): 359–69; Anderson, *Imperial Fora*, 136–7; Heinrich Bauer, "Kaiserfora und Janustempel," *RömMitt* 84 (1977): 302–3.

88 Serv. *Ad. Aen.* 7.607; Anderson, *Imperial Fora*, 137.

89 Anderson, *Imperial Fora*, 137.

90 D'Ambra, *Private Lives*, 29.

91 Bauer and Morselli, "Forum Nervae," 308; Anderson, "Domitian," 109–10.

92 Anderson, *Imperial Fora*, 134–5; Anderson, "Domitian," 108. Bauer and Morselli, "Forum Nervae," 308–9; von Blanckenhagen, *Flavische Architektur*, 16–17.

93 For detailed description of the architrave, see von Blanckenhagen, *Flavische Architektur*, 51–7; D'Ambra, *Private Lives*, 47–77 and appendix B.

94 Anderson, *Imperial Fora*, 135.

95 Eight sections of the frieze, about one and a half bays, remain. For a complete description, see von Blanckenhagen, *Flavische Architektur*, 116–27; D'Ambra, *Private Lives*, 112–26.

96 Bauer and Morselli, "Forum Nervae," 309; Ov. *Met.* 6.5–145.

97 A number of remains of the frieze were discovered in 1882 under a house at Via della Croce Bianca, 37. Rodolfo Lanciani, *Notes from Rome*, ed. Anthony L. Cubberley (Rome: British School at Rome, 1988), 115.

98 D'Ambra, *Private Lives*, 12, 47–8; Ov. *Met.* 6.5–145.

99 D'Ambra, *Private Lives*, 47–77; For information on looms in Rome, see Diane Lee Carroll, "Dating the Foot-Powered Loom: The Coptic Evidence," *AJA* 89 (1985): 168–73; and John Peter Wild, "The Roman Horizontal Loom," *AJA* 91 (1987): 459–71.

100 D'Ambra, *Private Lives*, 49–50.

101 Anderson, *Imperial Fora*, 132; Palladio, *Four Books*, pl. 4.12.

102 Anderson, *Imperial Fora*, 132; Colini, "Forum Pacis," fig. 20 and pl. 3.

103 Anderson, *Imperial Fora*, 132.

104 Meneghini and Ungaro, *The Imperial Forums*, 24. For drawing of the entablature of the Temple of Minerva by A. Coner, see Thomas Ashby, Jr., "Sixteenth-Century Drawings of Roman Buildings Atributed to Andreas Coner," *PBRS* 2 (1904): 46–7.

105 Bauer and Morselli, "Forum Nervae," 309.

106 MacKendrick, *The Mute Stones Speak*, 304–5.

107 Anderson, *Imperial Fora*, 138.

108 Southern, *Domitian*, 46–7, 121; Jones, *Emperor Domitian*, 100.

109 Jones, *Emperor Domitian*, 100.

110 Ibid. 47.

111 D'Ambra, *Private Lives*, 5.

112 Suet. *Dom.* 4.

113 Cass. Dio 67.

114 Jones, *Emperor Domitian*, 100; Suet. *Dom.* 4

115 Suet. *Dom*, 4; The college of the *Flaviales* was established for the worship of the deified Flavian emperors, as the *Augustales* had been for the deified Julio-Claudians.

116 Javier Arce, "Arcus Titi (Via Sacra)," in *LTUR*, vol. 1, 109–11.

117 Archaeological explorations have revealed that the foundations of the Arch of Titus overlays the Clivius Sacer of Augustus, which had been replaced by a straight road of Nero, a part of which descended through it to the Colosseum. See G. Lugli, *The Roman Forum and the Palatine* (Rome: Bardi Editore, 1964), 73; Luciani and Sperduti, *Foro Romano*, 147–9; Michael Pfanner, *Der Titusbogen: Mit Einer Bauaufnahme von Helmut Schwanke* (Mainz-am-Rhein: Verlag Philipp von Zabern, 1983), 91; Southern, *Domitian*, 38. In the Middle Ages, the arch was incorporated into a fortress of the Frangipane family, damaging the lower half of the triumph reliefs. It was not restored to its familiar form until 1821 by Valadier, who used travertine to distinguish the new from the original masonry. See C. Hülsen, *The Forum and the Palatine* (New York: A. Bruderhausen, 1928), 35. For a complete history of the arch, see Pfanner, *Der Titusbogen*, passim.

118 Arce, "Arcus Titi," 111.

119 For detailed description of the columns and the architrave, see von Blanckenhagen, *Flavische Architektur*, 62–4.

120 The inscription reads: SENATVS POPVLVSQVE ROMANVS DIVO D. VESPASIANI. F. VESPASIANO AVGVSTO (THE SENATE AND PEOPLE OF ROME DEDICATED THIS ARCH TO THE DEIFIED TITUS VESPASIANUS AUGUSTUS, SON OF THE DEIFIED VESPASIAN). Dudley, *Urbs Roma*, 115. The attic inscription on the west, facing the Forum Romanum, was added in a restoration of 1823 by Pius VII. See Arce, "Arcus Titi," 110.

121 Charles D. Curtis, "Roman Monumental Arches," *Supplement Papers American School of Classical Studies in Rome* 2 (1908), 49.

122 MacKendrick, *The Mute Stones Speak*, 296; Arce, "Arcus Titi," 111.

123 Richard Brilliant, *Roman Art from the Republic to Constantine* (London: Phaidon Press, 1974), 119.

124 Smith, *Architectural Symbolism*, 19.

125 Ibid.

126 Dion. Hal. *Rom. Ant.* 1: 409–11.

127 Thomas L. Donaldson, *Ancient Architecture on Greek and Roman Coins and Medals* (Chicago: Argonaut, 1966), 205–6; See also Ernst H. Kantorowicz, "The King's Advent and the Enigmatic Panels in the Doors of Santa Sabina," *ArtBul* 26 (1944): 212.

128 Donaldson, *Ancient Architecture*, 206.

129 Kantorowicz, "The King's Advent," 212.

130 The Arch of Titus was related further to a circular fountain monument called the Meta Sudans, located directly east in a space near the Colosseum. It marked the point where the Via Sacra turned southward and became the Via Trionfale. Built in A.D. 97 by Domitian, possibly on the site of an earlier fountain, the Meta Sudans was an important urban monument for the Flavian emperors; not only was it on axis with the Arch of Titus, it was also aligned axially with the more distant Templum Pacis and the Temple of Vespasian in the west end of the Forum Romanum. It was also located at the meeting point of five of the city's fourteen regions (I, II, III, IV, X) that had been established by Augustus between 10 and 4 B.C. Lanciani, *Ruins and Excavations*, 191, 87–9; and Ernest Nash, *Pictorial Dictionary of Ancient Rome*, vol. 2, (New York and Washington, DC: Praeger, 1962), 61.

10: THE FORUM TRAIANI

1 For Domitian's role in initiating work on a new forum complex northwest of the Forum of Augustus, see James E. Packer, *The Forum of Trajan in Rome: A Study of the Monuments*, vol. 1 (Berkeley and Los Angeles: University of California Press, 1996), 3–5; Anderson, *Imperial Fora*, 141–2.

2 For information on Trajan's adoption by Nerva and his early military career, see Julian Bennett, *Trajan Optimus Princeps: A Life and Times* (London: Routledge, 1997), 42–52; Cass. Dio 68.3.

3 Bennett, *Trajan Optimus Princeps*, 85–103; Cass. Dio 68.6–16.

4 For information on Apollodorus of Damascus, see William L. MacDonald, "Apollodorus," *MEA*, vol. 1, 9–94; MacDonald, *Architecture of the Roman Empire*, vol. 1, 129–37.

5 Cass. Dio 68.14; Bennett, *Trajan Optimus Princeps*, 101.

6 Cass. Dio 68.15; Bennett, *Trajan Optimus Princeps*, 102–3.

7 The precise location of the naumachia is unknown, although Bennett suggests it may have been on a site northeast of Castel Sant'Angelo, originally Hadrian's Mausoleum. There is evidence of a large basin with rounded corners measuring

100 meters wide by more than 300 meters long. It was lined with waterproofed walls, contained plumbing and drains, and was surrounded by vaulted corridors and *tabernae* that could have supported spectators' seating. Bennett, *Trajan Optimus Princeps*, 102, 148–9; Richardson, *Dictionary*, 266; Christian Hülsen, "Il Gaianum e la Naumachia Vaticana," *DissPontAcc* (1903): 373; Carlo Buzzetti, "Naumachia Traiani," *LTUR*, vol. 3, 338–9.

8 Bennett, *Trajan Optimus Princeps*, 144.

9 Ibid., 146–7, 150–2.

10 Anderson, *Imperial Fora*, 141–2.

11 Packer, *Forum of Trajan*, vol. 1, 3–5; Anderson, *Imperial Fora*, 141–2, 147–8, 151–6; Bennett, *Trajan Optimus Princeps*, 152; Leon, *Die Bauornamentik*, 47–9; Richardson, *Dictionary*, 175; Plin. *Paneg*. 51; *Ep*. 6–31; Aur. Vict. *Caes*. 13.5.

12 Packer, *Forum of Trajan*, vol. 1, 5; Bennett, *Trajan Optimus Princeps*, 153.

13 Cass. Dio, *Rom. Hist*. 68.16.3.

14 For a discussion of the date of Trajan's Column, see Anderson, *Imperial Fora*, 148, 154–9; Packer, *Forum of Trajan*, vol. 1, 5; F. A. Lepper, *Trajan's Parthian War* (London: Oxford University Press, 1948), 28; Anthony R. Birley, *Hadrian: The Restless Emperor* (London: Routledge, 1997), 64–5.

15 For a discussion of the date of the Temple of Divus Traianus, see Packer, *Forum of Trajan*, vol. 1, 5; Bennett, *Trajan Optimus Princips*, 157; Boatwright, *Hadrian and the City of Rome*, 92–8; *Hist. Aug. Had*. 6.1–3.

16 A treatise written by Apollodorus about the bridge is now lost. T. F. C. Blagg, "Apollodorus of Damascus," *DA*, vol. 2, 227.

17 Ibid.; MacDonald, "Apollodorus," 91–4; Henri von Blanckenhagen, "The Imperial Fora," *JSAH* 13 (1954): 21–6.

18 Anderson, *Imperial Fora*, 141.

19 Packer, *Forum of Trajan*, vol. 1, 4–5; Stambaugh, *The Ancient Roman City*, 75; Aul. Gell. 13.25.2; Sid. Apoll. *Carm*. 2.544–5.

20 Bennett states this was the first such example in Rome, but these activities had long been carried on in the Forum Romanum and its two basilicas. Bennett, *Trajan Optimus Princeps*, 154.

21 Anderson, *Imperial Fora*, 160–1; Aul. Gell. 13.25.1–3; Packer, *Forum of Trajan*, vol. 1, 276–83.

22 Packer, *Forum of Trajan*, vol. 1, 274.

23 Ibid., 276–83.

24 Anderson, *Imperial Fora*, 142; Bennett, *Trajan Optimus Princeps*, 154; Cass. Dio *Rom. Hist*. 69.4.1; Packer, *Forum of Trajan*, vol. 1, 4–5, 260–1.

25 As in all of the previous imperial fora, axiality and definition of a forum space by porticos were the dominant architectural and urbanistic motif. Packer, *Forum of Trajan*, vol. 1, 91–4.

26 Richardson, *Dictionary*, 175.

27 My discussion of the site is based on recently suggested reconstructions but cannot be considered definitive. Only further excavations of the site can reveal new evidence about the forum's overall composition.

28 Anderson, *Imperial Fora*, 143; Richardson, *Dictionary*, 176, Packer, *Forum of Trajan*, vol. 1, 95, n. 32; 261–2.

29 James Packer, "Forum Traiani," *LTUR*, vol. 2, 351; Packer, *Forum of Trajan*, vol. 1, 61–3; Anderson, *Imperial Fora*, 143–4; Richardson, *Dictionary*, 176; Strong, "Late Hadrianic Architectural Ornament," 120.

30 Strong, "Late Hadrianic Architectural Ornament," 120.

31 Packer, *Forum of Trajan*, vol. 1, 99–111; Bennett, *Trajan Optimus Princeps*, 154–5; Richardson, *Dictionary*, 176; Tac. *Ann*. 9.2. Anderson states there is no evidence to prove they were either roofed or not roofed. Anderson, *Imperial Fora*, 143. Packer points to the evidence of the beam sockets in surviving blocks of the upper attic as proof of a timber truss roof.

32 The existence of tree holes was found in excavations in 1982. See James E. Packer, Kevin Sarring, and Rose Mary Sheldon, "A New Excavation in Trajan's Forum," *AJA* 57 (1983): 165–72, pls. 21–3; Packer, *Forum of Trajan*, vol. 1, 95. The forum's marble slabs were each 1.20 by 2.35 meters (4 by 8 Roman feet). Packer, "Forum Traiani," 351.

33 For an image of the equestrian statue on a coin, see *BMCREmp*, vol. 3, 93, no. 445, pl. 16.18. For discussion of coin images, see Packer, *Forum of Trajan*, vol. 1, 95–6; and Paul Zanker, "Das Trajansforum in Rom," *AA* 85 (1970): 505, figs. 8 and 9.

34 The excavations of 1998–2000 uncovered the foundation of the equestrian statue of Trajan, placing it several yards to the southeast of the forum's centerpoint. Silvana Rizzo, "Il progetto Fori Imperiale," in *CBFI*, 73.

35 For a complete description of the composition of the southeast enclosure wall as it was thought to have been until the excavations of 1998–2000, see Packer, *Forum of Trajan*, vol, 1, 85–95, appendix 2: 417–18. For images of the Trajanic triumphal arch on coins see *BMCREmp*, vol. 3, 102, no. 509, pl. 18.3; 128, no. 665, pl. 21.15.

36 For discussion of the hypothesis that the Temple of Divus Traiani was located at the forum's southeast end, see Roberto Meneghini, "L'architettura del Foro di Traiano attraverso i ritrovamenti archeologici più recenti," *RömMitt* 105 (1998): 127–48. Earlier questions about the temple's location are raised in Roberto Meneghini, "Templum Divi Traiani," *BullCom* 97 (1996): 47–78.

37 For a discussion of tripartite forum complexes that could have served as precedents, see Eugenio La Rocca, "Il Foro di Traiano ed i fori tripartiti," *RömMitt* 105 (1998): 147–73; Meneghini, "L'architettura del Foro di Traiano," 146–7. Boatwright also discusses such precedents, although she believes the temple was located, as originally believed, northwest of Trajan's Column. See Boatwright, *Hadrian and the City of Rome*, 84.

38 Meneghini, "L'architettura del Foro di Traiano," 146–7.

39 Rizzo, "Il progetto Fori Imperiale," 73.

40 Ibid., 71–5, fig. 65.

41 Rizzo, "I cantieri di scavo dei Fori Imperiali," 204–5. For images of the arch on coins, see *BMCREmp*, vol. 3, no. 509, pl. 18.3; no. 984. For images of the temple on coins, see note 79.

42 For a discussion of examples of these plan types with basilicas at one end of the forum, see La Rocca, "Il Foro di Traiano," 147–73; Boatwright, *Hadrian and the City of Rome*, 84.

43 Boatwright, *Hadrian and the City of Rome*, 84; Zanker, "Trajansforum," 506.

44 Packer, *Forum of Trajan*, vol. 1, 229; Anderson, *Imperial Fora*, 144–5.

45 Packer, *Forum of Trajan*, vol. 1, 233.

46 The internal diameter of the basilica's apses is 22 meters; that of the forum hemicycles is 20 meters. See Packer, *Forum of Trajan*, vol. 1, 241–4; vol. 3, fol. 24; Anderson, *Imperial Fora*, 145.

47 See Packer, *Forum of Trajan*, vol. 1, 231–8, App. 7: 433–7; Packer, "Forum Traiani, 353.

48 Earlier reconstructions that suggest the Basilica Ulpia's façade was a wall include those by Jean-Baptiste-Cicéron Lesueur (1823), Angelo Uggeri (1833), Prosper-Mathieu Morey (1835), Fjodor Richter (1839), Luigi Canina (1830, 1848), Giuseppe Gatteschi (1924), Italo Gismondi (1939–40), and Carla Maria Amici (1970s). For a review of these early reconstructions, see Packer, *Forum of Trajan*, vol. 1, 139–215; James E. Packer, "Review of Carla Amici, *Foro di Traiano: Basilica Ulpia e Biblioteche*," in *AJA* 87 (October 1983): 570.

49 For Packer's reconstruction of the Basilica Ulpia with its columnar forum façade, see *Forum of Trajan*, vol. 1, 217–44; James Packer, "Trajan's Basilica Ulpia: Some Reconsiderations," *AJA* 86 (1982): 280; James Packer, "The Southeast Façade of the Basilica Ulpia in Trajan's Forum: The Evidence from the Northeast Colonnade," *AJA*, 90 (1986): 189–90; James Packer, "Trajan's Forum in 1989," *AJA* 96 (1992): 151–62. Among the earlier reconstructions, Julien Gaudet was the first to depict the main façade with columns alone; see "Mémoire de la restauration du Forum de Trajan," Manuscript nos. 207 (text), 2748 (drawings) (Paris: École des Beaux-Arts, 1867), pl. 30 and 32. See also P. Strack, *Untersuchungen zur römischen Reichsprägung des zweiten Jahrhunderts*, vol. 1 (Stuttgart, Kohlhammer, 1931), 204.

50 James E. Packer, "Numismatic Evidence for the Southeast (Forum) Façade of the Basilica Ulpia," in *Coins, Culture, and History in the Ancient World: Numismatic and Other Studies in Honor of Bluma L. Trell*, ed. Lionel Casson and Martin Price (Detroit: Wayne State University Press, 1981), 57–67; Packer, "Review of Amici, *Foro di Traiano*," 569–72; Packer, *Forum of Trajan*, vol. 1, 221–8, figs. 131, 132; M. Pensa, "L'architettura traianea attraverso le emissioni monetali coeve," *Centro Studi de Documentazione sull'Italia Romana, Atti*, 2 (1969–1970): 279–81. For further images of the Basilica Ulpia on coins, see, for instance, *BMCREmp*, vol. 3, 99, no. 492, pl. 17.15; 207, no. 982, pl. 38.8; *RIC*, vol. 2, 241, 261, nos. 246ff, pl. 9.150; 287, nos. 616ff.

51 Packer, *Forum of Trajan*, vol. 1, 219–28, appendix 5, 433–4; Packer, "Forum Traiani," 352.

52 Packer, *Forum of Trajan*, vol. 1, 221–8, App. 5: 433–4; Packer, "Forum Traiani," 352.

53 Packer, *Forum of Trajan*, vol. 1, 219–28; Packer, "Trajan's Forum in 1989," 151–62; Packer, "Forum Traiani," 352; Bennett, *Trajan Optimus Princeps*, 155; Richardson, *Dictionary*, 176.

54 For earlier reconstructions that suggest the Basilica Ulpia was two stories high plus a clerestory, see the restorations cited in note 48. See also Packer, *Forum of Trajan*, vol. 1, 139–215; Packer, "Review of Amici, *Foro di Traiano*," 570; Packer, "Trajan's Forum in 1989," 156–7.

55 Packer, *Forum of Trajan*, vol. 1, 228; Packer, "Review of Amici, *Foro di Traiano*," 570.

56 Packer, *Forum of Trajan*, vol. 1, 238–9, appendix 5: 435–7.

57 For discussion of Trajan's Column, see Sonia Maffei, "Forum Traiani: Columna," *LTUR*, vol. 2, 358. Amanda Claridge, "Hadrian's Column of Trajan," *JRA* 6 (1993): 5–9; Packer, *Forum of Trajan*, vol. 1, 115–19, appendix 7: 447–9; Mark Wilson Jones, "One Hundred Feet and a Spiral Stair: The Problem of Designing Trajan's Column," *JRA* 6 (1993): 24–38; Bennett, *Trajan Princeps Optimus*, 90.

58 Maffei, "Forum Traiani: Columna," 356; Cass. Dio 68.16.3. For the complete text of the inscription, see Packer, *Forum of Trajan*, vol. 1, 117, appendix 7: 447.

59 Claridge, "Hadrian's Column of Trajan," 5–6, 9. Excavations around the column in 1906 and 1928 suggest there was not as much excavated from the Esquiline as previously assumed. Maffei, "Forum Traiani: Columna," 357.

60 Wilson Jones, "Designing Trajan's Column," 24–38.

61 Claridge, "Hadrian's Column of Trajan," 5–6; Packer, *Forum of Trajan*, vol. 1, 117.

62 Amanda Claridge argues, in contrast, that it may not have been Trajan's intention to be buried in the column because Roman law normally forbade burial inside the city walls. It is possible, according to Claridge, that the Senate could have granted the right for his burial in the column after his death, but it is not likely that Trajan himself would have erected the column for that purpose. See Claridge, "Hadrian's Column of Trajan," 10–11; G. Boni, "Esplorazione del Forum Ulpium," *NSc* (1909): 361–410. Zanker, however, argues that because the table on which the ash urns of Trajan and Plotina once rested was carved from the same blocks of marble as the rest of the base, there must always have been the project of burying Trajan in the base. Zanker, "Das Trajansforum," 499–544. Packer states it was in fact the burial place of Trajan's ashes. See Packer, *Forum of Trajan*, vol. 1, 117. See also Birley, *Hadrian*, 99–100; Bennett, *Trajan Princeps Optimus*, 156; Boatwright, *Hadrian and the City of Rome*, 82–3.

63 Maffei, "Forum Traiano: Columna," 357–8; Claridge, "Hadrian's Column of Trajan," 10–11; Cass. Dio, *Rom. Hist.* 68.16.3, 69.2.3; Richardson, *Dictionary*, 176; Frank Lepper and Sheppard Frere, *Trajan's Column: A New Edition of the Cichorius Plates* (Wolfboro, NH: Alan Sutton, 1988), 21–2.

64 Claridge, "Hadrian's Column," 13.

65 Packer, *Forum of Trajan*, vol. 1, 115–16. Wilson Jones states the total height may be reconstructed as 144 feet, as mentioned in Eutropius. "Designing Trajan's Column," 27–8.

66 Maffei, "Forum Traiani: Columna," 357; Wilson Jones, "Designing Trajan's Column," 24–7; Bennett, *Trajan Princeps Optimus*, 90.

67 Packer, *Forum of Trajan*, vol. 1, 119, appendix 7, 448–9; Wilson Jones, "Designing Trajan's Column," 23–4; Maffei, "Forum Traiani: Columna," 357. For images of the column on coins, see, for instance, *RIC*, vol. 2, 260ff, nos. 235, 238–9, 292–3, 307, 313, 356, 579, 600–3, 677–80, 683; *BMCREmp*, vol. 3, 93, no. 449, pl. 16.19; 94, 454, pl. 17.1; 112, nos. 565–6, pls. 19.11–12; 128, no. 665, pl. 21.15; 210, nos. 994–5, pls. 39.4–5; 213, nos. 1002–3, pls. 40.1–2; 218, nos. 1024–25, pls. 41.7.

68 Maffei, "Forum Traiani: Columna," 357; Packer, *Forum of Trajan*, vol. 1, 119.

69 Claridge has proposed the theory that the column was initially designed to have a smooth shaft rather than the spiral reliefs

we see today. Given the fact that the friezes were carved in situ, they could have been carved any time in the years after Trajan's death, particularly, suggests Claridge, during the reign of Hadrian when it is known that the Temple of Divus Traianus was also built. See Claridge, "Hadrian's Column of Trajan," 5–22. Packer discounts this theory, arguing the column was integral to Trajan's program for propaganda. James E. Packer, "Trajan's Forum Again: The Column and the Temple of Trajan in the Master Plan Attributed to Apollodorus," *JRA* 7 (1994): 163. Peter Rockwell suggests that the carved frieze was executed from the bottom up, after the carving of the window frames, and that the carving of the joint lines of the drums corresponds perfectly, thus ruling out carving on the ground before erection. Peter Rockwell, "Preliminary Study of the Carving Techniques on the Column of Trajan," in *Marmi antichi*, ed. Patrizio Pensabene, *StudMisc* 26 (Rome, 1985): 101–11.

70 For a description of the reliefs, see Museum of Roman Civilization, *The Model of Rome and the Column of Trajan* (Rome: Editori Romani Associati, 1988), passim; Bennett, *Trajan Princeps Optimus*, 90–103.

71 Campbell, *The Emperor and the Roman Army*, 147; Richard Brilliant, *Gesture and Rank in Roman Art* (New Haven: Yale University Press, 1963), 107–9; Packer, *Forum of Trajan*, vol. 1, 119.

72 Campbell, *The Emperor and the Roman Army*, 147–8.

73 Packer, *Forum of Trajan*, vol. 1, 113–5, appendix 6: 444–6; Carla Maria Amici, *Foro di Traiano: Basilica Ulpia e Biblioteche* (Rome: X Ripartizione antichità belle arti e problemi di cultura, 1982), 68–9; Packer, "Forum Traiani," 353.

74 For discussion of the Trajanic libraries, see Cass. Dio 68.16.3; Packer, *Forum of Trajan*, vol. 1, 120–30, appendix 8, 450–4; Packer, "Trajan's Forum in 1989," 157–9; Amici, *Foro di Traiano*, 71–87; Packer, "Review of Amici, *Foro di Traiano*," 571; Packer, "Forum Traiani," 353.

75 Packer, *Forum of Trajan*, vol. 1, 5; Packer, "Trajan's Forum Again," 163; Boatwright, *Hadrian and the City of Rome*, 78; Henri von Blanckenhagen, "The Imperial Fora," *JSAH* 13 (1954): 23, 25–6.

76 For discussion of the Temple of Divus Traianus, see Packer, *Forum of Trajan*, vol. 1, 131–5, appendix 10: 457–61; Claridge, "Hadrian's Column of Trajan," 21; Boatwright, *Hadrian and the City of Rome*, 93–4.

77 For the complete inscription, see Packer, *Forum of Trajan*, vol. 1, 127, n. 31. He states there were three copies of the inscription, one on the temple, and two on the entrances into the temenos. See also Birley, *Hadrian*, 191; *Hist. Aug. Had.* 19.9; Boatwright, *Hadrian and the City of Rome*, 74–98.

78 See note 36 for the debate about the temple's location. Boatwright has analyzed other possible identities for the temple shown on imperial coins: a temple dedicated to Nerva, or Fortuna, Marciana, Trajan's natural father, or the Temple of Venus Genetrix, which he rededicated. Each is excluded in favor of the temple in Trajan's Forum. See Boatwright, *Hadrian and the City of Rome*, 88–90; and Packer, *Forum of Trajan*, vol. 1, 131, appendix 10.457.

79 Packer, "Forum Traiani," 354; Boatwright, *Hadrian and the City of Rome*, 77; Roberto Meneghini, "Nuovi dati sulle biblioteche e il Templum Divi Traiani nel Foro di Traiano," *BA* 19–21 (1993): 13–21; Roberto Meneghini, "Templum Divi Traiani," *BullCom* 97 (1996): 47–55. For images on coins of the temple and its flanking colonnades see, for instance, *BMCREmp*, vol. 3, 182, no. 863, pl. 32.8; *RIC*, vol. 2, 285, no. 577, pl. 10.186; Packer, *Forum of Trajan*, vol. 1, 131–5, appendix 11: 467–70, and fig. 81, pls. 68.1–70.1.

80 Packer, "Forum Traiani," 260–1; Carla Maria Amici, "Forum Traiani," *LTUR*, vol. 5, 259–60; Meneghini, "Nuovi dati sulle biblioteche e il Templum Divi Traiani," 13–21.

81 In comparison, the podium of the Temple of Mars Ultor was 4.23 meters high. Packer, *Forum of Trajan*, vol. 1, appendix 10: 457.

82 J. Theodore Peña, "*P. Giss.* 69: Evidence for the Supplying of Stone Transport Operations in Roman Egypt and the Production of Fifty-Foot Monolithic Column Shafts," *JRA* 2 (1989): 126–32.

83 Several fragments of the columns of the pronaos are still on the site. In all, about eight of the column shafts survive. Packer, *Forum of Trajan*, vol. 1, 131, n. 38, 311–12, appendix 10: 458; Boatwright, *Hadrian and the City of Rome*, 75; Gioia Piazzesi, "Gli edifici: ipotesi ricostruttive," in "Foro Traiano: Contributi per una ricostruzione storia e architettonica," ed. Patrizio Pensabene, *ArchCl* 41 (1989), 125–98; Packer, "Trajan's Forum in 1989," 161. Those who believe the temple was not constructed north of the column suggest the large granite column laying on the site was part of a colossal propylaeum just north of Trajan's Column. It would have provided an entrance from the Campus Martius. See Rizzo, "I cantieri di scavo dei Fori Imperiali," 204.

84 Packer, "Trajan's Forum in 1989," 162, n. 37; Packer, *Forum of Trajan*, vol. 1, appendix 10: 459.

85 Packer, *Forum of Trajan*, vol. 1, 131, appendix 10: 457–8; Packer, "Forum Traiani," 354–5.

86 Packer, *Forum of Trajan*, vol. 1, 134–5; Packer, "Forum Traiani," 355.

87 Packer, "Forum Traiani," 355. For images on coins, see note 79 and *BMCREmp*, vol. 3, 181, 857, pl. 32.5; 182, 859, pl. 32.7; 193, 915–16, pl. 35.3–4; 201, 955, pl. 37.7; Packer, *Forum of Trajan*, vol. 1, appendix 11: 467.

88 Packer, *Forum of Trajan*, vol. 1, 134–5; Packer, "Forum Traiani," 355.

89 Packer, *Forum of Trajan*, vol. 1, 134–5.

90 Strong, "Late Hadrianic Architectural Ornament," 120.

91 Packer, *Forum of Trajan*, vol. 1, 282–3.

92 Shils, *Center and Periphery*, 22–3.

93 Ibid., 154–5.

94 Bennett, *Trajan*, 190–202; Cass. Dio 68.17–33.

95 Bennett, *Trajan*, 201–2; Birley, *Hadrian*, 75–6.

96 Cass. Dio 417.

97 Bennett, *Trajan Optimus Princeps*, 202–4; Birley, *Hadrian*, 77–8.

11: HADRIAN'S PANTHEON

1 De Fine Licht, *The Rotunda*, 191; Wilson Jones, *Principles of Roman Architecture*, 179; MacDonald, *The Pantheon*, 77.

2 For biographical information on Hadrian's early years, see Stewart Perowne, *Hadrian* (London: Hodder and Stoughton,

1960), 22–34; Boatwright, *Hadrian and the City of Rome*, 1–32; Birley, *Hadrian*, 10–20.

3 *Hist. Aug. Had.* 2.10; Birley, Hadrian, 2; Perowne, Hadrian, 35.

4 *Hist. Aug. Had.* 3.3; Birley, *Hadrian*, 35–76; Perowne, *Hadrian*, 36–52.

5 Hadrian traveled to Selinous, on the southern coast of Turkey, to attend a memorial service to Trajan. The emperor's body was cremated, and the urn with his ashes was sent to Rome to be interred in the base of Trajan's Column in the Forum Traiani. Birley, *Hadrian*, 77; *Hist. Aug. Had.* 4.5; Perowne, *Hadrian*, 43–5.

6 *Hist. Aug. Had.* 6.1–5; Perowne, *Hadrian*, 45–6.

7 Birley, *Hadrian*, 104–41; Perowne, *Hadrian*, 67–74; Bernard W. Henderson, *The Life and Principate of the Emperor Hadrian A.D. 76–138* (London: Methuen, 1923), 75–101.

8 The Panhellenion was intended for an association of all the Hellenes. In creating this, Hadrian revived an aborted project of Pericles. Cass. Dio 69.16; Boatwright, *Hadrian and the City of Rome*, 205; Birley, *Hadrian*, 219.

9 *Hist. Aug. Had.* 13.4; Cass. Dio 69.16; Birley, *Hadrian*, 219, 264–6; Boatwright, *Hadrian and the Cities of the Roman Empire*, 150–53.

10 Hadrian died at Baia in the Gulf of Naples in July A.D. 138 Birley, *Hadrian*, 299–300.

11 Ibid., 158; Boatwright, *Cities of the Roman Empire*, 204–9.

12 Boatwright, *Cities of the Roman Empire*, 172–203.

13 Royston Lambert, *Beloved and God: The Story of Hadrian and Antinous* (London: Weidenfeld and Nicolson, 1984), 43.

14 Birley, *Hadrian*, 221.

15 Lambert, *Beloved and God*, 108–10; Birley, *Hadrian*, 233.

16 Lambert, *Beloved and God*, 109.

17 The majority of the brick stamps date from A.D., 123 to 125 thus much of the construction must have been done when Hadrian was in Rome from 125 to 128. Ziolkowski, "Pantheon," 54–5; de Fine Licht, *The Rotunda*, 186–90, 247–8, 285–91.

18 MacDonald, *The Pantheon*, 11.

19 David Watkin, *A History of Western Architecture* (New York and London: Thames and Hudson, 1986), 58–60.

20 M. AGRIPPA L. F. COS TERTIUM FECIT. See *Hist. Aug. Had.* 19.12; de Fine Licht, *The Rotunda*, 180; Claridge, *Rome*, 201.

21 *Hist. Aug. Had.* 19.10; Cass. Dio 53.27.2–3; Ziolkowski, "Pantheon," 54–5; Richardson, *Dictionary*, 283; Roddaz, *Marcus Agrippa*, 261.

22 De Fine Licht, *The Rotunda*, 186–8.

23 Ibid., 180–8; 285, n. 23.

24 For discussion of the earlier Pantheon structures, see Chapter 7 and Virgili and Battistelli, "Indagini in Piazza della Rotonda," 137–54.

25 Ibid., 142–5.

26 Roddaz, *Marcus Aggripa*, 261–5; Ziolkowski, "Pantheon," 55.

27 Thomas, "The Architectural History of the Pantheon," 170–1; Virgili and Battistelli, "Indagini in Piazza della Rotonda," 141.

28 De Fine Licht, *The Rotunda*, 192; Lambert, *Beloved and God*, 192–3; Thomas, "The Architectural History of the Pantheon," 170; Cass. Dio 53.27.2–4.

29 De Fine Licht, *The Rotunda*, 192–3; Cass. Dio 53.27.2–4; Godfrey and Hemsoll, "The Pantheon," 197; Thomas, "The Architectural History of the Pantheon," 170; MacDonald, *The Pantheon*, 77.

30 Cass. Dio 66.24.2; Ziolkowski, "Pantheon," 55; Richardson *Dictionary*, 283; Roddaz, *Marcus Agrippa*, 262.

31 Ziolkowski, "Pantheon," 55–66; Richardson, *Dictionary*, 283;

32 For discussion of Hadrian's forecourt to the Pantheon, see de Fine Licht, *The Rotunda*, 26, 32–3. Not all authors agree that the forecourt was 150 meters long. Richter and Ashby suggest that it was only 60 meters, thus making it square in shape. See Richter, *Topographie der Stadt Rom*, 239; Samuel Ball Platner and Thomas Ashby, *A Topographical Dictionary of Ancient Rome* (Oxford: Oxford University Press, 1929), 42.

33 Ziolkowski, "Pantheon," 57; de Fine Licht, *The Rotunda*, 26–31.

34 Ziolkowski, "Pantheon," 57; Sandro de Maria, *Gli archi onorari di Roma e dell'Italia romana* (Rome: 'L'Erma' di Bretschneider, 1988), 298f; de Fine Licht, *The Rotunda*, 26.

35 MacDonald, *The Pantheon*, 86; Thomas, "The Architectural History of the Pantheon," 169.

36 De Fine Licht, *The Rotunda*, 35–6.

37 Virgili and Battistelli, "Indagini in Piazza della Rotonda," 143, fig. 3.

38 These fountains are today covered over by the Piazza della Rotonda. Virgili and Battistelli, "Indagini in Piazza della Rotonda," 150–1; de Fine Licht, *The Rotunda*, 37; Ziolkowski, "Pantheon," 57.

39 Peña, "P. Giss' 69," 131. The columns on the east flank, along with their entablature, were badly damaged in the Middle Ages and replaced in 1625 and 1666 by Pope Urban VIII and Pope Alexander VII. They are possibly *spolia* from the Baths of Nero, which had been excavated from under the Piazza S. Luigi dei Francesi. The marble of the repaired architrave and cornice was taken from the Arcus Pietatis. De Fine Licht, *The Rotunda*, 40, 241; Ziolkowski, "Pantheon," 57; Wilson Jones, *Principles of Roman Architecture*, 208.

40 De Fine Licht, *The Rotunda*, 40. The capitals conform to the principles of Vitruvius in that the length of the diagonal of the abacus is twice the lower column diameter. Also conforming to Vitruvius is the fact that the total height of the columns excluding the plinth, is nine-and-a-half times the lower diameter. Paul Davies, David Hemsoll, and Mark Wilson Jones, "The Pantheon: Triumph of Rome or Triumph of Compromise?" *Art History* 10 (June 1987): 140–1.

41 De Fine Licht, *The Rotunda*, 40–1.

42 Ibid., 41–4.

43 See for instance, Lawrence, *Greek Architecture*, 169–82; Coulton, *Ancient Greek Architects at Work*, 107–9.

44 Davies, Hemsoll, and Wilson Jones, "The Pantheon," 133–53; Ziolkowski, "Pantheon," 58: Wilson Jones, *Principles of Roman Architecture*, 199–206.

45 It is this problem that led many architects, archaeologists, and historians to believe that the building represented separate building campaigns carried out by different emperors. It was only recently that detailed analysis of the building's construction, especially an identification of its brick stamps, proved conclusively that it was built in its entirety during the early years of Hadrian's reign. See Davies, Hemsoll, and Wilson

Jones, "The Pantheon" 134; Loerke, "Georges Chédanne and the Pantheon," 42–8; Thomas, "The Architectural History of the Pantheon," 165–7; Wilson Jones, *Principles of Roman Architecture*, 200–6.

46 Davies, Hemsoll, and Wilson Jones, "The Pantheon," 133–53.

47 The Temple of Divus Traianus, for instance, was under construction at the same time, and may have necessitated the diverting of larger columns away from the Pantheon. Davies, Hemsol, and Wilson Jones, "The Pantheon," 146; Wilson Jones, *Principles of Roman Architecture*, 209.

48 Davies, Hemsoll, and Wilson Jones use Greco-Roman feet in their discussion (1 Greco-Roman foot equals .296 meter). They suggest that the overall height of the order should have been 74 Greco-Roman feet as opposed to 59, and the height of the columns 60 feet as opposed to 48. See Davies, Hemsoll, and Wilson Jones, "The Pantheon," 135–8; Wilson Jones, *Principles of Roman Architecture*, 204–8.

49 The columns on the west side of the pronaos are closer together than those on the east side, possibly because of shifting of the foundations. Davies, Hemsoll, and Wilson Jones, "The Pantheon," 134, 148, n. 16; de Fine Licht, *The Rotunda*, 35–6.

50 These large fluted pilasters, which are aligned with the pronaos columns, were made of white marble, with bases and capitals similar to those of the columns. Their dimension remained consistent their entire height. For a discussion of the peculiarities in the size and details of these pilasters, see Davies, Hemsoll, and Wilson Jones, "The Pantheon," 134–5; de Fine Licht, *The Rotunda*, 69–72; Wilson Jones, *Principles of Roman Architecture*, 204–5.

51 Lothar Haselberger, "Deciphering a Roman Blueprint," *Scientific American* 272 (June 1995): 84–9. For discussion of the materials used in the construction of the pediment, see Antonio M. Colini, "Indagini sui frontoni dei templi di Roma," *BullCom* 51 (1924): 299–347.

52 Haselberger, "Deciphering a Roman Blueprint," 84–9.

53 Wilson Jones, *Principles of Roman Architecture*, 207.

54 De Fine Licht, *The Rotunda*, 46–7, 192–3; Lucos Cozza, "Le tegole di marmo del Pantheon," in *Città e architettura*, 109–18; Ziolkowski, "Pantheon," 61.

55 For the image of an eagle on Augustan coins, see *BMCREmp*, vol. 1, 93, no. 563, pl. 20, 21. For an oak wreath, see, for instance, *BMCREmp*, vol. 1, 60, no. 330, pl. 6, 10.

56 De Fine Licht, *The Rotunda*, 46, 192–3. A panel relief from the Forum Traiani showing an eagle in a wreath of oak leaves is in the church of SS. Apostoli.

57 Lambert, *Beloved and God*, 41, 46.

58 Originally there were eight of these panels in the entrance passage and ten on each side elevation, making twenty-eight in all. Thirteen of these are preserved well enough to identify the objects depicted. Two of the slabs from the entrance passage were removed during the Middle Ages but were discovered in excavations in 1874. They were later installed on the retaining wall west of the pronaos. De Fine Licht, *The Rotunda*, 80.

59 Ziolkowski, "Pantheon," 58.

60 De Fine Licht, *The Rotunda*, 80–2.

61 De Angeli, *Templum Divi Vespasiani*, 131–48; de Fine Licht, *The Rotunda*, 80–1.

62 Tod Marder, "Bernini and Alexander VII: Criticism and Praise of the Pantheon in the Seventeenth Century," *ArtBull* 71 (1989): 628–45; Lanciani, *Ruins and Excavations*, 481–3. The stories on the use of the melted down bronze from the Pantheon have been largely refuted. See de Fine Licht, *The Rotunda*, 51–8; M. E. Micheli, "Disiecta membra del Pantheon: 1747," *BullCom* 89 (1984): 56.

63 De Fine Licht, *The Rotunda*, 51–8; Thomas Ashby, "Addenda and Corrigenda to 'Sixteenth Century Drawings of Roman Buildings Attributed to Andreas Coner,'" *PBRS*, 6 (1913): 202–4.

64 MacDonald, *Architecture of the Roman Empire*, vol. 1, 98.

65 Palladio, *Four Books*, vol. 4, pl. 52.

66 Ziolkowski, "Pantheon," 59; MacDonald, *The Pantheon*, 85–6. Wilson Jones states that the diameter of the cylinder is about 147 feet, whereas the diameter of the cupola itself is nearer 150 feet. So, in fact, it is not a perfect sphere. Wilson Jones, *Principles of Roman Architecture*, 184–6.

67 There is a parallel between the rotunda plan and the large exedrae behind the colonnades of the Forum Augustum, which have a radius to their inner face of 23 meters. If they were joined together, they would have a diameter that is only slightly more than the Pantheon. The rotunda is essentially equivalent to the exedrae but a full circle in plan, transformed from a solid load-bearing wall of tufa in *opus quadratum* to a cavity-filled wall of brick and concrete. Ziolkowski, "Pantheon," 59; MacDonald, *The Pantheon*, 85–6; Thomas, "The Architectural History of the Pantheon," 169; Claridge, *Rome*, 204.

68 De Fine Licht, *The Rotunda*, 89–94; Ziolkowski, "Pantheon," 59.

69 For descriptions of the Pantheon's structural system, see MacDonald, *The Pantheon*, 28–33; Ziolkowski, "Pantheon," 59; Robert Mark and Paul Hutchinson, "On the Strucuture of the Roman Pantheon," *ArtBull* 68 (1986): 24–34; de Fine Licht, *The Rotunda*, 96–100.

70 De Fine Licht, *The Rotunda*, 136–7; Ziolkowski, "Pantheon," 59; Frank Sear, *Roman Architecture* (Ithaca: Cornell University Press, 1982), 167.

71 There have been arguments for marble cladding of the rotunda; however, there is no evidence of the clamps or brackets that would have been required to support marble slabs. De Fine Licht, *The Rotunda*, 106; Rodolfo Lanciani, *Storia degli scavi e notizia intorno le collezioni romane di antichità*, vol. 2 (Rome: E. Loescher, 1902), 237.

72 De Fine Licht, *The Rotunda*, 106–8.

73 Palladio, *Four Books*, vol. 4, pl. 53.

74 For an identification of the various types of marble used in the interior of the Pantheon, see Wilson Jones, *Principles of Roman Architecture*, 211.

75 For an analysis of the floor's geometry and its relationship to the pattern of the coffered dome, see William C. Loerke, "A Rereading of the Interior Elevation of Hadrian's Rotunda," *JSAH* 49 (March 1990): 35, 39–41. See also MacDonald, *The Pantheon*, 100–1; Wilson Jones, *Principles of Roman Architecture*, 194.

76 The floor was extensively restored in the nineteenth century, although similarly colored marbles were used. De Fine Licht, *The Rotunda*, 100–1; Wilson Jones, *Principles of Roman Architecture*, 184.

77 De Fine Licht, *The Rotunda*, 108; Wilson Jones, *Principles of Roman Architecture*, 222–3, Table 1.

78 De Fine Licht, *The Rotunda*, 108; G. P. Stevens, "Entasis of Roman columns," *MAAR* 4 (1924): fig. 18; Antoine Desgodetz, *Les édifices antiques de Rome* (Paris: n.p., 1779), 20.

79 De Fine Licht, *The Rotunda*, 124, fig. 33; Wilson Jones, *Principles of Roman Architecture*, 211.

80 Originally, all of the aedicule columns were porphyry. De Fine Licht, *The Rotunda*, 111; Wilson Jones, *Principles of Roman Architecture*, 196.

81 For a description of the aedicules in the cella of the Temple of Apollo Sosianus, see Viscogliosi, *Il Tempio di Apollo 'in Circo,'* 92–112.

82 De Fine Licht, *The Rotunda*, 109–10.

83 The coffering and crosses evident in the main exedra are from a later restoration. Ziolkowski, "Pantheon," 59; de Fine Licht, *The Rotunda*, 110.

84 MacDonald, *The Pantheon*, 37; Micheli, "Disiecta membra del Pantheon," 55–64.

85 Micheli, "Disiecta membra del Pantheon," 59.

86 De Fine Licht, *The Rotunda*, 115–18. For images of the original attic story, see Palladio, *Four Books*, vol. 4, pls. 57 and 58; Desgodetz, *Les édifices antiques de Rome*, pl 18; Micheli, "Disiecta membra del Pantheon," 59.

87 Loerke, "Hadrian's Rotunda," 29–30.

88 De Fine Licht, *The Rotunda*, 120.

89 Loerke, "Hadrian's Rotunda," 29–30; de Fine Licht, *The Rotunda*, 140–41, 200–1.

90 De Fine Licht, *The Rotunda*, 139–41.

91 Luca Beltrami, *Il Pantheon rivendicato ad Adriano* (Milan: n.p., 1929), fig. 7; de Fine Licht, *The Rotunda*, 140–1.

92 De Fine Licht, *The Rotunda*, 136; Ziolkowski, "Pantheon," 59; Wilson Jones, *Principles of Roman Architecture*, 187.

93 There is evidence in some of the coffers of hooks to fasten bronze ornaments. See de Fine Licht, *The Rotunda*, 145. Lanciani assumed the dome was only decorated with stucco and paint. Rodolfo Lanciani, "Prima e seconda relazione sugli scavi per lo isolamento del Pantheon," *NSc* (1881): 264.

94 Loerke, "Hadrian's Pantheon," 29–30; Wilson Jones, *Principles of Roman Architecture*, 187.

95 De Fine Licht, *The Rotunda*, 140–1.

96 Fausto Masi, *The Pantheon as an Astronomical Instrument* (Rome: Edizioni Internationali di Letteratura e Scienze, 1996), 7; Thomas, "The Architectural History of the Pantheon," 174.

97 De Fine Licht, *The Rotunda*, 200.

98 MacDonald, *The Pantheon*, 88–9. This idea was suggested earlier by Mommsen and supported by Hülsen and Platner and Ashby. See Thomas, "The Architectural History of the Pantheon," 172–3.

99 Thomas, "The Architectural History of the Pantheon," 173.

100 Ibid.; de Fine Licht, *The Rotunda*, 192.

101 Thomas, "The Architectural History of the Pantheon," 174.

102 Ibid., 173–4; Masi, *The Pantheon as an Astronomical Instrument*, 7.

103 De Fine Licht, *The Rotunda*, 140–1; Sperling, *Das Pantheon*, 28, 223–36.

104 Loerke, "Hadrian's Rotunda," 38–41. De Fine Licht discusses the presence of the twenty-four coffers but rejects any evidence for the number to have been related to the moon. De Fine Licht, *The Rotunda*, 200–01; Wilson Jones, *Principles of Roman Architecture*, 183.

105 Some scholars argue it was not a temple at all. See Ziolkowski, "Pantheon," 60; Giangiacomo Martines, "Argomenti di geometria antica a proposito della cupola del Pantheon," *QuadIstStArch* 13 (1991): 3–10. Others argue it was a temple only in the broadest sense and that it served many other functions. See Godfrey and Hemsoll, "The Pantheon," 205; Wilson Jones, *Principles of Roman Architecture*, 184.

106 Martines, "Argomenti di geometria," 3–10; Ziolkowski, "Pantheon," 61; Wilson Jones, *Principles of Roman Architecture*, 184; Archimedes, "De sphera et cylindro," in J. L. Heiberg, ed., *Archimedis opera omnia*, vol. 1, (Leipzig: n.p., 1910–1915), 229.

107 The sixteen-part geometry may have been related to the sixteen-part Etruscan sky, which would imply celestial connotations. De Fine Licht, *The Rotunda*, 195–8; Wilson Jones, *Principles of Roman Architecture*, 183.

108 Martines, "Argomenti di geometria," 3–10; Ziolkowski, "Pantheon," 61.

109 Paul Godfrey and David Hemsoll argue that because the Pantheon has a circular rather than rectangular cella, it was not an appropriate *templum*. See Godfrey and Hemsoll, "The Pantheon" 201; Ziolkowski, "Pantheon," 60–1.

110 Cass. Dio, *Rom. Hist.* 69.7.

111 Godfrey and Hemsoll, "The Pantheon" 201, 208, n. 52.

112 Wilson Jones suggests it may not have been a temple in the strict sense of the term, although this did not rule out a spiritual realm and temple-like associations. Wilson Jones, *Principles of Roman Architecture*, 179. Despite this suggestion, the presence of the sacral instruments is undeniable evidence of its function as a temple.

113 De Fine Licht, *The Rotunda*, 191.

114 Ibid.

115 Lambert, *Beloved and God*, 38.

116 Loerke, "Hadrian's Rotunda," 39–41.

117 Lambert, *Beloved and God*, 41.

118 Birley, *Hadrian*, 233; Boatwright, *Cities of the Roman Empire*, 153.

119 Lambert, *Beloved and God*, 109.

120 See Chapter 7 for discussion of the Pantheon's relation to the Mausoleum of Augustus and the Temple of Capitoline Jupiter.

121 De Fine Licht, *The Rotunda*, 202.

122 Thomas, "The Architectural History of the Pantheon," 180; de Fine Licht, *The Rotunda*, 192.

123 De Fine Licht, *The Rotunda*, 192.

124 Lambert, *Beloved and God*, 202.

125 Ibid., 42.

126 Ibid., 41.

12: HADRIAN AND THE ANTONINES

1 Birley, *Hadrian*, 112.

2 Alessandro Cassatella, "Venus et Roma, Aedes, Templum," *LTUR*, vol. 5, 121.

3 Birley, *Hadrian*, 233; Lambert, *Beloved and God*, 208–9.

4 Andrea Barattolo, "Il Tempio di Venere e di Roma: Un tempio 'Greco' nell'urbe," *RömMitt* 85 (1978): 397–410.

5 Boatwright, *Cities of the Roman Empire*, 150–3.

6 Lambert, *Beloved and God*, 45.

7 Cassatella, "Venus et Roma," 121; Richardson, *Dictionary*, 409–10.

8 Cassatella, "Venus et Roma," 121; *BMCREmp*, vol. 3, 328ff, nos. 700–3, 707; 334, nos. 750–6; R. Turcan, "La 'Fondation' du Temple de Venus et de Roma," *Latomus* 23 (1964): 44–8.

9 Boatwright, *Hadrian and the City of Rome*, 120–1.

10 The temple is represented on coins from A.D. 140 to 145. See *RIC*, vol 2, 110, nos. 622, 623; 113, no. 651; 114, no. 664; *BMCREmp*, vol. 4, 205–06, nos. 1279–85, pls. 29. 10–13, 30.1–3. Lanciani, *Ruins and Excavations*, 194–96; Henry J. Middleton, *The Remains of Ancient Rome*, vol. 2 (London and Edinburgh: Adam and Charles, 1892), 219–21; Boatwright, *Hadrian and the City of Rome*, 121–124.

11 For information on the Domus Aurea see P. Gregory Warden, "The Domus Aurea Reconsidered," *JSAH* 40 (December 1981): 271–8; MacDonald, *Architecture of the Roman Empire*, vol. 1, 20–46; Boëthius, *The Golden House of Nero*, passim.

12 The architect Decrianus moved the Colossus. *Hist. Aug. Had.* 19.12–13; Birley, *Hadrian*, 112; A. Carandini, "'*Domus et insulae*' sulla pendici settentrionali del Palatino," *BullCom* 91 (1986): 263–74; Lanciani, *Ruins and Excavations*, 190; Plin. *Nat. Hist.* 34.18.43–47.

13 Brick stamps in the platform's foundations date from A.D. 123 Boatwright, *Hadrian and the City of Rome*, 120–1; Barattolo, "Il Tempio di Venere e Roma," 399.

14 Boatwright, *Hadrian and the City of Rome*, 128.

15 Cassius Dio relates the story that Hadrian sent the plans of the building to Apollodorus and that he suggested setting the building high on a podium with hollowed out spaces underneath so that the building might be more conspicuous from the Via Sacra and its substructures might accommodate the machines for the Colosseum. The story that Hadrian ordered Apollodorus put to death for his criticisms is dubious. Cassatella, "Venus et Roma," 122; Boatwright, *Hadrian and the City of Rome*, 119; Cass. Dio, *Rom. Hist.* 69.4.4; Birley, *Hadrian*, 112.

16 Middleton, *The Remains of Ancient Rome*, vol. 2, 222.

17 Boatwright, *Hadrian and the City of Rome*, 127; Barattolo, "Tempio di Venere e Roma," 400, nos. 15 and 16.

18 Boatwright, *Hadrian and the City of Rome*, 127; Barattolo, "Tempio di Venere e Roma," 400.

19 A. Munoz, *La sistemazione del Tempio di Venere e Roma* (Rome, 1935), 16; Cassatella, "Venus et Roma," 122. For dimensions of the Temple of Olympian Zeus see Dinsmoor, *Ancient Greece*, 340 (41.11 by 107.89 meters); and Boatwright, *Cities of the Roman Empire*, 150–1 (ca. 44 by 110 meters).

20 The correct plan of the Temple of Veunus and Rome is published in Alessandro Cassatella and Stefania Panella, "Restituzione dell'impianto Adrianeo del Tempio di Venere e Roma," 52–4.

21 Del Monte states the columns were about 20 meters high, which is probably exaggerated. Claudia del Monte, "Tempio di Venere e Roma: Indagini e restauri," in *ArchGiub*, 164; Dinsmoor, *Ancient Greece*, 340–1.

22 Cassatella, "Venus et Roma," 122–3.

23 Strong, "Late Hadrianic Architectural Ornament," 130.

24 Ibid., 136.

25 Sear, *Roman Architecture*, 182–3.

26 Fred C. Albertson, "An Augustan Temple Represented on a Historical Relief Dating to the Time of Claudius," *AJA* 91 (1987): 445.

27 The bronze roof tiles remained in place until being stripped off by Pope Honorius I in the 630s for use on St. Peter's Basilica. Middleton, *The Remains of Ancient Rome*, vol. 2, 222.

28 Aur. Vict. *Caes.* 40.26; Cassatella, "Venus et Roma," 121–3; Boatwright, *Hadrian and the City of Rome*, 125.

29 Prud. *Sym.* 1.217s; Cassatella, "Venus et Roma" 121. Boatwright, *Hadrian and the City of Rome*, 125; del Monte, "Tempio di Venere e Roma," 164–9.

30 Middleton, *Ancient Rome*, vol. 2, 221; Andrea Barattolo, "Nuove ricerche sull'architettura del Tempio di Venere e di Roma in età Adrianea," *RömMitt* 80 (1973): 243–69; Andrea Barattolo, "Sulla decorazione delle celle del Tempio di Venere e di Roma all'epoca di Adriano," *BullCom* 84 (1974–5), 133–48; Barattolo, "Tempio di Venere e Roma," 245–7.

31 Cassatella, "Venus et Roma," 123.

32 Boatwright, *Hadrian and the City of Rome*, 125–7. Pausanius mentions four Greek temples that may have influenced the design of the Temple of Venus and Rome: Sicyon, Argos, Olympia, and Mantineia. Barattolo, "Il Tempio di Venere e Roma," 402–7.

33 Strong, "Late Hadrianic Architectural Ornament," 137.

34 Middleton, *Ancient Rome*, vol. 2, 221.

35 Roma is depicted on numerous reliefs, including the Ara Pacis, the Arch of Titus, and one of the Trajanic reliefs incorporated into the Arch of Constantine. Boatwright, *Hadrian and the City of Rome*, 129–30; Cornelius C. Vermeule, *The Goddess Roma in the Art of the Roman Empire* (Cambridge, MA: Spink, 1959), 29–42.

36 Boatwright, *Hadrian and the City of Rome*, 130.

37 Ibid., 132.

38 Frank E. Brown, "Hadrianic Architecture," in *Essays in Memory of K. Lehmann*, ed. L. F. Sandler (New York: n.p., n.d.), 56.

39 For images of the temple at the time of its dedication, see *RIC*, vol. 2, 327, 370 nos. 263, 265; 372, no. 280; *BMCREmp*, vol. 3, 328ff, nos. 700–3, 707; 334, nos. 750–6. See also Jocelyn M. C. Toynbee, *The Hadrianic School: A Chapter in the History of Greek Art* (Cambridge: Cambridge University Press, 1934), 137, 143; quoted in Lambert, *Beloved and God*, 168.

40 *Hist. Aug. Had.* 25.1–9; Cass. Dio 69.23; Birley, *Hadrian*, 300; Perowne, *Hadrian*, 179–80; Michael Grant, *The Antonines: The Roman Empire in Transition* (New York: Routledge, 1994), 11.

41 Birley, *Hadrian*, 300; Perowne, *Hadrian*, 180; Grant, *The Antonines*, 11.

42 The Temple of Matidia was a peripteral temple that stood in an enclosure surrounded by a portico. A fragment of the *Forma Urbis Romae* suggests it was eight by thirteen columns and that its portico covered about the same area as the Temple of Deified Hadrian. The columns had a diameter of 1.70 meters and a height of 13.70 to 17 meters, making it taller than the Pantheon. See Perowne, *Hadrian*, 180; Birley, *Hadrian*, 110; Francesca de Caprariis, "Matidia, Templum," *LTUR*, vol. 3, 233; Boatwright, *Hadrian and the City of Rome*, 58–61, Coarelli, *Roma*, 298; E. Rodriguez-Almeida, *Forma Urbis*

Marmorea, aggiornamento generale 1980 (Rome: n.p., 1981), 127; Richardson, *Dictionary*, 247.

43 De Caprariis, "Matitdia, Templum," 233.

44 Mafalda Cipollone, "Hadrianus, Divus, Templum; Hadrianeum," *LTUR*, vol. 3, 7–8; Claridge, *Rome*, 200; Richardson, *Dictionary*, 184.

45 Lucos Cozza, *Tempio di Adriano* (Rome: De Luca Editore, 1932), 7–8.

46 Cipollone, "Hadrianeum," 7–8; Strong, "Late Hadrianic Architectural Ornament," 123–5. For a discussion of the fluting of the column shafts, see Amanda Claridge, "Roman Methods of Fluting Columns and Pilasters," in *Città e architettura*, 119–28.

47 Wilson Jones, "Designing the Roman Corinthian Order," 39.

48 Ibid., 38; Strong, "Late Hadrianic Architectural Ornament," 123–4.

49 Strong, "Late Hadrianic Architectural Ornament," 130.

50 Strong states that the convex frieze was common in Asia Minor during the second century A.D., as seen, for instance, in the Temple of Apollo at Sagalassos from ca. A.D. 100. The convex frieze may have been developed from the S-curve frieze, which was first used in Syria, then in Asia Minor and Greece. An S-curve frieze is found on the west door of the Theater at Ephesus and in the interior Corinthian Order of the Tholos at Epidaurus. Ibid., 135–6.

51 Ibid., 123–6; Richardson, *Dictionary*, 184.

52 Strong, "Late Hadrianic Architectural Ornament," 126; Richardson, *Dictionary*, 184.

53 Sear, *Roman Architecture*, 166; Richardson, *Dictionary*, 184. Twenty-one of the figures of the provinces and nine trophy panels are known; twenty-three survive whole or in part. Cipollone suggests the sculpted panels were not on the podium, but inside the cella. Cipollone, "Hadrianeum," 8.

54 Cipollone, "Hadrianeum," 8.

55 Alessandro Cassatella, "Antoninus, Divus et Faustina, Diva, Aedes, Templum," *LTUR*, vol. 1, 46.

56 Ibid.; Coarelli, *Foro Romano*, vol. 2, 269ff; Luciani and Sperduti, *Foro Romano*, 132.

57 Cassatella, "Antoninus, Divus et Faustina," 46–7.

58 Claridge, *Rome*, 109. For images of the Temple of Antoninus and Faustina on coins, see *RIC*, vol. 3, 69ff, nos. 343, 354, 388, 396, 406A, 1115, 1137, 1148, 1168, 1195.

59 Cassatella, "Antoninus, Divus et Faustina," 47.

60 Ibid.

61 Wilson Jones, "Designing the Roman Corinthian Order," 39.

62 Claridge, *Rome*, 107; Cassatella, "Antoninus, Divus et Faustina," 8. The underside of the architrave had carved panels similar to those of the Pantheon, but executed badly. De Fine Licht, *The Rotunda*, 188.

63 Cassatella, "Antoninus, Divus et Faustina," 46.

EPILOGUE

1 Among the later temples constructed, most were relatively small or, in contrast, so large that they were never completed. The Temple of Heliogabalus, for instance, was built on the Palatine in A.D. 218–222. One of the largest temples to be started in Rome but never finished was the Temple of Hercules and Dionysius on the Quirinal, previously identified as the Temple of the Sun or Aurelian. Finally, there was the Temple of Serapis of Caracalla; see Richardson, *Dictionary*, 361. What were more often built after this time were commemorative columns, triumphal arches, and especially baths. Later temples were begun, but none were completed because the commitment to the gods had faded. For discussion of the Temple of Sol Heliogabalus, see Antonio F. Caiola, Maria A. Tomei, and Françoise Villedieu, "Ex Vigna Barberini: indagini archeologiche e restauri," in *ArchGiub*, 158–61; P. Bigot, "Le Temple de Jupiter Ultor et la Vigne Barberini," *BullCom* 39 (1911): 80–5; Filippo Coarelli, "Heliogabalus, Templum: Heliogabalium," *LTUR*, vol. 3, 10–11. For Temple of Sol built by Aurelian, see Jaqueline Calzini Gysens and Filippo Coarelli, "Sol, Templum," *LTUR*, vol. 4, 331–3.

2 Edwards, *Religion and Power*, 7.

3 De George, *The Nature and Limits of Authority*, 1.

4 Boring, "What Is Precedent," 260–3.

ABBREVIATIONS

AA	*Art and Archaeology*
ActaAArtH	*Acta ad archaeologiam et artium historiam pertinentia*
ArtBul	*Art Bulletin*
AH	*Architectural History*
AJA	*American Journal of Archaeology*
AJAH	*American Journal of Ancient History*
Ancient Rome	Coulston, Jon, and Hazel Dodge, eds., *Ancient Rome: The Archaeology of the Eternal City*. Dublin: Center for Mediterranean and Near Eastern Studies, Trinity College; Oxford: Oxford University School of Archaeology, 2000
ArchLaz	*Quaderni di archeologia etrusco-italica: archeologia laziale*
ArchGiub	Fedora Filippi, ed., *Archeologia e Giubileo; Gli interventi a Roma e nel Lazio nel piano per il grande giubileo del 2000*. Naples: Electa, 2000
ANRW	Temporini, H., and W. Haase, eds., *Aufstieg und Niedergang der römischen Welt*, 37 vols. Berlin and New York: Walter de Gruyter, 1978
ArchCl	*Archeologia Classica*
Atti CongrStArchit	*Atti del Congresso (nazionale) di storia dell'architettura*
AttiPontAcc	*Atti della Pontificia Accademia romana di archeologia*
BA	*Bollettino di Archeologia*
BMCREmp	Mattingly, Harold, *Coins of the Roman Empire in the British Museum*, 5 vols. London: British Museum, 1936–1966
BMCRR	Grueber, H. A., *Coins of the Roman Republic in the British Museum*. London: British Museum, 1910
BRE	Raaflaub, Kurt A., and Mark Toher, eds., *Between Republic and Empire: Interpretations of Augustus and His Principate*. Berkeley: University of California Press, 1990
BullArchGov	*Bullettino Archeologica Governatorato*
BullArchIt	*Bullettino Archeologico Italiano*
BullCom	*Bullettino della Commissione Archeologica Comunale di Roma*
CAH	Cook, S. A., F. E. Adcock, and M. P. Charlesworth, eds., *The Cambridge Ancient History*, 14 vols. Cambridge: Cambridge University Press, 1970–2000

CARI	De Fine Licht, Kjeld, ed., *Città e Architettura nella Roma imperiale: atti del seminario del 27 ottobre 1981 nel 250 anniversario dell'Accademia di Danimarca*. Rome: Analecta Romana Instituti Danici, suppl. 10, 1983
CBFI	Baiani, Serena, and Massimiliano Ghilardi, eds., *Crypta Balbi – Fori Imperiali: Archaeologia urbana a Roma e interventi di restauro nell'anno del Grande Giubileo*. Rome: Edizioni Kappa, 2000
CFIFT	Morselli, Chiara, and Edoardo Tortorici, eds., *Curia, Forum Iulium, Forum Transitorium*. Rome: De Luca Edizioni D'Arte, 1989
Classical Marble	Herz, Norman, and Marc Waelkens, eds., *Classical Marble: Geochemistry, Technology, Trade*. Dordrecht: Kluwer Academic, 1988
DA	Turner, Jane, ed., *The Dictionary of Art*, 34 vols. New York: Grove and MacMillan, 1996
ELA	Cristofani, M., ed., *Etruria e Lazio arcaico*. Rome: Atti Incontro di Studio Roma, 1987
FUR	Carettoni, Gianfilippo, Antonio M. Colini, Lucos Cozza, and Guglielmo Gatti, *La Pianta Marmorea di Roma antica (Forma Urbis Romae)*, 2 vols. Rome: Danesi, 1960
FT	Pensabene, Patrizio, et al., "Foro Traiano: Contributi per una ricostruzione storica e architettonica," *Archeologia Classica* 41 (1989): 27–292
Hephaistos	*Hephaistos: New Approaches in Classical Archaeology and Related Fields*
Hist. Aug.	*Historia Augusta*
Inscr. It.	Degrassi, A., *Fasti Anni Numani et Iuliani (Inscriptiones Italiae)*. Rome, 1963
JAIA	*Journal of the American Institute of Architects*
JDAI	*Jahrbuch des Deutschen Archäologischen Instituts*
JGH	*Journal of Garden History*
JRA	*Journal of Roman Archaeology*
JRIBA	*Journal of the Royal Institute of British Architects*
JRS	*Journal of Roman Studies*
JSAH	*Journal of the Society of Architectural Historians*
Kaiser Augustus	Heilmeyer, Wolf-Dieter, Eugenio La Rocca, and H. G. Martin, eds., *Kaiser Augustus und die verlorene Republik*. Berlin: Kulturstadt Europas, 1988
LTUR	Steinby, Eva Margareta, ed., *Lexicon Topographicum Urbis Roma*, 6 vols. Rome: Edizioni Quasar, 1993–2000
MEA	Placek, Adolph, ed., *Macmillan Encyclopedia of Architects*, 4 vols. New York: Free Press; London: Collier Macmillan, 1982
MemPontAcc	*Atti della Pontificia Accademia Romana di Archeologia: Memorie*
MAAR	*Memoirs of the American Academy in Rome*
MEFRA	*Mélanges de l'École Française à Rome: Antiquité*

MemLinc	*Memorie: Atti della Accademia Nazionale dei Lincei, Classe di scienze morali, storiche e filologiche*
MonLinc	*Monumenti antichi pubblicati per cura della Accademia Nazionale dei Lincei*
NSc	*Notizie degli scavi di antichità*
OHCW	Boardman, John, Jasper Griffin, Oswyn Murray, eds., *The Oxford History of the Classical World.* Oxford: Oxford University Press, 1986
PAAR	*Papers and Memoires of the American Academy in Rome*
PBSR	*Papers of the British School in Rome*
ProcBritAc	*Proceedings of the British Academy*
QuadIstStArch	*Quaderni dell'Istituto di Storia dell'Architettura*
QArchEtr	*Quaderni del Centro di Studio per l'Archeologia Etrusco-Italica*
RE	*Paulys Real-Encyclopädie der Classischen Altertumswissenschaft,* 66 vols. Stuttgart: Alfred Druckenmüller Verlag, 1893–1972
RendLinc	*Atti dell'Accademia Nazionale dei Lincei: Rendiconti*
RendPontAcc	*Atti della Pontificia Accademia Romana di Archeologia: Rendiconti*
RIC	Mattingly, Harold, and Edward A. Sydenham, *The Roman Imperial Coinage*, 9 vols. London: Spink and Son, 1923–1981
RivFil	*Rivista di filologia e d'istruzione classica*
Roman Questions	Linderski, Jerzy, *Roman Questions: Selected Papers.* Stuttgart: Franz Steiner Verlag, 1995
RRC	Crawford, Michael H., *Roman Republican Coinage*, 2 vols. New York: Cambridge University Press, 1974
RivStorIt	*Rivista Storica Italiana*
RömMitt	*Mitteilungen des Deutschen Archäologischen Instituts, Römische Abteilung*
StudMisc	*Studi miscellanei: Seminario di Archeologia e Storia dell'Arte Greca e Romana dell'Università di Roma*
TAPA	*Transactions of the American Philological Association*

WORKS CITED AND CONSULTED

Académie de France à Rome et al., *Roma Antiqua: 'Envois' degli architetti francesi (1786–1901), Grandi Edifici Pubblici*. Rome: Edizioni Carte Segrete, 1992.

Académie de France à Rome et al., *Roma Antiqua: 'Envois' des architects français (1788–1924), Forum, Colisée, Palatin*. Rome: Académie de France à Rome, École française de Rome, École nationale supérieure des Beaux-Arts, 1985.

Adam, Jean-Pierre, *Roman Building: Materials and Techniques*. Trans. Anthony Mathews. London: Batsford, 1994.

Le temple du Portunus au Forum Boarium. Rome: École Française, 1994.

Adkins, Lesley, and Roy A. Adkins, *Handbook to Ancient Life in Rome*. New York: Facts on File, 1994.

Aikin, Roger C., *The Capitoline Hill during the Reign of Sixtus V*. Ph.D. diss., University of California, Berkeley, 1977.

Albertson, Fred C., "An Augustan Temple Represented on a Historical Relief Dating to the Time of Claudius," *AJA* 91 (1987): 441–58.

Alföldi, Andreas, *Early Rome and the Latins*. Ann Arbor: University of Michigan Press, 1963.

Amici, Carla Maria, *Il Foro di Cesare*. Florence: Leo S. Olschki Editore, 1991.

Foro di Traiano: Basilica Ulpia e Biblioteche. Rome: X Ripartizione antichità belle arti e problemi di cultura, 1982.

"Forum Traiani," *LTUR*, vol. 5, 259–60.

Ammerman, Albert J., "On the Origins of the Forum Romanum," *AJA* 94 (1990): 627–45.

Amy, Robert, and Pierre Gros, *La Maison Carrée de Nîmes*. Paris: Editions du Centre National de la Recherche Scientifique, 1979.

Anderson, James C., Jr., "Domitian, the Argiletum and the Temple of Peace," *AJA* 86 (1982): 101–10.

The Historical Topography of the Imperial Fora. Brussels: Latomus, 1984.

Roman Architecture and Society. Baltimore: Johns Hopkins University Press, 1997.

Andrén, Arvid, *Architectural Terracottas from Etrusco-Italic Temples*, 2 vols. Lund: Haran Ohlsson, 1940.

Andreussi, Maddalena, "'Murus Servii Tullii:' Mura repubblicane," *LTUR*, vol. 3, 319–24.

Arce, Javier, "Arcus Titi (Via Sacra)," in *LTUR*, vol. 1, 109–11.

Archimedes, "De sphera et cylindro," in *Archimedis opera omnia*, vol. 1. Ed. J. L. Heiberg. Leipzig: n.p., 1910–1915, 229ff.

Arendt, Hannah, "What Was Authority?" in *Authority*. Ed. Carl J. Friedrich. Cambridge: Harvard University Press, 1958.

Arnold, William Thomas, *Studies of Roman Imperialism*. Manchester: University of Manchester Press, 1906.

Arnott, Peter D., *The Romans and Their World*. New York: St. Martin's Press, 1970.

Ascione, Enrico, *Roma 1450–1750*. Rome: Fratelli Palombi Editori, 1980.

Ashby, Thomas, "Addenda and Corrigenda to 'Sixteenth Century Drawings of Roman Buildings Attributed to Andreas Coner,'" *PBSR* 6 (1913): 202–04.

"Sixteenth-Century Drawings of Roman Buildings Attributed to Andreas Coner," *PBSR* 2 (1904): 46–7.

Auer, Hans, *Der Tempel des Vesta und das Haus der Vestalinnen am Forum Romanum*. Vienna: F. Tempsky, 1888.

Badian, Ernst, *Roman Imperialism in the Late Republic*. Pretoria: University of South Africa, 1967.

Bak, Janos M., ed., *Coronations: Medieval and Early Modern Monarchic Ritual*. Berkeley: University of California Press, 1990.

Baker, George Philip, *Augustus: The Golden Age of Rome*. London: Grayson and Grayson, 1937.

Balsdon, J. P. V. D., *The Emperor Gaius (Caligula)*. Oxford: Clarendon Press, 1964.

Banks, Edgar J., "The Seven Wonders of the Ancient World: The Mausoleum of Halicarnassus," *AA* 5 (March 1917): 137–41.

"The Seven Wonders of the Ancient World: The Temple of Diana at Ephesus," *AA* 5 (January 1917): 13–19.

Banti, Luisa, *Etruscan Cities and Their Culture*. Trans. Erika Bizzarri. Berkeley and Los Angeles: University of California Press, 1973.

Barattolo, Andrea, "Nuove ricerche sull'architettura del Tempio di Venere e di Roma in età Adrianea," *RömMitt* 80 (1973): 243–69.

"Sulla decorazione delle celle del Tempio di Venere e di Roma all'epoca di Adriano," *BullCom* 84 (1974–1975): 133–48.

"Il Tempio di Venere e di Roma: un tempio 'Greco' nell'urbe," *RömMitt* 85 (1978): 397–410.

Barker, Graeme, and Tom Rasmussen, *The Etruscans*. Malden, MA: Blackwell, 1998.

Barrett, Anthony A., *Caligula: The Corruption of Power*. New Haven: Yale University Press, 1989.

Barroero, Liliana, et al., *Via dei Fori Imperiali: La zona archeologica di Roma: Urbanistica, beni artistici e politica culturale*. Venice: Marsilia, 1983.

Barrow, Reginald Haynes, *The Romans*. Baltimore: Penguin Books, 1968.

Bartoli, Alfonso, "Il Tempio di Antonio e Faustina," *MonLinc* 23 (1914): 949–74.

Barton, Ian M., "Capitoline Temples, in Italy and the Provinces, especially Africa," in *ANRW*, vol. 2, 12.1 259–333.

"Religious Buildings," in *Roman Public Buildings*. Ed. Ian M. Barton. Exeter: University of Exeter Press, 1995.

Bauer, Heinrich, "Augustusforum, Hallen und Exedren," in *Kaiser Augustus*, 184–9.

"Il Foro Transitorio e il Tempio di Giano," *RendPontAcc* 49 (1976–1977): 117–49.

"Kaiserfora und Janustempel," *RömMitt* 84 (1977): 302–3.

"Das Kapitel des Apollo Palatinus-Tempels," *RömMitt* 76 (1969): 183–204.

"Porticus Absidata," *RömMitt* 90 (1983): 111–84.

and Chiara Morselli, "Forum Nervae," *LTUR*, vol. 2, 307–8.

Beard, Mary, John North, and Simon Price, *Religions of Rome: A History*, 2 vols. Cambridge: Cambridge University Press, 1999.

Beltrami, Luca, *Il Pantheon rivendicato ad Adriano*. Milan: Tipografia Umberto Allegretti, 1898.

Bender, Henry V., *The Civilization of Ancient Rome: An Archaeological Perspective*. Lanham, NY: University Press of America, 1985.

Bennett, Julian, *Trajan: Optimus Princeps*. London: Routledge, 1997.

Bianchi, Elisabetta, "I bolli laterizi del Foro di Traiano: Il catalogo del Bloch e rinvenimenti delle campagne di scavo 1991–1997 e 1998–2000," *BullCom* 102 (2001): 83–120.

Bigot, P., "Le Temple de Jupiter Ultor et la Vigne Barberini," *BullCom* 39 (1911): 80–5.

Birley, Anthony K., *Hadrian: The Restless Emperor*. London: Routledge, 1997.

Bittner, Herbert, and Ernest Nash, eds., *Rome*. Chicago: Henry Regnery, 1950.

Blagg, T. F. C., "Apollodorus of Damascus," *DA*, vol. 2, 227.

Blake, Marion Elizabeth, *Ancient Roman Construction in Italy from the Prehistoric Period to Augustus*. Washington, DC: Carnegie Institution, 1947.

Roman Construction in Italy from Nerva through the Antonines. Ed. Doris Taylor Bishop. Philadelphia: American Philosophical Society, 1973.

Blanckenhagen, Henri von, *Flavische Architektur und ihre Dekoration, untersucht am Nervaforum*. Berlin: Verlag Gebr. Mann, 1940.

"The Imperial Fora," *JSAH* 13 (1954): 23–6.

Bloch, Raymond, "Le départ des Étrusques de Rome et la dédicace du Temple de Jupiter Capitolin," *CARI* (1961): 62–70.

The Origins of Ancient Rome. New York: Praeger, 1960.

Boak, Arthur E. R., *A History of Rome to 565 A.D.* New York: Macmillan, 1943.

Boatwright, Mary Taliaferro, *Hadrian and the Cities of the Roman Empire*. Princeton: Princeton University Press, 2000.

Hadrian and the City of Rome. Princeton: Princeton University Press, 1987.

Boëthius, Axel, *Etruscan and Early Roman Architecture*. Baltimore: Penguin Books, 1978.

The Golden House of Nero: Some Aspects of Roman Architecture. Ann Arbor: University of Michigan Press, 1960.

"Veteris capitoli humilia tecta," *ActaAArtH* 1 (1962): 27–33.

and J. B. Ward-Perkins, *Etruscan and Roman Architecture*. Baltimore: Penguin Books, 1970.

et al., *Etruscan Culture, Land and People*. Trans. Nils G. Sahlin. New York: Columbia University Press; Malmo, Sweden: Alhem, 1962.

Bonardi, Ermete, "Le origini del Pantheon," *Forma Urbis* 1 (June 1996): 14–23.

Boni, Giacomo, *Aedes Vestae: Estratto della Nuova Antologia*. Rome: Direzione della Nuova Antologia, 1900.

"Esplorazione del Forum Ulpium," *NSc* (1909): 361–410.

"Nuove scoperte nella città e nel suburbio: Il sacrario di Vesta," *NSc* (1900): 159–91.

Boring, William A., "What Is Precedent Doing to American Architecture?" *JAIA* 12 (June 9, 1924): 260–3.

Bowder, Diana, ed., *Who Was Who in the Roman World*. New York: Washington Square Books, 1980.

Boyd, M. J., "The Porticoes of Metellus and Octavia and Their Two Temples," *PBSR* 21 (1953): 152–9.

Bradshaw, H. C., "Praeneste: A Study for Its Restoration," *PBSR*, 9 (1920): 233–62.

Brilliant, Richard, *The Arch of Septimius Severus in the Roman Forum*. Rome: n.p., 1967.

"Arcus: Septimius Severus (Forum)" *LTUR*, vol. 1, 103–5.

Gesture and Rank in Roman Art. New Haven: Yale University Press, 1963.

Roman Art from the Republic to Constantine. London: Phaidon Press, 1974.

Brown, Frank E., *Cosa: The Making of a Roman Town*. Ann Arbor: University of Michigan Press, ca. 1980.

Cosa I: History and Topography. Rome: American Academy in Rome, 1951.

Cosa II: The Temples of the Arx. Rome: American Academy in Rome, 1960.

"Hadrianic Architecture," in *Essays in Memory of K. Lehmann*. Ed. L. F. Sandler. New York: n.p., n.d.

"The Regia," *MAAR*, 12 (1935): 67–88.

"Vitruvius," in *MEA*, vol. 4, 335.

Brunt, P. A., *The Fall of the Roman Republic and Related Essays*. Oxford: Clarendon Press, 1988.

Buchan, John, *Augustus*. London: Hodder and Stoughton, 1937.

Buchner, Edmund, *Die Sonnenuhr des Augustus: Nachdruck aus RM 1976 und 1980 und Nachtrag über die Ausgrabung 1980/1981*. Mainz-am-Rhein: Verlag Philipp von Zabern, 1982.

"Horologium Augusti," *LTUR*, vol. 3, 35–7.

"Horologium Solarium Augusti: Vorbericht über die Ausgrabungen 1979/80," *RömMitt* 87 (1980): 355–73.

"Solarium Augusti und Ara Pacis," *RömMitt* 83 (1976): 319–65.

Bunsen, Christian K. J., *Les forums de Rome: restaurés et expliqués*. Rome, n.p., 1837.

Buzzetti, Carlo, "Claudius, Divus, Templum (Reg. II)," *LTUR*, vol. 1, 277–8.

"Naumachia Traiani," *LTUR*, vol. 3, 338–9.

"Portunus, Aedes," *LTUR*, vol. 5, 153–4.

Cafiero, Maria Laura, *Ara Pacis Augustae*. Rome: Fratelli Palombi Editori for Comune di Roma. Assessorato alla Cultura, Centro di Coordinamento Didattico, 1989.

Caiola, Antonio Federico, Maria Antonietta Tomei, and Françoise Villedieu, "Ex Vigna Barberini: Indagini archeologiche e restauri," in *ArchGiub*, 158–61.

Calzini Gysens, Jaqueline, and Filippo Coarelli, "Sol, Templum," *LTUR*, vol. 4, 331–2.
Camp, John M., *The Archaeology of Athens*. New Haven: Yale University Press, 2001.
Campbell, J. B., *The Emperor and the Roman Army: 31 B.C.–A.D. 235*. Oxford: Clarendon Press, 1984.
Canina, Luigi, *Architettura antica*, 2 vols. Rome: Canina, 1830–1840.
Cenni storici e ricerche iconografiche sul Teatro di Pompeo. Rome: n.p., 1835.
Gli edifizi di Roma Antica, 2 vols. Rome: Canina, 1848–1851.
Esposizione storica e topografica del Foro Romano e sue adiacenze. Rome: Tipi dello stesso Canino, 1845.
Esposizione storica e topografica del Foro Romano e sue adiacenze. Bologna: Arnaldo Forni, 1973.
Esposizione topografica di Roma antica: Distanta nelle tre prime epoche autoromana, reale e consolare. Rome: Tipi dello stesso Canino, 1845.
Indicazione dei principali edifizi di Roma antica: estratta dalla terza parte dell'architettura romana. Rome: Mercuri e Robaglia, 1830.
Cannadine, David, and Simon Price, eds., *Rituals of Royalty: Power and Ceremonial in Traditional Societies*. Cambridge: n.p., 1987.
Caraffa, Guido, *Il Tempio detto di Vesta nel Foro Boario*. Rome: V. Ferri Editore, 1948.
Carandini, A., "'Domus et insulae' sulla pendici settentrionali del Palatino," *BullCom* 91 (1986): 263–74.
Carettoni, Gianfilippo, "Die Bauten des Augustus auf dem Palatin," in *Kaiser Augustus*, 263–7.
"Roma – le costruzioni di Augusto e il Tempio di Apollo sul Palatino," *ArchLaz* 1 (1978): 67–74.
Carpiceci, A. C., and L. Pennino, *Paestum and Velia Today and 2500 Years Ago*. Salerno: Edition Matonti, 1989.
Carroll, Diane Lee, "Dating the Foot-Powered Loom: The Coptic Evidence," *AJA* 89 (1985): 168–73.
Cary, Max, *A History of Rome down to the Reign of Constantine*. London: Macmillan, 1938.
and Howard H. Scullard, *A History of Rome: Down to the Reign of Constantine*. London: Macmillan, 1979.
Cassatella, Alessandro, "Antoninus, Divus et Faustina, Diva, Aedes, Templum," *LTUR*, vol. 1, 46–7.
"Venus et Roma, Aedes, Templum," *LTUR*, vol. 5, 121–3.
and Stefania Pensabene, "Restituzione dell'impianto Adrianeo del Tempio di Venere e Roma," *ArchLaz* 10 (1990): 54.
Castagnoli, Ferdinando, *L'Angolo meridionale del Foro della Pace*. Spoleto and Rome: n.p., 1959.
"Campo Marzio," *Capitolium* 35.7 (1960): 93–113.
"Il Campo Marzio nell'antichità," *MAL* 8 (1947): 93–193.
Foro Romano. Milano: Domus, 1957.
Orthogonal Town Planning in Antiquity. Trans. Victor Caliandro. Cambridge: MIT Press, 1971.
"Peripteros sine postico," *RömMitt* 62 (1955): 139–43.
"Porticus Philippi," in *Città e architettura*, 93–118.
Progetto per lo scavo di un settore dei Fori di Cesare e di Nerva. Rome: De Luca, 1982.
Studi di urbanistica antica. Rome: n.p., 1966.
"Il Tempio dei Penati e la Velia," *RivFil* 74 (1946): 157–66.
"Sul tempio 'italico,'" *RömMitt* 73–74 (1966–1967): 14.
"Il tempio romano: questioni di terminologia e di typologia," *PBSR* 52 (1984): 7–9.
Topografia e urbanistica di Roma antica. Bologna: Licinio Cappelli Editore, 1969.
"Topografia romana e tradizione storiografica su Roma arcaica," *ArchCl* 25–6 (1973–1974): 123–31.
and Lucos Cozza, "L'angelo meridionale del Foro della Pace," *BullCom* 76 (1956–1958): 119–42.
Cecamore, Claudia, "Apollo e Vesta sul Palatino fra Augusto e Vespasiano," *BullCom* 96 (1994–1995): 9–32.
Chisholm, Kitty, and John Ferguson, *Rome: The Augustan Age*. Oxford: Oxford University Press, 1981.
Ciancio Rossetto, Paola, "Indagini e restauri nel Campo Marzio meridionale: Teatro di Marcello, Portico d'Ottavia, Circo Flaminio, Porto Tiberino," *ArchLaz* 12 (1995): 93–101.
"Theatrum Marcelli," *LTUR*, vol. 5, 31–5.
Cipollone, Mafalda, "Hadrianus, Divus, Templum; Hadrianeum," *LTUR*, vol. 3, 7–8.
Cipriano, Palmira, *Templum*. Rome: Università la Sapienza, 1983.
Claridge, Amanda, "Hadrian's Column of Trajan," *JRA* 6 (1993): 5–22.
Oxford Archaeological Guides: Rome. New York: Oxford University Press, 1998.
"Roman Methods of Fluting Corinthian Columns and Pilasters," in *Città e architettura*, 119–28.
Coarelli, Filippo, *Il Campo Marzio dalle origini alla fine della Repubblica*. Rome: Quasar, 1997.
"Il Campo Marzio occidentale. Storia e topografia," *Mélanges de l'École Française de Rome* 89 (1977): 807–46.
"Curia Hostilia," *LTUR*, vol. 1, 331–2.
Il Foro Boario dalle origini alla fine della Repubblica. Rome: Edizioni Quasar, 1992.
"Il Foro in età arcaica: Regia, Via Sacra, Comizio," *ArchLaz* 4 (1981): 241–8.
Il Foro Romano, 2 vols. Rome: Edizioni Quasar, 1983.
"Forum Holitorium," *LTUR*, vol. 2, 299.
Guida archeologica di Roma. Milan: Mondadori, 1975.
"Heliogabalus, Templum; Heliogabalium," *LTUR*, vol. 3, 10–11.
"Hercules Olivarius," *LTUR*, vol. 3, 20.
"Hercules Victor, Aedes (ad Portam Trigeminam)," *LTUR*, vol. 3, 22–3.
"Ianus, Aedes (Apud Forum Holitorium, ad Theatrum Marcelli)," *LTUR*, vol. 3, 90–1.
"Iuno Sospita (in Foro Holitorio), Aedes," *LTUR*, vol. 3, 128–9.
"Iuppiter Feretrius," *LTUR* 3, 135–6.
"Latiaris Collis," *LTUR*, vol. 3, 177.
Lazio: Guide archeologiche Laterza. Rome: Laterza, 1984.
"Moneta in Arce," *LTUR*, vol. 3, 279–80.
"Il Pantheon, l'apoteosi di Augusto e l'apoteosi di Romolo," in *CARI*, 41–6.
"Pax, Templum," *LTUR*, vol. 4, 67.
"Pons Aemilius," *LTUR*, vol. 4, 106–7.
"Pons Sublicius," *LTUR*, vol. 4, 112–13.
"Public Building in Rome between the Second Punic War and Sulla," *PBSR* 45 (1977): 1–23.
Roma: Guide archeologiche Laterza. Rome: Laterza, 1988.
"Roma Quadrata," *LTUR*, vol. 4, 207–9.
"Rostra (età repubblicana)," *LTUR*, vol. 4, 212–13.
I santuari del Lazio in età repubblicana. Rome: Nuova Italia Scientifica, 1987.

"Saturnus, Aedes," *LTUR*, vol. 4, 234–6.
"Spes, Aedes," *LTUR*, vol. 4, 336–7.
"Il Tempio di Bellona," *BullCom* 80 (1968): 37–72.
and Luisanna Usai, *Guida Archeologica di Roma*. Rome: Mondadori, 1974.
et al., *L'Area Sacra di Largo Argentina I*. Rome: X Ripartizione antichità belle arti e problemi di cultura, 1981.
Cody, Jane M., "New Evidence for the Republican 'Aedes Vestae,'" *AJA* 77 (1973): 43–50.
Colini, Antonio M., "Aedes Veiovis inter arcem et Capitolium," *BullCom* 70 (1944): 5–56.
"Il Foro di Augusto in Roma," in *Quaderni de 'La ricerca scientifica' 100: un decennio di ricerche archeologiche* 2 (1978): 443–5.
"Foro di Cesare," *BullCom* 61 (1933): 262–4.
"Forum Pacis," *BullCom* 65 (1937): 7–40.
"Indagini sui frontoni dei templi di Roma," *BullCom* 51 (1924): 299–347.
"Portus Tiberinus," *QArchEtr* 12 (1986): 157.
"Scavi dei Fori Imperiale," *BullCom* 61 (1933): 262–4.
"Scavo del Foro Transitorio," *BullCom* 62 (1934): 165–6.
"Scoperte presso Piazza Campitelli," *Capitolium* 16 (1941): 11, 385–93.
"Storia e topografia del Celio nell'antichità," *MemPontAcc* 7 (1944): 41–2.
Il Tempio di Apollo, *BullArchGov* 68 (1940): 9–41.
Il Tempio di Veiove; Aedes Veiovis inter arcem et Capitolium. Rome: Governatorato, 1943.
"Templum Apollinis Sosiani," *BullCom* 66 (1938): 259–60.
and Carlo Buzzetti, "Aedes Portuni in Portu Tiberino," *BullCom* 91 (1986): 7–30.
et al., "Area Sacra di S. Omobono," in *Lazio arcaico e mondo greco*. Rome: n.p., 1977, 9–61.
Colonna, Giovanni, "Etruria e Lazio nell'età dei Tarquini," in *ELA*, 64–6.
ed., *Santuari d'Etruria*. Milan: Electa, 1985.
"Tarquinio Prisco e il Tempio di Giove Capitolino," *La Parola del Passato* 36 (1981): 41–59.
Cornell, Tim J., *The Beginnings of Rome: Italy and Rome from the Bronze Age to the Punic Wars (c. 1000–264 B.C.)*. London and New York: Routledge, 1995.
"The City of Rome in the Middle Republic," in *Ancient Rome*, 42–60.
Coulton, J. J., *Ancient Greek Architects at Work: Problems of Structure and Design*. Ithaca: Cornell University Press, 1977.
The Architectural Development of the Greek Stoa. Oxford: Clarendon Press, 1976.
"Hermogenes of Priene," *MEA*, vol. 2, 359–61.
"Towards Understanding Greek Temple Design: General Considerations," in *Annual of the British School of Archaeology at Athens* 70 (1975): 66–74.
Coussin, J.-A., "Le Temple di Vesta nel Foro Boario," in *Restaurations des monuments antiques*. Paris: n.p., 1879.
Corso, Antonio, "Vitruvius and Attic Monuments," *The Annual of the British School in Athens* 92 (1997): 373–400.
Cozza, Lucos, "Le tegole di marmo del Pantheon," in *CARI*, 109–18.
Tempio di Adriano. Rome: De Luca Editore, 1932.
Craven, Brian, *The Punic Wars*. London: Weidenfeld and Nicolson, 1980.
Crawford, Michael, *The Roman Republic*. Cambridge: Harvard University Press, 1993.
Cressedi, G., "Il Foro Boario e il Velabro," *BullCom* 89 (1984): 249–96.
Cresy, Edward, and G. L. Taylor, *Architectural Antiquities of Rome*. London: G. L. Taylor and E. Cresy, 1822.
Cromer, Evelyn Basing, *Ancient and Modern Imperialism*. London: J. Murray, 1910.
Crozzoli, Aite L., "I tre templi del Foro Olitorio," *MemPontAcc* 13 (1981), tav. 1.
Curtis, Charles D., "Roman Monumental Arches," *Supplement Papers American School of Classical Studies in Rome* 2 (1908), 49.
Dalmazzoni, Angelo, *L'antiquario o sia la guida de forestieri*. Rome: Angelo Dalmazzoni, 1804.
D'Ambra, Eve, *Private Lives, Imperial Virtues: The Frieze of the Forum Transitorium in Rome*. Princeton: Princeton University Press, 1993.
Darwall-Smith, Robin Haydon, *Emperors and Architecture: A Study of Flavian Rome*. Brussels: Latomus, 1996.
Davies, Paul, David Hemsoll, and Mark Wilson Jones, "The Pantheon: Triumph of Rome or Triumph of Compromise?" *AH* 10 (June 1987): 133–53.
De Agostino, Alfredo, *Veio: La Storia – I Ruderi – Le Terracotte*. Rome: Istituto Poligrafico dello Stato, 1965.
De Angeli, Stefano, "Iuppiter Optimus Maximus Capitolinus, aedes (fasi tardo-repubblicane e di età imperiale)," *LTUR*, vol. 3, 148–53.
Templum Divi Vespasiani. Rome: De Luca Edizioni d'Arte, 1992.
"Vespasianus, Divus, Templum," *LTUR*, vol. 5, 124.
De Caprariis, Francesca, "Matidia, Templum," *LTUR*, vol. 3, 233.
De Fine Licht, Kjeld, *The Rotunda in Rome: A Study of Hadrian's Pantheon*. Copenhagen: Jutland Archeological Society, 1968.
De George, Richard T., *The Nature and Limits of Authority*. Lawrence: University of Kansas Press, 1985.
Degrassi, Attilio, "Esistette sul Palatino un Tempio di Vesta?" *RömMitt* 62 (1955): 144–57.
Inscriptiones Latinae: Liberae rei publicae. Florence: La Nuova Italia, 1963.
De Grummond, Nancy Thomson, ed., *An Encyclopedia of the History of Classical Archaeology*. Westport, CT: Greenwood Press, 1996.
DeLaine, Janet, "Building the Eternal City: The Construction Industry of Imperial Rome," in *Ancient Rome*, 119–41.
"Rabirius," *DA*, vol. 25, 835.
Delbrueck, Richard, *Hellenistische Bauten in Latium*, 3 vols. Strassburg: Karl J. Trubner, 1907.
Del Bufalo, Edmondo, *La Via Imperiale e il suo significato storico e politico*. Spoleto: Istituto di Studi Romani, 1940.
Del Monte, Claudia, "Tempio di Venere e Roma: Indagini e restauri," in *ArchGiub*, 164–9.
De Maria, Sandro, *Gli archi onorari di Roma e dell'Italia romana*. Rome: 'L'Erma' di Bretschneider, 1988.
De Nuccio, Matilde, "Tempio di Bellona: Studi preliminari," *ArchLaz* 12.1 (1995): 71–7.
Desgodetz, A., *Les édifices antiques de Rome*. Paris, n.p., 1779.
D'Espouy, Hector, ed., *Fragments from Greek and Roman Architecture: The Classical American Edition of Hector d'Espouy's Plates*. New York: Norton, 1981.
Monuments Antiques, vol. 2. Paris: Massin, n.d., 103–5.

DeWaele, Jos. A., "Satricum nel VI e V secolo A.C.: l'architettura templare," *ArchLaz* 4 (1981): 310–16.
Dickinson, John, *Death of a Republic: Politics and Political Thought at Rome 59–44 B.C.* New York: Macmillan, 1963.
Di Mino, Maria Rita, "Terracotte architettoniche dalla zona del monumento a Vittorio Emmanuele," *ArchLaz* 4 (1981): 119–25.
Dinsmoor, William Bell, *The Architecture of Ancient Greece.* New York: Norton, 1975.
Donaldson, Thomas L., *Ancient Architecture on Greek and Roman Coins and Medals.* Chicago: Argonaut, 1966.
Dorey, T. A., and Dudley, D. R., *Rome against Carthage.* London: Secker and Warburg, 1971.
Doxiades, C. A., *Architectural Space in Ancient Greece.* Trans. Jaqueline Tyrwhitt. Cambridge: MIT Press, 1972. (Originally published in German in 1937.)
Dudley, Donald R., *The Civilization of Rome.* New York and Toronto: New American Library, 1962.
The Romans. London: Hutchinson, 1970.
Urbs Roma: A Source Book of Classical Texts on the City and Its Monuments. London: Phaidon Press, 1967.
Dumbabin, T. J., *The Western Greeks.* London: Oxford University Press, 1948.
Dumézil, Georges, *Archaic Roman Religion,* vol. 1. Trans. Philip Krapp. Chicago: University of Chicago Press, 1970.
Dupont, Florence, *Daily Life in Ancient Rome.* Oxford and Cambridge, MA: Blackwell, 1993.
Dutert, Ferdinand, *Le Forum romain et les forums de Jules César, d'Auguste, de Vespasien, de Nerva et de Trajan.* Paris: A. Levy, 1876.
Dwyer, Eugene, "Vitruvius," in *DA,* vol. 32, 632–6.
Dyer, Thomas H., *A History of the City of Rome: Its Structures and Monuments.* London: Longmans, Green, 1865.
Earl, Donald, *The Age of Augustus.* London: Elek Books, 1968.
Eckstein, Arthur M., *Senate and General: Individual Decision Making and Roman Foreign Relations, 264–194 B.C.* Berkeley: University of California Press, 1987.
Edwards, Douglas, "Power and Politics: Jewish Defeats by the Romans in Iconography and Josephus," in *Diaspora Jews and Judaism: Essays in Honor of, and in Dialogue with, A. Thomas Kraabel.* Ed. J. A. Overman and R. S. MacLennan. Atlanta: Scholars Press, 1992, 293–310.
Religion and Power: Pagans, Jews, and Christians in the Greek East. New York and Oxford: Oxford University Press, 1996.
England, E. B., ed., *The Laws of Plato.* Manchester: University of Manchester Press; London: Longmans Green, 1921.
Fagerlind, Lars, "The Transformations of the Corinthian Capital in Rome and Pompeii during the Later Republican Period," in *Corolla archaeologica principi hereditario regni sueciae Gustavo Adolpho.* Lund: C. W. K. Gleerup, 1932, 118–31.
Fasolo, Furio, and Giorgio Gullini, *Il santuario della Fortuna Primigenia a Palestrina.* Rome: University of Rome, Istituto di Archeologia, 1953.
Fauno, Lucio, *De antiquitatibus urbis Romae (Delle antichità della città di Roma).* Venice: Michele Tramezzino, 1548.
Favro, Diane, "Pater urbis: Augustus as City Father of Rome," *JSAH* 51 (March 1992): 61.
The Urban Image of Augustan Rome. New York: Cambridge University Press, 1996.
Fea, Carlo, *Descrizione di Roma e suoi contorni abbellita della pianta e delle vedute le più interessanti della medesima.* Rome: Crispino Puccinella, 1824.
L'integrità del Pantheon rivendicata a Marco Agrippa. Rome: Francesco Eourlié, 1820.
Fears, J. R., "The Theology of Victory at Rome," *ANRW* 2 (1981): 827–948.
Ferguson, John, *The Religions of the Roman Empire.* New York: Thames and Hudson, 1970.
Ferguson, William Scott, *Greek Imperialism.* London: Constable, 1913.
Ferroni, Angela Maria, "Concordia, Aedes, *LTUR,* vol. 1, 316–17.
Fidenzoni, Paolo, *Il Teatro di Marcello.* Rome: Edizioni Liber, ca. 1960.
Fiechter, Ernst R., "Der Ionische Tempel am Ponte Rotto in Rom," *RömMitt,* 21 (1906): 220–79.
Finocchi, Paola, "Il 'Templum' di Iuppiter Latiaris sul Mons Albanus," *ArchLaz* 4 (1980): 156–8.
Flaccomio, Gabriella, Emilia Talamo, et al., *Il 'Tempio di Romolo' al Foro Romano.* Rome: Multigrafica Editrice, 1981.
Fowler, Warde W., "The Idea of the Man God," in *Roman Ideas of Deity in the Last Century before the Christian Era.* London: Macmillan, 1914, 81–106.
Frank, Tenney, *An Economic History of Rome.* London: Jonathan Cape, 1927.
"The First and Second Temples of Castor at Rome," *MAAR* 5 (1925): 79–102.
"Roman Buildings of the Republic: An Attempt to Date Them from Their Materials," *MAAR* 3 (1924), 1–136.
Roman Imperialism. New York: Macmillan, 1914.
Rome and Italy of the Empire. Baltimore: Johns Hopkins University Press, 1940.
Frazer, Alfred K., "Hadrian's Teatro Marittimo at Tivoli, and Pantheon," in *Architectural Studies in Memory of Richard Krautheimer.* Ed. Cecil L. Striker. Mainz-am-Rhein: Verlag Philipp von Zabern, 1996, 77–8.
Frederiksen, Martin, *Campania.* Ed. Nicholas Purcell. Rome: British School at Rome, 1984.
Frothingham, A. L., *A Revised List of Roman Memorial and Triumphal Arches.* Norwood, MA: Norwood Press, 1904.
Frutaz, Amato Pietro, *Le piante di Roma,* 3 vols. Rome: Istituto di Studi Romani, 1962.
Gaggiotti, Marcello, et al., *Umbria, Marche: Guide archeologiche Laterza.* Rome and Bari: Giuseppe Laterza, 1980.
Galinsky, Karl, *Augustan Culture: An Interpretive Introduction.* Princeton: Princeton University Press, 1996.
Gamucci, Bernardo, *Le antichità della città di Roma: raccolte sotto brevità da diversi antichi e moderni scrittori.* Venice: Appresso Giovanni Varisco, 1569.
Gansey, Peter, and Richard Saller, *The Roman Empire: Economy, Society and Culture.* London: Gerald Duckworth, 1987.
Ganzert, Joachim, *Der Mars-Ultor-Tempel auf dem Augustusforum in Rom. Beiheft Erläuterungen.* Mainz-am-Rhein: Verlag Philipp von Zabern, 1996.
and Valentin Kockel, "Augustusforum und Mars-Ultor-Tempel," in *Kaiser Augustus,* 149–72.
Garnsey, P. D. A., and C. R. Whittaker, eds., *Imperialism in the Ancient World: The Cambridge University Research Seminar in Ancient History.* New York: Cambridge University Press, 1978.

Garzetti, Albino, *From Tiberius to the Antonines: A History of the Roman Empire AD 14–192*. Trans. J. R. Foster. London: Methuen, 1974.

Gasparri, Carlo, *Aedes Concordiae Augustae*. Rome: Istituto di Studi Romani, 1979.

Gatteschi, Giuseppe, *Restauri della Roma Imperiale*. Genoa: Tipi della S.A.I.G.A. Barabine and Grave, 1924.

Gatti, Emanuele, "Saepta Julia," *LTUR*, vol. 4, 228–9.

Gatti, Guglielmo, "La ricostruzione dell'Arco di Augusto al Foro Romano," *RendPontAcc* 21 (1945–1946): 105–22.

Gaudet, Julien, "Mémoire de la restauration du Forum de Trajan," Manuscript nos. 207 (text), 2748 (drawings). Paris: École des Beaux-Arts, 1867.

Geertz, Clifford, "Centers, Kings and Charisma: Reflections on the Symbolics of Power," in *Culture and Its Creators: Essays in Honor of E. Shils*. Ed. J. Ben-David and T. N. Clark. Chicago: University of Chicago Press, 1977, 150–71.

The Interpretation of Cultures: Selected Essays. London: Fontana Press, 1993.

Gelzer, Matthias, *Caesar: Politician and Statesman*. Trans. Peter Needham. Oxford: Basil Blackwell, 1968.

Gibbon, Edward, *The Decline and Fall of the Roman Empire*. Baltimore: Penguin Books, 1980.

Giglioli, Giulio Quirino, "Le copie romane delle 'cariatidi' dell'eretteo nelle 'porticus' del Foro di Augusto," *RömMitt* 62 (1955): 153–9.

Giuliani, Cairoli F., "Architettura e tecnica edilizia," in *Roma repubblicana fra il 509 e il 270 A.C.* Ed. Patrizio Pensabene. Rome: Edizioni Quasar, 1982, 29–31.

Forma Italiae: Tibur. Rome: De Luca Editore, 1970.

"Mercati e Foro Traiano: Un fatto di attribuzione," *QuadIstStArch* 10 (1987): 25–8.

and Patrizia Verduchi, *L'area centrale del Foro Romano*. Florence: n.p., 1987.

"Basilica Iulia," *LTUR*, vol. 1, 177–8.

Gjerstad, Einar, "A proposito della ricostruzione del tempio arcaico di Giove Capitolino in Roma. Risposta ad Axel Boëthius," *ActaAArtH* 1 (1962): 35–40.

Early Rome: Fortifications, Domestic Architecture, Sanctuaries, Stratigraphic Excavations, vol. 3. Lund: C. W. K. Gleerup, 1960.

Early Rome: Synthesis of Archaeological Evidence, vol. 4. Lund: C. W. K. Gleerup, 1966.

Early Rome: Historical Survey, vol. 6. Lund: Berlingska Boktryckeriet, 1973.

"The Etruscans and Rome in Archaic Times," in *Etruscan Culture: Land and People*. Trans. Nils G. Sahlin. New York: Columbia University Press; Malmö, Sweden: Alhem, 1962.

"Die Ursprüngsgeschichte der römischen Kaiserfora," *OpArch* 3 (1944): 40–72

Gleason, Kathryn L., "'Porticus Pompeiana:' A New Perspective on the First Public Park of Ancient Rome," *JGH* 14 (January–March 1994): 13–27.

Godfrey, Paul, and David Hemsoll, "The Pantheon: Temple or Rotunda?" in *Pagan Gods and Shrines of the Roman Empire*. Ed. Martin Henig and Anthony King. Oxford: Oxford University Committee for Archaeology, 1986, 195–209.

Goldsberry, Mary A., *Sicily and Its Cities in Hellenistic and Roman Times*. Ph.D. diss., University of North Carolina, 1973.

Goldsworthy, Adrian, *The Punic Wars*. London: Cassell, 2000.

Goodyear, William Henry, *Greek Refinements: Studies in Temperamental Architecture*. New Haven: Yale University Press; London: Oxford University Press, 1912.

Graindor, Paul, *Athènes sous Hadrien*. Le Caire: Imprimerie Nationale, Boulac, n.d.

Granger, Frank, "Greek Origins of the Pantheon," *JRIBA* 40 (1933): 57–61.

Grant, Michael, *The Antonines: The Roman Empire in Transition*. London and New York: Routledge, 1994.

Cleopatra. London: Weidenfeld and Nicolson, 1972.

History of Rome. New York: Charles Scribner's Sons, 1978.

Julius Caesar. London: Weidenfeld and Nicolson, 1969.

Nero: Emperor in Revolt. New York: American Heritage Press, 1970.

The Roman Forum. London: Weidenfeld and Nicolson, 1970.

Greco, Emanuele, *Magna Grecia: Guide archeologiche Laterza*. Rome and Bari: Giuseppe Laterza and Sons, 1981.

and Dinu Theodorescu, Collection de l'École Française de Rome, *Poseidonia – Paestum*, 3 vols. Rome: École Française de Rome, 1980.

Greenhalgh, Peter, *Pompey: The Republican Prince*. London: Weidenfeld and Nicolson, 1981.

Gregorovius, Ferdinand, *The Emperor Hadrian: A Picture of the Graeco-Roman World in His Time*. Trans. Mary E. Robinson. London and New York: Macmillan, 1898.

Griffin, Miriam T., *Nero: The End of a Dynasty*. New Haven: Yale University Press, 1984.

Grimal, Pierre, *The Civilization of Rome*. Trans. W. S. Maguiness. London: Allen and Unwin, 1963.

Dictionary of Classical Mythology. Trans. A. R. Maxwell-Hyslop. Oxford: Blackwell, 1966.

Roman Cities. Trans. G. Michael Woloch. Madison: University of Wisconsin Press, 1983.

Gromort, Georges, *Choix d'éléments empruntés à l'architecture classique*, 2 vols. Paris: A. Vincent and Company, 1927.

Gros, Pierre, "Apollo Palatinus," *LTUR*, vol. 1, 54–7.

L'architecture romaine du début du IIIème siècle av. J.-C. à la fin du Haut-Empire I: Les monuments publics. Paris: Picard, 1996.

"Aurea Templa: Recherches sur l'architecture religieuse de Rome à l'époque d'Auguste," *BEFAR* 231 (1976): 221–6.

"Hermodorus et Vitruve," *MEFRA* 85 (1973): 137–61.

"Iulius, Divus, Aedes," *LTUR*, vol. 3, 116–19.

"Iuppiter Tonans, *LTUR*, vol. 3, 159–60.

"Theatrum Pompei," *LTUR*, vol. 5, 35–8.

and Jean P. Adam, "Temple ionique du Forum Boarium: Sondage Sud-Est," *BullCom* 91 (1986): 31–4.

Grossi, Olindo, "The Forum of Julius Caesar and the Temple of Venus Genetrix." *MAAR* 13 (1936): 215–20.

Gruen, Erich S., *Culture and National Identity in Ancient Rome*. Ithaca: Cornell University Press, 1992.

The Hellenistic World and the Coming of Rome, 2 vols. Berkeley: University of California Press, 1984.

ed., *Imperialism in the Roman Republic*. New York: Holt, Rinehart and Winston, 1970.

The Last Generation of the Roman Republic. Berkeley: University of California Press, 1974.

Studies in Greek Culture and Roman Policy: Cincinnati Classical Studies, vol. 7. Leiden: n.p., 1990.

Gualandi, M. L., "Pendici settentrionali del Palatino: Lo Scavo," *BullCom* 91 (1986): 429–34.

Guittard, Charles, *The Romans: Life in the Empire*. Brookfield, CT: Millbrook Press, 1992.

Hall, John F., *Etruscan Italy: Etruscan Influences on the Civilizations of Italy from Antiquity to the Modern Era*. Provo, UT: Brigham Young University and Museum of Art, 1996.

Hamilton, Edith, *Mythology*. New York: New American Library, 1964.

Hammond, Mason, *The Augustan Principate in Theory and Practice during the Julio-Claudian Period*. Cambridge: Harvard University Press, 1933.

Hannestad, Niels, *Roman Art and Imperial Policy*. Aarhus, Denmark: Aarhus University Press, 1986.

Hanson, John Arthur, *Roman Theater Temples*. Westport, CT: Greenwood Press, 1978.

Harris, William V., *War and Imperialism in Republican Rome 327–70 B.C.* Oxford: Clarendon Press, 1979.

Haselberger, Lothar, "Deciphering a Roman Blueprint," *Scientific American* 272 (June 1995): 84–9.

Hassel, Franz Josef, *Der Trajansbogen in Benevent: Ein Bauwerk des römischen Senates*. Mainz-am-Rhein: Verlag Philipp von Zabern, 1966.

Haynes, Sybille, *Etruscan Civilization: A Cultural History*. Los Angeles: J. Paul Getty Museum, 2000.

Helbig, Wolfgang, *Guide to the Public Collections of Classical Antiquities in Rome*, 2 vols. Trans. James F. and Findlay Muirhead. Leipzig: Baedeker, 1895–1896.

Henderson, Bernard, *The Life and Principate of the Emperor Hadrian A.D. 76–138*. London: Methuen, 1923.

Henig, Martin, and Anthony King, eds., *Pagan Gods and Shrines of the Roman Empire*. Oxford: Oxford University Committee for Archaeology, 1986.

Herz, Norman, and Marc Waelkens, eds., *Classical Marble: Geochemistry, Technology, Trade*. Dordrecht: Kluwer Academic, 1988.

Hesburg, Henner von, "Die Veränderung des Erscheinungsbildes der Stadt Rom unter Augustus," in *Kaiser Augustus*, 93–115.

"Mausoleum Augusti: Das Monument," *LTUR*, vol. 3, 234–7.

Heurgon, Jacques, *The Rise of Rome to 264 B.C.* Trans. James Willis. Berkeley and Los Angeles: University of California Press, 1973.

Hill, Herbert, *The Roman Middle Class in the Republican Period*. Oxford: Basil Blackwell, 1952.

Hill, Ida Thallon, *The Ancient City of Athens: Its Topography and Monuments*. London: Methuen & Co., 1953.

Hodge, Trevor A., *The Woodwork of Greek Roofs*. Cambridge: Cambridge University Press, 1960.

Holland, L. A., "Janus and the Bridge," *PAAR* 21 (1961): 141–78.

Holloway, R. Ross, *The Archaeology of Ancient Sicily*. London and New York: Routledge, 1991.

Homo, Léon, *Rome impériale et l'urbanisme dans l'antiquité*. Paris: Albin Michel, 1951.

Hopkins, Alfred, "Concrete Construction, the Testimony of the Roman Forum," *AR* 25 (February 1909): 95–102.

Houston, George W., "Tiberius on Capri," *Greece and Rome* 32 (October 1985) 179–96.

Hülsen, Christian, *Bilder aus der Geschichte des Kapitols*. Rome: Loescher, 1899.

The Forum and the Palatine. New York: A. Bruderhausen, 1928.

The Forum Romanum: Its History and Its Monuments. Rome: Loescher; New York: G. E. Stechert, 1909.

"Il Gaianum e la Naumachia Vaticana," *DissPontAcc* (1903): 373.

"Osservazioni sull' architettura del Tempio di Giove Capitolino," *RömMitt* 3 (1888): 150–5.

Hurwit, Jeffrey M., *The Athenian Acropolis: History, Mythology, and Archaeology from the Neolithic Era to the Present*. New York: Cambridge University Press, 2001.

Iacopi, Irene, "Basilica Sempronia," *LTUR*, vol. 1, 187–8.

et al., "La riscoperta del Foro nel secolo XIX," in *Forma: La città antica e il suo avvenire*. Rome: De Luca Editore, 1985, 63–71.

Ioppolo, Giovanni, "I reperti ossei animali nell'area archeologica di S. Omobono," *RendPontAcc* 44 (1971–1972): 3–19.

Isaac, Benjamin H., *The Limits of Empire: The Roman Army in the East*. Oxford: Oxford University Press, 1990.

Isabelle, M. E., *Les édifices circulaires et les domes*. N.p., 1855.

Jacobson, David M., "Hadrianic Architecture and Geometry," *AJA* 90 (1986): 69–85.

Johnson, Mark J., "The Mausoleum of Augustus: Etruscan and Other Influences on Its Design," in *Etruscan Italy: Etruscan Influences on the Civilization of Italy from Antiquity to the Modern Era*. Provo, UT: Brigham Young University and Museum of Art, 1996, 217–39.

Jolivet, Vincent, "Les cendres d'Auguste: Note sur la topographie monumentale du Champs de Mars septentrional," *ArchLaz* 9 (1988): 90–6.

Jones, Brian W., *The Emperor Domitian*. New York: Routledge, 1992.

The Emperor Titus. London: Croom Helm; New York: St. Martin's Press, 1984.

Jones, Stuart H., "Notes on Roman Historical Structures," *PBSR*, 3 (1905): 215–71.

"The Primitive Institutions of Rome," in *CAH*, vol. 7, 414ff.

"The Sources for the Tradition of Early Roman History," in *CAH*, vol. 7, 312–22.

Jordan, Henri, ed., *Forma urbis Romae: regionum XIIII*. Berolini: apud Weidmannos, 1874.

"Osservazioni sul Tempio di Giove Capitolino," *Annali dell'Istituto di Corrispondenza Archeologica* (1876): 145–72.

Der Tempel der Vesta und Das Haus der Vestalinnen. Berlin: Weidmannsche und Verlag, 1886.

Topographie der Stadt Rom im Alterthum, vol. 1. Berlin: Weidmannsche und Verlag, 1878.

Kähler, Hans, *Das Fortunaheiligtum von Palestrina Praeneste*. Frankfurt: n.p., 1957.

"Das Pantheon in Rom," in *Meitensteine der europäischer Kunst*, Ed. E. Steingräber. N.p., 1965, 47–75.

Kallet-Marx, Robert Morstein, *Hegemony to Empire: The Development of the Roman Imperium in the East from 148 to 62 B.C.* Berkeley: University of California Press, 1995.

Kantorowicz, Ernst H., "The King's Advent and the Enigmatic Panels in the Doors of Santa Sabina," *ArtBull* 26 (1944): 212.

Keaveney, Arthur, *Sulla: The Last Republican*. London and Canberra: Croom Helm, 1982.

Kellum, B. A., "The City Adorned: Programmatic Display at the 'Aedes Concordiae Augustae,'" in *BRE*, 277ff.

Kildahl, Phillip A., *Caius Marius*. New York: Twayne, 1968.

King, Anthony, *Roman Gaul and Germany*. London: British Museum, 1990.

Kleiner, Fred S., *The Arch of Nero in Rome: A Study of the Roman Honorary Arch before and under Nero*. Rome: Giorgio Bretschneider Editore, 1985.

"The Study of Roman Triumphal and Honorary Arches 50 Years after Kahler," *JRA* 1 (1988): 196–206.

Kockel, Valentin, "Forum Augustum," *LTUR*, vol. 2, 289–95.

Koldeway, Robert, and Otto Puchstein, *Die Griechischen Tempel in Unteritalien und Sicilien*. Berlin: A. Asher, 1899.

Kuttner, Ann L., *Dynasty and Empire in the Age of Augustus: The Case of the Boscoreale Cups*. Berkeley: University of California Press, 1995.

Krause, Bernd H., *Iuppiter Optimus Maximus Saturnus*. N.p., 1989.

Krauss, Friedrich, *Paestum: Die Griechischen Tempel*. Berlin: Verlag Gebr. Mann, 1943.

Kriesis, Anthony, *Greek Town Building*. Athens: National Technical University of Athens, 1965.

Krill, Richard M., "Roman Paganism under the Antonines and Severans," *ANRW* 2 (1978): 27–44.

La Blanchere, René, *Terracina e le terre pontine*. Gaeta: Altracittà, 1984.

Labrouste, Henri, *Les temples de Paestum*. Paris: Firmin-Didot, 1877.

Lacey, W. K., *Augustus and the Principate: The Evolution of the System*. Leeds: Francis Cairns, 1996.

Lake, Agnes Kirsopp, "The Archaeological Evidence for the 'Tuscan Temple,'" *MAAR* 12 (1935): 90–108.

Lambert, Royston, *Beloved and God: The Story of Hadrian and Antinous*. London: Weidenfeld and Nicolson, 1984.

Lancaster, Lynne, "Building Trajan's Markets," *AJA* 102 (April 1998): 283–308.

"The Date of Trajan's Markets: An Assessment in the Light of Some Unpublished Brick Stamps," *PBSR* 63 (1995): 25–40.

Lanciani, Rodolfo, "Ara di Vermino," *BullCom* 4 (January–March 1876): 31–6.

"Architectural Results of the Latest Excavations in the Forum at Rome," *JRIBA* 8 (1901): 25–35.

L'atrio di Vesta. Rome: Libreria Spithover, 1884.

I commentarii di Frontino intorno le acque e gli acquedotti. Rome, n.p., 1880.

"La controversia sul Pantheon," *BullCom* 20 (1892): 150–9.

"La controversia sul Pantheon," *JRIBA* 2 (1895): 175–82.

La distruzione dell'antica Roma. Rome: Armando Curcio Editore, 1986.

Forma Urbis Romae. Rome: Edizione Quasar, 1990.

New Tales of Old Rome. Boston: Houghton Mifflin, 1902.

Notes from Rome. Ed. Anthony L. Cubberley. Rome: British School at Rome, 1988.

Pagan and Christian Rome. London: Macmillan, 1895.

"Pantheon-Thermae Agrippae," in *Storia degli scavi e notizia intorno le collezioni romane di antichità*, vol. 2 (Rome: E. Loescher, 1902), 237.

"I portici dei Foro Olitorio e il tesseramento delle derrate nell'antica Roma," *BullCom* 45 (1918): 168–92.

"Prima e seconda relazione sugli scavi per lo isolamento del Pantheon," *NSc* (1881): 255–94.

"Il Tempio di Giove Ottimo Massimo," *BullCom* 3 (October–December 1875): 165–203.

The Ruins and Excavations of Ancient Rome. London: Macmillan, 1897.

The Ruins and Excavations of Ancient Rome. New York: Bell, 1979.

Rovine e scavi di Roma antica. Rome: Quasar, 1985.

La Rocca, Eugenio, *Amazzonomachia: Le sculture frontonali del Tempio di Apollo Sosiano*. Rome: De Luca Editore, 1985.

Ara Pacis Augustae: In occasione del restauro della fronte orientale. Rome: 'L'Erma' di Bretschneider, 1983.

"Der Apollo-Sosianus-Tempel," in *Kaiser Augustus*, 121–36.

I fori imperiali. Rome: Progetti Museali, 1995.

"Il Foro di Traiano ed i fori tripartiti," *RömMitt* 105 (1998): 147–73.

"Scultore frontonali del Tempio di Apollo Sosiano: notizia preliminare," *BullCom* 87 (1980–1981): 57–73.

Last, Hugh, "The Founding of Rome," in *CAH*, vol. 7, 333–68.

"The Kings of Rome," in *CAH*, vol. 7, 387–95.

Laurence, Ray, *Roman Pompeii: Space and Society*. London and New York: Routledge, 1994.

Lauter, Hans, "Porticus Metelli-Porticus Octaviae; die baulichen Reste," *BullCom* 87 (1980–1981): 37–46.

Lawrence, A. W., *Greek Architecture*. Baltimore: Penguin Books, 1973.

Lazenby, J. F., *Hannibal's War: A Military History of the Second Punic War*. Warminster, England: Aris and Phillips, 1978.

Lazzarini, L., et al., "Determination of the Provenance of Marbles Used in Some Ancient Monuments in Rome," in *Classical Marble*, 399–407.

Leach, John, *Pompey the Great*. London: Croom Helm, 1978.

Lega, Claudia, "Colossus Nero," *LTUR*, vol. 1, 295–8.

Le Glay, Marcel, et al., *A History of Rome*. Trans. Antonia Nevill. Malden, MA: Blackwell, 2001.

Leon, C. F., *Die Bauornamentik des Trajansforum und ihre Stellung in der früh-und mittelkaiser-zeitlichen Architektur-dekoration Roms*. Vienna: Böhlaus, 1971.

Lepper, Frank, *Trajan's Parthian War*. London: Oxford University Press, 1948.

and Sheppard Frere, *Trajan's Column: A New Edition of the Cichorius Plates*. Wolfboro, NH: Alan Sutton, 1988.

Lesueur, Jean-Baptiste-Cicéron, *La basilique Ulpienne (Rome) restauration exècute en 1823*. Paris: Firmin-Didot, 1877.

Levick, Barbara, *Claudius*. New Haven: Yale University Press, 1990.

Tiberius the Politician. New York: Routledge, 1999.

Vespasian. New York: Routledge, 1999.

Liebeschuetz, J. H. W. G., *Continuity and Change in Roman Religion*. Oxford: Clarendon Press, 1979.

Linderski, Jerzy, "Cicero and Roman Divination," in *Roman Questions*, 458–84.

"Roman Religion in Livy," in *Roman Questions*, 608–25.

"Watching the Birds: Cicero the Augur and the Augural *Templa*," in *Roman Questions*, 485–95.

Ling, Roger, "Hellenistic and Graeco-Roman Art," in *OHCW*, 495–530.

Lintott, Andrew, *'Imperium Romanum:' Politics and Administration*. New York: Routledge, 1993.

Loerke, William, "Georges Chédanne and the Pantheon: A Beaux-Arts Contribution to the History of Roman Architecture," *Modulus: University of Virginia School of Architecture Review* (1982): 42–8.

"A Rereading of the Interior Elevation of Hadrian's Rotunda," *JSAH* 49 (March 1990): 22–43.

Lucchini, Flaminio, *Pantheon*. Rome: La Nuova Italia Scientifica, 1996.

Luce, T. J., "Livy, Augustus, and the Forum Augustum," in *BRE*, 123–38.

Luciani, Roberto, and Leandro Sperduti, *Foro Romano*. Rome: Alma Venus, 1992.

Lugli, Giuseppe, *Itinerario di Roma antica*. Milan: n.p., 1970.

Roma Antica: Il Centro Monumentale. Rome: G. Bardi Editore, 1946.

The Roman Forum and the Palatine. Rome: G. Bardi Editore, 1964.

Lugli, Josephus, *Forma Italiae: Regio I, Latium e Campania*. Rome: Danesi, 1926.

Lyngby, Helge, and Giuseppina Sartorio, "Indagini archeologiche nell'area dell'antica Porta Trigemina," *BullCom* 80 (1968): 5–36.

Macauley, Thomas, *The Layers of Ancient Rome*. London: Cassel, 1907.

Macciocca, Maria, "Mausoleum Augusti: Le Sepolture," *LTUR*, vol. 3, 237–8.

MacDonald, William L., "Apollodorus," *MEA*, vol. 1, 91–4.

The Architecture of the Roman Empire: An Urban Appraisal, 2 vols. New Haven and London: Yale University Press, 1982 and 1986.

The Pantheon: Design, Meaning, and Progeny. Cambridge: Harvard University Press, 1976.

"Rabirius," *MEA*, vol. 3, 509–11.

MacKendrick, Paul, *The Mute Stones Speak: The Story of Archaeology in Italy*. New York: Norton, 1983.

MacNamara, Ellen, *The Etruscans*. Cambridge: Harvard University Press, 1991.

Maetzke, G., "Regione VIII: Area nord-occidentale del Foro Romano," *BullCom* 91 (1986): 373–80.

Maffei, Sonia, "Forum Traiani: Columna," *LTUR*, vol. 2, 356–9.

Magoffin, Ralph van Deman, *A Study of the Topography and Municipal History of Praeneste*. Baltimore: Johns Hopkins University Press, 1908.

Mambella, R., "Contributi alla problematica del tempio etrusco-italico," *RendPontAcc* 6 (1982): 35–42.

Maranón, Gregorio, *Tiberius: The Resentful Caesar*. New York: Duell, Sloan and Pearce, 1956, 65–6.

Marchetti-Longhi, G., *L'Area Sacra ed i templi repubblicani del Largo Argentina*. Milan and Rome: Casa Editrice d'Arte Bestetti and Tumminelli, 1929.

"Gli scavi del Largo Argentina: L'ara di aula Postumio Albino," *BullCom* 61 (1933): 163–94.

"Gli scavi del Largo Argentina: Tempio A," *BullCom* 64 (1936): 83–139.

"Gli scavi del Largo Argentina: Tempio C," *BullCom* 60 (1932): 253–346.

"Gli scavi del Largo Argentina: Le epigrafi," *BullCom* 71 (1943–1944): 57–95.

"Gli scavi del Largo Argentina: Il Tempio B," *BullCom* 76 (1956–1958): 45–118.

"Il tempio Ionico di Ponte Rotto: Tempio di Fortuna o di Portuno?" *RömMitt* 40 (1925): 319–30.

I templi della zona Argentina. Rome: Fratelli Palombi, 1929.

"Gli scavi del Largo Argentina: Evoluzione e trasformazione dell'area e dei templi dall'età imperiale all'inizio del Medioevo," *BullCom* 82 (1970–1971): 7–62.

"Theatrum Lapideum," *Capitolium: rassegna mensile di attività municipale* 2 (December 1926): 531–44.

Marconi, Pirro, *Agrigento: Topografia ed arte*. Florence: Vallecchi Editore, 1929.

Marder, Tod, "Bernini and Alexander VII: Criticism and Praise of the Pantheon in the Seventeenth Century," *ArtBull* 71 (1989): 628–45.

Mark, Robert, and Paul Hutchinson, "On the Structure of the Roman Pantheon," *ArtBull* 90 (1986): 69–85.

Marliano, Giovanni Bartolomeo, *Ritratto di Roma antica, formato nuovamente con la autorità di Bartolomeo Marliano, Alessandro Donati, e Faminio Nardini*. Rome: M. A. Rossi, 1689.

Urbis Romae topographia Italiano, m.c. 1560. Trans. M. Hercole Barbarasa da Terni. Rome: Antonio Blado, 1548.

Marta, Roberto, *Architettura Romana: Tecniche costruttive e forme architettoniche del mondo romano*. Rome: Edizioni Kappa, 1985.

Martines, Giangiacomo, "Argomenti di geometria antica a proposito della cupola del Pantheon," *QuadIstStArch* 13 (1991): 3–10.

Martínez-Pinna, Jorge, "Evidenza di un tempio di Giove Capitolino a Roma all inizio del VI sec. A.C." *Arch Laz* 4 (1981): 249–52.

Marucchi, Orazio, *Guida archeologica della città di Palestrina*. Rome: Edizioni Enzo Pinci, 1932.

Masi, Fausto, *The Pantheon as an Astronomical Instrument*. Rome: Edizioni Internazionali di Letteratura e Scienze, 1996.

Mattern, Torsten, "Der Magna-Mater-Tempel und die augusteische Architektur in Rom," *RömMitt* 107 (2000): 141–53.

McCann, Anna Marguerite, et al., *The Roman Port and Fishery of Cosa: A Center of Ancient Trade*. Princeton: Princeton University Press, 1987.

Meade, Wade C., *Ruins of Rome: A Guide to the Classical Antiquities*. Ruston, LA: Palatine, 1980.

Medri, Maura, "Suet., Nero, 31.1: Elementi e proposte per la ricostruzione del progetto della Domus Aurea," in *Meta Sudans I; Un area sacra in Palatio e la valle del Colosseo prima e dopo Nerone*. Ed. Clementina Panella. Rome: Istituto Poligrafico e Zecca dello Stato; Libreria dello Stato, 1996.

Meier, Christian, *Caesar: A Biography*. Trans. David McLintock. New York: Basic Books, 1982.

Meiggs, Russel, *Roman Ostia*. Oxford: Clarendon Press, 1960.

Trees and Timber in the Ancient Mediterranean World. Oxford: Oxford University Press, 1982.

Meiyer, Fik, *Trade, Transport, and Society in the Ancient World: A Sourcebook*. London: Routledge, 1992.

Mellor, Ronald, ed., *From Augustus to Nero: The First Dynasty of Imperial Rome*. East Lansing: Michigan State University Press, 1990.

Meneghini, Roberto, "L'architettura del Foro di Traiano attraverso i ritrovamenti archeologici più recenti," *RömMitt* 105 (1998): 127–48.

"I Fori Imperiali in età post-classica: I Fori di Augusto e di Traiano," in *CBFI*, 83–9.

Il Foro di Nerva. Rome: Fratelli Palombi Editori for the Commune di Roma Assessorato alla Cultura, 1991.

"Nuovi dati sulle biblioteche e il Templum Divi Traiani nel Foro di Traiano," *BA* 19–21 (1993): 13–21.

"Templum Divi Traiani," *BullCom* 97 (1996): 47–88.

and Lucrezia Ungaro, *The Imperial Forums and Trajan's Market*. Rome: Fratelli Palombi Editori, 1993.

Mereu, Honoré, "Roman Forum," *American Architect and Building News* 70 (1900): 5.

Merrill, E. T., "Some Observations on the Arch of Trajan at Beneventum," *TAPA* 32 (1901): 43–63.

Meyer, Hugo, "Antinous and the Greek Renascence: An Introduction," in *Der Obelisk des Antinous*. Munich: Wilhelm Fink Verlag, 1994.

Micheli, M. E., "Disiecta membra del Pantheon: 1747," *BullCom* 89 (1984): 55–64.

Middleton, J. Henry, *The Remains of Ancient Rome*, 2 vols. London and Edinburgh: Adam and Charles, 1892.

Millar, Fergus, ed., *Caesar Augustus: Seven Aspects*. Oxford and New York: Clarendon Press, 1984.

The Crowd in Rome in the Late Republic. Ann Arbor: University of Michigan Press, 1998.

"The Political Character of the Classical Roman Republic, 200–151 B.C.," *JRS* 74 (1984): 1–19.

Mommsen, Theodor, *The History of Rome*. Trans. William Purdie Dickinson. New York: Charles Scribner's Sons, 1898.

Morini, Mario, *Atlante di storia dell'urbanistica*. Milan: Editore Ulrico Hoepli, 1979.

Morgan, M. Gwyn, "The Portico of Metellus: A Reconsideration," *Hermes* 99 (1971): 480–505.

Morselli, Chiara, "Forum Iulium," *LTUR*, vol. 2, 299–306.

"Forum Transitorium," in *CFIFT*, 53–68.

and Tortorici, Edoardo, "B. Sintesi storico-topografica," in *CFIFT*, 218–61.

Munoz, Antonio, *Campidoglio*. Rome: A Cura del Governatorato di Roma, 1930.

La sistemazione del tempio di Venere a Roma. Rome: Tumminelli, 1935.

Via dei Trionfi: Isolamento del Campidoglio. Rome: A Cura del Governatorato di Roma, 1933.

Munn, Mary Lou Zimmerman. *Corinthian Trade with the West in the Classical Period*. Ph.D. diss., Bryn Mawr College, 1983.

Museum of Roman Civilization, *The Model of Rome and the Column of Trajan*. Rome: Editori Romani Associati, 1988.

Musti, Domenico, *Polibio e l'imperialismo romano*. Naples: Liguri, 1978.

Muzzioli, Maria Pia, "Fonti per la topografia della IX regione di Roma: Alcune osservazioni," *PBSR* 60 (1992): 179–211.

Napoli, Mario, *Guida degli scavi di Velia*. Cava de Tirreni: Di Mauro, 1972.

Nardi, Roberto, "Arco di Settimio Severo," in *Roma Archeologia nel centro*. Rome: De Luca Editore, 1985, 34–40.

Nardini, Faminio, *Roma antica*. Rome: Falco, 1666.

Roma antica, vol. 2. Ed. C. Barbiellini. Rome: Biblioteca di Archeologia e Storia dell'Arte, 1771.

Nash, Ernest, *Pictorial Dictionary of Ancient Rome*, 2 vols. New York and Washington, DC: Praeger, 1962.

Nawrath, Curtius, *Das Antike Rom*. Vienna and Munich: Verlag Anton Schroll, 1957.

Nibby, Antonio, *Del Foro Romano, della via Sacra, dell'anfiteatro Flavio e de' luoghi adjacenti*. Rome: Presso V. Poggioli, 1819.

Itinéraire de Rome et de ses environs. Rome: Augustin Valentini, 1849.

Tivoli e le sue vicinanze. Tivoli: R. Reputazione romana di storia patria, 1942.

Nichols, Francis Morgan, *The Roman Forum: A Topographical Study*. London: Longmans, 1877.

"Some Remarks on the Regia, the Atrium Vestae, and the Original Locality of the Fasti Capitolini," *Archaeologia*, vol. 50, 227–50.

Nicolet, Claude, *Space, Geography, and Politics in the Early Roman Empire*. Ann Arbor: University of Michigan Press, 1991.

Nielsen, Inge, "Castor, Aedes, Templum," *LTUR*, vol. 1, 242–4.

and Birte Poulsen, ed., *The Temple of Castor and Pollux I: The Pre-Augustan Temple Phases with Related Decorative Elements*. Rome: Edizioni de Luca, 1992.

Nilsson, Martin P., in "The Origin of the Triumphal Arch," *Corolla archaeologica principi hereditario regni sueciae Gustavo Adolpho*. Lund: C. W. K. Gleerup, 1932.

Nordh, A., "Libellus de Regionibus Urbis Romae," *Scrifter utgivna av Svenska Institut i Rom* 3 (1949): 91.

North, J. A., "Conservatism and Change in Roman Religion," *PBSR* 44 (1976): 1–12.

Nünnerich-Asmus, Annette, *Basilika und Portikus: Die Architektur der Säulenhallen als Ausdruck gewandelten Urbanität in später Republik und früher Kaiserzeit*. Cologne: Böhlaus Verlag, 1994.

Ochs, Donovan J., *Consolatory Rhetoric: Grief, Symbol, and Ritual in the Greco-Roman Era*. Columbia: University of South Carolina Press, 1900.

Ogilvie, Robert M., *Early Rome and the Etruscans*. Hassocks, England: Harvester Press, 1976.

The Romans and Their Gods in the Age of Augustus. New York: Norton, 1970.

Olinder, Björn, "Porticus Octavia in Circo Flaminio," in *Topographical Studies in the Campus Region of Rome*. Stockholm: Per Skr Svel. Rome: n.p., n.d.

Onians, J. B., *Bearers of Meaning: The Classical Orders in Antiquity, the Middle Ages, and the Renaissance*. Princeton: Princeton University Press, 1988.

Oswalt, Sabine G., *Concise Encyclopedia of Greek and Roman Mythology*. Glasgow and Chicago: William Collins Sons and Follett, 1965.

Packer, James E., "The Basilica Ulpia in Rome: An Ancient Architectural Experiment," *AJA* 77 (1973): 223.

"Forum Traiani," *LTUR*, vol. 2, 348–56.

The Forum of Trajan in Rome: A Study of the Monuments, 3 vols. Berkeley and Los Angeles: University of California Press, 1996.

"Numismatic Evidence for the Southeast (Forum) Façade of the Basilica Ulpia," in Lionel Casson and Martin Price, ed., *Coins, Culture and History in the Ancient World: Numismatic and Other Studies in Honor of Bluma L. Trell*. Detroit: Wayne State University Press, 1981, 57–67.

"'Plurima et Amplissima Opera:' Parsing Flavian Rome," in *Flavian Rome: Culture, Image, Text*. Ed. A. J. Boyle and W. J. Dominik. Leiden: Brill, 2003, 167–98.

"Review of Carla Maria Amici, *Foro di Traiano: Basilica Ulpia e Biblioteche*," in *AJA* 87 (October 1983): 569–72.

"The Southeast Façade of the Basilica Ulpia in Trajan's Forum: The Evidence from the Northeast Colonnade," *AJA* 90 (1986): 189–90.

"Trajan's Basilica Ulpia: Some Reconsiderations," *AJA* 86 (1982): 280.

"Trajan's Forum Again: The Column and the Temple of Trajan in the Master Plan Attributed to Apollodorus," *JRA* 7 (1994): 163–82.

"Trajan's Forum in 1989," *AJA* 96 (1992): 151–62.

"'Trajan's Forum in 1989,' Review of *Foro Traiano:* Contributi per una ricostruzione storica e architettonica," by Patrizio Pensabene et al., *ArchCl* 41 (1989): 27–291.

Kevin Sarring, and Rose Mary Sheldon, "A New Excavation in Trajan's Forum," *AJA* 87 (1983): 165–72.

Palladio, Andrea, *The Four Books of Architecture*, 4 vols. New York: Dover Publications, 1965.

Pallottino, Massimo, *The Etruscans*. Trans. J. Cremona. Baltimore: Penguin Books, 1956.

Palmer, Robert E. A., "Cults of Hercules, Apollo Caelispex and Fortuna in and around the Roman Cattle Market," review of Coarelli, *Il Foro Boario dalle origini alla fine della Repubblica* in *JRA* 3 (1990): 234–40.

Roman Religion and Roman Empire: Five Essays. Philadelphia: University of Pennsylvania Press, 1974.

"The 'Vici Luccei' in the 'Forum Boarium' and some Lucceii in Rome," *BullCom* 85 (1976–1977): 135–62.

Palumbi, Domenico, "Hercules Victor, Aedes et Signam," *LTUR*, vol. 3, 23–5.

Panella, Stefania, "Scavo nella platea del tempio di Venere e Roma," in *Roma archeologia nel centro*. Rome: De Luca Editore, 1985.

Panvinii, Onuphrii, *Veronensis, Fratris, Augustiniani, Eremitae, Civitas Romana*. Paris: Apud Egidium & Nicolaum Gillios, 1588.

Panvinio, Onofrio, and Jacques Boissard, *Romanae urbis topographiae e antiquitatum*. Frankfurt: Theodori de Bry, 1597.

Paribeni, Roberto, "Saggi di scavi nell'area del tempio di Giove Ottimo Massimo sul Campidoglio," *NSc* (1921): 38–49.

Parker, John Henry, *The Archaeology of Rome: The Forum Romanum and the Via Sacra*, vol. 2. Oxford: James Parker; London: John Murray, 1876.

The Archaeology of Rome; VI: The Via Sacra. London: J. Murray, 1876.

Pasquali, Susanna, *Il Pantheon: Architettura e antiquaria nel settecento a Roma*. Modena: Franco Cosimo Panini, 1996.

Pasquinucci, Montagna, "L'altare del tempio del Divo Giulio," *Athenaeum Pavia* 52 (1974): 144–55.

Passarelli, V., "Rilievo e studio di restituzione dell'Hadrianum," *Atti III CongrStArchit* (1938): 123ff.

Paul, Eberhard, *Antikes Rom*. Leipzig: Koehler and Amelang, 1970.

Pedley, John Griffiths, *Paestum: Greeks and Romans in Southern Italy*. London: Thames and Hudson, 1990.

Peña, J. Theodore, "'P. Giss' 69: Evidence for the Supplying of Stone Transport Operations in Roman Egypt and the Production of Fifty-Foot Monolithic Column Shafts," *JRA* 2 (1989): 126–32.

Pensa, M., "L'architettura traianea attraverso le emissioni monetali coeve," *Centro Studi e Documentazione sull'Italia Romana, Atti* 2 (1969–1970): 279–81.

Pensabene, Patrizio, "Magna Mater, Aedes," *LTUR*, vol. 3, 206–7.

"Roma – saggi di scavo sul Tempio della Magna Mater del Palatino," *ArchLaz* 1 (1978): 67–71.

"Scavi nell'area del Tempio della Vittoria e del Santuario della Magna Mater sul Palatino," *ArchLaz* 9 (1988): 54–67.

Tempio di Saturno: Architettura e decorazione. Rome: De Luca Editore, 1984.

"Testimonianze di scavo del XVIII e del XIX secolo sul Palatino," in *Roma antica: Gli orti Farnesiani sul Palatino*. Rome: École Française de Rome and Soprintendenza Archeologica di Roma, 1990.

"Victoria, Aedes," *LTUR*, vol. 5, 149–50.

"La zona sud-occidentale del Palatino," *ArchLaz* 3 (1980): 65–81.

et al., "Review of *Foro Traiano*: Contributi per una ricostruzione storica e architettonica," *ArchCl* 41 (1989): 27–291.

Perelli, Luciano, *Imperialismo, capitalismo e rivoluzione culturelle nella prima metà del IIo secolo a.c.* Turin: G. Giappichelli, 1975.

Perowne, Stewart, *Hadrian*. London: Hodder and Stoughton, 1960.

Petrignani, Marcello, "Il Portico d'Ottavia," *BullArchIt* 16 (1960): 37–56.

Pfanner, Michael, *Der Titusbogen: Mit einer Bauaufnahme von Ulrike Hess und Fotografien von Helmut Schwanke*. Mainz-am-Rhein: Verlag Philipp von Zabern, 1983.

Piazzesi, Gioia, "Gli edifici: Ipotesi ricostruttive," in *FT*, 125–98.

Pietilä-Castren, L., "Some Aspects of the Life of Lucius Mummius Archaicus," *Arctos* 12 (1978): 115–23.

Pinza, G., "Gabii ed i suoi monumenti," *BullCom* 31 (1903): 330–43.

Pirson, Felix, "Style and Message on the Column of Marcus Aurelius," *PBSR*, 64 (1996): 139–79.

Pisani Sartorio, Giuseppina, "Fortuna et Mater Matuta, Aedes," *LTUR*, vol. 2, 281–5.

Platner, Samuel Ball, *The Topography and Monuments of Ancient Rome*. Boston: Allyn and Bacon: 1904.

Platner, Samuel Ball, and Thomas Ashby, *A Topographical Dictionary of Ancient Rome*. Oxford: Oxford University Press, 1929.

Plommer, Hugh, *Ancient and Classical Architecture* (Simpson's History of Architectural Development, vol. I). London and New York: Longmans, Green, 1956.

Pollitt, J. J., *The Art of Rome, c.753 B.C.–A.D. 337; Sources and Documents*. New York: Cambridge University Press, 1998.

Potter, Timothy W., *Roman Italy*. Berkeley: University of California Press, 1987.

Poulton, Michael, *Life in the Time of Augustus and the Ancient Romans*. Austin, TX: Raintree/Steck-Vaugn, 1992.

Price, S. R. F., "Between Man and God: Sacrifice in the Roman Imperial Cult," *JRS* 70 (1980): 28–43.

Proietti, Giuseppe, ed., *Adriano: Architettura e progetto*. Milan: Electa, 2000.

Purcell, Nicholas, "Forum Romanum (the Imperial Period)," *LTUR*, vol. 2, 336–42.

"Forum Romanum (the Republican Period)," *LTUR*, vol. 2, 320–36.

"Rediscovering the Roman Forum," *JRA* 2 (1989): 156–66.

Raaflaub, Kurt A., "Born to be Wolves? Origins of Roman Imperialism," in *Transitions to Empire: Essays in Greco-Roman History, 360–146 B.C., in Honor of E. Badian*. Ed. Robert W. Wallace and

Edward M. Harris. Norman: University of Oklahoma Press, 1996.

and Mark Toher, eds., *Between Republic and Empire: Interpretations of Augustus and His Principate*. Berkeley: University of California Press, 1990.

Rakob, Friedrich, and Wolf-Dieter Heilmeyer, *Der Rundtempel am Tiber in Rom*. Mainz-am-Rhein: Verlag Philipp von Zabern, 1973.

Raspi Serra, Joselita, *Paestum: Idea e immagine. Antologia di testi critici e di immagini di Paestum 1750–1836*. Modena: Franco Cosimo Panini 1990.

"The Expansion of Rome," in *OHCW*, 417–37.

Intellectual Life in the Late Roman Republic. Baltimore: Johns Hopkins University Press, 1985.

Rawson, Elizabeth, *Roman Culture and Society: Collected Papers*. Oxford: Clarendon Press; New York: Oxford University Press, 1991.

Rebert, Homer F., and Henri Marceau, "The Temple of Concord in the Forum Romanum," *MAAR* 5 (1925): 53–7.

Rehak, Paul, "The Ionic Temple Relief in the Capitoline: The Temple of Victory on the Palatine?" *JRA* 3 (1990): 172–86.

Reusser, Christoph, *Der Fidestempel auf dem Kapitol in Rom und seine Ausstattung*. Rome: 'L'Erma' di Bretschneider, 1993.

Rhodes, Robin, *Architecture and Meaning on the Athenian Acropolis*. New York: Cambridge University Press, 1995.

Ribbeck, Otto, *Tragicum romanorum fragmenta*, 2 vols. Leipzig: n.p., 1897.

Ricci, Corrado, *Il Foro di Cesare*. Milan and Rome: Treves-Treccanii Tumminelli, 1932.

"Scavi dei Fori Imperiali," *Capitolium* 6 (1930): 157–89.

Rich, J., W. "Augustus's Parthian Honors, the Temple of Mars Ultor and the Arch in the Forum Romanum," *PBSR* 66 (1998): 71–128.

Richardson, Lawrence, Jr., "The Approach to the Temple of Saturn in Rome," *AJA* 84 (January 1980): 51–62.

"Curia Julia and Janus Geminus," *RömMitt* 85 (1978): 359–69.

"The Evolution of the Porticus Octaviae," *AJA* 80 (1976): 57–64.

"Hercules Musarum and the 'Porticus Philippi' in Rome," *AJA* 81 (1977): 355–61.

A New Topographical Dictionary of Ancient Rome. Baltimore: Johns Hopkins University Press, 1992.

"A Note on the Architecture of the 'Theatrum Pompei' in Rome," *AJA* 91 (1987): 123–6.

Pompeii: An Architectural History. Baltimore and London: Johns Hopkins University Press, 1988.

Richmond, O. L., "The Augustan Palatium," *JRS* 4 (1914): 200–6.

Richter, Fjodor, *Il restauro del Foro Trajano . . . con la dichiarazioni di Antonio Grifi*. Rome: Alessandro Monaldi, 1839.

Richter, Otto Ludwig, "Die Augustusbauten auf dem Forum Romanum," *JDAI* 4 (1889): 137–51.

"Der Castortempel am Forum Romanum," *JDAI* 13 (1898): 87–114.

Topographie der Stadt Rom, 3 vols. Munich: C. H. Beck, 1901.

Ridley, R. T., *The Eagle and Spade: The Archaeology of Rome during the Napoleonic Era, 1809–1814*. Cambridge: n.p., 1992.

Riemann, Hans, "Beiträge zur Römischen Topographie," *RömMitt* 76 (1969): 103–21.

"Pacis Forum," in *RE*, vol. 18, 2107–22.

Rizzo, Silvana, "I cantieri di scavo dei Fori Imperiali," in *ArchGiub*, 202–6.

"Fori Imperiali, i cantieri di scavo," *Archeo* 15.12: 34–45.

"Il progetto Fori Imperiali," in *CBFI*, 62–78.

Robertson, D. S., *A Handbook of Greek and Roman Architecture*. Cambridge: Cambridge University Press, 1954.

Rockwell, Peter, "Preliminary Study of the Carving Techniques on the Column of Trajan," in *Marmi antichi, StudMisc* 26 (1981–1983) Ed. Patrizio Pensabene (Roma 1985): 101–11.

Roddaz, Jean-Michel, *Marcus Agrippa*. Paris and Rome: École française de Rome, 1984.

Rodocanachi, Emmanuel Pierre, *Le capitole romain antique et moderne*. Paris: Hachette, 1905.

Rodriguez-Almeida, E., *Forma Urbis Marmorea, aggiornamento generale 1980*. Rome: n.p., 1981.

Romanelli, Pietro, *The Roman Forum*. Rome: Istituto Poligrafico dello Stato, ca. 1975.

Rosienski, Herbert, *Power and Human Destiny*. Ed. Richard P. Stebbins. New York: Praeger, 1965.

"Theatrum Marcelli," *LTUR*, vol. 5, 31–5.

Rossi, Lino, *Trajan's Column and Dacian Wars*. London: Thames and Hudson, 1971.

Rostovtzeff, M., *Rome*. Trans. J. D. Duff. London: Oxford University Press, 1960.

Rowe, Michael Patrick, *Etruscan Temples: A Study of the Structural Remains, Origins and Development*. Ph.D. diss., Florida State University, 1989.

Rowell, Henry T., "The Forum and the Funeral Images of Augustus," *MAAR* 17 (1940): 131–43.

Rome in the Augustan Age. Norman: University of Oklahoma Press, 1962.

Ruggieri, Gianfranco, *The Pantheon*. Ed. Alberto Bracci Testasecca. Rome: Editoriale Museum, 1990.

Ruggiero, Isabella, "Ricerche sul Tempio di Portuno nel Foro Boario: Per una rilettura del monumento," *BullCom* 94 (1991–1992): 253–86.

Ryberg, Inez Scott, *Rites of State Religion in Roman Art*. Rome: American Academy in Rome, 1955.

An Archaeological Record of Rome from the Seventh to the Second Century B.C. London: Christophers; Philadelphia: University of Pennsylvania Press, 1940.

Said, Edward, *Culture and Imperialism*. New York: Knopf, 1993.

Saller, Richard, "The Emperor's Men: Senators, Equestrians, Freedman and Slaves," in *From Augustus to Nero: The First Dynasty of Imperial Rome*. Ed. Ronald Mellor. East Lansing: Michigan State University Press, 1990.

Sallman, Henri, "The Pantheon Coffers: Pattern and Number," *Architettura* 18 (1988): 121.

Salmon, Edward Togo, *The Making of Roman Italy*. Ithaca: Cornell University Press, 1982.

The Nemesis of Empire. London and New York: Oxford University Press, 1974.

Sande, Siri, and Jan Zahle, "Der Tempel der Dioskuren auf dem Forum Romanum," in *Kaiser Augustus*, 213–24.

Sanfilippo, Mario, *La costruzione di una capitale 1911–1945*. Milan: Silvana Editoriale, 1993.

Scott, Russell T., "Lavori e ricerche nell'Area Sacra di Vesta, 1990–91," *ArchLaz* 11 (1993): 11–17.

"Regia," *LTUR*, vol. 4, 189–92.

"Regia-Vesta," *ArchLaz* 9 (1988): 18–26.

"Vesta, Aedes," *LTUR*, vol. 5, 125–8.

Scranton, Robert L., *Greek Architecture*. New York: George Braziller, 1967.

Scullard, Howard H., *Festivals and Ceremonies of the Roman Republic*. London: Thames and Hudson, 1981.

From the Gracchi to Nero: A History of Rome from 133 B.C. to A.D. 68. New York: Methuen, 1982.

A History of the Roman World from 753 to 146 B.C. London: Methuen, 1980; New York: Barnes and Noble, 1964.

Scurati-Manzioni, Pietro, *L'architettura romana dalle origini a Giustiniano*. Roma: Guerini Studio, 1991.

Seager, Robin, *Pompey: A Political Biography*. Berkeley: University of California Press, 1979.

Sear, Frank, *Roman Architecture*. Ithaca, NY: Cornell University Press, 1982.

Sestieri, Pellegrino Claudio, *Paestum: The City, the Prehistoric Necropolis*. Rome: La Libreria dello Stato, 1953.

Shils, Edward, *Center and Periphery: Essays in Macrosociology*. Chicago: University of Chicago Press, 1975.

Shipley, Frederick W., "Chronology of the Building Operations in Rome from the Death of Caesar to the Death of Augustus," *MAAR* 9 (1931).

Shoe, Lucy Taxis, *Etruscan and Republican Mouldings*. Rome: American Academy in Rome, 1965.

"Profiles of Western Greek Mouldings," *MAAR* 14 (1952), passim.

Sisson, M., "The Stoa of Hadrian at Athens," *PBSR* 2 (1927): 50–72.

Skutsch, O., *The Annals of Q. Ennius*. Oxford: Oxford University Press, 1995, 76–7.

Smith, Christopher John, *Early Rome and Latium: Economy and Society, c.1000 to 500 B.C.* Oxford: Clarendon Press, 1996.

Smith, Earl Baldwin, *Architectural Symbolism of Imperial Rome and the Middle Ages*. Princeton: Princeton University Press, 1956.

Smith, Thomas Gordon, *Classical Architecture: Rule and Invention*. Layton, UT: Gibbs M. Smith, 1988.

Sommella, Anna Maria, "'La grande Roma dei Tarquini.' Alterne vicende di una felice intuizione," *BullCom* 101 (2000): 7–26.

"Le recenti scoperte sul Campidoglio e la fondazione del tempio di Giove Capitolino," *RendPontAcc* 70 (1997–1998): 57–79.

"Tabularium," *LTUR*, vol. 5, 17–20.

"Il Tabularium: Progetto di consolidamento e restauro," *ArchLaz* 4 (1981): 126–31.

Southern, Pat, *Augustus*. New York: Routledge, 1998.

Domitian: Tragic Tyrant. London: Routledge, 1998.

Sperling, Gert, *Das Pantheon in Rom: Abbild und Mass des Kosmos*. Berlin: Ars Una, 1999.

Stambaugh, John, *The Ancient Roman City*. Baltimore: Johns Hopkins University Press, 1989.

"The Functions of Roman Temples," *ANRW* 2 (1978): 554–608.

Stamper, John W., "The Temple of Capitoline Jupiter in Rome: A New Reconstruction," *Hephaistos* 16/17 (1998–1999): 107–38.

Stefani, Enrico, "Orvieto: Osservazioni intorno alla struttura del tempio," *NSc* (1925): 158–61.

"Veio: Tempio dell'Apollo-Esplorazione e sistemazione del santuario, *NSc* 7 (1953–1954): 29–112.

Steinby, Margarita, "Basilica Aemelia," *LTUR*, vol. 1, 167–8.

Stierlin, Henri, *Hadrian et l'architecture romaine*. Frieburg: Office du Livre, 1984.

Stevens, G. P., "Entasis of Roman Columns," *MAAR* 4 (1924), 121–52.

Stewart, Henry Perone, *Hadrian*. London: Hodden and Stoughton, 1960.

Stockton, David, "The Founding of the Empire," in *OHCW*, 531–59.

The Gracchi. Oxford: Clarendon Press, 1979.

Strack, P., *Untersuchungen zur römischen Reichsprägung des zweiten Jahrhunderts*, vol. 1. Stuttgart: Kohlhammer, 1931.

Strong, Donald, "The Administration of Public Building in Rome during the Late Republic and Early Empire," *BICS* 15 (1968): 101.

"Late Hadrianic Architectural Ornament in Rome," *PBRS* 21 (1953): 118–51.

Roman Art. Baltimore: Penguin Books, 1976.

Roman Imperial Sculpture. Baltimore: Penguin Books, 1961.

"Some Early Examples of the Composite Capital," *JRS* 50 (1960): 119–28.

"Some Observations on Early Roman Corinthian," *JRS* 53 (1963): 73–84.

and J. B. Ward-Perkins, "The Round Temple in the Forum Boarium," *PBRS* 28 (1960): 6–32.

and J. B. Ward-Perkins, "The Temple of Castor in the Forum Romanum," *PBRS* 30 (1962): 1–30.

Suolahti, Jaakko, *The Roman Censors: A Study on Social Structure; Annales Academiae Scientiarum Fennicae*, vol. 117. Helsinki, Finland: Suomalainen Tiedeakatemia, 1963.

Tagliamonte, Gianluca, "Forum Romanum (fino alla prima età repubblicana)," *LTUR*, vol. 2, 313–25.

"Iuppiter Optimus Maximus Capitolinus, Aedes, Templum (fino alla 83 B.C.)," *LTUR*, vol. 3, 148–53.

Taylor, Lily Ross, *The Divinity of the Roman Emperor*. Philadelphia: Porcupine Press, 1975.

Roman Voting Assemblies: From the Hannibalic War to the Dictatorship of Caesar. Ann Arbor: University of Michigan Press, 1990.

Thedenat, Henry, *Le Forum Romain et les Forums Impériaux*. Paris: Librairie Hachette, 1904.

Thomas, Edmund, "The Architectural History of the Pantheon in Rome from Agrippa to Septimius Severus via Hadrian," *Hephaistos* 15 (1997): 163–86.

and Christian Witschel, "Constructing Reconstruction: Claim and Reality of Roman Rebuilding Inscriptions from the Latin West," *PBRS* 60 (1922): 135–77.

Thomsen, Rudi, "Studien über den ursprünglichen Bau des Caesarforums," *Skrifter utgivna av Svenska Institutet i Rom. Opuscula Archaeologica* 5 (1941): 195–218.

Tittoni, Maria Elisa, ed., *La facciata del Palazzo Sentorio in Campidoglio: Momenti di storia urbana di Roma*. Rome: Pacini Editore, 1994.

Todd, Malcolm, *The Walls of Rome*. London: Paul Elek, 1978.

Toebelmann, Fritz, *Römische Gebälke*. Heidelberg: Carl Winter, 1923.

Tomlison, R. A., *Greek Sanctuaries*. London: Paul Elek, 1976.

Torelli, Mario, "Augustus, Divus, Templum (Novum); Aedes," *LTUR* vol. 1, 145–6.
"Pax Augusta, Ara," *LTUR*, vol. 4, 70–4.
Typology and Structure of Roman Historical Reliefs, Jerome Lectures, ser. 14. Ann Arbor: University of Michigan Press, 1982.
Tortorici, Edoardo, *Argiletum: Commercio speculazione edilizia e lotta politica dall'analisi topografica di un quartiere di Roma di età repubblicana*. Rome: 'L'Erma' di Bretschneider, 1991.
"Argiletum," in *CFIFT*, 44–5.
"Argiletum," *LTUR*, vol. 1, 125–6.
"Curia Julia," *LTUR*, vol. 1, 332–4.
"Forum Iulium, Curia" in *CFIFT*, 15–44.
"Tempio di Giano," in *CFIFT*, 50–1.
Toynbee, Jocelyn M. C., *The Hadrianic School: A Chapter in the History of Greek Art*. Cambridge: Cambridge University Press, 1934.
Travlos, John, *Bildlexikon zur Topographie des Antiken Athens*. Tübingen: Verlag Ernst Wasmuth, 1971.
Turcan, R., "La 'Fondation' du Temple de Venus et de Roma," *Latomus* 23 (1964): 44–8.
Turfa, Jean MacIntosh, and Alwin G. Steinmayer, Jr., "The Comparative Structure of Greek and Etruscan Monumental Buildings," *PBRS* 64 (1996): 1–39.
Uggeri, Angelo, *Della Basilica Ulpia nel Foro Traiano: Istoria e ristaurazione*. Rome: n.p., n.d.
Ulrich, Roger B., "The Appiades Fountain of the Forum Iulium," *RömMitt* 93 (1986): 405–23.
"Julius Caesar and the Creation of the Forum Iulium," *AJA* 97 (1993): 49–80.
The Roman Orator and the Sacred Stage: The Roman Templum Rostratum. Brussells: Latomus, 1994.
"The Temple of Venus Genetrix in the Forum of Caesar in Rome: The Topography, History, Architecture, and the Sculptural Program of the Monument." Ph.D. diss., Yale University, 1984.
Ungaro, Lucrezia, *Il Foro di Augusto*. Rome: Fratelli Palombi Editori, 1997.
Vahlen, J., *Ennianae poesis reliquiae*. Leipzig; n.p., 1903.
Valadier, Giuseppe, "Tempio detto di Vesta in Roma," in *Raccolta della più insigni fabbriche di Roma antica*, vol. 3. Rome: n.p., 1813.
Valenzani, Riccardo Santangeli, "Serapis, Aedes, Templum," *LTUR*, vol. 4, 302–3.
Van Deman, Esther Boise, "Methods of Determining the Date of Roman Concrete Monuments," *AJA* 16 (1912): 230–51, 387–432.
"The Neronian Sacra Via," *AJA* 27 (1923): 383–424.
The Sullan Forum, reprinted from *JRS*. London: Society for the Promotion of Roman Studies, 1922.
Vendittelli, Laura, "Diana Aventina, Aedes," *LTUR*, vol. 2, 11–13.
Vermeule, Cornelius C., *The Goddess Roma in the Art of the Roman Empire*. Cambridge, MA: Spink, 1959.
Verrall, Margaret de Gaudrion Merrifield, and Jane E. Harrison, *Mythology and Monuments of Ancient Athens; Being a Translation of a Portion of the "Attica" of Pausanius*. New York: Macmillan, 1890.
Viale, Vittorio, and Mercedes Viale Ferrero, *Aosta: Roma e Medievale*. Turin: Istituto Bancario San Paolo di Torino, 1967.
Vighi, Roberto, *Il foro di Paestum e l'edificio teatrale di topi italico*. Rome: Danesi, 1947.
Virgili, Paola, "A proposito del Mausoleo di Augusto: B. Peruzzi aveva ragione," *ArchLaz* 6 (1984): 209–11.
and Paola Battistelli, "Indagini in Piazza della Rotonda e sulla fronte del Pantheon," *BullCom* 100 (1999): 137–54.
Viscogliosi, Alessandro, "Ad aedem Apollinis," *ArchLaz* 12.1 (1995): 71 7.
"Apollo, Aedes in Circo," *LTUR*, vol. 1, 49–54.
"Die Architektur-Dekoration der Cella des Apollo-Sosianus-Tempels," in *Kaiser Augustus*, 136–48.
"Bellona, Aedes in Circo," *LTUR*, vol. 1, 192.
"Circus Flaminius," *LTUR*, vol. 1, 269–72.
"Circus Maximus," *LTUR*, vol. 1, 272–7.
Il Tempio di Apollo 'in Circo' e la formazione del linguaggio architettonico Augusteo. Rome: 'L'Erma' di Bretschneider, 1996.
"Iuno Regina, Aedes in Campo, ad Circum Flaminium," *LTUR*, vol. 3, 126–8.
"Iuppiter Stator, Aedes ad Circum," *LTUR*, vol. 3, 157–9.
"Porticus Metelli," *LTUR*, vol. 4, 130–2.
"Porticus Octavia," *LTUR*, vol. 4, 139–41.
"Porticus Octaviae," *LTUR*, vol. 4, 141–5.
"Porticus Philippi," *LTUR*, vol. 3, 146–7.
Vitelli, Luca, "Il 'cantiere' del Tempio della Pace," in *CBFI*, 114–16.
Vitruvius, *The Ten Books on Architecture*. Ed. Morris Hickey Morgan. New York: Dover Publications, 1960.
Ten Books on Architecture. Trans. Ingrid D. Rowland. Cambridge University Press, 1999.
Vogel, Lise, *The Column of Antoninus Pius*. Cambridge: Harvard University Press, 1973.
Waele, Jos. A. de, "Satricum nel VI e V secolo a.c.: L'architettura templare," *ArchLaz*, 4 (1981): 310–16.
Walker, Susan, "The Moral Museum: Augustus and the City of Rome," in *Ancient Rome*, 61–75.
and Andrew Burnett, *The Image of Augustus*. London: British Museum, 1984.
Wallace-Hadrill, Andrew, *Augustan Rome*. London: Bristol Classical, 1993.
"The Emperor and His Virtues," *Historia* 30 (1981): 298–323.
"Image and Authority in the Coinage of Augustus," *JRS* 76 (1986): 66–87.
"Roman Arches and Greek Honours: The Language of Power at Rome," *Proceedings of the Cambridge Philological Society* n.s., 36 (1990): 143–81.
"The Social Structure of the Roman House," *PBSR* 43 (1988): 43–97.
Warden, P. Gregory, "The Domus Aurea Reconsidered," *JSAH* 40 (December 1981): 271–8.
Ward-Perkins, J. B., "An Early Augustan Capital in the Forum Romanum," *PBSR* 35 (1967): 22–8.
Roman Imperial Architecture. New York: Penguin Books, 1985.
"Veii: The Historical Topography," *PBSR*, 29 (1961).
and Amanda Claridge, *Pompeii AD 79: Exhibition. Royal Academy of Arts, Piccadilly, London*. London: Imperial Tobacco Limited, 1976.

Watkin, David, *A History of Western Architecture*. New York and London: Thames and Hudson, 1986.

Watson, Alan, *Rome of the XII Tables: Persons and Property*. Princeton: Princeton University Press, 1975.

Weber, Max, *Economy and Society: An Outline of Interpretive Sociology, II*. Ed. Guenther Roth and Claus Wittich. New York: Badminton Press, 1968.

Weinstock, Stefan, *Divus Julius*. Oxford: Clarendon Press, 1971.

Weller, Charles Heald, *Athens and Its Monuments*. New York: Macmillan, 1924.

Wellesley, Kenneth, "What Happened on the Capitolium in December AD 69?" *AJAH* 6 (1981): 166–90.

The Year of the Four Emperors. New York: Routledge, 2000.

Wild, John Peter, "The Roman Horizontal Loom," *AJA* 91 (1987): 459–71.

Wilentz, Sean, ed., *Rites of Power: Symbolism, Ritual, and Politics Since the Middle Ages*. Philadelphia: University of Pennsylvania Press, 1985.

Williams, Derek, *The Reach of Rome: A History of the Roman Imperial Frontier 1st–5th Centuries A.D.* London: Constable, 1997.

Wilson Jones, Mark, "Designing the Roman Corinthian Order," *JRA* 2 (1989): 35–69.

"One Hundred Feet and a Spiral Stair: The Problem of Designing Trajan's Column," *JRA* 6 (1993): 23–38.

"Principles of Design in Roman Architecture: The Setting Out of Centralised Buildings," *PBSR* 57 (1989): 106–151.

Principles of Roman Architecture. New Haven: Yale University Press, 2000.

"The Tempietto and the Roots of Coincidence," *AH* 33 (1990): 1–28.

Wilson, R. J. A., "Roman Art and Architecture," in *OHCW*, 771–806.

Sicily under the Roman Empire: The Archaeology of a Roman Province, 36 B.C.–A.D. 535. Wiltshire, England: Aris and Phillips, 1990.

Wiseman, T. P., "The Circus Flaminius," *PBSR* 42 (1974): 3–26.

"Flavians on the Capitoline," *AJAH* 3 (1978): 163–78.

"Two Questions on the Circus Flaminius," *PBSR* 44 (1976): 44–7.

Woodhead, A. G., *The Greeks in the West*. London: Thames and Hudson, 1962.

Wrightman, Greg, "The Imperial Fora of Rome: Some Design Considerations," *JSAH* 95 (March 1997): 64–85.

Zanker, Paul, "Der Apollontempel auf dem Palatin: Ausstattung und politische Sinnbezüge nach der Schlacht von Actium," in *Città e architettura*, 21–40.

"Das Trajansforum in Rom," *AA* 85 (1970): 499–544.

Pompeii: Public and Private Life. Trans. Deborah Lucas Schneider. Cambridge: Harvard University Press, 2000.

The Power of Images in the Age of Augustus. Trans. Alan Shapiro. Ann Arbor: University of Michigan Press, 1990.

Zevi, Fausto, "Il calcidico della Curia Iulia," *RAL* 26 (1971): 237–51.

"Mars in Circo," *LTUR*, vol. 3, 226–7.

Ziegler, Konrat, "Pantheon," *RE*, vol. 18, 697ff.

Ziolkowski, Adam, *The Temples of Mid-Republican Rome and Their Historical and Topographical Context*. Rome: 'L'Erma' di Bretschneider, 1992.

"Mummius' Temple of Hercules Victor and the Round Temple on the Tiber," *Phoenix* 42 (Winter 1988): 309–33.

"Pantheon," *LTUR*, vol. 4, 54–61.

"Was Agrippa's Pantheon the Temple of Mars in Campo?" *PBSR* 62 (1994): 267–82.

Zoch, Paul, *Ancient Rome: An Introductory History*. Norman: University of Oklahoma Press, 1998.

INDEX

26968217R00171

Made in the USA
San Bernardino, CA
23 February 2019

The ARCHITECTURE *of* ROMAN TEMPLES

The Republic to the Middle Empire

This book examines the development of Roman temple architecture from its earliest history in the sixth century B.C. to the reigns of Hadrian and the Antonines in the second century A.D. Although archaeologists, architects, and historians have studied these temples since the Renaissance, this book is unique for its specific analysis of Roman temples as a building type. John Stamper analyzes their formal qualities, the public spaces in which they were located, and, most importantly, the authority of precedent in their designs. The basis of that authority was the Temple of Jupiter Capitolinus, the city's first and most important temple. Stamper challenges the accepted reconstruction of this temple, proposing a new reconstruction and an assessment of its role in the transformation of Rome. He also traces Rome's temple architecture as it evolved over time and how it accommodated changing political and religious contexts, as well as the effects of new stylistic influences.

John W. Stamper is Associate Professor and Associate Dean in the School of Architecture at the University of Notre Dame. Both an architect and architectural historian, he is the author of *Chicago's North Michigan Avenue: Planning and Development, 1900–1930.*

Bài 1: AN TOÀN MÔI TRƯỜNG SALON

Trở thành người thợ chuyên nghiệp làm móng tay, có thể nói người thợ phải thành thạo trong kỷ thuật làm móng giả như bọc móng, sửa móng (nail wrap), bột acrylic, và gel. Từ kỷ thuật cao này, dĩ nhiên phải cần đến những hóa chất và cũng từ việc sử dụng kém khôn ngoan sẽ dẫn đến nguy hại sức khỏe cho khách và chính bạn.

Mặc dù các nhà sản xuất (manufacturer) cố gắng mức tối đa để bảo vệ, nhưng tốt nhất là thợ cần phải hiểu biết, học hỏi phương cách sử dụng hóa chất được an toàn.

Những hoá chất thường gặp trong kỷ thuật làm móng giả như:

- Bột acrylic (polymer)	*- Nước acrylic (monomer)*	*- Gel móng*
- Nước sơn (nail polish)	*- Chùi nước sơn (polish remover)*	*- Aceton*
- Chất kết dính (primer)	*- Chất làm khô (dehydrator)*	*- Đèn cực tím (U.V)*
- Keo dán móng, vá móng	*- Kem mềm da (cuticle softener)*	*- Alcohol70 %*
- Nước sơn lót (base coat)	*- Dầu thoa da (cuticle oil)*	*- Top coat*

Vì quá nhiều hóa chất trong kỷ nghệ làm móng tay hiện nay nên khi sử dụng cần học hỏi thế nào là sự tiếp xúc quá độ (overexposure).

Thông thường hóa chất xâm nhập vào cơ thể gây nguy hại sức khỏe qua:

-Hấp thụ qua tiếp xúc ở làn da

-Hóa chất vô ý vào lưỡi qua ngón tay đụng thức ăn (ăn hóa chất)

-Hít vào qua đường khí quản tiến vào phổi

Nếu biết kiểm soát qua những ngã xâm nhập này, sự nguy hại gần như không đáng kể cho sức khỏe của bạn và khách.

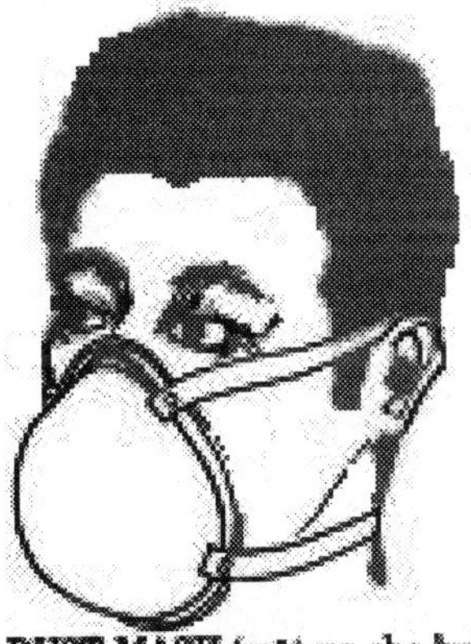

DUST MASK (mặt nạ che bụi)

Vài dấu hiệu cảnh giác về sự tiếp xúc nhiều hóa chất như:

- Uể oải	*- Chảy nước mũi, nước mắt*	*- Mệt, khó thở*
- Hơi nhức đầu	*- Mất ngủ*	*Nổi mụt nhỏ, ngứa rát da*
- Đau, khô cổ	*- Tê ngón chân*	*- Ngứa ngáy*

Sau khi nhận biết có những dấu hiệu trên, cần ngưng ngay và các dấu hiệu này sẽ nhanh chóng vượt qua bằng cách thay đổi chỗ làm việc được thoáng khí hơn.

Nếu trong một salon mà sự làm thông thoáng chỉ dùng air cleaner, mở cửa, quạt trần nhà,hoặc quạt để bàn.... , đây chỉ là hình thức làm không khí xoay chuyển quanh salon. Hệ thống thông hơi là phải làm hơi khí độc hại và bụi bậm được đẩy ra ngoài salon (good ventilation).

Hạn chế dùng bình hơi có sức ép như keo phun tóc, phun nước sơn nhanh khô, các sản phẩm từ hóa chất acrylic, gel, v.v... rất dễ bốc hơi, tạo làn hơi bụi đầy hóa chất quanh salon và ô nhiễm môi trường làm việc, rất khó kiểm soát sự nguy hại nếu không có hệ thống thông khí ra ngoài.

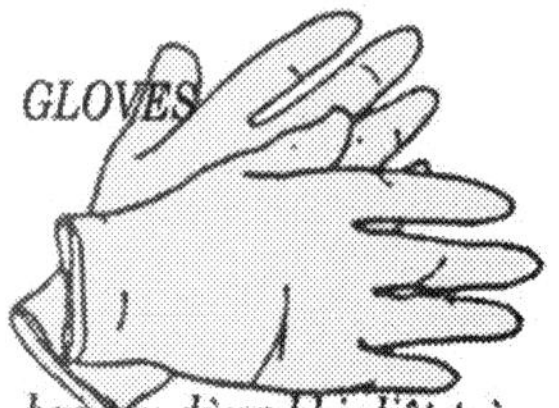

bao tay dùng khi diệt trùng

Để giảm bớt mức độ tiếp xúc hoá chất bằng cách:

- Đậy chặt bình chứa sau khi dùng
- Rót ra khối lượng nhỏ và có nắp đậy
- Hệ thống thoát hơi và hệ thống lọc khí bằng than thật tốt.

Theo luật định thì các nhà sản xuất phải cung cấp chỉ dẫn về an toàn vật liệu cho người tiêu thụ bằng bảng dữ kiện an toàn vật liệu (M.S.D.S).

Bảng M.S.D.S cho biết những chi tiết sau:

- *Nguy hại của hóa chất khi tiếp xúc trên làn da, đường hô hấp, rủi ro nuốt vào.*
- *Sự xâm nhập của hóa chất vào cơ thể chủ yếu qua đường miệng, da, và phổi*
- *Khả năng gây ung thư do hóa chất và cách cất giữ an toàn*
- *Sự nguy hại và lý do hóa chất nổ, cháy, và sự bốc hơi v.v...*
- *Nguy hại của sự tiếp xúc ngắn hạn hoặc dài hạn*
- *Tẩy rửa hóa chất chảy, đổ. Cách dùng thích hợp, an toàn cho sản phẩm đó Lời khuyên khi có cấp cứu, số điện thoại cần liên lạc*

Mùi hóa chất không liên quan đến sự an toàn. Vài chất nguy hiểm đôi khi có mùi thơm và ngay cả tiếp xúc nhiều với mùi thơm cũng có hại nữa. Mùi cảnh giác về nguy cơ tiếp xúc quá độ. Hơi khí hóa chất có thể tích tụ vào contact lens và ô nhiễm có thể gây hư hại đôi mắt. Dung dịch monomer, acetone, chất chùi nước sơn, cồn và sự rủi ro các chất ấy vấy vào mắt sẽ đau rát cần phải đi cấp cứu ngay. Gần 40% thương tật về mắt đều do sử dụng cẩu thả về hóa chất.

Phương cách giúp làm việc được an toàn:

- *Luôn rửa tay trước khi ăn bất cứ món nào. Nếu không, tay bạn cầm thức ăn và dẫn đến chính là bạn ăn hóa chất.*
- *Hướng dẫn cho khách trước khi cần chăm sóc chân (pedicure), không nên wax lấy lông chân hoặc cạo lông vì dễ nhiễm trùng. Thời gian cần ít nhất là 24 giờ và để ý tránh cào xước da khi cạo lông chân.*
- *Đừng để làn da tiếp xúc đến đầu cọ đắp bột acrylic, dung dịch acrylic, keo, acetone ... sẽ làm da khô và dị ứng.*
- *Không dùng sản phẩm không có nhãn hiệu, quá hạn.*
- *Đừng cất thức ăn, đồ uống chung cùng tủ lạnh với hóa chất hành nghề*
- *Sản phẩm có thể bốc cháy nếu gần đèn, lò gas, lò nhiệt hoặc sau thùng xe*
- *Liên lạc trung tâm kiểm soát chất độc, khi xảy ra tai nạn và cất giữ tờ M.S.D.S*
- *Đừng hút thuốc trong salon vì nhiều hóa chất rất dễ gây cháy*
- *Nên dùng thùng rác bằng kim loại và cần có nắp đậy để tránh bốc hơi*
- *Đừng ăn uống trong salon vì hóa chất, bụi bặm dễ bám vào thức ăn và đồ uống*

- *Nếu khách có bệnh tiểu đường mà họ cần làm pedicure thì nên ngâm chân vào nước ấm thôi khoảng 85- 90 độ F, không dùng nước nóng.*

Cơ quan quản trị an toàn nghề nghiệp (OSHA) luôn bảo vệ cho bạn và khách hàng. Vì thế, thợ chuyên nghiệp phải sử dụng những hóa chất được F.D.A chuẩn nhận, theo dõi tin tức, cập nhật hóa luật lệ và thay đổi việc sử dụng các hóa chất liên quan đến nghề nghiệp. Hiện nay nhiều tiểu bang áp dụng luật khắt khe vệ sinh cho bồn ngâm chân (pedicure spa). Trong quá khứ đã xảy ra nhiều bệnh cho khách, do đó thợ cần theo dõi luật tiểu bang về cách chùi rửa và tẩy trùng bồn ngâm chân và kèm theo bảng chi tiết trách nhiệm của người thợ sử dụng bồn ngâm.

Là một người thợ chuyên nghiệp cũng cần biết cách bảo vệ sức khỏe mình, đơn giản bằng cách giữa những lần hẹn khách, nên bước ra ngoài một ít phút để vận động và hít thở không khí tươi mát; mang mặt nạ che bụi; đừng để hướng gió thổi vào mặt khi xử dụng hóa chất. Điều này cũng phần nào giúp bớt đi tầm nguy hại cho sức khỏe.

TAI NẠN CÓ THỂ XẢY RA Ở SALON

- **Primer văng tóe vào da, vào mắt khách.**

Hóa tính primer giúp dính chặt giữa mặt móng và lớp bột móng khi làm móng acrylic. Primer là dạng acid mạnh, ăn mòn và bỏng cháy, lỡ nhiễu vào da, vào mắt cần cởi bỏ quần áo và dùng bông gòn hoặc khăn thấm nước mát lau ngay, lau nhiều lần nếu dính vào làn da. Nếu primer văng vào mắt phải giúp khách vốc nước mát rửa mắt trong 15 phút và gọi ngay cấp cứu.

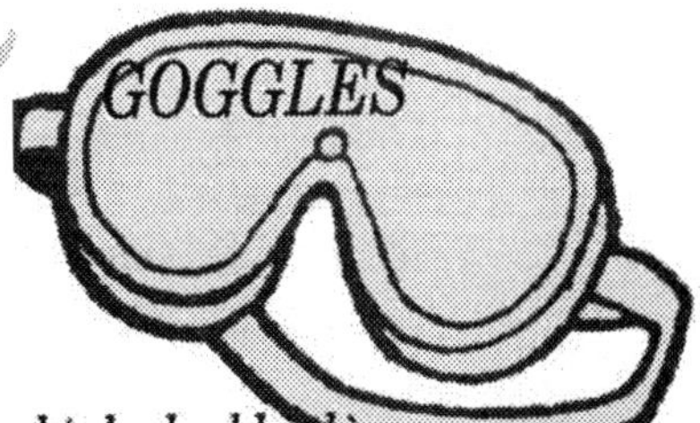

kính che khi dùng primer

- **Lỡ cắt đứt da**

Khách bị đứt tay khi làm móng, nên dẫn khách rửa tay sạch, lau khô, thoa chất sát trùng 3% Hydrogen Peroxide và băng lại. Đặc biệt nếu thợ bị đứt tay cũng làm tương tự như khách và mang bao tay làm tiếp. Bông gòn có máu bỏ vào bao nhựa kín vứt vào thùng rác và diệt trùng dụng cụ khoảng 15 phút bằng nước Quats

ĐỀ PHÒNG TAI NẠN Ở SALON

- Hiểu rõ sự nguy hại hóa chất, mở đóng nắp cẩn thận. Các lọ hóa chất cổ nhỏ tránh bốc hơi.
- Môi trường salon thông khí tốt, đặt hệ thống lọc khí, hút khí ra ngoài (ventilation system) và đặt hệ thống báo động khí độc (carbon monoxide alarm).
- Đeo kính an toàn khi gỡ móng acrylic, khẩu trang để tránh bụi bột acrylic. Dùng găng tay bằng nhựa vinyl, loại bao tay latex dễ gây dị ứng.
- Sử dụng sản phẩm đúng tiêu chuẩn qui định ngành thẩm mỹ tiểu bang. Bản thông tin an toàn sản phẩm chứa chất độc đặt nơi dễ thấy.

Ngành thẩm mỹ là ngành làm đẹp cho đời, tuy nhiên rất nhiều hóa chất trong ngành nails, đặc biệt các hóa chất cho móng acrylic, primer …. Nếu không xử dụng đúng sẽ tác hại vô cùng. Sự cẩu thả, thiếu vệ sinh chẳng những làm mất niềm tin cho khách, bị phạt tiền hoặc rút bằng hành nghề từ cơ quan kiểm tra mà còn làm ảnh hưởng kỷ nghệ thẩm mỹ, mà điều quan trọng trên hết là trực tiếp tác hại sức khỏe của khách hàng và chính chúng ta.

WORKING SAFETY

(An toàn nơi làm việc)

HYGIENCE *(Vệ Sinh)*

- **Do not bite your fingernails**. Nails should be manicured and well-groomed at all times. Always cover the mouth when sneezing or coughing; to prevent the spread of germs.
  Không nên cắn móng tay. Móng tay cần chăm sóc và luôn luôn gọn gàng. Luôn luôn che miệng khi hắt hơi hoặc ho để đề phòng việc lây lan vi trùng
- Do not lend or borrow personal items such as combs, drinking cups, brushes or cosmetics. Diseases or infections may be transmitted in this manner.
  Không nên cho mượn hoặc mượn vật dụng cá nhân như lược, ly uống nước, bàn chải hoặc mỹ phẩm. Bệnh hoặc nhiễm trùng có thể lây lan qua vật dụng này.

- **Keep articles** out of the mouth for sanitary reasons and to prevent accidental swallowing or injury. Use your own towel and wash cloth to prevent contact with germs. Bathe daily to keep the body clean and free from odor
  Đừng ngậm, giữ đồ vật bằng miệng vì lý do vệ sinh và cũng để ngăn ngừa sự rủi ro nuốt vào hoặc bị thương. Dùng khăn riêng và áo giặt sạch để ngăn ngừa tiếp xúc với vi trùng gây bệnh. Tắm rửa hằng ngày để giữ thân thể sạch và không có mùi
- To avoid body odors, deodorants or anti-perspirants should be used daily. Brush teeth and massage gums at least twice daily. Use mouth wash to prevent bad breath. Do not rub the eyes when trying to remove foreign matter from them.
  Đánh răng và massage lợi răng tối thiểu 2 lần một ngày. Nên súc miệng thường xuyên để ngăn ngừa mùi hôi. Để tránh thân thể có mùi, chất khử mùi và chống mồ hôi nên dùng hằng ngày. Đừng nên chà vào mắt trong lúc cố gắng lấy vật lạ dính vào mắt.

- **Maintain a healthy** body by exercise, adequate rest and a balanced diet. Wear clean undergarments and clean hose. To avoid fatigue, maintain correct posture when walking, standing or sitting.
  Mặc quần áo sạch và tất sạch Giữ cho cơ thể khỏe mạnh bằng cách tập thể dục, ngủ đủ và ăn uống điều độ. Để tránh mỏi mệt, giữ cơ thể cân bằng đúng cách khi đi bộ, đứng hoặc ngồi
- **Women should keep** her legs and armpits free of superfluous hair by using a safety razor or depilatories. Drink a sufficient quantity of water to keep the digestive system functioning properly and to promote better elimination.
  Phụ nữ nên dùng dao cạo hoặc phương pháp lấy lông nào để không có nhiều lông trên chân và nách. Uống đủ lượng nước cho cơ thể để giữ cho hệ thống tiêu hóa và bài tiết hoạt động tốt hơn.

- **Have a dental examination** at least every six months. Some clients are allergic to cigarette smoke; avoid smoking in salon and their presence.
  Nên khám răng định kỳ tối thiểu là mỗi 6 tháng. Một số khách dị ứng với khói thuốc, tránh hút thuốc ở tiệm và có sự hiện diện của họ.
- When bleeding, use powdered alum or alum solution not styptic pencil. Always wear gloves and safety glasses when using primer. Primers can cause serious, irreversible, damage to the eye and skin.
  Khi chảy máu, dùng bột phèn (alum) hoặc dung dịch alum cầm máu không nên dùng loại viết chì cầm máu. Luôn mang bao tay và kính an toàn khi dùng primer. Prime gây trầm trọng, không chữa trị được, hư mắt và da.

- **Do not re- use soiled linens**; place them in a covered container. Do not use any article dropped on the floor. It must be washed and sanitized before using again.
  Đừng dùng lại vải đã dùng rồi; bỏ chúng và thùng có nắp đậy. Không nên dùng bất cứ vật dụng gì rớt trên nền nhà. Vật đó phải được rửa và khử trùng trước khi dùng lại.
- Do not use in common a styptic alum stick for cuts. An infection may result. Do not use a common drinking utensil, powder puff, facial brush. Diseases may be spread from one person to another in this manner.
  Không nên dùng thỏi phèn chua cầm máu khi bị cắt đứt. Nhiễm trùng dễ xảy ra.
  Không nên dùng đi dùng lại cùng một ly uống nước, bông đánh phấn, bàn chải mặt. Bệnh có thể lây lan từ người sang người nếu dùng chung vật liệu đó.

- **Do not smell** the contents of a bottle in order to identify it. All bowls, containers, and shampoo sinks should be cleaned and sanitized after use. Place them in their proper places.
  Không nên ngửi dung dịch chứa trong bình để xác định chất đó. Tất cả các tô, đồ chứa và bồn gội tóc nên được giữ sạch và khử trùng sau khi dùng. Đặt chúng đúng vị trí.
- Remove cotton, oil or other liquids from the floor to prevent slipping or falling. Carefully read labels on jars and bottles before using contents
  Lấy, lau đi những bông gòn, dầu hoặc các hóa chất khác rớt trên nền nhà để đề phòng trơn trợt hoặc té ngã. Đọc kỹ nhản hiệu trên lọ hoặc bình chứa trước khi sử dụng chúng.
- Do not use contents of broken jars or bottles. Place in a paper bag, label broken glass, and place in trash container. Work only under adequate light. Improper lighting will result in eyestrain. Wear eyeglasses if prescribed.
  Không nên dùng chai, lọ bị vỡ. Đặt chúng trong bao giấy ghi vật dụng thủy tinh bị vỡ, và đặt trong thùng rác. Chỉ nên làm chỗ có đủ ánh sáng. Nếu không đủ sáng sẽ làm mắt mỏi mệt. Kính mắt được bác sĩ cấp.

- Wipe the cream or oil from the outside of bottles or jars. It will prevent the jars or bottles from slipping out of your hands. When sanitizing glass electrodes, using a pad of cotton dampened in 70% alcohol
  Lau sạch kem và dầu bên ngoài chai, lọ. Điều này đề phòng trợt tay khi đụng đến chai hoặc lọ.
  Khi khử trùng điện cực thủy tinh, nên dùng miếng bông gòn thấm ẩm cồn 70%.

- **The boiling or steaming time of water** and the immersion time of implements in a chemical solution should conform to the State Board of Cosmetology regulations issued by your State. Keep a complete first aid kit on hand.
  Thời gian nước sôi, xông hơi bằng nước và nhúng dụng cụ vào hóa chất diệt trùng do sự ấn định của ngành thẩm mỹ được điều hành bởi tiểu bang. Giữ đầy đủ dụng cụ cấp cứu trong tầm tay

- **Purchase chemicals** in small quantities and store them in a cool, dry place; otherwise they may deteriorate due to contact with air, light and heat. Alcohol evaporates quickly, has a cooling effect. Therefore, can apply alcohol to the acrylic nails when the acrylic nails get hot from the chemical action of the product.
  Mua hóa chất trong số lượng nhỏ và cất chúng vào nơi mát, khô; nếu không thì có thể phân hủy do tiếp xúc với không khí, ánh đèn và nóng. Cồn bay hơi nhanh, có tính làm mát, dịu lại. Vì vậy, có thể đắp cồn tới móng acrylic khi móng bột bị nóng do tác dụng của hóa chất.

MANICURING &PEDICURING *(Ngành chăm sóc tay và chân)*

- Handle sharp-pointed implements carefully and avoid dropping them. To prevent injury, avoid pushing the cuticle back too far.
  Giữ vật dụng bén nhọn cẩn thận và tránh rớt xuống. Đề phòng bị thương, tránh đẩy da lùi quá xa.
- Bevel a sharp toenail with an emery board. Do not use a sharp, pointed implement to clean under the nail. Don't file deeply into toenail and fingernail corners. Do not work on a hands or feet that are diseased or contain pus.
  Giũa nhẹ những cạnh bén ở móng chân với giũa giấy. Đừng dùng dụng cụ bén nhọn để làm sạch dưới móng. Đừng giũa sâu vào góc móng chân và móng tay. Đừng phục vụ cho khách có tay và chân bị bệnh hoặc có mủ.
- **Apply an antiseptic immediately** if the skin is accidentally cut. Apply styptic powder or alum solution to stop the bleeding from a small cut. Never use a styptic pencil. Avoid too much pressure at the base of the nail. Do not cut the cuticle, nip only any large hangnails.
  Thoa chất sát trùng ngay nếu da bị rủi cắt đứt. Thoa bột cầm máu hoặc dung dịch alum để ngưng máu từ các vết cắt nhỏ. Không bao giờ dùng viết chì cầm máu. Tránh ép nhiều ở nền móng. Đừng cắt da, chỉ tỉa bất cứ những miếng da xướt lớn.

- **Do not give a pedicure** to a person with a foot infection. If bleeding during a procedure, stop the service, wash client's hands, blot dry and apply styptic. The implement is cleaned and disinfected, or use another sanitized implement.
  Đừng làm pedicure với người có nhiễm trùng chân. Nếu chảy máu trong lúc làm, ngừng công việc, rửa tay khách, lau khô và thoa thuốc cầm máu. Dụng cụ được làm sạch và diệt trùng, hoặc dùng dụng cụ sạch khác.
- Add an antiseptic to the foot bath. Do not massage over the shin bone or above the knee. Insert cotton or toenail seperator between the toes before applying nail polish. This will prevent polish smear.
  Thêm chất sát trùng vào nước ngâm chân. Đừng massage trên xương ống hoặc trên đầu gối. Đưa bông gòn hoặc miếng ngăn giữa các ngón chân trước khi sơn móng. Điều này để đề phòng sơn lem vấy lên da.

- Never perform a manicure or pedicure on hands and feet with a contagious disease such as tinea or tinea pedis. Never massage for clients who have heart condition, had a stroke, and high blood pressure
  Không nên làm manicure hoặc pedicure trên tay và chân có bệnh truyền nhiễm như nấm vòng và nấm chân.
  Không bao giờ massage cho khách có bệnh tim, bị kích ngất đột quỵ, và máu cao

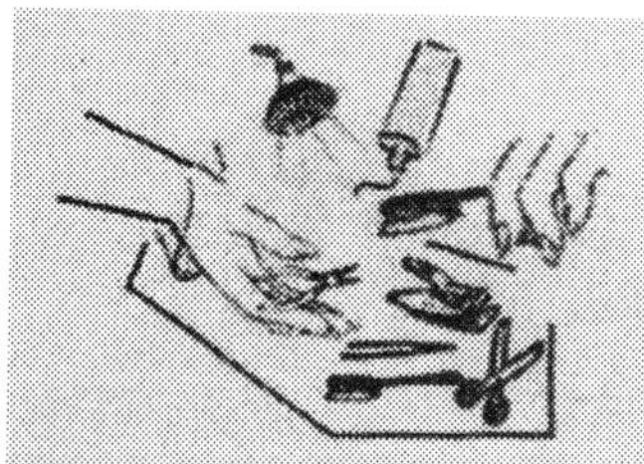

Brush with Liquid soap & warm water
Dùng bàn chải chà rửa dụng cụ

- **Moisture and dirt** may trap under the nail when acrylic nails lift, crack or grow out and are not maintained in a proper manner. **Calluses should be softened** and smoothed not removed; gentle rubbing with pumice powder or an abrasive.
  Chất ẩm và dơ có thể nhét bên dưới móng khi móng bột bị hở, nứt hoặc mọc dài ra và không được bảo trì đúng cách. Da chai cần được làm mềm và mịn không nên lấy đi; chà nhè nhẹ với đá bọt hoặc giũa
- Soften the edges on your abrasive when filing because a new file can etch a groove in the nail. If lifting is excessive, soak off the acrylic with aceton for 15 to 25 minutes and start fresh with a new acrylic nails.
  Làm mềm cạnh cây giũa khi cần giũa móng vì giũa mới có thể làm đứt rãnh móng. Nếu móng tay hở nhiều, nhúng bột acrylic vào aceton 15 đến 25 phút và bắt đầu làm bộ móng bột mới.

Bài 2: SIÊU VI KHUẨN HIV, BỆNH AIDS, VÀ VIÊM GAN

HIV (Human Immuno deficiency Virus) là siêu vi khuẩn tiêu diệt tính miễn nhiễm tự nhiên của cơ thể. Theo nghiên cứu siêu vi khuẩn HIV có từ 50 năm trước và khám phá từ loại khỉ xanh của người Phi Châu và năm 1959 phát hiện trong ngân hàng máu của người Phi Châu chứa rất nhiều vi khuẩn bệnh AIDS.

AIDS (Acquired Immune Deficiency Symdrome) là triệu chứng thiếu sót tính miễn nhiễm tự tạo trong cơ thể. AIDS là triệu chứng có nghĩa là tiếp nhận những dấu hiệu đáng lưu ý tạo bệnh chứ không phải bệnh. Ví dụ như đau cổ họng, nóng, đau khớp xương là những triệu chứng dẫn đến bệnh cúm (flu).

Một người có những nguyên nhân thiếu sót tính miễn nhiễm trong cơ thể (AIDS) là tạo ra HIV siêu vi khuẩn cực nhỏ, không thể thấy dễ dàng, là những siêu khuẩn tiêu diệt tính miễn nhiểm của người. Siêu vi khuẩn (virus) nhỏ hơn, đơn giản hơn, và khác hơn vi trùng (bacteria), vi trùng nhỏ hơn 100 lần so với đường kính của sợi tóc trong khi siêu vi khuẩn nhỏ hơn 50 lần vi trùng. Siêu vi khuẩn là ký sinh trùng, sống bên trong tế bào khác, chúng không thể sống và sinh sản tự chúng được, chúng phải làm nhiễm trùng vi trùng hoặc các mô tế bào để sống.

Triệu chứng AIDS có thể kéo dài hơn 10 năm tiến tới HIV sang giai đoạn nhiễm trùng. Thường dấu hiệu đầu tiên của HIV khoảng 3 tháng sau khi nhiễm trùng. Có dấu hiệu giống như bệnh cúm là tiêu chảy, buồn nôn, đau bắp thịt, thường xuyên mỏi mệt và cũng nhanh chóng biến mất.

Sự lây truyền HIV thường là do:

- Người có đời sống cẩu thả, sống ngoài lề đường, giao hợp bừa bãi với nhiều người khác nhau mà không mang dụng cu, bọc cao su bảo vệ, những người dùng thuốc kích thích, dùng chung kim chích, giao hợp bằng đường hậu môn nên vi khuẩn dễ xâm nhập qua những vết trầy xướt nhất là đối với phụ nữ, những người lạm dụng loại thuốc kích thích dễ gây nghiện, những người sống ở nơi nghèo khổ thiếu thông tin về vệ sinh ở những nước Phi Châu, Haiti

Tuy nhiên AIDS không thể lây truyền tay qua tay, ôm nhau, hôn hít, ăn uống chung, dùng cùng điện thoại và ngay cả ngồi cùng bồn cầu tiểu, tiện, hoặc luôn dùng bao condom khi giao hợp.

HEPATITIS (viêm gan)

Gan nằm bên phải, dưới lồng ngực nặng từ 2.5 pounds đến 4 pounds, là cơ quan chính thanh lọc độc tố, chuyển hóa thức ăn và giữ vai trò trọng yếu bảo trì sức khỏe. Gan phụ nữ nhỏ hơn gan đàn ông.
Năm 1930, khoa học đã khởi đầu khảo nghiệm gan và mãi đến 1973 mới tìm được viêm gan A phần nào hiểu được từ những chứng bệnh ngã nước bí ẩn xa xưa.

- **Viêm gan A** có thể lây lan qua mồ hôi, nước bọt, nước tiểu và nhiều nhất là phân người có bệnh và lây lan nhanh ở những nước nghèo, thiếu kiến thức vệ sinh.
- **Viêm gan B** thường gây ra cấp tính (acute hepatitis), mãn tính (chronic active hepatitis), chai gan (liver cirrhosis) và ung thư gan (liver cancer). Cứ 1 trong 3 người là có viêm gan B và hiện có khoảng 400 triệu người ở thời kỳ mãn tính. Vi khuẩn có trong máu, tinh dịch, nước tiểu, nước mắt, mồ hôi nhưng dễ dàng nhất là máu và tinh dịch.
- **Viêm gan C** cực kỳ nhỏ bé nhưng bọc bởi lớp vỏ cứng chắc rất khó chết ở điều kiện diệt trùng thông thường, khoảng 80% con người bệnh viêm gan C mãn tính. Viêm gan C xâm nhập tàn phá, tiêu hủy gan dẫn đến sưng gan và xơ gan (liver fibrosis), chai gan và ung thư gan. Cho đến nay chưa có thuốc trị.
- **Viêm gan D** là 1 dạng vi khuẩn đặc biệt sống nhờ vào vi khuẩn B gọi là vi khuẩn Delta. Đây là loại vi khuẩn nguy hiểm nhất, tàn phá mạnh lá gan và người bệnh chết rất nhanh.

MẶT TRƯỚC BỘ XƯƠNG

1. **Skull**: sọ
2. **Mandible**: xương hàm dưới
3. **Hyoid Bone**: xương yết hầu
4. **Cervical Vertebra**: đốt xương cổ
5. **Clavicle**: xương đòn
6. **Sternum**: xương ức
7. **Costal Cartilage**: sụn sườn
8. **Ribs**: xương sườn
9. **Scapula**: xương vai
10. **Humerus**: xương cánh tay trên
11. **Radius**: xương quay
12. **Ulna**: xương trụ
13. **Carpal Bones**: xương cổ tay
14. **Metacarpal Bones**: xương bàn tay
15. **Phalanges of Fingers**: các lóng ngón tay
16. **Thoracic Vertebra**: đốt xương trụ
17. **Lumbar Vertebra**: đốt xương thắt lưng
18. **Sacrum**: xương cùng
19. **Os Coxa**: xương khớp háng
20. **Femur**: xương đùi
21. **Patella**: xương đầu gối
22. **Tibia**: xương chày
23. **Fibula**: xương mác
24. **Tarsal Bones**: xương cổ chân
25. **Metatarsal Bones**: xương bàn chân
26. **Phalanges of Toes**: xương lóng ngón chân

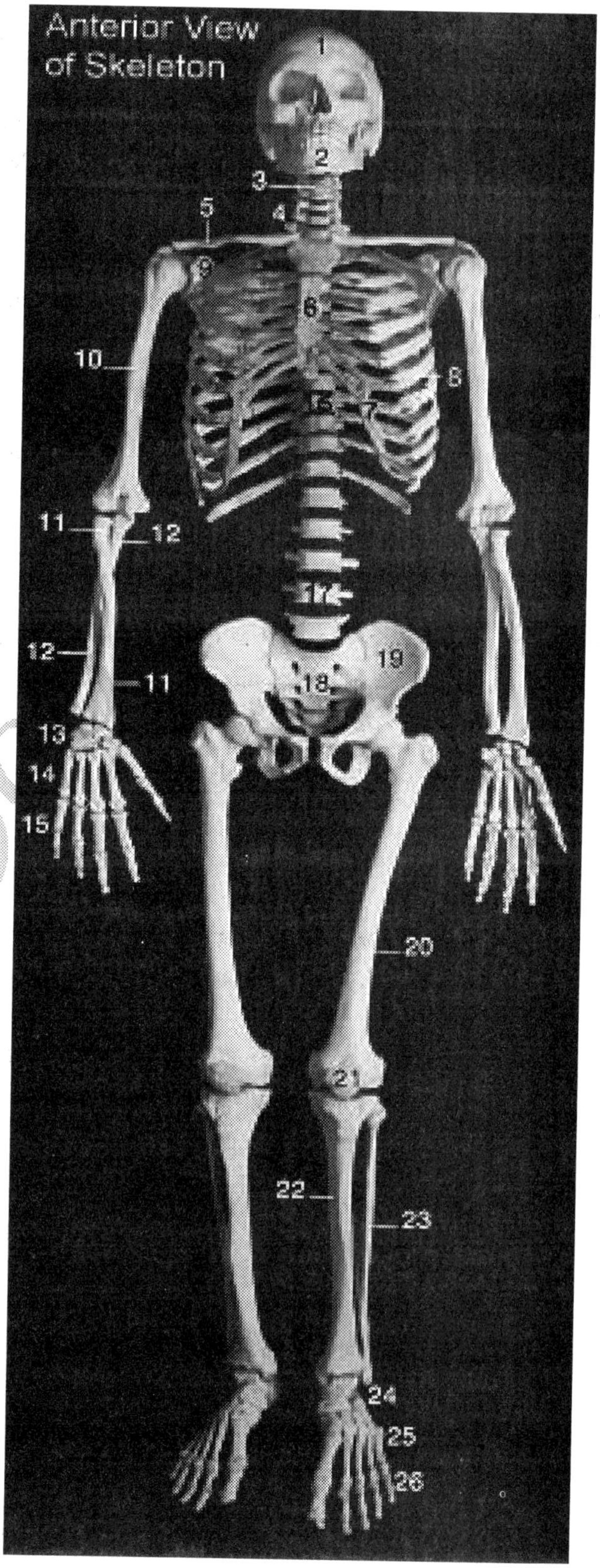

HIV/AIDS/ HEPATITIS

(Siêu vi khuẩn HIV-Bệnh AIDS-Bệnh viêm gan)

HIV- The cause of AIDS (*siêu vi khuẩn HIV là nguyên nhân gây bệnh AIDS).*

Africans see the disease as a product of Western lifestyles; they learned that one type of HIV is almost identical to a virus found in the African green monkey.
Người Phi châu xem bệnh này như là một sản phẩm của người phương Tây; họ học và biết được một loại HIV là vi khuẩn nhận biết qua từ loại khỉ xanh ở Phi châu.

Special studies on how HIV has evolved indicated that has existed for at least 50 years. AIDS is actually a syndrome, not a disease
Theo nghiên cứu đặc biệt HIV có dấu hiệu phát triển và tồn tại ít nhất là 50 năm. AIDS là triệu chứng chứ không phải bệnh

Further evidence has also been uncovered to support this idea. Stored, frozen blood samples taken from people in Africa in 1959 contained the AIDS-causing virus, HIV.
Những chứng minh thêm cũng chẳng khám phá để giúp cho ý kiến này. Máu đông cất giữ từ những người dân ở Phi Châu năm 1959 chứa nhiều bệnh AIDS.

Human Immunodeficiency Virus (HIV):_ *Siêu vi khuẩn tiêu diệt miễn nhiễm của con người*
Visual sign of HIV are tiny viruses, smaller than bacteria which are visible through a powerful electron microscope. Viruses are so simple they cannot live or reproduce on their own. To live, a virus must infect a bacteria or tissue
HIV là loại siêu vi trùng rất nhỏ chỉ thấy được nếu qua sự phóng cực đại từ kính hiển vi điện tử, nhỏ hơn cả vi trùng. Virus không thể sống hoặc tự sanh sản được. Để sống còn, siêu vi khuẩn phải tấn công & tạo sự nhiễm trùng vào các vi trùng hoặc các mô sống khác.

Acquired Immune Deficiency Syndrome (AIDS): *Triệu chứng thiếu sót miễn nhiễm tự tạo*
The collection of signs and symptoms that occur in such a case is called acquired immune deficiency syndrome or AIDS.
Sự thu thập dấu hiệu và triệu chứng xảy ra như trong trường hợp được gọi là triệu chứng thiếu sót miễn nhiễm tự tạo hoặc AIDS

AIDS is not a disease. It is a collection of symptoms that show that the body is no longer capable of protecting itself from infection or disease.
AIDS không phải là bệnh. Là một sự tập hợp các triệu chứng biểu hiện dấu hiệu cơ thể không có khả năng bảo vệ từ sự nhiễm trùng hoặc bệnh.

Transmitting the AIDS Virus *(Sự lan truyền của siêu vi khuẩn bệnh AIDS)*
Bacteria are 100 times smaller than the diameter of a human hair. Virus, however, are 50 times smaller than bacteria.
Vi trùng nhỏ hơn 100 lần so với đường kính của sợi tóc. Tuy nhiên siêu vi khuẩn lại 50 lần nhỏ hơn vi trùng.

Viruses are parasites. They can only live inside another cell called a host cell. Outside the host cell, viruses die quickly.
Siêu vi khuẩn là kí sinh trùng. Chúng có thể sống bên trong của một tế bào còn gọi là tế bào chủ (con tin)

Studies show that 99% of HIV is destroyed after several hours on dry surfaces.
In 1892, a young Russian scientist named Dimitrii Ivanovsky was the first to discover the existence of viruses.
Qua nghiên cứu có tới 99% siêu vi khuẩn bị tiêu hủy sau vài giờ trên bề mặt khô.
Năm 1892, nhà khoa học trẻ Dimitrii Ivanovsky, người Nga đầu tiên khám phá sự tồn tại của virus.

Viruses cause many human illnesses, such as influenza, measles, rubella, rabies, yellow fever, cold sores, herpes, mumps, chicken pox, warts, polio, AIDS and certain kinds of cancer.
Siêu vi khuẩn là nguyên nhân làm con người bệnh hoạn, như cúm (influenza), sởi (measles), bệnh phong chấn (rubella), bệnh dại (rabies), sốt vàng da (yellow fever), nấm lỡ miệng (cold sores), mụt giộp nước (herpes), bệnh quai bị (mumps), đậu mùa (chicken pox), mụn cóc (warts), tê liệt (polio), AIDS và một số bệnh ung thư khác.

Viruses enter the body it infects a tissues cell and once a cell is infected by a virus many things can happen. These viruses cause symptoms and disease very quickly. People infected with HIV usually don't show symptoms for 10 to 11 years.
Siêu vi khuẩn tiến vào cơ thể nhiễm trùng mô tế bào và tế bào bị nhiễm trùng do siêu vi khuẩn xảy ra nhiều biến chuyển. Những siêu vi khuẩn này là nguyên nhân gây triệu chứng và bệnh cực kỳ nhanh chóng. Con người nhiễm HIV thường thì chưa thấy được triệu chứng có đến 10, 11 năm sau đó.

Transmitting HIV *(lan truyền HIV)*

In the first 11 years of the epidemic over 57,000 heterosexual women and men in the United States have gotten AIDS by sharing needles.
Trong 11 năm đầu tiên bệnh dịch có hơn 57.000 trường hợp giao hợp nghịch giống đàn bà và đàn ông tại Hoa Kỳ mắc phải bệnh AIDS do dùng chung kim chích.

The second most risky type of behavior is anal sex. During anal sex, the virus may enter the blood stream through these small tears. Women are 2 – 3 times more likely to be infected if they participate in anal sex. Other studies have shown that over 90% of all new infections in gay men are a result of anal sex.
Sự nguy hiểm thứ nhì là dạng giao hợp bằng hậu môn. Trong thời kỳ đó, siêu vi khuẩn có thể tiến vào dòng máu qua những vết rách trầy nhỏ. Phụ nữ tăng từ 2 đến 3 lần hơn về tính nhiễm trùng nếu họ cho giao hợp bằng hậu môn. Một số nghiên cứu khác cho biết hơn 90 % sự nhiễm trùng của người đồng tính là kết quả của giao hợp bằng hậu môn

And:

- Blood to blood contact
  Tiếp xúc từ máu sang máu
- Share needles when injecting drug
  Kim chích từ người này sang người khác
- Sex with an HIV injected person
  Tình dục với người nhiễm trùng HIV

Sexually Transmitted Diseases (STDs) *Bệnh lây lan qua tình dục*

All anal sex is risky and dangerous. Some examples of STDs are: *Tất cả sự giao hợp qua hậu môn đều rủi ro và nguy hiểm. Vài ví dụ về bệnh lây lan qua tình dục (STDs) là:*

- Hepatitis B *(viêm gan B)*
- Genital warts *(Bệnh bứu sinh dục)*
- Syphilis *(bệnh giang mai)*
- Gonorrhea *(Bệnh lậu mủ)*
- Pelvic inflammatory disease *(sưng xương chậu)*

Bisexual men rarely transmit HIV to women. Out of the first 174,893 AIDS cases reported only 544 women became infected by having sex with a bisexual male.
Đàn ông giao hợp cả 2 giới ít khi lây truyền HIV tới phụ nữ. Trong số 174,893 người bệnh AIDS được báo cáo chỉ có 544 đàn bà bị nhiễm trùng do có giao hợp với đàn ông lưỡng tính.

Causes of STDs *(Nguyên nhân STDs)*

Living in poverty, have sex with people who inject drugs, male homosexuals or sex with prostitutes (sex for money).

Sống ở vùng nghèo khổ, tình dục với những người dùng cần sa, hút, chích thuốc phiện, đồng tính hoặc mua bán tình dục.

Smart Sex *(giao hợp khôn khéo)*

Using condoms is smart for many reasons. In 1991 over half a million people (602,577) in the United States were treated for gonorrhea and another 41, 006 for syphilis.

Dùng bao cao su khi giao hợp là một việc khôn khéo trong mọi lúc. Năm 1991 có hơn nữa triệu người (602.577) trong nước Mỹ bị bệnh lậu mủ và 41.006 bị bệnh giang mai.

HIV testing *(Thử nghiệm HIV)*

The most widely used test is the EIA (enzyme immunoassay) the immune system would not cause disease or fighting antibodies unless HIV was present.

Thử nghiệm được dùng rộng rãi là chất men thử hệ thống miễn nhiễm (EIA) sẽ không gây bệnh hay chống lại cơ thể con người trừ khi có siêu vi khuẩn HIV hiện diện

Signs and Symptoms of AIDS *(dấu hiệu và triệu chứng của AIDS)*

The symptoms of AIDS usually occur many years after infection. On the average, about 10 to 11 years will pass before infected individuals begin to show symptoms. Generally the first symptoms of HIV infection occur about three months after infection. Flulike symptoms with diarrhea, nausea, aching muscles and usually occur and quickly go away. Although infected with HIV, the person does not have AIDS. Many years may go by before AIDS symptoms appear.

Triệu chứng bệnh AIDS thường xảy ra nhiều năm sau khi nhiễm trùng. Trung bình 10 đến 11 năm trãi qua trước khi nhiễm trùng bắt đầu có triệu chứng. Dấu hiệu đầu tiên của nhiễm HIV xảy ra khoảng 3 tháng sau nhiễm trùng. Triệu chứng giống như cúm gồm tiêu chảy, nôn mửa, đau bắp thịt và thường xảy ra và thường nhanh chóng biến mất. Mặc dầu bị nhiễm trùng với HIV, con người không có bệnh AIDS. Nhiều năm có thể đi qua trước khi triệu chứng bệnh AIDS xuất hiện.

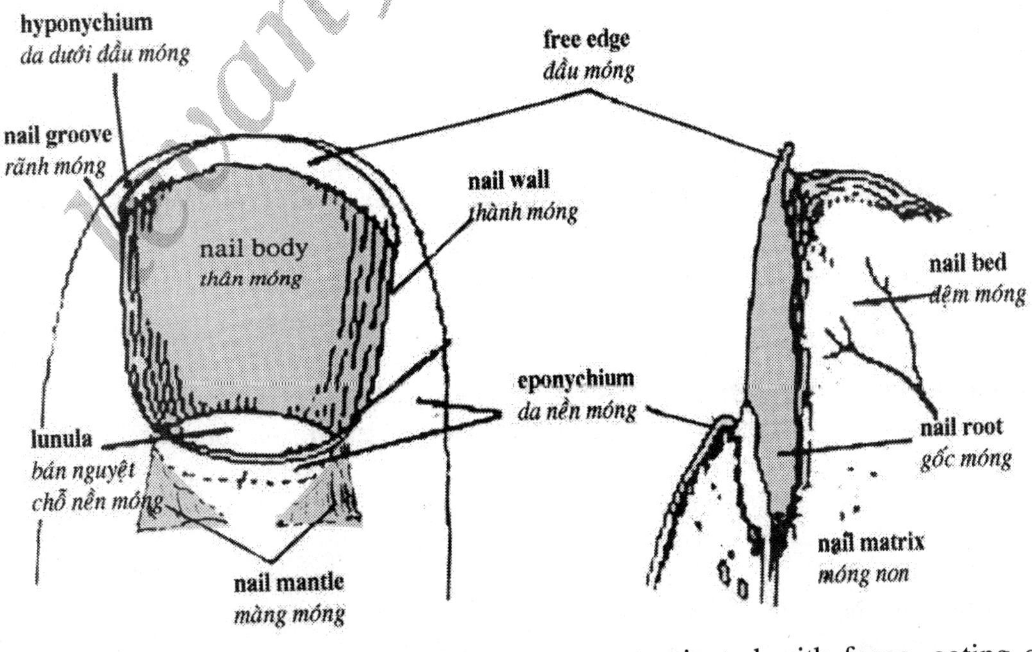

Hepatitis A *(viêm gan A)*

About 10 people per 100,000 become infected with hepatitis A. Hepatitis A is the least dangerous type. It is spread by water contaminated with feces, eating or drinking food. Increased numbers of cases are usually seen in areas where sanitation is poorest.

Khoảng 10/100,000 bị nhiễm với viêm gan A. Viêm gan A ít nguy hiểm hơn. Sự lây lan thường qua nước bị cáu bẩn, ăn hoặc uống bẩn. Số lượng bệnh viêm gan A tăng ở những vùng kém vệ sinh.

Hepatitis B *(viêm gan B)*

Any infection or inflammation of the liver. Hepatitis has two terms.

Là bất cứ sự nhiễm trùng hoặc chứng gây sưng nào ở lá gan. Bệnh viêm gan có hai giai đoạn.

- Acute hepatitis (short term)
  - Sưng gan cấp tính (ngắn hạn)
- Chronic hepatitis (last longer 6 months)
  - Sưng gan kinh niên (lâu hơn 6 tháng)

Most new infections are traced to sharing needles, anal and vaginal sex, and from mother to her newborn child are called Vertical transmission. Although Hepatitis is not spread by kissing but hepatitis can be transmitted through saliva.

Hầu hết sự nhiễm trùng phát sinh là do chích kim chung, giao hợp hậu môn, âm đạo, và từ người mẹ có bệnh truyền sang bé được gọi là lan truyền theo chiều dọc (vertical transmission). Mặc dùbệnh không lây lan qua hôn hít nhưng có thể lan truyền qua tiếp xúc đến nước bọt.

Hepatitis C *(viêm gan C)*

Hepatitis C is a serious illness, but much is still not understood. It can cause both acute and chronic disease and has also been linked to chronic liver desease and cancer. It can be as short as a few weeks or as long as one year.

Viêm gan C là bệnh trầm trọng, nhưng vẫn chưa rõ nguyên nhân. Nguyên nhân tạo nên cả bệnh cấp tính và kinh niên và có liên hệ tới bệnh viêm gan kinh niên và ung thư. Có thể xảy ra trong vài tuần hoặc lâu cả năm.

Hepatitis D *(viêm gan D)*

This virus can cause either acute or chronic infections, usually greatly increases the dangers. Hepatitis D especially common in the Middle East not United States

Đây là loại siêu vi khuẩn có thể là nhiễm trùng cấp tính và kinh niên, thường tăng lên đến nguy hiểm. Viêm gan D đặc biệt thường ở Trung Đông chứ không có ở Hoa Kỳ.

Hepatitis E *(viêm gan E)*

The symptoms are similar to hepatitis A. Hepatitis E especially common from Mexico, Africa, or Asia not occur in the United States

Triệu chứng viêm gan E giống như viêm gan A. Viêm gan E đặc biệt ở những nước Mễ tây cơ, Phi châu và Á châu chứ không có ở Hoa Kỳ.

Hepatitis spread the same ways as for AIDS *(cách lây lan vi khuẩn viêm gan giống như bệnh AIDS)*

Protection: *(bảo vệ)*

- Disinfection instruments (E.P.A registered)
  Diệt trùng dụng cụ được cơ quan E.P.A chuẩn nhận
- Wash off any blood drops in the premise of the salon immediately
  Lau sạch ngay bất cứ giọt máu nào nhiểu ở trong tiệm
- Receive hepatitis vaccine and give information, training
  Được chủng ngừa phòng bệnh viêm ganvà huấn luyện và thông tin đầy đủ
- Wear gloves if you have cuts or sores. Handle sharp instrument carefully
  Mang bao tay nếu bạn bị cắt đứt hoặc bị sưng da. Cẩn thận với những vật dụng bén nhọn

Disinfection *(Sự diệt trùng)*

High-quality disinfectants must perform several special jobs in the salon. They must be bactericides, fungicides and virucides. Disinfectants that perform both of these functions are called hospital level disinfectants.

Chất diệt trùng có chất lượng cao phải có nhiều công dụng cho salon. Chất diệt trùng phải diệt được các loại vi trùng, diệt nấm, và siêu vi khuẩn. Chất diệt trùng có được công dụng này gọi là chất diệt trùng cấp bệnh viện

Type of disinfectants: Các chất diệt trùng

- Quats — *Nước Quats*
- Phenols — *Phenols*
- Alcohol — *Cồn*
- UV rays — *Tia cực tím*
- Formalin — *Formalin*

The rights of people with AIDS: *Quyền của người bệnh AIDS*

Discriminating against an HIV-infected person is no different than discrimination based on race or sex. We must never forget that AIDS victim are people, just like us- except they are ill. They have mothers and fathers, friends and families, but more importantly, they have civil rights protected by the U.S. Constitution.

Kỳ thị chống lại người có bệnhy HIV là không khác gì sự kỳ thị về giống dân và phái tính. Chúng ta đừng bao giờ quên rằng nạn nhân của AIDS cũng là con người, như chúng ta ngoại trừ họ đang bệnh. Họ cũng có mẹ, cha, bạn và thân nhân, nhưng điều quan trọng hơn, họ cũng được hiến pháp Hoa Kỳ bảo vệ quyền dân sự.

Federal law also prohibits any salon employee from refusing service to an individual who is physically handicapped or infected with HIV.

Luật liên bang cũng cấm người thợ thẩm mỹ từ chối phục vụ tới bất cứ ai có khuyết tật về thể lý hoặc người nhiễm bệnh HIV

Ways to increase your risks from HIV *(những lý do tăng sự rủi ro mang nhiễm HIV)*

- Sharing needles and syringes *(dùng chung kim và ống chích)*
- Having anal sex *(giao hợp đường hậu môn)*
- Living in poor, inner cities *(sống nơi nghèo khổ, trong lòng phố)*
- Sex with people who are at risk *(sex với người có cuộc sống bừa bãi)*
- Not use condoms *(không dùng bọc cao su bảo vệ)*

Salon safety *(An toàn ở tiệm)*

- Wear gloves and safety glasses while mixing product
  Mang bao tay và kính an toàn khi pha trộn thuốc
- Weigh and measure all products
  Đo lường kỹ lưỡng các loại hóa chất khi dùng
- Store products away from food in cool, dark, and dry place
  Cất giữ hóa chất xa thực phẩm, ở chỗ mát, tối và khô ráo

Your responsibility as a professional *(Trách nhiệm của thợ chuyên nghiệp)*

- Don't take short-cuts when sanitation and disinfection for soil implements
  Đừng giảm bớt tiến trình cần thiết khi vệ sinh và diệt trùng dụng cụ
- Finally: You have a responsibility to your profession. Clients expect to see you act in a professional manner. This is how trust and respect can be earned from client.
  Cuối cùng bạn phải có trách nhiệm trong nghề nghiệp chuyên môn. Khách hàng mong đợi thấy ở bạn dùng đúng phương cách chuyên nghiệp. Đây là những điều tin cậy và kính trọng mà bạn sẽ đạt được từ khách hàng.
- Cosmetologists, nail technicians, and estheticians are exposed to dozens of people every day. If you are not careful, you could cause your own local epidemic
  Thợ thẩm mỹ, chuyên viên nail, và chuyên viên về da tiếp xúc hàng tá khách mỗi ngày. Nếu bạn không cẩn thận, bạn có thể tạo ra dịch bệnh.

Bài 3: NÉT CHUYÊN NGHIỆP CỦA THỢ THẨM MỸ

Luôn nhớ rằng, người khách có thể phán đoán qua phong cách hoạt động của bạn, từ cử chỉ đi, đứng, tư thế làm việc, ngồi, và ngay cả động tác nhặt một vật rơi trên nền salon nữa. Thêm vào đó sự tươm tất từ tóc, làn da, móng tay, quần áo gọn gàng, sạch sẽ, hơi thở tươi mát, thơm tho, xinh xắn, nói năng duyên dáng, và đầy vẻ hấp dẫn khi hiện diện trước khách hàng, chính là bạn đã tạo dựng được cho bạn niềm tự tin và là tác phong đúng cách đưa bạn đến thành công trong nghề thẩm mỹ.

Chuyên viên thẩm mỹ là công việc tiếp xúc rất nhiều người, nên cần có đạo đức trong nghề nghiệp:
Đối với người chủ và đồng nghiệp: nâng đỡ, hổ trợ học hỏi và đóng góp vào sự thành công của salon.

- *Không tạo sự mâu thuẩn với nhau, tạo sự bất hòa giữa đồng nghiệp, tung tin xấu hoặc xầm xì trước khách hàng về một đồng nghiệp nào đó, nịnh hót với chủ để tạo phần lợi về mình.*
- *Nhận trách nhiệm và thành thật, cố gắng giữ lời hứa, thông báo với chủ những sự việc khó giải quyết, đừng đổ lỗi cho đồng nghiệp, nên chịu trách nhiệm hành động của chính mình gây ra.*
- *Khi khách than phiền hoặc bất đồng về công việc của bạn đồng nghiệp nào đó, bạn nên đứng trung gian, không nên phê bình ác ý, bạn đề nghị khách cứ nói thẳng, nếu cần bạn chỉ đề nghị nhẹ nhàng sửa lại cho khách và tránh đổ lỗi cho bất cứ ai.*
- *Tôn trọng tài năng lẫn nhau, khen ngợi và khuyến khích*

Đối với khách hàng: có đạo đức bạn sẽ được khách tin tưởng, lời khen, là người sẽ mang khách đến cho bạn, và là nguồn quảng cáo tốt nhất.

- *Không nên nói xấu bất cứ người khách nào với khách thân quen của bạn, hoặc nói xấu người chủ, đồng nghiệp của bạn cho khách biết. Vì điều này làm khách sẽ ngại ngùng vì nghĩ rằng một lúc nào đó, bạn sẽ nói xấu họ.*
- *Phải biểu lộ cho khách biết bạn là người luôn tuân hành luật lệ ngành thẩm mỹ, luật vệ sinh. Đừng làm cẩu thả, vội vả hoặc rút ngắn tiến trình phục vụ vì khách sẽ nhận biết. Giữ lời hứa với khách và tôn trọng những đòi hỏi của khách.*
- *Luôn tạo cho khách sự thoải mái với công việc bạn làm. Nếu cần, giải thích công việc và đừng làm thêm những dịch vụ mà khách không cần, không muốn.*
- *Cần quan tâm đến khách hàng dù bạn thay đổi chỗ làm, giới thiệu khách với đồng nghiệp tin tưởng thay thế để phục vụ cho khách. Tạo cho khách thuận tiện dù bạn phải rời salon.*
- *Công bằng với khách, đừng tỏ lộ một đặc biệt cho khách người khách nào , hoặc bớt giá vô cớ.*
- *Nên giữ sự trung lập khi nghe có lời phê bình đến người thợ nào, tiệm nào, chủ nào, chỉ lắng nghe rút tỉa kinh nghiệm sống mà không cần cho ý kiến.*

Hình nét bên ngoài của thợ thẩm mỹ: thợ thẩm mỹ luôn tạo cảm giác cho khách thích nhìn bạn trong lúc phục vụ, ngồi đối diện với nhau, dáng vẻ, nét trang điểm của bạn sẽ luôn được khách chiếu cố và chính bạn cũng muốn người khác khen tặng vậy.
Những yếu tố cần thiết cho người thợ thẩm mỹ.

- *Lưu ý đến làn da chăm sóc mịn màng, mái tóc gọn gàng, móng tay phải sạch sẽ. Trông sao như có nét đẹp tự nhiên là tốt. Cơ thể cần phải tắm rửa mỗi ngày, súc miệng kỹ và khử mùi hôi, nhất là sau mỗi lần ăn v.v...*
- *Mặc quần áo thích hợp, sạch sẽ, hợp thời trang phản ảnh được sự tận tâm của nghề và tự tin khi tiếp xúc với khách hàng.*

- *Hơi thở không bay mùi nồng nặc, răng cần chăm sóc tốt, trắng đều, súc miệng và thuốc khử để chắc rằng lúc nào hơi thở cũng thơm tho. Khám răng định kỳ, hạn chế thức ăn có mùi, cần mang theo bàn chãi răng súc miệng sau khi ăn để giúp làn hơi dễ chịu khi giao tiếp với khách hàng.*

Ngay cả tư thế đứng, đi, ngồi, và nhặt đồ vật cũng phải tập theo tư thế lịch sự và đúng cách:

Lúc đứng: Nếu là nữ giới đứng xoay người 1 chút, vừa đẹp và trông hơi cao cao. Là một người thợ nữ thẩm mỹ khi đứng trên một bàn chân thẳng phía trước và bàn chân sau xéo góc 45 độ so với bàn chân trước. Nam giới thì đứng thẳng cân đối đều trên 2 chân và hai bàn chân cách nhau 12 inches.

Lúc đi: Nên di chuyển nhẹ nhàng, tay đong đưa nhẹ, lòng bàn tay xoay bên trong, chân đi song song, đừng tạo tiếng ồn, hai chân khép gần nhau khi đi

Lúc ngồi: Lưng thẳng, đầu thẳng, đầu gối kề nhau.

Lúc nhặt đồ: Đứng kề bên đồ vật để nhặt trông tư thế lịch sự và khi đứng lên dùng sức bắp thịt đùi đứng dậy. Vật nặng nhấc lên bằng bắp thịt ở chân chứ không dùng bắp thịt ở lưng.

Cách hành xử với chủ và đồng nghiệp trong ngành thẩm mỹ phải tạo được bầu khí hòa hợp, sự cạnh tranh với mục đích cùng nhau phát triển, đồng thời làm cho khách hàng vui thích môi trường làm việc của bạn mà trung thành.

- *Bày tỏ sáng kiến để cải tổ tốt nơi làm việc, vừa có lợi chung cho mọi người, kể cả người chủ*
- *Thành tâm công nhận điểm hay, giỏi trong chuyên môn của bạn đồng nghiệp.*
- *Chịu học hỏi điều hay, kỷ thuật mới, cởi mở đầu óc, sẵn sàng chấp nhận đề nghị, đừng cố chấp.*
- *Hiểu rõ sản phẩm mới trước khi bán hoặc giải thích sự ích lợi cho khách, đừng nài ép họ mua.*
- *Vấn đề cá nhân về việc làm nên trực tiếp nói thẳng chủ, đừng cho khách và đồng nghiệp biết.*
- *Tôn trọng ý kiến đồng nghiệp để có giải pháp tốt nhất, dù ý tưởng của bạn hay và quan trọng.*
- *Nâng đở học hỏi lẫn nhau để đáp ứng nhu cầu công việc và kỷ thuật mới nhằm phát triển salon.*
- *Lợi dụng tình cảm để hỏi mượn tiền, đồ vật của chủ và đồng nghiệp sẽ làm họ khó chịu và coi thường. Không đem chuyện cá nhân kể cho khách, đồng nghiệp và người chủ nghe, điều này chỉ dẫn đến sự phân tâm. Trừ trường hợp khẩn cấp, không nên dùng điện thoại salon giao tiếp với gia đình và bạn bè.*

Phong cách làm việc: Là cách làm việc và sinh hoạt có kế hoạch, sắp xếp lịch trình cá nhân và công việc sao cho không gây trở ngại việc hẹn khách đúng ngày giờ.

- Tạo cho khách cảm giác an toàn, chu đáo khi khách đến, gọi đúng tên, việc sẽ làm và làm đúng giờ đã hẹn. Chuẩn bị bàn, vật liệu, dụng cụ khử trùng và trong tư thế sẵn sàng phục vụ.
- Đừng cho khách thấy bạn nhai kẹo, ăn, gọi điện thoại làm cho khách khó chịu hoặc bạn hút thuốc dễ gây nguy hiểm vì hóa chất quanh bạn.
- Lịch hẹn khách thích hợp thời gian cho từng dịch vụ, đừng làm trể hẹn hoặc hẹn khách vào ngày khác. Nếu không làm được phải thông báo cho khách để khỏi mất thì giờ của họ mà họ vẫn thấy sự thành thật ở bạn.
- Tạo cho khách thoải mái khi đến salon, nên thân mật, vui vẻ và giúp họ cởi áo khoát nếu cần, mời họ ngồi hoặc hướng dẫn phòng vệ sinh. Thái độ khiêm tốn, quan tâm và lắng nghe khách.
- Đừng than phiền và tranh cãi với khách mà cần đề nghị và thảo luận để giúp ý kiến cho họ. Bạn nên giải thích ở mức độ nghề nghiệp là bạn đang làm gì cho họ và tại sao bạn làm vậy.

POSTURE AND PROFESSIONAL HEALTH

(Hình dáng và sức khỏe của thợ chuyên nghiệp)

- You should be a model of good grooming apart of the beauty industry. Client will want to look like you. It is necessary to maintain a professional appearance.
  Bạn sẽ là người gương mẫu tươm tất trong ngành thẩm mỹ. Khách muốn được giống như bạn. Đó là điều cần thiết để duy trì một nét chuyên nghiệp.
- **Your professional image** includes all of dressing professional, wearing make up and fresh breath, and use deodorant for your body.
  Hình thức chuyên nghiệp bao gồm đồng phục chuyên môn, trang điểm, hơi thở thơm tho, và dùng thuốc khử mùi cho cơ thể của bạn.
- The way in which you behave when you are working with clients, coworkers, and your employer in a salon is called professional ethics.
  Cách mà bạn biết tôn trọng trong lúc bạn đang phục vụ khách, đồng nghiệp, và người chủ ở trong tiệm được gọi là: đạo đức nghề nghiệp.
- Clients should always be called by their names
  Khách nên luôn luôn được gọi bằng chính tên của họ
- If you have a client that likes to gossip about other clients, coworkers, or employer, you should: remain neutral in conversation.
  Nếu bạn có người khách mà họ thích đồn nhảm về người khách khác, thợ, hoặc người chủ, bạn nên: giữ thái độ trung lập trong cuộc nói chuyện.
- **Before your clients** arrive for their appointment, you should: your station set up for service, all implements, and materials ready for use.
  Trước khi khách đến khi có hẹn, bạn nên: chuẩn bị nơi phục vụ, mọi dụng cụ và vật liệu sẵn sàng dùng cho khách.
- Good health is a basic element for living: *sức khoẻ tốt là yếu tố căn bản của cuộc sống*
- Hygiene is the branch of applied science that deals with healthful living.
  Vệ sinh là môn khoa học liên quan với cuộc sống khoẻ mạnh
- Public hygiene concerns the care taken by individuals to preserve health by following the rules of healthful living.
  Vệ sinh công cộng là những biện pháp do chính phủ ấn định để bảo vệ và phát triển sức khoẻ của dân chúng

- **The basic requirements for good personal hygiene are:**
  Những điều căn bản đòi hỏi cho vệ sinh cá nhân lành mạnh là:
  1- Take a daily shower, use a deodorant: *tắm rửa hằng ngày, thoa thuốc khử mùi hôi*
  2- Brush teeth after meals: *đánh răng sau mỗi bữa ăn*
  3- Keep clothing clean and neat: *mặc quần áo sạch sẽ và gọn gàng*
  4- Have regular medical and dental checkups: *khám bệnh định kỳ và khám răng đều*
  5- Keep hands and nails clean and well groomed: *giữ cho tay và móng luôn sạch sẽ và mịn*
  6- Follow a daily regiment of good diet, exercise, and adequate rest
  Hằng ngày phải theo cách ăn uống tốt, tập thể dục và ngủ nghĩ đủ

- **Attitude, thought, and emotion affect the body:**
  Thái độ, suy nghĩ, và xúc cảm mạnh ảnh hưởng đến cơ thể như sau:
  - Mental depression weakens the function of the organs, thereby lowering resistance of the body to disease.
    Tâm thần chán nản làm suy yếu nhiệm vụ của các chức năng, vì thế giảm đi sức đề kháng bệnh của cơ thể

- A thought may either stimulate or depress the functions of the body.
Sự suy nghĩ có thể vừa là kích thích hoặc căng thẳng các chức năng của cơ thể
- Strong emotions, such as worry, anger, and fear have a harmful effect on the heart, arteries, and glands.
Xúc cảm mạnh, như lo lắng, giận dữ, và sợ tạo nguy hại ảnh hưởng đến tim, động mạch và các tuyến.

- **The basic rules for maintaining good posture**:
Những điều căn bản để cho tư thế ngay ngắn.
  - Keep your shoulder's back, carry the weight on the balls of your feet, not on the heels, keep your knees slightly flexed.
  Giữ 2 vai ngã ra sau, giữ sức nặng của thân thể lên bàn chân, không phải gót chân, giữ hai đầu gối uyển chuyển.
  - A good standing posture*: một tư thế đứng đúng:*

  Benefits of correct posture are: Improved functioning of the internal organs, prevention of fatigue, improve personal appearance
  Những ích lợi với tư thế đúng cách là:Tăng thêm các hoạt động các chức năng bên trong, ngăn ngừa mỏi mệt, tăng thêm vẻ đẹp cá nhân

- **A good sitting posture is accomplished by***: tư thế ngồi đúng cách được thực hiện*
  - Allowing the feet to carry the weight of the thighs
  Để cho bàn chân chịu sức nặng của đùi
  - Sitting well back in the chair, never slouching
  Ngồi sát tựa vào ghế, đừng bao giờ ngồi thụn người xuống

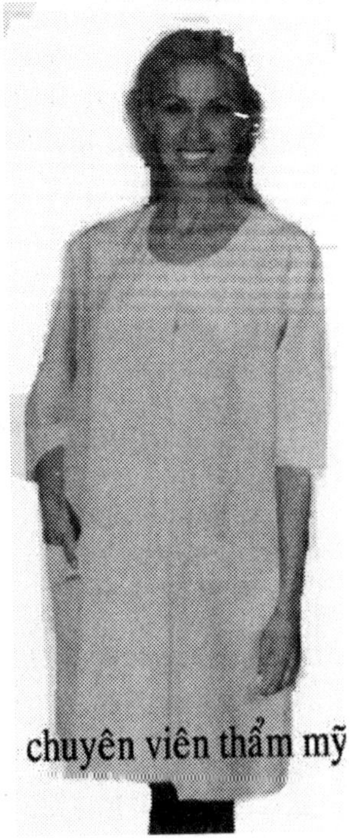
chuyên viên thẩm mỹ

- **The proper way to lift a heavy object is:**
Phương cách đúng để nâng một vật nặng là:
  - Lift with your back straight, push with the heavy thigh muscles, never back muscles:
  Giữ lưng thẳng khi nhấc đồ, chịu sức nặng trên bắp thịt đùi, không bao giờ dùng bắp thịt ở lưng.
  - Suggestion for hands and nails grooming are*:*
  chú ý cho đôi tay và móng mịn màng là:
  - Should not be too long and pointed nails shape*:*
  đừng để móng dài và nhọn
  - When you place your hands in harsh solutions, wear plastic or rubber gloves
  Khi tay bạn đụng vào dụng dịch mạnh, mang bao tay nhựa hoặc cao su
  - If you bite or pick your nails, you must break this habit
  Nếu bạn cắn hoặc xướt móng, nên bỏ thói quen này.

- **Three rules** of the "care of the feet" are: *ba điều trong cách "chăm sóc chân" là:*
  - Keep toenails filed smooth, wear shoes that fit correctly, give the feet daily care
  Giũa mịn các móng chân, mang giày vừa vặn, chăm sóc chân hằng ngày.

- **Some good topics** for conversation between a manicurist and a client are:
Những đề tài hấp dẫn trong đàm thoại giữa thợ thợ chăm sóc tay chân và khách là:
  - Travel, literature*: du lịch, văn chương*
  - Personal grooming and cosmetic needs*: cá nhân gọn gàng và mỹ phẩm cần thiết*

- Client's own activities: *các hoạt động riêng của khách*
- Fashions, client's personal interests: *thời trang, điều thích thú của khách*

- **Topic** to avoid when conversing with a client are personal problems, religions:
  Đề tài tránh nói chuyện với khách khó khăn cá nhân, tôn giáo
  - Other client's poor behavior: *tính không tốt của khách hàng khác*
  - Poor workmanship of co-workers: *những điều không tốt của bạn đồng nghiệp*
  - Health problems, financial status: *trở ngại sức khỏe, tình trạng tài chánh*
  - Confident information given to you by the client: *sự riêng tư mà khách đã tâm sự cho bạn biết.*

- **Rules for ethical behavior**: *nguyên tắc về tư cách đạo đức.*
  - Practice the highest standards of professionalism at all times
    Ứng dụng tiêu chuẩn thực hành cao nhất của nghề nghiệp tất cả mọi lúc
  - Be honest, but tactful, with all your clients
    Có sự thành thật mà tế nhị với tất cả mọi khách hàng
  - Treat all clients fairly, and with equal amounts of respect
    Đối xử công bằng và có sự kính trọng mọi người khách như nhau
  - Be dependable in all your dealing with co-workers, clients, and others
    Có thể tin cậy được trong cách xử thế với bạn đồng nghiệp, khách và mọi người
  - Take the initiative in solving problems for your clients and for your salon
    Cần có sự sáng kiến, chủ động giải quyết vấn đề đối với khách và đối với salon

The Manicurist's responsibilities are: *bổn phận của người chuyên viên về da là*

- Must know the laws, rules and regulations governing cosmetic, and must comply with them.
  Phải hiểu rõ luật, điều lệ và qui tắc ngành thẩm mỹ, và phải tuân hành luật
- A very easy way to lose your coworker respect is to borrow money from them
  Rất dễ mất đi sự kính trọng của người đồng nghiệp là mượn tiền của họ.
- You should never smoke when you are around chemical products, clients, coworkers
  Bạn không bao giờ hút thuốc khi chung quanh bạn là các hóa chất, khách hàng, các đồng nghiệp.

GUIDELINES:

Keep your energy up. Sleep well 6 -8 hours every night. Have a fitness program.
Giữ đủ năng lực. Mỗi đêm ngủ ngon giấc từ 6 -8 giờ. Có lập chương trình thể dục.

Respect others: avoid interupting, never discuss your personal life with a co-worker. When you treat other people well, they will respect you and build your self-esteem.

Tôn trọng mọi người: *tránh ngắt lời người khác, không nên thảo luận đời sống cá nhân mình với người đồng nghiệp. Khi bạn đối sử tốt với mọi người, họ sẽ tôn trọng bạn và tạo được niềm tin với bạn.*

Never take on more than you can handle
Không nên làm việc nhiều hơn khả năng mình.

Communication skills: communication is two sides, it ensures that your clients will understand your ideas and suggestions; you understand perfectly the needs and desires of the people around you.

Khả năng tiếp chuyện: đàm thoại gồm có hai khía cạnh, nó tạo cho người khách hiểu được ý kiến và sự gợi ý của bạn. Bạn hiểu được hoàn toàn những gì cần và ước muốn của mọi người chung quanh.

Bài 4: LIÊN HỆ VI TRÙNG VÀ SỰ LÂY TRUYỀN BỆNH

Có hơn 1 thế kỷ qua, nhà hóa học Pháp Louis Pasteur (1822 – 1895) khám phá vi sinh vật (microorganisms), nghĩa là ông tìm ra được một sự sống rất nhỏ mang ảnh hưởng vô cùng lớn. Có hơn 15.000 loại vi trùng tồn tại khắp nơi và sinh sản cực nhanh đến hàng triệu con trong 60 phút.

Active bacteria: vi trùng hoạt động, và phát triển là *(active stage).* Chúng tồn tại trong môi trường ấm, tối, bẩn, và ẩm. Hầu hết vi trùng tiến đến giai đoạn trưởng thành trong vòng 20 đến 30 phút và tiến sang giai đoạn sanh sản trực phân *(direct division or mitosis).*

Inactive bacteria: vi trùng không hoạt động được trong môi trường nhiều ánh sáng, nóng, thiếu thức ăn hoặc khô. Với điều kiện trên phần đông vi trùng sẽ chết hoặc biến sang giai đoạn không hoạt động, giai đoạn nghĩ ngơi *(inactive stage)*, và thành lập bào tử *(spore).* Bào tử có thể bay lẫn trong không khí và gặp điều kiện thuận lợi như ẩm mốc, tối thì chúng lại sinh sôi nẩy nở. Các chất diệt trùng mạnh cũng không đủ diệt được bào tử.

Là một chuyên viên về móng tay bạn cần cẩn thận hơn để tránh sự nhiễm trùng cho bạn, cho khách. Sự nhiễm trùng không nhất thiết do vi trùng, nấm mà một vài loại nhiễm trùng cho thể lây lan trong khi làm móng.

HAI LOẠI VI TRÙNG:

1. **Vi trùng không gây bệnh, vô hại, hoặc vi trùng có lợi (nonpathogenic):** Vi trùng không gây bệnh này chiếm 75%. Chúng sống trong đất, phân bón càng giúp cho thêm màu mỡ đất, và ở con người loại vi trùng này thường ở ruột và miệng giúp cho tiến trình tiêu hủy thức ăn và tiêu hóa.

2. **Vi trùng gây bệnh, có tác hại (pathogenic):** Loại vi trùng này được gọi là *(germ: vi khuẩn)* sinh sôi nẩy nở nhanh, tiết ra độc tố khi chúng xâm nhập ăn mất chất sống. Loại vi trùng gây bệnh này chiếm 30%. Vi khuẩn gây bệnh hay độc tố của chúng có trong máu hoặc các mô khác là **bị nhiễm khuẩn (sepsis)**, và không có vi trùng gây bệnh là **vô nhiễm khuẩn (asepsis).**

Cocci *vi trùng hình tròn*

Diplococci *(pnenomia) vi trùng hình tròn đi từng cập (sưng phổi)*

Streptococci *(strep throat) vi trùng hình tròn kết từng chuỗi (tạo mủ, đau cổ)*

Staphylococci *(pustules) vi trùn hình tròn kết chùm (áp xe, mụn nhọt)*

BA LOẠI VI TRÙNG GÂY BỆNH: ***Cocci*** *(cầu trùng)*, ***Bacilli*** *(hình que)*, ***và Spirilla*** *(hình xoắn).*

- ***CẦU TRÙNG*** *(cocci): vi trùng hình tròn trái berry, không di chuyển trong dung dịch, bay trong không khí, bụi. Có 3 loại vi trùng cocci:*
  - ***a. Streptococci****: vi trùng hình chuỗi thường ở trong hệ hô hấp và ruột, nhiễm độc máu, gây đau họng, sốt cảm cúm, nóng đau nhức.*

*b. **Staphylococci**: vi trùng phát triển từng chùm, từng bó (liên cầu trùng), là loại vi trùng mạnh không có vỏ bọc, gây nhiều bệnh lở da, mụt mủ, nhiễm độc thức ăn.*

*c. **Diplococci:** vi trùng đi từng cặp, gây bệnh sưng phổi, sởi, và cảm cúm.*

- ***VI TRÙNG HÌNH QUE** (bacilli): vi trùng có dạng như ống cuốn tóc, hình gậy (trực trùng). Trong điều kiện khắc nghiệt một số vi trùng này biến thành bào tử (spores). Loại bacilli này là nguyên nhân gây 1 số bệnh trầm trọng như cứng hàm, lao phổi, bạch hầu.*

***VI TRÙNG HÌNH XOẮN** (spirilla): có hình cong cong hoặc xoắn ốc, một trong số vi trùng xoắn là gây bệnh giang mai (Treponema pallidum)*

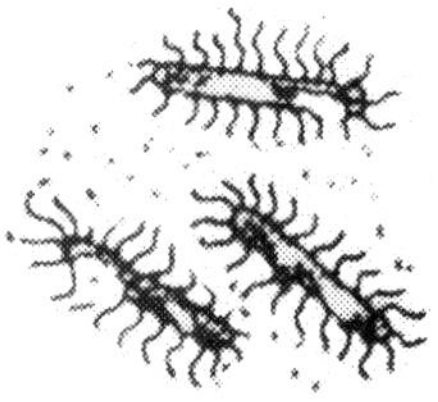

Typhoid bacilli *(influenza)*
Vi trùng hình que (thương hàn)

Bacilli *(tuberculosis)*
vì trùng hình que (lao phổi)

Sprilla *(syphilis)*
vì trùng hình xoắn (giang mai)

SỰ NHIỄM TRÙNG Ở SALON

1. Rủi ro đứt tay, nhiễm trùng từ người này sang người khác, vết thương mở miệng, bất cứ ai có ho, cảm cúm, nhảy mũi, chảy nước mắt, mũi…
2. Dễ gây nấm, mốc, vi trùng gây bệnh giữa móng giả và thật. Lây vi khuẩn từ khách
3. Tiếp xúc qua đồ vật ở tiệm như tay nắm cửa, điện thoại, chai, cọ sơn, khăn, bàn…
4. Dụng cụ không khử trùng, khăn bẩn, thùng rác bẩn, dũa, kềm…hoặc dùng lại vật liệu như dũa giấy, bông gòn.

THỢ THẨM MỸ CẦN NGĂN NGỪA SỰ NHIỄM TRÙNG Ở SALON

- *Tránh ép mạnh trên những nệm móng nhạy cảm, đánh buffer mạnh quá, dùng dũa máy cẩu thả, cắt da phao tay nhiều, rách da vì dũa sâu, ép mạnh làm da bị bầm.*
- *Phải có trách nhiệm nghề nghiệp, thực hành đúng phương cách khử trùng, đừng viện cớ sự bận rộn công việc mà làm tắt (short cut) trong tiến trình vệ sinh, khử trùng dụng cụ.*
- *Khi khách đã từng đề nghị đi bác sĩ chữa trị, do đó khi trở lại salon cần xem giấy giới thiệu an toàn. Không thể phục vụ cho khách khi biết họ đang mắc bệnh truyền nhiễm thông thường như cảm cúm, ngay cả bạn mắc bệnh cũng cần phải nghĩ ngơi và trị bệnh để tránh lây bệnh cho khách và đồng nghiệp nữa.*

SỰ NHIỄM TRÙNG VÀ GÂY BỆNH

Sự nhiễm trùng và bệnh xãy ra là lúc vi trùng gây bệnh *(pathogenic bacteria)* tấn cống cơ thể con người, lấn mạnh qua hệ thống phòng thủ của cơ thể và từ đó sản sinh độc tố *(toxin)* cực nhanh để gây bệnh.

Hai hình thức nhiễm trùng:

- **Local infection** là nhiễm trùng ở một vùng nhỏ như mụn nhọt *(pimples)*, hoặc vết cắt.
- **General infection** là nhiễm trùng trong dòng máu tiến đến các phần trên cơ thể, là hình thức nhiễm độc máu như bệnh giang mai *(syphilis)*.

Tuy nhiên cơ thể chúng ta cũng tạo một mạng lưới để bảo vệ sự tấn công của vi trùng. Một làn da lành lặn luôn là màng bảo vệ chính yếu cho cơ thể, nước mắt, nước bọt (miếng), lông mịn bên trong mũi và màng nhầy ẩm ướt giữ vi trùng nằm hẳn bên ngoài mũi, chất dịch acid trong bao tử tiêu diệt vi trùng và nguồn máu trắng *(white blood cells)* sẵn sàng tấn công các loại vi trùng gây bệnh xâm nhập cơ thể.

Vì thế khi nóng sốt chẳng hạn, cơ thể phản ứng chống lại làm nhiệt độ tăng lên và cơn sốt chính là lúc cơ thể đang tấn công tiêu diệt vi trùng.

SỰ MIỄN NHIỄM (immunity)

Miễn nhiễm là khả năng chống bệnh, tiêu diệt vi khuẩn khi vi trùng gây bệnh tấn công cơ thể. Có hai loại miễn nhiễm.

1. ***Miễn nhiễm tự nhiên*** *(natural immunity) là cơ thể có khả năng chống bệnh của con người sinh ra, hoặc do đặc tính di truyền, thể lực tốt, đời sống lành mạnh. Thêm vào đó các chất dịch cơ thể, mồ hôi, làm da lành lặn, hệ thống bạch cầu khỏe là phương tiện tốt tạo miễn nhiễm tự nhiên.*
2. ***Miễn nhiễm tự tạo hoặc nhân tạo*** *(acquired immunity) có được là do cơ thể sau khi trãi qua cơn bệnh đã tạo được loại kháng thể (protein molecule) để sẵn sàng chống trả khi bệnh đó trở lại gọi là miễn nhiễm có tính tự nhiên (natural acquired immunity), hoặc phải chủng ngừa (inoculation) để tạo kháng thể mà chúng ta biết qua hình thức đưa vào cơ thể một ít lượng vi trùng yếu để tạo hệ thống miễn nhiễm như chích ngừa cảm cúm (influenza), phong đòn gánh (tetanus), thương hàn (typhoid fever), trái rạ (chicken pox), ho gà(whooping cough) ...*

Vi trùng dễ lây lan qua không khí, qua tiếp xúc vật dụng bẩn, qua nước, chúng phát triển cực nhanh trong những nơi ấm, tối, ẩm mốc. Vi trùng sinh sản theo lối trực phân, khi chúng đủ điều kiện để trưởng thành phân chia hai và cứ thế sinh sản. Hơn nữa, chính vi trùng tự có khả năng di chuyển, đặc biệt loại vi trùng hình gậy *(bacilli)* và hình xoắn *(spirilla)* tự xoay, lắc qua lắc lại bằng những sợi lông như chân giả *(flagella or cilia)* trong chất dịch cơ thể để đẩy đi.

Là một chuyên viên về móng, không chỉ biết phục vụ khách mà còn phải biết phân tích bệnh cho khách biết và hiểu rõ cách phòng ngừa vì nhiều trường hợp gây bệnh là do thợ móng. Người thợ cần nhận biết khi móng đổi màu, biết móng bị nấm *(fungus)* có màu trắng quanh móng, móng bị mốc, thúi móng *(mold, mildew)* có màu xanh, vàng do vi khuẩn bài tiết, hoặc lâu ngày thành màu đen, có mùi ….., thợ cần phải biết và khuyên khách đi bác sĩ trị liệu.

Người thợ móng *(manicurist)* cần ý thức, trách nhiệm với nghề nghiệp bằng sự hiểu biết và thi hành luật vệ sinh, nếu không thì hình ảnh chuyên nghiệp của bạn sẽ tạo ảnh hưởng vô cùng xấu đối với khách của bạn và kỷ nghệ làm móng nói chung.

THE RELATIONSHIP OF BACTERIA AND SPREADING OF DISEASE

(Sự liên hệ vi trùng và lây bệnh)

- **Anton Van Leeuwenhock (1632 – 1723),** a Dutch naturalist discovered bacteria. Bacteria (germs or microbes) can exist on the skin, air, and decayed matter. They can be seen with the aid of a microscope.
  Nhà tự nhiên học người Hà Lan là Anton Van Leeuwenhock khám phá ra vi trùng
  Vi trùng (germs hoặc mirobes) có thể tồn tại trên da, không khí, vật mục nát. Chúng có thể thấy được với sự trợ giúp của kính hiển vi.
- **Bacteria** also named micro-organisms, germs or microbes are minute, one-celled vegetable. Bacteria are too small, about fifteen hundred-rod shaped bacteria barely reach access the head of a pin.
  Vi trùng cũng là micro-organisms, germs hoặc microbes là những đơn bào thực vật cực nhỏ Vi trùng rất nhỏ khoảng 1,500 con vi trùng hình gậy chỉ vỏn vẹn ở trên đầu mũi kim.
- **Pathogenic bacteria** are harmful, produce disease. **Non-pathogenic bacteria** are beneficial or harmless type, they are not produce disease. Hairlike projection attached to the bacteria and allow it to move is called a flagella (cilia)
  Vi trùng gây bệnh là vi trùng có hại, tạo bệnh. Vi trùng không gây bệnh là loại vi trùng có lợi hoặc dạng vô hại, chúng không sinh bệnh. Cấu trúc giống sợi tóc để vi trùng di chuyển gọi là chân giả, hoặc lông bơi..
- .**Cocci** bacteria are round shape; Bacilli are rod shape; Spirilla are curved or corkscrew shape. All of them are pathogenic.
  Cocci là vi trùng hình tròn; Bacilli là vi trùng hình que, trực trùng; Spirilla là vi trùng hình cong hoặc hình xoắn. Tất cả chúng là loại vi trùng gây bệnh.
- **Parasites** are bacterial that live on living matter. Saprophytes are bacteria that live on dead organic manner but help to improve soil fertility.
  Ký sinh trùng là vi trùng sống trên vật sống. Khuẩn hoại vật là vi trùng sống trên trên vật chết mà giúp tăng thêm màu mỡ cho đất.
- Bacteria grow in clusters or bunches are **staphylococci** cause pustules and boils; Bacteria grow in pair are **diplococci** cause pneumonia; Bacteria grow in chains are **streptococci** cause strep throat
  Vi trùng lớn lên thành bó hoặc chùm là staphylococci tạo mủ và mụt nhọt; Vi trùng lớn lên từng cặp là diplococci tạo sưng phổi. Vi trùng lớn lên từng chuỗi là streptococci nguyên nhân sưng cổ họng.
- Bacteria multiply by this manner; each organism divides in the middle, forming two daughter cells, which grow to full size and then reproduce again.
  Vi trùng phát triển như phép nhân; mỗi vi khuẩn tự chia đôi từ giữa, lập 2 tế bào con, lớn dần lên như tế bào mẹ và rồi tiếp tục sinh sản.
- **A local infection**, such as a boil that contains pus. **A general infection** such as blood poisoning, results when bacteria or their poisons enter the bloodstream. **A general infection** is syphilis by spirilla bacteria, also known as treponema pallida
  Nhiễm trùng tại chỗ như mụt nhọt có chứa mủ; Nhiễm trùng toàn bộ là nhiễm độc trong máu, kết quả là lúc vi trùng nhiễm độc vào trong dòng máu. Nhiễm trùng toàn bộ là bệnh giang mai do vi trùng hình xoắn là treponema pallida

- **Four common contagious** disease that prevent and esthetician from working are tuberculosis, virus infections, ringworm, and head lice. A certain kind of mosquito cause malaria
Bốn loại bệnh truyền nhiễm làm cản trở việc làm của thẩm mỹ viên là bệnh lao, nhiễm siêu vi khuẩn, nấm, và chí. Một điều chắc chắn con muỗi là nguyên nhân gây ra bệnh sốt rét
- **AIDS** (Acquired Immune Deficiency Syndrome) caused by the **HIV** (Human Immune deficiency Virus). The most tranmitting are: sexual contact with infected person; sharing needles for drugs
AIDS (Triệu chứng thiếu sót miễn nhiễm tự tạo) nguyên nhân do HIV (Siêu vi khuẩn tiêu diệt miễn nhiễm con người). Hầu hết sự lây lan là : tiếp xúc tình dục với người có bệnh; dùng chung kim chích thuốc phiện.

- **Four principal routes** through which bacteria can enter the body are through the mouth, nose, eyes, and breaks or wounds in the skin. The tough outer covering that bacteria create during the inactive stage is called a spore
Bốn nơi chính mà vi trùng xâm nhập vào cơ thể là qua miệng, mũi, mắt và da bị thương. Lớp bọc ngoài của vi trùng tạo ra trong giai đoạn thụ động được gọi là bào tử.
- **Four ways** the body resists infection are: - Unbroken skin; Body secretions such as perpiration; White blood cells; Antitoxins
Bốn cách mà cơ thể chống sự nhiễm trùng là: Làn da lành lặn; Cơ thể bài tiết như mồ hôi thoát ra; Tế bào bạch huyết; Kháng độc tố

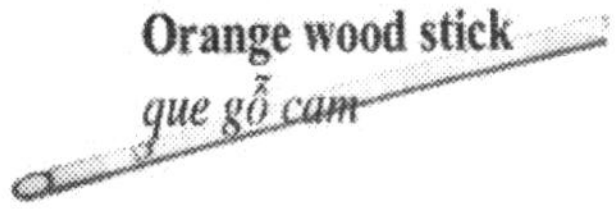
Orange wood stick
que gỗ cam

Cuticle nipper
kềm cắt da

Nails brush
bàn chãi nóng

Metal nail file
dũa kim loại

- **Immunity** is the ability of the body to fight and overcome certain disease caused by germs and their poisons.
Sự miễn nhiễm là khả năng của cơ thể chống lại sự nhiễm trùng và trãi qua cơn bệnh do vi trùng gây bệnh và chất độc của chúng.
- **Natural immunity** means natural resistance to disease to develop through hygienic living.
Miễn nhiễm tự nhiên là tự nhiên chống lại cơn bệnh được phát triển qua đời sống vệ sinh
- **Acquired immunity** is secured the body develops after it has overcome a diseases, or by injections of serum (inoculation).
Miễn nhiễm tự tạo là sự có được sau khi cơ thể trãi qua một cơn bệnh, hoặc do chích thuốc chủng ngừa.

- **A human disease** carried is a person who immune to the disease himself can infect other persons with the germs of the disease. Two examples are diphtheria and typhoid fever.
Một người bệnh truyền nhiễm là người đã qua cơn bệnh và tự miễn nhiễm có thể truyền bệnh người khác với vi trùng gây bệnh. Hai ví dụ đó là bệnh yết hầu và thương hàn.
- **Disinfectants,** intense the heat and ultra-violet rays can destroy bacteria
Chất diệt trùng, sức nóng và tia U.V có thể hủy diệt vi trùng.
- **Pediculosis** is also called head lice.
Pediculosis được gọi là chí ở trên đầu

SAFETY IN THE SALON *(An toàn trong tiệm)*

- **Chemical's gas** found in formalin is an active gas cause cancer and has prohibited by many states is formaldehyde.
Chất khí của hóa chất tìm thấy trong formalin là hơi khí hoạt động gây ung thư và bị cấm dùng ở nhiều tiểu bang là khí formadehyde.

- An antiseptic is a chemical agent that may kill or retards the growth of bacteria.
  Chất sát trùng là một hóa chất có thể giết hoặc làm yếu đi sự sinh sản của vi trùng
- **Asepsis** is freedom from disease causing germs. **Sepsis** is contamination due to pathogenic germs*: sự vô trùng là tuyệt đối không có vi trùng. Nhiễm trùng máu là nhiễm bẩn do vi trùng gây bệnh tạo ra.*
- Forms of heat sterilizing are*: các dạng dùng nhiệt để tiệt trùng là*
  - Dry heat from 320 – 338 degrees F at least 30 minutes or more depending on load
    Nhiệt khô từ 320 – 338 độ F tối thiểu 30 phút hoặc hơn tùy số lượng dụng cụ nhiều hay ít
  - Autoclave (steam) from 250 – 273 degrees F in 9 to 20 minutes
    Lò hơi tự động (hơi nóng) từ 250 – 273 độ F trong 9 đến 20 phút
- **Disinfectants** usually are stronger than antiseptics and destroy all bacteria as Quats, alcohol.
  Chất diệt trùng thường mạnh hơn loại sát trùng và hủy diệt các vi trùng như Quats, alcohol
- Two forms of radiation for disinfection are*: hai loại quang tuyến dùng cho diệt trùng là:*
  - **Ultra-violet radiation**, especially in the shorter wavelength, destroys most bacteria
    Tuyến tử ngoại cực tím (U.V) đặc biệt trong tần sóng ngắn, tiêu diệt hầu hết vi trùng
  - **Gamma ray radiation** destroys micro-organisms through the action of ionized particles
    Tuyến gamma tiêu diệt vi sinh vật qua tác động của các phân tử ion.

Emery board
dũa giấy

Metal pusher
cây xủi da

Chamois buffer
cây buffer bọc da dê

- **Bacteria** form spherical spores with tough covering during the inactive stage are anthrax and tetenus bacilli.
  Dạng vi trùng mà thành lập bào tử với lớp vỏ bọc trong suốt thời kỳ không hoạt động là loại vi trùng hình gậy anthrax và tetenus.
- ***Boils or pimples*** *that contain pus are signs of local infection*
  Nhọt và mụt có chứa mủ là dấu hiệu của nhiễm trùng tại chỗ
- 12.5 % solution of Quats mixed 1oz (ounce) of Quats to 1 gallon of water. The ideal temperature of the salon should be about 70 degrees F
  12.5 % dung dịch nước Quats trong 1 ounce pha với 1 gallon nước. Nhiệt độ thích hợp của salon nên giữ khoảng 70 độ F
- **Sterilization** is the process of making an object germ-free, by destroying all micro-organisms, both pathogenic and non-pathogenic includes spores as hospital level.
  Sự tiệt trùng là tiến trình làm vô trùng, hủy diệt tất cả vi sinh vật, cả hai loại vi trùng gây bệnh và không gây bệnh kể cả bào tử của vi trùng như cách diệt trùng cấp bệnh viện.
- **Sanitation** is the process of making object clean and safe for use, to prevent the growth of germs and to reduce the risk of infectious disease.
  Vệ sinh là tiến trình là cho vật được sạch sẽ và an toàn khi dùng, để ngăn ngừa sử nẩy nở của vi trùng và giảm bớt nguy cơ của sự nhiễm trùng bệnh.
- **OSHA** (Occupational Safety & Health Administration): *Quản trị an toàn sức khỏe nghề nghiệp*

Bài 5: VỆ SINH VÀ DIỆT TRÙNG Ở SALON

Luật lệ về vệ sinh và diệt trùng trên toàn khắp Hoa Kỳ rất nghiêm ngặt, đặc biệt các ngành nghề tiếp xúc cơ thể con người đều phải qua kỳ thi lấy giấy phép, và trong lãnh vực thẩm mỹ gồm có chuyên viên về móng *(manicurist),* chuyên viên săn sóc da, trang điểm *(esthetician),* chuyên viên lấy lông vĩnh viễn *(electrologist),* và thẩm mỹ toàn phần *(cosmetologist)* càng cần lưu ý hơn.

Người thợ tiếp xúc với khách, dụng cụ làm cho khách, do đó sự lây bệnh trực tiếp rất dễ dàng. Qua những xảy diễn nguy hại đến khách như trong việc làm các loại móng giả gây nhiễm trùng từ dụng cụ, thiếu phân tích, hoặc cẩu thả trước khi làm móng sẽ dẫn đến bị nấm, mốc hoặc ngay cả những thiết bị hiện đại giúp chăm sóc chân thoải mái hơn (*pedicure spa*) đã xảy ra một số trường hợp đáng tiếc, cũng chỉ vì thiếu kiến thức và trách nhiệm mà vệ sinh và diệt trùng không đúng cách.

VỆ SINH *(sanitation)*

Vệ sinh là cách làm hằng ngày của người thợ cần phải rửa tay thường xuyên sau khi tiếp xúc đồ vật, trước và sau khi ăn, sau khi đi tiểu, tiện, trước khi và sau khi phục vụ khách, vì qua rửa tay là loại đi những chất bẩn, vi khuẩn gây bệnh được tẩy đi phần mặt ngoài qua hình thức này.

Vệ sinh cũng là cách để duy trì một salon chuyên nghiệp luôn giữ cho salon sạch sẽ, an toàn phục vụ khách hàng.

Vì thế người thợ và chủ đều phải có trách nhiệm sau:

- *Salon luôn sạch sẽ không có bất cứ loại côn trùng nào như gián, chuột.*
- *Bụi, bột giũa rơi xuống nền, bay trong không khí, do đó cửa ra vào, bàn, tủ nên lau chùi thường xuyên, sàn nhà thường quét, hút bụi. Rác rưởi bỏ vào thùng có nắp đậy và đổ rác nhiều lần trong ngày để tránh ô nhiễm môi trường vì xử dụng nhiều hóa chất cho khách như alcohol, acetone.v.v...*
- *Cung cấp nước uống sạch, dùng loại ly giấy một lần vứt bỏ, xà phòng tẩy trùng, giấy lau tay, giấy vệ sinh, khăn giấy trải bàn làm cho khách, khăn giấy lót dụng cụ sạch và đầy đủ.*
- *Salon không nên dùng để ở, nấu nướng, thức ăn không đặt chung cùng sản phẩm làm móng trong cùng tủ. Không ăn, uống bừa bãi và tuyệt đối cấm hút thuốc tại salon theo luật liên bang.*
- *Các dung dịch làm móng đều có nhãn rõ ràng, đặt nơi thích hợp, các dụng cụ dùng lại như kềm cắt da, cây sủi kim loại cần diệt trùng và cất giữ đúng cách.*
- *Đừng cho bất cứ con vật nào vào salon để tránh ô nhiễm trừ khi con chó dẫn đường cho người mù. Quần áo người thợ luôn sạch, khử mùi hôi thân thể (deodorant) và súc miệng sau khi ăn.*

HÌNH THỨC KHỬ TRÙNG

Hội đồng thẩm mỹ và sức khỏe nêu ra những phương pháp cần thực hành ở salon đều được cơ quan quản trị về thực phẩm và thuốc *(FDA: Food and Drug Administration)* và trung tâm kiểm soát bệnh tật *(CDC: Center for Disease Control)* chuẩn nhận.

- ***SÁT TRÙNG*** *(antiseptic) có thể giết vi trùng hoặc làm chậm sự phát triển của vi trùng, là chất an toàn dùng trên da như Hydrogen Peroxide 3 – 5%; Boric Acid 2 - 5%; Cồn Isopropyl 60%; Tincture of Iodine 2%; Merthiolate sát trùng vết thương.*

- ***DIỆT TRÙNG*** *(disinfection) giết tất cả vi trùng cả vi trùng có lợi và gây bệnh, diệt vi trùng trên hầu hết bề mặt của dụng cụ nhưng không đủ khả năng diệt bào tử (spores) như Formalin từ 10%, Phenol 5%, Alcohol 70% v.v....*
- ***TIỆT TRÙNG*** *(sterilization) hiệu quả và dùng như diệt trùng, có khả năng diệt các loại vi trùng, bào tử vi trùng. Cách này không đòi hỏi xử dụng ở salon và thường được dùng trong bệnh viện. Đây là phương thức dùng nhiệt như sử dụng nồi hấp nhiệt độ cao (autoclave).*

PHƯƠNG PHÁP VỆ SINH KHI CHUẨN BỊ PHỤC VỤ KHÁCH

1. Sạch sẽ bàn làm móng bằng lau chùi, dùng dung dịch diệt trùng lau bàn hoặc bình xịt chất diệt trùng được chuẩn nhận từ EPA (Environment Protection Administration).
2. Dụng cụ làm cho khách phải được diệt trùng rồi theo phương cách từng bước một diệt trùng dụng cụ như sau: rửa sạch dụng cụ bằng nước ấm và xà phòng, xả sạch nước và lau khô, ngâm dụng cụ vào dung dịch diệt trùng theo qui định, xả sạch dụng cụ bằng nước, lau khô và cất giữ trong bao kín hoặc hộp kín cho đến khi dùng cho người khách mới.
3. Dùng khăn sạch, khăn giấy sạch trải bàn, gối lót tay, các vật liệu hoàn toàn mới cho mỗi người khách như dũa giấy, buffer, que gỗ cam (orange wood stick), bông gòn.
4. Tay bạn được rửa kỷ bằng xà phòng khử trùng và khi bắt tay cần thoa thêm loại gel chứa alcohol là chất khử trùng tốt để lau tay. Mọi việc bạn chuẩn bị đều được khách hàng quan sát và họ sẽ tin tưởng vào nghề nghiệp của bạn hơn.

HÓA CHẤT SÁT TRÙNG THÔNG THƯỜNG

- *Xà phòng, kem diệt vi khuẩn (antimicrobal soap, cream) 2%, dùng để rửa tay.*
- *Hóa chất formalin 5%, sát trùng bồn nước, bồn gội, lau tủ, bàn......*
- *Cồn Isopropyl 60% dạng dung dịch, gel, hoặc bọt dùng sát trùng tay, da, vết cắt nhỏ, nhưng không nên dùng nếu chỗ đó đang ngứa.*
- *Hydrogen Peroxide (H_2O_2) 3% – 5%, dạng dung dịch, dùng sát trùng da và vết cắt nhỏ*
- *Tincture of Iodine 2%, dạng dung dịch, dùng sát trùng vết cắt và vết thương*
- *Boric Acid 2 – 5%, dạng bột trắng pha loãng, dùng sát trùng mắt*

DỤNG CỤ VÀ CÁC CHẤT DIỆT TRÙNG CÓ HIỆU QUẢ

Diệt trùng có hiệu quả phải có những đặc tính, tiêu diệt hết mọi vi trùng *(bactericides)*, diệt nấm *(fungicides)*, và diệt được siêu vi khuẩn *(virucides)*.

- **Quats (Quaternary Ammonium Compounds)** là hổn hợp ammonium diệt trùng chuyên nghiệp thích hợp cho salon vì tác dụng nhanh, giá rẽ, ổn định, không bay hơi nhanh, không mùi. Nước Quats tiếp xúc trực tiếp với làn da lâu cũng gây ngứa da và sưng da. Độ mạnh của Quats 1/1000, thời gian 20 phút đủ khả năng diệt trùng.
  Cách pha chế nước Quats 1/1000 như sau:
  12.5% độ mạnh với 1 oz dung dịch (30ml) quat pha 1 galon (3 lit 8) nước.
  Công thức pha chế nước Quats hiện nay đều có chứa chất chống mòn, chống rỉ sét. Ngoài ra có thể dùng nước Quats lau chùi mặt bàn, tủ.

- **Phenol 5% (Carbolic Acid)** dạng dung dịch, dùng diệt trùng dụng cụ ngâm chìm ít nhất là 10 phút, các chất liệu như cao su có thể bị mềm và đổi màu với hóa chất này. Tránh để da tay tiếp xúc gây ngứa, hơi phenolics hít vào làm tổn thương màng mũi, cổ họng và phổi. Đây là hóa chất diệt trùng tốt nhưng giá cả mắc quá.

- **Alcohol Ethyl or Methyl 70% hoặc Alcohol Isopropyl 99%** dạng dung dịch, ngâm dụng cụ hoặc điện cực thủy tinh ít nhất 20 phút. Các loại cồn này tiếp xúc đều gây ngứa mắt, mũi, cổ họng, và phổi, ảnh hưởng trung khu thần kinh, ngứa da và sưng da. Sự bất tiện của cồn là dễ bay hơi, dễ bốc cháy, và ăn mòn dụng cụ.

- **Formalin** là dung dịch diệt trùng mạnh với **10% độ mạnh** cần ngâm dụng cụ diệt trùng trong 20 phút và **25% độ mạnh** cần ngâm dụng cụ trong 10 phút. Trong dung dịch formlin có chứa chất khí độc formaldehyde dễ gây ung thư, gây ngứa mắt, mũi, cổ họng, dị ứng da, và tạo hen suyển mà hiện bị cấm dùng ở một số tiểu bang. Formalin trong kỷ nghệ chứa 37% formaldehyde và dùng trong việc diệt mối, gián, và sâu bọ.

- **Sodium Hypochlorite 10%** dạng dung dịch để tẩy rửa nhà, chất này có khả năng chống lại siêu vi trùng HIV. Đây là 1 hóa chất mạnh, bào mòn dụng cụ bằng kim loại, gây bệnh gan. Dụng cụ diệt trùng cần ngâm ít nhất 10 phút.

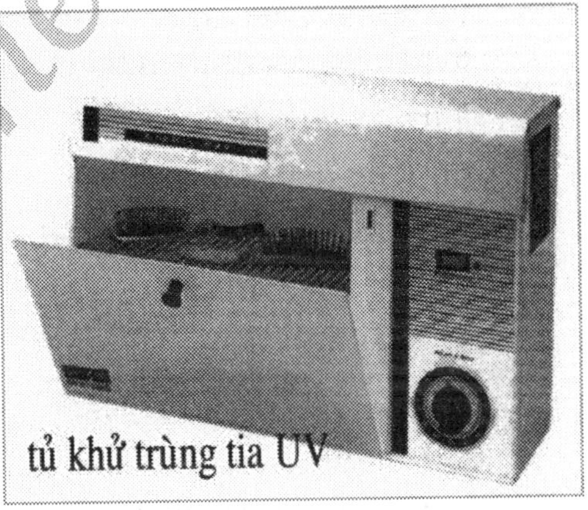
tủ khử trùng tia UV

- **Hấp dụng cụ bằng hơi nước sôi 100 độ C** *(212 độ F)* để diệt trùng và trong cơ sở y tế người ta dùng **Autoclave** là dụng cụ có sức ép và hơi nóng có sức diệt trùng hữu hiệu.

- **Tia cực tím Ultraviolet rays** diệt được nấm và vi trùng, khi xử dụng cần che mắt.

- **Hơi nhiệt** hình thức như hơ nóng, nướng.

- **Tủ khử trùng khô (dry cabinet sanitizer)** là tủ kín chứa khí formaldehyde tỏa mùi nồng nặc diệt trùng.

AN TOÀN NGHỀ NGHIỆP

Để tạo sự an toàn cho nghề nghiệp cần biết sử dụng từ những hóa chất sát trùng, diệt trùng, sạch sẽ cá nhân, giữ vệ sinh salon, mang bao tay, kính che mắt, biết phân biệt thế nào là sự xáo trộn thông thường về da, móng, thế nào là bệnh cần đưa đi bác sĩ.

Đừng ngửi hóa chất để xác định, đừng tự ý pha trộn sản phẩm riêng cho salon mình, đừng dùng ngón tay bạn để vuốt lông cọ ướt nước acrylic, gel, hoặc keo.

Các chai lọ hóa chất cần có nhãn hiệu rõ ràng, đậy chặt nắp hóa chất và cất giữ nơi khô ráo, tối, và mát, xa nguồn thức ăn, nước uống, xa tầm tay trẻ con, và ngay cả cần hộp cấp cứu đầy đủ ngay khi nguy cấp.

Khách hàng sẵn sàng lắng nghe về những giải thích trong sự hiểu biết thấu đáo về lãnh vực chuyên môn của bạn, hành xử chuyên nghiệp, bạn sẽ có được lòng tin, sự kính trọng và cuối cùng là ý thức trách nhiệm của một chuyên viên thẩm mỹ cần có.

SANITATION AND DISINFECTION IN THE SALON

Vệ sinh và diệt trùng ở salon

- Salon sanitation is lowest level as sanitized surfaces. Guidelines to keep the salon looking its best such as floors should be swept clean; employees must be worn clean attire; no pets or animals in salon (except for trained Seeing Eye Dogs); soiled linen are removed...
Vệ sinh ở tiệm là cấp thấp nhất trong các phương pháp như khử trùng bề mặt. Hướng dẫn giữ salon được sạch sẽ như: Nền lót phải được quét sạch; thợ mặc đồ sạch sẽ; không có thú vật nào trong tiệm (ngoại trừ con chó được huấn luyện dẫn đường cho người mù); khăn, vải dơ bẩn phải dọn dẹp sạch...

- **A good rule** to remember in caution wear gloves and safety glasses when apply primer; formalin and borax are a disinfectant and fumigant in dry cabinet sanitizer, formadehyde is the gas released from fomalin and can get cancer. Not suggest to use in salon
Một điều lệ đúng cần ghi nhớ là luôn lưu ý mang bao tay và kính an toàn khi thoa chất primer; formalin và borax là một chất diệt trùng, tạo xông hơi khí khô khử trùng trong tủ, formadehyde là chất khí thoát ra từ formalin và có thể gây ung thư. Không nên dùng ở salon.

- All disinfectant approved by the (E.P.A) and each state for proper use, safety precautions & important information sheet in (M.S.D.S) as hazard, combustion level ...
Các chất diệt trùng phải chuẩn nhận bởi (Cơ quan bảo vệ môi trường) và cách sử dụng từng mỗi tiểu bang, sự lưu ý an toàn và những tin tức quan trọng trong (bảng dữ kiện an toàn vật liệu) về sự nguy hại, mức độ bùng cháy...

1. **Antiseptic**: can kill bacteria or slow their growth and safe for skin.
Sát trùng: có thể giết vi trùng hoặc làm chậm sự phát triển của vi trùng và an toàn cho da.
2. **Disinfections**: kill all bacteria and on non-living surfaces but does not kill bacteria spores and use for instruments and implements.
Diệt trùng: giết tất cả vi trùng và các bề mặt dụng cụ nhưng không giết được các bào tử của vi trùng và diệt trùng cho dụng cụ và đồ nghề của thợ.
3. **Sterilization**: most effective, destroys all bacteria and bacteria spores. Bactericides, Fungicides, and Virucides are called hospital level disinfectants.
Tiệt trùng có hiệu quả tối đa, hủy diệt tất cả vi trùng và bào tử vi trùng. Diệt trùng, diệt nấm, và siêu vi khuẩn được gọi là chất diệt trùng bệnh viện.

- **O.S.H.A:** Occupation safety and health administration created as part of the U.S department of labor to regulate.
***O.S.H.A:** Quản trị về sức khỏe và an toàn cho nghề nghiệp điều hành do bộ lao động.*

Types of disinfectants: *Các chất diệt trùng*

- **Quats:** Quaternary ammonium compounds disinfect implements in 10 to 15 minutes.
Hổn hợp nước Quat diệt trùng dụng cụ từ 10 đến 15 phút.
- **Phenol:** (phenolic disinfectants) like Quats but disadvantage: rubber and plastic are softened and discolored.
Phenol hay chất diệt trùng phenolic cũng giống nước Quat nhưng bất tiện vì cao su và nhựa bị mềm và bay màu.
- **Alcohol has 3 types**: Methyl, Ethyl (or grain) and Isopropyl (from chemical) alcohol. To be affected for disinfection: ethyl and methyl 70% or Isopropyl 99%. Disadvantage of alcohol: flammable, evaporates quickly and corrode.
Cồn có 3 loại là Methyl, Ethyl (từ ngũ cốc) và Isopropyl (điều chế). Để được hữu hiệu diệt trùng loại ethyl, methyl 70% hoặc Isopropyl là 99%. Sự bất tiện của cồn là dễ cháy, bay hơi nhanh và ăn mòn.

- Bleach (sodium hypochlorite) uses household bleach.
  Chất tẩy (sodium hypochlorite) dùng tẩy nhà
- High frequency sound waves to create powerful combined disinfectants to clean nooks, crannies of implements is called ultrasonic cleaners.
  Dùng sóng cao tần tạo khả năng để kết hợp với chất diệt trùng để làm sạch các kẻ, hóc của dụng cụ được gọi là cách làm sạch ultrasonic.

- Use gloves, safety glasses, disinfectants, personal hygiene and salon cleanliness together is universal sanitation.
  Những cách sử dụng như dùng bao tay, kính an toàn, chất diệt trùng, vệ sinh cá nhân và làm sạch sẽ ở tiệm phối hợp với nhau được gọi là cách vệ sinh toàn bộ.

WORKING SAFETY: ***An toàn làm việc***

- **Overexposure** is a danger you need to avoid. Overexposure for prolonged period causes most of the problems. All of this product can be safe, but all can be dangerous if used incorrectly.
  Sự tiếp xúc nhiều hóa chất sẽ nguy hiểm bạn cần nên tránh. Sự tiếp xúc lâu dài là nguyên nhân tạo ra vấn đề. Tất cả sản phẩm có thể là an toàn, nhưng có thể là nguy hiểm nếu dùng không đúng cách.
- Your body will usually give you some early warning: *Cơ thể của bạn thường sẽ báo trước các dấu hiệu.*
  - Rash *(rát da)*
  - Lightheadedness *(đau đầu nhẹ)*
  - Tingling toes *(ngứa ngón chân)*
  - Breathing problems *(khó thở)*
  - Insomnia *(chứng mất ngủ)*
  - Watery eyes *(chảy nước mắt)*
  - Runny nose *(chảy nước mũi)*
  - Dry throat *(khô cổ họng)*
  - Irritability *(nóng nảy)*
  - Sore *(đau)*
  - Fatigue *(mệt mỏi)*
  - Sluggishness *(uể oải)*

M.S.D.S (material safety data sheet) contains the following information:
M.S.D.S là bảng dữ kiện an toàn vật liệu bao gồm những tin tức sau đây:

- Permissible exposure limits. Identify of chemical (hazardous ingredients)
  Giới hạn sự tiếp xúc cho phép. Nhận rõ hóa chất (thành phần độc hại)
- Primary routes of entry into the body: chemical entry through the skin, mouth or lungs.
  Đường đầu tiên vào cơ thể: hóa chất vào qua da, miệng hoặc phổi.
- Physical hazards; explosion; fire hazards; evaporate
  Nguy hại thể lý; sự bùng nổ; lửa cháy; bốc hơi
- You breathe them (inhalation), you contact through your skin and you eat them (ingestion)
  Bạn hít thở hóa chất, bạn tiếp xúc qua da và bạn ăn phải hoá chất (ăn vào bụng)

- **Primer, monomer**, adhesives or phenolic disinfectant solutions in the eye are worse. Wearing contacts in salon in risky because vapors will collect in soft contacts.
  Primer (chất kết dính), monomer (nước acrylic), keo hoặc chất diệt trùng phenolic gây nguy hại khi dính vào mắt. Mang contact lens dễ nguy hiểm vì hơi sẽ bám vào màng mắt kính mềm.

- **Prolonged inhalations** of excessive amounts of nail filing may be harmful. Always wear a dust mask when filing especially if you used a drill.
  Hít nhiều bột giũa móng lâu dài gây nguy hại. Luôn luôn mang mặt nạ che bụi khi giũa đặc biệt là khi dùng máy.

- **Charcoal filters** must be discarded after 20 hours to use. Your breathing zone is and invisible sphere in front your face but it is very important.
  Miếng lọc than ở bàn làm móng phải vứt bỏ sau 20 giờ xử dụng. Vùng hơi thở của bạn là khối cầu nhỏ trước mặt không thấy được nhưng rất quan trọng.

SAFETY IN THE SALON *(An toàn trong tiệm)*

- Chemical's gas found in formalin is an active gas cause cancer and has prohibited by many states is formaldehyde.
  Chất khí của hóa chất tìm thấy trong formalin là hơi khí hoạt động gây ung thư và bị cấm dùng ở nhiều tiểu bang là khí formadehyde.
- An antiseptic is a chemical agent that may kill or retards the growth of bacteria.
  Chất sát trùng là một hóa chất có thể giết hoặc làm yếu đi sự sinh sản của vi trùng
- Asepsis is freedom from disease causing germs. Sepsis is contamination due to pathogenic germs.
  Sự vô trùng là tuyệt đối không có vi trùng. Nhiễm trùng máu là nhiễm bẩn do vi trùng gây bệnh tạo ra.

- **Forms of heat sterilizing are:** *các dạng dùng nhiệt để tiệt trùng là*
  - Dry heat from **320 – 338 degrees F** at least **30 minutes** or more depending on load
    Nhiệt khô từ 320 – 338 độ F tối thiểu 30 phút hoặc hơn tùy số lượng dụng cụ nhiều hay ít
  - Autoclave (steam) from 250 – 273 degrees F in 9 to 20 minutes
    Lò hơi tự động (hơi nóng) từ 250 – 273 độ F trong 9 đến 20 phút
- Disinfectants usually are stronger than antiseptics and destroy all bacteria as Quats, alcohol.
  Chất diệt trùng thường mạnh hơn loại sát trùng và hủy diệt các vi trùng như Quats, alcohol

- **Two forms of radiation for disinfection are**: *hai loại quang tuyến dùng cho diệt trùng là:*
  - Ultra-violet radiation, especially in the shorter wavelength, destroys most bacteria
    Tuyến tử ngoại cực tím (U.V) đặc biệt trong tần sóng ngắn, tiêu diệt hầu hết vi trùng
  - Gamma ray radiation destroys micro-organisms through the action of ionized particles
    Tuyến gamma tiêu diệt vi sinh vật qua tác động của các phân tử ion.

- The ideal temperature of the salon should be about 70 degrees F
  Nhiệt độ thích hợp của salon nên giữ khoảng 70 độ F
- Which of the following bacteria form spherical spores with tough covering during the inactive stage are anthrax and tetenus bacilli.
  Dạng vi trùng mà thành lập bào tử với lớp vỏ bọc trong suốt thời kỳ không hoạt động là loại vi trùng hình gậy anthrax và tetenus.
- Boils or pimples that contain pus are signs of local infection
  Nhọt và mụt có chứa mủ là dấu hiệu của nhiễm trùng tại chỗ

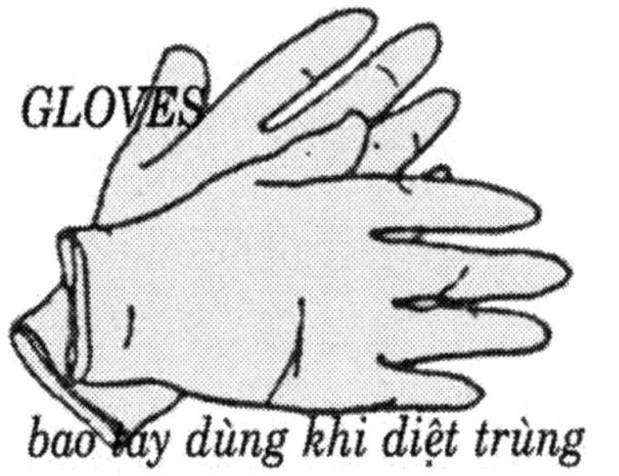

- **12.5 % solution of Quats mixed 1oz (ounce) of Quats to 1 gallon of water**
  12.5 % dung dịch nước Quats trong 1 ounce pha với 1 gallon nước
- OSHA (Occupational Safety & Health Administration):
  Quản trị an toàn sức khỏe nghề nghiệp

- **Sterilization** is the process of making an object germ-free, by destroying all micro-organisms, both pathogenic and non-pathogenic includes spores as hospital level.
  Sự tiệt trùng là tiến trình làm vô trùng, hủy diệt tất cả vi sinh vật, cả hai loại vi trùng gây bệnh và không gây bệnh kể cả bào tử của vi trùng như cách diệt trùng cấp bệnh viện.
- Sanitation is the process of making object clean and safe for use, to prevent the growth of germs and to reduce the risk of infectious disease.
  Vệ sinh là tiến trình là cho vật được sạch sẽ và an toàn khi dùng, để ngăn ngừa sử nẩy nở của vi trùng và giảm bớt nguy cơ của sự nhiễm trùng bệnh.

Bài 6: CHĂM SÓC TAY VÀ CHÂN

Ngành chăm sóc tay, chân xuất phát từ Trung Hoa và Ai Cập, tay chân được chãi chuốt, xoa bóp, và sơn màu, chính là để phân biệt giới quí tộc và hạng bình dân lao động. Thời đó móng tay cũng được cắt giũa, đánh bóng, và màu móng được nhuộm từ thảo mộc. Riêng phụ nữ Hoa Kỳ đến đầu thế kỷ 19 sơn móng đã thấy ở những phim trường điện ảnh, và đến năm 1920s, các salon đã phục vụ cho cả nam và nữ. Đến 1950s một số tiểu bang đòi hỏi giấy phép hành nghề, móng giả xuất hiện 1970s và kỷ nghệ móng tay mạnh từ 1980 đến nay.

Từ ngữ chăm sóc tay (manicuring) đến từ chữ Latin (***manus là tay, và cura là chăm sóc).*** Chăm sóc tay chính là giữ gìn đôi bàn tay mềm mại và đẹp.

Có 4 dạng móng tay căn bản, dựa vào chiều dài ngón tay, hình dáng bàn tay, và ngay cả tìm hiểu nghề nghiệp người khách để gợi ý kiểu móng.

1. **Móng bầu dục (OVAL)** *thường thấy ở bàn tay phụ nữ, nền móng tròn, dài trông đẹp hơn cho những người làm thương mãi, giáo chức, nghề nghiệp mua bán nhẹ nhàng, cần và thích khoe bàn tay. Đây là dạng móng tay đẹp, hấp dẫn.*
2. **Móng chữ nhật, vuông (SQUARE, RECTANGULAR)** *là móng trông có vẽ mạnh, chắc. Dạng móng này thích hợp cho người làm việc dùng đôi tay đánh computer, lắp ráp vật dụng.*
3. **Móng nhọn (POINT)** *là móng dũa dài hơn bình thường, trông mãnh mai, dễ yếu và gãy. Dạng móng này thích hợp cho bàn tay gầy và thân móng hẹp.*
4. **Móng tròn (ROUND)** *gọt tròn ở đầu móng hơi quá đầu ngón tay, trông tự nhiên. Dạng móng này thích hợp cho đàn ông*

Là người thợ chuyên nghiệp đều hiểu rõ từ các hóa phẩm, vật liệu, dụng cụ và trang bị chính yếu để chăm sóc đôi tay như:

- **Hóa phẩm (cosmetics):** dung dịch lau rửa nước sơn cũ không chứa acetone cho khách mang móng tay giả *(polish remover)*; cuticle solvent hay *cuticle remover chứa 2 – 5%* sodium, potassium hydroxide, và glycerin để làm mềm da tay dễ tỉa da chết.; *nail whitener* màu trắng phấn chứa zinc oxide hay titanium dioxide để che đậy dưới móng có đốm dễ sinh nấm, mốc; hoặc *nail strengthener* là các chất làm mạnh móng tay.
- **Vật liệu (materials):** các loại bột cầm máu *(alum)*, bông gòn, khăn vải, khăn giấy v.v…
- **Dụng cụ (implements):** các dụng cụ như sủi da kim loại *(metal pusher)*, cầm như nắm viết, dùng cây sủi đẩy da lùi ra sau để tỉa da chết; kềm cắt da chết *(cuticle nipper)* dùng cắt tỉa da thừa ở nền móng; nail brush bàn chãi móng; dũa giấy *(emery board)* một mặt nhám và mặt mịn dài cở 7 inch, đặt dũa góc 45 độ so với móng, ép nhẹ và dùng 1 lần bẻ đôi bỏ ngay vào túi rác. Không nên giữ lại dũa cũ dù chỉ dành cho người khách đó, cần tuân thủ luật vệ sinh của tiểu bang v.v…

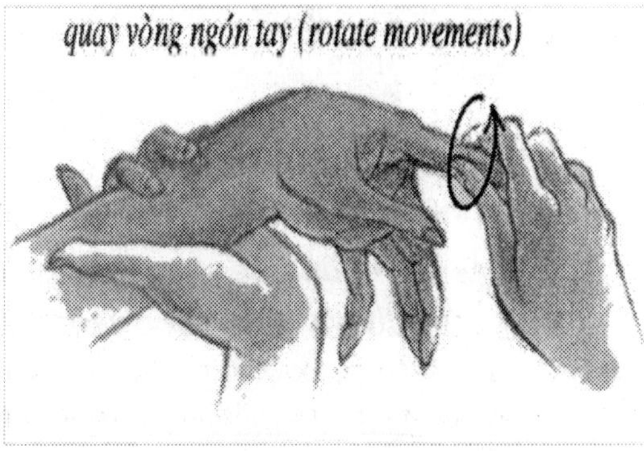

- **Trang bị (equipments):** là những thiết bị sử dụng lâu dài như bàn làm móng, đèn bàn loại 40 watts; tô ngâm tay *(fingerbowl)*; ghế của khách và thợ v.v…

HÌNH THỨC CHĂM SÓC TAY (PLAIN MANICURE)

1. **Móng tay nước (plain manicure)** là cách chăm sóc tay thông thường ngâm móng tay vào nước ấm. Theo cách thức làm manicure, người thợ cần ghi phiếu sức khỏe để kiểm tra để quyết định có hay không nên làm cho khách. Khi làm móng nhớ bắt đầu ngâm bàn tay thuận lâu hơn, vì bàn tay xử dụng nhiều hơn nên da chai tạo dày hơn.
2. **Móng tay dầu (hot oil manicure)** là cách dùng chất dầu olive hoặc lotion thoa tay đặt vào lò cho ấm lên thay vì dùng nước ấm và xà phòng, cách làm gần giống móng tay nước nhưng massage cho dầu thấm vào da và móng trước khi đẩy và cắt da chết. Móng dầu làm hàng tuần giúp cho loại móng dễ gãy, da khô quanh móng, tăng sự ẩm ướt cho da và móng, đặc biệt giúp cho người có thói quen cắn móng tay.
3. **Móng tay kiểu Pháp (French manicure)** là hình thức làm như móng tay nước nhưng khi sơn móng thì sau khi phết nước sơn lót, tiếp theo là sơn trắng, sơn lên đầu móng dạng chữ V hoặc tròn, và màu hồng nhạt hoặc nước trong phủ lên từ gốc móng đến đầu móng. Móng kiểu Pháp là kiểu nghệ thuật rất thích hợp cho khách vào những tháng hè và lễ, tiệc.
4. **Làm móng bằng giũa điện (electric manicure)** là dụng cụ motor xoay chạy bằng điện được gắn vào một số dụng cụ nhỏ để dũa móng, đẩy da, chãi móng, đánh bóng, và dụng cụ mài da chai. Cần đọc chỉ dẫn cẩn thận trước khi dùng và luật tiểu bang khi xử dụng.
5. **Dùng sáp (paraffin wax)** là dùng nhiệt từ 125 – 130 độ nóng chảy chất sáp paraffin trãi lên làn da bàn tay, móng tay, nhằm tăng lượng máu nuôi da và giúp da khô thêm ẩm ướt, mềm mại. . Đây là cách nhúng bàn tay hay bàn chân vào lò chứa paraffin lỏng, cứ cách vài giây nhúng một lần và khoảng 5 đến 7 lần nhúng, làn da được bọc sáp dày, rồi dùng plastic quấn lại và đặt tay vào bao cách nhiệt; khách thoải mái trong 10 phút rồi gỡ lớp sáp paraffin bỏ đi. Sáp paraffin giúp ích cho làn da tuổi già và người có chứng phong thấp.
6. **Làm móng cho đàn ông (men's manicure)** là cách làm giống như đàn bà, tuy nhiên đàn ông chỉ thích sơn màu trong suốt (top coat), tốt nhất là dùng bột đá (pumice powder) và cây buffer đánh bóng móng.
7. **Làm móng tay dã chiến (booth manicure)** là cách tiện lợi, không cần bàn làm móng vì làm móng tay trong lúc người khách đang làm một dịch vụ khác như nhuộm tóc, chãi sấy tóc v.v...

MASSAGE BÀN TAY VÀ CÁNH TAY (hand & arm massage)

Massage tay cũng là phần quan trọng cho mỗi dịch vụ chăm sóc tay. Không những là công việc tạo sự thoải mái xoa bóp bàn tay, cánh tay trước, cùi chỏ cho khách mà massage còn kích thích tuần hoàn máu, giữ cho đôi tay thêm mềm dẻo và làn da mịn màng.

Các tác động massage cần làm từ 3 đến 5 lần gồm:

- *Chuyển động nhẹ nhàng cổ tay, bẻ tới bẻ lui*
- *Thợ dùng ngón cái xoay tròn lòng bàn tay*
- *Chuyển động các ngón tay*
- *Chuyển động lưng bàn tay và cổ tay*
- *Chuyển động mặt dưới cánh tay trước*
- *Vặn ma sát cánh tay trước.....*
- *Nhồi bóp cánh tay*
- *Lắc cùi chỏ*
- *Chuyển động ma sát (friction movements)*

chà xoay xoay bàn tay (friction movements)

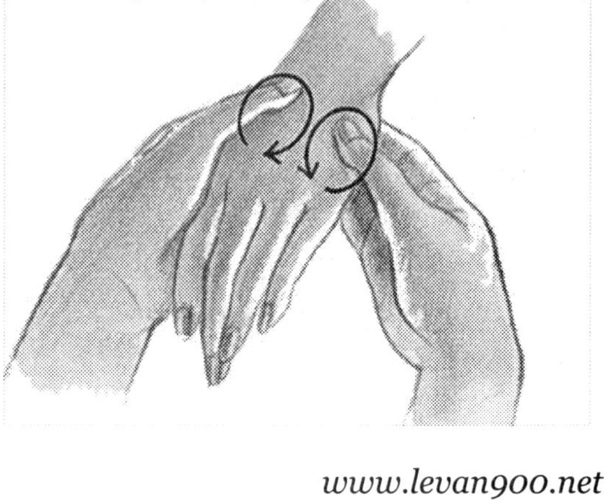

Khi massage cũng cần để ý như tránh massage mạnh ở những khớp nếu người khách bị bệnh đau khớp xương (arthritic). Không nên massage nếu khách có máu cao, bệnh tim, hoặc đã từng bị tai biến mạch máu (stroke), vì khi massage tăng sự tuần hoàn máu và có thể nguy hại đến khách hàng.

KHẢ NĂNG CỦA NGƯỜI THỢ GIỎI

Là người thợ chuyên nghiệp cần học hỏi kỷ năng chăm sóc tay, biết phương pháp chữa trị cho móng, và làn da bị xáo trộn, tìm hiểu rõ đặc tính của những dung dịch, hóa chất sử dụng hiệu quả lên da, móng của khách; hiểu biết về sự cấu trúc của xương, bàn tay, cánh tay, và móng tay; khả năng biết phân biệt giữa móng bị xáo trộn như da khô hoặc móng bị bệnh như nấm, đâm khóe để giới thiệu Bác sĩ chữa trị.

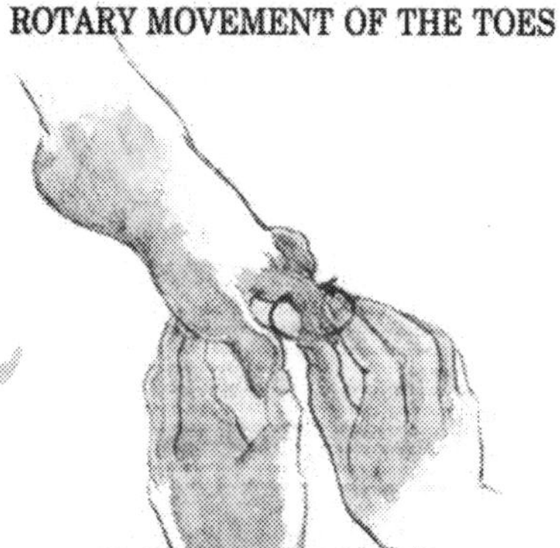

quay vòng các ngón chân

Đồng thời cũng hiểu biết về luật an toàn như:

- *Đừng giũa sâu vào góc móng*
- *Mài mòn nhẹ các dụng cụ bén bằng dũa trước khi làm*
- *Thoa sát trùng hoặc bột alum nếu có đứt tay, chảy máu*
- *Không nên làm nếu da tay sưng, hoặc nhiễm trùng*
- *Nếu khách chảy máu, ngưng làm việc, cầm máu, và thay đổi dụng cụ mới hoặc phải diệt trùng trước khi dùng lại.*

CHĂM SÓC CHÂN (PEDICURE)

Từ ngữ chăm sóc đôi chân *(pedicure),* gốc từ chữ Latin **pedis** có nghĩa là **chân**, và **cura** là **"chăm sóc".** Chăm sóc chân đơn giản là hình thức tạo sự thoải mái cho đôi chân đồng thời làn da được làm mịn với có thể giữ móng dài, trông đẹp hơn. Khách đến salon chăm sóc chân thường là hạng sang trọng, dịch vụ này giúp loại bỏ lớp da sần sùi, bàn chân và ngón chân được chăm sóc tăng thêm vẻ đẹp và giữ gìn cho chân luôn tốt.

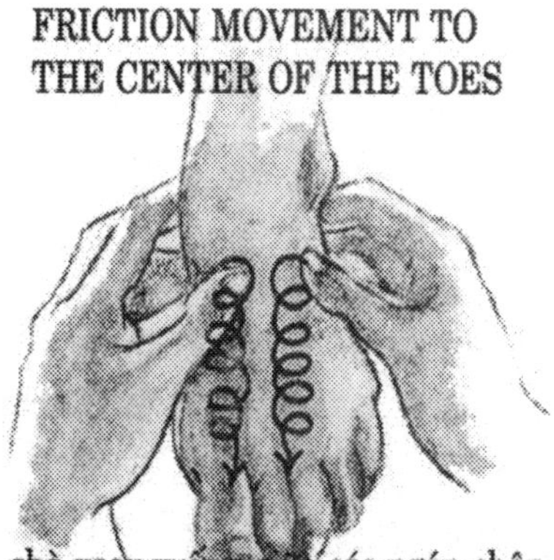

chà xoay xuống giữa các ngón chân

Chuẩn bị làm chân, người thợ cẩn thận quan sát nền nhà không bị ướt, có thể gây trơn trợt khi đem nước ấm pha xà phòng ngâm chân khách, hoặc thấy nước nhiểu cần lau khô ngay.

Khi bắt đầu làm chân, bạn có thể bảo khách tháo giày, tất, hoặc lăn đôi tất dài đến đầu gối. Xịt thuốc sát trùng và ngâm chân vào nước ấm xà phòng khoảng 5 đến 10 phút. Tuy nhiên, khi hẹn khách làm chân, nên báo cho khách mang sandals, giày trống ngón chân để khi sơn khỏi bị lem, vấy nước sơn….

Dưới bàn chân có da chai, cục chai *(corn),* thợ không nên dùng da lấy đi và ngay cả không nên dùng động tác thump compression để massage chân, sẽ làm cho khách đau và gây khó chịu.

Tuyệt đối không dùng dao *(credo knife)* chà, nạo da chai, vì dụng cụ này bén, dễ làm đứt da và không được phép xử dụng trong hội đồng thẩm mỹ tiểu bang.

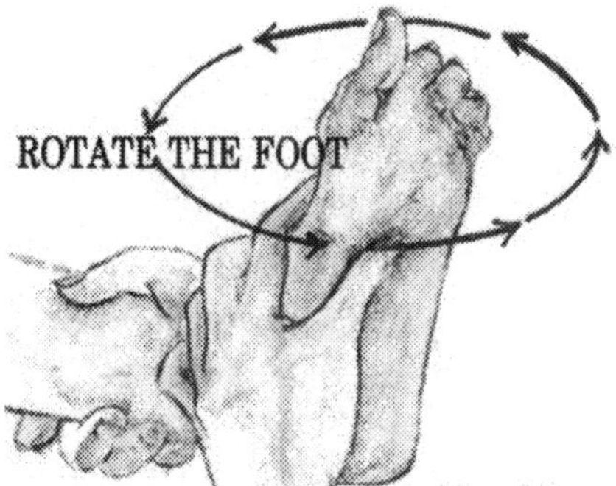

quay vòng bàn chân

MANICURING & PEDICURING

(Ngành học chăm sóc tay và chân)

•The ancients regarded long, polished, and colored fingernail as a mark of distinction between aristocrats and common laborers. The purpose of a manicure and a pedicure is to improve the appearance of the hands, feet and nails.
Từ xa xưa để móng tay dài, sơn bóng, là dấu hiệu phân biệt giữa giới quý tộc và bình dân lao động. Mục đích của chăm sóc tay và chân là nâng lên vẽ đẹp của tay, chân và móng.

A cosmetologist, manicurist should have: *(Thợ thẩm mỹ tổng quát và thợ nail cần phải)*

- Knowledge of the structure of the hands, arms and nails.
  Hiểu biết về cấu trúc của bàn tay, cánh tay, và móng.
- Knowledge of the composition of the cosmetic used.
  Hiểu biết về các thành phần mỹ phẩm được dùng .
- Knowledge of structure of the foot, ability pedicure.
  Hiểu biết cấu trúc của bàn chân, và tác dụng chăm sóc đôi chân.

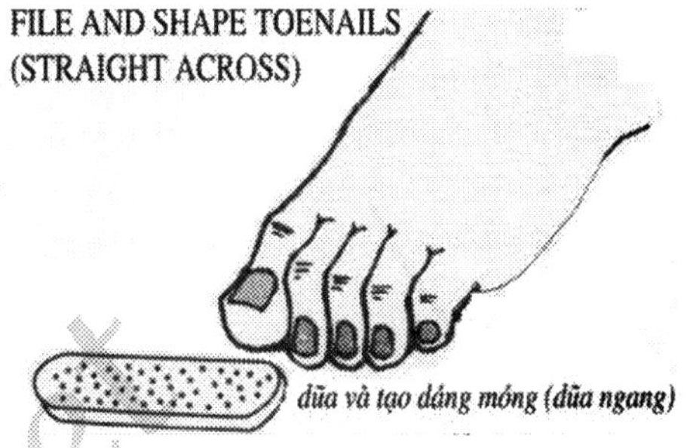

Shape of nails: *(Hình dáng của móng)*

* Square *(Vuông)* * Round *(Tròn)* * Oval *(Bầu dục)* * Pointed *(Nhọn)*

- In general, the oval-shaped nail, nicely rounded at the base and slightly pointed at the tips, fits most hands.
  Về phương diện tổng quát móng hình bầu dục tròn ở nền móng và hơi nhọn ở đầu móng thích hợp mọi bàn tay.
- People, who perform manual work, require shorter, more round-shaped nails in order to avoid nail breakage and injury.
  Những người làm việc bằng tay đòi hỏi móng ngắn hơi tròn để tránh gãy móng hoặc tổn thương đến móng.

Cosmetics in manicuring:
(Hóa mỹ phẩm trong ngành móng tay)

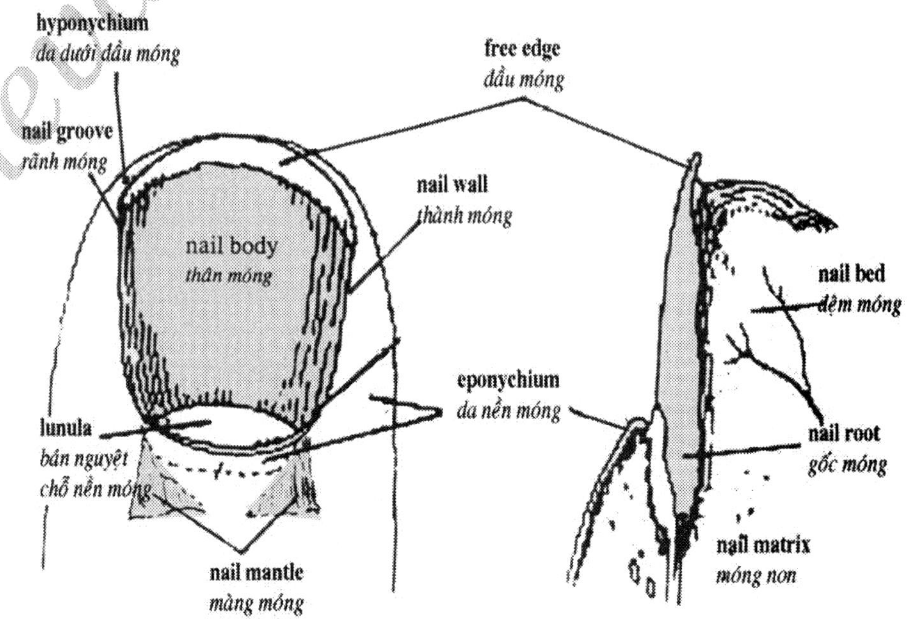

- Nail polish removers: Contain organic solvent, dissolve old polish on nails.
  Nail polish remover là chất chùi nước sơn chứa dung môi hữu cơ, hòa tan nước sơn cũ trên móng.
- Cuticle oil: soften and lubricates the skin.
  Cuticle oil là dầu thoa da vừa mềm vào trơn da
- Cuticle creams: (lanolin, petroleum, or beeswax) are used to prevent or correct brittle nails and dry cuticle.
  Kem thoa da có lanoloin (chất nhờn), petroleum (chất dầu có trong mỏ dầu hỏa), beeswax (sáp ong) được dùng đển chữa móng dòn và da khô.

- Cuticle-removers or solvents: Contain 2 - 5% sodium or potassium hydroxide, glycerin.
  Kem mềm da hoặc solvent chứa 2 - 5% chất sodium hydroxide hoặc potassium hydroxide và chất nhờn glycerin.
- Nail whiteners: (paste, cream and pencil form) contain zinc oxide or titanium dioxide, applied under the free edges.
  Nail whitetener (dạng sền sệt, kem và cây viết) là chất màu trắng chứa oxide kẽm hoặc titanium dioxide, thoa dưới đầu móng để diệt móng có đốm
- Powdered alum or solution: Used to stop the blending minor cuts.
  Bột phèn chua hoặc nước phèn chua dùng để thoa ngưng chảy máu những vết cắt nhỏ
- Adhesives or glue (cyanoacrylate) is formulated for professional salon use on the nail plate.
  Keo hoặc glue được dùng trong salon để thoa móng.

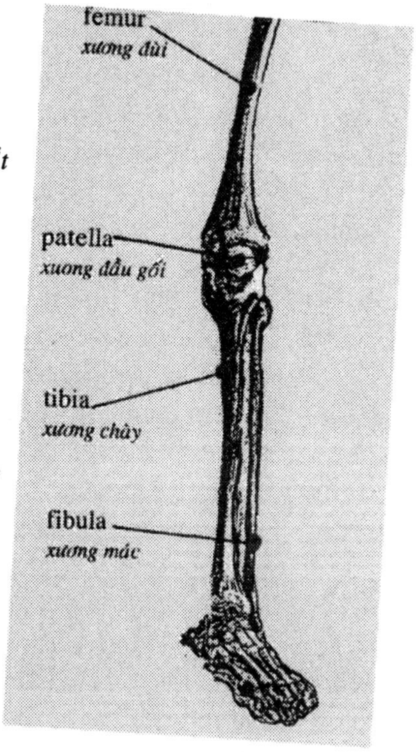

Preparation of the manicuring table: *(Chuẩn bị bàn làm móng tay)*
- Must be perfectly clean. Everything, including containers, bowls, instruments and materials, must be in perfect order. Sanitize manicuring implements after used.
  Mọi thứ phải sạch hoàn toàn kể cả lọ chứa, tô, dụng cụ và vật liệu phải thứ tự. Khử trùng dụng cụ sau khi dùng.

Plain manicure: ***Chăm sóc tay thông thường***
- Be extremely careful to avoid cutting the client's skin. However, if this occurs administer 3% hydrogen peroxide.
  Đặc biệt cẩn thận tránh việc cắt da tay khách. Tuy nhiên, nếu xảy ra thoa 3% H_2O_2
- Use light pressure when using a metal pusher or orangewood at the root of the nail. Hold the metal pusher as you hold a pen.
  Ép nhẹ khi dùng cây sủi hoặc que gỗ cam ở nền móng. Giữ cây sủi như nắm cây viết.
- To prevent the occurrence of such loose skin, trim the cuticle only enough to allow a tiny margin of cuticle.
  Đề phòng làm da bị lỏng, tỉa da vừa phải còn giữ lại viền da mỏng ở móng
- Callus growth at the fingertips can be softened by the application of cream or lotions. Skins on fingernails may be bleached with nail bleach or 6% peroxide.
  Da chai mọc đầu ngón tay thoa kem làm mềm da hoặc lotion. Da trên móng tay có thể tẩy với chất tẩy móng hoặc 6% peroxide.

Reconditioning hot oil manicure: ***Chăm sóc tay bằng dầu***
- Need electric heater and hot oil or cream (olive oil or hand lotion can also be used). Hot oil manicure is beneficial for ridged and brittle nails and dry cuticles. Improves the skin soft and pliable.
  Cần lò điện và dầu nóng hoặc kem (dầu olive hoặc kem thoa tay có thể dùng được). Chăm sóc tay bằng dầu giúp cho móng gợn và móng dòn và da khô. Làm cho da mềm và dẽo dai.

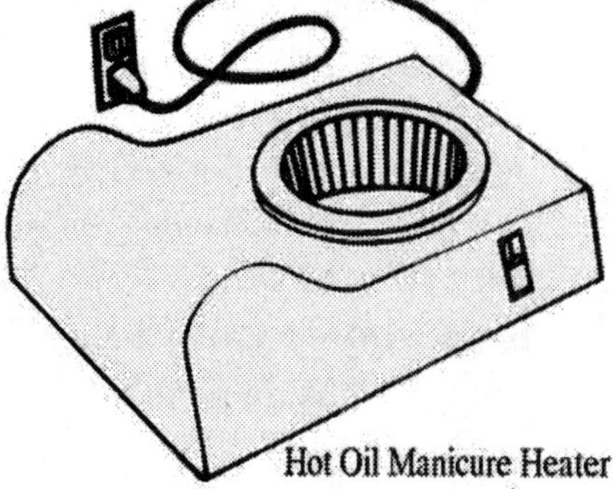

Hot Oil Manicure Heater
Lò làm móng tay dầu

- Electric manicure tool looks like a portable drill to file the nail
  Dụng cụ làm móng bằng điện như loại giũa máy nhỏ để giũa móng.

Booth manicure: ***Làm móng tay dã chiến (tạm thời)***

- Not at the manicuring table, while the client is receiving another service as hair permanent waving, color hair…

  Là dịch vụ không cần phải có bàn để làm móng tay, phục vụ khách trong khi họ đang uốn tóc hoặc nhuộm tóc…

Advanced nail techniques: ***Cách làm móng tay cao cấp***

- When a person cannot grow natural nails of the desired length and strength, could solve the problem with the help of advanced nail techniques: nail wrapping, sculptured nails, nail tipping or acrylic overlays.

  Khi người khách không có được móng thật dài và cứng chắc, có thể giải quyết vấn đề bằng cách làm thêm móng bao, móng bột, gắn tip hoặc gắn típ phủ bột.

Artificial nails may be use for the following purposes: ***Móng giả được làm theo các mục đích sau đây:***

- To mend or conceal broken, short, bad or damage nails

  Vá hoặc che đậy những móng gãy, ngắn, xấu hoặc hư)
- To help the habit of nail biting and protect split or breakage nails

  Giúp cho những người có thói quen cắn móng và bảo vệ móng chẻ hoặc gãy

Nail wrapping: ***Bọc móng***

- To mend torn, broken, or split nails and to fortify weak or fragile nails. Bolstering nails with mending tissue, silk, linen...

  Vá những móng rách, gãy, hoặc nứt và làm cứng chắc hơn những móng yếu hoặc dễ gãy. Bao móng lại với giấy vá, lụa hoặc vải dày…

Sculptured nails: ***Móng bột đắp trên form***

- Also known as build-on nails, are used when one or more nail are to be lengthened. Are made by combining a liquid and powder acrylic product to apply on nail forms.

  Được biết là build-on nails, đắp lên một hoặc nhiều móng để tăng độ dài, cách làm bằng cách dùng nước và bột acrylic đắp trên form móng.

First ball on free edge
viên bột thứ nhất lên đầu móng

Application acrylic form: ***Cách đắp móng bột***

* First, apply at free edge joins the nail form *(đầu tiên đắp ở đầu móng)*

* Second, apply on natural nail next to the free edge line *(kế đến đắp trên thân móng kế đầu móng)*

* Third, acrylic application near cutile, sidewall *(sau cùng đắp bột ở gần da và thành móng*

And then glide brush over nail to smooth *(dùng cọ vuốt nhẹ trên mặt móng cho mịn)*

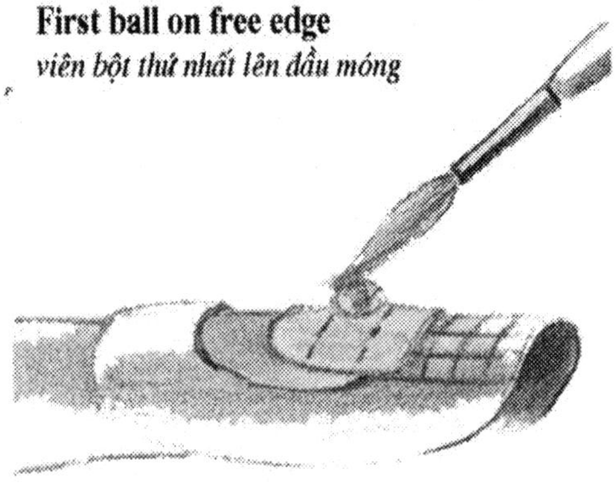

Second ball on center of nail
viên bột thứ hai lên giữa móng

Removing sculpture nails: ***Cách gỡ bỏ móng bột***

- Soak nails is an approved solvent specified, softened, remove them with acrylic nipper. Do not pry acrylic material from nail bed.

  Nhúng móng trong dung dịch hòa tan, mềm móng và gỡ bỏ với cây kìm gở móng. Đừng nạy móng bột từ đệm móng.

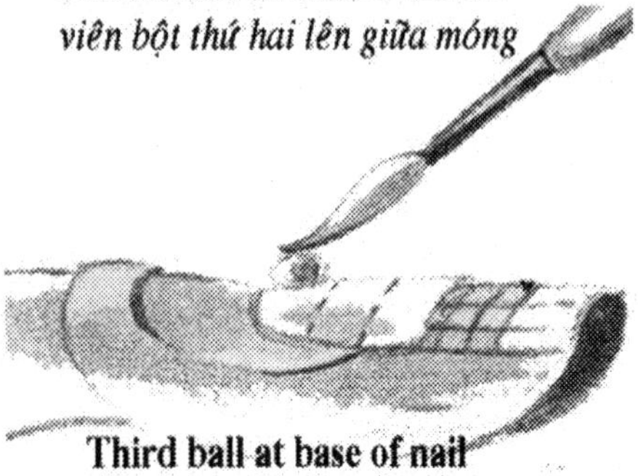

Third ball at base of nail
viên bột thứ ba lên nền móng

Acrylic overlays: ***Móng gắn típ đắp bột***

- Can strengthen weak nails or repair damaged one.
  Có thể làm mạnh những móng yếu hoặc sửa những móng hư

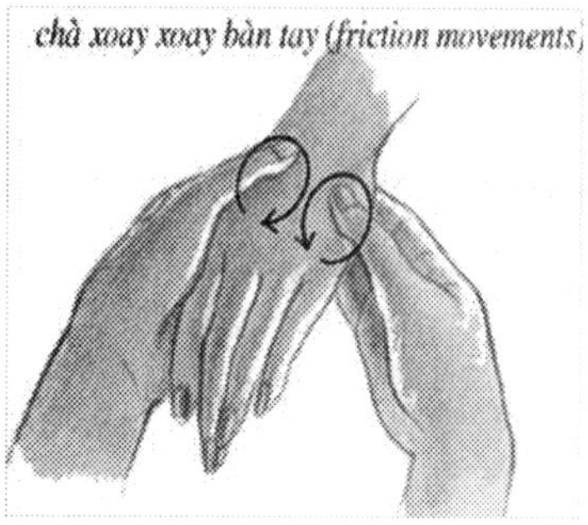

Press-on artificial nails (plastic or nylon): *Móng giả ép dán tạm thời (nhựa hoặc nhựa tổng hợp)*

- A convenient way to lengthen and beautify nails. They can be worn everyday or special occasions. It can remove with nail polish remover and gently lift from the side.
  Gắn móng tạm thời vừa dài và đẹp. Có thể mang móng thay đổi hằng ngày hoặc khi lễ hội. Móng có thể gỡ bỏ với chất chùi nước sơn và nhè nhẹ nâng lấy ra ở cạnh bên.

Nail tipping: ***Gắn tip***

- Anyone can have long-looking nails by simply extending the natural nail with nail tips.
  Bất cứ ai muốn cho móng dài trông tự nhiên bằng cách nối dài móng thật với móng tip

Pedicure: ***Chăm sóc chân***

- Pedicuring is the care of the feet, toes and toenails, foot care not only improves personal appearance, it also adds to the comfort of the feet.
  Ngành chăm sóc chân là chăm sóc đôi chân, ngón và móng chân, chăm sóc chân không những nâng lên vẽ đẹp mà còn giúp cho đôi chân cảm thấy dễ chịu, thoải mái.
- Abnormal foot conditions: corns, calluses, ingrown nail, are best treated by podiatrist
  Tình trạng chân bất thường: cục chai, da chai, móng đâm khóe, được chữa trị bởi Bác sĩ chuyên khoa chân
- Do not administer a manicure or pedicure on hands or feet with contagious disease (ringworm or athlete's foot).
  Đừng bao giờ phục vụ manicure và pedicure mà trên tay hoặc chân có bệnh lây lan như nấm ở tay (ringworm :nấm vòng tròn) hoặc nấm chân (athlete's foot)

Foot & leg massage***: Massage chân và bàn chân***

FRICTION MOVEMENT TO THE CENTER OF THE TOES

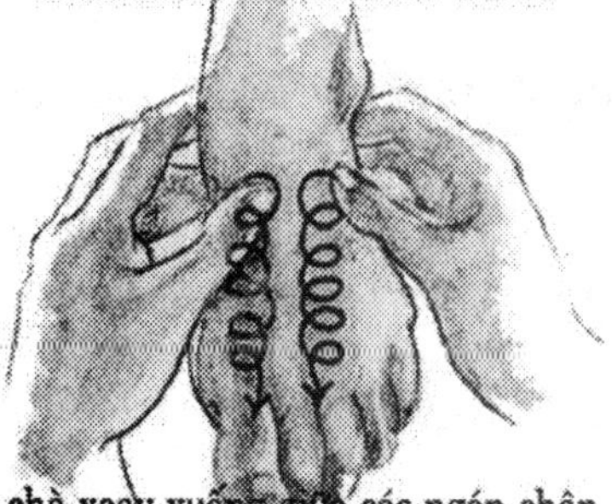

chà xoay xuống giữa các ngón chân

- The foot massage may be extended up to the knee. Apply rotary movement to feet and toes. Do not massage over the shinbone and above the knee.
  Massage chân có thể lên đến đầu gối. Dùng động tác xoay xoay cho chân và ngón chân. Đừng massage trên xương ống chân (tibia) và trên đầu gối.
- It is advisable to keep the pressure to the muscular tissue on either side of the shinbone.
  Nên dùng động tác ép mô bắp thịt ở 2 bên ống chân
- **The foot massages** from the heel and work down to the center of the toes. Do not use a credo knife to remove the callus
  Massage chân từ gót và tiến dần xuống trung tâm các ngón. Đừng bao giờ dùng dao nạo để lấy da chai
- Do not massage if your customer has heart condition, has had a stroke or high blood pressure because massage increases the blood circulation.
  Đừng massage nếu người khách có bệnh tim, bị stroke hoặc cao huyết áp vì massage làm tăng tuần hoàn máu.
- **Foot massag**e stimulates blood flow; clients consult a physician before receiving a massage.
  Massage chân tạo kích thích dòng máu, khách tham khảo bác sĩ trước khi muốn massage.

Bài 7: CÁC LOẠI BỆNH MÓNG

Móng tay, tóc đều là phần phụ thuộc của da, là loại đạm sừng **protein keratin**, tuy nhiên chất sừng trong da là keratin mềm *(soft keratin)*, tóc là keratin hơi cứng và móng là loại keratin cứng nhất *(hard keratin)*.

Móng bắt đầu mọc từ móng non **(matrix),** được nuôi dưỡng bằng mạch máu, bạch cầu và thần kinh, giữ nhiệm vụ tăng trưởng tế bào móng, nằm dưới gốc móng, như là phần chân lông **(papilla)**. Móng non rất dễ bị tổn thương và khi bị bệnh sẽ làm móng mọc bất thường, nên cần thận đừng đè ép móng. Vành trắng nữa vòng tròn là **lunula** ở gốc móng cũng là chỗ móng non nối liền nền móng.

HÓA TÍNH CỦA MÓNG

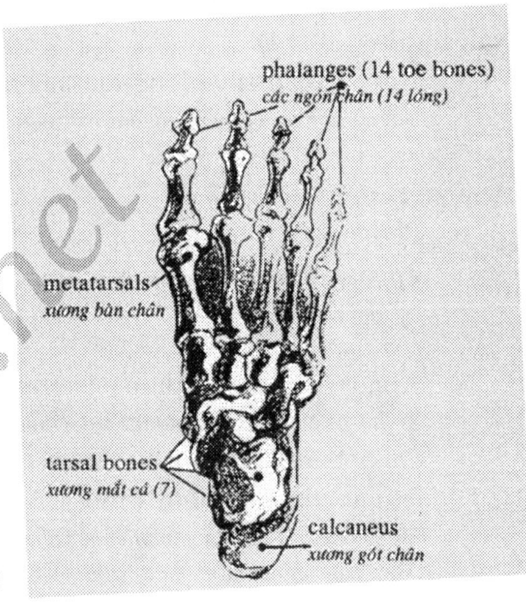

*Từ kỹ thuật về móng là **onyx**, và môn học tìm hiểu về móng và **onychology**. Móng có đặc tính thấm nước dễ hơn thấm vào làn da và lượng nước có ở móng cũng liên hệ đến sinh hoạt và môi trường sinh sống. Móng tay nhìn thấy khô, bề mặt cứng nhưng có chứa lượng nước từ **10% đến 30%,** móng bình thường chứa khoảng **18%** và lượng nước trong móng giữ nhiệm vụ làm móng có độ dẻo dai, móng thiếu lượng nước cần thiết sẽ dẫn đến móng đục và dòn, vì thế thoa lớp sơn lót, hoặc các chất tái tạo cho móng tốt chính là giúp móng bớt đi sự mất nước ở móng. Nồng độ hydrogen (pH) của móng thuộc acid từ **4.5 đến 5.5.***

*Một số nhà khoa học cũng đồng ý trong móng có **calcium** nhưng không hẳn giữ nhiệm vụ làm cho móng mạnh và cứng. Các nguyên tố vô cơ **(inorganic elements)** được tìm thấy trong móng gồm zinc, magnesium, potassium, iron, copper, sodium và các hợp tố hữu cơ **organic compounds** (amino acids) như sulfur va nitrogen cũng tìm thấy trong móng để tạo chất sừng đạm **(protein keratin).***

ĐẶC TÍNH CỦA MÓNG

Móng tay mọc chậm hơn tóc, sự tăng trưởng của móng, thực tế không có một chất nào thoa lên giúp cho móng mọc nhanh hơn, tuy nhiên việc ăn uống đúng cách *(good diet)* sẽ giúp cho móng mọc tốt, khỏe hơn.

Móng tay mọc nhanh vào mùa hè, và chậm hơn vào mùa đông, và từng ngón cũng có khác như ngón cái *(thumbnail)* mọc chậm hơn các ngón khác; ngón giữa *(middle fingernail)* mọc nhanh nhất. Móng trẻ em mọc nhanh hơn móng của người lớn và càng chậm dần khi về già. Móng chân mọc chậm hơn so với móng tay, tuy nhiên móng lại cứng hơn và dày hơn.

Móng tay giúp cho bàn tay nắm giữ đồ vật chặt hơn, dễ dàng hơn, nhất là các vật nhỏ, và bảo vệ đầu ngón tay. Móng chân giúp bảo vệ đầu ngón chân và đi đứng vững vàng hơn, bám chặt hơn.

Nhìn qua móng có thể nhận biết được tình trạng sức khỏe. Móng bình thường sẽ có bề mặt móng mịn, hơi cong, không dấu vết trên móng, màu hồng nhạt, hơi có chất dầu, không bị lõm, móng không dợn sóng, cứng chắc và sáng bóng.

Móng trung bình mọc 1/8 inch (0.31 cm) mỗi tháng, mọc với hình dáng vuông, bầu dục, nhọn, hay tròn là tùy mỗi cá nhân. Toàn bề mặt móng tay mọc dài cần thời gian từ 4 đến 6 tháng và móng chân cần từ 6 đến 12 tháng. Tuổi từ 10 đến 14 móng mọc mạnh nhất và yếu dần lúc đến tuổi già.

PHÂN BIỆT BỆNH MÓNG:

Nhìn qua **<u>màu móng</u>** người thợ có thể nhận biết như:

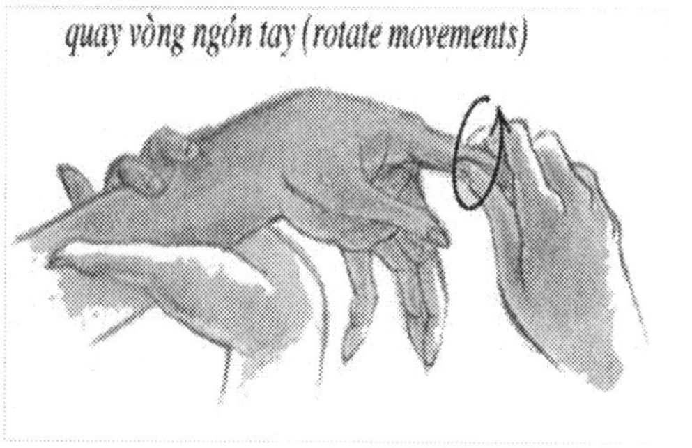

- **Màu trắng** là thiếu chất đạm, bị gan, và thận.
- **Màu vàng** là bệnh hệ thống bạch cầu, nhuộm tóc, chất nicotine thuốc lá.
- **Màu xanh** do nhiễm trùng.
- **Màu nâu đỏ** do nước sơn làm oxít móng, khô móng.
- **Màu nâu** do nấm, sưng nhiễm trùng lâu ngày.
- **Màu đen** do nấm lâu năm và thiếu trầm trọng vitamin 12.

Là chuyên viên móng *(manicurist)*, bạn phải hiểu biết để thông báo cho khách những bệnh móng không thể làm được mà giới thiệu khách đi bác sĩ chữa trị, cũng như móng nào an toàn làm được.

<u>Thợ không nên làm:</u> *một điều có thể nhận biết da và móng nếu có sưng dù nhiễm trùng hay không, rách, trầy xước, sưng đỏ (paronychia); đau, có mủ (onychia); lỏng móng (onycholysis); móng thúi do nấm chuyển từ vàng sang đen (mold); bị nấm vàng ký sinh có đốm trắng và đường sọc hơi vàng (onychomycosis); móng rụng do nóng sốt, giang mai (onychoptosis); sưng và có màu đỏ trong móng (pyogenic granuloma); hoặc móng sưng phồng, cong làn da nhô cao hơn (onychogryposis) là không thể làm được và khuyên họ cần đi bác sĩ trị liệu. Riêng loại móng bầm (bruised nail) có thể manicure, nhưng không nên làm móng giả lên móng bị bầm.*

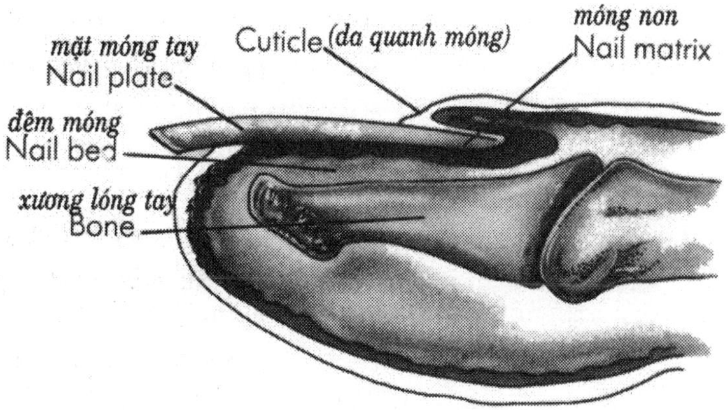

- ***<u>Thợ có thể làm:</u>*** *như móng gợn sóng (furrows); móng mỏng trắng vỏ trứng (eggshell nail); móng bị xước (hangnails hoặc agnails); móng dày (onychauxis hay hypertrophy); móng chẻ (onychorrhexis); móng mọc đâm khóe (ingrow nail hay onychocryptosis); móng có đốm trắng (leukonychia); móng có nốt ruồi đen, nâu (nevus); da mọc chồm lên móng (pterygium); móng bị teo nhỏ (onychatrophia hay atrophy); móng mất màu do tuần hoàn kém (discolored nail).*

CẤU TRÚC CỦA MÓNG

Móng tay chia 3 phần: **gốc móng** *(nail root)* là chỗ móng bắt đầu mọc, **thân móng** *(nail plate)* là phần chính móng dính vào da, **đầu móng** *(free edge)* là phần móng dài quá đầu ngón tay. Thân móng *(nail body)* thực tế là một kết hợp của nhiều lớp sừng đạm trở nên dày cứng.

Dưới móng tay gồm có:

- Nền móng **(nail bed)** chứa dây thần kinh, nhiều mạch máu dinh dưỡng cho sự phát triển móng.
- Móng non **(matrix)** là phần chính phát triển móng rất nhạy cảm, do đó người thợ móng cẩn thận đừng ép mạnh dễ bị tổn thương làm móng phát trưởng bất thường và gây bệnh. Móng chứa nhiều dây thần kinh, máu đỏ, bạch cầu kiểm soát mức tăng trưởng của móng. Móng non sẽ tiếp tục phát triển mạnh khi nhận đủ sự dinh dưỡng cho tế bào móng. Móng sẽ mọc chậm lại nếu sức khỏe kém hoặc tổn thương móng non
- Vòng bán nguyệt **(lunula)** là phần màu trắng lợt ở gốc móng, chỗ móng non nối liền nền móng.

Chung quanh móng tay *gồm có:*

- ***Eponychium*** *là da mọc ở gốc móng kéo dài lấn tới chỗ nữa mặt trăng* ***(lunula)***
- *Lớp da ngoại bì nằm chung quanh viền móng* ***(perionychium)***
- *Lớp da xếp sâu trong gốc móng* ***(mantle)***
- *Rãnh móng* ***(nail grooves)*** *là khe hở để móng mọc ra hai bên móng*
- *Thành móng* ***(nail walls)*** *là lớp da xếp chồng hai bên móng*
- *Lớp da chồng lên nhau bao quanh móng* ***(cuticle)***
- *Da ngoại bì dưới đầu móng* ***(hyponychium)***

Móng mọc nhanh lúc còn trẻ, lúc phụ nữ mang thai, chơi đàn piano, đánh máy vì có sự kích thích móng và ngược lại móng sẽ mọc chậm hơn vì thiếu dinh dưỡng, dùng thuốc kích thích như cần sa, thiếu máu, rối loạn nội tiết, xuống trọng lượng nhanh, đó là dấu hiệu của bệnh móng.

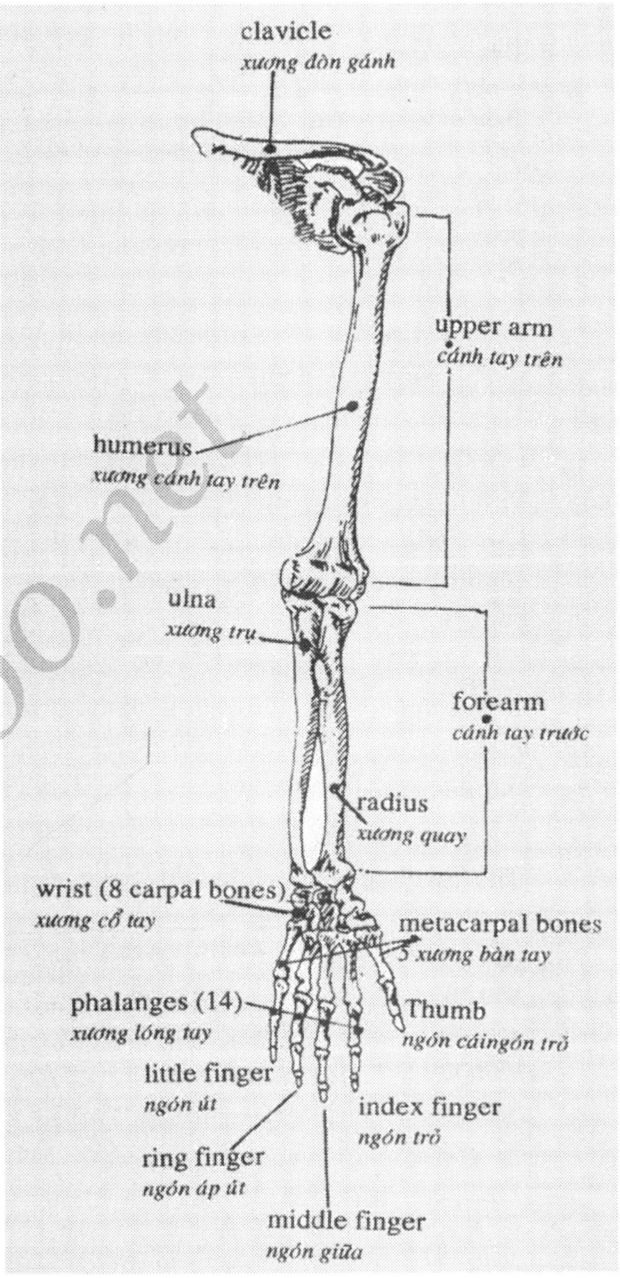

NAIL DISORDERS

(Bệnh móng)

Nail structure *(cấu trúc của móng)*

- The nail body extends from the root to the free edge. The nail is a horny, translucent plate, it is an appendage of the skin that protects the tip of finger and toes. Nails consist of nail root - nail body - free edge.
  Thân móng tay kéo dài từ gốc móng đến đầu móng. Móng là chất sừng, mặt móng trong suốt, là phần phụ thuộc của da để bảo vệ đầu móng tay và chân. Móng gồm có gốc móng, thân móng và đầu móng.
- Nail bed is a visible portion of the skin which the nail body rests. Has many bloods vessels that provide the nourishment necessary for the continued growth of the nail.
  Đệm móng là phần thấy được thuộc về da, nằm bên dưới thân móng. Có nhiều mạch máu bên trong cung cấp cho sự dinh dưỡng cần thiết cho móng mọc ra.
- Matrix is beneath the nail root to contain nerves. Lunula is called half moon is located at the base of the nail.
  Móng non bên dưới của gốc móng chứa nhiều thần kinh. Lunula còn gọi là nửa vầng trăng nằm ở nền móng.

Structure surrounding the nail *(cấu trúc chung quanh móng)*

- Consist of cuticle, eponychium, hyponychium, perionychium, nail wall, nail grooves, nail mantle (nail fold).
  Gồm có da quanh móng tay (cuticle), da mỏng ở nền móng (eponychium), da dưới đầu móng (hyponychium), da chung quanh sát móng tay (perionychium), da thành móng phía trước thuộc (nail wall), rãnh móng ở dưới và sau thành móng (nail grooses), màng móng hoặc lớp xếp tạo lập rãnh móng và giữ hình dáng cho móng (nail mantle).

Nail growth *(móng phát triển)*

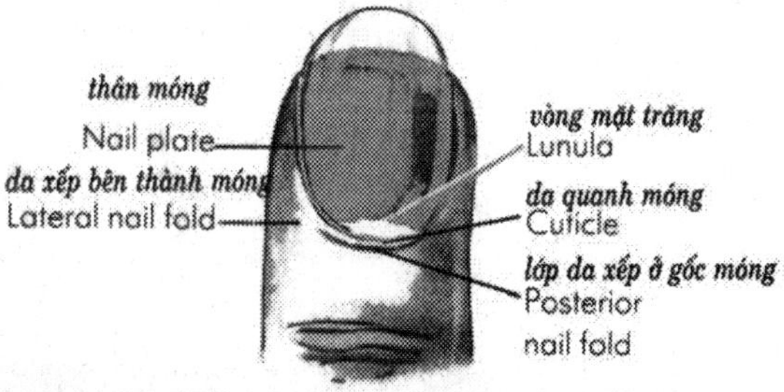

- Normal nail grows forward, starting at the matrix and extending over tip of the finger. The average rate of growth in normal adult is about 1/8"per month. Is influenced by nutrition, general health and disease.
  Móng bình thường mọc về phía trước, bắt đầu ở móng non vả kéo dài qua đầu móng. Trung bình móng mọc ở người lớn là 1/8 inch. Ảnh hưởng bởi sự dinh dưởng, sức khỏe tổng quát và bệnh tật.
- To replace a toenail it takes from 6 - 12 months and fingernail it takes about 4 - 6 months. Cold weather decrease the growth rate and the warm weather increase it. Men's nails grow faster the women. The age from 10 to 14 the growth fastest after that decreased with aging process.
  Để thay thế một móng chân từ 6 - 12 tháng và móng tay từ 4 - 6 tháng. Trời lạnh mọc chậm và thời tiết ấm mọc nhanh hơn. Móng đàn ông mọc nhanh hơn đàn bà. Tuổi từ 10-14 móng mọc nhanh nhất và giảm lần khi lớn lên.
- Nail malformation through injury becomes distored or discolored. The nail bed is injured after the loss of a nail will be badly formed.
  Móng biến dạng do bị thương trở nên hư và đổi màu. Đệm móng bị hư sau khi mất, móng sẽ mọc xấu hơn.

Nail disorder *(bệnh móng)*

- A nail disorder with infection or irritation should refer to a physician, never get treated by a nail technician or cosmetologist, but recognize normal or abnormal nail conditions.
  Sự xáo trộn móng có nhiễm trùng hoặc ngứa sẽ chuyển đến bác sĩ, không bao giờ chữa trị thợ móng tay hay thợ thẩm mỹ tổng quát, nhưng cần nhận rõ tình trạng bình thường hoặc bệnh móng tay.

Nail irregularities *(móng bất thường)*

- Corrugation (wavy ridges): are caused by uneven growth of the nails, result of illness or injury. Ridge filler can give a smooth look to the nail.
  Corrugation (móng gợn sóng) là móng mọc không đều, kết quả do bệnh hoặc bị thương. Dùng chất làm đầy gợn sóng (ridge filler) có thể làm mịn mặt móng.
- **Furrows** (corrugations) in the nails can run lengthwise or across the nail (depressions). Avoid the use of the metal pusher. Use cotton-tipped orange wood stick pushes around the cuticle.
  Furrows là gợn trong móng chạy theo đường dọc hoặc ngang móng (lõm xuống). Tránh dùng cây sủi kim loại. Dùng cây gỗ quấn bông gòn đẩy chung quanh da móng.
- Leuconychia (or white spots): Injury to the base of the nail or a bruise. It will grow out
  Leuconychia (đốm trắng) do tổn thương ở nền móng hoặc bị bầm. Đốm mọc dần dần ra khỏi móng.
- **Onychauxis** (hypertrophy): Overgrowth of the nail, thickening of the nail plate by internal imbalance or heredity, can buff it with pumice powder.
  Onychauxis (móng dày) là móng mọc quá độ, dày mặt móng, bệnh do không quân bình nội tạng hoặc do di truyền, có thể dùng buffer chà mịn với bột đá.
- Onychatrophia (atrophy) to lose its luster, become smaller, sometime be shed entirely, shrinks. It may be internal disease or injury to the matrix.
  Onychatrophia (atrophy) là móng bị đục, nhỏ dần, đôi khi bị rụng. Có thể do bệnh nội thương hoặc bị tổn thương ở móng non.

- **Pterygium:** Forward growth of the cuticle on the nail plate, can be treated by hot oi manicure.
  Pterygium là móng có da mọc chồm lên mặt móng, có thể chữa bằng cách làm móng tay dầu.
- Onychophagy (bitten nails) is a result of nervous habits. Can hide and beauty deformed nails with artificial tips or wraps.
  Onychophagy là bệnh cắn móng tay, hậu quả của tính lo sợ. Có thể che đậy hoặc làm đẹp bằng hình thức móng giả hoặc móng bao.
- **Onychorrhexis**: A split or brittle nail, by careless filing of the nails, vitamin deficiencies illness, frequent exposure to strong soap.
  Onychorrhexis là móng chẻ, móng dòn, do giũa móng cẩu thả, bệnh suy dinh dưỡng, và thường xuyên tiếp xúc xà phòng mạnh.
- Hangnail (agnail): Dryness of the cuticle, cutting off too much cuticle. Advise the client use hot oil manicures.
  Hangnail (agnail) là da khô ở quanh móng, do cắt quá nhiều da. Khuyên khách nên làm móng dầu.
- **Eggshell nails**: Thin, white nail plate, curves at free edge. This disorder can be caused by a chronic illness of systemic or nervous origin, improper diet. They are fragile and break easily.
  Eggshell nails là móng mỏng, màu trắng, cong ở đầu móng. Đây là do bệnh kinh niên bắt nguồn ở hệ thống thần kinh, suy dinh dưỡng. Móng dòn và gãy dễ dàng.
- Blue nails: Poor blood circulation or a heart disorder.
  Móng bị xanh là do tuần hoàn kém hoặc do bệnh tim
- Bruised nails: Dark, purplish to black due to bleeding in the nail bed. The dried blood attaches itself to the nail and grows out with it. Bruised nail is not worked for artificial nail services.
  Bruised nails là móng bị bầm có màu tím đậm đến màu đen do bị chảy máu trong đệm móng. Máu khô dính trong móng và đưa dần ra ngoài. Móng bầm không nên làm móng giả lên.

Fungus and mold *(nấm và mốc)*

- Fungi: Vegetable parasites including all types or fungus and mold. Both are contagious from the client to the nail technician.
  Fungi là kí sinh thực vật bao gồm nấm và mốc. Cả hai đều dễ lây lan từ người khách đến thợ

- Nail fungus: Appears as a discoloration in the nail that spreads toward the cuticle (hands, feet, nails). As the condition matures, the discoloration becomes darker.
  Nail fungus là nấm ăn móng có màu lợt trong móng và lây sang da (bàn tay và móng tay). Nếu không chữa trị để lâu, màu lợt sẽ biến dần màu đậm.
- Nail mold: Moisture is trapped between an unsanitized natural and products that are put over nail, such as tip, gels, acrylic nail products. It turns from yellow, green to black if not treated.
  Nail mold là móng bị mốc, ẩm ướt, bẩn giữa móng thật và sản phẩm móng giả như tip, gel, móng bột acrylic. Móng mốc đổi màu từ vàng, xanh tới đen nếu không được chữa trị.

Nail disease: *(Bệnh móng)*

- A person's occupation plays an important role in the cause of many nail infections. The manicurist and cosmetologist's hands are exposed daily to chemical materials, therefore hands and nails should be protected with gloves when working with chemicals.
  Nghề nghiệp của con người giữ vai trò quan trọng về nhiễm trùng móng. Đôi tay của người thợ thẩm mỹ tiếp xúc với hóa chất hằng ngày, vì thế bàn tay và móng nên được mang bao tay để bảo vệ khi tiếp xúc hóa chất.
- Onychosis (Nail disease)- *onychosis là tên kỹ thuật nói về bệnh móng*
- Onychomycosis: Tinea unguium or ringworm (by vegetable parasite); forms whitish patches.
  Onychomycosis là loại nấm hoặc vòng mụn nước (do kí sinh trùng thực vật) tạo mảng trắng.
- Ring worm (tinea) of the hands is a highly contagious disease. The principal symptoms are red lesions occurring in patches or rings over the hands.
  Ringworm là loại nấm ở đôi tay rất dễ lay lan. Triệu chứng chủ yếu là vết lỡ đỏ có từng mảng hoặc vòng trên tay.
- **Ringworm** of the foot (athlete's foot): The foot deeply itches and vesicles (blisters) appear. When the vesicles rupture, the skin becomes red and oozes. Fungus infection of the feet is likely to become chronic.
  Ringworm ở chân là athlete's foot. Có tính ngứa và nổi mụn nước. Khi mụn nước vỡ ra, da đỏ nước rỉ ra. Nhiễm trùng nấm ở chân có thể thành bệnh kinh niên.
- **Onychia:** An inflammation of the entire nail, pus may form, and shedding of the nail by improperly sanitized nail implements.
  Onychia là bệnh sưng móng có thể tạo mủ, và rụng móng do dụng cụ làm móng khử trùng không đúng cách.
- Paronychia (or felon): An inflammation condition of the tissues surrounding the nails. Paronychia can be caused by the use of unsanitary implements.
  Paronychia (felon) là nhiễm trùng các mô trung quanh móng. Có thể làm nguyên nhân dùng dụng cụ bẩn.

  Onychoptosis is the periodic shedding of one or more nails. This condition might follow certain diseases, such as syphilis. *Onychoptosis là bệnh rụng móng do bệnh giang mai từ vi trùng spirilla.*
- Oncholysis: Loosing of nail, without shedding (internal disorder).
  Oncholysis là bệnh lỏng móng mà không rụng (bệnh nội thương)
- **Onychophyma**: Denotes a swelling of the nail, more commonly referred to as onychauxis.
  Onychophyma là bệnh móng dày nổi lên còn gọi là onychauxis.
- Onychophosis: Growth of horny epithelium in the nail bed.
  Onychophosis là sừng móng mọc dày trong đệm móng
- **Onychogryposis** (onychogryphosis): Enlarged by increased curvature and thick of the nail, brownish in color, and one side of the nail grows faster then other side.
  Onychogryposis hoặc onychogryphosis là móng có độ cong nhiều và dày, màu hơi nâu, và một bên móng mọc nhanh hơn bên kia móng.
- **Onychocryptosis**: Ingrown nails (finger or toe). Filing the nail too much in the corners and poor-fitting shoes are causes of this disorder. The nail has grown deeply into the groove.
  Onychocryptosis là móng mọc đâm vào khóe (ngón tay hoặc ngón chân) do giũa móng sâu vào các góc móng và do mang giày quá chật. Móng mọc đâm sâu vào rãnh móng.

* A SERVICE CAN BE PERFORMED:

Tình trạng móng có thể phục vụ cho khách

- Leukonychia (white spot) : *đốm trắng*
- Onychatrophia (atrophy) : *rụng móng*
- Agnails (hangnails) : *xước da quanh móng*
- Furrows (corrugations) : *mặt móng gợn sóng*
- Onychauxis (hypertrophy) : *móng bị dày do bệnh nội thương, di truyền*
- Onychocryptosis (ingrown nails) : *móng mọc đâm khóe*
- Onychophagy (bitten nails) : *thói quen cắn móng*
- Eggshell nails : *trắng, mỏng cong đầu móng*
- Onychorrhexis (split nails) : *móng chẻ và dòn*
- Pterygium : *da mọc chồm lên móng*
- Onychophyma : *móng dày phồng lên*
- Discolored nails : *có màu, xanh, đỏ, tím do dùng thuốc, bệnh tim.*
- Onychophosis : *lớp sừng mọc dày ở nền móng*
- Nevus : *nốt ruồi nâu hoặc đen trong móng*
- Tile-shaped nails : *móng cong đều từ móng non đến đầu móng*
- Eponychial disorders (hyponychial) : *da mọc tràn lên mặt móng và dưới đầu móng*
- Melanonychia : *mặt móng có lằn sợi đen từ nền đến đầu móng.*
- Plicatured nail : *móng biến dạng từ móng non ngón chân, đầu móng có hình vuông*
- Bruised nails : *móng dập đông máu bên trong có màu tím (chỉ làm manicure thôi)*
- Onychogryphosis (onychogryposis) : *móng nâu, dày, dài, cong, cứng, do tổn thương đệm móng non.*
- Ram's horn nails (onychogryphosis) : *móng màu nâu cứng, dài cong như kèn do không chăm sóc, tổn thương móng non, nếu không nhiễm trùng thợ có thể chăm sóc*

* A SERVICE CANNOT BE PERFORMED:

Tình trạng móng không thể phục vụ

- Onychia : *sưng móng có mủ dẫn đến rụng móng*
- Paronychia : *sưng đỏ chung quanh móng*
- Pyogenic granuloma : *sưng tụ máu đỏ ở nền đệm móng đến thân móng*
- Mold (fungus) : *móng bị nấm, ẩm móng có màu vàng, xanh hoặc đen*
- Onychomycosis (tinea unguium) : *móng nhiễm trùng do nấm thực vật*
- Blue Nails : *móng đổi màu do tuần hoàn máu kém*
- Onycholysis : *móng nhiễm trùng từ đầu móng đến nền móng*
- Onychoptosis : *móng và ngón rụng, có bệnh giang mai (syphilis)*
- Onychomadesis : *mặt móng rụng do nhiễm trùng ở móng non*
- Trumpet (pincer nail) : *móng kèn mọc dài cuốn lại biến dạng ở ngón chân*
- Infected ingrown nails : *móng mọc đâm khóe bị nhiễm trùng*

Bài 8: HÌNH THỨC SẢN PHẨM VÀ THÀNH PHẦN HÓA HỌC

Điều quan trọng người thợ chuyên nghiệp không những có đôi tay khéo léo mà cần học hỏi để có được kiến thức. Các hóa chất cao cấp trong ngành thẩm mỹ hiện nay luôn có sự thay đổi mới, vì thế cần phải học và xử dụng chúng để tạo ích lợi cho khách hàng, và hiểu rõ về tiêu chuẩn an toàn, sức khỏe khi sử dụng hóa chất trong lúc làm cho khách.

Hóa học chia 2 lãnh vực:

- **Hóa học hữu cơ (organic chemistry):** là các dạng có chứa than (carbon). Than hiện diện trong cây cối, động vật, than mềm, chất khí thiên nhiên và nhiều dạng nhân tạo khác. Dạng hữu cơ như cỏ, cây, dầu … cháy được, không hòa tan trong nước nhưng có thể hòa tan trong dung môi như cồn (alcohol) và benzene.
- **Hoá học vô cơ (inorganic chemistry)** không cháy, hòa tan trong nước, không chứa than như nước, không khí, chì, sắt…

THAY ĐỔI HÓA TÍNH VÀ VẬT LÝ: *Vật chất có thể thay đổi theo 2 hình thức.*

*- **Thay đổi hóa tính** là có sự thay đổi khác với tính nguyên thủy ban đầu, ví dụ hai hoá chất pha trộn như pha H_2O_2 với thuốc nhuộm đó là sự oxýt hóa hoặc nước acrylic chấm vào bột acrylic là một sự kết dính của 2 hóa chất, tạo thành một dạng mới và không tách ra được như tình trạng ban đầu.*

*- **Thay đổi vật lý** là sự thay đổi hình thức của chất khí, chất đặc, và chất lỏng của 1 dạng mà không thay đổi bất cứ dạng mới nào ví như nước có thể đông thể đặc, tan chảy sang thể lỏng, và bốc hơi thành khí, hơi nước do đó nước không thay đổi tính hóa học mà chỉ thay đổi hình dạng bên ngoài.*

CÁC DẠNG VẬT CHẤT

Gồm nguyên tố (elements); hợp tố (compounds); và hỗn hợp (mixtures).

Nguyên tố (elements) hiện nay đã tìm được 109 nguyên tố và có ký hiệu bằng chữ như: Ag là bạc; Au là vàng; C là than; O là oxygen; H là hydrogen; Pb là chì; Zn là kẽm; Cl là chlorine; v.v…..

Nguyên tố là đơn vị căn bản của vật chất không thể phân chia thành 1 dạng nhỏ hơn.

Các nguyên tố có trong da, tóc và toàn cơ thể con người như sulfur; chlorine; carbon; oxygen; nitrogen; sodium; hydrogen; phosphorus.

- *Nguyên tử (atom)* là phần nhỏ nhất của một nguyên tố (element) và còn giữ đặc tính nguyên tố.
- *Phân tử (molecule)* gồm ít nhất 2 nguyên tử (atoms) cùng nhau hợp lại thành nguyên tố và 2 nguyên tử khác nhau sẽ thành hợp tố (compounds)

Hợp tố (compounds) là dạng kết hợp ít nhất từ 2 nguyên tố như 2 phân tử hydrogen kết với 1 phân tử oxygen thành hợp tố là nước (H_2O).

Các hợp tố xử dụng cho da và tóc như: hydrogen peroxide (H_2O_2); ammonium thioglycolate; alcohol; alkalies; water. Hợp tố chia làm 4 loại: Oxide như hydrogen peroxide; Acid như nitric acid (NHO); Alkaline (base) là chất kiềm như sodium hydroxide (NaOH); salt là muối như sodium chlorine (NaCl).

Hỗn hợp (mixtures) là một dạng pha trộn có tính vật lý hơn là hóa tính như khối bê tông là sự kết hợp của xi măng, sạn, cát. Thành phần của chất hỗn hợp không thay đổi đặc tính như hợp tố, nhưng vẫn giữ đặc tính riêng.

CÓ 3 DẠNG HÌNH THỂ CỦA VẬT CHẤT:

- ***Chất đặc** (SOLIDS) có trọng lượng nhất định, khối lượng, và hình dáng như cây kéo, cây kềm cắt da, dụng cụ cắt móng....*

- ***Chất lỏng*** *(LIQUIDS) có trọng lượng, và thể tích nhất định nhưng hình dáng không nhất định như thuốc duỗi tóc, nước sơn móng, acetone....*
- ***Chất khí*** *(GASES) có trọng lượng nhất định, nhưng thể tích và hình dáng không nhất định như hơi thở, sự ép khí từ keo xịt tóc....*

CHẤT DUNG MÔI & CHẤT HÒA TAN *(solvent &solute):* Nước, acetone là những chất dung môi tốt, dạng lỏng có khả năng làm tan được chất khác. Các chất tan được như muối, đường, nước sơn móng là những chất hòa tan. Dung môi tốt hay xấu la` khả năng tan được chất hòa tan chậm hay nhanh. Dung môi (solvent) được làm nóng lên như acetone đun nóng 105 độ F sẽ làm mềm móng nhanh hơn 30%, tuy nhiên nhiều chất dung môi dễ bốc cháy nên rất cẩn trọng khi xử dụng.

PRIMER là một chất giúp chất khác dính chặt vào thân móng, thoa trước lúc đắp bột acrylic vào móng. Primer là acid thoa lên mặt móng mà thôi vì đụng lên lớp da dễ ăn mòn và hại cho da. Thực chất primer không hại móng nếu đừng thoa nhiều quá, thường sự hư hại móng là do người thợ giũa mặt móng quá nhiều làm mỏng móng, yếu nên móng dễ gãy, và dễ bị nhiễm trùng....
Lớp sơn lót (base coat) giúp nước sơn dính chắc hơn, thoa trước khi sơn bóng là hình thức chất primer. Nước sơn móng, sơn lót và sơn phủ bề mặt không phải là polymer kết dính như bột acrylic với nước monomer. Nước sơn không có phản ứng hóa học, thành phần chỉ là chất làm tan dễ bốc hơi.

DỊ ỨNG HÓA CHẤT *là do sự tiếp xúc hóa chất nhiều lần và lâu từ 4 đến 6 tháng cả khách và thợ có thể gây dị ứng (overexposure). Dị ứng với người thợ vì thường có thói quen dùng ngón tay vuốt cọ đang ướt hóa chất, sờ lên má và mặt, dùng cọ cở lớn; trộn lẫn các sản phẩm để pha chế cho riêng mình v.v..., chính vì thế số thợ mắc phải dị ứng có tới 40% và một số đã phải bỏ nghề.v.v.... Dị ứng với khách thường xảy ra ở lớp da quanh móng, nền móng của khách hoặc đặt sản phẩm làm móng như gel lên quá dày, đặt dưới đèn UV không đúng cách, đúng thời gian.*
Lớp da bàn tay thường dễ tiếp xúc các hóa chất như keo, gel, các chất monomer, và ngay cả tiếp xúc lâu trong nước cũng khó chịu, nứt nẻ, do đó giữ tay khô, thoa ẩm da bù vào lớp dầu của da bị mất.

NỒNG ĐỘ ACID VÀ ALKALINE là số pH (nồng độ hydrogen), nếu từ 0 đến 6.9 là acid như hydrogen peroxide là 4; móng tay, da, tóc cở 4.5 – 5.5; nước cất là 7 ở mức trung hòa. Trị số từ 7.1 – 14 là alkaline như xà phòng là 8, thuốc nhuộm là 10 và tẩy tóc là 12, 13.

CÁC HÓA CHẤT THƯỜNG DÙNG TRONG KỶ NGHỆ NAILS NHƯ:
- **Nước (H_2O)** là hóa chất quan trọng phong phú chiếm 75% bề mặt quả đất và 70% cơ thể con người.
- **Alcohol** (cồn) là loại hoá chất không màu do lên men từ tinh bột, đường không dùng để khử trùng da
- **Alum** là **aluminum potassium** hoặc **ammonium sulphate**, bột trắng có tính se da, cầm máu.
- **Quaternary ammonium compounds (quats)** là chất sát trùng, bảo quản, khử trùng, diệt vi trùng
- **Zinc oxide** là chất trắng đục trong phấn thoa da mặt, phấn nền và whittener che đốm dưới đầu móng.
- **Glycerin** là chất nhờn chất không màu, không mùi trích từ dầu, mỡ, mật mía dùng làm dầu thoa da, mềm da, kem thoa mặt và một số dung dịch khác
- **Nail glue** là chất keo dán vào thân móng, loại keo kỷ thuật cao **cyanoacrylate** cho ngành thẩm mỹ.

HÓA CHẤT NGÀNH THẨM MỸ VÀ ẢNH HƯỞNG
Thẩm mỹ viên tiếp xúc với nhiều hóa chất nên cần giữ sự tiếp xúc có ảnh hưởng thấp nhất có thể được đặc biệt là những dạng độc chất.

Cơ quan OSHA luôn thông báo những sự giới hạn này gọi là PELs (Permissible Exposure Limits) với hàng trăm loại hóa chất khác nhau, có ảnh hưởng khác nhau qua mùi (odors), qua sự thở, hít vào phổi và di chuyển vào dòng máu truyền khắp cơ thể; nuốt (swallowing) hóa chất sự tiếp xúc các phân tử hóa chất (particles) qua ăn, uống, và hút thuốc nơi làm việc; hoặc màng nhầy cổ họng (mucus), vào mắt và thẩm thấu vào cơ thể mà thường không biết.

Qua bảng dữ kiện an toàn vật liệu (Material Safety Data Sheet) các hóa chất có ảnh hưởng.

- HÓA CHẤT LÀM MÓNG BỘT (SCULPTURED, ACRYLIC NAILS) gồm các chất Glycol ethers, Formadehyde, Ethyl acetate, Butyl acetate, Demethyl p- toluidine, Acetone, Xylen, Trichlorethane, Toluene, Methylene chloride, Methyl etyl ketone (MEK), Methacrylates.
  Các hóa chất này gây ngứa mắt, ngứa mũi, ngứa họng, ngứa phổi, phỏng da, phỏng mắt, ngứa da, sưng da, suyển, dị ứng, sưng thận và loét bao tử nếu nuốt vào, suyển (asthma), tác hại trung khu thần kinh tạo ra chóang váng (dizziness), ngây ngây muốn mữa (nausea), ảnh hưởng hệ thống sinh sản (reproductive problem), gây ung thư nếu dùng lâu năm.

Rất nhiều hóa chất kể trên chứa **FORMADEHYDE** dễ dẫn đến ung thư nếu tiếp xúc quá độ. Hóa chất ảnh hưởng sức khỏe tức thì **(Acute effects)** nhẹ như ngứa mắt, mũi, da hoặc nặng như hư mắt. Hóa chất ảnh hưởng lâu dài **(Chronic effects)** qua thời gian dài và nhiều lần sẽ dẫn đến ảnh hưởng bệnh nghiêm trọng khó chữa khỏi được.

5 CÁCH ĐỂ GIẢM BỚT ĐỘC HẠI CỦA HÓA CHẤT (FIVE WAYS TO REDUCE CHEMICAL HAZARDS)

1. **Gắn hệ thống thông khí, lọc khí tốt (ventilation)**: hệ thống đẩy hơi và bụi ra hẳn ngoài salon, kéo lượng hơi độc xa tầm mũi và miệng, hệ thống lọc bụi bậm lẫn độc tố qua miếng lọc than tạo không khí sạch cho salon, thường xuyên thay lọc khí, mở rộng cửa và cửa sổ để thông khí tự nhiên.
2. **An toàn nơi làm việc (work in a safe way):** đừng chứa các hoá chất gần thức ăn, gần nhiệt, hóa chất đậy chặt khi không dùng, vứt bỏ hóa chất dư thừa đúng cách, pha trộn hóa chất nơi riêng biệt và thông khí tốt, lau sạch hóa chất rơi nhiểu xuống nền, đừng ăn uống, hút thuốc gần hóa chất, kiểm soát hóa chất thường xuyên, thợ được hướng dẫn sự nguy hại độc tố và cách tự bảo vệ, có bình chữa lửa, chất rửa mắt và hộp cấp cứu.
3. **Tránh bớt sản phẩm độc hại (avoid hazardous chemicals):** cố gắng thay thế một số chất như dùng bình có nút bơm hoá chất thay vì bằng gas xịt, dùng chất gel dính tóc thay vì keo xịt, dùng nhiệt duỗi thẳng tóc thay vì dùng hóa chất duỗi tóc.
4. **Nơi dùng hóa chất cần cách riêng (isolate the work process):** có phòng riêng pha hóa chất và phòng riêng làm móng tay bằng bột acrylic có hệ thống thông khí tốt.
5. **Cần trang thiết bị bảo vệ cho bạn (use personal protective equipment):** mang tấm che bụi vào miệng, mũi khi làm móng, kính lồi che mắt (goggles) để phòng hóa chất và bụi văng vào mắt, chọn đúng loại bao tay cho loại hóa chất xử dụng xong rồi vứt bỏ ngay và rửa tay.

Nói chung càng sử dụng hóa chất là càng có cơ hội tác hại cho sức khỏe, vì thế cách tốt nhất để ngăn ngừa sự thương tổn do hóa chất là ngừng tiếp xúc chất độc hại hoặc phải thực hành các cách trên để giảm bớt tác hại của hóa chất thuộc lãnh vực nghề nghiệp cho sức khỏe.

PRODUCT FORMS AND CHEMISTRY SIMPLIFIED

(Hình thức sản phẩm và thành phần hóa học)

- Nail plates are 100% chemical. Nail plates also contain traces of iron, aluminum, copper, silver, gold and other chemicals.
  Mặt móng tay 100% hóa chất. Mặt móng tay chứa sắt, nhôm, đồng, bạc, vàng và một số hóa chất khác.
- Light, radio waves are are energy that they don't occupy space. Energy is not the matter, however, energy can affect matter in many ways.
  Ánh sáng, sóng vô tuyến là năng lượng, chúng không chiếm chỗ trong không gian. Năng lượng không phải là vật chất, tuy nhiên có thể ảnh hưởng đến vật chất trong nhiều cách.

- Forms of matter: ***Element***: S, O, or two same atoms; ***Atom***: smallest of element; ***Molecule***: *2 different atoms or* 2 same atoms are called elements; ***Mixture***: Concrete sand, gravel and cement; ***Compounds***: 2 or more different elements.
  Các dạng của vật chất: ***Nguyên tố*** *như S, O, hoặc 2 nguyên tử giống nhau;* ***Atom*** *là nguyên tử, phần nhỏ nhất của một nguyên tố;* ***Phân tử*** *là 2 nguyên tử khác nhau hoặc 2 nguyên tử giống nhau được gọi là nguyên tố;* ***Chất pha trộn*** *như sạn, sỏi và xi măng;* ***Hợp tố*** *là 2 hay nhiều nguyên tố khác nhau.*
- Four types of compounds: **Oxides**: H_2O_2 (hydrogen peroxide); **Acid**: Nitrogen+ Hydrogen+ Oxygen=Nitric acid (HNO); **Alkalis**: Sodium+ Oxygen +Hydrogen=Sodium hydroxide (NaOH); **Salts**: Hydrogen replaced by metal ($CuSO_4$) or NaCl.
  Bốn loại hợp tố: Oxides như hydrogen peroxide; Acid như nitơ +hydro + oxy; Alkalis (kiềm) như sút NaOH; Muối từ khí hydro được thay thế bằng kim loại như CuSO4 hoặc NaCl
- Chemical change: H_2O_2 +aniline derivative (oxidation creates color)
  Thay đổi hóa tính như Hydrogen peroxide +Aniline derivative (tạo oxide trong thuốc nhuộm tóc)
- Physical change: Ice (solid) melt and become a liquid and water freezes (solid) ...
  Thay đổi thể lý như viên đá lạnh chảy ra thành chất lỏng và đông lại thành chất đặc ...

Properties of matter: *Đặc tính riêng của vật chất*

a) Density: Water 62.4 lbs (cubic foot) .03m^3, volume of 1F^3
   Tỉ trọng (độ dày đặc): 1 cubic foot nước (1F3) =.03 mét khối nước nặng 62.4 lbs (cở 28 kílô)

b) Specific gravity: Lightness or heavy. Example: water = 0, copper = 8.9 times as dense as water
   Trọng lượng riêng: độ nhẹ hoặc độ nặng. Ví dụ: nước =0, đồng = 8.9 lần nặng hơn nước

b) Hardness: Resist scratching. Example: Diamond: 10; Knife: 6.2; Asphalt: 1.3
   Độ cứng: Độ chống cào xước. Ví dụ: Kim cương = 10; Dao = 6.2; Nhựa đường = 1.3

c) Odor: To identify ammonium thioglycolic, monomer from acrylic liquid
   Mùi: Nhận rõ mùi riêng biệt của thio, nước đắp bột acrylic

d) Color: Identify color of gold, silk and copper.
   Màu: Nhận rõ màu riêng biệt của vàng, bạc và đồng.

- Chemistry of water: Human body is 70% water and water covers almost 75% of the earth's surface.
  Hóa tính của nước: Cơ thể con người chiếm 70% nước và nước chiếm 75% bề mặt địa cầu.
- **Catalyst** is a chemical that can make a chemical reaction go faster. Solvent is dissolves another substance. An adhesives is a chemical that causes two surfaces to stick together
  Catalyst (chất xúc tác) là hóa chất có thể làm phản ứng hóa tăng nhanh hơn. Dung môi là chất hòa tan được với dạng khác. Keo là hóa chất làm cho bề mặt dính lại nhau.

- **Primers** are substances that improve adhesion. Base coats act as the "go-between" or "anchor." They still must be used with caution and skin contact must be avoided.
  Primer là chất tăng lên sự dính. Là lớp nền tác dụng như là "lớp gạch nối" hoặc "neo chặt". Được sử dụng phải cẩn thận, tránh tiếp xúc vào da.
- Do not touch any monomer liquids, gels or adhesives to the skin; never use monomer to "clean up" the edges, under the nail or sidewalls, *never* smooth the surface with monomer *and never* mix your own special product blends.
  Đừng đụng da vào chất nước acrylic, gel hoặc keo, không bao giờ dùng nước acrylic để làm sạch cạnh móng, dưới móng và thành móng; không bao giờ dùng nước acrylic để vuốt mặt móng và không bao giờ tự ý pha trộn sản phẩm với nhau.

- Desks, people, and cabinet have shape and volume, therefore they are examples of solids. Organic chemistry is the study of all substances containing carbon.
  Bàn, con người, và tủ đựng có hình dáng và thể tích, vì vậy đó là những ví dụ của thể đặc. Hóa học hữu cơ là môn học của tất cả các dạng chứa than.
- **A dilute solution** contains a small quantity of solute in proportion to the quantity of solvent.
  Một dung dịch pha loãng chứa một số lượng nhỏ chất hòa tan trong thành phần số lượng của dung môi.
- Two types of emulsions used in cosmetics are oil-in-water and water-in-oil.
  Có hai loại nhũ tương được dùng trong mỹ phẩm là dầu trong nước và nước trong dầu.
- Chemistry is the science that deals with the composition, structure and properties of matter and how matter changes under different conditions.
  Hóa học là môn khoa học liên hệ với thành phần, cấu trúc và đặc tính của vật chất và thay đổi dưới những điều kiện khác nhau.

- **The two branches** of chemistry are inorganic and organic. Substances that do not contain carbon (water, air…) are inorganic and substances that do contain carbon (desk, cabinet, food) are organic.
  Hai ngành hóa học là vô cơ và hữu cơ. Dạng không chứa than là vô cơ (nước, không khí) và dạng chứa than là hữu cơ (bàn, tủ, thức ăn...)
- There are 3 forms of matter as **solids, liquids, and gases**. Matter is anything that has mass and occupies space. Matter can be changed in two ways: either through physical or chemical means.
  Có 3 dạng vật chất là chất đặc, lỏng, và chất khí. Vật chất là bất cứ vật chất có khối lượng và chiếm chỗ trong không gian. Vật chất có thể thay đổi theo 2 cách vừa là thể lý và hóa tính.

  Example: physical change as ice melts into water and chemical change as soap is formed from the chemical reaction between an alkaline substance and oil or fat.
  Ví dụ: thay đổi thể lý như viên đá lạnh chảy ra thành nước và thay đổi hóa tính như xà phòng được tạo ra từ phản ứng giữa chất kiềm và dầu hoặc mỡ.

- **Silver, Zinc, Iron, Carbon** is all examples of elements. There are 109 known elements.
  Bạc, Kẽm, Sắt, Than là tất cả những ví dụ của những nguyên tố. Được biết có 109 nguyên tố.
- Oxides; Acids; Bases, and Salt are the four most important classes of compounds.
  Oxides (hợp tố chứa oxy); Acids (hợp tố thường có chứa hydro không kim loại); Bases or alkalies (hợp tố chứa hydro, kim loại, oxygen); Salt (hợp tố có phản ứng của acid và base) là 4 loại hợp tố quan trọng.
- Distilled or filtered water is used in most salon machines as facial machine.
  Nước cất hoặc nước lọc được dùng trong hầu hết các máy móc trong salon như máy facial
- **The pH** (potential Hydrogen) of the skin's acid mantle ranges from 4.5 to 5.5.
  Nồng độ hydrogen của màng acid da trong khoảng từ 4.5 đến 5.5.

THE EFFECT OF CHEMICAL PRODUCTS

Tác dụng của các hóa chất

alum solution: *muối alumium, chất cầm máu*
base coat: *chất không màu thoa lên móng thật trước khi sơn móng*
cuticle cream: *kem ngăn ngừa móng dòn, da khô chứa lanolin, petroleum, và sáp ong*
cuticle oil: *dầu làm mềm và trơn da thoa chung quanh móng tay, móng chân*
cuticle remover: *kem làm mềm để lấy da chết quanh móng; chứa alkali, dầu nhờn glycerin; chứa potassium hydroxide*
formadehyde hardeners: *chất làm mạnh móng tạo chất sừng; chứa 5% formadehyde*
formalin: *chất diệt trùng có chứa khí formadehyde trong dung dịch, với độ mạnh 5% để lau sạch bồn rửa tay, tủ, với độ mạnh 25% nhúng dụng cụ để diệt trùng trong 10 phút*
hand cream: *kem chứa chất nhờn, chất ẩm dùng cho da khô, da nứt và da ngứa*
hand lotion: *giống như hand cream nhưng chứa nhiều dầu hơn, ít đặc*
olive oil: *dầu olive vàng xanh dùng trong thức ăn và dùng trong hot oil manicure*
liquid nail polish: *chất hơi đặc để sơn hoặc bóng móng*
massage cream: *chất kem nhờn emollient chữa trị, trơn da, dinh dưỡng cho da.*
nail conditioner: *chất ẩm để chống móng khô và dòn*
nail dryer: *chất thoa để bảo vệ nước sơn khô nhanh chống dính*
nail hardener: *chất ngăn ngừa móng chẻ hoặc bị lột móng*
nylon fiber hardener: *chất làm cứng móng có trong nước sơn bóng, thoa theo chiều dọc hoặc ngang trên mặt móng.*
polish remover: *chất dung môi hữu cơ dùng làm hoà tan và chùi nước sơn cũ trên móng*
polish thinner: *chất dung môi để pha nước sơn có chứa aceton*
protein hardener: *chất đạm làm cứng móng có chất collagen có trong nước sơn bóng*
top coat or sealer: *nước sơn không màu phủ lên nước sơn đề phòng móng nứt và giúp bóng móng*
catalyst: *chất giúp tác dụng hóa chất nhanh hơn*
gel nail: *chất dẽo trong suốt đắp lên móng thật, cứng chắc và đẹp hơn bột acrylic*
light-cured gels: *loại gel đắp móng được cứng lại bằng tia đèn cực tím (ultra violet rays)*
no-light gels: *loại gel được cứng lại không cần dùng đèn U.V, cứng gel lại nhờ chất xúc tác hoặc ngâm vào nước*
liquid nail wrap: *hoá chất thoa tạo sợi làm cứng chắc mặt móng để giúp móng thật mọc dễ dàng*
monomer: *dung dịch acrylic là dạng nước có phân tử cực nhỏ để dễ kết với polymer*
polymer: *chất bột acrylic kết với monomer để giúp việc kết cứng lại*
primer: *chất giúp cho mặt móng kết dính chặt với chất đắp móng giả như gel, bột acrylic..*
hard water: *nước có nhiều tạp chất như nước rửa tay, tạo sự hạn chế tạo bọt ở xà phòng*
soft water: *nước được lọc sạch, nước mưa, hoặc nước cất dùng để pha chế sản phẩm, tạo xà phòng nhiều bọt*
dry nail polish: *bột khô đánh bóng mặt móng dùng với cây buffer da dê*
nail bleach: *chất tẩy trắng móng, ví dụ như 6% hydrogen peroxide (6% H_2O_2)*
solvent: *dung dịch để hoà tan chất khác*
solute: *là chất được hòa tan*
nail whitener: *chất làm trắng móng chứa oxýt kem và tatinium dioxide, thoa dưới đầu móng để che đốm*
adhesive: *chất keo để dán dính hai bề mặt với nhau*
phenolics: *chất diệt trùng mạnh làm mềm hoặc mất màu các vật bằng nhựa; độ mạnh 5% nhúng dụng cụ trong 10 phút.*
aceton: *hóa chất mạnh dùng ngâm mềm móng giả khi cần tháo gỡ, chất gây ngứa và dễ sưng da*
nail anamel: *nước sơn móng tay, móng chân*

suspension: *các chất lơ lửng được pha trộn trong một dung dịch như salad dressing oil pha với dấm*

emulsion: *nhiều chất không kết hợp được nhưng pha trộn và kết lại nhờ có chất kết dính tổng hợp như mayonnaise*

oil-in-water emulsion: *(O/W) kem có ít dầu trong thành phần sản phẩm chứa nhiều thành phần nước hơn như mayonnaise (nước sốt mayonne)*

water-in-oil emulsion: *(W/O) kem ít nước trong thành phẩm có chứa nhiều dầu như cold cream thích hợp cho da khô*

ammonia water: *dung dịch có khí nồng kết hợp từ hydrogen and nitrogen*

sodium hypochlorite: *chất tẩy lau nhà, với độ mạnh 10% nhúng dụng cụ trong 10 phút để diệt trùng*

boric acid: *chất bột trắng trong, nếu pha trộn từ 2 đến 5% độ mạnh dùng để làm sạch mắt*

tincture of iodin: *dung dịch với độ mạnh 2% để thoa sạch vết cắt và vết thương*

hydrogen peroxide: *dung dịch với độ mạnh từ 3 – 5% để thoa sát trùng da và vết cắt nhỏ*

quaternary ammonium compounds: *dung dịch diệt trùng với độ mạnh 1/1000 nhúng chìm dụng cụ trong 10 phút.*

DISPOSABLE IMPLEMENTS AFTER EACH CLIENT SUCH AS:

Vật liệu vứt bỏ sau mỗi lần làm cho khách như:

- **Orange wood sticks:** *que gỗ cam*
- **Emery boards:** *cây giũa giấy*
- **Black beauty files:** *cây giũa đen (giũa bột)*
- **Buffer:** *cây buffer chà mịn bóng móng*

REUSABLE IMPLEMENTS AND EQUIPMENTS AFTER EACH CLIENT

Dụng cụ xử dụng lại sau mỗi lần làm cho khách khi đã được diệt trùng

- **Tweezer:** *nhíp nhổ lông*
- **Fingerbowl:** *tô ngâm móng*
- **Metal nail file:** *giũa kim loại*
- **Ultra violet lamp:** *đèn cực tím*
- **Electric file:** *cây giũa máy*
- **Cuticle nipper:** *kềm cắt da*
- **Arm cushion:** *lót tay cở 8"X 12"*
- **Metal cuticle pusher or steel pusher:** *cây sủi da bằng kim loại*
- **Nail brush:** *bàn chãi móng*
- **Basin:** *thau ngâm chân*
- **Nails clippers:** *dụng cụ cắt móng tay*
- **Acrylic brush:** *cây cọ đắp bột*
- **Electric nail dryer:** *lò sấy khô móng tay*
- **Chamois buffer:** *cây buffer đánh bóng bọc da dê*
- **Chamois buffer:** *cây buffer bọc da dê*

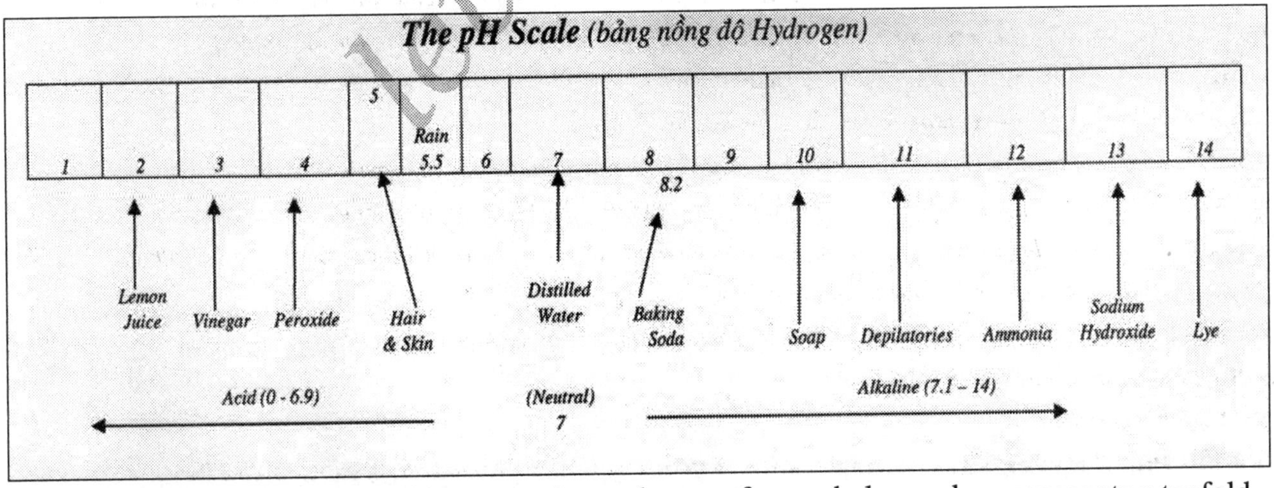

The pH scale is a loga scale. This means that a change of one whole number represents a tenfold change in pH. A pH of 8 is 10 times more alkaline than a pH of 7 and a pH of 9 is 100 times more alkaline than a pH of 7.

Bảng nồng độ Hydrogen gọi là trị số loga. Điều này được giải thích nếu trị số lớn hơn 1 là 10 lần hơn độ kiềm. Ví dụ:Nồng độ Hydrogen 8 là 10 lần độ kiềm lớn hơn 7 và nồng độ Hydrogen 9 là 100 lần độ kiềm lớn hơn 7.

Bài 9: TẾ BÀO, MÔ, BỘ PHẬN, HỆ THỐNG

Để duy trì sức khỏe lành mạnh, tươi trẻ cũng như có được làn mịn màng, móng tay, chân cứng chắc, tóc bóng mượt, con người cũng cần những loại thức ăn chính yếu mỗi ngày. Trong phần thức ăn cần thiết được chia làm từng nhóm sau:

CHẤT ĐẠM (PROTEIN): cung cấp lượng hoá chất cần thiết cho người từ bé cho đến tuổi già. Các **chất đạm động vật (amimal proteins)** như thịt, bơ, sữa, trứng, cá, gà vịt và **chất đạm thực vật (vegetable proteins)** như ngũ cốc, hạt, đậu,....Tuy nhiên chất đạm động vật cần thiết hơn đạm thực vật vì qua tiến trình hoạt động tạo nhiều **amino acid** cần thiết có cơ thể con người hơn.

CHẤT ĐƯỜNG, BỘT (CARBOHYDRATES): là nguồn năng lực nhiên liệu cung cấp cho cơ thể như bánh mì, khoai tây, ngũ cốc, gạo. Mặc dù có loại ít năng lượng nhưng dùng nhiều sẽ bị dư thừa thành chất béo và dễ tăng cân.

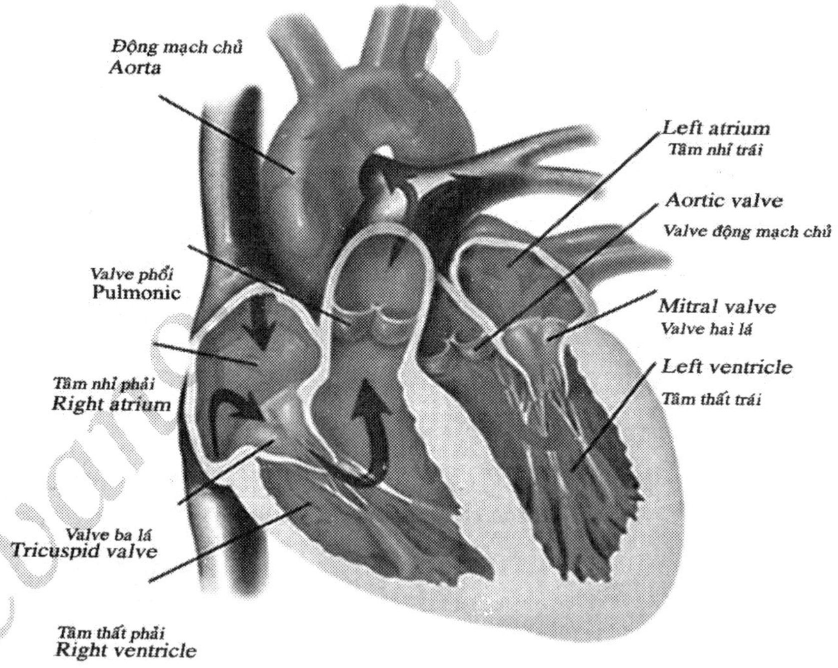

CHẤT KHOÁNG (MINERALS): có khả năng kiểm soát những nhiệm vụ các chức năng trong cơ thể cho sự phát triển răng, xương, bắp thịt, nội tạng, chất dịch gồm các chất calcium, potassium, phosphorus, đồng, sắc. Các chất này có trong thực phẩm như trứng, thịt, gan, tim, thận, gạo, bánh mì, sữa, trái cây và rau đậu.

CÁC CHẤT BỔ DƯỠNG *(VITAMINS): giúp chống bệnh, giữ sức khỏe tốt hơn, ngoài ra giúp làn da, mái tóc thêm đẹp, mịn màng, và móng tay chân cứng chắc nữa.*

- ***Vitamin A*** *có trong bơ, carrot, bí, lá xanh, mận có khả năng giúp làn da khỏe, tóc mướt, móng chắc.*
- ***Vitamin B*** *có trong bánh mì, sữa, thịt, rau, lá xanh có khả năng giúp hệ thống thần kinh và bệnh da.*
- ***Vitamin C*** *có trong nước chanh, cà chua, dưa, dâu có khả năng giúp nướu khỏe, răng cứng chắc.*
- ***Vitamin D*** *có trong sữa, gan, lòng đỏ trứng, nguồn mặt trời, nguồn U.V giúp da khỏe, mịn màng.*

MƯỜI HỆ THỐNG QUAN TRỌNG TRONG CƠ THỂ:

1. **Hệ thống bắp thịt** giúp tạo hình, nâng đỡ bộ xương, chuyển động. Cơ thể có hơn 500 cơ bắp, chiếm 40 đến 50% trọng lượng của cơ thể. Cơ bắp chia 3 phần: gốc (origin) dính chặt vào xương không cử động; ngọn (insertion) là phần lắp vào cử động; và bụng (belly) là phần giữa bắp thịt được nối lại bằng những sợi gân.

Bắp thịt có 3 loại:

- ***Cơ có vân, sợi (striated)*** *cử động theo ý muốn như cơ mặt, cánh tay.*
- ***Cơ không vân, mịn (non-striated)*** *cử động không theo ý muốn như cơ dạ dày, ruột.*
- ***Cơ tim (cardiac)*** *cơ đặc biệt chỉ có ở quả tim.*

2. **Hệ thống tuần hoàn** giúp luân chuyển máu cho động mạch, tĩnh mạch, mạch máu nhỏ khắp cơ thể. Sự tuần hoàn bao gồm tim, máu, và sự luân chuyển mạch máu kể cả bạch huyết.
   - ***Tim*** *như cái bơm bóp lại và buông máu ra từ tâm thất đến tâm nhĩ và phân phối khắp cơ thể. Tim hình chóp cở bằng nắm tay, mỗi phút bơm lượng máu khắp cơ thể từ 5 đến 6 quarts (4 đến 6 lít), nhịp đập lúc bình thường từ 72 đến 80 lần mỗi phút.*
   - ***Máu*** *có độ đậm đặc như nước ép cà chua. Trong động mạch máu đỏ tươi, tĩnh mạch màu đỏ sậm. Người lớn có lượng máu từ 8 đến 10 pints (3.8 lit đến 4.5 lit). Nhiệt độ máu 98.6 độ F (37 độ C). Máu đảm trách nhiều chức năng vì trong máu có huyết thanh (tiểu cầu) đông máu lại đóng kín vết thương;* ***bạch cầu*** *chống nhiễm trùng, các vi khuẩn gây bệnh;* ***huyết tương*** *chất dịch lỏng màu vàng nhạt mang thức ăn, oxygen, chất dịch đến nuôi dưỡng các tế bào cơ thể; máu điều hòa nhiệt độ cơ thể chống lạnh hoặc nóng; loại bỏ thán khí, bài tiết chất độc, chất bẩn, chất thừa qua phổi, da, ruột già, thận.*

3. **Hệ thống da** gồm 2 lớp ngoại, nội biểu bì, giúp bao bọc, điều hòa thân nhiệt, nhận rõ xúc cảm. Hệ thống da bao gồm tóc, lông, da, móng, các tuyến mồ hôi, tuyến dầu.
4. **Hệ thống nội tiết** tạo những tuyến không ống, tiết thẳng vào máu như chất hormon kích thích tố, ảnh hưởng đến sự biến thái cơ thể, kết hợp với hệ thần kinh điều hòa và phối hợp các cơ quan khác trong cơ thể.
5. **Hệ thống bài tiết** loại trừ chất thải khỏi cơ thể gồm có: phổi đẩy thán khí carbon dioxide ra ngoài; ruột già đẩy bỏ thức ăn không tiêu hóa và phân hóa ra; da thoát mồ hôi; gan lọc độc tố, tiết ra mật; và thận tiết nước tiểu.

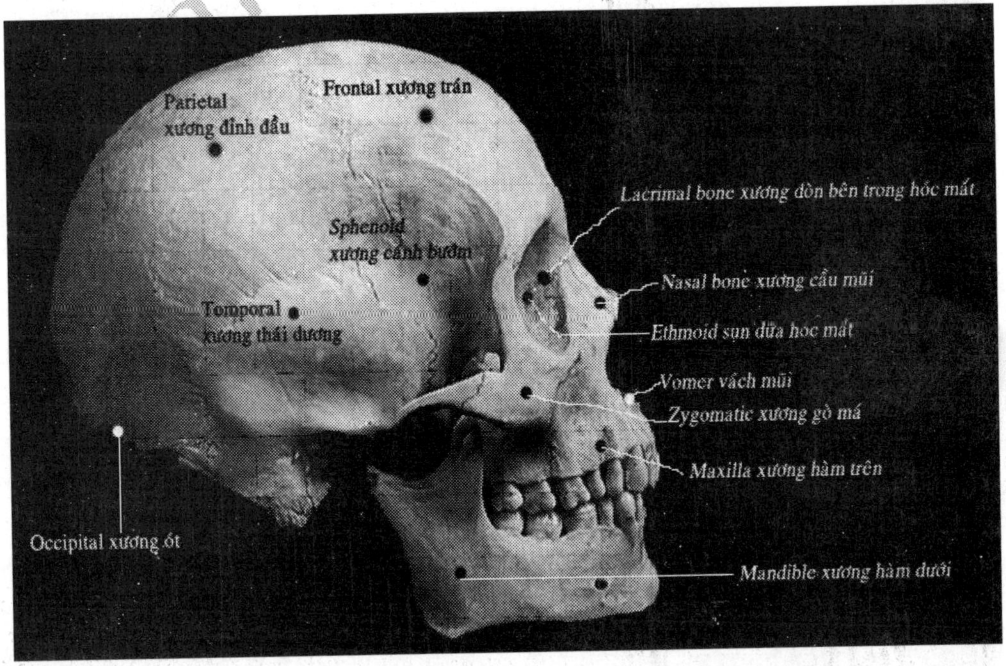

6. **Hệ thống tiêu hóa** giúp biến thức ăn nuôi dưỡng tế bào, sự tiêu hóa từ bao tử, ruột non và hấp thụ vào mạch máu nhờ chất men (enzyme) có trong dịch vị giúp chuyển đổi thức ăn nuôi dưỡng, sau đó chất thải, không tiêu hóa đẩy ra ruột già. Sự thoải mái, vui tươi sẽ giúp tiêu hóa tốt hoặc sự buồn phiền, trầm cảm gây xáo trộn và chậm tiêu hóa. Tiến trình tiêu hóa hoàn tất cần thời gian từ 8 đến 9 giờ.

7. **Hệ thống hô hấp** cung cấp oxy cho cơ thể nhờ phổi là cơ quan mô xốp thu nhận không khí trong lồng ngực. Khi thở ra là thải khí carbon dioxide và hít hơi vào là oxygen được hấp thụ. Hệ hố hấp hài hòa sự hoạt động của cơ thể. Hít hơi qua mũi không khí được thanh lọc qua màng nhầy, lông mũi giữ lại nhiều vi trùng và làm ấm hơi khi tiến vào phổi tốt hơn là thở bằng miệng.

8. **Hệ thống sinh dục** giúp cơ thể sinh sản.

9. **Hệ thống xương** như cái sườn giúp bảo vệ chức năng bên trong, chỗ bắp thịt bám vào, sản xuất tế bào máu trong tủy xương, nâng đỡ và chuyển động. Xương là những mô cứng của cơ thể chứa nhiều chất khoáng và muối. Có **206 xương** trong cơ thể gồm xương đầu, xương mặt, xương cổ, xương sống, sườn, xương tay, chân, ngoài ra còn có khớp xương, khớp trục, bản lề, khớp trợt như mắt cá, cổ tay…..
   Xương có màu trắng bên ngoài và đỏ sậm bên trong và cấu trúc liên kết xương gồm có **sụn (cartilage)** tạo bọc đệm cho xương và tạo hình bên ngoài như tai, mũi; **dây chằng (ligament)** là loại mô sợi giữ chặt xương; và **chất trơn nhờn (synovial fluid)** cung cấp cho sụn và giúp xương cử động dễ dàng.

10. **Hệ thống thần kinh** giúp kiểm soát và điều hợp, hài hòa chức năng của các hệ thống cơ thể. Hệ thần kinh gồm **não tủy trung khu thần kinh (não và tủy sống)** giúp kiểm soát hoạt động tinh thần, ý thức hoạt động bắp thịt, diễn tả nét mặt, kiểm soát 5 giác quan: nếm, sờ, nghe, thấy và ngửi. Và **thần kinh ngoại biên** giúp mang tín hiệu đi và đến não bộ; **thần kinh phản xạ** như nhịp tim, nhịp thở..
    *Mỗi một diện tích nhỏ trên cơ thể được cung cấp những sợi nhỏ thần kinh. Mô thần kinh lớn nhất là não trong hộp sọ nặng từ **44 đến 48 ounces** (khoảng 1.3 kg) và dây tủy sống bắt nguồn từ não chạy dọc khắp thân mình. Các loại dây thần kinh gồm **thần kinh cảm giác** giúp nhận biết nóng, lạnh, nếm, sờ, ép....; **thần kinh vận động** gây xung động đến cơ bắp tạo ra cử động; **thần kinh hỗn hợp** gởi và nhận tín hiệu vừa cảm giác và vận động; **thần kinh phản xạ** trực tiếp đến tủy sống và tạo phản xạ như giật tay, chân khi bất ngờ đụng vật quá nóng.*

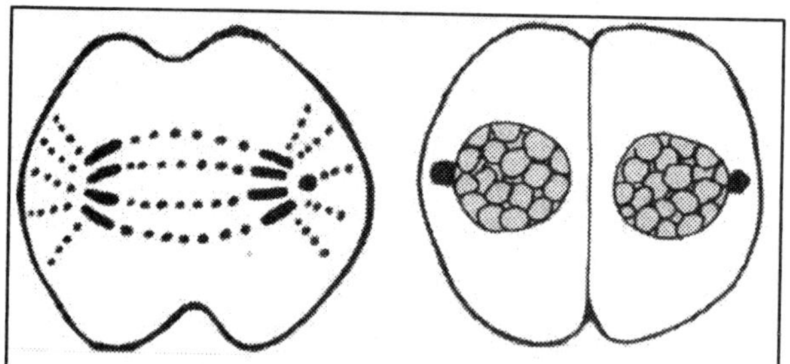

one cell has divided to create two cells
tế bào trưởng thành chia hai

PHÁT TRIỂN VÀ SINH THÁI TẾ BÀO

Tế bào là đơn vị nhỏ, căn bản của tất cả mọi sự sống từ thảo mộc, động vật và con người được cấu tạo bởi **nguyên sinh chất (protoplasm)** chứa thành phần dinh dưỡng; **chất phát triển (cytoplasm)** có khả năng tự điều chỉnh tế bào; **tích bào centrosome** bên trong cytoplasm ảnh hưởng sinh sản tế bào; và **nhân (nucleus)** là trung tâm và vai trò quan trọng tái sinh sản. Tế bào sinh sản theo lối phân chia gọi là trực phân (mitosis).

Tế bào biến đổi **(metabolism)** gồm 2 giai đoạn: **sự hấp thụ (anabolism)** tích trử nước, thức ăn, oxygen, nhiệt độ cần thiết cho sự phát triển; và **tiêu hao (catabolism)** phân hóa qua sự hoạt động co thắt, bài tiết. Hai giai đoạn cùng lúc xảy ra liên tục để duy trì ổn định cho cơ thể gọi là **homeostasis.**

CELLS, TISSUES, ORGANS, SYSTEMS

(Tế bào, Mô, Bộ phận, Hệ thống)

- The chemical process in which cells are nourished (store food and water) and carry out (release energy) their activities is metabolism
  Tiến trình hoá chất trong tế bào được nuôi dưỡng và giải thoát khi hoạt động là sự trao đổi chất của tế bào.
- **Catabolism** is the breaking down of cellular tissue (*sự dị hoá là giai đoạn tiêu hao các mô tế bào)*
- **Anabolism** is the building up of the tissue or store food and water
  Sự đồng hoá là giai đoạn tạo dựng các mô hoặc tích trữ thức ăn và nước
- Bone, catilage, tendons, ligament, and fat tissure are all example of connective tissue
  Xương, sụn, gân, dây chằng, và mô mỡ là những ví dụ của mô liên kết.
- Hyoid bone or the "U" shaped neck bone located in the front of the throat and is commonly called the "Adam's apple".
  Xương hyoid hoặc là xương cổ hình chữ "U" nằm ở phía trước cổ họng được thường gọi là "Adam's apple".
  The scapula forms the back of shoulder: *xương scapula thành lập phía sau bả vai*
  Various methods of muscles stimulation are: *các phương pháp kích thích bắp thịt là:*
    - * Moist heat - steamer or warm steam towels
      Nhiệt ẩm – hơi nước hoặc khăn hơi ẩm
    - * Dry heat - heating masks, heat lamp
      Nhiệt khô - mặt nạ nóng, đèn nhiệt
    - * Electric current- high-frequency, faradic
      Dòng điện – cao tần, dòng faradic (co thắt)
    - * Massage- Vibration machine, hand massage
      Xoa bóp – máy rung, massage bằng tay
    - * Chemical- acid and salt (*hóa chất – acid và muối*)
    - * Light rays- infrared rays and ultraviolet rays
      Tia đèn – tia đèn nhiệt màu đỏ và tia cực tím

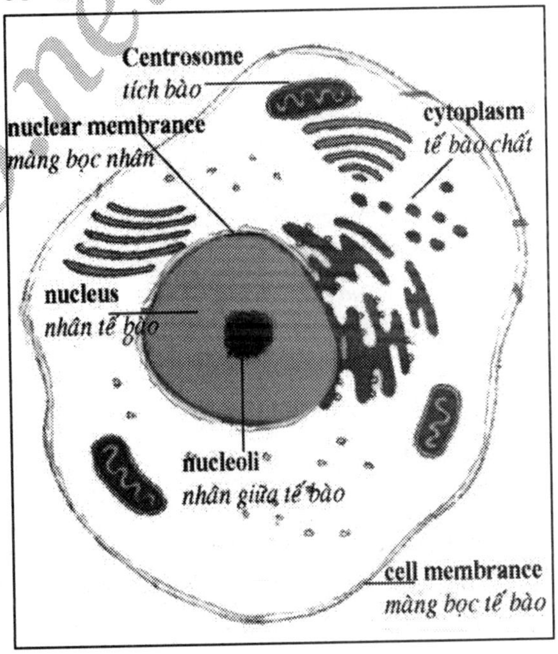

- The body's largest organ is the skin, the membranous tissue that covers the body
  Bộ phận trãi rộng nhất cơ thể là lớp mô da phủ khắp cơ thể.
- **A cell** is a minute portion of living substance consisting of protoplasm, which is living matter, surrounded by a membrane, containing a nucleus
  Tế bào là một phần rất nhỏ của vật chất sống gồm có nguyên sinh chất, là sự sống của tế bào, chung quanh bao bọc bởi màng bọc, chứa nhân tế bào.
- Structure of the cell*: cấu trúc của tế bào*
  - Cell membrane has protoplasm*: màng bọc có nguyên sinh chất*
  - Nucleus for reproduction*: nhân giữ việc sinh sản*
  - Cytoplasm for self –repair of the cell*: tế bào chất giữ việc tự điều chỉnh của tế bào*
  - Centrosome for maintaining of the original cell*: tích bào để duy trì tế bào gốc.*
- When a cell reaches maturity, it reproduces by mitosis or indirect division
  Khi tế bào tiến đến trưởng thành, sinh sản theo hình thức gián phân hoặc phân chia gián tiếp.
- **Metabolism** is a complex chemical process in which cells are nourished and supplied with energy needed to on these many activities.
  Sự biến hóa tế bào là tiến trình phức tạp về hóa tính mà tế bào được nuôi dưỡng và cung cấp năng lượng cần thiết cho hoạt động của cơ thể.

- The two phases of metabolism are anabolism, which builds up cellular tissues and catabolism, which breaks down cellular tissue.
  Hai giai đoạn biến hóa của tế bào là đồng hóa (tạo dựng) và dị hoá (tiêu hao tế bào).

- Body tissues are classified in five groups*: mô cơ thể được chia làm 5 nhóm*
  - **Connective tissue** binds together other tissues and bones of the body, supports, protect as cartilage, ligaments, tendons, and fat tissues are examples.
    Mô liên kết, nối liền các mô và xương của thân thể, giúp đỡ, bảo vệ ví dụ như sụn, dây chằng, gân và mô mỡ.
  - **Muscular tissue** contracts and allows movement in various parts of the body
    Mô bắp thịt co thắt và để tạo sự chuyển động các phần trong cơ thể.
  - **Nerve tissue** transmits messages to and from the brain and controls, coordinates all body functions.
    Mô thần kinh chuyển tin tức tới và từ bộ óc và kiểm soát, phối hợp tất cả các nhiệm vụ trong cơ thể.
  - **Epithelial tissue** is the protective covering on body surfaces. It includes the skin, mucous membranes, linings of the heart, digestive, respiration organs and glands.
    Mô bảo vệ là bề mặt bảo vệ cơ thể. Bao gồm da, màng nhầy, màng bọc tim, màng giúp tiêu hóa, cơ quan hô hấp và các tuyến.
  - **Liquid tissue** carries food, wasted products, and hormones. This type includes the blood and lymph.
    Mô dinh dưỡng mang thức ăn, chất thải và kích thích tố. Gồm máu đỏ và bạch cầu.

- The skin is both a tissue and an organ*: Da vừa là mô và là bộ phận*
- The skull has 2 parts: 8 cranium bones and 14 facial bones
  Xương sọ đầu có 2 phần: 8 xương sọ và 14 xương mặt
- Beside the teeth, bone is the hardest structure of the body. There are 206 bones in the body
  Ngoài răng ra, xương là phần cứng nhất của cơ thể. Có 206 cái xương trong cơ thể
  The thorax is made up of the breastbone; the spine; the ribs; the connective cartilage
- *Xương lồng ngực được cấu tạo của xương ức; xương sống; xương sườn; sụn liên kết*
  The chest is a elastic bony cage consist of 12 ribs on each side:
  Xương ngực là như cái lồng xương đàn hồi gồm có 12 cái xương sườn ở mỗi bên
- **The humerus** is the largest bone of the upper arm:
  Humerus là xương lớn nhất nằm ở cánh tay trên
- The metacarpal bones are the five long slender bones of the hand.
  Metacarpal là 5 xương dài thon cuả bàn tay

- The function of the muscular system is the produce all the movements of the body
  Nhiệm vụ của hệ thống bắp thịt là tạo ra mọi chuyển động của cơ thể
- **Myology** is the study of the structure, functions and diseases of the muscles
  Myology là môn học về cấu trúc, nhiệm vụ và bệnh của bắp thịt
- The cardiac is the heart muscle not found anywhere else.
  Cardiac là bắp thịt tim không thể có ở nơi khác
- **The muscle has 3 parts**: the origin (not move), the insertion (move), and the belly (middle)
  Bắp thịt có 3 phần: gốc (không di chuyển), ngọn (di chuyển), bụng bắp thịt (phần giữa)
- Three kinds of muscular tissue: Striated (voluntary muscle) as face, hand; Non-striated (involuntary muscle) as intestines; and Cardiac (heart muscle).
  Có 3 loại bắp thịt: có sợi (bắp thịt tự ý) như bắp thịt mặt, tay; không có sợi (bắp thịt không tự ý) như bắp thịt ruột; và Cardiac (bắp thịt tim).

- **The central nervous system** controls mental activities, five senses (hearing, smelling, tasting, feeling, and seeing) and facial, body movements.
  Hệ thống trung khu thần kinh kiểm soát các hoạt động tinh thần, ngũ quan (nghe, ngửi, nếm, cảm xúc, và thấy) và chuyển động của mặt và cơ thể.
- The main divisions of the central nervous system are brain, spinal cord, and nerves.
  Phần chính yếu của hệ thống trung khu thần kinh là bộ óc, tủy sống, và thần kinh.
- **The fifth cranial nerve** are affected by massage is the largest of cranial nerve that control chewing and also called trigeminal or trifacial nerve
  Thần kinh sọ thứ 5 ảnh hưởng đến massage là thần kinh lớn nhất ở thần kinh sọ, kiểm soát về nhai và cũng được gọi là thần kinh trigeminal hoặc trifacial.
- The blood vascular system consists of the heart and the blood vessels (arteries, and capillaries, veins) which carry blood from the heart to the body, and then back to the heart.
  Hệ thống bơm đẩy máu gồm có quả tim và các mạch máu (động mạch, mao mạch, tĩnh mạch) nhiệm vụ mang máu từ tim đến các phần của thân thể, và rồi trở về lại quả tim.

- **Arteries** (thick walled) carry pure blood from the heart to the tissues of the body
  Động mạch (thành dày) mang máu sạch từ quả tim đến các mô của cơ thể
- **Veins** (thin walled) carry impure blood from the tissues to the heart
  Tĩnh mạch (thành mỏng) mang máu dơ từ các mô trở lại tim
- **Capillaries** (minute, thin walled) connect the smaller arteries with the veins
  Mao mạch (mạch máu nhỏ, thành mỏng) nối liền các động mạch và tĩnh mạch nhỏ
- The blood circulation that goes from the heart to the lungs to be purified then back to the heart is called pulmonary circulation.
  Sự tuần hoàn máu đi từ tim đến phổi làm máu sạch lại rồi trở về tim gọi là tuần hoàn phổi.
- The lymphatic system is the waste disposal and drainage system for the body tissue
  Hệ thống bạch huyết là hệ thống thoát chất bả cho các mô tế bào của cơ thể
- The endocrine system is the body's chemical control system. The endocrine (ductless) put their secretions directly into the blood stream.
  Hệ thống nội tiết là hệ thống kiểm soát trao đổi hoá tính trong cơ thể. Nội tiết (tuyến không có ống) đem sự bài tiết trực tiếp bên trong dòng máu.
- **The skin** is considered part of the endocrine system because it produces vitamin D
  Da được xem là phần của hệ thống nội tiết bởi vì nó sản xuất chất vitamin D
- Kidneys, liver, skin, intestines and lungs are all part of the excretory system.
  Thận, gan, da, ruột và phổi là những bộ phận của hệ thống nội tiết.

- Nose breathing is healthier than mouth breathing because the air is warmed by the surface of the capillaries, and the bacteria in the air is caught by the hairs that line the nasal passages.
  Hít thở bằng mũi tốt hơn thở miệng vì không khí được làm ấm bằng bề mặt các lớp mao mạch, và vi trùng trong không khí được giữ lại bằng lớp lông mũi trên đường qua mũi.
- The size of the heart about a fist is a cardiac muscular; cone-shaped that contains 4 chambers: right and left atrium (2 upper thin walled chambers) and right and left ventricle (2 lower thick walled chambers).
  Hình dạng quả tim bằng nắm tay là loại bắp thịt cardiac hình nón, chứa 4 ngăn: tâm nhĩ phải và trái (2 ngăn trên thành mỏng) và tâm thất phải và trái (2 ngăn dưới thành dày).
- **Blood** contains red corpucles (carry oxygen) and white corpuscle (leucocytes–destroy germs), plasma (carries food, carbon dioxide), and platelets (clotting blood).
  Máu là một chất lỏng chứa hồng cầu (mang oxy) và bạch cầu (leucocystes –tiêu diệt vi trùng gây bệnh), huyết tương (mang chất nuôi dưỡng, loại bỏ độc tố), và huyết thanh (đông máu).

Bài 10: CẤU TRÚC CỦA DA

Dermatology là ngành học về cấu trúc, nhiệm vụ và bệnh da. Da có tính bền, đàn hồi và là cơ quan rộng nhất cơ thể với người lớn mô da có diện tích 20 square feet và trọng lượng từ 6 đến 7 lbs. Mí mắt là vùng da mỏng nhất và gót chân là vùng da dày nhất.
Da con người biểu hiện ví như tấm gương vì nhìn qua làn da khỏe mạnh có màu hồng, ẩm, mượt mà và nồng độ acid khoảng 4.5 đến 5.5 hoặc ngược lại làn da xám, khô tìm biểu lộ sự bệnh hoạn, thiếu oxygen v.v...

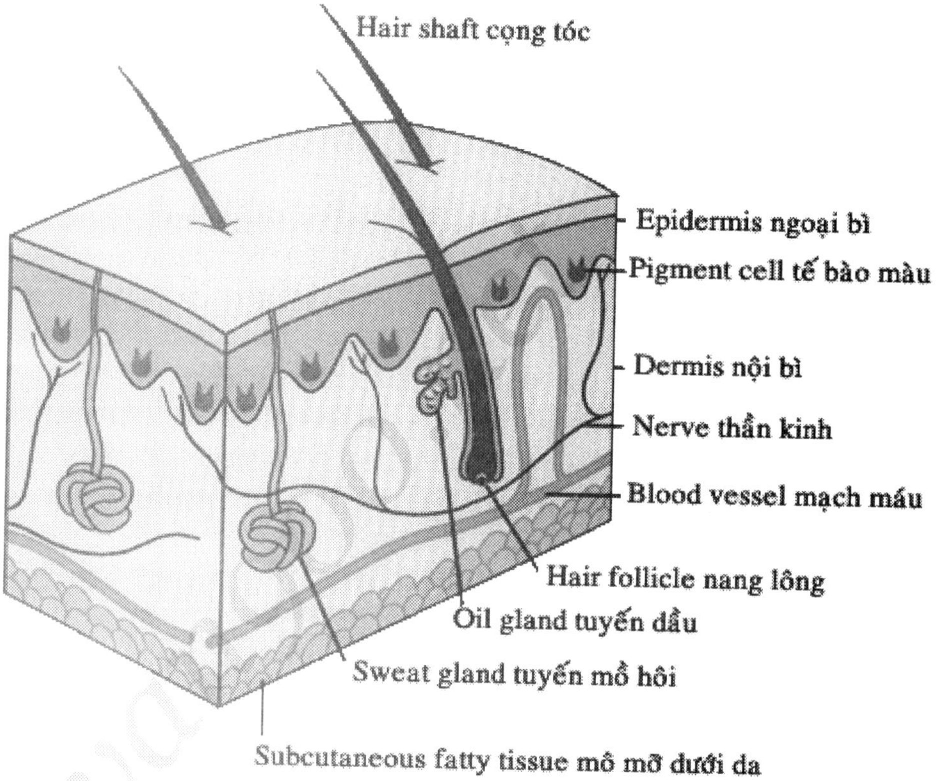

Màu da tùy thuộc vào nguồn cung cấp máu cho chất melanin tạo màu da. Tuy nhiên có nhiều trường hợp màu da bất thường. Ví dụ như chứng bạch tạng (albinism) thiếu sắc tố melanin bẩm sinh làm tóc trắng, da trắng hồng không ăn nắng; bớt (nevus) do sắc tố bất thường hoặc mao quản giãn nở, hoặc đồi mồi (chloasma); tàn nhang (freckle); hoặc mảng da lợt màu (vitiligo).

Nhiệm vụ của da giữ nhiệt cho cơ thể ở 98.6 độ F, ngay cả khi ảnh hưởng thời tiết bên ngoài quá lạnh hoặc nóng.

Da chia làm 2 lớp ngoại bì (epidermis) và nội bì (dermis).

- **Ngoại bì** là lớp mỏng bên ngoài không chứa mạch máu, chứa nhiều dây thần kinh còn gọi là lớp bọc (scarf skin) hoặc cuticle.

Ngoại bì (epidermis) mỏng nhưng chia làm 4 lớp:

1. *Lớp sừng ngoài cùng gọi là lớp horny **(stratum corneum):** là những tế bào sừng, vảy tạo chất karetin như móng, và tóc, lông được liên tục thay thế để tạo lớp sừng mới.*
2. *Lớp tế bào trong **(stratum lucidum)** là lớp tế bào mỏng trong suốt.*
3. *Lớp hạt **(stratum granulosum)** còn gọi là **stratum mucosum** là lớp có khuynh hướng đẩy tế bào chết ra bề mặt da thay lớp sừng mới.*
4. *Lớp nẩy mầm **(stratum germinativum)** là lớp sâu nhất chứa hạt màu melanin có nhiệm vụ bảo vệ tia U.V từ mặt trời. Lớp này đánh giá về màu da và nhiệm vụ phát triển lớp ngoại bì*

- **Nội bì** (dermis) sâu bên trong, dày hơn 25 lần ngoại bì. Nội bì chứa mạch máu, bạch cầu, thần kinh, mạch đàn hồi collagen, tuyến mồ hôi, tuyến dầu còn gọi da thật, derma, corium, cutis.

Nội bì (dermis) dày chia làm 2 lớp:

1. *Lớp nhú* ***papillary*** *có hình dạng chóp nhỏ duỗi thẳng tới lớp ngoại bì, chứa mạch máu nhỏ, đầu thần kinh và cũng chứa một ít sắc tố melanin*
2. *Lớp lưới chằng chịt* ***reticular*** *chứa tế bào mỡ, tuyến dầu, tuyến mồ hôi, mạch máu, bạch cầu, nang lông, và cơ dựng lông* ***(arrector pili muscles)***

NHIỆM VỤ CỦA DA:

1. Điều tiết lượng dầu **(secretion)** giúp trơn mịn da, giữ mềm mại, dẻo dai cho làn da. Phần lớn khắp cơ thể đều có tuyến dầu trừ lòng bàn tay, lòng bàn chân
2. Bài tiết mồ hôi **(excretion)** loại độc tố gồm chất muối và hoá chất qua làn da bằng hình thức ra mồ hôi. Phần lớn cơ thể có tuyến mồ hôi nhưng nhiều nhất là ở trán, nách, lòng bàn tay, lòng bàn chân. Ra nhiều mồ hôi gây mất nước cho cơ thể.
3. Điều hòa thân nhiệt **(heat regulation)** giúp bảo vệ cơ thể do môi trường quá nóng hoặc lạnh với sự trợ giúp của máu giữ cho nhiệt độ cơ thể ở 98.6 độ F (37 độ C).
4. Nhận biết cảm giác **(sensation)** nhờ thần kinh cuối ở da cảm nhận nóng, lạnh, sờ, ép hoặc đau đớn qua cào xướt, ngứa.
5. Bảo vệ cơ thể **(protection)** tránh tổn thương, xâm nhập của vi trùng, trầy trụa, tạo lớp dầu chống nước, hoặc các dạng hóa chất khác.
6. Hút thấm **(absorption)** vào da qua dạng thuốc thấm vào trong da, kích thích tố nữ, kem thoa mặt, kem nhờn tốt da và tốt tóc.

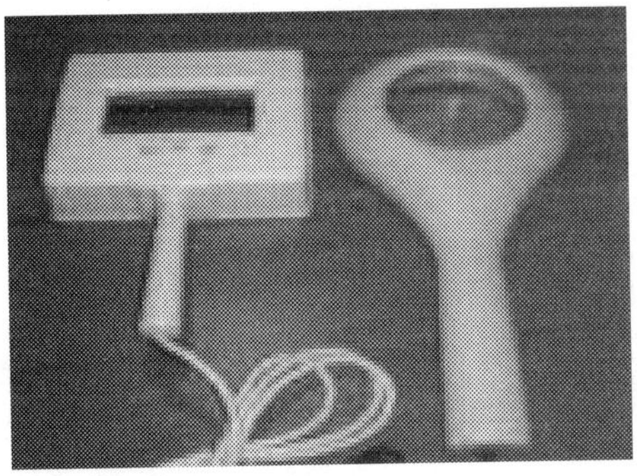

SỰ DINH DƯỠNG DA

Có hơn một nữa lượng máu trong cơ thể phân phối tới da. Da được nuôi dưỡng bởi hồng cầu, bạch cầu giúp cho sự tăng trưởng của da, tóc, và móng.

Da chứa 2 loại tuyến:

- *Tuyến mồ hôi (sudoriferous glands) giúp điều hòa thân nhiệt, loại chất thải qua sức nóng, thể dục v.v...Chất lỏng gọi là mồ hôi tiết từ 1 đến 2 pints thoát hằng ngày qua lỗ mồ hôi trên da.*
- *Tuyến dầu (sebaceous glands) tiết ra làm trơn da. Khắp cơ thể đều có tuyến dầu ngoại trừ lòng bàn tay, bàn chân. Làn da cần được làm sạch hằng ngày để khỏi bị nghẹt các tuyến dầu và đó là lý do tạo mụn đầu đen (blackheads). Làn da có sự đàn hồi vì thế nếu làn da bị ấn ép vẫn trở lại hình dáng ban đầu và sự đàn hồi mất dần khi tuổi càng cao.*

NHỮNG THƯƠNG TỔN VẾT LỠ DA VÀ NHIỄM TRÙNG

Với ngành thẩm mỹ, người thợ cũng rất dễ những bệnh về da do tiếp xúc các hóa chất làm sưng da do tiếp xúc (contact dermatitis), mẫn cảm một số thành phần hóa chất như thuốc uốn tóc, tẩy tóc, thuốc nhuộm, chất gel móng, nước acrylic, bột acylic, acetone v.v....

Sự dị ứng hóa chất cả khách và thợ nếu tiếp xúc thời gian dài từ hơn 4 tháng. Sự tiếp xúc lâu ngày, nhiều lần (overexposure), người thợ thường dị ứng ở giữa ngón cái và ngón trỏ, cổ tay, lòng bàn tay, hoặc người khách dị ứng ở vùng da quanh móng, đầu móng, đệm móng (nail bed).

Da tay ngâm trong nước quá lâu bị mất chất dầu tự nhiên, khô da, lỡ, nứt nẻ, nhức buốt.

Da bị nhiễm trùng cần được chuyển đến bác sĩ chuyên về da (dermatologist) điều trị như:

- ***Nấm ở chân*** *(tinea pedis; athlete's foot) nhận biết qua những chấm nhỏ màu hồng, mụn nước ở trên bàn chân hoặc lòng bàn chân, ngứa khó chịu và dễ lây lan.*
- ***Nấm ở tay*** *(tinea; ringworm) có đốm đỏ và rất ngứa ở bàn tay và dễ lây lan.*
- ***Nhiễm trùng ở vùng môi, mũi, và mặt*** *(herpes simplex) là nhiễm trùng siêu vi khuẩn có từng chùm mụt nước. Vi khuẩn cũng dễ biến mất 1 vài tuần sau đó, nhưng cũng dễ lây lan.*
- ***Vảy nến (psoriasis)*** *là chứng sưng da kinh niên thường ở vùng da đầu, ngực, lưng dưới, đầu gối, và cùi chỏ nhận dạng qua những mảng tròn dày, khô, vảy bạc, ngứa.*

Dấu hiệu hoặc triệu chứng ở da chia làm hai nhóm:

1. **Triệu chứng cảm thấy** (subjective symptoms) như đau quá, nhức quá, ngứa, nóng rát, khó chịu. Đây chỉ là sự cảm nhận không thấy được.
2. **Triệu chứng thấy được** (objective symptoms) như mụt nhọt có nước (bulla), mụt mủ bị sưng (pustule), viêm sưng do côn trùng cắn (wheals) xuất hiện những nốt nhỏ và ngứa.

Thường những vết lở này làm các mô da thay đổi. Là một thẩm mỹ viên cần phân biệt điều kiện da được phục vụ trong phạm vi nghề nghiệp hoặc cần phải chuyển đến bác sĩ điều trị.

STRUCTURE OF THE SKIN

(Cấu trúc của da)

- A fatal skin cancer that begins with a mole is melanotic sarcoma.
  Da ung thư gây chết người bắt đầu ở nốt ruồi là melanotic sarcoma.
- The skin has a slightly acid **(4.5 to 5.5 PH scale),** moist, soft, flexible covering of the body, and free from any disease, disorder is a healthy skin
  Làn da có tính acid nhe (4.5 đến 5.5 nồng độ Hydrogen), ẩm, mềm, uyển chuyển bao phủ cơ thể, và không có bệnh, lở loét là một làn da khỏe mạnh.
- The appearance of a good complexion is: *vẽ ngoài của một làn da khỏe mạnh là:*
  - Fine grained texture skin : *làn da mịn hạt nhỏ*
  - Healthy skin color : *màu da khỏe (tươi sáng)*
  - And free of blemishes : *không tì vết lở loét*
- **Two main division** of the skin are epidermis (outer layer) and dermis (inner layer): *hai lớp da chính của da là lớp ngoại bì mỏng nhất còn gọi là cuticle hoặc scarf skin lớp nội bì dày gấp 25 lần so với ngoại bì còn gọi là derma, corium, cutis, hoặc true skin.*

  - The layers of the epidermis are: *các lớp da của ngoại bì là:*
  - Stratum corneum (horny layer): *lớp sừng ngoài cùng chứa chất đạm keratin*
  - Stratum lucidum (clear layer): *lớp tế bào trong suốt, ánh sáng xuyên qua được*
  - Stratum granulosum (granular layer): *lớp hạt để thay thế lớp tế bào chết (lớp sừng)*
  - Stratum germinativum (deepest layer): *lớp nẩy mầm trong cùng của ngoại bì tạo màu cho da*

  - The dermis consists of two layers: the papillary or superficial layer, and the reticular or deeper layer (network). It is a highly sensitive and vascular layer of connective tissue. Within its structure are numerous blood vessels, lymph vessels, nerves, sweat glands, oil glands, hair follicles, errector pili muscles, and papillae.
  Lớp nội bì gồm 2 lớp: lớp nhủ hoặc lớp superficial, và lớp reticular hoặc lớp sâu bên trong kết như mạng lưới. Có tính nhạy cảm cao và là lớp nối kết mạch máu của mô liên kết. Cấu trúc bên trong là số lượng mạch máu, bạch cầu, thần kinh, tuyến mồ hôi, tuyến dầu, nang lông, cơ dựng lông, và chân lông.

- **The subcutaneous tissue** is below the dermis, it is also called adipose, or subcutis tissue and thinness and thickness depend on the age, sex, and general health . It function are:
  Mô dưới da là lớp bên dưới nội bì, cũng được gọi là adipose hoặc mô subcutis, mỏng hoặc dày tùy thuộc vào tuổi tác, giới tính, và sức khỏe tổng quát. Có nhiệm vụ là:
  - Give smoothness to the body: *tạo lớp bọc mịn màng cho cơ thể*
  - Contain fat for use as energy: *chứa lớp mỡ xử dụng như năng lượng*
  - Protective cushion for the outer skin: *màng đệm cho lớp da ngoài*
- Blood and lymph nourish the skin and about ½ to 2/3 of the entire blood supply in the body is distributed to the skin
  Hồng cầu và bạch cầu nuôi dưỡng da và khoảng từ ½ đến 2/3 lượng máu cung cấp cho cơ thể được phân phối đến da.

- Motor, sensory, and secretory nerve fibers are three types of nerve fibers found in the skin. Therefore, the skin reacts to five things: heat, cold, touch, pressure, and pain.
  Sợi thần kinh vận động, cảm giác và bài tiết là 3 loại sợi thần kinh tìm thấy ở trong da. Vì thế da có phản ứng với 5 điều: nóng, lạnh, sờ, ép, và đau.
- **The arrector pili muscles** are the motor nerve fibers attached to hair follicles.
  Cơ dựng lông là sợi thần kinh vận động dính liền với nang lông.

- **The melanin**, coloring matter of the skin is found in the basal layer or living stratum, and the blood supply determine the color of the skin.
Melanin, chất màu của da được tìm thấy trong lớp basal (lớp trong cùng của ngoại bì) hoặt là lớp sống và lượng máu cung cấp đánh giá màu của da.

- The stratum germinativum (stratum mucosum) is a single layer of cells to replace older cells that are being shed in twenty-eight days.
Lớp mầm sống (lớp màng nhầy) là lớp của tế bào, để thay thế lớp cũ rụng đi trong 28 ngày.

- **The average weigh** of the skin is 7 pounds and the skin cover about 18.2 square feet on adult body. The skin thickness from 1/12 to 1/5 inch.
Trong lượng trung bình của da là 7 pounds va da phủ khoảng 18.2 feet vuông trên cơ thể người lớn. Da dày từ 1/12 cho đến 1/5 inch.

- The functions of the nerve fibers distributed to sweat and oil gland as:
  - Regulation of the excretion of perspiration from sweat glands
  - Control the flow of sebum to the surface of the skin

Nhiệm vụ của những dây thần kinh phân phối đến tuyến mồ hôi và tuyến dầu như:
- Điều hòa việc tiết mồ hôi từ các tuyến mồ hôi
- Kiểm soát lượng dầu tiết ra bề mặt da

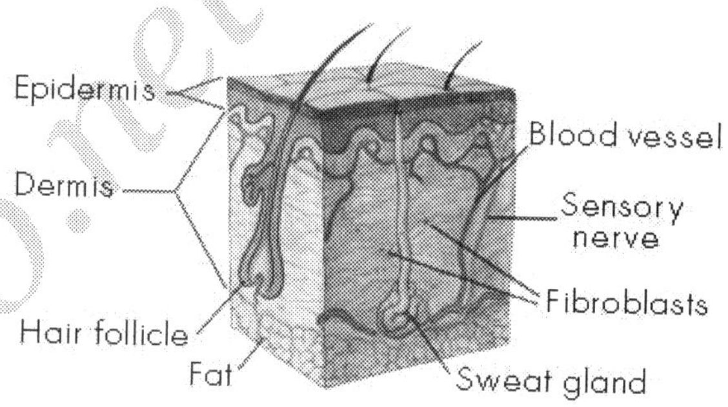

- **Each square inch of the skin contains**: 650 sweat glands; 95 oil glands; 65 hairs; 9,500,000 cells; 19 yard of blood vessels; 78 yard of nerves.
Mỗi inch vuông của da chứa: 650 tuyến mồ hôi; 95 tuyến dầu; 65 sợi lông; 9 triệu rưỡi tế bào; 19 yard mạch máu; 78 yard thần kinh.

- **Six important functions** of the skin are protection, sensation, heat regulation, secretion, excretion, and absorption
Sáu nhiệm vụ quan trọng của da là bảo vệ, cảm giác, điều hòa nhiệt độ, điều tiết, bài tiết và sự hút thấm.

- The sweat glands consist of a coiled base and a tube-like duct, with forms a pore at the surface of the skin. Sweat gland were found over the entire areas of the skin, more numerous on the palms, soles, forehead, and armpits
Tuyến mồ hôi gồm có cuộn mồ hôi và tuyến hình ống tạo ra lỗ chân lông ở bề mặt da. Tuyến mồ hôi được tìm thấy ở khắp làn da nhiều nhất là ở lòng bàn tay, bàn chân, trán và nách

- Functions of sweat glands are eliminating waste products. Four things capable of increasing the activity of sweat glands: heat, exercise, mental excitement, and certain drugs
Nhiệm vụ của tuyến mồ hôi là loại chất thải. Bốn điều có thể nâng lên hoạt động của tuyến mồ hôi là nhiệt độ, thể dục, hồi hộp và dược liệu.

- **Oil glands** are found in all parts of the body, with exception of the palms and soles. The chief function of sebum is lubricates the skin and hair, keeping them soft and pliable
Tuyến dầu được tìm thấy ở trên thân thể ngoại trừ lòng bàn tay và lòng bàn chân. Nhiệm vụ chính của tuyến dầu là làm trơn da và tóc, giữ mềm và uyển chuyển

DISEASE AND DISORDERS OF THE SKIN *(Bệnh và sự xáo trộn làn da)*

- Skin is the largest organ of the body. The study of the skin is known as dermatology. Dermatitis is a technical term to indicate an inflammatory condition of the skin.
  Da là bộ phận lớn nhất trong cơ thể. Môn học về da được biết là dermatology. Dermatitis là từ kỹ thuật biểu thị tình trạng sưng da.

- **A keloid** is an over-growth of scar tissue. The technical term for a wart is verruca.
  Keloid (thẹo lồi) là một loại mô nổi lên của thẹo. Tên kỹ thuật của mụn cóc là verruca.

- The technical name for the sweat gland is sudoriferous gland, and they secrete perspiration. A fundus is a coiled base at the end of the sudoriferous glands.
  Tên kỹ thuật cho tuyến mồ hôi là sudoriferous và tuyến tiết ra mồ hôi. Fundus là cuộn ống mồ hôi ở cuối tuyến suforiferous.

- **Fissure** is a crack in the skin, to penetrate into the dermis. A structural change in the tissues caused by injury or diseade is called a lesion.
  Fissure là vết nứt trong da, xâm nhập vào nội bì. Sự thay đổi cấu trúc trong các mô là nguyên nhân do bị thương hoặc bệnh được gọi là vết lở (lesion).

- A keratoma is commonly called a callous. A vesicle is a blister with clear fluid (example: poison ivy produces small vesicles). A bulla is similar to a vesicle, but larger.
  Keratoma là tên mà thông thường được gọi là da chai. Vesicle là mụn nước có chất nước trong (ví dụ: chất độc cây thường xuân tạo mụn nước). Bulla giống như vesicle nhưng lớn hơn

- **The manicurist, esthetician** should be able to recognize common skin disorders to help prevent their spread, and to avoid more serious conditions and refuses to treat a client with infectious diseases to safeguard herseft and the public's health.
  Chuyên viên về móng, da phải có khả năng nhận biết bệnh thông thường để giúp ngăn ngừa lây lan, và để tránh tình trạng trầm trọng hơn và nên khước từ chữa trị cho khách bị bệnh nhiễm trùng để an toàn cho thợ và cho sức khỏe công cộng.

- A dermatologist is a skin specialist. Dermatology is the study of the skin its nature, structure, functions, diseases and treatment
  Dermatologist là bác sĩ đặc biệt về da. Dermatology là môn học về tự nhiên về da, cấu trúc, nhiệm vụ, bệnh và chữa trị cho da.

- **An objectivc lesions** of the skin that can be seen as macule, papule, wheal, tubercle, tumor, vesicle, bulla, and pustule.
  Vết lở objective ở da là vết lở có thể thấy được như macule (đốm ở da như tàn nhang), wheal (ngứa, sưng do côn trùng cắn), tubercle (bướu đặc cở hạt đậu), tumor (bướu lớn), visicle (mụn nước), bulla (mụn nước lớn hơn vesicle), và pustule (mụt sưng có mủ).

- **Seven secondary lesions of skin** are scale, crust, excoriation., fissure, ulcer, scar, and skin stain. They develop in the later stages of the disease.
  Bảy vết lở cấp hai của da là ulcer (lở loét), scale (vẩy), stain (đốm), crust (vảy cứng), excoriation (vết trầy da), fissure (vết nứt), scar (thẹo). Chúng phát triển sau khi trãi qua bệnh.

Bài 11: MÓNG NHÂN TẠO

Móng tip, lụa, bột, gel

Móng nhân tạo là dùng vật liệu gắn, đắp, hoặc phủ lên móng thật. Móng giả có những đặc điểm, mục đích riêng khi dùng như bảo vệ móng, làm móng cứng chắc hoặc che đậy khuyết điểm móng thật, tạo được một bộ móng tay đẹp và thích hợp với các ngón của bàn tay.

1. ***Móng Tip:*** *là loại móng bằng plastic, nylon, acetate. Nếu chỉ gắn tip thôi thì chỉ là tạm thời vì móng rất yếu dễ gãy, vì thế tip gắn lên mặt móng thật thường được kèm theo phủ lụa (silk over lay) thì vừa nhẹ, tự nhiên mà vẫn có được bộ móng dài cứng chắc. Khách chỉ muốn gắn tip, vì họ chỉ muốn tăng chiều dài của móng theo ý riêng.*

   Có 2 loại tip: ***half well*** *là tip có vòng khuyết ngắn gắn vào phần đầu móng và* ***full well*** *là tip có phần khuyết lớn hơn và gắn chặt vào phần móng thật nhiều hơn. Tip được đánh số để dễ chọn lựa. Gắn tip không nên gắn quá nữa móng thật và gắn tip nghiêng 45 độ và well móng khớp với đầu móng thật, giữ tip từ 5 đến 10 giây là tip dính vào móng thật.*

   DRILL MACHINE FOR ARTIFICIAL NAILS

   máy dũa móng bột, móng gel

   Vật liệu làm móng tip cần: ***tip*** *đủ cở từ số 1 đến 10;* ***keo*** *dán móng tip vào móng thật; và* ***buffer*** *để đánh nhẵn lằn nối cho mịn đẹp.*

   Nếu khách chỉ gắn tip thôi thì dễ gãy, do đó cần trở lại salon để cho thêm keo vào lằn giữa móng tip và móng thật và buff lại cho láng. Khi cần lau chùi nước sơn cũ để thay nước sơn mới, nên dùng chất chùi nước sơn (polish remover) không có acetone, vì chất acetone sẽ làm mềm và chảy tan tip.

Carbide bit (đầu giũa dùng cắt móng)

2. **Móng lụa (silk wrap)** chỉ là một trong số các loại bọc bằng fabric. Trên thực tế thợ thường dùng lụa để bọc móng vì vừa chắc lại đẹp, dễ làm. Tuy nhiên còn có **thủy tinh sợi (fiberglass)** là chất liệu tổng hợp bọc móng với những sợi đan thưa, mỏng đẹp và cứng chắc hơn lụa (silk), và loại **vải dày (linen)** sợi dày, thô, chất liệu nặng, màu đục khi cho keo vào nhưng rất chắc. Móng bọc có thể bọc trên móng thật hoặc phủ lên móng đã gắn tip.

   Vì móng tăng trưởng 1/8 inch mỗi tháng nên móng bọc **(nail wrap)** cũng tiến dần phía đầu móng, do đó móng cần bảo trì bằng cách cho thêm keo sau 2 tuần và sau 4 tuần nên cắt lụa vá chỗ trống phía nền móng, thoa keo.

   <u>Vật liệu</u>: keo, kéo nhỏ cắt fabric, buffer, fabric (*lụa, linen, fiber glass*), chất làm keo mau khô).

   Ngoài ra còn một hình thức bọc **móng giấy (paper wrap),** dùng giấy mỏng phủ lên mặt móng và dưới móng. Loại giấy bọc **(mending tissues)** này chỉ dùng tạm thời vì chỉ thoa phết lên chất keo vá móng **(mending liquid)** trên mặt giấy. Chất keo vá dễ tan ra, tróc ra với chất chùi nước sơn acetone hoặc không acetone.

Keo dán móng (adhesive or glue): Keo dán móng hoặc trãi lên lụa thường dùng từng ống nhỏ cở 4 đến 6 gram. Keo giữ được cở 6 tháng tùy cách bảo quản, đầu keo thẳng lên và nên cất giữ trong phòng từ 60 đến 85 độ F.

3. ***Móng bột (nail acrylic)*** *là hình thức dùng loại hóa chất cứng lại để đắp lên móng thật, móng giả, và móng form để giúp móng dài ra, đẹp, và cứng chắc. Đây là sự kết hợp chất lỏng acrylic (**monomer**), bột acrylic (**polymer**) và chất xúc tác (**catalyst**) giúp tăng mau quá trình đông cứng (curing) và tiến trình cứng lại thành móng acrylic gọi là **polymerization**.*

   Có 2 cách đắp bột:
   - *Một màu bột có thể là bột trong suốt (**clear, crytal powder**), bột trắng **(white powder),** và bột hồng **(pink powder).***
   - *Hai màu bột **(French manicure)** là dùng bột trắng ở đầu móng và thân móng dùng bột trong hoặc bột hồng.*

Để có bộ móng bột trắng hồng đẹp mãi, cần hẹn khách trở lại khoảng 2, 3 tuần để refill phần bột hồng. Nhưng sau lần refill thứ hai khoảng 5, 6 tuần tính từ lúc đầu thì phần đầu móng đã dài ra nhiều phía đầu móng (free edge), và phần bột hồng dài ra theo. Bạn phải làm backfill cho khách bằng cách dùng viết chì vẽ lằn cong (smile line) và dùng giũa máy (electric filing) với đầu giũa kim loại nhỏ và dài dùng để cắt (carbide) hoặc đầu giũa nhỏ và ngắn hơn (backfill bit), ép đầu giũa cở 45 độ theo lằn cười khuyết lõm để refill bột trắng, và phần bột hồng vào phần móng mới mọc ra.

Cần dùng máy giũa điện (electric file) gắn đầu giũa (bit) để giũa tùy từng loại và vị trí giũa. Loại đầu giũa giấy dùng 1 lần phải loại bỏ (sanding bands or sander) có nhiều cở, loại 180 hạt là cở trung bình cho móng thật, loại 240 hạt (grid) là cở mịn trung bình để giũa mịn, và loại 350 hạt khá mịn dùng làm láng kết thúc chà móng. Độ hạt của đầu giũa giống như giũa thường và cục chà mịn bằng tay (buffer).

First ball on free edge
viên bột thứ nhất lên đầu móng

Cách làm bột trắng hồng và tuần tự hẹn khách như sau: lần đầu khoảng 2, 3 tuần là refill bột hồng, lần hai khoảng 2, 3 tuần nữa làm backfill cả bột hồng và trắng, lần ba khoảng thêm 2, 3 tuần nữa làm refill bột hồng và cứ thế tiếp tục.

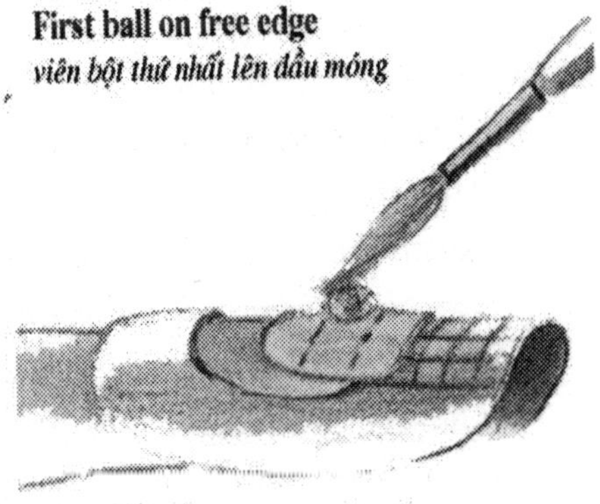

Second ball on center of nail
viên bột thứ hai lên giữa móng

Có thể dùng form và đắp bột cho khách hàng có thói quen cắn móng tay (onychophagy), sau một thời gian móng thật mọc dài ra, gở bỏ móng bột acrylic và khách sẽ bỏ tật cắn móng.

Trong khi mang móng acrylic nếu khách không chăm sóc đúng cách móng sẽ bị nứt, gãy, và hở vì vậy móng dễ bị dơ, ẩm và nấm (fungus). Do đó móng bột acrylic cũng cần bảo trì bằng cách đắp lên (fill) chỗ móng thật mọc ra mỗi 2 hoặc 3 tuần hoặc vá lại ngay chỗ nứt, gãy để móng giữ được lâu và đẹp.

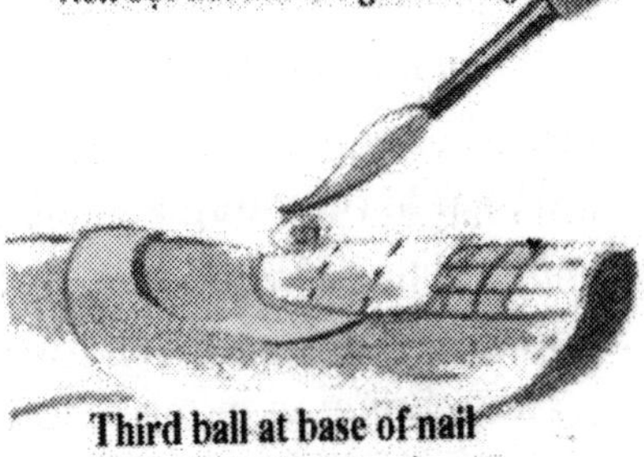

Third ball at base of nail
viên bột thứ ba lên nền móng

*Để cho chất acrylic dính chặt vào móng thật cần thoa chất **Primer** như là lớp lót để sát trùng và là lớp kết dính 2 mặt lại với nhau. Chất **primer** là hóa chất mạnh có thể làm cháy da và đặc biệt cẩn thận văng vào mắt. Khi sử dụng cần mang bao tay và kính an toàn.*

Khi cần tháo móng, tốt nhất là ngâm ngập đầu móng vào acetone, móng sẽ mềm dễ tháo ra. Da và móng sẽ rất khô sau khi gỡ bỏ acrylic. Vì vậy, nên cần thoa dầu (cuticle oil) để da mềm và khôi phục chất dầu của móng và da bị mất.

***Vật liệu** gồm có giũa nhám, buffer, bột acrylic, nước acrylic, cây cọ (brush), tip, nail form, lọ nhỏ, chất primer giúp móng acrylic dính chặt, chất sát trùng (antiseptic), dầu (cuticle oi)l.*

4. **Móng gel** là loại móng làm bằng chất dẽo trắng trong suốt, hoặc có màu trong suốt, dùng đắp móng vừa chắc, nhẹ hơn acrylic không cần phải sơn nếu khách thích loại màu trong này. Hiện nay thị trường sản xuất nhiều loại gel có màu nên kỷ thuật làm móng gel được xem có tính nghệ thuật cao trong ngành manicure. Gel là một hóa chất đậm đặc giống như acrylic và cũng cần chất xúc tác để cứng lại.

   Có hai loại gel:

   - ***Light-cured gel** là loại gel khi đắp lên cần phô móng ra nguồn sáng đặc biệt như nguồn đèn cực tím (Ultra violet), hoặc nguồn đèn halogen để cứng lại.*
   - ***No-light gel** là loại gel không cần đèn mà cần hoạt chất hổ trợ mới cứng được như chất thúc đẩy (activator) xịt lên hoặc nhúng vào nước.*

Gel có thể trãi phủ trên móng thật, móng tip. Trước khi trãi gel lên móng thật phải sạch, đẩy lùi da nền móng để tránh hở gel (lift). Đầu tiên trãi lớp gel mỏng đều lên móng thật hoặc móng có gắn tip, trãi đều nhẹ như sơn móng, tránh đừng thoa gel lên da quanh móng sẽ rất dễ tróc. Sau đó đặt móng đã thoa gel dưới đèn **Ultra Violet** để gel cứng lại gọi là **cure gel.** Tiếp tục móng được thoa lớp gel thứ hai, đặt dưới đèn U.V cứng lại. Làm gel là một nghệ thuật làm móng cao cấp nên cần thực tập nhiều lần mới có được tay nghề giỏi.

***Vật liệu** gồm có: tip, nail form, keo, cục chà nhám (block buffer), primer, cọ lấy gel (gel brush), gel (light-cured gel), đèn U.V để hơ cứng gel.*

<u>Lưu ý:</u> đèn (gel lamp) sẽ làm cứng cây cọ làm gel và gel nếu đặt quá gần đèn. Cách làm cứng móng bằng đèn tùy theo sản phẩm, có loại thoa từng móng gel đặt vào đèn, có loại thoa cả 4 móng gel rồi đặt vào đèn. Do đó luôn theo sự hướng dẫn nhà sản xuất.

Đặc biệt loại gel không cần đèn phải dùng activator là loại hóa chất xịt lên móng và phun xịt từ vòi đến mặt móng cách 8 inches (activator-cured), hoặc loại gel nhúng vào nước ấm từ 2 đến 5 phút để gel cứng lại (water-cured).

***CÁCH GỠ MÓNG GEL:** Ngâm vào acetone như acrylic khoảng 15 đến 25 phút, gel và acrylic sẽ mềm ra, hoặc dùng hóa chất lấy gel (gel remover) tùy theo nhà sản xuất, gel sẽ mềm và dễ dàng gỡ bỏ đi.*

Để được bộ móng gel nhẹ, đẹp có thể chọn cách làm **gel trên form**. Gắn form sát đầu móng và đặt gel tạo đầu móng mới (**free edge**) trước, đặt dưới đèn U.V cho cứng gel đầu móng, sau đó cho gel lên mặt móng thật, form móng, làm cứng mặt gel lại và lấy form ra, giũa móng…..

Theo thời gian móng thật mọc dài ra, do đó khách mang bộ móng tay gel cần bảo trì cứ mỗi 2 đến 3 tuần bằng cách giũa nhám chỗ móng thật mới mọc và thoa gel lên (fill gel), làm cứng gel, giũa gel, buff gel cho khớp với lớp gel cũ.

ARTIFICIAL NAILS (*TIP; WRAP; ACRYLIC & GEL NAILS)*

(Các loại móng giả (tip; bao; bột và móng gel)

NAIL TIPS: *Móng tip*

- Apply tips to the natural nail to add extra length, very weak if not wear overlay such as a fabric wrap or over acrylic nail.
  Gắn tip đến móng thật là tăng thêm chiều dài, rất yếu nếu không có lớp gì trãi lên như móng lụa hoặc bột acrylic.
- **Nail adhesive**: glue or bonding agent used to secure the nail tip to the natural nail. It can be very dangerous if glue drop in the eyes. A manicurist and the client should always wear safety goggles when using nail adhesives.
  Keo dán móng là loại keo kết chặc dùng để dán móng típ vào móng thật. Có thể rất nguy hiểm nếu keo nhiễu vào mắt. Thợ chăm sóc tay và khách nên mang kính lồi che mắt khi dùng keo móng.
- **Nail tips**: the tip should never cover more than ½ of the natural nail plate, all tips have a well that serves as the point of contact with the nail plate.
  Móng tip không bao giờ nên phủ lên hơn nữa móng thật, các móng tip có rãnh bên dưới tiếp giáp với móng thật.
- Although your client's tips blend perfectly with natural nails, tips are very seldom worn without an additional nail service such as wraps, acrylic nails, or gel nails.
  Mặc dầu móng tip gắn hoàn hảo với móng thật nhưng móng tip cần đắp thêm bao móng, bột hoặc gel.

  * Weekly or biweekly manicure for re-glue of rebuffing, most tips need none acetone polish remover because acetone remover dissolves the tips.
  Mỗi tuần hoặc 2 tuần một lần chăm sóc tay nên thêm keo và chà mịn lại, móng tip nên dùng chất chùi móng không có chất aceton vì chất aceton sẽ làm tan mềm móng tip.
- Tips that have been glued to the nail plate can cause damage if removed improperly. Use a glue remover or acetone to remove tips.
  Móng tip được gắn keo tới móng thật có thể bị hư nếu gỡ ra không đúng cách. Dùng chất làm mềm keo hoặc chất aceton để gỡ bỏ móng tip.

NAIL WRAP: *Móng bọc*

Nail wraps, sometimes called overlays, and are nail-sized pieces of cloth or paper with nail adhesive

Móng bao còn gọi là móng được phủ lên, và được dùng vải hoặc giấy với keo dán móng

- Fabric wraps are made form fiberglass, silk, or linen.
  Vật liệu bao móng được làm bằng thủy tinh sợi, lụa hoặc vải dày
  - **Fiberglass** (thin synthetic) is a loose weave. It makes easy for adhesive to penetrate.
    Thủy tinh sợi (sợi tổng hợp mỏng) là loại sợi đan thưa. Dễ dàng cho keo dính chặt vào
  - **Silk** is tight weave that very clear when glue is applied, silk is a thin material but strong, lightweight and smooth.
    Lụa là vật liệu có sợi đan chặt rất trong khi cho keo vào, lụa là vải mỏng nhưng cứng chắc, nhẹ và mịn màng.
  - **Linen** is a closely woven, heavy material. It is a strong wrap and thicker than silk or fiberglass.
    Vải thô là loại sợi đan dày, vật liệu thô. Bọc rất cứng chắc và dày hơn lụa và thủy tinh sợi

- Fabric wraps need regular maintenance to keep them looking fresh
  Loại bao móng bằng vải, lụa hoặc thủy tinh sợi bảo trì thường xuyên để luôn luôn trông đẹp.
  - Two weeks maintenance (1/16 inch with glue and buff)
    Bảo trì 2 tuần một lần (chỗ hở 1/16 inch thêm keo và chà mịn)
  - Four weeks maintenance (fill with adhesive and silk)

Bảo trì 4 tuần (keo và lụa và chà mịn)

* Liquid nail wrap is similar to nail hardener, but thicker, made up of tiny fibers designed to strengthen and preserve the natural nail as it grows.
Keo cho bao móng giống như chất làm cứng móng, nhưng đặc hơn, làm bằng những sợi nhỏ tạo ra cho mạnh móng và bảo quản móng thật lúc mọc ra.

- Paper wrap are made of very thin paper (mending tissues). It is dissolved in both acetone and non-acetone remover. Paper wraps are temporary to add strength for a short period of time.
  Bao giấy bằng loại giấy mỏng (giấy vá). Giấy bị tan trong aceton và chất lấy nước sơn không aceton. Giấy bao là loại dịch vụ tạm thời thêm vào độ mạnh cho móng trong khoảng thời gian ngắn.

ACRYLIC NAILS: *Móng bột*

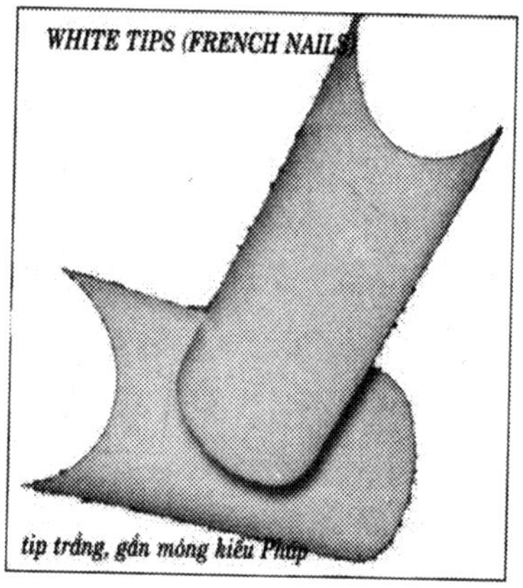

- Acrylic nails also known as sculptured or build-on nails are made by combining a liquid acrylic product with a powdered acrylic product.
  Móng bột cũng còn gọi là móng sculpture hoặc móng tự tạo ra được làm bằng sự kết hợp nước acrylic và bột acrylic.

- There are three basic ingredients in the acrylic nail process.
  Có 3 thành phần căn bản trong tiến trình làm móng bột.
  - Liquid acrylic is a type of monomer.
    Nước acrylic là dạng monomer (chất tạo sự kết dính)
  - Finished acrylic nail s are polymers. They are usually solid
    Hoàn tất móng là polymers (thành phần kết chuỗi). Thường là dạng đặc
  - A catalyst is an ingredient that speeds up the hardening process and make a chemical reaction go faster.
    Catalyst là chất xúc tác là thành phần thúc đẩy tiến trình cứng lại và tạo ra phản ứng hoá học được nhanh hơn.

- The process of forming the acrylic nail is called polymerization. Chemical reactions make polymers also are polymerizations that mean cure or hardening.
  Tiến trình tạo cứng móng bột được gọi là polymerization. Phản ứng hóa học làm polymer cũng là polymerization nghĩa là cứng lại (cure) hoặc đóng cứng lại (hardening).

- **There are two acrylic nail methods-one-color and two-color**. French acrylic nails is the two-color method uses white acrylic powder for the free edge and clear, or pink powder for the nail plate and needs no polish.
  Có 2 phương pháp làm móng bột là một màu và hai màu. Móng acrylic kiểu Pháp là phương pháp 2 màu, dùng bột trắng ở phần đầu móng và bột trong hoặc hồng ở thân móng
- Acrylic powder consist of white, clear, natural, and pink powder is available.
  Bột acrylic gồm có màu trắng, trong, tự nhiên và hồng.

- Primer applied to the natural nail so that the acrylic product will adhere to the natural nail. Primer can be etching primers and non-etching primer. **Etching primer** can burn the nail bed tissue and stronger than **non-eching primer**
  Chất primer thoa lên móng thật để giúp bột acrylic dính chặt vào móng thật. Primer có thể là loại etching và không etching. Loại eching primer có thể bỏng các mô của đệm móng và mạnh hơn không non-etching primer.

- **Eching primer** will not damage the nail plate but can damage to skin and eyes. Wear safety glasses and plastic gloves when apply primer to the nail plate.
  Eching primer không làm hư thân móng nhưng có thể làm hư hại đến da và mắt. Mang kính an toàn và bao tay khi thoa primer đến thân móng
- If the nails lift, crack, or grow out with no maintenance, moisture and dirt can trapped under acrylic nail and fungus can begin to grow.
  Nếu móng bị hở, tróc, hoặc mọc ra mà không bảo trì, chất ẩm và dơ có thể nhét bên dưới móng bột và nấm có thể phát triển ra.

- **Most odorless acrylics** are self-leveling. As the product sets, it automatically levels off, so there is less shaping required. Odorless acrylics are products that do not smell as strongly as traditional acrylic products.
  Hầu hết bột acrylic không mùi có đặc tính riêng của chúng. Khi dùng bột như tự động chảy vì thế chỉ dành cho móng muốn đắp thấp tự nhiên. Loại odorless acrylic không tạo mùi khó chịu như loại cũ thông thường (traditional acrylic).

- Never mix any acrylics liquid and any acrylics powder (odor or odorless) together. A fill-in will be necessary in two or three weeks, depending on how quickly the nails grow.
  Không bao giờ pha trộn bất cứ loại nước acrylic nào và bất kỳ loại bột nào với nhau. Cần bảo trì (fill-in) khoảng 2 hoặc 3 tuần, tùy theo móng mọc nhanh hay chậm.

GELS: *Móng gel*

- Gels are strong, durable artificial nails that are brushed on the nail plate like polish.
  Gel là loại tạo móng giả mạnh, bền chắc dùng cọ trãi gel lên mặt móng như thoa nước sơn
- There are two types of gels: *Có hai loại gel*
  - **Light-cured gels** harden when they are exposed to a special light source-either an ultraviolet light or a halogen light.
  Gel cứng lại cần đèn khi đưa móng vào nguồn đèn cực tím (ultraviolet) hoặc đèn nhiệt (halogen)
  - **No-light gels** harden when a gel activator (adhesive dryer) is sprayed or brushed on, hold it about 8 inches or when they are soaked in warm water from 2 to 5 minutes.
  Gel không cần đèn được cứng lại khi dùng chất gel xúc tác (chất khô keo) được xịt hoặc thoa lên, xịt cần giữ khoảng cách cở 8 inch từ móng khách hoặc nhúng vào nước ấm từ 2 đến 5 phút.
- Gels are available in colors that need no polish. Colored gels are a great base for nail art.
  Móng gel cũng có màu không cần phải sơn. Gel màu là một căn bản tuyệt vời của nghệ thuật móng

Be carcful not to damage the natural nail plate by buffing too roughly.
Cẩn thận hư móng thật do chà móng quá sần sùi

- To strengthen and lengthen their natural nails with a lightweight artificial nail may choose gel nails over forms.
  Để làm mạnh và dài cho móng trông nhẹ nhàng có thể chọn móng gel đắp trên miếng form.

- **Both light-cured** and non-light-cured gels should be maintained every two to three weeks, depending on how fast the client's nails grow.
  Cả 2 loại móng gel cần đèn và không cần đèn nên chăm sóc lại cứ mỗi 2 tới 3 tuần, tùy theo tốc độ móng mọc của khách.
- Use gel remover or aceton remove gel nails by soak client's nails for a few minutes in small glass bowl.
  Dùng chất gỡ gel hoặc aceton lấy gel móng bằng các nhúng móng vài phút trong tô thủy tinh nhỏ.

Bài 12: MÁY GIŨA ĐIỆN VÀ NGHỆ THUẬT TRÊN MÓNG

Xử dụng giũa máy điện **(electric file)** cần thành thạo, hiểu biết để tránh gây thương tổn cho khách. Trong khi giũa dễ tạo sức nóng khi ép mạnh với vòng quay quá nhanh.
Có nhiều loại giũa trong kỷ nghệ làm móng, có loại dùng chân đạp (foot pedals) để kiểm soát tốc độ quay, hoặc loại dùng pin, dây belt v.v....

Với loại giũa chuyên nghiệp vừa bền vừa tiện gọn để trên bàn làm móng, máy cũng khá đắt tiền từ $200 đến $700.

DRILL MACHINE FOR ARTIFICIAL NAILS

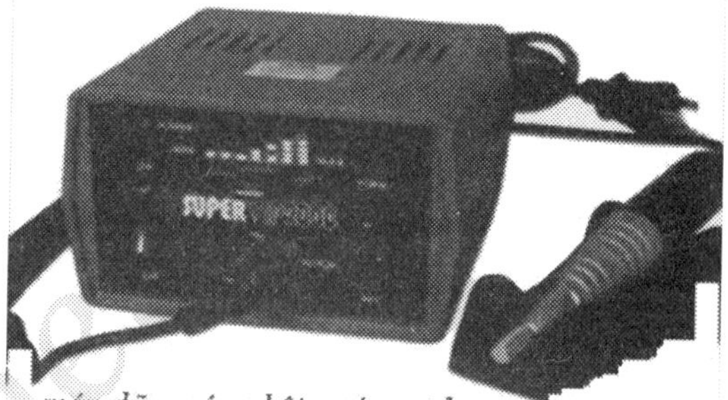

máy dũa móng bột, móng gel

Giũa máy cần chọn lựa kỹ sao cho hệ thống motor đủ mạnh, được thông khí không nóng, tốc độ quay cần thiết, sức ép của giũa trên mỗi inch vuông (horsepower). Máy giũa phải điều chỉnh tốc độ, chỉnh chiều quay dễ dàng trong từng vị trí trên móng nhân tạo. Người thuận tay trái thích hợp hơn vì chiều quay tới cũng như dễ tập hướng ngược lại hơn.

Tốc độ giũa máy có thể từ 100 RPMs đến 35.000 RPMs tùy theo ngành nghề ứng dụng. Để giũa móng bột acrylic, gel...., thợ móng chỉ cần độ vòng qua trong một phút từ 5.000 đến 15.000 vòng.
Ví dụ: *7.000 RPMs là số vòng quay cọ xát lên móng 7.000 lần trong một phút.*

RPMs: Revolutions Per Minute (vòng quay trong 1 phút)

Đầu giũa có nhiều loại, với loại hình ống tròng vào và chỉ dùng cho mỗi người khách phải vứt bỏ, loại hạt lớn nhỏ trên mỗi đầu giũa khác nhau. Hạt (grit) trị số càng lớn thì độ nhám nhiều, giũa mòn nhanh, càng nhiều hạt càng mịn.
Ví dụ: đầu giũa khoảng 100 hạt, hoặc 260 hạt làtính trên mổi square inch.

- **Các loại đầu giũa** kim loại, kim cương thì tính theo dạng và tác dụng khác nhau, loại này có thể diệt trùng và dùng lại.
- **Đầu kim cương** (diamond bit) cũng có loại mịn, nhám dùng trên bề mặt móng;
- **Đầu giũa làm móng chân** (pedicure bit) dạng tròn hình ống hoặc hình chóp dính hạt diamond thích hợp giũa da chai, móng dày.
- **Đầu giũa cắt móng** (carbitde bit) hoặc tạo lằn cong cười (backfill bit). Đầu giũa làm mịn bóng bằng cao su tổng hợp (natural nail bit),. Đầu giũa nhọn, dài để xỏ lỗ trên móng (jewelry bit).

CÁC ĐẦU GIŨA KỂ TRÊN DIỆT TRÙNG NHƯ CÁCH DIỆT TRÙNG DỤNG CỤ KHÁC.

Riêng loại bọc đầu giũa đen, nâu hình ống dễ làm nóng móng, mài nhanh **(sanding band)** và đầu đánh bóng với kem chà **(buffing bit)** cần **vứt bỏ sau mỗi lần làm cho khách.**
Trục đầu giũa cho các loại gắn vào motor giũa đường kính cở 3/32 inch (1/4 phân).
Khi giũa mặt móng luôn để ý đầu giũa cọ xát ngang bằng mặt móng, đi tới lui và tránh ép mạnh.

Đối với móng nứt, hở (lifted product) nên dùng đầu giũa lằn cong cười (French backfill bit) cắt cở 75% lõm xuống rồi đẩy ngược móng hở ra sau, không kéo mạnh.

Khi làm backfill là khách hàng đã làm móng bột trắng hồng từ 5-6 tuần, đã refill một lần bột trắng hồng cách lần đầu 2 – 3 tuần, nay phần móng trắng và hồng đã ra quá dài, do đó phải làm backfill, dùng viết chì vẽ lằn cong (smile line) và dùng giũa máy (electric filing) với đầu giũa kim loại nhỏ và dài dùng để cắt (carbide) hoặc đầu giũa nhỏ và ngắn hơn (backfill bit), ép đầu giũa cở 45 độ lõm theo lằn cười để refill bột trắng, và phần bột hồng vào phần móng mới mọc ra.

Trong kỷ thuật làm móng bột acrylic, móng gel, móng bột trắng hồng (pink and white acrylic) cần dùng máy giũa vừa nhanh, tạo dáng dễ dàng và đẹp hơn, vừa tiết kiệm thời gian năng lực.

NGHỆ THUẬT TRÊN MÓNG

Nguồn lợi tức không nhỏ đối với chuyên viên ngành chăm sóc tay chân là tạo kiểu, vẽ hình hoặc những chất liệu thêm vào trước khi và trong khi sơn móng. Khách ở những vùng nắng ấm thường khoe nét đẹp ở móng tay, chân, cũng là cơ hội để biểu hiện sự tươi mát bằng nghệ thuật lên móng như sơn móng kiểu Pháp *(French manicure);* xịt màu lên móng *(airbrush)* hòa lẫn nhiều màu sắc; vẽ cảnh *(freehand painting)*; chỉ có keo tạo sọc *(striping tape);* đá màu *(gem);* miếng kim loại vàng, bạc v.v.... Để tạo nghệ thuật vẽ, cần hiểu qui tắc về màu sắc (color theory):

- *Nhóm màu thứ NHẤT (**primary colors**): là những màu căn bản nguyên thủy, không phải pha trộn để có được là những màu **VÀNG, ĐỎ,** và **XANH**.*
- *Nhóm màu thứ NHÌ (**secondary colors**): là những màu được tạo thành từ sự pha trộn cùng số lượng của 2 màu thứ nhất và màu thứ hai đó cũng bổ sung cho màu thứ nhất đã tạo ra.*
  *<u>Ví dụ:</u> màu thứ NHÌ là **XANH LÁ CÂY** do pha trộn cùng số lượng của 2 màu nhóm thứ nhất là **VÀNG + XANH BIỂN**, hoặc màu thứ nhì là **CAM** do pha trộn của 2 màu **ĐỎ + VÀNG**, và màu thứ nhì là **TÍM** do pha trộn của 2 màu **ĐỎ + XANH BIỂN**.*
  *Vậy màu **XANH LÁ CÂY, CAM, TÍM** là thuộc nhóm màu thứ NHÌ.*
- *Nhóm màu thứ BA (**tertiary colors**): màu thứ nhất pha cùng số lượng màu thứ hai kế cận.*
  *<u>Ví dụ:</u> màu thứ nhất là **ĐỎ** pha với màu **CAM**; hoặc màu **CAM** pha với màu **VÀNG**; hoặc màu **VÀNG** pha với **XANH LÁ CÂY** v.v..... Đó là những màu (đỏ+cam); (cam + vàng); (vàng + xanh lá) ......thuộc nhóm màu thứ BA.*
- *Nhóm màu thứ TƯ (**complementary colors**): là màu trực tiếp đối diện trong bảng qui luật màu mà khi được pha trộn sẽ tạo màu trung hòa, nâu. Và những màu này đặt kề nhau sẽ nổi hẳn lên về nghệ thuật màu.*
  *<u>Ví dụ:</u> màu **XANH BIỂN** pha với màu đối diện là **CAM**; màu **ĐỎ** pha với màu đối diện là **XANH LÁ CÂY**; hoặc màu **VÀNG** pha với màu đối diện là **TÍM**.*
  *Riêng màu **ĐEN** và màu **TRẮNG** không được xem là màu. Tuy nhiên nhất định luôn có sự hiện diện những màu này trong nghệ thuật pha màu.*

* **FRENCH MANICURE** (*móng tay kiểu Pháp*): sơn 2 màu trên móng, thân móng màu hồng nhạt như màu nền, hoặc màu trong, vẽ màu trắng cong (smile line) ở đầu móng (free edge), hoặc dùng mẫu giấy cắt sẵn (stencil) để xịt bằng airbrush trông rất đẹp, ngoài ra cũng dùng cách này cho móng chân.

* **FREEHAND PAINTING** (*sơn móng tùy sáng kiến*): đó là cách dùng cọ nhỏ, cây que nhỏ, nhọn tạo hình hoa lá cành, hình lá cờ ngày lễ độc lập, con thú, hoặc ông già Noel v.v...

* **GEMS** (*gắn mãnh đá nhỏ lên móng*): móng sau khi sơn lót, sơn màu. Sau đó dùng que nhỏ chấm vào nước phủ bóng (top coat) để lấy mãnh đá đặt lên lớp sơn còn ướt, móng khô xong phũ lên top coat. Vàcũng có cách trãi lên móng những lá vàng hay bạc là những miếng kim loại mỏng như giấy.
Khi cần lau đi chỉ cần dùng chất chùi nước sơn hoặc chất nước mạnh hơn như acetone là lau ra ngay.

***STRIPING TAPE** (*chỉ màu có keo tạo vệt*): chỉ keo có nhiều màu trong cuộn, trãi lên ngang, dọc, xéo, dùng dao cắt theo ý, cách móng cở 1/16 inch, cần phủ lên chỉ keo nước bóng (top coat).

ELECTRIC FILING AND DESIGN TECHNIQUES ON NAILS

(Máy giũa điện và nghệ thuật trên móng)

Choosing an electric file has a high and low speed, adjusts forward and backward. Most electric files start 100 RPMs to 35,000 RPMs. The average manicurists choose from 5,000 to 15,000 RPMs. *Chọn máy giũa sao cho điều chỉnh được tốc độ cao thấp, tới lui. Hầu hết máy giũa có vòng quay từ 100 đến 35 ngàn vòng . Thợ làm móng nên chọn máy từ 5.000 tới 15.000 vòng trong một phút.*

RPMs: Revolutions Per Minute (vòng quay trong 1 phút)

The **bit** is just as important as the electric file you buy it. *(đầu giũa là phần quan trong của máy)*

- **Sanding bands** come in fine, coarse grids from 100 grids to 260 grids (on square inch), round, black, heat up faster than a metal bit. They are good for shotening nail acrylic, gel.
- **Buffing bits** such as chamois, brushes. These are great for high gloss shine on nail surface.

Đầu giũa nhám *có nhiều cở từ min đến lớn vàđộ hạt 100 đến 260 hạt trên 1 inch vuông, hình ống tròn, đen, dễ làm nóng móng hơn đầu kim loại. Tốt cho làm ngắn móng bột, gel. Đầu giũa chà bóng bọc da, vải giúp đánh bóng móng*

Sanding bands and buffing bits are discarded after each customer *(2 loại đầu giũa này vứt bỏ sau khi dùng)*

Diamond bits are made of metal and diamond come in extra fine to coarse grids. These are good for cut for artificial nails. **Carbide bits** are made of metal, very sharp and **Backfill bits** smaller good for trench out the growth at the smile line. **Pedicure bits** are a large barrel or cone shapes with diamond bits. This is good for dry callus.

Đầu giũa kim cương *làm bằng kim loại phủ hạt kim cương và có cở mịn đến hạt lớn. Loại này dùng để cắt móng giả.* ***Đầu giũa carbide*** *bằng kim loại, bén và loại* ***đầu giũa backfill*** *nhỏ hơn, giúp cho khoét mương mặt móng tạo lằn cong cười khi đắt thêm bột acrylic trắng.* ***Đầu giũa làm chân*** *có hình ống, hình chóp bằng kim loại bọc kim cương để mài da chai ở chân.*

Bits in nails industry for shank size of bits is 3/32 inch (1/4 centimetter)

Trục đầu giũa có đường kính cở 3/32 inch (1/4 phân)

All bits above have to disinfect the same as your implements after used *(cần diệt trùng sau khi dùng)*

Many companies that introduce some electric files much better equipment and guide line for their product how to use these machines safely. Educating your customers about electric file ia safe tool and never hurting them with a professional manicurist.

Nhiều nhà sản xuất máy giũa đã giới thiệu khá nhiều thiết bi giũa và kèm hướng dẫn cách dùng an toàn cho khách. Cần giải thích cho khách sự an toàn của máy giũa khi bạn dùng và không bao giờ bị tổn thương cho khách nếu thợ móng chuyên nghiệp.

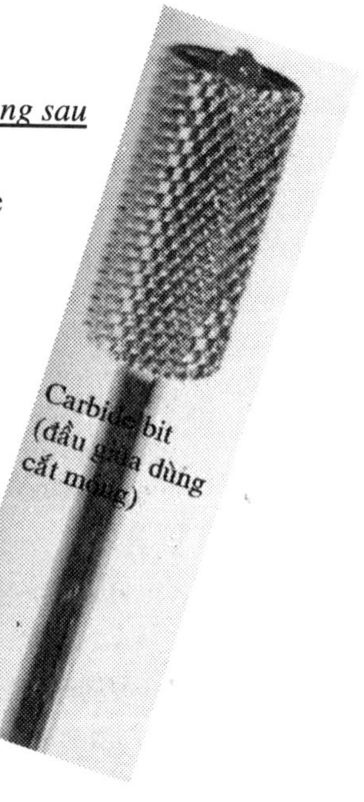

Carbide bit (đầu giũa dùng cắt móng)

DESIGN TECHNIQUES ON NAILS

- Gems, foiling, striping tape, gold leafing, color acrylic paiting, French manicure, two color fade... are the nails art. For example: red gel, polish half, stars, stripes, cats eyes, and tiger lilies., highlighted with a rhinestone dew drop.

  Đá quí, giấy kim loại, keo chỉ, lá vàng, bột acrylic màu, móng tay kiểu Pháp, hai màu chồng nhau... là nghệ thuật của móng. Ví dụ: gel đỏ, sơn ½ móng, ngôi sao, sọc, mắt mèo, và vằn cọp, làm sáng lên với loại đá lấp lánh như sương.

- **Gems** give sparkle; tiny rhinestones are popular nail art materials. Use a wet orange wood stick or tweezers to pick up small gems on the shiny side of the stone. Put them on while the top coat of the polish is still tacky so gems will adhere. Reapply top coat.
  Gems tạo sự lấp lánh, những viên đá nhỏ thông dụng cho nghệ thuật của móng. Dùng que gỗ cam hoặc nhíp để gắp những viên đá có mặt óng ánh. Đặt đá lên móng đã thoa nước bóng và sẽ dính đá lên đó. Thoa lại nước bóng.
- **Striping tape:** Tape has a tacky backing and is stuck to a dry then polish nail. Cut it 1/16 inch away from cuticle and free edge. Seal tape on nail with top coat and reapply top coat every three to four days.
  ***Keo chỉ sọc:** Keo có mặt sau dính và dán lên mặt móng khô và sơn móng. Cắt keo chỉ cách da 1/16 inch và đầu móng. Thoa lớp bóng cho dính chặt và cứ thoa thêm lớp bóng cách 3 tới 4 ngày.*
- **Foil** is very fragile leafing that is available in gold, silver and copper. Use tweezers to remove the pieces of foil on the tacky top coat. Seal the foil with a top coat and reapply the top coat.
  ***Foil** là lá kim loại dòn có thể là lá vàng, bạc, và đồng. Dùng nhíp gắp từng miếng nhỏ foil lên trên lớp sơn bóng. Thoa lớp bóng lên và thoa thêm lớp nữa.*
- **Gold leaf application:** Apply clear & nail polish on area you want covered. Use tweezers or orangewood stick, place bits of gold and press gold leaf flat on nail. Apply clear polish over gold leaf to seal. Let dry
  Gold leaf là nguyên chiếc lá vàng kim loại đặt lên lớp sơn bóng. Dùng nhíp hoặc que gỗ dính vào miếng lá vàng và ép miếng lá vàng lên móng. Thoa nước bóng lên lá vàng chặt lại. Đợi khô.
- **Airbrush** for nail art: You must use a design tool, stencil or mask paper. An airbrush looks like a small spray gun. It uses compressed air to force paint out of its tip creating a fine mist of paint.
  Dùng airbrush cho móng kiểu: Bạn phải dùng dụng cụ xịt sơn móng, mẫu hình kiểu hoặc miếng che xịt. Airbrush giống như súng xịt nhỏ. Ép không khí để đẩy sơn ra như sương xịt sơn.

PRIMARY COLORS *(màu thứ nhất)*

Three basic colors (*3 màu căn bản*)

BLUE RED YELLOW

SECONDARY COLORS *(màu thứ hai)*

Mixing equal portions of 2 primary colors
Trộn 2 màu căn bản đều nhau

Blue + Red	**VIOLET**
Blue + Yellow	**GREEN**
Red + Yellow	**ORANGE**

TERTIARY COLORS *(màu thứ ba)*

Mixing equal portions of 1 primary and 1 secondary color *(Trộn màu thứ 1& 2 đều nhau)*
Blue + Green; Blue + Violet; Green +Yellow...

COMPLEMENTARY COLORS *(màu thứ tư)*

Colors directly opposite each other, 2 complementary colors are mixed; they neutralize each other by creating brown
(2 màu đối diện trộn đều trung hòa nhau tạo màu nâu)

* ***Blue + Orange***	*NEUTRAL*	***Dark brown*** *(nâu đậm)*
* ***Red + Green***	*NEUTRAL*	***Reddish brown*** *(nâu đỏ)*
* ***Yellow + Violet***	*NEUTRAL*	***Golden brown*** *(nâu nhạt)*

If three primary colors such as (blue + red +yellow) are mixed in equal parts becomes black
(nếu 3 màu căn bản thứ nhất (xanh, đỏ, vàng) trộn đều

- **Two colors fade**: The color fade, or color blend, is one of the most used airbrushed nail color services.
  Xịt trộn 2 màu: Làm màu trộn với nhau, hoặc trộn haimàu lẫn lộn, là cách dùng airbrushed xịt lẫn với nhau.
- **Traditional French manicure:** The airbrushed French is easier, quicker & more attractive than the hand polished version.
  Loại chăm sóc móng tay kiểu Pháp: Dùng airbrush kiểu Pháp dễ hơn, nhanh hơn & hấp dẫn hơn cách sơn tay.
- Apply a clear base coat to the nail. French tip application with stencil. Mist paint then blow air to dry the nail tip and stencil. After completed, apply paint border and let it dry for 3 minutes. This procedure is easily accomplished on toe nails.
  Thoa lớp nước bóng lên móng. Dùng mẫu cắt sẵn để xịt viền trắng kiểu Pháp. Hơi sơn xịt thổi lên móng khô và mẫu cắt sẵn. Sau khi xong, thoa sơn viền móng và để khô khoảng 3 phút. Cách này cũng dễ xịt lên móng chân.

Bài 13: PHÁT TRIỂN SALON

Bạn đang hành nghề thẩm mỹ thì cũng nên nghĩ một lúc nào đó bạn trở thành chủ nhân một salon. Có thể là salon nhiều dịch vụ thẩm mỹ hoặc chỉ chuyên về nails. Kinh doan salon là mang trách nhiệm lớn, do đó cần có kiến thức về thương mãi, kế toán, bảo hiểm, luật địa phương, tiểu bang, và liên bang, đồng thời tâm lý cũng là những yếu tố cần yếu cho những ai khao khát trở thành chủ tiệm.

YẾU TỐ MỞ TIỆM:

1. ***Địa điểm*** *luôn là điều cần lưu ý như đông đúc dân chúng sống quanh vùng, salon nên gần những nơi hoạt động thương mãi phát triển, nhà hàng, chợ, và xe cộ qua lại nhiều. Đồng thời tìm hiểu sự tiêu dùng dân chúng quanh vùng, thu nhập cá nhân.... . Salon phải trong tầm nhìn, hấp dẫn và thu hút khách đi bộ. Chỗ đậu xe thuận tiện để khách không phải lo lắng. Và tránh sự cạnh tranh với đồng nghiệp.*
2. ***Bảng hợp đồng*** *ghi rõ salon có thay đổi hoặc cần sữa chữa cơ sở kinh doanh thế nào sau khi ký hợp đồng để tránh sự bất đồng, cần hiểu điều nào thuộc về chủ và về người thuê. Nếu cần thuê luật sư để thương lượng hợp đồng.*
3. ***Bảng kế hoạch kinh doanh*** *ghi chi tiết chi phí cho tiền lương, huê hồng, sữa chữa, quảng cáo, thuế, bảo hiểm, vật liệu tiêu dùng, lợi nhuận và thua lỗ, đủ nguồn vốn hoạt động, thời gian cần thiết tạo được lượng khách hàng thường xuyên, nói chung lập bảng kế hoạch kinh doanh để vay mượn vốn cần những yếu tố trên, tốt nhất nên tham khảo với chuyên viên kinh tế.*

NAILS SALON – FULL SERVICE SALON

Nails salon: có thể bạn chỉ mở tiệm làm móng tay chân mà thôi, như thế có lợi cho những người thợ chia xẻ, học hỏi, trao đổi kinh nghiệm công việc, dễ dàng thay thế khi có người nghĩ bệnh. Đồng thời khách đến chăm sóc móng cũng thích đến chuyên môn của tiệm và chuyên môn của người thợ sẽ dễ dàng tạo được lượng khách trung thành.

Full service salon: salon phục vụ nhiều việc như tóc, da, massage thì thường chỉ 1 hoặc 2 người thợ làm móng. Sự tiện lợi cho khách làm tóc, da mặt và làm móng tay chân tiết kiệm thì giờ vì khỏi phải đến nơi khác. Tuy nhiên cũng có bất tiện là khi đau bệnh khó có người thay thế và vì không cạnh tranh nên không học hỏi được nhiều kỹ thuật hay từ đồng nghiệp.

Dù bạn mở salon hình thức nào bạn cần có sự hiểu biết về căn bản thương mãi, luật, bảo hiểm và ngay cả tìm hiểu tâm lý người tiêu dùng nữa.

Salon cần trình bày đẹp và hợp lý, bàn của thư ký, nhận phone gọi hẹn là nơi quan trọng, là nguồn thu nhập của tiệm. Trên bàn tiếp khách nên chưng hoa, các lối đi trong salon thuận tiện, restroom sạch sẽ, salon cần thông thoáng tốt và nhất là trả lời thật chuyên nghiệp.

HÌNH THỨC LÀM CHỦ SALON

- ***Cá nhân (individual ownership):*** *là hình thức làm chủ chỉ một người, vừa quản lý và có thể là thợ. Đây là cách làm chủ lời ăn lỗ chịu, người chủ tự quyết định mọi việc của salon.*
- ***Hùm hạp (partnership):*** *là hình thức làm chủ từ 2 người trở lên. Lợi điểm của cách làm chủ này là có được nhiều vốn, chia xẻ công việc, trách nhiệm và cùng có quyết định chung phát triển salon.*
- ***Công ty (corporation):*** *là cách làm chủ từ 3 người trở lên, hình thức cổ phần. Công ty bắt buộc phải có điều lệ riêng chặt chẽ, có bảo hiểm hỏa hoạn, cắp, trộm, tai nạn do bất cẩn xảy ra cho khách. Với hình thức cổ phần không bị mất mát phần tài sản riêng nếu cơ sở làm ăn thua lỗ, chỉ mất cổ phần tham dự vào công ty.*

Dù hình thức nào, cơ sở kinh doanh cần phải hiểu biết điều lệ, luật, và bảo hiểm để hoạt động kinh doanh hợp pháp.

- Điều lệ địa phương (local regulations): sửa chữa, thay đổi về cấu trúc cơ sở.
- Luật tiểu bang (state laws): thuế bán, lệ phí giấy phép hành nghề, bồi thường nhân viên có thương tích.
- Luật liên bang (federal laws): an sinh xã hội, bồi thường thất nghiệp, pha chế mỹ phẩm, hóa chất, cơ quan bảo quản an toàn nghề nghiệp (OSHA).
- Luật thuế thu nhập (income tax laws): phụ trách cả tiểu bang và liên bang
- Bảo hiểm (insurance): rủi ro nghề nghiệp, bị hỏa hoạn, cướp, trộm, cơ sở tạm không hoạt động.

Giữ sổ sách salon là một trong yếu tố quan trọng để rõ sự chi tiêu, thu nhập, chi phí hàng ngày, tuần , tháng, như chi phí lặt vặt hàng ngày cần tổng kết giao cho người kế toán và cũng để định giá trị của salon từng năm và giá bán cho người có ý muốn mua cơ sở của bạn nữa.

Salon phục vụ khách được phép mở bán sản phẩm liên hệ đến dịch vụ làm đẹp (beauty supplies). Tuy nhiên để hợp thức hóa cơ sở cần xin giấy phép (sale permit), để tính phần thuế thanh toán lại sở thuế tiểu bang sau mỗi kỳ 3 tháng, cũng như nộp những chi phí được trừ ra từ nhân viên. Do đó cần có người trông coi về sổ sách kế toán cho salon (book keeping).

Sản phẩm trong tiệm gồm: thuốc, hóa chất, sản phẩm sử dụng, tiêu thụ cho nhu cầu khách hàng ***(consumption supplies)*** và sản phẩm để bán lẽ cho khách mang về sử dụng ***(retail supplies).***

Sản phẩm ở salon cần kiểm toán tồn kho để không bị thiếu sót trong khi sử dụng và dự trù cho những dịp lễ thường năm. Tuy nhiên cũng đừng ham rẻ mua số lượng lớn sản phẩm trở nên tồn đọng gây trở ngại nguồn vốn luân lưu và cất giữ lâu hóa chất mất tác dụng phải loại bỏ….

Chi phí salon được phân phối tương đối sau đây: tiền lương cho thợ hoặc ăn chia (commissions) khoảng 50% đến 60%; thuê địa điểm khoảng 13% đến 18% ; sản phẩm tiêu thụ dùng cho khách khoảng 5% đến 8%; quảng cáo khoảng 3% đến 5% và chi phí linh tinh cho salon khoảng 3%.......

Điều hành salon là thành viên của tiệm bao gồm: thư ký, thợ tay chân, thợ thẩm mỹ, chuyên viên về màu, thợ massage nếu là salon nhiều dịch vụ. Đồng thời rõ ràng về giá cả phục vụ và sổ hẹn khách bố trí thích hợp theo thời gian từng việc.

__Việc bán lẽ__ cho khách cũng là yếu tố quan trọng, người thợ cũng cần hiểu rõ sản phẩm để mô tả cho khách, không nói sai lệch và cũng cần có sự tế nhị khi gợi ý người khách mua sản phẩm.

Theo tâm lý khách mua hàng cũng cần sự thúc đẩy của thợ như giúp khách làm quyết định sản phẩm có lợi thế nào và kết quả. Đồng thời người thợ, người chủ cũng luôn biểu lộ nét tươi trẻ, gọn gàng, hợp thời để khách luôn xem mình là người mẫu cố vấn cho họ về phương diện thẩm mỹ.

Để tạo uy tín, niềm tin cho khách, yếu tố đầu tiên là phục vụ người khách được hài lòng và chính họ tự giới thiệu người thân quen. Tuy nhiên quảng bá cơ sở cũng là một phần quan trọng khác như quảng cáo trên báo, radio, hoặc gởi thư trực tiếp cũng làm cho người khách cảm thấy được chiếu cố hơn….

Để phát triển kinh doanh người chủ salon, người thợ thẩm mỹ cần hiểu rõ mọi đối tượng khách hàng từ giới trẻ đến người cao niên, từ người nhút nhác, nóng tính, đến cả người khách nhiều chuyện luôn cần tự chủ giải quyết công việc nhẹ nhàng, trôi chảy. Với kinh nghiệm nghề nghiệp, kiên nhẫn, và thành thật sẽ giúp cho quí vị thành công kinh doanh ngành thẩm mỹ.

HOW TO DEVELOP A SALON

(Làm thế nào phát triển salon)

- When planning to open a salon, careful consideration must be given to the selection of proper location. A good location is near a supermarket or a department store and attract the attention of pedestrians, should be clearly visible.
Khi có kế hoạch mở salon, cẩn thận xem xét nên chọn một địa điểm thích hợp. Một nơi tốt là gần nơi siêu thị hoặc tiệm bán nhiều hàng hóa và hấp dẫn sự chú ý của người đi bộ, nên ở nơi dễ thấy.

- Three types of ownership in a salon are: *ba hình thức làm chủ salon là:*
- Individual ownership: the proprietor is boss and manager, receives all profits and losses.
Làm chủ một người: người đứng tên là chủ và quản lý, thu nhận tất cả lợi nhuận và mất mác xảy ra.
- Partnership: from 2 or more people, more capital, profits and works are equally shared
Hợp tác làm chủ: từ 2 hay nhiều người, nhiều vốn, lợi nhuận và công việc chia đồng đều.
- Corporation: from 3 or more people, taxation and regulation by the state, the stockholder is not legally responsible for losses.
Công ty: từ 3 hay nhiều người hơn, thuế và điều lệ do tiểu bang, cổ phần viên không có trách nhiệm pháp lý về việc thiệt hại.

- Criteria when selecting employees for a salon is general skill level, overall attitude, and personality.
Các tiêu chuẩn để chọn nhân viên cho cơ sở thẩm mỹ kỹ năng tổng quát, thái độ mọi mặt và cá tính.
- The flow of operational service toward the reception room with amenities such as: phone, coffee, magazines, and pleasant music.
Một loạt các dịch vụ đều tập trung về nơi tiếp khách với những điều cần phục vụ như: điện thoại, coffee, tạp chí và âm nhạc thích hợp.

- **Insurance policies** are purchased by salon owner to protect themseves against suit for malpractice.
Bảng hợp đồng bảo hiểm được mua do chủ tiệm để bảo vệ cho chính họ chống lại những kiện tụng với những rũi ro do nghề nghiệp gây ra.

- A color scheme that is restful and flattering to males, females, and young adult to senior groups. Daily sales slips and petty cash book should be kept for at least 6 months.
Màu sắc hài hòa dễ chịu và đẹp mắt cho cả nam, nữ, và từ người trẻ đến thành phần cao niên. Hóa đơn bán hằng ngày, và sổ chi tiêu lặt vặt nên giữ tối thiểu là 6 tháng.
- Lost of income as a result of wasted time can be minimized by keeping an accurate appointment book.
Thiệt hại về thu nhập như là kết quả của lãng phí thời gian, có thể giảm thiểu bằng cách giữ chính xác sổ hẹn khách.

- **Consumption supplies** use in the daily business operation. **Retail supplies** is sold to clients
Vật liệu tiêu thụ dùng hằng ngày cho công việc. Vật dụng bán lẽ được bán cho khách hàng

- Plumbing, lighting, air conditioning, and heating are sufficient for satisfactory services. A clean rest room containing toilet and basin.
Hệ thống nước, điện, điều hòa, và nhiệt hữu hiệu cho công việc. Nhà vệ sinh phải sạch sẽ có cả bồn cầu và bể tắm.

DISPLAYS AND SERVICES *(Trình bày và phục vụ)*

- Promotions help introduce to clients to new products & services. For advertising to be effective, your efforts must be focused. The most effective advertising and promotion vehicle is client referrals, and word-of-mouth.
  Sự quảng cáo giúp giới thiệu khách hàng đến những sản phẩm mới và công việc. Để quảng cáo được hữu hiệu, sự tác động của bạn phải tập trung. Hầu hết việc quảng cáo hữu hiệu và phương tiện thúc đẩy cho sự phát triển là khách hàng giới thiệu và miệng truyền miệng.

- Direct mail is often seen as the most selective and efficient from of advertising for local businesses.
  Quảng cáo gởi tận nhà thường được ưa chuộng và hữu hiệu từ nguồn quảng cáo thương mãi địa phương.

- One the business is established, 2 to 3% is a normal expenditure for advertising
  Một cơ sở kinh doanh cần chi 2 đến 3 % thông thường cho quảng cáo.

- **The key points** in consultative selling are: *Các điểm chính trong việc tham khảo mua bán là:*
  - Experience is worth a thousand words : *kinh nghiệm đáng giá cả ngàn lời nói*
  - Know your products and services : *biết rõ sản phẩm và các dịch vụ*
  - Listen, analyze, question, and probe : *lắng nghe, phân tích, câu hỏi, thăm dò*
  - Be sensitive : *nhạy cảm*
  - Offer benefits, not products : *đưa ra lợi ích, không phải sản phẩm*
  - Close the sale : *kết thúc việc buôn bán*

- **Eight key points** in retail display are: *Tám điểm chính trong cách trình bày bán lẽ là:*
  - Supported by signage : *mọi lứa tuổi ủng hộ*
  - Supported by people : *dân chúng ủng hộ*
  - Well-stocked : *đủ hàng hóa*
  - Stocked with a variety of products : *có đủ các các loại hàng hóa*
  - Well organized and neat : *sắp xếp ngay ngắn và gọn gàng*
  - Well-lighted : *đủ ánh sáng*
  - Attractive and functional : *hấp dẫn và có tác dụng*
  - Visible : *thấy dễ dàng*

- Offer some advice and guidance. Suggest several courses of action that the client can take using your services and products.
  Có vài lời khuyên và hướng dẫn. Gợi ý nhiều hướng dẫn ứng dụng cho khách có thể phục vụ và sản phẩm liên hệ.
- Take a moment to be personal. Ask about the children, the job-anything that is of importance to the client. Be sure to thank the client for the call, remind the client about the appointment. If did not schedule, invite them to call.
  Dùng hình thức có tính cá nhân. Hỏi về các em bé, bất cứ điều gì có quan trong đến khách. Cảm ơn khách khi gọi đến, nhắc nhở khách về giờ hẹn. Nếu không lấy hẹn, mời họ gọi đến.

RULES AND REGULATIONS

(Luật và điều lệ)

1. **A duplicate license** shall be issued upon filing a statement explaining the loss verified by oath & accompanied by a fee. Every license holder shall display his or her license in a conspicuous place of business.
Giấy phép thứ hai sẽ được cấp lại nếu ghi trong tờ khai mất có xác nhận lời thề và kèm theo lệ phí cho giấy phép mới. Người có bằng sẽ trưng bày license ở nơi dễ thấy của tiệm

kính che khi dùng primer

2. Every establishment shall provide at least one public toilet, adequate hand washing facilities and drinking water. Implements are not to be placed in a uniform pocket
Mỗi cơ sở thẩm mỹ phải cung cấp nhà vệ sinh Chung, đủ dụng cụ rửa tay, và nước uống. Dụng cụ không được đặt trong túi áo choàng
3. **Each cosmological establishment** shall display a copy of sanitary rules in a conspicuous place. All precaution for safety, health regulations and sanitation are the responsibility of the establishment owner, the instructor and the operators
Mỗi cơ sở thẩm mỹ nên trưng bày bảng luật lệ vệ sinh ở nơi dễ thấy. Tất cả những điều về luật lệ an toàn, sức khỏe và vệ sinh là trách nhiệm của chủ tiệm, thầy, cô giáo, và người thợ

4. **Live animals** are not permitted to be brought into or remain except a sightless person with a trained dog. The main purpose of maintaining sanitary conditions of implements and work areas in an establishment is to prevent the spread of germs.
Thú vật sống không được mang vào tiệm hoặc giữ trừ trường hợp chó được huấn luyện dẫn đường cho người m.ù. Mục đích chính sự vệ sinh bảo quản dụng cụ và nơi làm việc trong tiệm là để ngăn ngừa lây lan của vi trùng gây bệnh
5. Which of the following are grounds for disciplinary action by the Board of Cosmetology: if continued practiced by a person having a infections disease.
Điều căn bản nào là vi phạm luật đối với ngành thẩm mỹ: nếu tiếp tục làm việc màcó mang bệnh nhiễm trùng.
6. **Towels** are being laundered in an establishment, the treatment should include: Washing in water temperature of **140 -160 degree F** for at least **15 minutes.**
Trong tiệm thẩm mỹ, khăn được giặt với nước nóng vừa, từ 140 đến 160 độ F tối thiểu là 15 phút

7. **Before using** on a patron, all non-electrical instrument shall be disinfected in the following manner: Washed with soap or detergent water, immerse in **E.P.A** disinfectant for a minimal **ten minutes**, and then stored on a clean, covered place.
Trước khi dùng cho khách, tất cả dụng cụ không phải bằng điện sẽ được diệt trùng bằng cách rửa xà phòng hoặc chất tẩy, nhúng chìm vào dung dịch diệt trùng E.P.A chuẩn nhận tối thiểu 10 phút, và giữ trong nơi sạch phủ kín.
8. All electrical instruments, such as clippers or vibrators shall be disinfected prior to each use by removing all matter and disinfected with **E.P.A** registered or according to manufacturer's instructions
Tất cả dụng cụ bằng điện như dụng cụ cắt tóc, lông hoặc máy rung được diệt trùng trước mỗi lần dùng bằng cách lấy rời ra và diệt trùng theo tiêu chuẩn E.P.A hoặc theo sự hướng dẫn của nhà chế tạo.

9. **All instruments** that have been used on a patron and soiled in any manner shall be placed in a properly labeled container. All bottles and containers shall be correctly labeled to disclose their content.
Tất cả mọi dụng cụ được sử dụng cho khách và dụng cụ dơ trong mọi hình thức sẽ đặt vào đúng chỗ đồ chứa vật dụng đó có dán nhãn. Tất cả chai, lọ và hộp chứa nên dán đúng nhãn hiệu như chất chứa bên trong.

bao tay dùng khi diệt trùng

10. **No school or establishment** shall have products containing hazardous substances which have been banned by: The food & Drug Administration (**F.D.A**)
Không có trường học hoặc cơ sở thẩm mỹ nào dùng hóa chất độc hại mà bị cấm bởi: Cơ quan quản trị thuốc và thực phẩm (F.D.A)

11. No school or establishment shall have on the premises any razor edged device or tool to remove calluses, or any needle like instruments for the purpose of extracting skin blemishes.
Không có trường học hoặc cơ sở thẩm mỹ sử dụng bất cứ dụng cụ bằng dao cạo hoặc bất cứ dụng cụ nào để cạo, cắt da chai hoặc bất cứ dùng loại kim nào vào mục đích để rạch da lấy mụn (chỗ bị lở)

12. Supplies, which use direct contact with a patron and can not be disinfected, shall be deposited in a wasted receptacle immediately.
Các vật dụng trực tiếp dùng cho khách và không thể diệt trùng được sẽ vứt bỏ trong thùng rác ngay.

13. **The attire of operators** in charge, while serving a patron shall at all times be kept clean. You must inform the Board of Barbering & Cosmetology for your changed of address within thirty days.
Quần áo của người thợ trong lúc đang phục vụ cho khách trong tất cả mọi lúc phải giữ sạch sẽ. Quí vị phải thông báo cho Hội đồng thẩm mỹ về thay đổi địa chỉ trong vòng 30 ngày.

14. All liquids, creams, and other cosmetic preparations shall be kept in clean and closed containers. Powders may be kept in clean shakers. Neck dusters and all other brushes used in an establishment or school on a customer shall be maintained in a clean and sanitary condition.
Các mỹ phẩm pha chế dạng lỏng, kem nên cất giữ trong hộp chứa sạch có nắp đậy; dạng bột nên cất giữ trong lo chai rắc sạch sẽ. Cây phủi ở cổ và cây cọ dùng cho khách phải giữ sạch và trong điều kiện vệ sinh.

tủ khử trùng tia UV

15. **No establishment or school** shall have on the premises cosmetic products containing hazardous substance which have been banned by the U.S. Food and Drug Administration for use in cosmetic products, including liquid methyl methacrylate monomer and methylene chloride. No product shall be used in a manner that is disapproved by the FDA.
Không có salon hoặc trường học nào có mặt hàng mỹ phẩm nào chứa dạng độc hại bị cấm bởi cơ quan F.D.A dạng mỹ phẩm đó bao gồm dung dịch đắp bột methyl methacrylate monomer and methylene chloride. Không một sản phẩm nào được dùng mà chưa được chuẩn nhận bởi FDA

16. Shampoo trays and bowls must be cleaned with soap and water or other detergent after each shampoo, kept in good repair and in asanitary condition at all times. Treatment tables must be covered with a clean sheet of examination paper for each patron.
Khay đựng dầu gội và tô phải được làm sạch với xà phòng và nước hoặc chất tẩy sau mỗi lần gội tóc, giữ trong tình trạng tốt và vệ sinh trong mọi lúc. Bàn dùng làm cho khách phải được phủ với giấy sạch cho từng người khách.

17. **When only a portion** of a cosmetic preparation is to be used on a patron, it shall be removed from the container in such a way as not to contaminate the remaining portion. Pencils cosmetics shall be sharpened before each use.
Khi chỉ dùng 1 ít mỹ phẩm dùng cho khách, kem phải được lấy từ lọra mà không làm bẩn phần còn lại. Loại viết chì màu dùng cho trang điểm nên làm bén lại sau mỗi lần dùng.

18. Establishment and school shall keep the floors, furniture, walls clean and in good repair; shall have a systerm of adequate ventilation; provided a supply of hot and cold running water; drinking water; hand washing facilities, and shall provide public toilet rooms.
Cơ sở thẩm mỹ và trường học phải giữ nền nhà, bàn tủ, vách tường sạch và luôn được bảo trì tốt; cần có hệ thống thông khí; cung cấp hệ thống nước nóng và lạnh; nước uống; chỗ rữa tay, và có nhà vệ sinh chung.

PRACTICAL TEST

Nails 900

<u>Sample</u>

APPOINTMENT SCHEDULE

Read instruction very carefully before doing any services

10:00 Disinfectant and sanitation preparation (Quat's solution)
* (<u>for the day's appointment</u>)

10:05 Give your client a complete manicure including hands & arms massage

10:35 Application of artificial nails

a. Do one acrylic nail form

b. Do one nail tip

c. Do one nail wrap (silk or paper)

d. Do one tip overlay with acrylic

APPLY POLISH TO ALL FINGERNAILS WHEN DONE

11:00 Demonstrate all sanitation and disinfectant technique at 10:05 (for manicure implements)

11:15 Give your client a complete pedicure ***(1foot only)***

11:45 Clean up & dismiss your model

• • • • • • • • • • • • • •

<u>Đề mẫu</u>

CHƯƠNG TRÌNH THI

Đọc cẩn thận trước khi làm

10:00: Pha chế dung dịch diệt trùng (nước quats)

10:05: Làm hoàn tất móng tay nước kể cả massage bàn tay và cánh tay

10:35: Làm các móng giả

a. 1 ngón đặt form, đắp bột giũa láng

b. 1 ngón dán tip, giũa láng

c. 1 ngón phủ lụa hoặc phủ giấy

d. 1 ngón dán tip, giũa láng đắp bột

LÀM XONG SƠN MÀU CÁC MÓNG TAY

11:00: Diệt trùng dụng cụ lúc 10:05 (dụng cụ móng tay nước)

11:15: Làm hoàn tất một chân kể cả massage

11:45: Dọn dẹp, nhớ lau bàn, gương sạch sẽ và cùng người mẫu rời phòng

HOW TO DO DISINFECTION & SANITATION TECHNIQUES

These are of practical importance to the Manicurist
- *To preserve the patron's health*
- *To keep all implements germ-free*
- *To prevent the spread of infectious disease*

A. MATERIAL

Liquid soap; Towel; Paper towels; Brush; Gloves; Cover container; Clean seal plastic bag; Quats (Quaternary ammonium compounds)

B. PROCEDURE

1. Technician wash hands with liquid soap and warm water
2. Set up area for disinfection
3. Prepare disinfectant solution (mix in box consist of 2/3 water + 1oz Quats)
4. Remove all foreign matter from implement or equipment
5. Brush with liquid soap & warm water then rinse by water
6. Pat & wipe with clean towels or paper towels
7. Totally immerse them in QUATS SOLUTION (10 minutes); E.P.A registers.
8. Wear gloves and remove them
9. Rinse & Wipe with towels or paper towels to dry
10. Put clean implements in seal plastic bag or covered container
11. Dispose Quats solution in shampoo bowl
12. Clean up your workstation

Brush with Liquid soap & warm water
Dùng bàn chải chà rửa dụng cụ

Sterilization: *Kill germ, bacteria and spores*
Disinfection: *Kill germ, bacteria (harmful or beneficial)*
Antiseptic : *May kill germ or retard the growth of bacteria*

- *All disinfectant solutions must be Environmental Protection Agency (E.P.A) registered and possess bactericidal, fungicidal and virucidal.*

Notice: Disinfectant solution must be changed at least daily or whenever visibly cloudy or dirty.

E.P.A: Environmental Protection Agency

CÁCH DIỆT TRÙNG DỤNG CỤ

Diệt trùng là tiến trình hủy diệt vi trùng những dụng cụ của người thợ để ngăn ngừa nhiễm trùng, lây lan, nhằm giữ gìn vệ sinh công cộng và tạo an toàn cho mọi người khách khi chúng ta phục vụ.

A. VẬT LIỆU

Xà phòng; Khăn; Khăn giấy; Bàn chải; Bao tay; Hộp chứa dung dịch; Bao nhựa sạch, kín; Nước QUATS (hợp chất diệt trùng)

B. CÁCH LÀM

1. *Thợ rửa tay với nước ấm và xà phòng*
2. *Dọn bàn, chuẩn bị trãi giấy để đặt dụng cụ diệt trùng*
3. *Pha chế dung dịch diệt trùng (2/3 nước sạch + 1oz Quat)*
4. *Lau và lấy sạch các chất bám vào dụng cụ*
5. *Dùng bàn chải chà rửa với xà phòng và nước ấm xong xả nước sạch*
6. *Vỗ bớt nước, lau khô với khăn giấy sạch*
7. *Nhúng chìm vào dung dịch QUATS 10 phút (E.P.A chuẩn nhận)*
8. *Mang bao tay lấy dụng cụ ra*
9. *Xả lại nước sạch, lau khô bằng khăn hoặc khăn giấy sạch*
10. *Bỏ vào bao nhựa dán kín hoặc hộp kín*
11. *Đổ bỏ nước Quats vào bồn gội tóc*
12. *Dọn dẹp chỗ làm*

* ***Sterilization:*** *Tiệt trùng là khả năng tiêu hủy vi trùng, vi khuẩn, nấm. Đặc biệt diệt cả bào tử của vi trùng (spores), tiệt trùng dụng cụ thường dùng ở bệnh viện.*

* ***Disinfection:*** *Diệt trùng là khả năng diệt vi trùng, vi khuẩn và nấm, được dùng diệt trùng dụng cụ ở salon, trường thẩm mỹ (Quats solution)*

Ngoài ra còn nhiều cách diệt trùng khác như xông hơi hóa chất; nước sôi ở 212 độ F (100 độ C) trong 20 phút; Sây nóng; Tia cực tím.

* ***Antiseptic:*** *Sát trùng là khả năng có thể giết vi trùng hoặc làm chậm phát triển của vi trùng, chất sát trùng thường dùng khi da bị trầy xước hoặc chảy máu nhẹ.*

- *Tại Salon hoặc School, nước QUATS diệt trùng mỗi ngày thay 1 lần hoặc thay bất cứ khi nào thấy đục hoặc dơ bẩn*
- *Tại trung tâm thi, diệt trùng dụng cụ xong đem dung dịch đổ đi vào bồn rửa tay hoặc đổ sau cuộc thi*

E.P.A: Environmental Protection Agency
Cơ quan bảo vệ môi trường

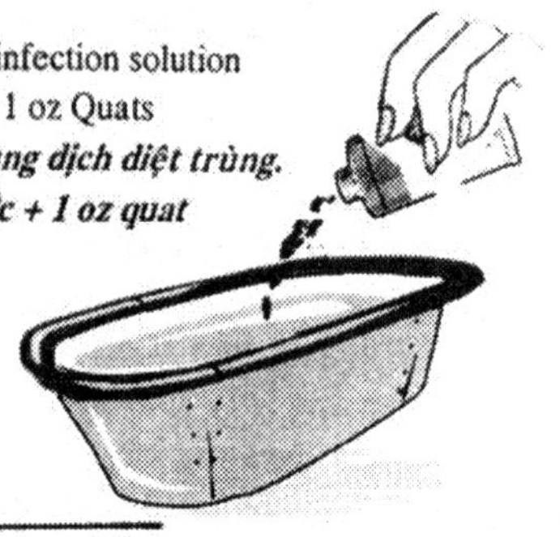

Prepare disinfection solution
2/3 water + 1 oz Quats
Pha chế dụng dịch diệt trùng.
lấy 2/3 nước + 1 oz quat

DISINFECTON & SANITATION TECHNIQUE

Cách diệt trùng dụng cụ

Brush with Liquid soap & warm water
Dùng bàn chải chà rửa dụng cụ

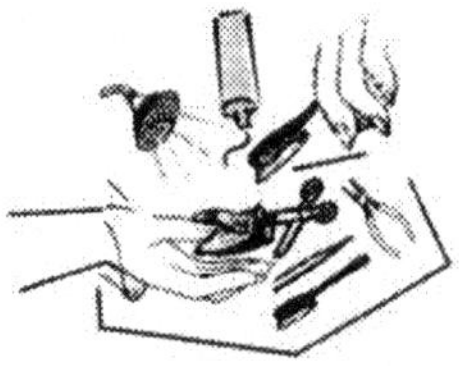

Rinse out with warm water
Rửa lại bằng nước cho sạch

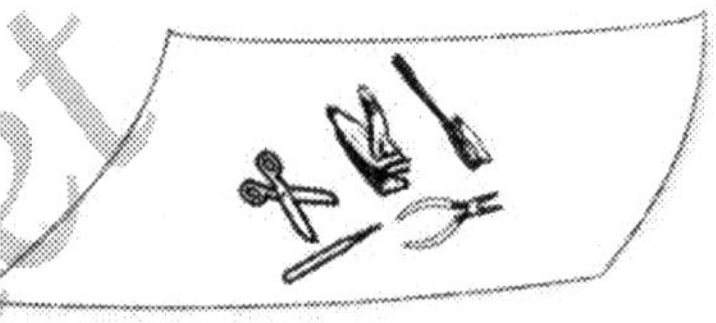

Wipe with clean paper towels
Lau khô với khăn giấy

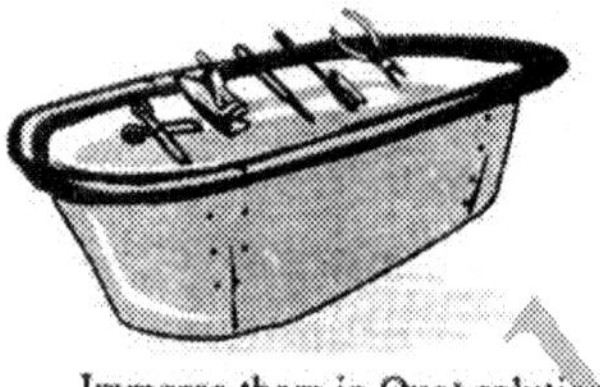

Immerse them in Quat solution 10 minutes
Nhúng vào dung dịch diệt trùng 10 phút

Wear gloves & remove implements out
Mang bao tay, lấy dụng cụ ra

Rinse out with water
Xả lại nước sạch

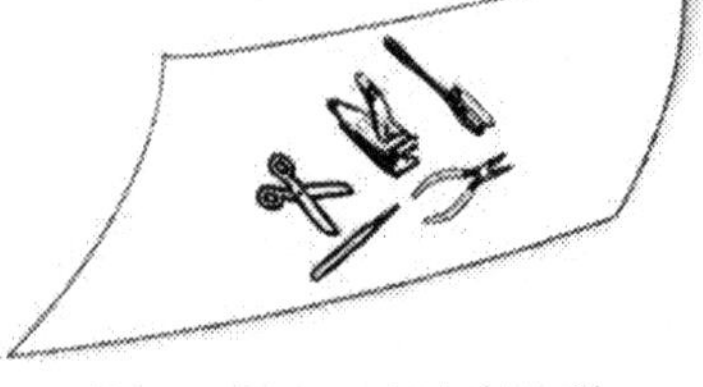

Wipe with clean paper towels
Lau khô với khăn giấy

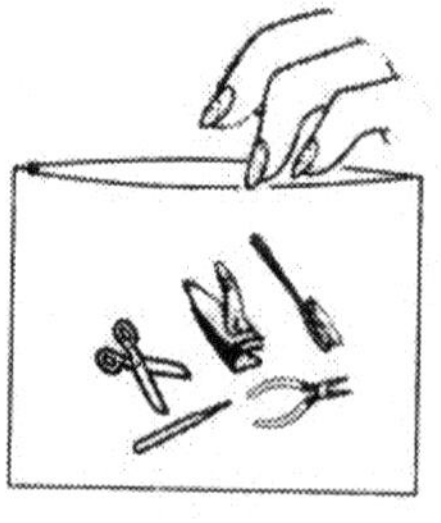

Putting seal plastic bag
Bỏ vào bao nhựa sạch

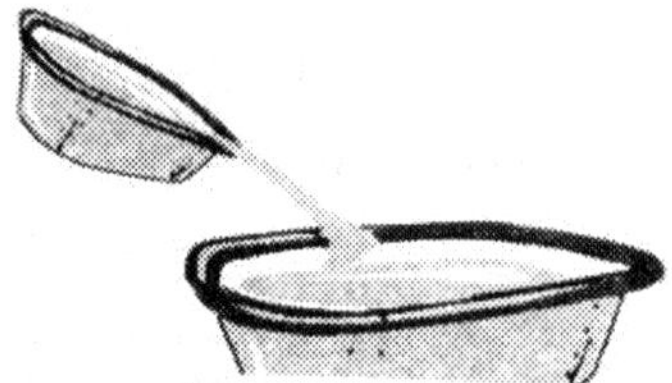

Dispose Quats solution
in shampoo bowl
Đổ bỏ nước Quats

HOW TO DO A PLAIN MANICURE

Manicure is the care of hands and nails. The word manicure is derived from the Latin. Word Manus meaning hand and Cura meaning care.
A plain manicure improves the appearance of the hands and nails because hands play an important role in both men and women appearance.

A. MATERIALS & IMPLEMENTS

Liquid soap; Trash bag; Soil container; Towels; Cushion; Paper towels; Cotton; Polish remover; Cuticle softener; Cuticle oil; Hand lotion; Nail brush; Finger bowl; Emery board; Orange wood stick; Metal pusher; Cuticle nipper; Nail clipper; Nail polish (base coat; color's polish; top coat).

B. PROCEDURE

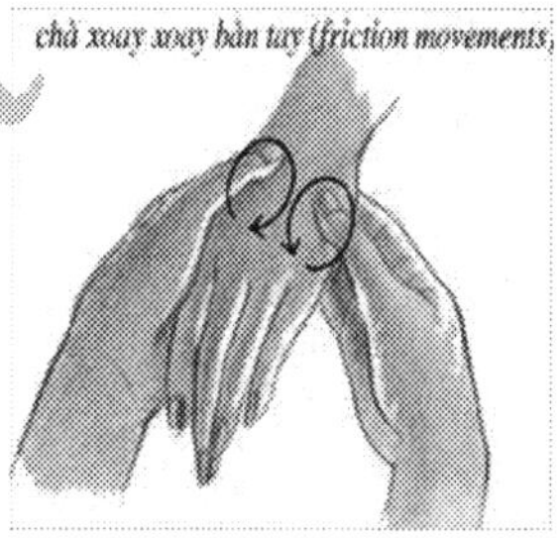

1. Technician wash hands with liquid soap and warm water
2. Set up manicure kit on sanitary maintenance area (SMA)
3. Wash patron's hands with liquid soap and warm water
   * *Mix some drops liquid soap + water into finger bowl*
4. Examine patron's hands (removes all jewelry on hands)
5. Remove old polish from fingernails
6. Shorten/trim the nails with nail clipper
7. File nail of the left hand (corner to center) then soak finger with soapy water into finger bowl
8. File nail of right hand
9. Remove left hand from finger bowl then blot dry with paper towel
10. Apply cuticle softener on cuticle around the nail plate
11. Push cuticle back in circular motion with flat side of metal pusher
12. Trim dead cuticle by cuticle nipper
    (to third finger; soak right hand into finger bowl)
13. Brush nail surface over plastic bowl with soapy water then blot dry
14. Apply cuticle oil around the nail plate & massage with rotary movement
15. Remove right hand, blot dry and repeat step 10 to 14 of right hand
16. Apply hand lotion; give a massage of both hands from finger to elbow (proper technique)
17. Clean the surface nails and underneath free edge of nails (from center to toward each side)
18. Apply nail polish (base coat; color's polish; top coat)
    * *Clean color's polish (if needed)*
19. Clean up your workstation.

When completed, discard emery board, orange wood stick, used paper towels in trash bag. Put soil implements in soil container, and then wash hands for next assignment.

CÁCH LÀM MÓNG TAY NƯỚC

Làm móng tay nước là cắt, tiả móng, da chết và massage đôi tay được đẹp và mềm mại. Hiện nay đàn ông và phụ nữ rất cần dịch vụ này. Chăm sóc đôi tay cũng thể hiện được vẽ ngoài và giữ một vai trò quan trọng trong đời sống.

A. VẬT LIỆU & DỤNG CỤ

Xà phòng nước; Bao rác; Hộp đựng đồ dơ; Khăn; Đệm lót; Khăn giấy; Bông gòn; Chất chùi nước sơn; Chất mềm da; Dầu thoa da; Kem massage; Bàn chải móng; Tô ngâm tay; Dũa giấy; Que gỗ cam; Cây sủi da; Kềm cắt da; Kềm cắt móng; Nước sơn (nước lót, nước màu, nước phủ).

B. CÁCH LÀM

1. *Thợ rửa tay bằng nước ấm và xà phòng*
2. *Dọn bàn, đặt dụng cụ làm móng tay lên tấm khăn có trãi giấy sạch*
3. *Đưa khách rửa tay và lấy tô ngâm tay pha nước ấm với 1 vài giọt xà phòng*
4. *Khám tay khách và bảo khách lấy nữ trang trên tay cất đi*
5. *Chùi nước sơn cũ*
6. *Cắt móng cả hai bàn tay bằng nail clipper*
7. *Giũa bàn tay trái trước (từ góc vào giữa) xong ngâm các ngón tay vào tô nước ấm*
8. *Giũa bàn tay phải*
9. *Lấy bàn tay trái ra khỏi tô nước, lau khô bằng giấy sạch*
10. *Thoa chất mềm da ở vùng da quanh móng*
11. *Dùng mặt bằng cây sủi xoay nhẹ, đẩy lùi da trên mặt móng*
12. *Dùng kềm cắt da tỉa da chết, da dư*
    (tỉa da đến ngón thứ 3 nhớ ngâm tay phải vào tô nước pha xà phòng)

13. *Dùng bàn chãi chà rửa mặt móng, lau khô*
14. *Thoa dầu vùng da chung quanh móng, xoa mặt móng*
15. *Lấy tay phải ra, lau khô (lập lại từ bước 10 - 14 trên tay phải)*
16. *Thoa kem massage, massage từ ngón đến khuỷu tay (đúng cách)*
17. *Chùi sạch mặt móng và dưới móng (từ giữa ra 2 bên móng)*
18. *Sơn móng (nước lót; nước sơn; nước phủ bóng)*
    * Lau vết sơn bị lem ra ngoài (nếu có)
19. *Dọn dẹp*

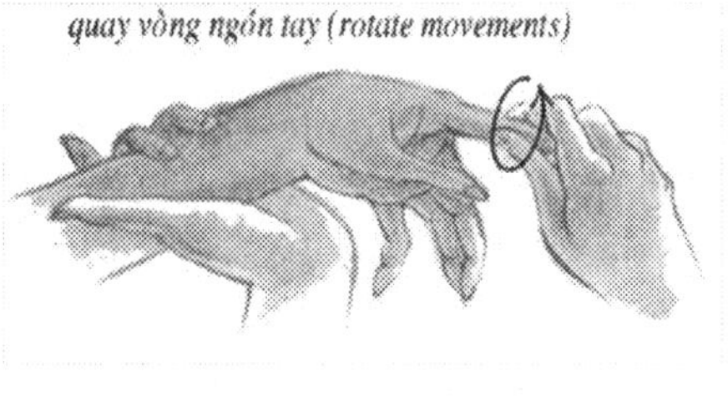

CẦN NHỚ:

Sau khi làm cho khách xong nhớ lấy dụng cụ đã dùng bỏ vào hộp đựng đồ dơ; vứt bỏ giũa, que gỗ và giấy dơ vào bao rác. Thợ rửa tay cho dịch vụ kế tiếp.

PLAIN MANICURE

(water manicure)

Cách làm móng tay nước

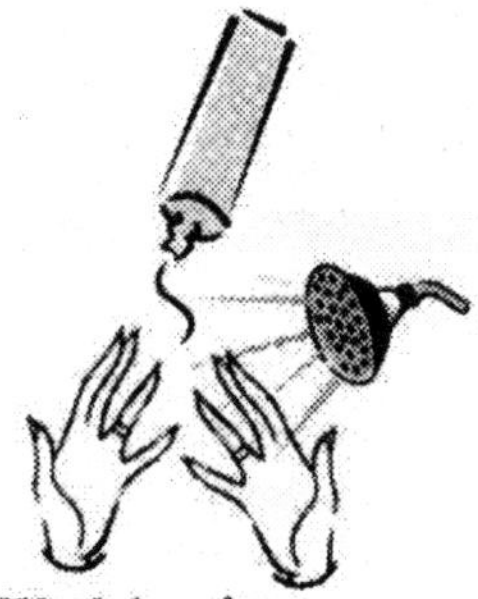

Wash hands

Thợ rửa tay

Set up table

Dọn bàn

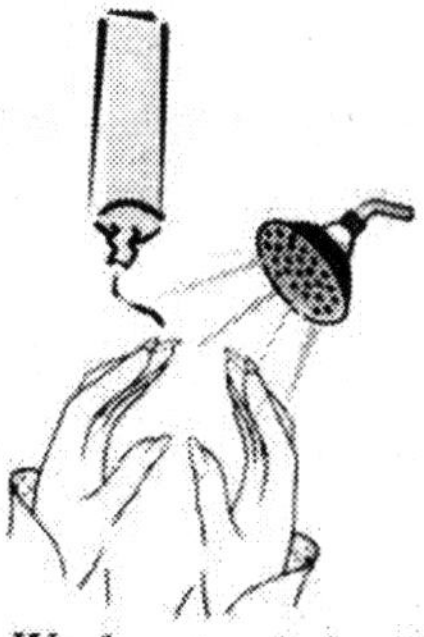

Wash patron's hands

khách rửa tay

Mix liquid soap
+ water into finger bowl

Lấy tô nước ngâm tay trộn xà phòng

Examine patron's hands

Khám 2 bàn tay khách

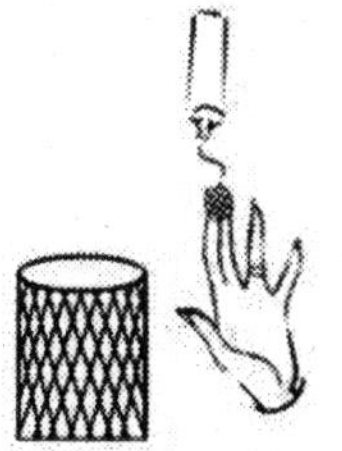

Remove old polish

Chùi nước sơn cũ

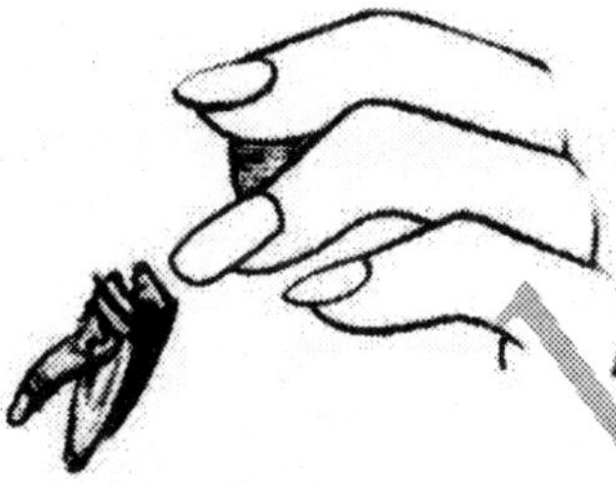

Shorten the nails

Cắt ngắn móng cả 2 bàn tay

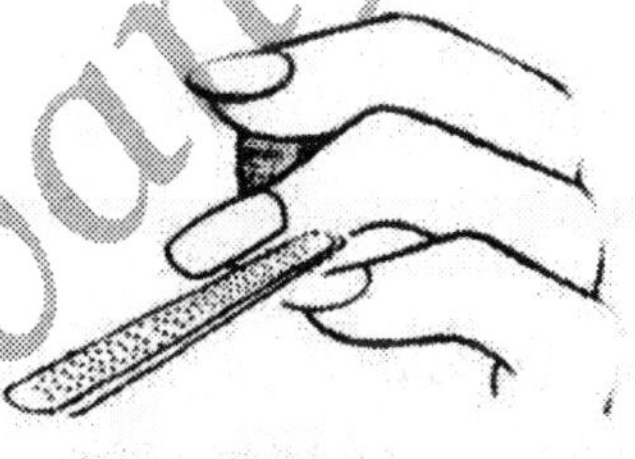

File nails (corner to center)

Dũa móng bàn tay trái (từ góc ra giữa)

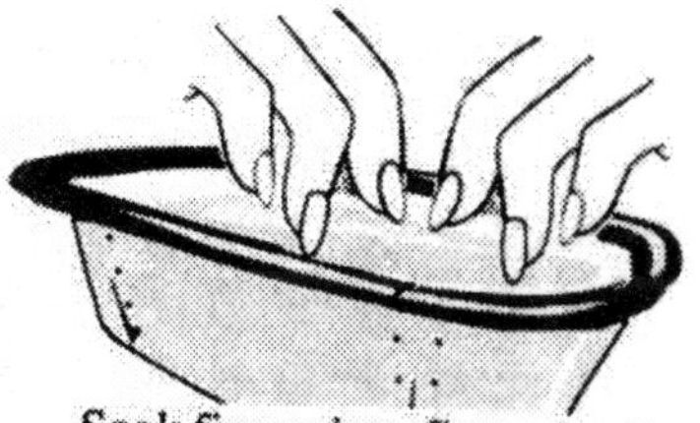

Soak finger into finger bowl

Ngâm móng vào tô

Blot dry with paper towel

Lau khô bằng giấy lau

Apply cuticle softener

Thoa chất mềm da

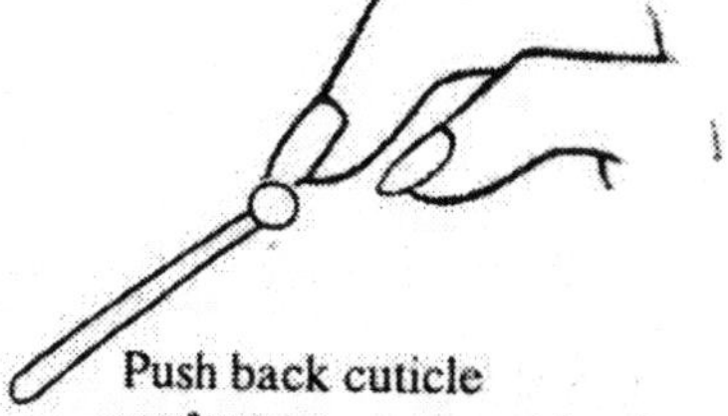

Push back cuticle

Đẩy lùi da trên mặt móng

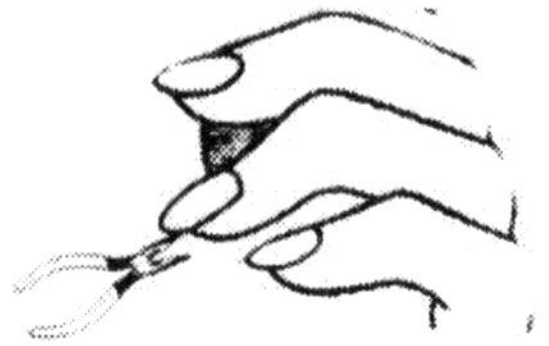

Trim dead cuticle to third finger,
soak finger at right hand
Tỉa da chết, da dư đến ngón thứ 3,
rồi ngâm tay phải

Brush nail surface, blot dry
Chà rửa mặt móng, lau khô

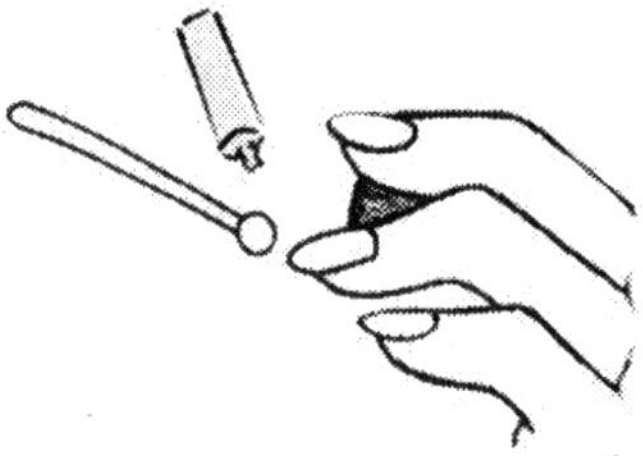

Apply cuticle oil, rotary movement
Thoa dầu, xoa mặt móng

Remove right hand, blot dry
(repeat as left hand)
lấy tay phải ra, lau khô (làm như tay trái)

Apply hand lotion, massage both hands
Thoa kem và massage cả 2 tay

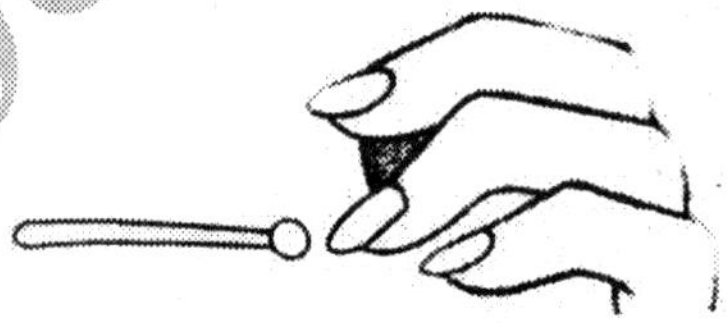

Clean the surface nail, under free
edge with polish remover
Lau sạch mặt móng, dưới móng
bằng chất chùi nước sơn (từ giữa ra 2 bên)

Apply nail polish
Sơn móng

Clean up:
-Throw away orange wood stick,
emery board in trash bag
Vứt bỏ que gỗ và dũa giấy vào túi rác

-Put soil implements in box
& wash hands
Đặt dụng cụ dơ vào hộp
và rửa tay

HOW TO DO A PEDICURE

Pedicure is the care of the feet, toes and toenails. The word pedicure is derived from the Latin word. Pedi means foot and Cura means care. In today's shoe fashions, toes and heels are often exposed. Neglected toenails and rough harsh heels distract from the beauty of the foot.

A. MATERIALS & IMPLEMENTS

Liquid soap; Trash bag; Soil container; 2 basins; Paper towels; Towels; Toenail clipper; Toe separators; Low tool (salon); Cotton; Polish remover; Cuticle softener; Cuticle oil; Massage lotion; Nail brush; Emery board; Orange wood stick; Metal pusher; Cuticle nipper; Nail polish.

B. PROCEDURE

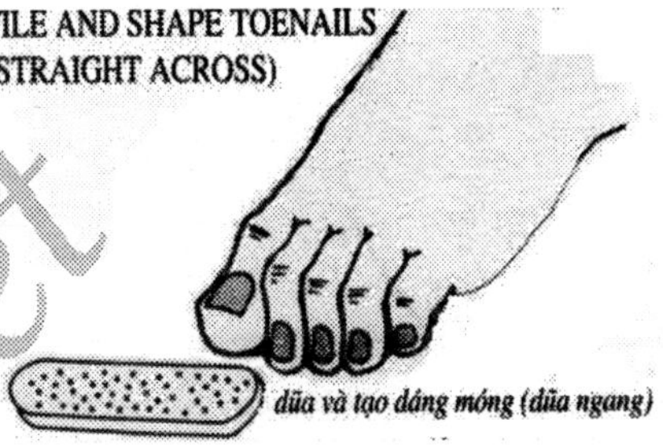

1. Technician wash hands with liquid soap and warm water
2. Set up pedicure kit on sanitary maintenance area
   * Prepare 2 basins (one warm water mix liquid soap and other one with clear water)
   * *Take off shoes or sandals of client.*
3. Soak patron's feet in basin warm water mix liquid soap
4. Brush toe nails and heels the both feet in basin with warm water mix liquid soap
5. Take the both feet out and rinse in basin with clear water and blot dry with towel
6. Examine patron's feet
7. Remove old polish from toenails
8. Shorten the toenails the both feet
9. File and shape toenails of left foot *(straight across)* and slighly file at each corner
10. Soak left foot into clear water basin
11. File and shape toenails of right foot
12. Remove left foot, blot dry then soak the right foot
13. Apply cuticle softener on toenail's surface of left foot
14. Push back cuticle with metal pusher
15. Trim dead cuticle with cuticle nipper
16. Brush toenails surface into clear water basin, blot dry
17. Apply cuticle oil and massage with rotary movement
18. Remove right foot from basin, blot dry with towel, and repeat step 13 - 17
19. Apply massage lotion and give a massage from toenails to knees *(proper technique)*
20. Clean toenails surface and under free edge the both feet
21. Put on toe separators *(insert toes)*
22. Apply nail polish *(base coat; color's polish; top coat)*
23. Clean up your workstation

When completed, discard emery board, orange wood stick, toe seperators, used paper towels in trash bag. Put soil implements in soil container, and then wash hands for next assignment.

CÁCH LÀM MÓNG CHÂN

Làm móng chân là nghệ thuật chăm sóc đôi chân, bàn chân, các móng chân được cắt tỉa gọn, sạch, mịn màng và đẹp.
Hiện nay với các kiểu giày, dép thời trang thường để lộ gót chân, móng chân nên pedicure rất cần để đôi chân thêm đẹp và duyên dáng.

A. VẬT LIỆU & DỤNG CỤ

Xà phòng; Bao rác; Hộp đựng đồ dơ; 2 thau; Khăn giấy; Khăn; Kềm cắt da; Dụng cụ cắt móng chân; Đồ ngăn chân; Ghế nhỏ (salon); Bông gòn; Chất chùi nước sơn; Chất mềm da; Nước sơn; Dầu thoa da; Kem massage; Bàn chải; Giũa; Que gỗ cam; Cây sủi da.

B. CÁCH LÀM

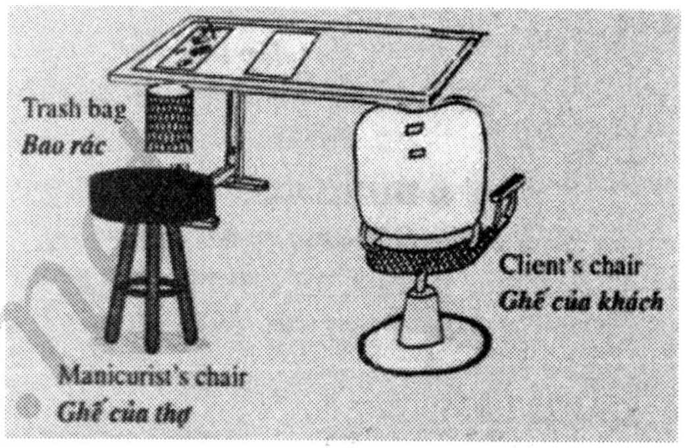

1. *Thợ rửa tay với nước ấm và xà phòng*
2. *Dọn bàn, đặt dụng cụ làm móng chân lên tấm khăn có trãi giấy sạch*
   - **Pha 1 thau nước ấm xà phòng và 1 thau nước trong**
   - **Tháo giày hoặc dép cho khách**
3. *Nhúng chân khách vào thau nước ấm xà phòng*
4. *Dùng bàn chải chà mặt móng, gót chân*
5. *Lấy chân ra, rửa chân ở thau nước trong và dùng khăn lau khô*
6. *Khám chân khách* (các ngón và bàn chân)
7. *Chùi nước sơn cũ trên mặt móng chân*
8. *Cắt móng chân cho cả hai bàn chân*
9. *Giũa móng từ ngón út bàn chân trái giũa ngang đầu móng và giũa nhẹ ở 2 góc móng*
10. *Nhúng chân trái vào thau nước trong*
11. *Giũa móng chân phải*
12. *Lấy chân trái ra lau khô và nhúng chân phải vào thau nước trong*
13. *Thoa chất mềm da trên mặt móng chân trái*
14. *Dùng cây sủi xoay nhẹ đẩy lùi da trên mặt móng*
15. *Tỉa da chết, da dư bằng kềm cắt da*
16. *Chà rửa mặt móng ở thau nước trong, lau khô*
17. *Thoa dầu chung quanh da, xoa mặt móng.*
18. *Lấy chân phải ra, lau khô và làm từ số 13 đến 17 trên chân phải*
19. *Thoa kem massage và massage cả 2 chân từ ngón đến đầu gối*
20. *Dùng que gỗ quấn bông gòn thấm chất chùi nước sơn, chùi mặt móng, dưới móng* (từ giữa ra 2 bên).
21. *Dùng miếng xốp ngăn ngón chân* (toe separators)
22. *Sơn móng chân* (nước lót, nước sơn, nước phủ bóng)
23. *Dọn dẹp chỗ làm*

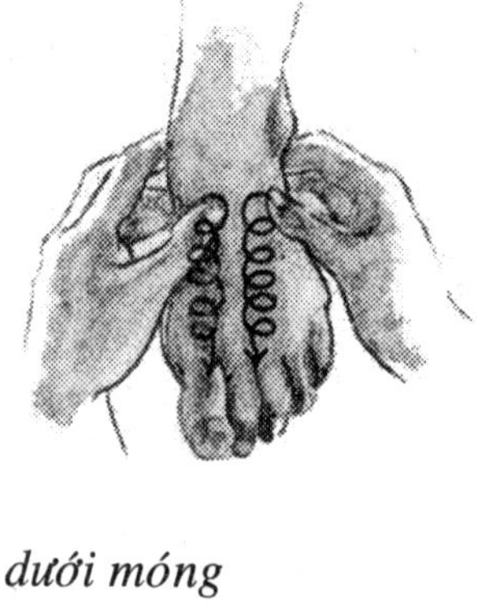

CẦN NHỚ:

***Vứt bỏ giũa giấy, que go, ngăn chân. Lấy dụng cụ đã dùng bỏ vào hộp dựng đồ dơ, vứt bỏ giấy trên bàn vào bao rác, và bưng từng thau đổ vào bồn và xả nước sạch.**

PEDICURE

Cách làm móng chân

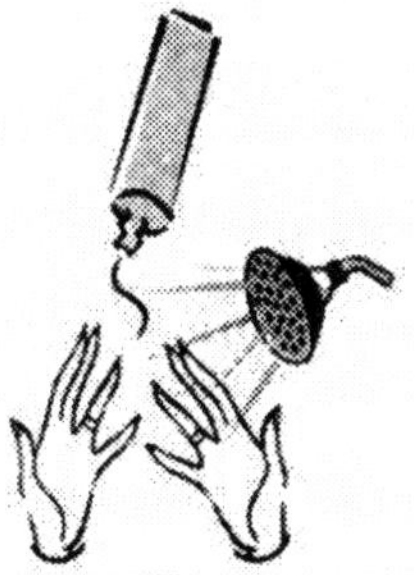

Wash hands

Thợ rửa tay

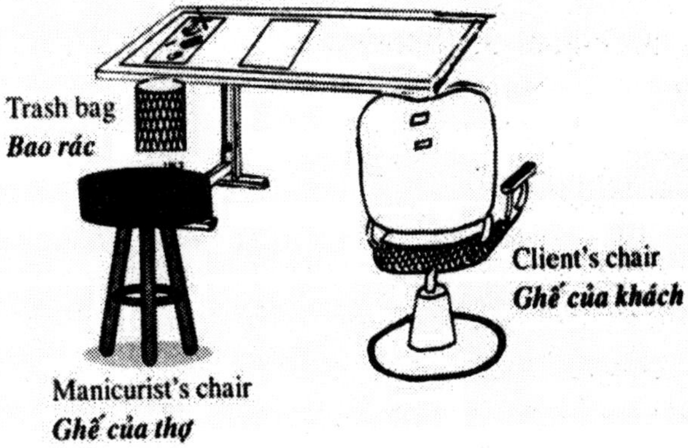

Mix some liquid soap with warm water

Pha vài giọt xa phòng với nước ấm

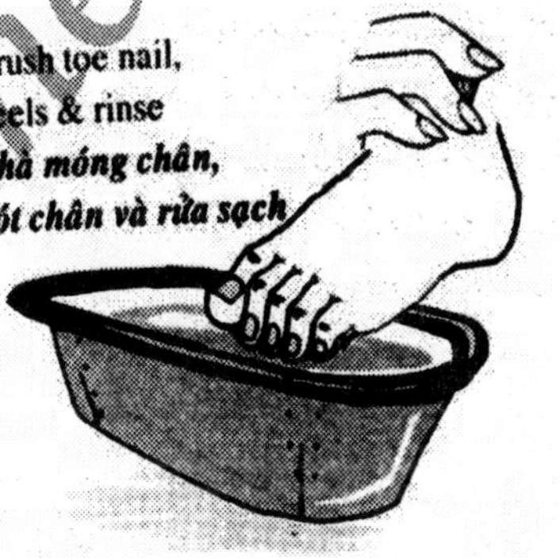

Brush toe nail, heels & rinse

Chà móng chân, gót chân và rửa sạch

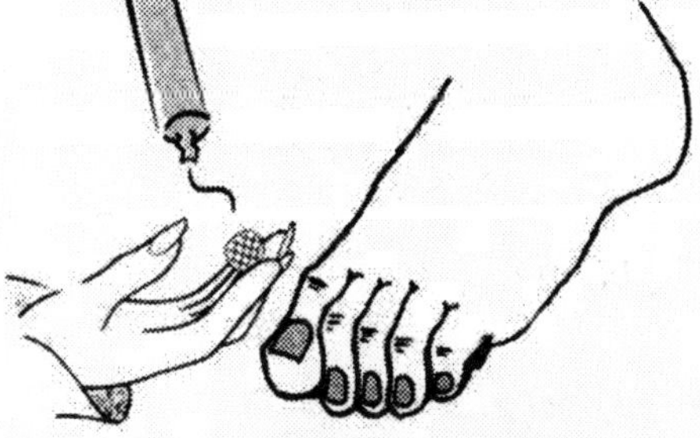

Remove old polish

Chùi nước sơn cũ

Shorten the nails

Cắt ngắn móng

File & shape toenail (straight across)

Dũa và tạo dạng móng chân (dũa ngang)

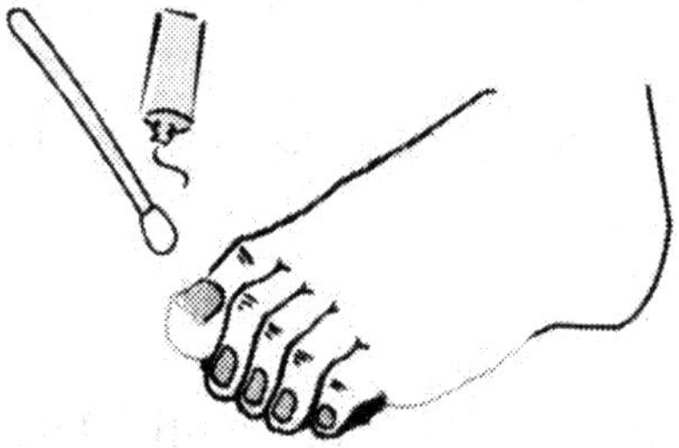

Apply cuticle softener
Thoa chất làm mềm da

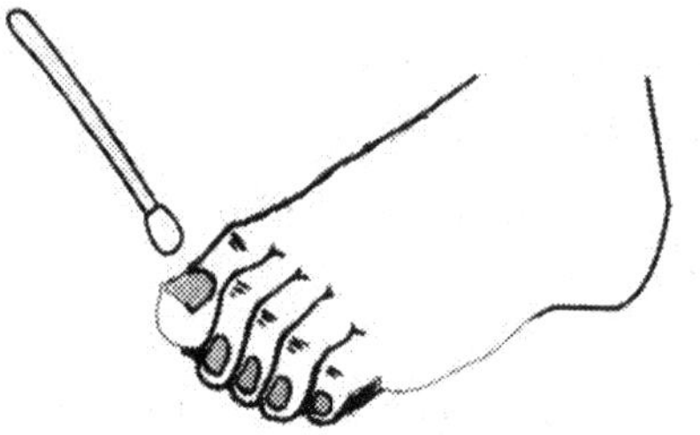

Push back cuticle
Đẩy lùi da mặt móng

Trim dead cuticle
Tỉa da chết quanh móng

Brush toe nail surface into clear water
Chà rửa mặt móng ở thau nước sạch

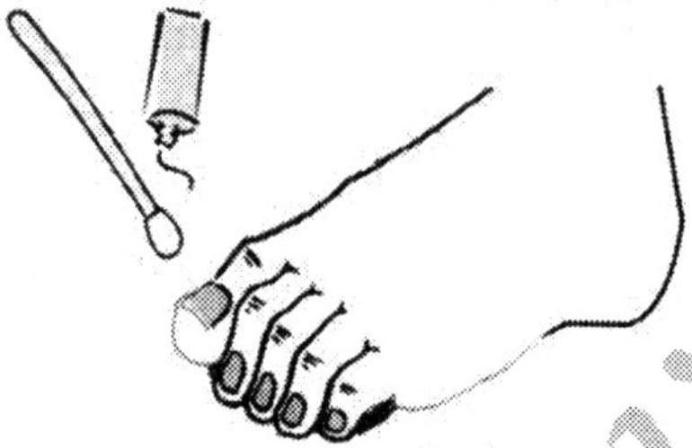

Apply cuticle oil
Thoa dầu cho da

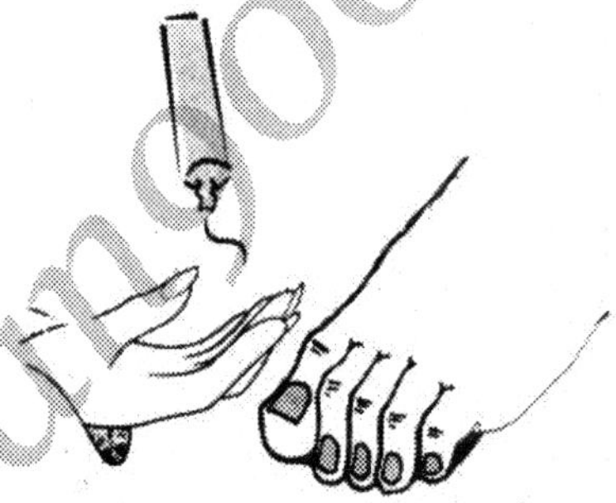

Apply massage lotion &
message from toenail to knee
Thoa kem massage và massage
từ ngón đến đầu gối

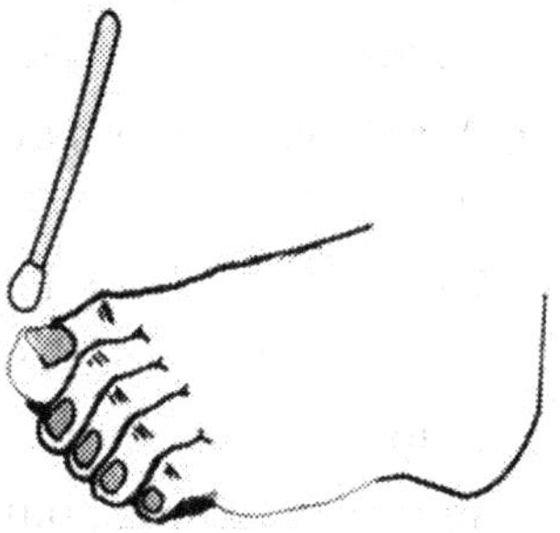

Clean toenail surface
& under free edge
Chà sạch mặt móng
và dưới móng

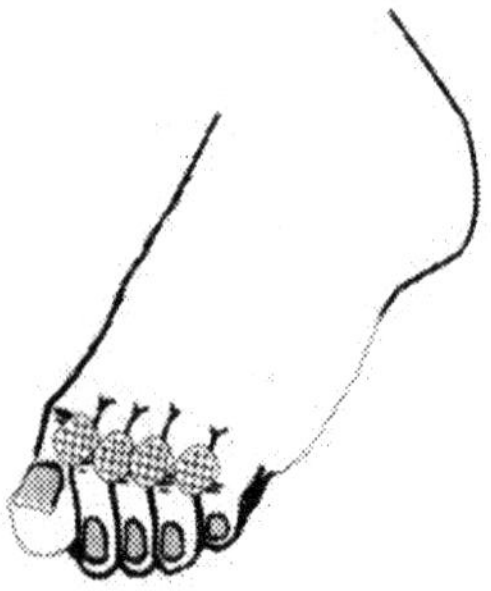

Put on toe separators
Gắn xốp ngăn ngón chân

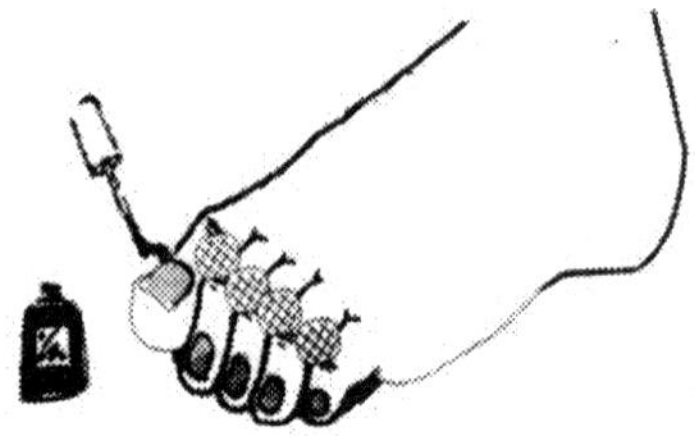

Apply nail polish
Sơn móng chân

Clean up:
Throw away emery board & orange wood stick, toe separators in trash bag, put some soil implements in soil instrument box & wash hands

Dọn dẹp:
Vứt bỏ dũa giấy, que gỗ, xốp ngăn ngón chân vào bao rác, lấy dụng cụ dơ bỏ vào hộp để diệt trùng, xong rửa tay

HOW TO DO AN APPLICATION OF ARTIFICIAL TIP

When a woman can not grow natural nails of the desired length, she may solve the problem by the application of artificial nail tips.
Nail tips are artificial nails made of plastic, nylon or acetate. Nail tips are applying to naisl to extend the natural nails.

A. MATERIALS & IMPLEMENTS

Liquid soap; Towels; Paper towels; Nail file (abrasive); Nail Clipper; Cotton; Nail tip; Thick & thin glue (adhesive); Buffer; Polish remover; Orange wood stick; Trash bag; Soil container.

B. PROCEDURE

1. Technician wash hands with liquid soap and warm water
2. Set up materials and implements on sanitary maintenance area
3. Wash patron's hands with liquid soap and warm water
4. Examine patron's hands
5. Remove old polish on finger nails
6. Trim, shape natural nail
7. Choose the tips that fit on natural nail
8. Rough all nails at free edges
9. Apply glue at the free edge of natural nails
10. Apply nail tip on natural nail, 45 degrees angle at well of tip, hold firm until it dry
11. Cut tip of nails to desired length
12. File nail at seam and leave resulting dust on nails
13. Apply glue at seam
14. File sides of tips, buff, shape tip blend with natural nails
    - *Can apply more glue & buff seam (invisible line)*

15. Apply cuticle oil around nails plate, massage finger nails with rotary movement
16. Patron washes hands, blot dry and clean underneath free edge of nails
17. Apply nail polish on fingernails
    (base coat; color's polish; top coat)
18. Clean up workstation.

Measure tip fit with natural nail
Đo tip vừa vặn với móng thật

<u>***REMEMBER:***</u>

When completed, put orange wood stick, buffer, file in trash bag. Some reused implements put in soil container.

CÁCH GẮN TIP

Khách muốn có đôi bàn tay móng dài trông như thật, chúng ta chỉ cần gắn móng giả (tip) giũa láng mịn ở lằn nối và sơn lên là có đôi bàn tay móng dài trông tự nhiên nhẹ nhàng mà duyên dáng.

A. VẬT LIỆU & DỤNG CỤ

Xà phòng; Khăn; Khăn giấy; Giũa; Đồ cắt móng; Bông gòn; Móng giả (tip); Keo đặc và keo lỏng; Giũa mịn chà láng; Chất chùi nước sơn; Nước sơn (lót, màu, phủ); Que gỗ; Túi rác; Hộp đựng đồ dơ.

B. CÁCH LÀM

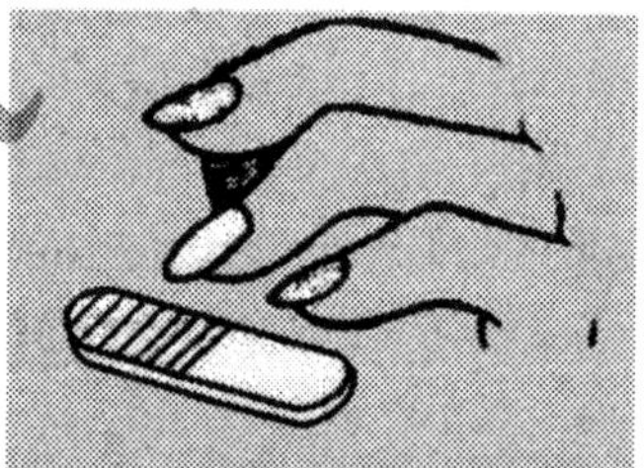
Buff on nail surface
Chà mịn mặt móng

1. *Thơ rửa tay với xà phòng và nước ấm*
2. *Dọn bàn, đặt dụng cụ và vật liệu lên khăn có trãi giấy sạch*
3. *Rửa tay khách với nước ấm và xà phòng*
4. *Khám tay khách*
5. *Chùi nước sơn cũ trên móng*
6. *Cắt và giũa tạo móng*
7. *Chọn tip vừa với móng thật*
8. *Chà nhám đầu móng*
9. *Chấm keo lên đầu móng thật*
10. *Gắn tip vào móng thật với góc 45 độ ngay chỗ khớp của tip; giữ móng chặc chờ khô keo*
11. *Cắt ngắn tip theo yêu cầu*
12. *Giũa chỗ khớp cho mịn và giử lại lớp bột giũa trên lần móng*
13. *Thêm keo lằn nối móng*
14. *Giũa cạnh móng, chà móng mịn chỗ khớp nối giữa tip và móng thật*
    - *Cho thêm keo, dùng buffer chà láng chỗ nối giữa tip và móng thật*

15. *Thoa dầu lên da chung quanh móng, xoa mặt móng*
16. *Khách rửa tay, lau khô*
17. *Sơn móng tay*
    (nước lót, màu sơn, nước bóng)
18. *Dọn dẹp chỗ làm*

CẦN NHỚ

Khi làm xong, bỏ que gỗ, buffer, giũa vào bao rác. Bỏ dụng cụ đã dùng vào hộp đựng đồ dơ.

NAIL TIP

Cách gắn móng giả

Rough all nails at free edge

Chà nhám đầu móng

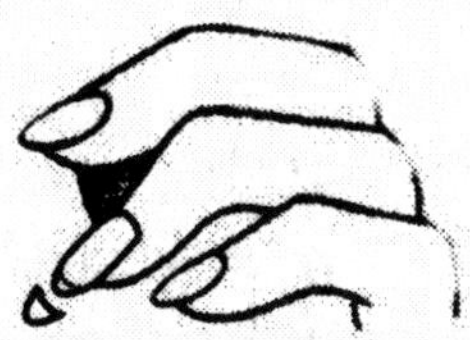

Tips match with natural nail

Móng giả vừa vặn móng thật

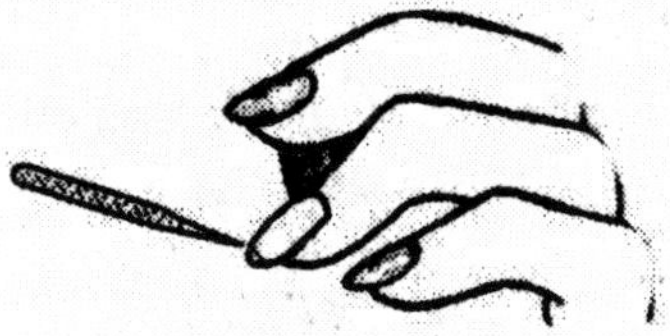

Apply glue at the free edge

Chấm keo lên móng thật

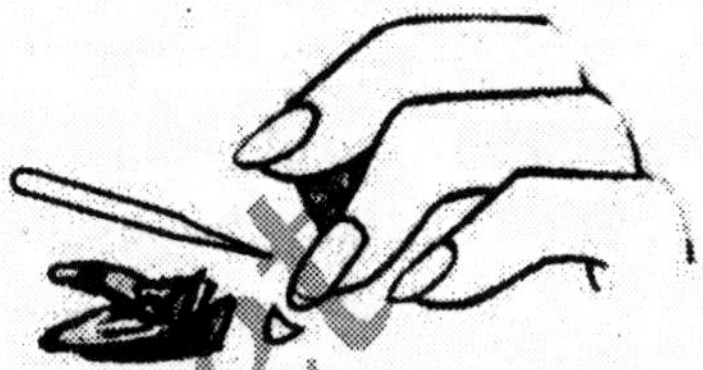

Apply nail tip on natural nail
& shorten the nail

Đặt tip vào móng thật & cắt ngắn

Shape nails & file nail at seam, apply
more glue at seam, apply cuticle oil

Tạo dáng móng, dũa ở lằn nối,
thêm keo, thoa dầu

Clean up:

Throw away orange wood stick
& file in trash bag

Vứt bỏ que gỗ và dũa

Manicurist washes hands

Thợ rửa tay

HOW TO DO A NAIL TIP WITH APPLICATION ACRYLIC OVERLAY

(Tip overlay)

When people desire long nails and they can not have it due to nail breakage or other factors, they will request the full set of tips with acrylic overlay to keep their nails in good shape. Models and actresses... request this service because they prefer long nails and this improves their hands appearance.

Tips are used to extend the natural naisl and the mixture of acrylic powder and acrylic liquid help to build over the nails. This is called "Tip Overlay or Full Set"

A. MATERIALS & IMPLEMENTS

Liquid soap; Towels; Paper towels; Nail tips; Glue (adhesive); Nail file 100 - 180 grids; Nail clipper; Acrylic brush; Acrylic liquid; Acrylic powder; 2 cups; Buffer; Cuticle oil; Nail polish (base coat, color's polish, top coat); Orange wood stick; Trash bag; Soil container.

B. PROCEDURE

1. Technician wash hands with liquid soap and warm water
2. Set up materials and implements on sanitary maintenance area
3. Wash patron's hands with liquid soap and warm water.
4. Examine patron's hands
5. Remove old nail polish
6. Measure all tips to fit natural nails
7. Rough on natural nails surface
8. Push back cuticle on nail plate
9. Glue tips to free edge of natural nails

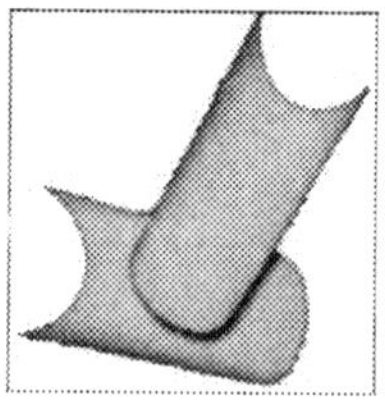

10. Apply nail tip on natural nail covering no more than 1/3, add more glue at seam
11. Shorten the tips if required
12. File sides, buff, shape tips and blend with natural nails, rough the tip surface
13. Apply primer on natural nails (salon)
14. Pour acrylic liquid & acrylic powder into cups
15. Apply each ball of acrylic on *(first at tip; second at nail plate; third at near cuticle),* wait until it dries; hear "click" sound when light beat by brush handle
16. File and shape all acrylic nails
17. Buff all finger nails
18. Apply cuticle oil around nail plate, massage with rotary movement
19. Take patron to wash their hands, blot dry &clean under nail tips with polish remover
20. Apply nail polish to all fingernails *(base coat, color's polish, top coat)*
21. Clean up your workstation

- ***When completed, put orange wood stick, buffer, file in trash bag. Some reused implements put in soil container. And pour remain acrylic liquid into cup of remain acrylic powder, remove it with paper towel, and discard them in trash bag.***

CÁCH GẮN TIP, PHỦ BỘT

Đây là móng gắn tip dài theo ý khách và phủ bột lên móng làm móng dài, cứng chắc, đẹp và duyên dáng thường gọi là Full Set hoặc Tip overlay. Dịch vụ này được khách ưa chuộng, giá cao. Vì thế, thợ thường chú trọng trau dồi trong lãnh vực này.

A. VẬT LIỆU & DỤNG CỤ

Xà phòng; Khăn; Khăn giấy; Tips; Keo; Giũa nhám; Giũa mịn; Đồ cắt móng tay; 2 ly; Bột acrylic; Nước acrylic; Cây cọ; Dầu thoa móng; Nước sơn (nước lót, màu sơn, nước bóng); Bao rác; Hộp đựng đồ dơ.

B. CÁCH LÀM

1. *Thợ rửa tay với nước ấm và xà phòng*
2. *Dọn bàn, đặt dụng cụ và vật liệu lên khăn có trãi giấy sạch*
3. *Rửa tay khách với nước ấm và xà phòng*
4. *Khám tay khách*
5. *Chùi nước sơn cũ*
6. *Đo tip vừa cở móng thật*
7. *Làm nhám mặt móng thật*
8. *Đẩy lùi da trên mặt móng thật*
9. *Chấm keo lên đầu móng thật*
10. *Dán móng giả (tip) vào móng thật, thêm keo chỗ nối*
11. *Cắt ngắn tip theo ý khách*
12. *Giũa 2 bên móng giả, tạo hình dạng móng, giũa trên lằn nối cho mịn, làm nhám mặt móng tip.*
13. *Thoa primer lên móng thật (salon)*
14. *Rót bột và nước acrylic vào 2 ly nhỏ*
15. *Đặt từng viên bột lên móng* (thứ 1 ở tip, thứ 2 ở mặt móng, thứ 3 ở chỗ gần da ở nền móng)*; đợi khô bằng cách gõ nhẹ đuôi cây cọ lên bột, nghe tiếng kêu "click" là khô*

16. *Giũa cong đều, tạo dáng cho móng*
17. *Dùng buffer chà móng cho mịn, bóng*
18. *Thoa dầu lên da quanh móng, massage mặt móng*
19. *Đưa khách rửa tay, lau khô, chùi sạch dưới tip với chất chùi nước sơn*
20. *Sơn móng tay* (nước lót, nước sơn, nước bóng*)*
21. *Dọn dẹp chỗ làm*

Làm xong, bỏ que gỗ, buffer, dũa vào bao rác. Dụng cụ đã dùng bỏ vào hộp đựng đồ dơ. Rót nước acrylic dư vào ly bột acrylic thừa, dùng giấy lau sạch bột trong ly vứt bỏ vào bao rác.

NAIL TIP OVERLAY WITH ACRYLIC

Cách thức gắn tip, phủ bột

Rough on natural nail surface
Chà nhám mặt móng thật

Measure tip fit with natural nail
Đo tip vừa vặn với móng thật

Glue tip, apply tip
Chấm keo, gắn móng

Shorten the tip & add more glue at seam
Cắt ngắn tip, thêm keo ở lằn nối

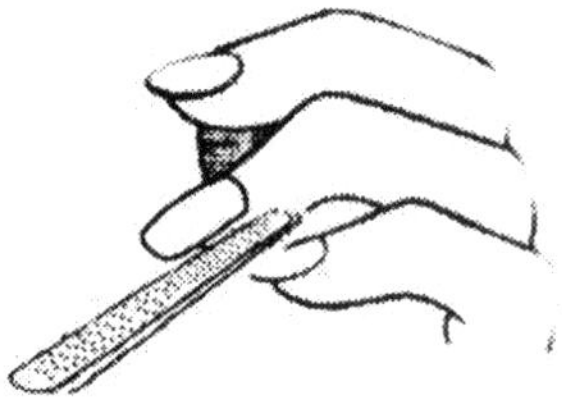

File both sides, seam & shape nail
Dũa 2 bên, lằn nối, và tạo dạng móng

Pump acrylic liquid into cup
Hút nước acrylic bơm ra cup

Pour acrylic powder into cup
Rót bột ra cup

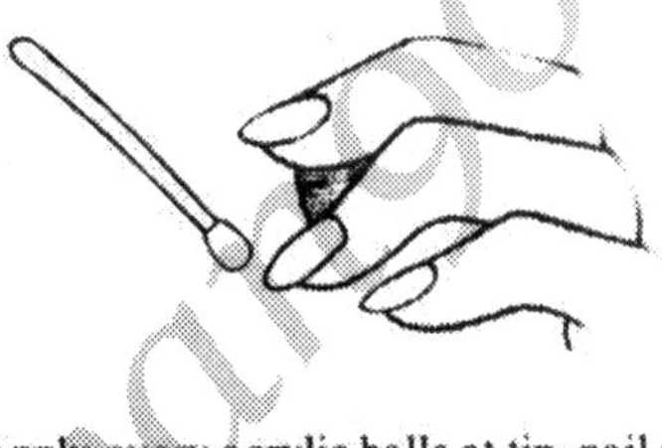

Apply every acrylic balls at tip, nail plate and near cuticle
Đặt từng viên bột lên móng ở tip, mặt móng thật và chổ gần da

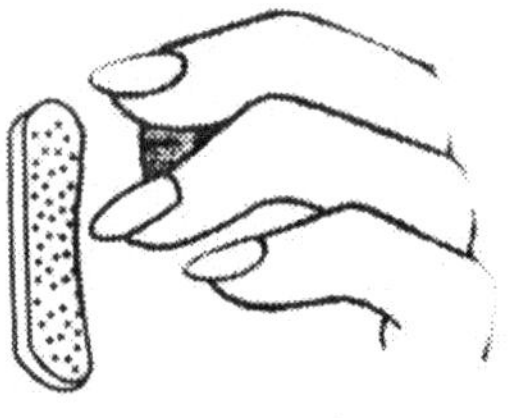

File & shape nail & buffing
Dũa tạo dạng móng và buff móng cho mịn

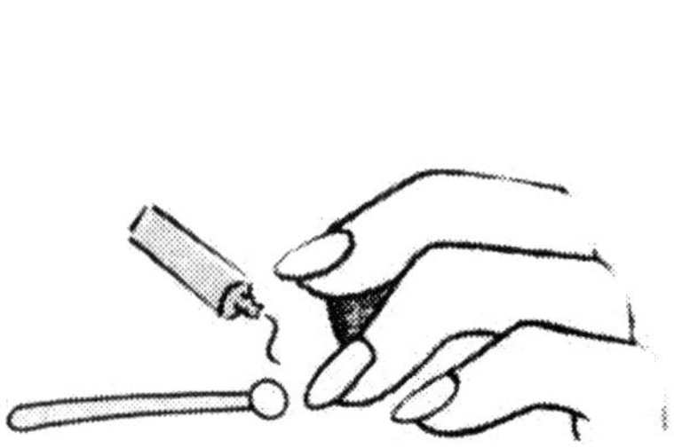

Apply cuticle oil
Thoa dầu lên da chung quanh móng

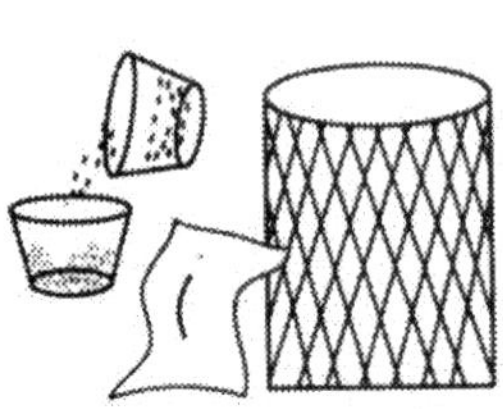

Clean up:
Throw away file, orange wood stick in trash bag. Pour extra liquid into acrylic powder. Remove it with paper, discard in trash bag
Dọn dẹp: ***bỏ dũa, que gỗ vào bao rác. Rót nước acrylic vào cup bột, dùng giấy lau, vứt bỏ vào bao rác***

HOW TO DO AN APPLICATION OF SCULPTURE NAIL

(Artificial nail; Acrylic nail; Brush on nail; Build on nail)

Sculpture nails are the extension of natural nail by acrylic form. By mixing a powder and a liquid chemical product, when it dries and forms a firm continues nail plate. Patrons who desire long nails and can not have it due to nail breakage or other factors, they will request the service of sculpture nails.

A. MATERIALS & IMPLEMENTS

Liquid soap; Cotton; Towels; Paper towels; Primer (salon); Acrylic liquid; Acrylic powder; Brush; File (black beauty file); Nail forms; 2 cups; Buffer; Finger nail clipper; Cuticle oil; Polish remover; Orange wood stick; Trash bag; Soil container.

B. PROCEDURE

1. Technician wash hands with liquid soap and warm water
2. Set up materials and implements on sanitary maintenance area
3. Wash patron's hands with liquid soap and water
4. Examine hands
5. Remove old nail polish
6. Push back cuticle on nail plates
7. Rough on natural nail surface
8. Apply nail form under free edge
9. Apply primer
10. Pour liquid and powder acrylic into cups
11. Apply every acrylic balls
    *(**First**: at form line; **Second**: at nail plate; **Third**: at base area (low half moon)*

Pump acrylic liquid into cup
Hút nước acrylic đơm ra cup

12. When acrylic completely dry and hear "click" sound when light beat by brush handle
13. Take nail form off
14. File and shape the acrylic nail to smooth, good shape
15. Buff nails and apply cuticle oil around cuticle
16. Take your patron to wash their nails; blot dry
17. Apply nail polish *(base coat, color's polish, top coat)*
18. Clean up your workstation

<u>REMEMBER:</u>

When completed, put orange wood stick, buffer, file in trash bag. Some reused implements put in soil container. And pour remain acrylic liquid into cup of remain acrylic powder, remove it with paper towel, and discard them in trash bag.

CÁCH GẮN MÓNG FORM ĐẮP BỘT

(Sculpture nails)

Đây là cách dùng form nhôm (mẫu sẵn) nối dài theo móng thật, sau đó đắp bột acrylic lên, móng sẽ dài cứng chắc. Cách làm móng kiểu này uyển chuyển theo dạng móng mà khách mong muốn.

A. VẬT LIỆU & DỤNG CỤ

Xà phòng; Bông gòn; Khăn; Khăn giấy; Primer (salon); Bột acrylic; Nước acrylic; Cây cọ; Giũa nhám; Buffer mịn; Form; 2 ly; Dụng cụ cắt móng; Dầu thoa da; Chất chùi nước sơn; Que gỗ; Bao rác; Hộp đựng đồ dơ.

B. CÁCH LÀM

First ball on free edge
viên bột thứ nhất lên đầu móng

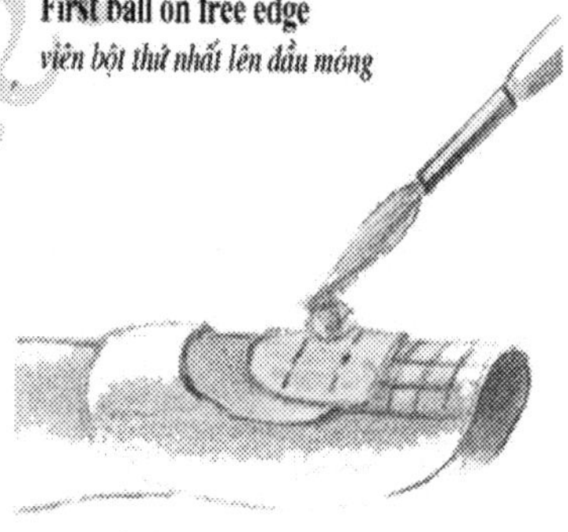

Second ball on center of nail
viên bột thứ hai lên giữa móng

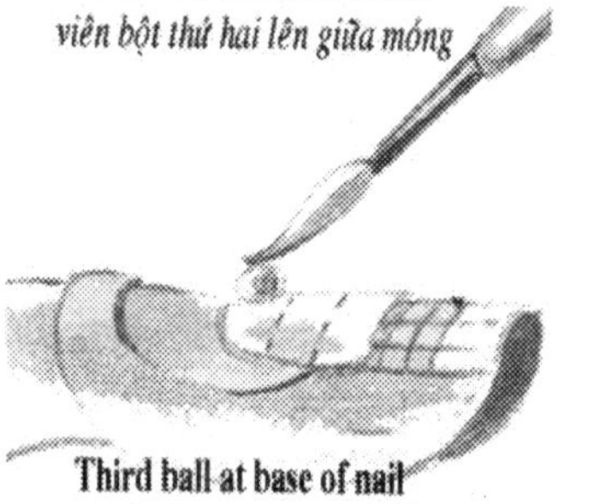

Third ball at base of nail
viên bột thứ ba lên nền móng

1. *Thợ rửa tay với nước ấm và xà phòng*
2. *Dọn bàn, đặt dụng cụ và vật liệu làm móng bột lên khăn có trãi giấy sạch*
3. *Đưa khách rửa tay*
4. *Khám tay khách*
5. *Chùi nước sơn cũ*
6. *Đẩy lùi da tay trên mặt móng*
7. *Giũa nhám mặt móng thật*
8. *Đặt form dưới đầu móng (free edge) bằng 2 tay*
9. *Thoa primer lên mặt móng thật*
10. *Rót nước và bột acrylic vào 2 ly nhỏ*
11. *Đặt từng viên bột* (**Thứ 1**: lần nối form móng; **Thứ 2**: giữa mặt móng; **Thứ 3**: nền móng gần cuticle vuốt ra).
12. *Đợi bột acrylic khô hoặc bằng cách gõ nhẹ đuôi cọ lên mặt móng bột, nghe kêu "click" là khô)*
13. *Lấy form ra khỏi đầu móng* (bằng 2 tay)
14. *Giũa nhẵn, mịn tạo dạng móng đẹp*
15. *Buff (chà) mịn móng và thoa dầu vùng da chung quanh móng*
16. *Dẫn khách đi rửa tay, lau khô*
17. *Sơn móng* (nước lót, màu sơn, nước bóng)
18. *Dọn dẹp chỗ làm*

<u>CẦN NHỚ</u>

- ***Làm xong, bỏ que gỗ, buffer, dũa vào bao rác. Bỏ dụng cụ đã dùng vào hộp đựng đồ dơ. Và rót nước acrylic dư vào ly bột acrylic thừa, dùng giấy lau sạch bột trong ly, và vứt bỏ vào bao rác.***

SCULPTURE NAIL

(form acrylic)

Cách đặt form phủ bột

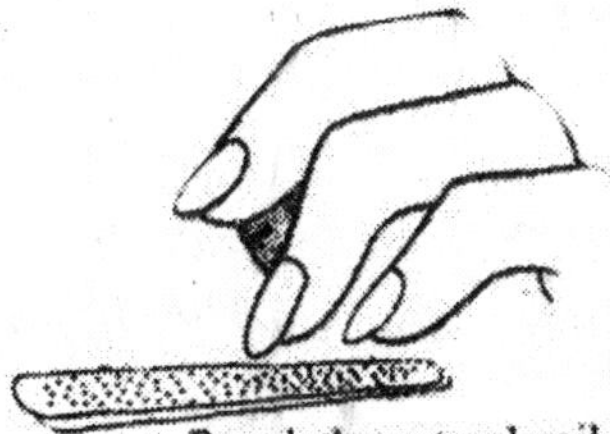

Rough the natural nail surface

Chà nhám mặt móng thật

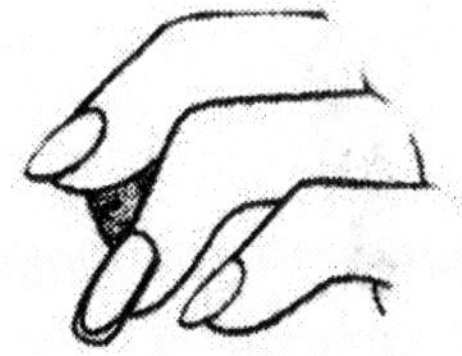

Apply nail form under free edge

Gắn form dưới đầu móng thật

Pour acrylic powder into cup

Rót bột ra cup

Pump acrylic liquid into cup

Hút nước acrylic bơm ra cup

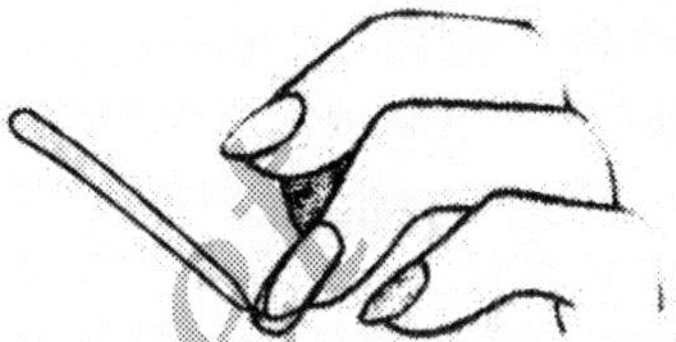

Apply every acrylic balls at form, nail plate, near cuticle

Đặt từng viên bột lên móng ở form, mặt móng thật, chỗ gần da

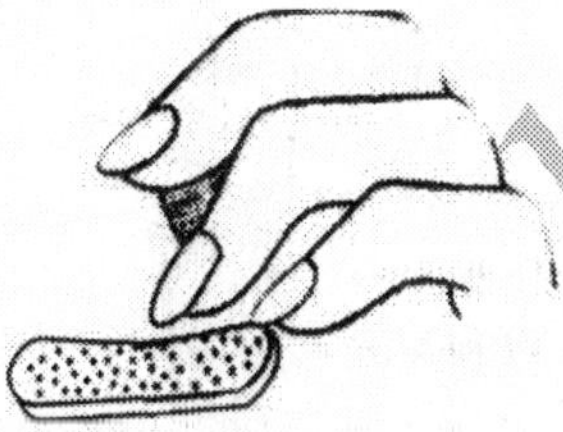

Wait until it dries, take nail form off & file nail. Apply cuticle oil

Đợi khô, lấy form ra, dũa móng, thoa dầu chung quanh móng

Pour extra liquid into acrylic powder. Remove it with paper towel, discard in trash bag.

Rót nước acrylic vào cup bột, dùng giấy lau, vứt bỏ vào bao rác

Clean up:

Throw away orange wood stick file, paper towel

Vứt bỏ que gỗ, dũa, giấy lau

HOW TO DO A SILK WRAP

When the people can not grow natural fingernails of the desired strength, silk wrap is used to fortify weak and fragile nails by silk.

A. MATERIALS & IMPLEMENTS

Liquid soap; Towels; Paper towels; Nail file; Silk; Glue; Scissor; Cotton; Cuticle oil; Buffer; Polish remover; Cushion; Nail clipper; Cuticle pusher; Orange wood stick; Nail polish; Trash bag; Soil container.

B. PROCEDURE

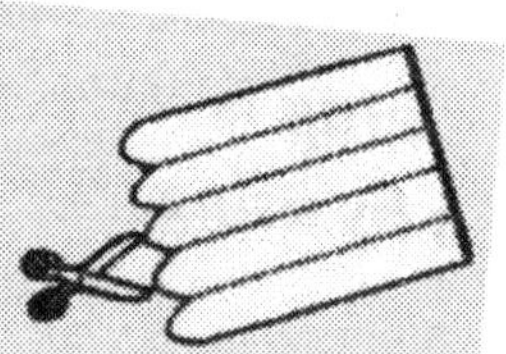

Cut silk
Cắt lụa

1. Technician washes hands with liquid soap and warm water
2. Set up silk wrap kits on sanitary maintenance area
3. Wash patron's hands
4. Examine patron's hands with liquid soap and warm water
5. Remove old nail polish
6. Push back cuticle
7. Rough on natural nail surface
8. Cut silk and apply on natural nail
   (1/16 inch away from the cuticle and edge nail plate)

9 Draw glue on silk
10 File excess silk wrap
11 Add more glue at free edge and shape nail
12 Buff all nails to smooth the nail plate
13 Apply cuticle oil around nails cuticle with rotary movement
14 Wash patron's hands, towel dry
15 Apply nail polish
- *Base coat*
- *Color's polish*
- *Top coat*

16 Clean up your work station

<u>REMEMBER</u>:

When completed, put orange wood stick, buffer, file in trash bag. Some reused implements put in soil container. We can use LINEN WRAP or FIBERGLASS WRAP to fortify weak and fragile nails

CÁCH LÀM MÓNG LỤA

Khi móng tay thật của khách không được cứng chắc như ý muốn hoặc bị tét, bạn có thể dùng lụa bọc lại, móng vẫn đẹp và chắc.

A. VẬT LIỆU & DỤNG CỤ

Xà phòng; Khăn; Khăn giấy; Giũa mịn; Giũa nhám; Lụa; Keo; Kéo; Bông gòn; Chất chùi nước sơn; Đệm tay; Dầu thoa da; Cây sủi da; Đồ cắt móng; Que gỗ; Nước sơn; Bao rác; Hộp đựng đồ dơ.

B. CÁCH LÀM

1. *Thợ rửa tay với xà phòng và nước ấm*
2. *Dọn bàn, chuẩn bị dụng cụ và vật liệu làm móng lụa trên khăn có trãi giấy sạch*
3. *Rửa tay khách với xà phòng và nước ấm*
4. *Khám tay khách*
5. *Chùi nước sơn cũ*
6. *Đẩy lùi da tay*
7. *Chà nhám mặt móng thật*
8. *Cắt lụa và dán lụa vào móng* (cách đều nền da cở 1/16 inch)
9. *Thoa keo lên khắp mặt móng phủ luạ*
10. *Giũa đứt lụa đầu móng*
11. *Cho thêm keo đầu móng và giũa tạo dáng*
12. *Chà (buff) mặt móng cho mịn*
13. *Thoa dầu chung quanh da trên móng tay với động tác xoa tròn nhẹ*
14. *Rửa tay khách, lau khô*
15. *Sơn móng tay*
    - Nước lót
    - Nước màu
    - Nước bóng
16. *Dọn dẹp chỗ làm*

<u>CẦN NHỚ</u>

Khi làm xong, bỏ que gỗ, buffer, gĩua vào bao rác. Bỏ dụng cụ đã dùng vào hộp đồ dơ.
Có thể dùng loại vải dày (linen) hoặc thủy tinh sợi (fiber glass) để bọc cho móng tay bị yếu hoặc dòn dễ gãy được cứng chắc hơn

SILK WRAP

Cách làm móng lụa

Rough on natural nail surface

Chà nhám mặt móng thật

Cut silk

Cắt lụa

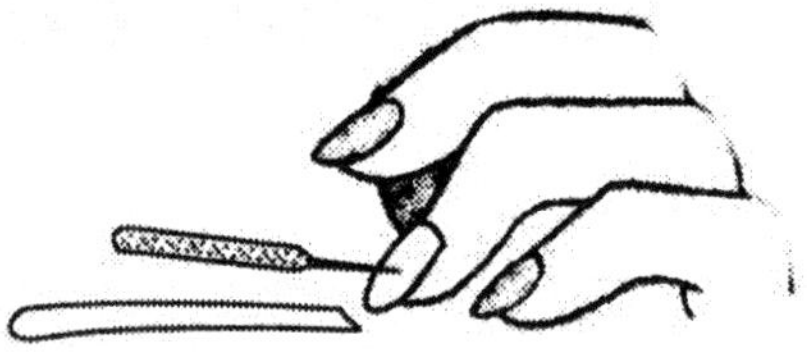

Apply silk on natural nail

Dán lụa lên móng thật

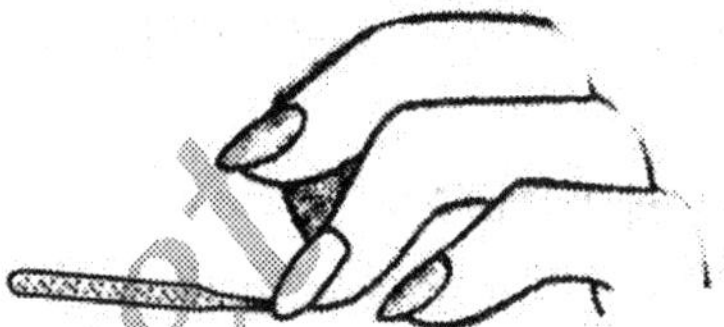

Draw glue on silk to avoid bubble

Thoa keo lên lụa tránh bọt khí

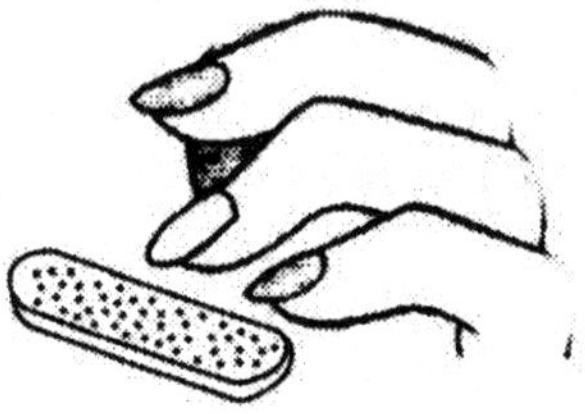

File to cut the silk mesh

Dũa đứt lụa đầu móng

Apply more glue & shape nail

Thêm keo, tạo dạng móng

Buff on nail surface

Chà mịn mặt móng

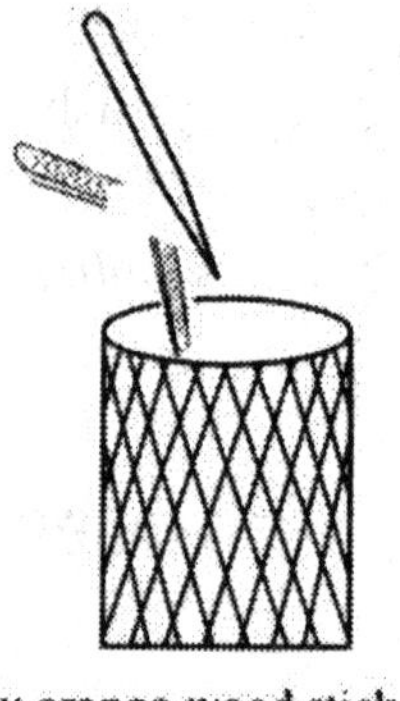

Clean up:
Throw away orange wood stick, file, paper towels

Dọn dẹp:
Vứt bỏ que gỗ, dũa, giấy lau

HOW TO DO A PAPER WRAP

Nail wrap is used to mend torn, broken or split nails and to fortify weak or fragile nails by using mending tissues and mending liquid

A. MATERIALS & IMPLEMENTS

Liquid soap; Towels; Paper towels; Cushion; File; Mending tissue; Mending liquid; Orange wood stick; Scissor; Nail polish; Polish remover; Cuticle pusher; Nail clipper; Cotton; Buffer; Trash bag; Soil container.

B. PROCEDURE

1 Techician washes hands with liquid soap and warm water
2 Set up all implements and materials for paper wrap on S.M.A
3 Wash patron's hands
4 Examine patron's hands
5 Remove old nail polish
6 Push back cuticle
7 Rough on natural nail surface
8 Cut mending tissue smaller than natural nail
(nails must have a visible free edge)
9 Apply paper on natural nail
10 Smooth down with orange wood stick
11 Cut paper in slits shape
12 Stick paper under free edge with orange stick
13 Apply mending liquid over entire tissue and under neath
14 Wait until it dries, buff on nails to smooth
15 Apply nail polish
- *Base coat*
- *Color's polish*
- *Top coat*

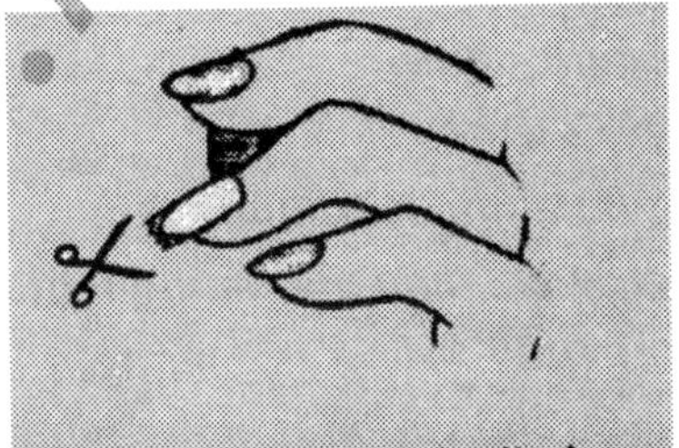

Cut paper in slit shape
Cắt giấy răng cưa

16 Clean up your work station

<u>*REMEMBER:*</u>

When completed, put orange wood stick, buffer, file in trash bag. Some reused implements put in soil container.

S.M.A: Sanitary Maintenance Area

CÁCH LÀM MÓNG GIẤY

Đôi tay sạch và đẹp là tăng thêm phần hấp dẫn cho phụ nữ. Cũng như chăm sóc tay là góp phần bảo vệ cho đôi bàn tay.
Vì nhiều lý do, nhưng nếu móng tay bị xước, rách và yếu muốn giữ móng được chắc, mọc dài ra bằng cách dùng giấy và keo vá móng để giữ tạm thời chờ móng dài ra.

A. VẬT LIỆU & DỤNG CỤ

Xà phòng; Khăn; Khăn giấy; Đệm lót; Giũa; Giấy vá; Que gỗ; Đồ sủi da; Đồ cắt móng; Bông gòn; Kéo; Chất chùi nước sơn; Giũa mịn; Keo vá móng; Nước sơn (nước lót; nước sơn; nước phủ); Bao rác; Hộp đựng đồ dơ

B. CÁCH LÀM

1. *Thợ rửa tay với nước ấm và xà phòng*
2. *Dọn bàn, đặt dụng cụ và vật liệu làm móng giấy lên tấm khăn có trãi giấy sạch*
3. *Rửa tay khách với nước ấm và xà phòng*
4. *Khám tay khách*
5. *Chùi nước sơn cũ*
6. *Đẩy lùi da tay*
7. *Chà nhám nhẹ mặt móng thật*
8. *Cắt giấy nhỏ hơn mặt móng thật một chút*
9. *Dán ép giấy xuống mặt móng*
10. *Sửa giấy cho vừa mặt móng bằng que gỗ*
11. *Cắt răng cưa giấy đầu móng*
12. *Nhét giấy dưới mặt móng với đầu que gỗ*
13. *Thoa keo vá móng lên giấy ở mặt trên và dưới mặt móng*
14. *Chờ khô dùng giũa mịn chà nhẹ lớp keo vá cho láng*
15. *Sơn móng*
    - Nước lót
    - Nước màu
    - Nước bóng
16. *Dọn dẹp*

CẦN NHỚ

Khi làm xong, bỏ que gỗ, buffer, gĩua vào bao rác. Bỏ dụng cụ đã dùng vào hộp đựng đồ dơ.

S.M.A: khu vực giữ vệ sinh

PAPER WRAP

Cách làm móng giấy

Rough on natural nail surface
Chà nhám mặt móng thật

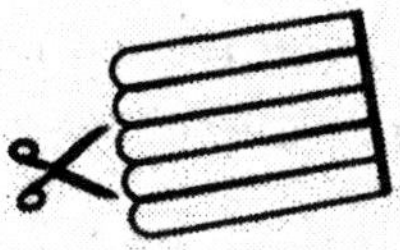

Cut paper wrap
Cắt giấy

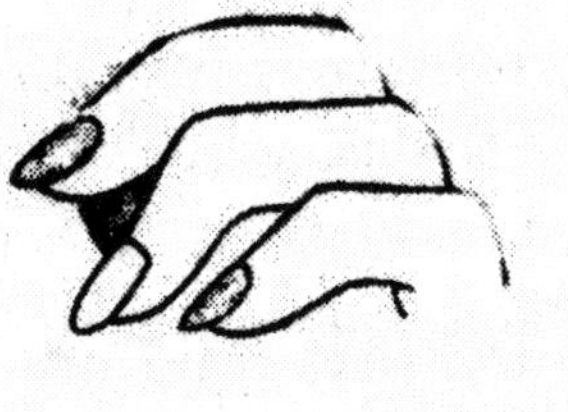

Apply paper on natural nail
Dán giấy lên móng thật

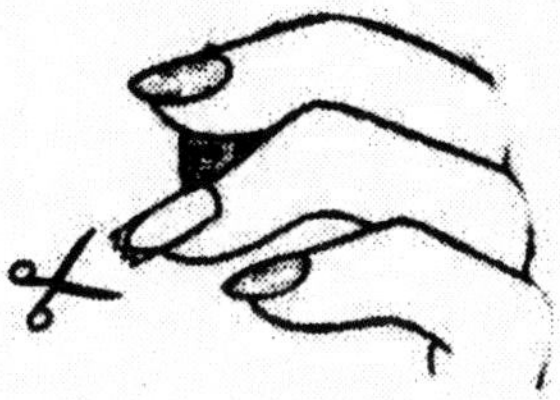

Cut paper in slit shape
Cắt giấy răng cưa

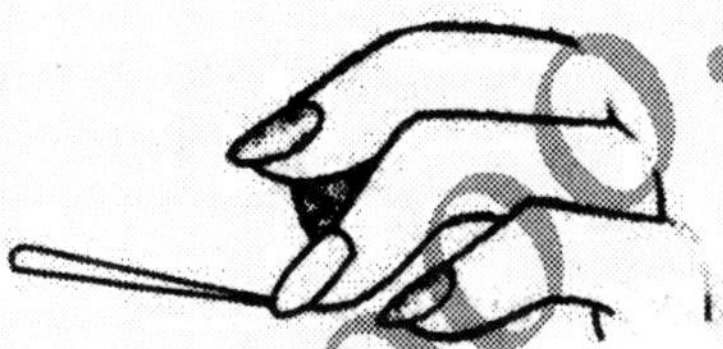

Stuck paper under free edge
Nhét giấy dưới đầu móng

Apply mending liquid
over paper wrap
Thoa keo vá móng lên giấy

Wait until it dries, buffer on nail to
smooth then apply nail polish
Đợi khô, dùng buffer chà mịn móng,
thoa nước sơn

Clean up:
Throw away orange wood stick, file,
and paper towels
Vứt bỏ que gỗ dũa và giấy lau

HOW TO DO A HOT OIL MANICURE

(Reconditioning hot oil manicure)

If clients have dry skin, brittle nails recommend them to do this service instead of plain manicure once a week.

A. MATERIAL, IMPLEMENTS & EQUIPMENT

Liquid soap; Towels; Spatula; Paper towels; Cushion; Orange wood stick; Polish remover; Nail brush; Bowl (hot oil heater); Emery board; Cuticle oil or olive oil; Cuticle nipper; Nail clipper; Nail polish; Cotton; Trash bag; Soil container.

B. PROCEDURE

1. Technician washes hands with liquid soap and warm water
2. Set up equipments and materials for hot oil manicure
   * *Prepare heater, lotion*
3. Wash patron's hands with liquid soap and warm water
4. Do client consultation about her dry skin or brittle nails
5. Remove old polish
6. Shorten the nail
7. File, shape nails on left hand
8. Put left hand in heater with hot oil lotion
9. File, shape nails on right hand
10. Remove left hand from heater and spread lotion on arm
11. Place right hand in oil heater
12. Spread more lotion on left hand & arm to the elbow
13. Hand, arm massage on left hand
14. Loosen cuticle use orange wood stick & cotton tip
15. Nip excess cuticles
16. Repeat on right hand (step 10 - 15)
17. Wipe hands and arms with warm towel and wipe off excess lotion
18. Wrap a cold towel on arms and hands *(gently press)* for close the pore
19. Remove traces of oil on nail surface and under free edge by polish remover
20. Apply polish *(base coat, color's polish, top coat)*
21. Clean up your workstation

<u>REMEMBER:</u>

When completed, put orange wood stick, buffer, file in trash bag. Hot oil and cup put in trash can and some reused implements put in soil container.

CÁCH LÀM MÓNG TAY DẦU

Nếu khách có da tay khô, móng tay dòn, xướt móng, tật cắn móng, da chồm lên mặt móng. Chúng ta nên khuyên họ làm dịch vụ này thay vì làm móng tay nước, nên làm móng dầu mỗi tuần một lần.

A. VẬT LIỆU & DỤNG CỤ

Xà phòng; Khăn; Khăn giấy; Đệm lót tay; Que gỗ; Chất chùi nước sơn; Tô ngâm tay hoặc lò ngâm bằng điện; Giũa giấy; Dầu olive; Đồ cắt móng; Kềm cắt da; bông gòn; Túi rác; Hộp đựng đồ dơ.

B. CÁCH LÀM

1. *Thợ rửa tay với nước ấm và xà phòng*
2. *Dọn bàn (làm ấm dầu trước vài phút)*
3. *Rửa tay khách với nước ấm và xà phòng*
4. *Thảo luận với khách về da khô, móng dòn*
5. *Chùi nước sơn cũ*
6. *Cắt ngắn móng tay*
7. *Giũa móng bàn tay trái*
8. *Ngâm bàn tay trái vào lò dầu ấm*
9. *Giũa móng ở bàn tay phải*
10. *Lấy tay trái ra khỏi lò và trãi dầu lên cánh tay*
11. *Đặt bàn tay phải vào lò dầu ấm*
12. *Trãi thêm dầu từ ngón đến khuỷu của tay trái*
13. *Massage bàn tay và cánh tay trái*
14. *Dùng que gỗ đẩy lùi da trên mặt móng*
15. *Cắt bớt da dư quanh móng*
16. *Lấy tay phải ra và lập lại từ bước 10 - 15*
17. *Dùng khăn ấm lau dầu dư trên da*
18. *Dùng khăn lạnh bọc cánh tay và bàn tay ép nhẹ để đóng lỗ chân lông*
19. *Lấy polish remover chùi vết dầu trên mặt móng, dưới đầu móng*
20. *Sơn móng* (nước lót, nước màu, nước phủ)
21. *Dọn dẹp chỗ làm*

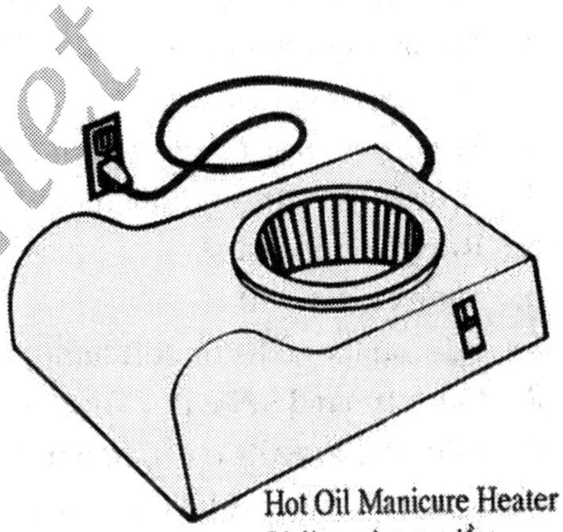

Hot Oil Manicure Heater
Lò làm móng tay dầu

<u>CẦN NHỚ</u>

Khi làm xong, bỏ que gỗ, buffer, gĩua vào bao rác. Dầu và cup đựng bỏ vào thùng rác và đặt dụng cụ đã dùng vào hộp đựng đồ dơ.

CLIENT RECORD CARD (*Hồ sơ khách hàng*)

FOR MANICURIST

This model is not under 15 years of age; and is not a current or former student in barbering or any branch of cosmetology; a current or former licensee of this state or any other; persons currently or formerly owners or employees of school of barbering, cosmetology, or electrology.
Người mẫu không dưới 15 tuổi; và không là đang học ngành thẩm mỹ; không là thợ thẩm mỹ trong tiểu bang này hoặc tiểu bang khác; không là người chủ và nhân viên của trường thẩm mỹ gồm cắt tóc, thẩm mỹ toàn phần, hoặc ngành lấy lông, tóc vĩnh viễn.

Candidate's name .... Application #. ....
Tên người dự thi — *Đơn thi số#*

Valid photographic I.D number .... Type of I.D. ....
Số thẻ chứng nhận giá trị có ảnh — *Loại thẻ chứng nhận*

Signature — Date
Chữ ký người dự thi — *Ngày*

Model's name ....
Tên khách (người mẫu)

Address ....
Địa chỉ

City: .... State .... Zipcode ....
Thành phố — *Tiểu bang* — *Zipcode*

Valid photographic I.D number .... Type of I.D ....
Số thẻ chứng nhận giá trị có ảnh — *Loại thẻ chứng nhận*

Signature
Chữ ký người mẫu

HANDS OR FEET CARE

(Chăm sóc tay hoặc chân)

Skin type ______________________ Shape of nail ----------------------------
Loại da — *Kiểu móng*

* SPECIALTY NAILS SERVICE (*Cách làm móng đặc biệt*)

Number of tips........................ Number of wraps.............................. Number of acrylics..............................
Móng tip — *Móng bọc* — *Móng bột acrylic*

WRITTEN TEST

Nails 900

MANICURIST EXAMINATION 1

1. A dry nail polish (paste or powder) is best for the nails that are:

a. Brittle | **c. Thin**
b. Sculptured | **d. Thick**

Chất đánh bóng móng khô (dạng sền sệt hoặc bột) tốt nhất dùng cho loại móng:

a. Dòn | *c. Mỏng*
b. Móng bột | *d. Dày*

2. How many times must be applied to create gel nail over form or over tip?

a. Two | **c. Four**
b. Three | **d. Following manufacture direction**

Cần bao nhiêu lớp gel để tạo móng gel qua form hoặc trên móng giả (tip)?

a. Hai | *c. Bốn*
b. Ba | *d. Theo hướng dẫn nhà sản xuất*

3. Which one of the following is not ground for disciplinary action by the Board of Cosmetology?

a. Failure to display license properly | **c. Not comply the rules sanitary conditions**
b. Failure to perform acts of manicuring after a reasonable length of time | **d. Performing acts of cosmetology outside licensed school or establishment**

Điều nào dưới đây không kể là vi phạm vào luật của ngành thẩm mỹ:

a. Không đặt bằng hành nghề đúng chỗ | *c. Không tuân luật lệ về điều kiện vệ sinh*
b. Không hành nghề nails trong một khoảng thời gian hợp lý | *d. Hành nghề bên ngoài trường thẩm mỹ hoặc tiệm*

4. Muscles extending down the forearm are called:

a. Flexors | **c. Both a & b**
b. Extensors | **d. Neither of the above**

Bắp thịt vươn dài xuống cánh tay trước được gọi là:

a. Cơ co cánh tay | *c. Cả hai a & b*
b. Cơ duỗi cánh tay | *d. Không có điều nào ở trên*

5. Linen wraps are not good service if client's hands are usually:

a. Held | **c. Photographed**
b. In water | **d. Touched**

Bao móng bằng vải dày (linen) không phải là cách tốt để làm cho khách nếu tay luôn luôn :

a. Nắm lại | *c. Chụp hình*
b. Trong nước | *d. Chạm đến (sờ)*

6. O.S.H.A stands for:

a. Occupied Safety Hazard Area | **c. Occupied Safety Health Agency**
b. Occupational Safety & Health Admisnitration | **d. On Safety Housing Agency**

O.S.H.A là các chữ viết tắt tượng trưng về:

a. Khu vực trở ngại an toàn nghề nghiệp | *c. Cơ quan sức khỏe an toàn*
b. Quản trị sức khỏe và an toàn nghề nghiệp | *d. Cơ quan an toàn nhà cửa*

7. When an accident happens during manicuring, three percent solution peroxide can be used for:

a. Disinfectant | **c. Germicide**

b. Antiseptic | **d. Hangnail**

Khi có tai nạn xảy ra trong khi làm móng tay, dung dịch peroxide 3% có thể được dùng cho việc:

a. Diệt trùng | *c. Diệt vi trùng gây bệnh*

b. Sát trùng | *d. Bệnh da xước*

8. The bulb of U.V lamp should be cleaned daily and changed at least:

a. Twice a year | **c. Every year**

b. Every 5 months | **d. Every 3 months**

Bóng của đèn UV (đèn cực tím) nên được làm sạch hằng ngày và thay tối thiểu:

a. Hai lần một năm | *c. Mỗi năm*

b. Mỗi 5 tháng | *d. Mỗi 3 tháng*

9. If the nail tip shows an air pocket, what should you do?

a. Apply polish remover | **c. Remove it and reapply it**

b. Apply base coat | **d. Apply top coat**

Nếu móng tip bị bọt không khí lọt vào giữa, bạn phải làm gì?

a. Dùng chất chùi nước sơn | *c. Tháo tip ra và làm lại*

b. Sơn nước lót | *d. Sơn nước bóng lên*

10. In order to apply the artificial nails, what do you use to roughen the surface of the nail?

a. Fine emery board | **c. Nippers**

b. File | **d. Pushers**

Để đắp móng bột, bạn dùng vật gì để làm nhám bề mặt móng?

a. Giũa giấy mịn | *c. Đồ cắt da*

b. Giũa | *d. Đồ đẩy da*

11. Why do you have to file the acrylic nails when it dries?

a. Because they lift | **c. Because they remove rough from nail's surface**

b. Because they split | **d. None of the above**

Tại sao bạn phải giũa móng bột khi khô?

a. Vì chúng tróc (hở) ra | *c. Vì chúng cần lấy đi lớp xù xì trên bề mặt móng*

b. Vì chúng bị nứt | *d. Không phải những điều trên*

12. When doing artificial nails, the work room must be:

a. Warmed | **c. On the second floor**

b. Well ventilated and light | **d. Have a large fan and light**

Khi làm móng bột, nơi làm việc phải:

a. Được sưởi ấm | *c. Nằm ở lầu hai*

b. Thoáng khí tốt và đủ sáng | *d. Có một quạt máy lớn và đèn lớn*

13. Where can you find out about the safety information of the product?

a. The M.S.S.D | **c. The M.D.S.S**

b. The M.S.D.S (Material Safety Data Sheet) | **d. The S.D.S.M**

Nơi đâu bạn có được những tin tức về sự sử dụng an toàn của sản phẩm?

a. Trong M.S.S.D | *c. Trong M.D.S.S*

b. Trong M.S.D.S (bảng kê an toàn vật liệu) | *d. Trong S.D.S.M*

14. Which of the following is the M.S.D.S. items:

a. Control and protection measures

b. Primary routes of entry into the body

c. Permissible exposure limits

d. All of the above

Điều nào dưới đây là một trong những nội dung của bản M.S.D.S?

a. Những cách thức an toàn sử dụng

b. Đường đầu tiên xâm nhập vào cơ thể

c. Độ tiếp xúc cho phép

d. Tất cả những điều trên

15. To protect your health while doing acrylic nails, when using acrylic liquid and powder you must:

a. Wear safety glasses

b. Wear contact lenses

c. Wear dust mask

d. Both "a" and "c"

Để bảo vệ sức khỏe của bạn khi làm móng bột acrylic, khi dùng dung dịch acrylic và bột, bạn phải:

a. Mang kính an toàn

b. Mang kính sát tròng

c. Mang miếng che bụi

d. Câu a và c

16. The portion of the skin under the free edge is called:

a. Hyponychium

b. Lunula

c. Eponychium

d. Nail mantle

Phần da nằm dưới đầu móng gọi là:

a. Hyponychium

b. Hình bán nguyệt (lunula)

c. Eponychium

d. Màng móng (mantle)

17. What kind of chemical do you use to remove old polish for customer who has artificial nails?

a. Acetone

b. None-acetone

c. Non-acetone polish remover

d. Polish remover

Bạn dùng hóa chất nào để chùi nước sơn cho khách có mang móng giả?

a. Acetone

b. Chất không có acetone

c. Chất chùi nước sơn không có acetone

d. Chất chùi nước sơn

18. Cosmetologist and manicurist should not work on patrons:

a. If keratoma is present

b. If verruca is present

c. If they have a common cold

d. If they have a carbuncle

Thợ làm tóc và thợ làm móng tay không nên phục vụ nếu khách:

a. Nếu có keratoma (bệnh da dày)

b. Nếu có mụn cóc

c. Nếu có cảm cúm

d. Bệnh thán thư (mụt lở dưới da)

19. You can eat your lunch:

a. In the salon

b. In the separated area of the salon

c. In the reception area

d. In any where in the salon

Bạn có thể ăn trưa:

a. Trong tiệm

b. Trong khu vực riêng biệt với chỗ làm

c. Trong khu vực tiếp khách

d. Bất cứ nơi nào trong tiệm

20. What is the chemical structure of acrylic liquid?

a. It is a monomer

b. It is a catalyst

c. It is a polymer

d. It is an acid

Cấu trúc hóa học của dung dịch acrylic là gì?

a. Là một chất monomer

b. Là một chất xúc tác

c. Là một chất polymer

d. Là một chất acid

21. **Supplies, which come into direct contact with a patron and can not be disinfected shall be:**

a. Wiped clean | **c. Disposed it in a waste receptacle immediately**

b. Soaked in alcohol | **d. Used as often as needed**

Vật liệu tiếp xúc trực tiếp với khách mà không thể diệt trùng, sẽ được:

a. Lau sạch | *c. Vứt bỏ vào thùng rác ngay*

b. Nhúng vào cồn (alcohol) | *d. Dùng thường xuyên khi cần*

22. **How do you hold the nail tip for application?**

a. Downward | **c. Upward**

b. Forward | **d. Backward**

Khi gắn móng tip, bạn giữ móng giả (tip) theo hướng nào?

a. Hướng xuống dưới | *c. Hướng lên trên*

b. Hướng về phía trước | *d. Hướng ra sau*

23. **How long after application of the artificial nails, you can fill them?**

a. 1 week | **c. 3 weeks**

b. 2 weeks | **d. 1 month**

Sau khi đắp móng giả, bao lâu thì bạn có thể refill (phủ bột vào phần nền móng mới mọc)?

a. Một tuần | *c. Ba tuần*

b. Hai tuần | *d. Một tháng*

24. **What is the use of primer?**

a. It is used as bonding substance | **c. It is used as glue**

b. It is used as tape | **d. None of the above**

Primer có tác dụng gì?

a. Dùng như một chất liên kết | *c. Dùng như keo*

b. Dùng như băng keo | *d. Không phải những điều trên*

25. **When the nail tip is larger than the real nail, you can adjust it by using _______?**

a. Cuticle nipper | **c. File**

b. Cuticle pusher | **d. Scissor and file**

Nếu móng tip lớn hơn móng thật, bạn dùng dụng cụ gì để điều chỉnh?

a. Đồ cắt da | *c. Giũa*

b. Đồ đẩy (sủi) da | *d. Kéo và giũa*

26. **Clients with sensitive skin generally show allergic symptoms after repeated exposure for:**

a. 4 to 6 months | **c. 15 days to 1 month**

b. 7 to 9 months | **d. 2 to 3 months**

Khách có da nhạy cảm thông thường biểu hiện triệu chứng dị ứng sau khi tiếp tục tiếp xúc từ:

a. 4 đến 6 tháng | *c. 15 ngày đến 1 tháng*

b. 7 đến 9 tháng | *d. 2 đến 3 tháng*

27. **Light bulb used for the manicure table is:**

a. 75 watts | **c. 120 watts**

b. 40 watts | **d. 60 watts**

Năng lượng của bóng đèn đặt (gắn) ở bàn làm móng tay là:

a. 75 watt | *c. 120 watt*

b. 40 watt | *d. 60 watt*

28. What would you do to the wet sanitize?

a. Keep the lid on at all time

b. Dumb them after using on one customer

c. Discard them after been used on 5 customers

d. Wait until end of the day and discard them

Bạn nên làm gì đối với hộp đựng dung dịch khử trùng?

a. Luôn luôn đậy nắp

b. Đổ bỏ sau khi dùng cho một khách hàng

c. Đổ bỏ đi sau khi dùng 5 người khách

d. Đợi đến cuối ngày rồi đổ bỏ

29. What action will dilute the acrylic powder?

a. Mix powder with alcohol

b. Mix liquid with alcohol

c. Mix liquid and powder

d. Mix liquid and powder and water

Tác dụng nào sẽ làm bột acrylic loãng ra:

a. Trộn bột với alcohol

b. Trộn dung dịch với cồn (alcohol)

c. Trộn dung dịch với bột

d. Trộn dung dịch với bột và nước

30. After you finish the acrylic nail you should:

a. Discard both liquid and powder

b. Mix them together then use paper towel to wipe and discard the neutralized product

c. Put them back to the container

d. Keep using on another customer

Sau khi bạn đã hoàn tất móng acrylic, bạn nên:

a. Đổ bỏ cả dung dịch và bột

b. Trộn bột với nước, dùng giấy lau vất bỏ đi sản phẩm đã trung hòa

c. Đổ chúng vào lại lọ chứa

d. Giữ lại để dùng cho người khách khác

31. It's important that when you are repairing acrylic nails or using chemicals such as primer and acetone. You must let your customer:

a. Close the eyes

b. Turn the customer head to the outer side

c. Wear safety glass

d. Tell the customer look up the ceiling

Điều quan trọng khi bạn sửa móng acrylic hoặc dùng những hóa chất như primer và acetone. Bạn phải cho khách:

a. Nhắm mắt lại

b. Quay đầu khách đi hướng khác

c. Mang kính an toàn

d. Bảo khách nhìn lên trần nhà

32. To use a registered E.P.A disinfectant to disinfect implements, you should:

a. Immerse the tips of implements only

b. Immerse implements include handle

c. Immerse half of the implements

d. Immerse the handle of implements only

Khi sử dụng chất diệt trùng đồ nghề theo tiêu chuẩn E.P.A, bạn nên:

a. Chỉ ngâm phần đầu của dụng cụ

b. Ngâm dụng cụ, kể cả tay cầm

c. Ngâm phân nữa thân dụng cụ vào

d. Chỉ ngâm phần tay cầm của dụng cụ

33. If the customer has athlete's foot, refer the client to a:

a. Dermatology physician

b. Pediatrist physician

c. Pedestrian

d. Pediculosis

Nếu khách có bệnh da chân mụn nước (nấm chân), bạn khuyên khách đến:

a. Bác sĩ khoa da

b. Bác sĩ khoa trẻ em

c. Khách bộ hành

d. Bệnh chấy rận

34. What are the signs of athlete's foot?

a. Callous

b. Corns

c. Blisters and fissures

d. Swelling foot

Dấu hiệu nào là của bệnh nấm da chân (athlete's foot):

a. Da chai

b. Cục chai

c. Mụt nước, nứt da

d. Chân phồng lên

35. If you want to take off acrylic or gel nails you should:

a. Immerse fingers in alcohol

b. Soak nails in acetone

c. Immerse fingers in polish remover

d. Immerse fingers in water

Nếu bạn muốn tháo móng acrylic hoặc móng gel, bạn nên:

a. Ngâm ngón tay vào alcohol

b. Ngâm móng vào acetone

c. Ngâm ngón tay vào chất chùi nước sơn

d. Ngâm ngón tay vào nước

36. If two containers have same color of chemicals but they are different substance you should:

a. Read M.S.D.S

b. Label each container if know the of chemicals

c. Discard all of them

d. Just use it

Bạn nên làm gì với hai lọ chứa đựng hai hóa chất khác nhau nhưng có cùng một màu?

a. Đọc M.S.D.S

b. Dán nhãn hiệu cho chúng, nếu biết

c. Đổ cả hai lọ ấy đi

d. Cứ sử dụng

37. What is the color of a primer when it is dry after being applied on a nail?

a. White

b. Yellow

c. Gray

d. Chalky white

Primer có màu gì lúc khô, khi được thoa lên móng?

a. Trắng

b. Vàng

c. Xám

d. Trắng phấn

38. When an artificial nail tip is not well applied, what may you see?

a. Air pocket

b. Air bubble

c. Balloon

d. "a" and "b"

Khi móng tip không được gắn đúng cách, bạn sẽ thấy:

a. Túi không khí

b. Bọt khí

c. Bong bóng

d. Câu a và b

39. What is the chemical structure of acrylic powder?

a. It is a combination of polymer and monomer

b. It is a combination of monomer and catalyst

c. It is a combination of ground up polymer and catalyst

d. It is a combination of powder and liquid

Bột acrylic có cấu trúc hóa chất gì?

a. Là sự kết hợp của polymer và mononer

b. Sự kết hợp monomer và chất xúc tác

c. Là sự kết hợp của polymer căn bản và chất xúc tác

d. Là sự kết hợp của bột và dung dịch

40. The ending process of acrylic nails, it is called ?

a. Polymerization **c. Reaction**

b. Catalyzing **d. All of the above**

Tiến trình kết thúc khi đắp móng acrylic, được gọi là?

a. Polymerization (phản ứng kết hợp) *c. Phản ứng*

b. Catalyzing (xúc tác) *d. Tất cả những điều trên*

41. When primer touches the skin, what may you feel?

a. Itching **c. Burn and irritation**

b. Burn **d. Irritation**

Khi chất primer dính lên da, bạn cảm thấy như thế nào?

a. Ngứa *c. Rát bỏng và khó chịu*

b. Bỏng *d. Khó chịu*

42. When working on male customer's nail, what do you use to hide spots?

a. Base coat **c. Nail bleach**

b. Nail whitener **d. Polish remover**

Khi làm móng tay cho phái nam, bạn dùng chất gì để che dấu những đốm (vết):

a. Nước sơn lót *c. Chất tẩy móng*

b. Chất làm trắng móng (zinc oxide) *d. Chất chùi nước sơn*

43. During the application of artificial nails, after applying tips on natural nails what is the next step?

a. Add more glue **c. Nail polish**

b. Apply base coat **d. Apply top coat**

Trong lúc đắp móng giả, sau khi đã đắp tip lên móng thật, bước kế tiếp là gì?

a. Cho thêm keo *c. Sơn móng*

b. Sơn nước lót *d. Sơn nước bóng*

44. Each establishment shall post:

a. A list of current prices for services **c. Owner's name and address**

b. A list of service and price **d. A copy of the sanitary rules**

Mỗi cơ sở hành nghề thẩm mỹ nên dán:

a. Bảng giá cả cho các dịch vụ *c. Tên và địa chỉ của chủ tiệm*

b. Danh sách và giá cả các dịch vụ *d. Bảng luật lệ vệ sinh*

45. While performing a pedicure on a client, you notice that his feet are full of water blister, you:

a. After the massage, wrap the feet in hot towels saturate with an antiseptic **c. Refuse to work on the feet until the condition is healed**

b. Pop/ break the blisters **d. Continue with the service**

Khi chăm sóc chân cho khách, bạn thấy chân người ấy nổi đầy mụn nước, bạn:

a. Sau khi xoa bóp, quấn chân khách trong khăn nóng có thấm chất sát trùng *c. Từ chối phục vụ, cho đến khi chân khách lành*

b. Bóp vỡ những mụn nước *d. Tiếp tục làm việc*

46. For pedicure, when offering a leg massage, do not:

a. Massage shinebone

b. Massage the side of the shinebone

c. Massage below the knee

d. Massage bebow the ankle

Đối với việc chăm sóc chân, khi làm thêm massage, đừng:

a. Massage xương ống chân

b. Massage hai bên xương ống chân

c. Massage dưới đầu gối

d. Massage dưới mắt cá chân

47. What is the technical term for split or brittle nail?

a. Onychorrhexis

b. Leuconychia

c. Pterygium

d. Hangnail

Danh từ chuyên môn cho móng tét hoặc móng giòn là:

a. Onychorrhexis

b. Leuconychia (hột gạo, đốm trắng)

c. Pterygium (da chồm lên nền móng)

d. Hangnail (da xước)

48. How do you hold an electric file (nail drill)?

a. Like to hold a pen

b. Thumb and ring finger

c. Between palm

d. Index and middle finger

Bạn giữ dụng cụ giũa máy như thế nào?

a. Như nắm viết

b. Ngón cái và ngón giữa

c. Giữa lòng bàn tay

d. Ngón trỏ và ngón giữa

49. Which of the following conditions, may you refuse service to?

a. Callous

b. Scar

c. Lesion

d. Furrow

Một trong những tình trạng dưới đây bạn không nên phục vụ:

a. Da chai

b. Thẹo

c. Vết lở

d. Móng bị gợn sóng

50. How do you remove acrylic nails if a client does not want to wear them any more?

a. Polish remover

b. Alcohol 99%

c. Quats solution

d. Acetone

Làm thế nào để lấy đi móng bột, nếu người khách không muốn mang móng nữa:

a. Chất lau nước sơn

b. Cồn 99%

c. Nước Quats diệt trùng

d. Acetone

51. A person with manicuring license is allowed to work with:

a. Hands and feet

b. Arms and hair

c. Nails and hair

d. Nails and face

Một người có bằng hành nghề chăm sóc tay được phép làm:

a. Tay và chân

b. Cánh tay và tóc

c. Móng tay và tóc

d. Móng tay và mặt

52. Leaving the cap off the acrylic nail liquid container will:

a. Cause the product to increase in volume

b. Cause the product to evaporate

c. Cause the product to be easier to apply

d. Cause the nail to be hard and brittle

Không đậy nắp dung dịch acrylic sẽ làm cho:

a. Sản phẩm tăng thể tích

b. Sản phẩm bay hơi

c. Sản phẩm dùng dễ dàng hơn

d. Làm móng tay cứng và dòn

53. The ratio between polymer and monomer should be:

a. Until it is moist **c. 5 cc**

b. Manucurist judgment **d. 3 cc**

Tỷ lệ giữa polymer (bột) và monomer (nước) sẽ là:

a. Độ ẩm vừa phải *c. 5 cc*

b. Phán đoán của thợ *d. 3 cc*

54. If you open a salon, the first requirements for the Board of Barbering and Cosmetology approved are:

a. Skin care license **c. Cosmetology license**

b. Manicure license **d. Business license**

Nếu bạn mở tiệm, những đòi hỏi đầu tiên của ngành thẩm mỹ là:

a. Bằng săn sóc về da *c. Bằng thẩm mỹ viên (tóc, da, nail)*

b. Bằng săn sóc tay chân *d. Giấy phép mở tiệm*

55. Where does glue overflow?

a. Nail mantle **c. Nail plate**

b. Nail body **d. Nail groove**

Keo thường bị chảy tràn lên:

a. Màng móng *c. Mặt móng*

b. Thân móng *d. Rãnh móng*

56. What condition should nail surface be when placing rhinestones?

a. Base coat shoul be tacky **c. Nail polish should be tacky**

b. Top coat should be tacky **d. None of the above**

Điều kiện nào của mặt móng nên đặt đá màu lóng lánh lên?

a. Lớp sơn lót còn dẻo *c. Lớp nước sơn còn ướt*

b. Lớp phủ bóng còn dẻo *d. Không phải những điều kể trên*

57. A manicurist license entitles the licensee to do all except one of the following:

a. Manicure in barber shop **c. Manicure in salon**

b. Remove rollers on client's hair when not busy **d. Handle appointment book in an establishment**

Bằng làm móng tay cho phép người có bằng làm tất cả các dịch vụ, ngoại trừ:

a. Làm móng tay trong tiệm cắt tóc *c. Làm móng tay trong salon*

b. Tháo ống cuốn tóc cho khách khi rảnh rỗi. *d. Quản lý sổ ghi hẹn cho khách trong tiệm.*

58. What would you do when glue overflows onto the skin in the application of nail tips:

a. Stop **c. Stop and clean up the glue with polish remover**

b. Remove tip **d. apply base coat**

Bạn sẽ làm gì khi keo chảy tràn lên da khách lúc đang gắn móng giả (tip):

a. Ngưng làm *c. Ngừng làm và lau sạch keo bằng chất chùi nước sơn* b.

Tháo tip ra *d. Sơn nước lót*

59. While cutting excess cuticle around the nail, you accidentally cut the client's skin so that it bleeds. What should you use to stop this bleeding?

a. Powder alum

b. Alcohol

c. Acetone

d. Non-Acetone

Khi cắt da dư quanh móng, bạn vô tình cắt phải da khách làm chảy máu, bạn sẽ dùng chất gì để cầm máu?

a. Powder alum (phèn bột)

b. Alcohol

c. Acetone

d. Non-acetone

60. What is catalyst?

a. It is an ingredient that speeds up the hardening process

b. It is an ingredient that slows the hardening process

c. It's an ingredient that makes the hardening of the polymer

d. None of the above

Chất xúc tác là gì?

a. Là chất giúp nhanh tiến trình làm cứng

b. Là chất làm chậm tiến trình cứng

c. Là chất làm polymer cứng lại

d. Không phải những điều trên

61. What is leuconychia?

a. Blue nail

b. White spot in the nail body

c. Yellow spot

d. None of the above

Leuconychia (móng hột gạo) là bệnh gì?

a. Móng bị xanh

b. Đốm trắng trên thân móng

c. Đốm vàng

d. Không phải những điều trên

62. What do you use mending paper for?

a. Covering nail surfaces

b. Covering some spots

c. Repairing split nails

d. Covering wavy ridge on nail surfaces

Bạn dùng giấy vá móng để làm gì?

a. Phủ mặt móng

b. Phủ đốm móng

c. Để sửa móng nứt

d. Phủ đường gợn trên mặt móng

63. What is the contraindication for application of artificial nails on a customer who never wear artificial nails before?

a. High sensitivity to artificial nail

b. Low sensitivity to artificial nails

c. No sensitive to artificial nails

d. None of the above

Người khách sẽ có phản ứng khó chịu gì khi làm móng giả mà trước đó họ chưa từng được mang loại móng này?

a. Rất nhạy cảm đối với móng giả

b. Ít nhạy cảm đối với móng giả

c. Không nhạy cảm đối với móng giả

d. Không phải những điều trên

64. If the client has callous, which instrument should not be used?

a. Pumice stone

b. Credoknife

c. Nail brush

d. Foot file

Nếu khách hàng có da chai, bạn không nên dùng dụng cụ nào:

a. Đá bọt

b. Dao nạo da

c. Bàn chải móng

d. Giũa chà da chân

65. When you save an emery board in a plastic bag for each client after service, it will cause the growth of?

a. Mildew **c. Bacteria**

b. Spirilla **d. None of the above**

Khi bạn giữ lại cây giũa giấy trong bao nylon sau mỗi lần làm khách, đó là nguyên nhân phát triển:

a. Mildew (mốc) *c. Vi trùng*

b. Vi trùng hình xoắn *d. Không phải những điều kể trên*

66. To avoid responsibility of client's allergy to a product, you have to:

a. Establish a health record card **c. Suggest self treatment**

b. Refer patron to a physician **d. Treat it with medicine**

Để khỏi mang trách nhiệm về việc khách hàng có phản ứng với một sản phẩm, bạn phải:

a. Lập hồ sơ sức khỏe *c. Khuyên khách tự chữa trị*

b. Khuyên khách đi khám bác sĩ *d. Chữa bằng thuốc men*

67. Warming the solvent to 105 degrees speeds removal time for removing artificial nail enhancement by

a. 30% **c. 50%**

b. 60% **d. 75%**

Làm ấm chất mềm móng giả lên 105 độ sẽ tăng nhanh thời gian gỡ bỏ móng nhân tạo (móng giả) thêm:

a. 30% *c. 50%*

b. 60% *d. 75%*

68. What happen when the acrylic nail is immersed too long in water?

a. There will be fungus growth **c. Fungus growth and infection**

b. There will be infection **d. There will be itching**

Điều gì sẽ xảy ra nếu móng acrylic ngâm quá lâu trong nước?

a. Nấm sẽ sinh sản *c. Nấm sẽ sinh sản và gây nhiễm trùng*

b. Gây nhiễm trùng *d. Gây ngứa*

69. What do you need to do before doing an artificial nail?

a. Discuss with the customer **c. Set up table**

b. Make record card **d. All of the above**

Bạn cần phải làm gì trước khi làm móng giả?

a. Thảo luận với khách *c. Chuẩn bị bàn làm việc*

b. Lập hồ sơ *d. Tất cả những điều trên*

70. What do you use to wipe (to clean) the manicure table?

a. Disinfectant **c. Alcohol**

b. Soap **d. Water**

Bạn dùng chất gì để lau sạch bàn làm móng tay:

a. Chất diệt trùng *c. Cồn*

b. Xà phòng *d. Nước*

71. What do you use to remove foot callouses?

a. Emery board **c. Cuticle nipper**

b. Foot file **d. Nail clipper**

Bạn dùng vật gì để lấy lớp chai da chân?

a. Giũa giấy *c. Đồ cắt da*

b. Giũa chà da chân *d. Đồ cắt móng*

72. **Where do you find lanolin and emollient?**

a. Hand lotion and cuticle cream
b. Alum solution
c. Oil and polish
d. All of the above

Chất lanolin và emollient có ở trong:

a. Kem thoa tay và kem thoa da
b. Dung dịch phèn cầm máu
c. Dầu và nước sơn móng
d. Tất cả những chất trên

73. **What product contains nitrocellulose?**

a. Polish remover
b. Hand lotion
c. Enamel
d. Soap

Sản phẩm nào chứa chất nitrocellulose?

a. Chất chùi nước sơn
b. Kem dùng massage
c. Nước sơn móng
d. Xà phòng

74. **Shaping is most often done before of the nail bath, as:**

a. Filing is less difficult on damp nail
b. Filing is more difficult on damp nail
c. Filing is more difficult on dry nail
d. Most patron's nails are already clean

Việc tạo dạng móng thường được làm trước khi ngâm tay, vì:

a. Giũa móng dễ hơn trên móng ẩm
b. Giũa móng khó hơn trên móng ẩm
c. Giũa móng khó hơn trên móng khô
d. Móng tay khách được sạch sẽ rồi

75. **What is the benefit of paper wraps (mending tissue)?**

a. Helps the nail grow faster
b. Strengthen the split nails
c. Smooth nails
d. Cover wavy ridges

Bao móng giấy (mending tissue) giúp ích gì?

a. Giúp móng mọc nhanh hơn
b. Làm chắc móng bị tét
c. Làm móng mịn màng
d. Che những đường gợn sóng

76. **To remove callous skin during a pedicure, use buffer with?**

a. Laundry powder
b. Baking powder
c. Pumice powder
d. Alum powder

Lấy đi lớp da chai trong lúc chăm sóc chân, sử dụng buffer với:

a. Bột giặt
b. Bột nổi làm bánh (baking soda)
c. Bột đá đánh bóng
d. Bột cầm máu

77. **When you apply acrylic nails, what is the use of the primer?**

a. Mending
b. Bonding
c. Remove stain
d. Strengthen nails

Khi bạn đắp móng bột, chất primer giúp cho việc?

a. Vá
b. Kết dính
c. Tẩy vết bẩn
d. Làm móng chắc

78. **Why do you have to discard the emery board after used?**

a. Bad
b. Cannot be sanitized
c. Thin
d. Coarse

Tại sao bạn phải vứt bỏ giũa giấy sau khi sử dụng?

a. Hư hỏng
b. Không thể khử trùng được
c. Mỏng
d. Dày (thô, nhám)

79. Why does acrylic nail lift easily?

a. Apply primer after applying powder | **c. Client changes polish at home**
b. Manicurist applies acrylic on cuticle | **d. Client's hands are wet**

Tại sao móng acrylic dễ tróc ra?
a. Thoa primer sau khi đắp bột
b. Thợ đắp bột dính lên da
c. Khách đổi nước sơn ở nhà
d. Tay khách ướt

80. How long do you immerse your client's feet in antiseptic solution when doing pedicure?

a. 10 minutes
b. 5 minutes
c. 15 minutes
d. 2 minutes

Khi làm dịch vụ về chân, bạn ngâm chân khách trong dung dịch sát trùng bao lâu?
a. 10 phút
b. 5 phút
c. 15 phút
d. 2 phút

81. What is the benefit of acrylic nail:

a. Cover up an infection
b. Strengthen and lengthen the nail
c. Make nail grows slower
d. Make nail grows faster

Móng acrylic có ích lợi gì?
a. Che đi chỗ nhiễm trùng
b. Làm móng chắc và dài
c. Làm móng mọc chậm đi
d. Làm móng mọc nhanh them

82. It is important to sanitize a client's nails before applying acrylic nails because the antiseptic will:

a. Dry the acrylic quickly
b. Help prevent fungus from forming
c. Softten the nail properly for acrylics
d. Adhere or attach the acrylic to the natural nail

Điều quan trọng khử trùng móng tay khách trước khi đắp bột bởi vì sự sát trùng móng sẽ:
a. Khô bột nhanh
b. Giúp ngăn ngừa nấm khi đắp bột
c. Mềm móng đúng cách cho đắp bột
d. Dính hoặc kết bột đến móng thật

83. What is the sign of fungus or mold?

a. When the nail lifts
b. When change the polish
c. When the nails is broken
d. When the nails turn into yellow or green

Dấu hiệu nào là của nấm hoặc mốc:
a. Khi móng tróc ra
b. Khi đổi màu sơn
c. Khi móng bị gãy
d. Khi móng đổi màu vàng hoặc xanh

84. To remove old polish on artificial nails, what should you use?

a. Nail solvent
b. Acetone polish remover
c. Non-acetone polish remover
d. Alcohol

Chùi nước sơn cũ trên móng giả, bạn nên dùng chất gì?
a. Nail solvent (chất làm mềm móng)
b. Chất chùi nước sơn có acetone
c. Chất chùi nước sơn không acetone
d. Cồn

85. Before trimming the cuticle, what do you do?

a. Apply acrylic nails
b. Apply cuticle oil
c. Apply cuticle solvent
d. Apply base coat

Trước khi tỉat da, bạn phải làm gì?
a. Đắp móng bột
b. Dùng dầu thoa da
c. Thoa chất làm mềm da
d. Sơn nước lót

86. Why do you have to fill acrylic nails?

a. Because the nail turns green **c. Because they lift**

b. Because the nail is split **d. None of the above**

Tại sao bạn phải làm fill cho móng bột?

a. Vì móng đổi màu xanh *c. Vì chúng tróc (hở ra)*

b. Vì móng bị nứt *d. Không phải những điều trên*

87. What kind of curing agent do you use when applying gel nails?

a. Blue light **c. Infrared light**

b. Red light **d. Ultra violet light**

Bạn dùng dụng cụ gì khi đắp móng gel?

a. Đèn xanh *c. Đèn hồng ngoại*

b. Đèn đỏ *d. Đèn cực tím*

88. For a more natural effect, the shape of the nail should conform to the:

a. Hand **c. Skin texture**

b.Cuticle **d. Fingertips**

Để nhìn được tự nhiên hơn, hình dạng của móng phải phù hợp với:

a. Bàn tay *c. Loại da*

b. Da ngón tay *d. Đầu ngón tay*

89. Watery blisters and thick white skin between the toes are signs of:

a. Pterygium **c. Pedicuring**

b. Onychia **d. Athlete's foot**

Mụt nước và da trắng dày giữa các ngón chân là dấu hiệu của:

a. Bệnh da mọc tràn ra móng *c. Môn học về chân*

b. Bệnh sưng móng non *d. Bệnh nấm ăn chân*

90. The active agent in nail bleach is usually:

a. Water **c. Hydrogen peroxide**

b. Soap **d. Detergent**

Thành phần chính trong chất tẩy móng thường là:

a. Nước *c. Hydrogen peroxide (H_2O_2)*

b. Xà phòng *d. Chất tẩy*

91. The manicurist can help in protecting the client's health by conducting the best:

a. Cosmetic products **c. Sanitary practices**

b. Professional instruments **d. Professional techniques**

Thợ làm móng có thể giúp bảo vệ sức khỏe khách bằng cách nào cho tốt nhất:

a. Mỹ phẩm *c. Các phương pháp vệ sinh*

b. Những dụng cụ chuyên môn *d. Kỹ thuật chuyên môn*

92. To push back cuticle you should use:

a. Metal pusher **c. Cuticle pusher**

b. Steel pusher **d. All of the above**

Bạn dùng cái gì để đẩy lùi da:

a. Dụng cụ đẩy da bằng kim loại *c. Đồ đẩy (xủi) da*

b. Dụng cụ đẩy da bằng thép *d. Tất cả những điều trên*

93. While performing a manicure, the technician accidentally cut into client's skin, what should he/she do immediately?

a. Refer to a physician
b. Use styptic pencil
c. Wash with warm water
d. Apply an antiseptic

Trong khi làm móng tay nước, người thợ rủi ro cắt đứt da tay khách chảy máu, ngay sau đó người thợ nên làm gì?

a. Khuyên khách đi bác sĩ
b. Dùng bút chì cầm máu
c. Rửa với nước ấm
d. Dùng chất sát trùng

94. Buffing the nails with pumice powder is used to treat:

a. Leuconychia
b. Pterygium
c. Onychophyma
d. Corrugation

Chà móng bằng bột đá bọt dùng để chữa trị:

a. Móng đốm trắng
b. Da mọc chồm lên móng
c. Onychophyma (móng lớn, dày & sưng)
d. Móng gợn sóng

95. If a patron's hands have ringworms, what should you do?

a. Wash patron's hands with disinfection solution
b. Apply antiseptic
c. Refuse to give service for client until it is healed
d. Keep on working

Nếu đôi tay khách bị nấm, bạn nên làm gì?

a. Rửa tay khách với dung dịch diệt trùng
b. Thoa chất sát trùng
c. Từ chối phục vụ khách cho đến khi lành lại
d. Tiếp tục làm

96. What's the last step for men manicure?

a. Apply nail polish
b. Apply nail bleach
c. Apply white nail polish
d. Apply dry polish

Giai đoạn cuối cùng làm móng tay cho nam giới là:

a. Sơn móng
b. Dùng chất tẩy móng
c. Thoa nước sơn trắng
d. Đánh bóng móng khô

97. What kind of chemical is flammable?

a. Cuticle cream
b. Cuticle solvent
c. Enamel
d. Hand lotion

Loại hóa chất nào dễ bắt lửa (dễ cháy)?

a. Kem thoa da
b. Chất làm mềm da
c. Nước sơn móng
d. Kem massage tay

98. Patron will respect and be loyal to a manicurist who is:

a. Arrogant
b. Illiterate
c. Sullen
d. Courteous

Khách sẽ kính trọng và trung thành với người thợ thẩm mỹ nào có:

a. Kiêu ngạo
b. Mù chữ, thất học
c. Cáu kỉnh
d. Nhã nhặn

99. Structures that are appendage to the skin are: hair, sweat glands, oil glands and:

a. Motor fiber | **c. Blood vessel**

b. Nails | **d. Sensory fibers**

Những cấu trúc phụ thuộc của da là: tóc, tuyến mồ hôi, tuyến dầu và:

a. Motor fibers (sợi thần kinh vận động) | *c. Mạch máu*

b. Móng | *d. Sensory fibers (sợi thần kinh cảm giác)*

100. White spots on the nails are known as:

a. Onychauxis | **c. Leuconychia**

b. Onychatrophia | **d. Hang nails**

Những đốm trắng trên móng có tên gọi:

a. Bệnh móng dày | *c. Móng hột gạo*

b. Bệnh teo móng | *d. Bệnh da xước*

MANICURIST EXAMINATION 2

1. **By removing the artificial nail product, you can cause damage to the natural nail due to:**
   a. Use a metal pusher **b. Pulling or twisting the product**
   c. Use aceton remover **d. Use cuticle softener**
   Nếu bạn tháo gỡ móng giả có thể làm hư móng thật do:
   a. Dùng cây sủi da bằng kim loại *b. Kéo hoặc vặn móng giả*
   c. Dùng chất aceton mềm móng *d. Dùng chất làm mềm da*

2. **The main ingredient of nail polish is:**
   a. 70 % alcohol **b. Glue**
   c. White lead **d. Nitro cellulose**
   Thành phần chính của nước sơn là:
   a. Cồn 70 % *b. Keo*
   c. Chì trắng *d. Nitro cellulose*

3. **When giving a manicure, if it is necessary to use a powdered astringent on a patron's skin to arrest bleeding , which of the following may be use to apply it:**
   a. Sterile gauze **b. Clean spatula**
   c. An antiseptic shaker dispenser **d. Any of the above**
   Khi làm móng, nếu cần thiết dùng bột se da để cầm máu trên da khách, vật nào sau đây được sử dụng:
   a. Vải thưa khử trùng *b. Que sạch*
   c. Hộp bột rắc sát trùng *d. Bất cứ loại nào kể trên*

4. **An inflammatory condition of the tissues surrounding the nail is known as:**
   a. Onychatrophia **b. Paronychia**
   c. Onychia **d. Onychoptosis**
   Tình trạng sưng chung quanh móng được biết là:
   a. Onychatrophia (rụng móng) *b. Paronychia*
   c. Onychia (nhiễm trùng móng) *d. Onychoptosis (móng rụng dần)*

5. **What happens when the brush and gel are placed close to curing light?**
   a. Soften of gel for 10 minutes **b. Harden of gel**
   c. Softening gel **d. Harden of gel in 20 mimutes**
   Xảy ra điều gì khi cây cọ gel và chất dẽo gel được đặt cạnh đèn gel móng?
   a. Mềm gel trong 10 phút *b. Cứng gel*
   c. Mềm gel *d. Cứng gel trong 20 phút*

6. **The ingredient of polish remover is:**
   a. Organic solvent and acetone **b. Zinc oxide**
   c. Resin **d. Mineral oil**
   Thành phần của chất chùi nước sơn là:
   a. Dung môi hữu cơ và acetone *b. Oxide kẽm*
   c. Nhựa resin *d. Dầu khoáng chất*

7. Rest and relaxation are very necessary to prevent:

a. Poor eating **b. Mental fatigue**

c. Poor oral hygiene **d. Bad body odors**

Sự nghĩ ngơi và thoải mái là rất cần thiết để ngăn ngừa:

a. Sự kém ăn *b. Tinh thần mệt mỏi*

c. Kém vệ sinh răng miệng *d. Mùi hôi của cơ thể*

8. Over-exertion and lack of rest tend to drain the body of its:

a. Efficiency and vitality **b. Nervous system**

c. Perpiration **d. Blood supply**

Gắng sức quá độ và nghỉ ngơi không đầy đủ có khuynh hướng làm cơ thể mất đi:

a. Hiệu năng và sức sống *b. Hệ thống thần kinh*

c. Mồ hôi *d. Lượng máu*

9. In case of a small cut, one of the following may be used:

a. Styptic pencil **b. 3% hydrogen peroxide**

c. Lump alum **d. Pumice powder**

Trong trường hợp da bị một vết cắt nhỏ, chất nào sau đây nên được sử dụng?

a. Bút chì cầm máu *b. 3% hydrogen peroxide*

c. Phèn cục *d. Bột đánh bóng*

10. Which one of the following qualifications is not necessary to be a successful manicurist?

a. Ability to identify nail disorders **b. Ability to treat common nail diseases**

c. Thorough knowledge of hands and arms **d. Understanding structures of the hand and arm**

Một trong những tiêu chuẩn nào sau đây không cần thiết cho sự thành công của thợ làm móng tay?

a. Khả năng nhận biết bệnh móng *b. Khả năng chữa bệnh móng thông thường*

c. Có kiến thức về bàn tay và cánh tay *d. Biết về cấu trúc của bàn tay và cánh tay*

11. Each licensed establishment is required to maintain the following minimum equipment:

a. 1 closed cabinet (for clean towels) **b. 1 airtight container**

c. 1 liquid sanitizer **d. All of the above**

Mỗi cơ sở kinh doanh có giấy phép, cần có số lượng vật dụng tối thiểu:

a. Một tủ đậy kín (cho khăn sạch) *b. Một đồ chứa kín hơi*

c. Một dung dịch khử trùng *d. Tất cả vật dụng trên*

12. Watery blisters and thick white skin between the toes are signs of:

a. Pterygium **b. Pedicuring**

c. Onychia **d. Athelete's foot**

Mụn nước và da trắng dày giữa các ngón chân là dấu hiệu của:

a. Da mọc chồm *b. Săn sóc chân*

c. Móng non sưng có mủ *d. Nấm ở chân*

13. To soften the cuticle, what solution should be added to the finger bowl?

a. Polish remover **b. Nail bleach**

c. Cuticle oil **d. Liquid soap**

Để làm mềm da phao tay, dung dịch nào cho vào tô nước ngâm tay:

a. Chất chùi nước sơn *b. Chất tẩy móng*

c. Dầu thoa da *d. Xà phòng nước*

14. Hangnails may be treated by softening the cuticle with:

a. Hot oil **b. Boric acid**

c. Strong soap **d. Polish remover**

Móng có da xước có thể được chữa trị bằng cách làm mềm da phao tay với:

a. Dầu ấm (làm móng tay dầu) *b. Chất sát trùng nhẹ (acid boric)*

c. Xà phòng mạnh *d. Chất chùi nước sơn*

15. Textbooks recommend that steel pusher should be used:

a. Flat, with gentle pressure, on a dry nail body **b. Flat, with gentle pressure, on a moist nail body**

c. At an angle, with pressure, on a dry nail **d. At an angle, light pressure, on moist nail**

Sách giáo khoa hướng dẫn nên dùng cây xủi da kim loại:

a. Nằm ngang, đè nhẹ nhàng trên thân móng khô *b. Nằm ngang, ép nhè nhẹ trên thân móng ẩm*

c. Nghiêng, đè mạnh trên móng khô *d. Nghiêng, ép nhẹ trên thân móng ẩm*

16. What material should never be used on plastic artificial nails?

a. Cuticle remover **b. Polish remover**

c. Aceton **d. Cuticle oil**

Chất liệu nào sẽ không bao giờ xử dụng trên móng nhân tạo?

a. Cuticle remover (mềm da) *b. Polish remover (chất chùi nước sơn)*

c. Aceton *d. Cuticle oil (dầu thoa da)*

17. If "Quats" are used to disinfect implements, it must possess which of the following properties to be in compliance with the law?

a. Bactericide **b. Virucide**

c. Fungicide **d. All of the above**

Nếu như Quats được dùng để diệt trùng dụng cụ, nó phải có những đặc điểm nào tuân theo như luật lệ đề ra?

a. Diệt vi trùng *b. Diệt siêu vi khuẩn*

c. Diệt nấm *d. Tất cả những tính chất trên*

18. Nail grow by constant multiplication of nail cells in the:

a. Eponychium **b. Cortex**

c. Matrix **d. Cuticle**

Móng mọc ra bằng sự phát triển liên tục của những tế bào ở:

a. Lớp da ở gốc móng *b. Lớp trong sợi tóc*

c. Móng non *d. Biểu bì*

19. Artificial nails help to:

a. Conceal broken nails **b. Cover up an inflammation**

c. Make nails grow faster **d. Prevent nail discoloration**

Móng nhân tạo giúp:

a. Che đậy chỗ móng gãy *b. Phủ lên chỗ sưng*

c. Làm móng mọc nhanh hơn *d. Ngăn ngừa móng nhạt màu*

20. Hygiene is:

a. Personal cleanliness

b. A science dealing with healthful living

c. Physiology and anatomy

d. A community practice

Vệ sinh là:

a. Sự sạch sẽ của cá nhân

b. Môn khoa học liên hệ sức khỏe đời sống

c. Khoa sinh lý và cơ thể học

d. Thực hành cộng đồng

21. Dead cuticles is easier to remove:

a. If it adheres to the nail body

b. When the nail is buffed first

c. After the softening action of cuticle solvent

d. When the patron does not wear polish

Da chết dễ dàng được lấy đi:

a. Nếu chúng dính vào thân móng

b. Nếu móng được đánh bóng trước

c. Sau khi thoa chất làm mềm da

d. Khi khách không có nước sơn trên móng

22. Which of the following procedures cannot be accomplish with nail mending:

a. Repairing split nails

b. Capping fragile nail tips

c. Reattaching the tip of a severed nail

d. Narrowing a tip of a thick nail

Dịch vụ nào dưới đây không nên vá móng:

a. Sữa chữa móng nứt

b. Phủ trên móng giòn

c. Sữa lại những móng bị tét, rách

d. Làm hẹp tip của móng tay dày

23. Scratches on a nail body could be the result from the use of:

a. Certain type of base coats

b. Strong polish remover

c. A steel pusher on a dry nail

d. The orangewood stick on a wet nail body

Những vết trầy trên thân móng là hậu quả của việc sử dụng:

a. Một số loại nước sơn lót

b. Chất chùi nước sơn quá mạnh

c. Dùng cây sủi kim loại trên móng khô

d. Dùng que gỗ trên thân móng ướt

24. You may use a steel file instead of an emery board to:

a. Remove a small amount of nail free edge

b. Give a smoother finish to the nail

c. Remove a large amount of nail free edge

d. Give a rough finish to the nail

Bạn có thể dùng cây giũa bằng kim loại thay cho cái dũa giấy để:

a. Giũa mòn một ít ở đầu móng

b. Làm cho móng mịn hơn

c. Giũa mòn nhiều ở đầu móng

d. Làm cho móng sần sùi

25. Cuticle cream are used to:

a. Treat brittle and dry cuticle

b. Encourage the growth of nails

c. Remove dead cuticle

d. Remove dry cuticle

Kem thoa da được dùng để:

a. Chữa trị móng dòn và da khô

b. Khuyến khích sự tăng trưởng của móng

c. Lấy đi da chết

d. Lấy đi da khô

26. Which one of the following is not benefit of hand massage:

a. Shiny nails

b. Increased circulation

c. Smooth skin

d. Flexible hands

Điều nào dưới đây không phải là một ích lợi cuả sự xoa bóp tay:

a. Móng sáng bóng

b. Tăng sự tuần hoàn

c. Da mịn màng

d. Tay mềm dẽo

27. Most nail textbook recommend that a cotton tipped orangewood stick be used to:

a. All of the following **b. Cuticle solvent**

c. Nail cream **d. Nail bleach**

Hầu hết sách giáo khoa ngành móng tay khuyến khích dùng cây gỗ quấn bông gòn để thoa:

a. Tất cả chất dưới đây *b. Chất làm mềm da*

c. Kem dưỡng móng *d. Chất tẩy móng*

28. The skin on which the nail body rest is known as the:

a. Matrix **b. Nail-bed**

c. Nail- groove **d. Nail- root**

Lớp da mà thân móng nằm lên được gọi là:

a. Móng non *b. Nền móng*

c. Nail-groove (rãnh móng) *d. Nail root (gốc móng)*

29. Nerves and blood vessels are found in the:

a. Nail plate **b. Lunula**

c. Nail matrix **d. Cuticle**

Dây thần kinh và mạch máu có trong:

a. Thân móng *b. Vòng trắng nền móng*

c. Móng non *d. Biểu bì*

30. Which one of these daily requirements for manicurist's good grooming is not required:

a. Daily bath and use body deodorant **b. Clean teeth and sweet breath**

c. Comfortable white shoes **d. Fresh, clean uniform**

Một trong những yêu cầu hằng ngày nào về sự tươm tất của người thợ mà không cần phải:

a. Tắm hằng ngày và khử mùi thân thể *b. Răng sạch sẽ, hơi thở trong lành*

c. Giày trắng vừa vặn *d. Đồng phục sạch sẽ*

31. Which of the following items is not an accepted sanitary procedure:

a. Wash hand before & after each manicure **b. Disinfect all used implements after used**

c. Use lump alum to stop minor bleeding **d. Use a clean towel for each patron**

Điều nào dưới đây không được chấp nhận là phương pháp vệ sinh:

a. Thợ rửa tay trước và sau khi làm *b. Diệt trùng dụng cụ sau khi làm*

c. Dùng phèn cục để cầm máu *d. Dùng khăn sạch cho mỗi khách hàng*

32. Manicure implement will be disinfected when immersed in 70% ethyl alcohol for a period of:

a. 2 minutes **b. 5 minutes**

c. 10 minutes **d. 25 minutes**

Dụng cụ làm móng sẽ được diệt trùng khi ngâm vào dung dịch ethyl alcohol 70% trong:

a. 2 phút *b. 5 phút*

c. 10 phút *d. 25 phút*

33. Before manicure implement are used on a client, they must be:

a. Wiped with 99% isopropyl alcohol **b. Dried with a clean towel**

c. Scrubbed and disinfected **d. Stop body odor**

Trước khi các dụng cụ làm móng được dùng trên khách, chúng phải được:

a. Lau sạch với isopropyl alcohol 99% *b. Lau khô với khăn sạch*

c. Được chà sạch và diệt trùng *d. Khử mùi thân thể*

34. Powdered alum is a styptic used to:

a. Destroy bacteria **b. Stop minor bleeding**

c. Sanitize implement **d. Stop body odor**

Phèn bột là chất cầm máu được dùng:

a. Diệt khuẩn *b. Cầm máu những vết thương nhẹ*

c. Khử trùng dụng cụ *d. Khử mùi thân thể*

35. The deep fold of a skin the nail root is lodged as known as:

a. Nail mantle **b. Nail groove**

c. Nail wall **d. Nail bed**

Lớp da nằm bọc sâu bên trong rễ móng được biết là:

a. Màng bọc móng *b. Rãnh móng*

c. Thành móng *d. Nền móng*

36. The movement of the hand is controlled by:

a. Supinators **b. Flexors**

c. Extensors **d. All of the above**

Cử động của bàn tay được điều khiển bởi:

a. Cơ lật bàn tay lên *b. Cơ co giật tay*

c. Cơ duỗi tay *d. Tất cả các cơ kể trên*

37. Biceps are muscle that covers the:

a. Forearm **b. Upper arm**

c. Hand **d. Wrist**

Bắp thịt hai đầu là bắp thịt bao bọc:

a. Cánh tay trước *b. Cánh tay trên*

c. Bàn tay *d. Cổ tay*

38. During a manicure, it would not be wise to:

a. File deeply into the corner of the free edge **b. Remove old polish before filing**

c. Soak fingertips before using the nail polish **d. Use the pusher before the nipper**

Trong khi làm móng tay, không nên:

a. Dũa sâu vào cạnh đầu móng *b. Chùi nước sơn trước khi giũa móng*

c. Ngâm tay trước khi sơn móng *d. Dùng xủi da trước khi tỉa da*

39. Drying nail polish with artificial heat can cause:

a. Add more shine to the finish **b. Cause the polish to run**

c. Make air bubbles **d. Lessen the completion time**

Làm khô nước sơn bằng sức nóng nhân tạo là nguyên nhân:

a. Tăng thêm độ bóng *b. Làm nước sơn chảy giọt*

c. Tạo bọt khí *d. Giảm lượng thời gian*

40. Adult nails grow at an average rate of:

a. 1/8" a week **b. 1/8" a month**

c. 1/16" a week **d. 1/16" a month**

Móng của người lớn mọc trung bình:

a. 1/8 inch mỗi tuần *b. 1/8 inch mỗi tháng*

c. 1/16 inch mỗi tuần *d. 1/16 inch mỗi tháng*

41. After the client is seated at the manicure table and their hands have been washed with soap and water normally the next step will be:

a. Applying the cuticle solvent **b. Applying hand lotion**

c. Removing the old polish **d. Placing one hand in the nail bath**

Sau khi khách đã rửa tay sạch với nước và xà phòng và ngồi vào bàn, thông thường, bước kế tiếp bạn làm là:

a. Thoa chất làm mềm da *b. Thoa kem thoa tay (hand lotion)*

c. Chùi nước sơn cũ *d. Đặt một bàn tay vào tô ngâm*

42. To clean under the free edge of the nail, manicurists usually use:

a. The finger bath brush **b. The pointed end of the pusher**

c. A cotton-tipped orangewood stick **d. A point of the nipper**

Để làm sạch dưới móng tay, thợ thường dùng:

a. Chà rửa ngón tay *b. Mũi nhọn của cây xủi da*

c. Que gỗ quấn bông gòn *d. Mũi nhọn của đồ cắt da*

43. The number of phalanges in the fingers of each hand are:

a. 10 phalanges **b. 5 phalanges**

c. 8 phalanges **d. 14 phalanges**

Số lượng (đốt) lóng tay của mỗi bàn tay là:

a. 10 đốt *b. 5 đốt*

c. 8 đốt *d. 14 đốt*

44. In manicuring, pumice powder may be used to:

a. Remove nail polish **b. Soften cuticle**

c. Soften nails **d. Smooth ridges**

Khi làm manicuring, bột đánh bóng được dùng để:

a. Chùi nước sơn *b. Làm mềm phao tay*

c. Làm mềm móng *d. Làm mịn đường gợn móng*

45. Who is liable for implements and maintaining the sanitary requirements in a licensed establishment?

a. The holder of the establishment license **b. The person in charge**

c. The licensed person working on permission **d. All of the above jointly**

Ai là người có trách nhiệm thi hành và duy trì luật vệ sinh trong cơ sở có giấy phép (trường và salon)?

a. Người chủ tiệm *b. Người quản lý*

c. Người có bằng và đang làm việc *d. Tất cả mọi người kể trên*

46. Pushing back the cuticles will:

a. Loosen the eponychium **b. Cause fungus on nails**

c. Not do any good **d. Slow down the nail growth**

Việc đẩy lùi da (sủi da) sẽ:

a. Làm lỏng lớp da ở gốc móng *b. Sinh sản nấm trên móng*

c. Không có ích lợi gì cả *d. Làm móng mọc chậm lại*

47. If not properly cared for, hangnails may:

a. Become spotted **b. Turn yellow**

c. Become infected **d. Become congenital**

Nếu không được săn sóc đúng cách, da xước có thể:

a. Trở nên lốm đốm *b. Ngã màu vàng*

c. Trở thành nhiễm trùng *d. Thành tật bẩm sinh*

48. When using an electric file (nail drill), you must use:

a. No pressure **b. Pumice powder**

c. Cuticle oil **d. Medium pressure**

Khi dùng máy giũa điện, bạn phải xử dụng:

a. Không sức ép *b. Bột đá đánh bóng*

c. Dầu thoa da *d. Ép trung bình*

49. If a slight cut occurs while giving a manicure, you should use:

a. An astringent **b. Styptic pencil**

c. Pumice stone **d. Lysol**

Nếu một vệt cắt nhẹ (đứt tay) xãy ra khi làm móng, bạn nên dùng:

a. Chất se da (đóng lỗ chân lông) *b. Bút chì cầm máu*

c. Đá bọt mài *d. Lysol*

50. The state board rule for handling emery board says that you should:

a. Wipe with 99% isopropyl alcohol **b. Discard after use on each client**

c. Store in plastic bag after use **d. Keep in dust-proof cabinet**

Luật của ngành thẩm mỹ tiểu bang, nói rằng dùng giũa giấy bạn phải:

a. Lau với isopropyl alcohol 99% *b. Hủy bỏ sau khi dùng cho mỗi khách*

c. Cất trong bao nylon sau khi dùng *d. Cất trong tủ kín tránh bụi*

51. Antiseptics are used to:

a. Disinfect manicure implements **b. Retard the growth of germs**

c. Destroy bacteria **d. Open pores of the skin**

Các chất sát trùng được dùng để:

a. Diệt trùng dụng cụ làm móng *b. Làm chậm sự phát triển vi trùng*

c. Diệt khuẩn *d. Làm nở lỗ chân lông*

52. During the application of acrylic nails, the powder on the brush should be:

a. Applied to all bristles **b. Worked into a thick paste**

c. Formed into a ball at the tip of the brush **d. Wet so it will stick to the brush**

Trong khi đắp bột, bột trên cọ nên:

a. Dính đều vào lông cọ *b. Nhồi thành sền sệt*

c. Tạo thành viên tròn trên đầu cọ *d. Làm ướt để dính vào cọ*

53. All bottles and containers used in the salon shall be:

a. Made of clear glass **b. Labeled only if poisonous**

c. Labeled as to their application **d. Labeled correctly, regardless of its contents**

Tất cả chai lọ dùng trong salon đều phải được:

a. Làm bằng thủy tinh trong suốt *b. Dán nhãn chỉ khi nào chúng chứa chất độc*

c. Dán nhãn theo công dụng của chúng *d. Dán nhãn đúng, không kể chứa chất gì*

54. Implements used with excessive pressure at the root of the nail might:

a. Remove excessive cuticle **b. Stimulate rapid nail growth**

c. Make the lunula visible **d. Injure live tissues**

Dụng cụ làm móng ép quá mạnh ở phần gốc móng có thể gây:

a. Lấy đi nhiều da *b. Kích thích móng mọc nhanh hơn*

c. Làm lộ hình bán nguyệt *d. Tổn thương những mô sống*

55. The manicure nippers are used for cutting dead cuticle and the proper use of the cuticle nippers will :

a. Not ruff up more cuticle **b. Leave cuticle free of snags**

c. Leave skin unbroken **d. All of the above**

Kềm cắt da được dùng cắt da chết và sử dụng đồ cắt da đúng cách sẽ:

a. Không cắt quá nhiều da *b. Làm phao tay không bị xơ*

c. Làm da không bị rách *d. Tất cả các điều trên*

56. To smooth out wavy ridges and add shine to the nail, you should use a:

a. Nail brush **b. Chamois buffer**

c. Block buffer **d. Black beauty file**

Để làm mịn móng gợn sóng và thêm bóng cho móng, bạn nên dùng:

a. Bàn chãi móng *b. Buffer bọc da dê*

c. Cục buffer *d. Dũa đen*

57. During a manicure, the instruments not in use should be kept:

a. In a clean manicure table drawer **b. In the sanitary maintenance area**

c. On top of the manicure table **d. In a labeled soiled instrument receptacle**

Khi làm móng, dụng cụ khi chưa dùng đến nên đặt :

a. Trong ngăn kéo sạch *b. Trong S.M.A (nơi giữ vệ sinh)*

c. Trên mặt bàn làm móng *d. Trong hộp đồ dơ có dán nhãn*

58. A manicurist's license entitles the licensee to do all except which one of the following?

a. Give a pedicure **b. Remove arm hair with wax**

c. Manicure in a salon **d. Manicure in barbershop**

Bằng hành nghề cho phép thợ làm móng phục vụ tất cả dịch vụ, ngoại trừ điều nào?

a. Săn sóc chân *b. Lấy lông cánh tay bằng sáp ong*

c. Làm móng tay ở tiệm thẩm mỹ *d. Làm móng tay trong tiệm cắt tóc*

59. Manicure implements when not in use should be sanitized and stored:

a. On an exposed shelf **b. In an open cabinet**

c. On the manicure table **d. In a closed container**

Dụng cụ làm móng khi chưa dùng đến nên được khử trùng và cất giữ:

a. Trên kệ *b. Trong thùng mở nắp*

c. Trên bàn làm móng *d. Trong hộp đậy kín*

60. The use of fingers to remove materials from a container is acceptable for client application if:

a. Container is not contaminated **b. Container contains semi-solids product**

c. If the fingers are covered with clean cotton **d. Both "b" and "c"**

Dùng ngón tay để lấy mỹ phẩm trong lọ có thể chấp nhận nếu:

a. Chất trong lọ không nhiễm bẩn *b. Lọ chứa chất sền sệt*

c. Nếu ngón tay được bọc bông gòn sạch *d. Cả hai câu "b" và "c"*

61. Which of the following is prohibited for use in a manicure:

a. Antiseptic lotion **b. Germicidal solution**

c. Powdered alum **d. Lump alum**

Chất liệu nào dưới đây bị cấm sữ dụng trong dịch vụ làm móng tay:

a. Dung dịch sát trùng *b. Dụng dịch diệt khuẩn*

c. Phèn bột (thuốc cầm máu) *d. Phèn cục*

62. Emery boards are discarded after each use because:

a. The abrasive is expended **b. They cannot be sanitized**

c. They are worn out **d. All of the above**

Giũa giấy phãi được hũy bỏ sau mỗi lần dùng vì:

a. Lớp nhám đã bị hỏng *b. Chúng không thể được khử trùng*

c. Chúng đã tróc ra *d. Tất cả các điều trên*

63. Thick nail polish may be thinned by adding:

a. More nail polish **b. Base coat**

c. Acetone, thinner **d. Sealer**

Nước sơn quá đặc có thể được làm loãng, bằng cách cho thêm:

a. Thêm nước sơn *b. Nước sơn lót*

c. Acetone, thinner *d. Sealer*

64. The abductor muscle are necessary for:

a. Bonding the wrist **b. Straightening the wrist**

c. Separating the fingers **d. Bending the elbow**

Bắp thịt abductor cần thiết cho:

a. Sự liên kết của cổ tay *b. Thẳng cổ tay*

c. Xòe các ngón tay *d. Gập cùi chỏ (khủyu tay)*

65. When buffing the nail, you should stroke from:

a. Side to side **b. Crisp, hard strokes, back and forth**

c. Front to back of nail **d. Back to front of nail**

Khi đánh bóng móng, bạn nên vuốt từ:

a. Cạnh đến cạnh *b. Chà vuốt mạnh, lui tới*

c. Đầu móng đến gốc móng *d. Từ gốc móng đến đầu móng*

66. Another name for cuticles is:

a. Hyponychium **b. Scarf skin**

c. Lunula **d. Mantle**

Một tên khác cho lớp da ngoài là:

a. Hyponychium (da dưới đầu móng) *b. Scarf skin (da bọc)*

c. Lunula (hình bán nguyệt) *d. Mantle (màng bọc)*

67. All manicure instruments must be disinfected before:

a. Putting them in a drawer **b. Leaving the salon**

c. Using them on another patron **d. The patron arrives**

Dụng cụ hành nghề móng tay phải được diệt trùng trước khi:

a. Được cất vào ngăn kéo *b. Rời khỏi tiệm*

c. Dùng chúng cho người khách khác *d. Khách đến*

68. **The product that must be used for disinfecting sharp instruments in a beauty salon is:**

a. 70% ethyl alcohol | **b. Dichloride of mercury**
c. Lanolin | **d. Boric acid**

Chất dùng để diệt trùng dụng cụ bén nhọn trong tiệm thẩm mỹ là:

a. Cồn ethyl 70% | *b. Thủy ngân*
c. Lanolin (chất nhờn) | *d. Boric acid*

69. **At the start of the manicure, the nipper, pusher, and orangewood stick should be:**

a. Handy and available to the manicurist | **b. In the manicure table drawer**
c. Laid out on the manicure table | **d. Kept in the sanitary maintenance area**

Khi bắt đầu làm dịch vụ về móng tay, đồ cắt da, cây đẩy da, và que gỗ nên được:

a. Để sẵn sàng cho thợ | *b. Trong ngăn kéo*
c. Đặt nằm trên bàn làm móng | *d. Để trong SMA (vùng vệ sinh)*

70. **Minor bleeding in manicuring is stopped best with:**

a. Alcohol | **b. Disinfectant**
c. Powdered alum | **d. Sealer**

Vết cắt nhẹ khi làm móng được cầm máu tốt nhất bằng:

a. Alcohol | *b. Chất diệt trùng*
c. Phèn bột alum | *d. Sealer (chất phủ bóng)*

71. **A hangnail condition may be corrected by trimming the hangnail and softening the surrounding skin with:**

a. Naphtha | **b. Cuticle oil**
c. Boric acid | **d. Polish remover**

Bệnh xước da ở móng tay (hangnail) có thể chữa trị bằng cách cắt da xước và làm mềm da quanh móng bằng:

a. Xà phòng naphtha | *b. Dầu thoa da*
c. Boric acid | *d. Chất chùi nước sơn*

72. **How far striping tape should be cut from the cuticle and free edge when design:**

a. 1/4 inch | **b. 1/8 inch**
c. 1/16 inch | **d. 1/32 inch**

Chỉ sọc tạo kiểu đường lằn trên móng được cắt cách da và đầu móng trong khi trình bày:

a. 1/4 inch | *b. 1/8 inch*
c. 1/16 inch | *d. 1/32 inch*

73. **The muscles that closes the fingers are called the:**

a. Adductors | **b. Extensor**
c. Abductors | **d. Phalanges**

Những bắp thịt dùng để khép các ngón tay được gọi là:

a. Adductors | *b. Extensor (cơ duỗi tay)*
c. Abductors (cơ xòe ngón) | *d. Phalanges (lóng tay)*

74. **A manicurist's license expired 6 months ago. To renew the license, the manicurist must know to:**

a. Retake the written part of the examination | **b. Retake both the written and practical**
c. Pay a delinquency fee in addition to renewal | **d. Pay just the renewal fee**

Bằng hành nghề móng tay hết hạn đã 6 tháng. Để lấy bằng mới, thợ phải:

a. Lấy lại phần thi viết | *b. Thi lại cả hai phần thi viết và thực hành*
c. Trả thêm tiền phạt và tiền đổi bằng mới | *d. Chỉ trả tiền đổi bằng mới*

75. Cosmetology textbooks recommend that a steel pusher be used on a moist nail:

a. To prevent scratching of the nail plate **b. To increase circulation**

c. So the mantle will not be disturbed **d. So the lunula can be seen**

Sách giáo khoa thẩm mỹ khuyên rằng dùng cây sủi da trên móng ẩm:

a. Để đề phòng trầy mặt móng *b. Tăng sự tuần hoàn*

c. Để không ảnh hưởng da bọc rễ móng *d. Để thấy lunula (hình bán nguyệt)*

76. The nail walls are small folds of skin overlapping the sides of the nail:

a. Mantle **b. Matrix**

c. Bed **d. Body**

Da thành móng là những lớp xếp nhỏ chồng lên cạnh của:

a. Da bọc rễ móng *b. Móng non*

c. Nền móng *d. Thân móng*

77. The nail root is lodged in the nail mantle at the:

a. Top of the nail **b. Base of nail**

c. Side of the nail **d. Tip of the nail**

Rễ móng nằm chặt vào màng bọc móng ở:

a. Trên móng *b. Nền móng*

c. Cạnh móng *d. Đầu móng*

78. The visible portion of the nail, resting upon the nail bed is the:

a. Nail body **b. Nail root**

c. Lunula **d. Free edge**

Phần nhìn thấy của móng, nằm trên đệm móng là:

a. Thân móng *b. Gốc móng*

c. Hình bán nguyệt *d. Đầu móng*

79. Which one of the following is not a main part of the fingernail:

a. Body **b. Root**

c. Mantle **d. Free edge**

Phần nào không là phần chính của móng tay:

a. Thân móng *b. Gốc móng*

c. Mantle (màng bọc móng) *d. Đầu móng*

80. Which of the following is not a nail disease:

a. Onychosis **b. Onychauxis**

c. Pterygium **d. Onychophagy**

Tình trạng nào sau đây không phải là bệnh móng:

a. Onychosis (móng biến dạng) *b. Onychauxis (móng dày)*

c. Pterygium (da chồm trên mặt móng) *d. Onychophagy (cắn móng tay)*

81. The nail root begins from an actively grow tissue called the:

a. Lunula **b. Matrix**

c. Hyponychium **d. Eponychium**

Rễ móng bắt đầu mọc từ mô sinh sản gọi là:

a. Lunula (hình bán nguyệt) *b. Móng non*

c. Hyponychium (da dưới đầu móng) *d. Eponychium (da trên mặt móng)*

82. Phalanges are found in the:

a. Nasal cavity **b. Root of the mouth**

c. Wrist **d. Digits**

Lóng tay được tìm thấy trong:

a. Nasal cavity (hốc mũi) *b. Hốc miệng*

c. Cổ tay *d. Ngón tay*

83. Split nails may be caused by:

a. Soaking too long **b. Use of the nail whitener**

c. Improper use of the buffer **d. Improper use of nail file**

Móng nứt có thể là nguyên nhân do :

a. Ngâm quá lâu *b. Dùng chất làm trắng móng*

c. Đánh bóng không đúng cách *d. Giũa không đúng cách*

84. The appearance of a healthy nail shows a:

a. Purple color **b. Slight pink color**

c. Yellowish color **d. Bluish color**

Bên ngoài của một móng tay khỏe mạnh biểu lộ:

a. Màu tím nhạt *b. Màu hồng lợt*

c. Màu vàng *d. Màu xanh tím*

85. If a client with nail fungus or mold, the only service you may be allowed to:

a. Fill in the new growth nail **b. Apply medicine treatment**

c. Remove artificial nails **d. Plain manicure**

Nếu người khách có móng bị nấm, mốc, bạn chỉ được phép làm:

a. Thêm ít bột vào chỗ móng mới mọc (fill in) *b. Thoa thuốc chữa trị*

c. Gỡ bỏ móng giả *d. Móng tay nước*

86. To prepare a 1000 p.p.m. solution of E.P.A. registered Quaternary ammonium compounds, using a 15% active ingredient, you would mix:

a. 11/4 ounce of "quats" to a gallon of water **b. 1 ounce of "quats" to a gallon of water**

c. 3/4 ounce of "quats" to a gallon of water **d. 1/2 ounce of "quats" to a gallon of water**

Để pha dung dịch diệt trùng Quats 1.000 p.p.m theo tiêu chuẩn của E.P.A dùng độ mạnh 15% của Quats, bạn sẽ cần:

a. 11/4 ounce Quats trong 1 gallon nước *b. 1 ounce Quats trong 1 gallon nước*

c. 3/4 ounce Quats trong 1 gallon nước *d. 1/2 ounce Quats trong 1 gallon nước*

87. Nail brushes and nail baths, used properly, help eliminate:

a. Ridges on the nails **b. Excess cuticle**

c. Stains on the nails **d. Dryness of nails**

Bàn chải móng và tô ngâm tay, dùng đúng cách giúp loại bỏ:

a. Gợn sóng trên móng *b. Da dư*

c. Vệt bẩn trên móng *d. Khô móng tay*

88. Blue nails are usually a sign of:

a. Worry | **b. Neuvous system**

c. Poor blood circulation | **d. Onychorrhexis**

Móng bị xanh thông thường là dấu hiệu về:

a. Lo lắng | *b. Hệ thống thần kinh*

c. Tuần hoàn máu kém | *d. Móng chẻ, nứt, dòn*

89. Which one of the following conditions the manicurist may not treat:

a. Agnails | **b. Paronychia**

c. Onychophagy | **d. Pterygium**

Tình trạng nào dưới đây thợ móng không nên chữa trị:

a. Agnails (xước da) | *b. Viêm da quanh móng*

c. Cắn móng tay | *d. Da mọc dư lên móng*

90. An abnormal overgrowth of the nail is known as:

a. Atrophy | **b. Hypertrophy**

c. Onychophagy | **d. Onychorrhexis**

Tình trạng móng mọc bất bình thường gọi là:

a. Bệnh rụng móng | *b. Hypertrophy (móng dày)*

c. Bệnh cắn móng tay | *d. Móng tét*

91. In manicuring, the nail buffer is used for tip and acrylic to:

a. Polish the nail | **b. Scrub the nails**

c. Remove eponychium | **d. Remove rough nail edges**

Khi làm móng, cây buffer sử dụng cho móng típ và bột được dùng để:

a. Đánh bóng móng | *b. Chà mịn móng giả*

c. Lấy da dư trên nền móng | *d. Chà mịn cạnh móng*

92. An abrasive to smooth nail ridges would be:

a. Powdered pumice | **b. Organic acid**

c. Nitro cellulose | **d. Castor oil**

Chất để chà nhám dùng làm mịn những móng gợn sóng là:

a. Bột đá đánh bóng | *b. Organic acid (acid hữu cơ)*

c. Nitro Cellulose (có trong sơn lót) | *d. Castor oil (thầu dầu)*

93. To remove stain from fingernails, use:

a. Nail polish remover | **b. Cuticle oil**

c. Nail whitener | **d. Nail bleach with 6% H_2O_2**

Để lấy đi vết bẩn trên móng tay, dùng:

a. Chất chùi nước sơn | *b. Dầu thoa da*

c. Chất thoa trắng móng | *d. Chất tẩy với 6% peroxide*

94. Which one of the following would not be a proper method of using a metal pusher?

a. Pointed end used to loosen cuticle | **b. Blade end follows the curve of the cuticle.**

c. Pusher is used from corner to base of the nail | **d. Pusher is used with gentle pressure.**

Phương pháp nào dưới đây là không đúng cách để dùng cây xủi kim loại?

a. Dùng mũi nhọn để xủi da | *b. Mặt bằng đẩy theo đường cong của da*

c. Cây xủi đẩy từ cạnh đến gốc móng | *d. Đẩy cây xủi với sức ép nhẹ*

95. A chamois is used:

a. To store implements **b. In a wet sanitizer**

c. To rest patron's hand **d. On the buffer**

Miếng da dê được dùng:

a. Để chứa dụng cụ *b. Trong dung dịch khử trùng*

c. Để khách dựa tay *d. Bọc cây buffer đánh bóng*

96. To retard polish chipping on the free edge:

a. Remove a hairline of polish at the tip **b. Leave the free edge exposed**

c. Leave the lunula exposed **d. Use only one layer of nail polish**

Để làm giảm lớp nước sơn tróc ở đầu móng:

a. Gạt đường viền mỏng nước sơn ở đầu móng *b. Chừa không sơn đầu móng*

c. Không sơn hình bán nguyệt *d. Chỉ dùng một lớp nước sơn*

97. For dry cuticles and brittle nails, it is best to give:

a. An oil manicure **b. A water manicure**

c. A plain booth manicure **d. A plain machine manicure**

Phương pháp tốt nhất cho da khô, móng dòn là:

a. Làm móng tay dầu *b. Làm móng tay nước*

c. Làm móng tay dã chiến *d. Làm móng bằng máy*

98. When removing acrylic nail enhancements, warming aceton to over 100 F degrees speeds removal time by:

a. 100 % **b. 20 %**

c. 50% **d. 30 %**

Để giúp dễ gỡ móng bột, làm ấm dung môi aceton hơn 100 độ F để ngâm móng, thời gian mềm móng nhanh hơn:

a. 100 % *b. 20 %*

c. 50 % *d. 30 %*

99. The bulb of Ultra Violet light cure gel on nail plate should be cleaned all the times and changed::

a. Every 6 months **b. Every 3 months**

c. Every year **d. Every month**

Bóng đèn cực tím (U.V) để làm cứng móng gel nên làm sạch thường xuyên và thay bóng:

a. Mỗi 6 tháng *b. Mỗi 3 tháng*

c. Mỗi năm *d. Mỗi tháng*

100. Irritation from damaged skin and low blood pressure by dilating the blood vessels, the immune system releases:

a. Histamines **b. Hormones**

c Plasma **d. Blood platelets**

Ngứa do làn da hư hại và có áp suất máu thấp do trương nở mạch máu, hệ thống miễn nhiễm sẽ tiết ra:

a. Chất histamines *b. Kích thích tố*

c. Huyết tương (tương bào) *d. Huyết thanh, tiểu cầu*

MANICURIST EXAMINATION 3

1. **Manicuring instruments may be disinfected by one of the following:**
   a. Hydrogen peroxide 6% **c. Liquid alum**
   b. 60% alcohol **d. Quats solution (1,000 p.p.m)**
   Dụng cụ làm móng tay có thể diệt trùng một trong những chất nào sau đây:
   a. Hydrogen peroxide 6% *c. Dung dịch phèn chua (chất cầm máu)*
   b. Cồn 60% *d. Dung dịch Quats 1.000 p.p.m*

2. **To draw with an airbrush, you need to used a/an:**
   a. Sponge **c. Nail pen**
   b. Design tools **d. Orange wood stick**
   Để vẽ bằng dụng cụ phun sơn (air brush), bạn cần xử dụng:
   a. Xốp *c. Viết móng tay*
   b. Dụng cụ vẽ kiểu *d. Que gỗ cam*

3. **When you apply artificial nails, hold the tip in place until it dries for.**
   a. 15 to 18 seconds **c. 5 to 10 seconds**
   b. 12 to 15 seconds **d. 2 to 4 seconds**
   Lúc bạn làm móng giả, giữ móng tip ở chổ cho đến khi khô khoảng.
   a. 15 đến 18 giây *c. 5 đến 10 giây*
   b.12 đến 15 giây *d. 2 đến 4 giây*

4. **A nail technician can recomend gel nails for the customer who wants lengh without:**
   a. Weight **c. Maintenance**
   b. Thick **d. Gem**
   Người thợ nail có thể khuyên khách làm móng gel vì muốn móng dài mà không:
   a. Nặng *c. Bảo trì*
   b. Dày *d. Đá quí*

5. **Three strengths of Quat solution are 10%; 12.5%; and 15%. When germicidal solution using 10% strength, how much Quat solution do you use in comparison with 12.5%, and 15% in one gallon.**
   a. Less solution **c. Same Amount**
   b. More solution **d. 70% alcohol**
   Ba nồng độ mạnh của dung dịch Quats là 10%, 12.5%, 15%. Khi xử dụng độ mạnh 10%, cần bao nhiêu dung dịch Quats so với 12.5% và 15% pha chế trong cùng một gallon:
   a. Ít dung dịch *c. Cùng số lượng*
   b. Nhiều dung dịch hơn *d. Cần 70%*

6. **Eyes can be damaged by improperly shielded when you use:**
   a. Autoclaves **c. Paper**
   b. Hand **d. Ultraviolet lamp**
   Mắt có thể bị hư vì che không đúng cách khi bạn dùng.
   a. Lò nấu tự động *c. Giấy*
   b. Bàn tay *d. Đèn cực tím (đèn U.V)*

7. **Another name for hives is:**

a. Hornets | **c. Keratoma**
b. Medulla | **d. Wheals**

Một tên khác của sưng da, ngứa da do côn trùng cắn là:
a. Tổ ong | *c. Da chai*
b. Medulla (lõi tóc) | *d. Wheals (mụn đỏ)*

8. **Clear cells are found in the skin layer called:**

a. Stratum corneum | **c. Melanin**
b. Stratum lucidum | **d. Stratum mucosum**

Lớp tế bào trong suốt được tìm thấy ở lớp da:
a. Stratum corneum (lớp sừng) | *c. Chất màu*
b. Stratum lucidum (lớp trong suốt) | *d. Lớp mầm sống chứa chất màu*

9. **A written description of services and prices is called the:**

a. Job description | **c. Service list**
b. Promotion ads | **d. Contract**

Bảng ghi về công việc và giá cả được gọi là:
a. Diễn tả công việc | *c. Bảng giá về việc làm*
b. Phát triển về quảng cáo | *d. Hợp đồng*

10. **A light-colored, slightly raised mark on the skin formed after an injury or lesion of the skin has healed is called a/an:**

a. Scar | **c. Abrasion**
b. Scratch | **d. Dry callus**

Một dấu nhạt, hơi nhô lên trên da sau khi bị thương tích hoặc vết lỡ được lành lại gọi là:
a. Thẹo | *c. Lỡ*
b. Cào xước | *d. Da chai khô*

11. **The practice of offering only selected clients reduced prices should be:**

a. Done discreetly | **c. Encouraged**
b. A weekly ritual | **d. Avoided**

Đặc biệt giảm giá cho một số khách hàng, nên:
a. Làm kín đáo | *c. Khuyến khích*
b. Một lần trong tuần | *d. Tránh*

12. **Acrylic nails must be removed by soaking fingertips in:**

a. Acetone | **c. Cuticle remover**
b. Polish remover | **d. Alcohol**

Muốn gở móng bột, nhúng móng tay vào:
a. Acetone | *c. Chất làm mềm da*
b. Chất chùi nước sơn | *d. Cồn*

13. Gel nails are applied by brushing the gel onto the:

a. Lunula **c. Entire nail**

b. Nail body **d. Free edge**

Móng gel là dùng cọ lấy gel cho lên

a. Hình bán nguyệt trên móng *c. Khắp mặt móng*

b. Thân móng *d. Đầu móng (phần móng mọc ngoài thân móng)*

14. The cuticle at the base overlapping the lunula is the:

a. Pterygium **c. Hyponychium**

b. Eponychium **d. Nail mantle**

Lớp da ở nền móng phủ lên lunula (nền móng có hình bán nguyệt) là:

a. Da mọc chồm lên mặt móng *c. Da dưới đầu móng*

b. Da ở nền móng *d. Màng móng*

15. The production of nail cells occurs in the nail:

a. Root **c. Matrix**

b. Bed **d. Cuticle**

Sự phát triển của tế bào móng xảy ra ở móng:

a. Gốc (rễ) móng *c. Móng non*

b. Nền móng (dưới mặt móng) *d. Lớp da ngoài*

16. The clicking sound made by gently tapping the brush handle on an applied acrylic nail indicates the nails are:

a. Dry **c. New**

b. Cracking **d. Need replacing**

Dùng cán cọ gõ nhẹ lên mặt móng bột nghe tiếng kêu "cách, cách" là dấu hiệu móng:

a. Khô *c. Mới*

b. Nứt *d. Cần thay đổi*

17. Honesty is the best policy when dealing with a client's:

a. Color's polish **c. Nail file**

b. Objections **d. Pedicure**

Thành thật là cách tốt nhất khi có đối phó với khách về:

a. Màu nước sơn *c. Giũa móng*

b. Sự bất bình *d. Chăm sóc chân*

18. Liquid soap, cotton balls used in a manicure service are classified as:

a. Materials **c. Soiled implements**

b. Lotion **d. Equipments**

Xà phòng nước, bông gòn xử dụng trong việc chăm sóc tay chân được phân loại như là:

a. Vật liệu tiêu thụ *c. Dụng cụ bẩn*

b. Dung dịch *d. Equipments (dụng cụ bền chắc)*

19. **What part of the nail is a pointed sander bit of electric file used for?**
a. Lunula
b. On the free edge
c. Under the free edge
d. Nail body
Phần nào của móng cần dùng đầu giũa nhọn của máy giũa điện?
a. Hình bán nguyệt ở nền móng
b. Trên đầu móng mọc ngoài thân móng
c. Dưới đầu móng (mọc ngoài thân móng)
d. Thân móng

20. **The fingerbowl used during a manicure contains water and:**
a. Cuticle cream
b. Antibacterial soap
c. Fungicide
d. Fumigants
Khi làm móng tô ngâm tay chứa nước và:
a. Kem dưỡng da
b. Xà phòng sát trùng
c. Diệt nấm
d. Khí diệt trùng (fumigant của diệt trùng khô)

21. **Metatarsal scissors petrissage is a massage movement which promotes:**
a. Blood flow to neck
b. Blood flow to legs
c. Cutting ability
d. Flexibility
Động tác cắt nhéo nhồi bóp là tác động massage để tăng lên:
a. Dòng máu ở cổ
b. Dòng máu ở chân
c. Tiêu hao khả năng
d. Sự dẻo dai

22. **An easy way for a nail technician to earn additional income is through:**
a. Retail sales
b. Double-booking clients
c. Cleaning houses
d. Changing professions
Một cách dễ dàng để cho người thợ tăng thêm thu nhập là:
a. Bán lẽ
b. Hẹn khách gấp đôi
c. Làm sạch nhà
d. Đổi nghề nghiệp

23. **The slits or tracks in the nail bed at the sides of nail on which the nail grows are called:**
a. Slim
b. Rails
c. Grooves
d. Furrows
Đường kẻ hai bên trong nền móng mà móng mọc ra gọi là:
a. Mỏng manh
b. Đường rầy
c. Đường rãnh móng
d. Đường gợn móng tay

24. **An airbrush can be used with colored polish in nail art to create:**
a. Shades and texture
b. Quick designs
c. Translucent applications
d. Gel nails base
Dùng màu phun xịt có thể dùng với màu sơn trong nghệ thuật móng tay để tạo ra:
a. Nét và độ mịn màng
b. Vẽ nhanh
c. Làm trong suốt
d. Nền móng gel

25. **A temporary artificial nail service is a:**
a. Silk overlay
b. Demonstration service
c. Tip with no overlay
d. Tip applied with no glue
Làm móng giả tạm thời là:
a. Phủ lụa
b. Diễn tả công việc
c. Móng giả không có gì phủ lên
d. Móng giả không cần keo

26. Rotation of elbow is a type of:

a. Chiropractic manipulation
b. Friction massages movement
c. Effleurage
d. Relaxer movement

Động tác vò tròn khuỷu tay là một kiểu của:
a. Nắn xương bằng tay
b. Động tác chà xoay (ma sát)
c. Xoa vuốt
d. Động tác êm dịu, thoải mái

27. By spraying the client's nails with water, you can reduce the heat generated during:

a. Buffing
b. Acrylic removal
c. Polishing
d. Filing

Dùng cách xịt nước lên móng khách, bạn có thể giảm bớt nhiệt trong lúc:
a. Chà bóng móng
b. Tháo móng bột
c. Sơn móng
d. Giũa móng

28. The half-moon shape at the base of the nail is called:

a. Mantle
b. Matrix
c. Lunula
d. Groove

Dạng nữa mặt trăng ở mặt móng được gọi là:
a. Lớp da bọc
b. Móng non
c. Lunula (hình bán nguyệt)
d. Rãnh móng

29. An advantage of Quats solution as a sanitation agent is their:

a. Stability
b. Weak solution
c. Odor
d. Antiseptic

Sự tiện lợi của dung dịch Quats được xem như là một chất khử trùng mà có:
a. Tính ổn định
b. Dung dịch yếu
c. Có mùi
d. Sát trùng

30. This substance can be in the stratum germinativum layer of the epidermis:

a. Elasticity
b. Mold
c. Herpes simplex
d. Melanin

Một dạng có trong lớp mầm sống ở trong cùng của ngoại bì có:
a. Sự đàn hồi
b. Mốc
c. Mụn giộp nước
d. Sắc tố

31. The service of trimming, shaping and polishing toenails, as will as performing foot massage, is called:

a. Podiatry
b. Manicure
c. Pedicure
d. Filing

Dịch vụ cắt, giũa, và sơn móng chân, cũng như làm thêm xoa bóp chân được gọi là:
a. Chữa trị chân
b. Chăm sóc tay
c. Săn sóc chân (pedicure)
d. Giũa

32. Circular movements in palm is effleurage and circular movements on wrist is a massage technique of:

a. Vibration
b. Tapping
c. Friction
d. Joint relaxer movements

Động tác xoay tròn lòng bàn tay là vuốt xoay và xoay tròn trên cổ tay là kỹ thuật massage của:
a. Rung
b. Vỗ
c. Xoay xoay ma sát
d. Giãn khớp xương

33. Only one third of the nail plate should be covered by a /an:

a. Glitter polish application
b. Artificial nail tip
c. French manicure polish
d. Buffer block

Chỉ có 1/3 mặt móng được phủ bởi:
a. Sơn kim tuyến
b. Móng giả
c. Sơn móng kiểu Pháp
d. Cục chà nhám

34. Crack repair of an acrylic nail is performed using:

a. Silk wrap
b. Mending tissue
c. Acrylic
d. Clear polish

Sửa móng bột acrylic bị nứt được làm bằng:
a. Phủ lụa
b. Giấy vá
c. Acrylic (bột)
d. Nước sơn trong

35. The epidermis contains no:

a. Cells
b. Blood vessels
c. Nerves
d. Keratin

Ngoại bì không có chứa:
a. Tế bào
b. Mạch máu
c. Thần kinh
d. Chất sừng

36. Questions about a client's job are part of the:

a. Health information
b. Service record
c. Friendship process
d. Client profile

Những câu hỏi về công việc làm của khách là yếu tố để:
a. Biết về sức khoẻ
b. Hồ sơ phục vụ khách
c. Tạo sự thân thiện
d. Ý niệm tiểu sử của khách

37. The blood and lymph circulation are stimulated by:

a. Massage
b. Tip application
c. Buffing
d. Filing

Sự tuần hoàn của máu và bạch cầu được kích thích bởi:
a. Xoa bóp
b. Gắn móng giả
c. Chà bóng
d. Giũa

38. Tuberculocidal disinfectants are used to clean:

a. Toilet seats
b. Visible blood spills
c. Bathroom floor
d. Cuticle nippers

Dung dịch diệt vi trùng lao (tuberculocidal) cần dùng để làm sạch:
a. Chỗ ngồi nhà vệ sinh
b. Giọt máu nhiễu
c. Nền phòng tắm
d. Kềm cắt da

39. The long, slender bones of the foot are called:

a. Metatarsals
b. Cartilage
c. Ligaments
d. Phalanges

Xương bàn chân dài thon được gọi là:
a. Metatarsals
b. Sụn
c. Dây chằng
d. Phalanges (lóng tay)

40. **The excess skin beneath a toenail's free edge may be softened by using:**

a. Alcohol
b. Silicone lotion
c. Cuticle solvent (cuticle softener)
d. Polish remover

Da dư bên dưới đầu móng chân có thể làm mềm bằng cách dùng:

a. Cồn
b. Dung dịch silicone
c. Chất dung môi (chất mềm da)
d. Chất chùi nước sơn

41. **To avoid smearing polish, especially in a pedicure application, the top coat should be followed by:**

a. Nail strengthener
b. A second top coat
c. Hot blowing air
d. Instant nail dry

Để tránh lem nước sơn, đặc biệt là sơn móng chân, lớp phủ trên cùng sẽ dùng:

a. Chất làm cứng móng
b. Lớp phủ bóng thứ hai
c. Thổi hơi nóng
d. Chất làm khô nhanh

42. **Hyponychium is the portion of the skin:**

a. Over the free edge
b. Under the free edge
c. Around the nail plate
d. At the base

Hyponychium là một phần của da:

a. Trên đầu móng
b. Dưới đầu móng
c. Chung quanh mặt móng
d. Ở nền móng

43. **Always begin a manicure by working with the client's hand that is:**

a. Not the favored one
b. Favored one
c. In worse shape
d. Closest

Luôn luôn làm móng tay bắt đầu với bàn tay nào của khách

a. Tay không thuận (trái)
b. Tay thuận (phải)
c. Hình dáng xấu
d. Gần nhất

44. **Skin that is red and sore is called:**

a. Healthy
b. Infected
c. Inflamed
d. Circulated

Da đỏ và đau nghiêm trọng được xem là:

a. Khỏe
b. Nhiễm trùng
c. Sưng
d. Tuần hoàn

45. **Gel nails stay the same color until:**

a. Removed
b. Water cured
c. Buffed
d. Filed

Làm gel là giữ cùng màu cho đến khi:

a. Lấy đi
b. Làm cứng bằng nước
c. Chà
d. Giũa

46. **Hangnails or agnails may be caused by the cuticle splits around the nail and a hardening of the:**

a. Lunula
b. Dermis
c. Medulla
d. Cuticle

Xước da móng tay hoặc agnail tạo ra do rách viền da quanh móng và chai cứng lại của:

a. Hình bán nguyệt trên móng
b. Nội bì
c. Lõi tóc
d. Da móng tay

47. Occupational disorders from ingredients in cosmetic and chemical can cause contact dermatitis or:

a. Irritant contact dermatitis

b. Eczema

c. Dermatitis venenata

d. Erythema

Bệnh nghề nghiệp do thành phần trong mỹ phẩm và hóa chất có thể gây nguyên nhân sưng da do tiếp xúc hoặc:

a. Ngứa sưng da do tiếp xúc

b. Eczema (chốc lỡ)

c. Dermatitis venenata

d. Sưng đỏ da

48. Replacement of an entire nail about ½ inch, take approximately:

a. 3 months

b. 4 months

c. 5 months

d. 6 months

Mặt móng được thay thế hoàn toàn ½ inch, cần khoảng:

a. 3 tháng

b. 4 tháng

c. 5 tháng

d. 6 tháng

49. The cells of the nail matrix are:

a. Constantly multiplying

b. Dead material

c. Found in the nail body

d. All clear and long

Tế bào của móng non:

a. Tiếp tục sinh trưởng

b. Vật đã chết

c. Thấy trong thân móng

d. Tất cả trong suốt và dài

50. An Infectious and inflammatory condition of the tissues surrounding the nail as known as:

a. Onychatrophia

b.Paronychia

c. Onychia

d. Onychoptosis

Tình trạng các mô chung quanh móng tay bị nhiễm trùng và sưng được biết là :

a. Móng tay teo nhỏ, khô

b. Sưng đỏ chung quanh móng

c. Móng non sưng đỏ có mủ

d. Rụng móng do nhiễm trùng

51. Filing deeply into the nail corners may cause:

a. Blue nails

b. Brittle nails

c. Ingrown nails

d. White spots

Giũa sâu vào góc móng có thể tạo ra:

a. Móng tay xanh

b. Móng tay dòn

c. Móng mọc đâm vô thịt

d. Đốm trắng (hột gạo)

52. What slows down the drying effect of the solvent in nail polish remover?

a. Oil

b. Pumice powder

c. Nail whitener

d. Nail bleach

Chất dung môi gì làm chậm khô trong dung dịch chùi nước sơn:

a. Dầu

b. Bột đá đánh bóng móng

c. Chất thoa trắng móng

d. Chất tẩy móng

53. In manicuring, softening the cuticle with cuticle oil is good treatment for:

a. White spots on nail

b. Hangnails

c. Cut or bleeding cuticle

d. Redness or swelling around the nail

Lúc làm manicure, dung dầu làm mềm da tốt cho việc chữa trị:

a. Đốm trắng trên móng

b. Xước da tay

c. Đứt da hoặc da chảy máu

d. Đỏ hoặc sưng chung quanh móng

54. Dead cuticle tissue is usually removed:

a. Just before the base coat is applied to nail
b. As the last step of the manicuring procedure
c. After the loosing of the cuticle by the pusher
d. Right after the soaking period

Da chết xung quanh móng tay thường được lấy đi:
a. Trước khi thoa sơn lót
b. Là động tác sau cùng của cách làm móng
c. Sau khi làm lỏng da bằng cây sủi
d. Ngay sau khi ngâm móng tay

55. Which one of the following qualifications is not necessary to be a successful manicurist:

a. Ability to identify nail disorders
b. Ability to treat common nail diseases
c. Thorough knowledge of hand cosmetics
d. Understanding of the structures of the hands

Điều kiện nào sau đây không cần thiết cho sự thành công của người thợ làm móng tay:
a. Khả năng biết sự xáo trộn móng
b. Khả năng chữa trị bịnh móng thông thường
c. Thông hiểu về mỹ phẩm thoa tay
d. Hiểu biết sự cấu tạo của bàn tay

56. Each license establishment is required to maintain the following minimum equipment:

a. 1 closet cabinet (for clean towel)
b. 1 airtight container (for clean instruments)
c. 1 liquid sanitizer box
d. All of the above

Mỗi cơ sở có giấy phép đòi hỏi việc bảo trì phải có tối thiểu những dụng cụ:
a. 1 tủ có cửa đóng kín (cho khăn sạch)
b. 1 hộp chứa đậy kín (cho dụng cụ sạch)
c. 1 hộp dung dịch khử trùng
d. Tất cả những câu trên

57. When giving a manicure, if it is necessary to use the styptic powder on a patron's skin to arrest bleeding, which of the following may be used to apply it:

a. Sterile gauze
b. Sterile spatula
c. A shaker dispenser
d. Any of the above

Khi làm móng tay, nếu cần thiết dùng bột cầm máu để chặn máu chảy trên da của khách, các thứ sau đây có thể được dùng là:
a. Gauze sạch được khử trùng
b. Que sạch khử trùng
c. Hộp thuốc rắc bột
d. Bất cứ thứ nào kể trên

58. To soften the cuticle, add to the water in the finger bowl a few drops of:

a. Polish remover
b. Nail bleach
c. Cuticle oil
d. Liquid soap

Để làm mềm da thêm vào nước trong tô ngâm móng tay vài giọt của:
a. Chất chùi nước sơn
b. Chất tẩy móng
c. Dầu thoa da
d. Xà phòng nước

59. Hangnails or agnails may be treated by softening the cuticle by:

a. Hot oil manicure
b. Boric acid
c. Strong soap
d. Polish remover

Xước da móng tay hoặc agnail có thể chữa trị bằng cách làm mềm da tay bằng
a. Làm móng tay dầu
b. Boric acid
c. Xà phòng mạnh
d. Chất chùi nước sơn

60. **How do you use to hold the nail tape (striping tape) to stay down?**

a. Apply small amount of nail polish
b. Apply top coat or clear polish
c. Apply color polish
d. Spray water

Bạn dùng cách gì để giữ sợi chỉ sọc có keo (tape tạo kiểu cho móng) dính sát mặt móng?

a. Thoa một ít nước sơn
b. Thoa nước bóng hoặc nước bóng trong suốt
c. Thoa nước sơn màu
d. Xịt nước

61. **Hot oil manicure that may receive for what nail condition?**

a. Paronychia
b. Onychia
c. Onychophagy
d. Onychosis

Móng tay dầu có thể được làm cho tình trạng móng tay loại nào?

a. Paronychia (sưng nhiễm trùng quanh móng)
b. Onychia (nhiễm trùng có mủ móng non)
c. Onychophagy (tật cắn móng)
d. Onychosis (bệnh móng)

62. **If "Quats" is used to disinfect implements, it must possess which of the following properties to be in compliance with the law?**

a. Bactericide
b. Virucide
c. Fungicide
d. All of the above

Nếu dùng "Quats" để diệt trùng dụng cụ, nó phải có đặc tính gì theo luật lệ ấn định:

a. Diệt vi trùng
b. Diệt siêu vi trùng
c. Diệt nấm
d. Tất cả những điều trên

63. **Nails grow by constant multiplication of the nail cells in the**

a. Eponychium
b. Nail grooves
c. Matrix
d. Cuticle

Móng tay mọc do sự sinh sản liên tục của những tế bào móng trong:

a. Da mọc chỗ nền móng
b. Rãnh móng
c. Móng non
d. Da chung quanh móng tay

64. **Artificial nails help a damaged or fragile nails, strenghen the nails, extend the nail, repair weak nails and:**

a. Conceal broken nails
b. Cover up an inflammation
c. Make nails grow faster
d. Prevent nail discoloration

Móng tay giả giúp phủ móng hư, móng dòn, làm mạnh móng, làm dài móng, sữa chữa móng yếu và:

a.Che đậy móng gãy
b. Che móng bi sưng
c. Làm móng mọc nhanh hơn
d. Ngăn ngừa móng tay phai màu

65. **Textbooks recommend a steel pusher be used:**

a. Flat, with gentle pressure on dry nail body
b. Flat, with gentle pressure on moist nail
c. At an angle, with pressure on a dry nail
d. At an angle, without pressure on moist nail

Sách giáo khoa khuyên nên dùng đồ sủi da bằng thép với:

a. Bề dẹp, với sức ép nhẹ trên móng khô
b. Bề dẹp, với sức ép nhẹ trên móng ẩm
c. Ở một góc, với sức ép trên móng khô
d. Ở một góc, không ép trên móng ẩm

66. **Dead cuticle is easier to remove:**

a. If it adheres to the nail body
b. When it is buffed first
c. After the softening action of cuticle solvent
d. When the patron does not wear nail polish

Da chết lấy đi dễ dàng hơn:
a. Nếu nó bám chặt vào thân móng
b. Khi nó được đánh bóng trước
c. Sau khi thoa lên chất mềm da
d. Khi khách hàng không sơn móng tay

67. **Which of the following procedures cannot be accomplished with nail mending?**

a. Repairing split nails
b. Capping fragile nail tips
c. Reattaching the tip of nails
d. Narrowing the tip of heavy nails

Một trong những cách nào không thể thực hiện với việc vá móng tay?
a. Sửa lại móng tay bị nứt
b. Bao đầu móng tay yếu dễ gãy
c. Gắn lại móng giả của đầu móng
d. Làm hẹp móng giả của móng tay dầy

68. **Scratches on nail body could result from the use of:**

a. Certain types of base coat
b. Strong polish remover
c. A steel pusher on a dry nail
d. The orangewood sticks on a wet nail body

Thân móng tay bị trầy có thể là kết quả từ việc dùng:
a. Dạng nước sơn lót
b. Chất chùi nước sơn mạnh
c. Cây thép xủi da trên móng tay khô
d. Que gỗ cam trên thân móng tay ướt

69. **You may use a steel file instead of an emery board to:**

a. Remove a small amount of nail
b. Give a smooth finish to the nail
c. Remove a large amount of the nail
d. Give a rough finish to the nail

Bạn có thể dùng giũa bằng thép thay vì giũa bằng giấy để:
a. Giũa mòn móng tay ít hơn
b. Làm cho móng tay mịn màng
c. Giũa mòn móng tay nhiều hơn
d. Làm nhám móng tay

70. **Cuticle creams are used to:**

a. Treat brittle nails and dry cuticle
b. Encourage the growth of nails
c. Remove dead cuticle
d. Remove dry cuticle

Kem thoa da được dùng để:
a. Chữa trị móng tay dòn và da khô
b. Kích thích sự tăng trưởng móng tay
c. Lấy đi da chết
d. Lấy đi da khô

71. **Which one of the following is not a benefit of hand massage?**

a. Shiny nails
b.Increased circulation
c. Smooth skin
d. Flexible hands

Điều nào sau đây không đem lại ích lợi của việc xoa bóp tay:
a. Móng bóng sáng
b. Tăng tuần hoàn
c. Da mịn màng
d. Tay mềm dẻo

72. **Most cosmetology textbooks recommend that a cotton tipped orangewood stick be used to apply:**

a. All of the following
b. Cuticle solvent, cuticle oil
c. Nail cream
d. Nail bleach

Hầu hết các sách giáo khoa ngành thẩm mỹ khuyên dùng đầu que gỗ cam quấn bông gòn để thoa:
a. Tất cả các việc sau
b. Chất mềm da tay, dầu thoa da
c. Kem móng tay
d. Chất tẩy móng tay

73. **The skin on which the nail body rests is known as the:**

a. Matrix
b. Nail bed
c. Nail groove
d. Root

Phần da mà thân móng tay nằm lên được biết là:

a. Móng non
b. Nền móng (đệm móng)
c. Rãnh móng
d. Gốc móng

74. **Nerves and blood vessels are found in the nail:**

a. Nail plate
b. Lunula
c. Matrix
d. Cuticle

Dây thần kinh và mạch máu tìm thấy ở trong:

a. Mặt móng
b. Nền móng tay hình bán nguyệt
c. Tế bào tăng trưởng (móng non)
d. Da chung quanh móng

75. **Which one of these daily requirements for a manicurist's good grooming is not required:**

a. Daily bath and use of underarm deodorant
b. Clean teeth and sweet breath
c. Comfortable white shoes
d. Fresh, clean uniform

Điều nào không cần thiết cho sự tươm tất hằng ngày của người thợ làm móng tay:

a. Tắm hằng ngày và thoa khử mùi nách
b. Đánh răng và hơi thở thơm tho
c. Giày trắng đúng cỡ
d. Đồng phục sạch sẽ, tươi mát

76. **Which of the following items is not an accepted sanitary procedure?**

a. Wash hands before and after each manicure
b. Disinfect all soiled implement after each used
c. Use lump alum to stop minor bleeding
d. Use a clean towel for each patron

Điều nào sau đây không được chấp nhận về phương thức vệ sinh khử trùng:

a. Rửa tay trước và sau mỗi lần làm móng tay
b. Diệt trùng dụng cụ bẩn sau mỗi lần dùng
c. Dùng cục phèn chua để cầm máu nhẹ
d. Dùng khăn sạch cho mỗi khách hàng

77. **Manicure implements will be disinfected when immersed in 99% isopropyl alcohol for a period of:**

a. 2 minutes
b. 5 minutes
c. 10 minutes
d. 20 minutes

Dụng cụ làm móng tay sẽ được diệt trùng khi ngâm vào cồn 99% isopropyl trong thời gian:

a. 2 phút
b. 5 phút
c. 10 phút
d. 20 phút

78. **Before manicure implements are used on a client, they must be:**

a. Wiped with 70% isopropyl alcohol
b. Dried with clean towel
c. Scrubbed and disinfected
d. Washed in warm soap water

Dụng cụ làm móng tay trước khi dùng cho khách, chúng phải được:

a. Lau với cồn 70 % isopropyl
b. Làm khô với khăn sạch
c. Chà rửa và diệt trùng
d. Rửa trong nước xà phòng ấm

79. **Powdered alum is styptic used to:**

a. Destroy bacteria
b. Stop minor bleeding
c. Sanitize implements
d. Stop body odor

Bột phèn chua là thuốc cầm máu dùng để:

a. Diệt vi trùng
b. Cầm máu nhẹ
c. Khử trùng dụng cụ
d. Khử mùi hôi thân thể

80. The deep fold of skin in which the nail root is lodged is called the:

a. Nail mantle

b. Nail groove

c. Nail wall

d. Nail bed

Lớp da xếp trong gốc móng tay gọi là:

a. Màng da bọc nền móng.

b. Đường rãnh thân móng tay

c. Thành móng tay

d. Nền móng tay (đệm móng tay)

81. The movement of the hand is controlled by:

a. Supinator

b. Flexors

c. Extensors

d. All of the above

Sự chuyển động của bàn tay được điều khiển bởi:

a. Cơ ngửa lòng bàn tay

b. Cơ gấp các khớp

c. Cơ duỗi tay

d. Tất cả những điều trên

82. The biceps is the muscle that covers the:

a. Forearm

b. Upper arm

c. Hand

d. Wrist

Cơ 2 đầu (biceps) là thịt bao bọc:

a. Cánh tay trước

b. Cánh tay trên

c. Bàn tay

d. Cổ tay

83. During a manicure, it would not be wise to:

a. File to free edge

b. Remove old polish before filing

c. Soak finger tips before using a pusher

d. Use the cuticle nipper before cuticle pusher

Trong lúc làm móng tay, không nên làm theo cách:

a. Giũa đầu móng tay

b. Chùi sơn cũ trước khi giũa

c. Ngâm móng tay trước khi sủi da tay

d. Dùng kềm cắt da trước khi sủi da

84. Anabolism and catabolism are two phases of :

a. Mitosis

b. Reproduction

c. Metabolism

d. Amitosis

Sự tiếp nhận năng lượng (đồng hóa) và tiêu hao năng lượng (dị hóa) là hai tiến trình (giai đoạn) của:

a. Gián phân

b. Sự sinh sản

c. Sự biến hóa tế bào

d. Trực phân

85. In shaping the fingernail, the nail is filled:

a. From corner to center

b. Straight across

c. From center to corner

d. From corner to corner

Tạo hình dạng móng tay, móng được giũa:

a. Từ góc vào giữa

b. Giũa ngang qua

c. Từ giữa ra góc

d. Từ góc này sang góc kia

86. After the client is seated at the manicure table and their hands have been washed with soap and warm water, normally the next step will be:

a. Applying cuticle solvent

b. Applying hand lotion

c. Removing the old polish

d. Placing one hand in the nail bath

Khi khách hàng ngồi vào bàn làm móng và tay họ đã được rửa sạch với xà phòng và nước, thông thường giai đoạn kế tiếp là:

a. Thoa chất làm mềm da tay

b. Thoa kem massage

c. Chùi nước sơn cũ

d. Đặt một bàn tay trong tô ngâm móng

87. To clean under the free edge of the nail, manicurists usually use:

a.The finger bath brush

b.The pointed end of the pusher

c. A cotton tipped orangewood stick

d. A point of the nipper blade

Để làm sạch phần dưới đầu móng tay, thợ thường dùng:

a. Bàn chải chà ngón tay

b. Đầu nhọn cây xủi da

c. Que gỗ quấn một ít bông gòn

d. Đầu nhọn của lưỡi kềm cắt da

88. In the application of liquid nail polish, best results are obtained if:

a. A thick nail polish is used

b. A thin nail polish is used

c. Some cuticle solvent is left on the nail

d. Brushes are clean and free from loose hairs

Trong tiến trình sơn móng tay, để đạt được kết quả tốt nhất nếu:

a. Dùng nước sơn dày

b. Dùng nước sơn mỏng

c. Còn sót chất mềm da trên móng

d. Cọ sạch sẽ và lông cọ không rụng

89. In manicuring, pumice powder may be used to:

a. Remove nail polish

b. Soften cuticle

c. Soften nail

d. Smooth ridges

Trong việc chăm sóc tay, bột đá bọt có thể dùng để:

a. Lấy đi nước sơn móng

b. Làm mềm da

c. Làm mềm móng tay

d. Làm mịn móng gợn sóng

90. Implements used with excessive pressure at the root of the nail may:

a. Remove excessive cuticle

b. Stimulate the nail to more rapid growth

c. Make the lunula visible

d. Injure live tissue

Dụng cụ dùng với sức ép mạnh ở gốc móng tay có thể:

a. Lấy đi da dư

b. Kích thích móng tay mọc nhanh hơn

c. Thấy rõ hình bán nguyệt trên móng

d. Làm tổn thương các mô sống

91. Pushing back of the cuticle:

a. Loosens the eponychium

b. File the finger tip

c. Cut dead cuticle

d. Slow nail growth

Đẩy lùi da tay là:

a. Làm lỏng da mọc lên nền móng

b. Giũa đầu móng tay

c. Cắt da chết

d. Làm chậm sự tăng trưởng móng tay

92. If not properly cared for, hangnails may:

a. Become spotted

b. Turn yellow

c. Become infected

d. Become congenital

Nếu không săn sóc đúng cách, da quanh móng bị xước có thể:

a. Thành lốm đốm

b. Chuyển màu vàng

c. Thành nhiễm trùng

d. Thành tật bẩm sinh

93. Polish remover may dry the cuticle if it is:

a. Used undiluted

b. Not washed off

c. Mixed with liquid polish

d. Applied with a brush

Chất chùi nước sơn có thể làm khô da tay nếu :

a. Dùng nguyên chất

b. Không rửa sạch

c. Trộn với nước sơn

d. Dùng với cây cọ

94. If a slight cut occurs while giving a manicure, you should use:

a. An astringent

b. Styptic pencil

c. Pumice stone

d. Lysol

Trong lúc chăm sóc tay nếu bị vết cắt nhẹ, bạn nên dùng:

a. Chất đóng lỗ chân lông (chất se da)

b. Viết chì cầm máu

c. Cục đá bọt

d. Lysol

95. The State Board of Cosmetology rule for handling emery board says that you should:

a. Wipe with 70% isopropyl alcohol

b. Discard after use on client

c. Store in plastic bag after use

d. Keep in dust-proof cabinet

Theo luật lệ của Hội Đồng Thẩm Mỹ Tiểu Bang nói rằng việc sử dụng giũa giấy bạn sẽ:

a. Lau với cồn 70 % isopropyl

b. Vứt bỏ sau khi dùng trên khách

c. Cất trong bao nhựa sau khi dùng

d. Giữ lại trong tủ không bụi

96. Antiseptic solution such as 3% hydrogen peroxide is used to:

a. Disinfect manicure implements

b. Retard the growth of germs

c. Destroy bacteria

d. Open pores of the skin

Dung dịch sát trùng như chất peroxide 3% được sử dụng để:

a. Diệt trùng dụng cụ làm móng tay

b. Làm chậm sự tăng trưởng của vi trùng

c. Tiêu diệt vi trùng

d. Làm nở lỗ chân lông của da

97. The powder on brush for the application of acrylic nail should be:

a. Applied to all bristles

b. Worked into a thick paste

c. Formed into a ball at the tip of the brush

d. Wet so it will stick to the brush

Dùng cọ lấy bột để đắp móng acrylic nên:

a. Dùng loại lông cứng

b. Làm cho bột sền sệt

c. Lấy bột từng viên trên đầu cọ

d. Ướt để bột dính vào cọ

98. What reasons the product are caused for allergic reactions to customers and manicurists:

a. Skin contact with monomers

b. Improper product

c. Overexposure

d. All of the above

Những lý do nào mà sản phẩm tạo những sự dị ứng cho khách và thợ chăm sóc tay chân:

a. Da tiếp xúc với nước acrylic

b. Sản phẩm không đúng cách

c. Tiếp xúc quá độ

d. Tất cả những điều trên

99. Overfilling on the nails will promote some problems except:

a. Infections

b. Loss the nail plate

c. Allergic reactions

d. Onychia

Giũa quá nhiều lên móng sẽ tạo ra những vấn đề ngoại trừ:

a. Nhiễm trùng

b. Mất nhiều mặt móng

c. Tạo ra dị ứng

d. Móng sưng có mủ

100. Proper use of the cuticle nippers will:

a. Not ruff up more cuticle

b. Leave cuticle free of snags

c. Leave skin unbroken

d. All of the above

Dùng đúng cách kềm cắt da tay sẽ:

a. Không có nếp gấp da nhiều

b. Giữ cho da trơn mịn (da không bị xừ)

c. Giữ cho da lành lặn

d. Tất cả những điều trên

MANICURIST EXAMINATION 4

1. **Scrubbing the nail plate and washing your hands removes:**
   a. Contaminant **b. Oil surface on nail**
   c. Fungal spores and bacteria **d. All of the above**
   Bạn chà mặt móng và rửa tay bạn là loại bỏ:
   a. Chất bẩn *b. Lớp dầu trên móng*
   c. Bào tử nấm và vi trùng *d. Tất cả các câu trên*

2. **How many percentage of manicurist affected by skin disorder on their hands:**
   a. 65% **b. 35%**
   c. 50% **d. 40%**
   Thợ làm móng tay bị ảnh hưởng xấu về da khoảng bao nhiêu phần trăm:
   a. 65% *b. 35%*
   c. 50% *d. 40%*

3. **The charcoal filter in a vented manicuring table must be changed every:**
   a. Month **b. 48 hours**
   c. 20 hours **d. One week**
   Miếng than lọc khí của bàn làm móng tay phải được thay mỗi:
   a. Một tháng *b. 48 giờ*
   c. 20 giờ *d. Một tuần*

4. **You hold the artificial tip in place until it dries for:**
   a. 15 to 25 seconds **b. 5 to 10 seconds**
   c. 14 to 20 seconds **d. 3 seconds**
   Bạn đặt móng giả nên giữ móng cho đến lúc khô khoảng:
   a. 15 đến 25 giây *b. 5 đến 10 giây*
   c. 14 đến 20 giây *d. 3 giây*

5. **Public hygiene also is known as sanitation and personal hygiene deals with the preservation of the well being of the:**
   a. Town **b. Society**
   c. Community **d. Individual**
   Vệ sinh công cộng được biết sự cải thiện vệ sinh chung và vệ sinh cá nhân là liên hệ về việc giữ gìn tốt cho:
   a. Thành phố *b. Xã hội*
   c. Cộng đồng *d. Chính người đó (cá nhân)*

6. **It is important to wash your hands often during flu season because good hygiene adds to:**
   a. Personal hygiene **b. Natural antibiotic**
   c. Natural immunity **d. Acquired immunity**
   Điều quan trọng việc rửa tay thường xuyên trong suốt mùa cúm bởi vì vệ sinh tốt là trợ giúp:
   a.Vệ sinh cá nhân *b. Kháng sinh tự nhiên*
   c. Miễn nhiễm tự nhiên *d. Miễn nhiễm tự tạo*

7. **Nail shapes should conform to the client's fingertips and make shape of the free edge with:**

a. Emery board | **b. Black file**

c. Chamois buffer | **d. Block buffer**

Hình dáng móng nên phù hợp với ngón tay của khách và tạo dạng đầu móng với:

a. Giũa giấy | *b. Giũa đen*

c. Buffer đánh bóng móng bằng da dê | *d. Cục buffer*

8. **Pterygium may be helped by hot oil manicure as it is:**

a. Caused by nail biting | **b. Softening of the nail**

c. An obstinate growth of cuticle at the base of the nail | **d. An ingrown nail**

Da chồm lên mặt móng có thể trị liệu bằng cách làm móng tay dầu, đó là:

a. Thói quen cắn móng tay | *b. Sự mềm móng*

c. Hiện tượng da mọc nhiều ở nền móng | *d. Móng mọc đâm khóe*

9. **Abnormal whiteness patches that is sometime found on patrons hand and arm is known as:**

a. Lentigo | **b. Chloasma**

c. Melanoderma | **d. Leucoderma**

Những mảng trắng bất thường đôi khi tìm thấy trên bàn tay và cánh tay khách được biết là:

a. Lentigo (tàn nhang) | *b. Chloasma (nám da)*

c. Melanoderma (mảng da sậm) | *d. Mảng da trắng do bẩm sinh(leucoderma)*

10. **A chiropodist is advised for:**

a. Nail discoloration | **b. Abnormal foot conditions**

c. Skin condition | **d. Scalp disorder**

Bác sĩ săn sóc chân cần thiết cho:

a. Sự biến màu của móng | *b. Tình trạng bất thường của chân*

c. Tình trạng của da | *d. Bệnh của da đầu*

11. **A properly given hand and arm massage will not:**

a. Relax and sooth the patron | **b. Increase the flexibility of the skin**

c. Increase the flow of blood to hands and arms | **d. Substitute for a poorly given manicure**

Xoa bóp (massage) cánh tay và bàn tay đúng cách sẽ không thể:

a. Làm khách dễ chịu, thoải mái | *b. Tăng sự đàn hồi của da*

c. Tăng sự tuần hoàn máu ở bàn tay và cánh tay | *d. Thay thế cho sự yếu kém khi làm móng tay nước*

12. **Nerves have their own origin in the:**

a. Connective tissue | **b. Brain and spinal cord**

c. Skeletal muscles | **d. Voluntary muscles**

Dây thần kinh bắt nguồn ở trong:

a. Mô liên kết | *b. Não bộ và tủy sống*

c. Những bắp thịt của bộ xương | *d. Bắp thịt tự ý (cơ tự quản)*

13. To file patron's nails use:

a. Steel files

b. Emery board

c. Black file

d. Both a & b

Khi giũa móng cho khách, dùng:

a. Giũa kim loại

b. Giũa giấy

c. Giũa đen

d. Cả hai a và b

14. The muscles extending down the forearm are called:

a. Extensors

b. Flexors

c. Both a & b

d. Neither of these

Bắp thịt vươn dài xuống cánh tay trước là:

a. Bắp thịt duỗi tay

b. Bắp thịt co tay

c. Cả hai a và b

d. Không phải những câu trên

15. There are three bones in each finger and two in each thumb. They are called:

a. Metacarpals

b. Phalanges

c. Carpus

d. Skeletal

Có ba lóng xương ở mỗi ngón, và 2 lóng ở ngón cái. Chúng được gọi là:

a. Xương lòng bàn tay

b. Xương ngón tay

c. Xương cổ tay

d. Bộ xương

16. What is the benefit of paper wraps (mending tissue)?

a. Help the nails grow faster

b. Strengthen the nails

c. Smooth nails

d. Cover wavy ridges

Bao móng bằng giấy (mending tissue) có lợi gì?

a. Giúp móng mọc nhanh hơn

b. Làm móng chắc

c. Làm cho móng mịn

d. Che đi những đường gợn sóng

17. When starting the pedicure, patron's feet should be:

a. Sterilized

b. Sanitized

c. Wiped with 70% alcohol

d. Dipped in bucket

Khi bắt đầu làm chăm sóc chân (pedicure), đôi chân khách nên được:

a. Tiệt trùng

b. Khử trùng

c. Lau bằng alcohol 70%

d. Ngâm vào chậu

18. When applying cuticle remover, use:

a. Cotton

b. Cuticle pusher

c. Cotton tipped orange wood stick

d. None of the above

Khi sử dụng chất làm mềm da, dùng:

a. Bông gòn

b. Cây xủi da

c. Cây gỗ quấn bông gòn

d. Không phải những điều trên

19. Patron's feet should be soaked in an antiseptic solution for ____ minute:

a. 10 to 15

b. 20

c. 3 to 5

d. 7 to 10

Đôi chân khách được ngâm trong dung dịch sát trùng bao nhiêu phút:

a. 10 đến 15 phút

b. 20 phút

c. 3 đến 5 phút

d. 7 đến 10 phút

20. **Before starting a pedicure, place instruments in a wet sanitizer containing 70% alcohol or:**

a. Formalin **b. 1,000 p.p.m of Quats solution**

c. Phenol **d. 500 p.p.m of Quats solution**

Trước khi chăm sóc chân, ngâm dụng cụ vào dung dịch khử trùng chứa 70% alcohol or:

a. Formalin *b. Dung dịch Quats 1.000 p.p.m*

c. Phenol *d. Dung dịch Quats 500 p.p.m*

21. **To render an object germ free is to practice:**

a. Sanitation **b. Sterilization**

c. Hygiene **d. Immunity**

Tiêu diệt hết vi trùng trên dụng cụ là thực hiện:

a. Sự khử trùng *b. Sự tiệt trùng*

c. Vệ sinh *d. Sự miễn nhiễm*

22. **Which one of the following is not a function of the nail:**

a. Protective covering **b. Covers nerves and delicate structures**

c. A protective covering of the humerus **d. Serve as a tool for grasping objects**

Điều nào dưới đây không phải là một chức năng của móng:

a. Bảo vệ *b. Bảo vệ dây thần kinh và cấu trúc li ti*

c. Bảo vệ xương cánh tay trên *d. Dùng như một dụng cụ nắm đồ vật*

23. **The visible portion of the nail bed is called:**

a. Lunula **b. Matrix**

c. Groove **d. Mantle**

Phần nhìn thấy được của nền móng gọi là:

a. Lunula (nữa vòng trắng mặt móng) *b. Móng non*

c. Rãnh móng *d. Màng móng*

24. **After use, manicure tables are required:**

a. To be put away **b. To be sterilized**

c. To be sanitized **d. None of the above**

Sau khi dùng, bàn manicure đòi hỏi phải:

a. Được cất đi *b. Được tiệt trùng*

c. Được khử trùng *d. Không phải những điều trên*

25. **The cuticle overlapping the lunula is the nail:**

a. Hyponychium **b. Eponychium**

c. Nail mantle **d. Nail groove**

Lớp da mọc nhiều lên viền hình bán nguyệt của móng là:

a. Da mọc nhiều dưới đầu móng (hyponychium) *b. Da mọc nhiều ở nền móng (eponychium)*

c. Màng móng *d. Rãnh móng*

26. **All floors, woodwork and furniture in a beauty shop should be:**

a. Washable **b. Modern**

c. Made of good material **d. Painted**

Nền nhà, vật dụng, bàn tủ trong viện thẩm mỹ nên dùng loại:

a. Có thể chùi rửa được *b. Hiện đại*

c. Làm bằng vật liệu tốt *d. Được sơn*

27. The nail include free edge, nail root, and:

a. Nail groove
b. Nail matrix
c. Nail bed
d. Nail body

Móng gồm có đầu móng, rễ móng, và:

a. Rãnh móng
b. Móng non
c. Nền móng
d. Thân móng

28. The medical term for brittle nails is:

a. Onychorrhexis
b. Onychophagy
c. Onychauxis (hypertrophy)
d. Onychatrophia (atrophy)

Danh từ y học cho móng dòn là:

a. Onychorrhexis
b. Onychophagy (cắn móng tay)
c. Onychauxis (móng lớn dày)
d. Atrophy (rụng móng)

29. The medical term for bitten nails is:

a. Leuconychia
b. Onychia
c. Onychauxis
d. Onychophagy

Danh từ y học cho tật cắn móng tay là:

a. Leuconychia (đốm trắng)
b. Onychia (sưng mủ móng non)
c. Onychauxis (móng lớn dày)
d. Onychophagy

30. All are nail diseases except:

a. Onychophagy
b. Paronychia
c. Onychia
d. Onycholysis

Tất cả những triệu chứng dưới đây là bệnh móng, ngoại trừ:

a. Tật cắn móng tay (onychophagy)
b. Paronychia (nhiễm trùng da quanh móng)
c. Onychia (sưng móng non)
d. Onycholysis (lỏng móng)

31. Organism that produce disease are:

a. Pathogenic
b. Non- pathogenic
c. Spores
d. Incubation

Những sinh vật gây bệnh là:

a. Pathogenic (vi trùng gây bệnh)
b. Non-pathogenic
c. Spores (bào tử)
d. Incubation (giai đoạn sinh bệnh)

32. The form bacteria take when it is in the resting stage is known as:

a. Cocci
b. Motile
c. Spores
d. Bacilli

Hình thái vi trùng trong giai đoạn nghỉ (không hoạt động) được biết là:

a. Cocci (cầu khuẩn)
b. Di động
c. Bào tử
d. Bacilli (vi trùng hình gậy)

33. How do you file with an electric file (nail drill), is not filing enough in one direction?

a. Back and forth movement
b. File on the opposite direction
c. Continue to file the same direction
d. Apply minimum pressure

Bạn dùng thế nào với máy giũa khi không giũa đủ theo một hướng?

a. Giũa tới lui
b. Giũa hướng ngược lại
c. Tiếp tục giũa cùng hướng
d. Boric acid 5%

34. **Which one of the following procedures will not make an article germ free:**

a. Boiling for two minutes
b. Wiping with 70% alcohol
c. Immersing in 1/1000 Quats solution for 10 minutes
d. Immersing in 5% formalin solution for 20 minutes

Phương pháp nào dưới đây sẽ không thể diệt trùng dụng cụ:
a. Đun sôi trong 2 phút
b. Lau bằng alcohol 70%
c. Ngâm trong dung dịch Quats 1/1000 trong 10 phút
d. Ngâm trong dung dịch formalin 5% trong 20 phút

35. **The two main divisions of the skin are the epidermis and:**

a. Subcutaneous tissue
b. Dermis
c. Corneum layer
d. Melanin

Hai thành phần chính của da là lớp ngoại bì và:
a. Mô mỡ (mô dưới da)
b. Nội bì
c. Lớp sừng
d. Sắc tố

36. **When performing a pedicure:**

a. Do not use antiseptic lotion
b. Do not massage feet
c. Do not apply top coat
d. Cuticle is not cut

Khi chăm sóc chân (pedicure):
a. Không dùng dung dịch sát trùng
b. Không nên massage chân
c. Không thoa chất phủ bóng móng
d. Da không được cắt

37. **The color of the skin depends on the blood supply to the skin and the coloring pigment is called:**

a. Keratin
b. Melanin
c. Fat
d. Moisture

Màu sắc của da phụ thuộc vào nguồn cung cấp máu đến da, chất màu được gọi là:
a. Keratin (chất sừng)
b. Melanin (sắc tố)
c. Fat (mỡ)
d. Moisture (hơi ẩm)

38. **The sebaceous glands secrete:**

a. Melanin
b. Saliva
c. Sebum
d. Perspiration

Tuyến dầu tiết ra:
a. Sắc tố
b. Nước bọt
c. Sebum
d. Mồ hôi (perspiration)

39. **The process used for making an object germ-free is known as:**

a. Germicide
b. Sterilization
c. Antiseptic
d. Suppuration

Tiến trình vô trùng một đồ vật được biết là:
a. Chất diệt trùng
b. Sự tiệt trùng
c. Sát trùng
d. Sự mưng mủ

40. The skin is lubricated by an oily substance known as:

a. Sweat **b. Sebum**

c. Hormone **d. Enzyme**

Da được trơn mịn là do một dạng dầu trong da được biết là:

a. Mồ hôi *b. Sebum*

c. Kích thích tố *d. Chất men*

41. Cuticle oil and cuticle solvent are used in manicure and pedicure:

a. The same effect **b. Not the same**

c. Both used for lubrication **d. Used to correct ridged nails**

Cuticle oil (dầu thoa da) và cuticle solvent (chất làm mềm da) được dùng cho chăm sóc tay và chân:

a. Có cùng một tác dụng *b. Là hai chất khác nhau*

c. Cả hai dùng cho trơn mịn *d. Dùng chữa trị móng bị gợn sóng*

42. Hot oil manicures are recommended for brittle nail and:

a. Broken nails **b. Dry cuticle**

c. Infections **d. Corrugated nails**

Cách săn sóc móng tay dầu giúp ích cho móng dòn và:

a. Móng gãy *b. Da khô*

c. Nhiễm trùng *d. Móng bị sọc dợn*

43. Ultra Violet ray may harm the:

a. Eyes **b. Head**

c. Hands **d. Legs**

Tia cực tím có thể gây tổn thương cho:

a. Mắt *b. Đầu*

c. Tay *d. Chân*

44. Where do you put you client's nails after applying gel?

a. Above the lamp **b. Next to the lamp**

c. Under the ultra violet lamp **d. None of the above**

Sau khi đắp móng gel, bạn phải đặt móng tay khách ở đâu?

a. Trên đèn *b. Bên cạnh đèn*

c. Dưới đèn cực tím *d. Không phải những điều trên*

45. Which one of the following does not apply to the use of pumice powder for manicuring:

a. Helps smooth roughness of nail **b. Helps correct atrophy of nail**

c. Sometimes used when buffing **d. Help to remove stains on the nails**

Điều nào dưới đây không nên xử dụng bột đá đánh bóng móng tay:

a. Giúp làm cho móng bóng láng *b. Giúp chữa trị móng tét*

c. Thỉnh thoảng dùng đánh bóng móng *d. Giúp lấy đi những vết bẩn trên móng*

46. The sweat glands of the skin excrete:

a. Sebum **b. Perspiration**

c. Oil **d. Oxygen**

Tuyến mồ hôi của da bài tiết:

a. Chất dầu trong tuyến dầu (sebum) *b. Perspiration*

c. Dầu *d. Khí Ôxy*

47. A hangnail is known as:

a. Onycholysis
b. Onychophagy
c. Agnail
d. Onychauxis

Bệnh da xước được biết với tên gọi:

a. Onycholysis (bệnh lở móng)
b. Onychophagy (móng tay bị cắn)
c. Agnail
d. Onychauxis (bệnh móng dày)

48. The sweat glands help to eliminate one of the followings from the body:

a. Oxygen
b. Waste products
c. Oil
d. Sebum

Tuyến mồ hôi giúp bài tiết chất gì ra khỏi cơ thể:

a. Ôxy
b. Chất cặn bã
c. Dầu
d. Chất dầu có trong tuyến dầu (sebum)

49. The skin is lubricated by glands called:

a. Sebaceous
b. Epidermis
c. Lymphatic
d. Sudoriferous (sweat glands)

Da được trơn mịn bởi những tuyến gọi là:

a. Tuyến dầu nhờn
b. Ngoại bì
c. Bạch huyết
d. Tuyến mồ hôi

50. The circulatory system or vascular system of the body is divided into two parts, they are:

a. White corpuscles or leucocytes
b. Blood platelets and plasma
c. Blood and lymphatic vascular
d. Red corpuscles or erythrocytes

Hệ thống tuần hoàn hoặc hệ thống bơm đẩy của cơ thể chia làm hai phần, đó là:

a. Những hạt máu trắng hoặc bạch cầu
b. Tiểu cầu (huyết thanh) và huyết tương
c. Hệ thống bơm máu và bạch huyết
d. Hạt máu đỏ hoặc hồng cầu

51. Excess fluids or lotions remaining in glass dish after treatment on patron shall be:

a. Poured back in bottle
b. Kept in closed cabinet until needed
c. Covered with sterile gauze
d. Discarded immediately

Những dung dịch hoặc lotion dư lại trong lọ thủy tinh sau khi phục vụ khách nên:

a. Rót lại vào bình chứa
b. Cất giữ trong tủ kín cho đến lúc cần
c. Phủ kín với vải thưa sạch
d. Vứt bỏ ngay

52. Which one of the arteries listed below supplies the structures on the little finger side of the forearm:

a. Ulnar
b. Radial
c. Brachial artery
d. Subclavian

Động mạch nào dưới đây cung cấp máu cho cấu trúc phía ngón út dọc theo cánh tay trước:

a. Ulnar (trụ)
b. Radial (quay)
c. Brachial (động mạch cánh tay trên)
d. Subclavian (dưới xương đòn gánh)

53. Every operator must thoroughly wash his or her hands:

a. Before starting work in the morning
b. Before going home at night
c. After manicure is completed
d. Before work on each patron

Mỗi người thợ phải hoàng toàn rửa tay sạch sẽ:

a. Vào buổi sáng trước khi làm việc
b. Vào buổi tối trước khi về nhà
c. Sau khi làm móng cho khách
d. Trước khi làm trên mỗi người khách

54. The skin is nourished by:

a. Water fluid
b. Blood and lymph
c. Body gases
d. Chemical solutions

Da được nuôi dưỡng bởi:

a. Nước
b. Máu đỏ và máu trắng
c. Thể hơi trong cơ thể
d. Các dung dịch hóa chất

55. Melanin protects the skin from the harmful action of excessive:

a. Bacteria
b. Pressure
c. Ultraviolet rays
d. Electrical current

Sắc tố bảo vệ làn da bị hư hại do tiếp xúc quá độ:

a. Vi trùng
b. Áp suất
c. Tia cực tím
d. Dòng điện

56. Blood vessels, nerves, sweat and oil glands are found in the:

a. Epidermis
b. Dermis
c. Cuticle layer
d. Scarf layer

Mạch máu, dây thần kinh, tuyến mồ hôi và tuyến dầu được tìm thấy trong:

a. Ngoại bì
b. Nội bì
c. Lớp biểu bì
d. Lớp da bọc ngoài

57. What type of air system is used in airbrush technique for your customer's fingernails?

a. Hydrogen
b. Oxygen
c. Nitrogen
d. Carbonic

Loại hơi khí nào được dùng trong kỷ thuật thổi xịt màu cho móng tay của khách?

a. Khí hydro
b. Khí ôxy
c. Khi Nitơ
d. Khí than

58. Manicurists are allowed to massage:

a. Neck & head
b. Back & shoulder
c. Leg & back
d. Hands & legs

Thợ móng tay được phép xoa bóp:

a. Cổ và đầu
b. Lưng và vai
c. Chân và lưng
d. Tay và chân

59. If the patron has a skin disease, the manicurist should:

a. Treat it with medicine
b. Refer that patron to a physician
c. Overlook it
d. Suggest self treatment

Nếu khách có bệnh về da, thợ móng tay nên:

a. Dùng thuốc chữa trị
b. Khuyên khách đi bác sĩ
c. Xem nhẹ bệnh đó
d. Gợi ý nên tự chữa trị

60. After each manicure emery boards are to be:

a. Placed in a tightly closed cabinet
b. Immersed in disinfectant solution
c. Wiped off with 70% alcohol
d. Discarded immediately

Sau mỗi lần làm móng tay, emery board (giũa giấy nhỏ) nên được:

a. Cất vào tủ kín
b. Ngâm vào dung dịch diệt trùng
c. Chùi rửa với cồn 70%
d. Vất bỏ ngay

61. After articles have been sanitized in quaternary ammonium compounds, they must next be:

a. Washed with laundry soap
b. Immersed in a antiseptic
c. Rinsed in clean water
d. Placed in a closed dust free cabinet

Sau khi các vật dụng đã được khử trùng trong dung dịch Quat, chúng phải được làm gì kế tiếp:

a. Rửa với xà phòng giặt
b. Ngâm vào dung dịch sát trùng
c. Xả với nước sạch
d. Cất và tủ kín tránh bụi

62. Which one of the following is not a division of the nail:

a. Free edge
b. Cuticle
c. Nail body
d. Nail root

Phần nào dưới đây không thuộc về móng:

a. Free edge (đầu móng)
b. Da quanh móng
c. Thân móng
d. Rễ móng

63. Using an antiseptic spray for pedicuring has a/an:

a. Antibacterial soap
b. Zinc oxide
c. Antifungal agent
d. Athlete's foot

Dùng hóa chất xịt sát trùng cho việc chăm sóc chân có:

a. Xà phòng sát trùng
b. Oxýt kẽm
c. Tính chống nấm
d. Nấm ở chân

64. Which one of the following will not destroy bacteria:

a. Boiling
b. Baking
c. Germicides
d. Styptics

Phương pháp nào dưới đây không giết được vi trùng:

a. Đun sôi
b. Nướng
c. Chất diệt khuẩn
d. Chất cầm máu

65. One of the following is not a function of the skin:

a. Protection
b. Elimination
c. Absorption
d. Digestion

Chức năng nào dưới đây không phải nhiệm vụ của da:

a. Bảo vệ
b. Bài tiết
c. Hấp thụ (thẩm thấu)
d. Tiêu hóa

66. The skin covering the body is:

a. Rigid and inflexible
b. Elastic and flexible
c. Dry and slightly rough
d. Tight and inelastic

Lớp da bao bọc cơ thể có tính:

a. Rắn, không co giãn
b. Mềm mại, co giãn
c. Khô, hơi nhám
d. Chặc, không co giãn

67. What happens if you leave imperfections when applying second coat of gel?

a. Thick
b. Not harden
c. Glossy finish
d. Not smooth

Xảy ra điều gì nếu lớp gel đầu trãi không đều khi cho thêm lớp gel thứ nhì?

a. Dày
b. Không cứng lại
c. Bóng sáng
d. Không mịn

68. A healthy nail is smooth and has no:

a. Spots or wavy ridges | **b. Flexibility**

c. Firmness | **d. Color**

Một móng tay khỏe mạnh thì láng mịn và không có:

a. Đốm hoặc sọc gợn sóng | *b. Dẻo (co giãn)*

c. Chắc chắn | *d. Màu*

69. Polish will last longer if the manicurist:

a. Does not take off hairline tip after each coat of polish

b. Takes off the hairline tip after each coat of polish

c. Takes off the hairline tip after applying the top coat

d. Takes off the hairline tip of the base coat

Nước sơn sẽ giữ lâu (bền) hơn nếu như thợ móng tay:

a. Không gạt bớt đường viền đầu móng sau mỗi lớp nước sơn

b. Gạt bớt đường viền đầu móng sau mỗi lớp nước sơn

c. Gạt bớt đường viền đầu móng sau lớp bóng

d. Gạt bớt đường viền đầu móng lớp sơn lót

70. No light gel. What do you use to harden the gel after applying on client's nails?

a. Acetone | **b. Water**

c. Quick dry nail polish | **d. Top coat**

Loại gel không cần đèn. Bạn phải dùng chất gì để làm cứng gel trên móng tay khách:

a. Aceton | *b. Nước*

c. Nước sơn loại mau khô | *d. Nước sơn bóng*

71. The eight carpal bones are classified as:

a. Round shape | **b. Flat shape**

c. Irregular shape | **d. Long shape**

Tám cục xương cổ tay được xem là:

a. Dạng tròn | *b. Dạng phẳng*

c. Dạng không đều | *d. Dạng dài*

72. Normal healthy skin is usually:

a. Slightly moist | **b. Slighly acid**

c. Soft, flexible | **d. All of the above**

Một làn da bình thường khỏe mạnh luôn luôn:

a. Hơi ẩm | *b. Có tính acid nhẹ*

c. Mềm mại, đàn hồi | *d. Tất cả những điều trên*

73. Where can you find out about the safety's information of the product?

a. M.S.S.D | **b. M.D.S.S**

c. M.S.D.S | **d. S.D.S.M**

Nơi nào bạn có thể tìm hiểu về những qui tắc an toàn sử dụng của sản phẩm:

a. M.S.S.D | *b. M.D.S.S*

c. M.S.D.S | *d. S.D.S.M*

74. **A solution of sodium hydroxide or potassium hydroxide is likely to be found in:**

a. Cuticle cream | **b. Cuticle oil**
c. Cuticle remover | **d. Nail whitener**

Dung dịch sodium hydroxide hoặc potassium hydroxide có thể tìm thấy trong:
a. Kem thoa da | *b. Dầu thoa da*
c. Chất làm mềm da | *d. Chất trắng thoa dưới đầu móng*

75. **Using powdered alum to stop bleeding is:**

a. Recommended | **b. Not used**
c. Prohibited | **d. Required**

Việc dùng bột phèn để cầm máu là:
a. Điều nên làm | *b. Không nên làm*
c. Bị cấm | *d. Yêu cầu*

76. **What is M.S.D.S?**

a. It stands for Material Safety Data Sheet | **b. Brand name of product**
c. Manufacture's direction | **d. None of the above**

M.S.D.S là gì?
a.Viết tắt của Material Safety Data Sheet | *b. Tên đặc biệt của sản phẩm*
c. Sự hướng dẫn của nhà sản xuất | *d. Không phải những điều trên*

77. **What information can you find in the M.S.D.S:**

a. Keep product off the skin | **b. Identification of hazardous chemicals**
c. Safety required for handling materials | **d. Sanitized implements**

Bạn tìm hiểu được điều gì trong M.S.D.S:
a. Tránh được sản phẩm tiếp xúc với da | *b. Phân biệt được chất nào là độc hại*
c. Đòi hỏi an toàn khi xử dụng hoá chất | *d. Khử trùng dụng cụ*

78. **The longest and largest bone of the upper arm is the:**

a. Ulna | **b. Radius**
c. Humerus | **d. Clavicle**

Xương dài và lớn nhất của cánh tay trên là:
a. Ulna (xương trụ) | *b. Radius (xương quay)*
c. Humerus (xương cánh tay trên) | *d. Clavicle (xương đòn gánh)*

79. **The radius is the small bone on the thumb side of the:**

a. Upper arm | **b. Forearm**
c. Wrist | **d. Hand**

Xương quay là xương nhỏ phía bên ngón cái của:
a. Cánh tay trên | *b. Cánh tay trước*
c. Cổ tay | *d. Bàn tay*

80. **The dermis is also known as the corium, cutis, derma or:**

a. Cuticle | **b. False skin**
c. True skin | **d. Fatty tissue**

Nội bì được biết đến với những tên gọi như corium, cutis, derma, hay là:
a. Biểu bì | *b. Da giả*
c. Lớp da thật | *d. Mô mỡ*

81. The portion of the nail that extends over the finger tips is called the:

a. Free edge **b. Matrix**

c. Nail root **d. Nail bed**

Phần kéo dài móng tay qua đầu ngón tay được gọi là:

a. Đầu móng *b. Matrix (móng non)*

c. Rễ móng *d. Nail bed (đệm móng)*

82. The hair contains hard karetin and the nails are also hard karetin with translucent plate. The both of them are:

a. Layers **b. Nodules**

c. Sheathes **d. Skin's appendages**

Tóc chứa chất sừng cứng và móng cũng là sừng cứng với bề mặt trong suốt. Cả hai loại đều là:

a. Các lớp *b. Nodules (bướu)*

c. Màng bọc (sheathes) *d. Các phần phụ thuộc của da*

83. Each M.S.D.S must contain the basic information of:

a. Physical and chemical characteristic **b. Physical hazard**

c. Health hazard **d. All of the above**

Mỗi bản M.S.D.S phải bao gồm những căn bản tin tức nói về:

a. Lý tính và hóa tính *b. Tác hại về thể lý*

c.Tác hại đến sức khỏe *d. Tất cả những điều trên*

84. Where can you get M.S.D.S:

a. At the manufacture's direction **b. At the F.M.D**

c. At your local distributor of beauty supplies **d. None of the above**

Bạn có được M.S.D.S ở đâu?

a. Từ sự chỉ dẫn của nhà sản xuất *b. Ở F.M.D*

c. Từ nơi phân phối sản phẩm ở địa phương *d. Không phải những nơi kể trên*

85. To prevent the rusting of instruments when disinfect manicuring equipment you should add which of the following to the disinfection solution?

a. 0.5 % of sodium nitrite **b. 70% alcohol**

c. Either of the above **d. Neither of the above**

Để ngăn ngừa rỉ sét khi diệt trùng dụng cụ chăm sóc tay, bạn nên cho thêm chất gì vào dung dịch:

a. 0.5 % sodium nitrite (chất chống rỉ) *b. Cồn 70%*

c. Cả hai chất trên *d. Không phải hai chất kể trên*

86. Buffing the nails gives them a:

a. Natural gloss **b. Rough appearance**

c. Both of the above **d. None of the above**

Việc đánh bóng móng làm cho chúng:

a. Bóng sáng có vẻ tự nhiên *b. Nhám bên ngoài*

c. Cả hai điều trên *d. Không phải hai điều trên*

87. In the manicuring procedure, the patron's hands are placed in the soap bath:

a. Just before using the pusher **b. Just after removing the nail polish**

c. Just after filing the nails **d. According to condition of nails**

Trong cách làm móng tay, tay khách được ngâm vào tô nước xà phòng:

a. Ngay trước khi dùng đồ đẩy da *b. Ngay sau khi chùi nước sơn*

c. Ngay sau khi giũa móng *d. Tùy theo tình trạng của móng*

88. A manicurist should never use styptic pencil because it is:

a. Expensive **b. Solid**

c. Not sanitary **d. Too strong**

Thợ làm móng tay không bao giờ nên dùng bút chì cầm máu bởi vì chúng:

a. Đắt tiền *b. Rắn (thể đặc)*

c. Không hợp vệ sinh *d. Quá mạnh*

89. Every beauty salon establishments should have a:

a. Wet sanitizer **b. Dry sanitizer**

c. Cabinet sterilizer **d. All of the above**

Mỗi thẩm mỹ viện nên có một:

a. Dung dịch diệt trùng *b. Khử trùng khô*

c. Tủ tiệt trùng *d. Tất cả những dụng cụ trên*

90. When your license expires, it must be renewed within:

a. 30 days **b. 1 year**

c. 5 years **d. 10 years**

Khi giấy phép hành nghề (license) hết hạn, bạn phải đổi bằng mới trong vòng:

a. 30 ngày *b. 1 năm*

c. 5 năm *d. 10 năm*

91. The best way to learn about the potential hazard and proper handling for any product is to:

a. Reading the manufacture's direction **b. Reading M.S.D.S**

c. Reading M.S.A **d. Reading S.M.A**

Cách tốt nhất để biết về tính độc hại cũng như cách dùng đúng cho bất cứ sản phẩm nào là:

a. Đọc chỉ dẫn của nhà sản xuất *b. Đọc M.S.D.S (bảng an toàn vật liệu)*

c. Đọc M.S.A *d. Đọc S.M.A (vùng giữ gìn vệ sinh)*

92. Which nerve extends down the middle of the arm and forearm to the hand and supplies the little finger and palm of the hand?

a. Radial nerve **b. Ulnar nerve**

c. Median nerve **d. Palmar**

Dây thần kinh nào vươn dài xuống từ giữa cánh tay và cánh tay trước đến bàn tay và cung cấp cho ngón út và lòng bàn tay:

a. Radial (thần kinh quay) *b. Ulnar (thần kinh trụ)*

c. Thần kinh cánh tay và bàn tay *d. Palmar (lòng bàn tay)*

93. Which can cause onychorrhexis?

a. Excessive use of nail polish remover
b. Careless filing
c. Excessive use of cuticle solvent
d. All of the above

Nguyên nhân nào có thể gây bệnh móng tét?

a. Dùng nhiều chất chùi nước sơn
b. Giũa móng cẩu thả
c. Dùng nhiều chất làm mềm da
d. Tất cả những điều trên

94. What is one of the causes of the nail matrix becoming infected and inflamed?

a. Excessive use of strong solutions
b. Usually following an illness
c. Improper sanitation of nail implements and bacterial infection
d. All of the above

Một trong số những nguyên nhân nào làm móng non bị nhiễm trùng và sưng?

a. Dùng quá nhiều hóa chất mạnh
b. Thông thường do sau khi bệnh
c. Khử trùng dụng cụ làm móng không đúng và bị nhiễm trùng
d. Tất cả những điều trên

95. Primer is chemical product that apply to the natural nail when apply acrylic overlay to:

a. Adhere
b. Prevent fungus
c. Dry properly
d. Both a & b

Primer là một hóa chất thoa lên mặt móng thật khi đắp bột acrylic:

a. Dính chặt
b. Đề phòng nấm
c. Khô đúng cách
d. Cả hai câu a &b

96. Hangnail may be corrected by trimming the hangnail and softening the surrounding skin with:

a. Naphtha soap
b. Cuticle oil
c. Boric acid
d. Polish remover

Da xước có thể điều trị bằng cách cắt tỉa bỏ phần da xước và làm mềm da chung quanh với:

a. Xà phòng Naphtha
b. Dầu thoa da
c. Boric acid (sát trùng nhẹ)
d. Chất chùi nước sơn

97. Each beauty salon that offers artificial nail service (silk, tip, gel, acrylic ...) must have:

a. Adequate ventilation
b. Adequate heat
c. Supply of cold water
d. Comfortable chairs

Tiệm thẩm mỹ làm móng nhân tạo (lụa, tip, gel, bột acrylic ...) phải có:

a. Hệ thống thoáng khí đầy đủ
b. Nguồn nhiệt đủ ấm
c. Cung cấp nước lạnh
d. Các ghế ngồi thoải mái

98. In manicuring, the chamois buffer covered with a removable cover that can be disinfected. It is used to:

a. Polish the nails
b. Scrub the nails
c. Remove eponychium
d. Remove rough nail edges

Trong công việc làm móng tay, chamois buffer là cục đánh bóng được bọc một lớp da dê có thể tháo gỡ và có thể diệt trùng dùng lại. Được xử dụng để:

a. Đánh bóng móng
b. Chà mặt móng
c. Lấy da trên móng
d. Lấy lớp da xù xì ở cạnh móng

99. The main purpose of the nail wraps is to:

a. Extend nail length

b. Smooth nail surface

c. Reduce rough free edge

d. Strengthen the nail

Mục đích chính của móng bao (gói) là để:

a. Móng dài thêm

b. Bề mặt móng láng mịn

c. Giảm xù xì ở đầu móng

d. Móng cứng, chắc

100. According to the rules of the Board of Barbering and Cosmetology, before a manicure, you must first:

a. Disinfect the entire set of instruments & clean manicuring table with Quats solution

b. Return instruments to storage

c. Keep the instruments in the wet sanitizer

d. Changes the wet sanitizer solution

Theo luật của Hội đồng thẩm mỹ, trước khi làm một dịch vụ chăm sóc tay, đầu tiên bạn phải:

a. Diệt trùng toàn bộ dụng cụ và lau sạch bàn làm móng với dung dịch Quats

b. Cất hết dụng cụ vào nơi chứa đồ

c. Cất dụng cụ trong dung dịch diệt trùng

d. Thay dung dịch diệt trùng

MANICURIST EXAMINATION 5

1. **Control and protection measures include:**
   a. Safety glasses **b. Protecting clothes**
   c. Gloves **d. All of the above**
   Kiểm soát và mức độ bảo vệ nghề nghiệp bao gồm:
   a. Kính an toàn *b. Bảo vệ quần áo*
   c. Bao tay *d. Tất cả các điều trên*

2. **Horizontal uneven lines across the nail plate are caused by minor injury to the nail or:**
   a. Incorrect filing **b. Weak eyes**
   c. Thickening of the nail plate **d. Internal disease**
   Các lần gợn sóng ngang không đều ở mặt móng là nguyên nhân do tổn thương nhẹ ở móng hoặc:
   a. Giũa không đúng cách *b. Đôi mắt yếu*
   c Mặt móng dày *d. Bệnh nội thương*

3. **One of the following is an accepted method for the laundering of towel**
   a. 160 F degrees in 5 minutes during the washing **b. 140 F degrees in 15 minutes during the washing**
   c. Both a and b **d. None of the above**
   Một trong những điều sau đây là phương pháp chấp nhận cho việc giặt khăn:
   a. 160 độ F giặt trong 5 phút *b. 140 độ F giặt trong 15 phút*
   c. Cả hai câu a và b *d. Không có các điều trên*

4. **The main ingredient in cuticle remover is:**
   a. Potassium hydroxide **b. Hydrogen peroxide**
   c. Lanolin **d. Resin**
   Thành phần chính trong chất làm mềm da là:
   a. Potassium hydroxide *b. Hydrogen peroxide (H_2O_2)*
   c. Chất nhờn có trong kem dưỡng da *d. Nhựa resin*

5. **The science that deal with the prevention of disease by the individual is:**
   a. Good grooming **b. Self-preservation**
   c. Personal hygiene **d. Personal development**
   Khoa học liên hệ đến việc ngăn ngừa bệnh của mỗi người là:
   a. Ăn mặc chỉnh tề *b. Tự gìn giữ*
   c. Vệ sinh cá nhân *d. Phát triển cá nhân*

6. **How do you pick up very small gems when using rhinestones?**
   a. Wet orange wood stick **b. Tweezer**
   c. Wet cuticle pusher **d. Q-tip**
   Cách nào bạn nhặt những viên đá quí rất nhỏ khi cần tạo móng nghệ thuật óng ánh?
   a. Chấm ướt đầu que gỗ cam *b. Nhíp nhổ lông*
   c. Cây sủi da ướt *d. Que bông gòn nhỏ (Q-tip)*

7. When doing fills, great care must be taken not to injure the:

a. Cuticle **b. Nail bed**

c. Nail walls **d. All of the above**

Khi fill móng (phủ kín nơi móng mới mọc), thật cẩn thận không làm tổn thương:

a. Da quanh móng *b. Nền móng*

c. Thành móng *d. Tất cả những điều trên*

8. If a patron has a condition known as onychophagy (result of an acquired nervous habit to chew the nail or the hardened cuticle), you should:

a. Send her to a physician **b. File nail very short**

c. Give oil manicure to promote grow **d. Buff well**

Nếu khách hàng cóvấn đề được biết là onychophagy (kết quả do thói quen lo sợ, cắn móng tay hoặc làm lớp da tay cứng lại), bạn nên:

a. Khuyên khách đi bác sĩ *b. Giũa móng thật ngắn*

c. Làm móng tay dầu giúp móng mọc nhanh *d. Đánh bóng móng thật mịn*

9. Cuticle removers usually contain:

a. Potassium hydroxide **b. Lanolin**

c. Silicone **d. Zinc oxide**

Chất làm mềm da thường có chứa:

a. Potassium hydroxide *b. Lanolin (chất nhờn)*

c. Silicone *d. Zinc oxide (oxide kẽm)*

10. The technical term for nail is onyx. Nails are composed of chemical substance called:

a. Keratin **b. Corium**

c. Carbon **d. Protein**

Tên kỷ thuật của móng tay là onyx. Móng tay được cấu tạo của một dạng hóa chất gọi là:

a. Keratin (chất sừng) *b. Corium (nội bì)*

c. Carbon (than) *d. Protein (chất đạm)*

11. No person training or working in cosmetology establishment uses lump alum or styptic pencils to:

a. Sterilize the skin **b. Bleach under nails**

c. Arrest bleeding **d. Mask odors**

Không người nào đang học hoặc làm ở thẩm mỹ viện được dùng phèn cục hoặc viết chì cầm máu để:

a. Tiệt trùng da *b. Tẩy phần dưới móng*

c. Chận đứng máu chảy *d. Tẩy mùi hôi*

12. No person working or training in a cosmetology establishment shall be permitted to carry instruments or supplies:

a. On tray **b. In the hands**

c. In uniform pockets **d. On clean towels**

Không một ai đang hành nghề hoặc đang học trong trường thẩm mỹ được phép mang những dụng cụ hoặc đem những vật dụng:

a. Trên khay *b. Tay*

c. Túi áo choàng *d. Khăn sạch*

13. **Nail antiseptic is used:**

a. With the cuticle nippers **b. To clean cuticle**
c. To prevent molds and mildews **d. With a circular motion**

Chất sát trùng móng được dùng:
a. Với dụng cụ cắt da *b. Làm sạch da quanh móng*
c. Để ngăn ngừa nấm và mốc *d. Với động tác xoay tròn*

14. **If the skin is accidentally nipped while manicuring:**

a. Use a styptic pencil **b. Apply an antiseptic solution**
c. Use formalin disinfectant **d. Send patron to a physician**

Nếu có rủi phạm cắt vào da khi làm móng, bạn dùng:
a. Bút chì cầm máu *b. Dung dịch sát trùng*
c. Dùng chất diệt trùng formalin *d. Đưa khách đi bác sĩ*

15. **The ability of the body to withstand disease is called:**

a. Septicemia **b. Resistance**
c. Contagion **d. Contamination**

Khả năng của cơ thể chống cự lại bệnh tật gọi là:
a. Nhiễm trùng máu *b. Sự kháng bệnh*
c. Sự lây lan *d. Sự nhiễm bẩn*

16. **A general infection is:**

a. Confined to a small area **b. In the blood stream**
c. Around the nails **d. At the hair roots**

Nhiễm trùng toàn bộ là:
a. Nhiễm trùng một vùng nhỏ *b. Trong dòng máu*
c. Chung quanh móng tay *d. Ở gốc tóc*

17. **When pathogenic bacteria multiply rapidly, a disease becomes:**

a. Immune **b. Virulent**
c. Antitoxic **d. Antiseptic**

Khi vi trùng gây bệnh sinh sản nhanh chóng, cơn bệnh trở thành:
a. Miễn nhiễm *b. Nhiễm khuẩn trầm trọng*
c. Kháng độc *d. Sát trùng*

18. **Which of the following is not an antiseptic?**

a. Hydrogen peroxide 3% **b. Formalin 2%**
c. Powder alum **d. Boric acid 5%**

Chất nào dưới đây không phải là một chất sát trùng?
a. Hydrogen peroxide 3% *b. Formalin 2%*
c. Powder alum (bột cầm máu) *d. Boric acid 5%*

19. **The destruction of bacteria may be accomplished by:**

a. Chemical agents **b. Division of cells**
c. Animal parasites **d. Protozoa**

Sự tiêu diệt vi khuẩn có thể được làm bằng:
a. Các hóa chất *b. Sự phân chia của tế bào*
c. Ký sinh trùng động vật *d. Protozoa (động vật nguyên sinh)*

20. Articles such as metal files, nippers or steel pushers that drop on the floor may be used again, if they are:

a. Used on the same patron | **b. Wiped of with 70% alcohol**

c. Rinsed with hot water | **d. Sanitized with a germicide**

Vật dụng như giũa kim loại, đồ cắt da, hoặc cây xủi thép bị rớt xuống sàn nhà có thể dùng lại nếu chúng được:

a. Dùng cùng một người khách | *b. Lau bằng alcohol 70%*

c. Xả bằng nước nóng | *d. Khử trùng bằng chất diệt trùng*

21. If nail mold is not treated, it can cause the nail to turn green or black and:

a. Split | **b. Pterygium**

c. Smell bad | **d. Harden skin**

Móng bị mốc không được chữa trị, có thể là nguyên nhân làm móng đổi màu xanh hoặc đen và:

a. Nứt, chẻ | *b. Da mọc chồm*

c. Có mùi hôi | *d. Da cứng lại*

22. The fingernail must be prepared or the acrylic nail will:

a. Lift | **b. Crack**

c. Peel | **d. Dissolve**

Móng tay phải được chuẩn bị kỹ, nếu không thì móng bột sẽ:

a. Tróc, hở | *b. Nứt*

c. Lột ra | *d. Hòa tan*

23. Which one of the following is caused by an infection?

a. Onychorrhexis | **b. Onychophagy**

c. Pterygium | **d. Paronychia**

Bệnh nào dưới đây gây ra do nhiễm trùng?

a. Móng tét (onychorrhexis) | *b. Móng tay bị cắn do thói quen (onychophagy)*

c. Da mọc chồm lên mặt móng | *d. Paronychia (bệnh nhiễm trùng quanh móng)*

24. Liquid and powder of acrylic should be used:

a. 2 cc | **b. 1cc**

c. Until it is moist | **d. Following manufacture directions**

Nước và bột đắp móng giả nên được dùng:

a. 2 cc | *b. 1 cc*

c. Còn ẩm ướt | *d. Theo hướng dẫn của nơi chế tạo*

25. For the intended operation, mending tissue should be:

a. Cut to the correct size | **b. Torn to the correct size**

c. Trimmed | **d. Prepared**

Để chuẩn bị cho vá móng, giấy vá nên được:

a. Cắt cho đúng cỡ | *b. Xé ra cho đúng cỡ*

c. Tỉa bớt | *d. Chuẩn bị trước*

26. Which one of the following is not a form of hygiene?

a. Personal | **b. Public**

c. General | **d. Systemic**

Điều nào dưới đây không phải là một hình thức của sự vệ sinh?

a. Cá nhân | *b. Công cộng*

c. Tổng quát | *d. Hệ thống cơ thể*

27. **The transfer of specific disease from person to person is called:**
a. Systemic | **b. Contagion**
c. Toxaemia | **d. Susceptibility**
Sự truyền bệnh từ người này sang người khác được gọi là:
a. Thuộc về cơ thể | *b. Bệnh truyền nhiễm (trực tiếp hoặc gián tiếp)*
c. Nhiễm trùng máu | *d. Sự mẫn cảm*

28. **The hair-like organs that enable bacteria to move are called:**
a. Anthrax | **b. Flagella**
c. Both of a & b | **d. None of the above**
Cấu trúc như sợi tóc của vi trùng giúp chúng di chuyển được gọi là:
a. Vi trùng bệnh than (có mủ, lớn) | *b. Chân giả (lông bơi)*
c. Cả hai câu a và b | *d. Không phải các câu kể trên*

29. **Amotile bacteria are:**
a. Capable of moving | **b. Harmless**
c. Incapable of moving | **d. Capable of producing specific disease**
Loại vi khuẩn amotile là:
a. Có khả năng di chuyển | *b. Vô hại*
c. Không có khả năng di chuyển | *d. Có khả năng gây bệnh đặc biệt*

30. **Bacteria reproduce best in:**
a. Direct sunlight | **b. Closed cabinet**
c. Freezing temperature | **d. Warm, dark, damp and dirty places**
Vi khuẩn sinh sản tốt nhất nơi:
a. Trực tiếp ánh sáng mặt trời | *b. Trong tủ đóng kín*
c. Có độ đông lạnh | *d. Những chỗ ấm, tối, ẩm và dơ bẩn*

31. **Mending tissue should be smoothed and tucked under free edge with:**
a. Fingers | **b. Orange wood stick**
c. Metal pusher | **d. Both a & b**
Giấy vá móng sẽ làm mịn đều mặt móng và nhét xuống dưới đầu móng bằng:
a. Các ngón tay | *b. Que gỗ cam*
c. Cây xủi da | *d. Cả hai câu a và b*

32. **Additional layers of mending tissue for nails should be:**
a. Placed under | **b. Placed on cuticle**
c. Added as needed | **d. Dried**
Bọc thêm lớp giấy vá cho móng nên:
a. Đặt xuống dưới | *b. Đặt lên trên da*
c. Làm nếu cần thiết | *d. Để khô*

33. **Mending tissue should be slightly applied with:**
a. Mending liquid | **b. Glue**
c. Polish remover | **d. 6% Hydrogen peroxide**
Giấy vá móng nên được thoa phết nhè nhẹ với:
a. Keo vá móng | *b. Keo*
c. Chất chùi nước sơn | *d. Chất tẩy móng (6% H_2O_2)*

34. **The shape of the finger nails should conform to the:**

a. Hands | **b. Cuticle**
c. Skin texture | **d. Fingertips**

Hình dáng của móng tay nên phù hợp với:

a. Bàn tay | *b. Da quanh móng*
c. Loại da | *d. Đầu ngón tay*

35. **Nails are nourished by the blood and lymph in the:**

a. Nail cells | **b. Matrix**
c. Nail body | **d. Nail wall**

Móng tay được nuôi dưỡng do máu đỏ và bạch cầu trong:

a. Tế bào móng | *b. Móng non*
c. Thân móng | *d. Thành móng*

36. **The two headed muscles on the front of the arm which flexes the elbow and lift the forearm is the:**

a. Triceps | **b. Biceps**
c. Deltoid | **d. Flexors**

Bắp thịt có hai đầu, ở trước cánh tay giúp duỗi khuỷu tay và nhấc cánh tay trước là:

a. Triceps (ba đầu) | *b. Biceps*
c. Deltoid (thịt tam giác phủ bả vai) | *d. Flexors (cơ duỗi)*

37. **All disinfectant solutions should never be used on nails, human skin, and hair because:**

a. Strong odor | **b. Burn skin**
c. Darken skin | **d. Damage can result**

Tất cả các dụng dịch diệt trùng không bao giờ xử dụng trên móng tay, da, và tóc bởi vì:

a. Mùi nồng nặc | *b. Móng tay nước*
c. Đậm màu da | *d. Tai hại có thể xảy ra*

38. **Which one of the followings causes the nail matrix become infected and inflamed?**

a. Excessive use of strong solutions | **b. Usually follow an illness**
c. Improperly sanitized implements | **d. All of the above**

Điều nào sau đây là nguyên nhân móng non trở nên nhiễm trùng và sưng:

a. Dùng nhiều hoá chất mạnh | *b. Thường bệnh tật*
c. Khử trùng dụng cụ không đúng cách | *d. Tất cả những điều trên*

39. **What are the classifications of nail shapes:**

a. Square, oval | **b. Round, pointed**
c. All of the above | **d. None of the above**

Móng có những hình dạng nào:

a. Vuông, bầu dục | *b. Tròn, nhọn*
c. Tất cả những dạng trên | *d. Không có dạng nào kể trên*

40. **Nails are designed to protect the:**

a. Tips of the fingers | **b. Medial phalanxes**
c. Proximal phalanxes | **d. Metacarpal**

Móng được tạo ra để bảo vệ:

a. Đầu các ngón tay | *b. Medial phalanxes (các lóng giữa)*
c. Proximal phalanxes (các lóng tay trong) | *d. Xương bàn tay*

41. The technical term for nail is:

a. Pollex **b. Onyx**

c. Index **d. Cortex**

Danh từ chuyên môn cho móng tay là:

a. Pollex (ngón cái) *b. Onyx*

c. Ngón trỏ *d. Cortex (lớp chứa chất màu của tóc)*

42. On the outer surface nails are convex and on the inner surface nails are:

a. Concave **b. Curve**

c. Round **d. Flat**

Mặt ngoài của móng có dạng lồi và mặt trong của móng có dạng:

a. Lõm *b. Cong*

c. Tròn *d. Bằng*

43. When trimming the cuticle, be sure to remove it:

a. On one side at a time **b. As a single segment**

c. At the base only **d. In a small section**

Khi tỉa biểu bì (cuticle), chỉ nên tỉa lấy đi:

a. Ở một bên một lần *b. Từng miếng da nhỏ*

c. Ở nền móng *d. Từng phần nhỏ*

44. The root of the nail is soft and the root has:

a. Hard **b. Living part of the nail**

c. Rough **d. Nail body**

Phần gốc của móng có tính mềm và phần gốc móng có:

a. Cứng *b. Tế bào sống của móng*

c. Xù xì (nhám) *d. Thân móng*

45. For clients who work on computer and assembly line. What is the best shape?

a. Square **b. Pointed**

c. Oval **d. Round**

Đối với khách hàng dùng computer hoặc làm việc lắp ráp dây chuyền. Dạng móng nào là tốt nhất?

a. Vuông *b. Móng nhọn*

c. Móng oval (dạng móng lý tưởng) *d. Mòng tròn*

46. The nail grows from the:

a. Cuticle **b. Matrix**

c. Eponychium **d. Hyponychium**

Móng mọc ra từ:

a. Da phao tay *b. Móng non*

c. Da nền móng *d. Da dưới đầu móng*

47. Some acetone products may .... sculpture nail material:

a. Soften **b. Harden**

c. Thin **d. Thicken**

Một số hoá chất aceton có thể làm .... chất liệu để tạo thành móng bột:

a. Mềm *b. Rắn, cứng*

c. Mỏng *d. Dày*

48. Nails should be filed according to:

a. Manicurist's idea

b. Shape of the fingertips

c. Shape of the wrist

d. Shape of the arm

Móng tay sẽ được giũa tùy thuộc vào:

a. Ý muốn của thợ

b. Hình dạng của các đầu ngón tay

c. Hình dạng của cổ tay

d. Hình dạng của cánh tay

49. The matrix contains all the following except one:

a. Nerves

b. Lymph

c. Blood

d. Melanin

Móng non có chứa tất cả những điều dưới đây ngoại trừ:

a. Dây thần kinh

b. Bạch cầu

c. Máu

d. Sắc tố

50. Every salon should:

a. Keep door close all time

b. Be well ventilated

c. Have carpet on floor

d. None of the above

Mỗi thẩm mỹ viện (salon) nên:

a. Luôn luôn khép kín cửa

b. Được thoáng khí tốt

c. Có nền trải thảm

d. Không phải những điều trên

51. The normal growth of the nail is about:

a. 1/4 inch per week

b. 1/8 inch per week

c. 1/16 inch per week

d. 1/32 inch per week

Bình thường móng tay mọc khoảng:

a. 1/4 inch mỗi tuần

b. 1/8 inch mỗi tuần

c. 1/16 inch mỗi tuần

d. 1/32 inch mỗi tuần

52. The bones of the hand are called metacarpals and the bones of the wrist are called:

a. Hinge joint

b. Phalanges

c. Gliding joint

d. Pivot joint

Xương bàn tay được gọi là metacarpals và xương cổ tay được gọi là:

a. Hinge joints (khớp khủyu)

b. Phalanges (xương lóng tay)

c. Gliding joint (khớp trợt)

d. Pivot joint (khớp trục)

53. When giving a manicure or pedicure. Do not file into the nail corner because they will make:

a. New growth area

b. Ingrown nails

c. Dry cuticle

d. Proximal phalange

Khi làm manicure hoặc pedicure. Đừng giũa vào góc cạnh móng vì chúng sẽ tạo:

a. Vùng mới mọc

b. Móng mọc đâm khóe

c. Da khô

d. Proximal phalange (lóng trong cùng)

54. Which of the following terms mean finger?

a. Annularist

b. Lunate

c. Navicular

d. Phalanx

Từ nào theo sau đây có nghĩa là ngón tay:

a. Annularist (ngón thứ ba tay trái)

b. Lunate (xương bán nguyệt cổ tay)

c. Navicular (xương thuyền ở cổ tay)

d. Phalanx (lóng tay)

55. The cell of the nail matrix is:

a. Constantly multiplying **b. Dead material**

c. Found in the nail body **d. All clear and long**

Tế bào của móng non là:

a. Phát triển liên tục *b. Vật chết*

c. Thấy trong thân móng *d. Trong suốt và dài*

56. The number of bones in the hand and forearm are:

a. 8 **b. 13**

c. 27 **d. 29**

Số lượng xương của bàn tay và cánh tay trước là:

a. 8 *b. 13*

c. 27 *d. 29*

57. The hand consists of how many bones?

a. 7 bones **b. 17 bones**

c. 27 bones **d. 37 bones**

Bàn tay gồm bao nhiêu xương:

a. 7 xương *b. 17 xương*

c. 27 xương *d. 37 xương*

58. Metacarpal bones (body of the hand) consist of:

a. 8 bones **b. 5 bones**

c. 14 bones **d. 4 bones**

Các xương thân bàn tay (metacarpal bones) gồm có:

a. 8 xương *b. 5 xương*

c. 14 xương *d. 4 xương*

59. Toenails should be filed:

a. Corner to center **b. Center to corner**

c. Straight acros **d. Back and forth**

Móng chân được giũa:

a. Từ cạnh móng ra giữa móng *b. Từ giữa móng tới cạnh móng*

c. Thẳng ngang *d. Lui, tới*

60. Nails grow faster on children and in the:

a. Winter **b. Summer**

c. Fall **d. Spring**

Móng mọc nhanh hơn trên trẻ em và vào:

a. Mùa đông *b. Mùa hè*

c. Mùa thu *d. Mùa xuân*

61. Cocci are bacteria that produce diseases that appear singly or in groups with the shape of:

a. Rod **b. Cork screw**

c. Round **d. Square**

Cầu trùng (cocci) là loại vi trùng tạo bệnh thường xuất hiện từng con riêng hoặc từng nhóm có hình dạng:

a. Que (gậy) *b. Xoắn*

c. Tròn *d. Vuông*

62. **When placed in position, the end of the nail form should be:**

a. Vertical to nail **b. Horizontal with nail**

c. Slightly upward **d. Slightly downward**

Khi đặt đúng vị trí, phần cuối của miếng form nên:

a. Thẳng đứng với móng *b. Ngang bằng với móng*

c. Hơi hướng lên trên *d. Hơi hướng xuống dưới*

63. **Chemicals are best stored in:**

a. Sunshine area **b. Warm area**

c. Dark, cool and clean area **d. None of the above**

Tốt nhất, nên chứa hóa chất trong:

a. Nơi có ánh mặt trời *b. Nơi ấm áp*

c. Nơi tối, mát mẻ và sạch *d. Không phải những nơi trên*

64. **If the fungus growth appeared around the patron's nails, you should:**

a. Treat with H_2O_2 **b. Bathe in medical product**

c. Refer to a physician **d. Treat with alcohol**

Nếu có nấm mọc xung quanh móng của khách hàng, bạn nên:

a. Chữa trị với hydrogen peroxide *b. Ngâm vào thuốc*

c. Giới thiệu đến bác sĩ *d. Chữa trị bằng alcohol*

65. **Cocci bacteria have a round shape; Bacilli have a rod shape; and spirilla bacteria have the shape of:**

a. Oval **b. Cork screw**

c. Square **d. Both a & b**

Vi trùng cocci dạng hình tròn; Vi trùng bacilli dạng hình que; và vi trùng spirilla dạng hình:

a. Oval *b. Xoắn*

c. Vuông *d. Cả hai a & b*

66. **When disinfecting your instruments, you are:**

a. Killing harmful bacteria **b. Destroying beneficial bacteria**

c. Both a and b **d. Just a**

Khi diệt trùng dụng cụ, là bạn đang:

a. Giết vi trùng gây bệnh *b. Tiêu hủy vi trùng có ích*

c. Cả hai a và b *d. Chỉ câu a*

67. **Saprophyte bacteria are:**

a. Beneficial **b. Harmful**

c. Spirilla **d. All of the above**

Thực vật hoại sinh là loại vi trùng:

a. Có ích *b. Có hại*

c. Vi trùng hình xoắn *d. Tất cả những điều trên*

68. **Syphillis is disease caused by:**

a. Bacilli **b. Cocci**

c. Spirilla **d. All of the above**

Bệnh giang mai gây ra do:

a. Vi trùng hình que *b. Cầu trùng (vi trùng hình tròn)*

c. Vi trùng hình xoắn *d. Tất cả những câu trên*

69. Excessive heat causes nail product to dry:

a. Too slow **b. Too thick**

c. Too thin **d. Too fast**

Sức nóng quá độ là nguyên nhân làm hóa chất móng tay khô:

a. Quá chậm *b. Quá dày*

c. Quá mỏng *d. Quá nhanh*

70. The active stage or vegetative stage of bacteria occurs when they are:

a. Resting stage **b. Reproducing**

c. Both of the above **d. None of the above**

Giai đoạn hoạt động (active stage) hoặc giai đoạn sinh sản (vegetative stage) của vi trùng là khi chúng:

a. Thụ động (không hoạt động) *b. Sinh sôi nẩy nở*

c. Cả hai điều trên *d. Không phải điều trên*

71. Sepsis means having a disease and being immune to disease means:

a. Good health **b. Resistant to disease**

c. Asepsis **d. Both a and c**

Nhiễm trùng máu là có bệnh và miễn nhiễm bệnh là:

a. Sức khỏe tốt *b. Chống lại bệnh*

c. Vô trùng *d. Cả hai câu a và c*

72: Refill or repair is used to sculpture nail, block buffer is used to:

a. Buff acrylic nails to blend it **b. Thick the nail plate**

c. Reshape the free edge **d. Thin the nail plate**

Đắp thêm bột vào phần móng mới mọc hoặc sữa chữa cho móng bột, cây buffer được dùng:

a. Chà móng bột được mịn đều *b. Dày mặt móng*

c. Tạo dáng cho đầu móng *d. Mỏng ở đầu móng*

73. If the matrix is destroyed, the nail will:

a. Never grow again **b. Grow faster**

c. Grow slower **d. Continue to grow**

Nếu móng non chết, móng sẽ:

a. Không mọc nữa *b. Mọc nhanh hơn*

c. Mọc chậm hơn *d. Tiếp tục mọc*

74. Sculpture nail products should be applied:

a. In small balls **b. In circular motion**

c. Extremely moist **d. Extremely dry**

Hóa chất làm móng bột nên được đắp:

a. Từng viên nhỏ *b. Chuyển động tròn*

c. Thật ẩm ướt *d. Thật khô*

75. The clavicle is the key bone of the:

a. Forearm **b. Body of hand**

c. Shoulders **d. Fingers**

Xương đòn gánh là xương chính của:

a. Cánh tay trước *b. Thân bàn tay*

c. Bả vai *d. Ngón tay*

76. One of the following separates the fingers:

a. Pronators

b. Supinators

c. Abductors

d. Adductors

Bắp thịt nào có tác dụng xòe các ngón tay:

a. Cơ nội chuyển (úp bàn tay xuống)

b. Cơ ngoại chuyển (lật ngửa bàn tay)

c. Cơ xòe ngón

d. Cơ khép ngón

77. Ingrown toenails are caused by:

a. Using coarse side of the file

b. Using a steel file

c. Cutting the nail straight across

d. Clipping or filing into the corners

Móng chân mọc đâm khóe gây ra do:

a. Dùng mặt nhám của giũa

b. Sử dụng giũa kim loại

c. Cắt móng chân thẳng ngang

d. Cắt và giũa sâu vào khóe móng

78. In artificial nails, growth of fungus will occur when:

a. Air in-take

b. Acrylic too thick

c. Acrylic too thin

d. None of the above

Trong dịch vụ móng nhân tạo, sự phát triển nấm sẽ xảy ra khi:

a. Có bọt khí lọt vào

b. Lớp acrylic quá dày

c. Lớp acrylic quá mỏng

d. Không có các điều trên

79. Cosmetologist and manicurist should renew their license:

a. Every two years

b. Every three years

c. Every five years

d. January 31 of every year

Thẩm mỹ viên và thợ móng tay đổi lại bằng hành nghề khi hết hạn:

a. Hai năm một lần

b. Ba năm một lần

c. Năm năm một lần

d. Ngày 31 tháng 1 hằng năm

80. If the nail product is setting up too fast:

a. Add more liquid monomer

b. Add more polymer

c. Add more material

d. Add acetone

Nếu chất làm móng bột rắn (khô) quá nhanh:

a. Lấy thêm dung dịch (monomer)

b. Dùng thêm bột

c. Thêm vật liệu

d. Thêm acetone

81. To make the fumigant, mix:

a. Formalin with boric acid

b. Formalin with formaldehyde

c. Formalin with borax

d. Formalin with alum powder

Để tạo chất khí diệt trùng (fumigant), trộn:

a. Formalin và boric acid

b. Formalin và formaldehyde

c. Formalin và borax

d. Formalin và phèn bột cầm máu

82. Soiled towels should be kept:

a. In the corner

b. On an open shelf

c. In a closed container

d. In an open hamper

Khăn bẩn nên được chứa trong:

a. Góc tiệm

b. Trên kệ trống

c. Trong thùng đậy kín

d. Thùng không đậy nắp

83. Touching the natural nail with finger before applying artificial nails could cause:

a. Spots **b. Improper adherence**

c. Slow drying **d. Finger mark**

Chạm tay vào móng thật trước khi bắt đầu đắp móng giả sẽ gây ra:

a. Vết (đốm) *b. Móng dính không đúng cách*

c. Chậm khô *d. Dấu ngón tay*

84. Which of the following has the power to destroy all germs:

a. Disinfectant solution **b. Germicide**

c. Bactericide **d. All of the above**

Chất nào sau đây có khả năng tiêu diệt tất cả vi trùng:

a. Dung dịch diệt trùng *b. Chất diệt vi trùng gây bệnh*

c. Chất diệt vi trùng *d. Tất cả các chất trên*

85. The radial bone is on the side of the:

a. Pinkie **b. Shoulder**

c. Ulnar bone **d. Thumb**

Xương quay nằm về phía:

a. Ngón út *b. Vai*

c. Xương trụ *d. Ngón cái*

86. The skin is the thinnest on the eyelids and thickest on the:

a. Cheek **b. Palm and soles**

c. Forehead **d. Elbow**

Da mỏng nhất là trên mí mắt và dày nhất trên:

a. Gò má *b. Lòng bàn tay và gót chân*

c. Trán *d. Khủyu tay (cùi chỏ)*

87. The manicurist should not work on patron who has:

a. Fungus **b. Immune**

c. Asepsis **d. None of the above**

Thợ làm móng không nên phục vụ khách hàng nào có:

a. Bệnh nấm *b. Miễn nhiễm*

c. Vô trùng *d. Không phải những điều trên*

88. The tubes that carry blood from heart to the body are:

a. Arteries **b. Veins**

c. Both a and b **d. None of the above**

Ống dẫn máu từ tim đi khắp cơ thể là:

a. Động mạch *b. Tĩnh mạch*

c. Cả hai câu a và b *d. Không phải những câu trên*

89. Ulnar vein supplies the:

a. Pinkie **b. Index**

c. Thumb **d. All fingers**

Tĩnh mạch trụ cung cấp máu cho:

a. Ngón út *b. Ngón trỏ*

c. Ngón cái *d. Tất cả các ngón tay*

90. Another name for onychomycosis is:

a. Athlete foot | **b. Tinea**

c. Tinea unguium | **d. Onycholysis**

Một tên gọi khác cho bệnh mục móng do nấm (onychomycosis) là:

a. Nấm chân | *b. Tinea (vòng mụn nước)*

c. Tinea unguium | *d. Bệnh lỏng móng (không rụng)*

91. For clients with ridge and brittle nails or dry cuticles, recommend a/an:

a. Hot oil manicure | **c. Soak in soap liquid and warm water in 5 minutes**

b. Trim dead cuticles | **d. Nail wrapping**

Đối với khách có móng gợn và dòn hoặc da tay khô, khuyên nên:

a. Chăm sóc tay với dầu | *c. Nhúng trong xà phòng và nước ấm trong 5 phút*

b. Tỉa da chết | *d.Bọc móng*

92. The largest organ of the body is the:

a. Nails | **b. Heart**

c. Lungs | **d. Skin**

Cơ quan lớn nhất trong cơ thể là:

a. Móng | *b. Tim*

c. Phổi | *d. Da*

93. When giving a pedicure, legs are to be massaged from toe to knee, except:

a. Below the ankle | **b. Above the ankle**

c. Muscular tissue | **d. Shin-bone**

Đối với chăm sóc chân (pedicure), massage chân từ ngón đến đầu gối, ngoại trừ:

a. Dưới mắt cá chân | *b. Trên mắt cá chân*

c. Mô bắp thịt | *d. Xương ống chân (xương chày)*

94. The outer most layer of the skin is epidermis and the second layer of the skin is:

a. Dermis | **b. Epidermis**

c. Derma | **d. Dermal**

Lớp ngoài cùng của da là epidermis và lớp thứ hai của da là:

a. Nội bì | *b. Ngoại bì*

c. Da thật | *d. Thuộc về da*

95. The correct way to apply nail polish starting from base to free edge is to:

a. Use 3 short strokes | **b. Apply it quickly and lightly**

c. Work from center to each side | **d. Drop nail polish then spreading**

Cách đúng nhất là thoa nước sơn từ nền móng đến đầu móng là:

a. Thoa 3 đường vuốt | *b. Thoa nhanh và nhẹ*

c. Thoa từ giữa ra mỗi cạnh | *d. Rơi nhỏ giọt nước sơn và trãi ra*

96. Oil manicure helps to improve which one of the nail conditions:

a. Hangnails | **b. Onychorrhexis**

c. Brittle nails | **d. All of the above**

Làm móng dầu giúp ngăn ngừa tình trạng nào dưới đây:

a. Hangnails (da xước) | *b. Móng nứt*

c. Móng dòn | *d. Tất cả các điều trên*

97. The study of the muscle is called myology and the study of the blood is known as:

a. Trichology **b. Osteology**

c. Angiology **d. Neurology**

Môn học về bắp thịt được gọi là myology và môn học về máu được biết là:

a. Myology (bắp thịt) *b. Osteology (xương)*

c. Angiology *d. Neurology (Thần kinh học)*

98. Bones protect organs from injury, allow bodily movements, and also gives shape and strength to the body. The human skeleton consists of:

a. 206 bones **b. 210 bones**

c. 209 bones **d. 200 bones**

Xương bảo vệ các chức năng bên trong khi bị tổn thương, cho phép mọi chuyển động cơ thể, tạo hình dáng và sức mạnh cho cơ thể. Xương cơ thể con người có tổng cộng:

a. 206 xương *b. 210 xương*

c. 209 xương *d. 200 xương*

99. You must sanitize a customer's nails before applying acrylic nails because it will:

a. Help to prevent hangnails **c. Prevent fungus from forming**

b. Soften the nail properly for acrylics **d. Help to adhere acrylic to natural nail**

Bạn nên khử trùng móng cho khách trước khi đắp móng bột vì chúng sẽ:

a. Giúp ngăn ngừa xước da *c. Ngăn ngừa nấm khi đắp*

b. Làm mềm móng đối với bột acrylic *d. Giúp dính bột acrylic đến móng thật*

100. The study of the skin is called dermatology and the study of the nerves is called:

a. Osteology **c. Myology**

b. Neurology **d. Angiology**

Môn học về da có tên là dermatology và môn học về thần kinh có tên là:

a. Osteology (môn học về xương) *c. Myology (môn học về bắp thịt)*

b. Neurology *d. Angiology (môn học về máu)*

MANICURIST EXAMINATION 6

1. **Which of the following a chemical is easily flammable in a salon?**
   a. Cuticle cream
   b. Cuticle oil
   c. Hand lotion
   d. Enamel solvent
   Hóa chất nào sau đây dễ dàng bốc cháy trong tiệm thẩm mỹ?
   a. Kem thoa da
   b. Dầu thoa da
   c. Kem massage
   d. Chất nước sơn

2. **Sodium hypochlorite is commonly known as:**
   a. Formaldehyde
   b. Ammonia
   c. Salt
   d. Household bleach
   Chất sodium hypochloride thường được biết là:
   a. Hơi diệt trùng formaldehyde
   b. Chất ammonia
   c. Salt (muối)
   d. Chất tẩy lau nhà

3. **How many vegetable cells make up a microbe?**
   a. One cell
   b. Two cells
   c. Three cells
   d. Four cells
   Có bao nhiêu tế bào thực vật tạo thành vi khuẩn?
   a. Một tế bào
   b. Hai tế bào
   c. Ba tế bào
   d. Bốn tế bào

4. **Which of the following is not a protein food:**
   a. Poultry
   b. Bean
   c. Candy
   d. Beef
   Chất nào sau đây không phải là chất đạm:
   a. Gà vịt
   b. Đậu
   c. Kẹo
   d. Thịt bò

5. **What can be used to remove nail polish that accidentally got on the client's skin?**
   a. An orange wood stick with cotton and polish remover
   b. A cotton swab with nail cleanser
   c. An orange wood stick with cotton and cuticle oil
   d. A cotton ball with polish thinner
   Bạn dùng gì để chùi nước sơn nếu rủi ro dính lên da khách?
   a. Que gỗ quấn bông gòn và chất chùi nước sơn
   b. Cục bông gòn với chất chùi sạch móng
   c. Que gỗ quấn bông và dầu thoa da
   d. Cục bông gòn với chất pha loãng nước sơn

6. **70% of ethyl alcohol is equivalent to how much of isopropyl alcohol?**
   a. 70%
   b. 90%
   c. 99%
   d. 120%
   70 % cồn ethyl tương đương bao nhiêu so với độ mạnh cồn isopropyl?
   a. 70 %
   b. 90 %
   c. 99 %
   d. 120 %

7. Emery boards are discard after each use because:

a. The abrasive is expended

b. They cannot be disinfected

c. They are worn out

d. All of the above

Giũa giấy bị bỏ sau mỗi lần dùng vì:

a. Cây giũa hết nhám

b. Chúng không thể diệt trùng được

c. Chúng bị hư

d. Tất cả những điều trên

8. Repeated or prolonged contact with solvents will leave the skin:

a. Oily

b. Moisture

c. Damaged and dry

d. Burned

Sự tiếp xúc nhiều lần và lâu dài với dung dịch sẽ làm cho da:

a. Dầu

b. Ẩm

c. Hư hại và khô

d. Phỏng

9. Wary ridge on a fingernail may be improved by rubbing the nail with:

a. Pumice powder

b. Cream

c. Oil

d. Polish remover

Những đường gợn sóng trên móng tay có thể chữa lại bằng cách chà móng tay với:

a. Bột đá bọt

b. Chất kem

c. Chất dầu

d. Chất chùi nước sơn

10. The care of the feet, legs, and toenails is called:

a. Pedicure

b. Hygiene of feet and legs

c. Foot massage

d. Paronychia

Sự chăm sóc bàn chân, chân và ngón chân gọi là:

a. Pedicure

b. Vệ sinh đôi bàn chân và chân

c. Xoa bóp chân

d. Paronychia (sưng chung quanh móng)

11. Nail whiteners are available in the form of:

a. A liquid

b. A paste

c. A powder

d. An oil

Chất làm trắng móng ở dạng:

a. Thể lỏng

b. Thể sền sệt

c. Thể bột

d. Thể dầu

12. All manicure instruments must be disinfected before:

a. Putting them in a table drawer

b. Leaving the salon for the day

c. Using them on another patron

d. The patron arrives

Tất cả dụng cụ làm móng tay phải được diệt trùng trước khi:

a. Đặt vào trong ngăn kéo của bàn

b. Để trong tiệm suốt ngày

c. Dùng lại cho người khách khác

d. Khách hàng đến

13. The feet need to soak to antibacterial soap prior to the pedicure procedure because they are:

a. Sanitation

b. Brushing feet

c. Removing toenails's old polish

d. To soften hangnails

Đôi chân cần nhúng vào xà phòng diệt trùng trước khi làm pedicure bởi vì chân cần được:

a. Vệ sinh sạch sẽ

b. Chà chân

c. Lấy đi nước sơn cũ ở móng chân

d. Làm mềm da xướt

14. At the start of the manicure, the cuticle nipper, cuticle pusher, and orangewood stick should be:

a. Handy and available to the manicurist

b. In the manicure table drawer

c. Laid out on manicure table

d. Kept in the sanitary maintenance area

Lúc bắt đầu chăm sóc tay, kềm cắt da, cây xủi da, và que gỗ cam nên:

a. Trong tầm tay của thợ

b. Trong ngăn kéo bàn làm móng

c. Để trên mặt bàn

d. Để trên giấy giữ vệ sinh (S.M.A)

15. To prepared a 1000 P.P.M solution of E.P.A. registered Quaternary ammonium compound, using a 15% active ingredient you would mix:

a. 1 ¼ ounce of "Quats" to a gallon of water

b. 1 ounce of "Quats" to a gallon of water

c. 3/4 ounce of "Quats" to a gallon of water

d. ½ ounce of "Quats" to a gallon of water

Để pha chế nước Quats (Quaternary ammonium compounds) 1,000 phần triệu được E.P.A chuẩn nhận, xử dụng dung lượng 15 % bạn pha:

a. 1 ¼ ounce Quats cho 1 gallon nước

b. 1 ounce Quats cho 1 gallon nước

c. ¾ ounce Quats cho 1 gallon nước

d. ½ ounce Quats cho 1 gallon nước

16. A hangnail condition may be corrected by trimming the hangnail and softening the surrounding skin with:

a. Naphtha soap

b. Cuticle oil

c. Boric acid

d. Polish remover

Da tay bị xước có thể chữa bằng cách tỉa da xước và làm mềm chung quanh da với:

a. Xà phòng naphtha (sản phẩm từ dầu mỏ)

b. Dầu thoa da

c. Boric acid

d. Chất chùi nước sơn

17. A base coat is usually applied:

a. Over the top coat

b. After the nail polish

c. Before the nail polish

d. With short strokes

Sơn lót thường dùng:

a. Trên lớp sơn ngoài

b. Sau nước sơn móng

c. Trước nước sơn móng

d. Với những đường vuốt ngắn

18. Manicure implements should be wasted and disinfected:

a. Once a day

b. After each use

c. Every week

d. Twice a week

Dụng cụ làm móng tay sẽ được rửa và diệt trùng:

a. Mỗi ngày một lần

b. Sau mỗi lần dùng

c. Hằng tuần

d. Một tuần 2 lần

19. A manicurist's license expired 6 months ago, to renew the license, the manicurist must now:

a. Retake both the written and practical parts of the examination

b. Retake the written part of the examination:

c. Pay the delinquency fee in addition to renewal fee

d. Pay just the renewal fee

Bằng hành nghề làm nail hết hạn 6 tháng, muốn gia hạn, thợ làm móng tay phải làm ngay:

a. Thi viết và phần thực hành

b. Thi lại phần viết

c. Trả lệ phí quá hạn và gia hạn

d. Chỉ trả lệ phí gia hạn

20. Cosmetology textbooks recommend that a steel pusher be used on a moist nail:

a. To prevent scratching of the nail plate **c. So the mantle will not be disturbed**

b. To increase circulation **d. So the lunula can be seen**

Sách giáo khoa thẩm mỹ khuyên nên dùng cây thép xủi da trên móng tay ẩm:

a. Ngăn ngừa mặt móng trầy xước *c. Màng da sẽ không bị xước*

b. Tăng sự tuần hoàn *d. Thấy vòng trắng mặt móng*

21. The nail walls are small folds of skin overlapping the sides of the nail:

a. Mantle **c. Bed**

b. Matrix **d. Body**

Thành móng tay là những nếp xếp nhỏ được chồng lên nhau bên cạnh của:

a. Màng móng *c. Nền móng tay*

b. Móng non *d. Thân móng tay*

22. The nail root is lodge in the nail mantle at the:

a. Top of the nail **c. Side of the nail**

b. Base of the nail **d. Tip of the nail**

Rễ móng tay nằm trong màng móng ở:

a. Trên móng tay *c. Cạnh móng tay*

b. Nền móng tay *d. Chóp đầu móng tay*

23. The visible portion of the nail, resting upon the nail bed is the:

a. Nail body **c. Lunula**

b. Nail root **d. Free edge**

Phần móng tay thấy được nằm trên nền móng tay là:

a. Thân móng tay *c. Lunula (vòng trắng nhỏ ở mặt móng)*

b. Rễ móng tay *d. Đầu móng tay*

24. Which one of the following is not a main part of the finger nail?

a. Body **c. Mantle**

b. Root **d. Free edge**

Phần nào sau đây không phải là phần chính của móng tay?

a. Thân móng tay *c. Màng móng*

b. Rễ móng tay *d. Đầu móng tay*

25. The carpal bones are classed as:

a. Regular **c. Flat**

b. Irregular **d. Round**

Xương cổ tay được sắp xếp dạng:

a. Bình thường *c. Bằng phẳng*

b. Không đồng đều *d. Tròn*

26. The nail root begins from an actively growing tissue called the:

a. Lunula **c. Hyponichium**

b. Matrix **d. Eponychium**

Rễ móng tay bắt đầu từ tế bào tăng trưởng gọi là:

a. Lunula (hình bán nguyệt) *c. Phần da dưới đầu móng tay*

b. Móng non *d. Phần da ở nền móng tay*

27. Phalanges are found in the:

a. Hands

b. Forearm

c. Wrist

d. Digits

Xương lóng tay được tìm thấy trong:

a. Bàn tay

b. Cánh tay trước

c. Cổ tay

d. Các ngón tay

28. Split nails may be cause by:

a. Soaking too long

b. Use of nail whitener

c. Imroper use of the buffer

d. Improper use of nail file

Móng tay bị nứt có thể là nguyên nhân do:

a. Ngâm móng tay quá lâu

b. Dùng chất làm trắng móng

c. Dùng buffer không đúng cách

d. Dùng giũa không đúng cách

29. The appearance of a healthy nail shows a:

a. Purple color

b. Slight pink color

c. Yellowish color

d. Bluish color

Móng tay khỏe mạnh có dấu hiệu:

a. Màu tím

b. Màu hồng nhạt

c. Màu vàng vàng

d. Màu xanh xanh

30. The Board of Barbering and Cosmetology rules requires clean towels in a salon to be stored:

a. In the shampoo area

b. In the reception area

c. In a close cabinet

d. At each work station

Luật lệ của Hội động thẫm mỹ của tiểu bang đòi hỏi khăn sạch ở tiệm phải được cất giữ ở:

a. Nơi gội tóc

b. Khu vực tiếp khách

c. Trong tủ đóng kín

d. Ở mỗi bàn làm khách

31. Minor bleeding in manicuring is stopped best with:

a. 6% Hydrogen peroxide

b. Disinfectant

c. Powdered alum

d. Astringen lotion

Nếu bị chảy máu nhẹ trong lúc làm móng tay tốt nhứt là dùng với:

a. Chất tẩy móng 6% peroxide

b. Chất diệt trùng

c. Powder alum (phèn bột)

d. Chất se da (đóng lỗ chân lông)

32. Nail brushes and nail baths used properly, help eliminate:

a. Ridges on the nail

b. Excess cuticle

c. Stains on the nail

d. Dryness of nails

Chà và rửa móng tay đúng cách, giúp loại bỏ :

a. Đường gợn sóng trên móng tay

b. Da dư

c. Vết dơ trên móng tay

d. Móng tay khô

33. Blue nail are usually a sign of:

a. Wrist trouble

b. A stomach ailment

c. Poor blood circulation

d. A lung disorder

Móng có màu xanh là dấu hiệu của:

a. Đau nhức cổ tay

b. Bao tử khó tiêu

c. Kém tuần hoàn máu

d. Phổi khó thở

34. Which one of the following conditions may not be treated by the manicurist?

a. Agnails | **c. Onychophagy**
b. Paronychia | **d. Pterygium**

Trình trạng nào sau đây không nên điều trị bởi thợ làm móng tay:

a. Xước da móng tay | *c. Cắn móng tay*
b. Sưng đỏ chung quanh móng tay | *d. Da mọc chồm lên nền móng*

35. An abnormal overgrowth of nail is known as:

a. Atrophy | **c. Onychophagy**
b. Hypertrophy | **d. Onychorrhexis**

Móng tay mọc quá mức bình thường được biết như là:

a. Atrophy (móng tay teo nhỏ, mờ đục) | *c. Onychophagy (tật cắn móng tay)*
b. Hypertrophy | *d. Onychorrhexis (móng tay bị nứt, chẻ)*

36. In manicuring, the nail chamois buffer is used to:

a. Polish the nail | **c. Remove eponychium**
b. Scrub the nails | **d. Remove rough nail edges**

Làm móng tay, cục buffer bọc da dê đánh bóng móng được sử dụng:

a. Làm bóng móng tay | *c. Lấy đi da dư trên mặt móng*
b. Chà lên móng tay | *d. Lấy đi da sần sùi cạnh móng tay*

37. An abrasive to smooth nail ridges would be:

a. Powdered pumice | **c. Nitro cellulose**
b. Organic acid | **d. Castor oil**

Chất chà mòn, làm mịn cho móng tay bị gợn sóng là:

a. Bột đá bọt | *c. Nitro cellulose*
b. Acid hữu cơ | *d. Dầu thầu dầu*

38. To remove stain from fingernails, use:

a. Nail polish remover | **c. Nail whitener**
b. Cuticle oil | **d. Nail bleach**

Để lấy chất dơ từ móng tay dùng:

a. Chất chùi nước sơn móng tay | *c. Chất trắng oxýt kẽm che móng bị đốm*
b. Dầu thoa da | *d. Chất tẩy móng*

39. Which one of the following would not be a proper method of using a metal pusher?

a. Pointed end used to loosen cuticle | **c. Pusher is used from corner to base of nail**
b. Blade end follows the curve of the cuticle | **d. Pusher is used with gentle pressure**

Cách nào sau đây là dùng không đúng với cây xủi da móng tay bằng kim loại?

a. Đầu nhọn dùng để làm lỏng da móng | *c. Dùng cây xủi từ góc tới nền móng*
b. Đầu dẹp theo chiều cong của da móng | *d. Dùng cây xủi da với ép nhẹ*

40. **Pterygium may be helped by having a hot oil manicure and using the cuticle nippers carefully to remove the growth because:**

a. Cause by nail biting

b. Softening of the nail

c. An obstinate growth of cuticle at the base

d. An ingrown nail

Pterygium (da mọc chồm lên móng) có thể chữa trị nhờ cách làm móng tay dầu ấm và dùng kềm cắt chỗ da mọc cẩn thận vì:

a. Tạo ra do cắn móng

b. Làm mềm móng

c. Da mọc tràn lên ở nền móng

d. Móng mọc đâm vô thịt

41. **To slow polish chipping on the free edge:**

a. Remove hairline of polish at the tip

b. Leave the free edge expose

c. Leave the lunula exposed

d. Use only one coat of polish

Để giúp cho nước sơn lâu tróc ở đầu móng tay:

a. Lau đường viền nước sơn ở đầu móng

b. Không sơn đầu móng tay (free edge)

c. Không sơn vòng trắng bán nguyệt ở mặt móng (lunula)

d. Chỉ dùng một lớp nước sơn

42. **For dry cuticles and brittle nails, it is best to give:**

a. An oil manicure

b. A water manicure

c. A plan booth manicure

d. A plain manicure with electric file

Đối với da khô và móng tay dòn, tốt nhất là làm:

a. Móng tay dầu

b. Móng tay nước

c. Làm móng tay dã chiến (không bàn)

d. Làm móng tay nước với máy giủa điện

43. **The proper way to remove old nail polish is to:**

a. Moistened cotton with polish remover, hold some second on nails and draw it straight off

b. Cotton with polish remover and rub the nail

c. Soak nails in oil in which a few drops of polish remover have been added

d. Soak nails in polish remove

Cách đúng nhất chùi bỏ nước sơn cũ là:

a. Bông gòn thấm chất chùi nước sơn giữ vài giây trên móng và kéo thẳng xuống

b. Bông gòn với chất chùi sơn và chà móng

c. Ngâm móng trong dầu có pha vài giọt chất chùi nước sơn

d. Ngâm móng tay trong chất chùi nước sơn

44. **Nail bleaches usually contain:**

a. Zinc oxide

b. Cocoa butter

c. Glycerin

d. Hydrogen peroxide

Chất tẩy móng tay thường chứa:

a. Oxide kẽm

b. Bơ cocoa

c. Glycerine (dầu nhờn)

d. Hydrogen peroxide (H_2O_2)

45. **Nail whitener is applied:**

a. Over the lunula

b. On the top of the free edge of the nail

c. Under the free edge of the nail

d. On the sides of the nails

Chất trắng che móng bị đốm được thoa:

a. Phủ lên vòng bán nguyệt

b. Trên mặt phần đầu móng

c. Dưới đầu móng (phần móng mọc ngoài đệm móng)

d. Trên 2 cạnh của móng

46. Two- color acrylic application requires use of all the following except:

a. White powder
b. Yellow powder
c. Pink powder
d. Acrylic liquid

Bột acrylic hai màu phải dùng những thứ sau đây ngoại trừ:

a. Bột trắng đầu móng
b. Bột vàng
c. Bột hồng
d. Nước acrylic

47. The common name for onychocryptosis is:

a. Hangnails
b. Bitten nails
c. Ingrown nails
d. Bruise nails

Tên thường gọi móng mọc ngược vô da (onychocryptosis) là:

a. Hangnails
b. Cắn móng
c. Ingrown nails (móng mọc đâm khóe)
d. Móng tay bị bầm

48. Spraying nail antiseptic on finger nails, removes:

a. Cotton bits
b. Nail polish
c. Cuticle oil
d. Natural oil

Xịt chất sát trùng móng trên móng tay, lấy đi:

a. Một ít bông gòn
b. Nail polish (nước sơn)
c. Dầu thoa da
d. Lớp dầu tự nhiên

49. The HIV virus, which causes AIDS may lay dormant in an infected person's system for up to:

a. 20 years
b. 15 years
c. 50 years
d. 3 years

Nhiễm vi khuẩn HIV, mà nguyên nhân của bệnh AIDS có thể đã nằm ẩn trong người có bệnh đã lâu đến:

a. 20 năm
b. 15 năm
c. 50 năm
d. 3 năm

50. When giving a manicure always begin working on the:

a. Right hand
b. Unfavored hand
c. favored hand
d. Left hand

Khi làm chăm sóc tay luôn luôn bắt đầu trên:

a. Tay phải
b. Tay không thuận
c. Tay thuận
d. Tay trái

51. Chemicals from nail products can enter your body in all these ways except:

a. Inhalation
b. Ingestion
c. Injection
d. Skin contact

Hóa chất từ các sản phẩm về móng tay có thể thấm vào thân thể bằng nhiều cách ngoại trừ:

a. Hít vào
b. Ăn uống vào
c. Chích
d. Tiếp xúc của da

52. If pus is present, the skin or nail is:

a. Infected
b. To be soaked in alcohol
c. Bruised
d. Inflamed

Nếu da và móng có mủ là:

a. Nhiễm trùng
b. Nhúng vào alcohol
c. Móng bị bầm
d. Sưng

53. The technical name for athlete's foot is:

a. Vitiligo

b. Chloasma

c. Tinea pedis

d. Sarcode

Tên y học của nấm mọc ở chân (athlete's foot) là:

a. Vitiligo (trắng lan ben)

b. Chloasma (đốm lớn nâu, đen đậm)

c. Tinea pedis

d. Sarcode (chất nguyên sinh)

54. An important part of the consultation is to determine whether or not the home maintenance for a service fits the client's....:

a. Looks

b. Lifestyle

c. Budget

d. Ability

Điều quan trọng trong tham khảo là cần đánh giá có hay không nên phục vụ tại nhà là tùy theo điều gì . . . . . . của khách:

a. Nhìn

b. Đời sống

c. Ngân sách

d. Khả năng

55. Equipment is the term for items used in nail technology that are:

a. Expensive

b. Made of plastic

c. Disposable

d. Permanent

Equipment (dụng cụ bền chắc) là từ diễn tả dụng cụ xử dụng trong kỹ thuật làm móng, có tính chất:

a. Đắt tiền

b. Làm bằng nhựa

c. Có thể vứt bỏ

d. Lâu dài (bền)

56. When pedicuring, the proper time to insert toe separators is before toenail polish and:

a. Clipping nails

b. Polish finger nails

c. Filing toenails

d. Soaking feet in water

Khi săn sóc chân, lúc đặt miếng xốp ngăn ngón chân là trước khi sơn móng chân và:

a. Clipping nails (cắt móng)

b. Sơn móng tay

c. Giũa móng chân

d. Nhúng chân vào nước

57. The foot massage begins with:

a. Joint relaxer movement

b. Thumb compression

c. Metatarsal

d. Brisk rubbing

Xoa bóp chân bắt đầu:

a. Khớp chuyển động

b. Ép ngón cái

c. Xương bàn chân

d. Chà nhanh

58. Bacteria multiply at amazing speeds in only half a day, a single bacteria cell can produce this many more:

a. 6,000

b. 16 millions

c. 100,000

d. 25,000

Vi trùng sinh sản rất nhanh chỉ trong 12 giờ (1/2 ngày), một tế bào vi trùng có thể tạo ra hơn:

a. 6.000

b. 16 triệu

c. 100.000

d. 25.000

59. Albinism is the congenital absence of this substance from the body:

a. Albumin **c. Melanin**

b. Fungus **d. Vitamin C**

Bệnh bạch tạng do bẩm sinh (albinism) là tình trạng thiếu chất gì trong cơ thể:

a. Chất albumin (hóa chất rửa hình) *c. Sắc tố*

b. Nấm *d. Chất bổ C*

60. Performing a service on an infected nail could cause your client a great deal of:

a. Healing **c. Regrowth**

b. Pain **d. Stimulating**

Phục vụ trên móng bị nhiễm trùng có thể là nguyên nhân gây cho khách:

a. Lành lại *c. Mọc lại*

b. Đau đớn *d. Kích thích*

61. Phenolics are good for implement disinfection, but are:

a. Difficult to work with **c. Hard to find**

b. Unbalanced **d. Costly**

Chất phenolics tốt cho việc diệt trùng dụng cụ nhưng:

a. Khó làm *c. Khó tìm*

b. Không cân bằng *d. Mắc tiền*

62. Your best source of advertising to attract new clients is:

a. Radio **c. Newspapers**

b. Current satisfied **d. Coupon mailers**

Nguồn quảng cáo tốt nhất để hấp dẫn khách mới là:

a. Phát thanh *c. Báo chí*

b. Làm khách hài lòng *d. Gởi phiếu giảm giá*

63. A lamp bulb with high wattage will affect product performance when giving this service:

a. Sculptured nails **c. Polish change**

b. Gel nails **d. Fiberglass wrap**

Bóng đèn với độ sáng mạnh sẽ ảnh hưởng đến hóa chất khi làm:

a. Móng bột *c. Đổi màu nước sơn*

b. Móng gel *d. Boc móng bằng thủy tinh sợi (dày,chắc hơn lụa)*

64. The body is protected from harmful bacteria infection and through the white cells found in:

a. Urine **c. Intestines**

b. Blood **d. Plasma**

Khi nhiễm vi trùng gây bệnh cơ thể được bảo vệ bởi tế bào máu trắng (bạch cầu) tìm thấy ở:

a. Nước tiểu *c. Ruột*

b. Máu *d. Huyết tương*

65. A properly ventilated salon is one that vents fumes and vapors to the:

a. Reception area **c. Outside**

b. Bathroom **d. Haircolor area**

Tiệm có hệ thống thoáng khí đúng cách là cần có hệ thống thoát khói và hơi ra:

a. Nơi thư ký *c. Bên ngoài*

b. Phòng tắm *d. Khu vực nhuộm tóc*

66. The difference between being a professional nail technician and "doing nails" is what to the clients:

a. Tip

b. Referral network

c. Location

d. Consultation

Sự khác biệt giữa một chuyên viên về nail và một người "chỉ biết làm nail" là điều gì đối với khách:

a. Móng giả

b. Đưa ra hệ thống làm việc

c. Địa điểm

d. Tham khảo

67. To avoid ingrown toenails, file the nails straight across and:

a. Steel implements

b. Slightly rounded corners

c. Metal files

d. Chamois buffers

Để tránh móng chân mọc đâm vào, giũa móng thẳng ngang với:

a. Dụng cụ bằng thép

b. Hơi tròn ở các góc

c. Giũa kim loại

d. Cục đánh bóng bọc da dê

68. Healthy nails result from:

a. A general state of health

b. Regular trimming

c. Exercise

d. Drinking carrot juice

Móng khỏe mạnh là kết quả từ:

a. Tình trạng sức khỏe tổng quát

b. Tỉa da thường xuyên

c. Thể dục

d. Uống nước carrot

69. Fingernails grow faster than:

a. Hair

b. Baby

c. Toenails

d. Cells

Móng tay mọc nhanh hơn:

a. Tóc

b. Em bé

c. Móng chân

d. Tế bào

70. Paper wraps will dissolve in aceton and :

a. Water

b. Dishwashing liquid

c. Polish applications

d. Polish remover

Bọc móng bằng giấy sẽ hòa tan trong aceton và:

a. Nước

b. Chất rửa chén dĩa

c. Thoa nước sơn

d. Chất chùi nước sơn

71. To reseal wrap during a glue fill, apply adhesive to:

a. Any broken edges

b. Polish brush before application

c. Entire nail

d. Only thumbnails

Để phủ loại móng bọc, lúc thêm keo vào móng, keo được thoa:

a. Bất cứ cạnh bị rách

b. Chà bóng trước khi thoa

c. Khắp mặt móng

d. Chỉ các móng ngón cái

72. Finish acrylic nails are:

a. Polymers

b. Monomers

c. Polymerizations

d. Catalysts

Lúc hoàn tất acrylic là:

a. Polymers (phân tử bột kết lại)

b. Monomers

c. Tiến trình kết hợp acrylic

d. Chất xúc tác

73. Foil leaf is available in gold, silver and:

a. Bronze

b. Copper

c. Turquoise

d. Zinc

Lá kim loại dùng trang sức cho móng gồm có lá vàng, bạc và:

a. Đồng thiếc

b. Đồng

c. Ngọc lam

d. Kẽm

74. Nonpathogenic bacteria belong to the group of bacteria known as:

a. Spirilla

b. Viruses

c. Cocci

d. Saprophytes

Vi trùng không gây bệnh thuộc loại nhóm vi trùng được biết là:

a. Hình xoắn

b. Vi khuẩn

c. Hình tròn

d. Thực vật hoại sinh

75. Problems or questions about your job should be discussed with:

a. Co-worker

b. Best friend

c. Your employer

d. Psychologist

Những trở ngại hoặc thắc mắc về việc làm của bạn sẽ được thảo luận với:

a. Bạn đồng nghiệp

b. Bạn thân

c. Người chủ của bạn

d. Chuyên viên tâm lý

76. To ensure full potency, chemical agents for sanitation should be purchased:

a. In bulk

b. In a small quantities

c. By mail

d. On sunny days

Để giữ nồng độ cần thiết, các hóa chất vệ sinh khử trùng nên được mua:

a. Khối lượng lớn

b. Trong bình chứa nhỏ

c. Bằng thư

d. Những ngày nắng

77. If no overlay is applied, an artificial tip is very:

a. Weak

b. Colorful

c. Ugly

d. Natural-looking

Nếu móng giả mà không có chất gì phủ lên thì tip rất:

a. Yếu

b. Màu sắc

c. Xấu

d. Trông tự nhiên

78. Light-cured gel nails are hardened using an ultraviolet light or a/an:

a. Non-acetone remover

b. Oily polish remover

c. Flashlight

d. Halogen light

Móng gel cần dùng đèn cực tím U.V để làm cứng móng hoặc:

a. Chất chùi nước sơn không acetone

b. Chất chùi nước sơn dầu

c. Đèn pin

d. Đèn halogen (đèn sáng vàng)

79. Silk, linen, fiberglass, and paper are the form a protective coating for damaged and fragile nails, called :

a. Stencils

b. Nail wraps

c. Gem applications

d. Gel applications

Lụa, vải dày, thủy tinh sợi và giấy là tạo lớp bảo vệ cho móng hư và móng gãy, được gọi là:

a. Mẫu trang trí cắt sẵn

b. Bọc móng

c. Rắc rải đá quí trên móng

d. Thoa gel

80. The joints in the ankle and wrist are known as:

a. Ball joints

b. Cartilage

c. Gliding joints

d. Carpus

Khớp mắc cá chân và cổ tay được biết là:

a. Khớp tròn

b. Sụn

c. Khớp trượt

d. Khối xương cổ tay

81. Extra long natural nails are not suited for this service:

a. Paper wraps

b. Recondition hot oil manicure

c. French Manicure

d. Nail art

Móng thật quá dài không thích hợp cho việc:

a. Bọc móng giấy

b. Móng tay dầu chữa trị

c. Làm móng kiểu Pháp

d. Nghệ thuật sơn móng

82. Percussion movements are also called:

a. Drum symphonies

b. Tapotement movement

c. Tingle toes

d. Tapping touches

Động tác vỗ nhẹ (percussion) cũng còn gọi là:

a. Trống hòa âm

b. Động tác tapotement

c. Ngứa ngón chân

d. Vỗ nhẹ

83. In acrylic technique, when the sable brush is dipped into liquid, then powder, this forms:

a. Glue

b. Chalky white color

c. Baking soda

d. An acrylic ball

Trong kỷ thuật đắp bột, cây cọ lông chồn được nhúng vô nước acrylic rồi đặt vô bột acrylic để tạo thành dạng:

a. Keo

b. Màu trắng phấn

c. Baking soda

d. Viên bột

84. Store acrylic products:

a. On well-lit shelves

b. Near the manicure lamp

c. In covered containers

d. Near a heating unit

Cất giữ chất acrylic:

a. Trên kệ nhiều ánh sáng

b. Gần đèn bàn làm móng

c. Trong đồ chứa đậy kín

d. Gần nhiệt (chổ nóng)

85. Material Safety Data Sheet (M.S.D.S) can be obtained from your salon's:

a. Distributor

b. Main office

c. Cleaning person

d. Fire department

Bảng dữ kiện về an toàn vật liệu (M.S.D.S) có ở được là do:

a. Nơi phân phối sản phẩm

b. Văn phòng chính

c. Người dọn dẹp

d. Trạm chữa lửa

86. The deep layer of skin is made up of 2 layers: papillary and recticular. They are called:

a. Epidermis

b. Dermis

c. Subcutaneous tissue

d. Nutrient level

Lớp da sâu bên trong được cấu tạo gồm 2 lớp: lớp đệm nhủ và lớp dinh dưỡng. Chúng được gọi là:

a. Ngoại bì

b. Nội bì

c. Mô dưới da

d. Lượng dinh dưỡng

87. An orangewood stick is classified as a/an:

a. Nail file

b. Equipment

c. Implement

d. Reusable item

Cây que gỗ cam được phân loại là:

a. Nail file

b. Thiết bị (dụng cụ dùng lâu bền)

c. Đồ dùng

d. Đồ có thể dùng lại

88. The free edge of sculptured nails should be shaped with a/an:

a. Emery board

b. Cuticle nipper

c. Chamois buffer

d. Metal nail file or black file

Đầu móng bột sẽ được tạo dáng móng với:

a. Giũa giấy

b. Kềm cắt da

c. Buffer đánh bóng bằng da dê

d. Giũa kim loại hoặc giũa đen

89. Striping tape is used to create lines when doing:

a. Football field markings

b. Nail art

c. Toenail clipping

d. French manicure

Chỉ sọc có keo được dùng để tạo đường lằn khi làm:

a. Lằn vạch môn football

b. Móng kiểu (móng nghệ thuật)

c. Cắt móng chân

d. Móng tay kiểu Pháp

90. Onychauxis is the technical term for a nail's:

a. Overgrowth

b. Infection

c. Bruise

d. Removal

Onychauxis là tên khoa học cho loại móng:

a. Mọc quá độ (móng dày)

b. Nhiễm trùng

c. Móng bầm

d. Rụng đi

91. Chloasma is commonly known as:

a. Freckles

b. Birthmark

c. Liver spots

d. Tanning

Bệnh đốm nâu thường được biết là:

a. Tàn nhang

b. Cái bớt (dấu sanh)

c. Đốm bệnh gan

d. Rám nắng

92. An accidental splash of solvent or primer can seriously injure the:

a. Nails

b. Skin

c. Implements

d. Eyes

Nếu chất solvent (dung môi) hoặc primer đổ văng ra có thể làm thương tổn nghiêm trọng cho:

a. Móng tay

b. Da

c. Dụng cụ

d. Đôi mắt

93. Manicure friction massage involves a wringing movement on the:

a. Toe

b. Arm

c. Finger

d. Wrist

Săn sóc tay, động tác xoay ma sát kết hợp với massage vặn nhẹ ở trên:

a. Ngón chân

b. Cánh tay

c. Ngón tay

d. Cổ tay

94. When removing artificial tips, first soak them in aceton to:

a. Dissolve free edge

b. Remove polish

c. Soften them

d. Dissolve sidewalls

Khi gỡ móng giả, đầu tiên là nhúng nó trong chất hòa tan (aceton) để:

a. Tan đầu móng

b. Chùi nước sơn

c. Làm mềm chúng

d. Tan cạnh móng

95. The chalky white color of primer before acrylic application indicates the primer is:

a. Dry

b. Odorless

c. Old

d. Not properly mixed

Màu trắng phấn của primer trước lúc đặt bột acrylic là dấu hiệu của primer:

a. Khô

b. Không mùi

c. Cũ

d. Trộn không đúng cách

96. A second coat of product is often unnecessary for what artificial nail when applying:

a. Colored lacquer

b. No-light gels

c. Light-cured gels

d. Acrylic nails

Thoa lớp thứ hai của sản phẩm thường là không cần thiết phải thoa lên khi làm loại móng nhân tạo nào:

a. Phủ màu

b. Gel không cần đèn

c. Gel cần đèn

d. Móng bột

97. The polish top coat should be tacky when these are applied on:

a. Tips

b. Paper wraps

c. Gel nails

d. Gems

Lớp phủ bóng trên móng sẽ dính lại khi đặt lên:

a. Móng giả (tip)

b. Bao móng giấy

c. Móng tay gel

d. Các mảnh đá quí

98. Odorless acrylics are self-leveling, which means they require less:

a. Product

b. Acrylic brush

c. Curve shaping (molding)

d. Buffing

Loại bột không mùi có đặc tính riêng là chúng ít tạo:

a. Sản phẩm

b. Cọ đắp bột

c. Độ cong móng

d. Chà mịn

99. Consumption supplies are the supplies used to:

a. Provide services

b. Give as samples

c. Stock retail kits

d. Eat lunch

Nguồn vật liệu tiêu thụ là vật liệu dùng để:

a. Sử dụng phục vụ khách

b. Như là hàng mẫu

c. Dụng cụ dành bán lẻ

d. Ăn trưa

100. Short nail and natural-looking is the best nail choice for a person who is a:

a. Computer operator

b. Telephone receptionist

c. Pianist

d. Stockbroker

Móng ngắn và trông tự nhiên là cách chọn kiểu tốt nhất cho người:

a. Sử dụng computer

b. Thư ký trả lời điện thoại

c. Người đánh đàn piano

d. Người mua bán cổ phần chứng khoán

MANICURIST EXAMINATION 7

1. **The disease AIDS (Acquired Immune Deficiency Symdrom) is caused:**
   a. Spirilla **c. Saprophyte**
   b. Virus **d. Spore**
   Bệnh AIDS (triệu chứng thiếu sót miễn nhiễm tự tạo) là nguyên nhân do:
   a. Vi trùng hình xoắn *c. Thực vật hoại sinh*
   b. Siêu vi khuẩn *d. Bào tử (vi trùng nằm trong lớp bọc)*

2. **The nails turn black and ___ when advanded nail mold.**
   a. Split **c. Soften**
   b. Smell bad **d. Harden**
   Móng trở màu đen và . . . . khi móng bị mốc lâu ngày:
   a. Nứt *c. Mềm*
   b. Mùi hôi *d. Cứng*

3. **The time to set up your station and sanitized your instruments is when clients are:**
   a. Go home **c. Dinking coffee**
   b. Waiting **d. Not yet present**
   Thời gian chuẩn bị làm cho khách và khử trùng dụng cụ là lúc khách:
   a. Về nhà *c. Uống cà phê*
   b. Đang đợi *d. Chưa có mặt*

4. **The brush used to apply sculpture nail is made of:**
   a. Feather **c. Plastic**
   b. Sable **d. Fiberglass**
   Loại cọ dùng đắp móng bột được làm bằng:
   a. Lông chim *c. Nhựa*
   b. Lông chồn *d. Thủy tinh sợi*

5. **Which of the following is prohibited for use in a manicure:**
   a. Antiseptic lotion **c. Powder alum**
   b. Germicidal solution **d. Lump alum**
   Chất nào sau đây bị cấm trong việc chăm sóc móng tay:
   a. Dung dịch sát trùng *c. Bột cầm máu (bột phèn chua)*
   b. Dung dịch diệt trùng *d. Phèn cục*

6. **A manicurist's license permit them to do all except:**
   a. Manicure in full salon services **c. Manicure in the barbershop**
   b. Manicure in nails salon only **d. Remove eyebrow with wax**
   License của thợ làm móng tay được phép làm tất cả ngoại trừ:
   a. Làm nails trong tiệm có đủ dịch vụ *c. Làm nails trong tiệm chuyên về cắt tóc*
   b. Làm nails trong tiệm chuyên về nails *d. Dùng sáp ong nhổ lông mày*

7. The transfer of the HIV (Human Immune Deficiency Virus) is through:

a. Sneezing **c. Touching**

b. Common cold **d. Bodily fluids**

Sự lây lan HIV (vi khuẩn tiêu diệt sự miễn nhiễm của người) là qua:

a. Nhảy mũi *c. Sờ mó*

b. Cảm lạnh *d. Chất dịch trong cơ thể*

8. Nail Fungus usually appears as a discoloration on the nail that spread toward the:

a. Cuticle **c. Nail bed**

b. Tip **d. Center**

Nấm ở móng thường thấy như làm lợt màu móng tay, sự lây lan tiến tới:

a. Biểu bì (lớp da) *c. Đệm móng*

b. Đầu móng *d. Giữa móng*

9. Early stage bacterial infection can be identified as a spot which is colored:

a. Black **c. Yellow - green**

b. Blue **d. Purple**

Sự nhiễm trùng có thể nhận biết sớm như một đốm mà có màu:

a. Đen *c. Vàng - xanh lá cây*

b. Xanh *d. Tím nhạt*

10. Clients with fungus or bacterial infection should be treated by a:

a. Manicurist **c. Cosmetologist**

b. Optometrist **d. Physician**

Khách bị nấm hoặc nhiễm trùng sẽ được chữa trị bởi:

a. Thợ móng tay *c. Thẩm mỹ viên*

b. Bác sĩ mắt *d. Bác sĩ*

11. The transfer of infected fluids between technician and clients is accomplished through:

a. Drinking glasses **c. Coughing**

b. Open wounds **d. Brushes**

Sự lây lan chất dịch nhiễm trùng giữa thợ và khách bị xảy ra qua:

a. Ly uống nước *c. Ho*

b. Vết thương để hở *d. Bàn chải*

12. The ability of the body to resist disease is called:

a. Rickettsia **c. Organisms**

b. Infection **d. Immunity**

Khả năng của cơ thể chống bệnh được gọi là:

a. Bệnh còi xương *c. Chất hữu cơ*

b. Nhiễm trùng *d. Sự miễn nhiễm*

13. Bacteria and germs multiply rapidly on:

a. Nail files **c. Towels**

b. Cuticle nippers **d. All a, b & c**

Vi trùng và mầm bệnh sinh sản nhanh trên:

a. Giũa móng tay *c. Khăn*

b. Kềm cắt da *d. Tất cả các câu a, b & c*

14. The removal of artificial nails from a client with nail fungus or bacterial infection should be accomplished wearing:

a. Gown

b. Gloves

c. Mask

d. Goggles (safety glasses)

Tháo gỡ móng giả cho tay khách bị nấm hoặc bị nhiễm trùng phải mang:

a. Áo choàng

b. Bao tay

c. Mặt nạ

d. Kính lồi (kính an toàn)

15. The nail technician with a contagious common illness should:

a. Stay home

b. Work quickly

c. Drink juice

d. Take a nap

Người thợ mắc bệnh thông thường dễ lây lan nên:

a. Ở nhà

b. Làm việc nhanh hơn

c. Uống nước trái cây

d. Ngủ 1 chút

16. Persons liable for implementing and maintaining sanitary rules in a salon are:

a. The holders of the establishments license

b. The operator in charge of business

c. The manicurist

d. All of the above

Người có trách nhiệm thi hành và bảo quản luật vệ sinh ở tiệm là:

a. Người có phép mở tiệm

b. Người thợ làm ở tiệm

c. Thợ chăm sóc tay, chân

d. Tất cả các câu trên

17. The rule and regulations of the Board of Barbering and Cosmetology:

a. Do not list minimum number and kinds of sanitary equipment

b. Do not cover the sanitary equipment

c. List minimum number and kinds of sanitary equipment

d. List minimum number of equipment

Luật và điều lệ của ngành thẩm mỹ tiểu bang:

a. Không cần tối thiểu số dụng cụ vệ sinh

b. Không bao gồm dụng cụ vệ sinh

c. Cần có tối thiểu các dụng cụ vệ sinh

d. Cần tối thiểu số dụng cụ

18. Objects dropped on the floor should be picked up and:

a. Washed and disinfected before reusing

b. Wiped with a towel

c. Wiped with a clean paper

d. Sanitized with a clean towels

Vật dụng rớt trên nền nhà sẽ nhặt lên và:

a. Rửa sạch và diệt trùng trước khi dùng lại

b. Lau với khăn

c. Lau với giấy sạch

d. Khử trùng với khăn sạch

19. A permissible styptic is:

a. Styptic pencil

b. Lump alum

c. Boric acid crystals

d. Alum powder

Chất cầm máu có thể được phép dùng là:

a. Viết chì cầm máu

b. Cục phèn chua

c. Tinh thể boric acid

d. Alum powder (bột phèn chua)

20. Storage place for clean implements may not be:

a. Plastic closed container **c. Closed cabinet**

b. Your kit **d. Dry sterilizer**

Nơi chứa dụng cụ sạch không phải là:

a. Hộp nhựa có nắp kín *c. Tủ kín*

b. Đồ nghề của bạn *d. Khử trùng khô*

21. Eldena is performing a pedicure on a client, how should she file the toenails?

a. Pointed **c. Round**

b. Oval **d. Straight across**

Eldena săn sóc chân cho khách, cô ấy sẽ giũa móng chân như thế nào:

a. Nhọn *c. Tròn*

b. Hình trái xoan *d. Ngang qua*

22. While cutting excessive cuticle around the nail, Annie accidentally cuts the client's skin so that it bleeds. What should Annie use to stop this bleeding?

a. Alum powder **c. Acetone**

b. Alcohol **d. Polish remover**

Trong lúc cắt quá nhiều da dư quanh móng của khách, Annie rủi cắt đứt da chảy máu. Annie sẽ dùng gì để cầm máu:

a. Alum powder *c. Aceton (chất làm mềm móng giả)*

b. Cồn *d. Chất chùi nước sơn*

23. Which of the following can Gwendolyn use to sanitize her manicuring implements?

a. Disinfectant solution **c. Formaldehyde basic**

b. Antiseptic **d. Non-acetone**

Chất gì mà Gwendolyn có thể dùng để khử trùng dụng cụ làm móng của cô:

a. Dung dịch diệt trùng *c. Formaldehyde căn bản*

b. Sát trùng *d. Chất không chứa aceton*

24. Katherine's nail salon offers nail acrylic that uses a portable device with a small motor. What type of device is it?

a. Oil **c. Electric file**

b. Booth **d. Airbrush machine**

Tiệm nails của Katherine dùng thiết bị gọn gàng với trục xoay nhỏ để làm móng bột. Kiểu dụng cụ này là:

a. Dầu *c. Máy giũa điện*

b. Làm dã chiến (tạm thời) *d. Máy phun sơn móng nghệ thuật*

25. Lucy is just beginning a basic manicure. What is the proper procedural order that he is to follow?

1. Shape nail **2.Polish the nail** **3. Remove old polish**

4. Loosen cuticle, trim cuticle **5. Soak in finger bowl** **6. Brush the surface nail**

a. 1, 2, 3, 4, 5, 6 **c. 3, 1, 5, 4, 6, 2**

b. 5, 3, 1, 2, 4, 6 **d. 1, 5, 4, 2, 6, 3**

Lucy theo tiến trình chăm sóc tay, Cách nào đúng theo thứ tự cần làm theo sau đây:

1. Tạo dáng cho móng *2. Sơn bóng móng* *3. Chùi nước sơn cũ*

4. Đẩy lùi da, tỉa da *5. Nhúng móng vào tô ngâm* *6. Chà rửa mặt móng*

a. 1, 2, 3, 4, 5, 6 *c. 3, 1, 5, 4, 6, 2*

b. 5, 3, 1, 2, 4, 6 *d. 1, 5, 4, 2, 6, 3*

26. **The thin line of skin at the base of the nail that extends from the skin at the nail wall is the:**

a. Eponychium
b. Hyponychium
c. Free edge
d. Nail groove

Đường da mỏng ở nền móng kéo dài từ da ở thành móng là:
a. Eponychium
b. Hyponychium (da dưới mặt móng)
c. Đầu móng tay
d. Nail groove (rãnh móng tay)

27. **The type of bacteria that does not produce disease and is often beneficial is:**

a. Spirilla
b. Bacilla
c. Pathogenic
d. Non - pathogenic

Loại vi trùng không tạo ra bệnh và thường có lợi là:
a. Vi trùng hình xoắn
b. Vi trùng hình gậy (que)
c. Pathogenic (vi trùng gây bệnh)
d. Non- pathogenic

28. **Parker is receiving a pedicure. His toenails should be shaped:**

a. Straight cross and slight at corners
b. Into a curved shape
c. Center to corner
d. Into a pointed shape

Parker là khách đến tiệm làm pedicure. Móng chân Parker sẽ được giũa theo cách:
a. Giũa ngang và vuốt nhẹ 2 cạnh
b. Vòng cung
c. Từ giữa ra góc
d. Giũa nhọn

29. **On a nail tip, the point where the tip meets the nail plate before it is glued to the nail is called the:**

a. Buffer block
b. Position stop
c. Half well
d. Full well

Trên móng giả (tip), vị trí mà móng tip gắn vào móng thật trước khi chấm keo ở móng được gọi là:
a. Cục chà mịn
b. Điểm dừng
c. ½ vành lõm dưới móng giả
d. Vành lõm lớn dưới móng giả

30. **Another name for a kneading massage movement is:**

a. Effleurage
b. Friction
c. Tapotement
d. Petrissage

Một tên khác của động tác kneading (nhồi bóp) là:
a. Effleurage (vuốt)
b. Xoay tròn (ma sát)
c. Topotement (gõ đệm ngón tay)
d. Petrissage

31. **Jessica has nail wraps on her nails that are opaque & need colored polish on them. This type of wrap is:**

a. Linen
b. Fiberglass
c. Silk
d. None of the above

Jessica bọc móng bằng vật liệu vải dày đục và cần sơn móng phủ lên. Kiểu bọc vải loại này là:
a. Vải sợi dày (linen)
b. Thủy tinh sợi
c. Lụa (silk)
d. Không có thứ nào kể trên

32. **Polish will not stain the nails if the nail technician applies:**

a. A top coat
b. Less than two coats of color polish
c. Non-acetone polish remover
d. A base coat

Nước sơn không có vết (lằn dợn) trên móng nếu thợ móng tay thoa:
a. Phủ lớp bóng
b. Ít hơn hai lớp sơn
c. Chất chùi nước sơn không aceton
d. Sơn lớp lót

33. **Pat is studying myology, which is the study of:**

a. Nerves
b. Bones
c. Skin
d. Muscles

Pat đang học về môn myology, đó là môn học:
a. Thần kinh
b. Xương
c. Da
d. Bắp thịt

34. **The two layers of skin are:**

a. Papillary and dermis
b. Papillary and strarum corneum
c. Dermis and epidermis
d. Epidermis and stratum corneum

Hai lớp của da là:
a. Lớp nhủ bên dưới và nội bì
b. Lớp nhủ dưới và lớp sừng
c. Nội bì và ngoại bì
d. Ngoại bì và lớp sừng

35. **Foot files are used to remove:**

a. Warts
b. Hangnails
c. Callus growths
d. Fungus

Giũa chà chân được dùng để lấy
a. Mụn cóc
b. Xướt da quanh móng
c. Da mọc dày (da chai)
d. Nấm

36. **Annie uses odorless acrylic nails. A difference between odorless and traditional acrylics is that odorless nails:**

a. Dry faster than traditional acrylics
b. Can be mixed with any traditional acrylic
c. Have no residue when they dry
d. Are self-leveling

Annie dùng acrylic không mùi. Sự khác biệt giữa acrylic không mùi và acrylic thông thường ở salon là loại không mùi:
a. Khô nhanh hơn loại thường
b. Có thể trộn với bột thường
c. Không dính khi khô
d. Có đặc tính riêng

37. **Gwendolyn, a salon owner, is adding the money she has spent on equipment, supplies, and uniforms. She is totaling her.**

a. Profit and loss comparisons
b. Income
c. Expenses
d. Net worth

Gwendolyn là chủ, cô dùng tiền chi tiêu cho dụng cụ, vật liệu và đồng phục. Tổng số tiền đó là:
a. So sánh lời và lỗ
b. Thu nhập
c. Chi phí
d. Tổng giá trị

38. **During a pedicure procedure, the feet are soaked:**

a. After the nails are shaped
b. At the beginning of the pedicure service
c. After the feet are massaged
d. Immediately before the top coat is applied

Trong cách thức chăm sóc đôi chân, chân được nhúng:
a. Sau khi móng được giũa
b. Lúc bắt đầu chăm sóc chân
c. Sau khi chân được massage
d. Làm ngay trước khi phủ sơn bóng

39. An example of a vegetable parasite is:

a. Pediculosis

b. Ringworm

c. Scabies

d. Lice

Một ví dụ của ký sinh thực vật là:

a. Pediculosis (chí)

b. Vòng mụn nước ở tay hoặc chân

c. Ghẻ ngứa

d. Chí

40. David's nail salon has installed new ventilation. This ventilation is important for manicurists and customers because nail products:

a. Are flammable

b. Only come in aerosol sprays

c. Can cause viral infections

d. Enter the body through inhalation

Salon của David gắn hệ thống thoát hơi mới. Hệ thống thông khí này quan trọng, giúp ích cho thợ và khách bởi vì hóa các sản phẩm về móng:

a. Dễ cháy

b. Chỉ là loại hơi xịt

c. Có thể nhiễm vi khuẩn

d. Xâm nhập vào cơ thể do hít thở

41. Jess's acrylics nails are curing. This means that they are

a. Softening

b. Weakening

c. Hardening

d. Shrinking

Móng bột của Jess kết lại có nghĩa là chúng:

a. Mềm

b. Yếu

c. Cứng

d. Co lại

42. The hairlike projections by which bacteria move are called

a. Mitosis

b. Cocci

c. Staphylococci

d. Flagella

Cấu trúc giống sợi tóc mà vi trùng di chuyển được gọi là:

a. Gián phân

b. Vi khuẩn hình tròn (tụ cầu)

c. Liên tụcầu (vi trùng hình chùm)

d. Flagella (chân giả, lông bơi)

43. Annie has white spots on her little finger. Annie's condition is called:

a. Onychauxis

b. Leukonychia

c. Onychorrhexis

d. Agnails

Annie có những chấm trắng trên ngón út. Trường hợp của Annie được gọi là:

a. Móng dày

b. Leukonychia

c. Móng tét dòn

d. Agnails (da xướt)

44. David's feet have ringworm. It is called:

a. Nail mold

b. Onychia

c. Tinea pedis

d. Onychogryposis

Bàn chân của David có vòng mụt nước. Được gọi là:

a. Móng bị mốc

b. Móng sưng có mủ

c. Tinea pedis

d. Onychogryposis (móng dày và cong)

45. Helen has bitten, deformed nail is called:

a. Onychophagy

b. Nail mold

c. Leukonychia

d. Paronychia

Helen có thói quen (tật) cắn móng tay, móng bị biến dạng được gọi là:

a. Onychophagy

b. Móng bị mốc

c. Móng có đốm trắng

d. Sưng chung quanh móng

46. The nail service where acrylic is added to Cindy's new growth area is called

a. Lifting

b. Rebalancing

c. Crack repair

d. Acrylic beads

Thêm bột vào chỗ móng mới mọc cho Cindy được gọi là:

a. Hở (bị tróc ra)

b. Cân bằng lại (fill)

c. Sửa chổ nứt

d. Giọt bột

47. Nails of adults grow at an average of:

a. 1/8 of an inch per week

b. 1/8 of an inch per month

c. 1/20 of an inch per week

d. 1/16 of an inch per month

Móng tay người lớn mọc trung bình:

a. 1/8 inch mỗi tuần

b. 1/8 inch mỗi tháng

c. 1/20 inch mỗi tuần

d. 1/16 inch mỗi tháng

48. In the matrix blood vessels and .... can be found?

a. Lunula

b. Nerves

c. Hyponychiums

d. Cartilage

Ở móng non tìm thấy có mạch máu và ....?

a. Lunula (hình bán nguyệt)

b. Tế bào thần kinh

c. Da dưới đầu móng

d. Sụn

49. An infected nail should be treated by a:

a. Nail technician

b. Physician

c. Pharmacist

d. Cosmetologist

Móng tay nhiễm trùng sẽ được chữa trị bởi:

a. Thợ móng tay

b. Bác sĩ

c. Dược sĩ

d. Thợ thẩm mỹ

50. In most states, instruments sanitized with hospital-grade disinfectant should be immersed in germicidal solution for ______ minutes:

a. 8

b. 10

c. 20

d. 30

Hầu hết các tiểu bang khử trùng dụng cụ cao cấp chất khử trùng cấp bệnh viện, dụng cụ sẽ được nhúng vô dung dịch diệt trùng ______ phút:

a. 8

b. 10

c. 20

d. 30

51. **The purpose of buffing the nail before applying an acrylic nail is to:**

a. Remove natural oil
b. Add color to the nail
c. Remove acrylic residue
d. Add gloss to the nail

Mục đích của chà móng trước khi đắp bột là để:
a. Lấy đi lớp dầu tự nhiên của móng
b. Thêm màu cho móng
c. Lấy bột còn sót
d. Thêm bóng móng

52. **Hangnails are treated by softening the cuticle with:**

a. Hot oil manicure
b. Polish remover
c. Pumice powder
d. Alum solution

Xước da tay được chữa trị bằng cách làm mềm da với:
a. Móng tay dầu
b. Chất chùi nước sơn
c. Bột đá
d. Nước phèn chua (chất cầm máu)

53. **The digital bones of the fingers are called:**

a. Metatarsi
b. Metacarpi
c. Phalanges
d. Clavicles

Xương digital của ngón tay được gọi là:
a. Xương bàn chân
b. Xương bàn tay
c. Lóng tay
d. Xương đòn gánh

54. **The nevus on Vern's nail was probably caused by:**

a. High blood pressure
b. A pigmented mole that occurs in the nail
c. Poor blood circulation
d. The natural immune system

Vết nâu đen trên móng tay Vern là nguyên nhân do:
a. Áp suất máu cao
b. Nốt ruồi đậm màu trong móng
c. Tuần hoàn kém
d. Hệ thống miễn nhiễm tự nhiên

55. **Kathy's local beauty supply distributor has given her a Material Safety Data Sheet for the product she uses. This sheet provides information for the products:**

a. Instructions on how to apply the product
b. Chemistry, hazards, &handling procedure
c. Required sanitation policies and procedure
d. Percentage of allergic reactions to it

Kathy có tờ M.S.D.S về cách dùng hóa chất từ nơi cung cấp vật liệu, tờ giấy này cung cấp về những điều gì của sản phẩm:
a. Hướng dẫn thế nào cách dùng sản phẩm
b. Hóa chất, độc hại và cách thức bảo trì
c. Đòi hỏi cách vệ sinh và cách làm
d. Số lượng phần trăm về dị ứng

56. **Gwendolyn has a light-cured gel system in her salon. Two light sources for these gels are:**

a. Ultraviolet and halogen
b. Ultraviolet and infrared
c. Infrared and halogen
d. Infrared

Ở tiệm Gwendolyn dùng đèn để làm gel. Hai loại đèn để làm gel này là:
a. Đèn cực tím và đèn trắng halogen
b. Đèn cực tím và đèn hồng ngoại
c. Đèn hồng ngoại và đèn trắng halogen
d. Đèn hồng ngoại

57. The technical term for the nail is:

a. Hyponychium

b. Onyx

c. Matrix

d. Cura

Tên y học của móng tay là:

a. Da dưới móng tay

b. Onyx

c. Móng non

d. Chăm sóc

58. Kristy's nails will grow faster

a. In the winter

b. In the autum

c. In the summer

d. On her feet

Móng của Kristy sẽ mọc nhanh hơn:

a. Vào mùa đông

b. Vào mùa thu

c. Vào mùa hè

d. Trên chân cô ấy

59. All of the following statements are true concerning AIDS except that it:

a. Attacks the body's immune system

b. Is caused by a virus

c. Lies dormant for many years

d. Is caused by bacteria

Tất cả những điều lo ngại về bệnh AIDS là đúng. Ngoại trừ đó là:

a. Tấn công hệ thống miễn nhiễm cơ thể

b. Nguyên nhân do vi khuẩn

c. Nằm ẩn qua nhiều năm

d. Nguyên nhân do vi trùng

60. Cindy is explaining to Cheryl that a particular hand lotion will meet all of Cheryl's needs for her dry hands. Cindy, the nail technician is discussing the hand lotion's:

a. Disadvantages

b. Benefits

c. Wrap- ups

d. Feature

Cindy giải thích cho cô Cheryl đặc điểm của chất kem thoa da tay khô mà cô ấy cần đến. Cindy, là người thợ chăm sóc móng đang thảo luận điều gì của chất kem đó:

a. Bất tiện

b. Tiện lợi (ích lợi)

c. Bọc lại

d. Miêu tả

61. The part of Peggy's nail plate that extends over her fingertips is called the

a. Free edge

b. Matrix

c. Hyponychium

d. Nail bed

Một phần mặt móng của Peggy kéo dài quá đầu móng được gọi là:

a. Đầu móng (móng mọc ngoài thân móng)

b. Móng non

c. Da dưới móng tay

d. Nền móng

62. The ulna is the large bone of the forearm, attached to the wrist and located on the side of the:

a. Thumb

b. Hand

c. Upper arm

d. Little finger

Ulna là xương lớn của cánh tay trước, dính liền cổ tay và nằm dọc theo:

a. Ngón cái

b. Bàn tay

c. Cánh tay trên

d. Ngón út

63. **Before using any manicuring implement, Sandy should**

a. Wipe it with tissue

b. Wipe it with a towel

c. Disinfect it

d. Wash it with soap and hot water

Trước khi dùng dụng cụ làm móng tay Sandy nên:

a. Lau dụng cụ với giấy

b. Lau dụng cụ với khăn

c. Diệt trùng dụng cụ

d. Rửa với xà phòng và nước nóng

64. **Helen is performing a manicure using hot by electric heater. This type of manicure is hot oil manicure, which performing is:**

a. Plain water

b. French

c. Reconditioning

d. Electric

Helen làm ấm dầu bằng lò điện để làm móng tay. Kiểu chăm sóc tay của Helen là làm móng tay dầu, được làm để:

a. Móng tay nước

b. Pháp

c. Chữa trị cho da và móng

d. Điện

65. **When moisture is trapped between unsanitized natural nail and artificial nail. It can turn from yellow to black. This is known as:**

a. Nail mold

b. Carcinogenic

c. Tinea pedis

d. Onychophagy

Khi chất ẩm nhét giữa móng thật bị bẩn và móng giả. Móng có thể đổi màu từ màu vàng đến màu đen. Điều này được biết là:

a. Nail mold (móng bị mốc)

b. Chất sinh ung thư

c. Nấm chân

d. Bệnh cắn móng

66. **If nails have molds and fungus, the nail technician should:**

a. Work on nails after washing them with an antibacterial soap

b. Soak her nails in alcohol for 20 minutes

c. First soak her nails in acetone for 20 minutes

d. Not work on these nails

Nếu móng bị mốc và nấm, thợ sẽ:

a. Làm được sau khi rửa xà phòng sát trùng

b. Nhúng móng tay vào cồn trong 20 phút

c. Nhúng tay khách vào acetone 20 phút

d. Không làm trên loại móng tay này

67. **Parker's wrist bone is called:**

a. Carpus

b. Metacarpus

c. Digit

d. Radius

Xương cổ tay của Parker được gọi là:

a. Carpus

b. Metacarpus (xương bàn tay)

c. Digit (ngón)

d. Radius (xương quay)

68. **Poor- fitting shoes may cause**

a. Pterygium

b. Onychophagy

c. Ingrown nails

d. Brittle nails

Giày quá chật có thể gây ra:

a. Da chồm lên móng

b. Bệnh cắn móng tay

c. Móng mọc đâm vô thịt

d. Móng dòn

69. For light-cured gel and no-light gel, after apply antiseptic to nails then pushing back the cuticles, what is the next step?

a. Apply gel on each nail then cure gel

b. Apply each tip then cure gel

c. Apply all forms then gel

d. Buff natural nails to remove shine

Đối với gel cần đèn và gel không cần đèn, sau khi thoa sát trùng lên móng và đẩy lùi da tay, kế đến là bạn làm gì?

a. Trãi gel lên từng móng và cứng gel

b. Trải từng tip và cứng gel

c. Gắn form móng và trãi gel

d. Chà nhẹ mặt móng để loại bỏ chất dầu trên móng

70. The type of polish remover to use on clients who have artificial nails is

a. Aceton

b. Non- acetone

c. Alcohol

d. Hydrogen peroxide

Chất để chùi nước sơn cho khách mang móng giả là:

a. Aceton

b. Không aceton

c. Cồn

d. Hydrogen peroxide (H_2O_2)

71. Sanding bands (paper files) and buffing bits should be disposed of between clients. How do you disinfect for other bits of electric file?

a. The same procedure as nail implements

b. Wipes with 70% alcohol

c. Soaking in antiseptic solution

d. Soaking in 6% hydrogen peroxide

Đầu giũa giấy đen bọc ngoài trục và vòng da đánh bóng móng nên vứt bỏ sau mỗi người khách. Bạn diệt trùng thế nào đối với các loại đầu giũa khác?

a. Cùng cách diệt trùng dụng cụ làm móng

b. Lau với cồn 70%

c. Nhúng vào dung dịch sát trùng

d. Nhúng vào 6% peroxide (chất tẩy móng)

72. While performing a pedicure, what should Anita use to separate her client's toes:

a. Paper towels

b. Her fingers

c. Toe separators

d. The orangewood stick

Trong lúc làm chân, Anita sẽ dùng cái gì để ngăn ngón chân của khách:

a. Khăn giấy

b. Ngón tay của cô

c. Toe separators

d. Cây que gỗ cam

73. When using Quarternary ammonium compounds, one important step is to:

a. Measure it carefully

b. Change it after each use

c. Change it daily

d. Dilute it to an antiseptic strength

Khi dùng nước Quats một điều quan trọng là:

a. Đo lường cẩn thận

b. Thay sau mỗi lần dùng

c. Thay đổi hằng ngày

d. Pha loãng thành chất sát trùng mạnh

74. The nail technician should file Tim's fingernails

a. From center to each corner

b. From each corner to the center

c. Straight across

d. Back and forth

Thợ làm móng sẽ giũa móng tay của Tim:

a. Từ giữa ra mỗi góc

b. Từ mỗi góc ra giữa

c. Giũa ngang

d. Giũa lui tới

75. Victoria uses quats solution to disinfect her implements. Another complete name for quats is

a. Sodium hypochlorite compounds
b. Formaldehyde
c. Quaternary ammonium compounds
d. Ethyl alcohol

Victoria dùng dung dịch Quats để diệt trùng dụng cụ. Tên gọi đầy đủ của Quats là:

a. Hỗn hợp thuốc tẩy
b. Formaldehyde (hơi khử trùng khô)
c. Quaternary ammonium compounds
d. Cồn ethyl

76. Tammy is applying a form of nail art that uses very fragile leafing. This type of nail art is:

a. Gems
b. Striping tape
c. Foil
d. Air- brushing

Tammy làm móng kiểu với mỹ thuật dùng những lá dòn xếp. Kiểu này là:

a. Đá quí
b. Chỉ sọc
c. Lá kim loại
d. Xịt phun màu

77. Tinea pedis is another name for:

a. Hangnails
b. Ingrown nails
c. Athlete's foot
d. Brittle nails

Tinea pedis là tên của:

a. Xước da
b. Móng mọc đâm vô thịt
c. Nấm ở chân (athlete's foot)
d. Móng dòn

78. The ulnar nerve supplies the

a. Thumb side of the arm
b. Little finger side of the arm
c. Fingers
d. Wrist

Thần kinh xương trụ cung cấp:

a. Ngón cái dọc theo cánh tay
b. Ngón út dọc theo cánh tay
c. Các ngón tay
d. Cổ tay

79. The deep fold of skin in which Rose's nail root is lodges is called the:

a. Nail fold or mantle
b. Nail groove
c. Eponychium
d. Lunula

Lớp xếp da trong gốc móng tay của Rose được gọi là:

a. Lớp da xếp hoặc màng bọc móng
b. Rãnh móng
c. Eponychium (da trên mặt móng)
d. Chỗ vành trắng móng

80. It is important to sanitize a client's nails before applying acrylic nails because the antiseptic will

a. Adhere the acrylic to the natural nail
b. Soften the properly for acrylic nail
c. Help to prevent fungus
d. Dry the acrylics quickly

Nên khử trùng móng tay khách trước khi làm móng bột vì điều quan trọng sát trùng sẽ:

a. Bột dính tới móng thật
b. Mềm móng bột đúng cách
c. Giúp ngăn ngừa nấm
d. Bột khô nhanh

81. Massage servive should not performed on a client who had stroke, heart condition, and:

a. Scar
b. High blood pressure
c. Cough
d. Dry skin

Massage không nên làm trên người khách có bịnh kích ngất, bệnh tim, và:

a. Thẹo
b. Cao máu
c. Ho
d. Da khô

82. For No-light gel, after you apply gel then cure gel. How far and how long you use activator or water?

a. Spray activator 8 inches away from nails

b. Spray activator then immerse in water

c. Immerse nails in lukerwarm water for 2- 5 minutes

d. Both "a" and " c" are correct

Gel không cần đèn, sau khi trãi gel và làm cứng. Xịt activator cách móng bao xa và nhúng nước bao lâu?

a. Xịt activator cách móng 8 inches (2tất)

b. Xịt activator rồi nhúng nước

c. Nhúng móng vào nước ấm từ 2 đến 5 phút

d. Cả hai "a" và "b" đều đúng

83. The parts of a muscle are

a. Origin, digits, and belly

b. Origin, insertion, and belly

c. Digits, insertion, and phalanges

d. Insertion, belly, and phalanges

Các phần của bắp thịt là:

a. Gốc, các ngón, bụng

b. Gốc, ngọn và bụng

c. Các ngón, ngọn và lóng tay

d. Ngọn, bụng và lóng tay

84. Gwendolyn, a nail technician, should apply nail polish in strokes that are:

a. Rough and jerky

b. Quick and smooth

c. Short and dry

d. Long and excessively wet

Gwendolyn là thợ nails, sẽ sơn móng theo những đường vuốt:

a. Nhám và giật giật

b. Nhanh và mịn

c. Ngắn và khô

d. Dài và thật ướt

85. Parker should store his dirt / soiled towels in .... until he has time to launder them:

a. A bin at the shampoo area

b. An open container for soiled items

c. A closed container for soiled items

d. The manicuring table drawer

Parker bỏ khăn dơ, khăn bẩn trong ....cho đến khi giặt:

a. Thùng ở nơi gội đầu

b. Đồ chứa khăn dơ mở nắp

c. Đồ đựng khăn dơ có nắp đậy

d. Ngăn kéo của bàn làm móng

86. What does a disinfectant do to bacteria?

a. Kills all bacteria

b. Kills only pathogenic bacteria

c. Retards bacteria growth

d. Retards only pathogenic bacteria growth

Chất diệt trùng là làm gì với vi trùng:

a. Giết tất cả vi trùng

b. Chỉ giết loại vi trùng gây bệnh

c. Làm chậm phát triển của vi trùng

d. Làm chậm phát triễn vi trùng gây bệnh

87. Annie's rubber implements should not be disinfected with:

a. Phenolics

b. Quaternary ammonium compounds

c. Sodium hypochlorite compounds

d. Fumigant

Vật dụng làm bằng cao su (nhựa) của Annie sẽ không nên diệt trùng với:

a. Phenolics

b. Hổn hợp nước Quats

c. Hổn hợp thuốc tẩy

d. Khử trùng khô bằng hơi

88. The nail plate is made up of a protein called:

a. Collagen

b. Melanin

c. Keratin

d. Sebum

Mặt móng tay được cấu tạo bởi thành phần protein gọi là:

a. Chất da

b. Sắc tố (chất màu của da)

c. Chất sừng

d. Dầu ở da

89. **Jessica, a nail technician, has just completed a manicure and is cleaning up on her table area. Jessica discardes all of the following used items except the:**

a. Cuticle nipper — **c. Orangewood stick**
b. Emery board — **d. Used cotton ball**

Jessica, là thợ làm xong móng tay và cô ấy dọn dẹp trên bàn của cô. Jessica vứt bỏ mọi vật liệu đã dùng ngoại trừ:
a. Kềm cắt da — *c. Que gỗ cam*
b. Giũa giấy — *d. Bông gòn bẩn*

90. **Nail technicians use nail forms when they apply:**

a. Nail tips — **c. Mending tissue**
b. Acrylic nails — **d. Acrylic over nail tips**

Thợ móng tay dùng forms (khuôn giấy nhôm) khi họ làm:
a. Móng giả — *c. Giấy vá móng*
b. Móng bột — *d. Bột đắp lên móng giả*

91. **The nail plate, or body, extends from the nail root to the:**

a. Lunula — **c. Nail bed**
b. Matrix — **d. Free edge**

Mặt móng hoặc thân móng kéo dài từ gốc móng đến:
a. Nơi hình bán nguyệt — *c. Nền móng*
b. Móng non — *d. Đầu móng (phần móng mọc ngoài thân móng)*

92. **While nipping her client's cuticles, accidently cuts into skin, and it begins to bleed. Helen, nail technician what should she apply to the cut:**

a. Alum powder — **c. 70% ethyl alcohol**
b. Disinfectant solution — **d. A styptic pencil**

Trong lúc cắt da tay khách, lỡ bị chảy máu, Helen là thợ, cô ấy sẽ thoa gì đến chỗ bị cắt:
a. Alum powder — *c. Cồn ethyl 70%*
b. Dung dịch diệt trùng — *d. Viết chì cầm máu*

93. **Smith's sudoriferous glands help:**

a. Regulate his body temperature — **c. Empty into his hair follicles**
b. Are commonly known as oil glands — **d. Secrete sebum**

Các tuyến mồ hôi của Smith giúp:
a. Điều hòa thân nhiệt — *c. Khoang trốngtrong nang lông*
b. Thường được biết là tuyến dầu — *d. Điều tiết chất dầu*

94. **In some states, formalin:**

a. Can not be used — **c. Is used to sanitize hands**
b. Is the safest disinfectant — **d. Must be F.D.A registered**

Một vài tiểu bang chất diệt trùng formalin:
a. Không được sử dụng — *c. Được dùng khử trùng đôi tay*
b. Là chất diệt trùng an toàn nhất — *d. Được cơ quan F.D.A chuẩn nhận*

95. The nail grooves are indentations found at the. . . . of the nail

a. Base **c. Root**

b. Sides **d. Free edge**

Rãnh móng tay được nhận biết ở _______ của móng:

a. Nền *c. Gốc*

b. Cạnh *d. Đầu móng (free edge)*

96. The maintenance of normal, internal stability in the organisms of Helen's body is known as:

a. Homeostasis **c. Carcinogenic**

b. Leukonychia **d. Onychogryposis**

Thân thể của Helen được ổn định và hoạt động bình thường được biết là :

a. Homeostasis (quân bình nội tạng) *c. Carcinogenic (chất sinh ung thư)*

b. Đốm trắng *d. Onychogryposis (móng dày và cong)*

97. Thomas is putting an antiseptic on his client's nails in preparation for artificial nails. An antiseptic:

a. Kills only pathogenic bacteria **c. Kills all bacteria**

b. Kills only nonpathogenic bacteria **d. Slows bacteria growth**

Thomas thoa chất sát trùng trên móng tay cho khách để chuẩn bị làm móng nhân tạo (tip, bột, lụa . . .) . Chất sát trùng:

a. Chỉ giết vi trùng gây bệnh *c. Giết các loại vi trùng*

b. Chỉ giết vi trùng không gây bệnh *d. Làm chậm phát triển vi trùng*

98. Annie is preparing her client's natural nails for acrylics. Which of the following must Annie does to the natural nails before applying the acrylic?

a. Soften it with skin cream **c. Soak it with hot oil**

b. Buff it to remove the shine **d. Soak for 10 minutes in warm soapy water**

Annie chuẩn bị đắp bột trên móng thật của khách. Vậy cô phải làm gì trên móng thật trước khi đắp bột:

a. Thoa mềm da với cream *c. Nhúng trong dầu ấm*

b. Chà lấy đi lớp bóng trên móng *d. Nhúng 10 phút trong xà phòng nước ấm*

99. Katherine hears, smells, tastes, touches, and sees well. Her five senses are under the control of her . . . . .nervous system:

a. Peripheral **c. Central**

b. Neurological **d. Automatic**

Thính giác (nghe), khứu giác (ngửi), vị giác (nếm), xúc giác (sờ) và thị giác (nhìn) của Katherine đều tốt. Năm giác quan của cô được kiểm soát bởi hệ thống . . . . thần kinh:

a. Peripheral (lớp ngoại biên) *c. Trung khu*

b. Neurological (khoa thần kinh) *d. Tự động*

100. Katherin's salon and Patrick's salon all use the same disinfection method. The most common method that salons use is . . . . disinfection:

a. Physical **c. Chemical**

b. Steam or moist heat **d. Autoclave**

Salon của Katherine và salon của Patrick dùng cùng phương pháp diệt trùng. Phương pháp thông thường ở salon dùng . . . . diệt trùng:

a. Vật lý *c. Hóa chất*

b. Hơi và nhiệt ẩm *d. Lò tự động*

MANICURIST EXAMINATION 8

1. **Manicurist never pulls or twists the product when removal of any artificial nail product. It can cause:**

a. Break to the artificial nails
b. Damage to the natural nails
c. Damage to the artificial nails
d. Onychophagy

Thợ manicurist không bao giờ kéo hoặc vặn bột khi lấy bỏ chất làm móng giả. Có thể là nguyên nhân:
a. Gãy móng giả
b. Hư móng thật
c. Hư đến móng giả
d. Bệnh cắn móng

2. **The long and slender bones that form the palm of the hand are:**

a. Metacarpals
b. Digits
c. Phalanges
d. Radius

Các xương dài và thon tạo lòng bàn tay là:
a. Metacarpals
b. Digits (ngón tay)
c. Các lóng tay
d. Xương quay

3. **The long and slender bones that form the foot are:**

a. Patella
b. Femur
c. Calcaneus
d. Metatarsals

Các xương dài và thon tạo xương bàn chân là:
a. Patella (đầu gối)
b. Femur (xương đùi)
c. Calcaneus (xương gót chân)
d. Metatarsals

4. **Keeping clean implements in a sterilize box with ultraviolet rays can be good for:**

a. One week
b. Quats solution
c. Cranies and nook
d. Disposable part

Cất giữ sạch sẽ các dụng cụ trong tủ tiệt trùng có chiếu tia cực tím có thể làm sạch:
a. Một tuần
b. Dung dịch diệt trùng
c. Hóc và kẻ nhỏ của dụng cụ
d. Phần có thể vứt bỏ

5. **Net income is the money you make after you pay for:**

a. Groceries
b. Expenses
c. Income
d. Clothes

Khoảng thu nhập là số tiền bạn làm được sau khi bạn trừ:
a. Thực phẩm
b. Chi phí
c. Thu nhập
d. Quần áo

6. **During a manicure sessions, John accidentally minor cuts Jenny's skin and she bleeds. Jenny says that she has AIDS. What should John do?**

a. Refer her to medicine doctor
b. Apply antiseptic, tell the owner and then call 911
c. Apply alum powder and call her doctor
d. Bring the emergency kit and show her how to use it

Trong lúc làm nail, John rủi cắt đứt nhẹ da cô Jenny và chảy máu. Jenny nói cho biết rằng cô có bệnh AIDS. John sẽ làm gì:
a. Chuyển đi bác sĩ y khoa
b.Thoa thuốc sát trùng, nói cho chủ biết và sau đó gọi 911
c. Thoa bột cầm máu và gọi bác sĩ của cô
d. Đem hộp thuốc cấp cứu đến và chỉ cô ấy cách sử dụng

7. On an annual basis, the nail care industry annually does this much business:

a. $3 billion | **c. $2 billion**

b. $5 million | **d. $10 million**

Tính trên căn bản kỹ nghệ làm móng tay hàng năm lên đến:

a. 3 tỉ đồng | *c. 2 tỉ đồng*

b. 5 triệu đồng | *d. 10 triệu đồng*

8. A common condition in which the cuticles around the nail split is known as:

a. Hangnails | **c. Nail crack**

b. Skin overgrowth | **d. Callus**

Thông thường da chung quanh móng bị xước được biết là:

a. Hangnails (xước da tay) | *c. Móng nứt*

b. Da mọc nhiều | *d. Da dày (chai)*

9. Prevent chemical accident by never using a product if the container is not:

a. Sealed | **c. Full**

b. Sanitized | **d. Labeled**

Đề phòng rũi ro về hóa chất bằng cách không bao giờ dùng sản phẩm nếu đồ chứa không:

a. Đóng kín lại | *c. Đầy*

b. Khử trùng | *d. Nhãn hiệu*

10. It is dangerous to judge if a chemical is safe by it's:

a. Label | **c. Ingredient**

b. Odor | **d. M.S.D.S**

Rất nguy hiểm phán đoán sự an toàn của một hóa chất bằng:

a. Nhãn hiệu | *c. Thành phần*

b. Mùi | *d. M.S.D.S*

11. Clear, white and pink are color of:

a. Acrylic powder | **c. Toe separators**

b. Sable brushes | **d. Paper towel**

Chất màu trong, trắng và hồng là màu của:

a. Bột acrylic | *c. Miếng xốp ngăn ngón chân*

b. Cọ đắp bột bằng lông chồn | *d. Khăn giấy*

12. The tacky feel of the surface of odorless acrylic nail indicates the nail are:

a. Old | **c. Dry**

b. Separating from nail plate | **d. Needing a fill**

Lớp nhựa dẻo bề mặt của loại bột acrylic không mùi, là dấu hiệu móng:

a. Cũ | *c. Khô*

b. Mặt móng rời (bong) ra | *d. Cần làm fill*

13. The layer of epidermis has cells that look like granules:

a. Stratum corneum | **c. Stratum lucidum**

b. Stratum mucosum | **d. Stratum granulosum**

Lớp ngoại bì có các tế bào giống như những hạt nhỏ:

a. Stratum corneum (lớp sừng) | *c. Stratum lucidum (lớp trong suốt)*

b. Stratum mucosum (lớp có chất màu) | *d. Stratum granulosum*

14. **Nail which are thin, white and curved over the free edge are called:**

a. Furrowed | **c. Eggshell**
b. Normal | **d. Dry**

Móng tay mỏng, trắng và cong ở đầu móng tay được gọi là:

a. Móng gợn sóng | *c. Móng vỏ trứng*
b. Móng bình thường | *d. Móng khô*

15. **Base and gloss coat are added to the nail through application of:**

a. Colored polish | **c. Buffing compound**
b. Silk wrap | **d. Mending liquid**

Nước lót và nước bóng thoa thêm vào móng lúc:

a. Thoa nước sơn | *c. Hỗn hợp chà bóng*
b. Bao lụa | *d. Keo vá móng*

16. **The appearance of a properly applied second coat of gel looks like:**

a. Gelatin | **c. Glossy top coat**
b. Primer | **d. Cuticle oil**

Lớp nước bóng thứ hai của gel giống như:

a. Sự đông đặc | *c. Lớp phủ bóng*
b. Primer (chất sát trùng và kết dính) | *d. Dầu thoa da*

17. **Formalin contains formaldehyde which causes the following except:**

a. Pain muscle | **c. Rash**
b. Lung irritation | **d. Skin irritation**

Formalin chứa chất formaldehyde tạo nguyên nhân sau đây ngoại trừ:

a. Đau bắp thịt | *c. Rát da*
b. Ngứa phổi | *d. Ngứa da*

18. **To make them feel welcome, new clients should be:**

a. Greeted | **c. Escorted to station**
b. Give salon tour | **d. All of the above**

Để tạo cho người khách mới một cảm giác chào đón, khách sẽ được:

a. Chào hỏi | *c. Đưa họ đến chỗ ngồi làm móng*
b. Đưa xem salon | *d. Tất cả các điều trên*

19. **Most pedicure service are performed by starting with:**

a. Right foot, little toe | **c. Left foot, little toe**
b. Right foot, middle toe | **d. Left foot, big toe**

Hầu hết cách chăm sóc chân được bắt đầu bằng:

a. Chân phải, ngón út | *c. Chân trái, ngón út*
b. Chân phải, ngón giữa | *d. Chân trái, ngón cái*

20. **The client who want length without weight should receive:**

a. Paper wraps | **c. Linen wraps**
b. Gel nails | **d. Silk wraps**

Khách hàng muốn móng dài mà không nặng sẽ làm:

a. Bọc giấy | *c. Bọc vải dày*
b. Móng gel (gắn tip, phủ gel) | *d. Bọc lụa*

21. To give sparkle to a nail art design, use:

a. Gems **c. Sequins**

b. Metallic polish **d. Fine buffer block**

Để cho móng óng ánh trong nghệ thuật làm móng, dùng:

a. Mảnh đá quí (đá màu bóng) *c. Đồ trang sức*

b. Sơn kim loại *d. Cục buffer mịn*

22. If the nail or skin to be worked on is inflamed, broken, swollen or infected, the client must:

a. Be sanitize with alcohol **c. Need manicure**

b. Be referred to a physician **d. Scrub with soap**

Nếu móng tay hoặc da bị sưng, nứt nẻ, phồng lên hoặc nhiễm trùng, người khách nên:

a. Khử trùng với alcohol *c. Cần chăm sóc tay*

b. Đưa đi bác sĩ *d. Chà với xà phòng*

23. Expenses are defined as to money you:

a. Earn **c. Spend**

b. Save **d. Donate**

Sự chi tiêu được xác định là số tiền mà bạn:

a. Thu được *c. Chi phí*

b. Tiết kiệm *d. Tặng*

24. A technician who is a good salesperson and a skilled professional will also be:

a. Artistic **c. Good manager**

b. Good receptionist **d. Very successful**

Một người thợ vừa là người bán hàng giỏi và có tay nghề vững sẽ là người:

a. Nhà nghệ thuật *c. Quản lý giỏi*

b. Thư ký giỏi *d. Rất thành công*

25. A client may want to match nails with clothing for a/an:

a. Special occasion **c. Few weeks**

b. Few days **d. Entire year**

Người khách muốn hợp màu móng tay với quần áo cho:

a. Dịp đặc biệt *c. Vài tuần*

b. Vài ngày *d. Cả năm*

26. The "true skin" is the deep layer of skin which is called:

a. Cuticle **c. Epidermis**

b. Cutis **d. Nail mantle**

Lớp da thật là lớp da sâu bên trong được gọi là:

a. Lớp da *c. Ngoại bì*

b. Cutis *d. Màng móng*

27. To remove gel nails, soak in acetone or:

a. Alcohol **c. Gel remover**

b. Dishwashing liquid **d. Warm water**

Lấy (gở bỏ) gel trên móng, là nhúng vào acetone hoặc:

a. Alcohol *c. Chất lấy gel (mềm gel)*

b. Dung dịch rửa chén, đĩa *d. Nước ấm*

28. If a chemical agent gets on your clothing, immediately:

a. Dab with water **c. Use spot remover**

b. Blot with towel **d. Remove garment**

Nếu một hóa chất dính (vấy) vào quần hoặc áo, ngay lập tức:

a. Chậm (thấm) với nước *c. Dùng chất chùi vết, đốm*

b. Thấm với khăn *d. Thay quần, áo*

29. Natural nails can be lengthened by adding:

a. Artificial tips **c. Paper wraps**

b. Silk wraps **d. Nails art**

Móng tay thật có thể làm dài bằng cách nối thêm:

a. Móng giả *c. Phủ (bao) giấy*

b. Phủ lụa *d. Vẽ móng kiểu*

30. A primer is applied to the natural nail when given acrylic nails in order to:

a. Dry properly **c. Prevent fungus**

b. Polish easily **d. Dry slowly**

Chất primer thoa lên móng thật khi làm móng bột để:

a. Khô đúng cách *c. Ngăn ngừa nấm*

b. Sơn dễ dàng *d. Chậm khô*

31. A long acrylic nail may be the best choice for a woman who is a:

a. Guitar player **c. Gardener**

b. Pianist **d. Cosmetic salesperson**

Mang móng bột dài là cách chọn tốt nhất cho nữ giới mà họ là:

a. Người đàn guitar *c. Người làm vườn*

b. Người đàn piano *d. Người bán mỹ phẩm*

32. Dry cuticles can cause:

a. Nail biting **c. Hangnails**

b. Buffing problems **d. Hoi oil manicure**

Da khô có thể là nguyên nhân:

a. Cắn móng tay *c. Xước da tay*

b. Do chà móng *d. Móng tay dầu*

33. Most clients are relaxed for massage technique by:

a. Effleurage movement **c. Vibration movement**

b. Kneading movement **d. Friction movement**

Hầu hết khách cảm nhận sự thoải mái là massage bằng kỷ thuật:

a. Effleurage movement (vuốt nhẹ) *c. Tác động rung*

b. Tác động nhồi bóp *d. Friction movement (chà xát xoay tròn)*

34. Seven years is the amount of time you should keep business records which were used to:

a. Pay off loans **c. Pay employees**

b. Complete tax returns **d. Order supplies**

Bạn cần lưu giữ hồ sơ trong thời hạn 7 năm để cần dùng cho việc:

a. Trả dứt nợ *c. Trả lương thợ*

b. Hoàn chỉnh hồ sơ thuế *d. Đặt mua hàng (vật liệu)*

35. An acquired skin, round and thickened patch of epidermis due to pressure or friction on the hands or feet is called:

a. Cocci **c. Keratoma (callus)**

b. Eczema **d. Flagella**

Lớp da tự tạo, mảng tròn và dày ở lớp ngoại bì là do sức ép hoặc sự cọ sát của tay hoặc chân được gọi là:

a. Vi khuẩn tròn *c. Keratoma (da chai)*

b. Chốc lở kinh niên *d. Flagella (chân giả, lông bơi)*

36. Fabric wraps are not a good service choice for a client whose hands are frequently:

a. In gloves **c. Photographed**

b. Held **d. In water**

Móng bao vải là việc không nên làm cho khách có đôi bàn tay thường xuyên:

a. Mang găng tay *c. Chụp hình*

b. Cầm giữ *d. Trong nước*

37. Peak and slow months can be determined by reviewing your:

a. Monthly records **c. Customer list**

b. Tax withholding **d. Supply inventory**

Những tháng khách hàng đông và ế ẩm được đánh giá bằng cách xem lại:

a. Hồ sơ hàng tháng *c. Danh sách khách*

b. Khoản tiền đóng thuế *d. Tồn kho vật liệu*

38. A liquid that kills or retards bacterial growth is a/an:

a. Soap **c. Antiseptic**

b. Solution **d. Chemical**

Một dạng chất lỏng có khả năng giết hoặc làm chậm sự phát triển vi trùng là:

a. Xà phòng *c. Antiseptic*

b. Dung dịch *d. Hóa chất*

39. Airbrushing nails is a small compressor. How much pressure per square inch (psi) does a manicurist need to do airbrushing?

a. 5 to 10 pounds **c. 20 to 25 pounds**

b. 10 to 20 pounds **d. 25 to 35 pounds**

Máy phun màu sơn tạo kiểu lên móng và dụng cụ ép hơi nhỏ. Cần bao nhiêu sức ép trên mỗi inch vuông (psi) mà người thợ móng xử dụng máy?

a. 5 đến 10 pound *c. 20 đến 25 pound*

b. 10 đến 20 pound *d. 25 to 35 pound*

40. Chemical storage should be in cool area and away from:

a. Appliance or furnace with pilot light **c. Perm solutions**

b. Hair colors **d. Garbage cans**

Cất giữ hóa chất ở nơi mát mẻ và cách xa:

a. Đồ dùng bằng điện hoặc lò có ngòi lửa *c. Dung dịch uốn tóc*

b. Màu tóc *d. Thùng đựng rác*

41. To add shine to the nail, use a chamois buffer with pumice powder or:

a. Water | **c. Dry polish**
b. Cuticle oil | **d. Cuticle remover**

Để giúp cho bóng móng, dùng buffer da dê với bột đá bọt nghĩa là:

a. Nước | *c. Đánh bóng khô*
b. Dầu thoa da | *d. Chất làm mềm da*

42. An accounting service is often used to help salon keep:

a. Making a profit | **c. Making loan payments**
b. Accurate financial records | **d. Tax losses large money**

Công việc kế toán, đó là việc thường giúp cho tiệm giữ được:

a. Tạo lợi nhuận | *c. Kế hoạch trả nợ*
b. Chính xác hồ sơ tài chánh | *d. Mất khoản tiền lớn về thuế*

43. A catalyst is an ingredient which causes a process to:

a. Explode | **c. Speed up**
b. Slow down | **d. Remain static**

Chất xúc tác là thành phần tạo cho tiến trình:

a. Nổ | *c. Nhanh hơn*
b. Chậm lại | *d. Sự hút dính (tĩnh điện)*

44. How do you change the sanding bands (sander) when using a electric file (drill machine)?

a. Pull out by use screw driver | **c. Pull out then submerge into the disinfection solution**
b. Just pull out and discard after each client | **d. Press down then pull out**

Bạn thay đổi ống giũa giấy đen bọc đầu giũa (bit) khi dùng giũa điện bằng cách nào?

a. Kéo ra bằng dụng cụ mở ốc | *c. Kéo ra rồi nhúng vào dung dịch diệt trùng*
b. Chỉ kéo ra và vứt bỏ sau mỗi lần làm khách | *d. Ép xuống rồi kéo ra*

45. Plastic gloves and safety glasses should always be worn when working with:

a. Primer | **c. Air brushes**
b. Gel | **d. Acrylic powder**

Bao tay nhựa và kính an toàn sẽ luôn luôn được mang khi đang sử dụng:

a. Primer (chất sát trùng và kết dính) | *c. Air brushes (máy phun màu)*
b. Gel (chất dẻo phủ móng dùng với đèn) | *d. Bột acrylic*

46. The main part of the nail is attached to the skin at the tip of the finger which is called:

a. Nail root | **c. Nail body**
b. Nail bed | **d. Nail fold**

Phần chính của móng được dính vào da ở đầu ngón tay được gọi là:

a. Gốc móng tay | *c. Thân móng tay*
b. Nền móng tay | *d. Lớp xếp của thành móng*

47. The outermost layer of the skin is called the cuticle, scarf skin, and:

a. Dermis | **c. Subcutaneous tissue**
b. Epidermis | **d. Stratum corneum**

Lớp ngoài cùng của da được gọi là cuticle, scarf skin (lớp bọc), và:

a. Nội bì | *c. Mô dưới da*
b. Ngoại bì | *d. Stratum corneum (lớp sừng)*

48. The proper way to mix polish is to:

a. Mix with top coat **c. Tap bottle on table**

b. Shake vigorously **d. Roll bottle between palms**

Cách đúng nhất trộn đều nước sơn là:

a. Trộn với nước sơn bóng *c. Vỗ lọ nước sơn lên bàn*

b. Lắc mạnh *d. Lăn lọ nước sơn giữa lòng hai bàn tay*

49. A weekly reconditioning hot oil manicure will benefit clients with:

a. Dry cuticle, agnail **c. Paper wraps**

b. Gel nails **d. Arthritis**

Nên làm móng tay dầu hằng tuần sẽ giúp cho những người khách có:

a. Da khô, da xước *c. Bọc móng bằng giấy*

b. Móng gel *d. Đau nhức khớp xương (viêm khớp)*

50. Ultraviolet radiation is harmful to:

a. Bones **c. Eyes**

b. Nail polish **d. Acrylic tips**

Ánh sáng tia cực tím có hại đến

a. Xương *c. Mắt*

b. Nước sơn móng tay *d. Móng tip phủ bột*

51. Liquid acrylic is a type of:

a. Polymer **c. Catalyst**

b. Monomer **d. Curing**

Nước acrylic là một dạng của:

a. Polymer (chất kết hợp) *c. Chất xúc tác*

b. Monomer *d. Sự lưu hóa (cứng gel)*

52. A condition in which white spots appear on the nails is called:

a. Leukonychia **c. Nevus**

b. Atrophy (onychatrophia) **d. Corrugations**

Trường hợp mà đốm trắng xuất hiện trên móng được gọi là:

a. Leukonychia (đốm trắng) *c. Đốm nâu đen*

b. Atrophy (rụng, teo móng) *d. Móng gợn sóng*

53. State regulation expect a salon environment to be:

a. Sterile **c. Decorative**

b. Infectious **d. Sanitary**

Những qui định của luật lệ tiểu bang muốn môi trường ở tiệm phải được:

a. Vô trùng *c. Trang trí*

b. Nhiễm trùng *d. Vệ sinh*

54. By understanding body structure, you will be more proficient when doing:

a. Fiber wraps **c. Pedicure**

b. Basic manicure **d. Hand & arm massage**

Hiểu biết cấu trúc cơ thể, bạn sẽ tạo được hiệu quả hơn khi làm:

a. Phủ bằng thủy tinh sợi *c. Làm chân*

b. Làm móng tay thông thường *d. Massage tay và cánh tay*

55. All living things are made up of this basic unit, called the:

a. Cell | **c. Nucleus**
b. Protein | **d. Cytoplasm**

Đơn vị căn bản của tất cả sự sống (sinh chất) được gọi là:

a. Tế bào | *c. Nhân tế bào*
b. Chất đạm | *d. Tế bào chất*

56. How many types of bacteria can be found nearly everywhere?

a. 15,000 | **c. 10,000**
b. 5,000 | **d. 1,500**

Có bao nhiêu loại vi trùng có thể tìm thấy ở mọi nơi?

a. 15.000 | *c. 10.000*
b. 5.000 | *d. 1.500*

57. Which activity is dangerous around nail chemicals?

a. Gossiping | **c. Talking loudly**
b. Chewing gum | **d. Smoking**

Hành động gây nguy hiểm chung quanh các hóa chất làm móng là?

a. Đồn nhảm | *c. Nói chuyện lớn*
b. Nhai kẹo | *d. Hút thuốc*

58. This medical specialty focuses on skin problems:

a. Cardiology | **c. Esthetics**
b. Dermatology | **d. Podiatry**

Ngành y khoa đặc biệt chữa trị về da:

a. Bệnh tim | *c. Mỹ phẩm về da*
b. Chuyên khoa da | *d. Chữa trị về chân*

59. A client consultation is the conversation you have with the client before:

a. Starting the service | **c. They pay**
b. They make appointment | **d. They buy retail products**

Sự tham khảo với khách hàng là một cuộc đàm thoại giữa bạn với khách trước khi:

a. Bắt đầu công việc | *c. Họ trả tiền*
b. Họ làm hẹn | *d. Họ mua lẻ sản phẩm*

60. The manicure table should have a bulb of this wattage in the lamp:

a. 60 watts | **c. 40 watts**
b. 100 watts | **d. 150 watts**

Bóng đèn đặt ở bàn làm móng tay có công suất (watt) là:

a. 60 watts | *c. 40 watts*
b. 100 watts | *d. 150 watts*

61. Natural immunity is obtained by keeping the body:

a. Warm | **c. Underweight**
b. Healthy | **d. Overweight**

Sự miễn nhiễm tự nhiên có được bằng cách giữ cho thân thể:

a. Ấm | *c. Giảm trọng lượng*
b. Khỏe mạnh | *d. Tăng trọng lượng*

62. The condition in which the nail loosens from the nail bed is:

a. Paronychia

b. Onychophagy (bitten nail)

c. Onychia

d. Onycholysis

Tình trạng mà móng bị lỏng từ đệm móng là:

a. Paronychia (sưng đỏ)

b. Onychophagy (bệnh cắn móng)

c. Onychia (sưng có mủ)

d. Onycholysis (lỏng móng mà không rụng)

63. How far away should gel activator be hold it at least .... from the client's nails?

a. 8 inches

b. 10 inches

c. 12 inches

d. 24 inches

Hóa chất xịt làm cứng gel cần đặt bao xa để xịt lên móng khách?

a. 8 inches (2 tất)

b. 10 inches (2 tất rưỡi)

c. 12 inches (3 tất)

d. 24 inches (6 tất)

64. The recommended maintenance schedule for all acrylic nails is every:

a. Weekly

b. Two to three weeks

c. Monthly

d. Two months

Lịch trình hẹn cho việc bảo quản cho móng bột acrylic là cứ mỗi:

a. Hàng tuần

b. 2 đến 3 tuần

c. Hàng tháng

d. 2 tháng

65. Your sense of right and wrong when you interact with clients, employer and coworkers is called:

a. Honesty

b. Professional ethics

c. Moral values

d. Moodiness

Sự cảm nhận về điều đúng và sai khi bạn tiếp xúc với khách, chủ, và bạn đồng nghiệp được gọi là:

a. Thành thật

b. Đạo đức nghề nghiệp

c. Phẩm cách

d. Buồn chán

66. Massage, nerve impulses and light rays are some of the ways to stimulate:

a. Phalanges

b. Muscles

c. Sanitation

d. Eyes

Massage, làm rung nhịp đập và các tia đèn là những cách để kích thích:

a. Các đốt xương ngón tay

b. Bắp thịt

c. Vệ sinh

d. Đôi mắt

67. The muscles which can cause goose bumps are called the:

a. Arrector pili

b. Papillae

c. Goosli muscles

d. Lesion

Bắp thịt có thể đẩy dựng, nổi gai (nổi da gà) được gọi là:

a. Arrector pili (cơ dựng lông)

b. Lớp nhủ ở chân lông

c. Bắp thịt goosli

d. Vết lở

68. An emergy board is an example of an item that is:

a. Wet sanitized

b. Heat sanitized

c. Disposable

d. Reused

Cái giũa giấy, đó là ví dụ của một món đồ mà:

a. Khử trùng bằng dung dịch

b. Khử trùng bằng nhiệt

c. Có thể vứt bỏ

d. Xử dụng lại

69. If the nail tip covers the nail plate from sidewall to sidewall, it is:

a. Too wide — **c. Too long**

b. Properly sized — **d. Too narrow**

Nếu móng tip phủ lên mặt móng từ cạnh này đến cạnh kia là:

a. Rộng quá — *c. Dài quá*

b. Đúng cở — *d. Hẹp quá*

70. The French manicure look can be created through the:

a. One- color acrylic method — **c. Proper buffing techniques**

b. Pink and red color acrylic method — **d. Two-color acrylic method**

Kiểu French manicure có thể tạo ra qua dạng:

a. Phương pháp bột một màu — *c. Chà (buff) móng đúng cách*

b. Phương pháp bột màu hồng và đỏ — *d. Phương pháp bột hai màu*

71. In acrylic applications the free edge is formed with the:

a. First acrylic ball — **c. Nail file**

b. Third acrylic ball — **d. Second acrylic ball**

Trong cách đắp bột, phần móng ngoài đầu móng được tạo với:

a. Viên bột đầu tiên — *c. Giũa móng*

b. Viên bột thứ ba — *d. Viên bột thứ hai*

72. Soaking in water hardens:

a. Acrylic ball — **c. No- light gels**

b. Rhinestone applications — **d. Acrylic residue**

Nhúng vào nước làm cứng lại là:

a. Viên bột — *c. Gel không cần đèn*

b. Gắn đá lóng lánh — *d. Bột còn sót lại*

73. When you apply for manicure, soft or fragile nails should be filed using a/an:

a. Emery board — **c. Chamois buffer**

b. Metal file — **d. Nail brush**

Khi bạn làm móng tay nước, móng mềm và dòn sẽ được giũa với:

a. Giũa giấy — *c. Buffer bọc da dê (đánh bóng)*

b. Giũa kim loại — *d. Bàn chãii móng*

74. Hypoallergenic products are used for the client's:

a. Scar — **c. Safety**

b. Skin cancer — **d. Acne**

Chất giảm dị ứng được xử dụng làm điều gì cho khách:

a. Thẹo — *c. An toàn*

b. Ung thư da — *d. Mụn bọc*

75. The movements of the body are controlled by the:

a. Efferent nerves — **c. Blood**

b. Peripheral system — **d. Central nervous system**

Sự chuyển động thân thể được điều khiển bởi:

a. Efferent nerve (thần kinh vận động) — *c. Máu*

b. Hệ thống ngoại biên — *d. Hệ trung khu thần kinh*

76. Mending liquid is a heavy adhesive used to apply:

a. Silk wraps **c. Paper wraps**

b. Linen wraps **d. Nail gems**

Chất vá móng là loại keo đặc, dùng để thoa lên:

a. Bọc lụa *c. Bọc giấy*

b. Bọc vải dày (linen) *d. Gắn đá quí cho móng*

77. Non-acetone remover is used to remove polish from:

a. Hangnails **c. Toenails**

b. Artificial tips **d. Accidental spills on clothes**

Lấy nước sơn bằng chất non - acetone cho:

a. Xước da tay *c. Móng chân*

b. Móng giả (móng nhân tạo) *d. Vấy nhiễu lên quần áo*

78. A repair patch is a piece of fabric (silk, fiber glass, linen) cut to:

a. Nail's shape **c. Completely cover crack or break**

b. Look like a daisy **d. ½ inch by ½ inch**

Miếng vá là nguyên liệu vải (lụa, thủy tinh sơi, vải dày) được cắt để:

a. Dạng của móng tay *c. Phủ lên chổ móng nứt hay gãy*

b. Giống như hoa *d. Cở ½ inch vuông*

79. Insomnia, watery eyes and sluggishness are symptoms of chemical:

a. Overexposure **c. Burn**

b. Inhalation **d. Poisoning**

Mất ngủ, chảy nước mắt và uể oải là các biến chứng của hóa chất do:

a. Tiếp xúc quá nhiều *c. Cháy, bỏng*

b. Sự hít vào *d. Nhiễm độc*

80. In order to have a good working relationship with co-workers, you should:

a. Respect their opinions **c. Ask their opinions**

b. Familiar attitude **d. Point out mistakes**

Để có sự liên hệ tốt với đồng nghiệp, bạn phải:

a. Tôn trọng ý kiến của họ *c. Hỏi ý kiến họ*

b. Thái độ thân mật *d. Chỉ ra những lỗi lầm*

81. Liquid nail wrap is used to:

a. Speed silk wrap procedure **c. Strengthen natural nail**

b. Preserve nail art **d. Cover fungi**

Chất keo để làm bao móng được sử dụng để:

a. Cách bao lụa được nhanh *c. Làm mạnh móng thật*

b. Giữ gìn móng kiểu *d. Che phủ nấm*

82. The opaqueness of linen wraps requires that they be covered with:

a. Glitter **c. Clear polish**

b. Mending tissue **d. Colored polish**

Bọc bằng vải linen có màu trắng đục nên nó được thoa phủ lên mặt móng bằng:

a. Lấp lánh *c. Sơn bóng*

b. Giấy vá *d. Nước sơn màu*

83. Always refuse service and refer a client to a physician if they have a skin or nail:

a. Hangnail | **c. Bruise**

b. Inflammation | **d. Callus**

Luôn luôn từ chối và bảo khách đi bác sĩ nếu da hoặc móng tay của khách bị:

a. Xước da tay | *c. Bầm đen*

b. Sưng lên | *d. Chai da*

84. Tanning is caused by exposing skin to the sun's:

a. Ultraviolet rays | **c. Vitamin D**

b. Keratoma | **d. Carotene**

Tạo cho làn da sậm là do da tiếp xúc đến ________ của mặt trời:

a. Tia cực tím | *c. Vitamin D*

b. Mảng da chai | *d. Carotene (như vitamin A có trong cà rốt)*

85. Learning about other services offered at the salon, such as hair and skin care, and then telling your clients about them, is called salon:

a. Performance | **c. Networking**

b. Show off | **d. Promotion**

Hiểu biết thêm những công việc khác của salon như về tóc và chăm sóc da mặt để nói chuyện với khách, được gọi là gì ở salon:

a. Trình diễn | *c. Mạng lưới làm việc*

b. Khoe khoang | *d. Thăng tiến nghề nghiệp*

86. The hardening process in acrylic nails is know as:

a. Catalyst | **c. Curing**

b. Polymerization | **d. Monomer**

Tiến trình làm cứng móng bột được biết là:

a. Xúc tác | *c. Làm cứng (sự lưu hóa)*

b. Polymerization (tiến trình bột cứng lại) | *d. Monomer (nước acrylic)*

87. The best way to protect yourself and your clients against infection is to:

a. Ask if they have an infection | **c. Sanitize implements properly**

b. Wear masks | **d. Sanitize 3 times a day**

Cách tốt nhất bạn bảo vệ chính bạn và khách chống lại nhiễm trùng là:

a. Hỏi khách có nhiễm trùng không? | *c. Khử trùng dụng cụ đúng cách*

b. Mang miếng che miệng | *d. Khử trùng 3 lần một ngày*

88. When conditions are unfavorable for reproduction, bacteria will go dormant after forming a tough covering called a:

a. Shell | **c. Mitosis**

b. Spore | **d. Flagella**

Khi điều kiện không thích hợp cho việc sinh sản, vi trùng sẻ trú núp, sau đó tạo lớp vỏ bọc gọi là:

a. Vỏ bọc | *c. Gián phân*

b. Bào tử | *d. Flagella (chân giả, lông bơi)*

89. After removing an artificial nail, any remaining glue residue is removed by using a/an:

a. Emery board | **c. Steel pusher**
b. Oily remover | **d. Fine buffer block**

Sau khi gỡ bỏ móng giả keo còn sót lại được lấy đi bằng cách dùng:

a. Giũa giấy | *c. Cây sủi bằng thép*
b. Chất chùi dầu | *d. Cục (khối) buffer mịn*

90. The technical name for callus is:

a. Freckle | **c. Keratoma**
b. Stratum lucidum | **d. Mole**

Danh từ y khoa của da chai (callus) là:

a. Tàn nhang | *c. Keratoma*
b. Lớp trong suốt của ngoại bì | *d. Nốt ruồi*

91. Bacilli and spirilla propel themselves with hairlike projections known as:

a. Flagella | **c. Mitosis**
b. Propellants | **d. Cocci**

Vi trùng bacilli và spirilla tự di chuyển giống như các vảy cấu tạo của sợi tóc được biết là:

a. Flagella (chân giả hoặc lông bơi) | *c. Gián phân*
b. Đẩy đi, trườn | *d. Vi trùng hình tròn*

92. To protect hands and nails when doing housework, clients should wear:

a. Silicone lotion | **c. Clear polish**
b. Rubber gloves | **d. Dust mask**

Để bảo vệ tay và móng khi làm công việc nhà, người khách sẽ mang:

a. Dung dịch silicon | *c. Nước sơn bóng*
b. Bao tay cao su | *d. Mặt nạ che bụi*

93. Linen wraps are the:

a. Hardest to do | **c. Closely woven, heavy material**
b. Easiest to rip or tear | **d. Hardest to maintain**

Vải bọc dày (linen) là:

a. Cứng nhất | *c. Vải dày, sợi đan chặc*
b. Rất dễ chẻ hoặc xé | *d. Giữ cứng nhất*

94. The nerve which supplies impulses to the top of the foot is the:

a. Dorsal | **c. Saphenous**
b. Digital | **d. Ulnar**

Thần kinh cung ứng nhịp đập ở mặt bàn chân là:

a. Dorsal | *c. Thần kinh ở da chân và đùi*
b. Ngón tay | *d. Thần kinh trụ*

95. Unsanitary implements can cause these nail diseases:

a. Onychomycosis | **c. Onychia and paronychia**
b. Mold | **d. Nevus**

Dụng cụ không sạch có thể là nguyên nhân gây bệnh móng:

a. Onychomycosis (mảng da trắng do nấm) | *c. Sưng đỏ và nhiễm trùng quanh móng*
b. Mốc meo | *d. Nevus (cái bớt lúc sanh)*

96. Cuticle pushers are also known as metal pusher or:

a. Nippers **c. Emery boards**

b. Orange wood stick **d. Steel pushers**

Đồ dụng cụ đẩy da cũng được biết là cây sủi kim loại hoặc:

a. Đồ cắt da *c. Giũa giấy*

b. Que gỗ cam *d. Steel pushers*

97. Men generally need more work done on their cuticle and the most common nail shape for male clients is:

a. Rectangular **c. Round**

b. Oval **d. Square**

Thông thường khách nam giới muốn được cắt bớt lớp da chết ở quanh viền mặt móng và hầu hết tạo hình dạng móng cho khách nam giới là:

a. Hình chữ nhật *c. Tròn*

b. Oval (trái soan) *d. Vuông*

98. To prevent contamination of the disinfectant solution, disinfection containers should be kept:

a. Warm **c. Cold**

b. In cupboards **d. Covered**

Để phòng dơ bẩn dung dịch diệt trùng, hộp chứa dung dịch diệt trùng nên giữ:

a. Ấm *c. Lạnh*

b. Trong ngăn tủ *d. Kín (nắp đậy lại)*

99. Client service records are usually kept on:

a. Pink paper **c. Triplicate forms**

b. Blue paper **d. Index cards**

Hồ sơ làm cho khách thường được giữ:

a. Giấy hồng *c. Mẫu hồ sơ gồm ba bản*

b. Giấy xanh *d. Thẻ giấy nhỏ ghi chi tiết việc làm*

100. Foot files are used to remove:

a. Warts **c. Fungus**

b. Hangnails **d. Callus growths**

Giũa chà chân được dùng để lấy:

a. Bướu *c. Nấm*

b. Xước da tay *d. Da chai phát triển*

MANICURIST EXAMINATION 9

1. **Infection with an inflammed with pus formation affecting the tissue at the nail base may be red and swollen. Which is caused by improper sanitized manicuring implements is called:**

a. Onychophagy **b. Onychauxis**
c. Onychorrhexis **d. Onychia**

Nhiễm trùng sưng lên và có mũ làm nền móng đỏ và sưng thường là do dụng cụ bẩn khi làm móng tay :
a. Onychophagy (móng cắn do thói quen) *b. Onychauxis (móng dày bất thường)*
c. Onychorrhexis (móng dòn, chẻ) *d. Onychia*

2. **Cleanse and sanitize a customer's nails before applying artificial nails because::**

a. Attach the artificial nail **b. To prevent fungus**
c. Adhere acrylic to the real nails **d. Harden the acrylic nails**

Làm sạch và vệ sinh móng cho khách trước khi gắn móng giả bởi vì:
a. Dính vào móng giả *b. Ngăn ngừa nấm*
c. Dính bột vào móng thật *d. Cứng bột lại*

3. **The ingredient in top coat is:**

a. Palm oil **b. Styptic**
c. Vitamin E **d. Polyester resin**

Thành phần có trong nước sơn phủ bóng là:
a. Dầu cây dứa (palm oil) *b. Chất cầm máu*
c. Vitamin E *d. Chất nhựa dẻo polyester*

4. **Polish remover used in salons for customers who wear nail tip or acrylic is:**

a. Alcohol **b. Primer**
c. Aceton **d. Non - aceton**

Chất chùi nước sơn ở tiệm dùng cho khách mang móng típ hoặc móng bột là:
a. Cồn *b. Primer*
c. Aceton *d. Non - aceton*

5. **A pH scale of 7 indicates a neutral solution such as pure water. What does the pH scale tell you?**

a. Acidity or alkalinity **b. Acid only**
c. Low or high volume **d. Alkaline only**

Bảng nồng độ hydrogen (pH) với số 7 là biểu hiện dung dịch trung hòa như nước trong suốt. Bảng nồng độ pH cho bạn biết điều gì?
a. Acid và alkaline *b. Chỉ có acid*
c. Độ thấp và cao *d. Chỉ có alkaline*

6. **When towels are being laundered in an establishment, the treatment should include:**

a. Washing a 140-160 degree water for at least fifteen minutes. **b. Washed in cold water as not to cause discoloring.**
c. Washed in warm soapy water. **d. None of the above.**

Khi khăn dơ đem đi giặt, điều kiện giặt khăn ở tiệm nên:
a. Giặt ở nhiệt độ từ 140 - 160 độ F, tối thiểu 15 phút *b. Giặt nước lạnh để tránh khỏi phai màu.*
c. Giặt trong nước xà phòng ấm. *d. Không phải các câu trên.*

7. What slows down the drying effect of the solvent in nail polish remover?

a. Oil | **b. Base coat**

c. Nail whitener | **d. Nail bleach**

Chất nào làm chậm đi sự mau khô của chất chùi nước sơn?

a. Dầu | *b. Nước sơn lót*

c. Chất trắng phủ móng có đốm | *d. Thuốc tẩy móng*

8. In manicuring, softening the cuticle with cuticle oil is good treatment for:

a. White spot on nail | **b. Hangnails**

c. Cut or bleeding cuticle | **d. Redness or swelling around a nail**

Trong lúc săn sóc móng tay, việc làm mềm phao tay bằng dầu là cách chữa trị tốt cho:

a. Những đốm trắng trên móng | *b. Móng có da xướt*

c. Da bị đứt hoặc chảy máu | *d. Sưng đỏ hoặc phồng quanh móng.*

9. One of the major elements required for good health is:

a. Freedom from canities | **b. Styptic form**

c. A well balanced diet | **d. Personal disinfection**

Một trong những yếu tố chính cần thiết giúp cho sức khỏe tốt là:

a. Không có tóc bạc | *b. Sự cầm máu*

c. Sự kiêng ăn đúng cách | *d. Sự diệt trùng cá nhân*

10. For a good and comfortable sitting posture, keep the sole of the feet on the floor and keep:

a. The feet and knees close together | **b. Chin out**

c. Chest relaxed | **d. Arms close together**

Để ngồi với một tư thế đúng và thoải mái, giữ hai bàn chân trên nền nhà và giữ:

a. Hai chân và đầu gối gần nhau | *b. Cằm ngẩng lên*

c. Ngực thoải mái | *d. Hai cánh tay khép vào nhau*

11. You may be allowed to service a client with nail mold or fungus is to:

a. Massage hands only | **b. Remove artificial nails**

c. Apply nail polish | **d. Refer your client to a physician**

Bạn có thể được phép phục vụ cho khách với loại móng bị mốc hoặc bị nấm là:

a. Chỉ massage đôi tay | *b. Gỡ móng giả ra*

c. Thoa nước sơn móng | *d. Chuyển khách đến bác sĩ*

12. What time of brush works the best for gel nails as blending and shading:

a. Large round sable brush | **b. Round sable brush**

c. Small flat synthetic brush | **d. Large flat sable brush**

Loại cây cọ nào tốt nhất cho gel móng để trãi đều và tạo dáng:

a. Cây cọ lông chồn lớn tròn | *b. Cây cọ tròn lông chồn*

c. Cây cọ nhỏ dẹp bằng sợi tổng hợp | *d. Dép mang trong nhà*

13. Water-cured is the technique cure gel by immerse nails in lukewarm water for 2 - 5 minutes is also called:

a. Gel application | **b. Gel activator**

c. Heat activator | **d. Light-cured gel**

Làm cứng bằng nước là kỹ thuật cứng gel bằng cách nhúng gel vào nước ấm 2 – 5 phút được gọi là:

a. Trãi gel | *b. Làm cứng gel*

c. Làm cứng bằng nhiệt | *d. Cứng gel bằng đèn*

14. Never use the back muscles to pick up an article on the floor, so what muscles should be used?

a. Ankles **b. Back**

c. Legs and buttocks **d. Calves**

Không bao giờ dùng những bắp thịt lưng nâng lên một vật từ nền nhà vậy bắp thịt nào cần được dùng:

a. Mắt cá chân *b. Lưng*

c. Chân và mông *d. Bắp chân*

15. When you lift a heavy object, lift with your back straight and push with:

a. Calves **b. Back**

c. Heavy arm muscles **d. Heavy thigh muscles**

Khi bạn nâng một vật nặng, nâng với lưng thẳng và kéo đồ vật lên bằng:

a. Bắp chân *b. Lưng*

c. Chịu đựng của bắp thịt cánh tay *d. Chịu đựng của bắp thịt đùi*

16. The outward reflection of a person's inner feelings is called:

a. Personality **b. Personal vitality**

c. Good grooming **d. Courtesy**

Phản ảnh bên ngoài nói lên nội tâm của một người là:

a. Tư cách *b. Nội lực*

c. Sự ăn mặc gọn gàng *d. Sự nhã nhặn*

17. It will be helpful to a student's success to develop a:

a. List of good stories **b. Positive attitude**

c. Pleasing personality **d. Business attitude only**

Để giúp cho sự thành công của học viên, cần biểu hiện hơn:

a. Nhiều câu chuyện hay *b. Thái độ tích cực*

c. Cách làm vừa lòng khách *d. Hình thái kinh doanh*

18. A very important attribute of a pleasing personality is a good:

a. List of stories **b. Financial standing**

c. Loud voice **d. Sense of humor**

Một yếu tố quan trọng góp phần vào việc làm vừa lòng khách là thể hiện tốt :

a. Nhiều câu chuyện *b. Khả năng tài chánh*

c. Giọng lớn *d. Tính hài hước, vui vẻ*

19. Good topic for salon conversation should be:

a. Debatable **b. Political**

c. Religious **d. Non-controversial**

Đề tài thích hợp để nói chuyện trong tiệm nên là

a. Chuyện có thể tranh luận *b. Chính trị*

c. Tôn giáo *d. Chuyện không gây tranh cãi*

20. If the client feels burned while manicurist uses electric file with too much pressure:

a. Spray with cold water **b. Apply antiseptic solution**

c. Immerse Quats solution **d. Spray with 70% alcohol**

Nếu người khách cảm thấy bỏng khi người thợ xử dụng máy giũa điện với nhiều sức ép::

a. Xịt nước lạnh *b. Thoa dung dịch sát trùng*

c. Nhúng vào Quat diệt trùng *d. Xịt cồn 70%*

21. Good conversation involves the use of a pleasant voice, good choice of words, intelligence, charm, and:

a. Grooming **b. Impatience**

c. Personality **d. Profanity**

Cuộc nói chuyện hấp dẫn là cần có được giọng nói hay, chọn từ ngữ, khéo léo, duyên dáng và:

a. Tươm tất *b. Thiếu kiên nhẫn*

c. Tư cách *d. Sĩ nhục (lời tục tỉu)*

22. Proper conduct in relation to employer and co-worker is called professional:

a. Ethics **b. Personality**

c. Courtesy **d. Honesty**

Sự cư xử đúng cách trong quan hệ người chủ và bạn đồng nghiệp được gọi là:

a. Đạo đức *b. Cá tính*

c. Sự nhã nhặn *d. Sự thành thật*

23. Extravagant claims and unfulfilled promises are examples of:

a. Great ability **b. Ethical conduct**

c. Poor ethics **d. Good personality**

Sự yêu cầu quá đáng và không giữ lời hứa là ví dụ của:

a. Khả năng cao *b. Cư xử có đạo đức*

c. Kém đạo đức *d. Tư cách tốt*

24. One important ingredient of a proper professional attitude is:

a. Arrogance **b. Posture**

c. Punctuality **d. Antecedents**

Một phần quan trọng trong thái độ chuyên nghiệp là:

a. Kiêu ngạo *b. Vóc dáng*

c. Sự đúng giờ giấc *d. Thành tích*

25. What is a nail condition that may receive a manicure:

a. Onycholysis **b. Onychia**

c. Paronychia **d. Onychophagy**

Điều kiện nào của móng mà có thể chăm sóc tay được:

a. Onycholysis (lỏng đầu móng đến nền móng) *b. Onychia (móng sưng có mũ)*

c. Paronychia (móng sưng đỏ chung quanh) *d. Onychophagy (thói quen cắn móng)*

26. All patrons must be treated honestly and fairly, without any demonstration of:

a. Courtesy **b. Confidence**

c. Dignity **d. Favoritism**

Mọi khách hàng phải được đối xử một cách thành thật, công bằng, mà không có bất cứ biểu hiện nào của:

a. Nhã nhặn *b. Tự tin*

c. Trang nghiêm *d. Thiên vị*

27. To be liked, it is important to handle patron with:

a. Tact **b. Familiarity**

c. Disdain **d. Arrogance**

Để được ưa thích, điều quan trọng là phục vụ cho khách với:

a. Sự tế nhị *b. Sự thân mật*

c. Khinh bỉ *d. Kiêu ngạo*

28. **The only true living part of the nail is the:**

a. Free edge | **b. Lunula**
c. Nail body | **d. Nail root**

Phần có sự sống của móng là:
a. Đầu móng (phần mọc ngoài thân móng) | *b. Hình bán nguyệt chỗ nền móng*
c. Thân móng | *d. Gốc móng*

29. **The scientific study of micro-organism is known as:**

a. Biology | **b. Pathology**
c. Bacteriology | **d. Genealogy**

Khoa học về vi sinh vật cực nhỏ được biết là:
a. Sinh vật học | *b. Bệnh lý học*
c. Vi trùng học | *d. Khoa phả hệ học*

30. **Most pathogenic bacteria are especially:**

a. On a clean body | **b. On sterile implement**
c. In dirty place | **d. On clean towels**

Hầu hết vi khuẩn gây bệnh đặc biệt nhiều ở:
a. Thân thể sạch | *b. Dụng cụ tiệt trùng*
c. Nơi dơ bẩn | *d. Trên khăn sạch*

31. **Harmful bacteria such as cocci, bacilli, and spirilla are referred to as:**

a. Pathogenic | **b. Saprophytes**
c. Non-pathogenic | **d. Protozoa**

Vi khuẩn gây hại như vi trùng hình tròn (cầu khuẩn), hình que (trực trùng), và vi trùng cong xoắn được xem là:
a. Vi trùng gây bệnh | *b. Thực vật hoại sinh*
c. Vi trùng không gây bệnh | *d. Động vật nguyên sinh*

32. **Non-pathogenic bacteria such as saprophytes lives on dead matter are referred to as:**

a. Germs | **b. Harmful**
c. Harmless | **d. Disease producing**

Vi trùng không gây bệnh ví như thực vật hoại sinh là vi trùng sống nhờ trên vật chết được xem là:
a. Vi trùng | *b. Có hại*
c. Vô hại | *d. Gây bệnh*

33. **Pathogenic bacteria are commonly known as:**

a. Antiseptic | **b. Disinfectant**
c. Germs or microbes | **d. Beneficial bacteria**

Vi trùng gây bệnh thường được biết là:
a. Sát trùng | *b. Diệt trùng*
c. Mầm bệnh hoặc vi khuẩn | *d. Vi trùng có lợi*

34. **Bacteria are best seen with the aid of:**

a. A microscope | **b. A telescope**
c. Regular eyeglasses | **d. Sunglasses**

Vi trùng được quan sát rõ nhất với sự trợ giúp của:
a. Kính hiển vi | *b. Kính viễn vọng*
c. Kính đeo mắt thường | *d. Kính mát*

35. Bacilli are bacteria with a:

a. Corkscrew shape
b. Round shape
c. Rod shape
d. Curved shape

Trực trùng (bacilli) là loại vi trùng có dạng:

a. Hình xoắn
b. Hình tròn (cầu khuẩn)
c. Hình que (gậy)
d. Hình cong

36. The cell of the bacteria reproduce by simply dividing in:

a. Half
b. Fungi
c. Microbes
d. Verruca

Tế bào của vi trùng sinh sản bằng sự phân chia:

a. Làm đôi
b. Nấm
c. Vi khuẩn
d. Mụn cóc

37. Before applying acrylic nails, the natural nails need to be buffed. What is the purpose for this service?

a. Add shiny to the nails
b. Prevent fungus
c. Remove natural oil
d. Apply manicure

Trước khi làm móng bột acrylic, móng thật cần làm nhám mặt móng. Làm điều này có mục đích gì?

a. Thêm bóng móng
b. Ngăn ngừa nấm
c. Lấy chất dầu tự nhiên
d. Chăm sóc tay

38. Some forms of bacteria have the ability to move with the aid of:

a. Flagella
b. Spores
c. Motility
d. Viruses

Vài loại vi khuẩn có khả năng di chuyển với sự trợ giúp của:

a. Chân giả (lông bơi)
b. Bào tử
c. Di chuyển
d. Siêu vi khuẩn

39. The inactive phase in the life cycle of bacteria is known as the:

a. Pathogenic stage
b. Spore-forming stage
c. Disease-producing stage
d. Non- pathogenic stage

Chu kỳ sống của vi trùng trong thời kỳ không hoạt động được biết là:

a. Thời kỳ vi trùng gây bệnh
b. Thời kỳ lập bào tử (vi trùng ẩn trong vỏ bọc)
c. Thời kỳ tạo bệnh
d. Thời kỳ không gây bệnh

40. A communicable disease is:

a. Not transferred to another
b. Not responsible for an epidemic
c. Transmitted to another
d. Caused by non-pathogenic bacteria

Bệnh truyền nhiễm là:

a. Không truyền qua người khác
b. Không ảnh hưởng lây lan
c. Truyền nhiễm sang người khác
d. Gây bởi vi trùng có lợi

41. A boil is an example of:

a. A general infection
b. A local infection
c. A non-pathogenic bacteria
d. A non-contagious disease

Mụn nhọt là một ví dụ của:

a. Sự nhiễm trùng toàn thể
b. Sự nhiễm trùng tại chỗ
c. Vi khuẩn không gây bệnh
d. Bệnh không truyền nhiễm

42. Resistance to disease is known as:

a. Immunity **b. Infection**

c. A parasite **d. A fungus**

Khả năng kháng bệnh (chống lại vi trùng gây bệnh) còn gọi là:

a. Sự miễn nhiễm *b. Sự nhiễm trùng*

c. Ký sinh trùng *d. Nấm*

43. An example of a general infection is:

a. A boil **b. Blood poisoning**

c. A verruca **d. Skin lesion**

Một ví dụ của sự nhiễm trùng toàn bộ là:

a. Mụt nhọt *b. Sự nhiễm độc máu*

c. Mụn cóc *d. Vết lở da*

44. Sterilization is the process of:

a. Keeping bacteria alive **b. Destroying only beneficial bacteria**

c. Destroying offensive odor **d. Killing both harmful and beneficial bacteria**

Sự tiệt trùng là tiến trình:

a. Giữ cho vi khuẩn sống *b. Chỉ tiêu diệt vi trùng có lợi*

c. Tẩy mùi hôi *d. Tiêu diệt vi trùng gây hại và có lợi*

45. For better adhesion of acrylic, tips, and nail wraps, natural oils should be removed and the nail should be dehydrated, using?

a. Nail antiseptic **b. 70% alcohol**

c. Nail bleach (6% peroxide) **d. Polish remover**

Để cho việc kết dính móng bột, móng tip, và móng bao, mặt móng nên lấy đi chất dầu tự nhiên trên móng và chất ẩm của móng, dùng:

a. Dung dịch sát trùng móng *b. 70% alcohol*

c. Chất tẩy móng 6% peroxide *d. Chất chùi nước sơn*

46. A Quaternary ammonium compounds 1,000 part per million (p.p.m) is commonly used as a disinfectant solution is also called:

a. Wet sanitizer **b. Dry sanitizer**

c. Antiseptic **d. Deodorant**

Hợp chất Quaternary ammonium 1.000 phần triệu (1.000 p.p.m) thường được dùng như là một dung dịch diệt trùng cũng còn được gọi là:

a. Chất khử trùng ướt *b. Chất khử trùng khô*

c. Chất sát trùng *d. Chất khử mùi hôi*

47. Nail bleach or 6% peroxide may remove some stains on fingernails. An optional step in a manicure is to apply nail bleach or peroxide to wipe:

a. Dry nail polish **b. On eponychium**

c. Under free edge **d. On hyponychium**

Chất tẩy móng hoặc 6% peroxide có thể lau đốm dơ ở trên móng tay. Một cách làm thêm trong việc chăm sóc tay là dùng chất tẩy móng hoặc peroxide để lau:

a. Khô nước sơn *b. Trên da ở nền móng tay*

c. Dưới đầu móng *d. Trên da ở dưới đầu móng tay*

48. Most beauty salons use which of the following sanitizing agent:

a. Dry heat | **b. Baking in oven**
c. Chemical agent | **d. Steam pressure sanitizes**

Các thẩm mỹ viện thường dùng phương pháp nào để khử trùng:

a. Hơi nóng | *b. Nướng trong lò*
c. Hóa chất | *d. Khử trùng bằng áp suất hơi nước*

49. Sharp metalic instruments may be sanitized with:

a. 50% alcohol | **b. 65% alcohol**
c. 70% alcohol | **d. 100% alcohol**

Những dụng cụ kim loại bén nhọn có thể được khử trùng bằng:

a. 50% alcohol | *b. 65% alcohol*
c. 70% alcohol | *d. 100% alcohol*

50. Before sanitizing any implements, it should be washed with:

a. Formaldehyde | **b. Warm water**
c. Cold water | **d. Soap and warm water**

Trước khi khử trùng bất cứ một dụng cụ nào, rửa sạch dụng cụ đó với:

a. Chất khí Formaldehyde | *b. Nước ấm*
c. Nước lạnh | *d. Xà phòng và nước ấm*

51. A dry sanitizer is most effective when it contain a formalin, borax and create:

a. Alcohol 70% | **b. Active fumigant**
c. Styptic | **d. Deodorant**

Khử trùng khô có tác dụng hữu hiệu khi nó chứa chất formalin, borax và tạo:

a. Cồn 70% | *b. Xông hơi diệt trùng (chất hoạt khí)*
c. Chất cầm máu | *d. Chất khử mùi*

52. Chemical solutions used in a beauty salon should be:

a. Heat cabinets | **b. Dry sanitizer**
c. Labled properly | **d. Wet sanitizer**

Dung dịch hóa học dùng trong thẩm mỹ viện nên:

a. Tủ nung nóng | *b. Khử trùng khô*
c. Dán đúng nhãn hiệu | *d. Dung dịch khử trùng*

53. Clients who wear tips need to come back to the salon for service weekly because tips should be:

a. Wrapped with silk | **b. Applied primer**
c. Reapplied tips | **d. Reglued at seam**

Khách mang móng tip cần trở lại salon hàng tuần bởi vì móng tip cần:

a. Bọc với lụa | *b. Thoa primer*
c. Gắn lại tip | *d. Thoa thêm keo ở lằn nối*

54. In order for a wet sanitizer to be effective, the objects being sanitized must be:

a. Made of metal | **b. Toxic**
c. Completely immersed | **d. Corrosive**

Để cho dung dịch khử trùng có hiệu nghiệm, các dụng cụ cần khử trùng phải:

a. Làm bằng kim loại | *b. Độc tố*
c. Ngâm toàn bộ | *d. Chất ăn mòn*

55. As disinfectant, a Quaternary ammonium compounds is considered to be:

a. Corrosive **b. Strongest solution**

c. Colorless and unstable **d. Odorless and stable**

Là chất diệt trùng, hợp chất Quaternary ammonium được xem là:

a. Chất ăn mòn *b. Dung dịch mạnh nhất*

c. Chất không màu và không ổn định *d. Chất không mùi và ổn định*

56. For effective disinfection, a Quaternary ammonium requires:

a. Long contact time **b. Triple strength**

c. Short contact time **d. Mixing with soap**

Để diệt trùng hiệu nghiệm, hợp chất Quaternary ammonium compounds cần:

a. Ngâm thời gian lâu *b. Nồng độ gấp ba lần*

c. Ngâm thời gian ngắn *d. Trộn với xà phòng*

57. For effective sanitation, the strength of Quats should be at least how many p.p.m (p.p.m: part per million)?

a. 1:1000 solution or 1,000p.p.m **b. 1: 2000 solution or 2,000 p.p.m**

c. 1:3000 solution or 3,000 p.p.m **d. 1: 4000 solution or 4,000 p.p.m**

Để khử trùng hữu hiệu, độ mạnh của nước Quats tối thiểu: (p.p.m: trên phần triệu)

a. Dung dịch 1/1.000 hoặc 1.000 p.p.m *b. Dung dịch 1/2.000 hoặc 2.000 p.p.m*

c. Dung dịch 1/3.000 hoặc 3.000 p.p.m *d. Dung dịch 1/4.000 hoặc 4.000 p.p.m*

58. To remove stains from the nails, use:

a. Nail polish remover **b. Aceton**

c. Nail whitener **d. Nail bleach or 6% H_2O_2**

Để tẩy vết trên móng, dùng:

a. Chất chùi nước sơn *b. Aceton*

c. Chất trắng thoa móng có đốm *d. Nail bleach hoặc 6% H_2O_2*

59. Which of the following has the same germ killing properties as a germicide?

a. Disinfectant **b. Antiseptic**

c. Deodorant **d. Anesthetic**

Loại nào sau đây có cùng đặc tính tiêu diệt vi khuẩn như là chất germicide?

a. Chất diệt trùng *b. Chất sát trùng*

c. Chất khử mùi *d. Chất gây tê*

60. Stain and discoloration may be removed from the skin and nails with:

a. Boric acid **b. Hydrogen peroxide**

c. White iodine **d. Dichloride of mercury**

Những vết bẩn và vết bạc màu có thể lấy đi trên da và móng với:

a. Acid boric (sát trùng nhẹ) *b. 6% Hydrogen peroxide (H_2O_2)*

c. White iodine (iốt trắng) *d. Dichloride of mercury (thủy ngân)*

61. A vapor use in a dry sanitizer to keep clean objects sanitary is a:

a. Germicide **b. Fumigant**

c. Disinfectant **d. Sepsis**

Chất khí dùng trong khử trùng khô để giữ vật dụng vệ sinh được sạch là:

a. Chất diệt khuẩn gây bệnh *b. Khí diệt trùng*

c. Chất diệt trùng *d. Nhiễm trùng máu*

62. A freshly laundered towel should be used:

a. For every two patrons

b. For each patron

c. Until it gets soiled

d. Whenever patron request it

Khăn giặt sạch sẽ được dùng:

a. Cho mỗi hai người khách

b. Cho mỗi người khách

c. Cho đến khi bẩn

d. Bất cứ lúc nào khách cần

63. Objects dropped on the floor should not be used again until they are thoroughly:

a. Washed with soap and cold water

b. Washed with a tissue

c. Sanitized

d. Wiped with a towel

Vật dụng rớt xuống sàn nhà không nên đem dùng lại, cho đến khi chúng được hoàn toàn:

a. Rửa xà phòng và nước lạnh

b. Lau sạch bằng giấy

c. Khử trùng

d. Lau sạch với khăn

64. Cream may be removed from jar with:

a. The end of a used towel

b. Finger tip

c. A clean spatula

d. Cotton

Kem nên được lấy khỏi lọ chứa bằng:

a. Mép khăn bẩn

b. Đầu ngón tay

c. Cây que sạch

d. Bông gòn

65. A chemical solution used to prevent the growth of bacteria is called a:

a. Fumigant

b. Astringent

c. Antiseptic

d. Deodorant

Dung dịch hóa chất dùng để ngăn ngừa sự phát triển của vi trùng được gọi là:

a. Chất khí diệt trùng

b. Chất làm se da

c. Chất sát trùng

d. Chất khử mùi

66. A chemical agent that destroys all germs is called:

a. Antiseptic

b. Disinfectant

c. Fumigant

d. Sepsis

Hóa chất dùng để tiêu diệt tất cả vi khuẩn được gọi là:

a. Chất sát trùng

b. Chất diệt trùng

c. Chất khí diệt trùng

d. Nhiễm trùng máu

67. To create vapor in a dry cabinet sanitizer, place one tablespoon of formalin in a tray with one tablespoon of:

a. Styptic

b. Alcohol

c. Lysol

d. Borax

Để tạo ra hơi khí trong tủ khử trùng khô, đặt một thìa formalin vào khay với một thìa:

a. Chất cầm máu

b. Alcohol (cồn)

c. Lysol (hóa chất lau nền nhà)

d. Borax (hàn the)

68. Objects that have been sanitized are kept clean by ultra violet rays or by:

a. Alcohol

b. Boric acid

c. Boiling water

d. Chemical vapor

Vật dụng đã được khử trùng nên được giữ sạch bằng tia cực tím hoặc:

a. Alcohol

b. Acid boric

c. Nước sôi

d. Hơi hóa chất

69. Before and after each use, the shampoo bowl (sink) should be:

a. Sanitized **b. Sterilized**

c. Fumigated **d. Vaporized**

Trước và sau khi sử dụng, bồn gội tóc (bồn rửa tay) nên được:

a. Khử trùng *b. Tiệt trùng*

c. Xông khí khử trùng *d. Làm bay hơi*

70. The skin under the nail's free edge is hyponychium and the skin that surrounds the nail area is called:

a. Eponychium **b. Perionychium**

c. Mantle **d. Eggshell nail**

Da dưới đầu móng tay là hyponychium và da chung quanh mặt móng tay là:

a. Eponychium (da nền móng) *b. Perionychium*

c. Màng móng *d. Móng mỏng trắng hơi cong*

71. Emery boards are used to shape the:

a. Side of nails **b. Lunula**

c. Free edge of nail **d. Cuticle**

Giũa giấy được dùng để tạo dáng:

a. Cạnh móng *b.Hình bán nguyệt (vòng trắng nền móng)*

c. Đầu móng *d. Da chung quanh móng*

72. Nail mending tissue is used to:

a. Soften cuticles **b. Repair split nails**

c. Removed nail polish **d. Polish the nail**

Giấy vá móng được dùng:

a. Mềm da *b. Sửa móng nứt*

c. Chùi nước sơn *d. Sơn móng*

73. Before using manicuring implements, they should be:

a. Wiped with tissue **b. Wiped with towel**

c. Cleansed and sanitized **d. Dipped with warm water**

Trước khi xử dụng, dụng cụ làm móng nên:

a. Lau bằng giấy *b. Lau bằng khăn*

c. Rửa sạch và khử trùng *d. Ngâm vào nước ấm*

74. Brittle nails and dry cuticles are treated with:

a. Oil manicure **b. Top coat**

c. Regular manicure **d. Machine manicure**

Móng dòn và da khô được chữa trị với:

a. Làm móng tay dầu *b. Chất phủ bóng nước sơn*

c. Làm móng tay nước *d. Máy giũa móng*

75. Manicuring implements should be sanitized (washed & disinfected):

a. Once a day **b. After each use**

c. Every week **d. Biweekly**

Dụng cụ làm móng phải được khử trùng (rửa sạch và diệt trùng):

a. Mỗi ngày một lần *b. Sau mỗi lần dùng*

c. Hàng tuần *d. Hai tuần một lần*

76. While giving a pedicure/manicure, nail implements such as cuticle nipper, metal pusher should be kept in:

a. Manicuring table drawer **b. In an open cabinet sanitizer**
c. A dry cabinet sanitizer **d. Alcohol jar sanitizer**

Trong lúc chăm sóc chân hoặc chăm sóc tay, dụng cụ làm móng như kềm cắt da, cây sủi nên được giữ trong:

a. Ngăn kéo bàn làm móng *b. Hộp khử trùng mở nắp*
c. Hộp khử trùng khô *d. Lọ alcohol khử trùng*

77. When shaping the fingernail, the nail is filed from:

a. Corner to center **b. Straight cross**
c. Center to corner **d. Corner to corner**

Khi tạo hình dạng móng tay, móng được giũa từ:

a. Cạnh đến giữa móng *b. Giũa ngang*
c. Giữa đến cạnh móng *d. Cạnh đến cạnh*

78. The instrument used for trimming the cuticle is a:

a. Nail buffer **b. Metal pusher**
c. Cuticle nipper **d. Nail brush**

Dụng cụ dùng tỉa da là:

a. Đồ chà mịn móng *b. Cây xủi da bằng kim loại*
c. Kềm cắt da *d. Bàn chải móng*

79. The correct way to apply nail polish (from base to free edge) is to:

a. Use thick polish **b. Use short, jerky strokes**
c. Apply three coats **d. Apply quickly and lightly**

Cách sơn móng đúng cách là từ gốc đến đầu móng:

a. Dùng sơn đặc *b. Vuốt từng vệt ngắn, chồng nhau*
c. Sơn ba lớp *d. Sơn nhanh và mịn nhẹ*

80. A cosmetic products applied over the nail polish to minimize chipping or cracking is a/an:

a. Base coat **b. Sealer**
c. Lacquer **d. Abrasive**

Loại mỹ phẩm phủ lên nước sơn để giảm nứt sơn và tróc sơn là:

a. Nước sơn lót *b. Nước phủ sơn cho bóng chắc*
c. Lớp phủ bề mặt *d. Giũa chà móng*

81. It is best to apply nail polish on:

a. Over the top coat **b. Over the base coat**
c. After the sealer **d. Before the base coat**

Cách tốt nhất là sơn móng trên:

a. Phủ lên lớp bóng ngoài *b. Lên lớp sơn lót*
c. Sau lớp sơn bóng *d. Trước lớp sơn lót*

82. The ideal nail shape is:

a. Taper **b. Rectangular**
c. Oval **d. Round**

Hình dáng lý tưởng của móng tay là:

a. Nhọn, túm *b. Chữ nhật*
c. Bầu dục *d. Tròn*

83. Wavy ridges may be improved by buffing the nail with:

a. Pumice powder **b. Cream**

c. Oil **d. Polish remover**

Móng có gợn móng có thể làm bằng cách chà móng với:

a. Bột đá *b. Kem*

c. Dầu *d. Chất chùi nước sơn*

84. A nail chamois buffer and buffing bits must not be used:

a. With paste polish **b. With dry polish**

c. Where not permit by law **d. Pumice powder**

Dụng cụ đánh mịn móng (buffer bằng da dê), và dầu đánh bóng bằng máy giũa không được dùng:

a. Với kem chà bóng *b. Đánh bóng móng khô*

c. Nơi luật lệ bị cấm *d. Bột đá đánh bóng*

85. For clients with ridges, brittle nails or dry cuticles, you should recommend:

a. Oil manicure **b. Electric manicure**

c. Both manicure **d. Nail wrapping**

Đối với những khách có móng gợn, móng dòn, và da khô, bạn nên khuyên:

a. Làm móng tay dầu *b. Làm móng với dụng cụ bằng điện*

c. Cả hai loại a & b *d. Dùng lụa hoặc giấy bọc móng*

86. The care of feet, legs, and toe nails is called:

a. Pedicure **b. Hypertrophy**

c. Manicure **d. Paronychia**

Chăm sóc bàn chân, đôi chân và các móng chân được gọi là:

a. Pedicure *b. Móng mọc dày*

c. Săn sóc tay *d. Nhiễm trùng da quanh móng*

87. To avoid ingrown toe nails, do not clip or file:

a. The free edge **b. In corner of toe nails**

c. Across the free edge **d. To round the nail**

Để tránh móng chân mọc đâm khóe, đừng cắt hoặc giũa:

a. Đầu móng chân *b. Sâu vào cạnh móng chân*

c. Ngang đầu móng *d. Làm tròn móng*

88. Another name for athlete's foot is:

a. Varicose **b. Pityriasis**

c. Tinea pedis **d. Pterygium**

Tên khác của chân bị nấm là:

a. Phồng lên *b. Lớp vảy mỏng*

c. Tinea pedis (mụn nước ngứa, nấm ở chân) *d. Pterygium (da mọc chồm lên mặt móng)*

89. Which of the following is located beneath the free edge:

a. Eponychium **b. Hyponychium**

c. Groove **d. Nail bed**

Phần da nằm dưới đầu móng là:

a. Eponychium (da ở chỗ vòng trắng lunula) *b. Hyponychium (da dưới đầu móng)*

c. Rãnh móng *d. Lớp thịt đệm móng*

90. Nail whitener are available in forms of cream, coating string, and paste, are applied:

a. Over the lunula | **b. On top of the free edge**
c. Under the free edge | **d. On the sides of the nail**

Chất trắng dùng phủ móng có đốm thường có dạng kem, sợi và sền sệt, được thoa:

a. Trên vòng trắng nền móng | *b. Ở trên đầu móng*
c. Dưới đầu móng | *d. Ở dọc cạnh móng*

91. Nail polish is protected from chipping by applying a:

a. Nail liquid polish | **b. Top coat**
c. Base coat | **d. Alum powder**

Nước sơn được bảo vệ cho khỏi tróc ra bằng cách thoa:

a. Nước sơn móng | *b. Lớp phủ bóng móng*
c. Lớp sơn lót | *d. Bột cầm máu*

92. Pumice powder is likely to be found in:

a. Cuticle cream | **b. Nail abrasive**
c. Hand cream | **d. Hand lotion**

Bột đá đánh bóng móng thường được thấy trong:

a. Kem thoa da quanh móng | *b. Chất đánh bóng móng*
c. Kem thoa da tay | *d. Kem massage tay*

93. Irregular nail ridges may be smoothen with:

a. Liquid lacquer | **b. Cuticle remover**
c. Nail solvent | **d. Pumice powder**

Những gợn sóng bất thường có thể làm láng, mịn với:

a. Chất phủ bóng mặt móng | *b. Chất làm mềm da*
c. Chất làm mềm móng | *d. Bột đá đánh bóng*

94. Soap is likely to be found in a:

a. Nail whitener | **b. Finger bath bowl**
c. Dry nail polish | **d. Liquid nail polish**

Xà phòng thường được dùng trong:

a. Chất trắng phủ móng có đốm | *b. Tô ngâm rửa tay*
c. Đánh bóng móng khô | *d. Nước sơn móng*

95. To prevent the nails from splitting, apply a nail:

a. Solvent | **b. Sealer**
c. Strengthener | **d. Abrasive**

Để ngăn ngừa móng tay khỏi nứt chẻ, thoa:

a. Dung môi | *b. Lớp phủ bóng*
c. Chất làm chắc móng | *d. Chà móng*

96. Healthy nails are curved, smooth and are not loose and without hollows and:

a. Flexibility | **b. Wavy ridges**
c. Firmness | **d. Color**

Móng tay tốt là cong, mịn, không lõm và không có:

a. Tính mềm dẻo | *b. Nhiều đường gợn*
c. Chắc chắn | *d. Màu*

97. When applying tips on natural nails, find stop line against the free edge at 45 degrees and hold the tip in place until dry for:

a. 5 to 10 seconds | **b. 10 to 15 seconds**

c. 15 to 20 seconds | **d. 1 minute**

Khi gắn tip lên trên móng thật, tìm lằn mức có điểm dừng dựa vào đầu móng góc 45 độ và giữ yên tip ở đó cho đến khi khô khoảng:

a. 5 đến 10 giây | *b. 10 đến 15 giây*

c. 15 đến 20 giây | *d. 1phút*

98. Nail salons need to install good ventilation systems. This is a very important for manicurists and customers because chemicals and products in salon can:

a. Cause irritation | **b. Cause viral infections**

c. Absorb the skin | **d. Absorb through inhalation and enter the body**

Salon cần lắp hệ thống thông khí (hút khí bẩn ra ngoài tiệm) tốt. Điều này quan trọng cho thợ và khách bởi vì hóa chất và sản phẩm ở trong salon có thể:

a. Nguyên nhân gây ngứa | *b. Nguyên nhân gây nhiễm trùng*

c. Có thể thấm qua da | *d. Thẩm thấu qua hít thở và xâm nhập vào cơ thể*

99. Origin, insertion, and belly are parts of the:

a. Heart | **b. Connective tissues**

c. Skeleton | **d. Muscle**

Phần gốc, phần ngọn và phần bụng là những phần của:

a. Quả tim | *b. Mô liên kết*

c. Bộ xương | *d. Bắp thịt*

100. Nail mold are caused when moisture is trapped between the acrylic nail products and unsanitized natural nails are called:

a. Virus infection | **b. Scabies**

c. Ringworm | **d. Fungus infection**

Móng tay bị nấm mốc là nguyên nhân do chất ẩm đọng ở giữa móng bột acrylic và móng thật bị dơ được gọi là:

a. Nhiễm trùng vi khuẩn | *b. Ghẻ ngứa*

c. Nấm vòng mụn nước | *d. Nấm nhiễm trùng*

MANICURIST TECHNICAL WORDS

Abdominoplasty: *lấy mỡ bụng*
Abductors: *cơ xoè ngón tay*
Abrasive stone bit: *trục giũa bằng đá tròn đều men màu hồng, xanh, trắng dùng bào mòn đều*
Accelerator: *chất thúc đẩy*
Accumulation: *chồng chất lên*
Aceton: *hóa chất mạnh dùng ngâm mềm móng giả khi cần tháo gỡ, chất gây ngứa và dễ sưng da*
Acid balance rinse: *chất xả ngừa lợt tóc*
Acid rinse: *chất phục hồi acid & lấy chất dơ tóc*
Acquire immunity: *miễn nhiễm tự tạo*
Acquisitiveness: *ham lợi*
Actinic ray (UV): *tia hóa tính không thấy được*
Activator-cured: *cách cứng gel không đèn, xịt lên gel hoặc chất thoa lên mặt gel cứng lại*
Acute disease: *bệnh cấp tính*
Adductors: *cơ khép ngón tay*
Adhesive: *chất keo để dán dính hai bề mặt với nhau*
Adipose tissue (subcutis): *mô mỡ dưới nội bì*
Affilating (slithering): *tỉa mỏng tóc đều bằng kéo*
Agae product: *chất khóang và kích thích tố thực vật tạo ẩm làn da*
Aggressiveness: *tính gây sự*
Agnails (hangnails): *xước da quanh móng*
AIDS: *bệnh do nhiễm vi khuẩn HIV*
Air hose: *ống dẫn hơi ép xịt phun sơn*
Albinism: *bệnh bạch tạng do bẩm sinh*
Algae products: *khoáng chất ở biển tạo ẩm làn da*
Allergic sensitizer: *dị ứng do tiếp xúc nhiều lần*
Allergy: *dị ứng*
Almond: *quả hạnh nhân có tính nhờn và giúp êm dịu*
Aloe: *cây lô hồi có tính nhờn, làm sạch da và lành da*
Alopecia areata: *sói tóc từng mảng*
Alopecia: *sói tóc*
Alphahydroxy: *chất acid lactic từ sữa giúp lột bỏ tế bào chết*
Alternating current: *dòng điện xoay chiều*
Alum root: *rễ alum có tính se da*
Alum solution: *muối alumium, chất cầm máu*
Aluminum oxide, crystals: *bột nhôm, mài da*
Anabolism: *tạo năng lượng*
Aluminum: *nhôm*
Amino dye: *thuốc nhuộm aniline*
Amitosis: *sinh sản trực phân*
Ammonia water: *dung dịch có khí nồng kết hợp từ hydrogen and nitrogen*
Ammonia: *khí của hydro và nitrogen mùi nồng*
Ammonium sulfite: *hỗn hợp ammonia và muối*
Ammonium thioglycolate: *chất uốn tóc alkaline*
Anagen: *giai đoạn tóc phát triển*
Anaphoresis: *điện cực âm đẩy alkaline vào da*
Androgenic alopecia: *tiến trình rụng sói tóc bình thường do gene di truyền*
Angular artery: *động mạch ở bên mũi*
Anhidrosis: *bệnh thiếu mồ hôi*
Animal parasite: *ký sinh trùng động vật*
Ankle: *mắt cá chân*
Anode: *cực dương*
Anterior auricular artery: *động mạch trước tai*
Anthrax: *bệnh than (mụt có mủ)*
Anti-perspirant: *chất đóng lỗ chân lông*
Antiseptics: *sát trùng*
Antitoxic: *kháng độc tố*
Apex: *phần tóc đỉnh đầu*
Apocrine: *tuyến mồ hôi dính với nang lông*
Apricot oil: *dầu mận, cho da tuổi già, da khô*
Arc base: *nền tóc hình cánh cung*
Aromatherapy: *hương liệu thảo mộc để chữa trị*
Aromatic: *hương liệu*
Arrector-pili muscle: *cơ dựng lông*
Arrogance: *kiêu ngạo*
Arteries: *động mạch mang máu từ tim tới cơ thể*
Aseptic: *vô trùng*
Assertiveness: *cương quyết*
Asteatosis: *bệnh thiếu dầu, vảy khô*
Astringents: *chất đóng lỗ chân lông*
Atheletes foot: *nấm ở chân*
Atom: nguyên tử
Atrium: *tâm nhĩ, ngăn trên, mỏng của tim*
Atrophy: *rung móng*
Auricularis anterior: *cơ trước tai*
Auricularis posterior: *cơ sau tai*
Auricularis superior: *cơ trên tai*
Auricularis: *cơ ở tai*
Auriculotemporal: *thần kinh ngoài tai, đỉnh đầu*
Autonomic nervous system: *hệ thần kinh tự động*
Avocado oil: *dầu trái bơ cho da thiếu nước*
Bacilli: *vi trùng hình ống, que (gây bệnh)*
Back brushing: *đánh rối bằng bàn chải tóc*

Back combing: *đánh rối bằng lược*
Backfill bit: *đầu giũa nhỏ tạo vòng cười cho móng pink and white*
Bacterial invasion: *tấn công của vi trùng*
Bactericidal: *chất có khả năng diệt trùng*
Bacteriology: *vi khuẩn học*
Balance diet: *kiêng ăn đúng cách*
Balayage: *cách dùng cọ chấm thuốc tẩy tóc lên từng*
Baldness: *sói tóc*
Balneology: *chữa trị bằng vòi phun nước khoáng*
Balneotherapy: *dùng chữa trị bỏng, rối loạn tâm thần cách massage bằng nước*
Barrel curl: *lọn tóc quấn bằng ngón tay*
Basal cell carcinoma: *ung thư da nhẹ có nốt màu lợt*
Basal layer: *lớp tế bào giữa ngoại bì và nội bì*
Base coat: *chất không màu thoa lên móng thật trước khi sơn móng*
Base pin curl: *nền tóc bên mặt tóc để tạo sọc*
Bee wax: *sáp ong*
Beehive: *kiểu lọn tóc tổ ong*
Belgium: *người Bỉ*
Belly (muscle): *phần giữa bắp thịt*
Beneficial bacteria: *vi trùng có lợi*
Biceps: *cơ hai đầu mặt trước của cánh tay trên*
Blemish: *khuyết điểm ở da*
Blender: *trộn lẫn đều nhau*
Blepharoplasty: *cắt mắt, giảm túi mỡ mắt*
Blood vascular system: *hệ thống bơm đẩy máu*
Bloodborne pathogens: *bệnh lây truyền qua máu*
Blow-dry styling: *chãi tóc bằng máy sấy*
Blowout waving: *sấy máy và lược tròn tạo sóng*
Bluing rinse: *thuốc xả tóc màu xanh biển*
Boiling point: *độ sôi (212 độ F; 100 độ C)*
Boils: *mụt mũ*
Boric acid: *chất bột trắng trong pha trộn từ 2 đến 5% độ mạnh dùng sát trùng nhẹ, làm sạch mắt*
Bounce hair: *tóc bồng bền*
Brass: *thau, hợp kim vàng nhạt cứng hơn đồng*
Brassy tone: *tóc có màu đỏ, cam và vàng hoe*
Brick brushing: *chãi tóc kiểu lát gạch*
Brohidrosis: *mồ hôi có mùi khó chịu ở nách*
Bruised nails: *móng bị dập đông máu bên trong có màu tím (chỉ làm manicure thôi)*
Buccal nerve: *thần kinh ảnh hưởng cơ ở miệng*
Buccinator: *bắp thịt mỏng ở má (cơ thổi hơi)*
Buffing bits: *trục vòng đầu giũa điện bằng da, vãi để đánh bóng, dùng 1 lần vứt bỏ*
Buld: *bầu tóc*
Bulla: *mụn nước nhỏ*
Bunch: *bó lại*
Bunions: *xương nhô ra ở đốt ngón chân cái*
Buttock: *mông*
Calamine lotion: *oxide kẽm trị sưng da có màu hồng*
Calcaneus: *xương gót chân*
Calves: *bắp chân*
Camomile flowers (azulene): *cúc La Mã có tính ẩm da, êm dịu, giúp lành da*
Camomile: *cúc vàng, chống sưng, tiêu hóa, êm dịu*
Camphor: *long não*
Capillaries: *mao quản (mạch máu nhỏ)*
Caraway: *hạt thơm làm gia vị ở Châu Âu*
Carbide bit: *trục giũa kim loại hình ống dài, nhỏ dùng cắt móng*
Carbon: *than*
Carbonic gas spray: *bình xịt khí carbonic trị da dầu, mụn đầu đen, và mụn bọc*
Carbuncle: *nhiễm trùng lỗ chân lông*
Cardiac muscle: *cơ tim*
Carpal bones: *xương cổ tay*
Carpal tunnel syndrome: *chứng đau tay và cổ tay*
Carpus: *xương cổ tay gồm 8 xương*
Cartilage: *sụn*
Cascarilla: *cỏ thơm ở Ấn độ*
Cassia oil: *dầu quế giúp tăng tuần hoàn*
Castor oil: *chất dầu từ cây thầu dầu*
Catabolism: *tiêu hao năng lượng*
Catagen: *giai đoạn ngưng phát triển*
Catalyst: *chất giúp tác dụng hóa chất nhanh hơn*
Cataphoresis: *tiến trình đẩy dung dịch bằng điện dương galvanic vào da*
Category: *phân loại*
Cathode: *cực âm*
Caustic: *chất ăn mòn*
Cedar: *một loại giống gỗ thông, lá xanh*
Cell membrane: *màng bọc tế bào*
Cell: *tế bào*
Central nervous system: *hệ trung khu thần kinh*
Centrosome: *tích bào, kiểm soát phân chia tế bào*
Ceresin: *chất nhựa nhuộm từ than đá như aniline*
Certified color: *màu tạm thời chấp nhận do FDA*
Cervical cutaneous nerve: *thần kinh bắp thịt cổ*
Cervical nerve: *thần kinh cổ*
Cervical vertebra: *đốt xương cổ*
Chamois buffer: *cục chà mịn móng bọc da dê*

Cheekbone: *xương gò má*
Chemical change: *thay đổi hóa tính thành chất mới*
Chemical compounds: *hợp tố hóa học*
Chemical exfoliation: *hóa chất lột tế bào chết*
Chemical reaction: *phản ứng hóa học*
Chloasma: *đốm nâu đen ở da*
Chronic disease: *bệnh kinh niên*
Cilia: *chân giả, lông bơi của vi trùng di chuyển*
Circle pin curl: *vòng tóc*
Circuit breaker: *dụng cụ tự động ngắt điện*
Circular friction: *chà xoay xoay*
Circular motion: *động tác xoay tròn*
Circulatory system: *hệ thống tuần hoàn tim, máu*
Civet cat: *chồn hôi ở Châu Phi*
Claustrophobia reaction: *phản ứng khó chịu, ngột ngạt*
Clavicle: *xương đòn gánh*
Clay masks: *mặt nạ đất sét*
Clove: *đinh hương nhiệt đới có tính sát trùng*
Coal tar product: *chất nhuộm từ than đá*
Coarse hair: *tóc cứng đường kính lớn*
Cocci: *vi trùng hình tròn*
Collagen: *chất đạm có sợi để tạo da*
Colloids: *chất keo da*
Color fade (color blend): *cách trộn 2 hoặc nhiều màu xịt trộn lẫn lên móng bằng máy phun sơn*
Color filer: *chất giúp đều màu cho tóc quá thấm*
Color rinse: *màu tạm thời*
Color wheel: *bảng chia loại màu*
Color wheel: *bảng hướng dẫn qui luật màu sắc*
Combustion: *sự oxid nhanh tạo nhiệt và ánh sáng*
Comfrey root (allantoin): *rễ cam thảo có tính se da, nhờn và êm dịu giúp mau lành da*
Common carotid arteries: *động mạch đầu, cổ*
Common cold: *cảm lạnh*
Communicable diseases: *bệnh truyền nhiễm*
Comomile flowers (azulene): *hoa cúc vàng La Mã có tính ẩm, lành da, và êm dịu*
Complementary color: *màu trung hòa, bổ sung*
Compound dye: *nhuộm tổng hợp*
Concealers: *mỹ phẩm để che chỗ khuyết điểm*
Conditioner filler: *chất làm tốt tóc*
Conditioner rinse: *kem xả mịn tóc*
Conductor: *chất dẫn điện*
Congenital disease: *bệnh bẩm sinh*
Congential: *bẩm sinh*
Congestion: *bị nghẽn máu*
Connective tissue: *mô liên kết (như xương, gân)*
Consumption supplies: *vật liệu tiêu thụ*
Contagion: *sự lây lan*
Contagious disease: *bệnh lây nhiễm*
Contagious: *truyền nhiễm*
Contaminant: *nhiễm bẩn*
Contamination: *sự nhiễm bẩn*
Contour: *lớp bọc viền ngoài*
Controversial: *tranh luận*
Converter: *biến điện từ DC qua AC*
Cool color: *màu mát (xanh, xanh lá, tím)*
Corium: *lớp nội bì*
Cornstarch: *bột bắp*
Corporation: *công ty từ ba người trở lên*
Corrosive: *chất ăn mòn, tiêu hủy chất khác*
Corrugator: *cơ chau mày tạo lằn ngang ở trán*
Cortex: *lớp giữa sợi tóc*
Cosmetics: *mỹ phẩm*
Cosmetology: *nghành thẩm mỹ học*
Costal cartilage: *sụn sườn*
Cotton strips: *dãi bông gòn*
Couperose skin: *da có nhiều mạch máu bị vỡ*
Courtesy: *sự nhã nhặn*
Cowlick: *xoáy bò, nhúm tóc dựng lên ở phía trước*
Cracking: *nứt*
Cranium: *xương sọ bảo vệ não*
Cream bleach: *kem tẩy*
Croquignole styling: *quấn tóc từ đuôi vào da đầu*
Crown area: *vùng đỉnh đầu*
Crushing: *sự vắt, ép*
Crust: *vảy cứng*
Cushion of the fingers: *đệm các đầu ngón tay*
Cuticle cream: *kem ngăn ngừa móng dòn, da khô chứa lanolin, petroleum, và sáp ong*
Cuticle oil: *dầu làm mềm và trơn da thoa chung quanh móng tay, móng chân*
Cuticle remover: *kem làm mềm để dễ lấy da chết chung quanh móng; chứa alkali, dầu nhờn glycerin; chứa potassium hydroxide*
Cuticle: *lớp ngoài cùng sợi tóc*
Cyst: *bướu nhỏ*
Cytoplasm: *tế bào chất*
dao có khung bảo vệ (guard)
Datatable story: *chuyện có thể tranh luận*
Dead cuticle: *da chết*
Debatable: *có thể thảo luận*
Decolorize: *tiến trình lợt màu tóc*

Decompose: *phân hủy*
Decontamination: *sự tẩy uế*
Deltoid: *thịt tam giác ở bả vai*
Demarcation: *đường viền*
Demi-permanent colors: *thuốc nhuộm oxýt hóa*
Dendrites: *tua thần kinh*
Density: *độ dày*
Deodorant: *chất khử mùi hôi*
Depilatory: *cách lấy lông tạm thời*
Depreciation: *sự giảm giá*
Depressor labii inferioris: *nâng môi dưới kéo xéo*
Dermabration: *mài da, chà sẹo*
Dermatitis venenata: *sưng da do hóa chất mỹ phẩm*
Dermatitis: *sưng da*
Dermatologist: *bác sĩ chuyên khoa da*
Dermatology: *ngành học về da*
Destruction: *sự tiêu diệt*
Detergent: *thuốc tẩy*
Detoxify: *loại độc tố*
Dexterity: *sự khéo léo*
Diabetic: *bệnh tiểu đường*
Diagnosis: *chẩn đoán bệnh*
Diameter: *đường kính*
Diamond bit: *trục giũa kim loại mặt ngoài có bụi diamond để mài móng*
Diathermy: *tạo nhiệt sâu trong mô bằng điện cao tần*
Diffuse melanin: *phân phối chất màu*
Diffusion: *sự phân tán*
Digestive system: *hệ thống tiêu hóa*
Digital nerve: *thần kinh cung cấp ngón tay và chân*
Digits: ngón tay
Diplococci: *cầu khuẩn đi từng đôi*
Discoloration: *sự nhạt màu*
Discolored nails: *có màu, xanh, đỏ, tím do dùng thuốc, bệnh tim.*
Disincrustation: *sự tan dầu trong nang lông*
Disintegrator: *sự phân hủy*
Distillation: *sự chưng cất*
Distilled water: *nước cất*
Double halo: *cở đầu lớn, chia tóc làm 8 phần*
Drab color: *màu nâu xám*
Dropped crown: *uốn viền tóc trước và ở gáy*
Dry nail polish: *bột khô đánh bóng mặt móng dùng với cây buffer da dê*
Dyskeratosis: *thiếu chất sừng ở ngoại bì*
Eccrine: *tuyến mồ hôi không dính với nang lông*
Eczema: *chốc lỡ*
Effilating (slithering): *tỉa mỏng đều bằng kéo*
Effleurage movement: *động tác vuốt, nhẹvà đều*
Eggshell nail: *móng mỏng như vỏ trứng, có màu trắng, và cong*
Egyptian: *người Ai Cập*
Elasticity: *độ đàn hồi*
Electric fill: *máy giũa móng bằng điện*
Electrologist: *thợ lấy lông vĩnh viễn*
Electrotherapy: *điện chữa trị dùng cho facial*
Element: *nguyên tố*
Elevation: *độ cao*
Emollient cream: *kem mềm và trơn da*
Emulsion: *nhủ tương, nhiều chất không kết hợp được nhưng pha trộn và kết lại nhờ có chất kết dính tổng hợp như mayonnaise*
Endocrine (ductless) glands: *tuyến nội tiết*
Energizer: *Tạo năng lực*
Enfleurage: *mỡ thấm hương liệu*
Environment: *môi trường*
Enzymes: *men tiêu hóa*
Epicranius: *bắp thịt phủ đỉnh đầu từ trán đến ót*
Epidemic: *bệnh dịch lây nhiễm nhiều người*
Epidermabrasion: *mài lớp ngoại bì*
Epidermal flakes: *bong da*
Epidermis: *lớp ngoại bì*
Epileptic: *động kinh*
Epithelial tissue: *mô ngoại biên*
Epizoon: *động vật ký sinh ngoài*
Eponychial disorders (hyponychial): *da mọc tràn lên mặt móng và dưới đầu móng*
Eponychium: *da mọc nền bán nguyệt móng tay*
Epricranium: *cơ phủ đỉnh đầu*
Estrogen: *kích thích tố nữ*
Ethmoid: *xương xốp giữa hóc mắt tạo xương mũi*
Etiology: *môn học về nguyên nhân bệnh*
Eucalyptus: *cây khuynh diệp (bạch dàn) có tính sát trùng, lành da, kích thích và hương thơm.*
Evaporate: *bay hơi, thay đổi thể lỏng sang thể khí*
Even color: *hòa đều màu*
Even porosity: *độ thấm đồng đều*
Excoriation: *da sưng và trầy xướt*
Excretory system: *hệ thống bài tiết*
Exfoliating: *mài da*
Exhalation: *sự thở ra*
Expression: *phương pháp ép dầu từ vỏ trái cây*
Extensor: *cơ duỗi cánh tay*
External carotid artery: *động mạch ngoài mặt, cổ*

***External jugular vein**: tĩnh mạch nằm một bên cổ*
***Extraction:** dung môi thấm vào thảo mộc*
***Eyebrows:** chân mày*
***Eyelashes:** lông mi*
***Face-lift:** căng da mặt*
***Facial artery**: động mạch của mặt, miệng, và mũi*
***Familliarity:** sự thân mật*
***Faradic current:** dòng điện co thắt bắp thịt*
***Femur**: xương đùi*
***Fennel**: có tính kích thích và hương thơm*
***Fermentation**: sự lên men*
***Fiberglass:** thủy tinh sợi*
***Fibula**: xương mác (xương nhỏ ở ống chân)*
***Fifth cranial nerve**: thần kinh thứ năm (ăn và nhai)*
***Final phase:** giai đoạn kết thúc*
***Fine curly hair:** tóc quăn mịn*
***Fine emery board:** giũa giấy mịn*
***Fissure**: da nứt sâu vào nội bì*
***Fitzpatrick scale:** bảng đo khả năng da dưới mặt trời của bác sĩ Thomas Fitzpatrick*
***Fixative:** chất chỉnh đốn*
***Flagella**: lông bơi nhỏ giúp vi trùng di chuyển*
***Flare-up:** lây ra, tăng thêm ra*
***Flexible hands:** đôi tay mềm dẻo*
***Flexible:** uyển chuyển*
***Flexor:** bắp thịt co tay*
***Fluid noozle**: đầu hình chóp máy phun sơn để giữ cho sơn phun ra bằng đầu kim bên trong*
***Fluorescent:** đèn huỳnh quang*
***Follicle:** nang lông, phần gốc tóc*
***Follicularis:** sưng lỗ chân lông*
***Forearm**: cánh tay trước*
***Formadehyde hardeners:** chất làm mạnh móng tạo chất sừng; chứa 5% formadehyde*
***Formaldehyde**: chất gây cancer có trong formalin*
***Formalin disinfectant:** chất diệt trùng formalin*
***Formalin:** chất diệt trùng có chứa khí formadehyde trong dung dịch, với độ mạnh 5% để lau sạch bồn rửa tay, tủ, với độ mạnh 25% nhúng dụng cụ để diệt trùng trong 10 phút*
***Fragile nail tips:** đầu móng dòn*
***Fragile:** dễ gãy*
***Freehand painting**: vẽ màu nghệ thuật tạo kiểu lên móng bằng cọ nhỏ và sơn*
***French twist:** xoắn tóc kiểu người Pháp*
***Friction (deep rubbing):** động tác ma sát, chà vòng*
***Friction movement:** động tác ma sát*
***Fringe area:** vùng tóc tam giác trước trán (bang)*
***Frizzy curl:** lọn tóc nhỏ, xoắn, tóc quăn xù*
***Frontal artery**: động mạch của trán và mí mắt trên*
***Frontal bone**: xương trán*
***Frontalis**: bắp thịt phía trước của da đầu*
***Frosting cap:** mũ nhựa trùm lên đầu dùng móc lấy tóc để nhuộm.*
***Fuller earth:** đất mùn*
***Fuller looking:** trông đầy đặn hơn*
***Fulling movement:** động tác kéo*
***Full-stem curl:** lọn tóc xa da đầu*
***Fumigant:** khí diệt trùng*
***Fumigation:** sự xông hơi*
***Fundus**: những cuộn ống mồ hôi*
***Fungal spores:** bào tử nấm*
***Fungi**: nấm ký sinh thực vật*
***Fungicidal**: khả năng tiêu diệt nấm*
***Furrows (corrugations)**: mặt móng gợn sóng*
***Furuncle**: dưới chân lông có mụn nhọt mủ*
***Galvanic current**: dòng điện Galvanic (D.C)*
***Gel nail:** chất dẽo trong suốt đắp lên móng thật, cứng chắc và đẹp hơn bột acrylic*
***Gems:** các mảnh đá qúi*
***General infection**: nhiễm trùng dòng máu*
***Gentian violet jelly:** kem thoa phỏng*
***Geranium**: lá đỏ thắm phong lữ có tính làm sạch da*
***Ginger**: gừng tạo hương thơm*
***Ginseng**: sâm có tính êm dịu và hương thơm*
***Glandular nervous system:** hệ thần kinh các tuyến*
***Glycerin:** chất dầu nhờn*
***Glyceryl monothioglycolate:** hóa chất uốn tóc acid*
***Glycosphingolipid:** màng mỡ kết dính mặt ngoài*
***Gonorrhea**: bệnh lậu mũ do vi trùng gonococci*
***Good penetration:** thấm dễ dàng*
***Good porosity:** độ thấm nhanh*
***Gossip:** tính đồn nhảm*
***Granule:** hạt*
***Granulosum:** lớp hạt thuộc ngoại bì*
***Grapeseed oil**: dầu massage hạt táo làm mịn da*
***Gravity-fed**: trọng lực đẩy ép sơn của máy airbrush*
***Greater auricular nerve**: thần kinh cổ tai, mặt*
***Greater occipital nerve**: thần kinh phía sau da đầu*
***Greek**: người Hy Lạp*
***Grids**: hạt cát chà dùng trên giũa giấy hoặc vòng bọc đầu giũa điện bằng giấy*
***Grinding:** sự tán nhỏ, nghiền nhỏ*
***Growing phase:** gia đoạn phát triển*

Hacking movement: *động tác chặt chặt*
Hair bulb: *bầu tóc*
Hair end: *đuôi tóc*
Hair papilla: *phần lõm dưới chân lông*
Hair tension: *căng tóc*
Hairline: *đường viền tóc*
Half off base: *lọn tóc quấn 90 độ*
Half-stem curl: *lọn tóc hơi gần da đầu*
Halogen bulb: *đèn halogen màu trắng vàng cứng gel*
Hand cream: *kem chứa chất nhờn, chất ẩm dùng cho da khô, da nứt và da ngứa*
Hand lotion: *giống như hand cream nhưng chứa nhiều dầu hơn, ít đặc*
Hard keratin: *chất sừng cứng (tóc)*
Hard water: *nước có nhiều tạp chất như nước rửa tay, tạo sự hạn chế tạo bọt ở xà phòng*
Harmful bacteria: *vi trùng có hại*
Harmless bacteria: *vi trùng vô hại*
Harsh alkali: *chất kiềm mạnh*
Hastened: *nhanh lên*
Heavy side of the hair: *bên tóc nhiều*
Hemoglobin (haemoglobin): *chất màu đỏ của máu*
Henna: *lá cây nhuộm tóc người Ai Cập thường dùng*
Hepatitis: *bệnh sưng gan*
Herbal jelly: *chất jell thảo mộc*
Heredity: *di truyền tổ tiên*
Herpes simplex: *mụn giộp nước*
High blood pressure: *áp suất máu cao*
High-frequency current: *dòng điện cao tần*
Hirsuties: *lông mọc nhiều*
Histamines: *hóa chất trương nở có trong máu*
Hollyhock: *cây thục quỳ có tính nhờn*
Homeostasis: *quân bình (cân bằng) nội tạng*
Horizontal position: *chiều ngang*
Hormones: *kích thích tố của tuyến nội tiết*
Hornet: *tổ ong*
Horsechestnut: *đậu ngựa làm chắc thành mạch máu*
Hue: *màu mắt tiếp nhận được*
Humectant: *chất ẩm*
Humerus: *xương lớn của cánh tay trên*
Hungarian: *người Hung gia lợi*
Hyaluronic acid: *acid hấp dẫn nước*
Hydrogen peroxide: *dung dịch với độ mạnh từ*
Hydrophilic: *phân tử hút nước*
Hydrotheraphy: *dùng nước trị bệnh*
Hyoid bone: *xương yết hầu, xương cổ chữ "U"*
Hyperhidrosis: *nhiều mồ hôi*
Hyperpigmentation: *Da đốm màu đậm*
Hypertrichosis: *lông mọc nhiều*
Hypertrophy: *móng mọc quá dày do di truyền*
Hyponychium: *da dưới đầu móng*
Hypopigmentation: *Da đốm màu lợt*
Immiscible: *chất không pha trộn được*
Immune: *miễn nhiễm*
Immunity: *sự miễn nhiễm tự nhiên hoặc tự tạo*
Immunocompromised: *tổn thương hệ miễn nhiễm*
Impetigo: *ghẻ lở*
Inactive stage: *giai đoạn không hoạt động*
Incandescent: *đèn nhiệt sáng vàng*
Index finger: *ngón trỏ*
Infected ingrown nail: *móng mọc đâm khóe bị nhiễm trùng*
Infectious disease: *bệnh lây lan do vi trùng*
Inferior labial artery: *động mạch của môi dưới*
Inflammation: *sự sưng phồng do ngứa, nhiễm trùng*
Infraorbital nerve: *thần kinh mí mắt dưới, bên mũi, môi trên và miệng*
Infra-red ray: *tia hồng ngoại*
Infratrochlear nerve: *thần kinh màng da mũi*
Ingrown nails: *móng mọc đâm khóe*
Inhalation: *sự hít vào*
Initiative: *sáng kiến*
Inorganic chemistry: *hóa vô cơ không chứa than*
Inorganic product: *sản phẩm vô cơ*
Insertion: *ngọn bắp thịt, phần di chuyển*
Insulator or nonconductor: *chất ngăn điện*
Insulator: *chất ngăn điện*
Integumentary system: *hệ thống vỏ bọc cơ thể*
Intense heat: *nhiệt độ cao*
Inventory system: *hệ thống tồn kho*
Iodine: *chất sát trùng iốt*
Ionization: *sự ion hóa*
Iontophoresis: *điện galvanic đẩy chất hòa tan vào da*
Jaundice: *bệnh da, nước tiểu, và mắt bị vàng*
Jawline: *đường hàm miệng*
Jewelry bit: *trục giũa nhỏ dài dùng khoan lỗ đeo vòng trang sức lên móng*
Jojoba: *loại đậu tính ẩm, nhờn, và trơn*
Kaolin: *đất sét trắng*
Keloid: *thẹo dày mảng trắng*
Keratin: *chất sợi (sừng) ở móng tay và tóc*
Keratinzation: *sự hóa sừng*
Keratoma: *da chai*
Kerosene: *dầu lửa*

Kinky: *tóc xoắn*
Knotted hair: *sợi tóc có nhiều gút*
Kojic acid*: chất làm sáng da*
Lacquer: *chất phủ bóng*
Lacrimal bone: *xương lệ ở hóc mắt*
Lancet*: dao rạch mụn*
Lanolin: *chất kem dưỡng da*
Lanugo: *lông tơ, lông măng*
Laser resurfacing: *dùng tia laser làm mờ vết nhăn, sẹo mụn*
LaStone massage: *dùng đá khoáng nóng và đá marble lạnh để massage*
Latissimus dorsi*: thịt phủ rộng phủ sau cổ và lưng, kiểm sóat bả vai và đong đưa cánh tay*
Lavender*: cây oải hương có tính sát trùng, kích thích và hương thơm*
Lavender*: nước hoa chống sưng, nhiễm trùng*
Leafing (nugget sheet)*: kim loại vàng, bạc, đồng dát mỏng tạo hình lên mặt móng*
Lemon*: chanh có tính se da*
Lemongrass*: cây sả nhiệt đới có tính làm sạch da*
Lentigines (freckle)*: tàn nhan*
Lentigo: *tàn nhan, đóm màu trên da*
Lettuce*: rau cải có tính êm dịu*
Leucocytes: *bạch cầu*
Leuconychia (white spot): *đốm trắng trên móng*
Leukoderma (leucoderma): *mảng trắng bẩm sinh*
Leukonychia (white spot)*: đốm trắng*
Levator anguli oris*: thịt nâng góc miệng, kéo vô*
Levator labii superioris*: thịt quanh môi trên, nở rộng mũi*
Licorice*: cam thảo, chất chống ngứa cho da nhạy ứng*
Ligament: *dây chằng*
Light-cured gels: *loại gel đắp móng được cứng lại bằng tia đèn cực tím (ultra violet rays)*
Lilac*: bông có màu hồng, tím, trắng*
Linen cape: *tấm choàng bằng vải thô*
Lipophilic*: phân tử hút mỡ và dầu*
Liposome*: mỡ chuyển hóa, chống độc tố trong da*
Liposuction: *hút mỡ*
Liquefy*: tan dầu*
Liquid nail polish: *chất hơi đặc để sơn hoặc bóng móng*
Liquid nail wrap: *hoá chất thoa tạo sợi làm cứng chắc mặt móng để giúp móng thật mọc dễ dàng*
Liquid tissue*: mô dinh dưỡng*
Local infection*: nhiễm trùng tại chỗ*
Lockjaw: *cứng hàm răng*
Loud noises: *tiếng động ồn ào*
Lovage root*: rễ lovage ở Châu Âu làm sạch da*
Lucas spray: *bình Lucas chứa thảo mộc pha nước cất xịt lên da khô, da có mạch mạch vỡ*
Lucidum: *lớp trong suốt thuộc ngoại bì*
Lumbar vertebra*: đốt xương thắt lưng*
Lump alum: *cục phèn cầm máu*
Lunula: *vòng trắng cong ở nền móng tay*
Lymph vascular system*: hệ thống đẩy bạch cầu*
Lymphatic drainage massage: *xoa bóp thông tuyến bạch huyết*
Lymphatic gland: *tuyến bạch cầu*
Maceration*: hoa nhúng vào dầu nóng có mùi thơm*
Macules: *đốm màu nhỏ ở da giống như tàn nhan*
Magnolia bark: *vỏ mộc lan giúp se da và kích thích*
Magnolia*: hoa mộc lan*
Malformation*: hình dạng bất thường*
Malignant melanoma: *đốm đen, nâu, nhô lên cở không đều (ung thư da nguy hiểm)*
Malnutrition*: dinh dưỡng kém*
Mammaplasty: *sửa ngực*
Mandible*: xương hàm dưới, mạnh và cứng nhất*
Marrow: *tủy xương*
Mask knife*: dùng dao nhỏ bén cắt mẫu tạo hình trên giấy, plastic để xịt sơn tạo hình lên móng*
Mask paper*: dùng giấy cắt tạo mẫu sẳn nghệ thuật*
Massage cream: *chất kem nhờn emollient chữa trị, trơn da, dinh dưỡng cho da.*
Massage cream: *chất kem nhờn emollient chữa trị, trơn da, dinh dưỡng cho da.*
Masseter*: bắp thịt nhai*
Matrix: *móng non*
Matter*: chất chiếm chỗ trong không gian*
Maxillae*: xương của hàm trên*
Mechanical reaction: *phản ứng cơ học*
Median nerve*: thần kinh cánh tay & bàn tay*
Medicated rinse: *chất xả tóc trị gàu ở da đầu*
Medulla*: lỏi tóc, tủy xương*
Melanin: *sắc tố*
Melanocytes*: chất màu thành tế bào*
Melanoma*: ung thư da*
Melanonychia*: mặt móng có lằn sợi đen từ nền đến đầu móng.*
Melanotic sarcoma: *nốt ruồi ung thư*
Membrane: *màng bọc*
Mental depression: *thần kinh suy sụp*

Mentalis: *bắp thịt nâng môi dưới, nhăn da cằm*
Mentoplasty: *sửa cằm*
Metabolism: *sự trao đổi chất của tế bào*
Metacarpal bones: *xương bàn tay*
Metatarsal bones: *xương bàn chân*
Methyl paraben: *chất bảo quản, chống vi trùng, chống nấm mốc*
Microbes (germ): *vi trùng gây bệnh*
Microbiology: *vi sinh vật học*
Microcomedone: *vi khuẩn mụn đầu đen*
Microdermabrasion: *ống hút da trộn với bột cát mịn aluminum dioxide loại bỏ da chết, đốm màu.*
Micromotor: *trục quay nhỏ của máy giũa móng*
Microorganism: *tế bào vi sinh động và thực vật*
Mildew: *ẩm mốc*
Milfoil: *cỏ thi có tính làm lành và sạch da*
Miliaria rubra: *rôm sởi, ngứa da do sức nóng*
Mineral hair dye: *chất khoáng nhuộm tóc*
Mineral oil: *dầu khoáng chất*
Miniaturization: *sự mất tóc, lông do di truyền, do kích thích tố*
Miscible solution: *dung dịch có thể pha trộn*
Miscible: *chất pha trộn được*
Mitosis: *sinh sản gián phân*
Mobility: *chuyển động*
Modelage mask (thermal mask): *mặt nạ nhiệt đắp cho da khô, da tuổi già*
Moderate heat: *nhiệt độ vừa phải*
Moisturize cream: *chất kem làm ẩm da*
Mold (fungus): *móng bị nấm, ẩm móng có màu vàng, xanh hoặc đen*
Molecule: *phân tử*
Monilethrix: *tóc nổi hạt dễ gãy*
Monomer: *dung dịch acrylic là dạng nước có phân tử cực nhỏ để dễ kết với polymer*
Motility: *tự di chuyển*
MSDS *(Material Safety Data Sheet): bảng dữ kiện an toàn vật liệu*
Musk deer: *sơn dương nhỏ*
Muslin: *vải mịn dùng để wax lấy lông*
Myology: *cấu trúc, nhiệm vu, và bệnh bắp thịt*
Naevaus: *dấu vết khi sinh ra*
Nail anamel: *nước sơn móng tay, móng chân*
Nail bed: *đệm móng*
Nail bleach: *chất tẩy trắng móng, ví dụ như 6% hydrogen peroxide (6% H202)*
Nail conditioner: *chất ẩm để chống móng khô và dòn*
Nail dryer: *chất thoa để bảo vệ nước sơn khô nhanh chống dính*
Nail grooves: *rãnh móng*
Nail hardener: *chất cứng móng,ngăn ngừa móng chẻ*
Nail matrix: *móng non*
Nail root: *gốc móng*
Nail walls: *thành móng*
Nail whitener: *chất oxýt kẽm và tatinium dioxide làm trắng móng, thoa dưới đầu móng để che đốm*
Nail-bed: *nền móng*
Nasal bones: *xương cầu mũi*
Nasal cavity: *hóc mũi*
Natural barrier: *màng bảo vệ mô da*
Natural immunity: *miễn nhiễm tự nhiên*
Natural nail bit: *trục đầu giũa bóng bằng cao su*
Needle: *kim bên trong vòi phun điều chỉnh sơn xịt*
Neurology: *cấu trúc, nhiệm vụ, bệnh hệ thần kinh*
Nevus: *nốt ruồi nâu hoặc đen trong móng*
Nipper: *dụng cụ cắt da móng tay*
Nitro cellulose: *chất sợi kết có trong nước sơn*
Nodules: *bướu nhỏ*
No-light gel: *gel phủ lên tip và dùng chất xịt hoặc nhúng nước làm gel cứng lại, không cần đèn*
No-light gels: *loại gel được cứng lại không cần dùng đèn U.V, cứng gel lại nhờ chất xúc tác hoặc ngâm vào nước*
Non- strip rinse: *chất xả tóc nhuộm không tạo sọc*
Non-contagious: *bệnh không lây lan*
Nonpathogenic: *vi trùng không gây bệnh*
No-stem curl: *lọn tóc sát da đầu*
Nucleus: *nhân tế bào*
Nylon fiber hardener: *chất làm cứng móng có trong nước sơn bóng, thoa theo chiều dọc hoặc ngang trên mặt móng.*
Oak bark: *vỏ gỗ oak có tính se da*
Objective symptom: *triệu chứng thấy được*
Occipital artery: *động mạch ót, sau đầu*
Occipital bone: *xương ót*
Occipitalis: *bắp thịt phủ phía sau da đầu*
Occupational disease: *bệnh nghề nghiệp*
Odorless: *không mùi*
Oil bleach: *thuốc tẩy có dầu*
Oil gland disorder: *xáo trộn tuyến dầu*
Oil-in-water emulsion: *(O/W) kem có ít dầu trong thành phần sản phẩm chứa nhiều thành phần nước hơn như mayonnaise (nước sốt mayonne)*

Oil-in-water: *dầu lơ lửng trong nước*
Ointment cream: *kem mỡ đặc*
Olive leaves: *lá cây olive có tính nhờn*
Olive oil: *dầu olive vàng xanh dùng trong thức ăn và dùng trong hot oil manicure*
On base: *lọn tóc quấn 135 độ so với da đầu*
Onychatrophia (atrophy): *rụng móng*
Onychauxis (hypertrophy): *móng bị dày do bệnh nội thương, di truyền*
Onychia: *móng non sưng có mủ dẫn đến rụng móng*
Onychocryptosis (ingrown nails): *móng đâm khóe*
Onychogryphosis (onychogryposis): *móng nâu, dày, dài, cong, cứng, do tổn thương móng non.*
Onycholysis: *móng nhiễm trùng từ đầu móng đến nền móng, móng lỏng không rụng*
Onychomadesis: *mặt móng rụng do nhiễm trùng ở móng non*
Onychomycosis (tinea unguium): *móng nhiễm trùng do nấm thực vật*
Onychomycosis (tinea unguium): *móng nhiễm trùng do nấm thực vật*
Onychophagy (bitten nails): *thói quen cắn móng*
Onychophosis: *lớp sừng mọc dày ở nền móng*
Onychophyma: *móng dày phồng lên*
Onychoptosis: *móng và ngón rụng do bệnh giang mai tạo bởi siêu vi khuẩn syphilis*
Onychoptosis: *móng.ngón rụng do bệnh giang mai*
Onychorrhexis (split nails): *móng chẻ và dòn*
Onychosis (onychopathy): *bệnh móng*
Opaque: *trắng đục*
Orange blossoms: *hoa cam tính ẩm da, hương thơm*
Orange: *cam tạo hương thơm*
Orbicularis oculi: *bắp thịt vòng hốc mắt, nhắm mắt*
Orbicularis oris: *bắp thịt vòng miệng, và đôi môi*
Organic chemistry: *hóa học hữu cơ có chứa than*
Organic solvent: *dung môi hữu cơ*
Origin: *gốc bắp thịt, phần cố định*
Os coxa: *xương khớp háng*
Osmidrosis: *mồ hôi mùi khó chịu ở nách*
Osteology: *học về cấu trúc và nhiệm vụ của xương*
Out off base: *lọn tóc quấn 45 độ*
Ovary: *tuyến sinh sản của phụ nự*
Overdirected base: *lọn tóc quấn 180 độ*
Overexposure: *tiếp xúc hóa chất lâu dài và nhiều lần*
Overlap: *chồng lên nhau*
Oxidation tint: *thuốc nhuộm oxýt hóa*
Ozone: ***khí quyển***

Pacemaker: *mang máy trợ tim*
Palmar: *lòng bàn tay*
Papaya: *chất men mủ đu đủ lột da nhẹ*
Papilary layer: *lớp nhủ đàn hồi*
Papilla: *hình chóp nhỏ dưới nang lông*
Papillary: *lớp nhủ dưới ngoại bì*
Parabens: *chất bảo quản mỹ phẩm và thực phẩm*
Paraffin wax masks: *mặt nạ sáp chứa paraffin*
Paraffin: *sáp làm ẩm da*
Para-phenylenediamine: *hóa chất nhuộm tóc*
Parasitic disease: *bệnh do ký sinh trùng*
Parietal artery: *động mạch đỉnh đầu*
Parietal bones: *xương đỉnh đầu*
Paronychia: *sưng đỏ chung quanh móng*
Partnership: *cách làm chủ từ hai người trở lên*
Patch test: *thử dị ứng*
Patella: *xương đầu gối*
Pathogenic: *vi trùng gây bệnh*
Pathology: *cấu trúc và nguyên nhân của bệnh*
Pectoralis major and minor: *thịt ngực giúp đong đưa cánh tay*
Pediculosis capitis: *chí truyền nhiễm, tạo mảng gàu*
Pedicure bit: *trục đầu giũa bọc diamond mài da chai*
Peppermint: *bạc hà, thông mũi, tiêu hóa, có tính sát trùng, lành da*
Percusion movement: *động tác vỗ nhẹ*
Peripheral nervous system: *hệ thần kinh ngoại biên*
Peroximeter: *đo nồng độ peroxide*
Personality: *nhân cách*
Perspiration: *sự ra mồ hôi*
Petrissage (kneading): *động tác nhồi bóp, vặn*
Petroleum cream: *kem bảo vệ da*
Phalanges of fingers: *xương lóng ngón tay*
Phalanges of toes: *xương lóng ngón chân*
Phalanges: *xương ngón tay và ngón chân*
Pharynx: *thực quản*
Phenol: *chất diệt trùng có tính độc, ăn mòn*
Phenolics: *chất diệt trùng mạnh làm mềm hoặc mất màu các đồ vật bằng nhựa; với độ mạnh 5% diệt trùng dụng cụ trong 10 phút*
Phonetician: *nhà ngữ âm học*
Physical reaction: *phản ứng thể lý*
Physically changed: *đổi thể lý không tạo chất mới*
Physiologist: *bác sĩ sinh lý học*
Physiology: *sinh lý học*
Phytotherapy (herbal therapy): *thảo mộc trị liệu da*
Piggy back: *kiểu 2 ống cuốn quấn chồng lên nhau*

Pigment: *hạt màu*
Pimple: *mụn nhọt*
Pinkeges: *viêm mắt cấp tính*
Pith: *lõi ở giữa*
Pityriasis capitis simplex: *gàu vảy khô*
Pityriasis steatoides: *gàu vảy dầu*
Pivot curl: *trục lọn tóc*
Plasma*: huyết tương nuôi tế bào và loại độc tố*
Platelets*: huyết thanh giữ nhiệm vụ đông máu*
Platysma*: bắp thịt rộng từ ngực và vai đến cằm*
Plicatured nail*: móng biến dạng từ móng non ngón chân, đầu móng có hình vuông*
Podiatrist: *bác sĩ về chân*
Polarity*: thay đổi điện cực*
Polish remover: *chất dung môi hữu cơ dùng làm hoà tan và chùi nước sơn cũ trên móng*
Polish thinner: *chất dung môi để pha nước sơn có chứa aceton*
Polymer: *chất bột acrylic kết với monomer để giúp việc kết cứng lại*
Polymerization*: tiến trình kết dính của hóa học*
Poor penetration: *thấm khó khăn*
Poor porosity: *độ thấm kém*
Porosity bond: *kết độ thấm*
Posterior auricular artery*: động mạch cung cấp máu đến da đầu phía sau và ở trên tai*
Posterior auricular muscle*: bắp thịt sau tai*
Posterior auricular nerve*: thần kinh sau tai và sọ*
Postpartum alopecia: *sói tóc, thiếu kích thích tố*
Potassium hydroxide: *hóa chất làm mềm da*
Powder bleach: *thuốc tẩy bột loại mạnh*
Predisposition test*: thử nghiệm dị ứng da*
Pre-lightening: *làm lợt trước*
Preservative: *chất bảo quản*
Pre-softening: *làm mềm trước*
Primary colors*: nhóm màu thứ 1: đỏ, vàng, xanh*
Primer: *chất giúp cho mặt móng kết dính chặt với chất đắp móng giả như gel, bột acrylic..*
Prism*: lăng kính*
Procerus*: thịt phủ cầu mũi, dưới chân mày*
Processing time: *thời gian phát triển*
Prognosis*: tiên đoán bệnh*
Progressive color: *màu tăng triển*
Pronators*: bắp thịt trở bàn tay vô và úp xuống*
Propylene glycol*: chất làm ẩm cho da khô, da nhạy cảm*
Protective base: *kem bảo vệ da, da đầu*
Protein hardener: *chất đạm làm cứng móng có chất collagen có trong nước sơn bóng*
Protoplasm*: nguyên sinh chất không màu như jelly*
Protozoa: *động vật nguyên sinh*
Psoriasis*: bệnh vảy nến có mảng đỏ và vảy bạc*
Psychiatrist: *bác sĩ tâm thần*
Psychologist: *bác sĩ tâm lý*
Psychotherapy*: tâm lý trị liệu*
Pterygium: *bệnh da chồm lên móng*
Puberty*: giai đoạn phát triển của thiếu niên*
Pull test: *kéo tóc để thử*
Pulmonary circulation*: sự tuần hoàn phổi*
Pyogenic granuloma*: sưng tụ máu đỏ ở nền đệm móng đến thân móng*
Quadratus*: bắp thịt vuông hàm dưới*
Quaternary ammonium compounds: *dung dịch ổn định và an toàn; với độ mạnh 1/1000 nhúng chìm dụng cụ trong 10 phút để diệt trùng*
Radish*: củ cải đỏ có tính se da*
Radius*: xương quay nhỏ của cánh tay trước*
Ram's horn nails (onychogryphosis)*: móng màu nâu cứng, dài cong như kèn do không chăm sóc, tổn thương móng non, nếu không nhiễm trùng thợ có thể chăm sóc*
Rating: *tỷ lệ*
Realistic expectation: *biểu hiện sự mong muốn*
Rectangular base: *lấy tóc nền chữ nhật*
Rectifier*: biến điện từ A.C qua D.C*
Red blood cells*: tế bào máu đỏ*
Rededial lotion: *chất giảm đau*
Reduction: *làm co lại*
Reflexology: *xoa bóp massage tay và chân*
Release oxygen: *giải thoát oxy*
Renaissance*: thời phục hưng*
Reproductive system*: hệ thống sinh sản*
Reservoir*: bình chứa*
Resilient curl: *lọn tóc đàn hồi*
Resin: *chất nhựa dẽo*
Respiration*: sự hô hấp*
Retail sale: *bán lẽ*
Retail supplies*: vật liệu để bán lẻ cho khách*
Retard: *chậm lại*
Retinoic acid*: kem trị mụn bọc (retin-A)*
Retrogress: *suy yếu*
Revert: ***trở lại***
Revolution Per Minute (RPMs)*: trị số vòng quay mỗi phút của máy sơn phun (airbrush)*

Rheostat: điều chỉnh độ mạnh dòng điện
Rhinoplasty: sửa, nâng sóng mũi
Rhytidectomy: căng mặt
Ribs: xương sường
Rickettsia: bệnh còi xương
Ridge curl: lọn tóc gợn nổi
Rimming: viền lề
Risorius: thịt kéo góc miệng ra sau, biểu lộ gầm gừ
Roller curl: lọn tóc bằng ống
Roman: người La mã
Rosasea: da vỡ mạch máu lâu ngày ở đôi má & mũi
Rose hips: cành hoa hồng có tính ẩm da
Rose leaves: lá hoa hồng có tính ẩm da
Rosemary: cây hương thảo có tính giảm đau, nghẽn máu kích thích và hương thơm
Rosewood: hồng mộc
Ruffing: đánh rối bằng bàn chãi
Sacrum: xương cùng
Sage: húng quế có tính sát trùng
Salicylic acid: acid sát trùng, làm mềm tế bào chết
Saliva: tuyến nước bọt
Salt glows: chà da bằng muối biển, dầu, và lotion da
Sandalwood: gỗ trầm hương có tính sát trùng và kích thích
Sanding bands: vòng màu nâu đen bọc đầu giũa điện, dùng 1 lần cần vứt bỏ
Sanitary Maintenance Area (S.M.A): nơi giữ vệ sinh
Saprophyte: thực vật hoại sinh
Sassafras bark: loại vỏ cây kích thích
Scabies: bệnh ghẻ ngứa lây lan
Scales: vảy
Scapula: xương vai
Scotch hose treatment: vòi nước nóng xịt lên lưng và các tuyến bạch huyết
Scratch: cào xướt
Sculpture curls: lọn tóc nắn bằng tay
Seasonal disease: bệnh do ảnh hưởng thời tiết
Seaweed: chất dinh dưỡng, kích thích, làm ẩm da từ rong biển
Sebaceous glands: tuyến dầu
Sebaceous secretion: điều tiết dầu
Seborrhea sicca: vảy dầu ở da đầu
Seborrhea: bệnh nhiều dầu
Sebum: chất dầu trong tuyến
Secondary colors: màu thứ 2: cam, xanh lá, tím
Semi-permanent colors: nhuôm bán vĩnh viễn
Senility: tuổi già
Sense of humor: tính hài hước
Sense of touch: cảm giác khi sờ đến
Sepsis: nhiễm trùng máu
Septicemia: nhiễm trùng máu
Sequins: đồ trang sức
Serenity: bình thản
Serratus anterior: thịt ngực giúp hơi thở và nâng cánh tay
Shadow wave: nắn tóc dợn sóng nhẹ ở mặt tóc ngoài
Shapeless: mất kiểu tóc
Shear: kéo tỉa
Shellfish: động vật biển có vỏ bọc (sò, tôm, cua...)
Shingling: cắt tóc từ gáy đến đỉnh đầu bằng kéo hoặc
Shiny nail: móng sáng bóng
Shrink: co lại
Single halo: cỡ đầu trung bình chia 9
Sinusoidal current: dòng điện hình Sin co thắt da
Skeletal system: hệ thống bộ xương
Skeletal: bộ xương
Skull: sọ
Slip: bột mịn cho da mặt
Slithering (effilating): tỉa mỏng tóc bằng kéo
Slouch slightly: hơi uể oải
Slouch: uể oải
Smooth skin: da mịn màng
Sneezing: nhảy mũi
Soap cape: trộn thuốc nhuộm và shampoo chãi tóc
Sodium bicarbonate (baking soda): tan da dầu
Sodium hypochlorite: chất tẩy, với độ mạnh 10% nhúng dụng cụ trong 10 phút để diệt trùng
Soft keratin: chất sừng mềm (da)
Soft water: nước được lọc sạch, nước mưa, hoặc nước cất dùng để pha chế sản phẩm, tạo xà phòng nhiều bọt
Solar spectrum: quang phổ mặt trời
Solute: dạng hòa tan trong dung dịch
Solvent: dung môi thường là chất lõng để pha trộn
Spectrum: quang phổ
Sorbitol: chất làm ẩm da
Spearmint: cây bạc hà lục có tính kích thích và hương thơm
Sphenoid bone: xương bướm, nối các xương đầu
Spinal cord: dây tủy sống
Spine: cột sống
Spingolipid: màng mỡ kết dính mặt trong
Spirilla: vi trùng hình xoắn gây bệnh giang mai
Split: nứt

Sponges: *xốp mềm*
Spores: *bào tử*
Springy curl: *lọn tóc co giãn không đều*
Squalane: *sản phẩm từ dầu olive, tạo nhờn*
Squalene: *dầu gan cá map, dầu mộng luá mì làm trơn và chất thơm*
Squamous cell carcinoma: *ung thư da trầm trọng có vảy đỏ, nốt sần dày*
Square base: *lấy tóc nền hình vuông*
Squoval: *móng hình vuông mà đầu móng oval*
Stabilizer solution: *chất ổn định*
Stack perm: *tóc chỉ uốn lọn tóc dài ở gáy)*
Stagger: *xếp lát gạch*
Staphylococci: *vi trùng hình tròn kết chùm có mủ*
Steatoma: *bướu dầu, hoặc buớu mỡ*
Steel pusher: *cây sủi kim loại*
Stem pin curl: *cọng tóc, từ nền đến vòng tóc*
Stencil: *mẫu hình cắt sẵn để xịt màu airbrush*
Stencil: *mẫu tạo hình cắt sẵn trên giấy, vãi, hoặc plastic cho nghệ thuật kiểu móng*
Sterno cleido mastoideu: *thịt vùng cổ và xoay đầu*
Sternocleidomastoideus: *bắp thịt cổ xoay đầu*
Sternum: *xương ức, xương ngực kết hợp xương sườn*
Stomach: *bao tử*
Stratum corneum: *lớp sừng bên ngoài của ngoại bì*
Stratum germinativum: *lớp mầm sống*
Stratum granulosum: *lớp hạt thuộc ngoại bì*
Stratum lucidum: *lớp trong suốt*
Stream hair: *dòng tóc, hướng tóc*
Stretch: *giãn*
Striated muscles: *bắp thịt có sợi, điều khiển do ý chí*
Structure: *cấu trúc*
Styptic pencil: *cây viết chì cầm máu*
Styptic powder: *bột cầm máu*
Styptics: *chất cầm máu*
Subcutaneous tissue (adipose): *mô mỡ dưới nội bì*
Subcutis (adipose): *mô mỡ*
Subjective symptoms: *triệu chứng cảm thấy (ngứa)*
Submandibular lipectomy: *chỉnh sửa cằm*
Subtraction: *loại bỏ đi*
Sudoriferous glands: *tuyến mồ hôi*
Sudoriferous secretion: *điều tiết mồ hôi*
Sulfonated oil: *dầu acid sulfuric*
Sulfur bonds: *cấu trúc chữ S của tóc*
Sunscreen oil: *dầu thoa chống nắng*
Supinator: *bắp thịt cánh tay trước đưa tay ra ngoài và lòng bàn tay ngửa lên*
Supra-orbital: *thần kinh trán, chân mày, da đầu*
Supra-trochlear: *thần kinh giữa đôi mắt*
Surfactant: *bề mặt*
Suseptibility: *sự mẫn cảm*
Suspension: *các chất lơ lửng được pha trộn trong một dung dịch như salad dressing oil pha với dấm*
Sweat gland disorder: *xáo trộn tuyến mồ hôi*
Swirl: *xoáy tóc*
Switch: *mớ tóc độn cao*
Sympathetic nervous system: *hệ thần kinh giao cảm*
Synthetic organic tint: *nhuộm tổng hợp*
Syphillis: *vi trùng giang mai hình xoắn*
Systemic disease: *bệnh do xáo trộn nội tiết*
Tact: *tế nhị*
Tang: *chuôi dao*
Tangled hair: *tóc rối*
Tapotement or percussion: *tác động vỗ nhẹ*
Tarsal bones: *xương mắt cá cổ chân*
Tartaric rinse: *kem xả có chất chua*
Tea tree: *cây trà có tính sát trùng*
Telogen: *giai đoạn tóc không hoạt động*
Temple area: *vùng thái dương*
Temporal bones: *xương thái dương*
Temporalis: *bắp thịt ở thái dương*
Temporary color: *thuốc nhuộm tạm thời*
Tendon: *sợi gân*
Terminal hair: *lông dài, mềm thường ở da đầu, chân, tay và cơ thể, cứng hơn lông măng*
Tertiary colors: *nhóm màu thứ ba (Red + Violet)*
Tesla high-frequency: *dòng điện cao tần tạo nhiệt dùng tia tím (violet rays)*
Testosterone: *kích thích tố nam*
Tetanus: *vi trùng phong đòn nghánh*
Texture: *cở kích sợi tóc*
Texturizing: *tỉa mỏng tóc xù xì bằng kéo tỉa hoặc*
Thalassotherapy: *trị liệu nước và sản phẩm biển*
Thermal iron styling: *kẹp nhiệt tạo lọn tóc*
Thermal styling: *chãi kiểu tóc bằng nhiệt*
Thermometer: *nhiệt độ kế*
Thermostat: *dụng cụ tự động điều hòa nhiệt độ*
Thigh: *đùi*
Thio relaxer: *chất duỗi tóc thio*
Thoracic Vertebra: *đốt xương trụ*
Thorax: *xương lồng ngực*
Thrombocytes: *nghẽn mạch máu*
Thyme: *cây xạ hương bạc hà để pha chế mỹ phẩm có tính sát trùng*

***Tibia**: xương chày (xương lớn ở ống chân)*
***Tighter curl:** lọn tóc quăn nhỏ*
***Tile-shaped nails**: móng cong đều từ móng non đến đầu móng*
***Tincture of iodin:** dung dịch với độ mạnh 2% để thoa sạch vết cắt và vết thương*
***Tinea capitis:** nấm có đốm đỏ, hở lỗ chân lông*
***Tinea favosa:** vảy nấm vòng nhô trên da đầu*
***Tissue:** mô*
***Titanium dioxide**: chất bột trắng có trong son môi*
***Tolegen effluvium:** rụng tóc do thuốc ngừa thai, thiếu vitamin*
***Toner:** màu thật nhạt, nhuộm sau khi tẩy tóc*
***Top coat or sealer:** nước sơn không màu phủ lên nước sơn để phòng nứt và giúp bóng móng*
***Topical antibiotic:** kem kháng sinh chống nhiễm trùng*
***Toxaemia:** nhiễm trùng máu*
***Toxins**: độc tố do siêu vi khuẩn*
***Tranquilizer**: thuốc an thần*
***Transconjunctival blepharoplasty:** cách lấy túi mỡ bên trong mí mắt dưới*
***Transition phase:** giai đoạn chuyển tiếp*
***Translucent powder:** bột trong cho trang điểm*
***Trapezius**: thịt phủ bả vai giúp đong đưa cánh tay*
***Traumatic alopecia:** sói tóc do hóa chất*
***Triangle base:** lấy tóc nền tam giác*
***Triceps**: thịt ba đầu phủ mặt sau cánh tay trên và kéo dài tới cánh tay trước*
***Trichloroacetic acid (TCA):** hóa chất lột da nhăn, da hư do nắng*
***Trichology:** ngành học về lông tóc*
***Trichorrhexis nodosa:** tóc có gút khô và dòn*
***Trumpet (pincer nail)**: móng kèn mọc dài cuốn lại biến dạng ở ngón chân*
***Tubercle**: bướu nhỏ đặc, hơi cứng*
***Tuberculocidal**: bệnh lao*
***Tumor**: bướu lớn*
***Turban**: khăn quấn tóc phụ nữ*
***Typhoid fever**: bệnh thương hàn do bacillus*
***Ulcer:** vết loét sâu có mủ*
***Ulna**: xương trụ cánh tay trước*
***Ultraviolet bulb**: tia violet bóng đèn làm gel cứng*
***Ultraviolet light (U.V)**: Tia cực tím*
***Universal sanitation**: vệ sinh toàn bộ*
***Up do:** bới tóc kiểu*
***Upper arm**: cánh tay trên*
***Urea:** chống sưng, chống mùi hô, và sát trùng*
***Vaccination (inoculation)**: chủng ngừa*
***Vaccine:** chủng ngừa*
***Vapor**: thể hơi*
***Varicella:** bệnh thủy đậu, đậu mùa trái rạ*
***Vellus:** lông tơ*
***Venereal disease**: bệnh hoa liễu*
***Ventricle:** tâm thất, ngăn dưới, dày của tim*
***Verruca (wart)**: mụn cóc*
***Vertex:** sói tóc ở đỉnh đầu dọc theo ót*
***Vertical position:** chiều dọc thẳng đứng*
***Vesicle**: mụn nước nhỏ*
***Vibration movement:** động tác rung một điểm*
***Vinegar rinse:** chất xả nước dấm*
***Virology**: môn học về siêu vi khuẩn*
***Virucidal**: chất diệt siêu vi khuẩn*
***Virulent:** nhiễm khuẩn trầm trọng*
***Vitiligo**: lang beng, đốm trắng, mất sắc tố ở da*
***Volatile**: chất dễ bay hơi*
***Voluntary muscles:** bắp thịt tự nguyện điều khiển do ý chí*
***Warm colors:** màu ấm (đỏ, vàng, cam)*
***Water-cured**: nhúng gel vào nước ấm cho cứng lại*
***Water-cured**: cách nhúng gel vào nước ấm từ 2 đến 5 phút làm cứng gel*
***Water-in-oil emulsion:** (W/O) kem có ít nước trong thành phần sản phẩm nhiều dầu như cold cream thích hợp cho da khô*
***Wax mask:** mặt nạ sáp*
***Weaving:** đan tóc để sáng tóc*
***Wen**: bướu dầu thường mọc ở da đầu*
***Wheals:** mẫn đỏ, sưng ngứa do côn trùng cắn*
***White willow bark**: vỏ cây liễu trắng có tính ẩm da*
***Whorl hair:** vòng tóc xoắn ở gần đỉnh đầu*
***Wintergreen**: cây lộc đề có tính kích thích*
***Witch hazel**: có tính se da, giúp sạch làn da*
***Wringing:** vặn, xoắn lại*
***Wrinkle skin:** da nhăn nheo*
***Wrist carpal bones**: xương cổ tay*
***Yeast**: men chứa nhiều vitamin B*
***Zinc oxide**: oxýt kẽm có tính sát trùng*
***Zygomatic or malar bones**: xương thành lập gò má*
***Zygomaticus**: thịt gò má đến miệng*

ANSWER KEYS

MANICURIST EXAMINATION 1

1. D	2. D	3. B	4. C
5. B	6. B	7. B	8. A
9. C	10. A	11. C	12. B
13. B	14. D	15. D	16. A
17. C	18. C	19. B	20. A
21. C	22. A	23. B	24. A
25. D	26. A	27. B	28. A
29. C	30. B	31. C	32. B
33. A	34. C	35. B	36. A
37. D	38. D	39. C	40. A
41. C	42. B	43. A	44. D
45. C	46. A	47. A	48. A
49. C	50. D	51. A	52. B
53. A	54. D	55. D	56. B
57. B	58. C	59. A	60. A
61. B	62. C	63. A	64. B
65. C	66. A	67. A	68. C
69. D	70. A	71. B	72. A
73. C	74. B	75. B	76. C
77. B	78. B	79. B	80. B
81. B	82. B	83. D	84. C
85. C	86. C	87. D	88. D
89. D	90. C	91. C	92. D
93. D	94. D	95. C	96. D
97. C	98. D	99. B	100. C

MANICURIST EXAMINATION 2

1. B	2. D	3. D	4. B
5. B	6. A	7. B	8. A
9. B	10. B	11. D	12. D
13. D	14. A	15. B	16. C
17. D	18. C	19. A	20. B
21. C	22. D	23. C	24. C
25. A	26. A	27. A	28. B
29. C	30. C	31. C	32. C
33. C	34. B	35. A	36. D
37. B	38. A	39. C	40. B
41. C	42. C	43. D	44. D
45. D	46. A	47. C	48. A
49. A	50. B	51. B	52. C
53. D	54. D	55. D	56. B
57. B	58. B	59. D	60. C
61. D	62. B	63. C	64. C
65. D	66. B	67. C	68. A
69. D	70. C	71. B	72. C
73. A	74. C	75. A	76. D
77. B	78. A	79. C	80. D
81. B	82. D	83. D	84. B
85. C	86. C	87. B	88. C
89. B	90. B	91. B	92. A
93. D	94. A	95. D	96. A
97. A	98. D	99. A	100. A

MANICURIST EXAMINATION 3

1. D	2. B	3. C	4. A
5. B	6. D	7. D	8. B
9. C	10. A	11. D	12. A
13. C	14. A	15. C	16. A
17. B	18. A	19. C	20. B
21. D	22. A	23. C	24. A
25. C	26. B	27. A	28. C
29. A	30. D	31. C	32. C
33. B	34. C	35. B	36. D
37. A	38. B	39. A	40. C
41. D	42. B	43. A	44. C
45. A	46. D	47. C	48. B
49. A	50. B	51. C	52. A
53. B	54. C	55. B	56. D
57. D	58. D	59. A	60. B
61. C	62. D	63. C	64. A
65. B	66. C	67. D	68. C
69. C	70. A	71. A	72. A
73. B	74. C	75. C	76. C
77. C	78. C	79. B	80. A
81. D	82. B	83. D	84. C
85. A	86. C	87. C	88. D
89. D	90. D	91. A	92. C
93. A	94. A	95. B	96. B
97. C	98. D	99. D	100. D

MANICURIST EXAMINATION 4

1. D	2. D	3. C	4. B
5. D	6. C	7. A	8. C
9. D	10. B	11. D	12. B
13. D	14. C	15. B	16. B
17. B	18. C	19. C	20. B
21. B	22. C	23. A	24. C
25. B	26. A	27. D	28. A
29. D	30. A	31. A	32. C
33. B	34. B	35. B	36. D
37. B	38. C	39. B	40. B
41. B	42. B	43. A	44. C
45. B	46. B	47. C	48. B
49. A	50. C	51. D	52. A
53. D	54. B	55. C	56. B
57. B	58. D	59. B	60. D
61. C	62. B	63. C	64. D
65. D	66. B	67. D	68. A
69. B	70. B	71. C	72. D
73. C	74. C	75. A	76. A
77. B	78. C	79. B	80. C
81. A	82. D	83. D	84. C
85. A	86. A	87. C	88. C
89. D	90. A	91. B	92. B
93. D	94. C	95. D	96. B
97. A	98. A	99. D	100. A

MANICURIST EXAMINATION 5

1. D	2. D	3. B	4. A
5. C	6. A	7. D	8. C
9. A	10. A	11. C	12. C
13. C	14. B	15. B	16. B
17. B	18. C	19. A	20. D
21. C	22. A	23. D	24. D
25. B	26. D	27. B	28. B
29. C	30. D	31. B	32. C
33. A	34. D	35. B	36. B
37. D	38. C	39. C	40. A
41. B	42. A	43. B	44. B
45. A	46. B	47. A	48. B
49. D	50. B	51. D	52. C
53. B	54. A	55. A	56. D
57. C	58. B	59. C	60. B
61. C	62. D	63. C	64. C
65. B	66. C	67. A	68. C
69. D	70. B	71. B	72. A
73. A	74. A	75. C	76. C
77. D	78. A	79. A	80. A
81. C	82. C	83. B	84. D
85. D	86. B	87. A	88. A
89. A	90. C	91. A	92. D
93. D	94. A	95. B	96. D
97. C	98. A	99. C	100. B

MANICURIST EXAMINATION 6

1. D	2. D	3. A	4. C
5. A	6. C	7. B	8. C
9. A	10. A	11. B	12. C
13. A	14. D	15. C	16. B
17. C	18. B	19. C	20. A
21. D	22. B	23. A	24. C
25. B	26. B	27. D	28. D
29. B	30. C	31. C	32. B
33. C	34. B	35. B	36. A
37. A	38. D	39. A	40. C
41. A	42. A	43. A	44. D
45. C	46. B	47. C	48. D
49. B	50. B	51. C	52. A
53. C	54. B	55. D	56. C
57. A	58. B	59. C	60. B
61. D	62. B	63. A	64. B
65. C	66. D	67. B	68. A
69. C	70. D	71. C	72. A
73. B	74. D	75. C	76. B
77. A	78. D	79. B	80. C
81. A	82. B	83. D	84. C
85. A	86. B	87. C	88. D
89. B	90. A	91. C	92. D
93. B	94. C	95. A	96. B
97. D	98. C	99. A	100. C

MANICURIST EXAMINATION 7

1. B	2. B	3. D	4. B
5. D	6. D	7. D	8. A
9. C	10. D	11. B	12. D
13. D	14. B	15. A	16. D
17. C	18. A	19. D	20. B
21. D	22. A	23. A	24. C
25. C	26. A	27. D	28. A
29. B	30. D	31. A	32. D
33. D	34. C	35. C	36. D
37. C	38. B	39. B	40. D
41. C	42. D	43. B	44. C
45. A	46. B	47. B	48. B
49. B	50. C	51. A	52. A
53. C	54. B	55. B	56. A
57. B	58. C	59. D	60. B
61. A	62. D	63. C	64. C
65. A	66. D	67. A	68. C
69. D	70. B	71. A	72. C
73. A	74. B	75. C	76. C
77. C	78. B	79. A	80. C
81. B	82. D	83. B	84. B
85. C	86. A	87. A	88. C
89. A	90. B	91. D	92. A
93. A	94. A	95. B	96. A
97. D	98. B	99. C	100. C

MANICURIST EXAMINATION 8

1. B	2. A	3. D	4. C
5. B	6. D	7. C	8. A
9. D	10. B	11. A	12. C
13. D	14. C	15. A	16. C
17. A	18. D	19. C	20. B
21. A	22. B	23. C	24. D
25. A	26. B	27. C	28. D
29. A	30. C	31. D	32. C
33. A	34. B	35. C	36. D
37. A	38. C	39. D	40. A
41. C	42. B	43. C	44. B
45. A	46. C	47. B	48. D
49. A	50. C	51. B	52. A
53. D	54. D	55. A	56. A
57. D	58. B	59. A	60. C
61. B	62. D	63. A	64. B
65. B	66. B	67. A	68. C
69. B	70. D	71. A	72. C
73. A	74. C	75. D	76. C
77. B	78. C	79. A	80. A
81. C	82. D	83. B	84. A
85. D	86. B	87. C	88. B
89. D	90. C	91. A	92. B
93. C	94. A	95. C	96. D
97. C	98. D	99. D	100. D

MANICURIST EXAMINATION 9

1. D	2. B	3. D	4. D
5. A	6. A	7. A	8. B
9. C	10. A	11. B	12. C
13. B	14. C	15. D	16. A
17. C	18. D	19. D	20. A
21. C	22. A	23. C	24. C
25. D	26. D	27. A	28. D
29. C	30. C	31. A	32. C
33. C	34. A	35. C	36. A
37. C	38. A	39. B	40. C
41. B	42. A	43. B	44. D
45. A	46. A	47. C	48. C
49. C	50. D	51. B	52. C
53. D	54. C	55. D	56. A
57. A	58. D	59. A	60. B
61. B	62. B	63. C	64. C
65. C	66. B	67. D	68. D
69. A	70. B	71. C	72. B
73. C	74. A	75. B	76. D
77. A	78. C	79. D	80. B
81. B	82. C	83. A	84. C
85. A	86. A	87. B	88. C
89. B	90. C	91. B	92. B
93. D	94. B	95. C	96. B
97. A	98. D	99. D	100. D

Vanle 900 Publisher

442 N. Rancho Santiago Blvd
Orange, CA 92869
(714) 878-2365

NAILS 900 BOOK

New edition
Vietnamese & English ($30.00)

900 questions
Practical test
Safety rules
Lesson review
Technical terms

(270 pages 8^1/2 x 11)

FACIAL 900 BOOK

New edition
Vietnamese & English ($35.00)

900 questions
Practical test
Safety rules
Lesson review
Technical terms

(310 pages 8^1/2 x 11)

HAIR 900 BOOK

New edition
Vietnamese & English ($40.00)

900 questions
Practical test
Safety rules
Lesson review
Technical terms

(368 pages 8 1/2 x11)

. thammy900@yahoo.com
. *cosmetology@levan900.net*

SÁCH & DVD STATE BOARD NGÀNH THẨM MỸ

NAILS DVD DEMO FOR PRACTICE

Vietnamese & English

Manicure
Pedicure
Artificial
Disinfection

(105 minutes) $15.00

FACIAL 900 DVD DEMO FOR PRACTICE

Vietnamese & English

Plain facial
Dermal light
Eyebrow
Eyelashes
Disinfection

(105 minutes) $15.00

HAIR 900 DVD DEMO FOR PRACTICE

Vietnamese & English

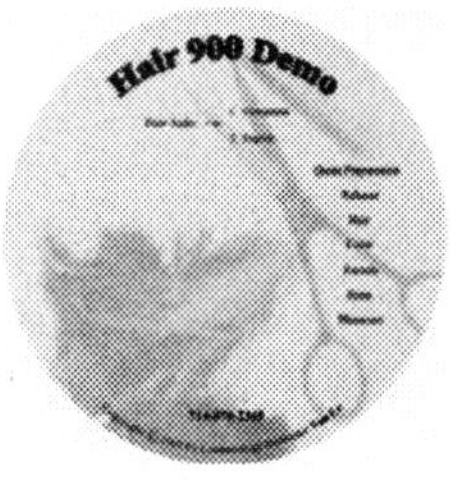

Bleach
Color
Relaxed
Hair cut
Wet set
Thermal

(120 minutes) $15.00

www.levan900.net

*STOMACH WRAP & REFLEXOLOGY

Vietnamese & English

(50 minutes) $15.00

*FACIAL MACHINE & DELUXE MASK FACIAL

Vietnamese & English

(60 minutes) $ 15.00

*FACE WRAP & BACK, HEAD MASSAGE

Vietnamese & English

(50 minutes) $15.00

GEL & ACRYLIC NAILS

(60 minutes) $15.00 each

Cosmetology Instructor Le Van
(714) 878-2365
Fax (714)532-5172

VAN LE 900
442 N. Rancho Santiago Blvd
Orange, CA 92869
Tel: (714) 878-2365& Fax: (714) 532-5172

Levan900.net
THE#1 GUIDE TO EFFECTIVE LEARNING SOLUTIONS

- *www.levan900.net*
- *E-mail: thammy900@yahoo.com*

ORDER FORM

Name: ....
Address: ....
....
Tel:

Amount		Price	Total
----	- *Hair 900 book (new edition)*	*$40.00*	**$** -------
	- *Facial 900 book (new edition)*	*$35.00*	
	- *Nails 900 book*	*$30.00*	
	- *Hair DVD 900 demo*	*$15.00*	
	- *Facial DVD 900 demo*	*$15.00*	
	- *Nails DVD 900 demo*	*$15.00*	
	- *Gel Nails DVD*	*$15.00*	
	- *Acrylic Nails DVD*	*$15.00*	
	- *Face, Back and Head Massage DVD*	*$15.00*	
	- *Stomach and Reflexology Massage DVD*	*$15.00*	
	- *Deluxe Facial DVD*	*$15.00*	
		Shipping & Handling First book or DVD **$3.00 each** additional book or DVD purchase	**$7.00**
		Total	

Make checks or money orders payable to ***Van Le 900***